mypoliscilab ™
Where participation leads to action!

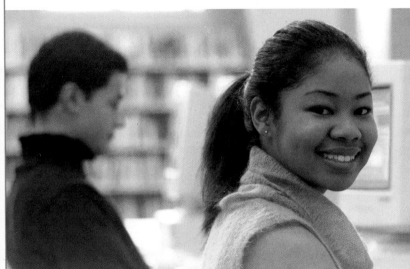

Welcome to MyPoliSciLab, where participation leads to action!

MyPoliSciLab is a state-of-the-art, interactive, and instructive online solution for introducing students to American Government. Designed to amplify and supplement a traditional lecture course or completely administer an online course, MyPoliSciLab combines multimedia — simulations, videos, news feeds and archives, quizzes and tests — to make teaching and learning more effective and fun!

WHAT STUDENTS ARE SAYING ABOUT ONLINE EXAMS AND QUIZZES

" I love it. I keep trying until I get a perfect grade and after a couple times you know the content like the back of your hand! "

" I liked being able to view the results of the quizzes immediately instead of having to wait for them to be graded by the instructor. "

WHAT STUDENTS ARE SAYING ABOUT ONLINE ACTIVITIES

" The activities were my favorite part of the course. They took a different approach to an interesting subject, and made it more applicable to real-life situations. This made the subject seem even more real than before. "

" I think they are a great tool to get students to interact with the material in a way you couldn't really do in class. "

ONE PLACE.
Everything your students need to succeed.

MyPoliSciLab is a state-of-the-art, interactive, and instructive online solution for your American Government course.

▶ Pre-Test, Post Test, and Chapter Exam
For each chapter of the printed textbook, students will navigate through a pre-test, post-test, and a full-chapter exam — all fully integrated with the online E-book so students can assess, review, and improve their understanding of the material in each chapter.

▶ Chapter Review
For each chapter, students will find additional resources such as a complete study guide, learning objectives, a summary.

▶ E-book.
Matching the exact layout of the printed textbook, the E-book contains multimedia icons in the margins that launch a wealth of exciting resources.

▶ The *New York Times* Online Feed & The *New York Times* Search by Subject™ Archive
Both provide free access to the full text of The *New York Times* and articles from the world's leading journalists of the *Times*. The online feed provides students with updated headlines and political news on an **hourly** basis.

▶ Online Administration
Instructors can easily track students' work on the site and monitor their progress on each activity. The *Instructor Gradebook,* which now includes upgraded functionality, provides maximum flexibility for allowing instructors to sort by student, activity, or to view the entire class in spreadsheet view.

▶ Research Navigator™
This database provides thousands of articles from journals as well as popular periodicals, such as *Newsweek* and *USA Today,* that give students and professors access to scholarly and topical content from a variety of sources.

▶ Interactive Activities
Students will find over 100 simulations, interactive timelines, videos, comparative exercises, and more — all integrated with the online E-book through icons that appear in the margins. Now fully updated with brand-new activities!

SIMULATION. Students are given a role to play — such as congress member, lobbyist, or police officer — so they can experience the challenges and excitement of politics firsthand.

TIMELINE. With an abundance of media and graphics, students can step through the evolution of an aspect of our political system.

VISUAL LITERACY. Students interpret and apply data about intriguing political topics. Each activity begins with an interactive primer on reading graphs and charts.

PARTICIPATION. Bringing the importance of politics home, these activities appear as three types: 1) Debates, 2) Surveys, and 3) "Get Involved" activities.

COMPARATIVE. Students compare the U.S. political system to those of other countries.

CONTINUOUSLY UPDATED MULTIMEDIA MAPPED TO CHAPTER CONTENT

NEW FEATURES

Student Polling
Updated weekly with timely, provocative questions, this new feature allows students to participate in nationwide polls on hot topics. Students are asked to vote on questions such as "Should flag burning be permitted?" Results of student responses around the country are immediately displayed.

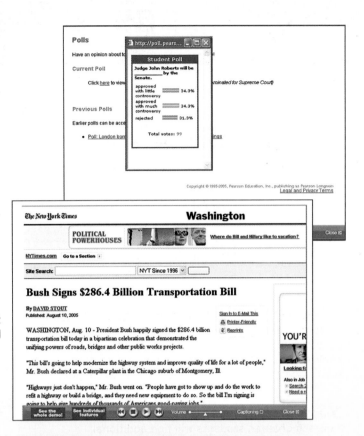

PoliSci News
PoliSci News contains 1) an online feed from The *New York Times* that is updated hourly, 2) an exclusive *New York Times* database that allows students to browse by subject area or search for a specific topic, and 3) PoliSci News Review — a series of articles selected by a political science professor that recap the previous week's most important political events and are followed by quizzes.

Roundtable Discussion Video Clips
Video clips consist of three professors discussing important concepts covered in the text. Key concepts such as campaign finance reform and critical questions such as "Is Federalism Dead?" are discussed from a wide range of perspectives and viewpoints — providing students with a balanced review of key course material. Each discussion is accompanied by critical thinking prompts, multiple choice questions, and a transcript for reference.

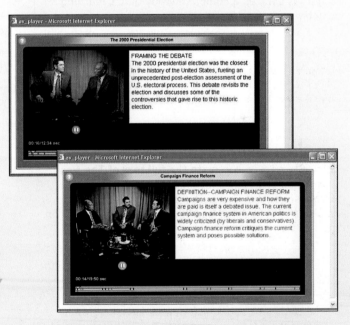

Debate Video Clips
Offering lively, challenging debates from two sides of an issue, these clips feature two professors discussing hot-button issues and answering pressing questions such as "Did George Bush steal the election?" Each discussion is accompanied by critical thinking prompts, multiple choice questions, and a transcript for reference.

INSTRUCTOR: WE CAN HELP YOU EASILY INTEGRATE THESE AMAZING ASSETS INTO YOUR COURSE...HOW?

Author's Choice
With so many incredible activities to assign, we have asked our authors to hand select one or two activities that best complement or amplify each chapter. You have the work done for you in easy-to-use, pre-packaged MyPoliSciLab assignments. If you only have time to assign and complete one activity for the chapter, the Author's Choice designation makes it easy!

Go to mypoliscilab.com to see a sample chapter!

Student Survey Results

Recently, Longman Publishers conducted a nationwide survey of students to determine just how useful they find MyPoliSciLab and its individual features. The sample included hundreds of students from both 2-year and 4-year schools.

The results are impressive. Not only do they show that students find MyPoliSciLab to be an effective supplement, but they show how each specific feature of MyPoliSciLab enhances students' learning experience and engages them with the course material. See for yourself!

Very low learning value →	1	2	3	4	5	4s & 5s
Online Quizzes	1.3%	1.3%	8.8%	26.8%	61.9%	88.7%
Chapter Exams	0.8%	5.0%	8.4%	18.4%	67.4%	85.8%
Debate Videos	2.2%	3.5%	15.8%	27.6%	50.9%	78.5%
Roundtable Videos	3.0%	3.0%	16.5%	32.0%	45.5%	77.5%
Chapter Activities	0.9%	5.2%	16.5%	23.9%	53.5%	77.4%
Online E-Book	5.4%	8.3%	15.1%	17.6%	53.7%	71.2%
PS News Review	5.0%	4.5%	23.2%	23.2%	44.1%	67.3%
Homepage Updates	8.0%	11.7%	16.9%	23.9%	39.4%	63.4%
Polling Questions	7.6%	9.0%	27.0%	20.9%	35.5%	56.4%

← Very high learning value

WHAT STUDENTS ARE SAYING ABOUT ONLINE E-BOOK

"It helped a lot, especially since you could magnify the words. Also, it was great to be able to type in a key word and see exactly where it appears in the text."

WHAT STUDENTS ARE SAYING ABOUT DEBATE VIDEOS

"All videos were fantastic and allowed each topic to be discussed from each viewpoint but was kept objective by the moderator."

WHAT STUDENTS ARE SAYING ABOUT POLISCI NEWS

"I really liked this feature. I don't get a chance to catch up on political news very often, so this was very helpful."

WHAT STUDENTS ARE SAYING ABOUT POLLING QUESTIONS

"The polling questions are fun. Sometimes I was very surprised at other students' responses."

PEARSON
Longman

American
GOVERNMENT
CONTINUITY AND CHANGE
★ 2008 Edition ★

KAREN O'CONNOR

Jonathan N. Helfat Distinguished Professor of Political Science
American University

LARRY J. SABATO

University Professor
and Robert Kent Gooch Professor of Politics
University of Virginia

PEARSON
Longman

New York San Francisco Boston
London Toronto Sydney Tokyo Singapore Madrid
Mexico City Munich Paris Cape Town Hong Kong Montreal

Editor-in-Chief: Eric Stano
Development Editor: Melissa Mashburn
Senior Marketing Manager: Elizabeth Fogarty
Supplements Editor: Brian Belardi
Senior Media Editor: Beth Strauss
Production Manager: Eric Jorgensen
Project Coordination, Text Design, and Electronic Page Makeup:
    Electronic Publishing Services Inc., NYC
Art Studio: Electronic Publishing Services Inc., NYC
Senior Cover Design Manager/Designer: Nancy Danahy
Cover images: Clockwise from upper left: American flag fence in Nebraska © Corbis; Stars and
Stripes © Veer/Getty Images; American flags, New York City, New York © Photodisc/Getty
Images; High angle view of a group of people holding a large American flag © Rubberball
Productions/Getty Images; American flag draped over a rural mailbox © Jupiter Images. Photo of
boxes © Nancy Danahy
Photo Researcher: Jody Potter
Senior Manufacturing Buyer: Alfred C. Dorsey
Printer and Binder: RR Donnelley & Sons Co.
Cover Printer: Phoenix Color Corp.

Library of Congress Cataloging-in-Publication Data

American government : continuity and change / Karen O'Connor…[et al.].—2008 ed.
        p. cm.
    Includes bibliographical references and index.
    ISBN 0-205-51141-4 (hardcover)
    1. United States—Politics and government.   2. Texas—Politics and government.
I. O'Connor, Karen, 1952–

JK276 .A45 2008
320 .473—dc22

                                                                        2006034938

Please visit us at www.ablongman.com.

ISBN 0–321–41533-7 (paperback)
ISBN 13 978-0-321-41533-2
ISBN 0–205–51141-4 (hardcover)
ISBN 13 978-0-205-51141-9
ISBN 0-13-1347624 (NASTA edition)
ISBN 13 978-0-13-1347625

1 2 3 4 5 6 7 8 9 10—DOW—10 09 08 07

To Meghan,
who grew up with this book

Karen O'Connor

To my Government 101 students
over the years, who all know that
"politics is a good thing"

Larry Sabato

★★★ Brief Contents

★★★ Detailed Contents

The Role of Political Parties in Organizing
   Congress   243
The Living Constitution *Article I, Section 8,*
   Clause 4   *244*
The House of Representatives   245
Join the Debate *Minority-Party Rights*
   in Congress   *248*
The Senate   250
The Committee System   251

The Members of Congress   **254**
   Global Perspective *Parliamentary Systems:*
      The Israeli Knesset   *255*
   Running for and Staying in Office   256
   Congressional Demographics   257
   Theories of Representation   258
   Analyzing Visuals *Approval Ratings of Congress*
      and Individual Representatives   *259*

How Members Make Decisions   **260**
   Party   260
   Constituents   261
   Colleagues and Caucuses   262
   Interest Groups, Lobbyists, and Political Action
      Committees   262
   Staff and Support Agencies   263
   Politics Now *Muslim Staffers Seek to Educate*
      Members of Congress   *264*

The Law-making Function of Congress   **264**
   How a Bill Becomes a Law: The Textbook
      Version   265
   How a Bill Really Becomes a Law: The China
      Trade Act of 2000   267
   American Values/American Voices *The Gang*
      of Fourteen and the Search for
      Compromise   *268*

Congress and the President   **271**
   The Shifting Balance of Power   271
   Congressional Oversight of the Executive
      Branch   272

Congress and the Judiciary   **275**

CHAPTER 8 The Presidency   **279**

The Origins of and Rules Governing the Office
   of President of the United States   **281**
   Presidential Qualifications and Terms of Office   282
   Rules of Succession   284
   The Living Constitution *Twenty-Fifth*
      Amendment, Section 2   *285*

The Constitutional Powers of the President   **286**
   The Appointment Power   286

The Power to Convene Congress   287
The Power to Make Treaties   287
Veto Power   288
The Power to Preside over the Military as
   Commander in Chief   289
Join the Debate *The War Powers Act*   *292*
The Pardoning Power   292

The Development and Expansion of Presidential
   Power   **294**
   Establishing Presidential Authority: The First
      Presidents   294
   Incremental Expansion of Presidential Powers:
      1809–1933   295
   The Growth of the Modern Presidency   296
   Politics Now *The Expansion of Presidential*
      Powers   *297*

The Presidential Establishment   **298**
   The Vice President   298
   The Cabinet   299
   The First Lady   300
   The Executive Office of the President (EOP)   301
   The White House Staff   302

The President as Policy Maker   **302**
   The President's Role in Proposing and
      Facilitating Legislation   303
   The Budgetary Process and Legislative
      Implementation   304
   Policy Making Through Regulation   305

Presidential Leadership and the Importance
   of Public Opinion   **306**
   Presidential Leadership   306
   American Values/American Voices *The*
      President and Moral Leadership   *307*
   Going Public: Mobilizing Public Opinion   307

The Public's Perception of Presidential
   Performance   **308**
   Global Perspective *North Korea's Kim Jong II*
      and Uncontrolled Executive Authority   *309*
   Analyzing Visuals *Presidential Approval*
      Ratings Since 1953, by Party   *310*

CHAPTER 9 The Executive Branch
and the Federal Bureaucracy   **315**

The Origins and Growth of the Federal
   Bureaucracy   **317**
   The Civil War and the Growth of Government   318
   From the Spoils System to the Merit System   318
   Regulating the Economy   319

★★★ Preface

It has happened again. As we have prepared every new edition of this book over the last decade, we find ourselves unfailingly surprised, challenged, and ultimately riveted by the dramatic changes that continue to take place across our political landscape. In 1992, the year this book first saw print, we experienced the "Year of the Woman" that produced record numbers of women elected to national office. Then, in 1994, we were greeted with the "Year of the Angry Male Voter" that produced a Republican revolution in Congress. The editions that followed those years appeared during various phases of the Clinton scandals, including the second impeachment trial of a U.S. president. Then came the 2000 election, with an outcome that remained in question until December and appeared to be decided by a single Supreme Court justice; the terrorist attacks of September 11, 2001; and the history-bucking 2002 midterm elections that returned control of both houses of Congress to the Republicans.

Little did we realize that, not long after those midterm elections, one of the longest, most expensive, divisive, and impassioned campaigns ever waged for the presidency was about to get underway. The 2004 national elections were dominated by heated discussion of the preemptive war in Iraq and debates about security and terrorism, the economy, and social issues such as same-sex marriage. A closely divided and hotly charged electorate returned George W. Bush to office for a second term with a majority of the popular vote and a solid win in the Electoral College. And, in 2006, concern over conduct of the war and corruption in Congress resulted in House and Senate Democrats winning control of both bodies and the election of the first female Speaker of the House.

It can never be said that American politics is boring. For every edition of this text, something unexpected or extraordinarily unusual has occurred, giving question to the phrase "politics as usual." At least on the national level, there appears to be little that is usual. Politics and policy form a vital, fascinating process that affects all our daily lives, and we hope that this text reflects that phenomenon and provides you with the tools to understand politics as an evolutionary process where history matters.

In less than a decade, our perceptions of politics, the role of the media, and the utility of voting appear to have undergone tremendous change. Since its inception, this text has tried diligently to reflect those changes and to present information about politics in a manner that actively engages students—many of whom have little interest in politics when they come into the classroom. In this edition, we build on a solid, tried-and-true base and at the same time present information about how politics now seems to be changing ever more rapidly. Thus, we present new information that we hope will whet students' appetites to learn more about politics while providing them with all of the information they need to make informed decisions about their government, politics, and politicians. We very much want our students to make such decisions. We very much want them to *participate*. Our goal with this text is to transmit just this sort of practical, useful information while creating and fostering student interest in American politics despite growing national skepticism about government and government officials at all levels. In fact, we hope that this new edition of our text will explain the national mood about politics and put it in a better context for students to understand their important role in a changing America.

Approach

WE BELIEVE that one cannot fully understand the actions, issues, and policy decisions facing the U.S. government, its constituent states, or "the people" unless these issues are examined from the perspective of how they have evolved over time. Consequently, the title of this book is *American Government: Continuity and Change*. In its pages, we try to examine how the United States is governed today by looking not just at present structures and behavior but also at the *Framers' intentions and how they have been implemented and adapted over the years*. For example, we believe that it is critical to an understanding of the role of political parties in the United States to understand the Framers' fears of factionalism, how parties evolved, and when and why realignments in party identification occurred.

To understand all levels of American government, students must appreciate its constitutional underpinnings. Our text includes a full, *annotated* Constitution of the United States and a boxed feature, "The Living Constitution," to ensure that students understand and appreciate the role of the Constitution in American government and their everyday lives. (More on this in the "Features" section of this Preface.)

In addition to the constitutional and historical origins of American government, we explore issues that the Framers could never have envisioned, and how the basic institutions of government have changed in responding to these new demands. For instance, no one more than two centuries ago could have foreseen election campaigns in an age when nearly all American homes contain television sets, and the Internet allows instant access to information from across the nation and across the globe. Moreover, citizen demands and expectations routinely force government reforms, making an understanding of the dynamics of change essential for introductory students.

Our overriding concern is that students understand their government as it exists today, so that they may become better citizens and make better choices. Careful updating in every edition to reflect the significant events that affect government and citizens alike is crucial to insuring a book that accurately communicates where the United States is as a nation. We believe that by providing students with information about government, and by explaining why it is important and why their participation counts, students will come to see that politics can be a good thing.

In writing this book, we chose to put the institutions of government (Part II) before political behavior (Part III). Both sections, however, were written independently, making them easy to switch for those who prefer to teach about the actors in government and elections before discussing its institutions. To test the book, each of us has taught from it in both orders, with no pedagogical problems.

What's Changed in This Edition?

IN THIS 2008 EDITION of *American Government: Continuity and Change,* we have retained our basic approach to the study of politics as a constantly changing and often unpredictable enterprise. But, we also discuss the dizzying array of important events that have taken place since the preceding edition of the book was published. Most importantly, we include in-depth coverage of the 2006 midterm elections and results. We also discuss the issues that have been the subject of heated debate through the 2004 and 2006 elections and are likely to continue to be debated as we head toward the 2008 presidential election, including the wars in Iraq and Afghanistan, the treatment of those suspected of or accused of terrorism, the federal deficit, and issues such as same-sex marriage. We examine the lobbying and ethics scandals that shook Congress prior to the 2006 elections, as well as government's failed response to Hurricane

Katrina, as of November 2006 the most significant disaster to face the United States since the September 11, 2001, terrorist attacks.

CHAPTER CHANGES

Many of these changes and others are reflected in this 2008 Edition. **Chapter 1** now includes a subsection that discusses the importance of religious faith as an element of shared political culture in the United States, along with updated demographic data and an expanded discussion of the aging U.S. population. The ideology section now discusses the functions of ideology and contrasts traditional conservatism with social conservatism. **Chapter 2** includes new coverage of the Iraqi Constitution and how it compares with the U.S. Constitution. **Chapter 3** opens with a new vignette about governmental responses to Hurricane Katrina and includes an updated discussion of judicial devolution and the Roberts Court. **Chapter 4** covers state-level outcomes in the 2006 midterm elections and how party control of state government can have national ramifications. State minimum wage increase initiatives are also discussed. **Chapter 5** includes an expanded discussion of freedom of assembly in light of protests related to the Iraq War, immigration policy, and genocide in Darfur, Sudan. Key 2006 Supreme Court rulings related to civil liberties (including *Hamdan* v. *Rumsfeld*) and congressional response to those decisions (including the Military Commissions Act) are also covered. **Chapter 6** has been revised to include coverage of civil rights enforcement at the U.S. Department of Justice, 2006 Supreme Court rulings related to civil rights, and living wage campaigns on college campuses. **Chapter 7** includes complete coverage of the outcome of the 2006 midterm elections and the makeup of the 110th Congress, and it features an expanded congressional oversight section. **Chapter 8** considers the impact of approval ratings on President George W. Bush's second-term policy initiatives. **Chapter 9** begins with a new vignette on avian flu planning. It also reflects second-term Bush administration Cabinet reshuffling, including the resignation of Secretary of Defense Donald Rumsfeld following the 2006 elections. **Chapter 10** offers updates on the Supreme Court's 2005–2006 term, including the addition of Chief Justice John G. Roberts Jr. as well as Justice Samuel A. Alito to the Court. **Chapter 11** has been restructured to begin with a thorough discussion of political socialization, polling, and opinion formation, followed by the effects of public opinion and polling on government. **Chapter 12** has been streamlined and extensively updated to reflect the impact of technology and campaign finance reform on party activities. Realignment, critical elections, and secular realignment discussions have been moved to this chapter from Chapter 13. **Chapter 13** features new data and updated figures on election results, voter turnout, and demographics in the 2006 midterm elections, and considers recent efforts to reform the electoral process. **Chapter 14** has a new opening vignette discussing the run-up to the 2008 presidential election and includes an updated and expanded campaign finance discussion. **Chapter 15** features expanded coverage of current media trends, a new section discussing the rules governing the media, an expanded discussion of media effects, and an updated section on debates surrounding media bias. **Chapter 16** includes coverage of lobbying scandals in the 109th Congress and an updated discussion of interest groups' use of the courts to challenge Bush administration policies. **Chapter 17** includes updated coverage of social welfare policies today, including a discussion of the new Medicare Prescription Drug Improvement and Modernization Act and coverage of President George W. Bush's efforts to privatize Social Security. **Chapter 18** includes an updated discussion of the economic policies of the George W. Bush administration, including the economic repercussions of environmental policy related to global warming. **Chapter 19** reflects recent Bush foreign policy efforts, including developments in the Middle East and Asia. Expanded discussions of homeland security efforts, the controversy over the NSA surveillance program, and the impact of reorganization efforts on U.S. intelligence operations are also included.

Features

THE 2008 EDITION has retained the best features and pedagogy from previous editions, enhanced or revised others, and added exciting new ones.

HISTORICAL PERSPECTIVE

Every chapter uses history to serve three purposes: first, to show how institutions and processes have evolved to their present states; second, to provide some of the color that makes information memorable; and third, to provide students with a more thorough appreciation that our government was born amid burning issues of representation and power, issues that continue to smolder today. A richer historical texture helps to explain the present.

COMPARATIVE PERSPECTIVE

Changes in the Middle East, Russia and Eastern Europe, North America, South America, and Asia all remind us of the preeminence of democracy, in theory if not always in fact. As new democratic experiments spring up around the globe (e.g., Iraq), it becomes increasingly important for students to understand the rudiments of presidential versus parliamentary government and of multiparty versus two-party systems. *Global Perspective* boxes, all of which have been substantially revised or written new for this edition, compare issues, politics, and institutions in the United States with those of both industrialized democracies and non-Western countries, such as Iraq and North Korea.

ENHANCED PEDAGOGY

We have revised and enhanced many pedagogical features to help students become stronger political thinkers and to echo the book's theme of evolution and change.

Preview and Review To pique students' interest and draw them into each chapter, we begin each chapter with a contemporary vignette. These vignettes deal with current issues of high interest to students and are intended to whet their appetites to read the rest of the chapter. Each vignette is followed by a bridge paragraph linking the vignette with the chapter's topics and by an outline previewing the chapter's major headings. Chapter summaries at the conclusion of each chapter restate the major points made under each of these same major headings.

Key Terms All boldfaced key terms are defined in the margin of the text where the term appears. Key terms are listed at the end of each chapter, with page references for review and study. An end-of-text glossary of the text's key terms is also provided.

Special Features The text is supported and enhanced by a number of boxed features. These features are designed to enhance student understanding of the political processes, institutions, and policies of American government. Features include:

- *American Values/American Voices.* New to this edition, these features examine the shared values that unite American citizens. American political culture, with its emphasis on liberty, equality, and individualism, as well as other values, is the glue that holds Americans together. Differing views of what it means to adhere to these values, however, often create conflict and division—especially in the policy arena. American Values/American Voices boxes are intended to help students understand the passionate beliefs and common concerns that underlie the controversies being debated on Capitol Hill, in the media, and in statehouses and homes across the United States. Topics discussed include U.S. efforts to promote democracy abroad, changes in government policy related to the establishment clause, voting rights for ex-felons, and Iraq War veterans running for office in the 2006 midterm elections.

- *Annotated Constitution of the United States.* Appearing between chapters 2 and 3, this copy of the Constitution features comprehensive commentary on the meaning and context of the most significant articles, sections, and amendments. These annotations allow students to understand not only the Constitution's language, but also *why* it was fashioned as it was and its continued relevance today. For instance, students learn everything from why Article I is the longest and most detailed portion of the Constitution to why the "full faith and credit" clause, rarely controversial, now becomes so in the context of same-sex marriage. The Constitution was annotated with the significant help of a constitutional expert and dedicated undergraduate teacher, Gregg Ivers, of American University.

- *The Living Constitution.* These boxes, which appear in every chapter, examine the constitutional context of each chapter's topic. Every box excerpts and explains a relevant portion of the Constitution, analyzes what the Framers were responding to when it was written, and examines how it is still relevant today. For instance, chapter 5 includes a box on the Ninth Amendment, a discussion of the impossibility of enumerating every fundamental liberty and right, and the Supreme Court's ruling—nonetheless—in favor of a host of fundamental liberties since 1965.

- *On Campus.* These popular boxes, which appear in most chapters, focus in particular on material that we believe will be of great interest to college students. To that end, this feature examines issues of concern to college campuses, as well as issues, events, and legislation that were initiated on college campuses and that had an impact on the larger arena of American politics. Chapter 6, for example, discusses living wage campaigns on campus. Chapter 16 discusses the impact of conservative interest groups on campus.

- *Join the Debate.* To engage students in critical thinking, foster interest in important issues, and help inspire their participation through involvement in decision making, we developed the *Join the Debate* feature. Heavily revised to remain current and resonant to both instructors and students, this feature introduces provocative issues under debate today and explores those issues by suggesting arguments for and against them. Topics such as chapter 7's minority party rights in Congress and chapter 10's Senate advise and consent are accompanied by supporting questions and selected reading suggestions from the authors. These features are designed to prompt students to examine various arguments in the debate, consider larger context, and take a position on issues that matter in American government today.

- *Global Perspective.* Recognizing that students benefit from understanding the commonalities and differences between the United States and other nations, Global Perspective boxes provide students with a comparative perspective on a range of issues. Some features examine a key topic such as freedom of the press, economic freedom, or American exceptionalism, while others focus on comparing an element of a foreign nation with a corresponding aspect of the United States. Features new to this edition include examinations of the Iraqi Constitution (chapter 2), the Mexican federal system (chapter 3), the Israeli Knesset (chapter 7), and the North Korean executive (chapter 8).

- *Politics Now.* These boxes provide in-depth examinations of contemporary issues, showcasing the book's currency and serving as a counterbalance to the text's thorough treatment of America's origins and history. Chapter 7, for example, discusses the efforts of a group of Muslim congressional staffers to educate members of

Congress about their religion, while chapter 10 examines the new Roberts Court and its likely impact on American jurisprudence.

■ *Analyzing Visuals.* These boxed features appear in every chapter and ask students to closely examine and assess a variety of different types of images, including photographs, tables, bar graphs, line graphs, and maps. Students are encouraged to analyze and interpret the visual information themselves, using the introductory paragraph and critical thinking questions provided to guide them. An introductory primer, *Analyzing Visuals: A Brief Guide* (see pages xxxiv–xxxvii), offers a foundation for analyzing and interpreting different kinds of visuals that students will encounter in the text and in their daily lives.

■ *Web Explorations.* The end of each chapter contains relevant links to the World Wide Web. Web Explorations encourage students to learn more and think critically about the key concepts in each chapter.

■ *MyPoliSciLab.* Throughout the text, students will find icons (see pages xxvii–xxviii for samples) in the text margins that direct them to relevant simulations, visual literacy exercises, and other activities that appear in Longman's online resource, MyPoliSciLab (see below).

The Ancillary Package

THE ANCILLARY PACKAGE for *American Government: Continuity and Change,* 2008 Edition, provides instructors and students with materials that allow them to augment, review, and better understand the materials covered in the textbook. We strive for comprehensiveness and accuracy, while seeking to provide a range of options suited for instructors and students at a variety of institutions.

INSTRUCTOR SUPPLEMENTS FOR QUALIFIED COLLEGE ADOPTERS

Instructor's Manual (ISBN 0-321-48137-2) Written by Sue Davis of Denison University, this comprehensive manual is designed to help instructors prepare lectures, classroom activities, and assignments. The manual features chapter outlines and summaries, a broad range of teaching suggestions, ideas for student research, and suggestions for discussion that complement text themes.

Test Bank written by author Karen O'Connor of American University (ISBN 0-321-47998-X) Contains hundreds of multiple choice, true-false, and essay questions along with an answer key. The test bank has been completely rewritten for this edition, and all questions have been written, reviewed, and class tested by Karen O'Connor herself. The test questions offer a range of difficulty from which instructors can choose, and they cover each chapter (including boxed features) comprehensively.

TestGen-EQ Computerized Testing System (ISBN 0-321-48298-0) This flexible, easy-to-master computerized test bank includes all the test items in the printed test bank. The software allows professors to edit existing questions and to add their own items. Tests can be printed in several different formats and can include features such as graphs and tables. It is available for Windows and Macintosh computers.

Digital Media Archive CD-ROM (ISBN 0-321-27068-1) This complete multimedia presentation tool for instructors includes more than 150 maps, graphs, and charts; 100 photos; and 50 video clips—all on one CD-ROM and ready for inclusion in an instructor's online course, PowerPoint® presentations, and websites. It was developed in consultation with Kurt Cline, California State University, Fresno; Martin S. Edwards, Texas Tech University; Scott R. Furlong, University of Wisconsin, Green Bay; James M. Lutz, Indiana University Purdue University, Fort Wayne; and John David Rausch, Jr., West Texas A&M University.

American Government Study Site (www.longmanamericangovernment.com) This online course companion provides a wealth of resources for students and instructors using Longman American government texts. Containing practice tests, flashcards, and Web explorations, the Study Site for American government helps students quickly master the fundamentals, review a subject for understanding, or prepare for an exam.

PowerPoint® Presentation A lecture-outline presentation to accompany all the chapters of this new edition along with complete graphics from the book. Visit the Instructor Resource Center at **www.ablongman.com/irc** to download the presentations. Contact your local Longman representative to gain access to the site.

Transparencies (ISBN 0-321-48134-8) Full-color acetates of the figures from all chapters of the book.

Longman Political Science Video Program Qualified adopters can peruse our list of videos for the American government classroom. Contact your local Allyn & Bacon/Longman representative for more information.

STUDENT SUPPLEMENTS FOR QUALIFIED COLLEGE ADOPTERS

MyPoliSciLab This state-of-the-art, interactive, online solution for the American government course, fully integrated in the course management system of your choice—CourseCompass®, WebCT, or Blackboard—or as an independent website free of a course management system altogether, is available at no additional charge when bundled with a copy of this text and contains the following features:

- *Assessment.* For each chapter of the text, students will navigate through a comprehensive pre-test, post-test, and a full chapter exam, all fully integrated with an online e-book version of this text so students can assess, review, and improve their understanding of the text chapters.

- *Interactive Activities.* Developed and revised by a team of more than 15 political science faculty, *MyPoliSciLab* features more than 100 highly interactive activities, all updated and revised—including comparative activities, visual literacy exercises, interactive timelines, participation exercises, and **more than 30 simulations**—for all of the major topics in the course.

- *Roundtable Discussion Video Clips.* Added and updated throughout the semester, these 10- to 12-minute video clips consist of three professors discussing important concepts covered in the text. Dozens of key concepts (such as campaign finance reform) and critical questions (such as, "Is Federalism Dead?") are discussed from a wide range of perspectives and viewpoints, providing students with a balanced review of key course material. Each discussion is accompanied by critical thinking prompts, multiple-choice questions, and transcripts for reference.

- *Debate Video Clips.* Updated throughout the semester and offering lively, challenging debates from two sides of an issue, these 10- to 12-minute clips feature two professors discussing hot-button issues and answering pressing questions such as, "Does the Patriot Act Violate American Civil Liberties?" Each discussion is accompanied by critical thinking prompts, multiple-choice questions, and transcripts for reference.

- *Student Polling.* Updated weekly with timely, provocative questions, this new feature allows students to participate in nationwide polls on hot topics. Students are asked to vote on questions such as, "Should flag burning be permitted?" Results of the thousands of student responses around the country are immediately displayed.

- *PoliSci News.* PoliSci News contains an online feed from the *New York Times* that is updated *hourly*; an exclusive *New York Times* database that allows students to browse by subject area or search for a specific topic; and PoliSci News Review, a series of articles selected by a political science professor that recaps the previous week's most important political events and are followed by quizzes and critical thinking questions.

- *Author's Choice.* With so many incredible activities to assign, the authors of this book have hand selected one or two activities that best complement or amplify each chapter. You have the work done for you in easy-to-use, prepackaged My-PoliSciLab assignments. If you only have time to assign and complete one activity for the chapter, the Author's Choice designation makes it easy!

- *Author Podcasts.* Throughout the 2007-2008 academic year, podcasts of author lectures will be added to MyPoliSciLab, giving you the opportunity to expose your students to dynamic new voices and offer "guest lecturers" on key topics. Contact your local Longman representative for more information.

- *Research Navigator™.* The EBSCO ContentSelect Academic Journal Database content is collected from thousands of articles organized by discipline and fully searchable. Articles in popular periodicals such as *Newsweek* and *USA Today* are included as well, giving students and professors access to topical content from a variety of sources.

- *Link Library.* Offers editorially selected "Best of the Web" sites. Libraries are continually scanned and kept up-to-date, providing the most relevant and accurate links for research assignments.

- *Writing Resources.* Topics include Avoiding Plagiarism, Finding Sources, Using Your Library, Start Writing, Internet Research, and Citing Sources.

- *Online e-Book.* Matching the exact layout of the printed textbook, the online e-book contains multimedia icons in the margins that launch to exciting resources (e.g., simulations or videos), which expand on key topics students encounter as they read through the text.

- *Online Administration.* Instructors can easily track student work on the site and monitor students' progress on each activity. The *Instructor Gradebook*, which includes upgraded functionality to ensure a truly seamless experience for users, provides maximum flexibility allowing instructors to sort by student, activity, or to view the entire class in spreadsheet view.

See the advertisement at the front of this text for more information.

Great Questions in Politics Written by some of the most influential scholars and thinkers in political science, each book in this series examines a major question in American politics, offers a new perspective on our political system, and challenges conventional wisdom and prevailing attitudes.

Package any of the Great Questions in Politics books with this book and receive a 10 percent discount.

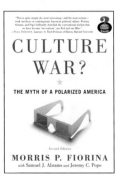

- *Culture War? The Myth of a Polarized America,* Morris. P. Fiorina, Stanford University; Samuel J. Abrams, Harvard University; and Jeremy C. Pope, Stanford University (ISBN 0-321-36606-9) This text combines polling data with a compelling narrative to debunk commonly believed myths about American politics—particularly the claim that Americans are deeply divided in their fundamental political views.

■ *Governing by Campaigning: The Politics of the Bush Presidency*, 2007 Edition, George C. Edwards III, Texas A&M University (ISBN 0-205-52962-3) This brief volume, by one of the foremost experts on the presidency, explores how the Bush administration has attempted sweeping changes in public policy—without broad support for doing so—by taking its case to the American public more than any other president in history.

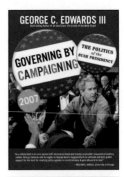

■ *A Divider, Not a Uniter: George W. Bush and the American People: The 2006 Election and Beyond*, Gary C. Jacobson, University of California, San Diego (ISBN 0-205-52974-7) This brief, engaging book is rich in data and analyzes the reasons the public is so divided along party lines about George W. Bush.

■ *Is Voting for Young People? with Postscript on New Forms of Citizen Engagement*, Martin P. Wattenberg, University of California, Irvine (ISBN 0-205-51807-9) This accessible, provocative, and brief book explores the reasons the young are less and less likely to follow politics and vote in the United States, as well as many other established democracies, and suggests ways of changing that.

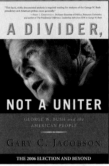

■ *Seven Sins of American Foreign Policy*, Loch K. Johnson, University of Georgia (ISBN 0-321-41585-X) This brief, accessible book by renowned intelligence and foreign policy expert, Loch Johnson, examines seven major shortcomings—"sins"—in American foreign policy over several administrations that have generated pervasive negative attitudes toward the United States, cost us friendship and support, and impaired our ability to advance our international interests.

■ *Congressional Travels: Places, Connections, and Authenticity*, Richard F. Fenno Jr., University of Rochester (ISBN 0-321-47071-0) This book argues that authenticity—knowing what a representative is like in his or her district and looking beyond mere roll-call voting—contributes significantly to understanding the full body of work done by our members of Congress. It further posits, by recounting Fenno's life's work, that the best way to gain a sense of authenticity is to do what Fenno is most famous for—making multiple trips and spending a great deal of time observing representatives at home, with their constituents, in their districts.

Study Site for American Government (www.longmanamericangovernment.com) This online course companion provides a wealth of resources for students and instructors using Longman American government texts. Containing practice tests, flashcards, and Web explorations, the Study Site for American government helps students quickly master the fundamentals, review a subject for understanding, or prepare for an exam.

Study Guide (ISBN 0-321-47995-5) Written by John Ben Sutter of Houston Community College. The printed study guide features chapter outlines, key terms, a variety of practice tests, and critical thinking questions to help students learn.

Research Navigator and Research Navigator Guide Research Navigator is a comprehensive website comprising four exclusive databases of credible and reliable source material for research and for student assignments: EBSCO's ContentSelect Academic Journal Database, the *New York Times* Search by Subject Archive, the *Financial Times* Article Archive and Company Financials, "Best of the Web" Link Library. The site also includes an extensive help section. The Research Navigator Guide provides your students with access to the Research Navigator website and includes reference material and hints about conducting online research. Available at no additional charge to qualified college adopters when packaged with the text.

Voices of Dissent: Critical Readings in American Politics, Seventh Edition (ISBN 0-205-56001-6) Edited by William F. Grover, St. Michael's College, and Joseph G. Peschek, Hamline University, this collection of critical essays goes beyond the debate between mainstream liberalism and conservatism to fundamentally challenge the status quo. Available at a discount when ordered packaged with the text.

You Decide! Current Debates in American Politics, 2007 Edition

(ISBN: 0-321-43016-6) Edited by John T. Rourke, University of Connecticut, this exciting debate-style reader is updated annually and examines provocative issues in American politics *today*. The topics have been selected for their currency, importance, and student interest, and the pieces that argue various sides of a given issue come from recent journals, congressional hearings, think tanks, and periodicals.

American Government: Readings and Cases, Seventeenth Edition

(ISBN: 0-321-47314-0) Edited by Peter Woll, Brandeis University, this longtime best-selling reader provides a strong, balanced blend of classic readings and cases that illustrate and amplify important concepts in American government, alongside extremely current selections drawn from today's issues and literature. Available at a discount when ordered packaged with this text.

Ten Things That Every American Government Student Should Read

(ISBN 0-205-28969-X) We asked American government instructors across the country to vote for 10 things beyond the text that they believe every student should read and put them in this brief and useful reader edited by Karen O'Connor of the American University. Available at no additional charge when ordered packaged with the text.

Choices: An American Government Database Reader

This customizable reader allows instructors to choose from a database of more than 300 readings to create a reader that exactly matches their course needs. Go to www.pearsoncustom. com/database/choices.html for more information.

Newsweek Magazine Discount Subscription

Students receive 12 issues of Newsweek at more than 80 percent off the regular price. An excellent way for students to keep up with current events.

New York Times Discount Subscription

A 10-week subscription for only $20! Contact your local Allyn & Bacon/Longman representative for more information.

Penguin-Longman Value Bundles

Longman offers 25 Penguin Putnam titles at more than a 60 percent discount when packaged with any Longman text. A totally unique offer and a wonderful way to enhance students' understanding of concepts in American government. Please go to **www.ablongman.com/penguin** for more information.

Writing in Political Science, Third Edition

(ISBN 0-321-21735-7) Written by Diane Schmidt, California State University-Chico, this guide takes students step-by-step through all aspects of writing in political science. Available at a discount when ordered packaged with any Longman textbook.

LONGMAN STATE POLITICS SERIES

Texas, Fourth Edition

(ISBN 0-321-38459-8) Written by Debra St. John, this is a 90-page primer on state and local government and political issues in Texas. Available at no additional cost when shrink-wrapped with the text.

Annotated 1876 Texas Constitution

(ISBN 0-321-35533-4) Annotated by Stefan D. Haag, Austin Community College, this supplement offers the full 1876

Texas Constitution integrated with a detailed primer examining the meaning and context of the Constitution's most significant language. This ancillary helps give students a deep understanding of what the 1876 Texas Constitution says, why it included the language it did, and what role this seminal document plays in the lives of Texans today.

California, **Fifth Edition** (ISBN 0-321-42764-5) Written by Barbara Stone, this is a 70-page primer on state and local government and political issues in California. Available at no additional cost when shrink-wrapped with the text.

Florida (ISBN 0-321-42763-7) Written by George Gonzalez, this is a 50-page primer on state and local government and political issues in Florida. Available at no additional cost when shrink-wrapped with the text.

Georgia (ISBN 0-321-42765-3) Written by Said L. Sewell and F. Carl Walton, this is a 70-page primer on state and local government and political issues in Georgia. Available at no additional cost when shrink-wrapped with the text.

Acknowledgments

Karen O'Connor thanks the thousands of students in her American Government courses at Emory and American University who, over the years, have pushed her to learn more about American government and to have fun in the process. She especially thanks her American University colleagues who offered books and suggestions for this most recent revision—especially David Lublin. Her former professor and longtime friend and co-author, Nancy E. McGlen, has offered support for more than two decades. Her former students, too, have contributed in various ways to this project, especially John R. Hermann, Paul Fabrizio, Bernadette Nye, Sue Davis, Laura van Assendelft, and Sarah E. Brewer.

For the last two editions of the book, Alixandra B. Yanus of the University of North Carolina, Chapel Hill, has offered invaluable assistance and unflagging support. Her fresh perspectives on politics and ideas about things of interest to students, as well as her keen eye for the typo, her research abilities, and her unbelievably hard work, have made this a much better book.

Larry J. Sabato would like to acknowledge all of the students from his University of Virginia Introduction to American Politics classes and the many student interns at the UVA Center for Politics who have offered many valuable suggestions and an abundance of thoughtful feedback. A massive textbook project like this one needs the very best assistance an author can find, and this author was lucky enough to find some marvelously talented people. Howard Ernst, associate professor of political science at the United States Naval Academy, and Zach Courser, a former University of Virginia graduate student who is now teaching at Claremont McKenna College, worked endless hours researching the new edition and weaving together beautifully constructed sections on recent American politics. In addition, Drew Kurlowski, a Ph.D. candidate at the University of Virginia, took great care in updating sections related to the 2006 midterm elections. Other current and former Center for Politics staff members, interns, and colleagues who helped with this and previous editions include, but are not limited to, Colin Allen, Molly Clancy, Bruce Larson, Gregg Lindskog, James Patterson, Ryan Rakness, Joshua Scott, Greg Smith, Matthew Smyth, and Matthew Wikswo. Finally, Larry extends his thanks to the faculty and staff of the Department of Politics at UVA, especially Debbie Best and Sid Milkis, chair of the department.

Particular thanks from both of us go to Dennis L. Dresang at the University of Wisconsin, Madison, who has once again brought a keen eye and insightful analysis to chapter 4 (State and Local Government); Christopher Borick at Muhlenberg College, who thoroughly revised chapters 17 and 18 (Social Welfare Policy and Economic Policy); and Kiki Caruson of the University of South Florida, who tackled the rapidly shifting landscape of chapter 19 (Foreign and Defense Policy) for this edition. Our continued thanks go to Steven Koven at the University of Louisville and Daniel S. Papp of the University System of Georgia, whose earlier work on these chapters continues to serve as such a strong foundation. We also thank Brian Bearry of the University of Texas at Dallas for his help with many of the Join the Debate and Global Perspective features.

In the now many years we have been writing and rewriting this book, we have been blessed to have been helped by many people at Macmillan, Allyn & Bacon, and now Longman. Eric Stano has been a fantastic editor as well as fun to work with. Our new development editor, Melissa Mashburn, has been a stern taskmaster with a political junkie's eye for extensive updating. Our marketing manager, Elizabeth Fogarty, has done a terrific job. We would also like to acknowledge the tireless efforts of the Longman sales force. In the end, we hope that all of these talented people see how much their work and support have helped us to write a better book.

Many of our peers reviewed past editions of the book and earned our gratitude in the process:

Danny Adkison, *Oklahoma State University*

Weston H. Agor, *University of Texas at El Paso*

Victor Aikhionbare, *Salt Lake Community College*

James Anderson, *Texas A&M University*

Judith Baer, *Texas A&M University*

Ruth Bamberger, *Drury College*

Christine Barbour, *Indiana University*

Ken Baxter, *San Joaquin Delta College*

Brian Bearry, *University of Texas at Dallas*

Jon Bond, *Texas A&M University*

Stephen A. Borrelli, *University of Alabama*

Ann Bowman, *University of South Carolina*

Robert C. Bradley, *Illinois State University*

Gary Brown, *Montgomery College*

John Francis Burke, *University of Houston–Downtown*

Kevin Buterbaugh, *Northwest Missouri State University*

Mark Byrnes, *Middle Tennessee State University*

Greg Caldeira, *Ohio State University*

John H. Calhoun, *Palm Beach Atlantic University*

David E. Camacho, *Northern Arizona University*

Alan R. Carter, *Schenectady County Community College*

Carl D. Cavalli, *North Georgia College and State University*

Steve Chan, *University of Colorado*

Richard Christofferson Sr. *University of Wisconsin–Stevens Point*

David Cingranelli, *SUNY Binghamton*

Clarke E. Cochran, *Texas Tech University*

Paul W. Cook, *Cy-Fair College*

Kevin Corder, *Western Michigan University*

Anne N. Costain, *University of Colorado*

Cary Covington, *University of Iowa*

Lorrie Clemo, *SUNY Oswego*

Stephen C. Craig, *University of Florida*

Lane Crothers, *Illinois State University*

Abraham L. Davis, *Morehouse College*

Robert DiClerico, *West Virginia University*

John Dinan, *Wake Forest University*

John Domino, *Sam Houston State University*

Keith L. Dougherty, *University of Georgia*

David E. Dupree, *Victor Valley College*

Craig F. Emmert, *Texas Tech University*

Walle Engedayehu, *Prairie View A&M University*

Alan S. Engel, *Miami University*

Timothy Fackler, *University of Nevada, Las Vegas*

Frank B. Feigert, *University of North Texas*

Terri S. Fine, *University of Central Florida*

Evelyn Fink, *University of Nebraska*

Scott R. Furlong, *University of Wisconsin–Green Bay*

James D. Gleason, *Victoria College*

Dana K. Glencross, *Oklahoma City Community College*
Sheldon Goldman, *University of Massachusetts, Amherst*
Doris Graber, *University of Illinois at Chicago*
Jeffrey D. Green, *University of Montana*
Roger W. Green, *University of North Dakota*
James Michael Greig, *University of North Texas*
Charles Hadley, *University of New Orleans*
Mel Hailey, *Abilene Christian University*
William K. Hall, *Bradley University*
Robert L. Hardgrave Jr. *University of Texas at Austin*
Chip Hauss, *George Mason University/University of Reading*
Stacia L. Haynie, *Louisiana State University*
John R. Hermann, *Trinity University*
Marjorie Hershey, *Indiana University*
Justin Holmes, *University of Minnesota*
Steven Alan Holmes, *Bakersfield College*
Tim Howard, *North Harris College*
John C. Hughes, *Oklahoma City Community College*
Jon Hurwitz, *SUNY Buffalo*
Thomas Hyde, *Pfeiffer University*
Joseph Ignagni, *University of Texas at Arlington*
Willoughby Jarrell, *Kennesaw State College*
Susan M. Johnson, *University of Wisconsin–Whitewater*
Dennis Judd, *University of Missouri–St. Louis*
Carol J. Kamper, *Rochester Community College*
David Kennedy, *Montgomery College*
Kenneth Kennedy, *College of San Mateo*
Donald F. Kettl, *University of Wisconsin*
Quentin Kidd, *Christopher Newport University*
John Kincaid, *Lafayette College*
Karen M. King, *Bowling Green State University*
Alec Kirby, *University of Wisconsin–Stout*
John F. Kozlowicz, *University of Wisconsin–Whitewater*
Jonathan E. Kranz, *John Jay College of Criminal Justice*
John C. Kuzenski, *The Citadel*
Mark Landis, *Hofstra University*
Sue Lee, *North Lake College*

Ted Lewis, *Collin County Community College*
Brad Lockerbie, *University of Georgia*
Cecilia Manrique, *University of Wisconsin–La Crosse*
Larry Martinez, *California State University–Long Beach*
Lynn Mather, *SUNY Buffalo*
Laurel A. Mayer, *Sinclair Community College*
Steve Mazurana, *University of Northern Colorado*
Clifton McCleskey, *University of Virginia*
Percival Robert McDonagh, *Catholic University*
James L. McDowell, *Indiana State University*
Carl E. Meacham, *SUNY Oneonta*
Stephen S. Meinhold, *University of North Carolina–Wilmington*
John Mercurio, *San Diego State University*
Mark C. Miller, *Clark University*
Kenneth F. Mott, *Gettysburg College*
Joseph Nogee, *University of Houston*
John O'Callaghan, *Suffolk University*
Bruce Oppenheimer, *Vanderbilt University*
Richard Pacelle, *Georgia Southern University*
Marian Lief Palley, *University of Delaware*
David R. Penna, *Gallaudet University*
Richard M. Pious, *Columbia University*
David H. Provost, *California State University–Fresno*
Lawrence J. Redlinger, *University of Texas at Dallas*
James A. Rhodes, *Luther College*
Leroy N. Rieselbach, *Indiana University*
David Robertson, *Public Policy Research Centers, University of Missouri–St. Louis*
David Robinson, *University of Houston–Downtown*
Norman Rodriguez, *John Wood Community College*
David W. Rohde, *Duke University*
Frank Rourke, *Johns Hopkins University*
Donald Roy, *Ferris State University*
Ronald Rubin, *City University of New York, Borough of Manhattan Community College*
Bruce L. Sanders, *MacComb Community College*

Denise Scheberle, *University of Wisconsin–Green Bay*

Gaye Lynn Scott, *Austin Community College*

Martin P. Sellers, *Campbell University*

Daniel M. Shea, *University of Akron*

John N. Short, *University of Arkansas–Monticello*

Michael Eric Siegel, *American University*

Mark Silverstein, *Boston University*

James R. Simmons, *University of Wisconsin–Oshkosh*

Andrea Simpson, *University of Richmond*

Philip M. Simpson, *Cameron University*

Elliott E. Slotnick, *Ohio State University*

Michael W. Sonnleitner, *Portland Community College*

Frank J. Sorauf, *University of Minnesota*

Gerald Stanglin, *Cedar Valley College*

C. S. Tai, *University of Arkansas–Pine Bluff*

Leena Thacker-Kumer, *University of Houston–Downtown*

Richard J. Timpone, *SUNY Stony Brook*

Albert C. Waite, *Central Texas College*

Brian Walsh, *University of Maryland*

Shirley Anne Warshaw, *Gettysburg College*

Matt Wetstein, *San Joaquin Delta College*

Richard Whaley, *Marian College*

Rich Whisonant, *York Technical College*

Martin Wiseman, *Mississippi State University*

Kevan Yenerall, *Bridgewater College*

Finally, we'd also like to thank our peers who reviewed and aided in the development of the current edition:

William Arp, *Southern University, Baton Rouge*

Vanessa Baird, *University of Colorado, Boulder*

Holly Brasher, *University of Alabama, Birmingham*

Michelle Brophy-Baermann, *University of Wisconsin*

Tracy Cook, *Central Texas College*

Jerry Hopkins, *East Texas Baptist University*

Ngozi Kamalu, *Fayetteville State University*

Ken Kennedy, *College of San Mateo*

Aaron Knight, *Houston Community College*

Matt Lindstrom, *St. John's University*

Susan MacFarland, *Gainesville College*

Ron Pettus, *St. Charles Community College*

Thomas Rowan, *Chicago State University*

David Sprick, *University of Missouri, Kansas City*

Harold Wingfield, *Kennesaw State University*

Analyzing Visuals: A Brief Guide

The information age requires a new, more expansive definition of literacy. Visual literacy—the ability to analyze, interpret, synthesize, and apply visual information—is essential in today's world. We receive much information from the written and spoken word, but much also comes from visual forms. We are used to thinking about reading written texts critically—for example, reading a textbook carefully for information, sometimes highlighting or underlining as we go along—but we do not always think about "reading" visuals in this way. We should, for images and informational graphics can tell us a lot if we read and consider them carefully. In order to emphasize these skills, this edition of *American Government: Continuity and Change* contains an *Analyzing Visuals* feature in each chapter. The features are intended to prompt you to think about the images and informational graphics you will encounter throughout this text, as well as those you see every day in the newspaper, in magazines, on the Web, on television, and in books. We provide critical thinking questions to assist you in learning how to analyze visuals. Though we focus on one visual in each chapter, we encourage you to examine carefully and ask similar questions of *all* the visuals in this text, and those you encounter elsewhere in your study of and participation in American government.

We look at several types of visuals in the chapters: tables, graphs and charts, maps, news photographs, and political cartoons. This brief guide provides some information about these types of visuals and offers a few questions to guide your analysis of each type.

Tables

Tables are the least "visual" of the visuals we explore. Tables consist of textual information and/or numerical data arranged in tabular form, in columns and rows. Tables are frequently used when exact information is required and when orderly arrangement is necessary to locate and, in many cases, to compare the information. For example, a table comparing Supreme Court decisions to public opinion poll information makes comparisons of the data visually accessible.

TABLE 10.8 **THE SUPREME COURT AND THE AMERICAN PUBLIC**			
In recent years, the Court's rulings have agreed with or diverged from public opinion on various questions, such as:			
Issue	*Case*	*Court Decision*	*Public Opinion*
Should homosexual relations between consenting adults be legal?	*Lawrence v. Texas* (2003)	Yes	Maybe (50%)
Should members of Congress be subject to term limits?	*U.S. Term Limits v. Thornton* (1995)	No	Yes (77% favor)
Is affirmative action constitutional?	*Grutter v. Bollinger* (2003) *Gratz v. Bollinger* (2003)	Yes	Yes (64%)
Before getting an abortion, whose consent should a teenager be required to gain?	*Williams v. Zbaraz* (1980)	One parent	Both parents (38%) One parent (37%) Neither parent (22%)
Is the death penalty constitutional?	*Gregg v. Georgia* (1976)	Yes	Yes (72% favor)
Source: Table compiled from Lexis-Nexis RPOLL.			

Here are a few questions to guide your analysis:

- What is the purpose of the table? What information does it show? There is usually a title that offers a sense of the table's purpose.

- What information is provided in the column headings (provided in the top row)? How are the rows labeled?

- Is there a time period indicated, such as January to June 2007? Or, are the data as of a specific date, such as June 30, 2007?

- If the table shows numerical data, what do these data represent? In what units? Dollars a special interest lobby provides to a political party? Percentages of men and women responding in a particular way to a poll question about the president's performance? Estimated life expectancy in years?

- What is the source of the information presented in the table?

Charts and Graphs

Charts and graphs depict numerical data in visual forms. The most common kinds of graphs plot data in two dimensions along horizontal and vertical axes. Examples that you will encounter throughout this text are line graphs, pie charts, and bar graphs. These kinds of visuals emphasize data relationships: at a particular point in time, at regular intervals over a fixed period of time, or, sometimes, as parts of a whole. Line graphs show a progression, usually over time (as in Social Security Costs and Revenues, 1970–2080). Pie charts (such as the distribution of federal civilian employment) demonstrate how a whole (total federal civilian employment) is divided into its parts (employees in each branch). Bar graphs compare values across categories, showing how proportions are related to each other (as in the numbers of women and minorities in Congress). Bar graphs can present data either horizontally or vertically.

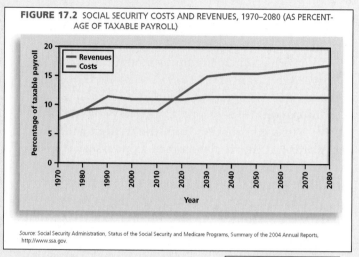

FIGURE 17.2 SOCIAL SECURITY COSTS AND REVENUES, 1970–2080 (AS PERCENTAGE OF TAXABLE PAYROLL)

Source: Social Security Administration, Status of the Social Security and Medicare Programs, Summary of the 2004 Annual Reports, http://www.ssa.gov.

Here are a few questions to guide your analysis:

- What is the purpose of the chart or graph? What information does it provide? Or, what is being measured? There is usually a title that indicates the subject and purpose of the figure.

- Is there a time period shown, such as January to June 2007? Or, are the data as of a specific date, such as June 30, 2007? Are the data shown at multiple intervals over a fixed period, or at one particular point in time?

- What do the units represent? Dollars a candidate spends on a campaign? Number of voters versus number of nonvoters in Texas? If there are two or more sets of figures, what are the relationships among them?

- What is the source? Is it government information? Private polling information? A newspaper? A private organization? A corporation? An individual?

- Is the type of chart or graph appropriate for the information that is provided? For example, a line graph assumes a smooth progression from one data point to the next. Is that assumption valid for the data shown?

- Is there distortion in the visual representation of the information? Are the intervals equal? Does the area shown distort the actual amount or the proportion?

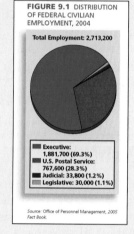

FIGURE 9.1 DISTRIBUTION OF FEDERAL CIVILIAN EMPLOYMENT, 2004

Total Employment: 2,713,200

- Executive: 1,881,700 (69.3%)
- U.S. Postal Service: 767,600 (28.3%)
- Judicial: 33,800 (1.2%)
- Legislative: 30,000 (1.1%)

Source: Office of Personnel Management, *2005 Fact Book.*

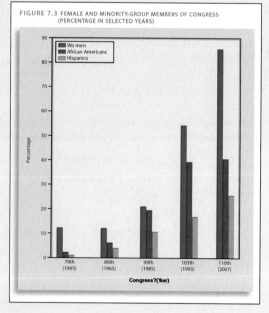

FIGURE 7.3 FEMALE AND MINORITY-GROUP MEMBERS OF CONGRESS (PERCENTAGE IN SELECTED YEARS)

Maps

Maps—of the United States, of particular regions, or of the world—are frequently used in political analysis to illustrate demographic, social, economic, and political issues and trends.

Here are a few questions to guide your analysis:

- Is there a title that identifies the purpose or subject of the map?

- What does the map key/legend show? What are the factors that the map is analyzing?

- What is the region being shown?

- What source is given for the map?

- Maps usually depict a specific point in time. What is the point in time being shown on the map?

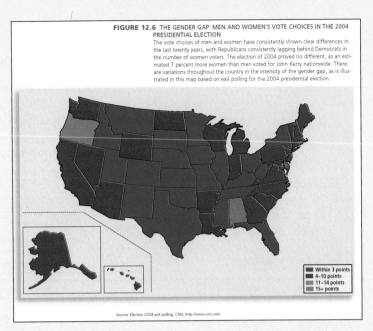

FIGURE 12.6 THE GENDER GAP: MEN AND WOMEN'S VOTE CHOICES IN THE 2004 PRESIDENTIAL ELECTION

The vote choices of men and women have consistently shown clear differences in the last twenty years, with Republicans consistently lagging behind Democrats in the number of women voters. The election of 2004 proved no different, as an estimated 7 percent more women than men voted for John Kerry nationwide. There are variations throughout the country in the intensity of the gender gap, as is illustrated in this map based on exit polling for the 2004 presidential election.

Within 3 points
4–10 points
11–14 points
15+ points

Source: Election 2004 exit polling, CNN, http://www.cnn.com.

News Photographs

If a picture is worth a thousand words, it is no wonder that our newspapers, magazines, and television news broadcasts rely on photographs as well as words to report and analyze the news. Photos can have a dramatic—and often immediate—impact on politics and government. Think about some photos that have political significance. For example, do you remember photos from the September 11, 2001, terrorist attack on the World Trade Center? Visual images usually evoke a stronger emotional response from people than do written descriptions. For this reason, individuals and organizations have learned to use photographs as a means to document events, make arguments, offer evidence, and even in some cases to manipulate the viewer into having a particular response.

Here are a few questions to guide your analysis:

- When was the photograph taken? (If there is no date given for the photograph in its credit line or caption, you may be able to approximate the date according to the people or events depicted in the photo. If the photograph appears in a newspaper, you can usually assume that the shot is fairly current with publication.)

- What is the subject of the photograph?

- Why was the photo taken? What appears to be the purpose of the photograph?

- Is it spontaneous or posed? Did the subject know he or she was being photographed?

- Who was responsible for the photo? (An individual, an agency, or organization?) Can you discern the photographer's attitude toward the subject?

- Is there a caption? If so, what kind of information does it provide? Does it identify the subject of the photo? Does it provide an interpretation of the subject?

Political Cartoons

Political cartoons have a long history in America. Some of the most interesting commentary on American politics takes place in the form of political cartoons, which usually exaggerate physical and other qualities of the persons depicted and often rely on a kind of visual shorthand to announce the subject or set the scene—visual cues, clichés, or stereotypes that are instantly recognizable. For example, a greedy corporate executive might be depicted as an individual in professional clothing with paper currency sticking out of his or her pockets.

DOONESBURY Garry Trudeau

In another cartoon, powdered wigs and quill pens might signal a historical setting. The cartoonist's goal is to comment on and/or criticize political figures, policies, or events. The cartoonist uses several techniques to accomplish this goal, including exaggeration, irony, and juxtaposition. For example, the cartoonist may point out how the results of governmental policies are the opposite of their intended effects (irony). In other cartoons, two people, ideas, or events that don't belong together may be joined to make a point (juxtaposition). Because cartoons comment on political situations and events, you generally need some knowledge of current events to interpret political cartoons.

Here are a few questions to guide your analysis:

- Study the cartoon element by element. Political cartoons are often complex. If the cartoon is in strip form, you also need to think about the relationship of the frames in sequence.

- What labels appear on objects or people in the cartoon? Cartoonists will often label some of the elements. For example, a building with columns might be labeled "U.S. Supreme Court." Or, an individual might be labeled "senator" or "Republican."

- Is there a caption or title to the cartoon? If so, what does it contribute to the meaning or impact of the cartoon?

- Can you identify any of the people shown? Presidents, well-known members of Congress, and world leaders are often shown with specific characteristics that help to identify them. Jimmy Carter was often shown with an exaggerated, toothy smile. George W. Bush is often shown with large ears, small eyes, and bushy eyebrows—sometimes with a "W" or a "43" label.

- Can you identify the event being depicted? Historical events, such as the American Revolution, or contemporary events, such as the 2004 presidential election, are often the subject matter for cartoons.

- What are the elements of the cartoon? Objects often represent ideas or events. For example, a donkey is often used to depict the Democratic Party. Or, an eagle is used to represent the United States.

- How are the characters interacting? What do the speech bubbles contribute to the cartoon?

- What is the overall message of the cartoon? Can you determine what the cartoonist's position is on the subject?

American
GOVERNMENT

THE POLITICAL LANDSCAPE

1

We the People of the United States, in Order to form a more perfect Union, establish Justice, insure domestic Tranquility, provide for the common defence, promote the general Welfare, and secure the Blessings of Liberty to ourselves and our Posterity, do ordain and establish this Constitution for the United States of America.

THESE ARE THE WORDS that begin the Preamble to the United States Constitution. Written in 1787 by a group of men we today refer to as the Framers, this document has guided our nation, its government, its politics, its institutions, and its inhabitants for over 200 years.

When the Constitution was written, the phrases "We the People" and "ourselves" meant something very different from what they do today. After all, voting largely was limited to property-owning white males. Indians, slaves, and women could not vote. Today, through the expansion of the right to vote, the phrase "the People" encompasses men and women of all races, ethnic origins, and social and economic statuses—a variety of peoples and interests. The Framers could not have imagined the range of people today who are eligible to vote.

In the goals it outlines, the Preamble to the Constitution describes what the people of the United States can expect from their government. Still, some citizens question how well the U.S. government can deliver on the goals set out in the Preamble. Few Americans today classify the union as "perfect"; many feel excluded from "Justice" and the "Blessings of Liberty," and even our leaders do not believe that our domestic situation is particularly tranquil, as evidenced by the creation of the Department of Homeland Security and the naming of a national intelligence director. Furthermore, as recent poll results and economic statistics indicate, many Americans believe that their general welfare is not well promoted by their government. Others simply do not care much at all about government. Many believe that they have no influence in its decision making, or they do not see any positive benefits from it in their lives. Yet, ironically, in times of emergency, be it a terrorist attack or the devastation of a hurricane or earthquake, many people immediately look to their government for help.

If there has been one constant in the life of the United States, it is change. The Framers would be astonished to see the current forms and functions of the institutions they so carefully outlined in the Constitution, as well as the number of additional political institutions that have arisen to support and fuel the functioning of the national government. The Framers also would be amazed at the array of services and programs the government—especially the national government—provides. They further would be surprised to see how the physical boundaries and the composition of the population have changed over the past 200 plus years. And, they might well wonder, "How did we get here?"

It is part of the American creed that each generation should hand down to the next not only a better America, but an improved economic, educational, and social status. In general, Americans long have been optimistic about our nation, its institutions, and its future. Thomas Jefferson saw the United States as the world's "best hope"; Abraham Lincoln echoed these sentiments when he called it the "last, best hope on earth."[1] But, while most Americans' lives are better than their parents', in the wake of the war in Iraq, political scandals, and natural disasters such as Hurricane Katrina, many Americans are uncertain about what the future holds and concerned about the direction of the nation.

I N THIS TEXT, WE PRESENT you with the tools that you need to understand how our political system has evolved and to prepare you to understand the changes that are yet to come. If you approach the study of American government and politics with an open mind, it should help you become a better citizen. We hope that you learn to ask questions, to understand how various issues have come to be important, and to see why a particular law was enacted and how it was implemented. With such understanding, we further hope that you will learn not to accept at face value everything you see on the television news, hear on the radio, or read in the newspaper and on the Internet, especially in the blogosphere. Work to understand your government, and use your vote and other forms of participation to help ensure that your government works for you.

We recognize that the discourse of politics has changed dramatically even in the last few years, and that many Americans—especially the young—are turned off by politics, especially at the national level. We also believe that a thorough understanding of the workings of government will allow you to question and think about the system—the good parts and the bad—and decide for yourself the advantages and disadvantages of possible changes and reforms. Equipped with such an understanding, we hope you will become better informed and more active participants in the political process.

Every long journey begins with a single step. In this chapter, we will examine the following topics:

- First, we will discuss *the origins of American government: what it is and why we need it*. Governments perform a range of well-known and not so well-known functions that affect citizens' lives on a daily basis.

- Second, we will look at *the roots of American government*. To understand how the U.S. government and our political system work today, it is critical to understand the philosophies that guided the American colonists as they created a system of governance different from those then in existence.

- Third, we will explore *American political culture and the characteristics of American democracy*. Several enduring values have defined American democracy since its beginning and continue to influence our nation's government and politics today.

- Fourth, we will explore *the changing characteristics of the American people*. Because the government derives its power from the people, an understanding of who the

American people are and their changing age, racial, and ethnic composition is critical to an understanding of American politics.

- Fifth, we will discuss *political ideology, its role in the world, and in politics.* Political ideology has a profound impact on the government policies that Americans support or oppose.

- Finally, we will discuss *current attitudes toward American government* and the role that government plays in people's lives.

The Origins of American Government: What It Is and Why We Need It

THROUGHOUT HISTORY, ALL SORTS OF SOCIETIES have organized themselves into a variety of governments, small and large, simple and complex, democratic and nondemocratic, elected and nonelected. **Governments** are the vehicles through which policies are made and affairs of state are conducted. In fact, the term "government" is derived from the Greek for "to pilot a ship," which is appropriate, since we expect governments to guide "the ship of state." As we explore throughout this text, governments are often a result of trial and error, experiment, compromise, and sometimes bloodshed.

government
The formal vehicle through which policies are made and affairs of state are conducted.

Unlike schools, banks, or corporations, the actions of government are binding on all of its citizens. **Citizens,** by law, are members of the political community who by nature of being born in a particular nation or having become a naturalized citizen are entitled to all of the freedoms guaranteed by the government. In exchange for these freedoms, citizens must obey the government, its laws, and its constitution. Citizens also are expected to support their government through exercising their right to vote, paying taxes due, and, if they are eligible, submitting themselves to military service.

citizen
Member of the political community to whom certain rights and obligations are attached.

Only governments can legitimately use force to keep order, and without governments, societies may descend into chaos. The sectarian violence seen in Iraq following the end of Saddam Hussein's regime vividly portrays the need for a strong government to enforce the rule of law.

As we explore American government in this text, we are referring to the web of formal administrative structures that exist on the national, state, and local levels. But, these governments do not exist in a vacuum. A variety of external forces such as the media, political parties, and interest groups influence the day-to-day workings of governments. Thus, we explore government in the context of **politics,** the study of what has been called "who gets what, when, and how," or more simply, the process of how policy decisions get made.

politics
The study of who gets what, when, and how—or how policy decisions are made.

The study of "who gets what, when, and how" can be a fascinating process. While all governments share to greater or lesser degrees the need to provide certain key functions, to whom they provide these benefits, which benefits they provide, when they provide them, and how they are provided vary tremendously across as well as within nations. One need only look to recent debates on tax policy and health care to realize that there are many questions involving who, what, when, and how during policy debates.

Comparing Political Landscapes

FUNCTIONS OF GOVERNMENT

The Framers of the U.S. Constitution clearly recognized the need for a new government. As our opening vignette underscores, in attempting "to form a more perfect Union," the Framers set out several key functions of government that continue to be relevant today. As discussed below, several of the Framers' ideas centered on their belief that the major function of government was creating mechanisms to allow individuals to solve conflicts in an orderly and peaceful manner. Just how much authority one must give up to governments in exchange for this kind of security, however, has vexed political philosophers as well as politicians for ages.

Establishing Justice One of the first things expected from governments is a system of laws that allows individuals to abide by a common set of principles. Societies adhering to what is called the rule of law allow for the rational dispensing of justice by acknowledged legal authorities. Thus, today, the Bill of Rights entitles people to a trial by jury, to know what the charges against them are, and to be tried in a courtroom presided over by an impartial judge. The U.S. Constitution created a federal judicial system to dispense justice, but the Bill of Rights specified a host of rights guaranteed to all citizens in an effort to establish justice.

Ensuring Domestic Tranquility As we will discuss throughout this text, the role of government in ensuring domestic tranquility is a subject of much debate. In times of crisis such as the terrorist attacks of September 11, 2001, the U.S. government, as well as state and local governments, took extraordinary measures to contain the threat of terrorism from abroad as well as within the United States. The creation of the Department of Homeland Security as well as the passage of legislation giving the national government nearly unprecedented ability to ferret out potential threats shows the degree to which the government takes seriously its charge to preserve domestic tranquility. On an even more practical front, local governments have police forces, the states have national guards, and the federal government can always call up troops to quell any threats.

Providing for the Common Defense The U.S. Constitution calls for the president to be the commander in chief of the armed forces, and the Congress is given the authority to raise an army. The Framers recognized that one of the major purposes of government is to provide for the defense of its citizens. As highlighted in Figure 1.1, the defense budget is a considerable (and growing) proportion of all federal outlays.

Promoting the General Welfare When the Framers added "promoting the general Welfare" to their list of key government functions, they never envisioned how the involvement of the government at all levels would expand so tremendously. In fact, promoting the general welfare was more of an ideal than a mandate for the new national government. Over time, however, our notions of what governments should do have expanded along with the number and size of governments. As we discuss throughout this text, however, there is no universal agreement on the scope of what governments should do. There is no doubt that Social Security income programs as well as governmental programs providing health care are designed to promote the general welfare. These programs also make up a significant proportion of the federal budget, as highlighted in Figure 1.1.

Securing the Blessings of Liberty A well-functioning government that enjoys the support of its citizenry is one of the best ways to "secure the Blessings of Liberty" for its people. In a free society, citizens enjoy a wide range of liberties and freedoms and feel free to prosper. They are free to criticize the government as well as to petition it when they disagree with its policies or have a grievance.

Taken together, these principal functions of government permeate our lives. Whether it is your ability to obtain a low-interest student loan, buy a formerly prescription-only allergy drug such as Claritin or Plan B over the counter, or drive a car at a particular age, government has played a major role. Similarly, without

FIGURE 1.1 ALLOCATION OF THE FEDERAL BUDGET, 2007

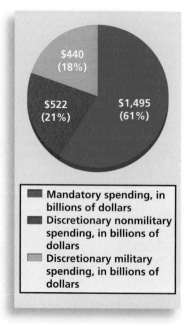

■ Mandatory spending, in billions of dollars
■ Discretionary nonmilitary spending, in billions of dollars
■ Discretionary military spending, in billions of dollars

$440 (18%)
$522 (21%)
$1,495 (61%)

Source: Fiscal Year 2007 Budget, http://www.whitehouse.gov/omb/budget/fy2007/pdf/spec.pdf.

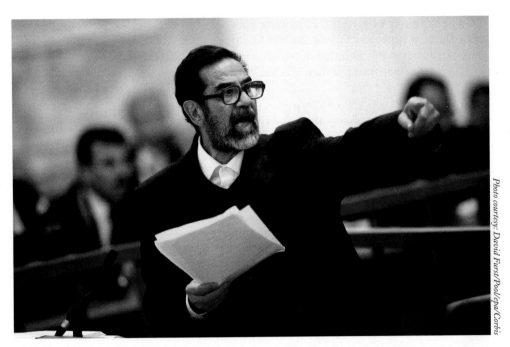

Former Iraqi President Saddam Hussein ruled Iraq as a totalitarian state. Here, in court, Hussein objects to the lengthy list of charges against him. In November of 2006, he was convicted by an Iraqi tribunal of more than 2,500 crimes against humanity and sentenced to death by hanging.

Photo courtesy: David Furst/Pool/epa/Corbis

government-sponsored research, we would not have cellular telephones, the Internet, four-wheel-drive vehicles, or even Velcro.

TYPES OF GOVERNMENT

As early as Plato and Aristotle, theorists have tried to categorize governments by who participates, who governs, and how much authority those who govern enjoy. As revealed in Table 1.1, a **monarchy,** the type of government explicitly rejected by the Framers, is defined by the rule of one in the interest of all of his or her subjects. The Framers also rejected adopting an aristocracy, which is defined as government by the few in the service of the many. The least appealing of Aristotle's classifications of government is **totalitarianism,** a form of government that he considered rule by "tyranny." Tyrants rule their countries to benefit themselves. This was the case in Iraq under Saddam Hussein. In tyrannical or totalitarian systems, the leader exercises unlimited power and individuals have no personal rights or liberties. Generally, these systems tend to be ruled in the name of a particular religion or orthodoxy, an ideology, or a personality cult organized around the supreme leader. Another unappealing form of government, an **oligarchy,** occurs when a few people rule in their own interest. In an oligarchy, participation in government is conditioned on the possession of wealth, social status, military position, or achievement. Oligarchies are rare today.

Aristotle called rule of the many for the benefit of all citizens a "polity" and referred to rule of the many to benefit themselves as a "democracy." The term **democracy** is derived from the Greek words *demos* (the people) and *kratia* (power or authority), and may be used to refer to any system of government that gives power to the people, either directly, or indirectly through elected representatives. Ironically, Aristotle was quite troubled by the idea of democracy, although he believed it better than tyranny or oligarchy. He strongly believed that the collective judgment of the many was preferable to that of a few.

monarchy
A form of government in which power is vested in hereditary kings and queens who govern in the interests of all.

totalitarianism
A form of government in which power resides in a leader who rules according to self-interest and without regard for individual rights and liberties.

oligarchy
A form of government in which the right to participate is conditioned on the possession of wealth, social status, military position, or achievement.

democracy
A system of government that gives power to the people, whether directly or through elected representatives.

TABLE 1.1 ARISTOTLE'S CLASSIFICATIONS OF GOVERNMENT

		In Whose Interest?	
		Public	Self
Rule by:	One	Monarchy	Tyranny
	The Few	Aristocracy	Oligarchy
	The Many	Polity	Democracy

Source: Aristotle, Politics 3, 7.

The majority of governments worldwide are democracies to one extent or another. In most democracies, contrary to Aristotle's fears, the "many"—or in the case of the United States and as noted in our chapter opening vignette, "the People"—are the ruling power, albeit through their elected leaders.

■ Isaac Newton and other Enlightenment thinkers challenged people's ideas about the nature of government.

Photo courtesy: E.R.L./Sipa

The Roots of American Government: Where Did the Ideas Come From?

THE CURRENT AMERICAN POLITICAL SYSTEM did not spring into being overnight. It is the result of philosophy, trial and error, and even luck. (See Global Perspective: American Uniqueness in the World: Are We Number One?) To begin our examination of why we have the type of government we have today, we will look at the theories of government that influenced the Framers who drafted the Constitution and created the United States of America.

THE REFORMATION AND THE ENLIGHTENMENT: QUESTIONING THE DIVINE RIGHT OF KINGS

In the third century, as the Roman Empire began to fall, kings throughout Europe began to rule their countries absolutely, claiming their right to govern came directly from God. Thus, since it was thought to be God's will that a particular monarch ruled a country, the people in that country had no right to question their monarch's authority or agitate for a voice in their government's operation.

During the Enlightenment period, the ideas of philosophers and scientists such as Isaac Newton (1642–1727) radically changed people's views of government. Newton and others argued that the world could be improved through the use of human reason, science, and religious toleration. He and other theorists directly challenged earlier notions that fate alone controlled an individual's destiny and that kings ruled by divine right.

The intellectual and religious developments of the Reformation and Enlightenment periods of the sixteenth and seventeenth centuries encouraged people to seek alternatives to absolute monarchies and to ponder new methods of governance. In the late sixteenth century, radical Protestants split from the Church of England, which was created by King Henry VIII when the Roman Catholic Church forbade him to divorce and remarry. These new Protestants or Puritans believed in their ability to speak one on one to God and established self-governing congregations. They were persecuted for their religious beliefs by the English monarchy. The Pilgrims were the first group of these Protestants to flee religious persecution and settle in America. There they established self-governing congregations and were responsible for the first widespread appearance of self-government in the American colonies. The Mayflower Compact, the document setting up their new government, was deemed sufficiently important to be written while the Pilgrims were still at sea. It took the form of a **social contract,** or agreement between the people and their government signifying their consent to be governed.

Self-Government

social contract
An agreement between the people and their government signifying their consent to be governed.

HOBBES, LOCKE, AND A SOCIAL CONTRACT THEORY OF GOVERNMENT

Two English theorists of the seventeenth century, Thomas Hobbes (1588–1679) and John Locke (1632–1704), built on conventional notions about the role of government and the relationship of the government to the people in proposing a **social contract theory** of government. They argued that all individuals were free and equal by natural right. This freedom, in turn, required that all men and women give their consent to be governed.

Hobbes was greatly influenced by the chaos of the English Civil War during the mid-seventeenth century. Its impact is evident in his most famous work, *Leviathan* (1651), a treatise on governmental theory that states his views on humanity and citizen. *Leviathan* is commonly described as a book about politics, but it also deals with religion and moral philosophy. In *Leviathan*, Hobbes argued pessimistically that humanity's natural state was one of war. Government, Hobbes theorized, particularly a monarchy, was necessary to restrain humanity's bestial tendencies because life without government was but a "state of nature." Without written, enforceable rules, people would live like animals—foraging for food, stealing, and killing when necessary. To escape the horrors of the natural state and to protect their lives, Hobbes argued, people must give up certain rights to government. Without government, Hobbes warned, life would be "solitary, poor, nasty, brutish, and short"—a constant struggle to survive against the evil of others. For these reasons, governments had to intrude on people's rights and liberties to better control society and to provide the necessary safeguards for property.

Hobbes argued strongly for a single ruler, no matter how evil, to guarantee the rights of the weak against the strong. Leviathan, a biblical sea monster, was his characterization of an all-powerful government. Strict adherence to Leviathan's laws, however all-encompassing or intrusive on liberty, was but a small price to pay for living in a civilized society.

In contrast to Hobbes, John Locke, like many other political philosophers of the era, took the basic survival of humanity for granted. Locke argued that a government's major responsibility was the preservation of private property, an idea that ultimately found its way into the U.S. Constitution. In two of his works (*Second Treatise on Civil Government* [1689] and *Essay Concerning Human Understanding* [1690]), Locke not only denied the divine right of kings to govern but argued that individuals were born equal and with natural rights that no king had the power to void. Under Locke's conception of social contract theory, the consent of the people is the only true basis of any sovereign's right to rule. According to Locke, people form governments largely to preserve life, liberty, and property, and to assure justice. If governments act improperly, they break their contract with the people and therefore no longer enjoy the consent of the governed. Because he believed that true justice comes from the law, Locke argued that the branch of government that makes laws—as opposed to the one that enforces or interprets laws—should be the most powerful.

Locke believed that having a chief executive to administer laws was important, but that he should necessarily be limited by law or by the social contract with the governed. Locke's writings influenced many American colonists, especially Thomas Jefferson, whose original draft of the Declaration of Independence noted the rights to "life, liberty, and property" as key reasons to separate from England.[2] This document was "pure Locke" because it based the justification for the split with England on the English government's violation of the social contract with the American colonists.

social contract theory
The belief that people are free and equal by God-given right and that this in turn requires that all people give their consent to be governed; espoused by John Locke and influential in the writing of the Declaration of Independence.

■ The title page from Thomas Hobbes's *Leviathan* (1651) depicts a giant ruler whose body consists of the bodies of his subjects. This is symbolic of the people coming together under one ruler.

Global Perspective

AMERICAN UNIQUENESS IN THE WORLD: ARE WE NUMBER ONE?

Is the United States unique—or is it merely ordinary? Most Americans consider this question at some point in their lives as they ponder the meaning and significance of their citizenship and identity. After all, if the United States is ordinary, then by implication Americans are probably ordinary, too. Most Americans, not satisfied with this answer, prefer to think of their country as unique.

In fact, American uniqueness—or exceptionalism—has been a pervasive theme in American political rhetoric since before the founding. Americans in the nineteenth century routinely described the nation as a "City on a Hill"—a reference to a passage in the New Testament in which Jesus Christ urges his followers to be an example for the rest of the world. U.S. foreign policy has for many years been guided by the idea that America is "bound to lead"—in the dual sense that America's leadership is both an obligation it owes to the world and an inevitable role, given the nation's size, wealth, and power.

How does the United States compare to the rest of the world in key areas, and what do these comparisons tell us about America's role in the world? The United States is one of the top ten countries with regard to landmass, population, gross domestic product (GDP), and GDP per capita. Surprisingly, given the tremendous amount of wealth, technology, and natural resources at the United States' disposal, the health and well-being of the American people in many respects are merely average. As of 2006, for example, the United States has a lower life expectancy at birth than more than forty other nations and has a higher unemployment rate than forty-eight other nations. And, it seems odd that the United States, one of the world's leaders in medical technological research, should rank forty-second in infant deaths, with countries such as Cuba and Slovenia having lower rates. Can the American people, acting privately or through government, change these rankings, or are they the product of structural forces that are impervious to change?

Throughout this text we will consider questions similar to this as we compare political aspects of the United States and other nations. As you study each chapter of this text, consider whether the differences between the United States and other countries stem from choice, unique circumstance, or some combination of the two.

QUESTIONS

1. What surprised you about the rankings discussed above? What rankings didn't come as a surprise? Is the United States better or worse off than you originally thought?
2. What in your own experience suggests that America is exceptional? What in your experience discounts this notion?

Source: CIA World Factbook, http://www.cia.gov/cia/publications/factbook.

DEVISING A NATIONAL GOVERNMENT IN THE AMERICAN COLONIES

Although social contract theorists agreed on the need for government, they did not necessarily agree on the form that a government should take. Thomas Hobbes argued for a single leader; John Locke and Jean-Jacques Rousseau (1712–1778), a French philosopher, saw the need for less centralized power.

The American colonists rejected a system with a strong ruler, like the British monarchy, when they declared their independence. Many of the colonists had fled Great Britain to avoid religious persecution and other harsh manifestations of power wielded by King George II, whom they viewed as a malevolent despot who failed to govern in their interests. They naturally were reluctant to put themselves in the same position in their new nation.

The colonists also were fearful of replicating the landed and titled system of the British aristocracy. They viewed the formation of a representative form of government as far more in keeping with the ideas of social contract theorists.

As evidenced by the creation in 1619 of the Virginia House of Burgesses as the first representative assembly in North America, and its objections to "taxation without representation," the colonists were quick to create participatory forms of government in which most men were allowed to take part. The New England town meeting, where all citizens gather to discuss and decide issues facing the town, today stands as a surviving example of a **direct democracy,** such as was used in ancient Greece when all free, male citizens came together periodically to pass laws and elect leaders by lot.

Direct democracies, in which the people rather than their elected representatives make political decisions, soon proved unworkable in the colonies. But, as more and more settlers came to the New World, many town meetings were replaced by a system called an **indirect democracy** (this is also called representative democracy). This system of government, in which representatives of the people are chosen by ballot, was considered undemocratic by ancient Greeks, who believed that all citizens must have a direct say in their governance.[3] Later, in the 1760s, Jean-Jacques Rousseau also argued that true democracy is impossible unless all citizens participate in governmental decision making. Nevertheless, indirect democracy was the form of government used throughout most of the colonies.

Representative or indirect democracies, which call for the election of representatives to a governmental decision-making body, were formed first in the colonies and then in the new union. Many citizens were uncomfortable with the term democracy because it implied a direct democracy that conjured up Hobbesian fears of the people and mob rule. Instead, they preferred the term **republic,** which implied a system of government in which the interests of the people were represented by more educated or wealthier citizens who were responsible to those who elected them. Today, representative democracies are more commonly called republics, and the words democracy and republic often are used interchangeably.

direct democracy
A system of government in which members of the polity meet to discuss all policy decisions and then agree to abide by majority rule.

indirect (representative) democracy
A system of government that gives citizens the opportunity to vote for representatives who will work on their behalf.

republic
A government rooted in the consent of the governed; a representative or indirect democracy.

American Political Culture and the Characteristics of American Democracy

VIDEO DEBATE
American Democracy and Human Rights

AS SHOWN ABOVE, the Framers devised a representative democratic system to govern the United States. This system is based on a number of underlying concepts and distinguishing characteristics that sometimes conflict with one another. Taken together, these ideas lie at the core of American political culture. More specifically, **political culture** can be defined as commonly shared attitudes, beliefs, and core values about how government should operate. American political culture emphasizes the values of personal liberty, equality, popular consent and majority rule, popular sovereignty, civil society, individualism, and religious faith.

political culture
Commonly shared attitudes, beliefs, and core values about how government should operate.

PERSONAL LIBERTY

Personal liberty is perhaps the single most important characteristic of American democracy. The Constitution itself was written to ensure life and liberty. Over the years, however, our concepts of liberty have changed and evolved from freedom *from* to freedom *to.* The Framers intended Americans to be free from governmental infringements on freedom of religion and speech, from unreasonable searches and seizure, and so on (see chapter 5). The addition of the Fourteenth Amendment to the Constitution and its emphasis on due process and on equal protection of the laws as well as the subsequent passage of laws guaranteeing civil rights, however, expanded Americans' concept of liberty to include demands for freedom to work or go to school without discrimination. Debates over how much the government should do to guarantee these rights or liberties illustrate the conflicts that continue to occur in our democratic system.

personal liberty
A key characteristic of U.S. democracy. Initially meaning freedom from governmental interference, today it includes demands for freedom to engage in a variety of practices free from governmental interference or discrimination.

political equality
The principle that all citizens are equal in the political process that is implied by the phrase "one person, one vote."

popular consent
The idea that governments must draw their powers from the consent of the governed.

majority rule
The central premise of direct democracy in which only policies that collectively garner the support of a majority of voters will be made into law.

popular sovereignty
The notion that the ultimate authority in society rests with the people.

natural law
A doctrine that society should be governed by certain ethical principles that are part of nature and, as such, can be understood by reason.

civil society
Society created when citizens are allowed to organize and express their views publicly as they engage in an open debate about public policy.

EQUALITY

Another key characteristic of our democracy is **political equality.** This emphasis reflects Americans' stress on the importance of the individual. Although some individuals clearly wield more political clout than others, the adage "one person, one vote" implies a sense of political equality for all.

POPULAR CONSENT AND MAJORITY RULE

Popular consent, the idea that governments must draw their powers from the consent of the governed, is one distinguishing characteristic of American democracy. Derived from John Locke's social contract theory, the notion of popular consent was central to the Declaration of Independence. A citizen's willingness to vote represents his or her consent to be governed and is thus an essential premise of democracy. Growing numbers of nonvoters can threaten the operation and legitimacy of a truly democratic system.

   Majority rule, another core political value, means that the majority (normally 50 percent of the total votes cast plus one) of citizens in any political unit should elect officials and determine policies. This principle holds for both voters and their elected representatives. Yet, the American system also stresses the need to preserve minority rights, as evidenced by the myriad protections of individual rights and liberties found in the Bill of Rights.

   The concept of the preservation of minority rights has changed dramatically in the United States. It wasn't until after the Civil War that slaves were freed and African Americans began to enjoy minimal citizenship rights. By the 1960s, however, anger at America's failure to guarantee minority rights in all sections of the nation fueled the civil rights movement. This ultimately led to congressional passage of the Civil Rights Act of 1964 and the Voting Rights Act of 1965, both designed to further minority rights.

POPULAR SOVEREIGNTY

Popular sovereignty, or the notion that the ultimate authority in society rests with the people, has its basis in **natural law.** Ultimately, political authority rests with the people, who can create, abolish, or alter their governments. The idea that all governments derive their power from the people is found in the Declaration of Independence and the U.S. Constitution, but the term popular sovereignty did not come into wide use until pre-Civil War debates over slavery. At that time, supporters of popular sovereignty argued that the citizens of new states seeking admission to the union should be able to decide whether or not their states would allow slavery within their borders.

CIVIL SOCIETY

Several of these hallmarks of our political culture also are fundamental to what many commentators now term **civil society.** This term is used to describe the society created when citizens are allowed to organize and express their views publicly as they engage in an open debate about public policy.[4] The fall of the Soviet Union "accelerated the global trend toward democracy . . . which pushed democracy to the top of the political agenda."[5] In Russia, for example, the U.S. government has used a variety of initiatives to train people how to act in a new democratic system.

   Independent and politically active citizens are key to the success of any democracy, yet people who have not lived in democratic systems often are unschooled, reluctant, or afraid to participate after years in communist or totalitarian systems. The U.S. government routinely makes grants to nongovernmental organizations, professional associations, civic education groups, and women's groups to encourage the kind of participation in the political system that Americans often take for granted. U.S. efforts to assist Afghanistan and Iraq, for example, include not only public works projects but also development of the new democratic government. (See American Values/American Voices: Exporting Democracy.)

VIDEO DEBATE

Exporting American Democracy

American Values/American Voices

EXPORTING DEMOCRACY

During his second inaugural address, delivered in January 2005, President George W. Bush made it clear that spreading the value of American democracy abroad was to be a major goal of the United States. The president's goal is not a new one for the United States. President Woodrow Wilson tried and failed after World War I to establish a democratic world order through the League of Nations. Harry Truman's administration had greater success after World War II when both Japan and West Germany were transformed into democratic nations. Supporters of U.S. efforts to export democracy to other nations cite scholarship that suggests democracies are less likely to go to war with one another.[a] Critics, however, charge that America's democratic impulse in foreign policy matters has led in the past and is likely to lead again to unforeseen and disastrous consequences.[b] Since President Bush identified spreading democracy abroad as one of the United States' major goals, many oppressed peoples have been given hope. However, the idealism of the president's agenda has often conflicted with U.S. foreign policy realities and other policy priorities.[c]

In the Middle East, for example, the administration has promoted elections in Afghanistan and Iraq to mixed success. The Iraqi Parliament's initial failure to agree on key ministerial positions dealing with foreign policy is just one indicator that American democracy might not work for everyone. And, in the Palestinian territories, U.S. efforts to prevent the radical Islamic group Hamas from winning control of the government were rebuffed by the electorate in a carefully monitored democratic election. As a result, the United States found itself in the ironic position of refusing to negotiate with a democratically elected government, albeit one with a history of terrorist attacks.

In other places, however, the United States has enjoyed greater success. In Kyrgyzstan, the U.S. government funded pro-democracy groups and provided generators to print an opposition newspaper before its peaceful revolution. Edil Baisalov, director of the Coalition for Democracy and Civil Society, can quote extensively from the Bush inaugural speech. "The Kyrgyz people are much, much better off today than they were a year ago, and I think the U.S. government should take pride in taking credit for that," he said. "And [it] should never apologize that it wants the people to be free."[d]

"The administration deserves credit," said Jennifer Windsor, executive director of Freedom House, a group that promotes democracy, "but it's just a start."[e] At the same time, however, Human Rights Watch criticized the Bush administration for undermining its credibility in promoting democracy and freedom abroad by attempting to identify terrorists and gain information through the use of abusive interrogation tactics at Guantanamo Bay, and by deporting detainees to countries where more brutal interrogation techniques could be used.

Outside the United States, officials also question the sincerity of the Bush administration's rhetoric while commending its efforts to speak out. "All they do is talk right now," said Gulam Umarov, the son of the leader of Uzbekistan's Sunshine Coalition. "I don't know what actual moves they take. But they are talking, which is really good."[f]

QUESTIONS

1. Is America's brand of democracy easily exportable? What pitfalls exist for nations with little experience in democracy?
2. Do highly religious Muslim nations or factions pose special problems to American efforts to bring democracy to the Middle East?

[a] G. John Ikenberry, "Why Export Democracy? The 'Hidden Grand Strategy' of American Foreign Policy," *Wilson Quarterly* 23: 2 (1999).

[b] Paul D. Carrington, "Exporting Democracy to Iraq," *Perspectives* 4: 1 (2003), http://www.oycf.org/Perspectives/20_033103/contents.htm.

[c] This feature draws heavily on Peter Baker, "The Realities of Exporting Democracy," *Washington Post* (January 25, 2006): A1.

[d] Quoted in Baker, "The Realities of Exporting Democracy."

[e] Quoted in Baker, "The Realities of Exporting Democracy."

[f] Quoted in Baker, "The Realities of Exporting Democracy."

INDIVIDUALISM

Although many core political values concern protecting the rights of others, tremendous value is placed on the individual in American democracy. All individuals are deemed rational and fair, and endowed, as Thomas Jefferson proclaimed in the Declaration of Independence, "with certain unalienable rights." Even today, many view individualism, which holds that the primary function of government is to enable the individual to achieve his or her highest level of development, as a mixed blessing. It is also a concept whose meaning has changed over time. The rugged individualism of the western frontier, for example, was altered as more citizens moved westward, cities developed, and demands for government services increased as many individuals no longer could exist independently of others.

SIMULATION

What Are American Civic Values?

■ Many religious people attempt to share their faith and message with others. Here, a woman in a New York City subway station shares her belief in the power of prayer.

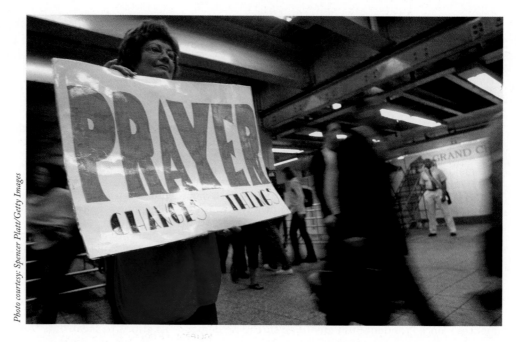

Photo courtesy: Spencer Platt/Getty Images

RELIGIOUS FAITH

Today, religion and religious faith are often at the forefront of how Americans perceive political and policy issues. As the nation waged war in Iraq and attempted to export democracy to the Middle East, an increasing number of Americans, for example, considered Islam "a religion that encourages violence" and did not view Islam as having much in common with their own religion.[6] Still, many Americans are quite comfortable with religion playing an important role in public policy. President George W. Bush's frequent references to his faith as guiding his decisions received the support of 62 percent of the American public in one poll.[7] In fact, although the First Amendment to the Constitution creates a wall of separation between church and state (see chapter 5), 72 percent agreed with the statement "The president should have strong religious beliefs."[8]

Most Americans profess to have strong religious beliefs, and the United States is the most churchgoing nation in the world. It is overwhelmingly Christian, with a growing number of Christian evangelicals who, since 1980, have played an exceptionally important role in American politics, defining the political positions of the Republican Party, in particular. People of religious faith often have very firm beliefs on social issues such as contraception and abortion, same-sex marriage, the right of homosexual people to adopt children, and the use of stem cells for medical research. The concerns of people of strong religious faith continue to play a major role in shaping the political agenda of the nation.

Changing Characteristics of the American People

AMERICANS HAVE MANY THINGS IN COMMON in addition to their political culture. Most Americans share a common language—English—and have similar aspirations for themselves and their families. Most agree that they would rather live in the United States than anywhere else, and that democracy, with all of its warts, is still the best system of government. Most Americans highly value education and want to send their children to the best schools possible, viewing a good education as the key to success.

Despite these similarities, politicians, media commentators, and even the citizenry itself tend to focus on differences among Americans, in large part because these differences contribute to political conflicts among the electorate. Although it is true that the United States and its population are undergoing rapid change, this is not necessarily a new phenomenon. It is simply new to most of us. In the pages that follow, we take a look at some of the characteristics of the American populace. Because the people of the United States are the basis of political power and authority, their characteristics and attitudes have important implications for how America is governed and what policies are made.

CHANGING SIZE AND POPULATION

One year after the Constitution was ratified, fewer than 4 million Americans lived in the thirteen states. They were united by a single language, most shared a similar Protestant-Christian heritage, and those who voted were white male property owners. The Constitution mandated that each of the sixty-five members of the original House of Representatives should represent 30,000 people. However, because of rapid population growth, that number often was much higher.

As the nation grew larger with the addition of new states, as revealed in Figure 1.2, the population also grew. Although the size of the United States has remained

FIGURE 1.2 U.S. POPULATION, 1880–2040

Since around 1890, when large numbers of immigrants began arriving in America, the United States has seen a sharp increase in population. The major reasons for this increase are new births and increased longevity, although immigration has also been a contributing factor.

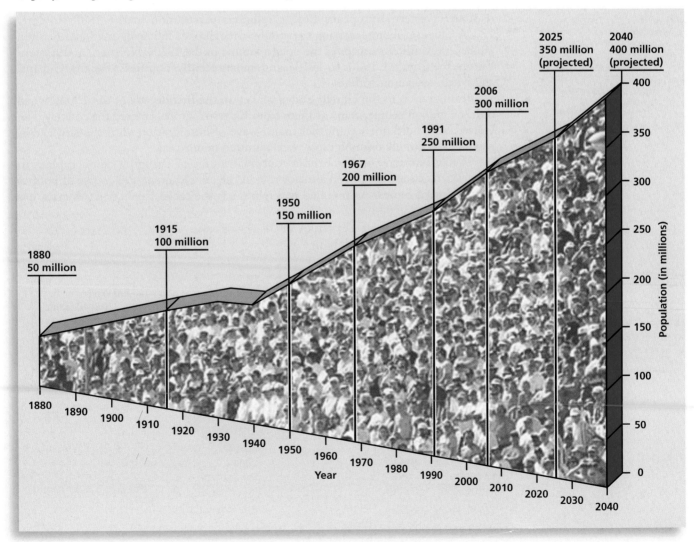

Source: USA Today (July 5, 2006):1A.

stable since the addition of Alaska and Hawaii in 1959, in 2006 there were more than 299 million Americans and a single member of the House of Representatives from Montana represented more than 927,000 people. As a result of this growth, most citizens today feel far removed from the national government and their elected representatives. Members of Congress, too, feel this change. Often they represent diverse constituencies with a variety of needs, concerns, and expectations, and they can meet only a relative few of these people face to face.

CHANGING DEMOGRAPHICS OF THE U.S. POPULATION

VISUAL LITERACY

Understanding Who We Are

As the physical size and population of the United States have changed, so have many of the assumptions on which it was founded. Much of this dynamism actually stems from changes in the demographics, the characteristics of the American population, that have occurred throughout our history. Below, we look at some demographic characteristics and then discuss some of the implications of these changes for how our nation is governed.

Changes in Racial and Ethnic Composition From the start, the American population has been altered constantly by the arrival of immigrants from various regions—Western Europeans fleeing religious persecution in the 1600s to early 1700s, Chinese laborers arriving to work on the railroads following the Gold Rush in 1848, Irish Catholics escaping the potato famine in the 1850s, Northern and Eastern Europeans from the 1880s to 1910s, and, most recently, Southeast Asians, Cubans, and Mexicans, among others.

Immigration to the United States peaked in the first decade of the 1900s, when nearly 9 million people, many of them from Eastern Europe, entered the country. The United States did not see another major wave of immigration until the late 1980s, when nearly 2 million immigrants were admitted in one year.

While immigration has been a continual source of changing demographics in America, race has also played a major role in the development and course of politics in the United States. As revealed in Figure 1.3, the racial balance in America has

FIGURE 1.3 RACE AND ETHNICITY IN AMERICA: 1967 AND 2006

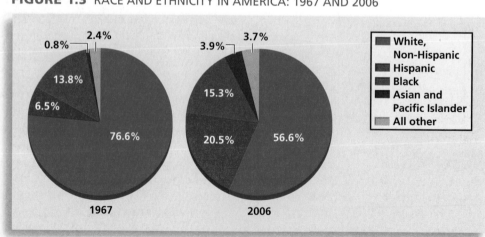

Source: U.S. Census Bureau.

THE HIGH TIDE OF IMMIGRATION—A NATIONAL MENACE.

Immigration statistics for the past year show that the influx of foreigners was the greatest in our history and that the hard-working peasants are now being supplanted by the criminals and outlaws of all Europe.

Photo courtesy: The New York Public Library/Art Resource, NY

■ Concern over immigration is not a new phenomenon, as this cartoon from the early 1900s depicts.

changed dramatically, with the proportion of Hispanics growing at the quickest rate. More importantly, what the figure does not show is that 40 percent of Americans under age twenty-five are members of a minority group, a fact that will have a significant impact on the demographics of the American polity. (See Join the Debate: The Huntington Theory of Hispanization.)

Changes in Age Cohort Composition Just as the racial and ethnic composition of the American population is changing, so too is the average age of the population. "For decades, the U.S. was described as a nation of the young because the number of persons under the age of twenty greatly outnumber[ed] those sixty-five and older," but this is no longer the case.[9] (See Figure 1.4.) Because of changes in patterns of fertility, life expectancy, and immigration, the nation's age profile has changed drastically.[10] When the United States was founded, the average life expectancy was thirty-five years; by 2006, it was eighty years for women and seventy-five years for men.

An aging population produces a host of new and costly demands on the government. In 2008, the first of what social scientists call "Baby Boomers" (the 76.8 million people who were born between 1946 and 1964) will reach age sixty-two and qualify for Social Security; in 2011, they will reach sixty-five and qualify for Medicare.[11] As Analyzing Visuals: Health Improvements Costly in the Long Run reveals, an aging America poses a great financial burden on working Americans, whose proportion of the population is rapidly declining.

These dramatic changes could potentially pit younger people against older people and result in dramatic cuts in benefits to the elderly and increased taxes for younger workers. Moreover, the elderly often vote against programs favored by younger voters, such as money for new schools and other items that they no longer view as important. At the same time, younger voters are less likely to support some things important to seniors, such as Medicaid and prescription drug reform, and have favored the Bush administration's plans for Social Security reform in higher numbers than seniors, presumably because they want to be sure the system is still viable when they retire.

SIMULATION

How to Satisfy Aunt Martha

FIGURE 1.4 AMERICA IS GETTING OLDER

America is aging—and doing so rapidly. By 2050, as shown below, more than 20 percent of the U.S. population will be senior citizens, with about 65 million people aged 65–84 and about 20 million people 85 and older.

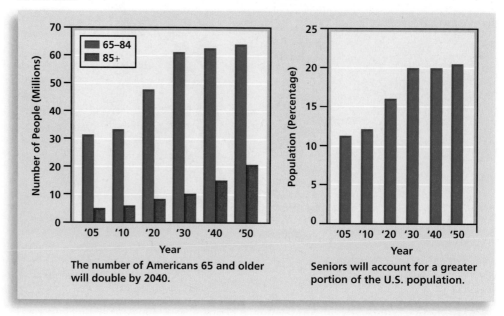

The number of Americans 65 and older will double by 2040.

Seniors will account for a greater portion of the U.S. population.

Source: USA Today (October 25, 2005): 2B.

■ With the tagline "Everyone has a little dirty laundry," the hit television show *Desperate Housewives* satirizes the idea of the perfect suburban family. The plot revolves around the concept that if a family seems ideal on the outside, there is most likely much hidden behind the façade.

Photo courtesy: ABC Photography Department

Changes in Family and Family Size Family size and household arrangements can be affected by several factors, including age at first marriage, divorce rates, economic conditions, longevity rates, and improvements in health care. In the past, familial gender roles were clearly defined. Women did housework and men worked in the fields. Large families were imperative; children were a source of cheap farm labor.

Industrialization and knowledge of birth control methods began to put a dent in the size of American families by the early 1900s. No longer needing children to work for the survival of the household unit on the farm, couples began to limit the sizes of their families.

By 1949, 49 percent of those polled thought that four or more children was the "ideal" family size; in 2004, only 12 percent favored large families, and 52 percent responded that no children to two children were the "best."[12] As chronicled in the popular press as well as by the U.S. Department of Commerce, the American family no longer looks like *The Cosby Show* or even *The Brady Bunch*. In 1940, nine out of ten households were traditional family households. By 2004, just 67.8 percent of children under eighteen lived with both parents. In fact, almost 20 percent of children under eighteen lived with just one of their parents, with the majority of those children (more than 80 percent) living with their mother. Moreover, by 2004, more than 26 percent of all households consisted of a single person, a trend that is in part illustrative of the aging American population and declining marriage rate.

These changes in composition of households, lower birthrates, and prevalence of single-parent families affect the kinds of demands people place on government as well as their perceptions of the role that government should play in their lives. Single-parent families, for example, may be more likely to support government-subsidized day care or after-school programs.

Analyzing Visuals

HEALTH IMPROVEMENTS COSTLY IN THE LONG RUN

One often thinks of advances in society as improving society. And, on the individual level, that is often true. If you, your parents, or grandparents are the victim of a stroke, you will be thrilled with recent advances such as a new drug that reduces cell death after a stroke and thus minimizes damage. But, the availability of new treatments such as this come with huge societal costs. The cost of just this one new intervention,

for example, will add over $28,000 per year per life of additional costs to Medicare. As you examine the costs associated with each new medical intervention, which ones do you think the government should supply for its citizens? Should access to the newest technologies be limited to those who can afford them? What about making treatments available to those who have smoked or otherwise abused their health?

COSTS PER NEW MEDICAL INTERVENTION

Treatment	What It Does or Would Do	Cost to Medicare per Additional Year of Life
Anti-aging compound for healthy people	$1-a-day compound adds 10 years to life	$11,245
Treatment for acute stroke	New drug reduces cell death after stroke	$28,024
Anti-aging compound for unhealthy people	$1-a-day compound adds 10 years to life	$38,105
Alzheimer's prevention	New drug delays onset of disease	$102,774
Implantable cardioverter defibrillator	Controls heart rhythm	$131,892
Diabetes prevention	Insulin-sensitizing drug reduces disease	$188,316
Pacemakers for atrial fibrillation	New generation of pacemakers	$1,795,850

Source: Rand and *USA Today* (October 25, 2005): 2B.

IMPLICATIONS OF THESE CHANGES

Today, 90 percent of Americans believe that illegal immigration is a serious problem, and several states have attempted to deny drivers licenses or access to other public services to undocumented immigrants.[13] Many believe that the numbers of immigrants, legal and illegal, arriving at our shores will lead to disastrous consequences.

PARTICIPATION

The Debate Over Immigration

Such anti-immigration sentiments are hardly new. In fact, American history is replete with examples of Americans set against any new immigration. In the 1840s, for example, the Know Nothing Party arose in part to oppose immigration from Roman Catholic nations, charging that the pope was going to organize the slaughter of all Protestants in the United States. In the 1920s, the Ku Klux Klan, which had over 5 million members, called for barring immigration to stem the tide of Roman Catholic and Jewish immigrants into the nation.

Changing racial, ethnic, and even age and family demographics also seem to intensify—at least for some—an us versus them mentality. For example, government affirmative action programs, which were created in the 1960s to redress decades of overt racial discrimination, continue to be under attack. As discussed in chapter 6, vocal critics of affirmative action believe that these programs give minorities and women unfair advantages in the job market, as well as in access to higher education.

Demographics also affect politics and government because an individual's perspective influences how he or she hears debates on various issues. Thus, African Americans, for example, viewed the government's initial slow response to the plight of the poor and displaced after Hurricane Katrina more unfavorably than whites.[14]

These cleavages and the emphasis many politicians put on our demographic differences play out in many ways in American politics. Baby Boomers and the elderly

Join the Debate

THE HUNTINGTON THEORY OF HISPANIZATION

OVERVIEW: Many observers of American culture and politics argue that one of the United States' greatest strengths is its ability to absorb and assimilate into the social body the diverse customs and values of different peoples. These commentators highlight the contributions to politics, the arts and sciences, national defense and the common good made by various waves of immigrants—and by those brought against their will during the years of slavery. Traditionalists such as Harvard professor Samuel Huntington contend that the American melting pot has been successful in part because, historically, the new Americans have absorbed the fundamental political principles of the United States as their own. Though there are numerous cultures within the country, Huntington insists that there is one shared American culture based on the values espoused in the Declaration of Independence—that is, American political culture is based on the fundamental principles of equality, individual rights, and government by consent. In order for the love of freedom and self-government to be nurtured and maintained, American core principles must be accepted and protected by all citizens.

Huntington argues that during the latter part of the twentieth and into the twenty-first century, there has been a new wave of immigration into the United States unlike any other; he considers immigration from Mexico in particular, and Latin America in general, to be potentially destructive of original American political principles. According to Huntington's highly controversial thesis, this immigration wave is unique in that there is a political agenda within part of the Hispanic community to "reclaim" the lands ceded to the United States after both the Texas war for independence and the Mexican-American War.

Furthermore, Huntington argues, no other nation has had to contend with a long, contiguous border that immigrants can cross rather freely to maintain familial, economic, and cultural ties, thereby fostering a type of dual national or cultural allegiance (or, at worst, immigrant loyalty to the home country) that can weaken ties to American core values. Finally, he contends, Hispanic immigrants have created linguistic and cultural enclaves within the United States (Los Angeles and Miami, for example) in which there is no need to learn the language, history, and political values of their adopted nation, thus further eroding social and political bonds between citizens.

Huntington's thesis raises serious questions. Are American core ideals so exceptional that only persons who share those values should be allowed citizenship? Can immigrants whose political and social beliefs differ from or oppose America's core values be assimilated into American society? If not, what corrective policy measures should be implemented? Has American history shown that, ultimately, most immigrants and their descendents embrace the principles that underlie the U.S. Constitution and American political culture?

ARGUMENTS FOR HUNTINGTON'S THESIS

■ **The core political values found in the Declaration of Independence and the Constitution are essential to maintain freedom and protect rights.** It may be that original American principles run the risk of being replaced by ideals that advocate forms of government or politics opposed to liberty, self-government, and individual

---

object to any changes in Social Security or Medicare, while those born in the 1960s and 1970s vote for politicians who support change, if they vote at all. Many policies are targeted at one group or the other, further exacerbating differences—real or imagined—and lawmakers often find themselves the target of many different factions. This diversity can make it difficult to devise coherent policies to "promote the general Welfare," as promised in the Constitution.

Political Ideology: Its Role in the World and in American Politics

ON SEPTEMBER 11, 2001, NINETEEN TERRORISTS, all of Middle Eastern origin and professing to be devout Muslims engaged in a "holy war" against the United States,

rights, thus changing the character of the American regime.

- **American institutions and political culture pursue "Justice as the end of government . . . as the end of civil society."** American ideals can be a guide for all to live together effectively in peace and harmony, rather than an end in themselves. These principles allow most individuals to pursue their unique conception of the American dream, relatively free from interference by the government and others.
- **A shared language and civic education bind citizens together.** Teaching multiple languages and cultural viewpoints while denying a common civic education and political origin can create competing sources of identity that will weaken citizens' attachments to one another and to their government.

ARGUMENTS AGAINST HUNTINGTON'S THESIS

- **Historically, certain waves of immigrants were incorrectly thought to be opposed to American values.** Benjamin Franklin expressed concerns that German immigrants could not be assimilated into colonial American life because of their culture and history, and Irish-Catholic immigrants were accused of both giving allegiance to the pope and of being anti-republican in political outlook—fears that proved to be unfounded.
- **Bilingualism in the Hispanic community does not indicate the creation of competing sources of social and political identity.** According to an opinion poll coordinated by the *Washington Post* in 2000, a mere 10 percent of second-generation Hispanic immigrants rely on speaking only Spanish, which follows the pattern of English language adoption by previous waves of immigration to the United States.

- **American political culture is more than its Anglo-Protestant core.** A strength of the American experience is its ability to absorb different cultures and values and transform them into one unique political society. It took both the successive waves of immigration and the freeing of the slaves to move the United States toward the realization of the ideals espoused in the Declaration of Independence.

QUESTIONS

1. Does the issue of Hispanic immigration threaten American sovereignty and values? Do demonstrations by pro- and anti-immigrant groups signal a significant shift in U.S. history?
2. Is American political culture more than its core principles and institutions? If so, what other values and institutions add to the United States' claim that it is a true "melting pot?"

SELECTED READINGS

Daniels, Roger. *Guarding the Golden Door: American Immigration Policy and Immigrants Since 1882*. New York: Hill and Wang, 2004.

Huntington, Samuel. *Who Are We? The Challenges to America's National Identity*. New York: Simon and Schuster, 2004.

---

hijacked four airplanes and eventually killed more than 3,000 people. The terrorists' self-described holy war, or *jihad*, was targeted at Americans, whom they considered infidels. Earlier, in 1995, a powerful fertilizer bomb exploded outside the Murrah Federal Building in Oklahoma City, killing nearly 170 people, including many children. This terrorist attack was launched not by those associated with radical Islam, but with an anti-government brand of neo-Nazism. Its proponents hold the U.S. government in contempt and profess a hatred of Jews and others they believe are "inferior" ethnic groups and races.

These are but two extreme examples of the powerful role of **ideologies** in the actions of individuals.[15] Ideologies are sets or systems of beliefs that shape the thinking of individuals and how they view the world, especially in regard to issues of "race, nationality, the role and function of government, the relations between men and women, human responsibility for the natural environment, and many other matters."[16] They have been increasingly recognized as a potent political force. Sir Isaiah Berlin, a noted historian and philosopher, noted that two factors above all others shaped human history in the twentieth century: one is science and

ideology
A set or system of beliefs that shapes the thinking of individuals and how they view the world.

technology; the other ideological battles— totalitarian tyrannies of both right and left and the explosions of nationalism, racism, and in places, of religious bigotry, which the most perceptive social thinkers of the nineteenth century failed to predict.[17]

Political scientists note that ideologies perform four key functions:

1. *Explanation.* Ideologies can provide us with reasons for why social and political conditions are the way they are, especially in time of crisis.
2. *Evaluation.* Ideologies can provide the standards for evaluating social conditions and political institutions and events.
3. *Orientation.* Ideologies can provide a sense of identity, whether you are male, female, native born, or foreign born, for example. Much like compasses, ideologies provide individuals with an orientation toward issues and a position within the world.
4. *Political Program.* Ideologies help people to make political choices and guide their political actions.

PREVAILING AMERICAN POLITICAL IDEOLOGIES

Today, in America, one most often hears about conservative, moderate, or liberal **political ideologies.** (Figure 1.5 shows the proportions of each group.) These ideologies often translate into political party support, which in turn affects how one votes at the polls. A small proportion of Americans also refer to themselves as **libertarians,** but pollsters rarely offer respondents the opportunity to label themselves as such.

Conservatism According to William Safire's *New Political Dictionary*, a **conservative** "is a defender of the status quo who, when change becomes necessary in tested institutions or practices, prefers that it come slowly, and in moderation."[18] Conservatives tend to believe that a government is best that governs least. They want less government, especially in terms of regulation of the economy. Conservatives favor local and state action over federal action, and emphasize fiscal responsibility, most

political ideology
The coherent set of values and beliefs about the purpose and scope of government held by groups and individuals.

libertarian
One who favors a free market economy and no governmental interference in personal libetties.

conservative
One thought to believe that a government is best that governs least and that big government can only infringe on individual, personal, and economic rights.

FIGURE 1.5 ADULT SELF-IDENTIFICATION AS LIBERAL, MODERATE, OR CONSERVATIVE, 1974–2006

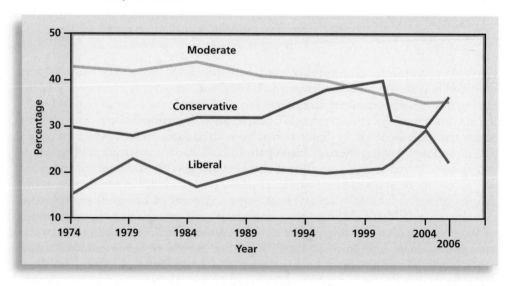

Source: Roper Center at the University of Connecticut, *Public Opinion Online.*

■ Speaker of the House Nancy Pelosi (D–CA) and House Minority Leader John Boehner (R–OH) represent vastly different ideological perspectives.

Photos courtesy: left, Greg Whitesell/UPI/Landov; right, Dennis Brack/Bloomberg News/Landov

notably in the form of balanced budgets. Conservatives are likely to support smaller, less activist governments and believe that domestic problems like homelessness, poverty, and discrimination are better dealt with by the private sector than by the government. Since the 1970s, **social conservatives** (sometimes referred to as the Religious Right) have increasingly affected politics and policies in the United States. Social conservatives believe that moral decay must be stemmed and that traditional moral teachings should be supported and furthered by the government. Social conservatives support government intervention to regulate sexual and social behavior and have mounted effective efforts to make abortion illegal and ban same-sex marriage. While a majority of social conservatives are evangelical Christians, some Jews and many Muslims are also social conservatives.

social conservative
One who believes that traditional moral teachings should be supported and furthered by the government.

Liberalism **Liberals** are identified as those who seek to change the political, economic, and social status quo to foster the development of equality and the well-being of individuals.[19] The meaning of the words liberal and liberalism have changed over time, but in the modern United States, liberals generally value equality over other aspects of shared political culture. They are supportive of well-funded government social welfare programs that seek to protect individuals from economic disadvantages or correct past injustices, and they generally oppose government efforts to regulate private behavior or infringe on civil rights and liberties.

liberal
One considered to favor governmental involvement in the economy and in the provision of social services and to take an activist role in protecting the rights of women, the elderly, minorities, and the environment.

PROBLEMS WITH POLITICAL LABELS

In a perfect world, liberals would be liberal and conservatives would be conservative. Studies reveal, however, that many people who call themselves conservative actually take fairly liberal positions on many policy issues. In fact, anywhere from 20 percent to 60 percent will take a traditionally conservative position on one issue and a traditionally liberal position on another.[20] People who take conservative stances against "big government," for example, often support increases in spending for the elderly, education, or health care. It is also not unusual to encounter a person who could be considered a liberal on social issues such as abortion and civil rights but a conservative on economic or pocketbook issues. And, as Figure 1.6 makes clear, states are not uniformly "red" or "blue," even though they are often portrayed that way in media reports. Today, most Americans' positions on specific issues cut across liberal/conservative ideological boundaries, and most people prefer to be categorized as moderates.

FIGURE 1.6 THE 2004 PRESIDENTIAL ELECTION RESULTS BY COUNTY

As the 2004 presidential election approached, analysts began to speak of a growing split in ideology occurring throughout the United States. After the election, a quick look at a U.S. map in which each state's Electoral College result was colored red (for George W. Bush) or blue (for John Kerry) made clear the split between voters on the West Coast and in the Northeast and those in the Southeast and Midwest. However, as this map showing the popular vote by county highlights, numerous blocks of counties within states such as Texas and Florida where Bush won the Electoral College votes actually went to Kerry. A similar pattern can be identified in blue states such as New York that went for Kerry: Bush won a significant number of counties there. What demographic factors might account for this? In a number of states—for example, Utah, Oklahoma, Nevada, Kansas, and Nebraska—Kerry won very few or no counties. Bush won few or no counties in Massachusetts and Vermont. What might account for these results?

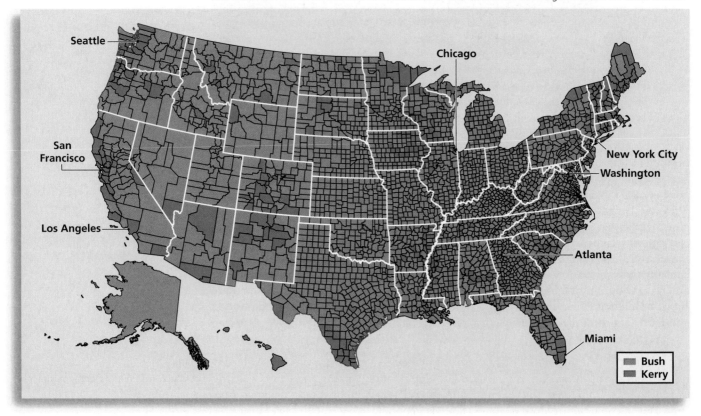

Sources: Associated Press; *Congressional Record*; Census Bureau.

Current Attitudes Toward American Government

AMERICANS' VIEWS ABOUT AND EXPECTATIONS OF government and democracy affect the political system at all levels. It has now become part of our political culture to expect negative campaigns, dishonest politicians, and political pundits who make their living bashing politicians and the political process. How Americans view politics, the economy, and their ability to achieve the **American dream**—an American ideal of a happy and successful life, which often includes wealth, a house, a better life for one's children, and, for some, the ability to grow up to be president—also is influenced by their political ideology as well as by their social, economic, educational, and personal circumstances.

Since the early 1990s, the major sources of most individuals' on-the-air news—the four major networks (ABC, CBS, FOX, and NBC) along with CNN and C-SPAN—have been supplemented dramatically as the number of news and quasi-news outlets has grown exponentially. First there were weekly programs such as *Dateline* on the regular networks. Next came FOX News, MSNBC, and CNBC—all competing for similar

American dream
An American ideal of a happy, successful life, which often includes wealth, a house, a better life for one's children, and, for some, the ability to grow up to be president.

audiences. During the 2006 election, for example, more people turned to a cable news program than to the regular networks for their political coverage. In addition, the Internet has quickly developed as an instantaneous source of news, as well as rumor, about politics. The growth of online diaries, usually called blogs, has accelerated this phenomenon.

As more and more news programs develop, the pressure on each network or news program to be the first with the news multiplies exponentially, as was illustrated on Election Night 2000 when all of the networks rushed to call states for a particular candidate and to be the first to predict the overall winner. The competition for news stories, as well as the instantaneous nature of these communications, often highlights the negative, the sensational, the sound bite, and the extreme. It's hard to remain upbeat about America or politics amidst the media's focus on personality and scandal. It's hard to remain positive about the fate of Americans and their families if you watch talk news shows that feature guests trying to outshout each other or watch campaign ads that highlight only the negative.

We also cannot ignore how Americans are now viewed abroad. For centuries, immigrants have come to our shores to be part of the American dream—but now, to some people in Europe, the Middle East, and elsewhere, America is no longer the beacon it once was. The spread of American culture as embodied by fast-food chains and American television programs such as *Sex and the City* and *Will and Grace* to other nations, along with the United States' unpopular involvement in Iraq, has intensified the stereotype of the "ugly American." Negative perceptions of the United States increasingly affect America's relations around the world, with important effects on Americans' expectations. When the cost of gasoline hit record levels in 2006, for example, an increasing number of Americans had to make difficult budgetary decisions in order to be able to commute to work.

Technological Innovations That Have Changed the American Political Landscape

HIGH EXPECTATIONS

In roughly the first 150 years of our nation's history, the federal government had few responsibilities, and its citizens had few expectations of it beyond national defense, printing money, and collecting tariffs and taxes. The state governments were generally far more powerful than the federal government in matters affecting the everyday lives of Americans (see chapters 3 and 4).

As the nation and its economy grew in size and complexity, the federal government took on more responsibilities, such as regulating some businesses, providing poverty relief, and inspecting food. Then, in response to the Great Depression of the 1930s, President Franklin D. Roosevelt's New Deal government programs proliferated in almost every area of American life, including job creation, income security, and aid to the poor. Since then, many Americans have looked to the government for solutions to all kinds of problems.

Politicians, too, have often contributed to rising public expectations by promising far more than they or government could deliver. Although President George W. Bush vowed to "leave no child behind," the high costs of waging war, a failing economy, and increases in the cost of homeland security left little money to fund that ambitious program to implement nationwide educational standards.

As voters look to governments to solve a variety of problems from education to terrorism, their expectations are not always met. Unmet expectations have led to cynicism about government and apathy, as evidenced in low voter turnout. It may be that Americans have come to expect too much from the national government and must simply readjust their expectations.

A MISSING APPRECIATION OF THE GOOD

Today, many Americans lack faith in the country's institutions and symbols. (See Figure 1.7.) This distrust makes it even easier for citizens to blame the government for all kinds of woes—personal as well as societal—or to fail to credit governments for the things they do well. Many Americans, for example, enjoy a remarkably high standard of living, and much of it is due to governmental programs and protections. (See Table 1.2 for quality of life measures.)

FIGURE 1.7 FAITH IN INSTITUTIONS

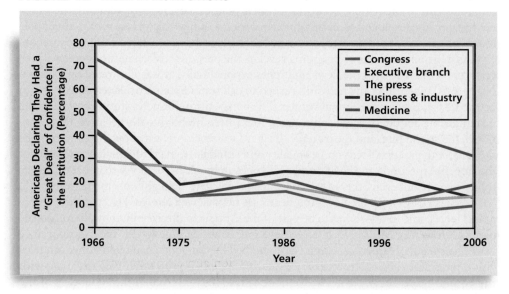

Sources: *Newsweek* (January 8, 1996): 32; *Public Perspective* 8 (February/March 1994): 4, Lexis-Nexis RPOLL, *Washington Post* (June 13, 2006): A2.

Even in the short time between when you get up in the morning and when you leave for classes or work, the government—or its rulings or regulations—pervades your life. The national or state governments, for example, set the standards for whether you wake up on Eastern, Central, Mountain, or Pacific Standard Time. The national government regulates the airwaves and licenses the radio or television broadcasts you might listen to or glance at as you eat and get dressed. States, too, regulate and tax telecommunications. Whether the water you use as you brush your teeth contains fluoride is a state or local governmental issue. The federal Food and Drug Administration inspects your breakfast meat and sets standards for the advertising on your cereal box, orange juice carton, and other food packaging. States set standards for food labeling. Are products really "lite," "high in fiber," or "fresh squeezed"? Usually, one or more levels of government are authorized to decide these matters.

Although all governments have problems, it is important to stress the good they can do. In the aftermath of the Great Depression in the United States, for example, the government created the Social Security program, which dramatically decreased poverty among the elderly. Our contract laws and judicial system provide an efficient framework for business, assuring people that they have a recourse in the courts should

TABLE 1.2 HOW ARE AMERICANS REALLY DOING?

	1945	1970	2005
Life expectancy	65.9	70.8	77.8
Per capita income (1999 constant dollars)	$6,367	$12,816	$27,240
Adults who are high school grads	25%[a]	52.3%	85.2%
Adults who are college grads	5%[a]	10.7%	27.7%
Households with phones	46%	87%	95.5%
Households with cable TV	0%	4%	69.8%
Women in labor force	29%	38%	58.9%
Own their own home	46%	63%	69%
Below poverty line	39.7%[b]	12.6%	12.7%

[a] 1940 figure.

[b] 1949 figure.

Source: U.S. Census Bureau, *2006 Statistical Abstract of the United States.*

someone fail to deliver as promised. Government-guaranteed student loan programs make it possible for many students to attend college. Government-sponsored research has also contributed to the development of new medicines to improve life expectancy. Thus, as Table 1.2 underscores, Americans live longer today than ever before, far more are high school graduates, and telephones and the development of cable television have dramatically changed how Americans live and work. And, as more women have entered the labor force, more families also own their own homes.

■ Former House Majority Leader Tom DeLay (R–TX) was forced to resign in the wake of an ethics scandal. Behavior such as DeLay's fuels Americans' misturst of many politicians.

Photo courtesy: Chip Somodevilla/Getty Images

MISTRUST OF POLITICIANS

One 2005 poll conducted by the Roper Center for Public Opinion Research at the University of Connecticut found that only 23 percent of Americans trust politicians.[21] A glance at the pages of any major newspaper offers a number of illustrations why this might be the case. Scandals involving advisers to President Bush, K Street lobbyists, and members of Congress are continually in the news. In one particularly striking example, House Majority Leader Tom DeLay (R–TX) was forced to resign first from his leadership position and later from the House altogether following allegations about the legality of a series of financial deals made by his associate, lobbyist Jack Abramoff, and several members of DeLay's congressional staff (see chapter 16). These allegations came on the heels of a redistricting scandal in DeLay's home state of Texas that led to several Democratic incumbents losing their seats in November 2004 general elections after they were pitted against Republican incumbents.

Despite scandals such as these, it is important to remember that most politicians do not conform to this mold. Instead, the great majority of politicians are hard-working individuals who pride themselves on being able to deliver programs and services to the members of their districts.

VOTER APATHY

Americans, unlike voters in many other societies, get an opportunity to vote on a host of candidates and issues, but some say those choices may just be too numbing. Responsible voters may simply opt not to go to the polls, fearing that they lack sufficient information regarding the vast array of candidates and issues facing them.

A Census Bureau report examining the reasons given by the millions of eligible voters who stayed home from the polls on Election Day in 2004 showed that being too busy was the single biggest reason Americans gave for not voting. The head of the Committee for the Study of the American Electorate thinks that time is just an excuse.[22] Instead, he believes many Americans don't vote because they lack real choices. Why vote, if your vote won't make much difference? In fact, Ralph Nader tried to run as an alternative to the two major parties in 2000 and 2004, arguing that there was little difference between Republicans and Democrats.

VIDEO ROUNDTABLE

Political Corruption

Some commentators have noted that nonvoting may even be a sign of contentment. If things are good, or you perceive that there is no need for change, why vote?

REDEFINING OUR EXPECTATIONS

Just as it is important to recognize that governments serve many important purposes, it is also important to recognize that government and politics are not static. Politics, moreover, involves conflicts over different and sometimes opposing ideologies, and these ideologies are very much influenced by one's racial, economic, and historical experiences. These divisions are real and affect the political process at all levels. It is clear to most Americans today that politics and government no longer can be counted on to cure all of America's ills. Government, however, will always play a major role. True political leaders will need to help Americans come to terms with America as it is to-day—not as it was in the past—real or imaginary. Perhaps a discussion on how "community" is necessary for everybody to get along (and necessary for democracy) is in order. Some democratic theorists suggest that the citizen-activist must bear ultimate responsibility for the resolution of these divisions.

The current frustration and dissatisfaction with politics and government may be just another phase, as the changing American body politic seeks to redefine its ideas about and expectations of government. This process is one that is likely to define politics well into the future, but the individualistic nature of the American system will have long-lasting consequences on how that redefinition can be accomplished. Americans want less government, but as they get older, they don't want less Social Security. They want lower taxes and better roads, but they don't want to pay for toll roads. They want better education for their children but lower expenditures on schools. They want greater security at airports but low fares and quick boarding. Some clearly want less for others but not themselves, a demand that puts politicians in the position of nearly always disappointing voters.

Politicians, as well as their constituents, are looking for ways to redefine the role of government, much in the same way that the Framers did when they met in Philadelphia to forge a solution between Americans' quest for liberty and freedom tempered by order and governmental authority. While citizens charge that it is still government as usual, a change is taking place in Washington, D.C. Sacrosanct programs such as Social Security and welfare are being continually reexamined, and some powers and responsibilities are being slowly returned to the states. Thus, the times may be different, but the questions about government and its role in our lives remain the same.

Although national crises such as the Civil War, the Great Depression, Watergate, and the 9/11 terrorist attacks created major turmoil, they demonstrated that our system can survive and even change in the face of enormous political, societal, and institutional pressures. Often, these crises have produced considerable reforms. The Civil War led to the dismantling of the slavery system and to the passage of the Thirteenth, Fourteenth, and Fifteenth Amendments (see chapter 6), which planted the seeds of recognition of African Americans as full American citizens. The Great Depression led to the New Deal and the creation of a government more actively involved in economic and social regulation. In the 1970s, the Watergate scandal and resignation of President Richard M. Nixon resulted in stricter ethics laws that have led to the resignation or removal of many unethical elected officials. Post 9/11, Americans seem more willing to accept limits on civil liberties to battle terrorism. At the same time, they are more aware of the nation's interdependence with the rest of the world.

Summary

IN THIS CHAPTER, we have made the following points:

1. **Government: What It Is and Why We Need It**
   Governments, which are made up of individuals and institutions, are the vehicles through which policies are made and affairs of state are conducted. We need governments to maintain order because governments alone can use force legitimately. Governments have many functions. In the U.S. context, most are included in the Preamble to the Constitution. Governments take many forms depending on the number who rule as well as whose interests are represented.

2. **Roots of American Government: Where Did the Ideas Come From?**
   The American political system is based on several principles that have their roots in classical Greek ideas. The ideas of social contract theorists John Locke and Thomas Hobbes, who held the belief that people are free and equal by God-given right, have continuing implications for our ideas of the proper role of government in our indirect democracy.

3. **American Political Culture and the Characteristics of American Democracy**
   Key characteristics of the political culture are personal liberty, equality, popular consent and majority rule, popular sovereignty, civil society, individualism, and religious faith.

4. **Changing Characteristics of the American People**
   Several characteristics of the American electorate can help us understand how the system continues to evolve and change. Chief among these are changes in size, population, and demographics.

5. **Political Ideology: Its Role in the World and in American Politics**
   Ideologies and ideas play a powerful role in politics here and abroad. Most Americans identify themselves as conservatives, liberals, or moderates.

6. **Current Attitudes Toward American Government**
   Americans have high and often unrealistic expectations of government. At the same time, they often fail to appreciate how much their government actually does for them. Some of this failure may be due to Americans' general mistrust of politicians, which may explain some of the apathy evidenced in the electorate.

KEY TERMS

American dream, p. 24
citizen, p. 5
civil society, p. 12
conservative, p. 22
democracy, p. 7
direct democracy, p. 11
government, p. 5
ideology, p. 21
indirect (representative) democracy, p. 11
liberal, p. 23
libertarian, p. 22
majority rule, p. 12
monarchy, p. 7
natural law, p. 12
oligarchy, p. 7
personal liberty, p. 11
political culture, p. 11
political equality, p. 12
political ideology, p. 22
politics, p. 5
popular consent, p. 12
popular sovereignty, p. 12
republic, p. 11
social conservative, p. 23
social contract, p. 8
social contract theory, p. 9
totalitarianism, p. 7

SELECTED READINGS

Almond, Gabriel A., and Sidney Verba. *Civic Culture: Political Attitudes and Democracy in Five Nations.* Princeton, NJ: Princeton University Press, 1963.

Ball, Terence, and Richard Dagger. *Political Ideologies and the Democratic Ideal,* 5th ed. New York: Longman, 2004.

Dahl, Robert A. *Polyarchy: Participation and Opposition.* New Haven, CT: Yale University Press, 1971.

Elshtain, Jean Bethke. *Democracy on Trial.* New York: Basic Books, 1995.

Fiorina, Morris P. *Culture War? The Myth of a Polarized America.* New York: Longman, 2004.

Fournier, Ron, Douglas B. Sosnick, and Matthew J. Dowd. *Applebee's America: How Successful Political, Business, and Religious Leaders Connect with the New American Community.* New York: Simon and Schuster, 2006.

Jamieson, Kathleen Hall. *Everything You Think You Know About Politics . . . and Why You're Wrong.* New York: Basic Books, 2000.

Hobbes, Thomas. *Leviathan.* Richard Tuck, ed. New York: Cambridge University Press, 1996.

Hochschild, Jennifer L. *Facing Up to the American Dream: Race, Class, and the Soul of the Nation.* Princeton, NJ: Princeton University Press, 1995.

Locke, John. *Two Treatises of Government.* Peter Lasleti, ed. New York: Cambridge University Press, 1988.

Nye, Joseph S., Jr. *The Paradox of American Power: Why the World's Superpower Can't Go It Alone.* New York: Oxford University Press, 2002.

Putnam, Robert D. *Bowling Alone: Collapse and Revival of the American Community.* New York: Simon and Schuster, 2000.

Skocpol, Theda, and Morris P. Fiorina, eds. *Civic Engagement in American Democracy.* Washington, DC: Brookings Institution Press, 1999.

Verba, Sidney, Kay Schlozman, and Henry Brady. *Voice and Equality: Civic Volunteerism in American Politics,* 2nd ed. Cambridge, MA: Harvard University Press, 2002.

Zakaria, Fareed. *The Future of Freedom: Illiberal Democracy at Home and Abroad.* New York: Norton, 2003.

WEB EXPLORATIONS

To connect with others who are interested in politics, see
http://www.pbs.org/news/news_government.html
For more on Thomas Hobbes and John Locke, see
http://www.iep.utm.edu/h/hobmoral.htm and
http://www.utm.edu/research/iep/l/locke.htm
To get a minute by minute update on U.S. population, see
http://www.census.gov/
For more detail on population projections, see
http://www.census.gov/population/www/projections/natsum.html
For more information on families and household composition, see
http://www.census.gov/population/socdemo/hh-fam/98ppla.txt
For more information on conservatives, see
http://www.conservative.org/
For more information on liberals, see
http://www.liberaloasis.com
To find out your ideological stance, go to
www.politicalcompass.org/index
For more information on the American electorate, see
http://www.census.gov/population/www/socdemo/voting/p20-542.html

We the People

insure domestic Tranquility, provide for the common

and our Posterity, do ordain and establish this Consti

Article I.

Section 1. All legislative Powers herein granted shall be vested in a Congress of the United States, which shall consist of a Se
of Representatives.

Section 2. The House of Representatives shall be composed of Members chosen every second Year by the People of the several Sta
in each State shall have Qualifications requisite for Electors of the most numerous Branch of the State Legislature.

No Person shall be a Representative who shall not have attained to the Age of twenty five Years, and been seven Years a Citizen
and who shall not, when elected, be an Inhabitant of that State in which he shall be chosen.

Representatives and direct Taxes shall be apportioned among the several States which may be included within this Union, according to
Numbers, which shall be determined by adding to the whole Number of free Persons, including those bound to Service for a Term of Years, and
not taxed, three fifths of all other Persons. The actual Enumeration shall be made within three Years after the first Meeting of the Congress
and within every subsequent Term of Ten Years, in such Manner as they shall by Law direct. The Number of Representatives shall not
fifty Thousand, but each State shall have at Least one Representative; and until such enumeration shall be made, the State of New Ham
shall to chuse three, Massachusetts eight, Rhode Island and Providence Plantations one, Connecticut five, New York

THE CONSTITUTION 2

AT AGE EIGHTEEN, all American citizens are eligible to vote in state and national elections. This has not always been the case. It took an amendment to the U.S. Constitution—one of only seventeen that have been added since the Bill of Rights was ratified in 1791—to guarantee the franchise to those under twenty-one years of age.

In 1942, during World War II, Representative Jennings Randolph (D–WV) proposed that the voting age be lowered to eighteen, believing that since young men were old enough to be drafted to fight and die for their country, they also should be allowed to vote. He continued to reintroduce his proposal during every session of Congress, and in 1954 President Dwight D. Eisenhower endorsed the idea in his State of the Union message. Presidents Lyndon B. Johnson and Richard M. Nixon—men who had also called upon the nation's young men to fight on foreign shores—echoed his appeal.[1]

During the 1960s, the campaign to lower the voting age took on a new sense of urgency as hundreds of thousands of young men were drafted to fight in Vietnam and thousands of men and women were killed in action. "Old Enough to Fight, Old Enough to Vote," was one popular slogan of the day. By 1970, four states—who under the U.S. Constitution are allowed to set the eligibility requirements for their voters—had lowered their voting ages to eighteen. Later that year, Congress passed legislation lowering the voting age in national, state, and local elections to eighteen.

The state of Oregon, however, challenged the constitutionality of the law in court, arguing that Congress had not been given the authority to establish a uniform voting age in state and local government under the Constitution. The U.S. Supreme Court agreed.[2] The decision from the sharply divided Court meant that those under age twenty-one could vote in national elections but that the states were free to prohibit them from voting in state and local elections. The decision presented the states with a logistical nightmare. States setting the voting age at twenty-one would be forced to keep two sets of registration books: one for voters twenty-one and over, and one for voters under twenty-one.

Jennings Randolph, by then a senator from West Virginia, reintroduced his proposed amendment to lower the national voting age to eighteen.[3] Within three months of the Supreme Court's decision, Congress sent

CHAPTER OUTLINE

- ✪ The Origins of a New Nation
- ✪ The First Attempt at Government: The Articles of Confederation
- ✪ The Miracle at Philadelphia: Writing a Constitution
- ✪ The U.S. Constitution
- ✪ The Drive for Ratification
- ✪ Methods of Amending the Constitution

the proposed Twenty-Sixth Amendment to the states for their ratification. The required three-fourths of the states approved the amendment within three months—making its adoption on June 30, 1971, the quickest in the history of the constitutional amending process.

However, young people never have voted in large numbers. In spite of issues of concern to those under the age of twenty-five, including a possible draft, Internet privacy, reproductive rights, credit card and cell phone rules and regulations, rising college tuition, and the continuance of student loan programs, until 2004 voter turnout among those age eighteen to twenty-four continued to decline. Voter registration drives and voter awareness campaigns by groups like Rock the Vote and Hip-Hop Summit Action Network produced record numbers of young voters in 2004. And, according to exit polls after the 2006 elections, the number of young voters was up by two percent over the youth turnout for the 2002 elections.

THE CONSTITUTION INTENTIONALLY WAS WRITTEN to forestall the need for amendment, and the process by which it could be changed or amended was made time consuming and difficult. Over the years, thousands of amendments—including those to prohibit child labor, provide equal rights for women, grant statehood to the District of Columbia, balance the federal budget, and ban flag burning—have been debated or sent to the states for their approval, only to die slow deaths. Only twenty-seven amendments have successfully made their way into the Constitution. What the Framers came up with in Philadelphia has continued to work, in spite of increasing demands on and dissatisfaction with our national government. Perhaps Americans are happier with the system of government created by the Framers than they realize.

The ideas that went into the making of the Constitution and the ways in which it has evolved to address the problems of a growing and changing nation are at the core of our discussion in this chapter.

- First, we will examine *the origins of a new nation* and the circumstances surrounding the Declaration of Independence and the break with Great Britain.
- Second, we will discuss *the first attempt at American government* created by the *Articles of Confederation.*
- Third, we will examine the circumstances surrounding *writing a Constitution* in Philadelphia.
- Fourth, we will review the results of the Framers' efforts—*the U.S. Constitution.*
- Fifth, we will present *the drive for ratification* of the new government.
- Finally, we will address *methods of amending the Constitution.*

The Origins of a New Nation

STARTING IN THE EARLY SEVENTEENTH CENTURY, colonists came to the New World for a variety of reasons. Often, as detailed in chapter 1, it was to escape religious persecution. Others came seeking a new start on a continent where land was plentiful. The independence and diversity of the settlers in the New World made the question of how best to rule the new colonies a tricky one. More than merely an ocean separated England from the colonies; the colonists were independent people, and it soon became clear that the crown could not govern its subjects in the colonies with the same close rein used at home. King James I thus allowed some local participation in decision making through arrangements such as the first elected colonial assembly, the Virginia House of Burgesses formed in 1619, and the elected General Court that governed the Massachusetts Bay colony after 1629. Almost all of the colonists agreed that the king ruled by divine right, but English monarchs allowed the colonists significant liberties in terms of self-government, religious practices, and economic organization. For 140 years, this system worked fairly well.[4]

By the early 1760s, however, a century and a half of physical separation, development of colonial industry, and the relative self-governance of the colonies led to weakening ties with—and loyalties to—the crown. By this time, each of the thirteen colonies had drafted its own written constitution, which provided the fundamental rules or laws for each colony. Moreover, many of the most oppressive British traditions—feudalism, a rigid class system, and the absolute authority of the king—were absent in the New World. Land was abundant. The guild and craft systems that severely limited entry into many skilled professions in England did not exist in the colonies. Although religion was central to the lives of most colonists, there was no single state church, and the British practice of compulsory tithing (giving a fixed percentage of one's earnings to the state-sanctioned and -supported church) was nonexistent.

TRADE AND TAXATION

Mercantilism, an economic theory designed to increase a nation's wealth through the development of commercial industry and a favorable balance of trade, justified Britain's maintenance of strict import/export controls on the colonies. After 1650, for example, Parliament passed a series of navigation acts to prevent its chief rival, Holland, from trading with the English colonies. From 1650 until well into the 1700s, England tried to regulate colonial imports and exports, believing that it was critical to export more goods than it imported as a way of increasing the gold and silver in its treasury. These policies, however, were difficult to enforce and were widely ignored by the colonists, who saw little self-benefit in them. Thus, for years, an unwritten agreement existed. The colonists relinquished to the crown and the British Parliament the authority to regulate trade and conduct international affairs, but they retained the right to levy their own taxes.

This fragile agreement was soon put to the test. The French and Indian War, fought from 1756 to 1763 on the western frontier of the colonies and in Canada, was part of a global war initiated by the British. This American phase of the Seven Years' War was fought between England and France with its Indian allies. In North America, its immediate cause was the rival claims of those two European nations for the lands between the Allegheny Mountains and the Mississippi River. The Treaty of Paris, signed in 1763, signaled the end of the war. The colonists expected that with the Indian problem on the western frontier now under control, westward migration and settlement could begin in earnest. In 1763, they were shocked when the crown decreed that there was to be no further westward movement by British subjects. Parliament believed that expansion into Indian territory would lead to new expenditures for the defense of the settlers, draining the British treasury, which had yet to recover from the high cost of waging the war.

To raise money to pay for the war as well as the expenses of administering the colonies, Parliament enacted the Sugar Act in 1764, which placed taxes on sugar, wine, coffee, and other products commonly exported to the colonies. A postwar colonial depression heightened resentment of the tax. Major protest, however, failed to materialize until imposition of the Stamp Act by the British Parliament in 1765. This law required that all paper items bought and sold in the colonies carry a stamp mandated by the crown. The tax itself was not offensive to the colonists. However, they feared this act would establish a precedent for the British Parliament not only to regulate commerce in the colonies, but also to raise revenues from the colonists without the approval of the colonial governments. Around the colonies, the political cry "no taxation without representation" became prominent. To add insult to injury, in 1765, Parliament passed the Quartering Act, which required the colonists to furnish barracks or provide living quarters within their own homes for British troops.

mercantilism
An economic theory designed to increase a nation's wealth through the development of commercial industry and a favorable balance of trade.

■ Today, Samuel Adams (1722–1803) is well known for the beer that bears his name. His original claim to fame was as a leader against the British and loyalist oppressors (although he did bankrupt his family's brewery business). As a member of the Massachusetts legislature, he advocated defiance of the Stamp Act. With the passage of the Townshend Acts in 1767, he organized a letter-writing campaign urging other colonies to join in resistance. Later, in 1772, he founded the Committees of Correspondence to unite the colonies.

Stamp Act Congress
Meeting of representatives of nine of the thirteen colonies held in New York City in 1765, during which representatives drafted a document to send to the king listing how their rights had been violated.

Committees of Correspondence
Organizations in each of the American colonies created to keep colonists abreast of developments with the British; served as powerful molders of public opinion against the British.

Most colonists, especially those in New England, where these acts hit merchants hardest, were outraged. Men throughout the colonies organized the Sons of Liberty, under the leadership of Samuel Adams and Patrick Henry. Women formed the Daughters of Liberty. Protests against the Stamp Act were violent and loud. Riots, often led by the Sons of Liberty, broke out. They were especially violent in Boston, where the colonial governor's home was burned by an angry mob, and British stamp agents charged with collecting the tax were threatened. A boycott of goods needing the stamps as well as British imports also was organized.

FIRST STEPS TOWARD INDEPENDENCE

In 1765, nine of the thirteen colonies sent representatives to a meeting in New York City, where a detailed list of crown violations of the colonists' fundamental rights was drafted. Known as the **Stamp Act Congress,** this gathering was the first official meeting of the colonies and the first step toward a unified nation. Attendees defined what they thought to be the proper relationship between colonial governments and the British Parliament; they ardently believed Parliament had no authority to tax them without representation in that body. In contrast, the British believed that direct representation of the colonists was impractical and that members of Parliament represented the best interests of all the English, including the colonists.

The Stamp Act Congress and its petitions to the crown did little to stop the onslaught of taxing measures. Parliament did, however, repeal the Stamp Act and revise the Sugar Act in 1766, largely because of the uproar made by British merchants who were losing large sums of money as a result of the boycotts. Rather than appeasing the colonists, however, these actions emboldened them to increase their resistance. In 1767, Parliament enacted the Townshend Acts, which imposed duties on all kinds of colonial imports, including tea. Responses from the Sons and Daughters of Liberty were immediate. Another boycott was announced, and almost all colonists gave up their favorite drink in a united show of resistance to the tax and British authority.[5] Tensions continued to run high, especially after the British sent 4,000 troops to Boston. On March 5, 1770, English troops opened fire on a mob that included disgruntled dock workers, whose jobs had been taken by British soldiers, and members of the Sons of Liberty, who were taunting the soldiers in front of the Boston Customs House. Five colonists were killed in what became known as the Boston Massacre. Following this confrontation, all duties except those on tea were lifted. The tea tax, however, continued to be a symbolic irritant. In 1772, at the suggestion of Samuel Adams, Boston and other towns around Massachusetts set up **Committees of Correspondence** to articulate ideas and keep communications open around the colony. By 1774, twelve colonies had formed committees to maintain a flow of information among like-minded colonists.

Meanwhile, despite dissent in England over the treatment of the colonies, Parliament passed another tea tax designed to shore up the sagging sales of the East India Company, a British exporter of tea. The colonists' boycott had left that British trading house with more than 18 million pounds of tea in its warehouses. To rescue British merchants from disaster, in 1773 Parliament passed the Tea Act, granting a monopoly to the financially strapped East India Company to sell the tea imported from Britain. The company was allowed to funnel business to American merchants loyal to the crown, thereby undercutting colonial merchants, who could sell only tea imported from other nations. The effect was to drive down the price of tea and to hurt colonial merchants, who were forced to buy tea at the higher prices from other sources.

When the next shipment of tea arrived in Boston from Great Britain, the colonists responded by throwing the Boston Tea Party. Similar tea parties were held in other colonies. When the news of these actions reached King George III, he flew into a rage against the actions of his disloyal subjects. "The die is now cast," the king told his prime minister. "The colonies must either submit or triumph."

King George's first act of retaliation was to persuade Parliament to pass the Coercive Acts of 1774. Known in the colonies as the Intolerable Acts, they contained a key provision calling for a total blockade of Boston Harbor until restitution was made for the tea. Another provision reinforced the Quartering Act. It gave royal governors the authority to house British soldiers in the homes of private citizens, allowing Britain to send an additional 4,000 soldiers to patrol Boston.

THE FIRST CONTINENTAL CONGRESS

The British could never have guessed how the cumulative impact of these actions would unite the colonists. Samuel Adams's Committees of Correspondence spread the word, and food and money were sent to the people of Boston from all over the thirteen colonies. The tax itself was no longer the key issue; now the extent of British authority over the colonies was the far more important question. At the request of the colonial assemblies of Massachusetts and Virginia, all but Georgia's colonial assembly agreed to select a group of delegates to attend a continental congress authorized to communicate with the king on behalf of the now-united colonies.

Photo courtesy: Collection of the New York Historical Society

■ Paul Revere's engraving of the Boston Massacre was potent propaganda. Five men were killed, not seven, as the legend states, and the rioters in front of the State House (left) were scarcely as docile as Revere portrayed them.

■ To hurt American merchants loyal to the crown, colonists threw a "Boston Tea Party" on December 16, 1773.

Photo courtesy: Bettmann/Corbis

First Continental Congress
Meeting held in Philadelphia from September 5 to October 26, 1774, in which fifty-six delegates (from every colony except Georgia) adopted a resolution in opposition to the Coercive Acts.

The **First Continental Congress** met in Philadelphia from September 5 to October 26, 1774. It was made up of fifty-six delegates from Connecticut, Delaware, Maryland, Massachusetts, New Hampshire, New Jersey, New York, North Carolina, Pennsylvania, South Carolina, Rhode Island, and Virginia. Only Georgia refused to send any delegates. The colonists had yet to think of breaking with Great Britain; at this point, they simply wanted to iron out their differences with the king. By October, they had agreed on a series of resolutions to oppose the Coercive Acts and to establish a formal organization to boycott British goods. The Congress also drafted a Declaration of Rights and Resolves, which called for colonial rights of petition and assembly, trial by peers, freedom from a standing army, and the selection of representative councils to levy taxes. The Congress further agreed that if the king did not capitulate to their demands, they would meet again in Philadelphia in May 1775.

THE SECOND CONTINENTAL CONGRESS

Second Continental Congress
Meeting that convened in Philadelphia on May 10, 1775, at which it was decided that an army should be raised and George Washington of Virginia was named commander in chief.

King George refused to yield, tensions continued to rise, and a **Second Continental Congress** was deemed necessary. Before it could meet, fighting broke out early in the morning of April 19, 1775, at Lexington and Concord, Massachusetts, with what Ralph Waldo Emerson called "the shot heard round the world." Eight colonial soldiers, called Minutemen, were killed, and 16,000 British troops besieged Boston.

When the Second Continental Congress convened in Philadelphia on May 10, 1775, delegates were united by their increased hostility to Great Britain. In a final attempt to avert conflict, the Second Continental Congress adopted the Olive Branch Petition on July 5, 1775, asking the king to end hostilities. King George rejected the petition and sent an additional 20,000 troops to quell the rebellion. As a precautionary measure, the Congress already had appointed George Washington of Virginia as commander in chief of the Continental Army. The selection of a southern leader was a strategic decision, because up to that time British oppression largely was felt in the Northeast. In fact, the war essentially had begun with the shots fired at Lexington and Concord in April 1775.

In January 1776, Thomas Paine, with the support and encouragement of Benjamin Franklin, issued (at first anonymously) *Common Sense*, a pamphlet forcefully arguing for independence from Great Britain. In frank, easy-to-understand language, Paine denounced the corrupt British monarchy and offered reasons to break with Great Britain. "The blood of the slain, the weeping voice of nature cries 'Tis Time to Part,' " wrote Paine. *Common Sense*, widely read throughout the colonies, was instrumental in changing minds in a very short time. In its first three months of publication, the forty-seven-page *Common Sense* sold 120,000 copies, the equivalent of almost 22 million books, given the current U.S. population. One copy of *Common Sense* was in distribution for every thirteen people in the colonies—a truly astonishing number, given the low literacy rate.

Common Sense galvanized the American public against reconciliation with England. On May 15, 1776, Virginia became the first colony to call for independence, instructing one of its delegates to the Second Continental Congress to introduce a resolution to that effect. On June 7, 1776, Richard Henry Lee of Virginia rose to move "that these United Colonies are, and of right ought to be, free and independent States, and that all connection

Photo courtesy: Bettmann/Corbis

■ After the success of *Common Sense*, Thomas Paine wrote a series of essays collectively entitled *The Crisis* to arouse colonists' support for the Revolutionary War. The first *Crisis* papers contain the famous words "These are the times that try men's souls."

between them and the State of Great Britain is, and ought to be, dissolved." His three-part resolution—which called for independence, the formation of foreign alliances, and preparation of a plan of **confederation**—triggered hot debate among the delegates. A proclamation of independence from Great Britain was treason, a crime punishable by death. Although six of the thirteen colonies had already instructed their delegates to vote for independence, the Second Continental Congress was suspended to allow its delegates to return home to their respective colonial legislatures for final instructions. Independence was not a move to be taken lightly.

confederation
Type of government where the national government derives its powers from the states; a league of independent states.

THE DECLARATION OF INDEPENDENCE

Committees were set up to consider each point of Richard Henry Lee's proposal. A committee of five was selected to begin work on a **Declaration of Independence.** The Congress selected Benjamin Franklin of Pennsylvania, John Adams of Massachusetts, Robert Livingston of New York, and Roger Sherman of Connecticut as members of the committee. Adams lobbied hard for a Southerner to add balance. Thus, owing to his southern origin as well as his "peculiar felicity of expression," Thomas Jefferson of Virginia was selected as chair.

Declaration of Independence
Document drafted by Thomas Jefferson in 1776 that proclaimed the right of the American colonies to separate from Great Britain.

On July 2, 1776, twelve of the thirteen colonies (with New York abstaining) voted for independence. Two days later, the Second Continental Congress voted to adopt the Declaration of Independence penned by Thomas Jefferson. On July 9, 1776, the Declaration, now with the approval of New York, was read aloud in Philadelphia.[6]

In simple but eloquent language, Jefferson set out the reasons for the colonies' separation from Great Britain. Most of his stirring rhetoric drew heavily on the works of seventeenth- and eighteenth-century political philosophers, particularly the English philosopher John Locke (see chapter 1). Locke had written South Carolina's first constitution, a colonial charter drawn up in 1663 when that colony was formed by King Charles II and mercantile houses in England. In fact, many of the words in the

Photo courtesy: Bob Brown/Richmond Times-Dispatch/AP/Wide World Photos

■ The author of the Declaration of Independence, Thomas Jefferson (1743–1826) was a philosopher, farmer, inventor, and diplomat. He also served as the third president of the United States. Although Jefferson considered liberty an unalienable right of humanity, he owned slaves his entire life. In 1998, DNA evidence combined with historical documentation convinced many scholars and members of the public that Jefferson had fathered at least one child, Eston Hemings, by his slave Sally Hemings. Here, descendents of that union celebrate those findings.

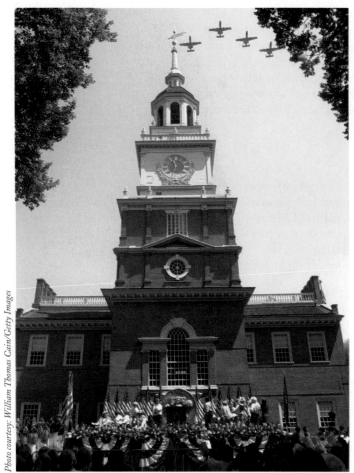

■ July 4th celebration at Independence Hall in Philadelphia, Pennsylvania, where the Declaration of Independence was first read aloud by Thomas Jefferson on July 9, 1776.

opening of the Declaration of Independence closely resemble passages from Locke's *Second Treatise on Civil Government*.

Locke was a proponent of social contract theory, a philosophy of government that held that governments exist based on the consent of the governed. According to Locke, people leave the state of nature and agree to set up a government largely for the protection of property rights included life, liberty, and material possessions. Furthermore, argued Locke, individuals who give their consent to be governed have the right to resist or remove rulers who deviate from those purposes. Such a government exists for the good of its subjects and not for the benefit of those who govern. Thus, rebellion was the ultimate sanction against a government that violated the rights of its citizens.

It is easy to see the colonists' debt to John Locke. In ringing language, the Declaration of Independence proclaims:

> We hold these truths to be self-evident, that all men are created equal, that they are endowed by their Creator with certain unalienable Rights, that among these are Life, Liberty and the pursuit of Happiness.

Jefferson and others in attendance at the Second Continental Congress wanted to have a document that would stand for all time, justifying their break with Great Britain and clarifying their notions of the proper form of government. So, Jefferson continued:

> That to secure these rights, Governments are instituted among Men, deriving their just powers from the consent of the governed. That whenever any Form of Government becomes destructive of these ends, it is the Right of the People to alter or abolish it, and to institute new Government, laying its foundation on such Principles and organizing its Powers in such form, as to them shall seem most likely to effect their Safety and Happiness.

After this stirring preamble, the Declaration enumerates the wrongs that the colonists had suffered under British rule. All pertain to the denial of personal rights and liberties, many of which would later be guaranteed by the U.S. Constitution through the Bill of Rights.

After the Declaration was signed and transmitted to the king, the Revolutionary War was fought with a greater vengeance. At a September 1776 peace conference on Staten Island (New York), British General William Howe demanded revocation of the Declaration of Independence. Washington's Continental Army refused, and the war raged on while the Continental Congress attempted to fashion a new united government.

The First Attempt at Government: The Articles of Confederation

AS NOTED EARLIER, the British had no written constitution. The delegates to the Second Continental Congress were attempting to codify arrangements that had never before been put into legal terminology. To make things more complicated, the delegates had to arrive at these decisions in a wartime atmosphere. Nevertheless, in late 1777, the **Articles of Confederation,** creating a loose "league of friendship" between the thirteen sovereign or independent states, were passed by the Congress and presented to the states for their ratification.

The Articles created a type of government called a confederation or confederacy. Unlike Great Britain's unitary system of government, wherein all of the powers of the government reside in the national government, the national government in a confederation derives all of its powers directly from the states. Thus, the national government in a confederacy is weaker than the sum of its parts, and the states often consider themselves independent nation-states linked together only for limited purposes such as national defense. So, the Articles of Confederation proposed the following:

- A national government with a Congress empowered to make peace, coin money, appoint officers for an army, control the post office, and negotiate with Indian tribes.
- Each state's retention of its independence and sovereignty, or ultimate authority, to govern within its territories.
- One vote in the Continental Congress for each state, regardless of size.
- The vote of nine states to pass any measure (a unanimous vote for any amendment).
- The selection and payment of delegates to the Congress by their respective state legislatures.

The Articles, finally ratified by all thirteen states in March 1781, fashioned a government that reflected the political philosophy of the times.[7] Although it had its flaws, the government under the Articles of Confederation saw the nation through the Revolutionary War. However, once the British surrendered in 1781, and the new nation found itself no longer united by the war effort, the government quickly fell into chaos.

PROBLEMS UNDER THE ARTICLES OF CONFEDERATION

In today's America, we ship goods, travel by car and airplane across state lines, make interstate phone calls, and more. Over 250 years ago, Americans had great loyalties to their states and often did not even think of themselves as Americans. This lack of national sentiment or loyalty in the absence of a war to unite the citizenry fostered a reluctance to give any power to the national government. By 1784, just one year after the Revolutionary Army was disbanded, governing the new nation under the Articles of Confederation proved unworkable.[8] In fact, historians refer to the chaotic period from 1781 to 1789 when the former colonies were governed under the Articles of Confederation as the "critical period." Congress rarely could assemble the required quorum of nine states to conduct business. Even when it did meet, there was little agreement among the states on any policies. To raise revenue to pay off war debts and run the government, various land, poll, and liquor taxes were proposed. But, since Congress had no specific power to tax, all these proposals were rejected. At one point, Congress was even driven out of Philadelphia (then the capital of the new national government) by its own unpaid army.

Although the national government could coin money, it had no resources to back up the value of its currency. Continental dollars were worth little, and trade between states became chaotic as some states began to coin their own money. Another weakness was that the Articles of Confederation did not allow Congress to regulate commerce among the states or with foreign nations. As a result, individual states attempted to enter into agreements with other countries, and foreign nations were suspicious of trade agreements made with the Congress of the Confederation. In 1785, for example, Massachusetts banned the export of goods in British ships, and Pennsylvania levied heavy duties on ships of nations that had no treaties with the U.S. government.

Articles of Confederation
The compact among the thirteen original states that was the basis of their government. Written in 1776, the Articles were not ratified by all the states until 1781.

VIDEO ROUNDTABLE

Articles of Confederation

Fearful of a chief executive who would rule tyrannically, the draftees of the Articles made no provision for an executive branch of government that would be responsible for executing, or implementing, laws passed by the legislative branch. Instead, the president was merely the presiding officer at meetings. John Hanson, a former member of the Maryland House of Delegates and of the First Continental Congress, was the first person to preside over the Congress of the Confederation. Therefore, he is often referred to as the first president of the United States.

The Articles of Confederation, moreover, had no provision for a judicial system to handle the growing number of economic conflicts and boundary disputes among the individual states. Several states claimed the same lands to the west, and Pennsylvania and Virginia went to war with each other.

The Articles' greatest weakness, however, was the lack of a strong central government. Although states had operated independently before the war, during the war they acceded to the national government's authority to wage armed conflict. Once the war was over, however, each state resumed its sovereign status and was unwilling to give up rights, such as the power to tax, to an untested national government. Consequently, the government was unable to force the states to abide by the provisions of the Treaty of Paris, signed in 1783, which officially ended the war. For example, states passed laws to allow debtors who owed money to Great Britain to postpone payment. States also opted not to restore property to citizens who had remained loyal to Britain during the war. Both actions violated the treaty.

The crumbling economy was made worse by a series of bad harvests that failed to produce cash crops, thus making it difficult for farmers to get out of debt quickly. George Washington and Alexander Hamilton, both interested in the questions of trade and frontier expansion, soon saw the need for a stronger national government with the authority to act to solve some of these problems. They were not alone. In 1785 and 1786, some state governments began to discuss ways to strengthen the national government.

■ With Daniel Shays in the lead, a group of Continental Army veterans marched on the courthouse in Springfield, Massachusetts, to stop the state court from foreclosing on the mortgages on their farms.

Photo courtesy: Bettmann/Corbis

SHAYS'S REBELLION

Before action to strengthen the government could take place, however, new unrest broke out in America. In 1780, Massachusetts adopted a constitution that appeared to favor the interests of the wealthy. Property-owning requirements barred the lower and middle classes from voting and office holding. And, as the economy of Massachusetts worsened, banks foreclosed on the farms of many Massachusetts Continental Army veterans who were waiting for promised bonuses that the national government had no funds to pay. The last straw came in 1786, when the Massachusetts legislature enacted a new law requiring the payment of all debts in cash. Frustration and outrage at the new law caused Daniel Shays, a former Continental Army captain, and 1,500 armed, disgruntled farmers to march to Springfield, Massachusetts. This group forcibly restrained the state court located there from foreclosing on the mortgages on their farms.

The Congress immediately authorized the secretary of war to call for a new national militia. A $530,000 appropriation was made for this purpose, but every state except Virginia refused Congress's request for money. The governor of Massachusetts then tried to raise a state militia, but because of the poor economy, the state treasury lacked the necessary funds to support his action. Frantic attempts to collect private financial support were made, and a militia finally was assembled. By February 4, 1787, this privately paid force put a stop to what was called **Shays's Rebellion.** The failure of the Congress to muster an army to put down the rebellion provided a dramatic example of the weaknesses inherent in the Articles of Confederation and shocked the nation's leaders into recognizing the new government's overwhelming inadequacies. And, it finally prompted several states to join together to call for a convention in Philadelphia in 1787.

Shays's Rebellion
A 1786 rebellion in which an army of 1,500 disgruntled and angry farmers led by Daniel Shays marched to Springfield, Massachusetts, and forcibly restrained the state court from foreclosing mortgages on their farms.

The Miracle at Philadelphia: Writing A Constitution

ON FEBRUARY 21, 1787, in the throes of economic turmoil and with domestic tranquility gone haywire, the Congress passed an official resolution. It called for a Constitutional Convention in Philadelphia for "the sole and express purpose of revising the Articles of Confederation."

However, many delegates that gathered in sweltering Philadelphia on May 25, 1787, were prepared to take potentially treasonous steps to preserve the union. For example, on the first day the convention was in session, Edmund Randolph and James Madison of Virginia proposed fifteen resolutions creating an entirely new government (later known as the Virginia Plan). Their enthusiasm, however, was not universal. Many delegates, including William Paterson of New Jersey, considered these resolutions to be in violation of the convention's charter, and proposed the New Jersey Plan, which took greater steps to preserve the Articles.

These proposals met heated debate on the convention's floor. Eventually the Virginia Plan triumphed following a declaration from Randolph that, "When the salvation of the Republic is at stake, it would be treason not to propose what we found necessary."

Though the basic structure of the new government was established, the work of the Constitutional Convention was not complete. These differences were resolved through a series of compromises, and less than one hundred days after the meeting convened, the Framers had created a new government to submit to the electorate for its approval.

THE CHARACTERISTICS AND MOTIVES OF THE FRAMERS

The fifty-five delegates who attended the Constitutional Convention labored long and hard that hot summer. Owing to the high stakes of their action, all of the convention's work was conducted behind closed doors. George Washington of Virginia, who was unanimously elected the convention's presiding officer, cautioned delegates not to reveal details of the convention even to their family members. Further, the delegates agreed to accompany Benjamin Franklin of Pennsylvania to all of his meals. They feared that the normally gregarious gentleman might get carried away with the mood or by liquor and inadvertently let news of the proceedings slip from his tongue.

All of the delegates to the Constitutional Convention were men; hence, they often are referred to as the "Founding Fathers." Most of them, however, were quite young; many were in their twenties and thirties, and only one—Franklin, at eighty-one—was quite old. A number owned slaves. Here, we generally refer to the delegates as the Framers, because their work provided the framework for our new government. The Framers brought with them a vast amount of political, educational, legal, and business experience. It is clear that they were an exceptional lot who ultimately produced a brilliant **constitution,** or document establishing the structure, functions, and limitations of a government. (See Analyzing Visuals: Who Were the Framers?)

VIDEO ROUNDTABLE

Intent of the Framers

constitution
A document establishing the structure, functions, and limitations of a government.

Analyzing Visuals

WHO WERE THE FRAMERS?

Who were the Framers of the U.S. Constitution? Of the fifty-five delegates who attended some portion of the Philadelphia meetings, seventeen were slaveholders who owned approximately 1,400 slaves. (George Washington, George Mason, and John Rutledge held the greatest number of slaves at the time of the convention.) In terms of education, thirty-one went to college; twenty-four did not. Most of those who did not attend college were trained as business, legal, and printing apprentices. Seven delegates signed both the U.S. Constitution and the Declaration of Independence. After studying the graph and the material on writing and signing the Constitution in this chapter, answer the following critical thinking questions: What is the relationship, if any, between the number of a state's delegates who served in the Continental Congresses and the number of the state's signers of the Constitution? What is the relationship, if any, between a state's population (shown in parentheses in the graph) and the number of the state's signers of the U.S. Constitution? What does that suggest about the conflict between the large states and small states? What is the relationship, if any, between the number of a state's delegates who were slaveholders and the number of the state's signers of the U.S. Constitution? What does that suggest about the conflicts over slavery at the convention?

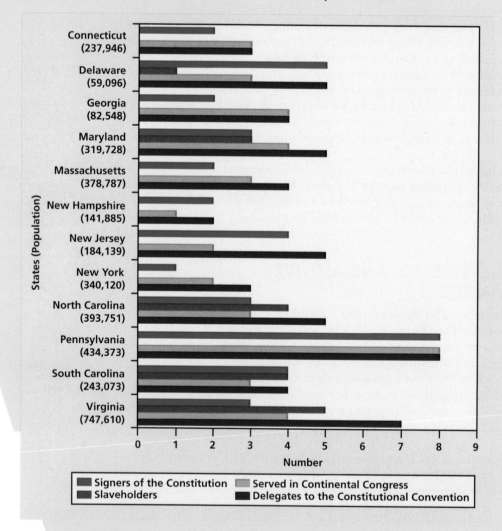

Sources: Clinton Rossiter, *The Grand Convention* (New York: Macmillan, 1966); National Archives and Records Administration, "The Founding Fathers: A Brief Overview," http://www.archives.gov/exhibit_hall/charters_of_freedom/constitution/founding_fathers_overview.html.

However, debate about the Framers' motives filled the air during the ratification struggle and has provided grist for the mill of historians and political scientists over the years. In his *Economic Interpretation of the Constitution of the United States* (1913), Charles A. Beard argued that the 1780s were a critical period not for the nation as a whole, but rather for businessmen who feared that a weak, decentralized government could harm their economic interests.[9] Beard argued that the merchants wanted a strong national government to promote industry and trade, to protect private property, and most importantly, to ensure payment of the public debt—much of which was owed to them. Therefore, according to Beard, the Constitution represents "an economic document drawn with superb skill by men whose property interests were immediately at stake."[10]

By the 1950s, this view had fallen into disfavor when other historians were unable to find direct links between wealth and the Framers' motives for establishing the Constitution and others faulted Beard's failure to consider the impact of religion and individual views about government.[11] In the 1960s, however, another group of historians began to argue that social and economic factors were, in fact, important motives for supporting the Constitution. In *The Anti-Federalists* (1961), Jackson Turner Main posited that while the Constitution's supporters might not have been the united group of creditors suggested by Beard, they were wealthier, came from higher social strata, and had greater concern for maintaining the prevailing social order than the general public.[12] In 1969, Gordon S. Wood's *The Creation of the American Republic* resurrected this debate. Wood deemphasized economics to argue that major social divisions explained different groups' support for (or opposition to) the new Constitution. He concluded that the Framers were representatives of a class that favored order and stability over some of the more radical ideas that had inspired the American Revolutionary War and the break with Britain.[13]

THE VIRGINIA AND NEW JERSEY PLANS

The less populous states were concerned with being lost in any new system of government where states were not treated as equals regardless of population. It is not surprising that a large state and then a small one, Virginia and New Jersey, respectively weighed in with ideas about how the new government should operate.

The **Virginia Plan,** proposed by James Madison and Edmund Randolph, called for a national system based heavily on the European nation-state model, wherein the national government derives its powers from the people and not from the member states.

Its key features included:

- Creation of a powerful central government with three branches—the legislative, executive, and judicial.
- A two-house legislature with one house elected directly by the people, the other chosen from among persons nominated by the state legislatures.
- A legislature with the power to select the executive and the judiciary.

In general, smaller states such as New Jersey and Connecticut felt comfortable with the arrangements under the Articles of Confederation. These states offered another model of government, the **New Jersey Plan.** Its key features included:

- Strengthening the Articles, not replacing them.
- Creating a one-house legislature with one vote for each state with representatives chosen by state legislatures.
- Giving Congress the power to raise revenue from duties on imports and from a postal service.
- Creating a Supreme Court with members appointed for life by the executive officers.

Virginia Plan
The first general plan for the Constitution, proposed by James Madison and Edmund Randolph. Its key points were a bicameral legislature, an executive chosen by the legislature, and a judiciary also named by the legislature.

New Jersey Plan
A framework for the Constitution proposed by a group of small states; its key points were a one-house legislature with one vote for each state, the establishment of the acts of Congress as the "supreme law" of the land, and a supreme judiciary with limited power.

CONSTITUTIONAL COMPROMISES

The most serious disagreement between the Virginia and New Jersey plans concerned state representation in Congress. When a deadlock loomed, Connecticut offered its own compromise. Representation in the House of Representatives would be determined by population and each state would have an equal vote in the Senate. Again, there was a stalemate.

A committee to work out an agreement soon reported back what became known as the **Great Compromise.** Taking ideas from both the Virginia and New Jersey plans, it recommended:

- In one house of the legislature (later called the House of Representatives), there would be fifty-six representatives—one representative for every 30,000 inhabitants. Representatives would be elected directly by the people.
- That house should have the power to originate all bills for raising and spending money.
- In the second house of the legislature (later called the Senate), each state should have an equal vote, and representatives would be selected by the state legislatures.
- In dividing power between the national and state governments, national power would be supreme.[14]

As Benjamin Franklin summarized it:

The diversity of opinions turns on two points. If a proportional representation takes place, the small states contend that their liberties will be in danger. If an equality of votes is to be put in its place, large states say that their money will be in danger. . . . When a broad table is to be made and the edges of a plank do not fit, the artist takes a little from both sides and makes a good joint. In like manner, both sides must part with some of their demands, in order that they both join in some accommodating position.[15]

The Great Compromise ultimately met with the approval of all states in attendance. The smaller states were pleased because they got equal representation in the Senate; the larger states were satisfied with the proportional representation in the House of Representatives. The small states then would dominate the Senate while the large states, such as Virginia and Pennsylvania, would control the House. But, because both houses had to pass any legislation, neither body could dominate the other.

The Great Compromise dealt with one major concern of the Framers—how best to treat the differences in large and small states—but other problems stemming largely from regional differences remained. Slavery, which formed the basis of much of the southern states' cotton economy, was one of the thorniest issues to address. To reach an agreement on the Constitution, the Framers had to craft a compromise that balanced southern commercial interests with comparable northern concerns. Eventually the Framers agreed that Northerners would support continuing the slave trade for twenty more years, as well as a twenty-year ban on taxing exports to protect the cotton trade, while Southerners consented to a provision requiring only a majority vote on navigation laws, and the national government was given the authority to regulate foreign commerce. Moreover, it was also agreed that the Senate would have the power to ratify treaties by a two-thirds majority, which assuaged the fears of southern states, who made up more than one-third of the nation.

Another sticking point concerning slavery remained: how to determine state population for purposes of representation in the House of Representatives. Slaves could not vote, but the southern states wanted them included for purposes of determining population. After considerable dissension, it was decided that population for purposes of representation and the apportionment of direct taxes would be calculated by adding the "whole Number of Free Persons" to "three-fifths of all other Persons." "All other Persons" was the delegates' euphemistic way of referring to slaves. Known as the **Three-Fifths Compromise,** this highly political deal assured that the South would

Great Compromise
A decision made during the Constitutional Convention to give each state the same number of representatives in the Senate regardless of size; representation in the House was determined by population.

Three-Fifths Compromise
Agreement reached at the Constitutional Convention stipulating that each slave was to be counted as three-fifths of a person for purposes of determining population for representation in the U.S. House of Representatives.

hold 47 percent of the House—enough to prevent attacks on slavery but not so much as to foster the spread of slavery northward.

UNFINISHED BUSINESS AFFECTING THE EXECUTIVE BRANCH

The Framers next turned to fashioning an executive branch. While they agreed on the idea of a one-person executive, they could not settle on the length of the term of office, nor on how the chief executive should be selected. With Shays's Rebellion still fresh in their minds, the delegates feared putting too much power, including selection of a president, into the hands of the lower classes. At the same time, representatives from the smaller states feared that the selection of the chief executive by the legislature would put additional power into the hands of the large states.

Amid these fears, the Committee on Unfinished Portions, whose sole responsibility was to iron out problems and disagreements concerning the office of chief executive, conducted its work. The committee recommended that the presidential term of office be fixed at four years instead of seven, as had earlier been proposed. By choosing not to mention a period of time within which the chief executive would be eligible for reelection, they made it possible for a president to serve more than one term.

The Framers also created the Electoral College and drafted rules concerning removal of a sitting president. The Electoral College system gave individual states a key role, because each state would select electors equal to the number of representatives it had in the House and Senate. It was a vague compromise that removed election of the president and vice president from both the Congress and the people and put it in the hands of electors whose method of selection would be left to the states. As Alexander Hamilton noted in *Federalist No. 68,* the Electoral College was fashioned to avoid the "tumult and disorder" that the Framers feared could result if the masses were allowed to vote directly for president. Instead, the selection of the president was left to a small number of men (the Electoral College) who "possess[ed] the information and discernment requisite" to decide, in Hamilton's words, the "complicated" business of selecting the president. (For details about the Electoral College, see chapter 13.)

■ The U.S. Constitution contains many phrases that are open to several interpretations. There are also omissions that raise questions about the democratic nature of the Constitution. The lingering question of how to interpret the Constitution still sparks debates among scholars and citizens. In this cartoon, Garry Trudeau pokes fun at the notion of the infallible Framers by imagining what a discussion leading up to the Three-Fifths Compromise might have sounded like.

DOONESBURY   Garry Trudeau

In drafting the new Constitution, the Framers also were careful to include a provision for removal of the chief executive. The House of Representatives was given the sole responsibility of investigating and charging a president or vice president with "Treason, Bribery, or other high Crimes and Misdemeanors." A majority vote then would result in issuing articles of impeachment against the president or vice president. In turn, the Senate was given sole responsibility to try the president or vice president on the charges issued by the House. A two-thirds vote of the Senate was required to convict and remove the president or the vice president from office. The chief justice of the United States was to preside over the Senate proceedings in place of the vice president (that body's constitutional leader) to prevent any conflict of interest on the vice president's part (see chapter 7).

The U.S. Constitution

Comparing Constitutions

AFTER THE COMPROMISE ON THE PRESIDENCY, work proceeded quickly on the remaining resolutions of the Constitution. The Preamble to the Constitution, the last section to be drafted, contains exceptionally powerful language that forms the bedrock of American political tradition The Preamble originally read:

> We the people of the States of New Hampshire, Massachusetts, Rhode Island and the Providence Plantations, Connecticut, New Jersey, New York, Pennsylvania, Delaware, Maryland, Virginia, North Carolina, South Carolina and Georgia, do ordain, declare and establish the following Constitution for the government of ourselves and our Posterity.

Its opening line, "We the People," ended, at least for the time being, the question of from where the government derived its power: it came directly from the people. This phrase was later followed by "the United States" instead of a list of the individual states. This substitution boldly proclaimed that a loose confederation of states no longer existed. Instead, there was but one American people and one nation.

The Constitution's final draft next explained the need for the new outline of government: "in Order to form a more perfect Union" indirectly acknowledged the weaknesses of the Articles of Confederation in governing a growing nation. Next, the optimistic goals of the Framers for the new nation were set out: to "establish Justice, insure domestic Tranquility, provide for the common defence, promote the general Welfare, and secure the Blessings of Liberty to ourselves and our Posterity"; followed by the formal creation of a new government: "do ordain and establish this Constitution for the United States of America."

On September 17, 1787, the Constitution was approved by the delegates from all twelve states in attendance. While the completed document did not satisfy all the delegates, of the fifty-five delegates who attended some portion of the meetings, thirty-nine ultimately signed it. The sentiments uttered by Benjamin Franklin probably well reflected those of many others: "Thus, I consent, Sir, to this Constitution because I expect no better, and because I am not sure that it is not the best."[16]

THE BASIC PRINCIPLES OF THE CONSTITUTION

The proposed structure of the new national government owed much to the writings of the French philosopher Montesquieu (1689–1755), who advocated distinct functions for each branch of government, called **separation of powers,** with a system of **checks and balances** between each branch. The Constitution's concern with the distribution of power between states and the national government also reveals the heavy influence of political philosophers, as well as the colonists' experience under the Articles of Confederation.[17]

separation of powers
A way of dividing power among three branches of government in which members of the House of Representatives, members of the Senate, the president, and the federal courts are selected by and responsible to different constituencies.

checks and balances
A governmental structure that gives each of the three branches of government some degree of oversight and control over the actions of the others.

Federalism The question before and during the convention was how much power states would give up to the national government. Given the nation's experiences under the Articles of Confederation, the Framers believed that a strong national government was necessary for the new nation's survival. However, they were reluctant to create a powerful government after the model of Britain, the country from which they had just won their independence. Its unitary system was not even considered by the colonists. Instead, they employed a system (now known as the **federal system**) that divides the power of government between a strong national government and the individual states. This system was based on the principle that the federal, or national, government derived its power from the citizens, not the states, as the national government had done under the Articles of Confederation.[18]

Opponents of this system feared that a strong national government would infringe on their liberty. But, supporters of a federal system, such as James Madison, argued that a strong national government with distinct state governments could, if properly directed by constitutional arrangements, actually be a source of expanded liberties and national unity. The Framers viewed the division of governmental authority between the national government and the states as a means of checking power with power, and providing the people with double security against governmental tyranny. Later, the passage of the Tenth Amendment, which stated that powers not given to the national government were reserved by the states or the people, further clarified the federal structure (see chapter 3).

federal system
Plan of government created in the U.S. Constitution in which power is divided between the national government and the state governments and in which independent states are bound together under one national government.

Separation of Powers Madison and many of the Framers clearly feared putting too much power into the hands of any one individual or branch of government. Madison's famous words, "Ambition must be made to counteract ambition," were widely believed at the Constitutional Convention.

Separation of powers is simply a way of parceling out power among the three branches of government. Its three key features are:

1. Three distinct branches of government: the legislative, the executive, and the judicial.
2. Three separately staffed branches of government to exercise these functions.
3. Constitutional equality and independence of each branch.

As illustrated in Figure 2.1, the Framers were careful to create a system in which law-making, law-enforcing, and law-interpreting functions were assigned to independent branches of government. On the national level (and in most states), only the legislature has the authority to make laws; the chief executive enforces laws; and the judiciary interprets them. Moreover, initially, members of the House of Representatives, members of the Senate, the president, and members of the federal courts were selected by and were therefore responsible to different constituencies. Madison believed that the scheme devised by the Framers would divide the offices of the new government and their methods of selection among many individuals, providing each office holder with the "necessary means and personal motives to resist encroachment" on his or her power. The Constitution originally placed the selection of senators directly with state legislators, making them more accountable to the states. The Seventeenth Amendment, ratified in 1913, however, called for direct election of senators by the voters, making them directly accountable to the people, thereby making the system more democratic.

The Framers could not have foreseen the intermingling of governmental functions that has since evolved. Locke, in fact, cautioned against giving a legislature the ability to delegate its powers. In Article I of the Constitution, the legislative power is vested in the Congress. But, the president is also given legislative power via his ability to veto legislation, although his veto can be overridden by a two-thirds vote in Congress. Judicial interpretation, including judicial review, a process cemented by the 1803

FIGURE 2.1 SEPARATION OF POWERS AND CHECKS AND BALANCES UNDER THE U.S. CONSTITUTION

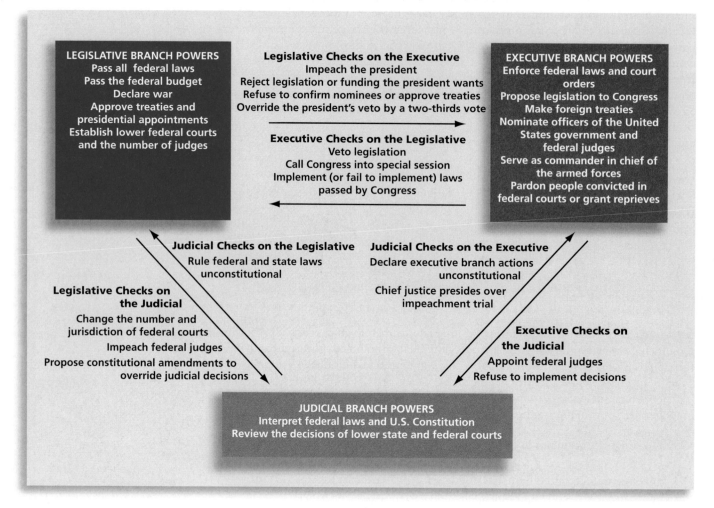

decision in *Marbury* v. *Madison,* then helps to clarify the implementation of legislation enacted through this process.

So, instead of a pure system of separation of powers, a symbiotic, or interdependent, relationship among the three branches of government has existed from the beginning. Or, as one scholar has explained, there are "separated institutions sharing powers."[19] While Congress still is entrusted with making the laws, the president, as a single person who can easily capture the attention of the media and the electorate, retains tremendous power in setting the agenda and proposing legislation. And, although the Supreme Court's major function is to interpret the law, its involvement in areas such as the 2000 presidential election, criminal procedure, abortion, and other issues has led many to charge that it has surpassed its constitutional authority and become, in effect, a law-making body.

Checks and Balances　The separation of powers among the three branches of the national government is not complete. According to Montesquieu and the Framers, the powers of each branch (as well as the two houses of the national legislature and between the states and the national government) could be used to check the powers of the other two branches of government. The power of each branch of government is checked, or limited, and balanced because the legislative, executive, and judicial branches share some authority and no branch has exclusive domain over any single activity. The creation of this system allowed the Framers to minimize the threat of tyranny from any one branch. Thus, for almost every power granted to one branch, an equal control was established in the other two branches. For example, although the president, as the commander in chief, has the power to deploy American troops, as George W. Bush did to Iraq in 2003, he needed authorization from the Congress to keep the troops in the Middle East for longer than ninety days. Similarly, to pay for this mission, the president had to ask Congress to appropriate funds, which it did in the form of an initial $87 billion supplemental appropriations bill and additional funds.

The American System of Checks and Balances

THE ARTICLES OF THE CONSTITUTION

The document finally signed by the Framers condensed numerous resolutions into a Preamble and seven separate articles. The first three articles established the three branches of government, defined their internal operations, and clarified their relationships with one another. All branches of government were technically considered equal, yet some initially appeared more equal than others. The order of the articles, and the detail contained in the first three, reflects the Framers' concern that these branches of government might abuse their powers. The four remaining articles define the relationships among the states, declare national law to be supreme, and set out methods of amending the Constitution.

Article I: The Legislative Branch
Article I vests all legislative powers in the Congress and establishes a bicameral legislature, consisting of the Senate and the House of Representatives. It also sets out the qualifications for holding office in each house, the terms of office, the methods of selection of representatives and senators, and the system of apportionment among the states to determine membership in the House of Representatives. Article I, section 2, specifies that an "enumeration" of the citizenry must take place every ten years in a manner to be directed by the U.S. Congress.

One of the most important sections of Article I is section 8. It carefully lists the powers the Framers wished the new Congress to possess. These specified or **enumerated powers** contain many key provisions that had been denied to the Continental Congress under the Articles of Confederation. For example, one of the major weaknesses of the Articles was Congress's lack of authority to deal with trade wars. The Constitution remedied this problem by authorizing Congress to "regulate Commerce with foreign Nations, and among the several States." Congress was also given the authority to coin money.

After careful enumeration of seventeen powers of Congress in Article I, section 8, a final, general clause authorizing Congress to "make all Laws which shall be necessary and proper for carrying into Execution the foregoing Powers" was added to Article I. Often referred to as the elastic clause, the **necessary and proper clause** has been a source of tremendous congressional activity never anticipated by the Framers, including the passage of laws that regulate the environment, welfare programs, education, and communication.

The necessary and proper clause, also called the elastic clause, is the basis for the **implied powers** that Congress uses to execute its other powers. Congress's enumerated power to regulate commerce has been linked with the necessary and proper clause in a variety of Supreme Court cases. As a result, laws banning prostitution where travel across state lines is involved, regulating trains and planes, establishing federal minimum-wage and maximum-hour laws, and mandating drug testing for certain workers have passed constitutional muster.

enumerated powers
Seventeen specific powers granted to Congress under Article I, section 8, of the U.S. Constitution; these powers include taxation, coinage of money, regulation of commerce, and the authority to provide for a national defense.

necessary and proper clause
The final paragraph of Article I, section 8, of the U.S. Constitution, which gives Congress the authority to pass all laws "necessary and proper" to carry out the enumerated powers specified in the Constitution; also called the elastic clause.

implied powers
Powers derived from the enumerated powers and the necessary and proper clause. These powers are not stated specifically but are considered to be reasonably implied through the exercise of delegated powers.

Join the Debate

THE "EQUAL OPPORTUNITY TO GOVERN" AMENDMENT

OVERVIEW: Article II, section 1, clause 5, of the U.S. Constitution declares: "No person except a natural-born citizen, or a citizen of the United States at the time of the Adoption of this Constitution, shall be eligible to the Office of President." Why would the Founders put such a restriction on the qualifications for president of the United States? In a letter to George Washington, John Jay argued that the duty of commander in chief was too important to be given to a foreign-born person—the potential for conflict of interest, danger, and appearance of impropriety in matters of war and foreign policy should not be left to chance. Charles Pinckney, a South Carolina delegate to the Constitutional Convention, expressed concern that foreign governments would use whatever means necessary to influence international events, and he cited the example of Russia, Prussia, and Austria manipulating the election of Stanislaus II to the Polish throne—only to divide Polish lands among themselves. Furthermore, Pinckney contended that the clause would ensure the "experience" of American politics and principles and guarantee "attachment to the country" so as to further eliminate the potential for mischief and foreign intrigue.

The election of Austrian-born Arnold Schwarzenegger and of Canadian-born Jennifer Granholm to the governorships of California and Michigan, respectively, reopened the debate concerning the citizenship requirement for president. Why shouldn't naturalized citizens be eligible for president? Many naturalized citizens have performed great service to their adopted country; both Henry Kissinger (born in Germany) and Madeleine Albright (born in Czechoslovakia) performed admirably as secretary of state, and over 700 foreign-born Congressional Medal of Honor recipients have demonstrated patriotism and the willingness to die for the country they embraced. With these viewpoints in mind, in July 2003, Senator Orrin Hatch (R–UT) introduced the Equal Opportunity to Govern Amendment to strike the natural-born–citizen clause from the Constitution. The proposed amendment takes into account the Framers' fear of foreign intervention and of divided loyalty by placing a lengthy citizenship requirement—twenty years—before naturalized citizens become eligible to run for presidential office.

Should a nation whose fundamental principle is equality of citizens have a constitutional clause that denies some citizens the presidency? Doesn't the Constitution allow the means to adapt to changes in history and social mores? On the other hand, doesn't the clause help prevent corruption from foreign sources?

ARGUMENTS FOR THE EQUAL OPPORTUNITY TO GOVERN AMENDMENT

- **The United States is in part composed of its immigrant population and they should have a share in all political offices.** America is a nation of immigrants and many of the original Founders were foreign born, notably Alexander Hamilton, who helped shaped Washington's administration and the executive branch. The Constitution allows for naturalized citizens to attain other high political office such as Speaker of the House, senator, or Supreme Court justice; why should naturalized citizens be denied the presidency?

Article II: The Executive Branch Article II vests the executive power, that is, the authority to execute the laws of the nation, in a president of the United States. Section 1 sets the president's term of office at four years and explains the Electoral College. It also states the qualifications for office and describes a mechanism to replace the president in case of death, disability, or removal.

The powers and duties of the president are set out in section 3. Among the most important of these are the president's role as commander in chief of the armed forces, the authority to make treaties with the consent of the Senate, and the authority to "appoint Ambassadors, other public Ministers and Consuls, the Judges of the supreme Court, and all other Officers of the United States." Other sections of Article II instruct the president to report directly to Congress "from time to time," in what has come to be known as the State of the Union Address, and to "take Care that the Laws be faithfully executed." Section 4 provides the mechanism for removal of the president, vice president, and other officers of the United States for "Treason, Bribery, or other high Crimes and Misdemeanors" (see chapter 8).

- **The natural-born-citizen clause has outlived its usefulness.** The problems that existed in 1787 either have changed or do not exist in the twenty-first century. The amendment process was created to allow for historical and political change, and ratification of the Equal Opportunity to Govern Amendment will increase the talent pool of presidential nominees, thus increasing the quality and choice of presidential aspirants for the American people.
- **The natural-born-citizen clause is discriminatory.** The clause is un-American in that it denies equality of opportunity for all American citizens. Naturalized citizens serve in the military, pay taxes, run for local, state, and federal office, endure the same national hardships and crises, and add to the overall quality of American life; thus, naturalized citizens should have the same rights and privileges as the native born.

ARGUMENTS AGAINST THE EQUAL OPPORTUNITY TO GOVERN AMENDMENT

- **Foreign governments still attempt to have undue influence in American politics.** The Framers were correct in assuming foreign governments attempt to manipulate American politics. For example, in 1999, the Democratic National Committee returned over $600,000 in campaign contributions to Chinese nationals attempting to gain influence with the Clinton administration. The clause was meant to be another institutional safeguard against presidential corruption.
- **Running for president is not a right.** The office of the President is an institution designed for republican purposes. The Founders strongly believed foreign influence

within the U.S. government must be restricted (the language was unanimously adopted by the Constitutional Convention) and thus they did not grant a right to run for presidential office.

- **There is no public movement or outcry to remove this clause from the Constitution.** Many constitutional scholars argue the Constitution should be amended only for pressing reasons, and amendments should be construed with a view to the well-being of future generations. Foreign policy and events are too fluid and too volatile to risk undermining the president's foreign policy and commander-in-chief authority. Until the American people determine otherwise, the clause should remain.

QUESTIONS

1. Is the natural-born clause discriminatory? If so, should the Constitution be amended to realize the principle of political equality?
2. Were the Framers wise in their analysis of foreign influence on American politics? Did they create a true institutional barrier to help prevent corruption by foreign governments?

SELECTED READINGS

Amar, Akhil Reed. "Natural Born Killjoy: Why the Constitution Won't Let Immigrants Run for President, and Why That Should Change," *Legal Affairs,* March/April, 2004.

Breyer, Stephen. *Active Liberty: Interpreting Our Democratic Constitution.* New York: Knopf, 2005.

Because Article II limits the presidency to natural-born citizens, a new amendment would be needed to change that qualification. (See Join the Debate: The "Equal Opportunity to Govern" Amendment.)

Article III: The Judicial Branch Article III establishes a Supreme Court and defines its jurisdiction. During the Philadelphia meeting, the small and large states differed significantly as to the desirability of an independent judiciary and on the role of state courts in the national court system. The smaller states feared that a strong unelected judiciary would trample on their liberties. In compromise, Congress was permitted, but not required, to establish lower national courts. Thus, state courts and the national court system would exist side by side with distinct areas of authority. Federal courts were given authority to decide cases arising under federal law. The Supreme Court was also given the power to settle disputes between states, or between a state and the national government. Ultimately, it was up to the Supreme Court to determine what provisions of the Constitution actually meant.

■ Article II of the Constitution instructs the president to report directly to Congress "from time to time." Here, President George W. Bush delivers his 2006 State of the Union Address to a joint session of Congress.

Photo courtesy: Chris Kleponis/Bloomberg News/Landov

Although some delegates to the convention urged that the president be allowed to remove federal judges, ultimately judges were given appointments for life, presuming "good behavior." And, like the president's, their salaries cannot be lowered while they hold office. This provision was adopted to ensure that the legislature did not attempt to punish the Supreme Court or any other judges for unpopular decisions.

Articles IV Through VII The remainder of the articles in the Constitution attempted to anticipate problems that might occur in the operation of the new national government as well as its relations to the states. Article IV begins with what is called the full faith and credit clause, which mandates that states honor the laws and judicial proceedings of the other states. Article IV also includes the mechanisms for admitting new states to the union.

Article V (discussed in greater detail on p. 58) specifies how amendments can be added to the Constitution. The Bill of Rights, which added ten amendments to the Constitution in 1791, was one of the first items of business when the First Congress met in 1789. Since then, only seventeen additional amendments have been ratified.

supremacy clause
Portion of Article VI of the U.S. Constitution mandating that national law is supreme to (that is, supersedes) all other laws passed by the states or by any other subdivision of government.

Article VI contains the supremacy clause, which asserts the basic primacy of the Constitution and national law over state laws and constitutions. The **supremacy clause** provides that the "Constitution, and the laws of the United States" as well as all treaties are to be the supreme law of the land. All national and state officers and judges are bound by national law and take oaths to support the federal Constitution above any state law or constitution. Because of the supremacy clause, any legitimate exercise of national power supersedes any state laws or action, in a process that is called preemption, further discussed in chapter 3. Without the supremacy clause and the federal court's ability to invoke it, the national government would have little actual enforceable power; thus, many commentators call the supremacy clause the linchpin of the entire federal system.

Mindful of the potential problems that could occur if church and state were too enmeshed, Article VI also specifies that no religious test shall be required for holding any office. This mandate strengthens the separation of church and state guarantee that was quickly added to the Constitution when the First Amendment was ratified.

VIDEO DEBATE
Church and State

Global Perspective

BUILDING A NATION: THE IRAQI CONSTITUTION

The United States and its allies' forces invaded Iraq and overthrew Saddam Hussein and his Baath Party regime in 2003. In 2005, members of the Iraqi Transitional Government drafted a constitution to replace the Law of Administration for the State of Iraq for the Transitional Period that had been put in force by the Coalition Provisional Authority after the overthrow of Hussein's government. Iraqi voters ratified the constitution in October 2005.

On a basic level, the Iraqi Constitution shares many similarities with the U.S. Constitution. Both the American and Iraqi constitutions set up a federal form of government, in which power rests with the people and is shared between the states—or in Iraq, "governorates"—and a central government. Iraqi federalism is designed to accommodate Iraq's ethnic and religious diversity at the governorate level while securing national interests such as defense and trade at the federal level. Similarly, the U.S. Framers sought to balance the interests of large and small and northern and southern states while also providing for a strong central government that would protect the new nation from internal and external strife. Both constitutions also guarantee democratic forms and institutions. For example, Article 2 of the Iraqi Constitution promises that no law will contravene "the principles of democracy," and Article IV of the U.S. Constitution assures the American people that states must conform to "republican government."

Though both constitutions share certain fundamental principles, there are significant differences as well. Most of these differences relate to the religious and cultural differences between the two nations. While the First Amendment of the U.S. Constitution guarantees there will be no state establishment of religion, Article 2 of the Iraqi Constitution makes Islam "the official religion of the State and . . . a fundamental source of legislation," and notes that "no law that contradicts the established provisions of Islam may be established." Another significant difference between the two constitutions is that the Iraqi Constitution speaks to the social and economic welfare of the nation's polity, but the United States' constitution does not. Article 30 of Iraq's constitution guarantees the Iraqi people "social and health security" and "a suitable income and appropriate housing," and Article 31 gives "every citizen . . . the right to health care." These provisions are at least partly indicative of the contemporary nature of the Iraqi Constitution, but more importantly, they reflect Islam's traditional emphasis on caring for the less fortunate.

Like the Framers of the U.S. Constitution, the men and women who drafted the new Iraqi Constitution face great uncertainty and an uphill battle to secure their new nation's stability and sovereignty. Although it would be nearly a hundred years before divisions in the United States led to the U.S. Civil War, the Iraqi people were already facing what many experts considered a civil war at the time of their constitution's ratification.

QUESTIONS

1. What principles must a constitution embrace for a government to be considered truly democratic?
2. To what extent can a written constitution help a people overcome obstacles to national sovereignty and stability?

Sources: The Constitution of the United States of America; the Iraqi Constitution, Draft Document Ratified in a Popular Referendum on October 15, 2005. Translated from the Arabic by the United Nations' Office for Constitutional Support; translation subsequently approved by the Iraqi government. Available online at http://www.washingtonpost.com/wp-dyn/content/article/2005/10/12/AR2005101201450.html.

The seventh and final article of the Constitution concerns the procedures for ratification of the new Constitution: nine of the thirteen states would have to agree to, or ratify, its new provisions before it would become the supreme law of the land.

The Drive for Ratification

WHILE DELEGATES TO THE CONSTITUTIONAL CONVENTION labored in Philadelphia, the Congress of the Confederation continued to govern the former colonies under the Articles of Confederation. The day after the Constitution was signed, William Jackson, the secretary of the Constitutional Convention, left for New York City, then the nation's capital, to deliver the official copy of the document to the Congress. He also took with him a resolution of the delegates calling upon each of the states to vote on the new Constitution. Anticipating resistance from the representatives in the state legislatures, however, the Framers required the states to call special ratifying conventions to consider the proposed Constitution.

Jackson carried a letter from General George Washington with the proposed Constitution. In a few eloquent words, Washington summed up the sentiments of the Framers and the spirit of compromise that had permeated the long weeks in Philadelphia:

> That it will meet the full and entire approbation of every state is not perhaps to be expected, but each [state] will doubtless consider, that had her interest alone been consulted, the consequences might have been particularly disagreeable or injurious to others; that it is liable to as few exceptions as could reasonably have been expected, we hope and believe; that it may promote lasting welfare of that country so dear to us all, and secure her freedom and happiness is our ardent wish.[20]

The Second Continental Congress immediately accepted the work of the convention and forwarded the proposed Constitution to the states for their vote. It was by no means certain, however, that the new Constitution would be adopted. From the fall of 1787 to the summer of 1788, the proposed Constitution was debated hotly around the nation. State politicians understandably feared a strong central government. Farmers and other working-class people were fearful of a distant national government. Those who had accrued substantial debts during the economic chaos following the Revolutionary War feared that a new government with a new financial policy would plunge them into even greater debt. The public in general was very leery of taxes—these were the same people who had revolted against the king's taxes. At the heart of many of their concerns was an underlying fear of the massive changes that would be brought about by a new system. Favoring the Constitution were wealthy merchants, lawyers, bankers, and those who believed that the new nation could not continue to exist under the Articles of Confederation. For them, it all boiled down to one simple question offered by James Madison: "Whether or not the Union shall or shall not be continued."

FEDERALISTS VERSUS ANTI-FEDERALISTS

Federalists
Those who favored a stronger national government and supported the proposed U.S. Constitution; later became the first U.S. political party.

Anti-Federalists
Those who favored strong state governments and a weak national government; opposed the ratification of the U.S. Constitution.

Almost as soon as the ink was dry on the last signature to the Constitution, those who favored the new strong national government chose to call themselves **Federalists.** They were well aware that many still generally opposed the notion of a strong national government. Thus, they did not want to risk being labeled nationalists, so they tried to get the upper hand in the debate by nicknaming their opponents **Anti-Federalists.** Those put in the latter category insisted that they were instead Federal Republicans, who believed in a federal system. As noted in Table 2.1, Anti-Federalists argued that they simply wanted to protect state governments from the tyranny of a too powerful national government.[21]

Federalists and Anti-Federalists participated in the mass meetings that were held in state legislatures to discuss the pros and cons of the new plan. Tempers ran high at public meetings, where differences between the opposing groups were highlighted. Fervent debates were published in newspapers, which played a powerful role in the adoption process. The entire Constitution, in fact, was printed in the *Pennsylvania Packet* just two days after the convention's end. Other major papers quickly followed suit. Soon, opinion pieces on both sides of the adoption issue began to appear around the nation, often written under pseudonyms such as "Caesar" or "Constant Reader," as was the custom of the day.

THE FEDERALIST PAPERS

One name stood out from all the rest: "Publius" (Latin for "the people"). Between October 1787 and May 1788, eighty-five articles written under that pen name routinely

TABLE 2.1 FEDERALISTS AND ANTI-FEDERALISTS COMPARED

	Federalists	Anti-Federalists
Who were they?	Property owners, landed rich, merchants of Northeast and Middle Atlantic states	Small farmers, shopkeepers, laborers
Political philosophy	Elitist: saw themselves and those of their class as most fit to govern (others were to be governed).	Believed in the decency of "the common man" and in participatory democracy; viewed elites as corrupt; sought greater protection of individual rights.
Type of government favored	Powerful central government; two-house legislature; upper house (six-year term) further removed from the people, whom they distrusted.	Wanted stronger state governments (closer to the people) at the expense of the powers of the national government; sought smaller electoral districts, frequent elections, referendum and recall, and a large unicameral legislature to provide for greater class and occupational representation.
Alliances	Pro-British, Anti-French	Anti-British, Pro-French

appeared in newspapers in New York, a state where ratification was in doubt. Most were written by Alexander Hamilton and James Madison. Hamilton, a young, fiery New Yorker born in the British West Indies, wrote fifty-one; Madison, a Virginian who later served as the fourth president, wrote twenty-six; and jointly they penned another three. John Jay, also of New York, and later the first chief justice of the United States, wrote five of the pieces. These eighty-five essays became known as *The Federalist Papers*.

Today, *The Federalist Papers* are considered masterful explanations of the Framers' intentions as they drafted the new Constitution. At the time, although they were reprinted widely, they were far too theoretical to have much impact on those who would ultimately vote on the proposed Constitution. Dry and scholarly, they lacked the fervor of much of the political rhetoric that was then in use. *The Federalist Papers* did, however, highlight the reasons for the structure of the new government and its benefits. According to *Federalist No. 10*, for example, the new Constitution was called "a republican remedy for the disease incident to republican government." These musings of Madison, Hamilton, and Jay continue to be the clearest articulation of the political theories and philosophies that lie at the heart of our Constitution.

Forced on the defensive, the Anti-Federalists responded to *The Federalist Papers* with their own series of letters written by Anti-Federalists adopting the pen names of "Brutus" and "Cato," two ancient Romans famous for their intolerance of tyranny. These letters (actually essays) undertook a line-by-line critique of the Constitution.

Anti-Federalists argued that a strong central government would render the states powerless.[22] They stressed the strengths the government had been granted under the Articles of Confederation, and argued that the Articles, not the proposed Constitution, created a true federal system. Moreover, they argued that the strong national government would tax heavily, that the Supreme Court would overwhelm the states by invalidating state laws, and that the president eventually would have too much power, as commander in chief of a large and powerful army.[23]

In particular, the Anti-Federalists feared the power of the national government to run roughshod over the liberties of the people. They proposed that the taxing power of Congress be limited, that the executive be curbed by a council, that the military consist of state militias rather than a national force, and that the jurisdiction of the Supreme Court be limited to prevent it from reviewing and potentially overturning the decisions of state courts. But, their most effective argument concerned the absence of a bill of rights in the Constitution. James Madison answered these criticisms in *Federalist Nos. 10 and 51*. (The texts of these two essays are printed in Appendices III and IV.) In *Federalist No. 10*, Madison pointed out that the voters would not always succeed in electing "enlightened statesmen" as their representatives. The greatest

The Federalist Papers
A series of eighty-five political papers written by John Jay, Alexander Hamilton, and James Madison in support of ratification of the U.S. Constitution.

■ Alexander Hamilton (left), James Madison (center), and John Jay (right) were important early Federalist
leaders. Jay wrote five of *The Federalist Papers* and Madison and Hamilton wrote the rest. Hamilton became the first secretary of the treasury (1789–1795). He was killed in 1804 in a duel with Vice President
Aaron Burr, who was angered by Hamilton's negative comments about his character. Madison served in
the House of Representatives (1789–1797) and as secretary of state in the Jefferson administration
(1801–1808). In 1808, he was elected fourth president of the United States and served two terms
(1809–1817). Jay became the first chief justice of the United States (1789–1795) and negotiated the Jay
Treaty with Great Britain in 1794. He then served as governor of New York from 1795 to 1801.

threat to individual liberties would therefore come from factions within the government, who might place narrow interests above broader national interests and the
rights of citizens. While recognizing that no form of government could protect the
country from unscrupulous politicians, Madison argued that the organization of the
new government would minimize the effects of political factions. The great advantage
of a federal system, Madison maintained, was that it created the "happy combination"
of a national government too large to be controlled by any single faction, and several
state governments that would be smaller and more responsive to local needs. Moreover, he argued in *Federalist No. 51* that the proposed federal government's separation
of powers would prohibit any one branch from either dominating the national government or violating the rights of citizens.

RATIFYING THE CONSTITUTION

SIMULATION
You Are James Madison

Debate continued in the thirteen states as votes were taken from December 1787 to
June 1788, in accordance with the ratifying process laid out in Article VII of the proposed Constitution. Three states acted quickly to ratify the new Constitution. Two
small states, Delaware and New Jersey, voted to ratify before the large states could rethink the notion of equal representation of the states in the Senate. Pennsylvania,
where Federalists were well organized, was also one of the first three states to ratify.
Massachusetts assented to the new government but tempered its support by calling
for an immediate addition of amendments, including one protecting personal rights.
New Hampshire became the crucial ninth state to ratify on June 21, 1788. This action
completed the ratification process outlined in Article VII of the Constitution and
marked the beginning of a new nation. But, New York and Virginia, which at that
time accounted for more than 40 percent of the new nation's population, had not yet
ratified the Constitution. Thus, the practical future of the new nation remained in
doubt.

Hamilton in New York and Madison in Virginia worked feverishly to convince delegates to their state conventions to vote for the new government. In New York, sentiment against the Constitution ran high. In Albany, fighting resulting in injuries and death broke out over ratification. When news of Virginia's acceptance of the Constitution reached the New York convention, Hamilton finally was able to convince a majority of those present to follow suit by a narrow margin of three votes. Both states also recommended the addition of a series of structural amendments and a bill of rights.

North Carolina and Rhode Island continued to hold out against ratification. Both had recently printed new currencies and feared that values would plummet in a federal system where the Congress was authorized to coin money. On August 2, 1788, North Carolina became the first state to reject the Constitution on the grounds that no Anti-Federalist amendments were included. Soon after, in September 1789, owing much to the Anti-Federalist pressure for additional protections from the national government, Congress submitted the **Bill of Rights** to the states for their ratification. North Carolina then ratified the Constitution by a vote of 194–77. Rhode Island, the only state that had not sent representatives to Philadelphia, remained out of the new nation until 1790. Finally, under threats from its largest cities to secede from the state, the legislature called a convention that ratified the Constitution by only two votes (34–32)—one year after George Washington became the first president of the United States.

Bill of Rights
The first ten amendments to the U.S. Constitution.

AMENDING THE CONSTITUTION: THE BILL OF RIGHTS

Once the Constitution was ratified, elections were held. When Congress convened, it immediately sent a set of amendments to the states for their ratification. An amendment authorizing the enlargement of the House of Representatives and another to prevent members of the House from raising their own salaries failed to garner favorable votes in the necessary three-fourths of the states. (See On Campus: A Student's Revenge: The Twenty-Seventh [Madison] Amendment.) The remaining ten amendments, known as the Bill of Rights, were ratified by 1791 in accordance with the procedures set out in the Constitution. Sought by Anti-Federalists as a protection for individual liberties, they offered numerous specific limitations on the national government's ability to interfere with a wide variety of personal liberties, some of which were already guaranteed by many state constitutions (see chapters 5 and 6).

The Bill of Rights includes numerous specific protections of personal rights. Freedom of expression, speech, press, religion, and assembly are guaranteed by the First Amendment. The Bill of Rights also contains numerous safeguards for those accused of crimes.

Two of the amendments of the Bill of Rights were reactions to British rule—the right to bear arms (Second Amendment) and the right not to have soldiers quartered in private homes (Third Amendment). More general rights are also included in the Bill of Rights. The Ninth Amendment notes that these enumerated rights are not inclusive, meaning they are not the only rights to be enjoyed by the people, and the Tenth Amendment states that powers not given to the national government are reserved by the states or the people.

Methods of Amending the Constitution

THE FRAMERS DID NOT WANT to fashion a government that could be too influenced by the whims of the people. Therefore, they made the formal amendment process a slow one to ensure that the Constitution was not impulsively amended. In keeping with this intent, only seventeen amendments have been added since the

On Campus

A STUDENT'S REVENGE: THE TWENTY-SEVENTH (MADISON) AMENDMENT

On June 8, 1789, in a speech before the House of Representatives, James Madison stated:

> there is a seeming impropriety in leaving any set of men without controul to put their hand into the public coffers, to take out money to put into their pockets. . . . I have gone therefore so far as to fix it, that no law, varying the compensation, shall operate until there is a change in the legislation.

When Madison proposed that any salary increase for members of Congress could not take effect until the next session of Congress, he had no way of knowing that more than two centuries would pass before his plan, now known as the Twenty-Seventh Amendment, would become an official part of the Constitution. In fact, Madison deemed it worthy of addition only because the conventions of three states (Virginia, New York, and North Carolina) demanded that it be included.

By 1791, when the Bill of Rights was added to the Constitution, only six states had ratified Madison's amendment, and it seemed destined to fade into obscurity. In 1982, however, Gregory Watson, a sophomore majoring in economics at the University of Texas–Austin, discovered the unratified compensation amendment while looking for a paper topic for an American government class. Intrigued, Watson wrote a paper arguing that the proposed amendment was still viable because it had no internal time limit and, therefore, should still be ratified. Watson received a C on the paper.

Despite his grade, Watson began a ten-year, $6,000 self-financed crusade to renew interest in the compensation amendment. Watson and his allies reasoned that the amendment should be revived because of the public's growing anger with the fact that members of Congress had sought to raise their salaries without going on the record as having done so. Watson's perseverance paid off.

Photo courtesy: Ziggy Kaluzny/People Magazine Syndication

■ Gregory Watson with a document that contains the first ten amendments to the Constitution, as well as the compensation amendment ("Article the second: No law varying the compensation for services of the Senators and Representatives shall take effect until an election of Representatives shall have intervened"), which finally was ratified in 1992 as the Twenty-Seventh Amendment.

On May 7, 1992, the amendment was ratified by the requisite thirty-eight states. On May 18, the United States Archivist certified that the amendment was part of the Constitution, a decision that was overwhelmingly confirmed by the House of Representatives on May 19 and by the Senate on May 20. At the same time that the Senate approved the Twenty-Seventh Amendment, it also took action to ensure that a similar situation would never occur by declaring four other amendments dead.

Sources: Fordham Law Review (December 1992): 497–539; and Anne Marie Kilday, "Amendment Expert Agrees with Congressional Pay Ruling," *Dallas Morning News* (February 14, 1993): 13A.

---

addition of the Bill of Rights. However, informal amendments, prompted by judicial interpretation and cultural and social change, have had a tremendous impact on the Constitution.

FORMAL METHODS OF AMENDING THE CONSTITUTION

SIMULATION

You Are Proposing a Constitutional Amendment

Article V of the Constitution creates a two-stage amendment process: proposal and ratification.[24] The Constitution specifies two ways to accomplish each stage. As illustrated in Figure 2.2, amendments to the Constitution can be proposed by: (1) a vote of two-thirds of the members in both houses of Congress; or, (2) a vote of two-thirds of the state legislatures specifically requesting Congress to call a national convention to propose amendments. (See The Living Constitution.)

FIGURE 2.2 METHODS OF AMENDING THE CONSTITUTION

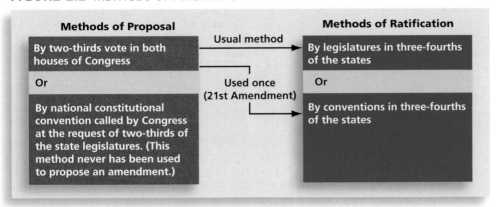

The second method has never been used. Historically, it has served as a fairly effective threat, forcing Congress to consider amendments that might otherwise never have been debated. In the 1980s, for example, several states called on Congress to enact a balanced budget amendment. To forestall the need for a special constitutional convention, in 1985, Congress enacted the Gramm-Rudman-Hollings Act, which called for a balanced budget by the 1991 fiscal year. But, Congress could not meet that target. The act was amended repeatedly until 1993, when Congress postponed the call for a balanced budget, the need for which faded in light of surpluses that occurred during the Clinton administration. The act also was ruled unconstitutional by a three-judge district court that declared that the law violated separation of powers principles.

The ratification process is fairly straightforward. When Congress votes to propose an amendment, the Constitution specifies that the ratification process must occur in one of two ways: (1) a favorable vote in three-fourths of the state legislatures; or, (2) a favorable vote in specially called ratifying conventions in three-fourths of the states.

The Constitution itself was ratified by the favorable vote of nine states in specially called ratifying conventions. The Framers feared that the power of special interests in state legislatures would prevent a positive vote on the new Constitution. Since ratification of the Constitution, however, only one ratifying convention has been called. The Eighteenth Amendment, which outlawed the sale of alcoholic beverages nationwide, was ratified by the first method—a vote in state legislatures. Millions broke the law, others died from drinking homemade liquor, and still others made their fortunes selling bootleg or illegal liquor. After a decade of these problems, Congress decided to act. An additional amendment—the Twenty-First—was proposed to repeal the Eighteenth Amendment. It was sent to the states for ratification, but with a call for ratifying conventions, not a vote in the state legislatures.[25] Members of Congress correctly predicted that the move to repeal the Eighteenth Amendment would encounter opposition in the statehouses, which were largely controlled by conservative rural interests. Thus,

Photo courtesy: Hulton Archive/Getty Images

■ For all its moral foundation in groups such as the Women's Christian Temperance Union (WCTU), whose members invaded bars to protest the sale of alcoholic beverages, the Eighteenth (Prohibition) Amendment was a disaster. Among its side effects was the rise of powerful crime organizations responsible for illegal sales of alcoholic beverages. Once proposed, it took only ten months to ratify the Twenty-First Amendment, which repealed the Prohibition Amendment.

The Living Constitution

The Congress, whenever two-thirds of both houses shall deem it necessary, shall propose amendments to this Constitution, or, on the application of the legislatures of two thirds of the several states, shall call a convention for proposing amendments, which, in either case, shall be valid to all intents and purposes, as part of this Constitution, when ratified by the legislatures of three fourths of the several states, or by conventions in three fourths thereof, as the one or the other mode of ratification may be proposed by the Congress.

—ARTICLE V

With this article, the Framers acknowledged the potential need to change or amend the Constitution. This article provides for two methods to propose amendments: by a two-thirds vote of both houses of Congress or by a two-thirds vote of the state legislatures. It also specifies two alternative methods of ratification of proposed amendments: by a three-quarters vote of the state legislatures, or by a similar vote in state ratifying conventions.

During the Constitutional Convention in Philadelphia, the Framers were divided as to how frequently or how easily the Constitution was to be amended. The original suggestion was to allow the document to be amended "when soever it shall seem necessary." Some delegates wanted to entrust this authority to the state legislatures; however, others feared that it would give states too much power. James Madison alleviated these fears by suggesting that both Congress and the states have a role in the process.

In the late 1960s and early 1970s, leaders of the new women's rights movement sought passage of the Equal Rights Amendment (ERA). Their efforts were rewarded when the ERA was approved in the House and Senate by overwhelming majorities in 1971 and then sent out to the states for their approval. In spite of tremendous lobbying, a strong anti-ERA movement emerged and the amendment failed to gain approval in three-quarters of the state legislatures. While it is not unusual to have over 100 potential amendments introduced in each session of Congress, actions that ban same-sex marriage, stop flag burning, and allow naturalized citizens to become president are some of the most frequently mentioned proposals.

The failed battles for the ERA as well as other amendments, including one to prohibit child labor and another to grant statehood to the District of Columbia, underscore how difficult it is to amend the Constitution. Thus, unlike the constitutions of individual states or many other nations, the U.S. Constitution rarely has been amended.

American Values/American Voices

BASEBALL, APPLE PIE, AND THE FLAG: THE POLITICS OF AMENDING THE CONSTITUTION

The American flag symbolizes the United States and is held as near and dear to most Americans as baseball, and certainly apple pie. We salute the flag at sporting events, begin the school day and many events pledging our allegiance to it, and men and women have died defending its honor. Thus, it should not be surprising that many people were outraged when the U.S. Supreme Court ruled in *Texas* v. *Johnson* (1989) that burning the American flag was a form of speech protected under the First Amendment.

Since the Court's initial ruling, passing a constitutional amendment to prohibit flag burning has become one of the social issues Republicans have used to mobilize their base. So far, Republicans have been unsuccessful at passing an anti–flag burning amendment. While the House of Representatives passed such an amendment, it has yet to garner the required two-thirds vote necessary for passage in the more moderate Senate.

In 2006, many political observers were surprised when a Republican bill that would ban some forms of flag burning had one Democratic co-sponsor: Senator Hillary Rodham Clinton (D–NY). Many political observers believe that Clinton is carefully positioning herself to the center in preparation for a run for the presidency in 2008, and thus is supporting a bill that would make it a crime to burn a flag to intimidate someone, burn someone else's flag, or destroy a flag on federal property. The bill co-sponsored by Clinton does not mention a constitutional amendment, and critics are divided as to whether this bill, written to meet many of the criticisms voiced by the majority of the Supreme Court, will withstand judicial review. Still, it is a bill popular with the general public, many of whom view the Court's decision as an attack on patriotic values.

QUESTIONS

1. Why are flags, national or state, the object of such emotional attachment?
2. If the First Amendment protects political speech, can you think of a way that could justify special protections for the flag beyond the ones currently in force, such as how it is to be displayed or disposed of— which, ironically, is by burning?

Congress's decision to use the convention method led to quick approval of the Twenty-First Amendment.

The intensity of efforts to amend the Constitution has varied considerably, depending on the nature of the change proposed. Whereas the Twenty-First Amendment took only ten months to ratify, an equal rights amendment (ERA) was introduced in every session of Congress from 1923 until 1972, when Congress finally voted favorably for it. Even then, years of lobbying by women's groups were insufficient to garner necessary state support. By 1982, the congressionally mandated date for ratification, only thirty-five states— three short of the number required—had voted favorably on the amendment.[26]

One of the most recent, concerted efforts would amend the Constitution to prohibit flag burning, as described in American Values/American Voices: Baseball, Apple Pie, and the Flag: The Politics of Amending the Constitution.

The History of Constitutional Amendemts

INFORMAL METHODS OF AMENDING THE CONSTITUTION

The formal amendment process is not the only way that the Constitution has been changed over time. Judicial interpretation and cultural and social change also have had a major impact on the way the Constitution has evolved.

Judicial Interpretation As early as 1803, the Supreme Court declared in *Marbury* v. *Madison* that the federal courts had the power to nullify acts of the nation's government when they were found to be in conflict with the Constitution.[27] Over the years, this check on the other branches of government and on the states has increased

Politics Now

POLITICS AND AMENDING THE CONSTITUTION

"The union of a man and a woman is the most enduring human institution, honored and encouraged in all cultures and by every religious faith." So spoke President George W. Bush in announcing his initial support of congressional action to amend the Constitution to ban same-sex marriages. He did not endorse a specific amendment but instead called upon Congress to take action and endorse an amendment in the wake of the specter of the thousands of same-sex marriages that were conducted in San Francisco, California in early 2004 (these were later ruled invalid by that state's Supreme Court).

At the time of the president's announcement, a resolution prohibiting same-sex marriage was already pending before the 108th Congress. This bill, which defined marriage as a union between a man and a woman, had first been introduced in the House of Representatives in May of 2003. A companion resolution was introduced in the Senate in November of 2003.

In the Senate, the amendment was killed for the 108th session in July when a procedural vote to get the resolution to the floor failed on a 48–50 vote—12 votes shy of the 60 votes required by Senate rules. (Sixty-seven votes are necessary for a constitutional amendment to be approved by the Senate.) Six Republicans and one Independent voted with 43 Democrats to kill the amendment. The White House issued a statement noting the president's "disappointment" and urged the House to take up the measure, which it did a few days later. The resolution did come to a floor vote there, but the 227–186 vote tally failed to reach the two-thirds required.

The measure was reintroduced in the 109th Congress. With an extremely competitive election on the horizon, many conservative Republicans saw the amendment as an opportunity to energize their base for the upcoming contest.[a] Prohibiting same-sex marriage was a staple of the Republican Party's "American Values Agenda" for the 2006 midterm elections, and leaders believed that even if the amendment did not pass both houses, forcing incumbent members of Congress to take a position on the bill could pay big dividends in the November elections.[b]

As expected, the amendment once again failed on a procedural vote in the Senate, and did not receive a two-thirds majority in the House of Representatives. Although President Bush expressed his disappointment at the amendment's defeat, he noted his continued dedication to putting such a provision in the constitution, noting, "Our nation's founders set a high bar for amending our Constitution—and history has shown us that it can take several tries before an amendment builds the two-thirds support it needs in both houses of Congress."[c]

Opponents of same-sex marriage have had greater success in amending state constitutions. In 2004, for example, eleven states approved varying forms of state constitutional amendment provisions, all by significant margins. Moreover, efforts to prohibit same-sex marriage in crucial swing states such as Ohio and Michigan are credited with delivering a victory for President Bush. Studies conducted after the election concluded that focus on same-sex marriage and moral values drew some African American voters who generally opposed same-sex marriage to the polls—diminishing traditional Democratic Party strength and energizing in all eleven states the Republican Party's conservative base.

Eight additional states—Arizona, Colorado, Idaho, South Carolina, South Dakota, Tennessee, Virginia, and Wisconsin—considered gay marriage amendments in the 2006 midterm elections. The Arizona amendment failed and a number of the other amendments passed by smaller margins than those passed in 2004. Many commentators prior to the election noted the increasing organization of gay rights groups.[d] Perhaps as a result of this increased organization, public support for prohibitions on same-sex marriage was also dropping in the general public. One survey by the Pew Research Center conducted in March 2006, for example, showed that only 51 percent of respondents favored prohibiting gay marriage. Two years earlier, that number stood at 63 percent of respondents.[e]

The increasing favorability of state supreme courts to gay rights claims also affected groups' efforts to prohibit same-sex marriage. The 2003 Massachusetts Supreme Judicial Court decision that legalized same-sex marriage in that state and the October 2006 New Jersey Supreme Court decision granting same sex couples expanded benefits, although not actual marriage, put gay rights groups' arguments for marriage equality squarely in the public eye.

Finally, some observers have suggested that the general public is simply "burned out" on the issue of same-sex marriage.[f] Increasing violence in Iraq and the series of ethics scandals in Washington, D.C. took attention away from the gay marriage issue in 2006 and allowed congressional Democrats to win majorities in the House and Senate. The implications of these and other changes for the future of a federal marriage amendment, however, remain to be seen.

QUESTIONS

1. Historically, issues about marriage have been left to the states. How appropriate do you think it is to alter the Constitution to take authority over marriage away from the states? Can you think of other instances in which authority has been taken away from the states?

2. Why do you think that ballot measures prohibiting same sex marriage in individual states lost steam between 2004 and 2006? What effect did the defeat of the federal marriage amendment have on this change?

[a]Andrea Stone, "GOP Still Plans to Make Issue of Gay Marriage: Amendment Falls Far Short in Senate Vote." *USA Today* (June 8, 2006): 6A.

[b]Mike Soraghan, "Musgrave's Gay Marriage Ban Defeated: Democrats Called the Vote Political Posturing." *Denver Post* (July 29, 2006): A8.

[c]Quoted in Craig Gilbert, "Gay Marriage Amendment Fails in Senate: Measure Falls Far Short of 60 Votes Needed to Keep it Alive." *Milwaukee Journal Sentinel* (June 8, 2006): A3.

[d]Kirk Johnson, "Gay Marriage Losing Punch as Ballot Issue." *New York Times* (October 14, 2006): A5.

[e]Stone, "GOP Still Plans to Make Issue of Gay Marriage."

[f]Johnson, "Gay Marriage Losing Punch"

the authority of the Court and significantly has altered the meaning of various provisions of the Constitution, a fact that prompted Woodrow Wilson to call the Supreme Court "a constitutional convention in continuous session." (More detail on the Supreme Court's role in interpreting the Constitution is found in chapters 5, 6, and 10 especially, as well as in other chapters in this book.)

Today, some analysts argue that the original intent of the Framers, as evidenced in *The Federalist Papers,* as well as in private notes taken by James Madison at the Constitutional Convention, should govern judicial interpretation of the Constitution.[28] Others argue that the Framers knew that a changing society needed an elastic, flexible document that could adapt to the ages.[29] In all likelihood, the vagueness of the document was purposeful. Those in attendance in Philadelphia recognized that they could not agree on everything and that it was wiser to leave interpretation to future generations.

Recently, law professor Mark V. Tushnet has offered a particularly stinging criticism of judicial review and our reliance on the courts to interpret the law. He believes that under our present system, Americans are unwilling to enforce the provisions of the Constitution because they believe this is the sole province of the court system. If we were to eliminate the deference given to court decisions, Tushnet argues, citizens would be compelled to become involved in enforcing their Constitution, thereby creating a system of populist constitutional law, and a more representative government.[30]

Social and Cultural Change   Even the most far-sighted of those in attendance at the Constitutional Convention could not have anticipated the vast changes that have occurred in the United States. For example, although many were uncomfortable with the Three-Fifths Compromise and others hoped for the abolition of slavery, none could have imagined that Colin Powell and Condoleezza Rice would each serve a term as the U.S. secretary of state. Likewise, few of the Framers could have anticipated the diverse roles that women would play in American society. The Constitution has evolved to accommodate such social and cultural changes. Thus, although there is no specific amendment guaranteeing women equal protection of the law, the federal courts have interpreted the Constitution to prohibit many forms of gender discrimination, thereby recognizing cultural and societal change. But, some change is resisted, as illustrated in Politics Now: Politics and Amending the Constitution.

Social change has also caused changes in the way institutions of government act. As problems such as the Great Depression appeared national in scope, Congress took on more and more power at the expense of the states to solve economic and social crises. In fact, Yale law professor Bruce Ackerman argues that on certain occasions, extraordinary times call for extraordinary measures such as the New Deal that, in effect, amend the Constitution. Thus, congressional passage (and the Supreme Court's eventual acceptance) of sweeping New Deal legislation that altered the balance of power between the national government and the states truly changed the Constitution without benefit of amendment.[31] Still, in spite of massive changes such as these, the Constitution survives, changed and ever changing after more than 200 years.

Summary

THE U.S. CONSTITUTION has proven to be a remarkably enduring document. In explaining how and why the Constitution came into being, this chapter has covered the following points:

1. The Origins of a New Nation
While settlers came to the New World for a variety of reasons, most remained loyal to Great Britain and considered themselves subjects of the king. Over the years, as new generations of Americans were born on colonial soil, those ties weakened. A series of taxes levied by the crown ultimately led the colonists to convene a Continental Congress and to declare their independence.

2. The First Attempt at Government: The Articles of Confederation
The Articles of Confederation (1781) created a loose league of friendship between the new national government and the states. Numerous weaknesses in the

new government became apparent by 1784. Among the major flaws were Congress's inability to tax or regulate commerce, the absence of an executive to administer the government, the lack of a strong central government, and no judiciary.

3. The Miracle at Philadelphia: Writing a Constitution
When the weaknesses under the Articles of Confederation became apparent, the states called for a meeting to reform them. The Constitutional Convention (1787) quickly threw out the Articles of Confederation and fashioned a new, more workable form of government. The Constitution was the result of a series of compromises, including those over representation, over issues involving large and small states, and over how to determine population. Compromises were also made about how members of each branch of government were to be selected. The Electoral College was created to give states a key role in the selection of the president.

4. The U.S. Constitution
The proposed U.S. Constitution created a federal system that drew heavily on Montesquieu's ideas about separation of powers. These ideas concerned a way of parceling out power among the three branches of government, and checks and balances to prevent any one branch from having too much power.

5. The Drive for Ratification
The drive for ratification became a fierce fight between Federalists and Anti-Federalists. Federalists lobbied for the strong national government created by the Constitution; Anti-Federalists favored greater state power.

6. Methods of Amending the Constitution
The Framers did not want to fashion a government that could respond to the whims of the people. Therefore, they designed a deliberate two-stage formal amendment process that required approval on the federal and state levels; this process has rarely been used. However, informal amendments, prompted by judicial interpretation and by cultural and social change, have had a tremendous impact on the Constitution.

KEY TERMS

Anti-Federalists, p. 54
Articles of Confederation, p. 39
Bill of Rights, p. 57
checks and balances, p. 46
Committees of Correspondence, p. 34
confederation, p. 37
constitution, p. 41

Declaration of Independence, p. 37
enumerated powers, p. 49
federal system, p. 47
The Federalist Papers, p. 55
Federalists, p. 54
First Continental Congress, p. 36
Great Compromise, p. 44
implied powers, p. 49
mercantilism, p. 33
necessary and proper clause, p. 49
New Jersey Plan, p. 43
Second Continental Congress, p. 36
separation of powers, p. 46
Shays's Rebellion, p. 41
Stamp Act Congress, p. 34
supremacy clause, p. 52
Three-Fifths Compromise, p. 44
Virginia Plan, p. 43

SELECTED READINGS

Ackerman, Bruce. *We the People: Transformations.* Cambridge, MA: Belknap Press, 2000.

Bailyn, Bernard. *The Ideological Origins of the American Revolution.* Cambridge, MA: Belknap Press, 1967.

Beard, Charles A. *An Economic Interpretation of the Constitution of the United States,* reissue ed. Mineola, NY: Dover, 2004.

Bernstein, Richard B., with Jerome Agel. *Amending America,* reissue ed. Lawrence: University Press of Kansas, 1995.

Bowen, Catherine Drinker. *Miracle at Philadelphia.* Boston: Little, Brown, 1986.

Brinkley, Alan, Nelson W. Polsby, and Kathleen M. Sullivan. *New Federalist Papers: Essays in Defense of the Constitution.* New York: Norton, 1997.

Dahl, Robert A. *How Democratic is the American Constitution?* New Haven, CT: Yale University Press, 2002.

Hamilton, Alexander, James Madison, and John Jay. *The Federalist Papers.* New York: Bantam Books, 1989 (first published in 1788).

Kyvig, David E. *Explicit and Authentic Acts: Amending the U.S. Constitution, 1776–1995.* Lawrence: University Press of Kansas, 1996.

Lynch, Joseph M. *Negotiating the Constitution: The Earliest Debates over Original Intent.* Ithaca, NY: Cornell University Press, 2005.

Main, Jackson Turner. *The Anti-Federalists: Critics of the Constitution, 1781–1788.* Chapel Hill: University of North Carolina Press, 2004.

———. *The Social Structure of Revolutionary America.* Princeton, NJ: Princeton University Press, 1965.

Rossiter, Clinton. *1787: Grand Convention,* reissue ed. New York: Norton, 1987.

Simon, James F. *What Kind of Nation: Thomas Jefferson, John Marshall, and the Epic Struggle to Create a United States.* New York: Simon and Schuster, 2003.

Stoner, James R., Jr. *Common Law and Liberal Theory.* Lawrence: University Press of Kansas, 1992.

Storing, Herbert J. *What the Anti-Federalists Were For.* Chicago: University of Chicago Press, 1981.

Sunstein, Cass R. *Designing Democracy: What Constitutions Do.* New York: Oxford University Press, 2001.

Tushnet, Mark. *Taking the Constitution Away from the Courts.* Princeton, NJ: Princeton University Press, 2000.

Tushnet, Mark, ed. *The Constitution in Wartime: Beyond Alarmism and Complacency.* Durham, NC: Duke University Press, 2005.

Vile, John R. *Encyclopedia of Constitutional Amendments, and Amending Issues, 1789–1995.* Santa Barbara, CA: ABC-CLIO, 1996.

Wood, Gordon S. *The Creation of the American Republic, 1776–1787,* reissue ed. New York: Norton, 1993.

WEB EXPLORATIONS

For more information on the work of the Continental Congress, see
http://lcweb2.loc.gov/ammem/bdsds/intro01.html

For a full text of the Articles of Confederation, see
http://www.usconstitution.net/articles.html

For demographic background on the Framers, see
http://www.usconstitution.net/constframedata.html

To compare *The Federalist Papers* with *The Anti-Federalist Papers,* see
http://www.law.emory.edu/FEDERAL/federalist/ and
http://wepin.com/articles/afp/index.htm

For the text of failed amendments to the U.S. Constitution, see
http://www.usconstitution.net/constamfail.html

The Constitution of the United States of America

We the People of the United States, in Order to form a more perfect Union, establish Justice, insure domestic Tranquility, provide for the common defence, promote the general Welfare, and secure the Blessings of Liberty to ourselves and our Posterity, do ordain and establish this Constitution for the United States of America.

ARTICLE I

Section 1.

All legislative Powers herein granted shall be vested in a Congress of the United States, which shall consist of a Senate and House of Representatives.

Article I is the longest and most detailed of any of the articles, sections, or amendments that make up the United States Constitution. By *enumerating* the powers of Congress, the Framers attached limits to the enormous authority they had vested in the legislative branch. At the same time, the allocation of certain powers to Congress ensured that the legislative branch would maintain control over certain vital areas of public policy and that it would be protected from incursions by the executive and judicial branches. Moreover, by clearly vesting Congress with certain powers (for example, the power to regulate interstate commerce), Article I established a water's edge for the exercise of state power in what were now national affairs.

Originally, Article I also contained restrictions limiting the amendment of several of its provisions, a feature found nowhere else in the Constitution. Section 4 prohibited Congress from making any law banning the importation of slaves until 1808, and section 9 prohibited Congress from levying an income tax on the general population. Neither section is operative any longer. Section 4 expired on its own, and section 9 was modified by passage of the Sixteenth Amendment, which established the income tax (see page 88).

Despite the great care the Framers took to limit the exercise of congressional authority to those powers enumerated in Article I, the power of Congress has grown tremendously since the nation's founding. Under Chief Justice John Marshall (1801–1835), the U.S. Supreme Court interpreted the Constitution to favor the power of the national government over the states and to permit

Congress to exercise both its *enumerated* (the power to regulate interstate commerce) and *implied* (the necessary and proper clause) powers in broad fashion. With only the occasional exception, the Court has never really challenged the legislative power vested in Congress to engage in numerous areas of public policy that some constitutional scholars (and politicians and voters) believe are the province of the states. Perhaps the only area in which legislative power has diminished over the years has been the war-making power granted to Congress, something that lawmakers, for all their occasional criticism of presidential conduct of foreign policy, have ceded to the executive branch rather willingly.

Section 2.

The House of Representatives shall be composed of Members chosen every second Year by the People of the several States, and the Electors in each State shall have the Qualifications requisite for Electors of the most numerous Branch of the State Legislature.

No person shall be a Representative who shall not have attained to the Age of twenty five Years, and been seven Years a Citizen of the United States, and who shall not, when elected, be an Inhabitant of that State in which he shall be chosen.

The qualifications clause, which sets out the age and residency requirements for individuals who wish to run for the House of Representatives, became the centerpiece of a national debate that emerged during the late 1980s and early 1990s over term limits for members of Congress. In *U.S. Term Limits* v. *Thornton* (1995), the Supreme Court ruled that section 2, clause 2, did not specify any other qualification to serve in the House other than age and residency (as did section 3, clause 3, to run for the Senate). Thus, no state could restrict an individual's right to run for Congress. The Court ruled that any modification to the qualifications clause would have to come through a constitutional amendment.

Representatives and direct Taxes shall be apportioned among the several States which may be included within this Union, according to their respective Numbers which shall be determined by adding to the whole Number of free Persons, including those bound to Service for a Term of Years, and excluding Indians not taxed, three fifths of all other Persons. The actual Enumeration shall be made within three Years after the first Meeting of the Congress of the United States, and within every subsequent Term ten Years, in such Manner as they shall by Law direct. The Number of Representatives shall not exceed one for every thirty Thousand, but each State shall have at Least one Representative; and until such enumerations shall be made, the State of New Hampshire shall be entitled to chuse three, Massachusetts eight, Rhode-Island and Providence Plantations one, Connecticut five, New-York six, New Jersey four, Pennsylvania eight, Delaware one, Maryland six, Virginia ten, North Carolina five, South Carolina five, and Georgia three.

Under the Articles of Confederation, "direct" taxes (such as taxes on property) were apportioned based on land value, not population. This encouraged states to diminish the value of their land in order to reduce their tax burden. Prior to the Constitutional Convention of 1787, several prominent delegates met to discuss—and ultimately propose—changing the method for direct taxation from land value to the population of each state. A major sticking point among the delegates on this issue was how to count slaves for taxation purposes. Southern states wanted to diminish the value of slaves for tax purposes, while northern states wanted to count slaves as closer to a full person. On the other hand, southern states wanted to count slaves as "whole persons" for purposes of representation to increase their power in the House of Representatives, but northern states rejected this proposal. Ultimately, the delegates settled on the "Three-Fifths Compromise," which treated each slave as three-fifths of a person for tax and representation purposes.

At the beginning, the Three-Fifths Compromise enhanced southern power in the House. In 1790, when the 1st Congress convened, the South held 45 percent of the seats, despite a significantly smaller free population than the North. Over time, however, the South saw its power in the House diminish. By the 1830s, the South held just over 30 percent of House seats, which gave it just enough power to thwart northern initiatives on slavery questions and territorial issues, but not enough power to defeat the growing power of the North to control commercial and economic policy. This standoff between the North and South led to such events as South Carolina Senator John C. Calhoun's doctrine of nullification and secession, which argued that a state could nullify any federal law not consistent with regional or state interests. By the 1850s, the Three-Fifths Compromise had made the South dependent on expanding the number of slaveholding territories eligible for admission to the union and a judicial system sympathetic to slaveholding interests. The Three-Fifths Compromise was repealed by section 2 of the Fourteenth Amendment (see pages 86–87).

When vacancies happen in the Representation from any State, the Executive Authority thereof shall issue Writs of Election to fill such Vacancies.

This clause permits the governor of a state to call an election to replace any member of the House of Representatives who is unable to complete a term of office due to death, resignation, or removal from the House. In some cases, a governor will appoint a successor to fill out a term; in other cases, the governor will call a special election. A governor's decision is shaped less by constitutional guidelines and more by partisan interests. For example, a Democratic governor might choose to appoint a Democratic successor if he or she believes that a Republican candidate might have an advantage in a special election.

The House of Representatives shall chuse their speaker and other Officers; and shall have the sole Power of Impeachment.

Clause 5 establishes the only officer of the House of Representatives—the Speaker. The remaining offices (party leaders, whips, and so on) are created by the House.

The House also has the sole power of impeachment against members of the executive and judicial branches. The House, like the Senate, is responsible for disciplining its own members. In *Nixon* v. *U.S.* (1993), the Supreme Court ruled that government officials who are the subject of impeachment proceedings may not challenge them in court. The Court ruled that the sole power given to the House over impeachment precludes judicial intervention.

Section 3.

The Senate of the United States shall be composed of two Senators from each State chosen by the Legislature thereof, for six Years; and each Senator shall have one Vote.

The provision of this clause establishing the election of senators by state legislatures was repealed by the Seventeenth Amendment (see page 88).

Immediately after they shall be assembled in Consequence of the first Election, they shall be divided as equally as may be into three Classes. The Seats of the Senators of the first Class shall be vacated at the Expiration of the second year, of the second Class at the Expiration of the fourth Year, and of the third Class at the Expiration of the sixth Year, so that one third may be chosen every second Year and if Vacancies happen by Resignation, or otherwise, during the Recess of the Legislature of any State, the Executive thereof may make temporary Appointments until the next Meeting of the Legislature, which shall then fill such Vacancies.

Vacancies for senators are handled the same way as vacancies for representatives—through appointment or special election. The Seventeenth Amendment modified the language authorizing the state legislature to choose a replacement for a vacant Senate position.

No Person shall be a Senator who shall not have attained to the Age of thirty Years, and been nine Years a Citizen of the United States, and who shall not, when elected, be an Inhabitant of that State for which he shall be chosen.

The Vice President of the United States shall be President of the Senate, but shall have no Vote, unless they be equally divided.

Clause 4 gives the vice president the authority to vote to break a tie in the Senate. This is the only constitutional duty the Constitution specifies for the vice president. As president of the Senate, the vice president also presides over procedural matters of that body, although this is not a responsibility that vice presidents really have ever shouldered.

The Senate shall chuse their other Officers, and also a President pro tempore, in the Absence of the Vice President, or when he shall exercise the Office of President of the United States.

Clause 5 creates the position of *president pro tempore* (the president of the time), the only Senate office established by the Constitution to handle the duties of the vice president set out in section 3, clause 4.

The Senate shall have the sole Power to try all Impeachments. When sitting for that Purpose, they shall be on Oath or Affirmation. When the President of the United States is tried, the Chief Justice shall preside: And no Person shall be convicted without the Concurrence of two thirds of the Members present.

Judgment in Cases of Impeachment shall not extend further than to removal from Office, and disqualification to hold and enjoy any Office of honor, Trust or Profit under the United States; but the Party convicted shall nevertheless be liable and subject to Indictment, Trial, Judgment and Punishment, according to law.

Just as the House of Representatives has the sole power to bring impeachment against executive and judicial branch officials, the Senate has the sole power to try all impeachments. Unless the president is facing trial in the Senate, the vice president serves as the presiding officer. In 1998, President Bill Clinton was tried on two articles of impeachment (four were brought against him in the House) and found not guilty on each count. The presiding officer in President Clinton's impeachment trial was Chief Justice William H. Rehnquist.

A conviction results in the removal of an official from office. It does not prohibit subsequent civil or criminal action against that individual. Nor does it prohibit an impeached and convicted official from returning to federal office. In 1989, Alcee Hastings, a trial judge with ten years experience on the U.S. District Court for the Southern District of Florida, was convicted on impeachment charges and removed from office. In 1992, he ran successfully for the 23rd District seat of the U.S. House of Representatives, where he continues to serve as of this writing.

Section 4.

The Times, Places and Manner of holding Elections for Senators and Representatives, shall be prescribed in each State by the Legislature thereof; but the Congress may at any time by Law make or alter such Regulations, except as to the Places of chusing Senators.

The Congress shall assemble at least once in every Year, and such Meeting shall be on the first Monday in December, unless they shall by Law appoint a different Day.

Section 4 authorizes the states to establish the rules governing elections for members of Congress, but Congress has never hesitated to exercise its law-making power in this area when it has believed that improvements were necessary to improve the electoral process. The first such action did not come until 1842, when Congress passed legislation making elections to the House based on single-member districts, not from the general population. By the turn of the twentieth century, Congress had passed legislation establishing additional criteria such as the rough equality of population among districts and territorial compactness and contiguity. Article I, section 4, is one of the three main areas from which Congress derives the power to regulate the electoral process. The other two are the necessary and proper clause of Article I, section 8, clause 3, and section 2 of the Fifteenth Amendment.

Section 5.

Each House shall be the Judge of the Elections, Returns and Qualifications of its own Members, and a Majority of each shall constitute a Quorum to do business; but a smaller Number may adjourn from day to day, and may be authorized to compel the Attendance of absent Members, in such Manner, and under such Penalties as each House may provide.

Each House may determine the Rules of its Proceedings, punish its Members for disorderly Behaviour, and with the Concurrence of two thirds, expel a Member.

Clause 2 gives power to the House and Senate to establish the rules and decorum for each chamber. Expulsion from either the House or the Senate does not preclude a member from running for congressional office again or serving in any other official capacity. In *Powell v. McCormack* (1969), the Supreme Court ruled that the House's decision to exclude an individual from the chamber despite having been elected was different from the expulsion of a sitting representative.

Each House shall keep a Journal of its Proceedings, and from time to time publish the same, excepting such Parts as may in their judgment require Secrecy; and the Yeas and Nays of the Members of either House on any question shall, at the Desire of one fifth of those present, be entered on the Journal.

The *Congressional Record* is the official journal of Congress. Justice Joseph Story, in his much praised scholarly treatment of the U.S. Constitution, *Commentaries on the Constitution* (1833), said the purpose of this clause was "to insure publicity to the proceedings of the legislature, and a correspondent responsibility of the members to their respective constituents." Recorded votes (and yea-or-nay voice votes, if agreed to by one-fifth of the House or Senate), speeches, and other public business are contained in the *Congressional Record*.

Neither House, during the Session of Congress, shall, without the Consent of the other, adjourn for more than three days, nor to any other Place than that in which the two Houses shall be sitting.

Section 6.
The Senators and Representatives shall receive a Compensation for their Services, to be ascertained by Law, and paid out of the Treasury of the United States. They shall in all Cases, except Treason, Felony and Breach of the Peace, be privileged from Arrest during their Attendance at the Session of their respective Houses, and in going to and returning from the same; and for any Speech or Debate in either House, they shall not be questioned in any other Place.

The Twenty-Seventh Amendment, ratified in 1992, now governs the procedures for compensation of members of Congress. From the nation's founding until 1967, Congress had determined the salaries of its members. Then, Congress passed legislation giving the president the responsibility to recommend salary levels for members of Congress, since the president already had the responsibility to recommend pay levels for other federal officials. In 1989, as part of the Ethics Reform Act, Congress established a new system of pay raises and cost-of-living adjustments based on a particular vote.

Clause 1 also protects the right of senators and representatives from criminal prosecution for any "Speech or Debate" made in Congress. This protection stemmed from lessons drawn from the persistent conflicts between the House of Commons and the Tudor and Stuart monarchies in Great Britain, who used their power to bring civil and criminal actions against legislators whose opinions were deemed seditious or dangerous. The 1689 English Bill of Rights contained protection for legislators to conduct their business in Parliament free from such fears, and the Framers believed that such protection was essential for Congress under the Constitution. The Supreme Court has held, however, in *Gravel v. U.S.* (1972), that the speech or debate clause does not immunize senators or representatives from criminal inquiry if their activities in the Senate or House are the result of alleged or proven illegal action.

The privilege from arrest clause has little application in contemporary America. The clause applies only to arrests in civil suits, which were fairly common when the Constitution was ratified. The Court has interpreted the phrase "except Treason, Felony or Breach of the Peace" to make members eligible for arrest for crimes that would fall into that category. For example, a member of Congress is eligible if he or she commits a serious traffic offense, such as drunk or reckless driving, on the way to or from legislative business.

No Senator or Representative shall, during the Time for which he was elected, be appointed to any civil Office under the Authority of the United States, which shall have been created, or the Emoluments whereof shall have been encreased during such time; and no Person holding any Office under the United States, shall be a Member of either House during his Continuance in Office.

Clause 2 prohibits any senator or representative from holding a simultaneous office in the legislative or executive branches. This is one of the least controversial provisions of the Constitution. Indeed, there is no judicial interpretation of its meaning.

The general purpose of this clause is to prevent one branch of government from having an undue influence on another by creating dual incentives. It is also another safeguard in the separation of powers.

Section 7.
All Bills for raising Revenue shall originate in the House of Representatives; but the Senate may propose or concur with Amendments as on other Bills.

The power to raise revenue found in clause 1 is unique to the House of Representatives. In *Federalist No. 58*, James Madison argued that vesting such authority in the House was a key feature of the separation of powers. No bill either raising or lowering taxes may originate in the Senate. Legislation that creates incidental revenue may begin in the Senate, as long as the legislation does not involve taxation.

Every Bill which shall have passed the House of Representatives and the Senate, shall, before it become a Law, be presented to the President of the United States; If he approve he shall sign it, but if not he shall return it, with his Objections to that House in which it shall have originated, who shall enter the Objections at large on their Journal, and proceed to reconsider it. If after such Reconsideration two thirds of that House shall agree to pass the Bill, it shall be sent, together with the Objections, to the other House, by which it shall likewise be reconsidered, and if approved by two thirds of that House, it shall become a Law. But in all such Cases the Votes of both Houses shall be determined by Yeas and Nays, and the Names of the Persons voting for and against the Bill shall be entered on the Journal of each House respectively. If any Bill shall not be returned by the President within ten Days (Sundays excepted) after it shall have been presented to him, the Same shall be a Law, in like Manner as if he had signed it, unless the Congress by their Adjournment prevent its Return, in which Case it shall not be a Law.

This clause establishes several key features of presidential-congressional relations in the flow of the legislative process. For a bill to become law, it must be passed by the House and Senate, and it must be signed by the president. The Supreme Court has ruled that the veto regulations outlined in this clause serve two purposes. First, by giving the president ten days to consider a bill for approval, clause 2 provides the president with ample time to consider legislation and protects him from having to approve legislation in the wake of congressional adjournment. But clause 2 also provides Congress with a countervailing power to override a presidential veto, a procedure that requires a two-thirds vote in each chamber.

Every Order, Resolution, or Vote to which the Concurrence of the Senate and House of Representatives may be necessary (except on a question of Adjournment) shall be presented to the President of the United States; and before the Same shall take Effect, shall be approved by him, or being disapproved by him, shall be repassed by two thirds of the Senate and House of Representatives, according to the Rules and Limitations prescribed in the Case of a Bill.

Clause 3 covers the presentation of resolutions, not actual legislation. For any resolution to have the force of law, it must be presented to the president for approval. Should the president veto the resolution, Congress may override this veto in the same manner expressed in section 7, clause 2. Resolutions that do not have the force of law do not require presidential approval. Preliminary votes taken on constitutional amendments and other legislative matters covered by clause 3 do not require presentation to the president.

This clause has been the subject of two major Supreme Court decisions dealing with the separation of powers. In *I.N.S.* v. *Chadha* (1983), the Court ruled that the House-only legislative veto, a practice begun during the 1930s to give Congress power to control power delegated to a rapidly expanding executive branch, violated both the bicameralism principles of Article I, section 1, and the presentment clause of section 7, clause 3. At the time, the ruling struck down about 200 legislative vetoes that had been included in various pieces of congressional legislation. In *Clinton* v. *New York* (1998), the Court ruled that the line-item veto passed by Congress to give the president the power to veto specific provisions of legislation rather than an entire bill violated the presentment clause of Article I, section 7, clause 3. The Court claimed that the line-item veto permitted the president to "repeal certain laws," a power that belonged to Congress and not the president.

Section 8.

The Congress shall have Power To lay and collect Taxes, Duties, Imposts and Excises, to pay the Debts and provide for the common Defence and general Welfare of the United States; but all Duties, Imposts and Excises shall be uniform throughout the United States;

To borrow Money on the credit of the United States;

To regulate Commerce with foreign Nations, and among the several States, and with the Indian Tribes;

To establish a uniform Rule of Naturalization, and uniform Laws on the subject of Bankruptcies throughout the United States;

To coin Money, regulate the Value thereof, and of foreign Coin, and fix the Standard of Weights and Measures;

To provide for the Punishment of counterfeiting the Securities and current Coin of the United States;

To establish Post Offices and post Roads;

To promote the Progress of Science and useful Arts, by securing for limited Times to Authors and Inventors exclusive Right to their respective Writings and Discoveries;

To constitute Tribunals inferior to the supreme Court;

To define and punish Piracies and Felonies committed on the high Seas, and Offences against the Law of Nations;

To declare War, grant Letters of Marque and Reprisal, and make rules concerning Captures on Land and Water;

To raise and support Armies, but no Appropriation of Money to that Use shall be for a longer Term than two Years;

To provide and maintain a Navy;

To make Rules for the Government and Regulation of the land and naval Forces;

To provide for calling forth the Militia to execute the Laws of the Union, suppress Insurrections and repel Invasions;

To provide for organizing, arming, and disciplining, the Militia, and for governing such Part of them as may be employed in the Service of the United States, reserving to the States respectively, the Appointment of the Officers, and the Authority of training the Militia according to the discipline prescribed by Congress;

To exercise exclusive Legislation in all Cases whatsoever, over such District (not exceeding ten Miles square) as may, by Cession of particular States, and the Acceptance of Congress, become the Seat of the Government of the United States, and to exercise like Authority over all Places purchased by the Consent of the Legislature of the State in which the Same shall be for the Erection of Forts, Magazines, Arsenals, dock-Yards, and other needful Buildings;—And

Article I, section 8, clause 1, is, in many ways, the engine of congressional power. First, clause 1 gives Congress the power to tax and spend, a power the Supreme Court has interpreted as "exhaustive" and "reaching every subject." Second, in giving Congress the power to provide for the common defense and general welfare, it offers no specific constraint on what Congress may spend public funds for and how much it may spend. Third, section 8 gives Congress complete authority in numerous areas of policy that affect Americans at home and abroad on a massive scale. These powers include the power to regulate interstate commerce (which Congress has relied on to establish federal civil rights law), to make war (a power that Congress, since the end of World War II in 1945, has increasingly deferred to the president), and to establish the federal judicial system.

Clause 1 is often cited by constitutional scholars as an example of how the Constitution constrains legislative power by limiting the powers that Congress may exercise. To a certain extent, this is true. But, it is also true that the Court has granted Congress extensive power to legislate in certain areas that bear only a tangential relationship to the specific language of some of the provisions of clause 1. For example, in *Katzenbach* v. *McClung* (1964), the Court turned back a challenge to the constitutionality of the Civil Rights Act of 1964, which Congress had passed

under its authority to regulate interstate commerce. The Court ruled that racial discrimination had an adverse effect on the free flow of commerce.

Clause 2 establishes the seat of the federal government—first New York City, now Washington, D.C. The clause also makes Congress the legislative body of the nation's capital, a power that extends to other federal bodies, such as forts, military bases, and other places where federal buildings are located.

To make all Laws which shall be necessary and proper for carrying into Execution the foregoing Powers, and all other Powers vested by this Constitution in the Government of the United States, or in any Department or Officer thereof.

Better known as the necessary and proper clause, this provision of Article I was one of the most contested points between Federalists and Anti-Federalists during the ratification debates over the Constitution. Anti-Federalists feared that the language was too broad and all-encompassing, and, if interpreted by a Supreme Court sympathetic to the nationalist ambitions of the Federalist Party, would give Congress limitless power to exercise legislative authority over state and local matters. In *McCulloch* v. *Maryland* (1819), Chief Justice John Marshall offered what constitutional scholars believe remains the definitive interpretation of the necessary and proper clause. While *McCulloch* certainly did cement the power of Congress in the federal system, the expansive definition given the necessary and proper clause by the Court is also testament to the flexible nature of the Constitution, and why so few amendments have been added to the original document.

Section 9.

The Migration or Importation of such Persons as any of the States now existing shall think proper to admit, shall not be prohibited by the Congress prior to the Year one thousand eight hundred and eight, but a Tax or duty may be imposed on such Importation, not exceeding ten dollars for each Person.

Like the other provisions of the Constitution that refer to slavery, such as the Three-Fifths Compromise, section 9 creates policy governing the institution without ever mentioning the word. The importation clause was a compromise between slave traders, who wanted to continue the practice, and opponents of slavery, who needed southern support to ratify the Constitution. In 1808, Congress passed legislation banning the importation of slaves; until then, Congress used its power to tax slaves brought to the United States.

The Privilege of the Writ of Habeas Corpus shall not be suspended, unless when in Cases of Rebellion or Invasion the public Safety may require it.

Clause 2 is the only place where the writ of habeas corpus—the "Great Writ," as it was known to the Framers—is mentioned in the Constitution. Only the federal government is bound by clause 2. The writ may only be suspended in times of crisis and rebellion, and then it is Congress that has the power, not the president. Thus, the Military Commissions Act, which gives power to the president to suspend the writ of *habeas corpus*, may be constitutionally suspect.

No Bill of Attainder or ex post facto Law shall be passed.

A bill of attainder is a legislative act punishing a person with "pains and penalties" without the benefit of a hearing or trial. The fundamental purpose of the ban on bills of attainder is to prevent trial by legislature and other arbitrary punishments for persons vulnerable to extra-judicial proceedings. An *ex post facto law* is one passed making a previously committed civil or criminal action subject to penalty. In *Calder v. Bull* (1798), the Court ruled that the ban on *ex post facto* laws applied only to penal and criminal actions. A similar restriction on the states is found in Article I, section 10, clause 1.

No Capitation, or other direct, Tax shall be laid, unless in Proportion to the Census or Enumeration herein before directed to be taken.

This clause, which originally prohibited Congress from levying an income tax, was modified by the Sixteenth Amendment, passed in 1913 (see page 88).

No Tax or Duty shall be laid on Articles exported from any State.

Clause 5 prohibits Congress from levying a tax on any good or article exported from a state to a foreign country or to another state. Many southern states feared that northern members of Congress would attempt to weaken the South's slave-based economy by taxing exports. This clause prohibited such action. Congress may prohibit the shipment of certain items from one state to another and to other countries.

No Preference shall be given by any Regulation of Commerce or Revenue to the Ports of one State over those of another: nor shall Vessels bound to, or from, one State, be obliged to enter, clear, or pay Duties in another.

Congress is prohibited from making laws regulating trade that favor one state over another. Clause 6 also prohibits Congress from establishing preferences for certain ports or trade centers over others, although it may, under its power to regulate interstate commerce, pass laws that incidentally benefit certain states or maritime outlets. The Supreme Court has ruled that states are not bound by the limitations on Congress expressed in this clause.

No money shall be drawn from the Treasury, but in Consequence of Appropriations made by Law; and a regular Statement and Account of the Receipts and Expenditures of all public Money shall be published from time to time.

Clause 7 serves two fundamental purposes. First, the clause prohibits any governmental body receiving federal funds from spending those funds without the approval of Congress. Once Congress has determined that federal funds are to be spent in a certain way, the executive branch may not exercise any discretion over that decision. Second, by restricting executive control of spending power, the clause firmly reinforces congressional authority over revenue and spending, a key feature of the separation of powers.

No Title of Nobility shall be granted by the United States: And no Person holding any Office of Profit or Trust under them, shall, without the Consent of the Congress, accept of any present, Emolument, Office, or Title, of any kind whatever, from any King, Prince, or foreign State.

This provision is among the first school-taught lessons about the Constitution. To reinforce the commitment to representative democracy, the Framers prohibited a title of nobility from being conferred on any public official. This clause also prohibits any government official from accepting compensation, gifts, or similar benefits from any foreign government for services rendered without the consent of Congress.

Section 10.

No state shall enter into any Treaty, Alliance, or Confederation; grant Letters of Marque and Reprisal; coin Money; emit Bills of Credit; make any Thing but gold and silver Coin a Tender in Payment of Debts; pass any Bill of Attainder, ex post facto Law, or Law impairing the Obligation of Contracts, or grant any Title of Nobility.

This clause denies several powers to the states that were once permissible under the Articles of Confederation, and it emphasizes the Framers' commitment under the Constitution to a strong national government with Congress as the centrifugal force. During the Civil War, the Union relied on this clause in support of its view that the Confederate states had no legal existence but instead were merely "states in rebellion" against the United States.

The restrictions on states passing either bills of attainder or ex post facto laws have come into play at various points in American history. During Reconstruction, several states enacted legislation prohibiting any individual who aided the Confederacy from entering certain professions or enjoying other benefits available to citizens who remained loyal to the Union. The Supreme Court struck down these laws on the grounds that they violated this clause.

The provision prohibiting states from passing any law "impairing the Obligation of Contracts," better known as the contract clause, has been the subject of considerable litigation before the Supreme Court. The contract clause was intended to bar the states from interfering in private contracts between consensual parties and was considered an important limit on the power of states to restrict the fledgling national economic order of the early republic. Early on, the Court considered many laws that restricted the terms set out in private contracts as unconstitutional. But as the United States became a more industrial society, and as citizen demands grew for government regulation of the economy, the environment, and social welfare benefits, the Court softened its position on the contract clause to permit states to make laws that served a reasonable public interest. A key case involving the contract clause is *Home Building and Loan Association* v. *Blaisdell* (1934). In *Blaisdell*, the Court ruled that a Depression-era law passed by the Minnesota legislature forgiving mortgage payments by homeowners to banks did not violate the contract clause.

No State shall, without the Consent of the Congress, lay any Imposts or Duties on Imports or Exports, except what may be absolutely necessary for executing its inspection Laws: and the net Produce of all Duties and Imposts, laid by any State on Imports or Exports, shall be for the Use of the Treasury of the United States, and all such Laws shall be subject to the Revision and Controul of the Congress.

No state may tax goods leaving or entering a state, although it may charge reasonable fees for inspections considered necessary to the public interest. The restriction on import and export taxes applies only to those goods entering from or leaving for a foreign country.

No State shall, without the Consent of Congress, lay any Duty of Tonnage, keep Troops, or Ships of War in time of Peace, enter into any Agreement or Compact with another State, or with a foreign Power, or engage in War, unless actually invaded, or in such imminent Danger as will not admit of delay.

Clause 3 cements the power of Congress to control acts of war and make treaties with foreign countries. The Framers wanted to correct any perception to the contrary gained from the Articles of Confederation that states were free to act independently of the national government on negotiated matters with foreign countries. They also wanted to ensure that any state that entered into a compact with another state—something this clause does not prohibit—must receive permission from Congress.

ARTICLE II

Section 1.

The executive Power shall be vested in a President of the United States of America. He shall hold his Office during the Term of four Years, and, together with the Vice President, chosen for the same Term, be elected as follows.

In *Federalist No. 70,* Alexander Hamilton argued for an "energetic executive" branch headed by a single, elected president not necessarily beholden to the majority party in Congress. Hamilton believed that a nationally elected president would not be bound by the narrow, parochial interests that drove legislative law-making. The president would possess both the veto power over Congress and a platform from which to articulate a national vision in both domestic and foreign affairs.

Hamilton believed that the constitutional boundaries placed on executive power through the separation of powers and the fact that the president was accountable to a national electorate constrained any possibility that the office would come to resemble the monarchies of Europe. However, most presidential scholars agree that the modern presidency has grown in power precisely because of the general nature of the enabling powers of Article II.

Each State shall appoint, in such Manner as the Legislature thereof may direct, a Number of Electors, equal to the whole Number of Senators and Representatives to which the State may be entitled in the Congress; but no Senator or Representative, or Person holding an Office of Trust of Profit under the United States, shall be appointed an Elector.

Clause 2 established the Electoral College and set the number of electors from each state at the total of senators and representatives serving in Congress.

The Electors shall meet in their respective States, and vote by Ballot for two Persons, of whom one at least shall not be an Inhabitant of the same State with themselves. And they shall make a List of all the Persons voted for, and, of the Number of Votes for each; which List they shall sign and certify, and transmit sealed to the Seat of the Government of the United States, directed to the President of the Senate. The President of the Senate shall, in the Presence of the Senate and House of Representatives, open all the Certificates, and the Votes shall then be counted. The Person having the greatest Number of Votes shall be the President, if such Number be a Majority of the whole Number of Electors appointed; and if there be more than one who have such Majority, and have an equal Number of Votes, then the House of Representatives shall immediately chuse by Ballot one of them for President; and if no Person have a Majority, then from the five highest on the List the said House shall in like Manner chuse the President. But in chusing the President, the Votes shall be taken by States, the Representation from each State having one Vote; A quorum for this Purpose shall consist of a Member or Members from two thirds of the States, and a Majority of all the States shall be necessary to a Choice. In every Case, after the Choice of the President, the Person having the greatest Number of Votes of the Electors shall be the Vice President. But if there should remain two or more who have equal Votes, the Senate shall chuse from them by Ballot the Vice President.

This provision of section 1 described the rules for calling the Electoral College to vote for president and vice president. Originally, the electors did not vote separately for president and vice president. After the 1800 election, which saw Thomas Jefferson and Aaron Burr receive the identical number of electoral votes even though it was clear that Jefferson was the presidential candidate and Burr the vice presidential candidate, the nation ratified the Twelfth Amendment (see page 85).

The Twelfth Amendment did not resolve what many constitutional scholars today believe are the inadequacies of the Electoral College system. In 1824, the presidential election ended in a four-way tie, and the House of Representatives elected second-place finisher John Quincy Adams president. In 1876, Benjamin Harrison lost the popular vote but won the presidency after recounts awarded him an Electoral College majority. But perhaps the most controversial election of all came in 2000, when George W. Bush, who lost the popular contest to Al Gore by approximately 500,000 votes, was named the presidential victor after a six-week court battle over the vote count in Florida. After the Supreme Court ruled against the position of Al Gore that a recount of the Florida popular vote should continue until all votes had been counted, an outcome that would have left the nation without a president-elect for several more weeks, Bush was awarded Florida's electoral votes, which gave him 271, just one more than he needed to win the office. Outraged Democrats pledged to mount a case for Electoral College reform, but, as was so often the case before, nothing happened.

The Congress may determine the Time of chusing the Electors, and the Day on which they shall give their Votes; which Day shall be the same throughout the United States.

No Person except a natural born Citizen, or a Citizen of the United States, at the time of the Adoption of this Constitution, shall be eligible to the Office of President; neither shall any Person be eligible to that Office who shall not have attained to the Age of thirty five Years, and been fourteen Years a Resident within the United States.

This provision of Article II is referred to as the presidential eligibility clause. In addition to setting out the age and resident requirements of presidential aspirants, this clause defines who may *not* run for president—any foreign-born individual who has nonetheless obtained United States citizenship. For example, Michigan Governor Jennifer Granholm, who has lived in the United States since she was four years old, may not run for president because she was born in Canada. The same is true for California Governor Arnold Schwarzenegger, who was born in Austria but has lived in the United States his entire adult life. Judicial interpretation of the presidential eligibility clause has not resolved the question of whether children born to U.S. citizens are eligible to run for president if they meet the residency requirements.

In Case of the Removal of the President from Office, or of his Death, Resignation, or Inability to discharge the Powers and Duties of the said Office, the Same shall devolve on the Vice President, and the Congress may by Law provide for the Case of Removal, Death, Resignation or Inability, both of the President and Vice President, declaring what Officer shall then act as President, and such Officer shall act accordingly, until the Disability be removed, or a President shall be elected.

This presidential succession clause has been modified by the Twenty-Fifth Amendment (see page 92).

The President shall, at stated Times, receive for his Services, a Compensation, which shall neither be encreased nor diminished during the Period for which he shall have been elected, and he shall not receive within that Period any other Emolument from the United States, or any of them.

Presidential compensation, like compensation for members of Congress, may not be increased for the current occupant of the office. The president is not eligible for any other public compensation during time in office. However, the president may continue to receive income such as interest on investments or book royalties.

Before he enter on the Execution of his Office, he shall take the following Oath or Affirmation:—"I do solemnly swear (or affirm) that I will faithfully execute the Office of President of the United States, and will to the best of my Ability, preserve, protect and defend the Constitution of the United States."

Since George Washington's inaugural in 1789, each president has added the phrase "so help me God" to the end of the presidential oath. Although Abraham Lincoln cited the oath to justify his suspension of the writ of *habeas corpus* during the Civil War, no other president has relied on the oath to justify action that stretched the boundaries of executive power. Presidents taking extraordinary action either at home or abroad have relied on either the commander in chief clause of section 2, clause 1, or the provision of section 3 authorizing the president to "faithfully execut[e]" the laws of the United States.

Section 2.

The President shall be Commander in Chief of the Army and Navy of the United States, and of the Militia of the several States, when called into the actual Service of the United States; he may require the Opinion, in writing, of the principal Officer in each of the executive Departments, upon any Subject relating to the Duties of their respective Offices, and he shall have Power to grant Reprieves and Pardons for Offences against the United States, except in Cases of Impeachment.

Section 2, clause 1, establishes the president as commander in chief of the Army and Navy of the United States. In modern times, that authority has extended to the Air Force, the Marines, and all other branches of the armed forces operating under the command of the United States, including state militias, reserve units, and national guards. Article I provides that Congress, and not the president, has the power to declare war. But, since World War II, no American president has received or requested a declaration of war to commit the armed forces to military conflicts, including those clearly acknowledged as large-scale war (Korea, Vietnam, the 1991 Persian Gulf War, Afghanistan, and the Iraq War). For these conflicts, the president received congressional *authorization* to use force, but not an Article I declaration.

Although the Supreme Court has ruled that the president has *inherent* power—that is, power to carry out the essential functions of his office in times of crisis, war or emergencies that are not *expressly* spelled out under Article II—it has not concluded that such power is unlimited. In *Youngstown Sheet & Tube* v. *Sawyer* (1952), the Court ruled that President Harry S Truman did not have the power to seize control of the nation's steel mills to continue the production of munitions and other war supplies without congressional authorization. More

recently, the Court ruled in *Hamdan* v. *Rumsfeld* (2006) that President George W. Bush exceeded his authority when he established military commissions that had not been approved by Congress to try detainees and other "enemy combatants" captured in the War on Terror. The Court ruled that since Congress had not approved of President Bush's system of military tribunals, prisoners were entitled to the protections of the Geneva Convention and the procedural rights of the Uniform Code of Military Justice. Congress passed the Military Commissions Act to address the Court's concerns.

Clause 1 also implicitly creates the Cabinet by authorizing the president to request the opinion "in writing" of the principal officers of the executive branch. The power to create Cabinet-level offices resides with Congress, not the president.

Presidential power to pardon is broad and limited only in cases of impeachment. Perhaps the most controversial pardon in American political history was President Gerald R. Ford's decision to pardon former President Richard M. Nixon, who resigned his office on August 8, 1974, after news reports and congressional inquiries strongly implicated him in the Watergate scandal. A real possibility existed that President Nixon could be tried on criminal charges as the result of his alleged activities during the Watergate scandal.

He shall have Power, by and with the Advice and Consent of the Senate, to make Treaties, provided two thirds of the Senators present concur; and he shall nominate, and by and with the Advice and Consent of the Senate, shall appoint Ambassadors, other public Ministers and Consuls, Judges of the supreme Court, and all other Officers of the United States, whose Appointments are not herein otherwise provided for, and which shall be established by Law: but the Congress may by Law vest the Appointment of such inferior Officers, as they think proper, in the President alone, in the Courts of Law, or in the Heads of Departments.

The President shall have Power to fill up all Vacancies that may happen during the Recess of the Senate, by granting Commissions which shall expire at the End of their next Session.

Clause 2 describes several powers the president may exercise in conjunction with the advice and consent of the Senate. These powers include the power, upon the approval of two-thirds of the Senate, to make treaties with foreign countries. But, the Constitution is silent on the question of whether a president (or Congress) may terminate a treaty by refusing to honor it or simply repealing it outright. When President Jimmy Carter terminated a treaty with China over the objection of Congress, several members sought a judicial resolution

of the action; the Court, however, did not decide the case on the merits and offered no resolution on the matter. The president does not require a two-thirds majority for approval of appointments to the federal judiciary, foreign ambassadorships, Cabinet-level positions, high-ranking positions in non-Cabinet agencies, and high-level military offices. But, the fact that the Senate must approve presidential appointments in these areas provides Congress (senators often listen to the constituents of House members on controversial choices) with an important check on presidential power to shape the contours of the executive branch.

Section 3.

He shall from time to time give to the Congress Information of the State of the Union, and recommend to their Consideration such Measures as he shall judge necessary and expedient; he may, on extraordinary Occasions, convene both Houses, or either of them, and in Case of Disagreement between them, with Respect to the Time of Adjournment, he may adjourn them to such Time as he shall think proper; he shall receive Ambassadors and other public Ministers; he shall take Care that the Laws be faithfully executed, and shall Commission all the Officers of the United States.

The president is required to deliver a State of the Union message to Congress each year. The nation's first two presidents, George Washington and John Adams, delivered their addresses in person. But the nation's third president, Thomas Jefferson, believed that the practice too closely resembled the Speech from the Throne delivered by British royalty. Instead, Jefferson prepared remarks for recitation before Congress by an assistant or clerk of Congress. Every American president after Jefferson followed suit until Woodrow Wilson renewed the original practice after his first year in office. Now, the State of the Union Address is a major media event, although it is less an assessment of the nation's health and happiness and more a presidential wish-list for policy initiatives and the touting of partisan accomplishments.

The final provision of section 3 authorizing the president to faithfully execute the laws of the United States has proven controversial over the years. Presidents have cited this broad language to justify such far-reaching action as the suspension of the writ of *habeas corpus*, as President Abraham Lincoln did during the Civil War before being rebuffed by the Supreme Court in *Ex parte McCardle* (1867), and the doctrine of executive privilege, which, as asserted by various presidents, permits the executive branch to withhold sensitive information from the public or the other branches of government for national security reasons. The Court has been of two

minds about the doctrine of executive privilege. On the one hand, the Court has said in such cases as *New York Times* v. *U.S.* (1971) and *U.S.* v. *Nixon* (1974) that the president has the power to withhold information to protect vital secrets and the nation's security. On the other hand, the Court has said, in ruling against the assertion of executive privilege in these two cases, that only an exceptional and demonstrated case can justify allowing the president to withhold information.

Section 4.

The President, Vice President and all civil Officers of the United States, shall be removed from Office on Impeachment for, and Conviction of, Treason, Bribery, or other High Crimes and Misdemeanors.

Presidential impeachment, like impeachment of the other described offices in section 4, is the responsibility of the House of Representatives. There is no judicial definition to what constitutes a high crime or misdemeanor. Complicating the matter further is that only the House and Senate are given responsibility over the impeachment process. No federal official subject to impeachment may challenge the action in federal court, as the Supreme Court has ruled that the rules governing impeachment are not actionable in court. Only two presidents, Andrew Johnson in 1868 and Bill Clinton in 1998, have ever been impeached. Neither president was convicted by the Senate of the charges brought against them.

ARTICLE III

Section 1.

The judicial Power of the United States, shall be vested in one supreme Court, and in such inferior Courts as the Congress may from time to time ordain and establish. The Judges, both of the supreme and inferior Courts, shall hold their Offices during good Behaviour, and shall, at stated Times, receive for their Services, a Compensation, which shall not be diminished during their Continuance in Office.

Like the power of Congress and the executive branch under Articles I and II, respectively, of the Constitution, the power of the federal judiciary has developed as the result of constitutional silences and ambiguities. Article III establishes only one federal court, the Supreme Court, and leaves to Congress the power to establish "inferior" courts as it deems necessary. Many students are surprised to learn that the power of judicial review was established by Congress, not the Supreme Court. Although the Court did articulate the power of judicial review in *Marbury* v. *Madison* (1803), that decision only applied to the power of the federal courts to review federal laws. The power of the federal courts to review state laws that allegedly trespassed upon the Constitution was established by the Judiciary Act of 1789. But, on the fundamental question of what constitutes the foundation and scope of judicial power, there is little doubt that the Court, not Congress, has been the foremost exponent of its own authority. Often, the Court has justified its authority to limit the power of the other branches to regulate its affairs by pointing to other provisions of the Constitution, most notably the supremacy clause of Article VI and section 5 of the Fourteenth Amendment, as well as Article III.

Section 2.

The judicial Power shall extend to all Cases, in Law and Equity, arising under this Constitution, the Laws of the United States, and Treaties made, or which shall be made, under their Authority;—to all Cases affecting Ambassadors, other public Ministers and Consuls;—to all Cases of admiralty and maritime Jurisdiction;—to Controversies to which the United States shall be a Party;—to Controversies between two or more States;—between a State and Citizens of another State;—between Citizens of different States;—between Citizens of the same State claiming Lands under Grants of different States,—and between a State, or the Citizens thereof, and foreign States, Citizens or Subjects.

In all Cases affecting Ambassadors, other public Ministers and Consuls, and those in which a State shall be Party, the supreme Court shall have original Jurisdiction. In all the other Cases before mentioned, the supreme Court shall have appellate Jurisdiction, both as to Law and Fact, with such Exceptions, and under such Regulations as the Congress shall make.

The Trial of all Crimes, except in Cases of Impeachment, shall be by Jury; and such Trial shall be held in the State where the said Crimes shall have been committed; but when not committed within any State, the Trial shall be at such Place or Places as the Congress may by Law have directed.

Section 1 invests the judicial power in "one Supreme Court," but it is in section 2 that we find the source of much of the controversy of the exercise of this power since *Marbury* was decided. By extending the judicial power to all "Cases, in Law and Equity, arising under the Constitution, [and] the laws of the United States," section 2 authorizes the Court to both decide matters of law and, if necessary, mandate a remedy commensurate with the degree of a constitutional violation. For example, in *Swann* v. *Charlotte-Mecklenburg Board of Education* (1971), the Court ruled that a lower court, having found that a school system had failed to meet desegregation requirements, had the power to order busing and other remedies to the constitutional violations it found in *Brown* v. *Board of Education* (1954).

Federal judicial power no longer extends to cases involving lawsuits between a state and citizens of another state. This provision was superceded by the Eleventh Amendment.

Section 2 also includes the exceptions and regulations clause. This clause has been used by congressional opponents of some of the Court's more controversial and generally liberal decisions. Although most scholars believe the clause limits the power of Congress to create broad jurisdiction for the courts it creates, others have argued that it permits Congress to strip the federal courts of jurisdiction to hear particular cases. Some opponents of the Court's decisions legalizing abortion, authorizing school busing, and upholding affirmative action have attempted to curb the power of federal courts to rule in such areas by stripping them of jurisdiction in such cases. To date, no president has ever signed such legislation.

Section 3.

Treason against the United States, shall consist only in levying War against them, or in adhering to their Enemies, giving them Aid and Comfort. No Person shall be convicted of Treason unless on the Testimony of two Witnesses to the same overt Act, or on Confession in open Court.

The Congress shall have Power to declare the Punishment of Treason, but no Attainder of Treason shall work Corruption of Blood, or Forfeiture except during the Life of the Person attainted.

Article III defines the only crime mentioned by the Constitution: treason.

ARTICLE IV

Section 1.

Full Faith and Credit shall be given in each State to the public Acts, Records, and judicial Proceedings of every other State. And the Congress may by general Laws prescribe the Manner in which such Acts, Records and Proceedings shall be proved, and the Effect thereof.

The full faith and credit clause rests on principles borrowed from international law that require one country to recognize contracts made in another country absent a compelling public policy reason to the contrary. Here, this principle, referred to in the law as comity, applied to the relationship between the states. For example, a driver's license issued in Ohio is good in Montana. The full and faith credit clause also requires a state to recognize public acts and court proceedings of another state. For the most part, interpretation of the full faith and credit clause has not been controversial.

That may well change, as advocates of same-sex marriage have suggested that such a marriage performed in one state must be recognized in another state, as is the case with heterosexual marriage. A constitutional challenge to the clause may well center on the public policy exception recognized in other areas of law.

Section 2.

The Citizens of each State shall be entitled to all Privileges and Immunities of Citizens in the several States.

A Person charged in any State with Treason, Felony, or other Crime, who shall flee from Justice, and be found in another State, shall on Demand of the executive Authority of the State from which he fled, be delivered up, to be removed to the State having Jurisdiction of the Crime.

The extradition clause requires that the governor of one state deliver a fugitive from justice to the state from which that fugitive fled. Congress passed the Fugitive Act of 1793 to give definition to this provision, but the federal government has no authority to compel state authorities to extradite a fugitive from one state to another. A state may, however, sue another state in federal court to force the return of a fugitive.

No Person held to Service or Labour in one State under the Laws thereof, escaping into another, shall, in Consequence of any Law or Regulation therein, be discharged from such Service or Labour, but shall be delivered up on Claim of the Party to whom such Service or Labour may be due.

The fugitive slave clause, which required any state, including those outside the slave-holding states of the South, to return escaped slaves to their owners, was repealed in 1865 by the Thirteenth Amendment. Prior to 1865, Congress passed laws in 1793 and 1850 to enforce the clause, leaving states without power to make concurrent laws on the subject, ensuring that the southern states would always have the Constitution on their side to protect slavery.

Section 3.

New States may be admitted by the Congress into this Union; but no new State shall be formed or erected within the Jurisdiction of any other State; nor any State be formed by the Junction of two or more States, or Parts of States, without the Consent of the Legislatures of the States concerned as well as of the Congress.

The Congress shall have Power to dispose of and make all needful Rules and Regulations respecting the Territory or other Property belonging to the United States; and nothing in this Constitution shall be so construed as to Prejudice any Claims of the United States, or of any particular State.

Section 4.

The United States shall guarantee to every State in this Union a Republican Form of Government, and shall protect each of them against Invasion; and on Application of the Legislature, or of the Executive (when the Legislature cannot be convened) against domestic Violence.

ARTICLE V

The Congress, whenever two thirds of both Houses shall deem it necessary, shall propose Amendments to this Constitution, or, on the Application of the Legislatures of two thirds of the several States, shall call a Convention for proposing Amendments, which, in either Case, shall be valid to all Intents and Purposes, as Part of this Constitution, when ratified by the Legislatures of three fourths of the several States, or by Conventions in three fourths thereof, as the one or the other Mode of Ratification may be proposed by the Congress; Provided that no Amendment which may be made prior to the Year One thousand eight hundred and eight shall in any Manner affect the first and fourth Clauses in the Ninth Section of the first Article; and that no State, without its Consent, shall be deprived of its equal Suffrage in the Senate.

Changes to the Articles of Confederation had required the unanimous approval of the states. But, Article V of the U.S. Constitution offers multiple options—none of which require unanimity—for constitutional change. Article V was quite crucial to the ratification of the Constitution. Federalists who supported the Constitution wanted to ensure that any additions or modifications to the nation's charter would require the approval of more than a simple majority of citizens. This is why any amendment coming out of Congress requires two-thirds of the House and Senate for approval. The same is true for the rule requiring three-fourths of the states to ratify an amendment (either through conventions or state legislative action). Anti-Federalists who either opposed the Constitution or had reservations about key sections of it were soothed by the prospect of an amending process that did not require the unanimous approval of the states.

Only twenty-seven amendments since 1789 have been added to the Constitution, the first fifteen of which were added by 1870. Since 1933, when the nation repealed Prohibition by passing the Twenty-First Amendment, the Constitution has been amended only six

times. In the modern constitutional era, efforts to amend the Constitution generally have centered on unhappiness with Supreme Court decisions (on school prayer, flag burning, school busing, abortion rights) or state court rulings with national implications (such as same-sex marriage) rather than any structural defect in the original Constitution (unlike woman suffrage or presidential succession) or a seismic political event (the Civil War). To date, none of these efforts have been successful.

ARTICLE VI

All Debts contracted and Engagements entered into, before the Adoption of this Constitution, shall be as valid against the United States under this Constitution, as under the Confederation.

This Constitution, and the Laws of the United States which shall be made in Pursuance thereof; and all Treaties made, or which shall be made, under the Authority of the United States, shall be the supreme Law of the Land; and the Judges in every State shall be bound thereby, any Thing in the Constitution or Laws of any State to the Contrary notwithstanding.

The Senators and Representatives before mentioned, and the Members of the several State Legislatures, and all executive and judicial Officers, both of the United States and of the several States, shall be bound by Oath or Affirmation, to support this Constitution; but no religious Test shall ever be required as a Qualification to any Office or public Trust under the United States.

Article VI made the national government responsible for all debts incurred by the Revolutionary War. This ensured that manufacturing and banking interests would be repaid for the losses they sustained during the conflict. But the most important provisions of Article VI by far are contained in its second and third clauses.

Clause 2 took another major step forward for national power and away from the confederate approach to government structure of the Articles of Confederation. By making "this Constitution" and all laws made under its authority the "supreme Law of the Land," Article VI created what constitutional scholars call the supremacy clause. The Supreme Court has invoked the supremacy clause on several occasions to rebut challenges mounted

by states to its decisions or acts of Congress. Among the more notable decisions by the Supreme Court that have cited the supremacy clause to mandate compliance with a previous ruling is *Cooper* v. *Aaron* (1958). In *Cooper*, the Court cited the supremacy clause in rejecting the argument of Governor Orval Faubus of Arkansas claiming that local schools were not obligated to follow the *Brown* v. *Board of Education* (1954) ruling. The Court said that *Brown* was the law of the land and, as such, all school boards were required to comply with its requirement to desegregate their schools.

Although most Americans rightly point to the First Amendment as the baseline for the guarantee for religious freedom, clause 3 of Article VI contains an important contribution to this principle—the ban on religious tests or qualifications to hold public office. Holders of public office, no matter how great or small, were required to affirm their allegiance to the Constitution and the laws of the United States, but they could not be required to profess a belief in God or meet any other religious qualification. Numerous states nonetheless ignored this requirement until 1961, when the Supreme Court ruled in *Torcaso* v. *Watkins* that states could not administer religious oaths to holders of public office.

ARTICLE VII

The Ratification of the Conventions of nine States, shall be sufficient for the Establishment of this Constitution between the States so ratifying the Same.

Done in Convention by the Unanimous Consent of the States present the Seventeenth Day of September in the Year of our Lord one thousand seven hundred and Eighty seven and of the Independence of the United States of America the Twelfth. IN WITNESS whereof We have hereunto subscribed our Names,

G. WASHINGTON,
Presid't. and deputy from Virginia

Attest
WILLIAM JACKSON,
Secretary

DELAWARE
George Read
Gunning Bedford, Jr.
John Dickinson
Richard Basset
Jacob Broom

MASSACHUSETTS
BAY
Nathaniel Gorham
Rufus King

CONNECTICUT
William Samuel
 Johnson
Roger Sherman

NEW YORK
Alexander Hamilton

NEW JERSEY
William Livingston
David Brearley
William Paterson
Jonathan Dayton

PENNSYLVANIA
Benjamin Franklin
Thomas Mifflin
Robert Morris
George Clymer
Thomas FitzSimons
Jared Ingersoll
James Wilson
Gouverneur Morris

NEW HAMPSHIRE
John Langdon
Nicholas Gilman

MARYLAND
James McHenry
Daniel of St. Thomas
 Jenifer
Daniel Carroll

VIRGINIA
John Blair
James Madison, Jr.

NORTH CAROLINA
William Blount
Richard Dobbs
 Spaight
Hugh Williamson

SOUTH CAROLINA
John Rutledge
Charles Cotesworth
 Pinckney
Charles Pinckney
Pierce Butler

GEORGIA
William Few
Abraham Baldwin

Articles in addition to, and amendment of the Constitution of the United States of America, proposed by Congress and ratified by the Legislatures of the several states, pursuant to the Fifth Article of the original Constitution.

(The first ten amendments were passed by Congress on September 25, 1789, and were ratified on December 15, 1791.)

AMENDMENT I

Congress shall make no law respecting an establishment of religion, or prohibiting the free exercise thereof; or abridging the freedom of speech, or of the press; or the right of the people peaceably to assemble, and to petition the Government for a redress of grievances.

For many Americans, the First Amendment represents the core of what the Bill of Rights stands for: limits on government power to limit or compel religious beliefs, the right to hold political opinions and express them, protection for a free press, the right to assemble peaceably, and the right to petition, through protest or the ballot, the government for a redress of political grievances. But it is also important to remember that the First Amendment, like most of the Bill of Rights, did not apply to state governments until the Supreme Court began to apply their substantive guarantees through the Fourteenth Amendment, a process that did not begin until 1925 in *Gitlow* v. *New York*.

Until then, state and local governments often failed to honor the rights and liberties that Congress, and by extension the national government, was expressly forbidden by the Constitution from withholding. For example, southern states, prior to the Civil War, outlawed pro-abolition literature; numerous states continued to collect taxes on behalf of state-sponsored churches and religious education; newspapers often were forbidden from publishing exposes on industry or political leaders because such speech was considered seditious and thus subject to prior restraint; and public protests on behalf of unpopular causes were often banned by state breach of peace laws.

The Supreme Court has recognized other important rights implied by the enumerated guarantees of the First Amendment. These include the right to association, even when such association might come in the form of clubs or organizations that discriminate on the basis of race, sex, or religion, and the right to personal privacy, which the Supreme Court held in *Griswold* v. *Connecticut* (1965) was based in part on the right of married couples to make decisions about contraception, a decision protected by one's personal religious and political beliefs.

AMENDMENT II

A well regulated Militia, being necessary to the security of a free State, the right of the people to keep and bear Arms, shall not be infringed.

Few issues in American politics generate as much emotional heat as the extent to which Americans have a right to keep and bear arms. Supporters of broad gun ownership rights, such as the National Rifle Association, argue that the Second Amendment protects an almost absolute individual right to own just about any small arm that can be manufactured, whether for reasons of

sport or self-defense. Proponents of gun control, such as the Brady Campaign to Prevent Gun Violence, argue that the amendment creates no such individual right, but refers instead to the Framers' belief—now outdated—that citizen militias had the right to form to protect themselves against other states and, if need be, the national government. Under this view, Congress and the states are free to regulate gun ownership and use as they see fit, provided that the national and state governments are within their constitutional orbit of power to do so.

The Supreme Court has not offered much help on the meaning of the Second Amendment. It has handed down only one case truly relying on the amendment, *U.S.* v. *Miller* (1939). There, a unanimous Court upheld a federal law requiring the registration of sawed-off shotguns purchased for personal use. While the Court rejected the position that the Second Amendment established an individual right to keep and bear arms, it did not close the door on individual gun ownership. This remains the constitutional baseline from which legislative battles over gun control legislation continue to be fought.

AMENDMENT III

No Soldier shall, in time of peace be quartered in any house, without the consent of the Owner, nor in time of war, but in a manner to be prescribed by law.

Among the complaints directed at King George III in the Declaration of Independence was the colonial-era practice of quartering large numbers of troops in private homes. The practice of quartering soldiers, along with the forced maintenance of British standing armies in times of peace without the consent of the colonial legislatures, formed a major component of the political grievances directed at the British crown. The Third Amendment was intended to protect individuals and their property from the abuse common to the practice of quartering soldiers.

AMENDMENT IV

The right of the people to be secure in their persons, houses, papers, and effects, against unreasonable searches and seizures, shall not be violated, and no warrants shall issue, but upon probable cause, supported by Oath or affirmation, and particularly describing the place to be searched, and the persons or things to be seized.

Although the Fourth Amendment is often discussed in tandem with the Fifth, Sixth, and Eighth Amendments—the other major provisions of the Bill of Rights outlining the criminal due process guarantees of citizens—it shares a similar undercurrent that motivated the adoption of the Third Amendment: to eliminate the practice of British officers from using the general writ of

assistance to enter private homes, conduct searches, and seize personal property. British officers had not been required to offer a specific reason for a search or justify the taking of particular items. In most cases, the writ of assistance was used to confiscate items considered to have violated the strict British customs laws of the colonial era.

The twin pillars of the Fourth Amendment, the probable cause and warrant requirements, are a direct reflection of the disdain the Framers had for the Revolutionary-era practices of the British. But, like the First Amendment, the guarantees of the Fourth Amendment did not apply to state and local law enforcement practices until well after the ratification of the Fourteenth Amendment. Until *Wolf* v. *Colorado* (1949), when the Court ruled that the Fourteenth Amendment made the Fourth Amendment binding on the states, evidence seized in violation of the probable cause or warrant requirements could be used against a criminal suspect. The Court's best-known decision on the Fourth Amendment, *Mapp* v. *Ohio* (1961), which established the exclusionary rule, also marked the high-water point in the rights afforded to criminal suspects challenging an unlawful search. Since the late 1970s, the Court has steadily added exceptions to the Fourth Amendment to permit law enforcement officers to engage in warrantless searches and seizures, provided that such practices meet a threshold of reasonableness in the context of the circumstances under which they are undertaken.

AMENDMENT V

No person shall be held to answer for a capital, or otherwise infamous crime, unless on a presentment or indictment of a Grand Jury, except in cases arising in the land or naval forces, or in the Militia, when in actual service in time of War or public danger; nor shall any person be subject for the same offence to be twice put in jeopardy of life or limb; nor shall be compelled in any criminal case to be a witness against himself, nor be deprived of life, liberty, or property, without due process of law; nor shall private property be taken for public use, without just compensation.

The Fifth Amendment, along with the Sixth Amendment, is the legacy of the ruthless and secretive tactics that figured prominently in the colonial-era system of British justice. By requiring that no person could be held for a "capital, or otherwise infamous" crime except upon indictment by a grand jury, the Fifth Amendment took an important step toward making the criminal indictment process a public function. Along with the public trial and trial by jury guarantees of the Sixth Amendment, the grand jury provision of the Fifth Amendment established that the government would have to make its case against the accused in public. Also, by guaranteeing that no person could be compelled to testify against himself or herself in a criminal proceeding, the Fifth Amendment highlighted the adversarial nature of the American criminal justice system, a feature that is distinct from its British counterpart. "Pleading the Fifth" is permissible in any criminal, civil, administrative, judicial, or investigatory context. *Miranda* v. *Arizona* (1966), one of the most famous rulings of the Supreme Court, established a right to silence that combined the ban against self-incrimination of the Fifth Amendment with the Sixth Amendment's guarantee of the assistance of counsel. The right to silence, unlike the ban against self-incrimination, extends to any aspect of an interrogation.

The Fifth Amendment also forbids double jeopardy, which prohibits the prosecution of a crime against the same person in the same jurisdiction twice, and prevents the government from taking life, liberty, or property without due process of law. This phrase was reproduced in the Fourteenth Amendment, placing an identical set of constraints on the states. The Court has applied all the guarantees of the Fifth Amendment, with the exception of the grand jury provision, to the states through the due process clause of the Fourteenth Amendment. Some constitutional scholars also consider the due process clause of the Fifth Amendment to embrace an equal protection provision when applied to federal cases.

The final provision of the Fifth Amendment prohibits the government from taking private property for public use without just compensation. Litigation on the takings clause, as some scholars refer to this provision, has generally centered on two major questions. The first is what constitutes a taking, either by the government's decision to seize private property or by regulating it to the point where its value is greatly diminished. The second question centers on what the appropriate level of compensation is for owners who have successfully established a taking.

The Supreme Court has taken an expansive definition of what it means to "take" private land for "public use." In *Kelo* v. *New London* (2004), the Court ruled that government could take private property and then sell it to private developers so long as that property was slated for economic development that would benefit the surrounding community. This marked the first time the Court had authorized a taking for something other than public use by governmental authorities.

AMENDMENT VI

In all criminal prosecutions, the accused shall enjoy the right to a speedy and public trial, by an impartial jury of the State and district wherein the crime shall have been committed, which district shall have been previously ascertained by law, and to be informed of the nature and cause of the accusation; to be confronted with the witnesses against him; to have compulsory process for obtaining witnesses in his favor, and to have the assistance of counsel for his defence.

The centerpiece of the constitutional guarantees afforded to individuals facing criminal prosecution, the Sixth Amendment sets out eight specific rights, more than any other provision of the Bill of Rights. As with the Fifth Amendment, the core features of the Sixth Amendment build upon the unfortunate legacy of the repressive practices of colonial-era Britain. The very first provision of the Sixth Amendment mandates that individuals subject to criminal prosecution receive "a speedy and public trial"; it then requires that all such trials take place in public, with the defendant informed of the cause and nature of the accusation against him or her. The common theme underlying these sections of the Sixth Amendment, as well as those requiring witnesses for the prosecution to testify in public, allowing the defendant to produce witnesses on his or her own behalf, and securing the assistance of counsel, is that any citizen threatened with the deprivation of liberty is entitled to have the case made against him or her in public. The Fifth Amendment also required the government to produce evidence that did not rely on confessions and self-incrimination. And, it required that any such evidence must be acquired lawfully and with the knowledge of a public magistrate. The Sixth Amendment establishes, in principle, the American criminal justice system as one that is open and public.

Since the vast majority of criminal prosecutions in the United States are undertaken by state and local authorities, the parchment promises of the Sixth Amendment did not extend to most Americans until the Supreme Court began incorporating the guarantees of the Bill of Rights to the states through the Fourteenth Amendment. Perhaps the best-known case involving the Sixth Amendment is *Gideon* v. *Wainwright* (1963), which held that all persons accused of a serious crime are entitled to an attorney, even if they cannot afford one, a rule that was soon extended to cover misdemeanors as well. Three years later, the Supreme Court fused the right to counsel rule established in *Gideon* with the Fifth Amendment ban against self-incrimination to create the principles animating *Miranda* v. *Arizona*. For a long time, the Court had never interpreted the Fifth and Sixth Amendments to mean that individuals had rights to criminal due process guarantees if they did not know about them or could not afford them. Decisions such as *Gideon* and *Miranda* offered a clear departure from this position.

The speedy and public trial clauses only require that criminal trials take place in public within a reasonable amount of time after the period of indictment, and that juries in such cases are unbiased. Americans also often cite the Sixth Amendment as entitling them to a trial by a "jury of one's peers." This is true to the extent individuals are entitled to a trial in the jurisdiction where the crime is alleged to have been committed. It does not mean, however, that they are entitled to a trial by persons of a similar age or background, for example.

AMENDMENT VII

In Suits at common law, where the value in controversy shall exceed twenty dollars, the right of trial by jury shall be preserved, and no fact tried by a jury, shall be otherwise re-examined in any Court of the United States, than according to the rules of the common law.

One feature of the British courts that the Framers sought to preserve in the American civil law system was the distinction between courts of common law and courts of equity. Common law courts heard cases involving strict legal rules, while equity courts based their decisions on principles of fairness and totality of circumstances. Common law courts featured juries that were authorized to return verdicts entitling plaintiffs to financial compensation for losses incurred, whereas equity courts relied upon judges to make determinations about appropriate relief for successful parties. Relief in equity courts did not consist of monetary awards, but injunctions, cease-and-desist orders, and so on. The Seventh Amendment carried over this British feature into the Constitution.

In 1938, Congress amended the Federal Rules of Civil Procedure to combine the function of civil common law and equity courts. In cases involving both legal and equitable claims, a federal judge must first decide the issue of law before moving to the equitable relief, or remedy, component of the trial. Judges are permitted to instruct juries on matters of law and fact, and may emphasize certain facts or legal issues to the jury in their instructions to the jury. But, the jury alone decides guilt or innocence. In some extraordinary cases, a judge may overturn the verdict of a jury. This happens only when a judge believes the jury has disregarded completely the facts and evidence before it in reaching a verdict.

Congress has also changed the $20 threshold for the right to a trial by jury. The amount is now $75,000. Finally, the Seventh Amendment has never been incorporated to the states through the Fourteenth Amendment.

AMENDMENT VIII

Excessive bail shall not be required, nor excessive fines imposed, nor cruel and unusual punishments inflicted.

For an amendment of so few words, the Eighth Amendment has generated an enormous volume of commentary and litigation since its ratification. This should not be surprising, as the three major provisions of the amendment deal with some of the most sensitive and emotionally charged issues involving the rights of criminal defendants.

The origin of the excessive bail clause stems from the reforms to the British system instituted by the 1689 English Bill of Rights. Having had limited success in preventing law enforcement officials from detaining suspects by imposing outrageous bail requirements, Britain amended previous laws to say that "excessive bail ought not to be required." Much like the British model, the Eighth Amendment does not state what an "excessive bail" is or the particular criminal offense that warrants a high bail amount. The Supreme Court has offered two fundamental rules on the excessive bail clause. First, a judge has the discretion to decide if a criminal offense is sufficiently serious to justify high bail. Second, a judge has the power, under *U.S.* v. *Salerno* (1987), to deny a criminal defendant bail as a "preventative measure." In both such cases, a judge's action must be considered proportionate to the nature of the criminal offense for which an individual stands accused.

Like the excessive bail clause, the excessive fines clause is rooted in the English Bill of Rights. The clause applies only to criminal proceedings, not civil litigation. For example, a tobacco company cannot appeal what it believes is an excessive jury award under this clause. An indigent criminal defendant, however, can challenge a fine levied in connection with a criminal conviction.

The most controversial section of the Eighth Amendment is the clause forbidding cruel and unusual punishments. The absence of such a guarantee from the Constitution was a major impetus for the adoption of the Bill of Rights. While most historians agree that the Framers wanted to prohibit barbaric forms of punishment, including torture, as well as arbitrary and disproportionate penalties, there is little consensus on what specific punishments met this definition. By the late 1800s, the Supreme Court had ruled that such punishments as public burning, disembowelment, and drawing and quartering crossed the Eighth Amendment barrier. In *Weems* v. *U.S.* (1910), the Court went the additional of step of concluding that any punishment considered "excessive" would violate the cruel and unusual punishment clause. And, in *Solem* v. *Helm* (1983), the Court developed a "proportionality" standard that required punishments, even simple incarceration, to bear a rational relationship to the offense.

The Court has never ruled, however, that the death penalty per se violates the Eighth Amendment. It has developed certain rules and exceptions governing the application of the death penalty, such as requiring a criminal defendant actually to have killed, or attempted to have killed, a victim. It has also ruled that the mentally retarded, as a class, are exempt from the death penalty. But it has also issued highly controversial decisions concluding, for example, that neither racial disparities in the application of capital punishment nor juvenile status at the time the offense was committed violate the Eighth Amendment. Except for a four-year ban on the practice between 1972 and 1976, the death penalty has always been an available punishment in the American criminal justice system.

AMENDMENT IX

The enumeration in the Constitution, of certain rights, shall not be construed to deny or disparage others retained by the people.

A major point of contention between the Federalists and Anti-Federalists was the need for a bill of rights. In *Federalist No. 84,* Alexander Hamilton argued that a bill of rights was unnecessary, as there was no need to place limits on the power of government to do things that it was not authorized by the Constitution to do. Hamilton also argued that it would be impossible to list all the rights "retained by the people." Protecting some rights but not others would suggest that Americans had surrendered certain rights to their government when, in Hamilton's view, the Constitution did nothing of the sort.

Given his well-deserved reputation for unbridled national power, Hamilton's views have often been dismissed as a cynical ploy to sidestep any meaningful discussion of the Bill of Rights and speed along the ratification process. But, James Madison, along with Thomas Jefferson, held a much deeper belief in the need for a bill of rights. Madison also believed that the enumeration of certain rights and liberties in the Constitution should not be understood to deny others that exist as a condition of citizenship in a free society. Madison, the primary author of the Bill of Rights, included the Ninth Amendment to underscore this belief.

The Supreme Court has never offered a clear and definitive interpretation of the Ninth Amendment, primarily because it has been wary of giving such general language any substantive definition. The amendment has been cited in such decisions as *Griswold* v. *Connecticut* (1965) and *Richmond Newspapers* v. *Virginia* (1980) along with other constitutional amendments to bolster the case on behalf of an asserted constitutional right. The difficulty in constructing a specific meaning for the Ninth Amendment can be illustrated by the fact that both supporters and opponents of legal abortion have cited it to defend the feasibility of their respective positions.

AMENDMENT X

The powers not delegated to the United States by the Constitution, nor prohibited by it to the States, are reserved to the States respectively, or to the people.

The Tenth Amendment generated little controversy during the ratification process over the Bill of Rights. As the Supreme Court later ruled in *U.S.* v. *Darby Lumber Co.* (1941), the Tenth Amendment states a truism about the relationship between the boundaries of national and state power—that the states retain those powers not specifically set out in the Constitution as belonging to the national government. There is little in the history in the debate over the Tenth Amendment to suggest that its language is anything other than declaratory. Indeed, the refusal of the 1st Congress to insert the word "expressly" before "delegated" strongly suggests that James Madison, who offered the most thorough explanation of the amendment during the floor debates, intended to leave room for this relationship to evolve as future events made necessary.

The earliest political and constitutional developments involving the Tenth Amendment tilted the balance of power firmly in favor of national power. Alexander Hamilton's vision for a national bank to consolidate the nation's currency and trading position was realized in *McCullough* v. *Maryland* (1819), in which the Court held that Article I granted Congress broad power to make all laws "necessary and proper" to the exercise of its legislative power. By no means, however, did *McCullough* settle the argument over the power reserved to the states. Led by Chief Justice Roger B. Taney, the Court handed down several decisions in the three decades leading up to the Civil War that offered substantial protection to the southern states on the matters closest to their hearts: slavery and economic sovereignty. From the period after the Civil War until the New Deal, the Court continued to shield states from congressional legislation designed to regulate the economy and promote social and political reform. After the constitutional revolution of 1937, when the Court threw its support behind the New Deal, Congress received a blank constitutional check to engage in the regulatory action that featured an unprecedented level of federal intervention in economic and social matters once the purview of the states, one that would last almost sixty years.

Beginning in *New York* v. *U.S.* (1992), however, the Court, in striking down a key provision of a federal environmental law, began to revisit the New Deal assumptions that underlay its modern interpretation of the Tenth Amendment. A few years later, in *U.S.* v. *Lopez* (1995), it invalidated a federal gun control law on the ground that Congress lacked authority under the commerce clause to regulate gun possession. And, in *U.S.* v. *Printz* (1997), the Tenth Amendment explicitly was cited to strike down an important section of the Brady Bill, a congressional law that required states to conduct background checks on prospective gun buyers. Although the Court has not returned to the dual federalism posture on the Tenth Amendment that it built from the years between the Taney Court and the triumph of the New

Deal, these decisions make clear that the constitutional status of the states as actors in the federal system has been dramatically strengthened.

AMENDMENT XI
(Ratified on February 7, 1795)

The Judicial power of the United States shall not be construed to extend to any suit in law or equity, commenced or prosecuted against one of the United States by Citizens of another State, or by Citizens or Subjects of any Foreign State.

The Eleventh Amendment was prompted by one of the earliest notable decisions of the Supreme Court, *Chisolm* v. *Georgia* (1793). In *Chisolm*, the Court held that Article III and the enforcement provision of the Judiciary Act of 1789 permitted a citizen of one state to bring suit against another state in federal court. Almost immediately after *Chisolm*, the Eleventh Amendment was introduced and promptly ratified, as the states saw this decision as a threat to their sovereignty under the new Constitution. The amendment was passed in less than a year, which, by the standards of the era, was remarkably fast.

The Eleventh Amendment nullified the result in *Chisolm* but did not completely bar a citizen from bringing suit against a state in federal court. Citizens may bring lawsuits against state officials in federal court if they can satisfy the requirement that their rights under federal constitutional or statutory law have been violated. The Eleventh Amendment has not been extensively litigated in modern times, but the extent to which states are immune under federal law from citizen lawsuits has reemerged as an important constitutional question in recent years. For example, the Court has said in several cases that the doctrine of sovereign immunity prevents citizens from suing state agencies under the Americans with Disabilities Act of 1990. But, as recently as 2003, the Court, in *Nevada* v. *Hibbs*, ruled that the Family and Medical Leave Act of 1993 did not immunize state government agencies against lawsuits brought by former state employees. States are also free to waive their immunity and consent to a lawsuit.

AMENDMENT XII
(Ratified on June 15, 1804)

The Electors shall meet in their respective states, and vote by ballot for President and Vice-President, one of whom, at least, shall not be an inhabitant of the same state with themselves; they shall name in their ballots the person voted for as President, and in distinct ballots the person voted for as Vice-President, and they shall make distinct lists of all persons voted for as President, and of all persons voted for as Vice-President, and of the number of votes for each, which lists they shall sign and certify, and transmit sealed to the seat of the government of the United States, directed to the President of the Senate;—The President of the Senate shall, in the presence of the Senate and House of Representatives, open all the certificates and the votes shall then be counted;—The person having the greatest number of votes for President, shall be the President, if such number be a majority of the whole number of Electors appointed; and if no person have such majority; then from the persons having the highest numbers not exceeding three on the list of those voted for as President, the House of Representatives shall choose immediately, by ballot, the President. But in choosing the President, the votes shall be taken by states, the representation from each state having one vote; a quorum for this purpose shall consist of a member or members from two-thirds of the states, and a majority of all the states shall be necessary to a choice. And if the House of Representatives shall not choose a President whenever the right of choice shall devolve upon them, before the fourth day of March next following, then the Vice-President shall act as President, as in the case of the death or other constitutional disability of the President.—The person having the greatest number of votes as Vice-President, shall be the Vice-President, if such number be a majority of the whole number of Electors appointed, and if no person have a majority, then from the two highest numbers on the list, the Senate shall choose the Vice-President; a quorum for the purpose shall consist of two-thirds of the whole number of Senators, and a majority of the whole number shall be necessary to a choice. But no person constitutionally ineligible to the office of President shall be eligible to that of Vice-President of the United States.

The Twelfth Amendment was added to the Constitution after the 1800 presidential election was thrown into the House of Representatives. Thomas Jefferson and Aaron Burr, running on the Democratic-Republican Party ticket, each received seventy-three electoral votes for president, even though everyone knew that Jefferson was the presidential candidate and Burr the vice presidential candidate. This was possible because Article II, section 1, did not require electors to vote for president and vice president separately. The Twelfth Amendment remedied this deficiency by requiring electors to cast their votes for president and vice president separately.

Whether it intended to or not, the Twelfth Amendment took a major step toward institutionalizing the party system in the United States. The 1796 election yielded a president and vice president from different parties, a clear indication that partisan differences were emerging in a distinct form. The 1800 election simply highlighted the problem further. By requiring electors to make their presidential and vice presidential choices separately, the Twelfth Amendment conceded that a party system in American politics had indeed evolved, an inevitable but nonetheless disappointing development to the architects of the original constitutional vision.

AMENDMENT XIII
(Ratified on December 6, 1865)

Section 1.

Neither slavery nor involuntary servitude, except as a punishment for crime whereof the party shall have been duly convicted, shall exist within the United States, or any place subject to their jurisdiction.

Section 2.

Congress shall have power to enforce this article by appropriate legislation.

The Thirteenth, Fourteenth, and Fifteenth Amendments are known collectively as the Civil War Amendments.

In anticipation of a Union victory, the Thirteenth Amendment was passed by Congress and sent to the states for ratification before the end of the Civil War. The amendment not only formally abolished slavery and involuntary servitude; it also served as the constitutional foundation for the nation's first major civil rights legislation, the Civil Rights Act of 1866. This law extended numerous rights to African Americans previously held in servitude as well as those having "free" status during the Civil War, including the right to purchase, rent, and sell personal property, to bring suit in federal court, to enter into contracts, and to receive the full and equal benefit of all laws "enjoyed by white citizens." The Thirteenth Amendment overturned the pre–Civil War decision of the Supreme Court, *Dred Scott* v. *Sandford* (1857), which held that slaves were not people entitled to constitutional rights, but property subject to the civil law binding them to their masters.

In modern times, the Court has ruled that the Thirteenth Amendment prohibits any action that recognizes a "badge" or "condition" of slavery, such as housing discrimination and certain forms of employment discrimination. The Department of Justice also has used the Thirteenth Amendment to file lawsuits against manufacturing sweatshops and other criminal enterprises in which persons are forced to work without compensation.

AMENDMENT XIV
(Ratified on July 9, 1868)

Section 1.

All persons born or naturalized in the United States, and subject to the jurisdiction thereof, are citizens of the United States and of the State wherein they reside. No State shall make or enforce any law which shall abridge the privileges or immunities of citizens of the United States; nor shall any State deprive any person of life, liberty, or property, without due process of law; nor deny to any person within its jurisdiction the equal protection of the laws.

Many constitutional scholars believe the Fourteenth Amendment is the most important addition to the Constitution since the Bill of Rights was ratified in 1791. In addition to serving as a cornerstone of Reconstruction policy, section 1 eliminated the distinction between the rights and liberties of Americans as citizens of their respective states and those to which they were entitled under the Bill of Rights as citizens of the United States. The Republican leadership that drafted and steered the Fourteenth Amendment to passage left no doubt that the three major provisions of section 1, which placed express limits on state power to abridge rights and liberties protected as a condition of national citizenship, were intended to make the Bill of Rights binding upon the states, thus overruling *Barron* v. *Baltimore* (1833). Although the Supreme Court has never endorsed this view, the selective incorporation of the Bill of Rights to the states during the twentieth century through the Fourteenth Amendment ultimately made the Reconstruction-era vision of the Republicans a reality. The former Confederate states were required to ratify the Fourteenth Amendment to qualify for readmission into the Union.

Section 2.

Representatives shall be apportioned among the several States according to their respective numbers, counting the whole number of persons in each State, excluding Indians not taxed. But when the right to vote at any election for the choice of electors for President and Vice President of the United States, Representatives in Congress, the Executive and Judicial officers of a State, or the members of the Legislature thereof, is denied to any of the male inhabitants of such State, being twenty-one years of age, and citizens of the United States, or in any way abridged, except for participation in rebellion, or other crime, the basis of representation therein shall be reduced in the proportion which the number of such male citizens shall bear to the whole number of male citizens twenty-one years of age in such State.

Section 2 established two major changes to the Constitution. First, by stating that representatives from each state would be apportioned based on the number of "whole" persons in each state, section 2 modified the Three-Fifths Compromise of Article 1, section 2, clause 3, of the original Constitution. Note, however, that section 2 still called for the exclusion of Indians "not taxed" from the apportionment criteria. Second, section 2, for the first time anywhere in the Constitution, mentions that only "male" inhabitants of the states age twenty-one or older would be counted toward representation in the House of Representatives and eligible to vote.

The Military Reconstruction Act of 1867 had strengthened Republican power in the southern states by stripping former Confederates of the right to vote, a law that, in conjunction with the gradual addition of blacks to the voting rolls, made enactment of the Fourteenth Amendment possible. Section 2 temporarily solidified the Republican presence in the South by eliminating from apportionment counts any person that participated in the rebellion against the Union.

Section 3.

No person shall be a Senator or Representative in Congress, or elector of President and Vice President, or hold any office, civil or military, under the United States, or under any State, who, having previously taken an oath, as a member of Congress, or as an officer of the United States, or as a member of any State legislature, or as an executive or judicial officer of any State, to support the Constitution of the United States, shall have engaged in insurrection or rebellion against the same, or given aid or comfort to the enemies thereof. But Congress may by a vote of two-thirds of each House, remove such disability.

Section 3 also reflected the power of the Reconstruction-era Republicans over the South. By eliminating the eligibility of former Confederates for public office or to serve as an elector for president or vice president, the Republicans strengthened their presence in Congress and throughout national politics. This measure also allowed African Americans to run for and hold office in the South, which they were doing by 1870, the same year the Fifteenth Amendment was ratified.

In December 1868, five months after the ratification of the Fourteenth Amendment, President Andrew Johnson declared universal amnesty for all former Confederates. This measure had the effect of returning white politicians and by extension the Democratic Party to power in the South. Republican concern over this development was a major force behind the adoption of the Fifteenth Amendment, which was viewed as an instrument to protect Republican political power by securing black enfranchisement. However, Republican president Ulysses S. Grant, who defeated Johnson in 1868, pardoned all but a few hundred remaining Confederate sympathizers by signing the Amnesty Act of 1872. Decisions such as these began the gradual undoing of Republican commitment to black civil rights in the South.

Section 4.

The validity of the public debt of the United States, authorized by law, including debts incurred for payment of pensions and bounties for services in suppressing insurrection or rebellion, shall not be questioned. But neither the United States nor any State shall assume or pay any debt or obligation incurred in aid of insurrection or rebellion against the United States, or any claim for the loss or emancipation of any slave, but all such debts, obligations and claims shall be held illegal and void.

Section 4 repudiated the South's desire to have Congress forgive the Confederacy's war debts. It also rejected any claim that former slaveholders had to be compensated for the loss of their slaves.

Section 5.

The Congress shall have power to enforce, by appropriate legislation, the provisions of this article.

By giving Congress the power to enforce the provisions of the Fourteenth Amendment, section 5 reiterated the post–Civil War emphasis on national citizenship and the limit on state power to deny individuals their constitutional rights. Section 5 also extended congressional law-making power beyond those areas outlined in Article I. But, the Court has taken a mixed view of the scope of congressional power to enforce the Fourteenth Amendment. In *Katzenbach* v. *Morgan* (1966), for example, the Supreme Court offered a broad ruling on the section 5 power of Congress. It held that Congress could enact laws establishing rights beyond what the Court said the Constitution required, as long as such laws were designed to establish a remedial constitutional right or protect citizens from a potential constitutional violation. In other cases, such as *City of Boerne* v. *Flores* (1997) and *U.S.* v. *Morrison* (2000), the Court ruled that Congress may not intrude upon the authority of the judicial branch to define the meaning of the Constitution or intrude on the power of the states to make laws within their own domain.

AMENDMENT XV
(Ratified on February 3, 1870)

Section 1.

The right of citizens of the United States to vote shall not be denied or abridged by the United States or by any State on account of race, color, or previous condition of servitude.

Section 2.

The Congress shall have power to enforce this article by appropriate legislation.

The Fifteenth Amendment was the most controversial of the Civil War Amendments, both for what it did and did not do. Although the adoption of the Thirteenth and Fourteenth Amendments made clear that blacks could not be returned to their pre–Civil War slavery, enthusiasm for a constitutional right of black suffrage, even among the northern states, was another matter. On the one hand, the extension of voting rights to blacks was the most dramatic outcome of the Civil War. The former Confederate states had to ratify the Fifteenth Amendment as a condition for readmission into the Union. On the other hand, the rejection of proposed language forbidding discrimination on the basis of property ownership, education, or religious belief gave states the power to regulate the vote as they wished. And, with the collapse of Reconstruction after the 1876 election, southern states implemented laws created by this opening with full force, successfully crippling black voter registration for generations to come in the region where most African Americans lived. Full enfranchisement for African Americans would not arrive until the passage of the Voting Rights Act of 1965, almost one hundred years after the ratification of the Fifteenth Amendment.

The Fifteenth Amendment also divided woman's rights organizations that had campaigned on behalf of abolition and black enfranchisement. Feminists such as Elizabeth Cady Stanton and Susan B. Anthony were furious over the exclusion of women from the Fifteenth Amendment and opposed its ratification, while others, such as Lucy Stone, were willing to support black voting rights at the expense of woman suffrage, leaving that battle for another day. The Supreme Court sided with those who opposed female enfranchisement, ruling in *Minor* v. *Happersett* (1875) that the Fourteenth Amendment did not recognize among the privileges and immunities of American citizenship a constitutional right to vote.

AMENDMENT XVI
(Ratified on February 3, 1913)

The Congress shall have power to lay and collect taxes on incomes, from whatever source derived, without apportionment among the several States, and without regard to any census or enumeration.

The Sixteenth Amendment was a response to the Supreme Court's sharply divided ruling in *Pollock* v. *Farmers' Loan & Trust Co.* (1895), which struck down the Income Tax Act of 1894 as unconstitutional. The Court, by a 5–4 margin, held that the law violated Article I, section 9, which prevented Congress from enacting a direct tax (on individuals) unless in proportion to the U.S. Census. In some ways, this was a curious holding, since the Court had permitted

Congress to enact a direct tax on individuals during the Civil War. Between the *Pollock* decision and the enactment of the Sixteenth Amendment, the Court approved of taxes levied on corporations, as such taxes were not really taxes but "excises" levied on "incidents of ownership."

Anti-tax groups have claimed the Sixteenth Amendment was never properly ratified and is thus unconstitutional. The federal courts have rejected that view and have sanctioned and fined individuals who have brought such frivolous challenges to court.

AMENDMENT XVII
(Ratified on April 8, 1913)

The Senate of the United States shall be composed of two Senators from each State, elected by the people thereof, for six years; and each Senator shall have one vote. The electors in each State shall have the qualifications requisite for electors of the most numerous branch of the State legislatures.

When vacancies happen in the representation of any State in the Senate, the executive authority of such State shall issue writs of election to fill such vacancies: Provided, That the legislature of any State may empower the executive thereof to make temporary appointments until the people fill the vacancies by election as the legislature may direct.

This amendment shall not be so construed as to affect the election or term of any Senator chosen before it becomes valid as part of the Constitution.

The Seventeenth Amendment repealed the language in Article I, section 3, of the original Constitution, which called for the election of U.S. senators by state legislatures. This method had its roots in the selection of delegates to the Constitutional Convention, who were chosen by the state legislatures. It was also the preferred method of the Framers, who believed that having state legislatures elect senators would strengthen the relationship between the states and the national government, and also contribute to the stability of Congress by removing popular electoral pressure from the upper chamber.

Dissatisfaction set in with this method during the period leading up to the Civil War, especially by the 1850s. Indiana, for example, deeply divided between Union supporters in the northern part of the state and Confederate sympathizers in the southern part, could not agree on the selection of senators and was without representation for two years. After the Civil War, numerous Senate elections were tainted by corruption, and many more resulted in ties that prevented seating senators in a timely fashion. In 1899, Delaware's election was so mired in controversy that it did not have representation in the Senate for four years.

The ratification of the Seventeenth Amendment was the result of almost two decades of persistent efforts at reform. By 1912, twenty-nine states had changed their election laws to require the popular election of senators. In the years before that, constitutional amendments were introduced on a regular basis calling for the popular election of senators. Although many powerful legislators entrenched in the Senate resisted such change, the tide of reform, now aided by journalists and scholars sympathetic to the cause, proved too powerful to withstand. One year after the Seventeenth Amendment was sent to the states for ratification, all members of the Senate were elected by the popular vote.

AMENDMENT XVIII
(Ratified on January 16, 1919)

Section 1.

After one year from the ratification of this article the manufacture, sale, or transportation of intoxicating liquors within, the importation thereof into, or the exportation thereof from the United States and all territory subject to the jurisdiction thereof for beverage purposes is hereby prohibited.

Section 2.

The Congress and the several States shall have concurrent power to enforce this article by appropriate legislation.

Section 3.

This article shall be inoperative unless it shall have been ratified as an amendment to the Constitution by the legislatures of the several States, as provided in the Constitution, within seven years from the date of the submission hereof to the States by the Congress.

The Eighteenth Amendment was the end result of a crusade against the consumption of alcoholic beverages than began during the early nineteenth century. A combination of Christian organizations emboldened by the second Great Awakening and women's groups, who believed alcohol contributed greatly to domestic violence and poverty, campaigned to abolish the manufacture, sale, and use of alcoholic beverages in the United States. Their campaign was moderately successful in the pre–Civil War era. By 1855, thirteen states had banned the sale of "intoxicating" beverages. By the end of the Civil War, however, ten states had repealed their prohibition laws.

Another wave of anti-alcohol campaigning soon emerged, however, as the Women's Christian Temperance Union, founded in 1874 and 250,000 strong by 1911, and the Anti-Saloon League, founded in 1913, pressed the case for Prohibition. Among the arguments offered by supporters of Prohibition were that the cereal grains used in the manufacture of beer and liquor diverted valuable resources from food supplies and that the malaise of drunkenness sapped the strength of manufacturing production at home and the conduct of America's soldiers in World War I. Underneath the formal case for Prohibition was a considerable anti-immigrant sentiment, as many Prohibitionists considered the waves of Italian, Irish, Poles, and German immigrants unduly dependent on alcohol.

In 1919, Congress passed the Eighteenth Amendment over President Woodrow Wilson's veto. That same year, Congress passed the Volstead Act, which implemented Prohibition and authorized law enforcement to target illegal shipments of alcohol into the United States (mostly from Canada, which, ironically, also mandated Prohibition in most of its provinces during this time) as well as alcoholic beverages illegally manufactured in the United States. Evidence remains inconclusive over just how successful the Eighteenth Amendment was in reducing alcohol consumption in the United States. More certain was the billion-dollar windfall that Prohibition created for organized crime, as well as small-time smugglers and bootleggers.

AMENDMENT XIX
(Ratified on August 18, 1920)

The right of citizens of the United States to vote shall not be denied or abridged by the United States or by any State on account of sex.

Congress shall have power to enforce this article by appropriate legislation.

The two major woman's rights organizations of the nineteenth century most active in the battle for female enfranchisement were the National Woman Suffrage Association (NWSA) and the American Woman Suffrage Association (AWSA). NWSA campaigned for a constitutional amendment modeled on the Fifteenth Amendment, which had secured African American voting rights, while AWSA preferred to pursue women's voting rights through state-level legislative initiatives. In 1890, the two organizations combined to form the National American Woman Suffrage Association. By 1919, the NAWSA, the newer, more radical National Woman's Party, and other activists had secured congressional passage of the Nineteenth Amendment by a broad margin. It was ratified by the states just over a year later.

The Nineteenth Amendment, however, did not free black women from the voting restrictions that southern states placed in the way of African Americans. They and other minorities were not protected from such restrictions until the passage of the Voting Rights Act of 1965.

AMENDMENT XX
(Ratified on February 6, 1933)

Section 1.

The terms of the President and Vice President shall end at noon on the 20th day of January, and the terms of Senators and Representatives at noon on the 3d day of January, of the years in which such terms would have ended if this article had not been ratified; and the terms of their successors shall then begin.

Section 2.

The Congress shall assemble at least once in every year, and such meeting shall begin at noon on the 3d day of January, unless they shall by law appoint a different day.

Section 3.

If, at the time fixed for the beginning of the term of the President, the President elect shall have died, the Vice President elect shall become President. If a President shall not have been chosen before the time fixed for the beginning of his term, or if the President elect shall have failed to qualify, then the Vice President elect shall act as President until a President shall have qualified; and the Congress may by law provide for the case wherein neither a President elect nor a Vice President elect shall have qualified, declaring who shall then act as President, or the manner in which one who is to act shall be selected, and such person shall act accordingly until a President or Vice President shall have qualified.

Section 4.

The Congress may by law provide for the case of the death of any of the persons from whom the House of Representatives may choose a President whenever the rights of choice shall have devolved upon them, and for the case of the death of any of the persons from whom the Senate may choose a Vice President whenever the right of choice shall have devolved upon them.

Section 5.

Sections 1 and 2 shall take effect on the 15th day of October following the ratification of this article.

Section 6.

This article shall be inoperative unless it shall have been ratified as an amendment to the Constitution by the legislatures of three-fourths of the several States within seven years from the date of its submission.

The Twentieth Amendment is often called the lame duck amendment because its fundamental purpose was to shorten the time between the November elections, particularly in a presidential election year, and the starting date of the new presidential term and the commencement of the new congressional session. The amendment modified section 1 of the Twelfth Amendment by moving the beginning of the annual legislative session from March 4 to January 3. This change meant that the newly elected Congress would decide any presidential election thrown into the House of Representatives. It also eliminated the possibility that the nation would have to endure two additional months without a chief executive.

The Twentieth Amendment also modified Article I of the Constitution by placing a fixed time—noon—to begin the congressional session.

AMENDMENT XXI
(Ratified on December 5, 1933)

Section 1.

The eighteenth article of amendment to the Constitution of the United States is hereby repealed.

Section 2.

The transportation or importation into any State, Territory, or possession of the United States for delivery or use therein of intoxicating liquors, in violation of the laws thereof, is hereby prohibited.

Section 3.

This article shall be inoperative unless it shall have been ratified as an amendment to the Constitution by conventions in the several States, as provided in the Constitution, within seven years from the date of the submission hereof to the States by the Congress.

The Twenty-First Amendment repealed the Eighteenth Amendment, which was the first and last time that a constitutional amendment has been repealed. The Twenty-First Amendment is also the only amendment to the Constitution approved by state ratifying conventions rather than a popular vote.

By the late 1920s, Americans had tired of Prohibition, and the arrival of the Great Depression in 1929 did nothing to lift their spirits. Few public officials, well aware of the extensive criminal enterprises that had grown up around Prohibition and had made a mockery of the practice, attempted to defend Prohibition as a success. Indeed, Franklin D. Roosevelt, in his initial bid for the presidency in 1932, made the repeal of Prohibition a campaign promise. In January 1933, Congress amended the Volstead Act to permit the sale of alcoholic beverages with an alcohol content of 3.2 percent. The ratification of the Twenty-First Amendment in December returned absolute control of the regulation of alcohol to the states. States are now free to regulate alcohol as they see fit. They may, for example, limit the quantity and type of alcohol sold to consumers, or ban alcohol sales completely. The Supreme Court, in

South Carolina v. *Dole* (1984), ruled that Congress may require the states to set a certain age for the consumption of alcohol in return for participation in a federal program without violating the Twenty-First Amendment.

AMENDMENT XXII
(Ratified on February 27, 1951)

Section 1.

No person shall be elected to the office of the President more than twice, and no person who has held the office of President, or acted as President, for more than two years of a term to which some other person was elected President shall be elected to the office of the President more than once. But this Article shall not apply to any person holding the office of President when this Article was proposed by the Congress, and shall not prevent any person who may be holding the office of President, or acting as President, during the term within which this Article becomes operative from holding the office of President or acting as President during the remainder of such term.

Section 2.

This article shall be inoperative unless it shall have been ratified as an amendment to the Constitution by the legislatures of three-fourths of the several States within seven years from the date of its submission to the States by the Congress.

Thomas Jefferson, who served as the third president of the United States, was the first person of public stature to suggest a constitutional provision limiting presidential terms. "If some termination to the services of the chief Magistrate be not fixed by the Constitution," said Jefferson, "or supplied by practice, his office, nominally four years, will in fact become for life." Until Ulysses S. Grant's unsuccessful attempt to secure his party's nomination to a third term, no other president attempted to extend the two-term limit that had operated in principle. Theodore Roosevelt, having ascended to the presidency after the assassination of William McKinley in 1901, was elected to his second term in 1904. He then sat out a term, and then ran against Woodrow Wilson in the 1912 election and lost.

The first president to serve more than two terms was Franklin D. Roosevelt, and it was his success that inspired the enactment of the Twenty-Second Amendment. In 1946, Republicans took control of Congress for the first time in sixteen years and were determined to guard against such future Democratic dynasties. A year later, Congress, in one of the most party-line votes in the history of the amending process, approved the Twenty-Second Amendment. Every Republican member of the House and Senate who voted on the amendment voted for it. The remaining votes came almost exclusively from southern

Democrats, whose relationship with Roosevelt was never more than a marriage of convenience. Ironically, some Republicans began to call for the repeal of the Twenty-Second Amendment toward the end of popular Republican Dwight D. Eisenhower's second term in 1956. A similar movement emerged in the late 1980s toward the end of Republican Ronald Reagan's second term. The American public at large, however, has shown little enthusiasm for repealing the Twenty-Second Amendment.

AMENDMENT XXIII
(Ratified on March 29, 1961)

Section 1.

The District constituting the seat of Government of the United States shall appoint in such manner as the Congress may direct:

A number of electors of President and Vice President equal to the whole number of Senators and Representatives in Congress to which the District would be entitled if it were a State, but in no event more than the least populous State; they shall be in addition to those appointed by the States, but they shall be considered, for the purposes of the election of President and Vice President, to be electors appointed by a State; and they shall meet in the District and perform such duties as provided by the twelfth article of amendment.

Section 2.

The Congress shall have power to enforce this article by appropriate legislation.

Article II, section 2, of the Constitution limits participation in presidential elections to citizens who reside in the states. The Twenty-Third Amendment amended this provision to include residents of the District of Columbia. Since the District was envisioned as the seat of the national government with a transient population, the Constitution afforded no right of representation to its residents in Congress. By the time the Twenty-Third Amendment was ratified, the District had a greater population than twelve states.

In 1978, Congress introduced a constitutional amendment to give the District of Columbia representation in the House and the Senate. By 1985, the ratification period for the amendment expired without the necessary three-fourths approval from the states.

AMENDMENT XXIV
(Ratified on January 23, 1964)

Section 1.

The right of citizens of the United States to vote in any primary or other election for President or Vice

President, for electors for President or Vice President, or for Senator or Representative in Congress, shall not be denied or abridged by the United States or any State by reason of failure to pay any poll tax or other tax.

Section 2.

The Congress shall have power to enforce this article by appropriate legislation.

The Twenty-Fourth Amendment continued the work of the Fifteenth Amendment. By abolishing the poll tax, the amendment eliminated one of the most popular tools used by voting registrars to prevent most African Americans and other minorities from taking part in the electoral process. Property ownership and literacy tests as conditions of the franchise extended back to the colonial era and were not particular to any region of the United States. But, the poll tax was a southern invention, coming after the enactment of the Fifteenth Amendment. By the fall of Reconstruction in 1877, eleven southern states had enacted poll tax laws. The poll tax was disproportionately enforced against poor African American voters and, in some cases, poor whites.

Congress had begun to debate a constitutional amendment to abolish the poll tax as far back as 1939, but it took the momentum of the civil rights movement to move this process forward. Shortly after the ratification of the Twenty-Fourth Amendment, Congress enacted the Civil Rights Act of 1964, the most sweeping and effective federal civil rights law to date. By the time of ratification of the Twenty-Fourth Amendment, only five states had poll taxes on their books. Spurred on by the spirit of the times, Congress enacted the Voting Rights Act of 1965, which enforced the poll tax ban of the Twenty-Fourth Amendment and also abolished literacy tests, property qualifications, and other obstacles to voter registration. In 1966, in *Harper* v. *Board of Elections,* the Supreme Court rejected a constitutional challenge to the historic voting rights law.

AMENDMENT XXV
(Ratified on February 10, 1967)

Section 1.

In case of the removal of the President from office or of his death or resignation, the Vice President shall become President.

Section 2.

Whenever there is a vacancy in the office of the Vice President, the President shall nominate a Vice President who shall take office upon confirmation by a majority vote of both Houses of Congress.

Section 3.

Whenever the President transmits to the President pro tempore of the Senate and the Speaker of the House of Representatives his written declaration that he is unable to discharge the powers and duties of his office, and until he transmits to them a written declaration to the contrary, such powers and duties shall be discharged by the Vice President as Acting President.

Section 4.

Whenever the Vice President and a majority of either the principal officers of the executive departments or of such other body as Congress may by law provide, transmit to the President pro tempore of the Senate and the Speaker of the House of Representatives their written declaration that the President is unable to discharge the powers and duties of his office, the Vice President shall immediately assume the powers and duties of the office as Acting President.

Thereafter, when the President transmits to the President pro tempore of the Senate and the Speaker of the House of Representatives his written declaration that no inability exists, he shall resume the powers and duties of his office unless the Vice President and a majority of either the principal officers of the executive department or of such other body as Congress may by law provide, transmit within four days to the President pro tempore of the Senate and the Speaker of the House of Representatives their written declaration that the President is unable to discharge the powers and duties of his office. Thereupon Congress shall decide the issue, assembling within forty-eight hours for that purpose if not in session. If the Congress, within twenty-one days after receipt of the latter written declaration, or, if Congress is not in session, within twenty-one days after Congress is required to assemble, determines by two-thirds vote of both Houses that the President is unable to discharge the powers and duties of his office, the Vice President shall continue to discharge the same as Acting President; otherwise, the President shall resume the powers and duties of his office.

Several tragedies to the men who occupied the offices of president and vice president and the lack of constitutional clarity about the path of succession in event of presidential and vice presidential disability spurred the enactment of the Twenty-Fifth Amendment.

Whether the vice president was merely an acting president or assumed the permanent powers of the office for the remainder of the term upon the death of a

president was answered in 1841 when John Tyler became president upon the death of William Henry Harrison, who died only a month after his inauguration. Seven more presidents died in office before the enactment of the Twenty-Fifth Amendment, and in each case the vice president assumed the presidency without controversy. What this amendment answered that the original Constitution did not was the method of vice presidential succession. The vice presidency often went unfilled for months at a time as the result of constitutional ambiguity. Since the enactment of the amendment, there have been two occasions when the president appointed a vice president. Both took place during the second term of President Richard M. Nixon. For the first time in United States history, the nation witnessed a presidential term served out by two men, President Gerald R. Ford and Vice President Nelson A. Rockefeller, neither of whom had been elected to the position.

The Twenty-Fifth Amendment also settled the path of succession in the event of presidential disability. This provision of the amendment was prompted by the memories of James Garfield lying in a coma for eighty days after being struck by an assassin's bullet and Woodrow Wilson's bedridden state for the last eighteen months of his term after a stroke. The first president to invoke the disability provision of the Twenty-Fifth Amendment was Ronald Reagan, who made Vice President George Bush acting president for eight hours while he underwent surgery. The only other time a president invoked this provision came in 2002, when George W. Bush underwent minor surgery and transferred the powers of his office to Vice President Dick Cheney.

The provision authorizing the vice president, in consultation with Congress and members of the Cabinet, to declare the president disabled has never been invoked.

AMENDMENT XXVI
(Ratified on July 1, 1971)

Section 1.

The right of citizens of the United States, who are eighteen years of age or older, to vote shall not be denied or abridged by the United States or by any State on account of age.

Section 2.

The Congress shall have power to enforce this article by appropriate legislation.

The Twenty-Sixth Amendment was a direct response to the unpopularity of the Vietnam War and was spurred by calls to lower the voting age to eighteen so that draft-eligible men could voice their opinion on the war through the ballot box. In 1970, Congress had amended the Voting Rights Act of 1965 to lower the voting age to eighteen in all national, state, and local elections. Many states resisted compliance, claiming that Congress, while having the power to establish the voting age in national elections, had no such authority in state and local elections. In *Oregon* v. *Mitchell* (1970), the Supreme Court agreed with that view. Congress responded by drafting the Twenty-Sixth Amendment, and the states ratified it quickly and without controversy.

AMENDMENT XXVII
(Ratified on May 7, 1992)

No law, varying the compensation for the services of the Senators and Representatives shall take effect until an election of Representatives shall have intervened.

The Twenty-Seventh Amendment originally was introduced in 1789 during the 1st Congress as one of the original twelve amendments to the Constitution. Only six of the necessary eleven (of thirteen) states had ratified the amendment by 1791. As more states came into the union, the prospect of the amendment's passage only dwindled. No additional state ratified the amendment until 1873, when Ohio approved its addition to the Constitution.

Sometime in the early 1980s, a University of Texas student discovered the amendment and launched an intensive effort to bring it to the public's attention for ratification. The amendment's core purpose, preventing members of Congress from raising their salaries during the terms in which they served, meshed well with another grassroots movement that began during this time, the campaign to impose term limits on members of the House and Senate. Nothing in the nation's constitutional or statutory law prohibited the resurrection of the Twenty-Seventh Amendment for voter approval. In 1939, the Supreme Court had ruled in *Coleman* v. *Miller* that amendments could remain indefinitely before the public unless Congress had set a specific time limit on the ratification process. By 1992, the amendment had received the necessary three-fourths approval of the states, making it the last successful effort to amend the Constitution. The Twenty-Seventh Amendment has not, however, barred Congress from increasing its compensation through annual cost-of-living-adjustments.

Photo courtesy: Susan Walsh/AP Wide World Photos

FEDERALISM

ON AUGUST 26, 2005, as New Orleans, Louisiana, and other low-lying Gulf Coast areas in Mississippi and Alabama braced for what could possibly be a Category 5 hurricane named Katrina, Louisiana Governor Kathleen Blanco declared a state of emergency and requested troop assistance from the U.S. Department of Defense. On August 27, as Governor Haley Barbour declared a state of emergency in Mississippi, Governor Blanco asked President George W. Bush to declare a federal state of emergency in Louisiana, believing that "effective response is beyond the capabilities of the State and affected local governments."

The White House responded by authorizing the Federal Emergency Management Agency (FEMA) "to identify, mobilize, and provide at its discretion, equipment and resources necessary to alleviate the impacts of the emergency." On Sunday, August 28, Mayor Ray Nagin issued the first-ever mandatory evacuation of New Orleans amid warnings that the levees, built by the U.S. Army Corps of Engineers, might not hold, thereby flooding the city. As massive evacuations of the coast occurred, Marty Bahamonde, a Boston-based FEMA official, was sent to New Orleans to be the eyes and ears of FEMA Director, Michael Brown. The Louisiana National Guard asked FEMA for 700 buses to help evacuate the poor who had no other method of transportation; FEMA sent 100.

When the storm first hit land on August 29, it looked as if it might not be as bad as predicted. Still, thousands of largely poor and elderly New Orleans citizens were forced to take refuge in the Superdome and the Convention Center. As feared, the levees gave way, flooding entire sections of New Orleans and basically destroying one of the poorest areas of the city. Many residents were stranded in their homes, some on their rooftops.

The situation quickly deteriorated even further when a large proportion of New Orleans police failed to show up for work, and Mayor Nagin and Governor Blanco seemed unable to agree on strategies to deal with the colossal disaster. Both, however, pleaded for more federal assistance, but their pleas fell on deaf ears as President Bush continued to attend to other business. Bush, for example, discussed immigration with Secretary of Homeland Security Michael Chertoff, posed for a birthday photo op with Senator John McCain, visited an Arizona resort to discuss prescription drugs, and attended a San Diego Padres baseball game.[1]

CHAPTER OUTLINE

- ⭐ The Origins of the Federal System: Governmental Powers Under the Constitution

- ⭐ Federalism and the Marshall Court

- ⭐ Dual Federalism: The Taney Court, Slavery, and the Civil War

- ⭐ Cooperative Federalism: The New Deal and the Growth of National Government

- ⭐ New Federalism: Returning Power to the States?

The president was not alone in his passive reaction. Various levels of government appeared either paralyzed or unaware of the disaster in Louisiana and other coastal areas. One government official who was not able to ignore the situation was FEMA agent Bahamonde, who sent increasingly desperate e-mails back to the FEMA director. Using his Blackberry, Bahamonde, who was in the Superdome with thousands of evacuees, told Brown: "Sir, I know that you know the situation is past critical. . . . Hotels are kicking people out, thousands gathering in the streets with no food or water. . . . Estimates are that many will die within hours. We are out of food and running out of water."

Three hours later, the FEMA director's press secretary responded to Bahamonde that Brown needed time to eat in Baton Rouge, where good restaurants were filling up. Bahamond wrote back, "OH MY GOD!!!!!" adding, "I just ate an MRE [a prepackaged meal used by the military] and crapped in the hallway of the Superdome along with 30,000 other close friends so I understand [the] concern about busy restaurants."

In the wake of the September 11, 2001, terrorist attacks, tremendous emphasis had been put on the need for local, state, and national officials to be able to work together in a time of national emergency. Katrina was the first major disaster after 9/11, and it quickly became apparent that no level of government in the federal system was adequately addressing the crisis. By Thursday, September 1, New Orleans Homeland Security Director Terry Ebbert said, "This is a national disgrace. FEMA has been here three days yet there is not command and control." Mayor Nagin sent out an SOS to FEMA and was told by FEMA Director Brown that Brown had heard "no reports of unrest."

With many local and state employees without homes or ways to get to work, and with nearly all forms of communication failing, hundreds died in New Orleans. The official response made clear that there was no effective coordination between the local, state, and national governments, nor any real agreement as to which level of government was responsible for what in this tragedy. In such a crisis, what is the role of a mayor? What role should a governor play? To what extent was the president responsible for FEMA's failures? These questions continue unresolved, yet they highlight some of the difficulties related to the federal system created by the U.S. Constitution.[2]

FROM ITS VERY BEGINNING, the challenge for the United States of America was to preserve the traditional independence and rights of the states while establishing an effective national government. In *Federalist No. 51*, James Madison highlighted the unique structure of governmental powers created by the Framers: "The power surrendered by the people is first divided between two distinct governments, and then . . . subdivided among distinct and separate departments. Hence, a double security arises to the rights of the people."

The Framers, fearing tyranny, divided powers between the state and the national governments. At each level, moreover, powers were divided among executive, legislative, and judicial branches. The people are the ultimate power from which both the national government and the state governments derive their power.

Although most of the delegates to the Constitutional Convention favored a strong federal government, they knew that some compromise about the distribution of powers would be necessary. Some of the Framers wanted to continue with the confederate form of government defined in the Articles of Confederation; others wanted a more centralized system, similar to that of Great Britain. Their solution was to create the world's first federal system (although the word "federal" never appears in the U.S. Constitution). The thirteen sovereign or independent states were bound together under one national government.

Today, the Constitution ultimately binds more than 87,000 different governments at the national, state, and local levels (see Figure 3.1). The Constitution lays out the duties, obligations, and powers of each of these units. Throughout history, however, this relationship has been reshaped continually by crises, historical evolution, public expectations, and judicial interpretation. All these forces have had tremendous influence on who makes policy decisions and how these decisions get made, as is underscored in our opening vignette.

Issues involving the distribution of power between the national government and the states affect you on a daily basis. You do not, for example, need a passport to go from Texas to Oklahoma. There is but one national currency and a national minimum wage. But, many differences exist among the laws of the various states. The age at which you may marry is a state issue, as are laws governing divorce, child custody, and most criminal laws, including how—or if—the death penalty is implemented. Other policies or programs, such as air traffic regulation, are solely within the province of the national government.[3] In areas such as education, however, the national and state governments work together in a system of shared powers.

FIGURE 3.1 NUMBER OF GOVERNMENTS IN THE UNITED STATES

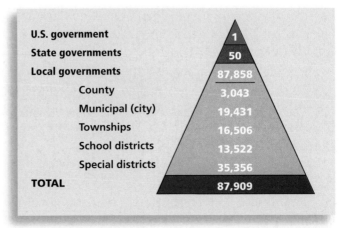

Source: U.S. Census Bureau, http://ftp2.census.gov/govs/cog/2002cogprelim.report.pdf.

To understand the current relationship between the states and the federal government and to better grasp some of the issues that arise from this constantly changing relationship, in this chapter, we will examine the following topics:

- First, we will look at *the origins of the federal system* and *governmental powers under the Constitution* created by the Framers.

- Second, we will explore the relationship between *federalism and the Marshall Court.*

- Third, we will examine the development of *dual federalism* before and after the *Civil War.*

- Fourth, we will analyze *cooperative federalism and the growth of national government.*

- Finally, we will discuss *new federalism,* the movement toward *returning power to the states.*

The Origins of the Federal System: Governmental Powers Under the Constitution

AS DISCUSSED IN CHAPTER 2, the United States was the first country to adopt a **federal system** of government. This system of government, where the national government and state governments derive all authority from the people, was designed to remedy many of the problems experienced under the Articles of Confederation. Under the Articles, the United States was governed as a **confederation** where the national government derived all of its powers from the states. This led to a weak national government that was often unable to respond to even small crises, such as Shays's Rebellion.

The new system of government also had to be different from the **unitary system** found in Great Britain, where the local and regional governments derived all their power from a strong national government. (Figure 3.2 illustrates these different forms of government.) Having been under the rule of English kings, whom they considered tyrants, the Framers feared centralizing power in one government or institution.

federal system
System of government where the national government and state governments share some powers, derive all authority from the people, and the powers of the national government are specified in the U.S. Constitution.

confederation
Type of government where the national government derives its powers from the states; a league of independent states.

unitary system
System of government where the local and regional governments derive all authority from a strong national government.

FIGURE 3.2 THE FEDERAL, UNITARY, AND CONFEDERATE SYSTEMS OF GOVERNMENT
The source of governmental authority and power differs dramatically in various systems of government.

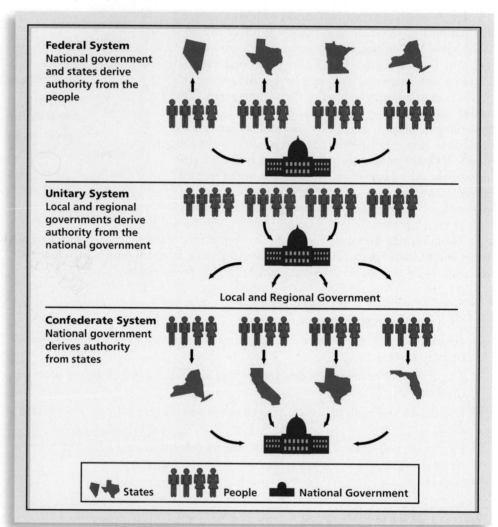

Comparing Federal and Unitary Systems

enumerated powers
Seventeen specific powers granted to Congress under Article I, section 8, of the U.S. Constitution; these powers include taxation, coinage of money, regulation of commerce, and the authority to provide for a national defense.

necessary and proper clause
The final paragraph of Article I, section 8, of the U.S. Constitution, which gives Congress the authority to pass all laws "necessary and proper" to carry out the enumerated powers specified in the Constitution; also called the elastic clause.

Therefore, they made both the state and the federal government accountable to the people at large. While the governments shared some powers, such as the ability to tax, each government was supreme in some spheres, as depicted in Figure 3.3 and described in the following section.

The federal system as conceived by the Framers has proven tremendously effective. Since the creation of the U.S. system, many other nations, including Canada (1867), Mexico (1917), and Russia (1993), have adopted federal systems in their constitutions. (See Global Perspective: American and Mexican Federalism.)

NATIONAL POWERS UNDER THE CONSTITUTION

Chief among the exclusive powers of the national government are the authorities to coin money, conduct foreign relations, provide for an army and navy, declare war, and establish a national court system. All of these powers set out in Article I, section 8, of the Constitution are called **enumerated powers.** Article I, section 8, also contains the **necessary and proper clause,** (also called the elastic clause), which gives Congress the authority to

FIGURE 3.3 THE DISTRIBUTION OF GOVERNMENTAL POWER IN THE FEDERAL SYSTEM

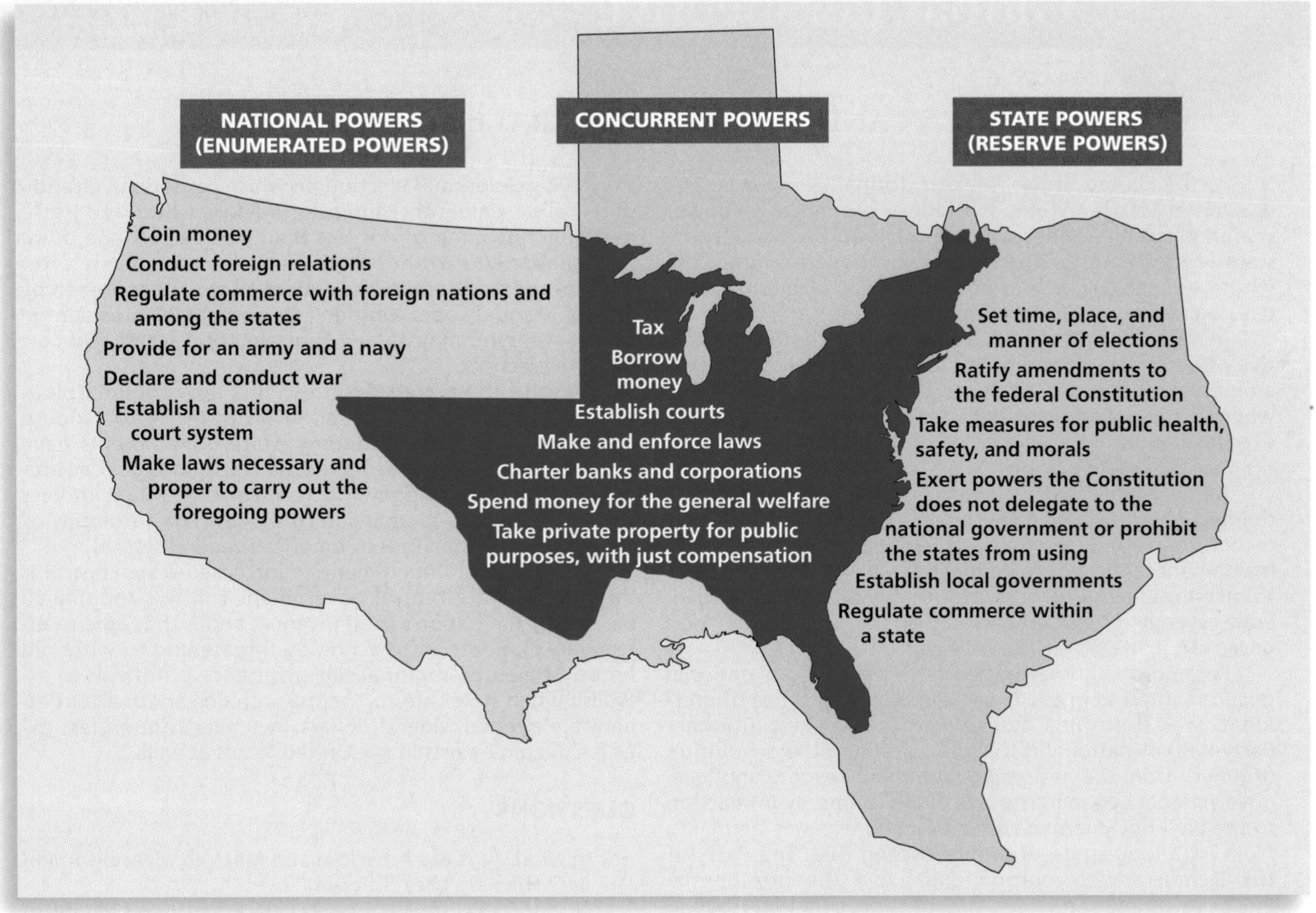

NATIONAL POWERS (ENUMERATED POWERS)

- Coin money
- Conduct foreign relations
- Regulate commerce with foreign nations and among the states
- Provide for an army and a navy
- Declare and conduct war
- Establish a national court system
- Make laws necessary and proper to carry out the foregoing powers

CONCURRENT POWERS

- Tax
- Borrow money
- Establish courts
- Make and enforce laws
- Charter banks and corporations
- Spend money for the general welfare
- Take private property for public purposes, with just compensation

STATE POWERS (RESERVE POWERS)

- Set time, place, and manner of elections
- Ratify amendments to the federal Constitution
- Take measures for public health, safety, and morals
- Exert powers the Constitution does not delegate to the national government or prohibit the states from using
- Establish local governments
- Regulate commerce within a state

enact any laws "necessary and proper" for carrying out any of its enumerated powers. These powers derived from enumerated powers and the necessary and proper clause are known as **implied powers.**

The federal government's right to tax was also clearly set out in the Constitution. The Framers wanted to avoid the financial problems that the national government experienced under the Articles of Confederation. If the national government was to be strong, its power to raise revenue had to be unquestionable. Although the new national government had no power under the Constitution to levy a national income tax, that was changed by the passage of the Sixteenth Amendment in 1913. Eventually, as discussed later in this chapter, this new taxing power became a powerful catalyst for further expansion of the national government.

Article VI of the federal Constitution underscores the notion that the national government is to be supreme in situations of conflict between state and national law. It declares that the U.S. Constitution, the laws of the United States, and its treaties are to be "the supreme Law of the Land; and the Judges in every State shall be bound thereby."

In spite of this explicit language, the meaning of what is called the **supremacy clause** has been subject to continuous judicial interpretation. In 1920, for example, Missouri sought to prevent a U.S. game warden from enforcing the Migratory Bird Treaty Act of 1918, which prohibited the killing or capturing of many species of birds as they made their annual migration across the international border from Canada to parts of the United States.[4] Missouri argued that the Tenth Amendment, which

implied powers
Powers derived from enumerated powers and the necessary and proper clause. These powers are not stated specifically but are considered to be reasonably implied through the exercise of delegated powers.

supremacy clause
Portion of Article VI of the U.S. Constitution mandating that national law is supreme to (that is, supersedes) all other laws passed by the states or by any other subdivision of government.

Global Perspective

AMERICAN AND MEXICAN FEDERALISM

Like the United States, Mexico, formally known as the United Mexican States, is a federal republic with power shared between a federal government and self-governing states. Mexico's thirty-one *estados* have separate state constitutions and their governments are organized into executive, legislative, and judicial branches.

In the United States, the authority of each state's executive office is determined by the state's constitution; for example, the governor of Texas is constitutionally weak, whereas the governor of New York has considerably more executive authority. In Mexico, all of the governors are given significant executive clout.

Mexican municipalities, like their cousins to the north, are charged with providing public services like police and fire protection, waste and sewage management, and park and road maintenance. And, the municipalities are likewise authorized to collect user fees and local taxes, though their ability to generate revenue is considerably less than that of American local government, in part due to Mexico's high poverty rate.

For more than seventy years, the Mexican national government (and in particular, the powerful office of president) was controlled by the Institutional Revolutionary Party (PRI). A national discussion regarding the devolution of power from the national government to state and local governments began in the late 1980s, primarily in reaction to the well-documented corruption and excesses stemming from PRI's long spate of uninterrupted rule. The Party of the Democratic Revolution (PRD) lost the presidential elections under suspicious circumstances in 1988, but in 2000, the opposition National Action Party (PAN) elected its candidate, Vicente Fox, to a six-year term as president, ushering in a new era of what many hoped would be contested, fair, and free elections in Mexico. The outcome of the 2006 presidential election, in which conservative candidate Felipe Calderón Hinojosa (PAN) was declared President Elect by a margin of less than one percentage point has dampened such hopes. Calderón's victory came after widespread and sometimes violent protests organized by Andrés Manuel López Obrador, the leftist PRD presidential candidate, who maintained that electoral fraud had cost him the election.

Despite these controversies, it is now commonplace for candidates running for all levels of office to espouse enthusiasm for local autonomy. State governments have also been clamoring for increased state and local autonomy and are now beginning to receive it, albeit in very small measures in comparison to the level of autonomy of states and municipalities in America's federal system.

A significant impediment to increased state control is the fact that the central government controls roughly 90 percent of the nation's total revenue, and is thus able to effectively mandate state action by threatening to withhold funds. Moreover, regional self-sufficiency is difficult to establish when states are competing with one another for desperately needed federal dollars. A similar though less extreme dynamic exists in the United States as well.

QUESTIONS

1. In what ways are American and Mexican federalism similar? How are they different?
2. Does federalism necessarily guarantee the exercise of local democracy? Why or why not?

Sources: The Economist (March 27, 2003); Library of Congress, Country Studies: Mexico; CIA World Factbook, http://www.cia.gov.

---

reserved a state's powers to legislate for the general welfare of its citizens, allowed Missouri to regulate hunting. But, the Court ruled that since the treaty was legal, it must be considered the supreme law of the land. (See also the discussion of *McCulloch* v. *Maryland* [1819] that follows later in the chapter.)

STATE POWERS UNDER THE CONSTITUTION

Because states had all the power at the time the Constitution was written, the Framers felt no need, as they did for the new national government, to list and restate the powers of the states. Article I, however, allows states to set the "Times, Places, and Manner, for holding elections for senators and representatives." This article also guarantees each state two members in the Senate and prevents Congress from limiting the slave trade before 1808. Article II requires that each state appoint electors to vote for president. Article IV provides each state a "Republican Form of Government," meaning one that represents the citizens of the state. It also assures that the national government will protect the states against foreign attacks and domestic rebellion.

Here, in an example of concurrent state and national power, birds are protected by both governments.

Photo courtesy: Judy Gelles/Stock Boston

It was not until the **Tenth Amendment,** the final part of the Bill of Rights, that the states' powers were described in greater detail: "The powers not delegated to the United States by the Constitution, nor prohibited by it to the States, are reserved to the States respectively, or to the people." (See The Living Constitution: Tenth Amendment.) These powers, often called the states' **reserve** or **police powers,** include the ability to legislate for the public health, safety, and morals of their citizens. Today, the states' rights to legislate under their police powers are used as the rationale for many states' restrictions on abortion. Similarly, some states now fund stem-cell research, in sharp contrast to the federal government. Police powers are also the basis for state criminal laws, including varied laws concerning the death penalty. As long as the U.S. Supreme Court continues to find that the death penalty does not violate the U.S. Constitution, the states may impose it, be it by lethal injection, gas chamber, or the electric chair.

Tenth Amendment
The final part of the Bill of Rights that defines the basic principle of American federalism in stating: "The powers not delegated to the United States by the Constitution, nor prohibited by it to the States, are reserved to the States respectively, or to the people."

reserve (or police) powers
Powers reserved to the states by the Tenth Amendment that lie at the foundation of a state's right to legislate for the public health and welfare of its citizens.

CONCURRENT POWERS UNDER THE CONSTITUTION

As revealed in Figure 3.3, national and state powers overlap. The area where the systems overlap represents **concurrent powers**—powers shared by the national and state governments. States already had the power to tax; the Constitution extended this power to the national government as well. Other important concurrent powers include the right to borrow money, establish courts, and make and enforce laws necessary to carry out these powers.

concurrent powers
Authority possessed by both the state and national governments that may be exercised concurrently as long as that power is not exclusively within the scope of national power or in conflict with national law.

POWERS DENIED UNDER THE CONSTITUTION

Some powers are explicitly denied to the national government or the states under Article I of the Constitution. In keeping with the Framers' desire to forge a national economy, for example, states are prohibited from entering treaties, coining money, or impairing obligation of contracts. States also are prohibited from entering into compacts with other states without express congressional approval. In a similar vein, Congress is barred from favoring one state over another in regulating commerce, and it cannot lay duties on items exported from any state.

State governments (as well as the national government) are denied the authority to take arbitrary actions affecting constitutional rights and liberties. Neither national

The Living Constitution

The Powers not delegated to the United States by the Constitution, nor prohibited by it to the States, are reserved to the states respectively, or to the people.

—TENTH AMENDMENT

This amendment to the Constitution—a simple affirmation that any powers not specifically given to the national government are left to the province of the states or to the citizenry—was actually unnecessary and added nothing to the original document. During the ratification debates, however, Anti-Federalists continued to be concerned that the national government would claim powers not intended for it at the expense of the states. Still, during the debates over this amendment, both houses of Congress rejected efforts to insert the word "expressly" before the word delegated. Thus, it was clear that the amendment was not intended to be the yardstick by which to measure the powers of the national government. This was reinforced by comments made by James Madison during the debate that took place over Alexander Hamilton's efforts to establish a national bank. "Interference with the power of the States was no constitutional criterion of the power of Congress," said Madison.

By the end of the New Deal, the Supreme Court had come to interpret the Tenth Amendment to allow Congress, pursuant to its authority under the commerce clause, to legislate in a wide array of areas that the states might never have foreseen when they ratified the amendment. In fact, until the 1970s, Congress's ability to legislate to regulate commerce appeared to trump any actions of the states. Since the mid-1970s, however, the Court has been very closely divided about how much authority must be reserved to the states vis-à-vis their authority to regulate commerce, especially when it involves regulation of activities of states as sovereign entities. The Court now requires Congress to attach statements of clear intention to tread on state powers. It is then up to the Court to determine if Congress has claimed powers beyond its authority under the Constitution.

---

bill of attainder
A law declaring an act illegal without a judicial trial.

ex post facto law
Law passed after the fact, thereby making previously legal activity illegal and subject to current penalty; prohibited by the U.S. Constitution.

nor state governments may pass a **bill of attainder,** a law declaring an act illegal without a judicial trial. The Constitution also bars the national and state governments from passing *ex post facto* **laws,** laws that make an act punishable as a crime even if the action was legal at the time it was committed. (For more on civil rights and liberties, see chapters 5 and 6.)

RELATIONS AMONG THE STATES

In addition to delineating the relationship of the states with the national government, the Constitution provides a mechanism for resolving interstate disputes and facilitating relations among states. To avoid any sense of favoritism, it provides that disputes between states be settled directly by the U.S. Supreme Court under its original jurisdiction as mandated by Article III of the Constitution (see chapter 10). Moreover, Article IV requires that each state give "Full Faith and Credit . . . to the public Acts, Records and judicial Proceedings of every other State." The **full faith and credit clause** ensures that judicial decrees and contracts made in one state will be binding and enforceable in another, thereby facilitating trade and other commercial relationships.

In 1997, the Supreme Court ruled that the full faith and credit clause mandates that state courts always must honor the judgments of other state courts, even if to do so is against state public policy or existing state laws. Failure to do so would allow a single state to "rule the world," said Supreme Court Associate Justice Ruth Bader Ginsburg during oral argument.[5] Full faith and credit cases continue to make their way through the judicial system. For example, a state's refusal to honor same-sex marriage contracts poses interesting constitutional questions. States can vary considerably on social issues; see American Values/American Voices: Legislating for One America or for Individual States?

Article IV contains the **privileges and immunities clause,** guaranteeing that the citizens of each state are afforded the same rights as citizens of all other states. Article IV also contains the **extradition clause,** which requires states to extradite, or return, criminals to states where they have been convicted or are to stand trial.

To facilitate relations among states, Article 1, section 10, clause 3, of the U.S. Constitution sets the legal foundation for interstate cooperation in the form of **interstate compacts,** contracts between states that carry the force of law. It reads, "No State shall, without the consent of Congress . . . enter into any Agreement or Compact with another state." Before 1920, interstate compacts were largely bistate compacts that addressed boundary disputes or acted to help two states accomplish some objective.

More than 200 interstate compacts exist today. While some deal with rudimentary items such as state boundaries, others help states carry out their policy objectives, and they play an important role in helping states carry out their functions. Although several bistate compacts still exist, other compacts have as many as fifty signatories.[6] The Drivers License Compact, for example, was signed by all fifty states to facilitate nationwide recognition of licenses issued in the respective states.

States today find that interstate compacts help them maintain state control because compacts with other states allow for sharing resources, expertise, and responses that often are available more quickly than those from the federal government. The Emergency Management Assistance Compact, for example, allows states to cooperate and to share resources in the event of natural and man-made disasters. After the terrorist attacks on September 11, assistance to New York and Virginia came from a host of states surrounding the areas of the attacks. (For more on compacts, see Table 3.1.)

full faith and credit clause
Section of Article IV of the Constitution that ensures judicial decrees and contracts made in one state will be binding and enforceable in any other state.

privileges and immunities clause
Part of Article IV of the Constitution guaranteeing that the citizens of each state are afforded the same rights as citizens of all other states.

extradition clause
Part of Article IV that requires states to extradite, or return, criminals to states where they have been convicted or are to stand trial.

interstate compacts
Contracts between states that carry the force of law; generally now used as a tool to address multistate policy concerns.

TABLE 3.1	COMPACTS BY THE NUMBERS
Interstate compacts with 25 or more members	13
Least compact memberships by a state (HI & WI)	14
Most compact memberships by a state (NH & VA)	42
Average compact memberships by a state	27
Compacts developed prior to 1920	36
Compacts developed since 1920	150+
Interstate compacts currently in operation	200+

Source: Council of State Governments, http://www.csg.org.

RELATIONS WITHIN THE STATES: LOCAL GOVERNMENT

The Constitution gives local governments, including counties, municipalities, townships, and school districts, no independent standing. Thus, their authority is not granted directly by the people but through state governments, which establish or charter administrative subdivisions to execute the duties of the state government on a smaller scale. For more information on the relationship between state and local governments, see chapter 4.

American Values/American Voices

LEGISLATING FOR ONE AMERICA OR FOR INDIVIDUAL STATES?

When the Framers were drafting the U.S. Constitution, they firmly believed that each state would at times exhibit its own unique political culture, a phenomenon that has been noted by many political scientists who study states within the federal system. Today, for example, we often talk about red states, blue states, and even purple states. But, how different are the states? Are those who live in the southern Bible Belt really more religious than their neighbors in other states? And, if so, how universal are "American values"?

A 2005 study published in the *Atlantic Monthly*, with tongue-in-cheek commentary by satirist P. J. O'Rourke, underscores how different are the political cultures of the various states.[a] For example, the ratio of married to divorced people is far lower in what New Englander O'Rourke refers to as the western "flyover" states that stretch from North Dakota down to western Texas. In parts of California, Florida, Tennessee, and Maine, more than 12 percent of the population has been divorced. And, while many parts of the South contain the poorest citizens in the nation, those same people often give a higher proportion of their income to charity than citizens in wealthier parts of the country.

Crime is another area where state differences are vast. Parts of Florida, South Carolina, and California have among the highest crime rates per 100,000 residents in the country.

Rourke's cheeky explanation for this pattern is that "retirees are America's secret criminal class." He continues, "this would explain the felonious Sunshine State and the great American Crescent of Crime that begins in seniors-friendly New Mexico, sweeps through the golden-age communities of Arizona and southern Nevada and continues up the Winnebago-frequented Pacific Coast."[b]

Differences in issues such as crime often lead to very different approaches to solving social problems and reflect local values. For many years New York State, often regarded as liberal, had no death penalty. Texas, regarded as conservative, not only has the highest proportion of inmates on death row but leads all states yearly in the number of inmates put to death.

QUESTIONS

1. Are there state or local values that make it difficult for us to discuss American values? Explain.
2. What basic shared attitudes are so fundamental that they must be a part of any discussion of American values?

---

[a]P. J. O'Rourke, "Continental Divides," *Atlantic Monthly* (January/February, 2005): 128–131.

[b]O'Rourke, "Continental Divides," 129.

Federalism and the Marshall Court

Federalism and the Supreme Court

THE NATURE OF FEDERALISM, including its allocation of power between the national government and the states, has changed dramatically over the past two hundred years. Much of this change is due to the rulings of the U.S. Supreme Court, which has played a major role in defining the nature of the federal system because the distribution of power between the national and state governments is not clearly delineated in the Constitution. Few Supreme Courts have had a greater impact on the federal/state relationship than the one headed by Chief Justice John Marshall (1801–1835). In a series of decisions, he and his associates carved out an important role for the Court in defining the balance of power between the national government and the states. Two rulings in the early 1800s, *McCulloch* v. *Maryland* (1819) and *Gibbons* v. *Ogden* (1824), were particularly important.

MCCULLOCH V. MARYLAND (1819)

McCulloch v. *Maryland* (1819) was the first major Supreme Court decision of the Marshall Court to define the relationship between the national and state governments. In 1816, Congress chartered the Second Bank of the United States. (The charter of the First Bank had been allowed to expire.) In 1818, the Maryland state

McCulloch v. Maryland (1819)
The Supreme Court upheld the power of the national government and denied the right of a state to tax the federal bank using the Constitution's supremacy clause. The Court's broad interpretation of the necessary and proper clause paved the way for later rulings upholding expansive federal powers.

legislature levied a tax requiring all banks not chartered by Maryland (that is, the Second Bank of the United States) to: (1) buy stamped paper from the state on which the Second Bank's notes were to be issued; (2) pay the state $15,000 a year, or, (3) go out of business. James McCulloch, the head cashier of the Baltimore branch of the Bank of the United States, refused to pay the tax, and Maryland brought suit against him. After losing in a Maryland state court, McCulloch appealed his conviction to the U.S. Supreme Court by order of the U.S. secretary of the treasury. In a unanimous opinion, the Court answered the two central questions that had been put to it: Did Congress have the authority to charter a bank? If it did, could a state tax it?

Chief Justice John Marshall's answer to the first question—whether Congress had the right to establish a bank or another type of corporation, given that the Constitution does not mention such a power explicitly—continues to stand as the classic exposition of the doctrine of implied powers and as a reaffirmation of the propriety of a strong national government. Although the word "bank" cannot be found in the Constitution, the Constitution enumerates powers that give Congress the authority to levy and collect taxes, issue a currency, and borrow funds. From these enumerated powers, Marshall found, it was reasonable to imply that Congress had the power to charter a bank, which could be considered "necessary and proper" to the exercise of its aforementioned enumerated powers.

Marshall next addressed the question of whether a federal bank could be taxed by any state government. To Marshall, this was not a difficult question. The national government was dependent on the people, not the states, for its powers. In addition, Marshall noted, the Constitution specifically calls for the national law to be supreme. "The power to tax involves the power to destroy," wrote Marshall.[7] Thus, the state tax violated the supremacy clause, because individual states cannot interfere with the operations of the national government, whose laws are supreme.

The Court's decision in *McCulloch* has far-reaching consequences even today. The necessary and proper clause is used to justify federal action in many areas, including education, health, and welfare. Furthermore, had Marshall allowed the state of Maryland to tax the federal bank, it is possible that states could have attempted to tax all federal agencies located within their boundaries, a costly proposition that could have driven the federal government into insurmountable debt.

GIBBONS V. *OGDEN* (1824)

Shortly after *McCulloch*, the Marshall Court had another opportunity to rule in favor of a broad interpretation of the scope of national power. *Gibbons v. Ogden* (1824) involved a dispute that arose after the New York State legislature granted to Robert Fulton the exclusive right to operate steamboats on the Hudson River. Simultaneously, Congress licensed a ship to sail on the same waters. By the time the case reached the Supreme Court, it was complicated both factually and procedurally. Suffice it to say that both New York and New Jersey wanted to control shipping on the lower Hudson River. But, *Gibbons* actually addressed one simple, very important question: what was the scope of Congress's authority under the commerce clause? The states argued that "commerce," as mentioned in Article I, should be interpreted narrowly to include only direct dealings in products. In *Gibbons*, however, the Supreme Court ruled that Congress's power to regulate interstate commerce included the power to regulate commercial activity as well, and that the commerce power had no limits except those specifically found in the Constitution. Thus, New York had no constitutional authority to grant a monopoly to a single steamboat operator, an act that interfered with interstate commerce.[8] Like the necessary and proper clause, today the commerce clause is used to justify a great deal of federal legislation, including regulation of highways, the stock market, and violence against women.

Gibbons v. Ogden (1824)
The Supreme Court upheld broad congressional power to regulate interstate commerce. The Court's broad interpretation of the Constitution's commerce clause paved the way for later rulings upholding expansive federal powers.

Dual Federalism: The Taney Court, Slavery, and the Civil War

IN SPITE OF NATIONALIST Marshall Court decisions such as *McCulloch* and *Gibbons*, strong debate continued in the United States over national versus state power. It was under the leadership of Chief Justice Marshall's successor, Roger B. Taney (1835–1863), that the Supreme Court articulated the notions of concurrent power and **dual federalism.** Dual federalism posits that having separated and equally powerful state and national governments is the best arrangement. Adherents of this theory typically believe that the national government should not exceed its constitutionally enumerated powers, and, as stated in the Tenth Amendment, all other powers are, and should be, reserved to the states or the people.

dual federalism
The belief that having separate and equally powerful levels of government is the best arrangement.

DRED SCOTT AND THE QUESTION OF SLAVERY

During the Taney Court era, the comfortable role of the Supreme Court as the arbiter of competing national and state interests became troublesome when the justices were called upon to deal with the controversial issue of slavery. In cases such as *Dred Scott* v. *Sandford* (1857), the Court tried to manage the slavery issue by resolving questions of ownership, the status of fugitive slaves, and slavery in the new territories.[9] These cases generally were settled in favor of slavery and states' rights within the framework of dual federalism. In *Dred Scott*, for example, the Taney Court, in declaring the Missouri Compromise unconstitutional, ruled that Congress lacked the authority to ban slavery in the territories. This decision seemed to rule out any nationally legislated solution to the slavery question, leaving the problem in the hands of the state legislatures and the people, who did not have the power to impose their will on other states.

THE CIVIL WAR, ITS AFTERMATH, AND THE CONTINUATION OF DUAL FEDERALISM

The Civil War (1861–1865) forever changed the nature of federalism. In the aftermath of the war, the national government grew in size and powers. It also attempted to impose its will on the state governments through the Thirteenth, Fourteenth, and Fifteenth Amendments. These three amendments, known collectively as the Civil War Amendments, prohibited slavery and granted civil and political rights (including the franchise for males) to African Americans.

The U.S. Supreme Court, however, continued to adhere to its belief in the concept of dual federalism. Therefore, in spite of the growth of the national government's powers, the importance of the state governments' powers was not diminished until 1933, when the next major change in the federal system occurred. Generally, the Court upheld any laws passed under the states' police powers, which allow states to pass laws to protect the general welfare of their citizens. These laws included those affecting commerce, labor relations, and manufacturing. After the Court's decision in *Plessy* v. *Ferguson* (1896), in which the Court ruled that state maintenance of "separate but equal" facilities for blacks and whites was constitutional, most civil rights and voting cases also became state matters, in spite of the Civil War Amendments.[10]

Photo courtesy: Missouri Historical Society

■ Dred Scott, born into slavery around 1795, became the named plaintiff in a case with major ramifications for the federal system. In 1833, Scott was sold by his original owners, the Blow family, to Dr. Emerson in St. Louis, Missouri. When Emerson died in 1843, Scott tried to buy his freedom. Before he could, however, he was transferred to Emerson's widow, who moved to New York, leaving Scott in the custody of his first owners, the Blows. Some of the Blows (Henry Blow later founded the anti-slavery Free Soil Party) and other abolitionists gave money to support a test case seeking Scott's freedom. They believed that Scott's residence with the Emerson family in Illinois and later in the Wisconsin Territory, which both prohibited slavery, made Scott a free man. After many delays, the U.S. Supreme Court ruled 7–2 in 1857 that Scott was not a citizen of the United States. "Slaves," said the Court, "were never thought of or spoken of except as property." Despite this ruling, Dred Scott was given his freedom later in 1857, when the Emerson family permanently returned him to the anti-slavery Blows. He died of tuberculosis one year later.

The Court also developed legal doctrine in a series of cases that reinforced the national government's ability to regulate commerce. By the 1930s, these two somewhat contradictory approaches led to confusion: states, for example, could not tax gasoline used by federal vehicles,[11] and the national government could not tax the sale of motorcycles to the city police department.[12] In this period, the Court, however, did recognize the need for national control over new technological developments, such as the telegraph.[13] And, beginning in the 1880s, the Court allowed Congress to regulate many aspects of economic relationships, such as monopolies, an area of regulation formerly thought to be in the exclusive realm of the states. Passage of laws such as the Interstate Commerce Act in 1887 and the Sherman Anti-Trust Act in 1890 allowed Congress to establish itself as an important player in the growing national economy.

Despite finding that most of these federal laws were constitutional, the Supreme Court did not enlarge the scope of national power consistently. In 1895, for example, the United States filed suit against four sugar refiners, alleging that their sale would give their buyer control of 98 percent of the U.S. sugar-refining business. The Supreme Court ruled that congressional efforts to control monopolies (through passage of the Sherman Anti-Trust Act) did not give Congress the authority to prevent the sale of these sugar-refining businesses, because manufacturing was not commerce. Therefore, the companies and their actions were beyond the scope of Congress's authority to regulate.[14]

SETTING THE STAGE FOR A STRONGER NATIONAL GOVERNMENT

In 1895, the U.S. Supreme Court found a congressional effort to tax personal incomes unconstitutional, although an earlier Court had found a similar tax levied during the Civil War constitutional.[15] Thus, Congress and the state legislatures were moved to ratify the **Sixteenth Amendment.** The Sixteenth Amendment gave Congress the power to levy and collect taxes on incomes without apportioning them among the states. The revenues taken in by the federal government through taxation of personal income "removed a major constraint on the federal government by giving it access to almost unlimited revenues."[16] If money is power, the income tax and the revenues it generated greatly enhanced the power of the federal government and its ability to enter policy areas where it formerly had few funds to spend.

The **Seventeenth Amendment,** ratified in 1913, similarly enhanced the power of the national government at the expense of the states. This amendment terminated the state legislatures' election of senators and put their election in the hands of the people. With senators no longer directly accountable to the state legislators who elected them, states lost their principal protectors in Congress. Coupled with the Sixteenth Amendment, this amendment paved the way for more drastic changes in the relationship between national and state governments in the United States.

Sixteenth Amendment
Authorized Congress to enact a national income tax.

Seventeenth Amendment
Made senators directly elected by the people; removed their selection from state legislatures.

Cooperative Federalism: The New Deal and the Growth of National Government

THE ERA OF DUAL FEDERALISM came to an abrupt end in the 1930s. While the ratification of the Sixteenth and Seventeenth Amendments set the stage for expanded national government, the catalyst for dual federalism's demise was a series of economic events that ended in the cataclysm of the Great Depression:

- Throughout the 1920s, bank failures were common.
- In 1921, the nation experienced a severe slump in agricultural prices.

- In 1926, the construction industry went into decline.
- In the summer of 1929, inventories of consumer goods and automobiles were at an all-time high.
- On October 29, 1929, stock prices, which had risen steadily since 1926, crashed, taking with them the entire national economy.

Despite the severity of these indicators, Presidents Calvin Coolidge and Herbert Hoover took little action, believing that the national depression was an amalgamation of state economic crises that should be dealt with by state and local governments. However, by 1933, the situation could no longer be ignored.

THE NEW DEAL

Rampant unemployment (historians estimate it was as high as 40 to 50 percent) was the hallmark of the Great Depression. In 1933, to combat severe problems facing the nation, newly elected President Franklin D. Roosevelt (FDR) proposed a variety of innovative programs under the rubric of "the New Deal" and ushered in a new era in American politics. FDR used the full power of the office of the president as well as his highly effective communication skills to sell the American public and Congress on a new level of government intervention intended to stabilize the economy and reduce suffering. Most politicians during the New Deal period (1933–1939) agreed that to find national solutions to the Depression, which was affecting the citizens of every state in the union, the national government would have to exercise tremendous authority.

In the first few weeks of the legislative session after FDR's inauguration, Congress passed a series of acts creating new federal agencies and programs proposed by the president. These new agencies, often known by their initials, created what many termed an alphabetocracy. Among the more significant programs were the Federal Housing Administration (FHA), which provided federal financing for new home construction; the Civilian Conservation Corps (CCC), a work relief program for farmers and homeowners; and the Agricultural Adjustment Administration (AAA) and the National Recovery Administration (NRA), which imposed restrictions on production in agriculture and many industries while also providing subsidies to farmers.

The New Deal programs forced all levels of government to work cooperatively with one another. Indeed, local governments—mainly in big cities—became a third partner in the federal system as FDR relied on big-city Democratic political machines to turn out voters to support his programs. For the first time in U.S. history, in essence, cities were embraced as equal partners in an intergovernmental system and became players in the national political arena because many in the national legislature wanted to bypass state legislatures, where urban interests usually were underrepresented significantly.

New Deal programs also enlarged the scope of the national government. Those who feared this unprecedented use of national power quickly challenged the constitutionality of the programs in court. And, at least initially, the Supreme Court often agreed with them.

Through the mid-1930s, the Supreme Court continued to rule that certain aspects of the New Deal went beyond the authority of Congress to regulate commerce. The Court's *laissez-faire,* or hands-off, attitude toward the economy was reflected in a series of decisions ruling various aspects of New Deal programs unconstitutional.

FDR and the Congress were outraged. FDR's frustration with the Court prompted him to suggest what ultimately was nicknamed his "Court-packing plan." Knowing that he could do little to change the minds of those already on the Court, FDR suggested enlarging its size from nine to thirteen justices. This would have given

This cartoon pokes fun at FDR (with his aide, Harold Ickes) and their unpopular "Court-packing plan" to expand the size of the Supreme Court to allow FDR to add justices to undo the majority's anti–New Deal decisions.

him the opportunity to pack the Court with a majority of justices predisposed toward the constitutional validity of the New Deal.

Even though Roosevelt was popular, the Court-packing plan was not. Congress and the public were outraged that he even suggested tampering with an institution of government. Nevertheless, the Court appeared to respond to this threat. In 1937, it reversed its series of anti-New Deal decisions, concluding that Congress (and therefore the national government) had the authority to legislate in any area so long as what was regulated affected commerce in any way. The Court also upheld the constitutionality of the bulk of the massive New Deal relief programs, including the National Labor Relations Act of 1935, which authorized collective bargaining between unions and employees in *NLRB* v. *Jones and Laughlin Steel Co.* (1937);[17] the Fair Labor Standards Act of 1938, which prohibited the interstate shipment of goods made by employees earning less than the federally mandated minimum wage;[18] and the Agricultural Adjustment Act of 1938, which provided crop subsidies to farmers.[19] Congress then used this newly recognized power to legislate in a wide array of areas, including maximum hour and minimum wage laws and regulation of child labor.

THE CHANGING NATURE OF FEDERALISM: FROM LAYER CAKE TO MARBLE CAKE

Before the Depression and the New Deal, most political scientists likened the federal system to a layer cake: each level or layer of government—national, state, and local—had clearly defined powers and responsibilities. After the New Deal, however, the nature of the federal system changed. Government now looked something like a marble cake:

> Wherever you slice through it you reveal an inseparable mixture of differently colored ingredients. . . . Vertical and diagonal lines almost obliterate the horizontal ones, and in some places there are unexpected whirls and an imperceptible merging of colors, so that it is difficult to tell where one ends and the other begins.[20]

cooperative federalism
The relationship between the national and state governments that began with the New Deal.

The metaphor of marble cake federalism refers to what political scientists call **cooperative federalism,** a term that describes the intertwined relationship among the national, state, and local governments that began with the New Deal. States began to take a secondary, albeit important, cooperative role in the scheme of governance, as did many cities. Nowhere is this shift in power from the states to the national government clearer than in the growth of federal grant programs that began in earnest during the New Deal. Between the New Deal and the 1990s, the tremendous growth in these programs, and in federal government spending in general, changed the nature and discussion of federalism from "How much power should the national government have?" to "How much say in the policies of the states can the national government buy?" During the 1970s energy crisis, the national government initially imposed a national 55 mph speed limit on the states, for example. Subsequent efforts forced states to adopt minimum-age drink restrictions in order to obtain federal transportation funds.

FEDERAL GRANTS AND NATIONAL EFFORTS TO INFLUENCE THE STATES

As early as 1790, Congress appropriated funds for the states to pay debts incurred during the Revolutionary War. But, it wasn't until the Civil War that Congress enacted its first true federal grant program, which allocated federal funds to the states for a specific purpose. Most commentators believe the start of this redistribution of funds began with the Morrill Land Grant Act of 1862, which gave each state 30,000 acres of public land for each representative in Congress. Income from the sale of these lands was to be earmarked for the establishment and support of agricultural and mechanical arts colleges. Sixty-nine land-grant colleges—including Texas A&M University, the University of Georgia, and Michigan State University—were founded or significantly assisted, making this grant program the single most important piece of education legislation passed in the United States up to that time.

As we have seen, Franklin D. Roosevelt's New Deal program increased the flow of federal dollars to the states with the infusion of massive federal dollars for a variety of public works programs, including building and road construction. In the boom times of World War II, even more new federal programs were introduced. By the 1950s and 1960s, federal grant-in-aid programs were well entrenched. They often defined federal/state relationships and made the national government a major player in domestic policy. Until the 1960s, however, most federal grant programs were constructed in cooperation with the states and were designed to assist the states in the furtherance of their traditional responsibilities to protect the health, welfare, and safety of their citizens.

categorical grant
Grant for which Congress appropriates funds for a specific purpose.

Most of these programs were **categorical grants,** ones for which Congress appropriates funds for specific purposes. Categorical grants allocate federal dollars by a precise formula and are subject to detailed conditions imposed by the national government, often on a matching basis; that is, states must contribute money to match federal funds, although the national government may pay as much as 90 percent of the total.

By the early 1960s, as concern about the poor and minorities rose, and as states (especially in the South) were blamed for perpetuating discrimination, those in power in the national government saw grants as a way to force states to behave in ways desired by the national government.[21] If the states would not cooperate with the national government to further its goals, it would withhold funds.

In 1964, the Democratic administration of President Lyndon B. Johnson (LBJ) launched its "Great Society" program, which included what LBJ called a "War on Poverty." The Great Society program was a broad attempt to combat poverty and discrimination. In a frenzy of activity in Washington not seen since the New Deal, federal funds were channeled to states, to local governments, and even directly to citizen action groups in an effort to alleviate social ills that the states had been unable or unwilling to remedy. There was money for urban renewal, education, and poverty programs, including Head Start and job training. The move to fund local groups directly was made by the most liberal members of Congress to bypass not only conservative state legislatures, but also conservative mayors and councils in cities such as Chicago, who were perceived as disinclined to help their poor, often African American, constituencies. Thus, these programs often pitted governors and mayors against community activists, who became key players in the distribution of federal dollars.

These new grants altered the fragile federal/state balance of power that had been at the core of many older federal grant programs. During the Johnson administration, the national government began to use federal grants as a way to further what federal (and not state) officials perceived to be national needs. Grants based on what states wanted or believed they needed began to decline, while grants based on what the national government wanted states to do to foster national goals increased dramatically. From pollution to economic development and law enforcement, creating a federal grant seemed like the perfect solution to every problem.[22] (See Politics Now: Bringing Home the Bacon.)

Not all federal programs mandating state or local action came with federal money, however. And, while presidents during the 1970s voiced their opposition to big government, their efforts to rein it in were largely unsuccessful.

New Federalism: Returning Power to the States?

IN 1980, former California Governor Ronald Reagan was elected president, pledging to advance what he called a **New Federalism** and a return of power to the states. This policy set the tone for the federal/state relationship that was maintained from the 1980s until 2001. Presidents and Congresses, both Republican and Democrat, took steps to shrink the size of the federal government in favor of programs administered by state governments. President Bill Clinton lauded the demise of big government. And, on the campaign trail in 2000, George W. Bush also seemed committed to this devolution. The September 11 terrorist attacks, however, have led to substantial growth in the power and scope of the federal government.

New Federalism
Federal/state relationship proposed by Reagan administration during the 1980s; hallmark is returning administrative powers to the state governments.

THE REAGAN REVOLUTION

The Republican Reagan Revolution had at its heart strong views about the role of states in the federal system. While many Democrats and liberal interest groups argued that federal grants were an effective way to raise the level of services provided to the poor, others, including Reagan, attacked them as imposing national priorities on the states. In part to curtail federal spending, Reagan almost immediately proposed mas-

Politics Now

BRINGING HOME THE BACON

In the wake of the September 11 terrorist attacks on the World Trade Center in New York and the Pentagon in the Washington, D.C., area, Congress passed extraordinary appropriations bills to beef up national security at home. Many of these bills allowed the Department of Homeland Security to disperse almost unlimited funds to communities across the country.

Few small towns anticipated the federal government largess that was to flow to them as a result of the attacks. Bellows Falls, Vermont, a small town with only eight full-time police officers, for example, received a homeland security grant that allowed it to set up sixteen surveillance cameras costing $15,000 each. These cameras were intended to watch intersections twenty-four hours a day, as well as the town square and a local sewage plant. In Ridgely, Maryland, population 1,300, its police chief found it "difficult to find something to use the money for." The Departments of Homeland Security and Justice were unable to compile information about how many small-town camera projects the agencies funded.[a]

Ironically, Bellows Falls was to receive only three fewer cameras than the District of Columbia, which has a population nearly 200 times that of the sleepy Vermont town. But, the citizens of Bellows Falls, once they recognized the possibility that "big government" could be watching them, ended up pressuring town trustees to reject the money that would have funded the surveillance cameras. While many federal grants are the impetus for local programs that are not necessarily at the top of anyone's list, but are still a source of funding for towns with small budgets, the citizens of Bellows Falls saw more pitfalls than positives in accepting the federal money. In late December, the local paper ran the headline "Spy Cameras Coming to BF." Several residents and the local American Civil Liberties Union protested. One trustee, for example, voiced her belief that "tapes of civic demonstrations would be kept by the federal government and used against citizens."[b]

Federal grants gradually are changing the way that small communities police themselves, another irony given that policing historically has been a function of state and local governments in the federal system. Still, whether towns put their homeland security dollars into surveillance cameras, and how they use those cameras, largely depends on local mores. In Washington, D.C., for example, the police use cameras only

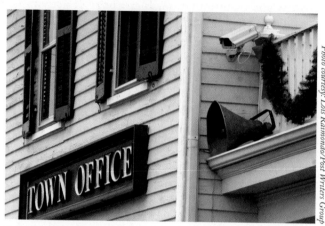

■ Surveillance cameras like this one have been installed throughout the United States thanks to post-9/11 federal funds.

during demonstrations and emergency situations. In some areas of the United States, however, local police use cameras with little or no rationale, causing privacy advocates to worry about Americans' civil liberties. This is especially true since congressional passage and presidential approval of the Military Commissions Act of 2006, which allows citizens to be detained indefinitely with no access to a lawyer and without knowledge of the charges against them if they are designated possible terrorists or believed to be aiding terrorists.

QUESTIONS

1. Should the federal government control how homeland security dollars are spent, or should state and local governments use such grants as they see fit?
2. How do such disparities arise in the federal system when funds are disbursed to states and communities?

[a]This feature draws heavily on David A. Farenthold, "Federal Grants Bring Surveillance Cameras to Small Towns," *Washington Post* (January 19, 2006): A1.

[b]Diann Daniel, "No Candid Cameras: After Outcry, Vermont Village Rejects Federally Funded Security Surveillance," CSOonline.com.

block grant
Broad grant with few strings attached; given to states by the federal government for specified activities, such as secondary education or health services.

sive cuts in federal domestic programs and drastic income tax cuts. Declining federal revenues dramatically altered the relationships among federal, state, and local governments. For the first time in thirty years, federal aid to state and local governments declined.[23] Reagan persuaded Congress to consolidate many categorical grants (for specific programs that often require matching funds) into far fewer, less restrictive **block grants**—broad grants to states for specific activities such as secondary education or health services, with few strings attached. He also ended general revenue sharing, which had provided significant restricted funds to the states.

By the end of the presidencies of Ronald Reagan and George Bush in 1993, most block grants fell into one of four categories: health, income security, education, or transportation. Yet, many politicians, including most state governors, urged the consolidation of even more programs into block grants. Calls to reform the welfare system, particularly to allow the states more latitude in an effort to get back to the Hamiltonian notion of states as laboratories of experiment, seemed popular with citizens and governments alike. New Federalism had taken hold.

THE DEVOLUTION REVOLUTION

In 1992, Bill Clinton was elected president—the first Democrat in twelve years. Although Clinton was a former governor, he was more predisposed to federal programs than his Republican predecessors. His ability to make changes in the federal system, however, was limited.

In 1994, Republican candidates for the House of Representatives joined together in their support for the Contract with America, a campaign document proposed by then House Minority Whip Newt Gingrich (R–GA). In it, Republican candidates pledged to force a national debate on the role of the national government in regard to the states. A top priority was scaling back the federal government, an effort that some commentators called the devolution revolution.

Running under a clear set of priorities contained in the Contract, Republican candidates took back the House of Representatives for the first time in more than forty years. A majority of the legislative proposals based on the Contract passed the House of Representatives during the first one hundred days of the 104th Congress. However, very few of the Contract's proposals, including acts requiring a balanced budget, tax reforms, and term limits, passed the Senate and became law.

On some issues, however, the Republicans were able to achieve their goals. For example, before 1995, **unfunded mandates,** national laws that direct state or local governments to comply with federal rules or regulations (such as clean air or water standards) but contain no federal funding to defray the cost of meeting these requirements, absorbed nearly 30 percent of some local budgets. Republicans in Congress, loyal to the concerns of these governments, secured passage of the Unfunded Mandates Reform Act of 1995. This act prevented Congress from passing costly federal programs without debate on how to fund them and addressed a primary concern for state governments.

Another important act passed by the Republican-controlled Congress and signed into law by President Bill Clinton was the Personal Responsibility and Work Opportunity Reconciliation Act of 1996. This legislation replaced the existing welfare program, known as Aid to Families with Dependent Children (AFDC), with a program known as Temporary Assistance for Needy Families (TANF). TANF returned much of the administrative power for welfare programs to the states and became a hallmark of the devolution revolution.

In the short run, these and other programs, coupled with a growing economy, produced record federal and state budget surpluses. States were in the best fiscal shape they had been in since the 1970s. According to the National Conference of State Legislatures, total state budget surpluses in 1998 exceeded $30 billion. These tax surpluses allowed many states to increase spending, while other states offered their residents

Photo courtesy: K. M. Cannon/Nevada Appeal/AP Wide World Photos

■ Interstate speed limits pose federalism questions. The National Highway System Designation Act of 1995 allows states to set their own speed limits, reversing an earlier national law that set 55 mph as a national standard. State limits now range from 55 to 75 mph.

unfunded mandates
National laws that direct states or local governments to comply with federal rules or regulations (such as clean air or water standards) but contain little or no federal funding to defray the cost of meeting these requirements.

VISUAL LITERACY
Federalism and Regulation

Photo courtesy: Jerry S. Mendoza/AP Wide World Photos

■ Michigan Democratic Governor Jennifer Granholm heads a state hard hit by cuts in some federal programs and the loss of jobs. Granholm was reelected to a second term in 2006.

preemption
A concept derived from the Constitution's supremacy clause that allows the national government to override or preempt state or local actions in certain areas.

VIDEO ROUNDTABLE
Contemporary Federalism

steep tax cuts. Mississippi, for example, increased its per capita spending by 42.4 percent, while Alaska opted to reduce taxes by 44.2 percent.[24]

Despite these strong economic conditions, Vice President Al Gore failed to turn the success of the Clinton administration into a Gore presidency in 2000. His opponent, Texas Governor George W. Bush, campaigned on a platform of even more limited federal government, arguing that state and local governments should have extensive administrative powers over programs such as education and welfare.

FEDERALISM UNDER THE BUSH ADMINISTRATION

On the campaign trail, President George W. Bush could not have foreseen the circumstances that would surround much of his presidency. A struggling economy, terrorist attacks on the World Trade Center and the Pentagon, and the rising costs of education and welfare produced state and federal budget deficits that would have been unimaginable only a few years before.

By 2003, many state governments faced budget shortfalls of more than $30 billion. Because state governments, unlike the federal government, are required to balance their budgets, governors and legislators struggled to make ends meet. Some states raised taxes, and others cut services, including school construction and infrastructure repairs. These dramatic changes helped nearly all of the states to project surpluses—albeit small—for fiscal year 2006.

The federal government was not so lucky; it struggled with a $427 billion budget deficit in 2005. This deficit had a number of sources, including President Bush's 2001 tax cuts, spending on the war in Iraq, costs associated with the dramatic expansion of the federal government after the September 11 terrorist attacks and Hurricanes Katrina and Rita. In addition, the No Child Left Behind Act, which imposed a host of federal requirements on everything from class size to accountability testing, increased burdens on the federal coffers.

The No Child Left Behind Act was viewed by many as an unprecedented usurpation of state and local powers. However, this trend of **preemption,** or allowing the national government to override state or local actions in certain areas, is not new. The phenomenal growth of preemption statutes, laws that allow the federal government to assume partial or full responsibility for state and local governmental functions, began in 1965 during the Johnson administration. Since then, Congress routinely has used its authority under the commerce clause to preempt state laws. However, until recently, preemption statutes generally were supported by Democrats in Congress and the White House, not Republicans. The Bush administration's support of this law reflects a new era in preemption. (See Join the Debate: The No Child Left Behind Act.)

THE SUPREME COURT: A RETURN TO STATES' RIGHTS?

The role of the Supreme Court in determining the parameters of federalism cannot be underestimated. Although Congress passed sweeping New Deal legislation, it was not until the Supreme Court finally reversed itself and found those programs constitutional that any real change occurred in the federal/state relationship. From the New Deal until the 1980s, the Supreme Court's impact on the federal system generally was to expand the national government's authority at the expense of the states.

Beginning in the late 1980s, however, the Court's willingness to allow Congress to regulate in a variety of areas waned. Once Ronald Reagan was elected president, he attempted to appoint new justices committed to the notion of states' rights and to rolling back federal intervention in matters that many Republicans believed properly resided within the province of the states and not Congress or the federal courts.

Mario M. Cuomo, a former Democratic New York governor, has referred to the decisions of what he called the Reagan-Bush Court as creating "a kind of new judicial federalism." According to Cuomo, this new federalism could be characterized by the Court's withdrawal of "rights and emphases previously thought to be national."[25] Illustrative of this trend is the Supreme Court's decision in *Webster* v. *Reproductive Health Services* (1989).[26] In *Webster*, the Court first gave new latitude—and even encouragement—to the states to fashion more restrictive abortion laws. Since *Webster*, most states have enacted new restrictions on abortion, with parental consent, informed consent or waiting periods, or bans on late-term or "partial birth" abortions being the most common. (See Analyzing Visuals: State-by-State Report Card on Access to Abortion.) The Court consistently has upheld the authority of the individual states to limit a minor's access to abortion through imposition of parental consent or notification laws. Still, as discussed in chapter 5, in *Stenberg* v. *Carhart* (2000) the Supreme Court ruled that the state law limiting "partial birth" abortions without any provision to save a woman's health was unconstitutional.[27] And, in 2006, a unanimous Roberts Court ruled that states seeking to restrict minors' access to abortion must allow for some exceptions for medical emergencies.[28]

The addition of two justices by President Bill Clinton did little to stem the course of a Court bent on rebalancing the nature of the federal system. Since 1989, the Supreme Court has decided several major cases dealing with the nature of the federal system. Most of these have been 5–4 decisions and most have been decided against increased congressional power or in a manner to provide the states with greater authority over a variety of issues and policies. (See On Campus: Legislating Against Violence Against Women.) In *U.S.* v. *Lopez* (1995), which involved the conviction of a student charged with carrying a concealed handgun onto school property, a five-person majority of the Court ruled that Congress lacked constitutional authority under the commerce clause to regulate guns within 1,000 feet of a school.[29] The majority concluded that local gun control laws, even those involving schools, were a state, not a federal, matter.

One year later, again a badly divided Court ruled that Congress lacked the authority to require states to negotiate with Indian tribes about gaming.[30] The U.S. Constitution specifically gives Congress the right to deal with Indian tribes, but the Court found that Florida's **sovereign immunity** protected the state from this kind of congressional directive about how to conduct its business. In 1997, the Court decided two more major cases dealing with the scope of Congress's authority to regulate in areas historically left to the province of the states: zoning and local law enforcement. In one, a majority of the Court ruled that sections of the Religious Freedom Restoration

"I GUESS I JUST HADN'T NOTICED IT BEFORE"

SUPREME COURT OF THE VARIOUS STATES.

OVERRULING OF CONGRESS ON STATE EMPLOYEES RIGHTS

©2000 HERBLOCK

Photo courtesy: Herblock/The Herb Block Foundation

■ Since 1989, the Supreme Court has often deferred to state courts as well as judgments of the state legislatures.

sovereign immunity
The right of a state to be free from lawsuit unless it gives permission to the suit. Under the Eleventh Amendment, all states are considered sovereign.

Join the Debate

THE NO CHILD LEFT BEHIND ACT

OVERVIEW: The U.S. Constitution is silent in regard to educating American citizens. According to traditional interpretations of the Constitution, the Ninth and Tenth Amendments give the states and American people rights and powers not expressly mentioned or prohibited by the Constitution. It was the Framers' belief that the federal principle would allow for and accommodate diverse opinions regarding life, liberty, and happiness—and it was the responsibility of the individual states to educate citizens accordingly. Historically, the states have assumed this task relatively free from federal interference, but over the last fifty years, declining educational attainment, coupled with the inability of the states to address the problem, has put education policy at the forefront of domestic policy debate. To correct this problem, the No Child Left Behind Act (NCLB) was signed into law in January 2002. NCLB was a controversial piece of legislation giving the national government substantial authority over state educational establishments; several years after enactment, NCLB is still controversial.

Though many educators and politicians agree on the goals set by the No Child Left Behind Act (NCLB)—higher educational standards, greater school accountability, ensuring qualified teachers, closing the gap in student achievement—NCLB is criticized by the two major political parties, even though significant congressional majorities of both parties voted for the act. Republicans complain that NCLB impermissibly allows federal intrusion into the educational rights of states, and Democrats worry that the federal government is not providing enough funding to meet NCLB's

strict guidelines. Nevertheless, in practice, both parties seem to have switched ideological positions in regard to the federal government's role. Though the Republicans in 1996 advocated eliminating the Department of Education and reducing federal education expenditures, the Bush administration has significantly increased education funding; conversely, Democrats, who traditionally have advocated an increased federal role in education, now advocate state control (though with increased federal spending as well). Four years after NCLB was signed into law, the National Assessment of Educational Progress (or NAEP, considered the nation's report card), announced general across-the-board improvement in student achievement scores. The NAEP also reported that the achievement gap between white and minority students had narrowed. Policy makers, however, continue to debate the true effectiveness of NCLB.

In the Information Age, it is imperative that all citizens have the requisite skills to survive and thrive in the new economy. With this in mind, what is the best way to ensure a quality education for all Americans? Where does proper authority to educate children lie? How can the federal government determine the best way to educate children in a nation in which there are numerous ethnicities, religions, and cultures, all having differing views on educational priorities? However, since the federal government in part funds state educational establishments, shouldn't it have a say in how its funds are spent? And, since American educational achievement lags behind education in other advanced democracies, shouldn't school systems and teachers be held accountable, and if so, what is the best way to address this problem?

ARGUMENTS FOR THE NO CHILD LEFT BEHIND ACT

- **NCLB gives state and local school districts the flexibility to meet its requirements.** The law gives states the liberty to define standards and the means to meet and

SIMULATION

You Are a Federal Judge

Act were unconstitutional because Congress lacked the authority to meddle in local zoning regulations, even if a church was involved.[31] Another 5–4 majority ruled that Congress lacked the authority to require local law enforcement officials to conduct background checks on handgun purchasers until the federal government was able to implement a national system.[32] In 1999, in another case involving sovereign immunity, a slim majority of the Supreme Court ruled that Congress lacked the authority to change patent laws in a manner that would negatively affect a state's right to assert its immunity from lawsuits.[33]

While it looked as if the Rehnquist Court (1986–2005) was well on its way to supporting Congress's devolution revolution, many commentators now question

measure them. As long as NCLB guidelines are met, the states may innovate, educate, and test according to their needs.

- **NCLB is not an unfunded mandate.** The Government Accountability Office has ruled that NCLB does not meet the description of an unfunded mandate as defined by the 1995 Unfunded Mandates Reform Act, primarily because state school systems have the option of accepting or rejecting NCLB funding. Federal spending accounts for only 8 percent of all educational expenditures in the United States.
- **NCLB represents federal responsiveness to the needs of parents with children in public schools.** Not only have the states failed to meet the guidelines set forth by various federal policy initiatives, but they have failed the expectations of parents as well. For example, Goals 2000 (1994) mandated a 90 percent high school graduation rate by 2000 and a number one rank in math and science for American students internationally. By 2000, the graduation rate was only 75 percent and American students ranked not first but nineteenth in math and eighteenth in science.

ARGUMENTS AGAINST THE NO CHILD LEFT BEHIND ACT

- **NCLB requirements force school districts to teach to the test.** Rather than teaching analytical and creative thinking, the testing requirements force school districts to have students cram for the exam, thus undermining the primary goal of a true education.
- **NCLB does not distinguish between disabled and non-English-speaking students and those students proficient in English.** A primary problem with NCLB is that it combines all students, regardless of their language level

or other core educational proficiencies. This is an unfair burden on educators in school systems with a disproportionate number of disabled or non-English-speaking students, as NCLB's punitive sections assume a homogenous, English-speaking student body.

- **NCLB should be considered an impermissible intrusion on the prerogatives of state educational establishments.** A primary concern of the Framers was excessive federal control over state policy. NCLB erodes the line separating federal and state authority. If school systems are not addressing the concerns of parents and educational problems, it is the proper duty of the states to address these issues. Federal educational spending has increased dramatically since the passage of NCLB, and many believe this gives the federal government too much control over a traditional state policy domain.

QUESTIONS

1. Does NCLB place too many guidelines on state educational establishments? If so, what is the best way to ensure higher standards and school accountability?
2. Does NCLB give the federal government too much authority over a policy domain that has traditionally belonged to the states? Since school districts reflect local mores and attitudes, are students best educated based on local guidelines?

SELECTED READINGS

Hess, Frederick M., and Michael J. Petrilli. *No Child Left Behind.* New York: Peter Lang, 2006.

Peterson, Paul E., and Martin R. West, eds. *No Child Left Behind? The Politics and Practice of School Accountability.* Washington, DC: Brookings Institution, 2003.

what was really happening. The addition of two new justices, Chief Justice John G. Roberts Jr. and Associate Justice Samuel A. Alito Jr., makes the future direction of the Court less certain. As *New York Times* Supreme Court reporter Linda Greenhouse once noted, "a hallmark of the Rehnquist Court has been a re-examination of the country's most basic constitutional arrangements, resulting in decisions that demanded a new respect for the sovereignty of the states and placed corresponding restrictions on the powers of Congress."[34] A careful analysis of Figure 3.5 demonstrates this point. During the 2002–2003 term, however, the Court took an unexpected turn in its federalism devolution revolution.[35] In a case opening states to lawsuits for alleged violations of the federal Family and Medical Leave Act

PARTICIPATION

Is Federalism Dead and Should It Be?

Analyzing Visuals

STATE-BY-STATE REPORT CARD ON ACCESS TO ABORTION

A liberal interest group, NARAL Pro-Choice America, rates each state and the District of Columbia in fourteen categories related to abortion access, bans on late-term or "partial birth" abortion procedures, counseling, clinic violence, the length of waiting periods, access for minors, and public funding, which it then translates into grades. NARAL gives an A only to states it evaluates as pro-choice on every issue on its agenda. After studying the map, answer the following critical think-

ing questions: What do the states that receive A's have in common? How might factors such as political culture, geography, and social characteristics of the population influence a state's laws concerning abortion? If a group that opposes abortion, such as the National Right to Life Committee, were to grade the states, would its ratings include the same categories or factors? Explain your answer. See Analyzing Visuals: A Brief Guide for additional guidance in analyzing maps.

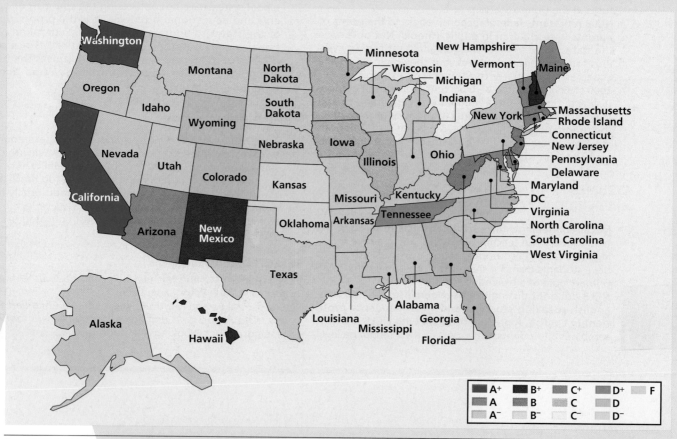

Legend: A+ B+ C+ D+ F / A B C D / A− B− C− D−

Source: NARAL Pro-Choice America/NARAL Foundation, "Who Decides? A State-by-State Review of Abortion and Reproductive Rights, 2006," http://www. prochoiceamerica.org. Reprinted by permission.

(FMLA), writing for a six-person majority, Chief Justice William H. Rehnquist rejected Nevada's claim that it was immune from suit under FMLA. Rehnquist noted that the law was an appropriate exercise of Congress's power to combat sex-role stereotypes about the domestic responsibilities of female workers and "thereby dismantle persisting gender-based barriers that women faced in the workplace."[36] And, in 2005, the Court upheld the power of Congress to prohibit states from allowing the use of medical marijuana.[37] But, as also is reflected in Figure 3.5, the Roberts Court's first decision involving federalism limited the federal government's right to block Oregon's physician assisted suicide law.[38]

FIGURE 3.4 THE REHNQUIST AND ROBERTS COURTS AND FEDERALISM

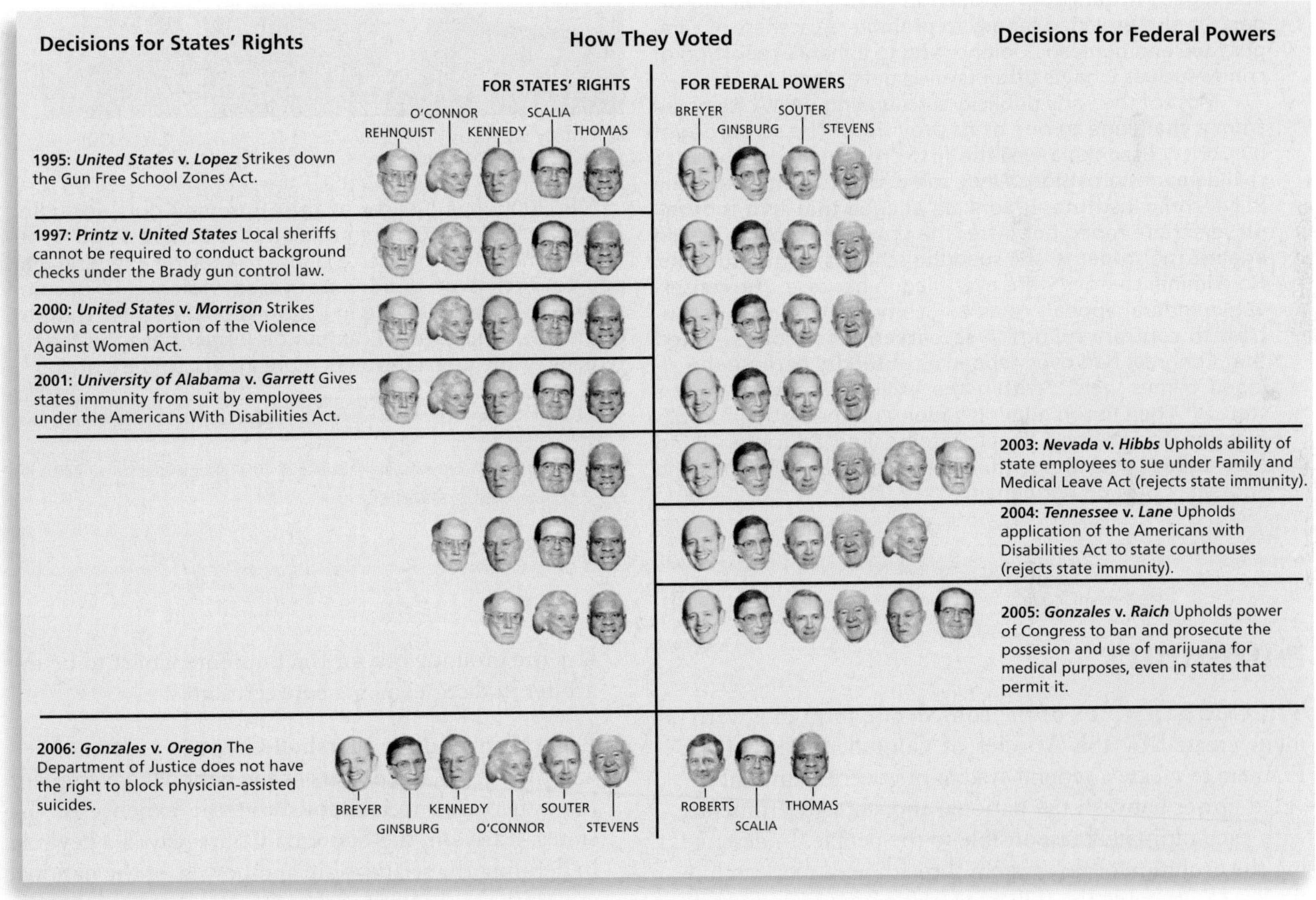

Decisions for States' Rights	How They Voted	Decisions for Federal Powers

FOR STATES' RIGHTS — REHNQUIST, O'CONNOR, KENNEDY, SCALIA, THOMAS

FOR FEDERAL POWERS — BREYER, GINSBURG, SOUTER, STEVENS

1995: *United States v. Lopez* Strikes down the Gun Free School Zones Act.

1997: *Printz v. United States* Local sheriffs cannot be required to conduct background checks under the Brady gun control law.

2000: *United States v. Morrison* Strikes down a central portion of the Violence Against Women Act.

2001: *University of Alabama v. Garrett* Gives states immunity from suit by employees under the Americans With Disabilities Act.

2003: *Nevada v. Hibbs* Upholds ability of state employees to sue under Family and Medical Leave Act (rejects state immunity).

2004: *Tennessee v. Lane* Upholds application of the Americans with Disabilities Act to state courthouses (rejects state immunity).

2005: *Gonzales v. Raich* Upholds power of Congress to ban and prosecute the possesion and use of marijuana for medical purposes, even in states that permit it.

2006: *Gonzales v. Oregon* The Department of Justice does not have the right to block physician-assisted suicides.

BREYER, GINSBURG, KENNEDY, O'CONNOR, SOUTER, STEVENS

ROBERTS, SCALIA, THOMAS

Source: New York Times (June 12, 2005): 3; *New York Times* (July 2, 2006): A18; Legal Information Institute at Cornell University Law School.

On Campus

LEGISLATING AGAINST VIOLENCE AGAINST WOMEN: A CASUALTY OF THE DEVOLUTION REVOLUTION?

As originally enacted in 1994, the Violence Against Women Act (VAWA) allowed women to file civil lawsuits in federal court if they could prove that they were the victims of rape, domestic violence, or other crimes motivated by gender. VAWA was widely praised as an effective mechanism to combat domestic violence. In its first five years, $1.6 million was allocated for states and local governments to pay for a variety of programs, including a national toll-free hotline for victims of violence that averages 13,000 calls per month, funding for special police sex crime units, and civil and legal assistance for women in need of restraining orders.[a] It also provided money to promote awareness of campus rape and domestic violence and to enhance reporting of crimes such as what is often termed date rape.

Most of the early publicity surrounding VAWA stemmed from a challenge to one of its provisions. The suit brought by Christy Brzonkala was the first brought under the act's civil damages provision. While she was a student at Virginia Polytechnic Institute, Brzonkala alleged that two football players there raped her. After the university took no action against the students, she sued the school and the students. No criminal charges were ever filed in her case. The conservative federal appeals court in Richmond, Virginia—in contrast to contrary rulings in seventeen other courts—ruled that Congress had overstepped its authority because the alleged crimes were "within the exclusive purview of the states."[b] The Clinton administration and the National Organization for Women Legal Defense and Education Fund (now called Legal Momentum) appealed that decision to the Supreme Court on her behalf.

Photo courtesy: Cindy Pinkston

■ Christy Brzonkala, the petitioner in *U.S. v. Morrison* (2000).

In 2000, five justices of the Supreme Court, including Justice Sandra Day O'Connor, ruled that Congress had no authority under the commerce clause to provide a federal remedy to victims of gender-motivated violence, a decision viewed as greatly reining in congressional power.[c] Thus, today, students abused on campus no longer have this federal remedy as the Court devolves more power to the states.

[a]Juliet Eilperin, "Reauthorization of Domestic Violence Act Is at Risk," *Washington Post* (September 13, 2000): A6.

[b]Tony Mauro, "Court Will Review Laws of Protection," *USA Today* (September 29, 1999): 4A.

[c]*U.S. v. Morrison*, 529 U.S. 598 (2000).

Summary

THE INADEQUACIES of the confederate form of government created by the Articles of Confederation led the Framers to create a federal system of government that divided power between the national and state governments, with each ultimately responsible to the people. In describing the evolution of this system throughout American history, we have made the following points:

1. The Origins of the Federal System: Governmental Powers Under the Constitution

The national and state governments have both enumerated and implied powers under the Constitution. The national and state governments share some concurrent powers. Other powers are expressly denied to both governments, although the national government is ultimately declared supreme. The Constitution also lays the groundwork for the Supreme Court to be the arbiter in disagreements between states.

2. Federalism and the Marshall Court

Over the years, the powers of the national government have increased tremendously at the expense of the states. Early on, the Supreme Court played a key role in defining the relationship and powers of the national government through its broad interpretations of the supremacy and commerce clauses.

3. Dual Federalism: The Taney Court, Slavery, and the Civil War

For many years, dual federalism, as articulated by the Taney Court, tended to limit the national government's authority in areas such as slavery and civil rights, and was the norm in relations between the national and state governments. However, the beginnings of a departure from this view became evident with the ratification of the Sixteenth and Seventeenth Amendments in 1913.

4. Cooperative Federalism: The New Deal and the Growth of National Government

The notion of a limited federal government ultimately fell by the wayside in the wake of the Great Depression and Franklin D. Roosevelt's New Deal. This growth in the size and role of the federal government escalated during the Lyndon B. Johnson administration and into the mid to late 1970s. Federal grants became popular solutions for a host of state and local problems.

5. New Federalism: Returning Power to the States?

After his election in 1980, Ronald Reagan tried to shrink the size and powers of the federal government through what he termed New Federalism. This trend continued through the 1990s, most notably through a campaign document known as the Contract with America. Initially, the George W. Bush administration seemed committed to this devolution, but the September 11 terrorist attacks led to substantial growth in the size of the federal government.

KEY TERMS

bill of attainder, p. 102
block grant, p. 112
categorical grant, p. 110
concurrent powers, p. 101
confederation, p. 97
cooperative federalism, p. 110
dual federalism, p. 106
enumerated powers, p. 98
ex post facto law, p. 102
extradition clause, p. 103
federal system, p. 97
full faith and credit clause, p. 103
Gibbons v. *Ogden* (1824), p. 105
implied powers, p. 99
interstate compacts, p. 103
McCulloch v. *Maryland* (1819), p. 104
necessary and proper clause, p. 98
New Federalism, p. 111
preemption, p. 114
privileges and immunities clause, p. 103
reserve (or police) powers, p. 101
Seventeenth Amendment, p. 107
Sixteenth Amendment, p. 107
sovereign immunity, p. 115
supremacy clause, p. 99
Tenth Amendment, p. 101

unfunded mandates, p. 113
unitary system, p. 97

SELECTED READINGS

Bowman, Ann O'M., and Richard C. Kearney. *State and Local Government*, 6th ed. Boston: Houghton Mifflin, 2005.

Campbell, Tom. *Separation of Powers in Practice.* Stanford, CA: Stanford University Press, 2004.

Derthick, Martha. *The Influence of Federal Grants.* Cambridge, MA: Harvard University Press, 1970.

Elazar, Daniel J., and John Kincaid, eds. *The Covenant Connection: From Federal Theology to Modern Federalism.* Lexington, MA: Lexington Books, 2000.

Finegold, Kenneth, and Theda Skocpol. *State and Party in America's New Deal.* Madison: University of Wisconsin Press, 1995.

Grodzins, Morton. *The American System: A View of Government in the United States.* Chicago: Rand McNally, 1966.

Kincaid, John. *The Encyclopedia of American Federalism.* Washington, DC: CQ Press, 2005.

McCabe, Neil Colman, ed. *Comparative Federalism in the Devolution Era.* Lanham, MD: Rowman and Littlefield, 2003.

Nagel, Robert F. *The Implosion of American Federalism.* New York: Oxford University Press, 2002.

Stephens, G. Ross, and Nelson Wikstrom. *American Intergovernmental Relations: A Fragmented Federal Polity.* New York: Oxford University Press, 2006.

Zimmerman, Joseph F. *Interstate Cooperation: Compacts and Administrative Agreements.* New York: Praeger, 2002.

WEB EXPLORATIONS

For a directory of federalism links, see
http://govinfo.library.unt.edu/amcouncil/federalism.html
For more on your state and local governments, see
http://www.statelocalgov.net/
For scholarly works on federalism, see
http://www.temple.edu/federalism and
http://www.cato.org/pubs/ and
http://www.urban.org
For perspectives on the federal system, see
http://www.usembassy.beusa/usapolitical.htm
For more information on interstate compacts, see
http://ssl.csg.org/compactlaws/comlistlinks.html
For the full text of *McCulloch* v. *Maryland* (1819), see
http://www.landmarkcases.org/mcculloch/home.html
For the full text of *Gibbons* v. *Ogden* (1824), see
http://www.landmarkcases.org/gibbons/legacy.html
For more information on the Great Depression, see
http://newdeal.feri.org/
For more on the devolution revolution, see
http://www.brookings.edu/comm/policybriefs/pb03.htm
To analyze where your state stands relative to other states, see
http://www.taxfoundation.org/statefinance.html
For more information on state abortion restrictions, see
http://www.prochoiceamerica.org/ or
http://www.NRLC.org

STATE AND LOCAL GOVERNMENT

4

ELIOT SPITZER WON THE NEW YORK GOVERNOR'S RACE in November 2006 with 68.9 percent of the votes cast—the largest margin of victory in the state's history. As Attorney General of New York, Spitzer waged a visible and effective war against unethical corporate behavior on Wall Street and vowed to make New York state government cleaner and better. Spitzer's victory ended 12 years of Republican occupancy of the governor's mansion.

New York voters generally favored Democrats in the 2006 midterm elections. They objected to scandals in Washington, as well as on Wall Street, and most of all, they expressed disapproval of President George W. Bush and the war in Iraq. Republicans lost three Congressional seats to Democrats and narrowly held on to another three. U.S. Senator Hillary Clinton easily won re-election to a second term, defeating her Republican opponent 66.5 percent to 31.4 percent.

New York was not the only state demanding change in 2006. Democrats took control of the U.S. Congress, the U.S. Senate, the majority of gubernatorial offices, and the majority of state legislatures. It was the largest sweep of party victories since the Republicans took control of Congress and state governments in 1994. Going into the elections, there was parity in party control of state governments. After the votes were counted, Democrats held 28 gubernatorial offices and controlled legislatures in 23 states, compared to 16 state legislatures under Republican control. Ten states have split party control and Nebraska's single legislative chamber is nonpartisan.

In some states, there were local scandals that also fueled the mood for change. A series of state-level political scandals, as well as the economy, affected voting in Ohio, for example. While local factors and the characteristics of individual candidates are always important, however, the Democratic victories in the fall of 2006 were heavily influenced by a national mood. Public opinion polls as well as campaign speeches clearly demonstrated national discontent. A common and effective strategy of Democrats at all levels of government was to link their Republican opponent to the President, the Iraq War and to national scandals.

Party control in state governments have national as well as local implications. State governments draw the boundaries for congressional as well as state legislative districts. As the 2010 census approaches, state governments

CHAPTER OUTLINE

- ✪ The Evolution of State and Local Governments
- ✪ State Governments
- ✪ Local Governments
- ✪ Grassroots Power and Politics
- ✪ Relations with Indian Nations
- ✪ State and Local Finances

123

can be expected to draw these boundaries in ways that bring advantage to the parties in control.

Presidential elections are also affected by what happens in the states. Governors have long been a source of presidential candidates. Two-term Iowa governor Tom Vilsack announced his intention to run for president in 2008 shortly after the 2006 elections, while Governor Mitt Romney of Massachusetts and Governor Bill Richardson of New Mexico are also likely candidates for the 2008 race. Moreover, potential presidential candidates drawn from Congress, including Senator John McCain (R–AZ), Senator Hillary Clinton (D–NY), and Senator Barack Obama (D–IL), help get governors elected as a way of building their own bases of support.

Likewise, in states where voters can put an issue on the ballot and get a proposal enacted into law, the outcomes can extend to other states and to the country as a whole. In 2006, for example, six states approved initiatives to increase the minimum wage. They joined 22 states that had already enacted minimum wage increases and helped catapult this issue to the top of the agenda for the newly elected Democratic majorities in the U.S. Senate and House of Representatives. State politics affect national politics, just as surely as national politics affect state politics. And changes in a number of state policies often serve as a signal to Congress that they need to act at the national level.

STATE AND LOCAL politics plays a critical role in the governance of our country. Widespread Democratic victories at the state level in 2006 are likely to have significant repercussions for national policies, as well as the 2008 presidential election. State and local government, moreover, is crucial to the health, safety, and security of the American people. State and local officials—on their own and at times in partnership with the federal government—educate our children, maintain law and order, care for those in need, clean and maintain the streets, license healthcare, legal, and other professionals, and generally provide for many of the basic services and structures we rely on.

This chapter will present the basic patterns and principles of state and local governance so that you may readily understand how public policies in your community are made and applied.

- First, we will review *the evolution of state and local governments*.
- Second, we will describe the major institutions of *state governments*, including trends in state elections.
- Third, we will examine the different types of *local governments* and explain the bases for their authority as well as the special traits of their institutions.
- Fourth, we will identify the nature of *grassroots power and politics*.
- Fifth, we will discuss federal and state government *relations with Indian nations*.
- Finally, we will explain the budgeting process for *state and local finances*.

The Evolution of State and Local Governments

AS POINTED OUT IN CHAPTER 3, the basic, original unit of government in this country was the state. The thirteen colonial governments became thirteen state governments, and their constitutions preceded the U.S. Constitution. The states initially were loosely tied together in the Articles of Confederation but then formed a closer union and more powerful national government.

State governments, likewise, determined the existence of local governments. As we will later discuss in more detail, in some cases—such as counties and, for most states, school districts—state laws *create* local governments. In others, such as towns and cities, states *recognize* and *authorize* local governments in response to petitions from citizens.

In other words, although the power of governments at all levels is derived from the people, governmental institutions in the United States are not built from the bottom. Local towns, villages, school districts, and similar smaller units do not form states that then form the United States. Instead, states are the basic units that on the one hand establish local governments and on the other hand are the building blocks of the federal government.

In the past, state and local governments were primarily part-time governments. Initially, almost all state and local elected officials were part-time. Except for governors and a handful of big-city mayors, people in office were farmers, teachers, lawyers, and shop owners who did public service during their spare time. This was true as well for many judges and local government bureaucrats.

As the responsibilities and challenges of government grew, more state and local jobs became full-time. Increases in the need for urban services led to more full-time local governments. Despite this trend, states with high levels of urbanization did not always have governments that responded to the specific needs of urban populations. The boundaries of districts from which state legislators got elected did not change in response to population shifts in the post–Civil War period. As a result, state legislatures did not represent the character of their respective states. One legislator from a rural area might represent 50,000 people, whereas a legislator from an urban setting might represent as many as 500,000 constituents. Such a pattern led to low priority for urban needs.

This kind of misrepresentation remained in place until the 1960s. The ruling by the U.S. Supreme Court in *Baker* v. *Carr* (1962) became a watershed in the evolution of state and local governments. The Court applied the Fourteenth Amendment of the U.S. Constitution and decreed that equal protection and the **one-person, one-vote** principles required that there be the same number of people in each of the legislative districts within a single state. As a result, state legislatures became more representative, and the agendas of state governments became much more relevant to the needs of all constituents.

one-person, one-vote
The principle that each legislative district within a state should have the same number of eligible voters so that representation is equitably based on population.

The 1960s and 1970s were a period in which the federal government added to the responsibilities of state and local governments. Federal programs to combat poverty, revitalize urban areas, and protect the environment were designed to be administered by state and local officials rather than federal agencies. With these programs came federal assistance and sometimes mandates to improve the capacities and the efficiency of subnational governments.

Since the 1970s, some trends in federalism have enhanced the importance of state and local governments while others have expanded the scope of the federal government. Conscious efforts since the Nixon administration were made to reverse the aggregation of power and authority in Washington, D.C. In part, this was philosophical, but it was also necessary. During the Reagan administration, the debt of the federal government more than tripled, and the flow of federal money and mandates that fueled much of the growth of state and local governments was reduced.

But, as noted in chapter 3, not all recent developments have enhanced the powers of state and local governments. In 2002, President George W. Bush signed a law that allows the federal government to force state and local authorities to turn over public schools to private businesses to manage if the schools are considered failing. In response to the terrorist attacks of September 11, 2001, the federal government expanded its role in domestic security, traditionally the responsibility of state and local police and public health officials.

Despite the conflicting messages, it is still clear that state and local governments have roles and responsibilities of increasing importance. For the most part, the political leaders of these jurisdictions relish these developments. Some states and cities, for example, are taking bold initiatives and even establishing direct ties with foreign countries in order to spur economic growth.[1] Others, especially in smaller and medium-sized communities, are overwhelmed with all there is to do.

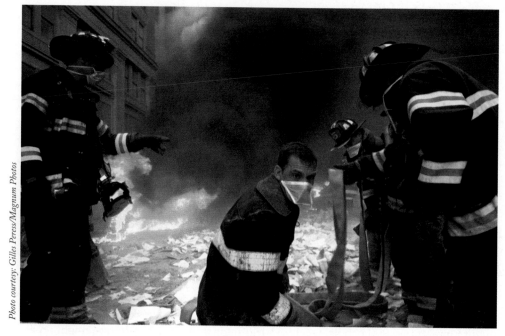

Photo courtesy: Gilles Peress/Magnum Photos

■ The heroic work of New York City firefighters and rescue workers in response to the 9/11 terrorist attacks was a vivid reminder of the importance of state and local governments. We depend heavily on state and local agencies for our safety and for services that affect our daily living.

PARTICIPATION

Explore Your
State
Constitution

state constitution
The document that describes the basic policies, procedures, and institutions of the government of a specific state, much as the U.S. Constitution does for the federal government.

State Governments

STATE GOVERNMENTS have primary responsibility for education, public health, transportation, economic development, and criminal justice. The state is also the unit of government that licenses and regulates various professions, such as doctors, lawyers, barbers, and architects. More recently, state governments have been active in welfare and the environment, in part as agents administering federal policies and programs and in part on their own. (For some of the tensions that exist between the federal and state governments, see The Living Constitution: Eleventh Amendment.)

STATE CONSTITUTIONS

Whereas a major goal of the writers of the U.S. Constitution in 1787 was to *empower* the national government, the authors of the original **state constitutions** wanted to *limit* government. The Constitutional Convention in Philadelphia was convened, as you recall from chapter 2, because of the perception that the national government under the Articles of Confederation was not strong enough. The debates were primarily over how strong the national, or federal, government should be.

In contrast, the assumption of the authors of the first thirteen state constitutions, based on their backgrounds in the philosophy and experiences of monarchical rule, was that government should not be all-powerful, and so the question was how to limit it. The state constitutions were written and adopted before the Constitutional Convention and included provisions that government may not interfere with basic individual liberties. Although these provisions were integral parts of each of the state constitutions, they were added to the federal constitution as the first ten amendments: the Bill of Rights.

The first state constitutions provided for the major institutions of government, such as executives (the governors), legislatures, and courts, with an emphasis on limiting the authority of each institution.[2] The office of governor was designed to be particularly weak. The most powerful institution was each state's legislature. These constitutions did not, moreover, fully embrace the principle of checks and balances that is found in the U.S. Constitution. For example, initially only South Carolina, New York, and Massachusetts gave their governors the authority to veto legislation.

The Living Constitution

The Judicial Power of the United States shall not be construed to extend to any suit in law or equity, commenced or prosecuted against one of the United States by Citizens of another State, or by Citizens or Subjects of any foreign State.

—ELEVENTH AMENDMENT

The Eleventh Amendment to the U.S. Constitution has been interpreted to grant the several states *sovereign immunity;* that is, a state cannot be sued in federal or state court without its consent. This amendment further defines the distribution of authority between federal and state governments, and it has been construed to give the states protection from the encroachment of federal power.

The Eleventh Amendment was a response to the angry public outcry regarding the Supreme Court's decision in *Chisholm* v. *Georgia* (1793)—a decision in which the Court held that the Judiciary Act of 1789 gave it original jurisdiction in cases regarding suits between states and citizens of other states. The *Chisholm* decision was not only widely regarded as being an untenable intrusion on state authority, but it was also considered a confirmation of Anti-Federalist fears that such a reading of Article III would "prove most pernicious and destructive" to states' rights.

The amendment was proposed at the very first meeting of Congress following the *Chisholm* decision in March 1794, and it was consequently ratified with "vehement speed" by February 1795. Interpretation of the Eleventh Amendment has subsequently been subject to inconsistent and obscure construction, and it has been a source of considerable dispute for constitutional scholars. Beginning with the New Deal, however, the federal government began to use the commerce clause to considerably expand its authority; the result was the increasing centralization and importance of the national government at the expense of substantial state power.

The Eleventh Amendment has received mounting scrutiny over the last decade because of the Rehnquist Court's use of the amendment to return numerous powers to the states, and thus to alter fundamentally the relationship the states have had with the federal government for over half a century. The trend of the increasingly conservative Court has been to reestablish a strong state sovereignty within the federal system.

The first state constitutions set the pattern for what was to come. In one of its last actions, the national congress under the Articles of Confederation passed the Northwest Ordinance of 1787, which addressed how new states might join the union. Lawmakers were responding primarily to settlers in what is now Ohio, but they extended coverage to the territory that includes Wisconsin, Illinois, Michigan, and Indiana—which the people in the original thirteen states considered the "northwest." The basic blueprint included in the ordinance was that a territory might successfully petition for statehood if it had at least 60,000 free inhabitants (slaves and American Indians did

**Explaining
Differences in
State Laws**

political machine
An organization designed to solicit votes from certain neighborhoods or communities for a particular political party in return for services and jobs if that party wins.

Progressive movement
Advocated measures to destroy political machines and instead have direct participation by voters in the nomination of candidates and the establishment of public policy.

**You Are
Attempting to
Revise the
California State
Constitution**

not count) and a constitution that was both similar to the documents of existing states and compatible with the national constitution. The first white settlers in the territory covered by the Northwest Ordinance were primarily from New York and Massachusetts. Not surprisingly, the initial constitutions of these states were almost identical to those of New York and Massachusetts.[3]

The Civil War had a profound impact on the constitutions of southern states. Southern states adopted new constitutions when they seceded and formed the Confederacy. After the Civil War, they had to adopt new constitutions acceptable to the Republican-controlled Congress in Washington, D.C. These Reconstruction-era constitutions typically provided former slaves with considerable power and disenfranchised those who had been active in the Confederacy. Because they divorced political power from economic wealth and social status and formal authority from informal influence, these were not workable constitutions. White communities simply ignored government and ruled themselves informally as much as possible. After less than ten years, whites reasserted political control and rewrote state constitutions.

The new documents reflected white distrust of government control and provided for a narrow scope of authority for state governments. Governors could serve for only two-year terms. Legislatures could meet for only short periods of time and in some cases only once every other year. Law enforcement authority, both police and justices of the peace, rested squarely in local community power structures.

Western states entered the union with constitutions that also envisioned weak governments. Here the central concern was to avoid the development of **political machines,** organizations that solicit votes from certain neighborhoods or communities for a particular political party in return for services and jobs if that party wins. (Political machines are discussed more fully later in the chapter.) In large cities in the Northeast and Midwest, machines based on bloc voting by new immigrants wrested political control from traditional elites. New states in the West sought to keep machine politics from ever getting started in the first place.

The most effective national anti-machine effort was the **Progressive movement,** led by such figures as Woodrow Wilson, Theodore Roosevelt, and Robert M. La Follette, who advocated changes that involved direct voter participation and bypassed traditional institutions.[4] These reforms included the use of primaries for nominating candidates instead of closed party processes, the initiative for allowing voters to enact laws directly rather than go through legislatures and governors, and the recall for constituents to remove officials from office in the middle of a term. Progressives succeeded in getting their proposals adopted as statutes in existing states and in the constitutions of new states emerging from western territories. In California, progressive reforms allowed state residents to recall their governor, Gray Davis, in 2003 and replace him with movie star Arnold Schwarzenegger. Schwarzenegger ran for reelection in 2006 and won handily against challenger Phil Angelides, the State Treasurer.

Though weak state government institutions may have been a reasonable response to earlier concerns, the trend since the 1960s, throughout the United States, has been to amend state constitutions in order to enhance the ability of governors, legislatures, and courts to address problems. In the 1970s alone, over 300 amendments to state constitutions were adopted. Most were to lengthen the terms of governors and provide chief executives with more authority over spending and administration, to streamline courts, and to make legislatures professional and full-time.[5]

Constitutional changes have also reflected some ambivalence. While there has been widespread recognition that state governments must be more capable, there is also concern about what that might mean in taxes and in the entrenchment of power. Thus, reforms have included severe restrictions on the ability of state and local governments to raise taxes and limits on how long legislators in some states may serve. Historic distrust of a powerful government continues.

Compared with the U.S. Constitution, state constitutions are relatively easy to amend. Every state allows for the convening of a constitutional convention, and over

200 have been held. Also, every state has a process whereby the legislature can pass an amendment to the constitution, usually by a two-thirds or three-fourths vote, and then submit the change to the voters for their approval in a referendum. Seventeen states, mostly in the West, allow for amendments simply by getting the proposal on a statewide ballot, without involvement of the legislature or governor.

An implication of the relatively simple amendment processes is frequent changes. All but nineteen states have adopted wholly new constitutions since they were first admitted to the union, and almost 6,000 specific amendments have been adopted. Another effect of the process is that state constitutions tend to be longer than the U.S. Constitution and include provisions that more appropriately should be statutes or administrative rules. The California constitution, for example, not only establishes state government institutions and protects individual rights but also defines how long a wrestling match may be. Florida's constitution stipulates that it is a misdemeanor to confine a pregnant pig.

GOVERNORS

Governors have always been the most visible elected officials in state governments. Initially, that visibility supported the ceremonial role of governors as their primary function. Now that visibility serves governors as they set the agenda and provide leadership for others in state governments. (Figure 4.1 shows the party affiliations of governors in the fifty states.)

The most important role that current governors play is in identifying the most pressing problems facing their respective states and proposing solutions to those problems. Governors first establish agendas when they campaign for office. After inauguration, the most effective way for the chief executive to initiate policy changes is when submitting the budget for legislative approval.

Budgets are critical to the business of state governments. How money is raised and spent says a lot about the priorities of decision makers. Until the 1920s, state legislatures commonly compiled and passed budgets and then submitted them for gubernatorial approval or veto. As part of the efforts since the 1960s to strengthen the effectiveness of state governments, governors were, like presidents, given the major responsibility for starting the budget process. Now nearly all states have their governors propose budgets.

The role of governor as budget initiator is especially important when coupled with the governor's veto authority and executive responsibilities. Like presidents, governors have **package** or **general veto** authority, which is the power to reject a bill in its entirety. In addition, governors in all but seven states may exercise a **line-item veto** on bills that involve spending or taxing. A line-item veto strikes only part of a bill that has been passed by the legislature. It allows a chief executive to delete a particular program or expenditure from a budget bill and let the remaining provisions become law. The intent of this authority is to enable governors to revise the work of legislators in order to produce a balanced budget.

When Tommy Thompson, U.S. secretary of health and human services from 2001 to 2004, was governor of Wisconsin, he was the most extensive and creative user of the line-item veto. He reversed the intent of legislation by vetoing the word "not" in a sentence and created entirely new laws by eliminating specific letters and numerals to make new words and numbers. Voters in Wisconsin were so upset with this free use of the veto pen that in 1993 they passed the "Vanna White amendment" to the state constitution, prohibiting the governor from striking letters within words and numerals within numbers. Not to be outmaneuvered, Governor Thompson then used his veto authority to actually *insert* numbers in bills that had passed the legislature. The

Photo courtesy: Wisconsin Historical Society

■ Wisconsin's Robert M. La Follette, a Republican, championed Progressive reforms both as governor from 1901 to 1906 and as a U.S. senator for nearly twenty years.

governor
Chief elected executive in state government.

package or general veto
The authority of a chief executive to void an entire bill that has been passed by the legislature. This veto applies to all bills, whether or not they have taxing or spending components, and the legislature may override this veto, usually with a two-thirds majority of each chamber.

line-item veto
The authority of a chief executive to delete part of a bill passed by the legislature that involves taxing or spending. The legislature may override a veto, usually with a two-thirds majority of each chamber.

FIGURE 4.1 POLITICAL PARTY OF STATE GOVERNORS, 2007
Democrats picked up six governorships in the 2006 midterm elections and now
control the corner offices in twenty-eight states.

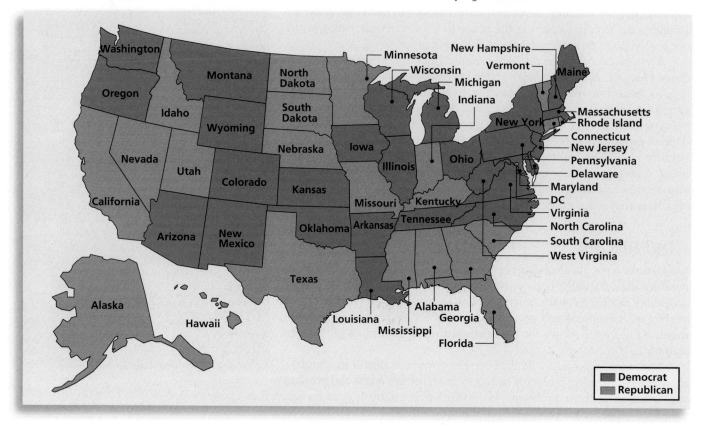

Source: National Council of State Legislatures, http://www.ncsl.org, and updates by the authors.

Wisconsin state supreme court, in 1995, upheld this interpretation of veto, as long as
the net effect of the vetoes was not to increase spending.

While the Wisconsin case is extreme, it illustrates the significant power that veto
authority can provide. Legislators can override vetoes, usually with a two-thirds vote
in each of the chambers, but this rarely happens. Only 6 percent of gubernatorial vetoes are overturned.[6]

The executive responsibilities of governors provide an opportunity to affect public
policies after laws have been passed. Agencies are responsible for implementing the
laws. That may mean improving a road, enforcing a regulation, or providing a service.
The speed and care with which implementation occurs are often under the influence
of the governor.[7] Likewise, governors can affect the many details and interpretations
that must be decided. State statutes require drivers of vehicles to have a license, but
they typically let an agency decide exactly what one must do to get a license, where
one can take the tests, and what happens if someone fails a test. Governors can influence these kinds of decisions primarily through appointing the heads of state administrative agencies.

One of the methods of limiting gubernatorial power is to curtail appointment authority.[8] Unlike the federal government, for example, states have some major agencies
headed by individuals who are elected rather than appointed by the chief executive.
Forty-three states, for example, elect their attorney general, secretary of state, treasurer, and auditor. Some states elect their head of education, agriculture, or labor. The
movement throughout states to strengthen the institutions of their governments has

included increasing the number of senior positions that are filled by gubernatorial appointments so that governors, like heads of major corporations, can assemble their own policy and management teams.

Another position that is filled by presidential appointment in the federal government but elected in most state governments is judge. This is one more example of approaches that have been taken to restrict the authority of governors. Nonetheless, governors are major actors in the judicial system. With the legislature, they define what a crime within a state is and attach penalties that should be meted out to those convicted of committing crimes. After being convicted, a person will be institutionalized or supervised by an agency that is, in every state, headed by a gubernatorial appointment. Moreover, governors have authority to grant a **pardon** to someone who has been convicted, thereby eliminating all penalties and voiding the court action on an individual's record. Governors may also **commute** all or part of a sentence, which leaves the conviction on record even though the penalty is reduced. In addition, governors grant **parole** to prisoners who have served part of their terms. Typically, governors are advised by a parole board on whether or not to grant a parole.

Finally, under the U.S. Constitution, governors have the discretion to **extradite** individuals. This means that a governor may decide to send someone, against his or her will, to another state to face criminal charges. When Mario Cuomo, who opposed the death penalty, was governor of New York, he refused an extradition request from a state that used capital punishment. That refusal became an issue in Cuomo's unsuccessful bid for reelection in 1994. The newly elected governor, George Pataki, ordered the extradition shortly after he was inaugurated. In fact, with the support of Governor Pataki, New York adopted the death penalty, although the state supreme court ruled that the law was unconstitutional.

Gubernatorial participation in the judicial process has led to some of the most colorful controversies in state politics. James E. Ferguson, as governor of Texas, granted 2,253 pardons between 1915 and 1917. His successor, William P. Hobby, granted 1,518 during the next two years, and then Governor Miriam "Ma" Ferguson outdid her husband by issuing almost 3,800 during her term. Texans were used to shady wheeling and dealing in politics, but this volume of pardons seemed a bit excessive. The Texas constitution was amended to remove authority to grant pardons and paroles from the governor; this power was placed in the hands of a board. Governors of the Lone Star State now have the lowest amount of authority among the fifty state chief executives to check actions of the judiciary.[9]

The general trend since the 1960s has been an increase rather than decrease in the power and authority of governors.[10] This enhancement of gubernatorial powers has come at the cost of the prerogatives of other institutions, especially state legislatures.

STATE LEGISLATURES

The principles of representative democracy are embodied primarily in the legislature. Legislatures, as mentioned above, were initially established to be the most powerful of the institutions of state government. In over half of the original states, legislatures began without the check of a gubernatorial veto. Until the twentieth century, most state legislatures were responsible for executive chores such as formulating a budget and making administrative appointments.

These tasks were, even more than was envisioned for the U.S. Congress, to be done by "citizen legislators" as a part-time responsibility. The image was that individuals would convene in the state capitol for short periods of time to conduct the state's business. State constitutions and statutes specified the part-time operation of the legislature and provided only limited compensation for those who served.

As mentioned earlier, the one-person, one-vote ruling of the U.S. Supreme Court in *Baker* v. *Carr* (1962) marked a turning point in the history of state legislatures, and state governments generally. Once legislatures more accurately

pardon
The authority of a governor to cancel someone's conviction of a crime by a court and to eliminate all sanctions and punishments resulting from the conviction.

commute
The action of a governor to cancel all or part of the sentence of someone convicted of a crime, while keeping the conviction on the record.

parole
The authority of a governor to release a prisoner before his or her full sentence has been completed and to specify conditions that must be met as part of the release.

extradite
To send someone against his or her will to another state to face criminal charges.

VIDEO ROUNDTABLE

Governors

Politics Now

GRADUATED DRIVER LICENSING

Once upon a time, young adults who were sixteen years old and could pass the required tests could get a driver's license. Now all but four states (Arizona, Kansas, Kentucky, and North Dakota) have graduated driver licensing (GDL) programs that put restrictions on those licenses. Specific provisions vary among the states, but generally teenage drivers may not drive unsupervised by an older adult for the first thirty to fifty hours after receiving their license, and even after that they may not drive unsupervised between 10 p.m. and 5 a.m. In fourteen states, teenagers who drive may not have more than two passengers, and in another ten states, they may not have anyone (other than family members) younger than twenty years old in the car with them.[a]

State legislatures responded to parents, insurance companies, and the federal Department of Transportation's National Highway Traffic Safety Administration in passing GDL programs. Car crashes are the leading killer of teenagers. This age group has the highest accident rate of any cohort, and sixteen-year-olds crash more than twice as often as eighteen- and nineteen-year-olds. After North Carolina adopted graduated driver licensing, it saw a 26 percent drop in crashes involving sixteen-year-olds. Michigan noted a 31 percent decrease.[b] These are impressive records.

But, placing restrictions on novice drivers has also met opposition. Opponents argue that it is not fair for all sixteen-year-olds to have limits because some are bad drivers. Some families need help from their new drivers, and the GDL rules limit young drivers' abilities to share driving responsibilities without supervision. Those in rural areas, often without access to public transportation, have been particularly unhappy with GDL legislation. In some states, the restrictions are stricter than what many states use as punishments for those convicted of drunk driving.

Despite these arguments, legislators in forty-six states have placed conditions on young drivers. Lawmakers in the remaining states are considering adopting graduated driver licensing programs. Legislators tend to propose graduated driver licensing in response to a specific tragedy involving a new driver. The tragedy sets the agenda. Then, the pressure of the federal government and local advocates, armed with data about the reduction in accidents where there are GDL laws, generates the support to enact the law.

[a]GDL Laws, Public Affairs Department, American Automobile Association, http://www.aaapublicaffairs.com.

[b]National Highway Traffic Safety Administration, State Legislative Fact Sheets, http://www.nhtsa.dot.gov/people/outreach/stateleg/graddriverlic.htm.

---

represented their states, agendas became more relevant and policies that were adopted reflected the needs and wishes of the people.[11] (See Politics Now: Graduated Driver Licensing.) State legislatures not only became more representative; they became more professional. Legislators worked more days—some of them full-time. In 1960, only eighteen state legislatures met annually. As of 2006, forty-three met every year and only seven every other year. Moreover, the floor sessions were longer, and between sessions legislators and their staff increasingly did committee work and conducted special studies.[12] In 2004, California's newly elected governor, Arnold Schwarzenegger, criticized the full-time role of state legislators, arguing that this made legislators think they had to enact more laws: "Spending so much time in Sacramento, without anything to do, then out of that comes strange bills."[13] His attempts to enact reforms, however, were decisively rejected by the people of California.

All states except Nebraska have two legislative houses. One, the senate, typically has fewer members than the other, usually called the "house" or the "assembly." The most common ratio between the two chambers is 1:3. In fourteen states the ratio is 1:2, and in New Hampshire it is 1:16. Another difference between the two bodies in thirty-four of the states is that senators serve four-year terms, whereas representatives in the larger house serve two-year terms. In eleven states, everyone in both houses serves two-year terms, and in the remaining five, including Nebraska, everyone serves for four years.

Although it has been common to have limits on how many terms someone may serve as governor, **term limits** for legislators did not gain widespread support until

term limits
Restrictions that exist in some states about how long an individual may serve in state or local elected offices.

STILL THE BEST CONGRESSIONAL TERM-LIMITING DEVICE.

■ Should voters force politicians out of office by refusing to reelect them, or should elected officials serve only for a period of time that is established by law? Is it realistic to think that incumbents can be beaten in their bids for reelection?

the 1980s and 1990s. By 1999, twenty states had laws limiting the number of years one might be a state legislator. Although there has been a slow but steady increase in the number of local governments with term limits, support for term limits in state legislatures has waned in recent years. By 2006, the number of states was down to fifteen. Depending on the state, limits vary between six and twelve years. (See Table 4.1.)

State legislatures are still primarily part-time, citizen bodies.[14] Every election puts new members in about one-fourth of the seats. Only a handful of legislators in each state envision careers as state lawmakers. Those with long-term political aspirations tend to view service in a state chamber as a step on a journey to some other office, in the state capital or in Washington, D.C. For some, their goal is to don a black robe and preside in a courtroom.

TABLE 4.1 STATES WITH TERM LIMITS FOR STATE LEGISLATORS

	House		Senate	
	Effective Date	Limit (years)	Effective Date	Limit (years)
Maine	1996	8	1996	8
California	1996	6	1998	8
Colorado	1998	8	1998	8
Arkansas	1998	6	2000	8
Michigan	1998	6	2002	8
Florida	2000	8	2000	8
Ohio	2000	8	2000	8
South Dakota	2000	8	2000	8
Montana	2000	8	2000	8
Arizona	2000	8	2000	8
Missouri	2002	8	2002	8
Oklahoma	2004	12	2004	12
Louisiana	2007	12	2007	12
Nebraska	n/a	n/a	2008	8
Nevada	2010	12	2010	12

ᵃBecause of special elections, term limits were effective in 1998 for one senator and in 2001 for five House members.

Source: National Council of State Legislatures, http://www.ncsl.org.

STATE COURTS

Almost everyone is in a courtroom at some point. It may be as a judge, a juror, an attorney, a court officer, or a litigant. It may also be for some administrative function such as an adoption, a name change, or the implementation of a will. Few of us will ever be in a federal court; almost all of us will be in a state court (except people who live in Washington, D.C., where *all* courts are federal courts).

The primary function of courts is to settle disputes, and most disputes are matters of state, not federal, laws. For the most part, criminal behavior is defined by state legislatures. Family law, dealing with marriage, divorce, adoption, child custody, and the like, is found in state statutes. Contracts, liability, land use, and much that is fundamental to everyday business activity and economic development also are part of state governance.

A common misunderstanding is that the courts in the United States are all part of a single system, with the U.S. Supreme Court at the head. In fact, state and federal courts are separate, with their own rules, procedures, and routes for appeal. The only time state and federal courts converge is when a case involves a claim that a state law or practice violates a federal law or the Constitution or a state court judge has interpreted the Constitution. (See chapter 10 for more on the judiciary.)

Sometimes federal and state laws are directly related. If there is a contradiction between the two, then federal law usually prevails. A state statute that allowed or encouraged racial discrimination, for example, would directly conflict with the 1964 federal Civil Rights Act and the Fourteenth Amendment to the U.S. Constitution. In 2006, North Dakota passed a law banning abortions that North Dakota legislators and the governor knew would not be enacted unless the Supreme Court changed the federal standard established in *Roe* v. *Wade* (1973). Through a rule known as **inclusion,** state courts are obliged to enforce the federal law. The state legislature passed the law with the hope that it would force the Court to overturn its previous ruling legalizing abortion.

Since the 1970s, the U.S. Supreme Court has generally taken the position that, especially with regard to individual rights protected in the Constitution, state courts should be encouraged to regard the federal government as setting minimums.[15] If state constitutions and laws provide additional protections or benefits, then state courts should enforce those standards.

Like other state government institutions, courts have modernized in the past few decades. Many states reorganized their court systems in the 1970s to follow a model that relied on full-time, qualified judges and simplified appeal routes, which enabled state supreme courts to have a manageable workload. Figure 4.2 illustrates the court structure that is now common among the states.

inclusion
The principle that state courts will apply federal laws when those laws directly conflict with the laws of a state.

FIGURE 4.2 STATE COURT STRUCTURE
Most state courts have the basic organization shown here.

	Jury or Bench Trials	Jurisdiction	Judges
STATE SUPREME COURT	Bench only	Appeal (limited)	Panel of judges, elected/appointed for fixed term
APPEALS COURTS	Bench only	Appeal (readily granted)	Panel of judges, elected/appointed for fixed term
CIRCUIT OR COUNTY COURTS	Jury and bench	Original and appeal	One judge per court, elected/appointed for fixed term
MUNICIPAL AND SPECIAL COURTS	Jury and bench	Original	One judge per court, elected/appointed for fixed term

Most court cases in urban areas begin in a court that specializes in issues such as family disputes, traffic, small claims (less than $500 or $1,000), or probate (wills) or in a general jurisdiction municipal court. Small towns and rural areas usually do not have specialized courts. If they do, the position of judge is part-time. Cases here start in county-level courts that deal with the full array of disputes.

Specialized courts do not use juries. A single judge hears the case and decides the case. General courts at this level do have juries if requested by the litigants (parties in a case). A major responsibility of the judges and juries that deliberate on cases when they are originated is to evaluate the credibility of the witnesses and evidence. When cases are heard on appeal, the only individuals making presentations are attorneys.

Appellate courts have panels of judges. There are no juries in these courtrooms. An important feature of the court reorganizations of the 1970s is that a court of appeals exists between the circuit or county courts and the state supreme court. This court is to cover a region in the state and is supposed to accept all appeals. In part, this appellate level is to allow supreme courts to decide whether or not they will hear a case. The basic principle is that all litigants should have at least one opportunity to appeal a decision. If the state supreme court is the only place where an appeal can be lodged, that court is almost inevitably going to have too heavy a caseload and unreasonable backlogs will develop.

Most state judges are elected to the bench for a specific term. This differs from the federal government, where the president appoints judges for indefinite terms. Only three states use gubernatorial appointments. The first states had their legislatures elect judges, and that is still the case in Connecticut, Rhode Island, South Carolina, and Virginia. As Table 4.2 shows, in thirteen states, voters elect judges and use party identification. In their efforts to limit and even destroy political machines, Pro-

TABLE 4.2 JUDICIAL SELECTION PATTERNS

Partisan Election	Nonpartisan Election	Election by Legislature	Appointment by Governor
Alabama	Arkansas	Connecticut	California
Arkansas	California	Rhode Island	Maine
Illinois	Florida	South Carolina	New Jersey
Indiana	Georgia	Virginia	
Kansas	Idaho		
Louisiana	Indiana		
Missouri	Kentucky		
New York	Michigan		
Ohio	Minnesota		
Pennsylvania	Mississippi		
Tennessee	Montana		
Texas	Nevada		
West Virginia	North Carolina		
	North Dakota		
	Oregon		
	South Dakota		
	Utah		
	Washington		
	Wisconsin		

Merit Plan

Alaska	Iowa	New York
Arizona	Kansas	Oklahoma
Colorado	Maryland	Rhode Island
Connecticut	Massachusetts	South Dakota
Delaware	Missouri	Tennessee
Florida	Nebraska	Vermont
Hawaii	New Hampshire	Wyoming
Indiana	New Mexico	

Note: Some states use different selection systems for different courts.

Source: Adapted from *The Book of the States, 2006* (Lexington, KY: Council of State Governments, 2006), 251–54.

Missouri (Merit) Plan
A method of selecting judges in which a governor must appoint someone from a list provided by an independent panel. Judges are then kept in office if they get a majority of "yes" votes in general elections.

gressives at the turn of the twentieth century advocated electing judges without party labels. Today, nineteen states use nonpartisan elections for selecting their judges. The remaining states went a step further and allowed for the election of judges but only after screening for qualifications. This process is referred to as the **Missouri** (or Merit) **Plan.** The governor selects someone from a list prepared by an independent panel and appoints him or her as a judge for a specific term of years. If a judge wishes to serve for an additional term, he or she must receive approval from the voters, who express themselves on a "yes/no" ballot. If a majority of voters cast a "no" ballot, the process starts all over. Six states (Kansas, Missouri, New York, Rhode Island, South Dakota, and Tennessee) use the Missouri Plan for some judicial positions and elections or appointments for the others.

ELECTIONS AND POLITICAL PARTIES

Elections are the vehicle for determining who will fill major state government positions and who will direct the institutions of state government. Almost all contests for state government posts are partisan. The major exceptions are judicial elections in many states, as noted above, and the senate in Nebraska's unicameral legislature. Although party labels are not used and political parties are not formally participants in nonpartisan races, the party identity of some candidates may be known and may have some influence.

Political parties have different histories and roles in the various states. The line graph in Analyzing Visuals: Patterns of Party Competition in State Legislatures shows the trends in the number of state legislative seats won by Republicans and Democrats. Most states have experienced significant competition between Republicans and Democrats since the Civil War. These states often have party control split between the two houses of the legislature and the governor's office or have frequent changes in party control of state government.

From 1994 to 2002, Republicans made gains in state elections. One of the reasons for Republican success is that voters in the South who had been voting for conservative Democrats began voting for conservative Republicans. Southerners have supported Republican presidential candidates since the Democratic Party began asserting leadership for civil rights following World War II. Alignment with Republicans in contests for state and congressional positions was a more gradual process, however. Today, Southerners no longer represent a significant minority within the national Democratic Party but instead are part of the majority within the Republican Party—nationally and regionally.

The period between 2002 and 2006 was one in which Republicans and Democrats equaled one another in their control of state legislatures. As indicated in the opening vignette, this changed with the fall 2006 elections. Six-hundred and sixty-one more Democrats than Republicans were elected to state legislative seats, and as a result Democrats seized control of an additional nine chambers. Democratic gains included all regions of the country and some overturned longstanding patterns. Democrats took control of the New Hampshire House for the first time since 1922, for example. They increased majorities they already had in states like Colorado and Massachusetts. The best showings for Republicans were in Montana and Oklahoma. Republicans also held control in the Michigan House and the New York Senate, despite the general success of Democrats in those states. Advantages of incumbency and personality can often trump party identity.

It is easy to exaggerate the importance of partisanship in state elections. While party labels and organizations matter, state campaigns are primarily centered on individual candidates. Voters often have an opportunity to meet face to face with those contending for state government offices, especially legislative offices. A common strategy of candidates is to downplay their party identification, both to emphasize their strengths as individuals and to appeal to independent voters. After the election,

Analyzing Visuals

PATTERNS OF PARTY COMPETITION IN STATE LEGISLATURES

This graph presents the trends of Republican and Democratic Party success in winning seats in state legislatures. Until the 1960s, the Democratic Party dominated the legislatures of southern states and the Republican Party did best outside that region. Based on the information presented in the graph and the chapter discussion on the parties in state legislatures, answer the following critical thinking questions: What trends do you see in the regional patterns of party competition? Do the regional trends allow you to make a summary statement about the national picture of parties in state legislatures? What major movement nationally led to the decline of Democratic dominance in southern states? What major national event contributed to a surge in Democratic strength in the mid-1970s? How would you explain the even competitiveness of the Republicans and Democrats since the mid-1990s?

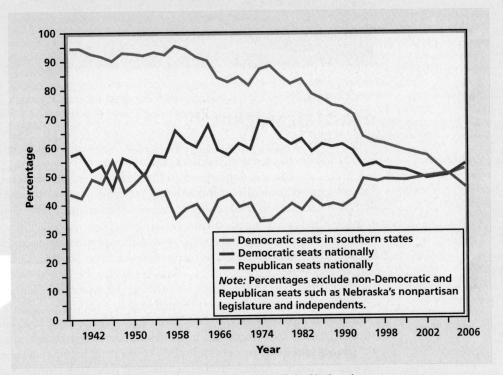

Source: National Conference of State Legislatures, http://www.ncsl.org. Updated by the authors.

party labels are important in determining who is in the majority in the legislature and therefore who will control committees and who will preside. That affects the agenda and the dynamics of policy making.

Elections since the 1960s have led increasingly to ethnic and racial and gender diversity among state and local officials. It is now common for African Americans, Hispanic Americans, and women to be mayors, including in some of the largest cities.

In November 2006, Massachusetts elected its first African American governor, Deval Patrick, and six of the 36 governors who won in that election were women. As of 2007, eight states had women governors. While women have made some gains in gubernatorial contests, there has been virtually no change in state legislatures, where women have held 22–24 percent of the seats since 1980.

■ In 2005, Los Angeles voters elected Antonio Villaraigosa, the son of a Mexican immigrant, as their mayor. Villaraigosa grew up in L.A.'s largely Hispanic eastside and has become nationally visible as a leader in the Democratic Party. Los Angeles has a mayor-council form of government.

Photo courtesy: Kevork Djansezian/AP Wide World Photos

DIRECT DEMOCRACY

As mentioned earlier, a Progressive reform meant to weaken parties and protect against the development of political machines was to provide opportunities for voters to legislate directly and not have to go through state legislatures and governors.[16] That process, known as the **direct initiative,** is available in eighteen states, most of them in the West. Citizens in these states have been able to enact laws as wide ranging as legalizing physician assisted suicide, limiting property taxes, building mass transit systems, protecting endangered species, establishing prison terms for certain criminal behaviors, and outlawing cock fighting. (See Join the Debate: Direct Democracy and State Government.)

direct initiative

A process in which voters can place a proposal on a ballot and enact it into law without involving the legislature or the governor.

A disadvantage of the direct initiative is the possibility that a law may be passed solely because of public opinion shaped largely by thirty-second television commercials and simplistic slogans. Unlike the process when a legislative body debates a measure, there is no opportunity for making amendments to direct initiatives.

Sometimes initiatives are passed and then set aside by courts because they violate the state or federal constitution or because the federal government preempts the state. When California, for example, passed Proposition 187 in 1994, denying most public services to unregistered immigrants, federal courts kept the state from implementing the law because it trespassed on federal immigration policy and violated the U.S. Constitution.

TIMELINE

The Initiative and Referendum

Debate, deliberation, and amendment are included in the **indirect initiative.** In this process, legislatures first consider the issue and then pass a bill that will become law if approved by the voters. The governor plays no role. Of the eleven states that have the indirect initiative, five also have the direct initiative.

indirect initiative

A process in which the legislature places a proposal on a ballot and allows voters to enact it into law, without involving the governor or further action by the legislature.

Voters in twenty-three states have the opportunity to veto some bills. In these states, voters may circulate a petition objecting to a particular law passed in a recent session of the legislature. If enough signatures are collected, then an item appears on the next statewide ballot, giving the electorate the chance to object and therefore veto the legislation. This is known as a **direct** or **popular referendum.**

All state and local legislative bodies may place an **advisory referendum** on a ballot. As the name implies, this is a device to take the pulse of the voters on a particular issue and has no binding effect. In addition, voter approval is required in a referendum to amend constitutions and, in some cases, to allow a governmental unit to borrow money through issuing bonds.

Finally, eighteen states provide for some form of **recall** election. Voters in these states have the power to petition for an election to remove an office holder before the next scheduled election. Judges, state legislators, and other office holders are occasionally the subject of a recall campaign. Most states require that the official serve in office for at least one year before being subject to a recall.[17]

direct (popular) referendum
A process in which voters can veto a bill recently passed in the legislature by placing the issue on a ballot and expressing disapproval.

advisory referendum
A process in which voters cast non-binding ballots on an issue or proposal.

recall
A process in which voters can petition for a vote to remove office holders between elections.

Local Governments

THE INSTITUTIONS AND POLITICS of local governance are even more individualized than those of state governments. In part this is because officials are friends, neighbors, and acquaintances living in the communities they serve. Except in large cities, most elected officials fulfill their responsibilities on a part-time basis. The personal nature of local governance is also due to the immediacy of the issues. The responsibilities of local governments include public health and safety in their communities, education of children in the area, jobs and economic vitality, zoning land for particular uses, and assistance to those in need. Local government policies and activities are the stuff of everyday living. (See American Values/American Voices: Rebuilding After Hurricane Katrina.)

CHARTERS

Romantic notions of democracy in America regard local governments as the building blocks of governance by the people. Alexis de Tocqueville, the critic credited with capturing the essence of early America, described government in the new country as a series of social contracts starting at the grass roots. He said, "the township was organized before the county, the county before the state, the state before the union."[18] It sounds good, but it's wrong. A more accurate description comes from Judge John F. Dillon, who in an 1868 ruling known as **Dillon's Rule** proclaimed: "The true view is this: Municipal corporations owe their origins to and derive their power and rights wholly from the [state] legislature. It breathes into them the breath without which they cannot exist. As it creates, so it may destroy. If it may destroy, it may abridge and control."[19] Dillon's Rule applies to all types of local governments.

There are many categories of local governments. Some of these are created in a somewhat arbitrary way by state governments. Counties and school districts are good examples. State statutes establish the authority for these jurisdictions, set the boundaries, and determine what these governments may and may not do and how they can generate funds.

Cities, towns, and villages are not established arbitrarily by state governments but emerge as people locate in a particular place. These local governments, however, need a **charter** that is acceptable to the state legislature, much as states must have a constitution acceptable to Congress in order to pass laws and levy taxes and fees. Charters describe the institutions of government, the processes used to make legally binding decisions, and the scope of issues and services that

Dillon's Rule
A court ruling that local governments do not have any inherent sovereignty but instead must be authorized by state government.

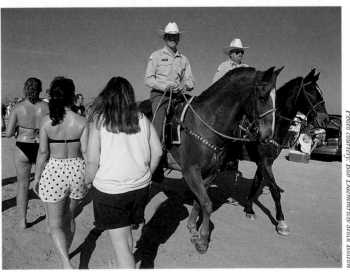

■ Responsibilities of local governments are wide ranging—from collecting the garbage in Minneapolis and filling potholes in Buffalo to patrolling the beach at Corpus Christi on spring break (shown here).

Join the Debate

DIRECT DEMOCRACY AND STATE GOVERNMENT: INITIATIVE AND REFERENDUM MOVEMENTS

OVERVIEW: In 1978, the passage of California's Proposition 13 sent a jolt through the nation's state legislatures and governors' offices. With a sluggish economy and high inflation, average California homeowners, reeling from the state's notoriously high property taxes, overwhelmingly voted for the "People's Initiative to Limit Property Taxation," more commonly known as Proposition 13, an initiative to lower and limit state property taxes. The passage of Proposition 13 demonstrated to the nation the power of direct democracy and initiative elections. Since 1978, states that use the initiative and referendum processes have dramatically increased the number of ballot proposals offered to their citizens. Proponents of the initiative and referendum maintain that these processes give Americans the means to directly affect government and policy by allowing them to create and vote on laws and state constitutional amendments they deem substantial and important.

Initiative and referendum mechanisms originated in the Progressive movement. Through the initiative process, citizens are able to place a proposal on a ballot and enact it into law; through the referendum process, voters can veto recently passed legislation. The first state to inaugurate an initiative and referendum system was South Dakota in 1898; eighteen other states soon followed suit. Currently, twenty-four states have some form of initiative and referendum system in place. Scholars offer different explanations for the use of these electoral processes. Some argue that the use of the initiative and referendum is a result of citizen grassroots mobilization to force action by unresponsive governments; others believe wealthy individuals and interest groups use

these mechanisms to gain from voters what legislators are unwilling to grant.

Detractors of the initiative and referendum argue that these processes do not truly facilitate quality democratic politics. They argue that most people have neither the time nor inclination to study and deliberate on proposed initiatives, and they point to the generally dismal turnout for state and local elections as proof of an apathetic citizenry. Why, they ask, should the important business of law-making and government be entrusted to those whose interests lie elsewhere? Critics maintain that if voters are truly unhappy with their government, all they have to do is show up at the ballot box and "throw the bums out." Critics also point out that states with numerous initiatives are currently trying to reform their respective systems, as voters are coming to the realization that policy-by-initiative is uniquely susceptible to the law of unintended consequences, not to mention that voters are also becoming disenchanted with long and confusing ballots and too many elections.

ARGUMENTS THAT INITIATIVES AND REFERENDUMS ENHANCE DEMOCRATIC PRACTICES

- **Initiative and referendum elections help circumvent an unresponsive state government.** Citizens can use the initiative process to implement new laws, policies, and constitutional amendments that legislators are unable or unwilling to implement, and they can use the referendum to reject legislation they don't like. Voters in California, Colorado, and Oklahoma used the initiative process to impose term limits on state legislators, and voters in Washington State approved a measure that requires performance audits of government agencies. Initiatives are thus a check on legislators and hold them accountable to their constituents.

---

charter
A document that, like a constitution, specifies the basic policies, procedures, and institutions of a municipality.

fall within the jurisdiction of the governmental body being chartered. There are five basic types of charters:

1. **Special charters.** Historically, as urban areas emerged, each one developed and sought approval for its own charter. To avoid inconsistencies, most state constitutions now prohibit the granting of special charters.

2. **General charters.** Some states use a standard charter for all jurisdictions, regardless of size or circumstance.

- **Initiative and referendum elections allow for the expansion of democratic processes.** The initiative and referendum allow average citizens to participate in law-making and policy-making processes. Voters have used these processes to control state tax and spending policy and to direct their governments on social policy. Voters in Washington State approved an initiative to ban smoking inside public facilities, and voters in Maine rejected a call to repeal their law prohibiting discrimination based on sexual orientation.
- **Initiative and referendum elections help voters counter the influence of powerful interest groups.** The influence of interest-group activities and expenditures on state and local government is undeniable. Initiative and referendum mechanisms give citizens a tool to circumvent the vote trading and logrolling that go on in the legislative process due to interest-group pressure. Laws passed through the initiative process do not have all the pork and amendments that typically come attached to legislation.

ARGUMENTS THAT INITIATIVE AND REFERENDUM HINDER DEMOCRATIC PRACTICES

- **Initiative and referendum elections impede effective government.** Initiatives and referendums prevent legislators from developing consistent and coherent policy. Initiatives that restrict legislatures from raising certain types of revenue may prevent legislators from adequately budgeting to meet changing needs and priorities. Many policy makers believe that because Proposition 13 limits the property-tax revenue stream, California state legislators have been unable to sufficiently fund the state's social service programs and educational system.
- **Initiatives and referendums may lead to unforeseen and undesirable consequences.** Many drafters of initiatives do not have the requisite legal or political expertise to skill-fully craft legislation. Legislators tend to make better laws, since they are usually expert in their office and have professional staffs for the research and drafting of legislation. Citizens do not have the necessary experience to understand the relationship between a given initiative and existing statutes and policy. This can result in implementation problems and poor and confused law.
- **Initiatives and referendums may be anti-democratic.** Paradoxically, initiatives and referendums may be anti-majoritarian and unrepresentative of a state's political culture. In states with historically low voter turnout, those who do vote may represent only small, well-organized groups or wealthy individuals who are able to unduly influence voters, and this can result in minority tyranny. *Congressional Quarterly* reports that roughly two-thirds of all money spent on initiatives in California in 1990 came from business interests.

QUESTIONS

1. Does the initiative and referendum system create bad law? Should citizens have such a direct input in drafting or rejecting legislation? Why or why not?
2. Do initiative and referendum mechanisms give citizens a way to restrain their government and counter the influence of interest groups, or are these instruments simply tools for organized interests? Explain your answer.

SELECTED READINGS

Ellis, Richard. *Democratic Delusions: The Initiative Process in the United States*. Lawrence: University Press of Kansas, 2002.
Schmidt, David D. *Citizen Lawmakers: The Ballot Initiative Revolution*. Philadelphia: Temple University Press, 1991.

3. **Classified charters.** This approach classifies cities according to population and then has a standard charter for each classification.

4. **Optional charters.** A more recent development is for the state to provide several acceptable charters and then let voters in a community choose from these.

5. **Home-rule charters.** Increasingly, states specify the major requirements that a charter must meet and then allow communities to draft and amend their own charters. State government must still approve the final product.

American Values/American Voices

REBUILDING AFTER HURRICANE KATRINA

As the 2006 hurricane season began, New Orleans was still far from recovering from Hurricane Katrina, which devastated Gulf Coast communities in September 2005. Levees essential to keeping neighborhoods at the delta of the Mississippi River from being under water were still not restored. Homes, furniture, cars, and appliances trashed by the hurricane remained strewn over vast areas of the city as if the hurricane had struck yesterday. Some businesses and schools were operating, and residents were trickling back, but they had to cope with periodic power outages, closed streets, and hazards from debris and polluted water.

Americans generally shared the frustrations of residents of New Orleans. In a national poll conducted by CBS News six months after Hurricane Katrina struck, only 5 percent expressed satisfaction with the progress that had been made in rebuilding New Orleans, 16 percent said they were angry, and another 43 percent were dissatisfied but not angry. Two-thirds of those polled agreed that the federal government should help with the rebuilding, and 64 percent disapproved of how President George W. Bush had responded. African Americans were especially critical of President Bush. While 60 percent of white respondents disapproved of the president's response regarding New Orleans, 90 percent of the African Americans polled voiced displeasure.

Moreover, following the devastation of Katrina, there was no single plan for rebuilding. President Bush, the U.S. House of Representatives, the State of Louisiana, and the City of New Orleans each established a separate commission to establish a plan, and each commission developed a different blueprint, based on different priorities and values.[a] President Bush emphasized the use of tax cuts and incentives to assist businesses in moving back into the area. Congressional inquiries and recommendations focused on housing issues—providing limited federal funding for individuals displaced by the hurricane and insisting that federal flood insurance be linked to locating and building homes in ways that do not make them vulnerable to storm damage. A major concern of Louisiana was to reestablish New Orleans as a tourist attraction and business center to generate tax revenues for the state treasury. And, the city itself had to address not only the obvious tasks of clearing debris but also how to balance the desires of families to rebuild their homes with the realities of probable storms and floods in the future.

Nongovernmental groups and panels have been active. Environmental advocates and professional associations, like the Urban Land Institute, volunteered their plans, which took into account the natural forces and needs of the delta area and the opportunity to bring new and different economic activities to New Orleans.[b] A green New Orleans, for example, would not use levees to keep water from where it would naturally flow or try to maintain an artificial shoreline. And, a new economy could be based on more than jazz and Cajun cooking. A study led by engineering faculty at the University of California, Berkeley, and supported by grants from the National Science Foundation targeted the design, construction, and maintenance of the levee system and urged rebuilding flood control that attended to technical details and not to costs. Professor Raymond B. Seed, chief author of the report, said, "People died because mistakes were made and because safety was exchanged for efficiency and reduced cost."[c]

Clearly decisions had to be made about how to proceed. But, while values and priorities were debated through 2005 and 2006, and plans were designed, the destruction brought by Hurricane Katrina remained, and the residents of New Orleans continued to suffer.

QUESTIONS

1. Should people be allowed to rebuild their homes on land that they own, even if it is vulnerable to floods? Should they be able to get flood insurance from the government?
2. When very poor people are affected by a disaster like Hurricane Katrina, what sort of assistance should they receive, and from what entities? What is their fate if the emphasis in rebuilding is on businesses and jobs that require skills they do not have?

---

[a]Manuel Roig-Franzia, "Who's in Charge of Rebuilding New Orleans?" *Washington Post* (November 4, 2005).

[b]"Moving Beyond Recovery to Restoration and Rebirth: Urban Land Institute Makes Recommendations on Rebuilding New Orleans," http://www.uli.org.

[c]John Schwartz, "New Study of Levees Faults Design and Construction," *New York Times* (May 22, 2006); and http://www.ce.berkeley.edu/-new_orleans/.

An important feature of home rule is that the local government is authorized to legislate on any issue that does not conflict with existing state or federal laws. Other charter approaches list the subjects that a town or city may address. (For an examination of one concern that a local government might have to address, see On Campus: College Towns and Binge Drinking.)

TYPES OF LOCAL GOVERNMENTS

There are about 87,000 local governments in the United States. The four major categories are as follows.

1. **Counties.** Every state has **counties,** although in Louisiana they are called parishes, and in Alaska, boroughs. With few exceptions, counties have very broad responsibilities and are used by state governments as basic administrative units for welfare and environmental programs, courts, and the registration of land, births, and deaths. County and city boundaries may overlap. State actions have merged city and county in New York, San Francisco, Denver, St. Louis, Nashville, and Honolulu.

2. **Towns.** In the first states and in the Midwest, "town" officially refers to a form of government in which everyone in a community is invited to an annual meeting to elect officers, adopt ordinances, and pass a budget.

3. **Municipalities.** Villages, towns, and cities are established as **municipalities** and authorized by state governments as people congregate and form communities. Some of the most intense struggles among governments within the United States are over the boundaries, scope of authority, and sources of revenue for municipal governments.

4. **Special Districts. Special districts** are the most numerous form of government. A special district is restricted to a particular policy or service area. School districts are the most common form of special district. Others exist for library service, sewerage, water, and parks. Special districts are governed through a variety of structures. Some have elected heads, and others, appointed. Some of these jurisdictions levy a fee to generate their revenues, whereas others depend on appropriations from a state, city, or county. A reason for the recent proliferation of special districts is to avoid restrictions on funds faced by municipalities, schools, or other jurisdictions. The creation of a special park district, for example, may enable the park to have its own budget and sources of funding and relieve a city or county treasury.

county
A geographic district created within a state with a government that has general responsibilities for land, welfare, environment, and, where appropriate, rural service policies.

municipality
A government with general responsibilities, such as a city, town, or village government, that is created in response to the emergence of relatively densely populated areas.

special district
A local government that is responsible for a particular function, such as K–12 education, water, sewerage, or parks.

■ One type of informal local government body is the neighborhood association. Whether such associations succeed in communicating clearly and resolving their problems is an open question.

Photo courtesy: Kevin Jacobus/The Image Works

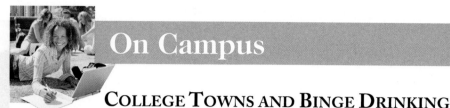

On Campus

COLLEGE TOWNS AND BINGE DRINKING

According to a study by the Harvard School of Public Health, 44 percent of U.S. college students engage in binge drinking.[a] Binge drinking is defined for men as having at least five drinks in a row, and for women, at least four drinks—a drink equals a twelve-ounce bottle of beer or wine cooler, a four-ounce glass of wine, or a shot of liquor, either by itself or in a mixed drink. A frequent binge drinker is someone who engages in this behavior at least three times in two weeks.

The Harvard study found that 50 percent of male college students and 39 percent of female students acknowledged that they were binge drinkers. Seventy-three percent of the men and 68 percent of the women said that the reason they drank alcoholic beverages was to get intoxicated.

There are no significant differences in the ages or classes of students and the pattern of binge drinking. Some binge drinkers are not yet twenty-one years old and therefore are breaking the law. Binge drinking, regardless of the legal drinking age, is associated with rowdiness, vandalism, fights, and sexual assault. The Harvard study demonstrated that binge drinkers are more likely than other students to miss class, get behind in school work, have unplanned sexual activity, engage in unprotected sex, damage property, and be hurt or injured.

Local and state governments are responsible for issuing licenses to sell alcoholic beverages. Inevitably, they must balance the pressure from bars and restaurants to do business freely and the need to ensure that alcohol is sold and consumed responsibly. An issue for local governments as well as for universities is that laws are broken when underage students drink and when binge drinking leads to assault and vandalism. Also, neighbors in campus areas want quieter, safer nights on the weekend. More central is the concern for health and safety—of the drinkers as well as of those around them.

An initial and obvious response of local governments has been to enhance policing focused on illegal drinking and unlawful behaviors related to the consumption of alcohol. Cities have revoked liquor licenses from businesses that make little effort to ensure that they are not serving underage drinkers. More innovative and proactive measures have included working with bar owners as well as fraternities and sororities to make sure that alcohol is not served to those who show signs of having had enough, educating students about the effects of binge drinking, eliminating sponsorship of events and programs by the alcohol industry, and sponsoring nonalcoholic alternatives for socializing and having fun. A few universities have sought to keep bars from having special deals during a "happy hour," since offering cheaper drinks in a relatively limited amount of time can encourage binge drinking from patrons trying to "get their money's worth." Some bar owners object strongly that these policing efforts interfere with their businesses.

Universities, health officials, police, and city governments all agree that binge drinking by college students is a serious problem. Attempts to curb the problem, however, have met with only limited success. Local government policies and university programs have not fared well as they confront business and individual choice.

[a] Henry Wechsler, George W. Dowdall, Andrea Davenport, and William DeJong, "College Alcohol Study," http://www.hsph.harvard.edu/cas/.

A particular municipality or special district may have been established for good reasons, but having multiple governments serving the same community and controlling the same area can create confusion. The challenge is to bridge the separation between municipalities, school districts, counties, and state agencies to effectively address an issue. A specific response to youth violence, for example, may be to provide a youth center or skateboard rink for young people in a community so they can hang out in a safe and healthy setting. Such a project poses questions about which jurisdictions will provide funding and ensure staffing. Land may have to be rezoned and building permits acquired. Will a park district be involved? Will schools count on this facility for after-school programming? What will be the role and approach of the police department? Who will be in charge? (For approaches to other issues, see Global Perspective: Urban Planning in Brazil.)

Formal and informal arrangements among local governments exist that allow them to cooperate and coordinate their work in a single area. Miami and Dade

Global Perspective

URBAN PLANNING IN BRAZIL

The impact of urbanization on resources and human health is an issue of increasing concern to nations around the world. While the explosive growth of cities was primarily a phenomenon of the late nineteenth and early twentieth centuries in the United States, other nations, like Brazil, have had to grapple with the host of problems accompanying urbanization much more recently, making city planning and urban development policy a priority.

Policy approaches vary according to resources, political culture, and geography, but urban development that takes environmental issues into account is increasingly important in most nations. Key aspects of environmentally friendly urban development includes the incorporation of "green space" into metropolitan areas, the integration of efficient, low-pollution mass transit, and effective zoning regulations. According to the International Platform for Sustainable Development (a global conference on international urban development held in Geneva, Switzerland), Curitiba, Brazil, provides one of the best examples of cutting-edge metropolitan planning. Aspects of the urban development plan for Curitiba are being emulated by a diverse array of American cities, including Portland, Oregon; Las Vegas, Nevada; and Denver, Colorado.

Curitiba was founded by Portuguese explorers in 1693 and is the capital of the Brazilian state of Paraná. Because of its location amid abundant natural resources, Curitiba became a thriving center of agricultural industry and experienced rapid growth in the mid-nineteenth century. Not only did Curitiba attract Brazilians, but it also attracted immigrants from places as diverse as Japan and Lebanon, and this population increase put considerable stress on the city's infrastructure. To address this, in 1968 Curitiba instituted the Curitiba Master Plan, an innovative urban-renewal approach that has received international plaudits. With 1.8 million inhabitants, Curitiba boasts 55 square meters of green space per resident, and the city possesses a novel rapid mass-transit system in which biarticulated buses (think of an elongated bus in three sections) travel in special lanes throughout the city. The city's residents work closely with the municipal government in major recycling enterprises where residents can exchange recyclables for fresh produce, and the city pays for the program by selling the recycled waste.

The Smart Growth initiative of Portland, Oregon, is modeled on aspects of Curitiba's master plan. Smart Growth policy limits the city's growth to predefined and continually modified limits, with the goal of directing development to maintain green and environmentally stable spaces while limiting new residents to "compact neighborhoods." For example, the Portland metro area converts a mere 10 acres of rural land to accommodate 100 new residents. According to the *Charlotte Observer*, this places Portland at the head of the land-use class in the United States, whereas Charlotte, North Carolina, converts 49 acres of country land for every 100 new residents to its metro area.

The trend globally is to follow Curitiba and Portland's lead in pursuing the conversion of a minimal amount of rural land to accommodate increased growth. Las Vegas and Denver, for example, are pursuing similar anti-sprawl measures. A growing international consensus is increasingly emphasizing the preservation of open spaces as a means to improve quality of life in urban areas. Cities like Curitiba and Portland have done much to shape that consensus.

QUESTIONS

1. Is it surprising to you that the global model for urban development is to be found in Brazil rather than the United States? Why do you think that is the case?
2. Does it seem the United States is joining other nations in pursuing ecologically sound living space? Why or why not?

Sources: Curitiba Institute of Research and Urban Planning; "The Portland Exception," Northwest Environment Watch, 2004; *Frontline*, PBS; and the World Bank.

County in Florida have been an early and visible example. The two jurisdictions have merged their public health services, jointly administer parks, operate a unified mass transit system, and together plan for development and land use. The establishment of the 911 emergency service can be a catalyst for cooperation by various police, fire, and paramedical agencies in a metropolitan area. Still, there continues to be conflict between governments on occasion and often a failure to even communicate. The past actions that created a local government can present a serious challenge for local officials and citizens alike.

COMPARATIVE

Comparing State and Local Governments

EXECUTIVES AND LEGISLATURES

town meeting
Form of local government in which all eligible voters are invited to attend a meeting at which budgets and ordinances are proposed and voted on.

Except for the traditional New England **town meeting,** where anyone who attends may vote on policy and management issues, local governments have some or all of the following decision-making offices:

- Elected executive, such as a mayor, village president, or county executive.
- Elected council or commission, such as a city council, school board, or county board.
- Appointed manager, such as a city manager or school superintendent.

Local government institutions are not necessarily bound to the principles of separation of powers or checks and balances that the U.S. Constitution requires of the federal government and most state constitutions require of their governments. School boards, for example, commonly have legislative, executive, and judicial authority. School board members are, with few exceptions, part-time officials, so they hire superintendents and rely heavily on them for day-to-day management and for new policy ideas. It is the school board, however, that makes the policies regarding instruction and facilities. The board also does the hiring and contracting to implement those policies. Similarly, the school board sets student conduct rules, determines if a student should be expelled, and then hears appeals from those who are disciplined.

The patterns of executive and legislative institutions in local government have their roots in the same profound events in our history that influenced state government. As mentioned earlier, the influx of immigrants into urban areas in the North after the Civil War prompted the growth of political machines.[20] New immigrants needed help getting settled. They naturally got much of that help from ethnic neighborhoods, where, for example, a family from Poland would find people who spoke Polish, restaurants with Polish food, and stores and churches with links to the old country. Politicians dealt with these ethnic neighborhoods. If the neighborhood voted to help provide victory for particular candidates for **mayor** (the chief elected official of a city) and **city council** (the legislature in a city government), then city jobs and services would be provided. Political machines were built on these quid pro quo arrangements. The bosses of those machines were either the elected officials or people who controlled the elected officials.

mayor
Chief elected executive of a city.

city council
The legislature in a city government.

manager
A professional executive hired by a city council or county board to manage daily operations and to recommend policy changes.

As part of their efforts to destroy the political machines, Progressives sought reforms that minimized the politics in local government institutions.[21] Progressives favored local governments headed by professional **managers** instead of elected executives. Managers would be appointed by councils, the members of which were elected on a nonpartisan ballot, thus removing the role of parties.

district-based election
Election in which candidates run for an office that represents only the voters of a specific district within the jurisdiction.

As another way of sapping the strength of ethnic bloc voting, Progressive reformers advocated that council members be elected from the city at large rather than from neighborhood districts. The choice between **district-based elections** and **at-large elections** now, however, raises concerns about discrimination against Hispanic Americans and African Americans. At-large elections may keep minority representatives from being elected. On the other hand, a city could be divided into districts that might have an ethnic group constitute a majority within a district. The at-large elections, in short, can have the same minimizing effect on these ethnic groups that was intended by Progressives on white ethnic groups.

at-large election
Election in which candidates for office must compete throughout the jurisdiction as a whole.

commission
Form of local government in which several officials are elected to top positions that have both legislative and executive responsibilities.

Progressives argued that the **commission** form of government was an acceptable alternative to mayors and boss politics. The commission evolved as a response to a hurricane in 1900 that killed almost 10,000 people in southern Texas. After the disaster, a group of prominent business leaders in Galveston formed a task force, with each member assuming responsibility for a specific area, such as housing, public safety, and finance. Task-force members essentially assumed the roles of both legislators making policy and managers implementing policy. The citizens of Galveston were so impressed with how well this worked that they amended their charter to replace the mayor and city council with a commission, elected at large and on a nonpartisan basis. The model spread quickly, and by 1917 almost 500 cities had adopted the commission form of government.

As Table 4.3 indicates, between 1984 and 2002 there was a trend away from the council–manager form of city government toward the mayor–council form. Now half of all U.S. cities have an elected mayor and a council. Mayors differ in how much authority they have. Some are strong and have the power to veto city council action, appoint agency heads, and initiate as well as execute budgets. The charters of other cities do not provide mayors with these formal powers. Except for the largest cities, mayors serve on a part-time basis.

Slightly more than one-third of the municipalities have the Progressive model of government, with an appointed, professional manager and an elected city council. This is the most common pattern among medium-sized cities, whereas the very large and the very small have mayors and councils. Some jurisdictions have both mayors and managers. Only 2 percent of U.S. cities use the commission form of government. Portland, Oregon, is the largest city run by a commission. Galveston, however, has abandoned this structure.

Over 1,800 of the almost 3,000 county governments are run by boards or councils that are elected from geographic districts and without any executive. Committees of the county board manage personnel, finance, roads, parks, social services, and the like. Almost 400 counties elect an executive as well as a board, and thus follow the mayor–council model. Almost 800 hire a professional manager.

School districts, with very few exceptions, follow the council–manager model. Other special districts have boards, sometimes called **public corporations** or **authorities,** that are elected or appointed by elected officials. If the district is responsible for services such as water, sewerage, or mass transit, the board is likely to hire and then supervise a manager.

Officials at the various levels of government also draw on a number of intergovernmental groups for information, expertise, and networking. See Table 4.4 for an overview of the top seven intergovernmental associations. These groups include the National Governors Association, the National Conference of State Legislatures, and the International City/County Management Association.

Photo courtesy: Bettmann/Corbis

■ In the aftermath of the devastating 1900 hurricane in Galveston, Texas, the commission form of city government came into being. Although later abandoned by Galveston, the model spread quickly, and by 1917, almost 500 cities had adopted the commission form of government.

public corporation (authority)
Government organization established to provide a particular service or run a particular facility that is independent of other city or state agencies and is to be operated like a business. Examples include a port authority or a mass transit system.

TABLE 4.3 MAJOR FORMS OF MUNICIPAL GOVERNMENT		
Form of Government	1984	2002
Council–Manager	3,387 (48.5%)	2,290 (34.7%)
Mayor–Council	3,011 (43.1%)	3,686 (55.8%)
Commission	143 (2.0%)	176 (2.7%)
Town Meeting	337 (4.8%)	370 (5.6%)
Representative Town Meeting	63 (.9%)	81 (1.2%)
Total[a]	6,981 (100%)	6,603 (100%)

[a]Totals for U.S. local governments represent only those municipalities with populations of 2,500 and greater. There are close to 30,000 local governments with populations under 2,500.

Source: Statistics from "Inside the Year Book: Cumulative Distributions of U.S. Municipalities," *The Municipal Year Books* 1984–2002, International City/County Management Association (ICMA), Washington, DC.

TABLE 4.4 **THE "BIG SEVEN" INTERGOVERNMENTAL ASSOCIATIONS**

Association	Date Founded	Membership
National Governors Association (NGA)	1908	Incumbent governors
Council of State Governments	1933	Direct membership by states and territories; serves all branches of government; has dozens of affiliate organizations of specialists
National Conference of State Legislatures (NCSL)	1948	State legislators and staff
National League of Cities (NLC)	1924	Direct membership by cities and state leagues of cities
National Association of Counties (NAC)	1935	Direct membership by counties; loosely linked state associations; affiliate membership for county professional specialists
United States Conference of Mayors (USCM)	1933	Direct membership by cities with population over 30,000
International City/County Management Association (ICMA)	1914	Direct membership by appointed city and county managers and other professionals

Source: Allan J. Cigler and Burdett A. Loomis, *Interest Group Politics*, 4th ed. (Washington, DC: CQ Press, 1995), 135. Reprinted by permission of Congressional Quarterly Inc.

Grassroots Power and Politics

POLITICAL PARTICIPATION in state and, especially, local politics is more personal and more issue-oriented than at the national level. Much of what happens is outside the framework of political parties. Elections for some state and local government offices, in fact, are **nonpartisan elections,** which means parties do not nominate candidates and ballots do not include any party identification of those running for office. Access and approaches are usually direct. School board members receive phone calls at their homes. Members of the city council and county board bump into constituents while shopping for groceries or cheering their children in youth sports. The concerns that are communicated tend to be specific and neither partisan nor ideological: a particular schoolteacher is unfair and ineffective; playground equipment is unsafe; it seems to be taking forever for the city to issue a building permit so that you can get started on a remodeling project.

In this setting, local news media invariably play a key role. The major newspaper in the state and what might be the only newspaper in a community can shape the agendas of government bodies and the images of government officials. The mere fact that a problem is covered by the media makes it an issue. If gang or cult activity is just a group of kids acting weird and dressing the same way, public officials might ignore it. News coverage of this or certainly of a violent incident involving members of such a group, on the other hand, assures attention. Then the question is how the media define the issue—as an isolated and unusual event or as a signal that certain needs are not being met?

The most powerful and influential people in a state or community are not necessarily those who hold offices in government. While there is always a distinction between formal and informal power, the face-to-face character of governance at the grassroots level almost invites informal ties and influence. The part-time officials in particular have a more ambiguous identity than do full-time government officials.

In small to medium-sized communities, it is common for a single family or a traditional elite to be the major decision maker, whether or not one of their members has a formal governmental position.[22] In another frequent pattern, the owners or managers of the major business in town dominate public decision making. If you want to advocate for some improvements in a local park, a curriculum change in the schools,

nonpartisan election
A contest in which candidates run without formal identification or association with a political party.

or a different set of priorities for the police department, it may be more important to get the support of a few key community leaders than the sympathy of the village president or the head of the school board. A newcomer interested in starting a business in a town likewise would be well advised to identify and court the informal elite and not just focus on those who hold a formal office.

Ad hoc, issue-specific organizations are prevalent in state and local governments.[23] Individuals opposed to the plans of a state department of transportation to expand a stretch of highway from two to four lanes will organize, raise funds, and lobby hard to stop the project. Once the project is stopped or completed, that organization will go out of existence. Likewise, neighbors will organize to support or oppose specific development projects or to press for revitalization assistance, and then they will disband once the decision is made. The sporadic but intense activity focused on specific local or regional concerns is an important supplement to the ongoing work of parties and interest groups in state and local governments. A full understanding of what happens at the grass roots requires an appreciation of ad hoc, issue-specific politics as well as the institutions and processes through which state and local governments make and implement public policies.

You Are a Restaurant Owner

domestic dependent nation
A type of sovereignty that makes an Indian tribe in the United States outside the authority of state governments but reliant on the federal government for the definition of tribal authority.

trust relationship
The legal obligation of the United States federal government to protect the interests of Indian tribes.

Relations with Indian Nations

TREATIES BETWEEN the federal government and American Indian nations directly affect thirty-four states. Most of these states are west of the Mississippi River, but New York, Michigan, Florida, Connecticut, and Wisconsin are also included. Although the treaties were signed by both the United States and an American Indian tribal nation, invariably the tribal leaders signed because of actual or threatened military defeat. The legal status of the various tribes in the United States is that of a **domestic dependent nation,** by which they retain their individual identity and sovereignty but must rely on the U.S. federal government for the interpretation and application of treaty provisions. Under the formal **trust relationship** between the United States and the Indian nations, the federal government is legally and morally obligated to protect Indian interests. State and local governments are clearly affected by federal–tribal relations but have little influence and virtually no legal authority over these relations.

The policy approach of the federal government toward Indians has varied widely (see Table 4.5). From 1830 to 1871, a major goal was to move all Indians to land west of the Mississippi. The policy between 1871 and 1934 was to assimilate Indians into the white culture of the United States. From 1934 until 1953 and then again from 1973 to today, the formal policy was to respect tribal customs, strengthen tribal governments, and promote economic self-determination. Between 1953 and 1973, the federal government terminated the legal status of various tribes, ended services to them, and refused to recognize their treaty rights. This generated protests and led to a resumption of the general policy begun in 1934.[24] While some would argue that the federal government has not been serious or effective enough in supporting treaty rights and self-determination, the current policy received new emphasis with

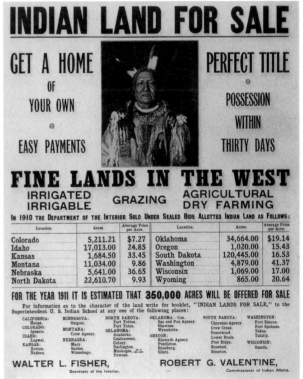

■ An advertisement from the Department of the Interior (c. 1911) luring individuals to purchase land designated as surplus after tribal allotments were made to Indians.

TABLE 4.5 **FEDERAL POLICIES TOWARD INDIAN NATIONS**	
Up to 1830	Mix conquest and coexistence. Make treaties.
1830–1871	Force all tribes west of Mississippi. Make treaties.
1871–1934	Assimilate Indians into white culture.
1934–1953	Respect tribal customs and government. Encourage economic self-determination.
1953–1973	Terminate legal status of tribes. Ignore treaty provisions.
1973 to present	Recognize tribes and treaty rights. Encourage constitutions and self-determination.

the inclusion of tribes in the devolution of responsibilities from Washington to states and local communities.

States are not parties to the treaties between the United States and American Indian nations and have no direct legal authority over tribes. The federal government has in several specific areas granted some powers to states. The Indian Gaming Regulatory Act of 1988, for example, gives state governments limited authority to negotiate agreements, called **compacts,** with tribes who wish to have casino gambling. Also, in 1953, Congress passed Public Law 280, which allows some states to pursue Indians suspected of criminal behavior even if they are on reservation land.

For the most part, however, federal–tribal relations provide given constraints and opportunities as states and communities engage in planning and problem solving. The two most important features of federal–tribal relations for state and local governments are land rights and treaty provisions for hunting, fishing, and gathering. Tribes have **reservation land** and **trust land,** neither of which is subject to taxation or regulation by state or local governments. The reservation land was designated in a treaty. Tribes can acquire trust land by purchasing or otherwise securing ownership of a parcel and then seeking to have it placed in trust status by the secretary of the Department of the Interior. The acquisition of trust land has the potential for disruption of a community's development plans or tax base and an obvious challenge to cordial, working relationships between tribes, the federal government, and state or local government.

Hunting, fishing, and gathering activities have important cultural and religious significance for many American Indian nations. Treaty provisions giving rights to tribes to hunt, fish, and gather wild rice or berries on their own land and on public lands and waterways in land they once owned are key to tribal identity and dignity. These treaty rights supersede state regulations enacted for environmental and recreational purposes. Non-Indian anglers and hunters sometimes protest that Indians have special privileges. Environmental planners worry about the potential implications of unregulated Indian activity. In 1999, for example, the Makah tribe in the Northwest celebrated the successful capture and killing of a whale. While the tribe applauded the preservation of an important cultural tradition, wildlife advocates bemoaned the treaty rights that allowed this destruction of a valued animal. Incidents like this notwithstanding, generally American Indian nations have a deeper commitment to environmental protection than the state and federal governments.

Since Congress passed the Indian Self-Determination and Education Assistance Act in 1975, the federal government has been trying to strengthen tribal governments by encouraging the adoption of constitutions. The Bureau of Indian Affairs offers assistance in writing the constitutions, and other federal agencies, such as the Environmental Protection Agency, are willing to devolve some of their authority for regulating water and air pollution to tribes that have constitutions.

While tribes may include some traditional patterns of governance in their constitutions, the basic concept of a constitution is alien to Indian tribes. The documents read very much like state constitutions, with preambles that espouse principles of

compact
A formal, legal agreement, as that between a state and a tribe.

reservation land
Land designated in a treaty that is under the authority of an Indian nation and is exempt from most state laws and taxes.

trust land
Land owned by an Indian nation and designated by the federal Bureau of Indian Affairs as exempt from most state laws and taxes.

democracy and clauses that provide for a familiar separation of powers among executive, legislative, and judicial branches. Not surprisingly, some nations struggle with the mandates of their constitutions and the informal but real power of traditional rule by elders.

State and Local Finances

STATE, TRIBAL, AND LOCAL GOVERNMENTS must, of course, have money. Getting that money is one of the most challenging and thankless tasks of public officials. Unlike the federal government, state and local governments must balance their budgets. Unlike private businesses, state and local governments may not spend less money than they have. Whereas the goal of a private business is to have significantly more income than expenses, a governor, mayor, or other local public executive would be criticized for taxing too heavily if something akin to profits appeared on the books.

The budgeting process involves making projections of expenses and revenues. State and local officials face some special uncertainties when they make these guesses. One important factor is the health of the economy. If one is taxing sales or income, those will vary with levels of employment and economic growth. Moreover, the public sector faces double jeopardy when the economy declines. Revenues go down as sales and incomes decline, and at the same time expenses go up as more families and individuals qualify for assistance during harsh times.

Another important factor affecting state and local government budgets is the level of funding that governments give to one another. States have been getting about one-fourth of their funds from Washington, D.C. That level has varied over time and, especially with federal deficit spending, is likely to decline. The amount of the decline will depend as much on political dynamics as it will on the health of the national economy. Local governments do not receive as much, but water and sewerage districts have been getting about 15 percent of their funds from the federal government. Local governments depend heavily on aid from state governments. The pattern varies from one state to another, but on average, school districts get slightly over half of their funds from state governments, counties get almost one-third, and cities about 20 percent.[25]

Not only is federal funding for state and local governments generally declining, but Congress and the president frequently require communities to spend their money for national programs and concerns. The National Governors Association, for example, estimated that states spend up to $4 billion each year to enhance security at airports, power plants, water sources, and vital infrastructure in the aftermath of the September 11 terrorist attacks.[26] The federal government has reimbursed state and local jurisdictions for less than one-third of their costs.

Different governments depend on different types of taxes and fees. Figure 4.3 presents the pattern of funding for state and local governments. Unlike the federal government, which relies primarily on the income tax, state governments rely almost equally on income taxes and sales taxes. States differ among themselves, of course. Alaska, Delaware, Montana, New Hampshire, and Oregon have no sales tax, whereas some of the southern states have a double-digit sales tax. Alaska, Florida, Nevada, New Hampshire, South Dakota, Tennessee, Texas, Washington, and Wyoming do not tax personal incomes. Tax rates differ among those states that do have an income tax, but the levels are generally less than 10 percent.

Tax increases pose risks for officials seeking reelection. More popular ways of getting needed revenues included using "rainy day funds" established in years when there

SIMULATION

You Are the Director of Economic Development for the City of Los Angeles, California

FIGURE 4.3 STATE AND LOCAL GOVERNMENT REVENUES (PERCENTAGE OF TOTAL REVENUES)

State governments depend primarily on sales and income taxes and funds from the federal government, while local governments are dependent on property taxes, user fees, and funds from state governments.

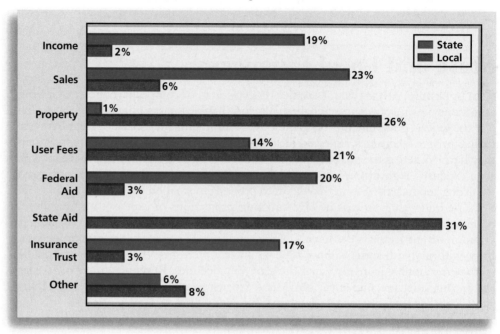

Source: *Statistical Abstract of the United States, 2006* (Washington, DC: Census Bureau, 2006), 291–300.

were surpluses, and selling to investors the rights to funds that states were to receive in a legal settlement with tobacco companies—investors paid states at the rate of $1 immediately in order to get $5 over twenty-five years. In response to serious budget shortfalls that occurred during the recession from 2001 to 2003, most states made tough adjustments to balance their budgets, typically opting for program cuts and fee increases rather than tax increases.[27] But the fear of severe damage to education, health care, and public safety led the Republican-dominated Virginia legislature to reverse course in the spring of 2004 and support a series of tax increases proposed by the Democratic governor, Mark Warner.[28]

Local governments rely primarily on property taxes, have little from levies on sales, and receive virtually nothing from income. Schools, in particular, depend on property taxes for funding. Both local and state governments levy user fees, such as admission to parks, licenses for hunting and fishing, tuition for public universities, and charges based on water use. States, more than local governments, administer retirement systems and insurance programs for public employees. Income from the investment of retirement funds is listed but is not generally available for any use other than paying retirement benefits. Similarly, user fees are typically placed in **segregated funds,** which means the funds are restricted to a specific use.

Most people accept user fees as the fairest type of taxation. The problem is that user fees do not generate very much revenue (usually less than 5 percent of a state's budget) and these fees can only be spent on the program or facility for which the fee was paid. A fishing license, for example, provides money to be used in stocking streams and conserving natural resources. The license revenue cannot be allocated for the general running of state government.

segregated funds
Money that comes in from a certain tax or fee and then is restricted to a specific use, such as a gasoline tax that is used for road maintenance.

In general, taxes can be evaluated according to how much money they can raise, whether the revenue is certain, and who bears the burden. Income taxes generate large sums of money, although the amount of money generated will fluctuate according to economic conditions and levels of employment. Of all the taxes, those based on income are the most **progressive taxes,** which means that they are based on the ability to pay.

Sales taxes also generate lots of money, and they vary with how well the economy is doing. These are not based on earnings, but on purchases. Since those with a low income must spend virtually all that they earn in order to live, sales taxes are **regressive taxes.** To counter the regressive nature of sales taxes, some states exempt food, medicine, clothing, and other necessities.

Property taxes vary with the value of one's property, not one's current income or spending. Thus, farmers and those with a fixed income, such as retired persons, may bear more of a burden than their current wealth suggests they should carry. The property tax can be a good revenue earner and is stable, since a jurisdiction can set a tax rate that virtually guarantees a certain level of revenue, regardless of economic trends. The local officials who set these rates invariably hear complaints about the regressive nature of property taxes.

progressive tax
The tax level increases with the wealth or ability of an individual or business to pay.

regressive tax
The tax level increases as the wealth or ability of an individual or business to pay decreases.

Summary

IN THIS CHAPTER we have examined the changing character of governance at the state and local levels in order to appreciate both the variation and the common patterns in subnational governments. We have made the following points:

1. Evolution of State and Local Governments
The initial intent was to limit the scope of state and local governments. That changed with the increased complexity of our society and economy and with the ruling of the U.S. Supreme Court that legislative districts within a state must each have the same number of people. The trend since the 1960s has been for more representative and more professional state and local governments. These jurisdictions and the federal government are forming partnerships with each other and with the private sector to address issues and provide services.

2. State Governments
State governments have traditionally had primary responsibility for criminal justice, education, public health, and economic development. Recently, state officials have assumed a larger role in welfare and environmental policy. State constitutions, which reflect major historical developments in American society, provide the basic framework of institutions and values in which state governments fulfill their roles. Since the 1960s, these governments have dramatically become more competent, professional, and accessible to the general public.

3. Local Governments
Local governance in the United States is conducted by a varied collection of over 87,000 units, most of which are run by part-time officials. These governments range from general jurisdictions covering densely urbanized areas to special districts functioning for a specific, narrow purpose. The forms of local governments also differ. There are town meetings in which all eligible voters in a community gather to conduct business, elected and appointed boards that have both executive and legislative powers, and governments with distinct legislative councils, elected executives, and professional managers. Local politics is frequently nonpartisan, thanks in part to conscious efforts to prevent control by political party machines.

4. Grassroots Power and Politics
Those who wield the most influence over the making and implementation of public policy in a community are not always the ones elected to formal offices. Sometimes power is in the hands of a family, a major business, a small number of individuals, or the local media. Whether or not those who are most powerful are the ones in government offices, governance at the grass roots is face to face, between neighbors, friends, and former high school classmates.

5. Relations with Indian Nations
American Indian nations obviously affect and are affected by state and local governments. But, due to treaty rights and the domestic dependent sovereignty of the tribes, the Indian nations have a special relationship with the federal government. Tribes

have important protections from the potential vagaries of state and local governments. Conversely, the special status of the tribes poses challenges to coherent and consistent policies in a community. Currently, the federal government is encouraging tribal governments to move to self-determination economically and politically and to enter into agreements with state and local governments on financial and policy matters.

6. State and Local Finances

Funding government is complex. Revenues are hard to project because governments tax personal and business incomes, sales, and property value—none of which governments can control. State, local, and tribal governments also rely heavily on money given to them by other jurisdictions, including the federal government. The challenge is, given these uncertainties and the general hostility toward taxes, to budget for required services and popular programs.

KEY TERMS

advisory referendum, p. 139
at-large election, p. 146
charter, p. 140
city council, p. 146
commission, p. 146
commute, p. 131
compact, p. 150
county, p. 143
Dillon's Rule, p. 139
direct initiative, p. 138
direct (popular) referendum, p. 139
district-based election, p. 146
domestic dependent nation, p. 149
extradite, p. 131
governor, p. 129
inclusion, p. 134
indirect initiative, p. 138
line-item veto, p. 129
manager, p. 146
mayor, p. 146
Missouri (Merit) Plan, p. 136
municipality, p. 143
nonpartisan election, p. 148
one-person, one-vote, p. 125
package or general veto, p. 129
pardon, p. 131
parole, p. 131

political machine, p. 128
Progressive movement, p. 128
progressive tax, p. 153
public corporation (authority) p. 147
recall, p. 139
regressive tax, p. 153
reservation land, p. 150
segregated funds, p. 152
special district, p. 143
state constitution, p. 126
term limits, p. 132
town meeting p. 146
trust land, p. 150
trust relationship, p. 149

SELECTED READINGS

Banfield, Edward C. *The Unheavenly City.* Boston: Little, Brown, 1970.

Benjamin, Gerald, and Michael J. Malbin, eds. *Limiting Legislative Terms.* Washington, DC: CQ Press, 1992.

Burns, Nancy E. *The Formation of American Local Governments: Private Values in Public Institutions.* New York: Oxford University Press, 1994.

Council of State Governments. *The Book of the States.* Lexington, KY: Council of State Governments, annual.

Crenson, Matthew A. *Neighborhood Politics.* Cambridge, MA: Harvard University Press, 1983.

Cronin, Thomas E. *Direct Democracy: The Politics of Initiative, Referendum, and Recall.* Cambridge, MA: Harvard University Press, 1999.

Dahl, Robert A. *Who Governs? Democracy and Power in an American City.* New Haven, CT: Yale University Press, 1961.

Erie, Steven P. *Rainbow's End: Irish Americans and the Dilemmas of Urban Machine Politics, 1840–1985.* Berkeley: University of California Press, 1988.

Erikson, Robert S., Gerald C. Wright, and John P. McIver. *Statehouse Democracy: Public Opinion and Policy in the American States.* Cambridge: Cambridge University Press, 1993.

Gerston, Larry N., and Terry Christensen. *Recall: California's Political Earthquake.* Armonk, NY: M. E. Sharpe, 2004.

Harrigan, John J., and David C. Nice. *Politics and Policy in States and Communities,* 8th ed. New York: Longman, 2004.

International City/County Management Association. *The Municipal Year Book.* Washington, DC: ICMA, annual.

Jewell, Malcolm E., and Marcia Lynn Whicker. *Legislative Leadership in the American States.* Ann Arbor: University of Michigan Press, 1994.

Renzulli, Diane. *Capitol Offenders: How Private Interests Govern Our States.* Washington, DC: Public Integrity Books, 2000.

Stone, Clarence N. *Regime Politics: Governing Atlanta, 1946–1988.* Lawrence: University Press of Kansas, 1989.

Woliver, Laura R. *From Outrage to Action: The Politics of Grass-Roots Dissent.* Urbana: University of Illinois Press, 1993.

WEB EXPLORATIONS

To find statistics on any branch of government in the fifty states, see the Council of State Governments at
http://www.csg.org

To learn about issues that governors nationwide deem most important, see the National Governor's Association at
http://www/nga.org

To learn about the policy issues being addressed in your state legislature, see the National Conference of State Legislatures at
http://www.ncsl.org

To understand how campaigns are financed in state governments, see the International City/County Management Association at
http://followthemoney.org

To learn more about the issues currently of concern to local government, see
http://www.1.icma.org/main/sc.asp?t=0

To learn more about American Indian nations and specific tribes, see
http://www.nativeweb.org

CIVIL LIBERTIES

THE FIRST AMENDMENT TO THE CONSTITUTION—passed by the Congress on September 25, 1789, and ratified by the states on December 15, 1791—boldly proclaims that "Congress shall make no law . . . abridging the freedom of speech . . . or the right of the people to peaceably assemble, and to petition the Government for a redress of grievances." However, when the Bill of Rights was drafted, approved by the Congress, and sent out to the states for their ratification, no one involved was thinking about protecting the political right to assembly as a means to petition the government about activities beyond American shores. The Framers, moreover, certainly would never have foreseen that Americans would take to the streets to petition their government and the United Nations to stop apartheid in South Africa, human rights violations in China, or genocide in Sudan's Darfur region.

While many Americans are unable to locate Darfur on maps of the African continent, for example, in late April 2006, massive "Stop Genocide" rallies were held all over the United States, urging President George W. Bush and his administration to take much stronger actions to prevent the widespread violence and killing in that region.

Since 2003, thousands of people in Darfur have been the target of Sudanese troops and pro-government Arab militias conducting a systematic campaign of killings and rapes.[1] In April 2006 alone, the United Nations estimated that 60,000 Darfuris had been displaced from their homeland. Thousands of Americans, including nearly 250 busloads of concerned activists from forty-one states, converged on the Mall in Washington, D.C., a site of frequent national protests, on April 30, 2006 to protest the actions and ask the president to intervene. Other Americans held rallies in seventeen other cities nationwide, and the combined effort resulted in the "largest public outcry for Darfur since the conflict began there."[2] Celebrities including actor George Clooney and a variety of elected representatives addressed those gathered at rallies around the nation. Some in the crowds carried signs reading "Never Again."[3] And, on the Mall, Representative Michael E. Capuano (D–MA) said, "you are here today to shine a bright light on the horrors and to show the world that America will not stand quietly by while the genocide continues. I am here to tell you your leaders are listening."[4]

CHAPTER OUTLINE

- ★ The First Constitutional Amendments: The Bill of Rights

- ★ First Amendment Guarantees: Freedom of Religion

- ★ First Amendment Guarantees: Freedom of Speech, Press, and Assembly

- ★ The Second Amendment: The Right to Keep and Bear Arms

- ★ The Rights of Criminal Defendants

- ★ The Right to Privacy

The rallies are not the only form of political expression that anti-genocide activists have taken. Because of student-led protest campaigns, Stanford and Harvard universities divested themselves of stock in companies doing business with or investing in Sudan. In addition, more than 750,000 American citizens coordinated by the Save Darfur Coalition have petitioned the U.S. government by sending postcards to President George W. Bush requesting that his administration do more to end the genocide. Without the guarantees of the First Amendment, these efforts by such diverse constituencies to convince the American government to help the embattled citizens of another country would never have been possible.

---

civil liberties
The personal guarantees and freedoms that the federal government cannot abridge by law, constitution, or judicial interpretation.

civil rights
The goverment-protected rights of individuals against arbitrary or discriminatory treatment.

SIMULATION

Balancing Liberty and Security at a Time of War

WHEN THE BILL OF RIGHTS, which contains many of the most important protections of individual liberties, was written, its drafters were not thinking about issues such as abortion, gay rights, physician assisted suicide, or any of the other personal liberties discussed in this chapter, let alone the rights of non-citizens, discussed in our opening vignette. As a result, the Constitution is nonabsolute in the nature of most **civil liberties,** personal guarantees and freedoms that the government cannot abridge, either by law or by judicial interpretation. Thus, when we discuss civil liberties such as those found in the Bill of Rights, we are concerned with limits on what governments can and cannot do. **Civil rights,** in contrast, are the goverment-protected rights of individuals against arbitrary or discriminatory treatment. (Civil rights are discussed in chapter 6.)

Questions of civil liberties often present complex problems. We must decide how to determine the boundaries of speech and assembly. We must also consider how much infringement on our personal liberties we want to give the police or other government actors. Moreover, in an era of a war on terrorism, it is important to consider what liberties should be accorded to those suspected of terrorist activity.

Civil liberties cases often fall to the judiciary, who must balance the competing interests of the government and the people. Thus, in many of the cases discussed in this chapter, there is a conflict between an individual or group of individuals seeking to exercise what they believe to be a liberty, and the government, be it local, state, or national, seeking to control the exercise of that liberty in an attempt to keep order and preserve the rights (and safety) of others. In other cases, two liberties are in conflict, such as a physician's and her patients' rights to easy access to a medical clinic versus a pro-life advocate's liberty to picket that clinic. Many of the Supreme Court's recent decisions, as well as actions of the George W. Bush administration in the aftermath of the September 11, 2001, terrorist attacks, are discussed in this chapter as we explore the various dimensions of civil liberties guarantees contained in the U.S. Constitution and the Bill of Rights.

- First, we will discuss *the Bill of Rights,* the reasons for its addition to the Constitution, and its eventual application to the states via the incorporation doctrine.
- Second, we will survey the meaning of one of *the First Amendment guarantees: freedom of religion.*
- Third, we will discuss the meanings of other *First Amendment guarantees: freedom of speech, press, and assembly.*
- Fourth, we will discuss *the Second Amendment* and *the right to keep and bear arms.*
- Fifth, we will analyze the reasons for many of *the rights of criminal defendants* found in the Bill of Rights and how those rights have been expanded and contracted by the U.S. Supreme Court.

- Finally, we will discuss the meaning of *the right to privacy* and how that concept has been interpreted by the Court.

The First Constitutional Amendments: The Bill of Rights

IN 1787, MOST STATE CONSTITUTIONS explicitly protected a variety of personal liberties such as speech, religion, freedom from unreasonable searches and seizures, and trial by jury. It was clear that in the new federal system, the new Constitution would redistribute power between the national government and the states. Without an explicit guarantee of specific civil liberties, could the national government be trusted to uphold the freedoms already granted to citizens by their states?

As discussed in chapter 2, recognition of the increased power that would be held by the new national government led Anti-Federalists to stress the need for a bill of rights. Anti-Federalists and many others were confident that they could control the actions of their own state legislators, but they didn't trust the national government to be so protective of their civil liberties.

The notion of adding a bill of rights to the Constitution was not a popular one at the Constitutional Convention. When George Mason of Virginia proposed that such a bill be added to the preface of the proposed Constitution, his resolution was defeated unanimously.[5] In the subsequent ratification debates, Federalists argued that a bill of rights was unnecessary. Not only did most state constitutions already contain those protections, but Federalists believed it was foolhardy to list things that the national government had no power to do.

Some Federalists, however, supported the idea. After the Philadelphia convention, for example, James Madison conducted a lively correspondence about the need for a national bill of rights with Thomas Jefferson. Jefferson was far quicker to support such guarantees than was Madison, who continued to doubt their utility. He believed that a list of protected rights might suggest that those not enumerated were not protected. Politics soon intervened, however, when Madison found himself in a close race against James Monroe for a seat in the House of Representatives in the First Congress. The district was largely Anti-Federalist. So, in an act of political expediency, Madison issued a new series of public letters similar to *The Federalist Papers* in which he vowed to support a bill of rights.

Once elected to the House, Madison made good on his promise and became the prime author of the Bill of Rights. Still, he considered Congress to have far more important matters to handle and viewed his work on the Bill of Rights as "a nauseous project."[6]

The insistence of Anti-Federalists on a bill of rights, the fact that some states conditioned their ratification of the Constitution on the addition of these guarantees, and the disagreement among Federalists about writing specific liberty guarantees into the Constitution led to prompt congressional action to put an end to further controversy. This was a time when national stability and support for the new government particularly were needed. Thus, in 1789, Congress sent the proposed Bill of Rights to the states for ratification, which occurred in 1791.

The **Bill of Rights**, the first ten amendments to the Constitution, contains numerous specific guarantees, including those of free speech, press, and religion (for the full text, see the annotated Constitution that begins on page 66). The Ninth and Tenth Amendments, in particular, highlight Anti-Federalist fears of a too-powerful

Bill of Rights
The first ten amendments to the U.S. Constitution, which largely guarantee specific rights and liberties.

Ninth Amendment
Part of the Bill of Rights that reads "The enumeration in the Constitution, of certain rights, shall not be construed to deny or disparage others retained by the people."

Tenth Amendment
Part of the Bill of Rights that reiterates powers not delegated to the national government are reserved to the states or to the people.

due process clause
Clause contained in the Fifth and Fourteenth Amendments. Over the years, it has been construed to guarantee to individuals a variety of rights ranging from economic liberty to criminal procedural rights to protection from arbitrary governmental action.

substantive due process
Judicial interpretation of the Fifth and Fourteenth Amendments' due process clause that protects citizens from arbitrary or unjust laws.

national government. The **Ninth Amendment,** strongly favored by Madison, makes it clear that this special listing of rights does not mean that others don't exist. The **Tenth Amendment** reiterates that powers not delegated to the national government are reserved to the states or to the people.

THE INCORPORATION DOCTRINE: THE BILL OF RIGHTS MADE APPLICABLE TO THE STATES

The Bill of Rights was intended to limit the powers of the national government to infringe on the rights and liberties of the citizenry. In *Barron* v. *Baltimore* (1833), the Supreme Court ruled that the national Bill of Rights limited only the actions of the U.S. government and not those of the states.[7] In 1868, however, the Fourteenth Amendment was added to the U.S. Constitution. Its language suggested the possibility that some or even all of the protections guaranteed in the Bill of Rights might be interpreted to prevent state infringement of those rights. Section 1 of the Fourteenth Amendment reads: "No State shall . . . deprive any person of life, liberty, or property, without due process of law." Questions about the scope of "liberty" as well as the meaning of "due process of law" continue even today to engage legal scholars and jurists.

Until nearly the turn of the century, the Supreme Court steadfastly rejected numerous arguments urging it to interpret the **due process clause** found in the Fourteenth Amendment as making various provisions contained in the Bill of Rights applicable to the states. In 1897, however, the Court began to increase its jurisdiction over the states.[8] It began to hold states to a **substantive due process** standard whereby states had the legal burden to prove that their laws were a valid exercise of their power to regulate the health, welfare, or public morals of their citizens. Interferences with state power, however, were rare. As a consequence, states continued to pass sedition laws (laws that made it illegal to speak or write any political criticism that threatened to diminish respect for the government, its laws, or public officials), anticipating that the Supreme Court would uphold their constitutionality. These expectations changed dramatically in 1925. Benjamin Gitlow, a member of the Socialist Party, was convicted of violating a New York law that prohibited the advocacy of the violent overthrow of the government. Gitlow had printed 16,000 copies of a manifesto in which he urged workers to rise up to overthrow the U.S. government. Although Gitlow's conviction was upheld, in *Gitlow* v. *New York* (1925), the Supreme Court noted that the states were not completely free to limit forms of political expression:

For present purposes we may and do assume that freedom of speech and of the press—which are protected by the First Amendment from abridgement by Congress—are among the *fundamental personal rights and "liberties"* protected by the due process clause of the Fourteenth Amendment from impairment by the states [emphasis added].[9]

Gitlow, with its finding that states could not abridge free speech protections, was the first step in the slow development of what is called the

■ Until *Gitlow* v. *New York* (1925), involving Benjamin Gitlow, the executive secretary of the Socialist Party, it generally was thought that the Fourteenth Amendment did not apply the protections of the Bill of Rights to the states. Here Gitlow, right, is shown testifying before a congressional committee that was investigating un-American activities.

Photo courtesy: AP Wide World Photos

incorporation doctrine. After *Gitlow,* it took the Court six more years to incorporate another First Amendment freedom—that of the press. *Near* v. *Minnesota* (1931) was the first case in which the Supreme Court found that a state law violated freedom of the press as protected by the First Amendment. Jay Near, the publisher of a weekly Minneapolis newspaper, regularly attacked a variety of groups—African Americans, Catholics, Jews, and labor union leaders. Few escaped his hatred. Near's paper was shut down under the authority of a state criminal libel law banning "malicious, scandalous, or defamatory" publications. Near appealed the closing of his paper, and the Supreme Court ruled that "The fact that the liberty of the press may be abused by miscreant purveyors of scandal does not make any the less necessary the immunity of the press from previous restraint."[10]

incorporation doctrine
An interpretation of the Constitution that holds that the due process clause of the Fourteenth Amendment requires that state and local governments also guarantee those rights.

SELECTIVE INCORPORATION AND FUNDAMENTAL FREEDOMS

Not all the specific guarantees in the Bill of Rights have been made applicable to the states through the due process clause of the Fourteenth Amendment, as revealed in Table 5.1. Instead, the Court has used the process of **selective incorporation** to limit the rights of states by protecting against abridgment of **fundamental freedoms**, those liberties defined by the Court as essential to order, liberty, and justice. Fundamental freedoms are subject to the Court's most rigorous strict scrutiny standard of review. (See chapter 6, pp. 220–21, for a more complete discussion of strict scrutiny and other standards of review.)

selective incorporation
A judicial doctrine whereby most but not all of the protections found in the Bill of Rights are made applicable to the states via the Fourteenth Amendment.

fundamental freedoms
Those rights defined by the Court to be essential to order, liberty, and justice and therefore entitled to the highest standard of review, strict scrutiny.

TABLE 5.1 THE SELECTIVE INCORPORATION OF THE BILL OF RIGHTS

Amendment	Right	Date	Case Incorporated
I	Speech	1925	*Gitlow* v. *New York*
	Press	1931	*Near* v. *Minnesota*
	Assembly	1937	*DeJonge* v. *Oregon*
	Religion	1940	*Cantwell* v. *Connecticut*
II	Bear arms		Not incorporated (A test has not been presented to the Court in recent history.)
III	No quartering of soldiers		Not incorporated (The quartering problem has not recurred since colonial times.)
IV	No unreasonable searches or seizures	1949	*Wolf* v. *Colorado*
	Exclusionary rule	1961	*Mapp* v. *Ohio*
V	Just compensation	1897	*Chicago, B&Q RR Co.* v. *Chicago*
	Self-incrimination	1964	*Malloy* v. *Hogan*
	Double jeopardy	1969	*Benton* v. *Maryland* (overruled *Palko* v. *Connecticut*)
	Grand jury indictment		Not incorporated (The trend in state criminal cases is away from grand juries.)
VI	Public trial	1948	*In re Oliver*
	Right to counsel	1963	*Gideon* v. *Wainwright*
	Confrontation of witnesses	1965	*Pointer* v. *Texas*
	Impartial trial	1966	*Parker* v. *Gladden*
	Speedy trial	1967	*Klopfer* v. *North Carolina*
	Compulsory trial	1967	*Washington* v. *Texas*
	Criminal jury trial	1968	*Duncan* v. *Louisiana*
VII	Civil jury trial		Not incorporated (Chief Justice Warren Burger wanted to abolish these trials.)
VIII	No cruel and unusual punishment	1962	*Robinson* v. *California*
	No excessive fines or bail		Not incorporated

Selective incorporation requires the states to respect freedoms of press, speech, and assembly, among other rights. Other guarantees contained in the Second, Third, and Seventh Amendments, such as the right to bear arms, have not been incorporated because the Court has yet to consider them sufficiently fundamental to national notions of liberty and justice.

The rationale for selective incorporation was set out by the Court in *Palko* v. *Connecticut* (1937).[11] Frank Palko was charged with first-degree murder for killing two Connecticut police officers, found guilty of a lesser charge of second-degree murder, and sentenced to life imprisonment. Connecticut appealed. Palko was retried, found guilty of first-degree murder, and sentenced to death. Palko then appealed his second conviction, arguing that it violated the Fifth Amendment's prohibition against double jeopardy because the Fifth Amendment had been made applicable to the states by the due process clause of the Fourteenth Amendment.

The Supreme Court upheld Palko's second conviction and the death sentence. They also chose not to bind states to the Fifth Amendment's double jeopardy clause and concluded that protection from being tried twice (double jeopardy) was not a fundamental freedom. Palko died in Connecticut's gas chamber one year later. *Palko* was overruled in 1969.

First Amendment

Part of the Bill of Rights that imposes a number of restrictions on the federal government with respect to the civil liberties of the people, including freedom of religion, speech, press, assembly, and petition.

establishment clause

The first clause in the First Amendment; it prohibits the national government from establishing a national religion.

■ HBO's popular *Big Love* depicts a polygamous family of one husband and three wives living in suburban Utah. The Mormon Church officially repudiated polygamy in 1890 and the practice is illegal, but various splinter groups continue to practice polygamy and insist that their family structures reflect God's will.

Photo courtesy: The Everett Collection

First Amendment Guarantees: Freedom of Religion

MANY OF THE FRAMERS were religious men, but they knew what evils could arise if the new nation was not founded with religious freedom as one of its core ideals. Although many colonists had fled Europe to escape religious persecution, most colonies actively persecuted those who did not belong to their predominant religious groups. Nevertheless, in 1774, the colonists uniformly were outraged when the British Parliament passed a law establishing Anglicanism and Roman Catholicism as official religions in the colonies. The First Continental Congress immediately sent a letter of protest announcing its "astonishment that a British Parliament should ever consent to establish . . . a religion [Catholicism] that has deluged [England] in blood and dispersed bigotry, persecution, murder and rebellion through every part of the world."[12]

The Framers' distaste for a national church or religion was reflected in the Constitution. Article VI, for example, provides that "no religious Test shall ever be required as a Qualification to any Office or Public Trust under the United States." This simple statement, however, did not completely reassure those who feared the new Constitution would curtail individual liberty. Thus, the First Amendment to the Constitution soon was ratified to allay those fears.

The **First Amendment** to the Constitution begins, "Congress shall make no law respecting an establishment of religion, or prohibiting the free exercise thereof." This statement sets the boundaries of governmental action. The **establishment clause** ("Congress shall make no law respecting an establishment of religion") directs the national government not to involve itself in religion. It creates, in Thomas Jefferson's words, a "wall of separation" between church and state. The **free exercise clause** ("or prohibiting the free exercise thereof") guarantees citizens that the national government will not interfere with their practice of religion. These guarantees, however, are not absolute. In the mid-1800s, Mormons traditionally practiced and preached polygamy, the taking of multiple wives. In 1879, when the Supreme Court was first called on to interpret the free exercise clause, it upheld the conviction of a Mormon under a federal law barring polygamy. The Court reasoned that to do otherwise would provide constitutional protections to a full range of religious beliefs, including those as extreme as human sacrifice. "Laws are made for the government of actions," noted the Court, "and while they cannot interfere with mere religious belief and opinions, they may with practices."[13] Later, in 1940, the Supreme Court observed that the First Amendment "embraces two concepts—freedom to believe and freedom to act. The first is absolute, but in the nature of things, the second cannot be. Conduct remains subject to regulation of society."[14]

free exercise clause
The second clause of the First Amendment; it prohibits the U.S. government from interfering with a citizen's right to practice his or her religion. Still, some forms of actual exercise of religion can be regulated.

THE ESTABLISHMENT CLAUSE

Over the years, the Court has been divided over how to interpret the establishment clause. Does this clause erect a total wall between church and state, or is some governmental accommodation of religion allowed? While the Supreme Court has upheld the constitutionality of many kinds of church/state entanglements such as public funding to provide sign language interpreters for deaf students in religious schools,[15] the Court has held fast to the rule of strict separation between church and state when issues of prayer in school are involved. In *Engel* v. *Vitale* (1962), the Court first ruled that the recitation in public school classrooms of a twenty-two-word nondenominational prayer drafted by the New Hyde Park, New York, school board was unconstitutional.[16] In 1992, the Court continued its unwillingness to allow organized prayer in public schools by finding unconstitutional the saying of prayer at a middle school graduation.[17] And, in 2000, the Court ruled that student-led, student-initiated prayer at high school football games violated the establishment clause.

The Court has gone back and forth in its effort to come up with a workable way to deal with church/state questions. In 1971, in *Lemon* v. *Kurtzman*, the Court tried to carve out a three-part test for laws dealing with religious establishment issues. According to the *Lemon* test, a practice or policy was constitutional if it: (1) had a secular purpose; (2) neither advanced nor inhibited religion; and, (3) did not foster an excessive government entanglement with religion.[18] But, since the early 1980s, the Supreme Court often has sidestepped the *Lemon* test altogether and has appeared more willing to lower the wall between church and state so long as school prayer is not involved.[19] In 1981, for example, the Court ruled unconstitutional a Missouri law prohibiting the use of state university buildings and grounds for "purposes of religious worship." The law had been used to ban religious groups from using school facilities.[20]

This decision was taken by many members of Congress as a sign that this principle could be extended to secondary and even primary schools. In 1984, Congress passed the Equal Access Act, which bars public schools from discriminating against groups of students on the basis of "religious, political, philosophical or other content of the speech at such meetings." The constitutionality of this law was upheld in 1990 when the Court ruled that a school board's refusal to allow a Christian Bible club to meet in a public high school classroom during a twice-weekly "activity period" violated the act. According to the decision, the primary effect of the act was neither to advance religion nor to excessively entangle government and religion—even though religious meetings would be held on school grounds with a faculty sponsor. The important factor seemed to be that the students had free choice in their selection of activities, including numerous nonreligious options from which to choose.[21] In 1993, the Court also ruled that religious groups must be allowed to use public schools after hours if that access is also given to other community groups.[22]

In 1995, the Court signaled that it was willing to lower the wall even further. In a case involving the University of Virginia, a 5–4 majority held that the university violated the free speech rights of a fundamentalist Christian group when it refused to fund the groups' student magazine. The importance of this decision was highlighted by Justice David Souter, who noted in dissent: "The Court today, for the first time, approves direct funding of core religious activities by an arm of the state."[23]

For more than a quarter century, the Supreme Court basically allowed "books only" as an aid to religious schools, noting that the books go to children, not to the schools themselves. This, however, seems to be changing. In 1997, in *Agostini* v. *Felton*, the Supreme Court approved of a New York program that sent public school teachers into parochial schools during school hours to provide remedial education to disadvantaged students. The Court concluded that this was not an excessive entanglement of church and state and therefore was not a violation of the establishment clause.[24] And, in 2000, the Court voted 6–3 to uphold the constitutionality of a federal aid provision that allowed the government to lend books and computers to religious schools.[25] Finally, in 2002, by a bitterly divided 5–4 vote, the Supreme Court in *Zelman* v. *Simmons-Harris* concluded that governments can give money to parents to allow them to send their children to private or religious schools.[26] The majority opinion, written by Chief Justice William H. Rehnquist, concluded that Cleveland's school voucher program gave families freedom of choice to send their children to the school of their choice. He concluded that the voucher system was neutral toward religion and, thus, was not an official sponsorship of religion prohibited by the establishment clause. In dissent, Justice David Souter called the opinion a "potentially tragic" error that "would force citizens to subsidize faiths they do not even share even as it corrupts religion by making it dependent on government."[27] Basically, the Court now appears willing to support programs so long as they provide aid to religious and nonreligious schools alike, and the money goes to persons who exercise free choice over how it is used.

Establishment issues, however, do not always focus on education. In 2005, for example, the Supreme Court in a 5–4 decision narrowly upheld the continued vitality of the *Lemon* test in holding that a privately donated courthouse display, which included the Ten Commandments and 300 other historical documents illustrating the evolution of American law, was a violation of the First Amendment's establishment clause. Court watchers now are waiting to see how the addition of two new justices to the Court will affect these closely divided opinions.[28] For example, in a case winding its way through the federal courts, a federal judge ruled in 2006 that Charles Colson's Prison Fellowship Ministries and the state of Iowa violated the religious establishment clause when it created a government-funded program intended to rehabilitate prisoners by total immersion in Christianity. (See American Voices/ American Values: Where's the Wall?) This case, brought by Americans United for Separation of Church and State, a liberal D.C.-based advocacy group, is "widely viewed as a major challenge to President Bush's faith-based initiatives, the White House's effort to deliver more government funding to religious groups that provide social services, especially in prisons."[29]

■ President George W. Bush addresses an audience at The White House National Conference on Faith-Based and Community Initiatives in 2006. The Bush administration's policies have paved the way for millions of dollars in public funds to go to religious organizations. Critics contend that some Bush policies run afoul of the Constitution's establishment clause.

Photo courtesy: Kimberlie Hewitt/The White House

THE FREE EXERCISE CLAUSE

The free exercise clause of the First Amendment proclaims that "Congress shall make no law . . . prohibiting the free exercise [of religion]." Although the free exercise clause of the First Amendment guarantees individuals the right to be free from governmental interference in the exercise of their religion, this guarantee, like other First Amendment freedoms, is not absolute. When secular law comes into conflict with religious law, the right to exercise one's religious beliefs is often denied—especially if the religious beliefs in question are held by a minority or by an unpopular or "suspicious" group.

The Supreme Court has interpreted the Constitution to mean that governmental interests can outweigh free exercise rights. State statutes barring the use of certain illegal drugs, snake handling, and polygamy—all practices of particular religious sects—have been upheld as constitutional when states have shown compelling reasons to regulate these practices. Nonetheless, the Court has made it clear that the free exercise clause requires that a state or the national government remain neutral toward religion. In 1993, for example, the Court ruled that members of the Santería Church, an Afro-Cuban religion, had the right to sacrifice animals during religious services. In upholding that practice, the Court ruled that a city ordinance banning such practices was unconstitutionally aimed at the group, thereby denying its members the right to free exercise of their religion.[30] Earlier, however, in 1990, the Court ruled that the free exercise clause allowed Oregon to ban the use of sacramental peyote (an illegal hallucinogenic drug) in some Native American tribes' traditional religious services. In upholding the state's right to deny unemployment compensation to two workers who had been fired by a private drug rehabilitation clinic because they had ingested peyote, a majority of the Court held that the state did not need to show a compelling interest to limit the free exercise of religion in this case.[31] This decision prompted a dramatic outcry. Congressional response was passage of the Religious Freedom Restoration Act, which specifically made the use of peyote in religious services legal.[32] Thus, as recently as 2006, the U.S. Supreme Court by a vote of 8–0, found that the use of hoasca tea, which is brewed from plants found in the Amazon River basin and which contains the controlled substance dimethyltryptamine (DMT), well-known for its hallucinogenic properties, was permissible free exercise of religion for members of the Brazilian-based O Centro Espirita Beneficente União Do Vegetal church (UDV). In *Gonzales v. O Centro Espirita Beneficente União Do Vegetal* (2006), the Court noted that Congress had overruled its earlier decision and specifically legalized the use of other sacramental substances including peyote. Queried Justice Ruth Bader Ginsburg regarding the religious uses of hoasca tea and peyote, "if the government must accommodate one, why not the other?"[33]

Although conflicts between religious beliefs and the government are often difficult to settle, the Court has attempted to walk the fine line between the free exercise and establishment clauses. In the area of free exercise, the Court often has had to confront questions of "What is a god?" and "What is a religious faith?"—questions that theologians have grappled with for centuries. In 1965, for example, in a case involving three men who were denied conscientious objector deferments during the Vietnam War because they did not subscribe to "traditional" organized religions, the Court ruled unanimously that belief in a supreme being was not essential for recognition as a conscientious objector.[34] Thus, the men were entitled to the deferments because their views paralleled those who objected to war and who belonged to traditional religions. In contrast, despite the Court's having ruled that Catholic, Protestant, Jewish, and Buddhist prison inmates must be allowed to hold religious services,[35] the Court ruled that Islamic prisoners can be denied the same right for security reasons.[36]

American Values/American Voices

WHERE'S THE WALL?

In President Thomas Jefferson's view, there was to be a near impenetrable wall between church and state. Subsequent presidents as well as U.S. Supreme Court justices have held to that view. But, the election of President George W. Bush, the second president to claim to be a born-again Christian (Jimmy Carter was the first), brought with it a new and what many critics have called an unprecedented entanglement of church and state. Immediately after he took office in 2001, President Bush created a new Office of Faith-Based Initiatives. In January 2004, he announced, "we want to fund programs that save Americans one soul at a time."[a] In his State of the Union message, the president urged the House and Senate to make his faith-based proposals permanent. The programs administered by this office represent some of the widest ranging entanglements of church and state in the history of the United States and are in many ways reflective of American values and the voices of the American people who believe that the United States would benefit from a closer connection between religious beliefs and governmental actions.

But, in making federal dollars available to religious groups for their programs, has the Bush administration left the Framers' intentions by the wayside? In 2003, for example, the administration announced that it would not withhold funding from religious groups that discriminate in hiring based on religious affiliation—thus reversing decades-old policies prohibiting religious discrimination by federally funded agencies. The Salvation Army, for example, not only received funding but was accorded greater freedom to exclude homosexuals from its workforce. In 2004, while Americorps was able to fund a day-care center run by the Roman Catholic Diocese of Providence, a Washington, D.C., mentoring program for children was abolished.[b] Justice Sunday III, a lobbying event designed to bring more conservative judges to the courts, discussed in greater detail in chapter 10, received $1 million in federal grants, some of which may have been used indirectly to lobby for Senate approval of Roman Catholic nominees to

the Supreme Court—Chief Justice John G. Roberts Jr. and Samuel A. Alito Jr., specifically.

Americans United for Separation of Church and State has been particularly critical of Bush's initiatives, especially those that have been accomplished through executive order and not through explicit congressional authorization. Abstinence-only sex-education programs for public schools, for example, have been a favorite of the Bush administration, but they have been barred from implementation by state judges—some of them conservatives—who believe that they contain too many "references to God, Jesus Christ, and the spiritual repercussions of sex before marriage."[c]

The separation of church and state has always been a thorny issue in American politics. A majority of Americans clearly value the moral teachings of most major religions, especially Christianity. U.S. coins are embossed with "In God We Trust." The U.S. Supreme Court asks God's blessing on the Court. Every session of the U.S. House and Senate begins with a prayer, and the House has its own chaplain. Yet, particularly when the United States is at war in an area of the world where religion often is at the core of nationalist pride and armed hostilities, it may be time to ponder once again the Framers' motives for including the establishment clause in the Constitution.

QUESTIONS

1. What reasons can you list in support of and in opposition to the United States embracing its Christian heritage more openly than ever before?
2. How does a diverse nation like the United States deal with clashes caused by citizens' sometimes competing religious values?

---

[a]"The Rise of the Religious Right in the Republican Administration," www.theocracywatch.org/faith_base.htm.

[b]"The Rise of the Religious Right in the Republican Administration."

[c]Theocracy Watch, http://www.theocracywatch.org.

First Amendment Guarantees: Freedom of Speech, Press, and Assembly

Comparing Civil Liberties

TODAY, SOME MEMBERS OF CONGRESS criticize the movie industry and reality television shows such as *Survivor* and *The Real World* for pandering to the least common denominator of society. Other groups criticize popular performers such as 50 Cent for lyrics that denigrate women. Such criticism often comes with calls for increased restrictions and greater regulation of media outlets. This leads many civil libertarians to believe that the rights to speak, print, and assemble freely are being seriously threatened.[37] (For more details on content regulation, see chapter 15.)

FREEDOM OF SPEECH AND THE PRESS

A democracy depends on a free exchange of ideas, and the First Amendment shows that the Framers were well aware of this fact. Historically, one of the most volatile areas of constitutional interpretation has been in the interpretation of the First Amendment's mandate that "Congress shall make no law . . . abridging the freedom of speech or of the press." Like the establishment and free exercise clauses of the First Amendment, the speech and press clauses have not been interpreted as absolute bans against government regulation. A lack of absolute meaning has led to thousands of cases seeking both broader and narrower judicial interpretations of the scope of the amendment. Over the years, the Court has employed a hierarchical approach in determining what the government can and cannot regulate, with some items getting greater protection than others. Generally, thoughts have received the greatest protection, and actions or deeds the least. Words have come somewhere in the middle, depending on their content and purpose. (See Global Perspective: Freedom of the Press for a worldwide look at press freedoms.)

The Alien and Sedition Acts When the First Amendment was ratified in 1791, it was considered only to protect against **prior restraint** of speech or expression, or to guard against the prohibition of speech or publication before the fact. However, in 1798, the Federalist Congress with President John Adams's blessings enacted the Alien and Sedition Acts, which were designed to ban any criticism of the Federalist government by the growing numbers of Democratic-Republicans. These acts made the publication of "any false, scandalous writing against the government of the United States" a criminal offense. Although the law clearly ran in the face of the First Amendment's ban on prior restraint, the Adams administration successfully prosecuted. Partisan Federalist judges imposed fines and jail terms on at least ten Democratic-Republican newspaper editors. The acts became a major issue in the 1800 presidential election campaign, which led to the election of Thomas Jefferson, a vocal opponent of the acts. He quickly pardoned all who had been convicted under their provisions and the Democratic-Republican Congress allowed the acts to expire before the Federalist-controlled Supreme Court had an opportunity to rule on the constitutionality of these serious infringements of the First Amendment.

Slavery, the Civil War, and Rights Curtailments After the public outcry over the Alien and Sedition Acts, the national government largely got out of the business of regulating speech. But, in its place, the states, which were not yet bound by the Bill of Rights, began to prosecute those who published articles critical of governmental policies. In the 1830s, at the urgings of abolitionists (those who sought an end to slavery), the publication or dissemination of any positive information about slavery became a punishable offense in the North. In the opposite vein, in the South, supporters of slavery enacted laws to prohibit publication of any anti-slavery sentiments. Southern postmasters refused to deliver northern abolitionist papers, a step that amounted to censorship of the mail.

During the Civil War, President Abraham Lincoln effectively suspended the free press provision of the First Amendment as well as the **writ of habeas corpus**—the right of a court to determine whether prisoners are being held lawfully and to free prisoners if the court determines they are not being held lawfully. He went so far as to order the arrest of the editors of two New York papers who were critical of him. Far from protesting against these blatant violations of the First Amendment, Congress acceded to them. In one instance, William McCardle, a Mississippi newspaper editor who had written in opposition to Lincoln and the Union occupation, was jailed by a military court without having any charges brought against him. He appealed his detainment to the U.S. Supreme Court, arguing that he was being held unlawfully. Congress, fearing that a victory for McCardle would hurt Lincoln's national standing and prompt other similarly treated Confederate editors to follow his lead, enacted legislation prohibiting the Supreme Court

prior restraint
Constitutional doctrine that prevents the government from prohibiting speech or publication before the fact; generally held to be in violation of the First Amendment.

Civil Liberties and National Security

writ of habeas corpus
A court order in which a judge requires authorities to prove that a prisoner is being held lawfully and that allows the prisoner to be freed if the judge is not persuaded by the government's case. Habeas corpus rights imply that prisoners have a right to know what charges are being made against them.

Global Perspective

FREEDOM OF THE PRESS

Americans are quite correctly proud of the independent voice exercised by the U.S. press. But, how do press freedoms in the United States compare with those found in other countries? And, just how free is the American press? Global comparisons can be made along three dimensions. First is the legal environment: what rules and regulations govern media content? Second is the political environment: how much political control is exercised over the content of the news media? Third is the economic environment: who owns the media and how are media outlets financed?

Using these three factors, Freedom House, a nonprofit organization that serves as a global civil liberties watchdog, issues a report each year on the degree of print, broadcast, and Internet freedom in every country in the world. The news media in each country are rated on a scale of 1–100, with those receiving a rating of 1–30 being considered free, those receiving a rating of 31–60 being considered partly free, and those receiving a rating of 61–100 being considered not free.

In 2005, the United States, along with neighboring Canada and four other nations, received a rating of 17; twenty other nations received ratings of 16 or higher, placing the news media in these nations in the free category. Finland, Iceland, and Sweden received ratings of 9, tying them for first place. Mexico, America's southern neighbor, received a rating of 42 in 2005, placing its press in the partly free category, primarily due to intimidation and violence against journalists sponsored by drug cartels and corrupt members of the police force or government. While media outlets in Mexico's large urban areas are relatively free from interference, journalists operating in more rural areas, especially along Mexico's border with the United States, are vulnerable to harassment and violence.

Russia's news media, with a rating of 68, is judged to be not free. The Russian government under the leadership of President Vladimir Putin has nearly complete control of the broadcast media, and Putin's government has passed laws and used financial pressure to restrict critical coverage of its policies. These restrictions are particularly true with respect to its handling of the long and bloody war in the breakaway province of Chechnya.

While Iraq's rating has improved significantly since Saddam Hussein was deposed in 2003, its media remain in the not free category. Moreover, its rating deteriorated somewhat from a 66 in 2004 to 70 in 2005, reflecting continued instability and violence, the targeting of journalists by extremists and occasionally government and coalition forces, and ambiguity surrounding the role of new institutions charged with regulating the media. Afghanistan's rating has similarly improved significantly since the overthrow of the Taliban regime in 2002, although its press, like Iraq's, received a rating in the not free range.

The five countries whose news media were rated least free in 2005 were Libya, Myanmar (Burma), Turkmenistan, Cuba, and North Korea (which came in last, with a rating of 97). Overall, 75 countries (39 percent) were judged to have a free press, 52 had a partly free press (27 percent), and 67 (34 percent) did not have a free press, a slight improvement over 2003 ratings of press freedom.

QUESTIONS

1. What factors would you look at in judging whether a country had a free press? Explain your reasoning.
2. Are economic, political, or cultural factors most important in making the press free? Why?

Sources: Freedom House, "Map of Press Freedom 2005" and "Freedom of the Press 2005: Press Freedom Rankings 1994–2005," both at http://www.freedomhouse.org.

---

from issuing a judgment in any cases involving convictions for publishing statements critical of the United States. Because Article II of the Constitution gives Congress the power to determine the jurisdiction of the Court, the Court was forced to conclude in *Ex parte McCardle* (1869) that it had no authority to rule in the matter.[38]

After the Civil War, states also began to prosecute individuals for seditious speech if they uttered or printed statements critical of the government. Between 1890 and 1900, for example, there were more than one hundred state prosecutions for sedition.[39] Moreover, by the dawn of the twentieth century, public opinion in the United States had grown increasingly hostile toward the commentary of Socialists and Communists who attempted to appeal to the growing immigrant population. Groups espousing socialism and communism became the targets of state laws curtailing speech and the written word. By the end of World War I, over thirty states had passed laws to punish seditious speech, and more than 1,900 individuals and over one hundred newspapers were prosecuted for violations.[40] In 1925, however, states' authority to regulate speech was severely restricted by the Court's decision in *Gitlow* v. *New York.* (For more on *Gitlow*, see p. 160.)

World War I and Anti-Governmental Speech The next major national efforts to restrict freedom of speech and the press did not occur until Congress, at the urging of President Woodrow Wilson during World War I, passed the Espionage Act in 1917. Nearly 2,000 Americans were convicted of violating its various provisions, especially those that made it illegal to urge resistance to the draft or to prohibit the distribution of anti-war leaflets. In *Schenck* v. *U.S.* (1919), the Supreme Court upheld this act, ruling that Congress had a right to restrict speech "of such a nature as to create a clear and present danger that will bring about the substantive evils that Congress has a right to prevent."[41] Under this test, known as the **clear and present danger test,** the circumstances surrounding an incident are important. Under *Schenck,* anti-war leaflets, for example, may be permissible during peacetime, but during World War I they were considered to pose too much of a danger to be permissible.

For decades, the Supreme Court wrestled with what constituted a danger. Finally, in *Brandenburg* v. *Ohio* (1969), the Court fashioned a new test for deciding whether certain kinds of speech could be regulated by the government: the **direct incitement test.** Now, the government could punish the advocacy of illegal action only if "such advocacy is directed to inciting or producing imminent lawless action and is likely to incite or produce such action."[42] The requirement of "imminent lawless action" makes it more difficult for the government to punish speech and publication and is consistent with the Framers' notion of the special role played by these elements in a democratic society. Passage of the Military Commissions Act in 2006, however, leaves this ruling in question.

PROTECTED SPEECH AND PUBLICATIONS

As discussed, the Supreme Court refuses to uphold the constitutionality of legislation that amounts to prior restraint of the press. Other types of speech and publication are also protected by the Court, including symbolic speech and hate speech.

Prior Restraint With only a few exceptions, the Court has made it clear that it will not tolerate prior restraint of speech. For example, in *New York Times Co.* v. *U.S.* (1971) (also called the Pentagon Papers case), the Supreme Court ruled that the U.S. government could not block the publication of secret Department of Defense documents illegally furnished to the *Times* by anti-war activists.[43] In 1976, the Supreme Court went even further, noting in *Nebraska Press Association* v. *Stuart* (1976) that any attempt by the government to prevent expression carried " 'a heavy presumption' against its constitutionality."[44] In this case, a trial court issued a gag order barring the press from reporting the lurid details of a crime. In balancing the defendant's constitutional right to a fair trial against the press's right to cover a story, the Nebraska trial judge concluded that the defendant's right carried greater weight. The Supreme Court disagreed, holding the press's right to cover the trial paramount. Still, judges are often allowed to issue gag orders affecting parties to a lawsuit or to limit press coverage of a case.

In 2005, however, the Court ruled that a trial judge's prohibition on defaming statements about a deceased public figure, in this case the high-profile attorney Johnnie Cochran, violated the First Amendment's protection of the right to free speech.[45] The Court found that Cochran's death diminished his need for protection, and thus the prohibition was an overly broad exercise of prior restraint.

Symbolic Speech In addition to the general protection accorded to pure speech, the Supreme Court has extended the

clear and present danger test
Test articulated by the Supreme Court in *Schenck* v. *U.S.* (1919) to draw the line between protected and unprotected speech; the Court looks to see "whether the words used" could "create a clear and present danger that they will bring about substantive evils" that Congress seeks "to prevent."

direct incitement test
A test articulated by the Supreme Court in *Brandenburg* v. *Ohio* (1969) that holds that advocacy of illegal action is protected by the First Amendment unless imminent lawless action is intended and likely to occur.

VISUAL LITERACY

What Speech Is Protected by the Constitution?

■ Defense attorney Johnnie Cochran was the posthumous respondent in a Supreme Court libel trial. Here, Cochran holds an autographed newspaper reporting the verdict in his most famous case—the murder trial of football star O.J. Simpson.

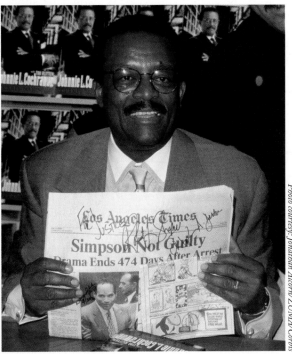

Photo courtesy: Jonathan Alcorn/ZUMA/Corbis

symbolic speech
Symbols, signs, and other methods of expression generally also considered to be protected by the First Amendment.

reach of the First Amendment to **symbolic speech,** a means of expression that includes symbols or signs. In the words of Justice John Marshall Harlan, these kinds of speech are part of the "free trade in ideas."[46] For more on symbolic speech, see On Campus: Political Speech and Mandatory Student Fees.

The Supreme Court first acknowledged that symbolic speech was entitled to First Amendment protection in *Stromberg* v. *California* (1931).[47] There, the Court overturned a communist youth camp director's conviction under a state statute prohibiting the display of a red flag, a symbol of opposition to the U.S. government. In a similar vein, the right of high school students to wear black armbands to protest the Vietnam War was upheld in *Tinker* v. *Des Moines Independent Community School District* (1969).[48]

Burning the American flag also has been held a form of protected symbolic speech. In 1989, a sharply divided Supreme Court (5–4) reversed the conviction of Gregory Johnson, who had been found guilty of setting fire to an American flag during the 1984 Republican National Convention in Dallas.[49] There was a major public outcry against the Court. President George Bush and numerous members of Congress called for a constitutional amendment banning flag burning. Others, including Justice William J. Brennan Jr., noted that if it had not been for acts similar to Johnson's, the United States would never have been created nor would a First Amendment guaranteeing the right of political protest exist.

Unable to pass a constitutional amendment, Congress passed the Federal Flag Protection Act of 1989, which authorized federal prosecution of anyone who intentionally desecrated a national flag. Johnson and his colleagues burned another flag and were again convicted. Their conviction was overturned by a 5–4 vote of the Supreme Court. The majority concluded that this federal law "suffered from the same fundamental flaw" as had the earlier Texas state law.[50] Since that decision, Congress has tried several times unsuccessfully to pass a constitutional amendment to ban flag burning.

Hate Speech

Hate Speech, Unpopular Speech, and Speech Zones "As a thumbnail summary of the last two or three decades of speech issues in the Supreme Court," wrote eminent First Amendment scholar Harry Kalven Jr. in 1966, "we may come to see the Negro as winning back for us the freedoms the Communists seemed to have lost for us."[51] Still, says noted African American scholar Henry Louis Gates Jr., Kalven would be shocked to see the stance that some blacks now take toward the First Amendment, which once protected protests, rallies, and agitation in the 1960s: "The byword among many black activists and black intellectuals is no longer the political imperative to protect free speech; it is the moral imperative to suppress 'hate speech.' "[52]

In the 1990s, a particularly thorny First Amendment area emerged as cities and universities attempted to prohibit what they viewed as offensive hate speech. In *R.A.V.* v. *City of St. Paul* (1992), a St. Paul, Minnesota, ordinance that made it a crime to engage in speech or action likely to arouse "anger," "alarm," or "resentment" on the basis of race, color, creed, religion, or gender was at issue. The Court ruled 5–4 that a white teenager who burned a cross on a black family's front lawn, thereby committing a hate crime under the ordinance, could not be charged under that law because the First Amendment prevents governments from "silencing speech on the basis of its content."[53] In 2003, the Court narrowed this definition, ruling that state governments could constitutionally restrict cross burning when it occurred with the intent of racial intimidation.[54]

Two-thirds of colleges and universities have banned a variety of forms of speech or conduct that creates or fosters an intimidating, hostile, or offensive environ-

On Campus

POLITICAL SPEECH AND MANDATORY STUDENT FEES

In March 2000, the U.S. Supreme Court ruled unanimously in *Board of Regents* v. *Southworth* that public universities could charge students a mandatory activity fee that could be used to facilitate extracurricular student political speech as long as the programs are neutral in their application.[a]

Scott Southworth, a law student at the University of Wisconsin, believed that the university's mandatory fee was a violation of his First Amendment right to free speech. He, along with several other law students, objected that their fees went to fund liberal groups. They particularly objected to the support of eighteen of the 125 various groups on campus that benefited from the mandatory activity fee, including the Lesbian, Gay, Bisexual, and Transgender Center, the International Socialist Organization, and the campus women's center.[b]

In ruling against Southworth and for the university, the Court underscored the importance of universities being a forum for the free exchange of political and ideological ideas and perspectives. The *Southworth* case performed that function on the Wisconsin campus even before it was argued before the Supreme Court. A student-led effort called the Southworth Project, for which over a dozen law and journalism students each earned two credits, was begun to make sure that the case was reported on campus in an accurate and sophisticated way. The Southworth Project, said a political science professor, gave "a tremendous boost to the visibility and the thinking process about the case."[c] In essence, the case made the Constitution and what it means come alive on the Wisconsin campus as students pondered the effects of First

■ Scott Southworth (right) defends his position on mandatory student fees in a 2003 debate at the University of Wisconsin with Journa Taylor (left), shared governance director of the University of Wisconsin Council.

Amendment protections on their ability to learn in a university atmosphere.

---

[a]*Board of Regents* v. *Southworth*, 529 U.S. 217 (2000).

[b]"U.S. Court Upholds Student Fees Going to Controversial Groups," *Toronto Star* (March 23, 2000): NEXIS.

[c]Mary Beth Marklein, "Fee Fight Proves a Learning Experience," *USA Today* (November 30, 1999): 8D.

---

ment on campus. To prevent disruption of university activities, some universities have also created free speech zones that restrict the time, place, or manner of speech. Critics, including the ACLU, charge that free speech zones imply that speech can be limited on other parts of the campus, which they see as a violation of the First Amendment. They have filed a number of suits in district court, but to date none of these cases has reached the Supreme Court.

UNPROTECTED SPEECH AND PUBLICATIONS

Although the Supreme Court has allowed few governmental bans on most types of speech, some forms of expression are not protected. In 1942, the Supreme Court set out the rationale by which it would distinguish between protected and unprotected speech. According to the Court, libel, fighting words, obscenity, and lewdness are not protected by the First Amendment because "such expressions are no essential part of any exposition of ideals, and are of such slight social value as a step to truth that any benefit that may be derived from them is clearly outweighed by the social interest in order and morality."[55]

Libel and Slander **Libel** is a written statement that defames the character of a person. If the statement is spoken, it is **slander.** In many nations—such as Great

libel
False written statements or written statements tending to call someone's reputation into disrepute.

slander
Untrue spoken statements that defame the character of a person.

Britain, for example—it is relatively easy to sue someone for libel. In the United States, however, the standards of proof are much more difficult. A person who believes that he or she has been a victim of libel must show that the statements made were untrue. Truth is an absolute defense against the charge of libel, no matter how painful or embarrassing the revelations.

It is often more difficult for individuals the Supreme Court considers "public persons or public officials" to sue for libel or slander. ***New York Times Co. v. Sullivan (1964)*** was the first major libel case considered by the Supreme Court.[56] An Alabama state court found the *Times* guilty of libel for printing a full-page advertisement accusing Alabama officials of physically abusing African Americans during various civil rights protests. (The ad was paid for by civil rights activists, including former First Lady Eleanor Roosevelt.) The Supreme Court overturned the conviction and established that a finding of libel against a public official could stand only if there was a showing of "actual malice," or a knowing disregard for the truth. Proof that the statements were false or negligent was not sufficient to prove actual malice.

In reality, the concept of actual malice can be difficult and confusing. In 1991, the Court directed lower courts to use the phrases "knowledge of falsity" and "reckless disregard of the truth" when giving instructions to juries in libel cases.[57] The actual malice standard also makes it difficult for public officials or persons to win libel cases. Still, many prominent people file libel suits each year; most are settled out of court. For example, actor Tom Cruise, who has won several lawsuits challenging a variety of European newspapers that have alleged he is gay, sued a U.S. porn star for $100 million in damages for alleging in U.S. tabloids that he is gay. A Los Angeles judge awarded Cruise $10 million when the defendant admitted his story was false and said that he would not defend himself against the suit.[58] Still, it is usually much easier for stars to sue for libel in British courts, where standards for proving libel are much less strict. Thus, in 2005, entertainer Justin Timberlake received "substantial damages" from a British newspaper after it published a made-up story alleging that he had sex with a supermodel.[59]

Fighting Words In the 1942 case of *Chaplinsky* v. *New Hampshire*, the Court stated that **fighting words**, or words that, "by their very utterance inflict injury or tend or incite an immediate breach of peace" are not subject to the restrictions of the First Amendment.[60] Fighting words, which include "profanity, obscenity, and threats," are therefore able to be regulated by the federal and state governments.

These words do not necessarily have to be spoken; fighting words can also come in the form of symbolic expression. For example, in 1968, a California man named Paul Cohen wore a jacket that said "Fuck the Draft. Stop the War" into a Los Angeles county courthouse. He was arrested and charged with disturbing the peace and engaging in offensive conduct. The trial court convicted Cohen, and this conviction was upheld by a state appellate court. However, when the case reached the Supreme Court in 1971, the Court reversed the lower courts' decisions and ruled that forbidding the use of certain words amounted to little more than censorship of ideas.[61]

Obscenity Through 1957, U.S. courts often based their opinions of what was obscene on an English common-law test that had been set out in 1868: "Whether the tendency of the matter charged as obscenity is to deprive and corrupt those whose minds are open to such immoral influences and into whose hands a publication of this sort might fall."[62] In *Roth* v. *U.S.* (1957), however, the Court abandoned this approach and held that, to be considered obscene, the material in question had to be "utterly without redeeming social importance," and articulated a new test for obscenity: "whether to the average person, applying contemporary community standards, the dominant theme of the material taken as a whole appeals to the prurient interests."[63]

In many ways, the *Roth* test brought with it as many problems as it attempted to solve. Throughout the 1950s and 1960s, "prurient" remained hard to define, as the

New York Times Co. v. Sullivan (1964)
The Supreme Court concluded that "actual malice" must be proved to support a finding of libel against a public figure.

fighting words
Words that, "by their very utterance inflict injury or tend to incite an immediate breach of peace." Fighting words are not subject to the restrictions of the First Amendment.

VIDEO ROUNDTABLE
Political Correctness

Supreme Court struggled to find a standard for judging actions or words. Moreover, it was very difficult to prove that a book or movie was "*utterly* without redeeming social value." In general, even some hardcore pornography passed muster under the *Roth* test, prompting some to argue that the Court fostered the increase in the number of sexually oriented publications designed to appeal to those living during the sexual revolution.

Richard M. Nixon made the growth in pornography a major issue when he ran for president in 1968. Nixon pledged to appoint to federal judgeships only those who would uphold law and order and stop coddling criminals and purveyors of porn. Once elected president, Nixon made four appointments to the Supreme Court, including Chief Justice Warren Burger, who wrote the opinion in *Miller* v. *California* (1973). There, the Court set out a test that redefined obscenity. To make it easier for states to regulate obscene materials, the justices concluded that lower courts must ask "whether the work depicts or describes, in a patently offensive way, sexual conduct specifically defined by state law." The courts also were to determine "whether the work, taken as a whole, lacks serious literary, artistic, political, or scientific value." And, in place of the contemporary community standards gauge used in *Roth*, the Court defined community standards to refer to the locality in question, under the rationale that what is acceptable in New York City might not be acceptable in Maine or Mississippi.[64]

Time and contexts clearly have altered the Court's and, indeed, much of America's perceptions of what works are obscene. But, the Supreme Court has allowed communities great leeway in drafting statutes to deal with obscenity and, even more importantly, other forms of questionable expression. In 1991, for example, the Court voted 5–4 to allow Indiana to ban totally nude erotic dancing, concluding that the statute furthered a substantial governmental interest, and therefore was not in violation of the First Amendment.[65] Since this case, the Court has largely stayed out of the fray of obscenity law. Congress, on the other hand, has continued to legislate on issues of obscenity.

Congress and Obscenity While lawmakers have been fairly effective in restricting the sale and distribution of obscene materials, Congress has been particularly concerned with obscenity and pornography on the Internet.

In 1990, concern over the use of federal dollars by the National Endowment for the Arts (NEA) for works with controversial religious or sexual themes led to passage of legislation requiring the NEA to "[take] into consideration general standards of decency and respect for the diverse beliefs and values of the American public" when it makes annual awards. Several performance artists believed that Congress could not regulate the content of speech solely because it could be offensive; they challenged the statute in federal court. In 1998, the Supreme Court upheld the legislation, ruling that, because decency was only one of the criteria in making funding decisions, the act did not violate the First Amendment.[66]

Monitoring the Internet has proven more difficult for Congress. In 1996, it passed the Communications Decency Act, which prohibited the transmission of obscene materials over the Internet to anyone under age eighteen. In 1997, the Supreme Court ruled in *Reno* v. *American Civil Liberties Union* that the act violated the First Amendment because it was too vague and overbroad.[67] In reaction to the decision, Congress passed the Child Online Protection Act (COPA) in 1998. The new law broadened the definition of pornography to include any "visual depiction that is, or appears to be, a minor engaging in sexually explicit conduct." The act also redefined "visual depiction" to include computer-generated images, shifting the focus of the law from the children who were involved in pornography to protection of children who could see the images via the Internet.[68] The act targeted material "harmful to minors" but applied only to World Wide Web sites, not chat rooms or e-mail. It also targeted only materials used for "commercial purposes."

The ACLU and online publishers immediately challenged the constitutionality of the act, and a U.S. court of appeals in Philadelphia ruled the law was unconstitutional because of its reliance on "community standards" as articulated in *Miller*, which are not enforceable on the Internet. While this case was on appeal to the Supreme Court, Congress enacted the Children's Internet Protection Act, which prohibited public libraries receiving federal funds from allowing minors access to the Web without anti-pornography filters. Meanwhile, in *Ashcroft* v. *Free Speech Coalition* (2002), the Court ruled that Congress had gone too far in a laudable effort to stamp out child pornography.[69] Six justices agreed that the law was too vague because "communities with a narrow view of what words and images are suitable for children might be able to censor Internet content, putting it out of reach of the entire country."[70]

Congressional reaction was immediate. Within two weeks of the Court's decision, lawmakers were drafting more specific legislation to meet the Court's reservations. New regulations were enacted in 2003 as part of an anti-crime bill. In this legislation, Congress further limited the kinds of cyber pornography subject to regulation and allowed those accused of creating and marketing such pornography to "escape conviction if they could show they did not use actual children to produce sexually explicit images."[71] In 2004, the Supreme Court struck down as unconstitutional Congress's latest effort to limit cyberporn. The Court also continued to block enforcement of COPA and Congress has continued to try to find ways to block children's access to Internet pornography.[72]

FREEDOMS OF ASSEMBLY AND PETITION

"Peaceful assembly for lawful discussion cannot be made a crime," Chief Justice Charles Evans Hughes wrote in the 1937 case of *DeJonge* v. *Oregon*, which incorporated the First Amendment's freedom of assembly clause.[73] Despite this clear declaration, and an even more ringing declaration in the First Amendment, the fundamental freedoms of assembly and petition have been among the most controversial, especially in times of war. As with other First Amendment freedoms, the Supreme Court often has become the arbiter between the freedom of the people to express dissent and government's authority to limit controversy in the name of national security.

Because the freedom to assemble is hinged on peaceful conduct, as underscored in our opening vignette on Darfur rallies, the freedoms of assembly and petition are

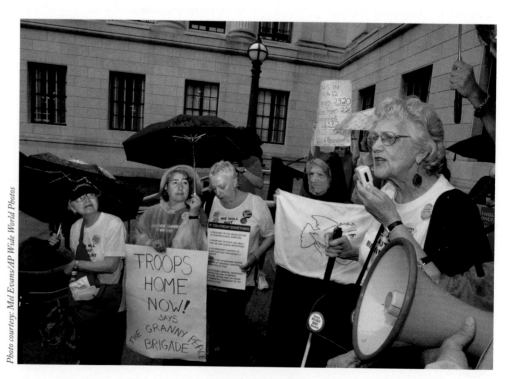

■ Members of an activist group calling itself the Granny Peace Brigade exercise their constitutional right to assemble in New York City to protest the Iraq War. In April of 2006, eighteen members of the group ranging in age from 59 to 91 were acquitted of two counts of disorderly conduct stemming from a protest against the war at a military recruitment center in Times Square. The judged ruled that the "grannies" had been wrongly arrested because there was credible evidence that they had left room for people to enter and leave the recruitment center.

Photo courtesy: Mel Evans/AP Wide World Photos

related directly to the freedoms of speech and of the press. If the words or actions taken at any event cross the line of constitutionality, the event itself may no longer be protected constitutionally. Absent that protection, leaders and attendees may be subject to governmental regulation and even criminal arrest, incarceration, or civil fines.

The Second Amendment: The Right to Keep and Bear Arms

DURING COLONIAL TIMES, the colonists' distrust of standing armies was evident. Most colonies required all white men to keep and bear arms, and all white men in whole sections of the colonies were deputized to defend their settlements against Indians and European powers. These local militias were viewed as the best way to keep order and protect liberty.

The Second Amendment was added to the Constitution to ensure that Congress could not pass laws to disarm state militias. This amendment appeased Anti-Federalists, who feared that the new Constitution would cause them to lose the right to "keep and bear arms" as well as an unstated right—the right to revolt against governmental tyranny.

Through the early 1920s, few state statutes were passed to regulate firearms (and generally these laws dealt with the possession of firearms by slaves). The Supreme Court's decision in *Barron* v. *Baltimore* (1833), which refused to incorporate the Bill of Rights to the state governments, prevented federal review of those state laws.[74] Moreover, in *Dred Scott* v. *Sandford* (1857) (see chapter 3), Chief Justice Roger B. Taney listed the right to own and carry arms as a basic right of citizenship.[75]

In 1934, Congress passed the National Firearms Act in response to the increase in organized crime that occurred in the 1920s and 1930s as a result of Prohibition. The act imposed taxes on automatic weapons (such as machine guns) and sawed-off shotguns. In *U.S.* v. *Miller* (1939), a unanimous Court upheld the constitutionality of the act, stating that the Second Amendment was intended to protect a citizen's right to own ordinary militia weapons and not unregistered sawed-off shotguns, which were at issue.[76] *Miller* was the last time the Supreme Court directly addressed the Second Amendment. In *Quilici* v. *Village of Morton Grove* (1983), the Supreme Court refused to review a lower court's ruling upholding the constitutionality of a local ordinance banning handguns against a Second Amendment challenge.[77]

In the aftermath of the assassination attempt on President Ronald Reagan in 1981, many lawmakers called for passage of gun control legislation. At the forefront of that effort was Sarah Brady, the wife of James Brady, the presidential press secretary who was badly wounded and left partially disabled by John Hinckley Jr., President Reagan's assailant. In 1993, her efforts helped to win passage of the Brady Bill, which imposed a federal mandatory five-day waiting period on the purchase of handguns.

In 1997, the U.S. Supreme Court ruled 5–4 that the section of the Brady Bill requiring state officials to conduct background checks of prospective handgun owners violated principles of state sovereignty.[78] The background check provision, while important, is not critical to the overall goals of the Brady Bill because a federal record-checking system went into effect in late 1998.

VIDEO DEBATE

Gun Control

Perhaps more important than the Brady Bill was the ban on assault weapons signed by President Bill Clinton as part of the Violent Crime Control and Law Enforcement Act in 1994. This provision, which prohibited Americans from owning many of the most powerful types of guns, carried a ten-year time limit. It expired just before the 2004 presidential and congressional elections. Neither President George W. Bush nor the Republican-controlled Congress made any serious efforts

■ President Bill Clinton signs the Brady Bill into law flanked by Vice President Al Gore, Attorney General Janet Reno, and James and Sarah Brady and their children.

Photo courtesy: Marcy Nighswander/AP Wide World Photos

to renew it, causing critics to charge that their inaction was political and prompted by anti-gun-control interests such as the National Rifle Association—a major donor to Republicans.

The Rights of Criminal Defendants

due process rights

Procedural guarantees provided by the Fourth, Fifth, Sixth, and Eighth Amendments for those accused of crimes.

THE FOURTH, FIFTH, SIXTH, AND EIGHTH Amendments supplement constitutional guarantees against writs of *habeas corpus, ex post facto* laws, and bills of attainder by providing a variety of procedural guarantees (often called **due process rights**) for those accused of crimes. Particular amendments, as well as other portions of the Constitution, specifically provide procedural guarantees to protect individuals accused of crimes at all stages of the criminal justice process. As is the case with the First Amendment, many of these rights have been interpreted by the Supreme Court to apply to the states. In interpreting the amendments dealing with what are frequently termed "criminal rights," the courts have to grapple not only with the meaning of the amendments but also with how their protections are to be implemented.

Over the years, many individuals criticized liberal Warren Court decisions of the 1950s and 1960s, arguing that its rulings gave criminals more liberties than their victims. The Warren Court made several provisions of the Bill of Rights dealing with the liberties of criminal defendants applicable to the states through the Fourteenth Amendment. It is important to remember that most procedural guarantees apply to individuals charged with crimes—that is, they apply before the individuals have been tried. These liberties were designed to protect those wrongfully accused, although, of course, they often have helped the guilty. But, as Justice William O. Douglas once noted, "Respecting the dignity even of the least worthy citizen . . . raises the stature of all of us."[79]

Many commentators continue to argue, however, that only the guilty are helped by the American system and that criminals should not go unpunished because of simple police error. The dilemma of balancing the liberties of the individual against those of society permeates the entire debate.

THE FOURTH AMENDMENT AND SEARCHES AND SEIZURES

The **Fourth Amendment** to the Constitution protects people from unreasonable searches by the federal government. Moreover, in some detail, it sets out what may not be searched unless a warrant is issued, underscoring the Framers' concern with possible government abuses.

> The right of the people to be secure in their persons, houses, papers, and effects, against unreasonable searches and seizures, shall not be violated, and no Warrants shall issue, but upon probable cause, supported by Oath or affirmation, and particularly describing the place to be searched, and the persons or things to be seized.

The purpose of this amendment was to deny the national government the authority to make general searches. The English Parliament often had issued general writs of assistance that allowed such searches. These general warrants were used against religious and political dissenters, a practice the Framers wanted banned. But, still, the language that they chose left numerous questions to be answered, including the definition of an unreasonable search.

Over the years, in a number of decisions, the Supreme Court has interpreted the Fourth Amendment to allow the police to search: (1) the person arrested; (2) things in plain view of the accused person; and, (3) places or things that the arrested person could touch or reach or are otherwise in the arrestee's immediate control. In 1995, the Court also resolved a decades-old constitutional dispute by ruling unanimously that police must knock and announce their presence before entering a house or apartment to execute a search. But, said the Court, there may be reasonable exceptions to the rule to account for the likelihood of violence or the imminent destruction of evidence.[80] But, in 2006, the Court ruled in a 5–4 decision that even if police refused to knock, evidence improperly seized could be used in cases where police had a valid warrant.[81]

Warrantless searches often occur if police suspect that someone is committing or is about to commit a crime. In these situations, police may stop and frisk the individual under suspicion. In 1989, the Court ruled that there need be only a "reasonable suspicion" for stopping a suspect—a much lower standard than probable cause.[82] Thus, a suspected drug courier may be stopped for brief questioning but only a frisk search (for weapons) is permitted. A person's answers to the questions may shift reasonable suspicion to probable cause, thus permitting the officer to search further. But, except at borders between the United States and Mexico and Canada (or international airports within U.S. borders), a search requires probable cause.

The Court also ruled in 2001 on a California policy that required individuals, as a condition of their probation, to consent to warrantless searches of their person, property, homes, or vehicles, thus limiting a probationer's Fourth Amendment protections against unreasonable searches and seizures.[83] The Court did not give blanket approval to searches; instead, a unanimous Court said that a probation officer must have a reasonable suspicion of wrongdoing—a lesser standard than probable cause afforded to most citizens.

Searches can also be made without a warrant if consent is obtained, and the Court has ruled that consent can be given by a variety of persons. It has ruled, for example, that police can search a bedroom occupied by two persons as long as they have the consent of one of them.[84] The same standard, however, does not apply to houses. In 2006, the Court ruled that the police could not conduct a warrantless search of a home if one of the occupants objected.[85]

In situations where no arrest occurs, police must obtain search warrants from a "neutral and detached magistrate" prior to conducting more extensive searches of houses, cars, offices, or any other place where an individual would reasonably have

Fourth Amendment
Part of the Bill of Rights that reads: "The right of the people to be secure in their persons, houses, papers, and effects, against unreasonable searches and seizures, shall not be violated, and no Warrants shall issue, but upon probable cause, supported by Oath or affirmation, and particularly describing the place to be searched, and the persons or things to be seized."

SIMULATION
You Are a Police Officer

Join the Debate

THE USA PATRIOT ACT

OVERVIEW: The Declaration of Independence forcefully espouses the principles that all individuals have "certain unalienable rights, that among these are Life, Liberty and the pursuit of Happiness," and that it is government's purpose to guarantee the secure enjoyment of these rights. To assure these liberties, government must necessarily use legitimate police force to ensure safety within its borders, and it must use military force to defend the state from outside aggression.

A considerable problem for democratic peoples in free and open societies is how to define the limits of government intervention in the private sphere. This problem becomes particularly acute during times of national crisis and armed conflict. Establishing the line between the government's constitutional duty to "provide for the common defence" and to "secure the blessings of liberty" is complicated. It becomes even more complex when those who threaten America's national security use the freedom and rights found in the United States as a means through which to wage war. To help defend against those wishing to use the openness of American society for harmful ends, the Uniting and Strengthening America by Providing Appropriate Tools Required to Intercept and Obstruct Terrorism Act of 2001, otherwise known as the USA Patriot Act, was signed into law on October 26, 2001, in response to the terrorist attacks on New York City and the Pentagon on September 11, 2001.

Sunset provisions of the USA Patriot Act that included amendments designed to address civil liberties concerns were renewed by Congress and signed into law by President George W. Bush in March 2006. Nevertheless, the act remains controversial. Does it help defend the United States against terrorist activity, or does it allow the government to abuse its power in the name of national security? Isn't it necessary that government narrow the scope of civil rights and liberties in times of national distress?

ARGUMENTS FOR THE USA PATRIOT ACT

- **The USA Patriot Act allows the government to use new technologies to address new threats.** Those engaged in terrorist activities today use sophisticated technologies. The USA Patriot Act allows the government to wage the war on terrorism by using the same and superior technologies to find and prosecute those engaged in terrorism and to help reduce the threat of terrorist attacks.
- **The USA Patriot Act dismantles the wall of legal and regulatory policies erected to sharply limit the sharing of information between intelligence, national security, and law enforcement communities.** Prior policy essentially prohibited various government agencies from communicating and coordinating domestic and national security activities, thus restricting the flow of valuable information that could prevent terrorist attacks. Now, government agencies can coordinate surveillance activities across domestic and national security policy domains.

VIDEO DEBATE

The Patriot Act

some expectation of privacy.[86] Police cannot get search warrants, for example, to require you to undergo surgery to remove a bullet that might be used to incriminate you, since your expectation of bodily privacy outweighs the need for evidence.[87] But, courts do not require search warrants in possible drunk driving situations. Thus, the police in some states can require you to take a Breathalyzer test to determine whether you have been drinking in excess of legal limits.[88] In other states, refusing a test may result in the automatic loss of your license.

Homes, too, are presumed to be private. Firefighters can enter your home to fight a fire without a warrant. But, if they decide to investigate the cause of the fire, they must obtain a warrant before their reentry.[89] In contrast, under the open fields doctrine first articulated by the Supreme Court in 1924, if you own a field, and even if you post "No Trespassing" signs, the police can search your field without a warrant to see if you are illegally growing marijuana, because you cannot reasonably expect privacy in an open field.[90]

■ **The USA Patriot Act allows government agencies to use the procedures and tools already available to investigate organized and drug crime.** The USA Patriot Act uses techniques already approved by the courts in investigating such crimes as wire fraud, money laundering, and drug trafficking. These techniques include roving wire taps and judicially approved search warrants, notice of which may be delayed in certain narrow circumstances.

ARGUMENTS AGAINST THE USA PATRIOT ACT

■ **Certain provisions of the USA Patriot Act may violate an individual's right to privacy.** For example, section 216 allows law enforcement officials to get a warrant to track which Web sites a person visits and to collect certain information in regard to an individual's e-mail activity. There need not be any suspicion of criminal activity—all law enforcement authorities need do is to certify that the potential information is relevant to an ongoing criminal investigation.

■ **The USA Patriot Act violates the civil rights and liberties of legal immigrants.** The act permits the indefinite detention of immigrants and other noncitizens. The U.S. Attorney General may detain immigrants merely upon "reasonable grounds" that one is involved in terrorism or engaged in activity that poses a danger to national security, and this detention may be indefinite until determination is made that such an individual threatens national security.

■ **Safeguards to prevent direct government surveillance of citizens have been reduced.** The Patriot Act repeals certain precautions in regard to the sharing of information between domestic law enforcement agencies and the intelligence community. These safeguards were put in place during the Cold War after the revelation that the Central Intelligence Agency (CIA) and the Federal Bureau of Investigation (FBI) had been conducting joint investigations on American citizens during the McCarthy era and civil rights movement—including surveillance of the Reverend Martin Luther King Jr.—for political purposes.

QUESTIONS

1. Does the USA Patriot Act balance liberty with security? If so, how does it strike that balance? If not, what do you think could be done to redress the imbalance?
2. Is the USA Patriot Act a necessary law? If so, what, in your view, can be done to rectify its flaws? If not, what should be done to ensure the security of the United States against terrorist activity?

SELECTED READINGS

Duncan, Stephen M. *War of a Different Kind: Military Force and America's Search for Homeland Security.* Annapolis, MD: United States Naval Institute, 2004.

Etzioni, Amitai. *How Patriotic Is the Patriot Act?* New York, NY: Routledge, 2004.

In 2001, in a decision that surprised many commentators, by a vote of 5–4, the Supreme Court ruled that drug evidence obtained by using a thermal imager (without a warrant) on a public street to locate the defendant's marijuana hothouse was obtained in violation of the Fourth Amendment.[91] In contrast, the use of low-flying aircraft and helicopters to detect marijuana fields or binoculars to look in a yard have been upheld because officers simply were using their eyesight, not a new technological tool such as the thermal imager.[92]

Cars have proven problematic for police and the courts because of their mobile nature. As noted by Chief Justice William H. Taft as early as 1925, "the vehicle can quickly be moved out of the locality or jurisdiction in which the warrant must be sought."[93] Over the years, the Court has become increasingly lenient about the scope of automobile searches.

In 2002, an unusually unanimous Court ruled that when evaluating if a border patrol officer acted lawfully in stopping a suspicious minivan, the totality of the circumstances had to be considered. Wrote Chief Justice William H. Rehnquist, the "balance between the public interest and the individual's right to personal security," tilts in favor of a "standard less than probable cause in brief investigatory stops." This ruling gave law enforcement officers more leeway to pull over suspicious motorists.[94] (See Join the Debate: The USA Patriot Act.)

Drug Testing   Testing for drugs is an especially thorny search and seizure issue. If the government can require you to take a Breathalyzer test, can it require you to be tested for drugs? In the wake of growing public concern over drug use, in 1986, President Ronald Reagan signed an executive order requiring many executive branch employees to undergo drug tests. In 1997, Congress passed a similar law authorizing random drug searches of all congressional employees.

While many private employers and professional athletic organizations routinely require drug tests upon application or as a condition of employment, governmental requirements present constitutional questions about the scope of permissible searches and seizures. In 1989, the Supreme Court ruled that mandatory drug and alcohol testing of employees involved in accidents was constitutional.[95] In 1995, the Court upheld the constitutionally of random drug testing of public high school athletes.[96] And, in 2002, the Court upheld the constitutionality of a Tecumseh, Oklahoma, policy that required mandatory drug testing of high school students participating in any extracurricular activities. Thus, prospective band, choir, debate, or drama club members were subject to the same kind of random drug testing undergone by athletes.[97]

In *Chandler* v. *Miller* (1997), the U.S. Supreme Court refused to allow Georgia to require all candidates for state office to pass a urinalysis drug test thirty days before qualifying for nomination or election, concluding that its law violated the search and seizure clause.[98] In general, all employers can require pre-employment drug screening. However, because governments are unconditionally bound by the constitutional search provisions of the Fourth Amendment, public employees enjoy more protection in the area of drug testing than do employees of private enterprises.[99]

Another issue is the constitutionality of compulsory drug testing for pregnant women. In 2001, in a 6-3 decision, the Court ruled that testing women for cocaine use and reporting positive results to law enforcement officials was unconstitutional. When pregnant women in South Carolina sought medical care for their pregnancies, they were not told that their urine tests were also tested for cocaine. Thus, some women were arrested after they unknowingly were screened for illegal drug use and then tested positive. The majority of the Court found that the immediate purpose of the drug test was to generate evidence for law enforcement officials and not to give medical treatment to the women. Thus, the women's right to privacy was violated unless they specifically consented to the tests.[100]

THE FIFTH AMENDMENT: SELF-INCRIMINATION AND DOUBLE JEOPARDY

Fifth Amendment
Part of the Bill of Rights that imposes a number of restrictions on the federal government with respect to the rights of persons suspected of committing a crime. It provides for indictment by a grand jury and protection against self-incrimination, and prevents the national government from denying a person life, liberty, or property without the due process of law. It also prevents the national government from taking property without fair compensation.

The **Fifth Amendment** provides that "No person shall be . . . compelled in any criminal case to be a witness against himself." "Taking the Fifth" is shorthand for exercising one's constitutional right not to self-incriminate. The Supreme Court has interpreted this guarantee to be "as broad as the mischief against which it seeks to guard," finding that criminal defendants do not have to take the stand at trial to answer questions, nor can a judge make mention of their failure to do so as evidence of guilt.[101] Moreover, lawyers cannot imply that a defendant who refuses to take the stand must be guilty or have something to hide.

This right not to incriminate oneself also means that prosecutors cannot use as evidence in a trial any of a defendant's statements or confessions that were not made voluntarily. As is the case in many areas of the law, however, judicial interpretation of the term voluntary has changed over time.

THE RIGHTS OF CRIMINAL DEFENDANTS

In earlier times, it was not unusual for police to beat defendants to obtain their confessions. In 1936, however, the Supreme Court ruled that convictions for murder based solely on confessions given after physical beatings were unconstitutional.[102] Police then began to resort to other measures to force confessions. Defendants, for example, were given the third degree—questioned for hours on end with no sleep or food, or threatened with physical violence until they were mentally beaten into giving confessions. In other situations, family members were threatened. In one case a young mother accused of marijuana possession was told that her welfare benefits would be terminated and her children taken away from her if she failed to talk.[103]

Miranda v. Arizona **(1966)** was the Supreme Court's response to these creative efforts to obtain confessions that were not truly voluntary. On March 3, 1963, an eighteen-year-old girl was kidnapped and raped on the outskirts of Phoenix, Arizona. Ten days later police arrested Ernesto Miranda, a poor, mentally disturbed man with a ninth-grade education. In a police-station lineup, the victim identified Miranda as her attacker. Police then took Miranda to a separate room and questioned him for two hours. At first he denied guilt. Eventually, however, he confessed to the crime and wrote and signed a brief statement describing the crime and admitting his guilt. At no time was he told that he did not have to answer any questions or that he could be represented by an attorney.

After Miranda's conviction, his case was appealed on the grounds that his Fifth Amendment right not to incriminate himself had been violated because his confession had been coerced. Writing for the Court, Chief Justice Earl Warren, himself a former district attorney and a former California state attorney general, noted that because police have a tremendous advantage in any interrogation situation, criminal suspects must be given greater protection. A confession obtained in the manner of Miranda's was not truly voluntary; thus, it was inadmissible at trial.

To provide guidelines for police to implement *Miranda,* the Court mandated that: "Prior to any questioning, the person must be warned that he has a right to remain silent, that any statements he does make may be used as evidence against him, and that he has a right to the presence of an attorney, either retained or appointed." In response to this mandate from the Court, police routinely began to read suspects what are now called their **Miranda rights,** a practice you undoubtedly have seen repeated over and over in movies and TV police dramas.

Although the Burger Court did not enforce the reading of *Miranda* rights as vehemently as had the Warren Court, Chief Justice Warren Burger, Warren's successor, acknowledged that they had become an integral part of established police procedures.[104] The Rehnquist Court, however, has been more tolerant of the use of coerced confessions and has employed a much more flexible standard to allow their admissibility. In 1991, for example, it ruled that the use of a coerced confession in a criminal trial does not automatically invalidate a conviction if its admission is deemed a "harmless error," that is, if the other evidence is sufficient to convict.[105]

But, in 2000, in an opinion written by Chief Justice William H. Rehnquist, the Court reaffirmed the central holding of *Miranda,* ruling that defendants must be read *Miranda* warnings. The Court went on to say that, despite an act of Congress that stipulated that voluntary statements made during police interrogations were admissible at trial, without *Miranda* warnings, no admissions could be trusted to be truly voluntary.[106]

In 2003, the Court was faced with a new twist on *Miranda* rights. Samuel Patane was arrested in his home for violating a restraining order taken out by his girlfriend. As he was being arrested and was about to be read his rights, Patane interrupted the officers, saying that he knew them. The officers subsequently found guns in Patane's home, which as an ex-felon he was not allowed to possess. Patane later argued that the search was illegal because he was not Mirandized. Although there was no majority opinion from the Court, a majority of the Justices still concluded that the guns could be used as evidence against Patane.[107]

Miranda v. Arizona **(1966)**
A landmark Supreme Court ruling that held the Fifth Amendment requires that individuals arrested for a crime must be advised of their right to remain silent and to have counsel present.

Miranda **rights**
Statements that must be made by the police informing a suspect of his or her constitutional rights protected by the Fifth Amendment, including the right to an attorney provided by the court if the suspect cannot afford one.

Photo courtesy: AP Wide World Photos

■ Even though Ernesto Miranda's confession was not admitted as evidence at his retrial, his ex-girlfriend's testimony and that of the victim were enough to convince the jury of his guilt. He served nine years in prison before he was released on parole. After his release, he routinely sold autographed cards inscribed with what are called the *Miranda* rights now read to all suspects. In 1976, four years after his release, Miranda was stabbed to death in Phoenix in a bar fight during a card game. Two *Miranda* cards were found on his body, and the person who killed him was read his *Miranda* rights upon his arrest.

double jeopardy clause
Part of the Fifth Amendment that protects individuals from being tried twice for the same offense.

The Fifth Amendment also mandates: "nor shall any person be subject for the same offense to be twice put in jeopardy of life or limb." This is called the **double jeopardy clause** and it protects individuals from being tried twice for the same offense. Thus, if a defendant is acquitted by a jury of a charge of murder, he or she cannot be retried for the offense even if new information is unearthed that could further point to guilt. In 2005, in *Smith* v. *Massachusetts,* for example, Justice Antonin Scalia, writing for a 5–4 majority concluded that double jeopardy applied when the trial judge ruled that the state's evidence was insufficient to maintain a prosecution but reversed herself later in the same trial when the prosecution produced more evidence that would have warranted finding the defendant guilty.[108]

THE FOURTH AND FIFTH AMENDMENTS AND THE EXCLUSIONARY RULE

exclusionary rule
Judicially created rule that prohibits police from using illegally seized evidence at trial.

In *Weeks* v. *U.S.* (1914), the U.S. Supreme Court adopted the **exclusionary rule,** which bars the use of illegally seized evidence at trial. Thus, although the Fourth and Fifth Amendments do not prohibit the use of evidence obtained in violation of their provisions, the exclusionary rule is a judicially created remedy to deter constitutional violations. In *Weeks,* for example, the Court reasoned that allowing police and prosecutors to use the "fruits of a poisonous tree" (a tainted search) would only encourage that activity.[109]

In balancing the need to deter police misconduct against the possibility that guilty individuals could go free, the Warren Court decided that deterring police misconduct was most important. In *Mapp* v. *Ohio* (1961), the Warren Court ruled that "all evidence obtained by searches and seizures in violation of the Constitution, is inadmissible in a state court."[110] This historic and controversial case put law enforcement officers on notice that if they found evidence in violation of any constitutional rights, those efforts would be for naught because the tainted evidence could not be used in federal or state trials. In contrast, the Burger and Rehnquist Courts and, more recently, Congress gradually have chipped away at the exclusionary rule.

In 1976, the Court noted that the exclusionary rule "deflects the truth-finding process and often frees the guilty."[111] Since then, the Court has carved out a variety of limited "good faith exceptions" to the exclusionary rule, allowing the use of tainted evidence in a variety of situations, especially when police have a search warrant and, in good faith, conduct the search on the assumption that the warrant is valid even though it is subsequently found invalid. Since the purpose of the exclusionary rule is to deter police misconduct, and in this situation there is no police misconduct, the courts have permitted the introduction at trial of the seized evidence. Another exception to the exclusionary rule is "inevitable discovery." Evidence illegally seized may be introduced if it would have been discovered anyway in the course of continuing investigation.

The Court, despite its conservative reputation, has continued to uphold the exclusionary rule. In a 2006 victory for advocates of defendants' rights, the Court ruled unanimously that the Fourth Amendment requires that any evidence collected under an anticipatory warrant—one presented by the police yet not authorized by a judge—would be inadmissible at trial as a violation of the exclusionary rule.[112]

VIDEO ROUNDTABLE

The Rights of the Accused

THE SIXTH AMENDMENT AND THE RIGHT TO COUNSEL

Sixth Amendment
Part of the Bill of Rights that sets out the basic requirements of procedural due process for federal courts to follow in criminal trials. These include speedy and public trials, impartial juries, trials in the state where crime was committed, notice of the charges, the right to confront and obtain favorable witnesses, and the right to counsel.

The **Sixth Amendment** guarantees to an accused person "the Assistance of Counsel in his defense." In the past, this provision meant only that an individual could hire an attorney to represent him or her in court. Since most criminal defendants are too poor to hire private lawyers, this provision was of little assistance to many who found themselves on trial. Recognizing this, Congress required federal courts to provide an attorney for defendants who could not to afford one. This was first required in capital cases (where the death penalty is a possibility); eventually, attorneys were provided to the poor in all federal criminal cases.[113] Similarly, in 1932, the Supreme Court directed states to furnish lawyers to defendants in capital cases.[114] It also began to expand the right to counsel to other state offenses but did so in a piecemeal fashion that gave the states little direction. Given the high cost of providing legal counsel, this ambiguity often made it cost-effective for the states not to provide counsel at all.

These ambiguities came to an end with the Court's decision in *Gideon* v. *Wainwright* (1963).[115] Clarence Earl Gideon, a fifty-one-year-old drifter, was charged with breaking into a Panama City, Florida, pool hall and stealing beer, wine, and some change from a vending machine. At his trial, he asked the judge to appoint a lawyer for him because he was too poor to hire one himself. The judge refused, and Gideon was convicted and given a five-year prison term for petty larceny. The case against Gideon had not been strong, but as a layperson unfamiliar with the law and with trial practice and procedure, he was unable to point out its weaknesses.

The apparent inequities in the system that had resulted in Gideon's conviction continued to bother him. Eventually, he requested some paper from a prison guard, consulted books in the prison library, and then drafted and mailed a petition to the U.S. Supreme Court asking it to overrule his conviction.

In a unanimous decision, the Supreme Court agreed with Gideon and his court-appointed lawyer, Abe Fortas, a future associate justice of the Supreme Court. Writing for the Court, Justice Hugo Black explained that "lawyers in criminal courts are necessities, not luxuries." Therefore, the Court concluded, the state must provide an attorney to indigent defendants in felony cases. Underscoring the Court's point, Gideon was acquitted when he was retried with a lawyer to argue his case.

In 1972, the Burger Court expanded the *Gideon* rule, holding that "even in prosecutions for offenses less serious than felonies, a fair trial may require the presence of a lawyer."[116] Seven years later, the Court clarified its decision by holding that defendants charged with offenses where imprisonment is a possibility but not actually imposed do not have a Sixth Amendment right to counsel.[117] Thirty years later, the Rehnquist Court expanded *Gideon* even further by revisiting the "actual imprisonment" standard announced in the 1972 and 1979 cases. In 2002, a 5–4 majority held that if a defendant received a suspended sentence and probation for a minor crime but could be sentenced in future if he or she violated the conditions of probation, then the defendant must be provided with a lawyer.[118]

The quality of counsel is an issue that has continued to vex courts. Various courts have held that lawyers who fell asleep during trial, failed to put on a defense, or were drunk during the proceedings were "adequate." In 2005, however, the Supreme Court ruled in a 5–4 opinion that the Sixth Amendment's guarantees required Ronald Rompilla's lawyers to examine files detailing Rompilla's criminal record, which the prosecution was likely to use during the sentencing phase of his trial. Because Rompilla's defense attorneys had not done this, Rompilla was granted a new sentencing hearing.[119]

■ When Clarence Earl Gideon wrote out his petition for a writ of certiorari to the Supreme Court (asking the Court, in its discretion, to hear his case), he had no way of knowing that his case would lead to the landmark ruling on the right to counsel, *Gideon* v. *Wainwright* (1963). Nor did he know that Chief Justice Earl Warren actually had instructed his law clerks to be on the lookout for a *habeas corpus* petition (literally, "you have the body," which argues that the person in jail is there in violation of some statutory or constitutional right) that could be used to guarantee the assistance of counsel for defendants in criminal cases.

Photo courtesy: Supreme Court Historical Society

Photo courtesy: Getty Images

■ In the wake of the 9/11 terrorist attacks, the U.S.-supported Afghani Northern Alliance captured a U.S. citizen, John Walker Lindh, and handed him over to U.S. forces. Lindh was returned to the United States, and a ten-count indictment charged him with conspiring with al-Qaeda to kill U.S. nationals. His confession allegedly occurred after a period during which he was left shackled and naked and denied food, water, and treatment for an injury. Additionally, he was questioned without a lawyer although his parents had requested that one be appointed for him. Lindh ultimately pled guilty to one count of "supplying services as a foot soldier," and was sentenced to up to twenty years in prison. The Military Commissions Act, passed by Congress and signed into law by President Bush just before the 2006 midterm elections, authorizes potentially harsher treatment of U.S. citizens accused of engaging in terrorist activities or aiding terrorists; civil liberties advocates question its constitutionality.

Eighth Amendment

Part of the Bill of Rights that states: "Excessive bail shall not be required, nor excessive fines imposed, nor cruel and unusual punishments inflicted."

THE SIXTH AMENDMENT AND JURY TRIALS

The Sixth Amendment (and, to a lesser extent, Article III of the Constitution) provides that a person accused of a crime shall enjoy the right to a speedy and public trial by an impartial jury—that is, a trial in which a group of the accused's peers act as a fact-finding, deliberative body to determine guilt or innocence. It also provides defendants the right to confront witnesses against them. The Supreme Court has held that jury trials must be available if a prison sentence of six or more months is possible.

Impartiality is a requirement of jury trials that has undergone significant change, with the method of selecting jurors being the most frequently challenged part of the process. Although potential individual jurors who have prejudged a case are not eligible to serve, no groups can be systematically excluded from serving. In 1880, for example, the Supreme Court ruled that African Americans could not be excluded from state jury pools (lists of those eligible to serve).[120] And, in 1975, the Court ruled that to bar women from jury service violated the mandate that juries be a "fair cross section" of the community.[121]

In 1986, the Court expanded the requirement that juries reflect a fair cross section of the community. Historically, lawyers had used peremptory challenges (those for which no cause needs to be given) to exclude African Americans from juries, especially when African Americans were criminal defendants. In *Batson* v. *Kentucky* (1986), the Court ruled that the use of peremptory challenges specifically to exclude African American jurors violated the equal protection clause of the Fourteenth Amendment.[122]

In 1994, the Supreme Court answered the major remaining unanswered question about jury selection: can lawyers exclude women from juries through their use of peremptory challenges? This question came up frequently because in rape trials and sex discrimination cases, one side or another often considers it advantageous to select jurors on the basis of their sex. The Supreme Court ruled that the equal protection clause prohibits discrimination in jury selection on the basis of gender. Thus, lawyers cannot strike all potential male jurors based on the belief that males might be more sympathetic to the arguments of a man charged in a paternity suit, a rape trial, or a domestic violence suit, for example.[123]

The right to confront witnesses at trial also is protected by the Sixth Amendment. In 1990, however, the Supreme Court ruled that this right was not absolute. In *Maryland* v. *Craig* (1990), the Court ruled that constitutionally the testimony of a six-year-old alleged child abuse victim via one-way closed circuit television was permissible. The clause's central purpose, said the Court, was to ensure the reliability of testimony by subjecting it to rigorous examination in an adversarial proceeding.[124] In this case, the child was questioned out of the presence of the defendant, who was in communication with his defense and prosecuting attorneys. The defendant, along with the judge and jury, watched the testimony.

THE EIGHTH AMENDMENT AND CRUEL AND UNUSUAL PUNISHMENT

The **Eighth Amendment** prohibits "cruel and unusual punishments," a concept rooted in the English common-law tradition. Interestingly, today the United States is the only Western nation to put people to death for committing crimes. Not surprisingly, there are tremendous regional differences in the imposition of the death penalty, with the South leading in the number of men and women executed each year.

In the 1500s, religious heretics and those critical of the English Crown were subjected to torture to extract confessions, and then were condemned to an equally hideous death by the rack, disembowelment, or other barbarous means. The English Bill of Rights, written in 1687, safeguarded against "cruel and unusual punishments" as a result of public outrage against those practices. The same language found its way into the U.S. Bill of Rights. Prior to the 1960s, however, little judicial attention was paid to the meaning of that phrase, especially in the context of the death penalty.

The death penalty was in use in all of the colonies at the time the U.S. Constitution was adopted, and its constitutionality went unquestioned. In fact, in two separate cases in the late 1800s, the Supreme Court ruled that deaths by public shooting[125] and electrocution were not "cruel and unusual" forms of punishment in the same category as "punishments which inflict torture, such as the rack, the thumbscrew, the iron boot, the stretching of limbs and the like."[126]

In the 1960s, the NAACP Legal Defense Fund (LDF), believing that the death penalty was applied more frequently to African Americans than to members of other groups, orchestrated a carefully designed legal attack on its constitutionality.[127] Public opinion polls revealed that in 1971, on the eve of the LDF's first major death sentence case to reach the Supreme Court, public support for the death penalty had fallen to below 50 percent. With the timing just right, in *Furman* v. *Georgia* (1972), the Supreme Court effectively put an end to capital punishment, at least in the short run.[128] The Court ruled that because the death penalty often was imposed in an arbitrary manner, it constituted cruel and unusual punishment in violation of the Eighth and Fourteenth Amendments. Following *Furman,* several state legislatures enacted new laws designed to meet the Court's objections to the arbitrary nature of the sentence. In 1976, in *Gregg* v. *Georgia,* Georgia's rewritten death penalty statute was ruled constitutional by the Supreme Court in a 7–2 decision.[129]

This ruling did not deter the LDF from continuing to bring death penalty cases before the Court. In *McCleskey* v. *Kemp* (1987), a 5–4 Court ruled that imposition of the death penalty—even when it appeared to discriminate against African Americans—did not violate the equal protection clause.[130] Despite the testimony of social scientists and evidence that Georgia was eleven times more likely to seek the death penalty against a black defendant, the Court upheld Warren McCleskey's death sentence. It noted that even if statistics show clear discrimination, there must be a showing of racial discrimination in the case at hand. Five justices concluded that there was no evidence of specific discrimination proved against McCleskey at his trial. Within hours of that defeat, McCleskey's lawyers filed a new appeal, arguing that the informant who gave the only testimony against McCleskey at trial had been placed in McCleskey's cell illegally.

Four years later, McCleskey's death sentence challenge again produced an equally important ruling on the death penalty and criminal procedure from the U.S. Supreme Court. In the second *McCleskey* case, *McCleskey* v. *Zant* (1991), the Court found that the issue of the informant should have been raised during the first appeal, in spite of the fact that McCleskey's lawyers initially were told by the state that the witness was not an informer. *McCleskey* v. *Zant* produced new standards designed to make it much more difficult for death-row inmates to file repeated appeals.[131] Justice Lewis Powell, one of those in the five-person majority, later said (after his retirement) that he regretted his vote and should have voted the other way.

The Supreme Court has exempted two key classes of people from the death penalty: those who are mentally retarded and those under the age of eighteen. In 2002, the Court ruled that mentally retarded convicts could not be executed.[132] This 6–3 decision reversed what had been the Court's position on executing the retarded since 1989, a thirteen-year period when several retarded men were executed. In 2005, the Court ruled in a 5–4 decision that standards of decency had evolved sufficiently in the United States, as well as internationally, so that executing those who committed murders as minors was against the Eighth Amendment's ban on cruel and unusual punishment.[133]

At the state level, a move to at least stay executions took on momentum in March 2000 when Governor George Ryan (R–IL) ordered a moratorium on all ex-

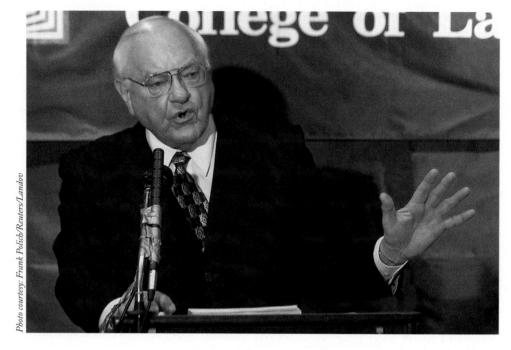

■ Amid questions about the fallibility of America's capital punishment system, Illinois Governor George Ryan commuted the sentences of 167 death-row inmates two days before leaving office in 2003. He had earlier declared a moratorium on execution in Illinois.

Photo courtesy: Frank Polich/Reuters/Landov

VISUAL LITERACY

Race and the
Death Penalty

ecutions. Ryan, a death penalty proponent, became disturbed by new evidence collected as a class project by Northwestern University students. The students unearthed information that led to the release of thirteen men on the state's death row. The specter of allowing death sentences to continue in light of evidence showing so many men were wrongly convicted prompted Ryan's much publicized action. Soon thereafter, the Democratic governor of Maryland followed suit after receiving evidence that blacks were much more likely to be sentenced to death than whites; however, the Republican governor who succeeded him lifted the stay. Before leaving office in January 2003, Illinois Governor Ryan continued his anti-death-penalty crusade by commuting the sentences of 167 death-row inmates, giving them life in prison instead. Ryan also pardoned another four men who had given coerced confessions. This action constituted the single largest anti-death-penalty action since the Court's decision in *Gregg,* and it spurred national conversation on the death penalty, which, in recent polls, has seen its lowest levels of support since 1978.

In another effort to verify that those on death row are not there wrongly, several states offer free DNA testing to death-row inmates. Over a hundred persons have been released from death row after DNA tests proved they did not commit the crimes for which they were convicted.[134] In New York, twenty individuals on death row were later found innocent with proof derived from evidence other than DNA.[135] (For the number of people executed each year in the United States, see Analyzing Visuals: U.S. Executions by Year, 1976–2006.) The U.S. Supreme Court recognized the potential exculpatory power of DNA evidence in *House* v. *Bell* (2006), in which the Court ruled a Tennessee death-row inmate who had exhausted other federal appeals was entitled to an exception to more stringent federal appeals rules due to DNA and related evidence suggesting his innocence.[136] The Court also revisited what can be considered cruel and unusual punishment in 2006 when it unanimously ruled that death-row inmates could challenge the drugs and procedures involved in lethal injections.[137]

Analyzing Visuals

U.S. EXECUTIONS BY YEAR, 1976–2006

The bar graph shows the total number of executions that have occurred in the United States since the Supreme Court ruled Georgia's rewritten death penalty statute constitutional in 1976. From 1976 through August 2006, 1,046 people accused of capital crimes as defined by the various states were executed. How would you explain the very low numbers of executions from 1976 to 1983? Given what you know about the legal appeals process, can the significantly higher number of executions from 1992 to 2002 be explained? What factors may have contributed to the decrease in the number of people executed over the past six years?

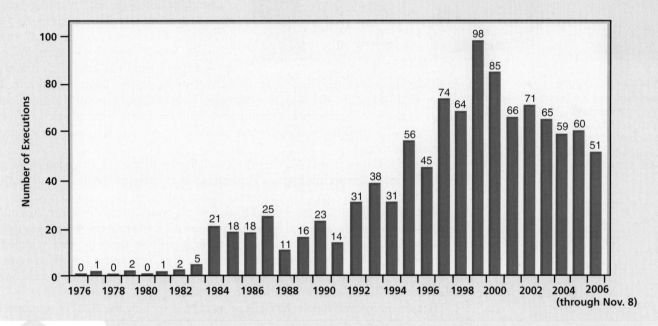

Source: http://www.deathpenaltyinfo.org/

The Right to Privacy

PARTICIPATION

Civil Liberties in Today's World: Privacy and the Rights of the Accused

TO THIS POINT, we have discussed rights and freedoms that have been derived fairly directly from specific guarantees contained in the Bill of Rights. However, the Supreme Court also has given protection to rights not enumerated specifically in the Constitution or Bill of Rights.

Although the Constitution is silent about the **right to privacy,** the Bill of Rights contains many indications that the Framers expected that some areas of life were off limits to governmental regulation. The liberty to practice one's religion guaranteed in the First Amendment implies the right to exercise private, personal beliefs. The guarantee against unreasonable searches and seizures contained in the Fourth Amendment similarly implies that persons are to be secure in their homes and should not fear that

right to privacy
The right to be let alone; a judicially created doctrine encompassing an individual's decision to use birth control or secure an abortion.

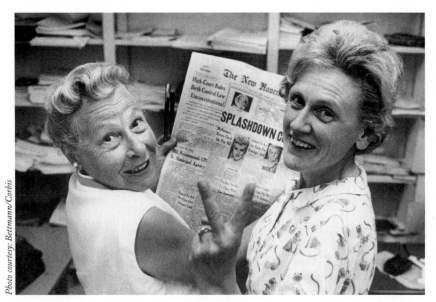

■ In this 1965 photo, Estelle Griswold (left), executive director of the Planned Parenthood League of Connecticut, and Cornelia Jahncke, its president, celebrate the Supreme Court's ruling *Griswold* v. *Connecticut* (1965).

Photo courtesy: Bettmann/Corbis

police will show up at their doorsteps without cause. As early as 1928, Justice Louis Brandeis hailed privacy as "the right to be left alone—the most comprehensive of rights and the right most valued by civilized men."[138] It was not until 1965, however, that the Court attempted to explain the origins of this right. (See The Living Constitution.)

BIRTH CONTROL

Today, most Americans take access to many forms of birth control as a matter of course. Condoms are sold in the grocery store, and some television stations air ads for them. Easy access to birth control, however, wasn't always the case. Many states often barred the sale of contraceptives to minors, prohibited the display of contraceptives, or even banned their sale altogether. One of the last states to do away with these kinds of laws was Connecticut. It outlawed the sale of all forms of birth control and even prohibited physicians from discussing it with their married patients until the Supreme Court ruled its restrictive laws unconstitutional.

Griswold v. *Connecticut* (1965) involved a challenge to the constitutionality of an 1879 Connecticut law prohibiting the dissemination of information about and/or the sale of contraceptives.[139] In *Griswold*, seven justices decided that various portions of the Bill of Rights, including the First, Third, Fourth, Ninth, and Fourteenth Amendments, cast what the Court called "penumbras" (unstated liberties on the fringes or in the shadow of more explicitly stated rights), thereby creating zones of privacy, including a married couple's right to plan a family. Thus, the Connecticut statute was ruled unconstitutional because it violated marital privacy, a right the Court concluded could be read into the U.S. Constitution through interpreting several amendments.

Later, the Court expanded the right of privacy to include the right of unmarried individuals to have access to contraceptives. "If the right of privacy means anything," wrote Justice William J. Brennan Jr., "it is the right of the individual, married or single, to be free from unwarranted governmental intrusion into matters so fundamentally affecting a person as the decision to bear or beget a child."[140] This right to privacy was to be the basis for later decisions from the Court, including the right to secure an abortion.

ABORTION

In the early 1960s, two birth-related tragedies occurred. Severely deformed babies were born to European women who had been given the drug thalidomide while pregnant, and, in the United States, a nationwide measles epidemic resulted in the birth of more babies with severe problems. The increasing medical safety of abortions and the growing women's rights movement combined with these tragedies to put pressure on the legal and medical establishments to support laws that would guarantee a woman's access to a safe and legal abortion.

By the late 1960s, fourteen states had voted to liberalize their abortion policies, and four states decriminalized abortion in the early stages of pregnancy. But, many women's rights activists wanted more. They argued that the decision to carry a pregnancy to term was a woman's fundamental constitutional right. In 1973, in one of the

The Living Constitution

The enumeration in the Constitution, of certain rights, shall not be construed to deny or disparage others retained by the people.

—NINcht AMENDMENT

This amendment simply reiterates the belief of many Federalists who believed that it would be impossible to enumerate every fundamental liberty and right. To assuage the concerns of Anti-Federalists, the Ninth Amendment underscores that rights not listed or spelled out are retained by the people.

James Madison, in particular, feared that the enumeration of so many rights and liberties in the first eight amendments to the Constitution would result in the denial of rights that were not enumerated. So, he drafted this amendment to clarify a rule about how the Constitution and Bill of Rights were to be construed.

Until 1965, the Ninth Amendment was rarely mentioned by the Court. In that year, however, it was used for the first time by the Court as a positive affirmation of a particular liberty—marital privacy. Although privacy is not mentioned in the Constitution, it was—according to the Court—one of those fundamental freedoms that the drafters of the Bill of Rights implied as retained. Since 1965, the Court has ruled in favor of a host of fundamental liberties guaranteed by the Ninth Amendment, often in combination with other specific guarantees, including the right to have an abortion.

most controversial decisions ever handed down, seven members of the Court agreed with this position.

The woman whose case became the catalyst for pro-choice and pro-life groups was Norma McCorvey, an itinerant circus worker. The mother of a toddler she was unable to care for, McCorvey could not leave another child in her mother's care. So, she decided to terminate her second pregnancy. She was unable to secure a legal abortion and was frightened by the conditions she found when she sought an illegal, back-alley abortion. McCorvey turned to two young Texas lawyers who were looking for a plaintiff to bring a lawsuit to challenge Texas's restrictive statute. The Texas law allowed abortions only when they were necessary to save the life of the mother. McCorvey, who was unable to obtain a legal abortion, later gave birth and put the baby up for adoption. Nevertheless, she allowed her lawyers to proceed with the case using her as their plaintiff. They used the pseudonym Jane Roe for McCorvey as they challenged the Texas law as enforced by Henry Wade, the district attorney for Dallas County, Texas.

When the case finally came before the Supreme Court, Justice Harry A. Blackmun, a former lawyer at the Mayo Clinic, relied heavily on medical evidence to rule

Roe v. Wade (1973)
The Supreme Court found that a woman's right to an abortion was protected by the right to privacy that could be implied from specific guarantees found in the Bill of Rights applied to the states through the Fourteenth Amendment.

that the Texas law violated a woman's constitutionally guaranteed right to privacy, which he argued included her decision to terminate a pregnancy. Writing for the majority in **Roe v. Wade (1973)**, Blackmun divided pregnancy into three stages. In the first trimester, a woman's right to privacy gave her an absolute right (in consultation with her physician), free from state interference, to terminate her pregnancy. In the second trimester, the state's interest in the health of the mother gave it the right to regulate abortions—but only to protect the woman's health. Only in the third trimester—when the fetus becomes potentially viable—did the Court find that the state's interest in potential life outweighed a woman's privacy interests. Even in the third trimester, however, abortions to save the life or health of the mother were to be legal.[141]

Roe v. *Wade* unleashed a torrent of political controversy. Anti-abortion groups, caught off guard, scrambled to recoup their losses in Congress. Representative Henry Hyde (R–IL) persuaded Congress to ban the use of Medicaid funds for abortions for poor women, and the constitutionality of the Hyde Amendment was upheld by the Supreme Court in 1977 and again in 1980.[142] The issue also polarized both major political parties.

From the 1970s through the present, the right to an abortion and its constitutional underpinnings in the right to privacy have been under attack by well-organized pro-life groups. The administrations of Ronald Reagan and George Bush were strong advocates of the anti-abortion position, regularly urging the Court to overrule *Roe*. They came close to victory in *Webster* v. *Reproductive Health Services* (1989).[143] In *Webster*, the Court upheld state-required fetal viability tests in the second trimester, even though these tests increased the cost of an abortion considerably. The Court also upheld Missouri's refusal to allow abortions to be performed in state-supported hospitals or by state-funded doctors or nurses. Perhaps most noteworthy, however, was that four justices seemed willing to overrule *Roe* v. *Wade* and that Justice Antonin Scalia publicly rebuked his colleague, Justice Sandra Day O'Connor, then the only woman on the Court, for failing to provide the critical fifth vote to overrule *Roe*.

After *Webster*, states began to enact more restrictive legislation. In *Planned Parenthood of Southeastern Pennsylvania* v. *Casey* (1992), the most important abortion case since *Roe*, Justices O'Connor, Anthony Kennedy, and David Souter, in a jointly authored opinion, wrote that Pennsylvania could limit abortions so long as its regulations did not pose "an undue burden" on pregnant women.[144] The narrowly supported standard, by which the Court upheld a twenty-four-hour waiting period and parental consent requirements, did not overrule *Roe*, but clearly limited its scope by abolishing its trimester approach and substituting the undue burden standard.

In 1993, newly elected pro-choice President Bill Clinton ended bans on fetal tissue research, abortions at military hospitals, and federal financing for overseas population control programs. He also lifted the federal gag rule, a regulation enacted in 1987 that barred public health clinics receiving federal dollars from discussing abortion. (These policies were later reversed by George W. Bush).[145] Clinton also ended the ban on testing RU-486, or mifepristone, a pill for medically induced, nonsurgical abortions, which ultimately was made available in the United States to women with a doctor's prescription late in 2000. President Clinton appointed two supporters of abortion rights, Ruth Bader Ginsburg and Stephen Breyer, to the Supreme Court.

While President Clinton was attempting to shore up abortion rights through judicial appointments, Republican Congresses made repeated attempts to restrict abortion rights. In March 1996 and again in 1998, Congress passed and sent to President Clinton a bill

■ A once very popular anti-abortion group, Operation Rescue, staged large scale protests in front of abortion clinics across the nation gaining a surprising new member—Norma McCorvey, the "Jane Roe" of *Roe* v. *Wade* (1973). In 1995, McCorvey announced that she had become pro-life and said she had been "used" by pro-choice groups.

Photo courtesy: LM Otero/AP Wide World Photos

to ban—for the first time—a specific procedure used in late-term abortions.[146] The president vetoed the Partial Birth Abortion Act over the objections of many of its supporters, including the National Right to Life Committee. Many state legislatures, however, passed their own versions of the act. In 2000, the Supreme Court, however, ruled 5–4 in *Stenberg* v. *Carhart* that a Nebraska partial birth abortion statute was unconstitutionally vague and therefore unenforceable, calling into question the laws of twenty-nine other states with their own bans on late-term procedures.[147]

By October 2003, however, Republican control of the White House and both houses of Congress facilitated passage of the federal Partial Birth Abortion Ban Act. Pro-choice groups such as Planned Parenthood, the Center for Reproductive Rights, and the American Civil Liberties Union immediately filed lawsuits challenging the constitutionality of this law. Also in 2003, the New Hampshire legislature enacted a law that made it illegal for physicians to perform an abortion on a woman under age eighteen unless her parents were notified in writing at least forty-eight hours before the procedure. While at least thirty-three states require abortion providers to notify a parent or obtain a parent's consent prior to the abortion, the Court has allowed these laws only if they contain a judicial bypass option, which provides minors seeking an abortion an alternative to obtaining their parents' consent or notifying them of their plans. The New Hampshire law went further than existing laws by stipulating that an abortion could not be performed unless the procedure was necessary to prevent the minor's death. It, like the federal Partial Birth Abortion Ban Act, failed to contain any provision concerning an exception to protect the health of the mother. The New Hampshire law was challenged immediately by Planned Parenthood of Northern New England. Eventually, the case was appealed to the U.S. Supreme Court, with the new Chief Justice John G. Roberts Jr. presiding. In an unusual move, the Court held oral arguments and released the tapes of them on the same day, November 30, 2005, possibly signaling a more press-friendly chief justice than Roberts's predecessor, William H. Rehnquist, who rarely released same-day tapes.

In a unanimous decision, the Court avoided the issue by sending the case back to the First Circuit—a move that favored Planned Parenthood. Still, said Justice Sandra Day O'Connor in her last official words on abortion: "We do not revisit our abortion

VIDEO DEBATE

Abortion

■ As several male members of Congress look on, President George W. Bush signs the Partial Birth Abortion Ban Act of 2003 at a special ceremony in Washington, D.C. Standing behind the president are, from left: House Speaker Dennis Hastert (R–IL), Senator Orrin Hatch (R–UT), Representative James Sensenbrenner (R–WI), Senator Rick Santorum (R–PA), Representative James Oberstar (D–MN), and Senator Mike DeWine (R–OH). The ceremony was held in front of leaders of the pro-life movement.

Photo courtesy: Pablo Martinez Monsivais/AP Wide World Photos

precedents today, but rather address a question of remedy: If enforcing a statute that regulated access to abortion would be unconstitutional in medical emergencies, what is the appropriate judicial response?"[148] The answer to her question was to come in the Court's decision regarding the constitutionality of the federal Partial Birth Abortion Ban Act. The Supreme Court heard oral argument on the challenge to the federal ban the day after the 2006 midterm elections, and Court watchers are anxious to see how the Court's two new appointees will vote.

HOMOSEXUALITY

It was not until 2003 that the U.S. Supreme Court ruled that an individual's constitutional right to privacy, which provided the basis for the *Griswold* (contraceptives) and *Roe* (abortion) decisions, prevented the state of Texas from criminalizing private sexual behavior. This monumental decision invalidated the laws of fourteen states.

In *Lawrence* v. *Texas* (2003), six members of the Court overruled its decision in *Bowers* v. *Hardwick* (1986) and found that the Texas law was unconstitutional; five justices found it violated fundamental privacy rights. [149] Justice Sandra Day O'Connor agreed that the law was unconstitutional, but concluded that it was an equal protection violation. (See chapter 6 for a detailed discussion of the equal protection clause of the Fourteenth Amendment.) Although Justice Antonin Scalia issued a stinging dissent, charging that "the Court has largely signed on to the so-called homosexual agenda," the majority of the Court was unswayed.[150]

THE RIGHT TO DIE

In 1990, the Supreme Court ruled 5–4 that parents could not withdraw a feeding tube from their comatose daughter after her doctors testified that she could live for many more years if the tube remained in place. Writing for the majority, Chief Justice William H. Rehnquist rejected any attempts to expand the right of privacy into this thorny area of social policy. The Court did note, however, that individuals could terminate medical treatment if they were able to express, or had done so in writing via a living will, their desire to have medical treatment terminated in the event they became incompetent.[151]

In 1997, the U.S. Supreme Court ruled unanimously that terminally ill persons do not have a constitutional right to physician assisted suicide. The Court's action upheld the laws of New York and Washington State that make it a crime for doctors to give life-ending drugs to mentally competent but terminally ill patients who wish to die.[152] But, Oregon enacted a right-to-die or assisted suicide law approved by Oregon voters that allows physicians to prescribe drugs to terminally ill patients.

In November 2001, however, Attorney General John Ashcroft issued a legal opinion determining that assisted suicide is not "a legitimate medical purpose," thereby putting physicians following the Oregon law in jeopardy of federal prosecution.[153] His memo also called for the revocation of the physicians' drug prescription licenses, putting the state and the national government in conflict in an area that Republicans historically have argued is the province of state authority. Oregon officials immediately (and successfully) sought a court order blocking Ashcroft's attempt to interfere with implementation of Oregon law.[154] Later, a federal judge ruled that Ashcroft had overstepped his authority on every point.[155]

The U.S. Supreme Court agreed with the lower court on many points. In *Gonzales* v. *Oregon* (2005), President Bush's new attorney general, Alberto Gonzales, argued that Oregon's Death with Dignity Act was a violation of the federal Controlled Substances Act (CSA) of 1970 and that the "Ashcroft directive" was consistent with the public interest.[156] The Court, however, disagreed and upheld Oregon's law by a 6–3 vote.[157] *Gonzales* v. *Oregon* was a case watched closely by groups on both sides of the right-to-die debate. (See Politics Now: The Right to Die?)

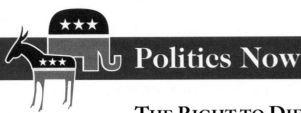

Politics Now

THE RIGHT TO DIE?

In the late 1990s, assisted suicide was a hot-button issue. Politicians and the media focused on controversial Jack Kevorkian, a Michigan physician who was eventually convicted of homicide for administering a lethal injection to a terminally ill patient. Following Kevorkian's 1999 conviction, the issue lost salience until a forty-one-year-old Florida woman thrust the right-to-die movement into the public eye once again in 2005.

Fifteen years earlier, Terri Schiavo had suffered cardiac-respiratory arrest, which left her comatose and incapacitated, although able to breathe on her own. Initially, her husband, Michael Schiavo, and her parents, Robert and Mary Schindler, worked together to pursue a variety of treatments and therapeutic options in an effort to restore Terri to her previous state. However, after about two years of experimental treatment and care that brought little improvement to Terri's mental and physical capabilities, her husband and parents began to turn against one another. The Schindlers wanted to continue as much therapy as possible, but Michael, Terri's court-appointed legal guardian, opposed such treatment, accepting the doctors' conclusion that she was in a persistent vegetative state from which she could never recover. In 1997, Michael hired a right-to-die attorney in an attempt to withdraw the feeding tube that kept his wife alive.

A series of trials and hearings in the Florida court system ensued; most of these hearings, including one in October 2003, were decided in favor of Michael. But, following this ruling, a special session of the Florida legislature passed a law allowing Governor Jeb Bush to sign an order reinstating Terri's nutrition. Michael challenged the law as unconstitutional. The Florida Supreme Court agreed, and after the U.S. Supreme Court refused to hear an appeal of the case, Terri's feeding tube was removed for the final time on March 18, 2005. Through unprecedented congressional action that many commentators and a majority of the American public viewed as an unnecessary politicization of a very private issue, the Schindlers were able to argue their case again in federal court. Nevertheless, Terri died thirteen days later of dehydration. An autopsy supported the conclusion that she could never have recovered or improved.

The controversy over Terri Schiavo's life, which received almost nonstop coverage for several months on cable news, continues to live on through a reinvigorated "will to live" movement. At the forefront of this movement is The Terri Schindler Schiavo Foundation, as well as the disabilities rights group Not Dead Yet.[a] Not Dead Yet, which was established following several of Dr. Kevorkian's initial assisted suicide cases and now has chapters in thirty states, has been an especially potent political force working to ensure full civil and medical rights for people with mental and physical disabilities. Members of Not Dead Yet argue that any action that jeopardizes the life of a disabled person, be it assisted suicide or violence against the disabled, violates the Americans with Disabilities Act and the Constitution's guarantee of equal protection of the law. (For more on equal protection and the civil rights of disabled Americans, see chapter 6.)

We live in an era of tremendous medical advancements that allow physicians to administer live-saving and life-preserving care to patients with severe illnesses and for a long amount of time. Questions about life and death have become more and more complicated. As one expert on these issues stated, "wonderful medical advances enable us to prolong the dying process. The first question is, Should we? And then come all the others: Who lives? Who dies? How do you decide? When do you decide? Who decides?"[b]

QUESTIONS

1. Are there any circumstances under which assisted suicide should be legal, or should the federal government prohibit assisted suicide in all cases as a way of ensuring the general welfare?
2. Do state legislatures and the U.S. Congress have the right to intervene in cases such as Schiavo? Explain your answer.

[a]See http://www.terrisfight.org and http://www.notdeadyet.org.

[b]Jeremy Pearce, "Ronald E. Cranford, 65, an Expert on Coma, Is Dead," *New York Times* (June 3, 2006): A14.

Summary

1. The First Constitutional Amendments: The Bill of Rights

Most of the Framers originally opposed the Bill of Rights. Anti-Federalists, however, continued to stress the need for a bill of rights during the drive for ratification of the Constitution, and some states tried to make their ratification contingent on the addition of a bill of rights. Thus, during its first session, Congress sent the first ten amendments to the Constitution, the Bill of Rights, to the states for their ratification. Later, the addition of the Fourteenth Amendment allowed the Supreme Court to apply some of the amendments to the states through a process called selective incorporation.

2. **First Amendment Guarantees: Freedom of Religion**
The First Amendment guarantees freedom of religion. The establishment clause, which prohibits the national government from establishing a religion, does not, according to Supreme Court interpretation, create an absolute wall between church and state. While the national and state governments may generally not give direct aid to religious groups, many forms of aid, especially many that benefit children, have been held to be constitutionally permissible. In contrast, the Court has generally barred organized prayer in public schools. The Court largely has adopted an accommodationist approach when interpreting the free exercise clause by allowing some governmental regulation of religious practices.

3. **First Amendment Guarantees: Freedom of Speech, Press, and Assembly**
Historically, one of the most volatile areas of constitutional interpretation has been in the interpretation of the First Amendment's mandate that "Congress shall make no law . . . abridging the freedom of speech or of the press." Like the establishment and free exercise clauses of the First Amendment, the speech and press clauses have not been interpreted as absolute bans against government regulation.

Some areas of speech and publication are unconditionally protected by the First Amendment. Among these are prior restraint, symbolic speech, and hate speech. Other areas of speech and publication, however, are unprotected by the First Amendment. These include libel, fighting words, and obscenity and pornography.

The freedoms of peaceable assembly and petition are directly related to the freedoms of speech and of the press. As with other First Amendment rights, the Supreme Court has often become the arbiter between the right of the people to express dissent and government's right to limit controversy in the name of security.

4. **The Second Amendment: The Right to Keep and Bear Arms**
Initially, the right to bear arms was envisioned as one dealing with state militias. Over the years, states and Congress have enacted various gun ownership restrictions with little Supreme Court interpretation as a guide to their ultimate constitutionality.

5. **The Rights of Criminal Defendants**
The Fourth, Fifth, Sixth, and Eighth Amendments provide a variety of procedural guarantees to individuals accused of crimes. In particular, the Fourth Amendment prohibits unreasonable searches and seizures, and the Court has generally refused to allow evidence seized in violation of this safeguard to be used at trial.

Among other rights, the Fifth Amendment guarantees that "no person shall be compelled to be a witness against himself." The Supreme Court has interpreted this provision to require that the government inform the accused of his or her right to remain silent. This provision has also been interpreted to require that illegally obtained confessions must be excluded at trial.

The Sixth Amendment's guarantee of "assistance of counsel" has been interpreted by the Supreme Court to require that the government provide counsel to defendants unable to pay for it in cases where prison sentences may be imposed. The Sixth Amendment also requires an impartial jury, although the meaning of impartial continues to evolve through judicial interpretation.

The Eighth Amendment's ban against "cruel and unusual punishments" has been held not to bar imposition of the death penalty.

6. **The Right to Privacy**
The right to privacy is a judicially created right carved from the penumbras (unstated liberties implied by more explicitly stated rights) of several amendments, including the First, Third, Fourth, Ninth, and Fourteenth Amendments. Statutes limiting access to birth control or abortion or banning homosexual acts have been ruled unconstitutional violations of the right to privacy. The Court, however, appears poised to allow some states to opt to allow their citizens the right to die under a physician's supervision.

KEY TERMS

Bill of Rights, p. 159
civil liberties, p. 158
civil rights, p. 158
clear and present danger test, p. 169
direct incitement test, p. 169
double jeopardy clause, p. 182
due process clause, p. 160
due process rights, p. 176
Eighth Amendment, p. 184
establishment clause, p. 162
exclusionary rule, p. 182
Fifth Amendment, p. 180
fighting words, p. 172
First Amendment, p. 162
Fourth Amendment, p. 177
free exercise clause, p. 163
fundamental freedoms, p. 161
incorporation doctrine, p. 161

libel, p. 171
Miranda rights, p. 181
Miranda v. *Arizona* (1966), p. 181
New York Times Co. v. *Sullivan* (1964), p. 172
Ninth Amendment, p. 160
prior restraint, p. 167
right to privacy, p. 187
Roe v. *Wade* (1973), p. 190
selective incorporation, p. 161
Sixth Amendment, p. 182
slander, p. 171
substantive due process, p. 160
symbolic speech, p. 170
Tenth Amendment, p. 160
writ of habeus corpus, p. 167

SELECTED READINGS

Abrams, Floyd. *Trials of the First Amendment.* New York: Viking, 2005.

Cole, David, and James X. Dempsey. *Terrorism and the Constitution: Sacrificing Civil Liberties in the Name of National Security,* 2nd ed. Washington, DC: First Amendment Foundation, 2002.

Etzoni, Amitai, and Jason H. Marsh, eds. *Rights vs. Public Safety after 9/11: America in the Age of Terrorism.* Lanham, MD: Rowman and Littlefield, 2003.

Fiss, Owen M. *The Irony of Free Speech,* reprint ed. Cambridge, MA: Harvard University Press, 1998.

Friendly, Fred W. *Minnesota Rag: Corruption, Yellow Journalism, and the Case That Saved Freedom of the Press,* reissue ed. Minneapolis: University of Minnesota Press, 2003.

Gates, Henry Louis, Jr., ed. *Speaking of Race, Speaking of Sex: Hate Speech, Civil Rights, and Civil Liberties.* New York: New York University Press, 1995.

Greenawalt, Kent. *Fighting Words: Individuals, Communities, and Liberties of Speech,* reprint ed. Princeton, NJ: Princeton University Press, 1995.

Ivers, Gregg, and Kevin T. McGuire, eds. *Creating Constitutional Change.* Charlottesville: University Press of Virginia, 2004.

Lewis, Anthony. *Gideon's Trumpet,* reissue ed. New York: Vintage Books, 1989.

————. *Make No Law: The Sullivan Case and the First Amendment,* reprint ed. New York: Random House, 1991.

O'Brien, David M. *Constitutional Law and Politics,* vol. 2: *Civil Rights and Civil Liberties,* 5th ed. New York: Norton, 2002.

————. *Animal Sacrifice and Religions Freedom:* Church of the Lukumi Babalu Aye *v.* City of Hialeah. Lawrence: University Press of Kansas, 2004.

O'Connor, Karen. *No Neutral Ground: Abortion Politics in an Age of Absolutes.* Boulder, CO: Westview, 1996.

Regan, Priscilla M. *Legislating Privacy: Technology, Social Values, and Public Policy.* Chapel Hill: University of North Carolina Press, 1995.

Weddington, Sarah. *A Question of Choice,* reprint ed. New York: Grosset/Putnam, 1993.

WEB EXPLORATIONS

To view an original copy of the Bill of Rights, see
http://www.archives.gov/national_archives_experience/charters/bill_of_rights.html

For groups with opposing views on how the First Amendment should be interpreted, see http://www.au.org/ and http://www.pfaw.org/ and http://www.aclj.org/

For more information on the *Agostini* v. *Felton* case, see
http://supct.law.cornell.edu/8080/supct/html/96-552.ZD.html

For more information on the National Endowment for the Arts, see http://www.arts.endow.gov/

For more information on *Chandler* v. *Miller,* see
http://supct.law.cornell.edu/supct/html/96-126.ZS.html

For other privacy issues, see http://www.epic.org/ and http://www.privacy.org/

To compare the different sides of the abortion debate, go to FLITE: Federal Legal Information Through Electronics at http://www.fedworld.gov/supcourt/ and Roe in a Nutshell at http://hometown.aol.com/abtrbng/roeins.htm

For more on gay rights and recent court cases, see http://www.hrc.org/

To learn more about the right-to-die movement, see http://www.hemlock.org/home.jsp

To learn more about the "will to live" movement, see http://notdeadyet.org/

Photo courtesy: UPI Photo/Roger L. Wollenberg/Landov

6

CIVIL RIGHTS

THE U.S. GOVERNMENT long has played an important role in enforcing civil rights in the nation. The passage of the Thirteenth, Fourteenth, and Fifteenth Amendments, for example, abolished slavery, guaranteed citizens equal protection of the laws, and granted the right to vote to newly free male slaves. Much later, after a prolonged civil rights movement sparked by years of discrimination against African Americans, particularly in the South, the U.S. Congress passed sweeping anti-discrimination legislation in the Civil Rights Act of 1964 and the Voting Rights Act of 1965. The Civil Rights Act, in particular, banned discrimination in employment, public accommodations, and education based on race, creed, color, religion, national origin, or sex. Over the years, Congress has added prohibitions based on pregnancy and disability to the act.

The Civil Rights Act and all federal statutes prohibiting discrimination are enforced by the Civil Rights Division of the Department of Justice. The division is headed by an assistant attorney general, a political appointee, who reports to the chief law enforcement official of the United States, the attorney general.

In 2006, the Civil Rights Division was in turmoil. Almost 20 percent of its lawyers, a record number, left in 2005 when many took advantage of a buy-out program that allowed them to retire early; other career lawyers took positions elsewhere because they were upset by what they perceived as the politicization of the division. Many of the lawyers, all career civil servants, believed they were being pressured to leave because they "did not share the administration's conservative view on civil rights laws."[1] Veteran lawyers charged that the political appointees in the division made hiring and policy decisions without consulting staff members with more expertise.

Significant statistical support for these perceptions exists. Since President George W. Bush took office and appointed those who shared his beliefs to key division spots, prosecutions of race and sex discrimination have decreased by 40 percent. Many division lawyers found their workloads shifted to immigration and deportation cases.[2]

Voting Rights Act enforcement, too, has been politicized, according to many nonpolitical career lawyers in the division's voting rights section. According to former lawyers in the section, attorneys "who remain are barred from offering recommendations in major voting rights cases."[3] And, when the section has involved itself in cases in Georgia, Mississippi, and Texas, it has supported actions that would favor the election of Republicans. With regard to the controversial Texas redistricting plan discussed in Chapter 13, for example, Attorney General Alberto Gonzales acknowledged in December 2005 that Department of Justice officials had overruled a unanimous finding by six lawyers and two analysts in the Civil Rights Division that aspects of the Texas plan would violate the Civil Rights Act of 1965.[4] In 2006, the U.S. Supreme Court ruled that states did not have to wait for a new U.S. Census to redraw district lines, supporting the administration's position. But, the Court also found that one of the districts diluted the voting power of Hispanics and thus violated the Voting Rights Act.[5]

When Gonzales became the nation's first Hispanic attorney general, observers thought that the Civil Rights Division would shift back to its traditional emphases. It did not, and morale among nonpolitical appointees continued to lag. The division's home page emphasized issues such as human trafficking and religious freedom, areas of concern that particularly interest the Republican Party's evangelical Christian base. This departure from the division's original focus demonstrates the significant impact a presidential administration may have on civil rights enforcement efforts.

---

civil rights
Refers to the government-protected rights of individuals against arbitrary or discriminatory treatment by governments or individuals based on categories such as race, sex, national origin, age, religion, or sexual orientation.

THE DECLARATION OF INDEPENDENCE, written in 1776, boldly proclaims: "We hold these truths to be self-evident, that all men are created equal, that they are endowed by their Creator with certain unalienable rights." And, although the Framers considered some equality issues, one entire class of citizens—slaves—were treated in the new Constitution more as property than as people. Delegates to the Constitutional Convention put political expediency before the immorality of slavery. Moreover, the Constitution considered white women full citizens for purposes of determining state population, but voting qualifications were left to the states, and none allowed women to vote at the time the Constitution was ratified.

Since the Constitution was written, concepts of **civil rights**, the government-protected rights of individuals against arbitrary or discriminatory treatment by governments or individuals based on categories such as race, sex, national origin, age, religion, or sexual orientation, have changed dramatically. The addition of the Fourteenth Amendment, one of three Civil War Amendments ratified from 1865 to 1870, introduced the notion of equality into the Constitution by specifying that a state could not deny "any person within its jurisdiction equal protection of the laws." Throughout history, the Fourteenth Amendment's equal protection guarantees have been the linchpin of efforts to expand upon the original intent of the amendment to allow its provisions to protect a variety of other groups from discrimination.

The Fourteenth Amendment has generated more litigation to determine and specify its meaning than any other provision of the Constitution. Within a few years of its ratification, women—and later, African Americans and other minorities and disadvantaged groups—took to the courts to seek expanded civil rights in all walks of life. But, the struggle to augment rights was not limited to the courts. Public protest, civil disobedience, legislative lobbying, and appeals to public opinion all have been part of the arsenal of those seeking equality.

Since passage of the Civil War Amendments, there has been a fairly consistent pattern of the expansion of civil rights to more and more groups. In this chapter, we will explore how notions of equality and civil rights have changed in this country.

- First, we will discuss *slavery, abolition, and winning the right to vote,* from *1800 to 1890.*

- Second, we will examine African Americans' and women's next *push for equality* from *1890 to 1954,* using two of the Supreme Court's most famous decisions, *Plessy* v. *Ferguson* (1896) and *Brown* v. *Board of Education* (1954), as bookends for our discussion.

- Third, we will analyze *the civil rights movement* and the Civil Rights Act of 1964 and its effects.

- Fourth, we will discuss the development of a new *women's rights movement* and its push for an equal rights amendment to the U.S. Constitution.

- Fifth, we will present the efforts of *other groups,* including Hispanic Americans, Native Americans, gays and lesbians, and Americans with disabilities, to *mobilize for rights* using methods often modeled after the actions of African Americans and women.

- Finally, we will explore *continuing controversies in civil rights,* including affirmative action and workplace discrimination.

Slavery, Abolition, and Winning the Right to Vote, 1800–1890

The Struggle for Equal Protecton

TODAY, WE TAKE THE RIGHTS of women and blacks to vote for granted. Since 1980, women have outvoted men at the polls in presidential elections; in the 1990s, African Americans and women became the core of the Democratic Party. But, it wasn't always this way. The period from 1800 to 1890 was one of tremendous change and upheaval in America. Despite the Civil War and the freeing of the slaves, the promise of equality guaranteed to African Americans by the Civil War Amendments failed to become a reality. Women's rights activists also began to make claims for equality, often using the arguments enunciated for the abolition of slavery, but they too fell far short of their goals.

SLAVERY AND CONGRESS

Congress banned the slave trade in 1808, after the expiration of the twenty-year period specified by the Constitution. In 1820, blacks made up 25 percent of the U.S. population and were in the majority in some southern states. By 1840, that figure had fallen to 20 percent. After the introduction of the cotton gin (a machine invented in 1793 that separated seeds from cotton very quickly), the South became even more dependent on agriculture and cheap slave labor as its economic base. At the same time, technological advances were turning the northern states into an increasingly industrialized region, which deepened the cultural and political differences and animosity between the North and the South.

As the nation grew westward in the early 1800s, conflicts between northern and southern states intensified over the admission of new states to the union with free or slave status. The first major crisis occurred in 1820, when Missouri applied for admission to the union as a slave state—that is, one in which slavery would be legal. Missouri's admission would have weighted the Senate in favor of slavery and therefore was opposed by northern senators. To resolve this conflict, Congress passed the Missouri Compromise of 1820. The Compromise prohibited slavery north of the geographical boundary at 36 degrees latitude. This act allowed Missouri to be admitted to the union as a slave state, and to maintain the balance of slave and free states, Maine was carved out of a portion of Massachusetts.

■ Frederick Douglass (1817–1895) was born into slavery but learned how to read and write. Once he escaped to the North (where 250,000 free blacks lived), he became a well-known orator and journalist. In 1847, he started a newspaper, the *North Star*, in Rochester, New York. The paper quickly became a powerful voice against slavery, and he urged President Abraham Lincoln to emancipate the slaves. Douglass was also a firm believer in woman's suffrage.

Photo courtesy: Library of Congress

■ This is the announcement that was placed in local newspapers about the upcoming 1848 Seneca Falls Woman's Rights Convention.

THE FIRST CONVENTION

EVER CALLED TO DISCUSS THE

Civil and Political Rights of Women,

SENECA FALLS, N. Y., JULY 19, 20, 1848.

———

WOMAN'S RIGHTS CONVENTION.

———

A Convention to discuss the social, civil, and religious condition and rights of woman will be held in the Wesleyan Chapel, at Seneca Falls, N. Y., on Wednesday and Thursday, the 19th and 20th of July current; commencing at 10 o'clock A. M. During the first day the meeting will be exclusively for women, who are earnestly invited to attend. The public generally are invited to be present on the second day, when Lucretia Mott, of Philadelphia, and other ladies and gentlemen, will address the Convention.*

———
* This call was published in the *Seneca County Courier*, July 14, 1848, without any signatures. The movers of this Convention, who drafted the call, the declaration and resolutions were Elizabeth Cady Stanton, Lucretia Mott, Martha C. Wright, Mary Ann McClintock, and Jane C. Hunt.

Photo courtesy: Library of Congress

THE FIRST CIVIL RIGHTS MOVEMENTS: ABOLITION AND WOMEN'S RIGHTS

The Missouri Compromise solidified the South in its determination to keep slavery legal, but it also fueled the fervor of those who opposed slavery. William Lloyd Garrison, a white New Englander, galvanized the abolitionist movement in the early 1830s. Garrison, a newspaper editor, founded the American Anti-Slavery Society in 1833; by 1838, it had more than 250,000 members. Given the U.S. population today, the National Association for the Advancement of Colored People (NAACP) would need 3.8 million members to have the same kind of overall proportional membership. (In 2006, NAACP membership exceeded 500,000.)

Slavery was not the only practice that people began to question in the decades following the Missouri Compromise. In 1840, for example, Garrison and Frederick Douglass, a well-known black abolitionist writer, left the Anti-Slavery Society when it refused to accept their demand that women be allowed to participate equally in all its activities. Custom dictated that women not speak out in public, and most laws made women second-class citizens. In most states, for example, women could not divorce their husbands or keep their own wages and inheritances. And, of course, they could not vote.

Elizabeth Cady Stanton and Lucretia Mott, who were to found the first women's rights movement, attended the 1840 meeting of the World Anti-Slavery Society in London with their husbands. After their long journey, they were not allowed to participate in the convention because they were women. As they sat in the balcony, apart from the male delegates, they paused to compare their status to that of the slaves they sought to free. They concluded that women were not much better off than slaves, and they resolved to meet to address these issues. In 1848, they finally sent out a call for the first woman's rights convention. Three hundred women and men, including Frederick Douglass, attended the first meeting for women's rights, which was held in Seneca Falls, New York.

The Seneca Falls Convention in 1848 attracted people from all over New York State and other states as well who believed that men and women should be able to enjoy all rights of citizenship equally. It passed resolutions calling for the abolition of legal, economic, and social discrimination against women. All of the resolutions reflected the attendees' dissatisfaction with contemporary moral codes, divorce and criminal laws, and the limited opportunities for women in education, the church, medicine, law, and politics. Ironically, only the call for "woman suffrage" failed to win unanimous approval. Most who attended the Seneca Falls meeting continued to press for women's rights along with the abolition of slavery.

THE 1850S: THE CALM BEFORE THE STORM

By 1850, much was changing in America: the Gold Rush had spurred westward migration, cities grew as people were lured from their farms, railroads and the telegraph increased mobility and communication, and immigrants flooded into the United States. The woman's movement gained momentum, and slavery continued to tear the nation apart. Harriet Beecher Stowe's *Uncle Tom's Cabin*, a novel that depicted the evils of slavery, further inflamed the country. *Uncle Tom's Cabin* sold more than 300,000 copies in 1852. Equivalent sales today would top 4 million copies.

The tremendous national reaction to Stowe's work, which later prompted President Abraham Lincoln to call Stowe "the little woman who started the big war," had not yet faded when a new controversy over the Missouri Compromise of 1820 became the lightning rod for the first major civil rights case to be addressed by the U.S. Supreme Court. As discussed in chapter 3, in *Dred Scott* v. *Sandford* (1857), the Court ruled that the Missouri Compromise, which prohibited slavery north of a set geographical boundary, was unconstitutional. Furthermore, the Court went on to add that slaves were not U.S. citizens, and as a consequence, slaves could not bring suits in federal court.

THE CIVIL WAR AND ITS AFTERMATH: CIVIL RIGHTS LAWS AND CONSTITUTIONAL AMENDMENTS

The Civil War had many causes, but slavery was clearly a key issue. During the war (1861–1865), abolitionists continued to press for an end to slavery. They were partially rewarded when President Abraham Lincoln issued the Emancipation Proclamation, which provided that all slaves in states still in active rebellion against the United States would be freed automatically on January 1, 1863. Designed as a measure to gain favor for the war in the North, the Emancipation Proclamation did not free all slaves—it freed only those who lived in the Confederacy. Complete abolition of slavery did not occur until congressional passage and ultimate ratification of the Thirteenth Amendment in 1865.

The **Thirteenth Amendment** was the first of the three Civil War Amendments. It banned all forms of "slavery [and] involuntary servitude." (See The Living Constitution: Thirteenth Amendment, Section 1.) Although southern states were required to ratify the Thirteenth Amendment as a condition of their readmission to the Union after the war, most of the former Confederate states quickly passed laws that were designed to restrict opportunities for newly freed slaves. These **Black Codes** prohibited African Americans from voting, sitting on juries, or even appearing in public places. Although Black Codes differed from state to state, all empowered local law-enforcement officials to arrest unemployed blacks, fine them for vagrancy, and hire them out to employers to satisfy their fines. Some state codes went so far as to require African Americans to work on plantations or to be domestics. The Black Codes laid the groundwork for Jim Crow laws, which later would institute segregation in all walks of life in the South.

An outraged Congress enacted the Civil Rights Act of 1866 to invalidate some state Black Codes. President Andrew Johnson vetoed the legislation, but—for the first time in history—Congress overrode a presidential veto. The Civil Rights Act formally made African Americans citizens of the United States and gave the Congress and the federal courts the power to intervene when states attempted to restrict the citizenship rights of male African Americans in matters such as voting. Congress reasoned that African Americans were unlikely to fare well if they had to file discrimination complaints in state courts, where most judges were elected. Passage of a federal law allowed African Americans to challenge discriminatory state practices in the federal courts, where judges were appointed for life by the president.

Because controversy remained over the constitutionality of the act (since the Constitution gives states the right to determine qualifications of voters), the **Fourteenth Amendment** was proposed simultaneously with the Civil Rights Act to guarantee, among other things, citizenship to all freed slaves. Other key provisions of the

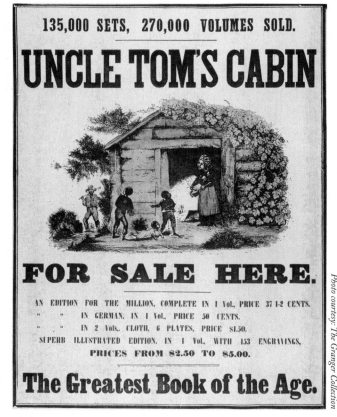

135,000 SETS, 270,000 VOLUMES SOLD.

UNCLE TOM'S CABIN

FOR SALE HERE.

AN EDITION FOR THE MILLION, COMPLETE IN 1 Vol., PRICE 37 1-2 CENTS.
" "   IN GERMAN. IN 1 Vol., PRICE 50 CENTS.
" "   IN 2 Vols., CLOTH, 6 PLATES, PRICE $1.50.
SUPERB ILLUSTRATED EDITION. IN 1 Vol., WITH 153 ENGRAVINGS,
PRICES FROM $2.50 TO $5.00.

The Greatest Book of the Age.

Photo courtesy: The Granger Collection

■ The original title page of *Uncle Tom's Cabin, or Life Among the Lowly,* by Harriet Beecher Stowe. By the 1960s, "Uncle Tom" had become a derogatory term for blacks who were perceived as subservient to whites.

Thirteenth Amendment
One of the three Civil War Amendments; specifically bans slavery in the United States.

Black Codes
Laws denying most legal rights to newly freed slaves; passed by southern states following the Civil War.

Fourteenth Amendment
One of the three Civil War Amendments; guarantees equal protection and due process of the laws to all U.S. citizens.

The Living Constitution

Neither slavery nor involuntary servitude, except as a punishment for crime whereof the party shall have been duly convicted, shall exist within the United States, or any place subject to their jurisdiction.

—THIRTEENTH AMENDMENT, SECTION 1

This amendment, the first of three Civil War Amendments, abolished slavery throughout the United States and its territories. It also prohibited involuntary servitude.

Based on his wartime authority, in 1863 President Abraham Lincoln issued the Emancipation Proclamation abolishing slavery in the states that were in rebellion against the United States. Because Congress was considered to lack the constitutional authority to abolish slavery, after one unsuccessful attempt to garner the two-thirds vote necessary, the proposed Thirteenth Amendment was forwarded to the states on February 1, 1865. With its adoption, said one of its sponsors, it relieved Congress "of sectional strifes." Initially, some doubted if any groups other than newly freed African slaves were protected by the provisions of the amendment. Soon, however, the Supreme Court went on to clarify this question by noting: "If Mexican peonage or the Chinese coolie labor system shall develop slavery of the Mexican or Chinese race within our territory, this amendment may safely be trusted to make it void."

In the early 1990s, the Supreme Court was called on several times to construe section 1 of the amendment, especially in regard to involuntary servitude. Thus, provisions of an Alabama law that called for criminal sanctions and jail time for defaulting sharecroppers were considered unconstitutional and Congress enacted a law banning this kind of involuntary servitude. More recently, the Court has found compulsory high school community service programs not to violate the ban on involuntary servitude.

The Supreme Court and a host of lower federal and state courts have upheld criminal convictions of those who psychologically coerced mentally retarded farm laborers into service or who lured foreign workers to the United States with promises of jobs and then forced them to work long hours at little or no pay. Human trafficking, in fact, has been targeted by the Bush administration as an especially onerous form of involuntary servitude. The U.S. Department of Justice has undertaken hundreds of investigations in an attempt to end this system.

Fourteenth Amendment barred states from abridging "the privileges or immunities of citizenship" or depriving "any person of life, liberty, or property without due process of law," or "deny any person within its jurisdiction the equal protection of the laws."

Unlike the Thirteenth Amendment, which had near-unanimous support in the North, the Fourteenth Amendment was opposed by many women because it failed to guarantee suffrage for women. During the Civil War, woman's rights activists put aside their claims for expanded rights for women, most notably the right to vote, and threw their energies into the war effort. They were convinced that once slaves were freed and given the right to vote, women similarly would be rewarded with the franchise. They were wrong.

In early 1869, after ratification of the Fourteenth Amendment (which specifically added the word "male" to the Constitution for the first time), woman's rights activists met in Washington, D.C., to argue against passage of any new amendment that would extend suffrage to black males and not to women. The convention resolved that "a man's government is worse than a white man's government, because, in proportion as you increase the tyrants, you make the condition of the disenfranchised class more hopeless and degraded."

In spite of these arguments, the **Fifteenth Amendment** was passed by Congress in early 1869. It guaranteed the "right of citizens" to vote regardless of their "race, color or previous condition of servitude." Sex was not mentioned.

Woman's rights activists were shocked. Abolitionists' continued support of the Fifteenth Amendment, which was ratified by the states in 1870, prompted many woman's rights supporters to leave the abolition movement and to work solely for the cause of women's rights. Twice burned, Susan B. Anthony and Elizabeth Cady Stanton decided to form their own group, the National Woman Suffrage Association (NWSA), to achieve that goal. (Another, more conservative group, the American Woman Suffrage Association, also was formed.) In spite of the NWSA's opposition, however, the Fifteenth Amendment was ratified by the states in 1870.

Fifteenth Amendment
One of the three Civil War Amendments; specifically enfranchised newly freed male slaves.

CIVIL RIGHTS, CONGRESS, AND THE SUPREME COURT

Continued southern resistance to African American equality led Congress to pass the Civil Rights Act of 1875, designed to grant equal access to public accommodations such as theaters, restaurants, and transportation. The act also prohibited the exclusion of African Americans from jury service. By 1877, however, national interest in the legal condition of African Americans waned. Most white Southerners and even some Northerners never had believed in true equality for "freedmen," as former slaves were called. Any rights that freedmen received had been contingent on federal enforcement. Federal occupation of the South ended in 1877. National troops were no longer available to guard polling places and to prevent whites from excluding black voters, and southern states quickly moved to limit African Americans' access to the ballot. Other forms of discrimination also were allowed by judicial decisions upholding **Jim Crow laws,** which required segregation in public schools and facilities, including railroads, restaurants, and theaters. Some Jim Crow laws, specifically known as miscegenation laws, barred interracial marriage.

All these laws, at first glance, appeared to conflict with the Civil Rights Act of 1875. In 1883, however, a series of cases decided by the Supreme Court severely damaged the vitality of the 1875 act. The ***Civil Rights Cases*** (1883) were five separate cases involving the convictions of private individuals found to have violated the Civil Rights Act by refusing to extend accommodations to African Americans in theaters, a hotel, and a railroad.[6] In deciding these cases, the Supreme Court ruled that Congress could prohibit only state or governmental action and not private acts of discrimination. The Court thus seriously limited the scope of the Civil Rights Act by concluding that Congress had no authority to prohibit private discrimination in public accommodations. The Court's opinion in the *Civil Rights Cases* provided a moral reinforcement for the Jim Crow system. Southern states viewed the Court's ruling as an invitation to gut the reach and intent of the Thirteenth, Fourteenth, and Fifteenth Amendments.

Jim Crow laws
Laws enacted by southern states that discriminated against blacks by creating "whites only" schools, theaters, hotels, and other public accommodations.

Civil Rights Cases **(1883)**
Name attached to five cases brought under the Civil Rights Act of 1875. In 1883, the Supreme Court decided that discrimination in a variety of public accommodations, including theaters, hotels, and railroads, could not be prohibited by the act because such discrimination was private discrimination and not state discrimination.

In devising ways to make certain that African Americans did not vote, Southerners had to avoid the intent of the Fifteenth Amendment. This amendment did not guarantee suffrage; it simply said that states could not deny anyone the right to vote on account of race or color. To exclude African Americans in a seemingly racially

■ Throughout the South, examples of Jim Crow laws abounded. One such law required separate public drinking fountains, shown here. Notice the obvious difference in quality.

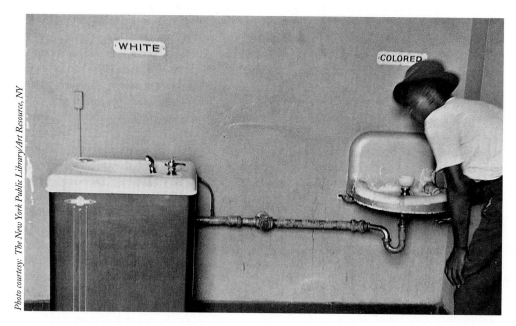

Photo courtesy: The New York Public Library/Art Resource, NY

poll tax
A tax levied in many southern states and localities that had to be paid before an eligible voter could cast a ballot.

neutral way, southern states used three devices before the 1890s: (1) **poll taxes** (small taxes on the right to vote that often came due when poor African American share-croppers had the least amount of money on hand); (2) some form of property-owning qualifications; and, (3) "literacy" or "understanding" tests, which allowed local voter registration officials to administer difficult reading-comprehension tests to potential voters whom they did not know.

These voting restrictions had an immediate impact. By the late 1890s, black voting fell by 62 percent from the Reconstruction period, while white voting fell by only 26 percent. To make certain that these laws did not further reduce the numbers of poor or uneducated white voters, many southern states added a **grandfather clause** to their voting qualification provisions, granting voting privileges to those who failed to pass a wealth or literacy test only if their grandfathers had voted before Reconstruction. Grandfather clauses effectively denied the descendents of slaves the right to vote.

grandfather clause
Voting qualification provision in many southern states that allowed only those whose grandfathers had voted before Reconstruction to vote unless they passed a wealth or literacy test.

While African Americans continued to face wide-ranging racism on all fronts, women also confronted discrimination. During this period, married women, by law, could not be recognized as legal entities. Women often were treated in the same category as juveniles and imbeciles, and in many states they were not entitled to wages, inheritances, or custody of their children.

VIDEO ROUNDTABLE

Equality

The Push for Equality, 1890–1954

THE PROGRESSIVE ERA (1890–1920) was characterized by a concerted effort to re-form political, economic, and social affairs. Evils such as child labor, the concentra-tion of economic power in the hands of a few industrialists, limited suffrage, political corruption, business monopolies, and prejudice against African Americans all were targets of progressive reform efforts. Distress over the inferior legal status of African Americans was aggravated by the U.S. Supreme Court's decision in ***Plessy v. Ferguson*** **(1896)**, a case that some commentators point to as the Court's darkest hour.[7]

In 1892, a group of African Americans in Louisiana decided to test the constitu-tionality of a Louisiana law mandating racial segregation on all public trains. They convinced Homer Plessy, a man of seven-eighths Caucasian and one-eighth African

***Plessy v. Ferguson* (1896)**
Plessy challenged a Louisiana statute requiring that railroads pro-vide separate accommodations for blacks and whites. The Court found that separate but equal accommoda-tions did not violate the equal pro-tection clause of the Fourteenth Amendment.

descent, to board a train in New Orleans and proceed to the "whites only" car.[8] He was arrested when he refused to take a seat in the car reserved for African Americans as required by state law. Plessy challenged the law, arguing that the Fourteenth Amendment prohibited racial segregation.

The Supreme Court disagreed. After analyzing the history of African Americans in the United States, the majority concluded that the Louisiana law was constitutional. The justices based their decision on their belief that separate facilities for blacks and whites provided equal protection of the laws. After all, they reasoned, African Americans were not prevented from riding the train; the Louisiana statute required only that the races travel separately. Justice John Marshall Harlan was the lone dissenter. He argued that "the Constitution is colorblind" and that it was senseless to hold constitutional a law "which, practically, puts the badge of servitude and degradation upon a large class of our fellow citizens."

Not surprisingly, the separate-but-equal doctrine enunciated in *Plessy* v. *Ferguson* soon came to mean only separate, as new legal avenues to discriminate against African Americans were enacted into law throughout the South. The Jim Crow system soon expanded and became a way of life and a rigid social code in the American South. Journalist Juan Williams notes in *Eyes on the Prize:*

> There were Jim Crow schools, Jim Crow restaurants, Jim Crow water fountains, and Jim Crow customs—blacks were expected to tip their hats when they walked past whites, but whites did not have to remove their hats even when they entered a black family's home. Whites were to be called "sir" and "ma'am" by blacks, who in turn were called by their first names by whites. People with white skin were to be given a wide berth on the sidewalk; blacks were expected to step aside meekly.[9]

By 1900, equality for African Americans was far from the promise first offered by the Civil War Amendments. Again and again, the Supreme Court nullified the intent of the amendments and sanctioned racial segregation while the states avidly followed its lead.[10]

THE FOUNDING OF THE NATIONAL ASSOCIATION FOR THE ADVANCEMENT OF COLORED PEOPLE

In 1909, a handful of individuals active in a variety of progressive causes, including woman suffrage and the fight for better working conditions for women and children, met to discuss the idea of a group devoted to the problems of the Negro. Major race riots recently had occurred in several American cities, and progressive reformers were concerned about these outbreaks of violence and the possibility of others. Oswald Garrison Villard, the influential publisher of the New York Evening Post—and the grandson of William Lloyd Garrison—called a conference to discuss the problem. This group soon evolved into the National Association for the Advancement of Colored People (NAACP). Along with Villard, its first leaders included W. E. B. DuBois, a founder of the Niagara Movement, a group of educated African Americans who took their name from their first meeting place in Niagara Falls, Ontario, Canada.

■ W. E. B. DuBois (second from right in the second row, facing left) is pictured with the other original leaders of the Niagara Movement. This 1905 photo was taken on the Canadian side of Niagara Falls because no hotel on the U.S. side would accommodate the group's African American members. At the meeting, a list of injustices suffered by African Americans was detailed.

KEY WOMEN'S GROUPS

The struggle for women's rights was revitalized in 1890 when the National and American Woman Suffrage Associations merged. The new organization, the National American Woman Suffrage Association (NAWSA), was headed by Susan B. Anthony. Unlike NWSA, which had sought a wide variety of expanded rights for women, this new association was devoted largely to securing woman suffrage. Its task was greatly facilitated by the proliferation of women's groups that emerged during the Progressive era. In addition to the rapidly growing temperance movement—the move to ban the sale of alcohol, which many women blamed for a variety of social ills—women's groups were created to seek protective legislation in the form of maximum hour or minimum wage laws for women and to work for improved sanitation, public morals, education, and the like. Other organizations that were part of what was called the club movement were created to provide increased cultural and literary experiences for middle-class women. With increased industrialization, for the first time some women found that they had the opportunity to pursue activities other than those centered on the home.

One of the most active groups lobbying on behalf of women during this period was the National Consumers' League (NCL), which successfully lobbied for Oregon legislation limiting women to eight hours of work a day. Soon after the law was enacted, Curt Muller was charged and convicted of employing women more than eight hours a day in his small laundry. When he appealed his conviction to the U.S. Supreme Court, the NCL sought permission from the state to conduct the defense of the statute.

At the urging of NCL attorney and future U.S. Supreme Court Justice Louis Brandeis, NCL members amassed an impressive array of sociological and medical data that were incorporated into what became known as the Brandeis brief. This contained only three pages of legal argument. More than a hundred pages were devoted to nonlegal, sociological data that were used to convince the Court that Oregon's statute was constitutional. In agreeing with the NCL in *Muller* v. *Oregon* (1908), the Court relied heavily on these data to document women's unique status as mothers to justify their differential legal treatment.[11]

■ In 1908, the U.S. Supreme Court ruled that Oregon's law barring women from working more than eight hours a day in laundries was constitutional. Thus, the conviction of Curt Muller (with arms folded), who owned the laundry where women worked twelve- and fourteen-hour days, was upheld. Ironically, one of the major goals of the later women's movement was to remove this kind of protective legislation.

Photo courtesy: Supreme Court Historical Society

Photo courtesy: Library of Congress

■ Suffragists demonstrating in the early 1900s for the franchise. Parades like this one took place in cities all over the United States. Other women took more militant action. Women in the National Woman's Party actually were jailed for demonstrating at the White House. They faced deplorable conditions while incarcerated and were force-fed after going on hunger strikes in protest.

Women seeking the vote used reasoning reflecting the Court's opinion in *Muller*. Discarding earlier notions of full equality, NAWSA based its claim to the right to vote largely on the fact that women, as mothers, should be enfranchised. Furthermore, although many members of the suffrage movement were NAACP members, the new women's movement—called the **suffrage movement** because of its focus on the vote alone and not on broader issues of women's rights—took on racist overtones. Suffragists argued that if undereducated African Americans could vote, why couldn't women? Some NAWSA members even argued that "the enfranchisement of women would ensure immediate and durable white supremacy."

Diverse attitudes clearly were present in the growing suffrage movement, which often tried to be all things to all people. Its roots in the Progressive movement gave it an exceptionally broad base that transformed NAWSA from a small organization of just over 10,000 members in the early 1890s to a true social movement of more than 2 million members in 1917. By 1920, a coalition of women's groups, led by NAWSA and the newer, more radical National Woman's Party, was able to secure ratification of the **Nineteenth Amendment** to the Constitution. It guaranteed all women the right to vote—fifty years after African American males were enfranchised by the Fifteenth Amendment.

After passage of the suffrage amendment in 1920, the fragile alliance of diverse women's groups that had come together to fight for the vote quickly disintegrated. Women returned to their home groups, such as the NCL or the Women's Christian Temperance Union, to pursue their individualized goals. In fact, after the tumult of the suffrage movement, widespread organized activity on behalf of women's rights did not reemerge until the 1960s. In the meantime, however, the NAACP continued to fight racism and racial segregation. In fact, its activities and those of others in the civil rights movement would later give impetus to a new women's movement.

suffrage movement
The drive for voting rights for women that took place in the United States from 1890 to 1920.

Nineteenth Amendment
Amendment to the Constitution that guaranteed women the right to vote.

LITIGATING FOR EQUALITY

During the 1930s, leaders of the NAACP began to sense that the time was right to launch a full-scale challenge in the federal courts to the constitutionality of *Plessy*'s separate-but-equal doctrine. Clearly, the separate-but-equal doctrine and the proliferation

American Values/American Voices

WHO IS ENTITLED TO VOTE?

Today, despite the significant progress that African Americans and other groups have made in securing civil rights, many voting rights advocates believe one growing group of disenfranchised individuals looms large: ex-felons. A question that goes to the heart of our criminal justice system and challenges American ideals of equality is this: once felons are convicted, should their civil rights, especially the right to vote, be sacrificed?

As of 2006, the answer appears to be yes. All but two states (Maine and Vermont) prohibit incarcerated felons from voting and thirty-six states prohibit felons from voting while they are on probation. Three states deny the vote to all ex-felons who have completed their sentences, and nine other states disenfranchise some categories of ex-offenders or allow convicted felons to apply for restoration of their voting rights only after they have served their sentence and have waited a specified number of years. According to Human Rights Watch and the Sentencing Project, nearly 5 million American citizens who have committed crimes are prevented from voting by state laws. Moreover, because a disproportionate percentage of ex-felons are African American males, many consider these voting prohibitions to be a form of government-sanctioned discrimination. In fact, one study estimates that nearly 15 percent of African American men cannot vote because of limitations on felons' voting rights.[a]

This issue is a concern not only to human rights groups but also to Democrats, who believe that many convicted felons would be more likely to vote Democratic. Some Republicans agree. According to Alabama Republican Party Chair Marty Connors, "As frank as I can be, we're opposed to [restoring voting rights] because felons don't tend to vote Republican." One study found that George W. Bush would have lost Florida, and therefore the presidential election in 2000, by 80,000 votes if ex-felons there had been allowed to vote.[b]

The Fourteenth Amendment, the locus of most civil rights laws, specifically allows states to deny voting rights to persons guilty of "participation in rebellion or other crimes." Supporters of voting rights for ex-felons argue that despite this constitutional authority, laws disenfranchising those who have paid their debt to society run counter to notions of equity in American society.

QUESTIONS

1. If a basic American value has been the continual expansion of voting rights, on what basis can those rights be denied to felons who have served their time? Is voting a civil right or a privilege?
2. In many states, jury service is linked to voting rights. Should convicted felons be allowed to serve on juries?

[a]Bryan Knowles, "Should Convicted Felons Have Voting Rights?" Speakout.com, June 9, 2000.

[b]Kevin Krajick, "Why Can't Ex-Felons Vote?" *Washington Post* (August 18, 2004): A19.

---

of Jim Crow laws were a bar to any hope of full equality for African Americans. Traditional legislative channels were unlikely to work, given blacks' limited or nonexistent political power. Thus, the federal courts and a litigation strategy were the NAACP's only hopes. The NAACP mapped out a long-range plan that would first target segregation in professional and graduate education.

Test Cases The NAACP opted first to challenge the constitutionality of Jim Crow law schools. In 1935, all southern states maintained fully segregated elementary and secondary schools. Colleges and universities also were segregated, but most states did not provide for postgraduate education for African Americans. NAACP lawyers chose to target law schools because they were institutions that judges could well understand, and integration there would prove less threatening to most whites.

Lloyd Gaines, a graduate of Missouri's all-black Lincoln University, sought admission to the all-white University of Missouri Law School in 1936. He was immediately rejected. In the separate-but-equal spirit, the state offered to build a law school at Lincoln (although no funds were allocated for the project) or, if he didn't want to wait, to pay his tuition at an out-of-state law school. Gaines rejected the offer, sued, lost in the lower courts, and appealed to the U.S. Supreme Court.

Gaines's case was filed at an auspicious time. As discussed in chapter 3, a constitutional revolution of sorts occurred in Supreme Court decision making in 1937.

Before this time, the Court was most receptive to and interested in the protection of economic liberties. In 1937, however, the Court reversed itself in a series of cases and began to place individual freedoms and personal liberties on a more protected footing. Thus, in 1938, Gaines's lawyers pleaded his appeal to a far more sympathetic Supreme Court. NAACP attorneys argued that the creation of a separate law school of a lesser caliber than that of the University of Missouri would not and could not afford Gaines an equal education. The justices agreed and ruled that Missouri had failed to meet the separate-but-equal requirements of *Plessy*. The Court ordered Missouri either to admit Gaines to the school or to set up a law school for him.[12]

Recognizing the importance of the Court's ruling, in 1939 the NAACP created a separate, tax-exempt legal defense fund to devise a strategy that would build on the Missouri case and bring about equal educational opportunities for all African American children. The first head of the NAACP Legal Defense and Educational Fund, commonly referred to as the LDF, was Thurgood Marshall, who later became the first African American to serve on the U.S. Supreme Court. Sensing that the Court would be more amenable to the NAACP's broader goals if it were first forced to address a variety of less threatening claims to educational opportunity, Marshall and the LDF brought a series of carefully crafted test cases to the Court.

The first case involved H. M. Sweatt, a forty-six-year-old African American mail carrier, who applied for admission to the all-white University of Texas Law School in 1946. Rejected on racial grounds, Sweatt sued. The judge gave the state six months to establish a law school or to admit Sweatt to the university. The state legislature saw the handwriting on the wall and authorized $3 million for the creation of the Texas State University for Negroes. One hundred thousand dollars of that money was to be for a new law school in Austin across the street from the state capitol building. It consisted of three small basement rooms, a library of 10,000 books, access to the state law library, and three part-time first-year instructors as the faculty. Sweatt declined the opportunity to obtain an education there and instead chose to continue his legal challenge.

While working on the Texas case, the LDF also decided to pursue a case involving George McLaurin, a retired university professor who had been denied admission to the doctoral education program at the University of Oklahoma. Marshall reasoned that McLaurin, at age sixty-eight, would be immune from the charges that African Americans wanted integration in order to intermarry with whites. After a lower court ordered McLaurin's admission, the university reserved a dingy alcove in the cafeteria for him to eat in during off-hours, and he was given his own table in the library behind a shelf of newspapers. In what surely "was Oklahoma's most inventive contribution to legalized bigotry since the adoption of the 'grandfather clause,'" McLaurin was forced to sit outside classrooms while lectures and seminars were conducted inside.[13]

The Supreme Court handled these two cases together.[14] The eleven southern states filed an *amicus curiae* (friend of the court) brief, in which they argued that *Plessy* should govern both cases. The LDF received assistance, however, from an unexpected source—the U.S. government. In a dramatic departure from the past, the administration of President

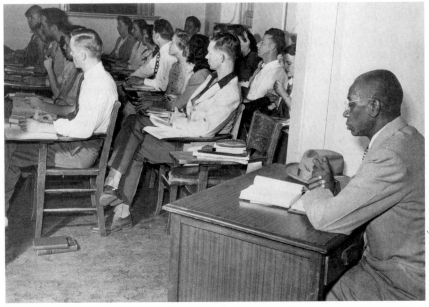

■ Here George McLaurin, the plaintiff in one of the LDF's challenges to "separate but equal doctrine," is shown outside the classroom. This was the university's shameful accommodation when a federal district court ordered his admission into the University of Oklahoma's doctoral program.

Photo courtesy: Bettmann/Corbis

Harry S Truman filed a friend of the court brief urging the Court to overrule *Plessy*. Earlier, Truman had issued an executive order desegregating the military.

Since the late 1870s, the U.S. government never had sided against the southern states in a civil rights matter and never had submitted an *amicus* brief supporting the rights of African American citizens. President Truman believed that because many African Americans had fought and died for their country in World War II, this kind of executive action was proper.

Although the Court did not overrule *Plessy*, the justices found that the measures taken by the states in each case failed to live up to the strictures of the separate-but-equal doctrine. The Court unanimously ruled that the remedies to each situation were inadequate to afford a sound education. In the *Sweatt* case, for example, the Court declared that the "qualities which are incapable of objective measurement but which make for greatness in a law school . . . includ[ing] the reputation of the faculty, experience of the administration, position and influence of the alumni, standing in the community, traditions and prestige" made it impossible for the state to provide an equal education in a segregated setting.[15]

In 1950, after these decisions were handed down, the LDF concluded that the time had come to launch a full-scale attack on the separate-but-equal doctrine. The decisions of the Court were encouraging, and the position of the U.S. government and the population in general appeared to be more receptive to an outright overruling of *Plessy*.

Brown v. Board of Education (1954)
U.S. Supreme Court decision holding that school segregation is inherently unconstitutional because it violates the Fourteenth Amendment's guarantee of equal protection; marked the end of legal segregation in the United States.

equal protection clause
Section of the Fourteenth Amendment that guarantees that all citizens receive "equal protection of the laws."

Brown v. Board of Education

Brown v. *Board of Education* (1954) actually was four cases brought from different areas of the South and border states involving public elementary or high school systems that mandated separate schools for blacks and whites.[16] In *Brown*, LDF lawyers, again led by Thurgood Marshall, argued that *Plessy*'s separate-but-equal doctrine was unconstitutional under the **equal protection clause** of the Fourteenth Amendment, and that if the Court was still reluctant to overrule *Plessy*, the only way to equalize the schools was to integrate them. A major component of the LDF's strategy was to prove that the intellectual, psychological, and financial damage that befell African Americans as a result of segregation precluded any court from finding that equality was served by the separate-but-equal policy.

In *Brown*, the LDF presented the Supreme Court with evidence of the harmful consequences of state-imposed racial discrimination. To buttress its claims, the LDF introduced the now-famous doll study, conducted by Kenneth Clark, a prominent African American sociologist who had long studied the negative effects of segregation on African American children. His research revealed that black children not only preferred white dolls when shown black dolls and white dolls, but that many added that the black doll looked "bad." This information was used to illustrate the negative impact of racial segregation and bias on an African American child's self-image.

The LDF's legal briefs were supported by important *amicus curiae* briefs submitted by the U.S. government, major civil rights groups, labor unions, and religious groups decrying racial segregation. On May 17, 1954, Chief Justice Earl Warren delivered the fourth opinion of the day, *Brown* v. *Board of Education*. Writing for the Court, Warren stated:

> To separate [some school children] from others . . . solely because of their race generates a feeling of inferiority as to their status in the community that may affect their hearts and minds in a way very unlikely ever to be undone. We conclude, unanimously, that in the field of public education the doctrine of "separate but equal" has no place.

There can be no doubt that *Brown* was the most important civil rights case decided in the twentieth century.[17] It immediately evoked an uproar that shook the nation. Some segregationists called the day the decision was handed down Black

Monday. The governor of South Carolina denounced the decision, saying, "Ending segregation would mark the beginning of the end of civilization in the South as we know it."[18] The LDF lawyers who had argued these cases as well as the cases leading to *Brown*, however, were jubilant.

Remarkable changes had occurred in the civil rights of Americans since 1890. Women had won the right to vote, and after a long and arduous trail of litigation in the federal courts, the Supreme Court had finally overturned its most racist decision of the era, *Plessy* v. *Ferguson*. The Court boldly proclaimed that separate but equal (at least in education) would no longer pass constitutional muster. The question then became how *Brown* would be interpreted and implemented. Could it be used to invalidate other Jim Crow laws and practices? Would African Americans ever be truly equal under the law?

The Civil Rights Movement

OUR NOTION OF CIVIL RIGHTS has changed profoundly since the *Brown* decision in 1954. (For more perspective on the outcome, see Join the Debate: *Brown* v. *Board of Education* After More than Fifty Years.) *Brown* served as a catalyst for change, sparking the development of the modern civil rights movement. Women's work in that movement and the student protest movement that arose in reaction to the U.S. government's involvement in Vietnam gave women the experience needed to form their own organizations to press for full equality. As African Americans and women became more and more successful, they served as models for other groups who sought equality—Hispanic Americans, Native Americans, homosexuals, the disabled, and others.

VIDEO ROUNDTABLE

Civil Rights Movement

SCHOOL DESEGREGATION AFTER *BROWN*

One year after *Brown*, in a case referred to as *Brown* v. *Board of Education II* (1955), the Court ruled that racially segregated systems must be dismantled "with all deliberate speed."[19] To facilitate implementation, the Court placed enforcement of *Brown* in the hands of appointed federal district court judges, who were considered more immune to local political pressures than were elected state court judges.

The NAACP and its LDF continued to resort to the courts to see that *Brown* was implemented, while the South entered into a near conspiracy to avoid the mandates of *Brown II*. In Arkansas, for example, Governor Orval Faubus, who was facing a re-election bid, announced that he would not "be a party to any attempt to force acceptance of change to which people are overwhelmingly opposed."[20] The day before school was to begin, he announced that National Guardsmen would surround Little Rock's Central High School to prevent African American students from entering. While the federal courts in Arkansas continued to order the admission of African American children, the governor remained adamant. Finally, President Dwight D. Eisenhower sent federal troops to Little Rock to protect the rights of the nine students attending Central High.

In reaction to the governor's outrageous conduct, the Court broke with tradition and issued a unanimous decision in *Cooper* v. *Aaron* (1958), which was filed by the Little Rock School Board asking the federal district court for a two-and-one-half-year delay in implementation of its desegregation plans. Each justice signed the opinion individually, underscoring his individual support for the notion that "no state legislator or executive or judicial officer can war against the Constitution without violating his undertaking to support it."[21] The state's actions thus were ruled unconstitutional and its "evasive schemes" illegal.

THE ARREST THAT CHANGED AMERICA

Photo courtesy: Roger Harvell/Editorial Cartoonists

Rosa
Parks
1913 ~ 2005

7053

■ Noted civil rights leader Rosa Parks died in 2005, leaving many editorial cartoonists with the occasion to comment on her historical significance.

A NEW MOVE FOR AFRICAN AMERICAN RIGHTS

In 1955, soon after *Brown II,* the civil rights movement took another step forward—this time in Montgomery, Alabama. Rosa Parks, the local NAACP's Youth Council adviser, decided to challenge the constitutionality of the segregated bus system. First, Parks and other NAACP officials began to raise money for litigation and made speeches around town to garner public support. Then, on December 1, 1955, Rosa Parks made history when she refused to leave her seat on a bus to move to the back to make room for a white male passenger. She was arrested for violating an Alabama law banning integration of public facilities, including buses. After she was freed on bond, Parks and the NAACP decided to enlist city clergy to help her cause. At the same time, they distributed 35,000 handbills calling for African Americans to boycott the Montgomery bus system on the day of Parks's trial. Black ministers used Sunday services to urge their members to support the boycott. On Monday morning, African Americans walked, carpooled, or used black-owned taxicabs. That night, local ministers decided that the boycott should be continued. A new, twenty-six-year-old minister, Reverend Martin Luther King Jr., was selected to lead the newly formed Montgomery Improvement Association.

As the boycott dragged on, Montgomery officials and local business owners began to harass the city's African American citizens. The residents held out, despite suffering personal hardship for their actions, ranging from harassment to job loss to bankruptcy. In 1956, a federal court ruled that the segregated bus system violated the equal protection clause of the Fourteenth Amendment. After a year of walking, black Montgomery residents ended their protest when city buses were ordered to integrate. The first effort at nonviolent protest had been successful. Organized boycotts and other forms of nonviolent protest, including sit-ins at segregated restaurants and bus stations, were to follow.

FORMATION OF NEW GROUPS

The recognition and respect that Reverend Martin Luther King Jr. earned within the African American community helped him to launch the Southern Christian Leadership Conference (SCLC) in 1957, soon after the end of the Montgomery bus boycott. Unlike the NAACP, which had northern origins and had come to rely largely on litigation as a means of achieving expanded equality, the SCLC had a southern base and was rooted more closely in black religious culture. The SCLC's philosophy reflected King's growing belief in the importance of nonviolent protest and civil disobedience.

On February 1, 1960, students at the all-black North Carolina Agricultural and Technical College participated in the first sit-in. The students marched to a local lunch counter, sat down, and ordered cups of coffee. They were refused service and sat at the counter until police arrived. When the students refused to leave, they were arrested and jailed. Soon thereafter, African American college students around the South did the same. Their actions were the subject of extensive national media attention.

Over spring break 1960, with the assistance of an $800 grant from the SCLC, 200 student delegates—black and white—met at Shaw University in North Carolina to consider recent sit-in actions and to plan for the future. Later that year, the Student Nonviolent Coordinating Committee (SNCC) was formed.

Whereas the SCLC generally worked with church leaders in a community, SNCC was much more of a grassroots organization. Always perceived as more radical than the SCLC, SNCC tended to focus its organizing activities on the young, both black and white.

In addition to joining the sit-in bandwagon, SNCC also came to lead what were called freedom rides, designed to focus attention on segregated public accommodations. Bands of college students and other civil rights activists traveled by bus throughout the South in an effort to force bus stations to desegregate. Often these protesters were met by angry mobs of segregationists and brutal violence, as local police chose not to defend protesters' basic constitutional rights to free speech and peaceful assembly. African Americans were not the only ones to participate in freedom rides; increasingly, white college students from the North began to play an important role in SNCC.

While SNCC continued to sponsor sit-ins and freedom rides, in 1963 Reverend Martin Luther King Jr. launched a series of massive nonviolent demonstrations in Birmingham, Alabama, long considered a major stronghold of segregation. Thousands of blacks and whites marched to Birmingham in a show of solidarity. Peaceful marchers were met there by the Birmingham police commissioner, who ordered his officers to use dogs, clubs, and fire hoses on the marchers. Americans across the nation were horrified as they witnessed the brutality and abuse heaped on the protesters on television. As the marchers hoped, the shocking scenes (see Analyzing Visuals: Police Confront Civil Rights Demonstrators in Birmingham) helped convince President John F. Kennedy to propose important civil rights legislation.

THE CIVIL RIGHTS ACT OF 1964

Both the SCLC and SNCC sought full implementation of Supreme Court decisions dealing with race and an end to racial segregation and discrimination. The cumulative effect of collective actions including sit-ins, boycotts, marches, and freedom rides—as well as the tragic bombings and deaths inflicted in retaliation—led Congress to pass the first major piece of civil rights legislation since the post–Civil War era, the Civil Rights Act of 1964, followed the next year by the Voting Rights Act. Several events led to the consideration of the two pieces of legislation.

In 1963, President John F. Kennedy requested that Congress pass a law banning discrimination in public accommodations. Seizing the moment, Reverend Martin Luther King Jr. called for a monumental march on Washington, D.C., to demonstrate widespread support for far-ranging anti-discrimination legislation. It was clear that national laws outlawing discrimination were the only answer: southern legislators would never vote to repeal Jim Crow laws. The March on Washington for Jobs and Freedom was held in August 1963, only a few months after the Birmingham demonstrations. More than 250,000 people heard King deliver his famous "I Have a Dream" speech from the Lincoln Memorial. Before Congress had the opportunity to vote on any legislation, however, John F. Kennedy was assassinated on November 22, 1963, in Dallas, Texas.

When Vice President Lyndon B. Johnson, a southern-born, former Senate majority leader, succeeded

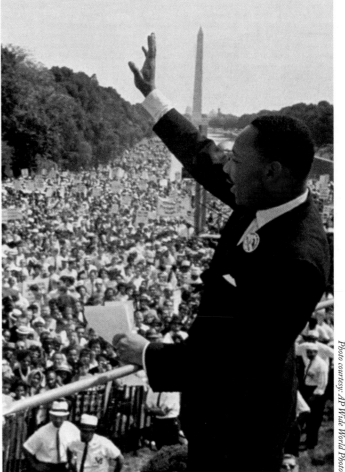

Photo courtesy: AP Wide World Photos

■ Reverend Martin Luther King Jr. delivers his famous "I Have a Dream" speech in Washington, D.C., on August 28, 1963. King was assassinated in 1968 at age thirty-nine in Memphis, Tennessee.

Join the Debate

BROWN V. BOARD OF EDUCATION AFTER MORE THAN FIFTY YEARS

OVERVIEW: It is difficult to overstate the impact of the Supreme Court decision in *Brown* v. *Board of Education* (1954) on American life. The *Brown* decision was instrumental in making civil rights the highest priority on the domestic policy agenda during the 1950s and 1960s, and it held out the promise of educational equality for all Americans. The Court in *Brown* held "education is perhaps the most important function of state and local governments," and that "In these days, it is doubtful . . . any child may reasonably be expected to succeed in life if he is denied the opportunity of an education"—which the Court believed is a right that "must be made available to all on equal terms." For American society to attain justice, the Court understood segregation had to end and that equal educational opportunity allowed all Americans the tools to survive and thrive in contemporary society.

After more than five decades, the results of the *Brown* decision have been mixed. The objective of *Brown* was to create equal educational opportunity; however, there is no constitutional mandate for such a prospect. The Constitution does not speak to education, so that right is given to the states to determine, and it follows that with vast discrepancies in wealth and resources between the states, educational establishments will be unequal as well. This problem is exacerbated when fewer funds are allocated to substandard school districts with significant minority populations. Additionally, many members of the middle class, predominately white, have been abandoning the inner cities, leaving poorer, minority populations in underfunded school districts, thus engendering *de facto* segregation. The

disparities in education reflect disparities in housing patterns and wealth, problems that are outside the authority of school administrators. Segregation is seen even in integrated schools when a disproportionate number of white and Asian Americans are found in advanced placement classes and a disproportionate number of black and Hispanic Americans are found in remedial and special-needs classes.

A principal effect of *Brown* was to highlight the disparity between the education of majority and minority America. More than fifty years later, however, it seems educational segregation may still be the rule rather than the exception. What is the best way to ensure equal educational opportunity for all Americans? Does a diverse classroom necessarily mean a quality education for all? If so, what is the best way to achieve this standard, and if not, what other policy alternatives are available? The 2000 National Assessment of Education Progress (NAEP) shows vast disparities in educational achievement between white and black America. Is segregation the problem, or are there other significant factors as well? What is the best way to ensure a level playing field in the education policy domain?

ARGUMENTS FOR THE EFFECTIVENESS OF *BROWN*

- ***Brown* has reframed the way Americans view educational integration.** The Court held in *Brown* that education is "necessary for good citizenship" and the only way to make American society more just is to provide all citizens the opportunity for a quality education in order for all to realize their ideal of the American Dream. Americans now understand that an equal education for all is necessary to improve the lives of individuals and to realize fundamental American political principles.
- ***Brown* signaled the end of racial segregation and helped usher in the civil rights movement.** *Brown* was

Kennedy as president, he put civil rights reform at the top of his legislative priority list, and civil rights activists gained a critical ally. Thus, through the 1960s, the movement subtly changed in focus from peaceful protest and litigation to legislative lobbying. Its focus broadened from integration of school and public facilities and voting rights to issues of housing, jobs, and equal opportunity.

The push for civil rights legislation in the halls of Congress was helped by changes in public opinion. Between 1959 and 1965, southern attitudes toward integrated schools changed enormously. The proportion of Southerners who responded that they would not mind their child's attendance at a racially balanced school doubled.

In spite of strong presidential support and the sway of public opinion, the Civil Rights Act of 1964 did not sail through Congress. Southern senators, led by South Carolina's Strom Thurmond, a Democrat who later switched to the Republican Party, conducted the longest filibuster in the history of the Senate. For eight

instrumental in creating the social context for the Civil Rights Acts of 1957, 1960, and 1964 and the Voting Rights Act of 1965. Though there is work yet to be done, the sum total of this legislation was to help further and partially realize the goals of social equality and equality before the law.

- **_Brown_ set the model for other social justice movements in the United States.** The legal approach by NAACP LDF lawyers has set the standard for other groups pursuing legal and social equality and inclusion. Supporters of women's rights, Hispanic and Native American rights, gay rights, and rights of the disabled may be said to owe a debt of gratitude to the constitutional interpretation and legal strategies offered by the legal team that argued for _Brown_ and the U.S. Supreme Court.

ARGUMENTS AGAINST THE EFFECTIVENESS OF _BROWN_

- **There are still vast disparities in educational attainment between minority and white students.** According to the NAEP, 63 percent of black, inner-city fourth-graders are unable to attain basic proficiency in reading. And, according to black educator Walter Williams, the average black high school graduate has achieved the educational equivalent of a seventh- or eighth-grade mastery of basic subjects and is thus ill prepared to enter the job market or a university.
- **The goal of _Brown_ has yet to be fully realized; instead of educational and social integration, segregation between the races is still a significant problem.** In 2004, approximately 70 percent of African American children attended public schools where greater than 50 percent of the student population is black—in Washington,

D.C., the student population is 85 percent black. One effect of the _Brown_ decision is "white flight"—the movement of the white middle class out of the inner cities to the suburbs and surrounding country.

- **The _Brown_ decision does not address other problems that affect educational attainment.** _Brown_ does not address other factors understood to affect social and educational achievement. For example, _Brown_ does not address issues such as the effect of high rates of illegitimacy in black communities on educational attainment. In a controversial speech to the NAACP, comedian Bill Cosby took black parents to task for not tending to the education of their children; after all, it is not funding or segregation keeping children from spending time doing their homework, from skipping school, and from reading.

QUESTIONS

1. Is integration in educational institutions the solution for academic achievement, or are there other, more significant solutions to help close the learning gap?
2. Will an attempt to realize educational equality across the states violate states' rights and the principle of federalism? What is the best way to ensure this equality?

SELECTED READINGS

Cottrol, Robert, et al. _Brown v. Board of Education: Caste, Culture and the Constitution._ Lawrence: University Press of Kansas, 2003.

Ogletree, Charles J. _All Deliberate Speed: Reflections on the First Half-Century of Brown v. Board of Education._ New York: Norton, 2004.

---

weeks, Thurmond led the effort to hold up voting on the civil rights bill until cloture (see chapter 7) was invoked and the filibuster ended. Once passed, the **Civil Rights Act of 1964:**

- Outlawed arbitrary discrimination in voter registration and expedited voting rights lawsuits.
- Barred discrimination in public accommodations engaged in interstate commerce.
- Authorized the Department of Justice to initiate lawsuits to desegregate public facilities and schools.
- Provided for the withholding of federal funds from discriminatory state and local programs.
- Prohibited discrimination in employment on grounds of race, color, religion, national origin, or sex.

Civil Rights Act of 1964
Legislation passed by Congress to outlaw segregation in public facilities and racial discrimination in employment, education, and voting; created the Equal Employment Opportunity Commission.

Analyzing Visuals

POLICE CONFRONT CIVIL RIGHTS DEMONSTRATORS IN BIRMINGHAM

Civil rights demonstrators in the 1960s sought national attention for their cause, and photos in the print media were a powerful tool in swaying public opinion. In the May 1963 photograph by Charles Moore reprinted here, dogs controlled by police officers in Birmingham, Alabama, attack civil rights demonstrators. This photograph first appeared in the May 17, 1963, issue of the very popular *Life* magazine as part of an eleven-page spread of Moore's photographs of the demonstration in Birmingham. The photo was reprinted often and even frequently mentioned on the floor of Congress during debates on the Civil Rights Act of 1964. After examining the photograph, answer the following critical thinking questions: What do you observe about the scene and the various people shown in the photograph? What do you notice about the man who is being attacked by the dogs? The other demonstrators? The police? What emotions does the picture evoke? Why do you think this image was an effective tool in the struggle for civil rights?

Photo courtesy: Charles Moore/Black Star/Stock Photo

- Created the Equal Employment Opportunity Commission (EEOC) to monitor and enforce the bans on employment discrimination.

As challenges were made to the Civil Rights Act of 1964, other changes continued to sweep the United States. African Americans in the North, who believed that their brothers and sisters in the South were making progress against discrimination, found themselves frustrated. Northern blacks were experiencing high unemployment, poverty, discrimination, and little political clout. Some, including Black Muslim leader Malcolm X, even argued that, to survive, African Americans must separate themselves from white culture in every way. These increased tensions resulted in riots in many major cities from 1964 to 1968, when many African Americans in the North took to the streets, burning and looting to vent their rage. The assassination of Reverend Martin Luther King Jr. in 1968 triggered a new epidemic of race riots.

THE IMPACT OF THE CIVIL RIGHTS ACT OF 1964

Many Southerners were adamant in their belief that the Civil Rights Act of 1964 was unconstitutional because it went beyond the scope of Congress's authority to legislate under the Constitution, and lawsuits were quickly brought to challenge the act. The Supreme Court upheld its constitutionality when it found that Congress was within the legitimate scope of its commerce power as outlined in Article I.[22]

Education   One of the key provisions of the Civil Rights Act of 1964 authorized the Department of Justice to bring actions against school districts that failed to comply with *Brown* v. *Board of Education*. By 1964, a full decade after *Brown*, fewer than 1 percent of African American children in the South attended integrated schools.

In *Swann* v. *Charlotte-Mecklenburg School District* (1971), the Supreme Court ruled that all vestiges of state-imposed segregation, called ***de jure*** discrimination, or discrimination by law, must be eliminated at once. The Court also ruled that lower federal courts had the authority to fashion a wide variety of remedies including busing, racial quotas, and the pairing of schools to end dual, segregated school systems.[23]

In *Swann*, the Court was careful to distinguish *de jure* from ***de facto*** discrimination, which is unintentional discrimination often attributable to housing patterns or private acts. The Court noted that its approval of busing was a remedy for intentional, government imposed or sanctioned discrimination only.

Over the years, forced, judicially imposed busing found less and less favor with the Supreme Court, even in situations where *de jure* discrimination had existed. In 1992, the Supreme Court ruled that an all-black school could continue to exist so long as the segregation was not a result of the school board's actions. In 1995, the Court ruled 5–4 that city school boards can use plans to attract white suburban students to mostly minority urban schools only if both city and suburban schools still show the effects of segregation, thus reversing a lower court desegregation order.[24] Today, the trend is toward dismantling court-ordered desegregation plans, although school districts remain under orders not to discriminate. Still, especially in the North, school segregation has increased steadily over the past fifteen years, especially when court-ordered busing ceased.[25] Many school districts now use magnet schools, for example, in lieu of busing, with permission from federal judges.

Employment Title VII of the Civil Rights Act of 1964 prohibits employers from discriminating against employees for a variety of reasons, including race, sex, age, and national origin. (In 1978, the act was amended to prohibit discrimination based on pregnancy.) In 1971, in one of the first major cases decided under the act, the Supreme Court ruled that employers could be found liable for discrimination if the effect of their employment practices was to exclude African Americans from certain positions.[26] African American employees were allowed to use statistical evidence to show that they had been excluded from all but one department of the Duke Power Company, because it required employees to have a high school education or pass a special test to be eligible for promotion.

The Supreme Court ruled that although the tests did not appear to discriminate against African Americans, their effects—that there were no African American employees in any other departments—were sufficient to shift to the employer the burden of proving that no discrimination occurred. Thus, the Duke Power Company would have to prove that the tests were a business necessity that had a "demonstrable relationship to successful performance" of a particular job.

The notion of "business necessity," as set out in the Civil Rights Act of 1964 and interpreted by the federal courts, was especially important for women. Women long

***de jure* discrimination**
Racial segregation that is a direct result of law or official policy.

***de facto* discrimination**
Racial discrimination that results from practice (such as housing patterns or other social or institutional, non-governmental factors) rather than the law.

■ In the late 1960s, court-ordered busing to achieve racial integration frequently required police escorts.

Photo courtesy: Bettmann/Corbis

had been kept out of many occupations on the strength of the belief that customers preferred to deal with male personnel. Conversely, males were barred from flight-attendant positions because the airlines believed that passengers preferred to be served by young, attractive women. Similarly, many large factories, manufacturing establishments, and police and fire departments refused to hire women by subjecting them to arbitrary height and weight requirements, which also disproportionately affected Hispanics. Like the tests declared illegal by the Court, these requirements often could not be shown to be related to job performance and were eventually ruled illegal by the federal courts.

The Women's Rights Movement

JUST AS IN THE ABOLITION MOVEMENT in the 1800s, women from all walks of life participated in the civil rights movement. Women were important members of new groups such as SNCC and the SCLC as well as more traditional groups such as the NAACP, yet they often found themselves treated as second-class citizens. At one point during a SNCC national meeting, its chair openly proclaimed: "The only position for women in the SNCC is prone."[27] Statements and attitudes like these led some women to found early women's liberation groups that were generally quite radical but small in membership. Others founded more traditional groups such as the National Organization for Women (NOW). Groups such as NOW sought improved rights for women through lobbying for specific laws or a constitutional amendment to guarantee women equal rights; others, following the model of the NAACP LDF, turned to the courts.

LITIGATION FOR EQUAL RIGHTS

As discussed earlier, initial efforts to convince the Supreme Court to declare women enfranchised under the equal protection clause of the Fourteenth Amendment were uniformly unsuccessful. The paternalistic attitudes of the Supreme Court, and perhaps society as well, continued well into the 1970s. As late as 1961, Florida required women who wished to serve on juries to travel to the county courthouse and register for that duty. In contrast, all men who were registered voters automatically were eligible to serve. When Gwendolyn Hoyt was convicted of bludgeoning her adulterous husband to death with a baseball bat, she appealed her conviction, claiming that the exclusion of women from her jury prejudiced her case. She believed that female jurors—her peers—would have been more sympathetic to her and the emotional turmoil that led to her attack on her husband and her claim of temporary insanity. She therefore argued that her trial by an all-male jury violated her rights as guaranteed by the Fourteenth Amendment.

In rejecting her contention, Justice John Harlan wrote in *Hoyt* v. *Florida* (1961): "Despite the enlightened emancipation of women from the restrictions and protections of bygone years, and their entry into many parts of community life formerly considered to be reserved to men, a woman is still regarded as the center of home and family life."[28]

These kinds of attitudes and decisions (*Hoyt* was unanimously reversed in 1975) were insufficient to forge a new movement for women's rights. Shortly after *Hoyt*, however, three events occurred to move women to action. In 1961, soon after his election, President John F. Kennedy created the President's Commission on the Status of Women, which was headed by former first lady Eleanor Roosevelt. The commission's report, *American Women*, released in 1963, documented pervasive discrimination against women in all walks of life. In addition, the civil rights movement and the publication of Betty Friedan's *The Feminine Mystique* (1963), which led some women to question their lives and status in society, added to their dawning recognition that something was wrong.[29] Soon after, the Civil Rights Act of 1964 prohibited discrimination based not only on race but also on sex. Ironically, that provision had been added to Title VII of the Civil Rights Act by southern Democrats. These senators saw a prohibition against sex discrimination in employment as a joke, and viewed its addition as a means to discredit the entire act and ensure its defeat. Thus, it was added at the last minute and female members of Congress seized the opportunity to garner support for the measure.

In 1966, after the **Equal Employment Opportunity Commission** failed to enforce the law as it applied to sex discrimination, female activists formed the National Organization for Women. NOW was modeled closely on the NAACP. Its founders sought to work within the system to prevent discrimination. Initially, most of this activity was geared toward two goals: achievement of equality either by passage of an equal rights amendment to the Constitution, or by judicial decision.

Not all women agreed with the notion of full equality for women. Members of the National Consumers' League, for example, feared that an equal rights amendment would invalidate protective legislation of the kind specifically ruled constitutional in *Muller* v. *Oregon* (1908). Nevertheless, from 1923 to 1972, a proposal for an equal rights amendment was made in every session of every Congress. Every president since Harry S Truman backed it, and by 1972 public opinion favored its ratification.

Finally, in 1972, in response to pressure from NOW, the National Women's Political Caucus, and a wide variety of other feminist groups, Congress voted in favor of the **Equal Rights Amendment** (ERA) by overwhelming majorities (84–8 in the Senate; 354–24 in the House). The amendment provided that:

> Equality of rights under the law shall not be denied or abridged by the United States or by any state on account of sex.
>
> The Congress shall have the power to enforce, by appropriate legislation, the provisions of this article.

Within a year, twenty-two states ratified the amendment, most by overwhelming margins. But, the tide soon turned. In *Roe* v. *Wade* (1973), the Supreme Court decided that women had a constitutionally protected right to privacy that included the right to terminate a pregnancy. Almost overnight, *Roe* gave the ERA's opponents political fuel. Although privacy rights and the ERA have nothing to do with each other, opponents effectively persuaded many people in states that had yet to ratify the amendment that the two were linked. They also claimed that the ERA and feminists were anti-family and that the ERA would force women out of their homes and into the workforce because husbands would no longer be responsible for their wives' support.

These arguments and the amendment's potential to make women eligible for the military draft brought the ratification effort to a near standstill. In 1974 and 1975, the amendment only squeaked through the Montana and North Dakota legislatures, and two states—Nebraska and Tennessee—voted to rescind their earlier ratifications. By 1978, one year before the deadline for ratification was to expire, thirty-five states had voted for the amendment—three short of the three-fourths necessary for ratification. Efforts in key states such as Illinois and Florida failed as opposition to the ERA intensified. Faced with the prospect of defeat, ERA supporters heavily lobbied Congress to extend the deadline for ratification. Congress extended the ratification period by three years, but to no avail. No additional states ratified the amendment and three more rescinded their votes.

What began as a simple correction to the Constitution turned into a highly controversial proposed change. Even though large numbers of the public favored

Equal Employment Opportunity Commission
Federal agency created to enforce the Civil Rights Act of 1964, which forbids discrimination on the basis of race, creed, national origin, religion, or sex in hiring, promotion, or firing.

Equal Rights Amendment
Proposed amendment that would bar discrimination against women by federal or state governments.

■ Members of Congress led by Representative Carolyn B. Maloney (D–NY) have reintroduced the Equal Rights Amendment in all recent sessions of Congress. Here, Representative Maloney (at podium), her co-sponsors, and women's groups hold a press conference in March of 2005 announcing the re-introduction of the ERA in the 109th Congress.

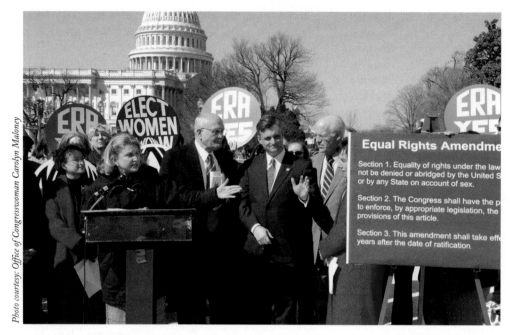

Photo courtesy: Office of Congresswoman Carolyn Maloney

the ERA, opponents needed to stall ratification in only thirteen states while supporters had to convince legislators in thirty-eight. The success that women's rights activists were having in the courts was hurting the effort. When women first sought the ERA in the late 1960s, the Supreme Court had yet to rule that women were protected by the Fourteenth Amendment's equal protection clause from any kind of discrimination, thus clearly showing the need for an amendment. But, as the Court widened its interpretation of the Constitution to protect women from some sorts of discrimination, in the eyes of many, the need for a new amendment became less urgent. The proposed amendment died without being ratified on June 30, 1982.

While several women's groups worked toward passage of the ERA (and continue to do so today), NOW and other groups, including the American Civil Liberties Union (ACLU), formed litigating arms to pressure the courts. But, women faced an immediate roadblock in the Supreme Court's interpretation of the equal protection clause of the Fourteenth Amendment.

THE EQUAL PROTECTION CLAUSE AND CONSTITUTIONAL STANDARDS OF REVIEW

The Fourteenth Amendment protects all U.S. citizens from state action that violates equal protection of the laws. Most laws, however, are subject to what is called the rational basis or minimum rationality test. This lowest level of scrutiny means that governments must allege a rational foundation for any distinctions they make. Early on, however, the Supreme Court decided that certain freedoms were entitled to a heightened standard of review. As early as 1937, the Supreme Court recognized that certain freedoms were so fundamental that a very heavy burden would be placed on any government that sought to restrict those rights. As discussed in chapter 5, when fundamental freedoms such as those guaranteed by the First Amendment or **suspect classifications** such as race are involved, the Court uses a heightened standard of review called **strict scrutiny** to determine the constitutional validity of the challenged practices, as detailed in Table 6.1.

suspect classification
Category or class, such as race, that triggers the highest standard of scrutiny from the Supreme Court.

strict scrutiny
A heightened standard of review used by the Supreme Court to determine the constitutional validity of a challenged practice.

TABLE 6.1　THE EQUAL PROTECTION CLAUSE AND STANDARDS OF REVIEW USED BY THE SUPREME COURT TO DETERMINE WHETHER IT HAS BEEN VIOLATED

Type of Classification (What kind of statutory classification is at issue?)	Standard of Review (What standard of review will be used?)	Test (What does the Court ask?)	Example (How does the Court apply the test?)
Fundamental freedoms (including religion, assembly, press, privacy) Suspect classifications (including race, alienage, and national origin)	Strict scrutiny or heightened standard	Is classification necessary to the accomplishment of a permissible state goal? Is it the least restrictive way to reach that goal?	*Brown* v. *Board of Education* (1954): Racial segregation not necessary to accomplish the state goal of educating its students.
Gender	Intermediate standard	Does the classification serve an important governmental objective, and is it substantially related to those ends?	*Craig* v. *Boren* (1976): Keeping drunk drivers off the roads may be an important governmental objective, but allowing eighteen-to twenty-one-year-old women to drink alcoholic beverages while prohibiting men of the same age from drinking is not substantially related to that goal.
Others (including age, wealth, mental retardation, and sexual orientation)	Minimum rationality standard	Is there any rational foundation for the discrimination?	*Romer* v. *Evans* (1996): Colorado state constitutional amendment denying equal rights to homosexuals is unconstitutional.

Beginning with *Korematsu* v. *U.S.* (1944), which involved a constitutional challenge to the internment of Japanese Americans as security risks during World War II, Justice Hugo Black noted that "all legal restrictions which curtail the civic rights of a single racial group are immediately suspect," and should be given "the most rigid scrutiny."[30] In *Brown* v. *Board of Education* (1954), the Supreme Court again used the strict scrutiny standard to evaluate the constitutionality of race-based distinctions. In legal terms, this means that if a statute or governmental practice makes a classification based on race, the statute is presumed to be unconstitutional unless the state can provide "compelling affirmative justifications": that is, unless the state can prove the law in question is necessary to accomplish a permissible goal and that it is the least restrictive means through which that goal can be accomplished. (In *Korematsu*, however, the Court concluded that the national risks posed by Japanese Americans were sufficient enough to justify their internment.)

During the 1960s and into the 1970s, the Court routinely struck down as unconstitutional practices and statutes that discriminated on the basis of race. "Whites-only" public parks and recreational facilities, tax-exempt status for private schools that discriminated, and statutes prohibiting racial intermarriage were declared unconstitutional. In contrast, the Court refused to consider whether the equal protection clause might apply to discrimination against women. Finally, in a case argued in 1971 by Ruth Bader Ginsburg (now an associate justice of the Supreme Court) as director of the Women's Rights Project of the ACLU, the Supreme Court ruled that an Idaho law granting a male parent automatic preference over a female parent as the administrator of their deceased child's estate violated the equal protection clause of the Fourteenth Amendment. *Reed* v. *Reed* (1971), the Idaho case, turned the tide in terms of constitutional litigation. Although the Court did not rule that sex was a suspect classification, it concluded that the equal protection clause of the Fourteenth Amendment prohibited unreasonable classifications based on sex.[31]

In 1976, the Court ruled that sex-discrimination complaints would be judged by a new, judicially created intermediate standard of review a step below strict

VIDEO ROUNDTABLE

Suspect Classifications and Gay Marriage

scrutiny.[32] In *Craig* v. *Boren* (1976), the Court carved out a new test to be used in examining claims of sex discrimination: "to withstand constitutional challenge, . . . classifications by gender must serve important governmental objectives and must be substantially related to achievement of those objectives." According to the Court, an intermediate standard of review was created within what previously was a two-tier distinction—strict scrutiny and rational basis.

Men, too, can use the Fourteenth Amendment to fight gender-based discrimination. Since 1976, the Court has applied the intermediate standard of constitutional review to most claims that it has heard involving gender. Thus, the following kinds of practices have been found to violate the Fourteenth Amendment:

- Single-sex public nursing schools.[33]
- Laws that consider males adults at twenty-one years but females at eighteen years.[34]
- Laws that allow women but not men to receive alimony.[35]
- State prosecutors' use of peremptory challenges to reject men or women to create more sympathetic juries.[36]
- Virginia's maintenance of an all-male military college, the Virginia Military Institute.[37]
- Different requirements for a child's acquisition of citizenship based on whether the citizen parent is a mother or a father.[38]

In contrast, the Court has upheld the following governmental practices and laws:

- Draft registration provisions for males only.[39]
- State statutory rape laws that apply only to female victims.[40]

The level of review used by the Court is crucial. Clearly, a statute excluding African Americans from draft registration would be unconstitutional. But, because gender is not subject to the same higher standard of review that is used in racial discrimination cases, the exclusion of women from the requirements of the Military Selective Service Act was ruled permissible because the government policy was considered to serve "important governmental objectives."[41]

This history has perhaps clarified why women's rights activists continue to argue that until the passage of an equal rights amendment, women will never enjoy the same rights as men. An amendment would automatically raise the level of scrutiny that the Court applies to gender-based claims, although there are clear indications that both Justices Ginsburg and Sandra Day O'Connor before her resignation favored requiring states to show "exceedingly persuasive justifications" for their actions.[42]

STATUTORY REMEDIES FOR SEX DISCRIMINATION

In part because of the limits of the intermediate standard of review and the fact that the equal protection clause applies only to governmental discrimination, women's rights activists began to bombard the courts with sex-discrimination cases. The Equal Pay Act, in 1963, requires employers to pay women and men equal pay for equal work. Women have won important victories under the act, but a large wage gap between men and women and men continues to exist, as underscored in Figure 6.1. Women in 2004 earned less than 77 percent of what men earned.

Other cases have been filed under Title VII of the Civil Rights Act, which prohibits discrimination by private (and, after 1972, public) employers. Key victories under Title VII include:

- Consideration of sexual harassment as sex discrimination.[43]
- Inclusion of law firms, which many argued were private partnerships, in the coverage of the act.[44]
- A broad definition of what can be considered sexual harassment, which includes same-sex harassment.[45]
- Allowance of voluntary affirmative action programs to redress historical discrimination against women.[46]

Other victories have come under **Title IX** of the Education Amendments of 1972, which bars educational institutions receiving federal funds from discriminating against female students. Holding school boards or districts responsible for sexual harassment of students by teachers, for example, was ruled actionable under Title IX by the U.S. Supreme Court.[47]

Title IX, which parallels Title VII, greatly expanded the opportunities for women in elementary, secondary, and postsecondary institutions. It bars educational institutions receiving federal funds from discriminating against female students. Since women's groups saw eradication of educational discrimination as key to improving other facets of women's lives, they lobbied for it heavily. Most of today's college students did not go through school being excluded from home economics or industrial arts or technology education classes because of their sex. Nor, probably, did many attend schools that had no team sports for females. Yet, this was commonly the case in the United States prior to passage of Title IX.[48] Nevertheless, sport facilities, access to premium playing times, and quality equipment remain unequal in many high schools and colleges. Moreover, the Bush administration has gone on record against many of Title IX's provisions, repeatedly allowing colleges and universities to reduce the number of women's sports teams, as well as scholarships and general spending on these teams.[49] (See chapter 9 for more on Title IX.)

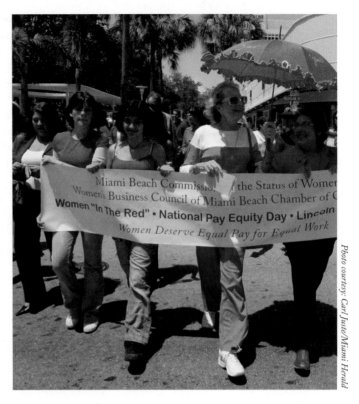

Photo courtesy: Carl Juste/Miami Herald

■ Women in Miami Beach, Florida, march to commemorate National Pay Equity Day. "Equal Pay Day" takes place each April—the month when women's wages theoretically catch-up to men's wages from the year before. Women are urged to wear red to symbolize the fact that women are "in the red" in comparison to men, who in 2004 earned $1.00 for every 77 cents earned by a woman.

Title IX
Provision of the Educational Amendments of 1972 that bars educational institutions receiving federal funds from discriminating against female students.

Other Groups Mobilize for Rights

AFRICAN AMERICANS AND WOMEN are not the only groups that have suffered unequal treatment under the law. Denial of civil rights has led many other disadvantaged groups to mobilize. Their efforts have many parallels to the efforts made by African Americans and women. Many of them also recognized that litigation and the use of test-case strategies would be key to further civil rights gains. Others have opted for more direct, traditional action.

HISPANIC AMERICANS

As noted in chapter 1, Hispanic Americans are the largest and fastest growing minority group in the United States. Until the 1920s, most Hispanics lived in the southwestern United States. These early groups, many of whom were from families who had owned land when parts of the Southwest were still in Mexico's control, formed the League of United Latin American Citizens (LULAC) in 1929. LULAC continues to be the largest Hispanic group in the United States, with local councils in every state and Puerto Rico.[50]

FIGURE 6.1 THE WAGE GAP, 1990–2004

The Equal Pay Act was passed in 1963; still women's wages continue to fall short of men's although the gap is closing among all women with the exception of Hispanic women. What factors might account for these glaring inequities?

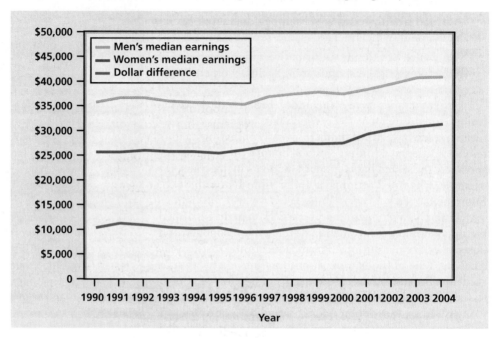

Sources: Census Bureau, Current Population Reports, Median Earning of Workers 15 Years Old and Over by Work Experience and Sex. Data from http://www.pay-equity.org/info-time.html.

As large numbers of immigrants from Mexico and Puerto Rico came to the United States, they quickly became a source of cheap labor, with Mexicans initially tending to settle in the Southwest, where they most frequently were employed as migratory farm workers, and Puerto Ricans mainly moving to New York City. Both groups tended to live in their own neighborhoods, where life was centered around the Roman Catholic Church and the customs of their homeland, and both groups largely lived in poverty.

Despite the income and language barriers faced by these immigrants, a push for greater Hispanic rights began in the mid-1960s, just as a wave of Cuban immigrants began to establish homes in Florida, dramatically altering the political and social climate of Miami and other neighboring towns and cities. This new movement, marked by the establishment of the National Council of La Raza in 1968, included many tactics drawn from the African American civil rights movement, including sit-ins, boycotts, marches, and other activities designed to attract publicity to their cause.[50] In one early example, in 1965, Cesar Chavez organized migrant workers into the United Farm Workers Union and led them in a strike against growers in California. This strike was eventually coupled with a national boycott of several farm products.

Hispanics also have relied heavily on litigation to secure legal change. Key groups are the Mexican American Legal Defense and Educational Fund (MALDEF) and the Puerto Rican Legal Defense and Educational Fund. MALDEF was founded in 1968 after members of LULAC met with NAACP LDF leaders and, with their assistance, secured a $2.2-million start-up grant from the Ford Foundation. MALDEF was originally created to bring test cases before the Supreme Court to force school districts to allocate more funds to schools with predominantly low-income minority populations, to implement bilingual education programs, to force employers to hire Hispanics, and to challenge election rules and apportionment plans that undercount or dilute Hispanic voting power.

MALDEF has been successful in its efforts to expand voting rights and opportunities to Hispanic Americans under the Voting Rights Act of 1965 (renewed in 2006 for ten years) and the U.S. Constitution's equal protection clause. In 1973, for example, it won a major victory when the Supreme Court ruled that multimember electoral districts (in which more than one person represents a single district) in Texas discriminated against African Americans and Hispanic Americans.[51] In multimember systems, legislatures generally add members to larger districts instead of drawing smaller districts in which a minority candidate could get a majority of the votes necessary to win.

MALDEF's success in educational equity cases came more slowly. In 1973, for example, the Supreme Court refused to find that a Texas law under which the state appropriated a set dollar amount to each school district per pupil, while allowing wealthier districts to enrich educational programs from other funds, violated the equal protection clause of the Fourteenth Amendment.[52] In 1989, however, MALDEF won a case in which a state district judge elected by the voters of only a single county declared the state's entire method of financing public schools to be unconstitutional under the state constitution.[53] And, in 2004, it entered into a settlement with the state of California in a case brought four years earlier to address, in MALDEF's words, "the shocking inequities facing public school children across the state."[54]

MALDEF continues to litigate in a wide range of areas of concern to Hispanics. High on its agenda today are affirmative action, the admission of Hispanic students to state colleges and universities, health care for undocumented immigrants, and challenging redistricting practices that make it more difficult to elect Hispanic legislators. It also litigates to challenge many state redistricting plans to ensure that Hispanics are adequately represented. In 2005, for example, MALDEF and other Hispanic rights groups played a major role in challenging a redistricting plan created by the Texas legislature, charging that the legislature's plan was designed intentionally to limit Hispanic representation in South Texas.[55,56]

MALDEF is also at the fore of legislative lobbying for expanded rights. Since 2002, it has worked to oppose restrictions concerning driver's license requirements for undocumented immigrants, to gain greater rights for Hispanic workers, and to ensure that redistricting plans do not silence Hispanic voters. It won a victory on this issue in California in 2004. MALDEF also focuses on the rights of Hispanic workers, an issue that attracted vast attention in 2006. In 2006, MALDEF, LULAC, and hundreds of ad hoc groups of Latinos, many encouraged from the pulpits of Roman Catholic Churches around the nation, rallied to show their concern about various governmental proposals being offered

■ More than a million immigrants and their supporters took to the streets across the nation to rally for immigrants' civil rights on May 1, 2006, in the wake of proposed immigration legislation in Congress that would crack down on illegal immigrants and toughen border security with Mexico. Here, an estimated 400,000 people march in Chicago, Illinois.

Photo courtesy John Zich/zimages.com

concerning immigrants. Not only had President George W. Bush proposed legislation that would affect immigration and strengthen the border with Mexico, but forty-three states were considering various laws to deal with illegal immigrants. Thus, on May 1, 2006, legal and illegal immigrants, supported by many American citizens, took the day off in what originally was to be an economic boycott called "Day Without an Immigrant."[57] Ultimately, more than 1 million marchers took to the streets in at least forty states to draw attention to the plight of immigrants, the vast majority of them of Hispanic origin.[58] Immigration issues continue to divide Americans. On October 26, 2006, President Bush signed a bill authorizing an additional 700 miles of fencing along the U.S. border with Mexico; 1.2 billion dollars was designated for enhanced border security. There is no mandate that these funds be used specifically to build the wall.

NATIVE AMERICANS

Native Americans are the first true Americans, and their status under U.S. law is unique. Under the U.S. Constitution, Indian tribes are considered distinct governments, a situation that has affected Native Americans' treatment by the Supreme Court in contrast to other groups of ethnic minorities. And, minority is a term that accurately describes American Indians. It is estimated that there were as many as 10 million Indians in the New World at the time Europeans arrived in the 1400s. The actual number of Indians is hotly contested, with estimates varying from a high of 150–200 million to a low of 20–50 million throughout North and South America.[59] By 1900, the number of Indians in the continental United States had plummeted to less than 2 million. Today, there are 2.8 million.

Many commentators would agree that for years Congress and the courts manipulated Indian law to promote the westward expansion of the United States. The Northwest Ordinance of 1787, passed by the Continental Congress, specified that "good faith should always be observed toward the Indians; their lands and property shall never be taken from them without their consent, and their property rights, and liberty, they shall never be invaded or disturbed, unless in just and lawful wars authorized by Congress." These strictures were not followed. Instead, over the years, "American Indian policy has been described as 'genocide-at-law' promoting both land acquisition and cultural extermination."[60] During the eighteenth and nineteenth centuries, the U.S. government isolated Indians on reservations as it confiscated their lands and denied them basic political rights. Indian reservations were administered by the federal government, and Native Americans often lived in squalid conditions.

With passage of the Dawes Act in 1887, however, the government switched policies to promote assimilation over separation. Each Indian family was given land within the reservation; the rest was sold to whites, thus reducing Indian lands from

■ Indian children were forcibly removed from their homes beginning in the late 1800's and sent to boarding schools where it was believed they could be forced to give up their cultural traditions and tribal languages. Here, young girls from the Yakima Reservation in Washington State are pictured in front of such a school in 1913.

Photo courtesy: Northwest Museum of Arts & Culture

Yakima School Girls   Ft Simcoe Wn

Politics Now

RECLAIMING RIGHTS: INDIANS USE DIVERSE WAYS TO REVERSE THE ECONOMIC ADVERSITY OF DISCRIMINATION

Under the U.S. Constitution, Indian tribes on tribal lands are treated as foreign nations and are therefore not subject to federal or state laws, which generally have prohibited gambling. Therefore, state governments and some Indian tribes have fashioned arrangements whereby in return for settlements of longtime land disputes, states have allowed Indians to build gambling casinos on their reservations. These agreements usually grant state governments a portion of the casinos' profits.

The profit-sharing relationship has been mutually beneficial. The state of Connecticut, for example, earned more than $400 million in 2003 from its revenue-sharing agreement. And, the Thunder Valley Casino has helped members of the United Auburn Indian Community in California to improve their living conditions drastically. Before the casino opened, not one of the 250 members of the tribe had ever attended college. Members of the tribe lived in slum conditions, nearly 80 percent did not know how to write a check, and many were unable to afford basic amenities such as running water and kitchen appliances.[a] Some were homeless. Now, the tribe has financial consultants to help its members. All get free medical, dental, and vision care. Special education and tutoring programs are helping the tribe's ninety-three children and their parents become more educated, as well as adjusted to the tremendous changes in their economic status.

These improvements in Indians' economic affairs have helped to increase their political clout. Tribes are donating to political campaigns of candidates who seem predisposed to policies favorable to tribes. The Agua Caliente Band of Cahuilla Indians, for example, donated $7.5 million to political campaigns in just one year alone. And, during the California governor recall of 2004, Indian tribes contributed over $11 million to candidates. These large expenditures, Indians claim, are legal, because as sovereign nations they are immune from federal and state campaign finance disclosure laws.[b] Meanwhile, Indian tribes seeking leverage for their casino operations were defrauded by lobbyist Jack Abramoff as part of an ongoing political scandal that pulled many Republican politicians into its wake (see chapter 16). It is likely that the political involvement of Indian tribes will continue to grow as their casinos—and the profits of those ventures—continue to proliferate.

[a]Louis Sahagun, "Tribes Fear Backlash to Prosperity," *Los Angeles Times* (May 3, 2004): B1.

[b]Sahagun, "Tribes Fear Backlash to Prosperity."

about 140 million acres to about 47 million. Moreover, to encourage Native Americans to assimilate, Indian children were sent to boarding schools off the reservation, and native languages and rituals were banned. Native Americans didn't become U.S. citizens nor were they given the right to vote until 1924.

At least in part because tribes were small and scattered (and the number of Indians declining), Native Americans formed no protest movement in reaction to these drastic policy changes. It was not until the 1960s that Indians began to mobilize. During this time, Indian activists, many trained by the American Indian Law Center at the University of New Mexico, began to file hundreds of test cases in the federal courts involving tribal fishing rights, tribal land claims, and the taxation of tribal profits. The Native American Rights Fund (NARF), founded in 1970, became the NAACP LDF of the Indian rights movement.[61]

Native Americans have won some very important victories concerning hunting, fishing, and land rights. Native American tribes all over America have sued to reclaim lands they say were stolen from them by the United States, often more than 200 years ago. Today, these land rights allow Native Americans to play host to a number of casinos across the country, a phenomenon that is explored in Politics Now: Reclaiming Rights.

One of the largest Indian land claims was filed in 1972 on behalf of the Passamaquoddy and the Penobscot tribes, which were seeking return of 12.5 million acres in Maine—about two-thirds of the entire state—and $25 billion in damages. The suit was filed by the Native American Rights Fund and the Indian Service Unit of a legal services office that was funded by the now defunct U.S. Office of Economic Opportunity. It took intervention from the White House before a settlement was reached in 1980, giving each tribe over $40 million.

Native Americans have not fared particularly well in areas such as religious free-dom, especially where tribal practices come into conflict with state law. As noted in chapter 5, the Supreme Court used the rational basis test to rule that a state could in-fringe on religious exercise (use of peyote as a sacrament in religious ceremonies) by a neutral law, and limited Indian access to religious sites during timber harvesting.[62] Congress attempted to restore some of those rights through passage of the Religious Freedom Restoration Act. Parts of the law, however, were later ruled unconstitutional by the Supreme Court.[63]

Like the civil rights and women's rights movements, the movement for Native American rights has had a radical as well as a more traditional branch. In 1973, for ex-ample, national attention was drawn to the plight of Indians when members of the radi-cal American Indian Movement took over Wounded Knee, South Dakota, the site of the massacre of 150 Indians by the U.S. Army in 1890. Just two years before the protest, the treatment of Indians had been highlighted in the best-selling *Bury My Heart at Wounded Knee*, which in many ways served to mobilize public opinion against the op-pression of Native Americans in the same way *Uncle Tom's Cabin* had against slavery.[64]

More recently, Indian tribes have found themselves locked in a controversy with the Department of the Interior over its handling of Indian trust funds, which are to be paid out to Indians for the use of their lands. In 1996, several Indian tribes filed suit to force the federal government to account for the billions of dollars it has col-lected over the years for its leasing of Indian lands, which it took from the Indians and has held in trust since the late nineteenth century, and to force reform of the system.[65] As the result of years of mismanagement, the trust, administered by the Department of the Interior, has no records of monies taken in or how they were disbursed. The on-going class action lawsuit includes 500,000 Indians, who claim that they are owed more than $10 billion. The trial judge found massive mismanagement of the funds, which generate up to $500 million a year, and at one time threatened to hold the sec-retary of the interior in contempt. Although this case has been largely deadlocked, in early 2004 a mediator was appointed to help bring greater resolution to the conflict.[66]

Indians also are attempting to have their voices heard by electing more Native Americans to office. In 2005, the Indigenous Democratic Network (INDN) was founded. Its campaign finance arm, INDN's List, is modeled after other political ac-tion committees (see chapter 16) and its purpose is to elect Indians and Democrats at the state and national level. INDN also trains candidates in "Campaign Camp" and encourages Indians to run for office.[67]

GAYS AND LESBIANS

Until very recently, gays and lesbians have had an even harder time than other groups in achieving anything approximating equal rights.[68] However, gays and lesbians have, on average, far higher household incomes and educational levels than these other groups, and they are beginning to convert these advantages into political clout at the ballot box and through changes in public opinion. As discussed in chapter 5, like African Americans and women, gays and lesbians initially did not fare well in the Supreme Court. In the late 1970s, the Lambda Legal Defense and Education Fund, the Lesbian Rights Project, and Gay and Lesbian Advocates and Defenders were founded by gay and lesbian activists dedicated to ending legal restrictions on the civil rights of homosexuals.[69] Although these groups have won important legal victories concerning HIV/AIDS discrimination, insurance policy survivor benefits, and even some employment issues, they generally were not as successful as other historically disadvantaged groups.[70]

In 1993, for example, President Bill Clinton tried to ban discrimination against ho-mosexuals in the armed services, who were subject to immediate discharge if their sex-ual orientation was discovered. Congressional and military leaders led the effort against Clinton's proposal. Eventually, Clinton and Senate leaders compromised on what was called the "Don't Ask, Don't Tell" policy. It stipulated that gays and lesbians would no longer be asked if they were homosexual, but they were barred from revealing their sexual orientation (under threat of discharge from the service).[71] Although this policy was initially viewed as a successful compromise, it has been called into question in recent years, as the wars in Iraq and Afghanistan have increased America's need for active-duty military personnel. Since the policy was adopted in 1994, at least 11,000 soldiers have been discharged for their sexual orientation.[72]

The public's views toward homosexuality have also changed, as signaled by the Court's 1996 decision in *Romer* v. *Evans*.[73] In this case, the Court ruled that an amendment to the Colorado constitution that denied homosexuals the right to seek protection from discrimination was unconstitutional under the equal protection clause of the Fourteenth Amendment.

In 2000, Vermont became the first state to recognize civil unions, marking another landmark in the struggle for equal rights for homosexuals. However, it was the Supreme Court's decision in *Lawrence* v. *Texas* (2003) that really put homosexual rights on the public agenda (see chapter 5). In this case, the Court reversed an earlier ruling by finding a Texas statute that banned sodomy to be unconstitutional. Writing for the majority, Justice Anthony Kennedy stated, "[homosexuals'] right to liberty under the due process clause gives them the full right to engage in their conduct without intervention of the government."[74]

PARTICIPATION

Civil Rights and Gay Adoption

Following the Court's ruling in *Lawrence*, many Americans were quick to call for additional rights for homosexuals. Many corporations also responded to this amplified call for equal rights. For example, Wal-Mart announced it would ban job discrimination based on sexual orientation. In addition, editorial pages across the country praised the Court's ruling, arguing that the national view toward homosexuality had changed.[75] In November 2003, the Massachusetts Supreme Court further agreed when it ruled that denying homosexuals the right to civil marriage was unconstitutional under the state's constitution. The U.S. Supreme Court later refused to hear an appeal of this case.

In 2004, many conservative groups and Republican politicians made same-sex marriage a key issue. Referendums or amendments prohibiting same-sex marriage were placed on eleven state ballots and all were passed overwhelmingly by voters.

President George W. Bush again renewed his call for a constitutional amendment to ban same-sex marriage in the summer of 2006. This effort failed in the U.S. Senate, where supporters did not gain a simple majority of votes in support of a ban, let alone the two-thirds vote necessary to send a proposed amendment to the states. Same-sex marriage bans were on several state ballots in the 2006 midterm elections, but the issue seemed to lack the emotional punch of the 2004 effort in the context of plummeting presidential approval and the ongoing war in Iraq.

■ George Lane, the appellant in the 2004 Supreme Court case of *Tennessee* v. *Lane*, which involved the scope of the Americans with Disabilities Act, was forced to crawl up two flights of stairs to attend a state court hearing on a misdemeanor charge. Had he not, Lane could have been jailed.

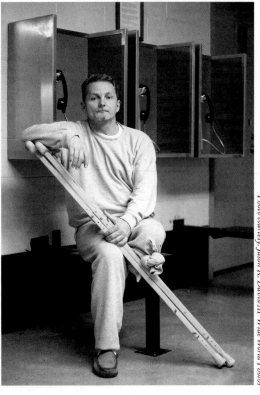

DISABLED AMERICANS

Disabled Americans also have lobbied hard for anti-discrimination legislation as well as equal protection under the Constitution. (See Global Perspective: Disability Rights for a discussion of European Union efforts in this area.) In the aftermath of World War II, many veterans returned to a nation unequipped to handle their disabilities. The Korean and Vietnam Wars made the problems of disabled veterans all the more clear. These veterans saw the successes of African Americans, women, and other minorities, and they too began to lobby for greater protection against discrimination.[76] In 1990, in coalition with other disabled people, veterans finally were able to convince Congress to pass the

Photo courtesy: Jason R. Davis/AP Wide World Photos

Global Perspective

DISABILITY RIGHTS

Securing the civil rights of people with disabilities is an increasingly important goal within the United States and throughout the world. While people with disabilities still face discrimination, conditions have improved markedly in the United States and many other nations. Redressing past discrimination is now a condition of European Union (EU) membership and is helping to raise awareness and improve conditions in nations who are seeking EU membership.

The American civil rights and women's rights movements gave rise to the U.S.-based disability rights movement in the 1960s and 1970s. The disabled in the United States first received limited protection in the Rehabilitation Act of 1973, yet it would be another seventeen years before America's disabled would receive comprehensive civil rights protection with the passage of the American with Disabilities Act (ADA). Similarly, during the European Union's 2003 "European Year of People with Disabilities," the European Parliament unveiled an action plan in which EU member states would update all disability laws to be in conformity with federation policy, as well as with current understandings of human rights.[a] The directive's goal is to "render discrimination of disabled people illegal in all areas of life." In addition to granting protections similar to those guaranteed to Americans by the ADA, the EU directive also regulates consumer product design to make products useful and accessible to people with disabilities and regulates how people with disabilities are portrayed in the media. The action plan's objective is to integrate Europe's disabled into social and economic life by "mainstreaming" disability issues into EU policy domains by 2010.

The EU's directive has provided disability rights groups with a useful bargaining chip in their efforts to further rights for the disabled in nations seeking EU membership. Mental Disability Rights International (MDRI), a nonprofit disability rights organization, released a report in September 2005 documenting the widespread use of electroshock therapy without anesthesia in Turkish psychiatric institutions. Turkey, which was just beginning membership talks with the European Union at the time of the report's release, has since ended the practice at its primary psychiatric facility and is also addressing other problems raised in the report.[b]

In May 2006, MDRI published a similar report, noting the significant institutional abuse against children with mental and physical disabilities in Romania, another nation seeking EU membership. Former Romanian dictator Nicolae Ceausescu's policies resulted in the neglect of nearly 200,000 children in state-run orphanages. Since Ceausescu's assassination and the end of Communist rule in 1989, the number of children in orphanages has dropped to approximately 30,000. According to MDRI's report, however, many of the children who remain in institutions have physical and mental disabilities and face decrepit and unsanitary conditions and extreme neglect. In some cases, children are being confined in adult facilities where they are permanently restrained.[c] MDRI and other human rights and disability rights groups are putting pressure on the EU to bar Romania's entrance until measures to address these problems are put in place and adequate resources are allocated to prevent further abuses. Though slow in coming, recognition of disability civil rights has gone global and increasingly nations will have to comply with an evolving understanding of human and civil rights.

QUESTIONS

1. What additional problems confront the disabled community around the globe? How can these problems be addressed?
2. Is the United States truly a leader in recognizing the civil rights of people with disabilities? Why or why not?

[a] European Disability Forum, news release, 2003.

[b] Craig S. Smith, "Romania's Orphans Face Widespread Abuse, Group Says," *New York Times* (May 10, 2006), http://select.nytimes.com.

[c] Mental Disability Rights International Report, May 2006.

You Are the Mayor

Americans with Disabilities Act (ADA). The statute defines a disabled person as someone with a physical or mental impairment that limits one or more "life activities," or who has a record of such impairment. It thus extends the protections of the Civil Rights Act of 1964 to all of those with physical or mental disabilities. It guarantees access to public facilities, employment, and communication services. It also requires employers to acquire or modify work equipment, adjust work schedules, and make existing facilities accessible. Thus, for example, buildings must be accessible to those in wheelchairs, and telecommunications devices must be provided for deaf employees.

In 1999, the U.S. Supreme Court issued a series of four decisions redefining and significantly limiting the scope of the ADA. The cumulative impact of these decisions was to limit dramatically the number of people who can claim coverage under the act. Moreover, these cases "could profoundly affect individuals with a range of impairments—from diabetes and hypertension to severe nearsightedness and hearing loss—who are able to function in society with the help of medicines or aids but whose impairments may still make employers consider them ineligible for certain jobs."[77] Thus, pilots who need glasses to correct their vision cannot claim discrimination when employers fail to hire them because of their correctable vision.[78] In the 2004 case of *Tennessee* v. *Lane*, however, the Court ruled 5–4 that disabled persons could sue states that failed to make reasonable accommodations to assure that courthouses are handicapped accessible.[79]

The largest national nonprofit organization lobbying for expanded civil rights for the disabled is the American Association of People with Disabilities (AAPD). Acting on behalf of the over 56 million Americans who suffer from some form of disability, it works in coalition with other disability organizations to assure that the ADA is implemented fully. AAPD was founded by activists who lobbied for the ADA and who recognized that "beyond national unity for ADA and our civil rights, people with disabilities did not have a venue or vehicle for working together for common goals."[80]

Civil rights groups such as the AAPD often find themselves working in concert with more radical disability rights groups such as Not Dead Yet. Not Dead Yet is one of many other disabilities groups actively opposing assisted suicide and euthanasia laws, believing that they infringe on the civil rights of people with disabilities, especially those who cannot advocate for themselves. Other groups, such as the National Right to Life Committee, also work to protect the rights of the disabled and elderly, believing that any attempts to withhold nourishment or treatment or to otherwise end life are basic violations of civil rights.

Continuing Controversies in Civil Rights

SINCE PASSAGE OF MAJOR CIVIL RIGHTS legislation in the 1960s and the Supreme Court's continued interest in upholding the civil rights of many groups, African Americans, women, Hispanics, Native Americans, gays and lesbians, and the disabled have come much closer to the attainment of equal rights. Yet, all of these groups still remain far from enjoying full equality under the Constitution in all areas of life. Enforcement of anti-discrimination laws varies, based on administration priorities as well as the resources of private individuals to fund challenges to perceived discriminatory practices. Private discrimination that cannot be legislated against is one major continuing source of discrimination. Gender equality, for example, has increased, but a 2006 poll shows that 38 percent of Americans do not think the country is ready for a woman president. More strikingly, in response to suggestions that an amendment be added to the Constitution to ban same-sex marriages, 55 percent of those polled in July 2005 favored this type of legislation.

Today, while most Americans agree that discrimination is wrong, most whites believe that affirmative action programs, which were designed in the late 1960s and early 1970s to remedy vestiges of discrimination against African Americans in particular, are no longer needed. White men are particularly opposed to principles of affirmative action, believing that qualified minorities should not receive preference over equally qualified white men.

AFFIRMATIVE ACTION

The civil rights debate centers on the question of equality of opportunity versus equality of results. Most civil rights and women's rights organizations argue that the lingering and pervasive burdens of racism and sexism can be overcome only by taking race or gender into account in fashioning remedies for discrimination. They argue that the Constitution is not and should not be blind to color or sex.

affirmative action
Policies designed to give special attention or compensatory treatment to members of a previously disadvantaged group.

VIDEO DEBATE

Affirmative Action

Other groups believe that if it was once wrong to use labels to discriminate against a group, it should be wrong to use those same labels to help a group. Laws should be neutral, or color-blind. According to this view, quotas and other forms of **affirmative action**, policies designed to give special attention or compensatory treatment to members of a previously disadvantaged group, should be illegal. (See Figure 6.2 for the results of one poll on the subject of affirmative action.)

The debate over affirmative action and equality of opportunity became particularly intense during the presidential administration of Ronald Reagan, in the wake of two court cases that were generally decided in favor of affirmative action shortly before Reagan's election. In 1978, the Supreme Court for the first time fully addressed the issue of affirmative action. Alan Bakke, a thirty-one-year-old paramedic, sought admission to several medical schools and was rejected because of his age. The next year, he applied to the University of California at Davis and was placed on its waiting list. The Davis Medical School maintained two separate admission committees—one for white students and another for minority students. Bakke was not admitted to the school, although his grades and standardized test scores were higher than those of all of the African American students admitted to the school. In *Regents of the University of California* v. *Bakke* (1978), a sharply di-

FIGURE 6.2 PUBLIC OPINION ON AFFIRMATIVE ACTION

These pie charts present the results of a Gallup Poll taken just before the Supreme Court handed down two major affirmative action cases in 2003. The poll queried non-Hispanic whites, blacks, and Hispanics about their opinions regarding affirmative action. Which group of those who were polled is most supportive of affirmative action? Which group is least supportive? What might explain these differences?

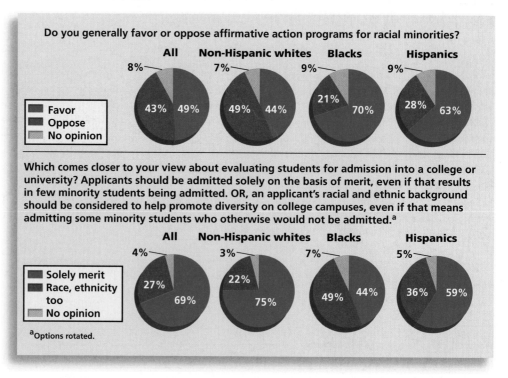

Note: N = 1,385 adults nationwide (MoE +/-3), including, with oversamples, 821 non-Hispanic whites (MoE +/-4), 241 blacks (MoE +/-7), and 266 Hispanics (MoE +/-7). Interviewing was June 12–15, 2003, for non-Hispanic whites, and June 12–18, 2003, for blacks and Hispanics.
Source: Gallup Poll, http://www.pollingreport.com.race.htm.

vided Court concluded that Bakke's rejection had been illegal because the use of strict quotas was inappropriate.[81] The medical school, however, was free to "take race into account."

Bakke was quickly followed by a 1979 case in which the Court ruled that a factory and a union could voluntarily adopt a quota system in selecting black workers over more senior white workers for a training program. These kinds of programs outraged blue-collar Americans who traditionally had voted for the Democratic Party. In 1980, they abandoned the party in droves to support Ronald Reagan, an ardent foe of affirmative action.

For a while, despite the addition of Reagan-appointed Justice Sandra Day O'Connor to the Court, the Court continued to uphold affirmative action plans, especially when there was clear-cut evidence of prior discrimination. In 1987, for example, the Court for the first time ruled that a public employer could use a voluntary plan to promote women even if there was no judicial finding or prior discrimination.[82]

In all these affirmative action cases, the Reagan administration strongly urged the Court to invalidate the plans in question, but to no avail. With changes on the Court, however, including the 1986 elevation to chief justice of William H. Rehnquist, a strong opponent of affirmative action, the continued efforts of the Reagan administration finally began to pay off as the Court heard a new series of cases signaling an end to the advances in civil rights law. In a three-month period in 1989, the Supreme Court handed down five civil rights decisions limiting affirmative action programs and making it harder to prove employment discrimination.

In February 1990, congressional and civil rights leaders unveiled legislation designed to overrule the Court's rulings, which, according to the bill's sponsor, "were an abrupt and unfortunate departure from its historic vigilance in protecting the rights of minorities."[83] The bill passed both houses of Congress but was vetoed by President Reagan's successor, George Bush, and Congress failed to override the veto. In late 1991, however, Congress and the White House reached a compromise on a weaker version of the civil rights bill, which was passed by overwhelming majorities in both houses of Congress. The Civil Rights Act of 1991 overruled the five Supreme Court rulings noted above, but it specifically prohibited the use of quotas.

The Supreme Court, however, has not stayed silent on the issue. In 1995, the Court ruled that Congress, like the states, must show that affirmative action programs meet the strict scrutiny test outlined in Table 6.1.[84] In 1996, the 5th U.S. Circuit Court of Appeals also ruled that the University of Texas Law School's affirmative action admissions program was unconstitutional, throwing the college and university admissions programs in Texas, Oklahoma, and Mississippi into turmoil. Later that year, the U.S. Supreme Court refused to hear the case, thereby allowing the Court of Appeals decision to stand.[85]

By 2002, the U.S. Supreme Court once again found the affirmative action issue ripe for review. In *Grutter* v. *Bollinger* (2003), the Court voted to uphold the constitutionality of the University of Michigan's law school admissions policy, which gave preference to minority applicants.[86] However, in a companion case, the Court struck down Michigan's undergraduate point system, which gave minority applicants twenty automatic points simply because they were minorities.[87]

Taken together, these cases set the stage for a new era in affirmative action in the United States. Although the use of strict quotas and automatic points is not constitutional, the Court clearly believes that there is a place for some preferential treatment, at least until greater racial and ethnic parity is achieved. However, as Justice Sandra Day O'Connor noted in *Grutter*, "a program must remain flexible enough to ensure that each applicant is evaluated as an individual and not in a way that makes an applicant's race or ethnicity the defining feature of his or her application."[88]

■ 1.6 million female Wal-Mart employees are presently engaged in a class action lawsuit, *Dukes v. Wal-Mart Stores, Inc.*, that accuses the retail giant of gender discrimination in wages and promotions. Wal-Mart's lawyers tried to argue against class action status by saying that a class composed of current and former women employees would be too large for one case to handle, but the judge emphatically disagreed. *Dukes v. Wal-Mart* is thus far the largest employment discrimination case in U.S. history.

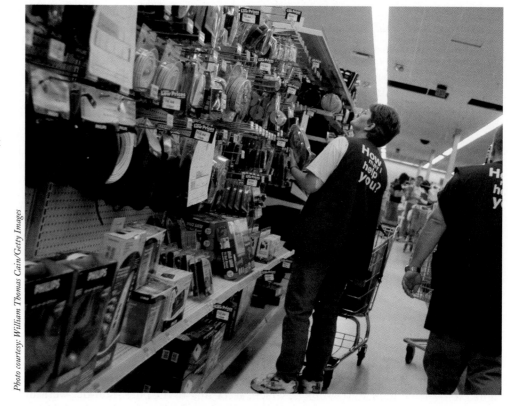

Photo courtesy: William Thomas Cain/Getty Images

Comparing Civil Rights

PAY EQUITY AND OTHER ISSUES OF WORKPLACE DISCRIMINATION

Race is not the only issue that continues to breed civil rights controversies. In fact, one of the largest barriers faced by minority groups living in the United States is the issue of pay equity, which, as already discussed, has an especially significant impact on female workers. The issue of pay equity for women has recently received national attention through a lawsuit filed against the nation's largest employer, Wal-Mart. Six California women filed a claim against the chain, charging that they were the victims of gender discrimination.[89] These women asserted that they were paid lower wages and offered fewer opportunities for advancement than their male colleagues. In June 2004, a federal judge broadened their class action suit to include 1.6 million women. The lawsuit is still pending before the ninth Circuit Court of Appeals. Meanwhile, similar suits have been filed by employees at other big box stores, including Costco.

Wal-Mart has also been involved in a lawsuit seeking pay equity for Hispanics. Nine illegal immigrants who worked as janitors at Wal-Marts in New Jersey are suing the company for discriminating against them by paying them lower wages and giving them fewer benefits based solely on their ethnic origin. Another group of Wal-Mart employees from twenty-one states is also suing the corporation, claiming that executives knowingly conspired to hire illegal immigrants and, in doing so, violated the workers' civil rights by refusing to pay Social Security and other wage compensation benefits.[90] These suits are representative of a growing trend in discrimination suits filed by immigrants who believe they have been persecuted or disadvantaged following changes in security and immigration law after the September 11 terrorist attacks. In fact, many of the Hispanics groups discussed in this chapter have been forced to devote significant portions of their time to immigration cases rather than workplace discrimination issues as the Civil Rights Division, as noted in our opening vignette,

On Campus

CAMPAIGNING FOR A LIVING WAGE

As a college student, you cross paths with a number of adults throughout the day. There are, of course, your parents and the professors, librarians, and administrators who control your academic life. But, there are also the food service workers who prepare food in the campus dining hall and the custodians who clean dorms, classrooms, and the student union. At many colleges and universities across the country, the latter are contract workers hired through companies such as Aramark and Sodexho. These cooks and cleaners—who are often minorities and immigrants—are not university employees, so they do not enjoy the tuition remission, health care, wage levels, or guaranteed employment given to professors and office staff. In fact, at many universities, these workers' salaries are insufficient to live on; one university janitor estimated that she made about $600 a month for her full-time job.[a]

Across the country, students have become aware of the low wages and little or no benefits given to service workers and have taken steps to lobby their universities' administrations for what is known as a living wage. The amount of this wage varies from municipality to municipality. It is calculated as the minimum hourly wage a person can earn and yet afford to pay for the basic essentials of life—food, water, shelter, utilities, and transportation—with a small amount left over for other expenditures. In Charlottesville, Virginia, home of the University of Virginia, for example, the living wage is $10.72 per hour.[b] In contrast, in Washington, DC, the living wage is $14 per hour.[c]

Currently, living wage campaigns are ongoing at about fifty universities across the country. Many of these efforts are coordinated by an interest group known as the Living Wage Action Coalition, which takes note of strategies used in successful living wage campaigns and has field organizers who travel around the country teaching students how to deploy these strategies at their own universities. The tactics used by living wage protestors are varied and can be extreme. At Georgetown University and the University of Miami, for example, students have gone on hunger strikes. At the University of Virginia and the University of Vermont, students have set up tent cities on their campus's main quads to bring attention to their cause. And, at Washington University in St. Louis, students set up residence inside the university's admissions building to get the attention of administrators, prospective students, and the public.

Success in adopting a living wage has been achieved at a number of campuses, including Georgetown, Stanford, Harvard, and Washington University. A number of municipalities, including San Francisco, California; Baltimore, Maryland; and Madison, Wisconsin, also have adopted living wage provisions. Even some states are now legislating minimum wages higher than federal levels. Observers, however, expect that this is only the beginning for living wage campaigns across the country as students demand moral action from universities that are being run more and more like corporations.[d]

---

[a] Jennifer Lenhart, "Georgetown Rally Presses Pay Issue: Students Join with Labor Officials," *Washington Post* (March 23, 2005): B3.

[b] Carol Morello and Susan Kinzie, "'Living Wage' Cry Still Piercing: U-VA Protestors Plan Next Round," *Washington Post* (April 19, 2006): B1.

[c] Lenhart, "Georgetown Rally Presses Pay Issue."

[d] Susan Kinzie, "GU Protestors Savor Win—and a Meal: Nine-Day Hunger Strike Resulted in Better Compensation for Contract Workers," *Washington Post* (March 25, 2005): B4.

---

continues to allocate lawyers' resources toward immigration issues. (For more on efforts to help minorities to overcome pay equity issues, see On Campus: Campaigning for a Living Wage.)

Summary

WHILE THE FRAMERS AND OTHER AMERICANS basked in the glory of the newly adopted Constitution and Bill of Rights, their protections did not extend to all Americans. In this chapter, we have shown how rights have been expanded to ever-increasing segments of the population. To that end, we have made the following points:

1. Slavery, Abolition, and Winning the Right to Vote, 1800–1890

When the Framers tried to compromise on the issue of slavery, they only postponed dealing with a volatile question that was later to rip the nation apart. Ultimately, the Civil War was fought to end slavery. Among its results were the triumph of the abolitionist position and adoption of the Thirteenth, Fourteenth, and Fifteenth Amendments. During this period, women also sought expanded rights, especially the right to vote, but to no avail.

2. The Push for Equality, 1890–1954

Although the Civil War Amendments were added to the Constitution, the Supreme Court limited their application. As Jim Crow laws were passed throughout the South, the NAACP was founded in the early

1900s to press for equal rights for African Americans. Women's groups also were active during this period, successfully lobbying for passage of the Nineteenth Amendment, which assured them the right to vote. Women's groups such as the National Consumers' League (NCL), for example, began to view litigation as a means to its ends, as it was forced to go to court to argue for the constitutionality of legislation protecting women workers.

3. The Civil Rights Movement

In 1954, the U.S. Supreme Court ruled in *Brown* v. *Board of Education* that state-segregated school systems were unconstitutional. This victory empowered African Americans as they sought an end to other forms of pervasive discrimination. Bus boycotts, sit-ins, freedom rides, pressure for voting rights, and massive nonviolent demonstrations became common tactics. This activity culminated in the passage of the Civil Rights Act of 1964, which gave African Americans another weapon in their legal arsenal.

4. The Women's Rights Movement

After passage of the Civil Rights Act, a new women's rights movement arose. Several women's rights groups were created, and while some sought a constitutional amendment, others attempted to litigate under the equal protection clause. Over the years, the Supreme Court developed different tests to determine the constitutionality of various forms of discrimination. In general, strict scrutiny, the most stringent standard, was applied to race-based claims. An intermediate standard of review was developed to assess the constitutionality of sex discrimination claims.

5. Other Groups Mobilize for Rights

Building on the successes of African Americans and women, other groups, including Hispanic Americans, Native Americans, gays and lesbians, and the disabled, organized to litigate for expanded civil rights as well as to lobby for anti-discrimination laws.

6. Continuing Controversies in Civil Rights

None of the groups discussed in this chapter has yet to reach full equality. One policy, affirmative action, which was designed to remedy education and employment discrimination, continues to be very controversial. And, gays, women, and immigrants continue to use the courts to seek remedies for costly employment discrimination.

KEY TERMS

affirmative action, p. 232
Black Codes, p. 201
Brown v. *Board of Education* (1954), p. 210
civil rights, p. 198

Civil Rights Act of 1964, p. 215
Civil Rights Cases (1883), p. 203
de facto discrimination, p. 217
de jure discrimination, p. 217
Equal Employment Opportunity Commission, p. 219
equal protection clause, p. 210
Equal Rights Amendment, p. 219
Fifteenth Amendment, p. 203
Fourteenth Amendment, p. 201
grandfather clause, p. 204
Jim Crow laws, p. 203
Nineteenth Amendment, p. 207
Plessy v. *Ferguson* (1896), p. 204
poll tax, p. 204
strict scrutiny, p. 220
suffrage movement, p. 207
suspect classification, p. 220
Thirteenth Amendment, p. 201
Title IX, p. 223

SELECTED READINGS

Delgado, Richard. *Justice at War: Civil Liberties and Civil Rights During Times of Crisis.* New York: New York University Press, 2005.

Eastland, Terry, *Ending Affirmative Action: The Case for Colorblind Justice.* New York: Basic Books, 1997.

Featherstone, Liza. *Selling Women Short: The Landmark Battle for Worker's Rights at Wal-Mart.* New York: Basic Books, 2005.

Freeman, Jo. *The Politics of Women's Liberation.* New York: Backinprint.com, 2000.

Garcia, John A. *Latino Politics in America: Community Culture and Interests.* Lanham, MD: Rowman and Littlefield, 2003.

Guinier, Lani, and Susan Sturm. *Who's Qualified?* Boston: Beacon Press, 2001.

Kluger, Richard. *Simple Justice,* reprint ed. New York: Vintage, 2004.

Mansbridge, Jane J. *Why We Lost the ERA.* Chicago: University of Chicago Press, 1986.

McClain, Paula D., and Joseph Stewart Jr. "Can We All Get Along?" *Racial and Ethnic Minorities in American Politics,* 4th ed. Boulder, CO: Westview, 2005.

McGlen, Nancy E., et al. *Women, Politics, and American Society,* 4th ed. New York: Longman, 2004.

Nobles, Melissa. *Shades of Citizenship: Race and the Census in Modern America.* Palo Alto, CA: Stanford University Press, 2000.

Reed, Adolph, Jr., ed. *Without Justice for All: The New Liberalism and Our Retreat from Racial Equity.* Boulder, CO: Westview, 1999.

Rodriguez, Clara E. *Changing Race: Latinos, the Census, and the History of Ethnicity in the United States.* New York: New York University Press, 2000.

Rosales, F. Arturo. *Chicano! The History of the Mexican American Civil Rights Movement.* Houston, TX: Arte Publico, 1996.

Williams, Juan. *Eyes on the Prize: America's Civil Rights Years, 1954–1965.* New York: Penguin, 1987.

Wilson, William Julius. *The Bridge over the Racial Divide: Rising Inequality and Coalition Politics,* 2nd ed. Berkeley: University of California Press, 2001.

WEB EXPLORATIONS

For more on civil rights generally, see
http://www.civilrightsproject.harvard.edu

For more on abolition, the American Anti-Slavery Society, and its leaders, see
http://www.loc.gov/exhibits/african/afam005.html

For more about the history of Jim Crow in the South, see
http://www.jimcrowhistory.org

To read the full text of *Brown* v. *Board of Education* (1954), see
http://caselaw.lp.findlaw.com/cgi-bin/getcase.pl?court=US&vol=347&invol=483

For more about the Montgomery bus boycott and Rev. Martin Luther King Jr., see
http://www.stanford.edu/group/King/about_king/encyclopedia/bus_boycott.html

For more about NOW and the EEOC, see
http://www.now.org and
http://www.eeoc.gov

For more about the Equal Rights Amendment, see
http://www.equalrightsamendment.org

For more about the ACLU Women's Rights Project, see
http://www.aclu.org/WomensRights/WomensRightsMain.cfm

To learn more about MALDEF, see
http://www.maldef.org

For more about the Native American Rights Fund, see
http://www.narf.org

For more about gay and lesbian rights groups, see
http://www.glaad.org

For more about disability advocacy groups, see
http://www.aapd-dc.org

CONGRESS

ON FEBRUARY 6, 2002, Representative Nancy Pelosi (D–CA) broke through a glass ceiling when she was sworn in as the Democratic House whip, becoming the first woman in history to win an elected position in the formal leadership of the U.S. House of Representatives.[1] The whip position has long been viewed as a stepping stone to becoming the Speaker of the House. House Speakers Tip O'Neill (D–MA) and Newt Gingrich (R–GA) were both former whips. As whip, it was Pelosi's responsibility to convince Democratic members of the House to vote together on the full range of bills before the 107th Congress.

First elected to Congress from California in 1986, Pelosi quickly made her mark as an advocate for human rights in China and as an effective fundraiser. Her fund-raising skills and years of experience in the House, in fact, helped her win the hotly contested race for the whip position. As part of the House leadership, she became the first woman to attend critical White House meetings, where, said Pelosi, "Susan B. Anthony and others are with me."[2]

Although the president's party traditionally loses seats in midterm elections, in 2002 House Republicans actually increased their majority. Critics charged that the Democrats lacked a consistent message. Therefore, soon after the election results were in, House Minority Leader Richard Gephardt (D–MO) resigned from his position, leaving Pelosi in line to succeed him. Representative Harold Ford (D–TN), one of the youngest members of the House, threw his hat into the ring to oppose Pelosi's campaign for the leader's position. Ford, a moderate, charged that Pelosi, who already was being referred to by conservatives as a "San Francisco liberal," was simply too liberal to lead the Democrats back to political viability in the 2004 elections. A majority of the members of the House Democratic Caucus, however, did not appear fazed by these charges; Pelosi was elected minority leader by an overwhelming majority of the caucus members.

In 2006, when Democrats regained control of Congress, Pelosi was catapulted into the role of Speaker. In shattering what she termed "the marble ceiling" as Speaker of the House, Pelosi became the first woman to hold that position and is second in line of succession to the presidency. Thus, more than 150 years after women first sought the right to vote, a female member of Congress now leads the House of Representatives.

CHAPTER OUTLINE

- ⭐ The Constitution and the Legislative Branch of Government

- ⭐ How Congress Is Organized

- ⭐ The Members of Congress

- ⭐ How Members Make Decisions

- ⭐ The Law-making Function of Congress

- ⭐ Congress and the President

- ⭐ Congress and the Judiciary

THE FRAMERS' ORIGINAL CONCEPTION of the representational function of Congress was much narrower than it is today. Instead of regarding members of Congress as representatives of the people, those in attendance at the Constitutional Convention were extremely concerned with creating a legislative body that would be able to make laws to govern the new nation. Over time, Congress has attempted to maintain the role of a law- and policy-making institution, but changes in the demands made on the national government have allowed the executive and judicial branches to gain powers at the expense of the legislative. Moreover, although the Congress as a branch of government has experienced a decline in its authority, the power and the importance of individual members have grown. Thus, the public doesn't think much about Congress itself, but somewhat ironically, citizens hold their own elected representatives in high esteem.

The dual roles that Congress plays contribute to this divide in public opinion. Members of Congress must combine and balance the roles of lawmaker and policy maker with being a representative of their district, their state, their party, and sometimes their race, ethnicity, or gender. Not surprisingly, this balancing act often results in role conflict.

In this chapter, we will analyze the powers of Congress and the competing roles members of Congress play as they represent the interests of their constituents, make laws, and oversee the actions of the other two branches of government. We will also see that as these functions have changed throughout U.S. history, so has Congress itself.

- First, we will examine what *the Constitution* has to say about Congress—*the legislative branch of government.*

- Second, we will describe *how Congress is organized.* We will compare the two chambers and how their differences affect the course of legislation.

- Third, we will look at *the members of Congress,* including how members get elected, and how they spend their days.

- Fourth, we will examine the various factors that influence *how members* of Congress *make decisions.*

- Fifth, we will outline *the law-making function of Congress.*

- Sixth, we will discuss the ever changing relationship between *Congress and the president.*

- Finally, we will review the relationship between *Congress and the judiciary.*

The Constitution and the Legislative Branch of Government

ARTICLE I OF THE CONSTITUTION describes the structure of the legislative branch of government we know today. As discussed in chapter 2, the Great Compromise at the Constitutional Convention resulted in the creation of an upper house, the Senate, and a lower house, the House of Representatives. Any two-house legislature, such as the one created by the Framers, is called a **bicameral legislature.** Each state is represented in the Senate by two senators, regardless of the state's population. The number of representatives each state sends to the House of Representatives, in contrast, is determined by that state's population.

The U.S. Constitution sets out the formal, or legal, requirements for membership in the House and Senate. As agreed to at the Constitutional Convention, House members are to be at least twenty-five years of age; senators, thirty. Members of the House are required to have resided in the United States for at least seven

bicameral legislature
A legislature divided into two houses; the U.S. Congress and the state legislatures are bicameral except Nebraska, which is unicameral.

years; those elected to the Senate, nine. Both representatives and senators must be legal residents of the states from which they are elected. Historically, many members of Congress have moved to their states specifically to run for office. U.S. Attorney General Robert Kennedy moved to New York to launch a successful campaign for the Senate, as did Hillary Rodham Clinton. Less successful was former Republican presidential hopeful Alan Keyes, who moved from Maryland to run unsuccessfully for the U.S. Senate in Illinois against Democrat Barack Obama.

Senators are elected for six-year terms, and originally they were elected by state legislatures because the Framers intended for senators to represent their states' interests in the Senate. State legislators lost this influence over the Senate with the ratification of the Seventeenth Amendment in 1913, which provides for the direct election of senators by voters. Then, as now, one-third of all senators are up for reelection every two years

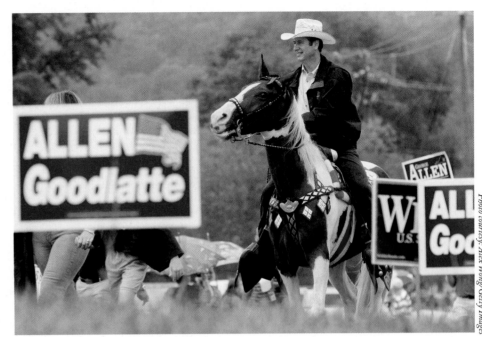

■ U.S. Sen. George Allen (R–VA), here seen riding a horse during a 2006 Labor Day parade, provided his Democratic challenger Jim Webb with an electoral opportunity when Allen referred to a Webb volunteer and native Virginian, S.R. Sidarth, as "Macaca"—a genus of monkeys. A video clip of the incident shows Allen saying, "Let's give a welcome to Macaca, here. Welcome to America and the real world of Virginia." Allen grew up in California and Illinois, but like many politicians prefers to present himself as a native of his chosen state, complete with a southern drawl. The "Macaca" video clip, which was posted on YouTube and viewed by tens of thousands, was credited, at least in part, with Allen's narrow defeat by Webb.

VIDEO DEBATE

Congressional Term Limits

Members of the House of Representatives are elected to two-year terms by a vote of the eligible electorate in each congressional district. The Framers expected that House members would be more responsible to the people both because they were elected directly by them and because they were up for reelection every two years.

The U.S. Constitution requires that a census, which entails the counting of all Americans, be conducted every ten years. Until the first census could be taken, the Constitution fixed the number of representatives in the House of Representatives at sixty-five. In 1790, then, one member represented about 30,000 people. As the population of the new nation grew and states were added to the union, the House became larger and larger. In 1910, it expanded to 435 members, and in 1929, its size was fixed at that number by statute. When Alaska and Hawaii became states in the 1950s, the number of seats was increased to 437. The number reverted back to 435 in 1963. In 2006, the average number of people in a district was 650,000.

Each state is allotted its share of these 435 representatives based on its population. After each U.S. Census, the number of seats allotted to each state is adjusted by a constitutionally mandated process called **apportionment**. After seats are apportioned, congressional districts must be redrawn by state legislatures to reflect population shifts to ensure that each member in Congress represents approximately the same number of residents. This process of redrawing congressional districts to reflect increases or decreases in the number of seats allotted to a state, as well as population shifts within a state, is called **redistricting**. The Supreme Court has ruled that states may redraw districts more frequently than after each U.S. Census. The legal controversies and effects of redistricting are discussed in chapter 13.

The Constitution specifically gives Congress its most important power: the authority to make laws. (See Table 7.1.) Both houses share this law-making power. For example,

apportionment
The process of allotting congressional seats to each state following the decennial census according to their proportion of the population.

redistricting
The redrawing of congressional districts to reflect increases or decreases in seats allotted to the states, as well as population shifts within a state.

TABLE 7.1 THE POWERS OF CONGRESS

The powers of Congress, found in Article I, section 8, of the Constitution, include the power to:

- Lay and collect taxes and duties
- Borrow money
- Regulate commerce with foreign nations and among the states
- Establish rules for naturalization (that is, the process of becoming a citizen) and bankruptcy
- Coin money, set its value, and fix the standard of weights and measures
- Punish counterfeiting
- Establish a post office and post roads
- Issue patents and copyrights
- Define and punish piracies, felonies on the high seas, and crimes against the law of nations
- Create courts inferior to (that is, below) the U.S. Supreme Court
- Declare war
- Raise and support an army and navy and make rules for their governance
- Provide for a militia (reserving to the states the right to appoint militia officers and to train militias under congressional rules)
- Exercise legislative powers over the seat of government (the District of Columbia) and over places purchased to be federal facilities (forts, arsenals, dockyards, and "other needful buildings")
- "Make all Laws which shall be necessary and proper for carrying into Execution the foregoing Powers, and all other Powers vested by this Constitution in the government of the United States" (Note: This "necessary and proper," or "elastic," clause has been interpreted expansively by the Supreme Court, as explained in chapter 2 and the Annotated Constitution.)

bill
A proposed law.

no **bill** (proposed law) can become law without the consent of both houses. Examples of other constitutionally shared powers include the power to declare war, raise an army and navy, coin money, regulate commerce, establish the federal courts and their jurisdiction, establish rules of immigration and naturalization, and "make all Laws which shall be necessary and proper for carrying into Execution the foregoing Powers." As interpreted by the U.S. Supreme Court, the necessary and proper clause, found at the end of Article I, section 8, when coupled with one or more of the specific powers enumerated in Article I, section 8, has allowed Congress to increase the scope of its authority, often at the expense of the states and into areas not necessarily envisioned by the Framers.

Congress alone is given formal law-making powers in the Constitution. But, it is important to remember that presidents issue proclamations and executive orders with the force of law (see chapter 8), bureaucrats issue quasi-legislative rules and are charged with enforcing laws, rules, and regulations (see chapter 9), and the Supreme Court and lower federal courts render opinions that generate principles that also have the force of law (see chapter 10).

Reflecting the different constituencies and size of each house of Congress (as well as the Framers' intentions), Article I gives special, exclusive powers to each house in addition to their shared role in law-making. For example, as noted in Table 7.2, the Constitution specifies that all revenue bills must originate in the House of Representatives. Over the years, however, this mandate has been blurred, and it is not unusual to see budget bills being considered simultaneously in both houses, especially since, ultimately, each must approve all bills, whether or not they involve revenues. The House also has the power to impeach: the authority to charge the president, vice president, or other "civil officers," including federal judges, with "Treason, Bribery, or other high Crimes and Misdemeanors." Only the Senate is authorized to conduct trials of **impeachment,** with a two-thirds yea vote being necessary before a federal official can be removed from office.

The House and Senate share in the impeachment process, but the Senate has the sole authority to approve major presidential appointments, including federal judges, ambassadors, and Cabinet- and sub-Cabinet-level positions. The Senate, too, must approve all presidential treaties by a two-thirds vote. Failure by the president to court the Senate can be costly. At the end of World War I, for example, President Woodrow Wilson worked hard to get other nations to accept the Treaty of Versailles, which contained the charter of the proposed League of Nations. He overestimated his

impeachment
The power delegated to the House of Representatives in the Constitution to charge the president, vice president, or other "civil officers," including federal judges, with "Treason, Bribery, or other high Crimes and Misdemeanors." This is the first step in the constitutional process of removing such government officials from office.

TABLE 7.2	KEY DIFFERENCES BETWEEN THE HOUSE OF REPRESENTATIVES AND THE SENATE

Constitutional Differences

House	Senate
435 voting members (apportioned by population)	100 voting members (two from each state)
Two-year terms	Six-year terms (one-third up for reelection every two years)
Initiates all revenue bills	Offers "advice and consent" on many major presidential appointments
Initiates impeachment procedures and passes articles of impeachment	Tries impeached officials Approves treaties

Differences in Operation

House	Senate
More centralized, more formal; stronger leadership	Less centralized, less formal; weaker leadership
Committee on Rules fairly powerful in controlling time and rules of debate (in conjunction with the Speaker of the House)	No rules committee; limits on debate come through unanimous consent or cloture of filibuster
More impersonal	More personal
Power distributed less evenly	Power distributed more evenly
Members are highly specialized	Members are generalists
Emphasizes tax and revenue policy	Emphasizes foreign policy

Changes in the Institution

House	Senate
Power centralized in the Speaker's inner circle of advisers	Senate workload increasing and institution becoming more formal; threat of filibusters more frequent than in the past
House procedures becoming more efficient	Becoming more difficult to pass legislation
Turnover is relatively high, although those seeking reelection almost always win	Turnover is moderate

support in the Senate, however. That body refused to ratify the treaty, dealing Wilson and his international stature a severe setback.

How Congress Is Organized

EVERY TWO YEARS, a new Congress is seated. After ascertaining the formal qualifications of new members, the Congress organizes itself as it prepares for the business of the coming session. Among the first items on its agenda are the election of new leaders and the adoption of rules for conducting its business. Each house has a hierarchical leadership structure that is closely tied to the key role of political parties in organizing Congress.

THE ROLE OF POLITICAL PARTIES IN ORGANIZING CONGRESS

As demonstrated in Figure 7.1, the organization of both houses of Congress is closely tied to political parties and their strength in each house. The basic division in Congress is between majority and minority parties. The **majority party** is the party in each house with the most members. The **minority party** is the party in each house with the second most members. Some of the implications of this split are discussed in Join the

majority party
The political party in each house of Congress with the most members.

minority party
The political party in each house of Congress with the second most members.

The Living Constitution

The Congress shall have power…to establish a uniform Rule of Naturalization.

—ARTICLE I, SECTION 8, CLAUSE 4

This article reiterates the sovereign power of the nation and places authority to draft laws concerning naturalization in the hands of Congress.

Congress's power over naturalization is exclusive—meaning that no state can bestow U.S. citizenship on anyone. Citizenship is a privilege and Congress may make laws limiting or expanding the criteria. The word *citizen* was not defined constitutionally until ratification in 1868 of the Fourteenth Amendment, which sets forth two kinds of citizenship: by birth and through naturalization. Throughout American history, Congress has imposed a variety of limits on naturalization, originally restricting it to "free, white persons." "Orientals" were excluded from eligibility in 1882. At one time those affiliated with the Communist Party and those who lacked "good moral character" (a phrase that was construed to bar homosexuals, drunkards, gamblers, and adulterers) were deemed unfit for citizenship. These restrictions no longer carry the force of law, but they do underscore the power of Congress in this matter.

Congress continues to retain the right to naturalize large classes of individuals, as it did in 2000 when it granted automatic citizenship rights to all minor children adopted abroad as long as both adoptive parents were American citizens. Naturalized citizens, however, do not necessarily enjoy the full rights of citizenship enjoyed by other Americans. Congress at any time, subject only to Supreme Court review, can limit the rights and liberties of naturalized citizens, especially in times of national crisis. In the wake of the September 11, 2001, terrorist attacks, when it was revealed that one-third of the forty-eight al–Qaeda-linked operatives who took part in some sort of terrorist activities against the United States were lawful permanent residents or naturalized citizens, Congress called for greater screening by the Immigration and Naturalization Service for potential terrorists.

TIMELINE

The Power of the Speaker of the House

Debate: Minority-Party Rights in Congress. (For the party breakdowns in the 110th Congress, see Figure 7.2.)

Parties play a key role in the committee system, an organizational feature of Congress that facilitates its law-making and oversight functions. The committees, controlled by the majority party in each house of Congress, often set the agendas, although in recent years chairs' power eroded substantially in the House of Representatives as the Speaker's power was enhanced.[3]

At the beginning of each new Congress—the 110th Congress, for example, will sit in two sessions, one in 2007 and one in 2008—the members of each party gather in their party caucus or conference. Historically, these caucuses have enjoyed varied powers, but today the party caucuses—now called caucus by House Democrats and conference by House and Senate Republicans and Senate Democrats—have several roles, including nominating or electing party officers, reviewing committee assignments,

FIGURE 7.1 ORGANIZATIONAL STRUCTURE OF THE HOUSE OF REPRESENTATIVES AND THE SENATE IN THE 110TH CONGRESS

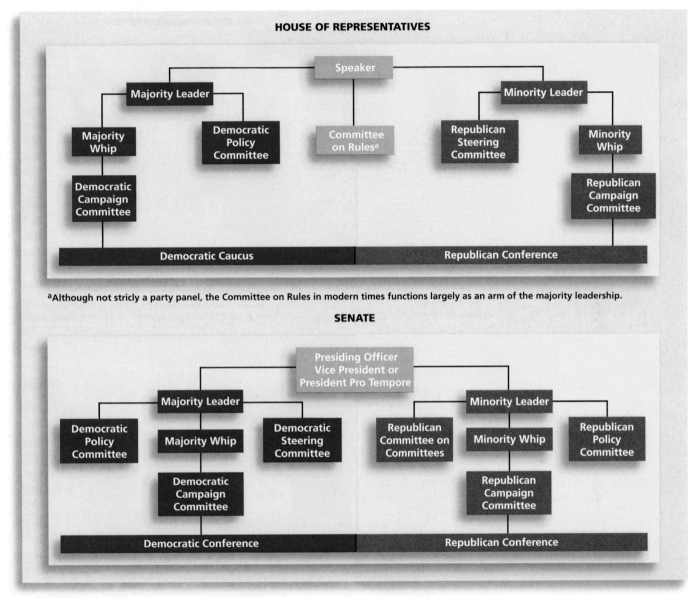

Source: Adapted from Roger H. Davidson and Walter J. Oleszek, *Congress and Its Members*, 10th ed. (Washington, DC: CQ Press, 2006.)

discussing party policy, imposing party discipline, setting party themes, and coordinating media, including talk radio. Conference and caucus chairs are recognized party leaders who work with other leaders in the House or Senate.[4]

Each caucus or conference has specialized committees that fulfill certain tasks. House Republicans, for example, have a Committee on Committees that makes committee assignments. The Democrats' Steering Committee performs this function. Each party also has a congressional campaign committee to assist members in their reelection bids.

THE HOUSE OF REPRESENTATIVES

Even in the first Congress in 1789, the House of Representatives was almost three times larger than the Senate. It is not surprising, then, that from the beginning the

FIGURE 7.2 THE 110TH CONGRESS

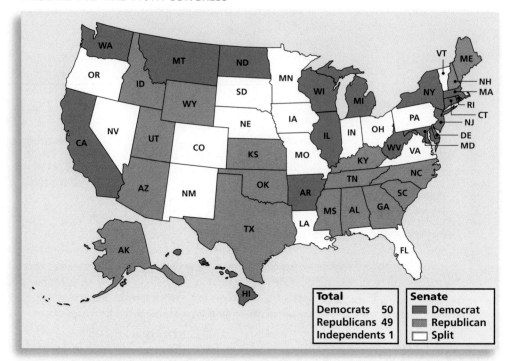

Total		Senate
Democrats	50	■ Democrat
Republicans	49	■ Republican
Independents	1	□ Split

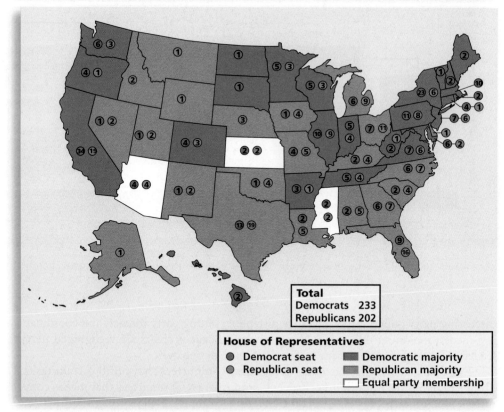

Total	
Democrats	233
Republicans	202

House of Representatives

● Democrat seat   ■ Democratic majority
● Republican seat   ■ Republican majority
□ Equal party membership

House has been organized more tightly, structured more elaborately, and governed by stricter rules. Traditionally, loyalty to the party leadership and voting along party lines has been more common in the House than in the Senate. House leaders also play a key role in moving the business of the House along. Historically, the Speaker of the House, the majority and minority leaders, and the Republican and Democratic House whips have made up the party leadership that runs Congress. This group now has been expanded to include deputy whips of both parties, as well as those who head the Democratic Caucus and the Republican Conference.

The Speaker of the House

The **Speaker of the House** is the only officer of the House of Representatives specifically mentioned in the Constitution. The office, the chamber's most powerful position, is modeled after a similar one in the British Parliament—the Speaker was the one who spoke to the king and conveyed the wishes of the House of Commons to the monarch.[5]

The entire House of Representatives elects the Speaker at the beginning of each new Congress. Traditionally, the Speaker is a member of the majority party, as are all committee chairs. Although typically not the member with the longest service, the Speaker generally has served in the House for a long time and in other House leadership positions as an apprenticeship. The current Speaker, Nancy Pelosi (D–CA), spent almost twenty years in the House and her predecessor Dennis Hastert (R–IL) was in office twelve years before being elected to the position.

The Speaker presides over the House of Representatives, oversees House business, and is the official spokesperson for the House, as well as being second in the line of presidential succession. Moreover, the Speaker is the House liaison with the president and generally has great political influence within the chamber. The Speaker is also expected to smooth the passage of party-backed legislation through the House.

The first powerful Speaker was Henry Clay (R–KY). Serving in Congress at a time when turnover was high, he was elected to the position in 1810, his first term in office. He was the Speaker of the House for a total of six terms—longer than anyone else in the nineteenth century.

By the late 1800s, the House ceased to have a revolving door and the length of members' average stays in the House increased. With this new professionalization of the House came professionalization in the position of Speaker. Between 1896 and 1910, a series of Speakers initiated changes that brought more power to the office as the Speaker largely took control of committee assignments and the appointing of committee chairs. Institutional and personal rule reached its height during the 1903–1910 tenure of Speaker Joe Cannon (R–IL).

Negative reaction to those strong Speakers eventually led to a revolt in 1910 and 1911 in the House and to a reduction of the formal powers of the Speaker. As a consequence, many Speakers between Cannon and Newt Gingrich, who became Speaker in 1995, often relied on more informal powers that came from their personal ability to persuade members of their party. Gingrich, the first Republican speaker in forty years, convinced fellow Republicans to return important formal powers to the position. These formal changes, along with his personal leadership skills, allowed Gingrich to exercise greater control over the House and its agenda than any other Speaker since the days of Cannon.

In time, Gingrich's highly visible role as a revolutionary transformed him into a negative symbol outside of Washington, D.C., and his public popularity plunged. Following a series of legislative and electoral failures, Gingrich resigned as Speaker in 1998 and later resigned from the House altogether.

Gingrich was replaced by a well-liked and respected former high school wrestling coach and social studies teacher, J. Dennis Hastert (R–IL). Hastert was a "pragmatic and cautious politician" known for his low-profile leadership style.[6] Hastert's passive style was, however, called into question just before the 2006 election when it appeared that he had failed to act when notified that Representative Mark Foley (R–FL)

Speaker of the House
The only officer of the House of Representatives specifically mentioned in the Constitution; elected at the beginning of each new Congress by the entire House; traditionally a member of the majority party.

Congressional Leadership

■ Throughout Congress's first several decades, partisan, sectional, and state tensions of the day often found their way onto the floors of the U.S. House and Senate. This eighteenth-century cartoon depicts a showdown that took place in the House on February 15, 1798, between Federalist Roger Griswold of Connecticut, and Republican Matthew Lyon of Vermont. Griswold, at right, is attempting to club Lyon with a hickory walking stick. Lyon, at left, is shown defending himself with a pair of fire tongs grabbed from the chamber's fireplace. The skirmish came as a surprise to few House members. Tensions between the two parties were high and attacks on the character of individual members often led to escalating violence.

Join the Debate

MINORITY-PARTY RIGHTS IN CONGRESS

OVERVIEW: After the closely contested 2000 and 2004 presidential elections, and with the outcome of the 2006 elections allowing Democrats to regain both chambers of Congress by winning what were in nearly every case close races, some political commentators have concluded that the United States may be viewed as divided into two significant minorities representing the Republican and Democratic Party faithful. It follows, so the logic goes, that in the event of close elections, the governing process should strive to reflect the policy and political desires of the relatively nonpartisan "moderate middle" of the American electorate. Representatives typically are chosen by partisans in primary elections, however, and elected officials are compelled to at least try to enact party preferences. Should law-making rules be written to prevent legislative majorities from enforcing their agendas over the objections of the minority party? What rights should the minority party in a two-party system have to pursue its interests? What does the Constitution say in regard to this dilemma?

Article I, section 5, of the Constitution gives both chambers of Congress the authority to "determine the Rules of its Proceedings" and declares that a "Majority of each [chamber] shall constitute a Quorum to do business" (a quorum is the number of members required to transact affairs). Other than giving a legislative minority the right to "compel the Attendance of absent Members" (to ensure there is a majority of representatives available to conduct legislative business), the Constitution does not speak to minority party rights. And, the language of the Constitution plainly gives each chamber the power to determine its own manners of procedure, and hence the power to make rules governing the legislative process. Thomas Jefferson and Supreme Court Justice Joseph Story, two commentators who had differing understandings of constitutional interpretation, were both in agreement that majority rule for law-making is a "natural right" and that giving legislative minorities the ability to frustrate law-making by a "natural majority" was tantamount to inviting rule by faction.

Discussions on this point in the Constitutional Convention show the Framers were concerned with legislative minorities having the ability to govern. They believed the majority principle was adequate to ensure legislation that reflected the will of the people, because in a country as large and diverse as the United States, compromise and conciliation between members of Congress would be unavoidable, given the diverse social, economic, and regional interests they would represent. This, they believed, would help foster decent law and policy. Nevertheless, the Framers did not foresee the rise of ideological political parties and their resulting political maneuvering. In fact, James Madison, in *Federalist No. 10,* argued that the Constitution would tend "to break and control the violence of faction." Many believe that minority safeguards like the Senate's filibuster rule may be necessary to ensure that congressional governance reflects the policy desires of the broad majority of American voters.

ARGUMENTS AGAINST MINORITY-PARTY RIGHTS IN CONGRESS

- **The Constitution is explicit where it requires supermajorities for political action.** The Constitution plainly states when a supermajority is necessary for an act of government, and there are seven instances in the Constitution where this is necessary. For example, Article I requires that a two-thirds vote of each chamber is necessary to override a presidential veto, and Article II requires that a two-thirds vote of the Senate is necessary to ratify treaties. If the Framers wanted more than a simple majority vote to make law and policy, it would be embodied in the Constitution's text.

party caucus or conference
A formal gathering of all party members.

majority leader
The elected leader of the party controlling the most seats in the House of Representatives or the Senate; is second in authority to the Speaker of the House and in the Senate is regarded as its most powerful member.

had made improper advances toward young male House pages. In 2007, Democrat Nancy Pelosi became the first female Speaker when Democrats won control of the House.

Other House Leaders After the Speaker, the next most powerful people in the House are the majority and minority leaders, who are elected in their individual **party caucuses** or **conferences.** The **majority leader** is the second most important person in the House; his or her counterpart on the other side of the aisle (the House is organized so that if you are facing the front of the chamber, Democrats sit on the left side and Republicans on the right side of the center aisle) is the

- **Voters have the ability to unseat members of Congress.** If voters don't care for the legislative and political agenda of the majority party in Congress, they are competent enough to vote the party out of power. Voter disaffection with forty years of Democratic Party dominance of Congress, for example, led to the party being voted out of majority status in the 1994 midterm elections. It is politically unwise to consider the electorate fools.
- **Giving a legislative minority authority to stop legislation frustrates the will of the electorate.** Even in a closely divided electorate, the majority principle remains. Echoing the sentiment expressed in the Constitutional Convention, Thomas Jefferson argued that majority rule must necessarily be the rule for democratic government because it is a self-evident part of natural justice—how else does one determine and act on the desires of the electorate? The Framers believed that giving legislative minorities rights was essentially giving democratic government over to the rule of small elites.

ARGUMENTS FOR MINORITY-PARTY RIGHTS IN CONGRESS

- **Legislative majorities can be unjust.** Many consider actions by legislative majorities to be harmful to the rights or lives of citizens. For example, some believe the Defense of Marriage Act, which gives the states the authority to deny the legitimacy of same-sex marriages made in other states, is an infringement on the rights of individual citizens to marry. Allowing a minority party the right to impede legislation could provide a means for preventing unjust or unfair legislation.
- **Giving the minority party legislative rights helps the deliberative process.** Better law would be the result of allowing a minority party the right to slow down the legislative process. Under Republican rule, Democrats frequently are not given the final text of bills until it is nearly time to vote on them. Giving the minority party assured rights would make certain there will be compromise and negotiation in the legislative process, and as a result, law and policy would be further filtered through deliberation and conciliation.
- **Legislation should reflect the preferences of the electorate as a whole.** Representative democracy means representation for all, not just for a political majority. Giving the minority party the right to block legislation will ensure legislation and policy are crafted in such a way as to reflect the diverse and broad policy preferences of the American electorate at large. Otherwise, legislation will reflect the ideological desires of only a portion of the American people.

QUESTIONS

1. Should minority parties have the right to slow down or derail the passage of legislation sponsored by the majority party? Is this a violation of the Framers' majority principle? Why or why not?
2. Given the fact that minority party representatives are nevertheless duly elected by a majority of their constituents, what minority-party protections, if any, seem appropriate?

SELECTED READINGS

Cox, Gary W., and Mathew D. McCubbins. *Setting the Agenda: Responsible Party Government in the U.S. House of Representatives.* New York, NY: Cambridge University Press, 2005.

Eilperin, Juliet. *Fight Club Politics: How Partisanship Is Poisoning the U.S. House of Representatives.* Lanham, MD: Rowman and Littlefield, 2006.

minority leader. The majority leader helps the Speaker schedule proposed legislation for debate on the House floor. In the past, both leaders worked closely with the Speaker. In recent Congresses, however, Republicans rarely have consulted Democratic Party leadership.[7]

The Republican and Democratic **whips,** who are elected by party members in caucuses, assist the Speaker and majority and minority leaders in their leadership efforts. The position of whip originated in the British House of Commons, where it was named after the "whipper in," the rider who keeps the hounds together in a fox hunt. Party whips—who were first designated in the U.S. House of Representatives in 1899 and in the Senate in 1913—do, as their name suggests, try to whip fellow

minority leader
The elected leader of the party with the second highest number of elected representatives in the House of Representatives or the Senate.

whip
Key representative who keeps close contact with all members and takes nose counts on key votes, prepares summaries of bills, and in general acts as communications link within the party.

Photo courtesy: Doug Mills/The New York Times

■ Head of the Democratic Senatorial Campaign Committee, Senator Charles Schumer (D–NY) and then Senate Minority Leader Harry Reid (D–NV) strategize after the Democratic Party picked up six seats from Republicans and recaptured the Senate majority in the 2006 election. Reid was chosen as Senate Majority Leader shortly after the election.

Congressional Partisanship

Democrats or Republicans into line on partisan issues. They try to maintain close contact with all members on important votes, prepare summaries of content and implications of bills, get "nose counts" during debates and votes, and in general get members to toe the party line. Whips and their deputy whips also serve as communications links, distributing word of the party line from leaders to rank-and-file members and alerting leaders to concerns in the ranks. Whips can be extraordinarily effective. In 1998, for example, President Bill Clinton was stunned to learn that moderate Republicans whom he had counted on to vote against his impeachment were "dropping like flies." The reason? Then House Republican Whip Tom DeLay (R–TX) had threatened Republicans that they would be denied coveted committee assignments and would even face Republican challengers in the next primary season unless they voted the party line.

THE SENATE

president pro tempore
The official chair of the Senate; usually the most senior member of the majority party.

The Constitution specifies that the presiding officer of the Senate is the vice president of the United States. Because he is not a member of the Senate, he votes only in the case of a tie. The official chair of the Senate is the **president pro tempore,** or pro tem, who is selected by the majority party and presides over the Senate in the absence of the vice president. The position of pro tem today is primarily an honorific office that generally goes to the most senior senator of the majority party. Once elected, the pro tem stays in that office until there is a change in the majority party in the Senate. Since presiding over the Senate can be a rather perfunctory duty, neither the vice president nor the president pro tempore actually perform the task very often. Instead, the duty of presiding over the Senate rotates among junior members of the chamber, allowing more senior members to attend more important meetings.

The true leader of the Senate is the majority leader, elected to the position by the majority party. Because the Senate is a smaller and more collegial body, operating without many of the more formal House rules concerning debate, the majority leader is not nearly as powerful as the Speaker of the House. The minority leader and the Republican and Democratic whips round out the leadership positions in the Senate and perform functions similar to those of their House counterparts. But, leading and whipping in the Senate can be quite a challenge. Senate rules always have given tremendous power to individual senators; in most cases senators can offer any kind of amendments to legislation on the floor, and an individual senator can bring all work on the floor to a halt indefinitely through a filibuster unless three-fifths of the senators vote to cut him or her off.[8]

Because of the Senate's smaller size, organization and formal rules never have played the same role that they do in the House. Through the 1960s, it was a gentlemen's club whose folkways—unwritten rules of behavior—governed its operation. One such folkway, for example, stipulated that political disagreements not become personal criticisms. A senator who disliked another referred to that senator as "the able, learned, and distinguished senator." A member who really couldn't stand another called that senator "my very able, learned, and distinguished colleague."

In the 1960s and 1970s, senators became more and more active on and off the Senate floor in a variety of issues, and extended debates often occurred on the floor without the rigid rules of courtesy that had once been the hallmark of the body. These changes weren't accompanied by giving additional powers to the Senate majority leader, who now often has difficulty controlling "the more active, assertive, and consequently less predictable membership" of the Senate.[9]

THE COMMITTEE SYSTEM

The saying "Congress in session is Congress on exhibition, whilst Congress in its committee rooms is Congress at work" may not be as true today as it was when Woodrow Wilson wrote it in 1885.[10] Still, "the work that takes place in the committee and subcommittee rooms of Capitol Hill is critical to the productivity and effectiveness of Congress."[11] Standing committees are the first and last places to which most bills go. Usually committee members play key roles in floor debate in the full House or Senate about the merits of bills that have been introduced. When different versions of a bill are passed in the House and Senate, a conference committee with members of both houses meets to iron out the differences. The organization and specialization of committees are especially important in the House of Representatives because of its size. The establishment of subcommittees allows for even greater specialization.

Congress created an institutionalized committee system in 1816, and more and more committees were added over time. The large number of committees resulted in duplication of duties and jurisdictional battles. When Republicans took control of the House in 1995, they cut several committees and subcommittees and reorganized (and renamed) several committees to highlight issues of importance to them.[12] Since 1995, many congressional scholars have reported that House committees have been weakened by several changes in the committee system, including how committee chairs are appointed, the devaluation of seniority, the shift of power from chairs to party leaders, a reduction in resources to subcommittee chairs, and the imposition of term limits on committee chairs.[13] It is expected that House Democrats will return to aspects of the pre-1995 committee structure in the 110th Congress.

Types of Committees There are four types of congressional committees: (1) standing; (2) joint; (3) conference; and, (4) select, or special.[14]

1. **Standing committees,** so called because they continue from one Congress to the next, are the committees to which bills are referred for consideration.

2. **Joint committees** are set up to expedite business between the houses and to help focus public attention on major matters, such as the economy, taxation, or scandals. They include members from both houses of Congress who conduct investigations or special studies.

3. **Conference committees** are special joint committees that reconcile differences in bills passed by the House and Senate. A conference committee is made up of those members from the House and Senate committees that originally considered the bill.

4. **Select (or special) committees** are temporary committees appointed for specific purposes. Generally such committees are established to conduct special investigations or studies and to report back to the chamber that established them.

standing committee
Committee to which proposed bills are referred.

joint committee
Includes members from both houses of Congress; conducts investigations or special studies.

conference committee
Joint committee created to iron out differences between Senate and House versions of a specific piece of legislation.

select (or special) committee
Temporary committee appointed for specific purpose, such as conducting a special investigation or study.

In the 109th Congress, the House had nineteen standing committees, as shown in Table 7.3, each with an average of thirty-one members. Together, these standing committees had a total of eighty-six subcommittees that collectively act as the eyes, ears, and hands of the House. They consider issues roughly parallel to those of the departments represented in the president's Cabinet. For example, there are committees on agriculture, education, the judiciary, veterans affairs, transportation, and commerce.

Although most committees in one house parallel those in the other, the House Committee on Rules, for which there is no counterpart in the Senate, plays a key role in the House's law-making process. Indicative of the importance of the Committee on Rules, majority party members are appointed directly by the Speaker. This committee reviews most bills after they come from a committee and before they go to the full chamber for consideration. Performing a traffic cop function, the Committee on Rules gives each bill what is called a rule, which contains the date the bill will come up for debate and the time that will be allotted for discussion, and often specifies what kinds of amendments can be offered. Bills considered under a closed rule cannot be amended.

Standing committees have considerable power. They can kill bills, amend them radically, or hurry them through the process. In the words of former President Woodrow Wilson, once a bill is referred to a committee, it "crosses a parliamentary bridge of sighs to dim dungeons of silence from whence it never will return."[15] Committees report out to the full House or Senate only a small fraction of the bills assigned to them. Bills can be forced out of a House committee by a **discharge petition** signed by a majority (218) of the House membership.

discharge petition
Petition that gives a majority of the House of Representatives the authority to bring an issue to the floor in the face of committee inaction.

TABLE 7.3	**COMMITTEES OF THE 109TH CONGRESS (WITH SUBCOMMITTEE EXAMPLES IN ITALICS)**

Standing Committees

House	Senate
Agriculture	Agriculture, Nutrition, and Forestry
Appropriations	Appropriations
Armed Services	Armed Services
Budget	Banking, Housing, and Urban Affairs
Education and the Workforce	Budget
Energy and Commerce	Commerce, Science, and Transportation
Financial Services	Energy and Natural Resources
Government Reform	Environment and Public Works
Homeland Security	Finance
House Administration	Foreign Relations
International Relations	Health, Education, Labor, and Pensions
Judiciary	Homeland Security and Governmental Affairs
Courts, the Internet, and Intellectual Property	Judiciary
Immigration, Border Security, and Claims	*Administrative Oversight and the Courts*
Commercial and Administrative Law	*Antitrust, Competition Policy, and Consumer Rights*
Crime, Terrorism, and Homeland Security	*The Constitution, Civil Rights, and Property Rights*
Constitution	*Corrections and Rehabilitation*
Resources	*Crime and Drugs*
Rules	*Immigration, Border Security, and Citizenship*
Science	*Intellectual Property*
Small Business	*Terrorism, Technology, and Homeland Security*
Standards of Official Conduct	Rules and Administration
Transportation and Infrastructure	Small Business and Entrepreneurship
Veterans Affairs	Veterans Affairs
Ways and Means	

Select, Special, and Other Committees

House	Senate	Joint Committees
Permanent Select Intelligence	Indian Affairs	Economics
Select Homeland Security	Select Ethics	Printing
Select Bipartisan Committee to Investigate the Preparation for and Response to Hurricane Katrina	Select Intelligence	Taxation
	Special Aging	Library

In the 109th Congress, the Senate had sixteen standing committees ranging in size from fifteen to twenty-nine members. It also had sixty-eight subcommittees, which allowed all majority party senators to chair at least one.

In contrast to the House, whose members hold few committee assignments (an average of 1.8 standing and three subcommittees), senators each serve on an average of three to four committees and seven subcommittees. Whereas the committee system allows House members to become policy or issue specialists, Senate members often are generalists. In the 109th Congress, Senator Kay Bailey Hutchison (R–TX), for example, served on several committees, including Appropriations; Commerce, Science, and Transportation; Veterans Affairs; and Rules. She served on even more subcommittees, chairing two of them, and was the vice chair of the Republican Conference.

Senate committees enjoy the same power over framing legislation that House committees do, but the Senate, being an institution more open to individual input than the House, gives less deference to the work done in committees. In the Senate, legislation is more likely to be rewritten on the floor, where all senators can participate and add amendments at any time.

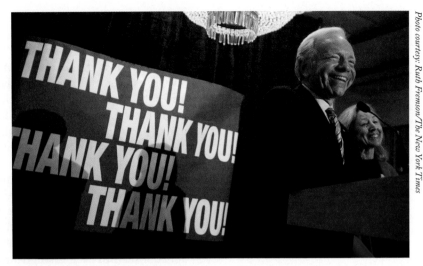

Photo courtesy: Ruth Fremson/The New York Times

■ Senator Joseph I. Lieberman of Connecticut, seen here celebrating his reelection with his wife, Hadassah, lost the Democratic primary in 2006 and ran and won the general election as an independent. After the 2006 election, the slim margin held by Senate Democrats hinged on Lieberman, who describes himself as an Independent Democrat, and Bernie Sanders, a Vermont independent. The fragility of this margin as well as the importance of every member was thrown into even sharper relief in December of 2006, when Senator Tim Johnson (D–SD) had emergency brain surgery.

Committee Membership Many newly elected members of Congress come into the body with their sights on certain committee assignments. Others are more flexible. Many legislators seeking committee assignments inform their party's selection committee of their preferences. They often request assignments based on their own interests or expertise or on a particular committee's ability to help their prospects for reelection. One political scientist has noted that committee assignments are to members what stocks are to investors—they seek to acquire those that will add to the value of their portfolios.[16]

Representatives often seek committee assignments that have access to what is known as **pork,** legislation that allows representatives to bring money and jobs to their districts in the form of public works programs, military bases, or other programs. In the past, a seat on the Armed Services Committee, for example, would allow a member to bring lucrative defense contracts back to his or her district, or to discourage base closings within his or her district or state. Many of these programs are called **earmarks** because they are monies that an appropriations bill designates—"earmarks"—for specific projects within a member's district or state.

Legislators who bring jobs and new public works programs back to their districts are hard to defeat when up for reelection. But, ironically, these are the programs that attract much of the public criticism directed at the federal government in general and Congress in particular. Thus, it is somewhat paradoxical that pork improves a member's chances for reelection.

Pork isn't the only motivator for those seeking strategic committee assignments.[17] Some committees, such as Energy and Commerce, facilitate reelection by giving House members influence over decisions that affect large campaign contributors. Other committees, such as Education and the Workforce or Judiciary, attract members eager to work on the policy responsibilities assigned to the committee even if the appointment does them little good at the ballot box. Another motivator for certain committee assignments is the desire to have power and influence within the chamber. The Appropriations and Budget Committees provide that kind of reward for some members, given the monetary impact of the committees. Congress can approve programs, but unless money for them is appropriated in the budget, they are largely symbolic.

VIDEO ROUNDTABLE
Contemporary Legislative Process

pork
Legislation that allows representatives to bring home the bacon to their districts in the form of public works programs, military bases, or other programs designed to benefit their districts directly.

earmark
Funds that an appropriations bill designates for a particular purpose within a state or congressional district.

In both the House and the Senate, committee membership generally reflects the party distribution within that chamber. For example, at the outset of the 110th Congress, Democrats held a narrow majority of House seats and thus claimed about a fifty-four percent share of the seats on several committees, including International Relations, Energy and Commerce, and Education and the Workforce. On committees more critical to the operation of the House or to the setting of national policy, the majority often takes a disproportionate share of the slots. Since the Committee on Rules regulates access to the floor for legislation approved by other standing committees, control by the majority party is essential for it to manage the flow of legislation. For this reason, no matter how narrow the majority party's margin in the chamber, it makes up more than two-thirds of the Committee on Rules membership.

Committee Chairs   Committee chairs enjoy tremendous power and prestige. They are authorized to select all subcommittee chairs, call meetings, and recommend majority members to sit on conference committees. Committee chairs may even opt to kill a bill by refusing to schedule hearings on it. They also have a large committee staff at their disposal and are often recipients of favors from lobbyists, who recognize the chair's unique position of power. Personal skill, influence, and expertise are a chair's best allies.

Historically, committee chairs were the majority party members with the longest continuous service on the committee. Committee chairs in the House, unlike the Senate, are no longer selected by **seniority,** or time of continuous service on the committee. When Republicans controlled the House, leaders interviewed potential chairs to ensure that candidates demonstrated loyalty to the party. The seniority system is also affected by term limits enacted by the House and Senate in 1995 and 1997, respectively. This term limit of six years for all committee chairs has forced many longtime committee chairs to step down or take over another committee. For example, Representative Henry Hyde (R–IL) stepped down as chair of the House Judiciary Committee in favor of a new position as chair of the International Relations Committee.

seniority
Time of continuous service on a committee.

The Members of Congress

TODAY, MANY MEMBERS OF CONGRESS find the job exciting in spite of public criticism of the institution. But, it wasn't always so. Until Washington, D.C., got air-conditioning and drained its swamps, it was a miserable town. Most representatives spent as little time as possible there, viewing the Congress, especially the House, as a stepping stone to other political positions back home. It was only after World War I that most House members became congressional careerists who viewed their work in Washington as long term.[18]

Many members of Congress clearly relish their work, although there are indications that political scandals, intense media scrutiny, the need to tackle hard issues, and a growth of partisan dissension are taking a toll on many members. Those no longer in the majority, in particular, often don't see their service in Congress as satisfying. Research by political scientists shows that "members voluntarily depart

■ Representative Charles B. Rangel (D–NY) became the chair of the powerful House Ways and Means Committee after Democrats won control of the House in the 2006 elections.

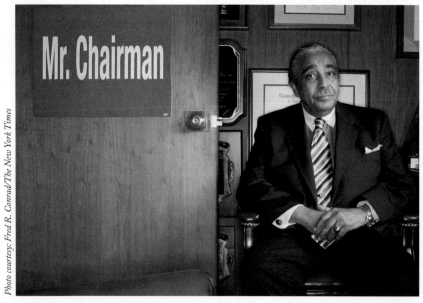

Photo courtesy: Fred R. Conrad/The New York Times

Global Perspective

PARLIAMENTARY SYSTEMS: THE ISRAELI KNESSET

When most Americans think of democratic law and policy making, they typically think of the U.S. Congress in action: bicameral in structure, controlled by two political parties, and limited by the Constitution's system of checks and balances. Writing in the early 1800s, Alexis de Tocqueville noted the U.S. Congress fits the genius, or political spirit, of the American people. But, he also wrote that different democratic states would require representative institutions that equally matched the genius of their peoples.

Democratic legislatures take diverse forms across the globe. Most of them are parliamentary systems in which the executive branch is dependent upon the legislative branch's—the parliament's—direct or indirect support. In the bulk of parliamentary systems, the head of government, generally referred to as the prime minister, is chosen by the governing party or coalition of parties in the parliament. This is a significant departure from America's co-equal executive and legislative branches of government. Another aspect of many parliamentary systems that differs markedly from the U.S. system is the employment of an electoral system of proportional representation in which legislative seats are awarded according to the proportion each party receives of the popular vote. In America's winner-take-all system, a one-vote majority determines a contest's winner. Nations relying on proportional representation tend to have a broad array of political parties with markedly different ideological outlooks and policy positions.

Almost no legislature could be more different from the American Congress than Israel's Knesset, the Middle East's longest-lived democratic legislature. With the exception of Turkey's National Assembly, no other legislative institution in the Middle East is typified by free and fair contested elections among formal opposition parties in well-established roles, as well as established minority parties.

The Knesset is unicameral, and Israel's elections guarantee proportional representation. Unlike the U.S. Congress in which the different chambers were designed to represent different interests (those of the people in the U.S. House of Representatives and those of the state governments in the Senate), the Knesset's single chamber can be said to approximate the ideal of direct democracy. The Israeli electoral system awards seats in the legislature to political parties in exact proportion to their share of the total vote. This means that any party able to gain a small plurality of votes will have representation. In 2006, the Knesset included representatives from twelve different parties, with no party holding a majority. Since the parties are so diverse in their views, compromise is often difficult to achieve. The Knesset's structure is significantly different from that of the U.S. Congress, where Democrats and Republicans control legislative and political activity and a party with only a one-seat advantage over its opposition holds significant power to influence legislation.

Significant differences in the political authority vested in the Knesset and the Congress exist as well, since the Knesset is not subject to the kind of checks and balances set out in the U.S. Constitution. For all practical purposes, the Knesset *is* the government. The Israeli prime minister cannot veto any legislative and policy action by the Knesset, and the Knesset is not subject to judicial review. In fact, the Knesset has the constitutional power to overrule Israeli Supreme Court decisions regarding legislative and governing action, even those that go against Israel's Basic Law. Despite this, in recent years Israel's Supreme Court has assumed an increased role in Israeli political affairs.

QUESTIONS

1. Does the principle of separation of powers help or hinder effective governance? In what ways?
2. What changes would be likely if the United States amended the Constitution and adopted a proportional representation electoral system?

when their electoral, policy, and institutional situations no longer seem desirable."[19] The increasing partisanship of the Congress also plays a role in many retirements. When asked why he was leaving the Senate, Warren Rudman (R–NH) remarked, "It's the whole atmosphere. It's become so partisan, so intense, in many ways it's just hateful."[20]

Former House and Senate members also can make a lot more money in the private sector. Former House Appropriations Committee Chair Robert Livingston built the tenth largest lobbying firm in D.C. in only four years, earning millions each year from clients who understand the access former members retain.[21] One recent study found that 43 percent of the 198 House members as well as 50 percent of the Senate members who left Congress between 1998 and 2004 registered as lobbyists.[22] In the wake of scandals and debates about how to deal ethically with the relationships between members of Congress and lobbyists, many of them

TABLE 7.4	A DAY IN THE LIFE OF A MEMBER OF CONGRESS
8:30 a.m.	Breakfast with a former member.
9:30 a.m.	Science Committee: Hearing.
10:00 a.m.	Private briefing by NASA officials for afternoon subcommittee hearing.
10:00 a.m.	Commerce Committee: Markup session of pending legislation.
12:00 p.m.	Photo opportunity with Miss Universe.
12:00 p.m.	Lunch with visiting friend at Watergate Hotel.
1:30 p.m.	Science Committee: Subcommittee hearing.
1:30 p.m.	Commerce Committee: Subcommittee markup session of pending legislation.
2:00 p.m.	House convenes.
3:00 p.m.	Meeting with National Alliance for Animal Legislation officials.
4:30 p.m.	Meeting with American Jewish Congress delegates.
5:00 p.m.	State University reception.
5:00 p.m.	Briefing by the commissioner of the Bureau of Labor Statistics on the uninsured.
5:30 p.m.	Reception/fundraiser for party whip.
6:00 p.m.	Reception/fundraiser for fellow member from the same state.
6:00 p.m.	Cajun foods reception sponsored by Louisiana member.
6:00 p.m.	Winetasting reception on behalf of New York wine industry, sponsored by New York member.
10:45 p.m.	House adjourns.

Source: C-SPAN.ORG/questions/week113.asp.

former colleagues, some members are opting not to take advantage of perks like private trips paid for by lobbyists. Such trips declined dramatically between 2005 and 2006. In March of 2005, for example, members took 146 trips financed by private interests. By March 2006, the number of trips was down to 29.[23]

Members must attempt to appease two constituencies—party leaders, colleagues, and lobbyists in Washington, D.C., and constituents at home.[24] In attempting to do so, members spend full days at home as well as in D.C. According to one study of House members in non-election years, average representatives made thirty-five trips back home to their districts and spent an average 138 days a year there.[25] One journalist has aptly described a member's days as a "kaleidoscopic jumble: breakfast with reporters, morning staff meetings, simultaneous committee hearings to juggle, back-to-back sessions with lobbyists and constituents, phone calls, briefings, constant buzzers interrupting office work to make quorum calls and votes on the run, afternoon speeches, evening meetings, receptions, fund-raisers, all crammed into four days so they can race home for a weekend gauntlet of campaigning. It's a rat race."[26] Table 7.4 shows a representative day in the life of a member of Congress.

RUNNING FOR AND STAYING IN OFFICE

Despite the long hours, hard work, and sometimes even abuse that senators and representatives experience, thousands aspire to these jobs every year. Yet, only 535 men and women (plus five nonvoting delegates) actually serve in the U.S. Congress. Membership in one of the two major political parties is almost always a prerequisite for election, because election laws in various states often discriminate against independents (those without party affiliation) and minor-party candidates. As discussed in chapter 14, money is the mother's milk of politics—the ability to raise money often is key to any member's victory, and many members spend nearly all of their free time on the phone dialing for dollars or attending fundraisers.

Incumbency helps members stay in office once they are elected.[27] It's often very difficult for outsiders to win because they don't have the advantages (enumerated in Table 7.5) enjoyed by incumbents, including name recognition, access to free media, inside track on fund-raising, and a district drawn to favor the incumbent. As illustrated in Analyzing Visuals: Approval Ratings of Congress and Individual Representatives, most Americans approve of their *own* members of Congress while having very low regard for Congress collectively.

It is not surprising, then, that from 1980 to 1990, an average of 95 percent of the incumbents who sought reelection won their primary and general election races.[28] More recent elections saw even higher proportions of incumbents returning to office. One study concluded that unless a member of Congress was involved in a serious scandal, his or her chances of defeat were minimal.[29] In 2006, more than twenty members seeking reelection lost, up from only seven in 2004. Many of these defeats were blamed on the president's unpopularity, the war in Iraq, and concerns over corruption.

incumbency
The fact that being in office helps a person stay in office because of a variety of benefits that go with the position.

VISUAL LITERACY
Why Is It So Hard to Defeat an Incumbent?

CONGRESSIONAL DEMOGRAPHICS

Congress is better educated, richer, more male, and more white than the rest of the United States. In fact, all but three senators are college graduates; 396 representatives share that honor. Over two-thirds of the members in each body also hold advanced degrees.[30] Many members of both Houses have significant inherited wealth, but given their educational attainment, which is far higher than the average American's, it is not surprising to find so many wealthy members of Congress.

Nearly two hundred of the members of Congress are millionaires. The Senate, in fact, is often called the Millionaires Club, and its members sport names including Rockefeller and Kennedy. In fact, twenty-one senators are worth at least $3.1 million. Twenty-nine members of the House have a net worth over that amount.[31]

The average age of senators is sixty. John E. Sununu (R–NH) is the youngest senator. The average age of House members is fifty-four; Representative Patrick McHenry (R–NC) was first elected to the House in 2004 at age twenty-nine and continues to be the youngest member of Congress.

As revealed in Figure 7.3, the 1992 elections saw a record number of women, African Americans, and other minorities elected to Congress. By the 110th Congress, the total number of women members increased to at least 70 in the House and sixteen in the Senate. In 2007, the number of African Americans serving in the House held steady at 40. Barack Obama (D–IL), elected to the Senate in 2004, continues to be the only African American to serve in that body. In the 110th Congress, only twenty-three Hispanics serve in the House. Three Hispanics serve in the Senate. Also serving in the 110th Congress are two members of Asian/Pacific Islander heritage in the Senate and five in the House of Representatives. Only one American Indian, Tom Cole (R–OK), serves in the 110th Congress.

Photo courtesy: Office of Representative Loretta Sanchez

■ In 2002, Representatives Loretta and Linda Sanchez (both D–CA) became the first sisters to serve together in the U.S. Congress. Since then, they have pushed for women's issues, such as enforcement of Title IX, research for breast cancer, and protections against sexual assault in the military. Here they are shown being sworn in by then Speaker of the House Dennis Hastert (R–IL).

TABLE 7.5 THE ADVANTAGES OF INCUMBENCY

- Name recognition gained through previous campaigns and repeated visits (many of them government paid) to the district to make appearances at various public events.
- Credit claimed for bringing federal money to the district in the form of grants and contracts.
- Positive evaluations from constituents earned by doing favors (casework) such as helping cut red tape and tracking down federal aid, and tasks handled by government-salaried professional staff members.
- Distribution of newsletters and other noncampaign materials free through the mails by using the "frank" (an envelope that contains the legislator's signature in place of a stamp).
- Access to media—incumbents are newsmakers who provide reporters with tips and quotes.
- Greater ease in fundraising—members' high reelection rates make them a good bet for people or groups willing to give campaign contributions in hopes of having access to powerful decision makers.
- Experience in running a campaign, putting together a campaign staff, making speeches, understanding constituent concerns, and connecting with people.
- Superior knowledge about a wide range of issues gained through work on committees, review of legislation, and previous campaigns.
- A record for supporting locally popular policy positions.
- In the House, a district drawn to enhance electability.

FIGURE 7.3 FEMALE AND MINORITY-GROUP MEMBERS OF CONGRESS, SELECTED YEARS

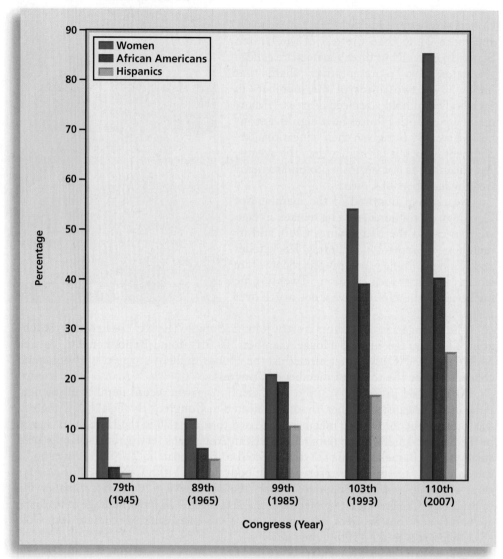

Occupationally, members of Congress no longer are overwhelmingly lawyers, although lawyers continue to be the largest single occupational group. In the 109th Congress, 275 were former state legislators and 111 were former congressional staffers. The number of veterans in Congress has continued to decline since the end of the Vietnam War. Still, 26 percent of those serving in the House or Senate are veterans, compared to 12 percent of the U.S. population.[32] In 2006, eleven Iraq war veterans ran; in Pennsylvania alone, three Democratic veterans unseated incumbent Republicans.

THEORIES OF REPRESENTATION

Over the years, political theorists have offered various ideas about how constituents' interests are best represented in any legislative body. Does it make a difference if the members of Congress come from or are members of a particular group? Are they bound to vote the way their constituents expect them to vote even if they personally favor another policy? Your answer to these questions may depend on your view of the representative function of legislators.

COMPARATIVE

Comparing Legislatures

Analyzing Visuals

APPROVAL RATINGS OF CONGRESS AND INDIVIDUAL REPRESENTATIVES

For many years, political scientists have noted that approval ratings of Congress as an institution are generally quite low, rarely exceeding 50 percent. On the other hand, the public's approval rating of its own member tends to be much higher, usually above 50 percent. The line graph demonstrates the differences between these ratings since 1990. Do the data for approval of Congress and approval of one's own representative follow similar trends over the period covered in the figure? What factors do you think account for the differences in the ratings of Congress and of one's own representative in 2006?

Note that the question regarding one's own representative was a slightly different one in 2004 from the earlier question—asking not just about approval but also about reelection. Do you think that this difference in wording affected the rating positively or negatively?

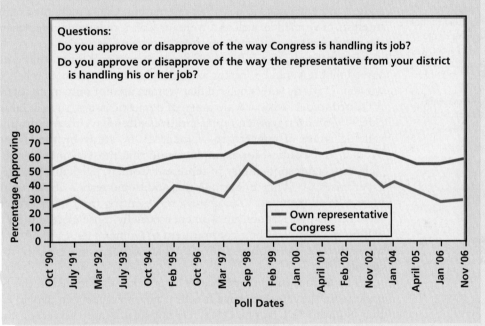

Questions:
Do you approve or disapprove of the way Congress is handling its job?
Do you approve or disapprove of the way the representative from your district is handling his or her job?

Source: Data derived from Lexis-Nexis RPOLL.

British political philosopher Edmund Burke (1729–1797), who also served in the British Parliament, believed that although he was elected from Bristol, it was his duty to represent the interests of the entire nation. He reasoned that elected officials were obliged to vote as they personally thought best. According to Burke, representatives should be **trustees** who listen to the opinions of their constituents and then can be trusted to use their own best judgment to make final decisions.

A second theory of representation holds that representatives are **delegates.** True delegates are representatives who vote the way their constituents would want them to, whether or not those opinions are the representative's. Delegates, therefore, must be ready and willing to vote against their conscience or personal policy preferences if they know how their constituents feel about a particular issue. Not surprisingly, members of Congress and other legislative bodies generally don't fall neatly into either category. It is often unclear how constituents feel about a particular issue, or there may be con-

trustee
Role played by elected representatives who listen to constituents' opinions and then use their best judgment to make final decisions.

delegate
Role played by elected representatives who vote the way their constituents would want them to, regardless of their own opinions.

Photo courtesy: Office of Senator Mikulski

■ Here the fourteen women senators in the 109th Congress meet. In 2006, two more were added to their ranks. Politically, eleven are Democrats and five are Republicans.

politico
Role played by elected representatives who act as trustees or as delegates, depending on the issue.

flicting opinions within a single constituency. With these difficulties in mind, a third theory of representation holds that **politicos** alternately don the hat of trustee or delegate, depending on the issue. On an issue of great concern to their constituents, representatives most likely will vote as delegates; on other issues, perhaps those that are less visible, representatives will act as trustees and use their own best judgment. Research by political scientists supports this view.[33]

How a representative views his or her role—as a trustee, delegate, or politico—may still not answer the question of whether it makes a difference if a representative or senator is male or female, African American, Hispanic, or Caucasian, young or old, gay or straight. Burke's ideas about representation don't even begin to address more practical issues of representation. Can a man, for example, represent the interests of women as well as a woman? Can a rich woman represent the interests of the poor? Are veterans more sensitive to veterans' issues?

Interestingly, one NBC/*Wall Street Journal* poll found that a majority of people agreed that it would be "better for society" if "most of the members of Congress were women."[34] Many voters believe that women are not only more interested in, but better suited to deal with, a wide range of domestic issues, such as education and health care.[35] Moreover, women representatives often have played prominent roles in advancing issues of concern to women.[36] One study by the Center for American Women and Politics, for example, found that most women in the 103rd Congress "felt a special responsibility to represent women, particularly to represent their life experiences. . . . They undertook this additional responsibility while first, and foremost, like all members of Congress, representing their own districts." However, research finds that Republican women, especially those elected more recently, "may be willing to downplay their commitment to women's issues in order to make gains on other district and policy priorities that conform more easily to the Republican agenda."[37]

The actions of the lone Native American who served in the Senate until 2005 underscore the representative function that members can play in Congress. Senator Ben Nighthorse Campbell (R–CO) not surprisingly served on the Committee on Indian Affairs. Earlier, as a member of the House, he fought successfully for legislation to establish the National Museum of the American Indian on the Mall in Washington, D.C. New African American and Hispanic senators are expected to be similarly responsive to issues of racial importance.

How Members Make Decisions

AS A BILL MAKES ITS WAY through the labyrinth of the law-making process described above, members are confronted with the question: "How should I vote?" Members adhere to their own personal beliefs on some matters, but their views often are moderated by other considerations. To avoid making any voting mistakes, members look to a variety of sources for cues.

PARTY

Members often look to party leaders for indicators of how to vote. Indeed, the whips in each chamber reinforce the need for party cohesion, particularly on issues of concern to the party. In fact, from 1970 to the mid-1990s, the incidence of party votes in which majorities of the two parties took opposing sides roughly doubled to more than 60 percent of all roll-call votes.[38] Describing this phenomenon, former political scientist turned representative David E. Price notes, "in rereading *Congressional Government* [written by then political scientist and later U.S. President Woodrow Wilson] certain Wilsonian themes struck me with much more force than they did [in 1994]: the balances of power between Congress and the executive in the federal government and between the committees and the parties within the Congress. Those balances were in better repair, I believe—not perfect repair, but better repair—in the 1990s than they are today."[39]

Photo courtesy: Office of Representative Nancy Pelosi

Under unified Republican control in the 107th Congress, for example, there was perfect party unity on all major votes taken in the House.[40] In the 108th Congress, Democratic senators demonstrated unanimity in filibustering several presidential judicial nominations to the U.S. Courts of Appeals. While some charged that this was not evidence of party unity, but instead elected officials taking their direction from major liberal special-interest groups, there can be no doubt that in both closely divided houses, party reigns supreme.[41]

With the election of George W. Bush, a Republican president determined to govern from the "right in" rather than the "center out," congressional Republicans, especially those in the House, took on a harder edge. New tactics were devised to eliminate dependence on or participation by Democrats. At the same time, members of the narrow Republican majority were kept in line largely by threats of poor committee assignments or loss of committee or subcommittee chairs. According to David E. Price, "Most obvious is the practice of going to the floor with a narrow whip count and holding the vote open as long as necessary to cajole the last few Republican members to vote yes. The most notorious example was the vote on the Republicans' privatized Medicare drug benefit, held open for almost three hours on November 22, 2003, but the tactic was [also] utilized . . . on the post-Katrina bill dealing with refinery construction and price-gouging."[42]

After years of Congress and the presidency being controlled by the Republican Party, in 2006, voters voiced their discontent over what many viewed as the excessive partisanship of the 109th Congress. A poll taken on Election Day 2006 found that 52 percent of voters would prefer **divided government,** the political condition in which different parties control the White House and Congress. Historically, divided government has lead to a situation called gridlock, which often results in very little important legislation being enacted into law. In an attempt to avert a gridlock scenario, Democratic Leader Nancy Pelosi (D–CA), soon to become the new Speaker of the House, met with President George W. Bush two days after the election.

■ Eager to regain a majority in Congress, House Democrats started a "30-Something Working Group" of younger House members designed to appeal to younger voters. Here Democratic Leader Nancy Pelosi (D–CA) along with Debbie Wasserman Schultz (D–FL) and Tim Ryan (D–OH) participate in the Rap, Rock 'n Roll Radio Row, talking about how Social Security will affect younger workers.

divided government
The political condition in which different political parties control the White House and Congress.

CONSTITUENTS

Constituents—the people who live and vote in the home district or state—are always in a member's mind when casting votes.[43] Studies by political scientists show that members vote in conformity with prevailing opinion in their districts about two-thirds of the time.[44] On average, Congress passes laws that reflect national public opinion at about the same rate.[45] It is rare for a legislator to vote against the wishes of his or her constituents regularly, particularly on issues of welfare rights, domestic policy, or other highly salient issues. For example, during the 1960s, representatives from southern states could not hope to keep their seats for long if they voted in favor of proposed civil rights legislation.

Gauging how voters feel about any particular issue often is not easy. Because it is virtually impossible to know how the folks back home feel on all issues, a representa-

PARTICIPATION

The Prepared Voter Kit

Photo courtesy: Nam Y. Huh/AP Wide World Photos

■ Senator Barack Obama (D–IL), seen here speaking at a church, campaigned extensively for Democratic candidates around the country in 2006 leading many to suspect he was testing the waters for a 2008 presidential run. Obama, who was elected to his first term in 2004, is the only African American senator in the 110th Congress.

logrolling
Vote trading, voting yea to support a colleague's bill in return for a promise of future support.

tive's perception of their constituents' preferences is important. Even when voters have opinions, legislators may get little guidance if their district is narrowly divided. Abortion is an issue about which many voters feel passionately, but a legislator whose district has roughly equal numbers of pro-choice and pro-life advocates can satisfy only a portion of his or her constituents.

In short, legislators tend to act on their own preferences as trustees when dealing with topics that have come through the committees on which they serve or with issues that they know about as a result of experience in other contexts, such as their vocation. On items of little concern to people back in the district or for which the legislator has little first-hand knowledge, the tendency is to turn to other sources for voting cues. But with regard to particularly charged topics like same-sex marriage, abortion restrictions, and flag burning—often called "wedge issues," given their ability to divide or drive a wedge between voters—members are always keenly aware of the consequences of voting against their constituents' views.

COLLEAGUES AND CAUCUSES

The range and complexity of issues confronting Congress mean that no one can be up to speed on more than a few topics. When members must vote on bills about which they know very little, they often turn for advice to colleagues who have served on the committee that handled the legislation. On issues that are of little interest to a legislator, **logrolling,** or vote trading, often occurs. Logrolling often takes place on specialized bills targeting money or projects to selected congressional districts. An unaffected member often will exchange a yea vote for the promise of a future yea vote on a similar piece of specialized legislation.

Members may also look to other representatives who share common interests. Special-interest caucuses created around issues, home states, regions, congressional class, or other commonalities facilitate this communication. Prior to 1995, the power of these groups was even more evident, as several caucuses enjoyed formal status within the legislative body and were provided staff, office space, and budgets. Today, however, all caucuses are informal in nature, although some, such as the Black and Hispanic Caucuses, are far more organized than others. The Congressional Women's Caucus, for example, has formal elections of its Republican and Democratic co-chairs and vice chairs, its members provide staff to work on issues of common concern to caucus members, and staffers meet regularly to facilitate support for legislation of interest to women.

INTEREST GROUPS, LOBBYISTS, AND POLITICAL ACTION COMMITTEES

A primary function of most lobbyists, whether they work for interest groups, trade associations, or large corporations, is to provide information to supportive or potentially supportive legislators, committees, and their staffs.[46] It is likely, for example, that a representative knows the National Rifle Association's (NRA) position on gun control legislation. What the legislator needs to get from the NRA is information and substantial research on the feasibility and impact of such legislation. How could the states implement such legislation? Is it constitutional? Will it really have an impact on violent crime or crime in schools? Organized interests can win over undecided legislators or confirm the support of their friends by providing information that legislators use to justify the position they have embraced. They also can supply direct campaign contributions, volunteers, and publicity to members seeking reelection. And, they may urge supporters to deluge their representatives with e-mails or even to visit members' D.C. or district offices.

Pressure groups also use grassroots appeals to pressure legislators by urging their members in a particular state or district to call, write, fax, or e-mail their senators or representatives. Lobbyists can't vote, but constituents back home can and do. Lobbyists and the corporate or other interests they represent, however, can contribute to political campaigns and are an important source of campaign contributions. Many have political action committees (PACs) to help support members seeking reelection.

While a link to a legislator's constituents may be the most effective way to influence behavior, it is not the only path of interest-group influence on member decision making.[47] The high cost of campaigning has made members of Congress, especially those without huge personal fortunes, attentive to those who help pay the tab for the high cost of many campaigns. The almost 5,000 PACs organized by interest groups are a major source of most members' campaign funding. When an issue comes up that is of little consequence to a member's constituents, there is, not surprisingly, a tendency to support the positions of those interests who helped pay for the last campaign. After all, who wants to bite the hand that feeds him or her? (Interest groups and PACs are discussed in detail in chapter 16. PACs are also discussed in chapter 14.)

SIMULATION
You Are an Informed Voter

STAFF AND SUPPORT AGENCIES

Members of Congress rely heavily on members of their staffs for information on pending legislation.[48] House members have an average of seventeen staffers; senators have an average of forty. Staff are divided between D.C. and district offices. Not only do staff members meet regularly with staffers from other offices about proposed legislation or upcoming hearings, but staff members also prepare summaries of bills and brief the representative or senator based on their research and meetings. Especially if a bill is nonideological or one on which the member has no real position, staff members can be very influential. In many offices, they are the greatest influence on their boss's votes. In many cases, lobbyists are just as likely to contact key staffers as they are members. And, in many of the recent major House lobbying scandals, it was staffers who ultimately faced criminal investigations or prosecutions for influence buying.

Congressional committees and subcommittees also have their own dedicated staff to assist committee members. Additional support for members comes from support personnel at the Congressional Research Service (CRS) at the Library of Congress, the Government Accountability Office (GAO), and the Congressional Budget Office (CBO) (see Table 7.6).

TABLE 7.6 **CONGRESSIONAL SUPPORT AGENCIES**		
Congressional Research Service (CRS)	*Government Accountability Office (GAO)*	*Congressional Budget Office (CBO)*
Created in 1914 as the Legislative Research Service (LRS), CRS is administered by the Library of Congress. It responds to more than a quarter of a million congressional requests for information each year. Its staff conducts non-partisan studies of public issues and conducts major research projects for committees at the request of members. The CRS also prepares summaries of all bills introduced and tracks the progress.	The Government Accountability Office (GAO) was established in 1921 as an independent regulatory agency for the purpose of auditing the financial expenditures of the executive branch and federal agencies. The GAO performs four additional functions: it sets government standards for accounting, it provides a variety of legal opinions, it settles claims against the government, and it conducts studies upon congressional request.	The CBO was created in 1974 to evaluate the economic effect of different spending programs and to provide information on the cost of proposed policies. It is responsible for analyzing the president's budget and economic projections. The CBO provides Congress and individual members with a valuable second opinion to use in budget debates.

Politics Now

MUSLIM STAFFERS SEEK TO EDUCATE MEMBERS OF CONGRESS

As the war in Iraq entered its second year, Representative Tom Tancredo (R–CO) gave a radio interview in July 2005 in which he suggested "bombing Islam's holy sites, including Mecca."[a] At that moment, Nayyera Haq, a spokesperson for Representative John Salazar (D–CO), realized that as a Muslim working on Capitol Hill, she could no longer stay quiet. By fall 2005, the twenty-four-year-old Haq organized with twenty-two mostly Democratic Muslims working in Congress to start the Congressional Muslim Staffers Association. Staff associations are not unusual. They are often formed around issue areas, sports teams (softball is a favorite), and other interests, including religion.

Haq's group was not the first Muslim group to form on Capitol Hill. Muslim staff members have been meeting together each Friday for prayer since 1998. That group, however, was inward looking and based on common interests. Haq's new group, on the other hand, comprised a cross-section of the American Muslim population, including whites, African Americans, South Asians, and Arab Americans, and had an external purpose. The association's goal is to educate other staffers, and through them, congressional members about Islam so that they might make more informed decisions about America's relationships with Islamic countries.

During spring 2006, for example, after violence was triggered around the world when cartoons caricaturizing Muhammad were printed in a Danish newspaper, the association hosted a lunchtime seminar open to other staffers and members of Congress. It dealt with the life of Muhammad and his critical importance to Muslims. The luncheon attracted over fifty non-Muslim staffers, and panelists now are regularly asked to talk to other off-Hill groups as Americans seek a better understanding of one of the world's oldest and largest religions.

The group also focuses on more general educational efforts, teaching staffers and members of Congress that Islam shares its roots with Judaism and Christianity, and providing them with a broader understanding of the breadth of Islamic beliefs. The association recognizes that theirs is an uphill battle. Still, Haq contends that her group has important work to do. "Being a Muslim staffer on the Hill is unique," says Haq. "In our offices there is a desire for knowledge about Islam. And there's a broad lack of understanding be-

■ Staffers Sarah Bassal (left) and Amina Rubin (right) prepare for a workshop on Muhammad intended to educate policymakers about Islam.

tween our government and others. It's almost a responsibility to speak up and not be silent as a progressive Muslim."[b] The 2006 election of the first Muslim member of Congress, Representative Keith Ellison (D–MN), is likely to provide additional opportunities for education and understanding about Islam in the 110th Congress.

QUESTIONS

1. To what extent are elected representatives responsible for educating themselves on major religions like Islam?

2. Staffers routinely play a key role in helping members of Congress draft legislation and determine policy positions, as well as how to vote on specific legislation. How appropriate is it for staffers to wield such influence?

[a]This feature draws heavily on Nela Banerjee, "Muslim Staff Members on Mission to Educate Congress," *New York Times,* (June 3, 2006): A11; and Pauline Jelinek, "Legislative Aides Aim to Lift Islam's Image," *Detroit Free Press* (June 3, 2006).

[b]Banerjee, "Muslim Staff Members on Mission to Educate Congress."

The Law-making Function of Congress

THE ORGANIZATION OF CONGRESS allows it to fulfill its constitutional responsibilities, chief among which is its law-making function. It is through this power that Congress affects the day-to-day lives of all Americans and sets policy for the future. Proposals for legislation—be they about terrorism, Medicare, or tax policy—can come from the president, executive agencies, committee staffs, interest groups, or even private individuals. Only members of the House or Senate, however, formally can submit a bill for congressional consideration (although many are initially drafted by lobbyists). Once a bill is introduced by a member of Congress, it usually reaches a dead end. Of the approximately 10,000 or so bills introduced during the 109th session of Congress, fewer than 250 were made into law.

It is probably useful to think of Congress as a system of multiple vetoes, which was what the Framers desired. They wanted to disperse power, and as Congress has evolved it has come closer and closer to the Framers' intentions. As a bill goes through Congress, numerous roadblocks to passage must be surmounted. In addition to realistic roadblocks, caution signs and other opportunities for delay abound. A member who sponsors a bill must get through every obstacle. In contrast, successful opposition means winning at only one of many stages, including: (1) the House subcommittee; (2) the full House committee; (3) the House Committee on Rules; (4) the House; (5) the Senate subcommittee; (6) the full Senate committee; (7) the Senate; (8) floor leaders in both Houses; (9) the House-Senate conference committee; and, (10) the president.

The story of how a bill becomes a law in the United States can be told in two different ways. The first is the textbook method, which provides a greatly simplified road map of the process to make it easier to understand. We'll review this method first.

HOW A BILL BECOMES A LAW: THE TEXTBOOK VERSION

A bill must survive several stages before it becomes a law. It must be approved by one or more standing committees and both chambers, and, if House and Senate versions differ, each house must accept a conference report resolving those differences. These multiple points of approval provide many opportunities for members to revise the content of legislation and may lead representatives to alter their views on a particular piece of legislation several times over. Thus, it is much easier to defeat a bill than it is to get one passed.

The House and Senate have parallel processes, and often the same bill is introduced in each chamber at the same time. A bill must be introduced by a member of Congress, but, in an attempt to show support for the aims of the bill, it is often sponsored by several other members (called co-sponsors).[49] Once introduced, the bill is sent to the clerk of the chamber, who gives it a number (for example, HR 1 or S 1—indicating House or Senate bill number one). The bill is then printed, distributed, and sent to the appropriate committee or committees for consideration.

The first action takes place within the committee, after it is referred there by the Speaker of the House or by the Senate majority leader. The committee usually refers the bill to one of its subcommittees, which researches the bill and decides whether to hold hearings on it. The subcommittee hearings provide the opportunity for those on both sides of the issue to voice their opinions. Most of these hearings are now open to the public because of 1970s sunshine laws, which require open sessions. After the hearings, the bill is revised in subcommittee, and then the subcommittee votes to approve or defeat the bill. If the subcommittee votes in favor of the bill, it is returned to the full committee. There, during **markup,** committee members can add items to the bill and send it to the House or Senate floor with a favorable recommendation. It can also reject the bill (see Figure 7.4).

The second stage of action takes place on the House or Senate floor. As previously discussed, in the House, before a bill may be debated on the floor, it must be approved by the Committee on Rules and given a rule and a place on the calendar, or schedule. (House budget bills, however, don't go to the Committee on Rules.) In the House, the rule given to a bill determines the limits on the floor debate and specifies what types of amendments, if any, may be attached to the bill. Once the Committee on Rules considers the bill, it is put on the calendar.

When the day arrives for floor debate, the House may choose to form a Committee of the Whole. This procedure allows the House to deliberate with only one hundred members present, to expedite consideration of the bill. On the House floor,

SIMULATION

You Are a Member of Congress

markup

A process in which committee members offer changes to a bill before it goes to the floor in either house for a vote.

FIGURE 7.4 HOW A BILL BECOMES A LAW

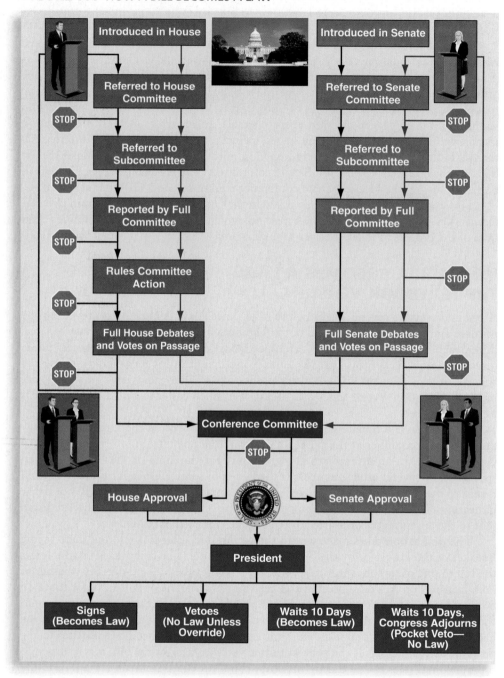

the bill is debated, amendments are offered, and a vote ultimately is taken by the full House. If the bill survives, it is sent to the Senate for consideration if it was not considered there simultaneously.

Unlike the House, where debate is necessarily limited given the size of the body, bills may be held up by a hold or a filibuster in the Senate. A **hold** is a tactic by which a senator asks to be informed before a particular bill is brought to the floor. This request signals the Senate leadership and the sponsors of the bill that a colleague may have objections to the bill and should be consulted before further action is taken.

Holds are powerful tools. In 2002, for example, Senator Joe Biden (D–DE) became so upset with congressional failure to fund Amtrak security (Biden takes Amtrak

hold
A tactic by which a senator asks to be informed before a particular bill is brought to the floor. This stops the bill from coming to the floor until the hold is removed.

back and forth to his home in Delaware when the Senate is in session) that he put holds on two Department of Transportation nominees, whom he called "fine, decent, and competent people." This meant that their nominations could not be considered until he removed his hold. In return, the Bush administration retaliated by withholding a third of the funding for a University of Delaware research project on high-speed trains. As the *Washington Post* noted in reporting this story, "Welcome to the wild wacky world of Washington politics, where people sometimes destroy a village to save it."[50]

Filibusters, which allow for unlimited debate on a bill (or on presidential appointments), grew out of the absence of rules to limit speech in the Senate. In contrast to a hold, a filibuster is a more formal and public way of halting action on a bill. There are no rules on the content of a filibuster as long as a senator keeps talking. A senator may read from a phone book, recite poetry, or read cookbooks to delay a vote. Often, a team of senators takes turns speaking to keep the filibuster going in the hope that a bill will be tabled or killed. In 1964, for example, a group of northern liberal senators continued a filibuster for eighty-two days in an effort to prevent amendments that would weaken a civil rights bill. Still, filibusters often are more of a threat than an actual event on the Senate floor, although members may use them in extreme circumstances. (See American Values/American Voices: The Gang of Fourteen and the Search for Compromise.)

There is only one way to end a filibuster. Sixteen senators must sign a motion for **cloture.** This motion requires the votes of sixty members to limit debate; after a cloture motion passes the Senate floor, members may spend no more than thirty additional hours debating the legislation at issue.

The third stage of action takes place when the two chambers of Congress approve different versions of the same bill. When this happens, they establish a conference committee to iron out the differences between the two versions. The conference committee, whose members are from the original House and Senate committees, hammers out a compromise, which is returned to each chamber for a final vote. Sometimes the conference committee fails to agree and the bill dies there. No changes or amendments to the compromise version are allowed. If the bill is passed, it is sent to the president, who either signs it or **vetoes** it. If the bill is not passed in both houses, it dies.

The president has ten days to consider a bill. He has four options:

1. The president can sign the bill, at which point it becomes law.

2. The president can veto the bill, which is more likely to occur when the president is of a different party from the majority in Congress; Congress may override the president's veto with a two-thirds vote in each chamber, a very difficult task.

3. The president can wait the full ten days, at the end of which time the bill becomes law without his signature if Congress is still in session.

4. If the Congress adjourns before the ten days are up, the president can choose not to sign the bill, and it is considered pocket vetoed.

A **pocket veto** figuratively allows bills stashed in the president's pocket to die. The only way for a bill then to become law is for it to be reintroduced in the next session and be put through the process all over again. Because Congress sets its own date of adjournment, technically the session could be continued the few extra days necessary to prevent a pocket veto. Extensions are unlikely, however, as sessions are scheduled to adjourn close to the November elections or the December holidays.

HOW A BILL REALLY BECOMES A LAW: THE CHINA TRADE ACT OF 2000

For each bill introduced in Congress, enactment is a long shot. A bill's supporters struggle to get from filing in both houses of Congress to the president's signature, and

filibuster
A formal way of halting action on a bill by means of long speeches or unlimited debate in the Senate.

cloture
Mechanism requiring sixty senators to vote to cut off debate.

veto
Formal constitutional authority of the president to reject bills passed by both houses of the legislative body, thus preventing their becoming law without further congressional activity.

pocket veto
If Congress adjourns during the ten days the president has to consider a bill passed by both houses of Congress, without the president's signature, the bill is considered vetoed.

American Values/American Voices

THE GANG OF FOURTEEN AND THE SEARCH FOR COMPROMISE

In early 2005, a bipartisan group of moderate senators successfully came together to negotiate a compromise over what was being called the "nuclear option" to abolish the filibuster.[a] The Gang of Fourteen, composed of seven Republicans and seven Democrats, led by Ben Nelson (D–NE) and John McCain (R–AZ), are sometimes called the "Mod Squad," as they are considered the Senate's moderates and often hold the power to cast the deciding votes on controversial pieces of legislation. By coming together, they effectively barred any change in Senate rules concerning the filibuster and forestalled the potential use of the nuclear option that would have allowed cloture on a filibuster to be ended by a simple majority vote, not the sixty votes required by current Senate rules.[b]

The group believes there is safety in numbers as its members often find themselves at odds with their increasingly partisan parties. As Democrats and Republicans have moved to the left and right respectively, the Gang of Fourteen argues that they more truly reflect American values and that it is their responsibility to give voice and power to the wishes of most Americans whose views, as reported by public opinion polls, are far more centrist than those of most elected officials in Washington, D.C.

In 2005, as acrimony increased in the Senate over the Democrats' use of the filibuster to prevent Senate votes on several controversial Bush administration nominees for vacancies on the federal courts, the Gang of Fourteen played an important role by entering into an agreement whereby the seven Democrats would no longer vote along with their party on filibustering judicial nominees except in "extraordinary circumstances." In turn, the seven Republicans would break with the Republican leadership and vote against the "nuclear option" if it was invoked. Because the Republicans' majority was so slim, the agreement effectively stopped the Republican leadership from changing Senate rules. More-

over, it prevented the Democrats from gaining the forty-one votes necessary to uphold a filibuster.

The informal group sprang to action again in July 2005, when it tried to advise President Bush on the choice of a nominee to replace retiring Supreme Court Justice Sandra Day O'Connor. In November 2005, the group met to discuss the nomination of Samuel A. Alito Jr. to the Supreme Court, and in January 2006, the members of the group unanimously supported a cloture vote in the Alito nomination, providing more than enough votes to prevent a filibuster. Alito was confirmed to take the much more moderate Justice O'Connor's place on the Court.

Many commentators now believe that in spite of their bipartisan intentions the "Gang of Fourteen" facilitated the confirmation of two conservatives to the Supreme Court—Alito and the new Chief Justice John G. Roberts Jr.—perhaps altering that Court's stance on a host of issues. Early votes by Roberts and Alito, especially in areas of criminal defendants' rights, support that view. Still, most Americans prefer not to see criminals go free over procedural issues. Thus, by facilitating the confirmation of these justices, the Gang of Fourteen may have been the true voice of American values in the Senate. In 2006, two Republicans in the Gang of Fourteen were defeated—Lincoln Chafee (R–RI) and Mike DeWine (R–OH). Joe Lieberman (D–CT) lost the Democratic primary but won in the general election. While the Gang of Fourteen has dissolved, the 2006 elections showed that the American public may largely prefer more moderate values.

[a]Jackie Kucinich and Jeffrey Young, "Social Security Is Next for Gang of Fourteen," *The Hill* (May 25, 2005): 1.

[b]James Kuhnhenn, "Appeals Picks Renew Battle: 'Gang of 14' May Intercede on 2 Judicial Nominees," *Pittsburgh Post-Gazette* (May 10, 2006): A8.

each bill follows a unique course. The progress of the trade legislation described below is probably even quirkier than most bills that actually become law.

Under the Trade Act of 1974, part of a two-decades-old American Cold War policy, the president of the United States was empowered to grant any nation "most favored" trade status, a designation that brings favorable U.S. tariff treatment. By law, however, the president was limited to extending that status to communist countries on a year by year (instead of permanent) basis subject to congressional review. Thus, since passage of that act, China, as a communist nation, could receive this status only a year at a time, even though it provided a huge potential market for U.S. goods. President Bill Clinton and many members of the business community wanted this year by year reauthorization dropped once China was scheduled to join the World Trade Organization. To do that required a new act of Congress. Ironically, the Clinton administration's push for this bill also allied President Clinton with many Republicans who favored opening trade to a nation with billions of new consumers. Many of the Republicans' biggest financial and political supporters would benefit from opening Chinese markets and removing barriers to service providers such as banks and telecommunications companies. In contrast, unions, a traditionally Democratic constituency, feared further loss of jobs to foreign shores.

Legislation to extend what is called permanent normal trade relations (PNTR) was viewed by Clinton as a means of putting "his imprint on foreign policy [as] the president who cemented in place the post-Cold-War experiment of using economic engagement to foster political change among America's neighbors and its potential adversaries."[51] He had begun this effort in 1993 after he pushed through Congress passage of the North American Free Trade Agreement (NAFTA) with Mexico and Canada. Now, as his time in office was coming to an end, he wanted Congress to act to allow him to cement PNTR with China.

As soon as the United States completed a bilateral agreement to make China a member of the World Trade Organization in November 1999 and early 2000, Clinton met with more than one hundred lawmakers individually or in groups, called scores more on the phone, and traveled to the Midwest and California to build support for the proposed legislation, which was necessary to implement this agreement. While Clinton was setting the stage for congressional action, the U.S. Chamber of Commerce and the Business Roundtable launched a $10 million ad campaign—the largest ever for a single legislative issue.[52]

On March 8, 2000, Clinton transmitted the text of legislation he was requesting to Congress. This proposed legislation, called S 2277, was formally introduced in the Senate on March 23 by Senator William Roth Jr. (R–DE). It was then read twice and referred to the Finance Committee. In the House, hearings on the China trade policy were held throughout the spring, even before the Clinton legislation formally was introduced. Anticipating concern from colleagues about China's human rights abuses, labor market issues, and the rule of law, some members proposed that Congress create (under separate legislation) a U.S. Congressional-Executive Commission on China to monitor those issues. HR 4444, the bill that Clinton sought, was introduced formally in the House on May 15, 2000, by Representative Bill Archer (R–TX). It was referred to the House Ways and Means Committee shortly thereafter and a mark-up session was held on May 17. It was reported out of committee on the same day by a vote of 34–4. On May 23, 2000, HR 4444 received a rule from the Committee on Rules allowing for three hours of debate. The bill was closed to amendments except motions to recommit, and the House Republican leadership "closed ranks behind the bill," claiming that economic change would foster political change.[53] But, they still had to sell this idea to their colleagues, many of whom balked at extending trade advantages to a communist government with a history of rights violations, including religious persecution and the denial of political rights to many. The rights legislation was designed to assuage those fears.

While the House Committee on International Relations was holding hearings (and even before), the Clinton administration sprang into action. Secretary of Commerce William Daley and several other Cabinet members were sent out to say the same thing over and over again: the bill will mean jobs for Americans and stability in Asia. Republican leaders got Chinese dissidents to say that the bill would improve human rights in China, and televangelist Billy Graham was recruited by the leadership to endorse the measure. At the same time, interest groups on both sides of the debate rushed to convince legislators to support their respective positions. Organized labor, still stinging from its NAFTA loss, was the biggest opponent of the bill. Teamsters and members of the United Auto Workers roamed the halls of Congress, trying to lobby members of the House.[54] Vice President Al Gore, knowing that he would need union support in the upcoming presidential election, broke ranks with the president and said that the bill would only serve to move American jobs to China.

On the other side, lobbyists from large corporations, including Procter & Gamble, and interest groups such as the Business Roundtable, used their cell phones and personal contacts to cajole legislators. "It's like a big wave hitting the shore," said one uncommitted Republican legislator from Staten Island, New York.[55] For the first time, he was lobbied by rank-and-file office workers at the request of their corporate offices, as well as union members. Another member of Congress was contacted by former President George Bush and Secretary of Defense William Cohen, and he received a special defense briefing from the Central Intelligence Agency. The president of the AFL-CIO also personally visited him. All stops were out, and this was the kind of treatment most undecided members received.

House debate on the bill began on May 24, 2000. That morning, House Republican Whip Tom DeLay (R–TX) didn't know if he had enough votes to support the measure to ensure its passage. The bare minimum he needed was 150 Republicans if he was to push the bill over the top.[56] DeLay lined up lots of assistance. Somewhat ironically, Texas Governor George W. Bush and retired General Colin Powell were enlisted to help convince wavering Republicans to support the Democratic president's goals. Powell, in particular, was called on to assuage national security concerns of several conservative representatives. Scores of pro-trade lobbyists spread out over Capitol Hill like locusts looking to light on any wavering legislators. A last-minute amendment to create a twenty-three-member commission to monitor human rights and a second to monitor surges in Chinese imports helped garner the votes of at least twenty more legislators.

Debate then came on a motion from House Democratic Whip David Bonior (D–MI) to recommit the bill to the Ways and Means and International Relations Committees to give them the opportunity to add an amendment to the bill to provide conditions under which withdrawals of normal trade relations with China could occur should China attack or invade Taiwan. This motion failed on a vote of 176–258. As lobbyists stepped up their efforts, their actions and those of the Republican leadership and the Clinton administration bore fruit. Every single uncommitted Republican voted for the bill, joining seventy-three Democrats to grant China permanent normal trade status as the bill passed by a surprisingly large margin of 237–197. "Frankly, they surprised me a bit. Members in the last few hours really turned around and understood how important this was," said DeLay. Stunned labor leaders admitted that they were outgunned. "The business community unleashed an unprecedented campaign that was hard for anyone to match," said the president of the United Auto Workers.[57]

As the bill was transmitted to the Senate, critics sprang into action. Senator Jesse Helms (R–NC), chair of the Foreign Relations Committee and a major critic of the Beijing government, immediately put fellow Republicans on notice that he would not rubber stamp the actions of the House. Although amendments were not allowed in the House, Senate rules that permit amendment were seen as a way of changing the nature of the bill and causing the amended version to go back to the House for a vote. Secretary Daley immediately went to see the Senate majority leader and members of the Senate Finance Committee, which had jurisdiction over the bill, to ask their assistance in fending off amendments.

While hearings on China were being held in the House, the Senate Finance Committee had been considering the bill. Once it passed the House, however, it was reported out of the Senate Finance Committee immediately on May 25. On that day, Senators Fred Thompson (R–TN) and Robert Torricelli (D–NJ) held a press conference to announce that they would offer parallel legislation based on their concerns about Chinese proliferation of weapons of mass destruction to continue a yearly review of China as a condition of open trade with that nation. They viewed the opening of PNTR to China as a national security as well as a trade issue.

The Senate began debating S 2277 on July 26, 2000. The next day, after a filibuster was begun by several opponents of the bill, including Senators Robert Byrd (D–WV), Jesse Helms (R–NC), Barbara Mikulski (D–MD), and Ben Nighthorse Campbell (R–CO), a move to invoke cloture was brought by the majority leader and several others. Cloture then was invoked by a vote of 86–12, well over the sixty votes required. The Senate recessed shortly thereafter. Debate on S 2277 began anew on September 5, after the Labor Day recess. At that time, until the final vote on September 19, 2000, scores of amendments were offered by senators; all failed by various margins. On September 19, 2000, the bill passed without amendment on an 83–15 vote with most senators voting as they had done on the cloture motion. Throughout that period, however, lobbyists kept up their pressure on the committed to make sure that no amendments were added to the bill that would require House reconsideration.

The bill was signed by President Clinton on October 10, 2000, amid considerable fanfare. Throughout the course of this bill becoming law, Clinton used his office in a way reminiscent of Lyndon B. Johnson's cajoling of recalcitrant legislators. One member got a new zip code for a small town and another got a natural gas pipeline for his district.[58] In the end, these kinds of efforts were crucial to House passage of the bill.

China became a member of the World Trade Organization on December 11, 2001. On December 28, 2001, President George W. Bush signed a formal proclamation granting normal trading status to China, ending annual reviews. In 2004, however, the United States and the European Union lodged WTO complaints against China, charging that it had failed to fulfill promises to open its markets to other nations.[59] Complaints from Washington and around the world have continued since that time. In early 2006, for example, President Bush filed a complaint with the WTO charging that Chinese officials were not fully opening their markets to American auto parts and manufacturers.[60]

Congress and the President

THE CONSTITUTION ENVISIONED that the Congress and the president would have discrete powers and that one branch would be able to hold the other in check. Over the years, and especially since the 1930s, the president often has held the upper hand. In times of crisis or simply when it was unable to meet public demands for solutions, Congress willingly has handed over its authority to the chief executive. Even though the chief executive has been granted greater latitude, Congress does, of course, retain ultimate legislative authority to question executive actions and to halt administration activities by cutting off funds for programs a president wants. Congress also wields ultimate power over the president, since it can impeach and even remove him from office.

THE SHIFTING BALANCE OF POWER

The balance of power between Congress and the executive branch has seesawed over time. The post–Civil War Congress attempted to regain control of the vast executive powers that President Abraham Lincoln, recently slain, had assumed. Angered at the refusal of Lincoln's successor, Andrew Johnson, to go along with its radical "reforms" of the South, Congress passed the Tenure of Office Act, which prevented the president, under the threat of civil penalty, from removing any Cabinet-level appointees of the previous administration. Johnson accepted the challenge and fired Lincoln's secretary of war, who many believed was guilty of heinous war crimes. The House voted to impeach Johnson, but the desertion of a handful of Republican senators prevented him from being removed from office. (The effort fell short by one vote.) Nonetheless, the president's power had been greatly weakened, and the Congress again became the center of power and authority in the federal government.

Beginning in the early 1900s, however, a series of strong presidents acted at the expense of congressional power. Theodore Roosevelt, Franklin D. Roosevelt, and Lyndon B. Johnson viewed the presidency as carrying with it enormous powers. Especially since the presidency of Franklin D. Roosevelt, Congress has ceded to the president a major role in the legislative process. Today, Congress often finds itself responding to executive-branch proposals. Critics of Congress point to its slow and unwieldy nature as well as the complexity of national problems as reasons that it often does not seem to act on its own. Many commentators have concluded that this power void allowed President George W. Bush to claim unprecedented presidential powers, as is discussed further below and in chapter 8.

The Bush administration has made it clear, more than any administration before it, that it believes Congress has limited oversight function, especially in times of war. In a further display of dominance, the Bush administration, which has refused to honor sub-poenas for information from Congress, was the first administration to enter a member of Congress's office to execute a search warrant. Eighteen FBI agents searched the office of Representative William J. Jefferson (D–LA) and removed files as part of an investigation of bribe-taking. This unprecedented action was criticized by House Speaker Dennis Hastert (R–IL), who "pushed Bush strongly on the issue" while on Air Force One.[61]

CONGRESSIONAL OVERSIGHT OF THE EXECUTIVE BRANCH

oversight
Congressional review of the activities of an agency, department, or office.

From the the 1960s through the election of President George W. Bush, Congress increased its **oversight** of the executive branch.[62] Oversight subcommittees became particularly prominent in the 1970s and 1980s as a means of promoting investigation and program review, to determine if an agency, department, or office is carrying out its responsibilities as intended by Congress.[63] Congressional oversight also includes checking on possible abuses of power by members of the military and governmental officials, including the president. The Republican-controlled Congress was especially mindful of its oversight duties during the Clinton administration. Not only did it regularly hold oversight hearings involving Cabinet secretaries, but it also launched several investigations of the Clintons' themselves, such as Travelgate, their investments in a failed Whitewater development in Arkansas, and, of course, President Bill Clinton's involvement with Monica Lewinsky that led to his impeachment in the House and trial in the Senate.

Historically, key to Congress's performance of its oversight function is its ability to question members of the administration to see if they are enforcing and interpreting the laws as intended by Congress. These committee hearings, now routinely televised, are among Congress's most visible and dramatic actions. The hearings are not used simply to gather information. Hearings may focus on particular executive-branch actions and often signal that Congress believes changes in policy need to be made before an agency next comes before the committee to justify its budget. Hearings also are used to improve program administration. Since most members of House and Senate committees and subcommittees are interested in the issues under their jurisdiction, they often want to help and not hinder policy makers.

Although most top government officials appear before various House and Senate committees regularly to update them on their activities, this is not necessarily the case for those who do not require Senate confirmation. Moreover, sometimes members of the administration are reluctant to appear before Congress.

With the election of President George W. Bush, a highly partisan, Republican-controlled Congress worked to lessen the oversight role of Congress as "centralized power was deployed uncritically in the service of the White House agenda."[64] A bipartisan team of congressional scholars concluded that the Bush administration has preferred to keep Democratic lawmakers out of the loop, and has "aggressively fought to expand executive power vis-à-vis congress. . . . Strong majority leadership in Congress has not led to vigorous exercise of Congressional authority and responsibility but to a general obeisance to presidential initiative and passivity in the face of presidential power."[65]

Thus, the Bush years have seen an unprecedented decline in congressional oversight. Democrats have been increasingly frus-

Photo courtesy: Chip Somodevilla/Getty Images

■ Then Senate Armed Services Committee Chairman John Warner (R–VA), committee ranking Democrat Carl Levin (D–MI), and committee members Senator Robert Byrd (D–WV) and Senator John McCain (R–AZ) caucus before holding a markup hearing about legislation related to military tribunals for enemy combatants and terrorism suspects on September 14, 2006. While some members of the committee fought for legislation that did not provide the far-reaching authority sought by the White House after the Supreme Court's ruling in Hamdan v. Rumsfeld (2006), the final legislation that was passed, the Military Commissions Act of 2006, provides the president with unprecedented powers to detain and interrogate citizens and non-citizens accused of terrorism. While some observers believed that the compromise eventually worked out between the White House and members of Congress indicated appropriate congressional oversight, others believe that a number of the act's provisions are unconstitutional.

trated by what they perceive as the majority's failure to investigate thoroughly a host of issues, including the September 11 terrorist attacks, Medicare prescription drug costs, abuse of detainees in Iraq and Afghanistan, and government failures in responding to Hurricanes Katrina and Rita. The 2007 Democratic House and Senate are likely to act immediately to reassert their responsibility to exercise this important constitutional check on the executive branch.

As Congress has moved to reclaim its traditional oversight function, members have additional means of oversight at their disposal. Legislators may augment their formal oversight of the executive branch by allowing citizens to appeal adverse bureaucratic decisions to agencies, Congress, and even the courts. The Congressional Review Act of 1996 allows Congress to nullify agency regulations by joint resolutions of legislative disapproval. This process, called **congressional review,** is another method of exercising congressional oversight.[66] The act provides Congress with sixty days to disapprove newly announced agency regulations, often passed to implement some congressional action. A regulation is disapproved if the resolution is passed by both chambers and signed by the president, or when Congress overrides a presidential veto of a disapproving resolution. Since its passage, only thirty-seven joint resolutions of disapproval relating to twenty-eight rules have been introduced.[67] To date, this act has been used only once—in 2001—when Congress reversed Clinton administration ergonomics regulations, which were intended to prevent job-related repetitive stress injuries.

Foreign Policy and National Security

The Constitution divides foreign policy powers between the executive and the legislative branches. The president has the power to wage war and negotiate treaties, whereas the Congress has the power to declare war and the Senate has the power to ratify treaties. The executive branch, however, has become preeminent in foreign affairs despite the constitutional division of powers. This supremacy is partly due to a series of crises and the development of nuclear weapons in the twentieth century; both have necessitated quick decision making and secrecy, which are much easier to manage in the executive branch. Congress, with its 535 voting members, has a more difficult time reaching a consensus and keeping secrets.

After years of playing second fiddle to a series of presidents from Theodore Roosevelt to Richard M. Nixon, a "snoozing Congress" was "aroused" and seized for itself the authority and expertise necessary to go head to head with the chief executive.[68] In a delayed response to Lyndon B. Johnson's conduct of the Vietnam War, in 1973 Congress passed the **War Powers Act** over President Nixon's veto. This act requires presidents to obtain congressional approval before committing U.S. forces to a combat zone. It also requires them to notify Congress within forty-eight hours of committing troops to foreign soil. In addition, the president must withdraw troops within sixty days unless Congress votes to declare war. The president also is required to consult with Congress, if at all possible, prior to committing troops.

The War Powers Act has been of limited effectiveness in claiming a larger congressional role in international crisis situations. Presidents Gerald Ford, Jimmy Carter, and Ronald Reagan never consulted Congress in advance of committing troops, citing the need for secrecy and swift movement, although each president did notify Congress shortly after the incidents. They contended that the War Powers Act was probably unconstitutional because it limits presidential prerogatives as commander in chief.

In 2001, when Congress passed a joint resolution authorizing the president to use force against terrorists, the resolution included language that met War Powers Act requirements and waived the sixty-day limit on the president's authority to involve U.S. troops abroad. This action prompted two senators who served in Vietnam, John McCain (R–AZ) and John Kerry (D–MA), to express concern over handing the president such open-ended use of military force. These concerns may have been valid, as some critics say President Bush took the congressional resolution as a blank check. Said one high-ranking Department of Justice official, "the president enjoys broad unilateral authority to use force in the war on terrorism—with or without specific congressional authorization."[69]

congressional review
A process whereby Congress can nullify agency regulations by a joint resolution of legislative disapproval.

War Powers Act
Passed by Congress in 1973; the president is limited in the deployment of troops overseas to a sixty-day period in peacetime (which can be extended for an extra thirty days to permit withdrawal) unless Congress explicitly gives its approval for a longer period.

Photo courtesy: left, Alex Wong/Getty Images; right: Office of Jay Rockefeller

July 17, 2003

Dear Mr. Vice President,

I am writing to reiterate my concerns regarding the sensitive intelligence issues we discussed today with the DCI, DIRNSA, Chairman Roberts and our House Intelligence Committee counterparts.

Most respectfully,

Jay Rockefeller

■ Senator Jay Rockefeller (D-WV) went public with his criticisms of the administration's domestic surveillance program in December of 2005. Rockefeller sent a handwritten letter voicing his concern to Vice President Cheney in 2003 (see excerpt at right), noting that he was placing a handwritten copy of the letter in a safe to insure that his concerns and recollection of events were recorded for posterity. When the administration subsequently argued that Congress had been adequately briefed on the program and implied members had raised no concerns about it, Rockefeller released his letter to the press.

The issue of oversight has become particularly thorny in a nation at war. As early as July 17, 2003, for example, Senator Jay Rockefeller (D–WV), the ranking member on the Senate Intelligence Committee, wrote to Vice President Dick Cheney that he was very troubled by what he had heard at a secret intelligence briefing. These secret briefings, which usually involved the White House revealing information to House and Senate members on the respective Intelligence Committees, are part of the oversight process, yet committee members are prohibited from telling anyone—even other members of Congress or key staffers—of the contents of the meetings. At this particular briefing, Rockefeller had been apprised that the National Security Agency was monitoring Americans' phone and e-mail communications without the judicial oversight called for by law. "Clearly," wrote Rockefeller, "the activities we discussed raise profound oversight issues."[70]

Confirmation of Presidential Appointments The Senate plays a special oversight function through its ability to confirm key members of the executive branch, as well as presidential appointments to the federal courts. As discussed in chapters 9 and 10, although the Senate generally confirms most presidential nominees, it does not always do so. A wise president considers senatorial reaction before nominating potentially controversial individuals to his administration or to the federal courts.

The Impeachment Process As discussed earlier, the impeachment process is Congress's ultimate oversight of the U.S. president (as well as of federal court judges). The U.S. Constitution is quite vague about the impeachment process, and much of the debate about it concerns what is an impeachable offense. The Constitution specifies that a president can be impeached for treason, bribery, or other "high crimes and misdemeanors." Most commentators agree that this phrase was meant to mean significant abuses of power. In *Federalist No. 65*, Alexander Hamilton noted his belief that impeachable offenses "are of a nature which may with peculiar propriety be denominated political, as they relate chiefly to injuries done immediately to society itself."

House and Senate rules control how the impeachment process operates (see Table 7.7). Yet, because the process is used so rarely, and under such disparate circumstances, there are few hard and fast rules. The U.S. House of Representatives has voted to impeach only seventeen federal officials. (Of those, seven were convicted and removed from office and three resigned before the process described below was completed.)

Only four resolutions against presidents have resulted in further action: (1) John Tyler, charged with corruption and misconduct in 1843; (2) Andrew Johnson, charged with serious misconduct in 1868; (3) Richard M. Nixon, charged with obstruction and the abuse of power in 1974; and, (4) Bill Clinton, charged with perjury and obstruction of justice in 1998. The House rejected the charges against Tyler; Johnson was acquitted

TABLE 7.7 THE EIGHT STAGES OF THE IMPEACHMENT PROCESS

1. **The Resolution.** A resolution, called an inquiry of impeachment, is sent to the House Judiciary Committee. Members also may introduce bills of impeachment, which are referred to the Judiciary Committee.
2. **The Committee Vote.** After the consideration of voluminous evidence, the Judiciary Committee votes on the resolution or bill of impeachment. A positive vote from the committee indicates its belief that there is sufficiently strong evidence for impeachment in the House.
3. **The House Vote.** If the articles of impeachment are recommended by the House Judiciary Committee, the full House votes to approve (or disapprove) a Judiciary Committee decision to conduct full-blown impeachment hearings.
4. **The Hearings.** Extensive evidentiary hearings are held by the House Judiciary Committee concerning the allegations of wrongdoing. Witnesses may be called and the scope of the inquiry may be widened at this time. The committee heard only from the independent counsel in the Clinton case.
5. **The Report.** The committee votes on one or more articles of impeachment. Reports supporting this finding (as well as dissenting views) are forwarded to the House and become the basis for its consideration of specific articles of impeachment.
6. **The House Vote.** The full House votes on each article of impeachment. A simple majority vote on any article is sufficient to send that article to the Senate for its consideration.
7. **The Trial in the Senate.** A trial is conducted on the floor of the Senate with the House Judiciary Committee bringing the case against the president, who is represented by his own private attorneys. The Senate, in essence, acts as the jury, with the chief justice of the United States presiding over the trial.
8. **The Senate Vote.** The full Senate votes on each article of impeachment. If there is a two-thirds vote on any article, the president automatically is removed from office and the vice president assumes the duty of the president. Both articles issued against President Clinton, charging him with lying to a grand jury and encouraging a grand jury witness to lie or mislead, were defeated in the Senate.

by the Senate by a one-vote margin; Nixon resigned before the full House voted on the articles of impeachment; and Clinton was acquitted by the Senate.

Congress and the Judiciary

AS PART OF OUR SYSTEM of checks and balances, the power of judicial review (discussed in chapters 2 and 10) gives the Supreme Court the power to review the constitutionality of acts of Congress. This is a potent power because Congress must ever be mindful to make sure that the laws that it passes are in accord with the U.S. Constitution. That is not to say, however, that Congress always does this. In spite of a 2000 Supreme Court case that indicated that a Nebraska state law banning partial birth abortion was unconstitutional, the U.S. Congress passed its own version outlawing the procedure despite extensive commentary that it would also be declared unconstitutional. Proponents wanted to get other members on record about their support or lack of support before the 2004 elections so that the issue could be used by Republicans to highlight the votes of Democrats—including John Kerry and John Edwards, who voted against the bill.

Congress exercises its control over the judiciary in a variety of ways. Not only does it have the constitutional authority to establish the size of the Supreme Court, its appellate jurisdiction, and the structure of the federal court system, and to allocate its budget, but the Senate also has the authority to accept or reject presidential nominees to the federal courts (as well as executive branch appointments).

In the case of federal district court appointments, senators often have considerable say in the nomination of judges from their states through **senatorial courtesy,** a process by which presidents generally defer to the senators who represent the state where the vacancy occurs. The judicial nominees of both Presidents Bill Clinton and George W. Bush have encountered a particularly hostile Senate. "Appointments have always been the battleground for policy disputes," says one political scientist. But now, "what's new is the rawness of it—all of the veneer is off."[71] (Nominations to the Supreme Court and lower federal courts are discussed in chapter 10.)

An equally potent form of congressional oversight of the judicial branch that involves both the House and the Senate is the setting of the jurisdiction of the federal courts.

senatorial courtesy
A process by which presidents, when selecting district court judges, defer to the senator in whose state the vacancy occurs.

Originally, the jurisdiction, or ability of the federal courts to hear cases, was quite limited. Over time, however, as Congress legislated to regulate the economy and even crime, the caseload of the courts skyrocketed. No matter how busy federal judges are, it is ultimately up to the Congress to determine the number of judges on each court.

During the 109th Congress, several members, unhappy with Supreme Court decisions and the Senate's failure to pass a proposed constitutional amendment to ban same-sex marriage, began to push for a bill to prevent federal courts from hearing challenges to the federal Defense of Marriage Act. In the House, the majority leader pledged to promote similar legislation to bar court challenges to the Pledge of Allegiance and other social issues, including abortion. When Congress rears the ugly head of jurisdiction, it is signaling to the federal courts that Congress believes federal judges have gone too far.

Summary

THE SIZE AND SCOPE OF CONGRESS, and the demands put on it, have increased tremendously over the years. In presenting the important role that Congress plays in American politics, we have made the following points:

1. **The Constitution and the Legislative Branch of Government**
The Constitution created a bicameral legislature with members of each body to be elected differently, and thus to represent different constituencies. Article I of the Constitution sets forth qualifications for office, states age minimums, and specifies how legislators are to be distributed among the states. The Constitution also requires seats in the House of Representatives to be apportioned by population. Thus, after every U.S. Census, district lines must be redrawn to reflect population shifts. The Constitution also provides a vast array of enumerated and implied powers to Congress. Some, such as law-making and oversight, are shared by both houses of Congress; others are not.

2. **How Congress Is Organized**
Political parties play a major role in the way Congress is organized. The Speaker of the House is traditionally a member of the majority party, and members of the majority party chair all committees. Because the House of Representatives is large, the Speaker enforces more rigid rules on the House than exist in the Senate. In addition to the party leaders, Congress has a labyrinth of committees and subcommittees that cover the entire range of government policies, often with a confusing tangle of shared responsibilities. Each legislator serves on one or more committees and multiple subcommittees. It is in these environments that many policies are shaped and that members make their primary contributions to solving public problems.

3. **The Members of Congress**
Members of Congress live in two worlds—in their home districts and in the District of Columbia. They must attempt to appease two constituencies—party leaders, colleagues, and lobbyists in Washington, D.C., and constituents in their home districts. Members, especially those in the House, never stop running for office. Incumbency is an important factor in winning reelection.

4. **How Members Make Decisions**
A multitude of factors affect legislators as they decide policy issues. These include political party, constituents, colleagues and caucuses, staff and support agencies and interest groups, lobbyists, and political action committees.

5. **The Law-making Function of Congress**
The road to enacting a bill into law is long and strewn with obstacles, and only a small share of the proposals introduced become law. Legislation must be approved by committees in each house and on the floor of each chamber. In addition, most House legislation initially is considered by a subcommittee and must be approved by the House Committee on Rules before getting to the floor. Legislation that is passed in different forms by the two chambers must be resolved in a conference before going back to each chamber for a vote and then to the president, who can sign the proposal into law, veto it, or allow it to become law without his signature. If Congress adjourns within ten days of passing legislation, that bill will die if the president does not sign it.

6. **Congress and the President**
Although the Framers intended for Congress and the president to have discrete spheres of authority, over time, power shifted between the two branches, with Congress often appearing to lose power to the benefit of the president. Still, Congress has attempted to oversee the actions of the president and the executive branch through committee hearings where members of the administration testify. Congress also uses congressional review to limit presidential power. Congress also has attempted to rein in presidential power through passage of the War Powers Act, to little practical effect. Congress, through the Senate, also possesses the power to confirm or reject presidential appointments. Its ultimate weapon is the power of impeachment and conviction.

7. **Congress and the Judiciary**
Congress exercises its control over the judiciary in a variety of ways. Not only does it have the constitutional authority to establish the size of the Supreme Court, its

appellate jurisdiction, and the structure of the federal court system, but the Senate also has the authority to accept or reject presidential nominees to the federal courts (as well as executive branch appointments).

KEY TERMS

apportionment, p. 241

bicameral legislature, p. 240

bill, p. 242

cloture, p. 267

conference committee, p. 251

congressional review, p. 273

delegate, p. 259

discharge petition, p. 252

divided government, p. 261

earmark, p. 253

filibuster, p. 267

hold, p. 266

impeachment, p. 242

incumbency, p. 256

joint committee, p. 251

logrolling, p. 262

majority leader, p. 248

majority party, p. 243

markup, p. 265

minority leader, p. 249

minority party, p. 243

oversight, p. 272

party caucus or conference, p. 248

pocket veto, p. 267

politico, p. 260

pork, p. 253

president pro tempore, p. 250

redistricting, p. 241

select (or special) committee, p. 251

senatorial courtesy, p. 275

seniority, p. 254

Speaker of the House, p. 247

standing committee, p. 251

trustee, p. 259

veto, p. 267

War Powers Act, p. 273

whip, p. 249

SELECTED READINGS

Adler, E. Scott, and John S. Lapinski. *The Macropolitics of Congress.* Princeton, NJ: Princeton University Press, 2006.

Bianco, William T., ed. *Congress on Display, Congress at Work.* Ann Arbor: University of Michigan Press, 2000.

Binder, Sarah A. *Stalemate: Causes and Consequences of Legislative Gridlock.* Washington, DC: Brookings Institute, 2003.

Campbell, Colton C., and Paul S. Herrnson. *War Stories from Capitol Hill.* New York: Pearson, 2003.

Cox, Gary W., and Matthew D. McCubbins. *Setting the Agenda: Responsible Party Government in the U.S. House of Representatives.* New York: Cambridge University Press, 2005.

Davidson, Roger H., and Walter Oleszek. *Congress and Its Members,* 10th ed. Washington, DC: CQ Press, 2005.

Deering, Christopher J., and Steven S. Smith, *Committees in Congress,* 3rd ed. Washington, DC: CQ Press, 1997.

Dodd, Lawrence C., and Bruce I. Oppenheimer, eds. *Congress Reconsidered,* 8th ed. Washington, DC: CQ Press, 2004.

Evans, Diana. *Greasing the Wheels: Using Pork Barrel Projects to Build Majority Coalitions in Congress.* New York: Cambridge University Press, 2004.

Fenno, Richard F., Jr. *Going Home: Black Representatives and Their Constituents.* Chicago: University of Chicago Press, 2003.

———— *Home Style: House Members in Their Districts,* reprint ed. New York: Longman, 2002.

Gertzog, Irwin N. *Women and Power on Capitol Hill: Reconstructing the Congressional Women's Caucus.* Boulder, CO: Lynne Rienner, 2004.

Mayhew, David R. *Congress: The Electoral Connection.* New Haven, CT: Yale University Press, 1974.

O'Connor, Karen, ed. *Women in Congress: Running, Winning, and Ruling.* New York: Haworth, 2004.

Oleszek, Walter J. *Congressional Procedures and the Policy Process,* 6th ed. Washington, DC: CQ Press, 2004.

Polsby, Nelson W. *How Congress Evolves: Social Bases of Institutional Changes,* new ed. New York: Oxford University Press, 2005.

Price, David E. *The Congressional Experience: A View from the Hill,* 3rd ed. Boulder, CO: Westview, 2005.

Quirk, Paul J., and Sarah A. Binder, eds. *Institutions of American Democracy: The Legislative Branch.* New York: Oxford University Press, 2006.

Quirk, Paul J., Sarah A. Binder, and Bert Rockman, eds. *Handbook of Political Institutions.* New York: Oxford University Press, 2006.

Rosenthal, Cindy Simon, ed. *Women Transforming Congress.* Norman: University of Oklahoma Press, 2003.

Schickler, Eric. *Disjointed Pluralism: Institutional Innovation and the Development of the U.S. Congress.* Princeton, NJ: Princeton University Press, 2001.

Swers, Michele. *The Difference Women Make: The Policy Impact of Women in Congress.* Chicago: University of Chicago Press, 2002.

Thurber, James A., ed. *Rivals for Power: Congressional Presidential Relations.* Lanham, MD: Rowman and Littlefield, 2001.

WEB EXPLORATIONS

To find out who your representative is and how he or she votes, see
http://www.thomas.loc.gov

To learn more about the legislative branch, see
www.senate.gov and
www.house.gov

To evaluate your own representative, see
http://scorecard.aclu.org/scorecardmain.html

To learn more about the 109th and 110th Congress, see
http://clerk.house.gov

For more on the offices of the Congress, including the Speaker of the House and his or her activities, see
http://speakernews.house.gov

For more information on minority-party rights and the Senate filibuster, see
http://www.americanprogress.org and
http://www.brookings.edu

Photo courtesy: Dennis Brack

THE PRESIDENCY

WHEN RONALD REAGAN DIED on June 5, 2004, many Americans, first in California and then in Washington, D.C., lined up for hours to pay their respects to the man who had been the fortieth president of the United States. Many people were able to see, for the first time in recent memory, the grandeur of a presidential state funeral. Reagan was the first president to lie in state in the Rotunda of the Capitol since Lyndon B. Johnson did in January 1973, and one of only nine American presidents to receive that honor.

The 200 plus years of presidential funerals underscore the esteem with which most Americans accord the office of the president, regardless of its occupant. Just before the first president, George Washington, died, he made it known that he wanted his burial to be a quiet one, "without parade or funeral oration." He also asked that he not be buried for three days; at that time, it was not without precedent to make this kind of request out of fear of being buried alive. Despite these requests, Washington's funeral was a state occasion as hundreds of soldiers, with their rifles held backward, marched to Mount Vernon, Virginia, where he was interred. Across the nation, imitation funerals were held, and the military wore black arm bands for six months.[1] It was during Washington's memorial service that Henry Lee declared that the former president was "first in war, first in peace, and first in the hearts of his countrymen."[2]

When Abraham Lincoln died in 1865 after being wounded by an assassin's bullet, more than a dozen funerals were held for him. Hundreds of thousands of mourners lined the way as the train carrying his open casket traveled the 1,700 miles to Illinois, where he was buried next to the body of his young son, who had died three years earlier. Most president's bodies were transported to their final resting place by train, allowing ordinary Americans the opportunity to pay their respects as the train traveled long distances. When Franklin D. Roosevelt died in Warm Springs, Georgia, his body was transported to Washington, D.C., and then to Hyde Park, New York, where he, like Washington, was buried on his family's estate.

Today, one of the first things a president is asked to do upon taking office is to consider his funeral plans. The military has a book 138 pages long devoted to the kind of ceremony and traditions that were so evident in the Reagan funeral: a horse-drawn caisson; a riderless horse with boots hung backward in the stirrups to indicate that the deceased will ride no more; a

CHAPTER OUTLINE

- ⭐ The Origins of and Rules Governing the Office of President of the United States

- ⭐ The Constitutional Powers of the President

- ⭐ The Development and Expansion of Presidential Power

- ⭐ The Presidential Establishment

- ⭐ The President as Policy Maker

- ⭐ Presidential Leadership and the Importance of Public Opinion

twenty-one-gun salute; a flyover by military aircraft. Each president's family, however, has personalized their private, yet also public opportunity to mourn. The Reagan family, for example, filed a 300-page plan for the funeral in 1989 and updated it regularly. Former presidents Gerald R. Ford, Jimmy Carter, and George Bush all have filed formal plans; Bill Clinton and George W. Bush have yet to do so.

The Reagan funeral also created a national time-out from the news of war, and even presidential campaigns were halted in respect for the deceased president. One historian commented that the event gave Americans the opportunity to "rediscover . . . what holds us together instead of what pulls us apart."[3] This is often the role of presidents—in life or in death.

VIDEO DEBATE

Presidential Power

THE AUTHORITY GRANTED TO the president by the U.S. Constitution and through subsequent congressional legislation makes it a position with awesome power and responsibility. Not only did the Framers not envision such a powerful role for the president, but they could not have foreseen the skepticism with which many presidential actions are now greeted in the press, on talk radio, and on the Internet. Presidents have gone into policy arenas never dreamed of by the Framers. Imagine, for example, what the Framers might have thought about President Bush's 2004 State of the Union message, in which he advocated colonizing Mars and addressed steroid use, or his 2006 address, in which he asked legislators to prohibit "the most egregious abuse of medical research—human cloning."

The modern media, used by successful presidents to help advance their agendas, have brought us closer to our presidents and made them seem more human, a mixed blessing for those trying to lead. Only two photographs exist of Franklin D. Roosevelt in a wheelchair—his paralysis was a closely guarded secret. Five decades later, Bill Clinton was asked on national TV what kind of underwear he preferred (briefs). Later, revelations about his conduct with Monica Lewinsky made this disclosure seem tame. This demystifying of the office of the president and increasing mistrust of government make governing a difficult job.

A president relies on more than the formal powers of office to lead the nation: public opinion and public confidence are key components of his ability to get his programs adopted and his vision of the nation implemented. As political scientist Richard E. Neustadt has noted, the president's power often rests on his power to persuade.[4] To persuade, he not only must be able to forge links with members of Congress, but he also must have the support of the American people and the respect of foreign leaders.

The abilities to persuade and to marshal the informal powers of the presidency have become more important over time. In fact, the presidency of George W. Bush and the circumstances that surround it are dramatically different from the presidency of his father George Bush (1989–1993). America is changing dramatically and so are the responsibilities of the president and people's expectations of the person who holds that office. Presidents in the last century battled the Great Depression, fascism, communism, and several wars involving American soldiers. With the Cold War over, until the war in Iraq, there were few chances for modern presidents to demonstrate their leadership in a time of crisis or threat.

The tension between public expectations about the presidency and the formal powers of the president permeate our discussion of how the office has evolved from its humble origins in Article II of the Constitution to its current stature. In this chapter:

■ First, we will examine *the origins of and rules governing the office of president of the United States* and discuss how the Framers created a chief executive officer for the new nation.

- Second, we will discuss *the constitutional powers of the president.*

- Third, we will examine *the development and expansion of presidential power* and a more personalized presidency. How well a president is able to execute the laws often depends strongly on his personality, popularity, leadership style, and view of the scope of presidential authority.

- Fourth, we will discuss the development of what is called *the presidential establishment.* Myriad departments, special assistants, and a staff of advisers help the president but also make it easier for a president to lose touch with the common citizen.

- Fifth, we will focus on *the president as policy maker.*

- Finally, we will examine *presidential leadership and the importance of public opinion,* including the effect that public opinion has on the American presidency and the role the president plays in molding public opinion.

The Origins of and Rules Governing the Office of President of the United States

THE EARLIEST EXAMPLE OF EXECUTIVE POWER in the colonies was the position of royal governor. These appointees of the king of England governed each colony and normally were entrusted with the "powers of appointment, military command, expenditure, and—within limitations—pardon, as well as with large powers in connection with the powers of law making."[5] Royal governors often found themselves at odds with the colonists and especially with elected colonial legislatures. As representatives of the crown, the governors were distrusted and disdained by the people, many of whom had fled from Great Britain to escape royal domination. Others, generations removed from England, no longer felt strong ties to the king and his power over them.

When the colonists declared their independence from England in 1776, their distrust of a strong chief executive remained. Most state constitutions reduced the once-powerful office of governor to a symbolic post elected annually by the legislature. However, some states did entrust wider powers to their chief executives. The governor of New York, for example, was elected directly by the people. Perhaps because he then was accountable to the people, he was given the power to pardon, the duty to execute the laws faithfully to the best of his ability, and the power to act as commander in chief of the state militia.

Under the Articles of Confederation, there was no executive branch of government; the eighteen different men who served as the president of the Continental Congress of the United States of America were president in name only—they held no actual authority or power in the new nation. When the delegates to the Constitutional Convention met in Philadelphia to fashion a new government, there was little dissention about the need for an executive branch to implement the laws made by Congress. Although some delegates suggested there should be multiple executives, eventually the Framers agreed that executive authority should be vested in one person. This agreement was relatively seamless because the Framers were sure that George Washington—whom they had trusted with their lives during the Revolutionary War—would become the first president of the new nation.

The Framers also had no problem in agreeing on a title for the new office. Borrowing from the constitutions of several states, the Framers called the new chief executive the president. How the president was to be chosen and by whom was a major stumbling block. James Wilson of Philadelphia suggested a single, more powerful president, who would be elected by the people and "independent of the legislature." Wilson also suggested giving the executive an absolute veto over the acts of Congress.

"Without such a defense," he wrote, "the legislature can at any moment sink it [the executive] into non-existence."[6]

The manner of the president's election haunted the Framers for some time, and their solution to the dilemma—the creation of the Electoral College—is described in detail in chapter 13. We leave the resolution of that issue aside for now and turn instead to details of the issues the Framers resolved quickly.

PRESIDENTIAL QUALIFICATIONS AND TERMS OF OFFICE

Comparing Chief Executives

The Constitution requires that the president (and the vice president, whose major function is to succeed the president in the event of his death or disability) be a natural-born citizen of the United States, at least thirty-five years old, and a resident of the United States for at least fourteen years. In the 1700s, those engaged in international diplomacy were often out of the country for substantial periods of time, and the Framers wanted to make sure that prospective presidents spent significant time on this country's shores before running for its highest elective office. Most presidents have prior elective experience, too, as revealed in Table 8.1. While there is no constitutional bar to a woman or member of a minority group seeking the presidency, no one other than a white male has been elected to this office.

Although only two of the last five presidents failed to win election to a second term, at one time the length of a president's term was controversial. Four-, seven-, and eleven-year terms with no eligibility for reelection were suggested by various delegates to the Constitutional Convention. The Framers ultimately reached agreement on a four-year term with eligibility for reelection.

The first president, George Washington (1789–1797), sought reelection only once, and a two-term limit for presidents became traditional. Although Ulysses S. Grant unsuccessfully sought a third term, the two terms established by Washington remained the standard for 150 years, avoiding the Framers' much-feared "constitutional monarch," a perpetually reelected tyrant. In the 1930s and 1940s, however, Franklin D. Roosevelt ran successfully in four elections as Americans fought first the Great Depression and then World War II. Despite Roosevelt's popularity, negative reaction to his long tenure in office ultimately led to passage (and ratification in 1951) of the **Twenty-Second Amendment.** It limits presidents to two four-year terms. A vice president who succeeds a president due to death, resignation, or impeachment is eligible for a total of ten years in office: two years of a president's remaining term and two elected terms, or more than two years of a president's term followed by one elected term.

Twenty-Second Amendment Adopted in 1951, prevents a president from serving more than two terms, or more than ten years if he came to office via the death or impeachment of his predecessor.

■ Senator Hillary Rodham Clinton (D–NY) waves goodbye after addressing the Campaign For America's Future 2006 "Take Back America" conference in Washington, DC. Senator Clinton and Secretary of State Condoleezza Rice have both been discussed as potential contenders for the presidency in 2008.

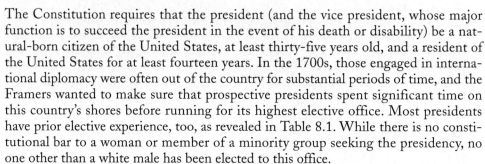

The Framers paid little attention to the office of vice president beyond the need to have an immediate official stand-in for the president. Initially, for example, the vice president's one and only function was to assume the office of president in the case of the death of the president or some other emergency. After further debate, the delegates made the vice president the presiding officer of the Senate (except in cases of presidential impeachment). They feared that if the Senate's presiding officer were chosen from the Senate itself, one state would be short a representative. However, the vice president was given the authority to vote in that body in the event of a tie.

Photo courtesy: Chip Somodevilla/Getty Images

TABLE 8.1   PERSONAL CHARACTERISTICS OF THE U.S.

President	Place of Birth	Higher Education	Occupation				
George Washington	VA	William & Mary	Farmer/surveyor				
John Adams	MA	Harvard	Farmer/lawyer				
Thomas Jefferson	VA	William & Mary	Farmer/lawyer				
James Madison	VA	Princeton	Farmer				
James Monroe	VA	William & Mary	Farmer/lawyer				
John Quincy Adams	MA	Harvard	Lawyer				
Andrew Jackson	SC	None	Lawyer				
Martin Van Buren	NY	None	Lawyer				
William H. Harrison	VA	Hampden	Military				
John Tyler	VA	William & Mary	Lawyer				
James K. Polk	NC	North Carolina	Lawyer				
Zachary Taylor	VA	None	Military				
Millard Fillmore	NY	None	Lawyer				
Franklin Pierce	NH	Bowdoin	Lawyer				
James Buchanan	PA	Dickinson	Lawyer				
Abraham Lincoln	KY	None	Lawyer				
Andrew Johnson	NC	None	Tailor	14	4		
Ulysses S. Grant	OH	West Point	Military	0	0	0	47
Rutherford B. Hayes	OH	Kenyon	Lawyer	3	6	0	55
James A. Garfield	OH	Williams	Educator/lawyer	18	0	0	50
Chester A. Arthur	VT	Union	Lawyer	0	0	1	51
Grover Cleveland	NJ	None	Lawyer	0	2	0	48
Benjamin Harrison	OH	Miami (Ohio)	Lawyer	6	0	0	56
Grover Cleveland	NJ	None	Lawyer	0	2	0	53
William McKinley	OH	Allegheny	Lawyer	14	4	0	54
Theodore Roosevelt	NY	Harvard	Lawyer/author	0	2	1	43
William H. Taft	OH	Yale	Lawyer	0	0	0	52
Woodrow Wilson	VA	Princeton	Educator	0	2	0	56
Warren G. Harding	OH	Ohio Central	Newspaper editor	6	0	0	56
Calvin Coolidge	VT	Amherst	Lawyer	0	2	3	51
Herbert Hoover	IA	Stanford	Engineer	0	0	0	55
Franklin D. Roosevelt	NY	Columbia	Lawyer	0	4	0	49
Harry S Truman	MO	None	Clerk/store owner	10	0	0	61
Dwight D. Eisenhower	TX	West Point	Military	0	0	0	63
John F. Kennedy	MA	Harvard	Journalist	14	0	0	43
Lyndon B. Johnson	TX	Southwest Texas State Teachers College	Educator	24	0	3	55
Richard M. Nixon	CA	Whittier/Duke	Lawyer	6	0	8	56
Gerald R. Ford	NE	Michigan/Yale	Lawyer	25	0	2	61
Jimmy Carter	GA	Naval Academy	Farmer/business owner	0	4	0	52
Ronald Reagan	IL	Eureka	Actor	0	8	0	69
George Bush	MA	Yale	Business owner	4	0	8	64
Bill Clinton	AR	Georgetown/Yale	Lawyer	0	12	0	46
George W. Bush	CT	Yale/Harvard	Business owner	0	6	0	54

ªAdams served in the U.S. House for six years after leaving the presidency.

Source: Adapted from *Presidential Elections Since 1789*, 4th ed. (Washington, DC: CQ Press, 1987), 4; Norman Thomas, Joseph Pika, and Richard Watson, *The Politics of the Presidency*, 3rd ed. (Washington, DC: CQ Press, 1993), 490; Harold W. Stanley and Richard G. Niemi, eds., *Vital Statistics on American Politics 2001–2002* (Washington, DC: CQ Press, 2001).

During the Constitutional Convention, Benjamin Franklin was a staunch supporter of including a provision allowing for **impeachment,** a process by which to begin to remove an official from office. He noted that "historically, the lack of power to impeach had necessitated recourse to assassination."[7] Not surprisingly, then, he urged the rest of the delegates to formulate a legal mechanism to remove the president and vice president.

The impeachment provision ultimately included in Article II was adopted as a check on the power of the president. As we discussed in detail in chapter 7, each

impeachment
The power delegated to the House of Representatives in the Constitution to charge the president, vice president, or other "civil officers," including federal judges, with "Treason, Bribery, or other high Crimes and Misdemeanors." This is the first step in the constitutional process of removing such government officials from office.

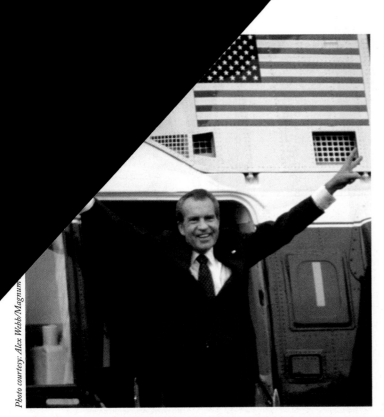

house of Congress was given a role to play in the impeachment process to assure that the chief executive could be removed only for "Treason, Bribery, or other high Crimes and Misdemeanors." The House is empowered to vote to impeach the president by a simple majority vote. The Senate then acts as a court of law and tries the president for the charged offenses. A two-thirds majority vote in the Senate on any count contained in the articles of impeachment is necessary to remove the president from office. Only two presidents, Andrew Johnson and Bill Clinton, have been impeached by the House of Representatives. Neither man, however, was removed from office by the Senate. (For more on how the impeachment process works, see Table 7.7: The Eight Stages of the Impeachment Process.)

In 1974, President Richard M. Nixon resigned from office rather than face the certainty of impeachment, trial, and removal from office for his role in covering up details about a break-in at the Democratic Party's national headquarters in the Watergate office complex. What came to be known simply as Watergate also produced a major decision from the Supreme Court on the scope of what is termed **executive privilege**. In *U.S. v. Nixon* **(1974),** the Supreme Court ruled unanimously that there was no overriding executive privilege that sanctioned the president's refusal to comply with a court order to produce information for use in the trial of the Watergate defendants.

■ President Richard M. Nixon gives one final salute as he leaves the White House after resigning from office.

executive privilege
An implied presidental power that allows the president to refuse to disclose information regarding confidential conversations or national security to Congress or the judiciary.

U.S. v. Nixon **(1974)**
Key Supreme Court ruling on power of the president, finding that there is no absolute constitutional executive privilege to allow a president to refuse to comply with a court order to produce information needed in a criminal trial.

RULES OF SUCCESSION

Through 2006, eight presidents have died in office from illness or assassination. William H. Harrison was the first president to die in office—he caught a cold at his inauguration in 1841 and died one month later. (John Tyler thus became the first vice president to succeed to the presidency.) In 1865, Abraham Lincoln became the first president to be assassinated.

The Framers were aware that a system of orderly transfer of power was necessary; this was the primary reason they created the office of the vice president. To further clarify the order of presidential succession, in 1947, Congress passed the Presidential Succession Act, which lists—in order—those in line (after the vice president) to succeed the president (see Table 8.2).

TABLE 8.2 PRESIDENTIAL LINE OF SUCCESSION

1. Vice President	10. Secretary of Commerce
2. Speaker of the House	11. Secretary of Labor
3. President Pro Tempore of the Senate	12. Secretary of Health and Human Services
4. Secretary of State	13. Secretary of Housing and Urban Development
5. Secretary of the Treasury	14. Secretary of Transportation
6. Secretary of Defense	15. Secretary of Energy
7. Attorney General	16. Secretary of Education
8. Secretary of the Interior	17. Secretary of Veterans Affairs
9. Secretary of Agriculture	

The Secretary of Homeland Security has not been put into the line of succession. Senate Bill 442, approved by the Senate in July of 2005, would place the Secretary of Homeland Security eighth in the line of succession, after the Attorney General, if it becomes law. A similar House bill, House Resolution 1455, is currently pending before the House Judiciary Committee.

The Living Constitution

Whenever there is a vacancy in the office of the Vice President, the President shall nominate a Vice President who shall take office upon confirmation by a majority vote of both Houses of Congress.

—TWENTY-FIFTH AMENDMENT, SECTION 2

This clause of the Twenty-Fifth Amendment allows a president to fill a vacancy in the office of vice president with the consent of a simple majority of both Houses of Congress. The purpose of this amendment, which also deals with vacancies in the office of the president, was to remedy some structural flaws in Article II. At the time of this amendment's addition to the Constitution in 1965, seven vice presidents had died in office and one had resigned. For over 20 percent of the nation's history there had been no vice president to assume the office of the president in case of his death or infirmity. When John F. Kennedy was assassinated, Vice President Lyndon B. Johnson became president and the office of vice president was vacant. Since Johnson had suffered a heart attack as vice president, members of Congress were anxious to remedy the problems that might occur should there be no vice president.

Richard M. Nixon followed Johnson as president, and ironically, during Nixon's presidency, the office of the vice president became empty twice! First, Nixon's vice president, Spiro T. Agnew, was forced to resign in the wake of charges of bribe taking, corruption, and income-tax evasion while an elected official in Maryland; he was replaced by popular House Minority Leader Gerald R. Ford (R–MI), who had no trouble getting a majority vote in both houses of Congress to confirm his nomination. When Nixon resigned rather than face sure impeachment, Ford became president and selected the former governor of New York, Nelson A. Rockefeller, to be his vice president. This chain of events set up for the first time in U.S. history a situation in which neither the president nor the vice president had been elected to those positions.

The Succession Act has never been used because there has always been a vice president to take over when a president died in office. The **Twenty-Fifth Amendment,** in fact, was added to the Constitution in 1967 to assure that this will continue to be the case. Should a vacancy occur in the office of the vice president, the Twenty-Fifth Amendment directs the president to appoint a new vice president, subject to the approval (by a simple majority) of both houses of Congress. (See The Living Constitution: Twenty-Fifth Amendment, Section 2.)

The Twenty-Fifth Amendment also contains a section that allows the vice president and a majority of the Cabinet (or some other body determined by Congress) to deem a president unable to fulfill his duties. It sets up a procedure to allow the vice president to become acting president if the president is incapacitated. The president also voluntarily can relinquish his power. In 2002, for example, President George W. Bush briefly made Vice President Dick Cheney acting president while he underwent a colonoscopy.

Twenty-Fifth Amendment
Adopted in 1967 to establish procedures for filling vacancies in the office of president and vice president as well as providing for procedures to deal with the disability of a president.

The Constitutional Powers of the President

THOUGH THE FRAMERS nearly unanimously agreed about the need for a strong central government and a greatly empowered Congress, they did not agree about the proper role of the president or the sweep of his authority. In contrast to Article I's laundry list of enumerated powers for the Congress, Article II details few presidential powers. Perhaps the most important section of Article II is its first sentence: "The executive Power shall be vested in a President of the United States of America." Nonetheless, the sum total of the president's powers, enumerated below, allows him to become a major player in the policy process.

THE APPOINTMENT POWER

To help the president enforce laws passed by Congress, the Constitution authorizes him to appoint, with the advice and consent of the Senate, "Ambassadors, other public Ministers and Consuls, judges of the supreme Court, and all other Officers of the United States, whose Appointments are not herein otherwise provided for, and which shall be established by Law." Although this section of the Constitution deals only with appointments, behind that language is a powerful policy-making tool. The president has the authority to make nearly 3,000 appointments to his administration (of which just over 1,000 require Senate confirmation),and he technically appoints more than 75,000 military personnel.[8] Many of these appointees are in positions to wield substantial authority over the course and direction of public policy. Although Congress has the authority "to make all laws," through the president's enforcement power—and his chosen assistants—he often can set the policy agenda for the nation. And, especially in the context of his ability to make appointments to the federal courts, his influence can be felt far past his term of office.

It is not surprising, then, that selecting the right people is often one of a president's most important tasks. Presidents look for a blend of loyalty, competence, and integrity. Identifying these qualities in people is a major challenge that every new president faces. Recent presidents, especially Bill Clinton and George W. Bush, have made an effort to create a Cabinet and staff that, in President Clinton's terms, looks "more like America," as is underscored in Table 8.3, which indicates the proportion of women appointed by recent presidents. In fact, of the first five major appointments announced by President George W. Bush during his first term, all but one were women or minorities: retired General Colin Powell (secretary of state), Condoleezza Rice (national security adviser), Texas Supreme Court Justice Alberto Gonzales (White House counsel), and longtime Bush adviser Karen Hughes (counselor to the president)—two blacks, two women, and a Hispanic. President Bush's early second-term Cabinet appointments were also historic and

SIMULATION

You Are Appointing a Supreme Court Justice

■ The president's power to nominate justices to the Supreme Court serves as a key check on the judiciary. In 2005, President Bush nominated White House counsel and longtime political aide Harriet E. Miers to replace Justice Sandra Day O'Connor. Miers later withdrew her name from consideration following questions from social conservatives about her policy positions and concern about her legal qualifications.

Photo courtesy: Morteza Nikoubazl/Reuters/Landov

TABLE 8.3	PRESIDENTIAL TEAMS (SENIOR ADMINISTRATIVE POSITIONS REQUIRING SENATE CONFIRMATION)		
	Total Appointments	Total Women	Percentage Women
Jimmy Carter	1,087	191	17.6%
Ronald Reagan	2,349	277	11.8%
George Bush	1,079	215	19.9%
Bill Clinton	2,479	1,125	45.0%
George W. Bush[a]	2,786	1,017	36.0%

[a]Bush data include all political appointees through 2005.

Sources: "Insiders Say White House Has Its Own Glass Ceiling," *Atlanta Journal and Constitution* (April 10, 1995): AF; Judi Hasson, "Senate GOP Leader Lott Says He'll Work with Clinton," *USA Today* (December 4, 1996): 8A; and "The Growth of Political Appointees in the Bush Administration," U.S. House of Representatives, Committee on Government Reform—Minority Staff, May 2006.

included the nomination of Rice as secretary of state and Gonzales as attorney general.

In the past, when a president forwarded a nomination to the Senate for its approval, his selections traditionally were given great respect—especially those for the **Cabinet,** an advisory group selected by the president to help him make decisions and execute the laws. In fact, until the Clinton administration, the vast majority (97 percent) of all presidential nominations were confirmed.[9]

Rejections of presidential nominees as well as onerous delays in their approval can have a major impact on the course of an administration. Rejections leave a president without first choices, affect a president's relationship with the Senate, and affect how the president is perceived by the public. Rejections and delays also have a chilling effect on other potential nominees. Still, President George W. Bush had little problem getting two nominees for the U.S. Supreme Court approved by the Republican-controlled Senate.

THE POWER TO CONVENE CONGRESS

The Constitution requires the president to inform the Congress periodically of "the State of the Union," and authorizes the president to convene either or both houses of Congress on "extraordinary Occasions." In *Federalist No. 77,* Hamilton justified the latter by noting that because the Senate and the chief executive enjoy concurrent powers to make treaties, "It might often be necessary to call it together with a view to this object, when it would be unnecessary and improper to convene the House of Representatives." The power to convene Congress was important when Congress did not sit in nearly year-round sessions. Today this power has little more than symbolic significance.

THE POWER TO MAKE TREATIES

The president's power to make treaties with foreign nations is checked by the Constitution's stipulation that all treaties must be approved by at least two-thirds of the members of the Senate. The chief executive can also "receive ambassadors," wording that has been interpreted to allow the president to recognize the existence of other nations.

Historically, the Senate ratifies about 70 percent of the treaties submitted to it by the president.[10] Only sixteen treaties that have been put to a vote have been rejected, often under highly partisan circumstances. Perhaps the most notable example of the Senate's refusal to ratify a treaty was its defeat of the Treaty of Versailles submitted by President Woodrow Wilson in 1919. The treaty was an agreement among the major nations to end World War I. At Wilson's insistence, it also called for the creation of the League of Nations—a precursor of the United Nations—to foster continued peace

Cabinet
The formal body of presidential advisers who head the fifteen executive departments. Presidents often add others to this body of formal advisers.

and international disarmament. In struggling to gain international acceptance for the League, Wilson had taken American support for granted. This was a dramatic miscalculation. Isolationists, led by Senator Henry Cabot Lodge (R–MA), opposed U.S. participation in the League on the grounds that the League would place the United States in the center of every major international conflict. Proponents countered that, League or no League, the United States had emerged from World War I as a world power and that membership in the League of Nations would enhance its new role. The vote in the Senate for ratification was very close, but the isolationists prevailed— the United States stayed out of the League, and Wilson was devastated.

The Senate also may require substantial amendment of a treaty prior to its consent. When President Jimmy Carter proposed the controversial Panama Canal Treaty in 1977 to turn the canal over to Panama, for example, the Senate required several conditions to be ironed out before approving the canal's return. Presidents may also "unsign" treaties, a practice often met with dismay from other signatories. For example, the Bush administration formally withdrew its support for the International Criminal Court (ICC). In a short, three-sentence letter to UN Secretary General Kofi Annan, the United States withdrew from efforts to create the first permanent court to prosecute war crimes, genocide, and other crimes against humanity. This treaty was formerly signed by President Bill Clinton and was scheduled to take effect July 1, 2002. Critics of the treaty argued that it could lead to politically motivated charges against U.S. troops in Afghanistan and Iraq.[11]

When trade agreements are at issue, presidents often are forced to be mindful of the wishes of Congress. What is called congressional "fast track" authority protects a president's ability to negotiate trade agreements with confidence that the accords will not be altered by Congress. Trade agreements submitted to Congress under fast track procedures bar amendments and require an up or down vote in Congress within ninety days of introduction.

Presidents also often try to get around the constitutional "advice and consent" of the Senate requirement for ratification of treaties and the congressional approval requirement for trade agreements by entering into an **executive agreement,** which allows the president to form secret and highly sensitive arrangements with foreign nations without Senate approval. Presidents have used these agreements since the days of George Washington, and their use has been upheld by the courts. Although executive agreements are not binding on subsequent administrations, since 1900 they have been used far more frequently than treaties, further cementing the role of the president in foreign affairs, as revealed in Table 8.4.

executive agreement
Formal government agreement entered into by the president that does not require the advice and consent of the U.S. Senate.

veto power
The formal, constitutional authority of the president to reject bills passed by both houses of Congress, thus preventing their becoming law without further congressional action.

VETO POWER

Presidents can affect the policy process through the **veto power,** the authority to reject any congressional legislation. The threat of a presidential veto often prompts members of Congress to fashion legislation that they know will receive presidential acquiescence, if not support. Thus, simply threatening to veto legislation often gives a president another way to influence law-making.

During the Constitutional Convention, proponents of a strong executive argued that the president should have an absolute and final veto over acts of Congress. Opponents of this idea, including Benjamin

TABLE 8.4 TREATIES AND EXECUTIVE AGREEMENTS CONCLUDED BY THE UNITED STATES, 1789–2006

Years	Number of Treaties	Number of Executive Agreements
1789–1839	60	27
1839–1889	215	238
1889–1929	382	763
1930–1932	49	41
1933–1944 (F. Roosevelt)	131	369
1945–1952 (Truman)	132	1,324
1953–1960 (Eisenhower)	89	1,834
1961–1963 (Kennedy)	36	813
1964–1968 (L. Johnson)	67	1,083
1969–1974 (Nixon)	93	1,317
1975–1976 (Ford)	26	666
1977–1980 (Carter)	79	1,476
1981–1988 (Reagan)	125	2,840
1989–1992 (Bush)	67	1,350
1993–2000 (Clinton)	209	2,047
2001–2006 (G.W. Bush)	45	612

Note: Number of treaties includes those concluded during the indicated span of years. Some of these treaties did not receive the consent of the U.S. Senate. Varying definitions of what an executive agreement comprises and their entry-into-force date make the above numbers approximate.

Sources: 1789–1980: *Congressional Quarterly's Guide to Congress,* 291; 1981–2002: Office of the Assistant Legal Adviser for Treaty Affairs. U.S. Department of State; 2002–2006: www.saramitchell.org/MarshallPrins.pdf/

Franklin, countered that in their home states the executive veto "was constantly made use of to extort money" from legislators. James Madison made the most compelling argument for a compromise on the issue:

> Experience has proven a tendency in our governments to throw all power into the legislative vortex. The Executives of the States are in general little more than Ciphers, the legislatures omnipotent. If no effectual check be devised for restraining the instability and encroachments of the latter, a revolution of some kind or other would be inevitable.[12]

line-item veto
The authority of a chief executive to delete part of a bill passed by the legislature that involves taxing or spending. The legislature may override a veto, usually with a two-thirds majority of each chamber.

In keeping with the system of checks and balances, then, the president was given the veto power, but only as a "qualified negative." Although the president was given the authority to veto any act of Congress (with the exception of joint resolutions that propose constitutional amendments), Congress was given the authority to override an executive veto by a two-thirds vote in each house. The veto is a powerful policy tool because Congress cannot usually muster enough votes to override a veto. Thus, in over 200 years, there have been approximately 2,500 presidential vetoes and only about a hundred have been overridden, as revealed in Table 8.5.

As early as 1873, in his State of the Union message, President Ulysses S. Grant proposed a constitutional amendment to give to presidents a **line-item veto,** a power enjoyed by many governors to disapprove of individual items within a spending bill and not just the bill in its entirety. Over the years, 150 resolutions calling for a line-item veto were introduced in Congress. Presidents from Gerald R. Ford to Bill Clinton supported the concept. Finally, in 1996, Congress enacted legislation that gave the president the authority to veto specific spending provisions within a bill without vetoing the bill in its entirety. This move allowed the president to project his policy priorities into the budget by vetoing any programs inconsistent with his policy goals. It also allowed President Clinton to do away with more outrageous examples of pork (legislators' pet projects that often find their way into a budget). The city of New York soon challenged the line-item veto law when the president used it to stop payment of some congressionally authorized funds to the city. In *Clinton* v. *City of New York* (1998), the U.S. Supreme Court ruled that the line-item veto was unconstitutional because it gave powers to the president denied him by the U.S. Constitution. Significant alterations of executive/congressional powers, said the Court, require constitutional amendment.[13]

THE POWER TO PRESIDE OVER THE MILITARY AS COMMANDER IN CHIEF

One of the most important constitutional executive powers is the president's authority over the military. Article II states that the president is "Commander in Chief of the Army and Navy of the United States." While the Constitution specifically grants Congress the authority to declare

TABLE 8.5	PRESIDENTIAL VETOES			
President	Regular Vetoes	Pocket Vetoes	Total Vetoes	Vetoes Overridden
Washington	2	.....	2	.....
J. Adams	.....	.....	.....	.....
Jefferson	.....	.....	.....	.....
Madison	5	2	7	.....
Monroe	1	.....	1	.....
J. Q. Adams	.....	.....	.....	.....
Jackson	5	7	12	.....
Buren	.....	1	1	.....
W. H. Harrison	.....	.....	.....	.....
Tyler	6	4	10	1
Polk	2	1	3	.....
Taylor	.....	.....	.....	.....
Fillmore	.....	.....	.....	.....
Pierce	9	.....	9	5
Buchanan	4	3	7	.....
Lincoln	2	5	7	.....
A. Johnson	21	8	29	15
Grant	45	48	93	4
Hayes	12	1	13	1
Garfield	.....	.....	.....	.....
Arthur	4	8	12	1
Cleveland	304	110	414	2
B. Harrison	19	25	44	1
Cleveland	42	128	170	5
McKinley	6	36	42	.....
T. Roosevelt	42	40	82	1
Taft	30	9	39	1
Wilson	33	11	44	6
Harding	5	1	6	.....
Coolidge	20	30	50	4
Hoover	21	16	37	3
F. Roosevelt	372	263	635	9
Truman	180	70	250	12
Eisenhower	73	108	181	2
Kennedy	12	9	21	.....
L. Johnson	16	14	30	.....
Nixon	26	17	43	7
Ford	48	18	66	12
Carter	13	18	31	2
Reagan	39	39	78	9
G. Bush[a]	29	15	44	1
Clinton	36	1	38	2
G. W. Bush[b]	1	.....	1	.....
Total	**1485**	**1066**	**2551**	**107**

[a]President George Bush attempted to pocket veto two bills during intrasession recess periods. Congress considered the two bills enacted into law because of the president's failure to return the legislation. The bills are not counted as pocket vetoes in this table.
[b]George W. Bush information as of December 2006.

Source: Congressional Research Service.

THE PRESIDENT'S MANY HATS

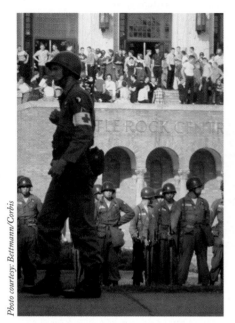

Photo courtesy: Bettmann/Corbis

■ Chief law enforcer: Troops sent by President Dwight D. Eisenhower enforce federal court decisions ordering the integration of public schools in Little Rock, Arkansas.

Photo courtesy: Matt Reinstein/The Image Works

■ Leader of the party: Ronald Reagan mobilized conservatives and changed the nature of the Republican Party.

Photo courtesy: Wally McNamee/Folio, Inc.

■ Commander in chief: President George Bush and his wife, Barbara, with troops in the Persian Gulf.

Photo courtesy: Bettmann/Corbis

■ Shaper of domestic policy: President Jimmy Carter announces new energy policies. Here, he wears a sweater to underscore that thermostats in the White House were turned down to save energy.

Photo courtesy: J. David Ake/AFP/Getty Images

■ Key player in the legislative process: President Bill Clinton meets with Speaker of the House Newt Gingrich (R–GA).

Photo courtesy: Bettmann/Corbis

■ Chief of state: President John F. Kennedy and his wife, Jacqueline, with the president of France and his wife during the Kennedys' widely publicized 1961 trip to that nation.

war, presidents since Abraham Lincoln have used the commander-in-chief clause in conjunction with the chief executive's duty to "take Care that the Laws be faithfully executed" to wage war (and to broaden various powers).

Modern presidents continually clash with Congress over the ability to commence hostilities. The Vietnam War, in which 58,000 American soldiers were killed and 300,000 were wounded, was conducted (at a cost of $150 billion) without a congressional declaration of war. In fact, acknowledging President Lyndon B. Johnson's claim to war-making authority, in 1964 Congress passed—with only two dissenting votes—the Gulf of Tonkin Resolution, which authorized a massive commitment of U.S. forces in South Vietnam.

During that highly controversial war, Presidents Johnson and then Nixon routinely assured members of Congress that victory was near. In 1971, however, publication of what were called *The Pentagon Papers* revealed what many people had suspected all along: Lyndon B. Johnson systematically had altered casualty figures and distorted key facts to place the progress of the war in a more positive light. Angered by this misinformation that had led Congress largely to defer to the executive in the conduct of the Vietnam War, in 1973 Congress passed the **War Powers Act** to limit the president's authority to introduce American troops into hostile foreign lands without congressional approval. President Richard M. Nixon vetoed the act, but it was overridden by a two-thirds majority in both houses of Congress.

Presidents since Nixon have continued to insist that the War Powers Act is an unconstitutional infringement of their executive power Still, in 2001, President George W. Bush complied with the act when he sought, and both houses of Congress approved, a joint resolution authorizing the use of force against "those responsible for the recent [September 11] attacks launched against the United States." This resolution actually gave the president more open-ended authority to wage war than his father had received in 1991 to conduct the Persian Gulf War or President Lyndon B. Johnson had received after the Gulf of Tonkin Resolution in 1964.[14] Later, in October 2002, after President Bush declared Iraq to be a "grave threat to peace," the House (296–133) and Senate (77–23) voted overwhelmingly to allow the president to use force in Iraq "as he determines to be necessary and appropriate," thereby conferring tremendous authority on the president to wage war. (See Join the Debate: The War Powers Act.)

SIMULATION

Presidential Leadership: Which Hat Do You Wear?

War Powers Act

Passed by Congress in 1973; the president is limited in the deployment of troops overseas to a sixty-day period in peacetime (which can be extended for an extra thirty days to permit withdrawal) unless Congress explicitly gives its approval for a longer period.

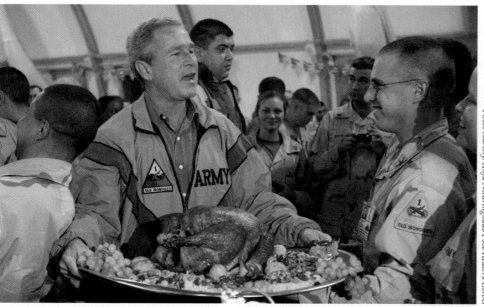

■ In 2003, President George W. Bush surprised American troops in Iraq on Thanksgiving Day.

Photo courtesy: Anja Niedringhaus/Pool/Reuters/Corbis

Join the Debate

THE WAR POWERS ACT

OVERVIEW: While the Constitution divides the power to wage war between Congress and the president, scholars and politicians disagree on the specifics of the division. They also disagree on how this division should play out in specific circumstances. The Constitution gives Congress the authority to declare war, to make the rules that govern military forces, and to provide appropriations to the armed services. Yet, the president's constitutional jurisdiction over war powers has steadily increased since the nation's founding. Although President James Madison would not go to war with Great Britain in 1812 without a war declaration from Congress, the last six major American conflicts—in Korea, Vietnam, the Persian Gulf, Kosovo, Afghanistan, and Iraq—were conducted without formal declarations of war.

The War Powers Act of 1973, passed in the aftermath of the Vietnam War, was an attempt to rein in the war-making authority of the president by demanding, among other things, that the executive notify Congress when committing the U.S. military to hostile action. The War Powers Act requires the president to report to Congress "in every possible instance" within forty-eight hours after deploying the armed forces in combat. Implied in the law is the understanding that the information Congress receives will be timely and accurate. President Richard M. Nixon's veto of the act was overridden by both houses of Congress, but presidential administrations since Nixon's, Democratic and Republican alike, have agreed that the act infringes on the president's constitutional duty as commander in chief.

The intelligence the president and Congress receive is critically important when determining whether or not to engage in and support armed conflict. The president's authority as commander in chief gives him access to significant intelligence resources needed to conduct foreign affairs, but sometimes these sources are flawed. For instance, in 1998,

President Bill Clinton ordered the destruction of a pharmaceutical plant in Sudan based on faulty intelligence that the site produced nerve gas. In 2002–2003, President George W. Bush made the case for invading Iraq by asserting that the country possessed weapons of mass destruction (WMDs) that posed an imminent threat to the United States. WMDs loomed large in the national debate regarding whether or not to intervene in Iraq.

Complying with the War Powers Act, the president asked for and received authorization from Congress to use military force against Iraq if diplomatic efforts failed. Critics have charged that congressional authorization would not have been as forthcoming had the president and his administration not ignored or downplayed intelligence reports that contradicted their beliefs in the existence of WMDs. The fact that such weapons were not found undermined the administration's credibility with many Americans, including members of Congress, as well as foreign nations. Some constitutional scholars have noted that intelligence failures and the rising death toll and costs related to military action in Iraq suggest it is time for Congress to increase its oversight of the executive in foreign policy matters. Other scholars disagree, siding with executive-branch officials who consider the War Powers Act an infringement on the president's constitutional authority.

Should a president, in times of crisis, be unlimited in his ability to defend the United States through the use of military force? To what extent should Congress be privy to the same intelligence reports available to the president and how much of a say should Congress have in decisions that will directly affect the lives of tens of thousands of Americans? What approach is most likely to ensure that when the United States goes to war, the war is not only necessary and just but is also conducted with the least amount of casualties and damage to all parties?

ARGUMENTS FOR THE WAR POWERS ACT

- **The War Powers Act reflects the will of the American people.** The doctrine of civilian supremacy places ultimate war-making authority with the American people, and the War Powers Act reflects the will of the people

THE PARDONING POWER

pardon
An executive grant providing restoration of all rights and privileges of citizenship to a specific individual charged or convicted of a crime.

Presidents can exercise a check on judicial power through their constitutional authority to grant reprieves or pardons. A **pardon** is an executive grant releasing an individual from the punishment or legal consequences of a crime before or after conviction, and restores all rights and privileges of citizenship. Presidents exercise complete pardoning power for federal offenses except in cases of impeachment, which cannot be pardoned. President Gerald R. Ford granted the most famous presidential pardon when he pardoned former President Richard M. Nixon—who had

as expressed through the representative institution of Congress.

- **The War Powers Act is an attempt by Congress to restore the balance of shared control of the military with the executive.** The act's stated purpose is to "fulfill the intent of the framers . . . and insure that the collective judgment of both the Congress and the President will apply to the introduction of United States Armed Forces into hostilities . . . and to the continued use of such forces." This is an attempt to return to the constitutional principle that waging war is to be shared by both branches of government.
- **The War Powers Act is an additional check on the president's authority as commander in chief.** The act is an attempt to prevent future presidents from engaging in hostilities of questionable importance to U.S. national security and to force deliberation within the government with regard to armed conflict. For example, had Congress known of President Lyndon B. Johnson's use of faulty or intentionally misleading information to increase U.S. military involvement in Vietnam, U.S. involvement in Southeast Asia may have taken a different, less costly path in both lives and expenditures.

ARGUMENTS AGAINST THE WAR POWERS ACT

- **International relations can be so volatile that the president must be able to act quickly without hindrance.** Alexander Hamilton argued that the reasons for war are "infinite" and that the United States must have an institution that can react quickly and with force to defend the United States. He found this energy in government in the executive—and the American executive was created in part to act quickly without relative interference during exceptional times of crisis.
- **The Supreme Court has upheld an expanded interpretation of the president's authority.** In *U.S.* v. *Curtiss-Wright* (1936), the Court argued that the president and "not Congress has the better opportunity of knowing the conditions which prevail in foreign countries, and especially this is true during times of war. He has his confidential

sources of information. . . . Secrecy in respect of information gathered by them may be highly necessary and the premature disclosure of it productive of harmful results." Thus, the Court concluded that the president is uniquely responsible in the area of foreign policy and war making.

- **It is the president's duty to "preserve, protect, and defend" the Constitution, and thus the country it governs, and it is the executive's prerogative to decide the means to do so, especially in times of conflict.** During extraordinary times, the president must take extraordinary means to defend the nation without undue interference from Congress. *Federalist No. 8* argues: "It is the nature of war to increase the executive at the expense of the legislative authority" as this is considered a natural shift in power. A historical example is President Abraham Lincoln's use of presidential power during the Civil War. A current example would be the Iraq War where National Intelligence Estimates released in 2006 conflicted with the intelligence shared with Congress by Bush administration officials prior to the onset of hostilities.

QUESTIONS

1. Is the War Powers Act constitutional? Does Congress have the power to limit the war-making power of the executive? If so, what implications does this have for U.S. national security?
2. Should Congress have access to the same information and intelligence regarding foreign-policy matters available to the president? Are there any circumstances where such information should be restricted to just the president and his closest advisers?

SELECTED READINGS

Fisher, Louis. *Presidential War Power.* Lawrence: University Press of Kansas, 2004.

Tushnet, Mark, ed. *The Constitution in Wartime: Beyond Alarmism and Complacency.* Durham, NC: Duke University Press, 2005.

not been formally charged with any crime—"for any offenses against the United States, which he, Richard Nixon, has committed or may have committed while in office." This unilateral, absolute pardon prevented the former president from ever being tried for any crimes he may have committed. It also unleashed a torrent of public criticism against Ford and questions about whether Nixon had discussed the pardon with Ford before Nixon's resignation. Many analysts attribute Ford's defeat in his 1976 bid for the presidency to that pardon.

Even though pardons are generally directed toward a specific individual, presidents have also used them to offer general amnesties. Presidents George Washington,

John Adams, James Madison, Abraham Lincoln, Andrew Johnson, Theodore Roosevelt, Harry S Truman, and Jimmy Carter used general pardons to grant amnesty to large classes of individuals for illegal acts. Carter, for example, incurred the wrath of many veterans' groups when he made an offer of unconditional amnesty to approximately 10,000 men who had fled the United States or gone into hiding to avoid being drafted for military service in the Vietnam War.

The Development and Expansion of Presidential Power

EVERY PRESIDENT BRINGS to the position not only a vision of America, but also expectations about how to use presidential authority. The forty-two men who have held the nation's highest office have been a diverse lot. (While there have been forty-three presidents, only forty-two men have held the office: Grover Cleveland served as the twenty-second and twenty-fourth president because he was elected to nonconsecutive terms in 1884 and 1892.) Most presidents find accomplishing their goals much more difficult than they envisioned. After President John F. Kennedy was in office two years, for example, he noted publicly that there were "greater limitations upon our ability to bring about a favorable result than I had imagined."[15] Similarly, as he was leaving office, President Harry S Truman mused about what surprises awaited his successor, Dwight D. Eisenhower, a former general: "He'll sit here and he'll say, 'Do this! Do that!' And nothing will happen. Poor Ike—it won't be a bit like the army. He'll find it very frustrating."[16]

A president's authority is limited by the formal powers enumerated in Article II of the Constitution and by the Supreme Court's interpretation of those constitutional provisions. How a president wields these powers is affected by the times in which the president serves, his confidantes and advisers, and the president's personality and leadership abilities. The 1950s postwar era of good feelings and economic prosperity presided over by the grandfatherly Eisenhower, for instance, called for a very different leader from the one needed by the Civil War–torn nation governed by Abraham Lincoln. Furthermore, not only do different times call for different kinds of leaders; they also often provide limits, or conversely, wide opportunities, for whoever serves as president at the time. Crises, in particular, trigger expansions of presidential power. The danger to the union posed by the Civil War in the 1860s required a strong leader to take up the reins of government. Because of his leadership during this crisis, Lincoln is generally ranked by historians as the best president (see Table 8.6).

ESTABLISHING PRESIDENTIAL AUTHORITY: THE FIRST PRESIDENTS

The first three presidents, and their conceptions of the presidency, continue to have a profound impact on American government. When President George Washington was sworn in on a cold, blustery day in New York City on April 30, 1789, he took over an office and a government that were yet to be created. Eventually, a few hundred postal workers were hired and Washington appointed a small group of Cabinet advisers and clerks. During Washington's two terms, the entire federal budget was only about $40 million, or approximately $10 for every citizen in

TABLE 8.6   THE BEST AND THE WORST PRESIDENTS

Who was the best president and who was the worst? Many surveys of scholars have been taken over the years to answer this question, and virtually all have ranked Abraham Lincoln the best. A 2000 C-SPAN survey of fifty-eight historians from across the political spectrum came up with these results:

Five Best Presidents	Five Worst Presidents
1. Lincoln (best)	1. Buchanan (worst)
2. F. Roosevelt	2. A. Johnson
3. Washington	3. Pierce
4. T. Roosevelt	4. Harding
5. Truman	5. W. Harrison

Source: C-SPAN Survey of Presidential Leadership. www.cspan.com.

America. In contrast, in 2007, the federal budget was $2.8 trillion, or $9,300, for every man, woman, and child.

George Washington set several important precedents for future presidents:

- He took every opportunity to establish the primacy of the national government. In 1794, for example, Washington used the militia of four states to put down the Whiskey Rebellion, an uprising of 3,000 western Pennsylvania farmers opposed to the payment of a federal excise tax on liquor. Leading those 1,500 troops was Secretary of the Treasury Alexander Hamilton, whose duty it was to collect federal taxes. Washington's action helped establish the idea of federal supremacy and the authority of the executive branch to collect the taxes levied by Congress.

PARTICIPATION
Rate the
Presidents

- He began the practice of regular meetings with his advisers (called the Cabinet), thus establishing the Cabinet system.

- He asserted the prominence of the role of the chief executive in the conduct of foreign affairs. He sent envoys to negotiate the Jay Treaty to end continued hostilities with Great Britain. Then, over senatorial objection, he continued to assert his authority first to negotiate treaties and then simply to submit them to the Senate for its approval. Washington made it clear that the Senate's function was limited to approval of treaties and did not include negotiation with foreign powers.

- He claimed the inherent power of the presidency as the basis for proclaiming a policy of strict neutrality when the British and French were at war. Although the Constitution is silent about a president's authority to declare neutrality, Washington's supporters argued that the Constitution granted the president **inherent powers**—that is, powers that belong to the national government simply because it is a sovereign state. Thus, they argued, the president's power to conduct diplomatic relations could be inferred from the Constitution. Since neither Congress nor the Supreme Court later disagreed, this power was implicitly added to the list of specific, enumerated presidential powers found in Article II.

inherent powers
Powers that belong to the national government simply because it is a sovereign state.

Like Washington, the next two presidents, John Adams and Thomas Jefferson, acted in ways that were critical to the development of the presidency as well as to the president's role in the political system. Adams's poor leadership skills, for example, heightened the divisions between Federalists and Anti-Federalists and probably quickened the development of political parties (see chapter 12). Jefferson took critical steps to expand the role of the president in the legislative process. Like Washington, he claimed that certain presidential powers were inherent and used those inherent powers to justify his expansion of the size of the nation through the Louisiana Purchase in 1803.

INCREMENTAL EXPANSION OF PRESIDENTIAL POWERS: 1809–1933

Although the first three presidents made enormous contributions to the office of the chief executive, the way government had to function in its formative years caused the balance of power to be heavily weighted in favor of a strong Congress. Americans routinely had close contacts with their representatives in Congress, while to most citizens the president seemed a remote figure. Members of Congress frequently were at home, where they were seen by voters; few citizens ever even gazed on a president. By the end of Jefferson's first term, it was clear that the Framers' initial fear of an all-powerful, monarchical president was unfounded. The strength of Congress and the relatively weak presidents who came after Jefferson allowed Congress quickly to assert itself as the most powerful branch of government.

Photo courtesy: Alexander Gardner/The Granger Collection

■ President Abraham Lincoln is widely regarded as the best president, largely because of his leadership during the Civil War. Here, Lincoln visits Union leaders at Antietam, Maryland, in 1862.

Andrew Jackson was the first president to act as a strong national leader who represented more than just a landed, propertied elite. By the time Jackson ran for president in 1828, eleven new states had been added to the union, and the number of white males eligible to vote had increased dramatically as property requirements for voting were removed by nearly all states. The election of Jackson, a Tennessean, as the seventh president signaled the end of an era: he was the first president not to be either a Virginian or an Adams. His election launched the beginning of Jacksonian democracy, a concept that embodied the western, frontier, egalitarian spirit personified by Jackson, the first common man to be elected president. The masses loved him, and legends were built around his down-to-earth image. Jackson, for example, once was asked to give a position to a soldier who had lost his leg on the battlefield and needed the job to support his family. When told that the man hadn't voted for him, Jackson responded: "If he lost his leg fighting for his country, that is vote enough for me."[17]

Jackson used his image and personal power to buttress the developing party system by rewarding loyal followers of his Democratic Party with presidential appointments. Frequently at odds with Congress, he made use of the veto power against twelve bills, surpassing the combined total of nine vetoes used by his six predecessors. Jackson also reasserted the supremacy of the national government (and the presidency) by facing down South Carolina's nullification of a federal tariff law.

Abraham Lincoln's approach to the presidency was similar to Jackson's. Moreover, the unprecedented emergency of the Civil War allowed Lincoln to assume powers that no president before him had claimed. Because Lincoln believed he needed to act quickly for the very survival of the union, he frequently took action without first obtaining the approval of Congress. Among many of Lincoln's legally questionable acts:

■ He suspended the writ of *habeas corpus,* which allows those in prison to petition to be released, citing the need to jail persons even suspected of disloyal practices.
■ He expanded the size of the U.S. army above congressionally mandated ceilings.
■ He ordered a blockade of southern ports, in effect initiating a war without the approval of Congress.
■ He closed the U.S. mails to treasonable correspondence.

Lincoln argued that the inherent powers of his office allowed him to circumvent the Constitution in a time of war or national crisis. Since the Constitution conferred on the president the duty to make sure that the laws of the United States are faithfully executed, reasoned Lincoln, the acts enumerated above were constitutional. He simply refused to allow the nation to crumble because of what he viewed as technical requirements of the Constitution.

THE GROWTH OF THE MODERN PRESIDENCY

Before the days of instantaneous communication, the nation could afford to allow Congress, with its relatively slow deliberative processes, to make most decisions. Furthermore, decision making might have been left to Congress because its members, and not the president, were closest to the people. As times and technology have

Politics Now

THE EXPANSION OF PRESIDENTIAL POWERS

The broad presidential powers claimed by Abraham Lincoln during the Civil War and Franklin D. Roosevelt (FDR) during the Great Depression illustrate just some of the ways that presidents have increased the powers of their office beyond what is explicitly written in the Constitution. President Richard M. Nixon, for example, also broadly interpreted executive powers in his attempts to wiretap suspected domestic terrorists' phones without a judge's permission, to block the release of papers regarding the Vietnam War and Watergate, and to impound federal funds.[a]

Like Lincoln, FDR, and Nixon, President George W. Bush has claimed greater administrative powers for the president and his advisers. Many of these powers, including authorizing secret wiretaps administered by the National Security Agency and permitting secret military tribunals for suspected terrorists imprisoned at Guantanamo Bay, have been claimed through relatively unchecked executive orders. Before ordering the invasion of Iraq, Bush worked with leaders in Congress to secure almost unprecedented authorization to circumvent the War Powers Act and run the military intervention through the White House rather than Congress. While the Supreme Court's ruling in *Hamdan* v. *Rumsfeld* (2006) provided a temporary check on the President's approach to detaining and trying detainees linked to the War on Terrorism, the Republican-led Congress rapidly provided Bush with the Military Commissions Act, which gave him the congressional authorization the Court had ruled he needed in order to continue his policies unabated.

How these widely criticized actions will affect the presidency as an institution—as well as President Bush's legacy—remains to be seen. Both Lincoln and FDR were criticized while in office. Today, their actions, which led to economic and military successes, receive wide praise from historians. Some scholars argue that Lincoln and FDR's actions can be viewed as an extension of presidential prerogative, a princi-

ple discussed in the works of British philosopher John Locke, whose writings informed much of the political philosophy of the Framers.[b] Under presidential prerogative, chief executives can act unilaterally in times of national emergency, as long as they have the consent of the governed and are acting in the people's best interests.

Nixon is not viewed as kindly by historians, who largely agree that even in the vague interest of national security, a number of Nixon's actions overstepped the acceptable boundaries of executive power. The Supreme Court, too, agreed with this interpretation: each of the attempts mentioned above to broadly interpret presidential power ended up before the Court; in each case, the Court ruled against Nixon.

The difference between Lincoln and FDR and Nixon seems to be one of how their expansions of presidential power fit within the big picture. As time passes, a similar standard will likely be used to examine Bush's actions. A judgment eventually will be made on whether Bush's expansion of powers provided the successful means to an important end, or whether his actions were unnecessary power-grabs with little clear justification.

QUESTIONS

1. What circumstances justify expansions of presidential power? What specific powers are most appropriate to be expanded?
2. How does the broadening of presidential powers affect the checks and balances and separation of powers systems conceived by the Framers? What can other branches do to rectify any imbalance that may exist?

[a]John W. Dean, "The U.S. Supreme Court and the Imperial Presidency," http://writ.news.findlaw.com/dean/20040116.html.

[b] Arthur M. Schlesinger, *The Imperial Presidency* (Boston: Houghton Mifflin, 1989).

---

changed, however, so have the public's expectations of anyone who becomes president. For example, the breakneck speed with which so many cable news networks and Internet sites report national and international events has intensified the public's expectation that, in a crisis, the president will be the individual to act quickly and decisively on behalf of the entire nation. Congress often is just too slow to respond to fast-changing events—especially in foreign affairs.

In the twentieth and twenty-first centuries, the general trend has been for presidential—as opposed to congressional—decision making to be more and more important. (See Politics Now: The Expansion of Presidential Powers.) The start of this trend can be traced to the four-term presidency of Franklin D. Roosevelt (FDR), who led the nation through several crises. This growth of presidential power and the growth of the federal government and its programs in general are now criticized by many people. To understand the basis for many of the calls for reform of the political

VIDEO ROUNDTABLE

Presidential Greatness

system being made today, it is critical to understand how the growth of government and the role of the president occurred.[18]

FDR took office in 1933 in the midst of a major crisis—the Great Depression—during which a substantial portion of the U.S. workforce was unemployed. Noting the sorry state of the national economy in his Inaugural Address, FDR concluded: "This nation asks for action and action now." To jump-start the American economy, FDR asked Congress for and was given "broad executive powers to wage a war against the emergency, as great as the power that would be given to me if we were in fact invaded by a foreign foe."[19]

Just as Abraham Lincoln had taken bold steps on his inauguration, Roosevelt also acted quickly. He immediately fashioned a plan for national recovery called the **New Deal,** a package of bold and controversial programs designed to invigorate the failing American economy (these are discussed in detail in chapter 3).

Roosevelt served an unprecedented twelve years in office; he was elected to four terms but died shortly after beginning the last one. During his years in office, the nation went from the economic war of the Great Depression to the real international conflict of World War II. The institution of the presidency changed profoundly and permanently as new federal agencies were created to implement New Deal programs as the executive branch became responsible for implementing a wide variety of new programs.

Not only did FDR create a new bureaucracy to implement his pet programs, but he also personalized the presidency by establishing a new relationship between the president and the people. In his radio addresses, or fireside chats, as he liked to call them, he spoke directly to the public in a relaxed and informal manner about serious issues.

To his successors, FDR left the modern presidency, including a burgeoning federal bureaucracy (see chapter 9), an active and usually leading role in both domestic and foreign policy and legislation, and a nationalized executive office that used technology—first radio, then television, and now the Internet—to bring the president closer to the public than ever before.

New Deal
The name given to the program of "Relief, Recovery, Reform" begun by President Franklin D. Roosevelt in 1933 to bring the United States out of the Great Depression.

The Presidential Establishment

AS THE RESPONSIBILITIES AND SCOPE of presidential authority grew over the years, so did the executive branch, including the number of people working directly for the president in the White House. The vice president and his staff, the Cabinet, the first lady and her staff, the Executive Office of the President, and the White House staff all help the president fulfill his duties as chief executive.

THE VICE PRESIDENT

For many years the vice presidency was considered a sure place for a public official to disappear into obscurity. When John Adams wrote to his wife, Abigail, about his position as America's first vice president, he said it was "the most insignificant office that was the invention of man . . . or his imagination conceived."[20]

Historically, presidents chose their vice presidents largely to balance—politically, geographically, or otherwise—the presidential ticket, with little thought given to the possibility that the vice president would become president. Franklin D. Roosevelt, for example, a liberal New Yorker, selected John Nance Garner, a conservative Texan, to be his running mate in 1932. After serving two terms, Garner—who openly disagreed with Roosevelt over many policies, including Roosevelt's decision to seek a third term—unsuccessfully sought the 1940 presidential nomination himself.

The Bush/Cheney ticket in 2000 showed an effort to balance the ticket in ways different from the past. Most commentators agreed that Dick Cheney was chosen to provide "gravitas"—a sense of national governmental experience, especially in foreign affairs, that Governor Bush neither had nor claimed. Similarly, the affable Senator John Edwards (D–NC) was selected as John Kerry's 2004 running mate to soften Kerry's somewhat aloof demeanor.

How much power a vice president has depends on how much the president is willing to give him. Jimmy Carter was the first president to give his vice president, Walter Mondale, more than ceremonial duties. In fact, Walter Mondale was the first vice president to have an office in the White House. No vice presidents, however, have ever enjoyed the access to, and ear of, the president to the extent of Vice President Cheney. Some commentators have even argued that Cheney has a clearer agenda of where the United States should be moving, especially in terms of foreign affairs, than the president. The vice president, for example, long believed it critical to end Saddam Hussein's regime in Iraq in order to build democracy in the Middle East, and there are questions as to whether Cheney and his now former top adviser, Lewis "Scooter" Libby, conspired to silence critics of the administration's justifications for war in Iraq.

Photo courtesy: Steve Sack

■ This political cartoon uses Vice President Dick Cheney's accidental shooting of a friend on a hunting trip to criticize the positions Cheney has taken on a host of policy issues. While Cheney has taken a less public role during President Bush's second term, commentators still credit him as being one of the most powerful vice presidents in American history.

THE CABINET

The Cabinet, which has no basis in the Constitution, is an informal institution based on practice and precedent whose membership is determined by tradition and presidential discretion. By custom, this advisory group selected by the president includes the heads of major executive departments. Presidents today also include their vice presidents in Cabinet meetings, as well as any other agency heads or officials to whom they would like to accord Cabinet-level status.

As a body, the Cabinet's major function is to help the president execute the laws and assist him in making decisions. Although the Framers had discussed the idea of some form of national executive council, they did not include a provision for one in the Constitution. They did recognize, however, the need for departments of government and departmental heads.

As revealed in Table 8.7, over the years the Cabinet has grown as new departments have accommodated for new pressures on the president to act in areas that initially were not considered within the scope of concern of the national government. As interest groups, in particular, pressured Congress and the president to recognize their demands for services and governmental action, they often were rewarded by the creation of an executive department. Since each was headed by a secretary who automatically became a member of the president's Cabinet, powerful groups including farmers (Agriculture), business people (Commerce), workers (Labor), and teachers (Education) saw the creation of a department as increasing their access to the president.

The size of the president's Cabinet has increased over the years at the same time that most presidents' reliance on their Cabinet secretaries has decreased, although some individual members of a president's Cabinet may be very influential. Many

TABLE 8.7 THE U.S. CABINET AND RESPONSIBILITIES OF EACH EXECUTIVE DEPARTMENT

Department Head	Department	Date of Creation	Responsibilities
Secretary of State	Department of State	1789	Responsible for the making of foreign policy, including treaty negotiation
Secretary of the Treasury	Department of the Treasury	1789	Responsible for government funds and regulation of alcohol, firearms, and tobacco
Secretary of Defense	Department of Defense	1789	Responsible for national defense; current department created by consolidating the former Departments of War, the Army, the Navy, and the Air Force in 1947
Attorney General	Department of Justice	1870	Represents U.S. government in all federal courts, investigates and prosecutes violations of federal law
Secretary of the Interior	Department of the Interior	1849	Manages the nation's natural resources, including wildlife and public lands
Secretary of Agriculture	Department of Agriculture	1889	Assists the nation's farmers, oversees food-quality programs, administers food stamp and school lunch programs
Secretary of Commerce	Department of Commerce	1903	Aids businesses and conducts the U.S. Census (originally the Department of Commerce and Labor)
Secretary of Labor	Department of Labor	1913	Runs labor programs, keeps labor statistics, aids labor through enforcement of laws
Secretary of Health and Human Services	Department of Health and Human Services	1953	Runs health, welfare, and Social Security programs; created as the Department of Health, Education, and Welfare (lost its education function in 1979)
Secretary of Housing and Urban Development	Department of Housing and Urban Development	1965	Responsible for urban and housing programs
Secretary of Transportation	Department of Transportation	1966	Responsible for mass transportation and highway programs
Secretary of Energy	Department of Energy	1977	Responsible for energy policy and research, including atomic energy
Secretary of Education	Department of Education	1979	Responsible for the federal government's education programs
Secretary of Veterans Affairs	Department of Veterans Affairs	1989	Responsible for programs aiding veterans
Secretary of Homeland Security	Department of Homeland Security	2002	Responsible for all issues pertaining to homeland security

commentators believe that Secretary of State Condoleezza Rice is especially influential in the Bush administration. (Chapter 9 provides a more detailed discussion of the Cabinet's role in executing U.S. policy.)

THE FIRST LADY

From the time of Martha Washington, first ladies (a term coined during the Civil War) have assisted presidents as informal advisers while making other, more public, significant contributions to American society. Abigail Adams, for example, was a constant sounding board for her husband, John. An early feminist, as early as 1776 she cautioned him "to Remember the Ladies" in any new code of laws. Edith Bolling Galt Wilson was probably the most powerful first lady. When President Woodrow Wilson collapsed and was left partly paralyzed in 1919, she became his surrogate and decided whom and what the stricken president saw. Her detractors dubbed her "Acting First Man."

Eleanor Roosevelt also played a powerful and much criticized role in national affairs. Not only did she write a nationally syndicated daily newspaper column, but she traveled and lectured widely, worked tirelessly on thankless Democratic Party matters, and raised six children. After FDR's death, she shone in her own right as U.S. delegate to the United Nations, where she headed the commission that drafted the covenant on human rights. Later, she headed John F. Kennedy's Commission on the Status of Women. More recently, Hillary Rodham Clinton, currently a U.S. senator from New York, played an active role in her husband's administration, most notably in defining a plan for health care reform that was widely criticized and never adopted.

Initially, Laura Bush, a former librarian, seemed to be following the path of her mother-in-law, former First Lady Barbara Bush. She adopted a behind-the-scenes role and made literacy the focus of her activities. In the aftermath of the tragedy of September 11, 2001, the first lady immediately took on a more public role, speaking out in support of improvements in the legal status of women in Afghanistan and Iraq. She also took to the campaign trail in 2002, 2004, and 2006, very effectively fund-raising on behalf of her husband as well as other Republican candidates.

THE EXECUTIVE OFFICE OF THE PRESIDENT (EOP)

The **Executive Office of the President (EOP)** was established by FDR in 1939 to oversee his New Deal programs. It was created to provide the president with a general staff to help him direct the diverse activities of the executive branch. In fact, it is a mini-bureaucracy of several advisers and offices located in the ornate Executive Office Building next to the White House on Pennsylvania Avenue, as well as in the White House itself, where the president's closest advisers often are located.

The EOP has expanded over time to include several advisory and policy-making agencies and task forces. Over time, the units of the EOP have become the prime policy makers in their fields of expertise as they play key roles in advancing the president's policy preferences. Among the EOP's most important members are the National Security Council, the Council of Economic Advisers, the Office of Management and Budget, the Office of the Vice President, and the Office of the U.S. Trade Representative.

The National Security Council (NSC) was established in 1947 to advise the president on American military affairs and foreign policy. The NSC is composed of the president, the vice president, and the secretaries of state and defense. The chair of the Joint Chiefs of Staff and the director of the Central Intelligence Agency also participate. Others such as the White House chief of staff and the general counsel may attend. The national security adviser runs the staff of the NSC, coordinates information and options, and advises the president.

Photo courtesy: Stock Montage, Inc.

■ In 1919, President Woodrow Wilson had what many believed to be a nervous collapse in the summer and a debilitating stroke in the fall that incapacitated him for several months. His wife, Edith Bolling Galt Wilson, refused to admit his advisers to his sickroom, and rumors flew about the "First Lady President," as many suspected it was his wife and not Wilson who was issuing the orders.

Executive Office of the President (EOP)
Created in 1939 to help the president oversee the executive branch bureaucracy.

Photo courtesy: The White House/Handout/Getty Images

■ President George W. Bush meets with his National Security Council in 2006. The Council's handling of the war in Iraq received a great deal of criticism during the 2006 midterm election campaign.

Although the president appoints the members of each of these bodies, they must perform their tasks in accordance with congressional legislation. As with the Cabinet, depending on who serves in key positions, these mini-agencies may not be truly responsible to the president.

Presidents can give clear indications of their policy preferences by the kinds of offices they include in the EOP. President George W. Bush, for example, not only moved or consolidated several offices when he became president in 2001, but he created a new Office of Faith-Based and Community Initiatives to help him achieve his goal of greater religious involvement in matters of domestic policy.

THE WHITE HOUSE STAFF

Often more directly responsible to the president are the members of the White House staff: the personal assistants to the president, including senior aides, their deputies, assistants with professional duties, and clerical and administrative aides. As personal assistants, these advisers are not subject to Senate confirmation, nor do they have divided loyalties. Their power is derived from their personal relationship to the president, and they have no independent legal authority.

Although presidents organize the White House staff in different ways, they typically have a chief of staff whose job is to facilitate the smooth running of the staff and the executive branch of government. Successful chiefs of staff also have protected the president from mistakes and helped implement policies to obtain the maximum political advantage for the president. Other key White House aides include the counselor to the president; domestic, foreign, and economic policy strategists; communications staff; White House counsel; and a lobbyist who acts as a liaison between the president and Congress.

As presidents have tried to consolidate power in the White House, and as public demands on the president have grown, the size of the White House staff has increased—from fifty-one in 1943, to 247 in 1953, to a high of 583 in 1972. Since that time, staffs have been trimmed, generally running around 500. During his 1992 presidential campaign, Bill Clinton promised to cut the size of the White House staff and that of the Executive Office of the President, and eventually he reduced the size of his staff by approximately 15 percent. The current White House has 435 staffers.

Although White House staffers prefer to be located in the White House in spite of its small offices, many staffers are relegated to the old Executive Office Building next door because White House office space is limited. In Washington, the size of the office is not the measure of power that it often is in corporations. Instead, power in the White House goes to those who have the president's ear and the offices closest to the Oval Office.

The President as Policy Maker

WHEN FDR SENT HIS first legislative package to Congress, he broke the traditional model of law-making.[21] As envisioned by the Framers, it was to be Congress that made the laws. Now FDR was claiming a leadership role for the president in the legislative process. Said the president of this new relationship: "It is the duty of the President to propose and it is the privilege of the Congress to dispose."[22] With those words and the actions that followed, FDR shifted the presidency into a law- and policy-maker role. Now the president and the executive branch not only executed the laws but generally suggested them, too.

Photo courtesy: Bettmann/Corbis

■ President Lyndon B. Johnson signs the long-awaited Civil Rights Act of 1964. Immediately to his right is Senator Edward Brooke (R–MA), the first African American to be popularly elected as a U.S. senator. On his left is Senator Walter Mondale (D–MN), who later served as vice president. Next to Mondale is Thurgood Marshall, whom Johnson later appointed to the U.S. Supreme Court, where he became its first African American member.

THE PRESIDENT'S ROLE IN PROPOSING AND FACILITATING LEGISLATION

From FDR's presidency to the Republican-controlled 104th Congress, the public looked routinely to the president to formulate concrete legislative plans to propose to Congress, which subsequently adopted, modified, or rejected his plans for the nation. Then, in 1994, it appeared for a while that the electorate wanted Congress to reassert itself in the legislative process. In fact, the Contract with America was a Republican call for Congress to take the reins of the law-making process. But several Republican Congresses failed to pass many of the items of the contract, and President Bill Clinton's continued forceful presence in the budgetary process made a resurgent role for Congress largely illusory. The same scenario holds true for President George W. Bush, although by 2006 even some Republicans were concerned with Bush's continued deficit spending requests.

Modern presidents continue to play a major role in setting the legislative agenda, especially in an era when the House and Senate are narrowly divided along partisan lines. Without working majorities, "merely placing a program before Congress is not enough," as President Lyndon B. Johnson (LBJ) once explained. "Without constant attention from the administration, most legislation moves through the congressional process at the speed of a glacier."[23] Thus, the president's most important power (and often the source of his greatest frustration), in addition to support of the public, is his ability to construct coalitions within Congress that will work for passage of his legislation. FDR and LBJ were among the best presidents at working Congress, but they were helped by Democratic majorities in both houses of Congress.[24]

On the whole, presidents have a hard time getting Congress to pass their programs.[25] Passage is especially difficult if the president presides over a divided government, which occurs when the presidency and Congress are controlled by different political parties (see chapter 7). Recent research by political scientists, however, shows that presidents are much more likely to win on bills central to their announced agendas, such as President George W. Bush's victory on the Iraq war resolution, than to secure passage of legislation proposed by others.[26]

Because presidents generally experience declining support for policies they advocate throughout their terms, it is important that a president propose key plans early in his administration, during the honeymoon period, a time when the goodwill toward the president often allows a president to secure passage of legislation that he would not be able to gain at a later period. Even President Lyndon B. Johnson, who was able to get nearly 60 percent of his programs through Congress, noted: "You've got to give it all you can, that first year . . . before they start worrying about themselves. . . . You can't put anything through when half the Congress is thinking how to beat you."[27]

patronage

Jobs, grants, or other special favors that are given as rewards to friends and political allies for their support.

Presidents can also use **patronage** (jobs, grants, or other special favors that are given as rewards to friends and political allies for their support) and personal rewards to win support. Invitations to the White House and campaign visits to the home districts of members of Congress running for office are two ways to curry favor with legislators, and inattention to key members can prove deadly to a president's legislative program. Former Speaker of the House Tip O'Neill (D–MA) reportedly was quite irritated when the Carter transition team refused O'Neill's request for extra tickets to Jimmy Carter's inaugural. This incident did not exactly get the president off to a good start with the powerful Speaker.

Another way a president can bolster support for his legislative package is to call on his political party. As the informal leader of his party, he should be able to use that position to his advantage in Congress, where party loyalty is very important. This strategy works best when the president has carried members of his party into office on his coattails, as was the case in the Johnson and Reagan landslides of 1964 and 1984, respectively. In fact, many scholars regard President Lyndon B. Johnson as the most effective legislative leader.[28] Not only had he served in the House and as Senate majority leader, but he also enjoyed a comfortable Democratic Party majority in Congress, and many Democrats owed their victories to his landslide win over his Republican challenger, Senator Barry Goldwater (R–AZ).[29]

THE BUDGETARY PROCESS AND LEGISLATIVE IMPLEMENTATION

Closely associated with a president's ability to pass legislation is his ability to secure funding for new and existing programs. A president sets national policy and priorities

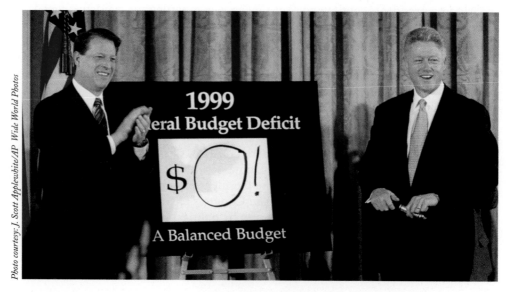

■ President Bill Clinton and Vice President Al Gore celebrate the first balanced budget in years, a feat not likely to be repeated soon in light of the federal tax cuts and huge spending increases under the next president, George W. Bush. In January 2006, the White House announced that the federal budget deficit was down from 2005's $432 billion to $248 billion.

Photo courtesy: J. Scott Applewhite/AP Wide World Photos

through his budget proposals and his continued insistence on their congressional passage. The budget proposal not only outlines the programs he wants but indicates the importance of each program by the amount of funding requested for each and for its associated agency or department.

Because the Framers gave Congress the power of the purse, Congress had primary responsibility for the budget process until 1930. The economic disaster set off by the stock market crash of 1929, however, gave FDR, once elected in 1932, the opportunity to assert himself in the congressional budgetary process, just as he inserted himself in the legislative process. In 1939, the Bureau of the Budget, which had been created in 1921 to help the president tell Congress how much money it would take to run the executive branch of government, was made part of the newly created Executive Office of the President. In 1970, President Nixon changed its name to the **Office of Management and Budget (OMB)** to clarify its function in the executive branch.

The OMB works exclusively for the president and employs hundreds of budget and policy experts. Key OMB responsibilities include preparing the president's annual budget proposal, designing the president's program, and reviewing the progress, budget, and program proposals of the executive department agencies. It also supplies economic forecasts to the president and conducts detailed analyses of proposed bills and agency rules. OMB reports allow the president to attach price tags to his legislative proposals and defend the presidential budget. The OMB budget is a huge document, and even those who prepare it have a hard time deciphering all of its provisions. Even so, the expertise of the OMB directors often gives them an advantage over members of Congress.

Office of Management and Budget (OMB)
The office that prepares the president's annual budget proposal, reviews the budget and programs of the executive departments, supplies economic forecasts, and conducts detailed analyses of proposed bills and agency rules.

POLICY MAKING THROUGH REGULATION

Proposing legislation and using the budget to advance policy priorities are not the only ways that presidents can affect the policy process, especially in times of highly divided government. Major policy changes have been made when a president has issued an **executive order,** a rule or regulation issued by the president that has the effect of law. While many executive orders are issued to help clarify or implement legislation enacted by Congress, other executive orders have the effect of making new policy. President Harry S Truman ordered an end to segregation in the military through an executive order, and affirmative action was institutionalized as national policy through Executive Order 11246, issued by Lyndon B. Johnson in 1966.

executive order
A rule or regulation issued by the president that has the effect of law. All executive orders must be published in the *Federal Register.*

Executive orders have been used since the 1980s to set national policies toward abortion. President Ronald Reagan, for example, used an executive order to stop federal funding of fetal tissue research and to end federal funding of any groups providing abortion counseling. President Bill Clinton immediately rescinded those orders when he became president. One of President George W. Bush's first acts upon taking office was to issue an executive order reversing those Clinton orders.

With the Stroke of a Pen: The Executive Order Over Time

Like presidents before him, George W. Bush has used executive orders to put his policy stamp on a wide array of important issues. After much soul searching, for example, he signed an executive order limiting federal funding of stem cell research to the sixty or so cell lines currently in the possession of scientific researchers.[30] An executive order also was used to allow military tribunals to try any foreigners captured by U.S. forces in Afghanistan or linked to the 9/11 terrorist acts. One of President Bush's more controversial executive orders eviscerated the 1978 Presidential Records Act, which "established that the records of presidents belong to the American people."[31] Now, scholars, journalists, and other interested persons must demonstrate a specific "need to know" when requesting presidential or vice presidential documents.[32] For whatever reason the order was issued, it demonstrates how easily presidents may thwart the wishes of Congress and substitute their own policy preferences through executive orders, which require congressional action to make them unenforceable.

Presidential Leadership and the Importance of Public Opinion

A PRESIDENT'S ABILITY to get his programs adopted or implemented depends on many factors, including his leadership abilities, his personality and powers of persuasion, his ability to mobilize public opinion to support his actions, the public's perception of his performance, and Congress's perception of his public support.

PRESIDENTIAL LEADERSHIP

Leadership is not an easy thing to exercise, and it remains an elusive concept for scholars to identify and measure, but it is important to all presidents seeking support for their programs and policies. Moreover, ideas about the importance of effective leaders have deep roots in our political culture. The leadership abilities of the great presidents—Washington, Jefferson, Lincoln, and FDR—have been extolled over and over again, leading us to fault modern presidents who fail to cloak themselves in the armor of leadership. (See American Values/American Voices: The President and Moral Leadership.) Americans thus have come to believe that "If presidential leadership works some of the time, why not all of the time?"[33] This attitude, in turn, directly influences what we expect presidents to do and how we evaluate them (see Table 8.8).

Research by political scientists shows that presidents can exercise leadership by increasing public attention to particular issues. Analyses of presidential State of the Union Addresses, for example, reveal that mentions of particular policies translate into more Americans mentioning those policies as the most important problems facing the nation.[34]

Frequently, the difference between great and mediocre presidents centers on their ability to grasp the importance of leadership style. Truly great presidents, such as Lincoln and FDR, understood that the White House was a seat of power from which decisions could flow to shape the national destiny. They recognized that their day-to-day activities and how they went about them should be designed to bolster support for their policies and to secure congressional and popular backing that could translate their intuitive judgment into meaningful action. Mediocre presidents, on the other hand, have tended to regard the White House as "a stage for the presentation of performances to the public" or a fitting honor to cap a career.[35]

Political scientist Richard E. Neustadt calls the president's ability to influence members of Congress and the public "the power to persuade." Neustadt believes this power is crucial to presidential leadership.[36]

TABLE 8.8 BARBER'S PRESIDENTIAL PERSONALITIES

Political scientist James David Barber defines presidential character as the "way the president orients himself toward life." Barber believes that there are four presidential character types, based on energy level (whether the president is active or passive) and the degree of enjoyment a president finds in the job (whether the president has a positive or negative attitude). Barber believes that active and positive presidents are more successful than passive and negative presidents. Active-positive presidents, he argues, approach the presidency with a characteristic zest for life and have a drive to lead and succeed. In contrast, passive-negative presidents find themselves reacting to circumstances, are likely to take directions from others, and fail to make full use of the enormous resources of the executive office.

	Active	Passive
Positive	F. Roosevelt	Taft
	Truman	Harding
	Kennedy	Reagan
	Ford	
	Carter[a]	
	G. Bush	
Negative	Wilson	Coolidge
	Hoover	Eisenhower
	L. Johnson	
	Nixon	

[a]Some scholars think that Carter better fits the active-negative typology.

Source: James David Barber, *The Presidential Character: Predicting Performance in the White House,* 4th ed. (Englewood Cliffs, NJ: Prentice Hall, 1992).

American Values/American Voices

THE PRESIDENT AND MORAL LEADERSHIP

In addition to the many formal roles that come with the office, the president of the United States is often expected to be the nation's moral leader and the chief enforcer of American values. Beginning in elementary school, for example, children learn not only about the contributions of great presidents to the betterment of the nation but also about these leaders' moral behavior. Students are taught that a young George Washington cut down a cherry tree against his parents' orders but could not lie to his father about his actions. Similarly, school children learn that Abraham Lincoln embraced American values of equality and fairness and as a result fought the Civil War to free the slaves and maintain the Union. But, neither of these stories is entirely correct. Washington most likely never cut down that cherry tree, and in recent years, scholars have questioned Lincoln's motives for the conduct of the Civil War. One researcher, for example, has claimed that Lincoln used the presidency to serve his own economic interests, as well as those of the railroad companies who had supported his political campaigns.[a]

The stories we learn as children help to increase the mythology of the American presidency. By telling tales of how the greatest presidents behaved during the nation's early years, Americans perpetuate the myth that presidents are exemplary figures born with moral compasses far superior to those possessed by the average citizen. And, in setting such a high bar for presidential actions, Americans also set themselves up for inevitable disappointment, expecting a level of perfection from presidents that no man or woman could possibly achieve.

Presidents, in truth, are just as likely as other citizens to suffer lapses of morality in both their professional and personal lives. President Bill Clinton, for example, was not the first president to be accused of adultery. He was just one president in a long line of predecessors including Thomas Jefferson, Andrew Jackson, Grover Cleveland, Franklin D. Roosevelt, and John F. Kennedy.

And, while President George W. Bush has been heavily criticized for his liberal use of executive orders for a variety of purposes, including establishing military tribunals and authorizing wiretaps of suspected terrorists, he is not the first president to use executive orders to achieve his policy goals. Presidents Franklin D. Roosevelt and Harry S Truman, for example, used executive orders to seize mills, mines, and factories whose production was crucial to the World War II and Korean War efforts. Roosevelt and Truman argued that these actions were necessary to preserve national security. The Supreme Court, however, eventually disagreed with the Truman administration in *Youngstown Sheet and Tube* v. *Sawyer* (1952). In that case, the Court unequivocally stated that Truman had overstepped the boundaries of his office as provided by the Constitution.[b]

It is important to remember that, whatever Americans are socialized to believe, presidents are not necessarily morally or ethically superior to average human beings. This idea was widely acknowledged by the Framers and was part of the reason the Constitution's authors relied so heavily on the concepts of checks and balances and separation of powers. No acknowledgment of this truth is more famous than that written by James Madison in *Federalist No. 51:* "If men were angels, no government would be necessary. If angels were to govern men, neither external nor internal controls on government would be necessary."

QUESTIONS

1. Why do you think presidents are expected to be moral leaders for the citizens of the United States? Do you think this expectation is a reasonable one? Why or why not?
2. What factors should be taken into consideration when judging the morality of presidential actions? Should presidents be held to a different moral or ethical standard than ordinary American citizens?

---

[a]Thomas DiLorenzo, *The Real Lincoln: A New Look at Abraham Lincoln, His Agenda, and an Unnecessary War*, reprint ed. (New York: Three Rivers Press, 2003).

[b]*Youngstown Sheet and Tube* v. *Sawyer*, 343 U.S. 579 (1952).

GOING PUBLIC: MOBILIZING PUBLIC OPINION

Historically, even before the days of radio, television, and the Internet, presidents tried to reach out to the public to gain support for their programs through what President Theodore Roosevelt called the bully pulpit. The development of commercial air travel and radio, newsreels, television, and computers have made direct communication to larger numbers of voters easier. Presidents, first ladies, and other presidential advisers

■ Most pundits as well as the public agree that President George W. Bush grew into his office in the aftermath of 9/11.

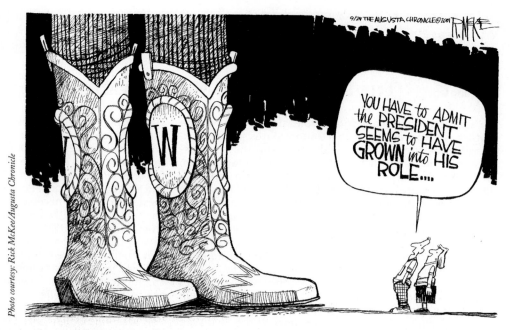

Photo courtesy: Rick McKee/Augusta Chronicle

■ President George W. Bush with former baseball great Cal Ripken and a former member of the original Girls Professional Baseball League (dramatized in the film *A League of Their Own*) at a T-Ball game on the White House lawn.

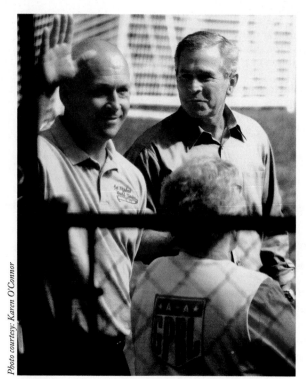

Photo courtesy: Karen O'Connor

travel all over the world to publicize their views and to build personal support as well as support for administration programs.

Direct, presidential appeals to the electorate like those often made by recent presidents are referred to as "going public."[37] Going public means that a president goes over the heads of members of Congress to gain support from the people, who can then place pressure on their elected officials in Washington.

Like most presidents, Bill Clinton was keenly aware of the importance of maintaining his connection with the public. Beginning with his 1992 campaign, Clinton often appeared on *Larry King Live* on CNN. Even after becoming president, Clinton continued to take his case directly to the people. He launched his health care reform proposals, for example, on a prime-time edition of *Nightline* hosted by Ted Koppel. Moreover, at a black-tie dinner honoring radio and television correspondents, Clinton responded to criticisms leveled against him for not holding traditional press conferences by pointing out how clever he was to ignore the traditional press. "You know why I can stiff you on the press conferences? Because Larry King liberated me from you by giving me to the American people directly," quipped Clinton.[38]

George W. Bush continued in the Clinton tradition of rarely holding press conferences yet trying to go directly to the people. He chose, for example, to give important speeches on the ongoing war in Iraq before receptive audiences at the National War College and the U.S. Air Force Academy.

THE PUBLIC'S PERCEPTION OF PRESIDENTIAL PERFORMANCE

Historically, a president has the best chances of convincing Congress to follow his policy lead when his public opinion ratings are

Global Perspective

NORTH KOREA'S KIM JONG IL AND UNCONTROLLED EXECUTIVE AUTHORITY

One of the Framers' biggest concerns was the potential for tyranny that a strong executive branch could present. As a result, the president's powers are subject to constitutional checks by the Congress and Supreme Court, as well as the will of the people, who vote in presidential elections every four years.

The difference between the American and North Korean executive could not be more extreme. The North Korean government is widely considered one of the world's most oppressive, and this is especially evident in the structure and function of its executive in relation to North Korea's institutions of government. North Korea—or, as it is formally known, the Democratic People's Republic of Korea (DPRK)—is a communist dictatorship that has been controlled by Kim Jong Il, the son of North Korea's founder, President Kim Il Sung, since the elder's death in 1994. The position of president essentially was abolished in North Korea in 1998 when Kim Il Sung was declared "eternal president of the republic."

Executive authority, political power, and governing right are vested in North Korea's only major political party, the Korean Workers' Party (KWP). Several minor parties exist, but they are controlled by the KWP and do not oppose its rule. Since 1997, Kim Jong Il's official titles have been general secretary of the KWP and chairman of the National Defense Commission. In 1998, Kim's latter position, which places him in control of North Korea's extensive military apparatus, was declared the "highest office of state," making him North Korea's official head of state.

Like the United States' Constitution, North Korea's Constitution calls for separation of power and checks and balances. However, due to the extremely secretive nature of the North Korean regime, little is known concerning the actual relationships between the executive, legislative, and judicial branches. The legislature, known as the Supreme People's Assembly, is understood to be a rubber-stamp assembly: it simply ratifies decisions made by executive institutions subject to KWP control. Since Kim Jong Il serves as both head of state and head of the party, the legislative authority of the assembly is considered nonexistent. North Korea's executive extensively interferes with the judiciary, and judges and prosecutors at all levels are chosen by KWP members, giving Kim Jong Il and his supporters *de facto* control over judicial operations.

The control Kim exercises over North Korea's economy is similar to his control of the nation's political and military institutions. Kim Il Sung's emphasis on building and maintaining an army, estimated to be as large as 1 million, resulted in a nation whose people depend on international aid for basic necessities. Widespread famine continues as Kim Jong Il's government allocates resources to building long-range missiles and developing chemical, biological, and nuclear weapons—an issue of great concern to the United States and other nations. The nation's domestic woes are likely to continue after the UN ordered additional sanctions when North Korea tested a nuclear bomb in October 2006, defying a UN directive not to do so.

QUESTIONS

1. Should absolute power be entrusted to a single political institution or individual? Why or why not?
2. How does the centralization of power in North Korea affect North Korea's citizens and other nations?

Sources: Library of Congress, "Country Notes, North Korea"; Freedom House, "North Korea"; *CIA World Factbook.*

---

high. Presidential popularity, however, generally follows a cyclical pattern. These cycles have been recorded since 1938, when pollsters first began to track presidential popularity.

Typically, presidents enjoy their highest level of public approval at the beginning of their terms and try to take advantage of this honeymoon period to get their programs passed by Congress as soon as possible. Each action a president takes, however, is divisive—some people will approve, and others will disapprove. Disapproval tends to have a negative cumulative effect on a president's approval rating.

Since Lyndon B. Johnson's presidency, only four presidents have left office with approval ratings of more than 50 percent. (See Analyzing Visuals: Presidential Approval Ratings Since 1953, by Party.) Many credit this trend to events such as Viet-

Presidential Success in Polls and Congress

Analyzing Visuals

PRESIDENTIAL APPROVAL RATINGS SINCE 1953, BY PARTY

Presidential approval ratings tend to follow a cyclical pattern. Presidents generally enjoy their highest ratings at the beginning of their terms and experience lower ratings toward the end. Presidents also typically receive higher rates of approval from members of their own party throughout their terms than from members of the opposing party. Presidents George Bush, Bill Clinton, and George W. Bush all enjoyed popularity surges during the course of their terms, and the drop-offs from those surges were generally much steeper among members of the other party than among members of their own party. President George W. Bush received a spectacular and sustained boost after September 11, 2001, but his approval ratings later dropped dramatically among voters affiliated with the Democratic Party, and he has received low marks from members of the Republican Party as well.

After viewing the line graph and reading the related chapter material, answer the following critical thinking questions about presidential approval patterns: What explains the cyclical pattern of presidential approval? Which presidents since Eisenhower have had the lowest ratings from members of the other party? By members of their own party? Which have had the highest ratings by members of the other party? By members of their own party? Do recent presidents' approval ratings follow the same overall pattern as those for presidents in the 1960s and 1970s?

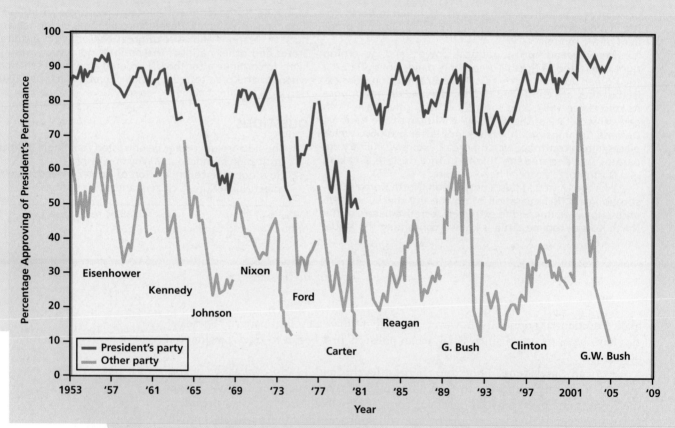

Source: Gary C. Jacobson, University of California at San Diego.

nam, Watergate, and the Iraq War, which have made the public increasingly skeptical of presidential performance.

However, recent presidents, including George Bush, Bill Clinton, and George W. Bush, have experienced a surge in their approval ratings during the course of their presidencies. Popularity surges allow presidents to achieve some policy goals that they believe are for the good of the nation, even though the policies are unpopular with the public. Usually coming on the heels of a domestic or international crisis such as the 1991 Persian Gulf War or the 9/11 terrorist attacks, these increased approval ratings generally don't last long, as the cumulative effects of governing once again catch up with the president.

President George Bush's rapid rise in popularity occurred after the major and, perhaps more important, quick victory in the 1991 Persian Gulf War. His popularity, however, plummeted as the good feelings faded and Americans began to feel the pinch of recession. In contrast, President Bill Clinton's approval scores skyrocketed after the 1996 Democratic National Convention. More interestingly, Clinton's high approval ratings continued in the wake of allegations of wrongdoing in the Oval Office, his eventual admission of inappropriate conduct, and through his impeachment proceedings. In fact, when Clinton went to the American public and admitted that he misled them about his relationship with Monica Lewinsky, an ABC poll conducted immediately after his speech showed a 10-point jump in his job approval rating.[39]

George W. Bush enjoyed one of the longest rallies in history. But, by 2005, his approval ratings once again hovered around 50 percent in the wake of personnel scandals, escalating violence in Iraq, and rising gas prices. The president's approval ratings dropped even lower in 2006; by the midterm elections they were a scant 35 percent. In many states, voters viewed the elections as a referendum on Bush, leading to widespread Democratic victories that resulted in Democrats gaining control of both the House and the Senate. The number of Democratic governors increased by seven in the 2006 elections, and Democrats also won control of nine additional chambers in the state legislatures.

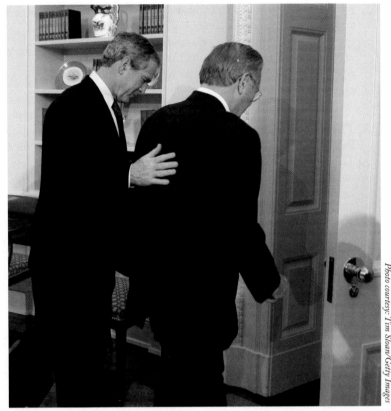

Photo courtesy: Tim Sloan/Getty Images

■ In the wake of Democratic wins that some attributed to President Bush's low approval ratings, Secretary of Defense Donald Rumsfeld surprised observers when he resigned a day after the 2006 midterm elections. Here, President Bush escorts Rumsfeld to the door of the Oval Office after the president introduced his nominee for Rumsfeld's replacement, Robert Gates.

Summary

BECAUSE THE FRAMERS FEARED a tyrannical monarch, they gave considerable thought to the office of the chief executive. Since ratification of the Constitution, the office has changed considerably—more through practice and need than from changes in the Constitution. In chronicling these changes, we have made the following points:

1. The Origins of and Rules Governing the Office of President of the United States

Distrust of a too powerful leader led the Framers to create an executive office with limited powers. They mandated that a president be at least thirty-five years old, a natural-born citizen, and a resident of the United States for at least fourteen years, and they opted not to limit the president's term of office. To further guard against tyranny, they made provisions for the removal of the president.

2. The Constitutional Powers of the President
The Framers gave the president a variety of specific constitutional powers in Article II, including the ap-

pointment power, the power to convene Congress, and the power to make treaties. The Constitution also gives the president the power to grant pardons and to veto acts of Congress. In addition, the president derives considerable power from being commander in chief of the military.

3. The Development and Expansion of Presidential Power

The development of presidential power has depended on the personal force of those who have held the office. George Washington, in particular, took several actions to establish the primacy of the president in national affairs and as true chief executive of a strong national government. But, with only a few exceptions, subsequent presidents often let Congress dominate in national affairs. With the election of FDR, however, the power of the president increased, and presidential decision making became more important in national and foreign affairs.

4. The Presidential Establishment

As the responsibilities of the president have grown, so has the executive branch of government. FDR established the Executive Office of the President to help him govern. Perhaps the most key policy advisers are those closest to the president: the vice president, the White House staff, some members of the Executive Office of the President, and sometimes, the first lady.

5. The President as Policy Maker

Since FDR, the public has looked to the president to propose legislation to Congress. Through proposing legislation, advancing budgets, and involvement in the regulatory process, presidents make policy.

6. Presidential Leadership and the Importance of Public Opinion

To gain support for his programs or proposed budget, the president uses a variety of skills, including personal leadership and direct appeals to the public. How the president goes about winning support is determined by his leadership and personal style, affected by his character and his ability to persuade. Since the 1970s, however, the American public has been increasingly skeptical of presidential actions, and few presidents have enjoyed extended periods of the kind of popularity needed to help win support for programmatic change.

KEY TERMS

Cabinet, p. 287
executive agreement, p. 288
Executive Office of the President (EOP), p. 301
executive order, p. 305
executive privilege, p. 284
impeachment, p. 283
inherent powers, p. 295
line-item veto, p. 289
New Deal, p. 298
Office of Management and Budget (OMB), p. 305
pardon, p. 292
patronage, p. 304
Twenty-Fifth Amendment, p. 285
Twenty-Second Amendment, p. 282
U.S. v. *Nixon* (1974), p. 284
veto power, p. 288
War Powers Act, p. 291

SELECTED READINGS

Barber, James David. *The Presidential Character: Predicting Presidential Performance in the White House,* 4th ed. Englewood Cliffs, NJ: Prentice Hall, 1992.

Campbell, Karlyn Kohr, and Kathleen Hall Jamieson. *Deeds Done in Words: Presidential Rhetoric and the Genres of Governance.* Chicago: University of Chicago Press, 1990.

Cooper, Philip J. *By Order of the President: The Use and Abuse of Executive Direct Action.* Lawrence: University Press of Kansas, 2002.

Cronin, Thomas E., and Michael A. Genovese. *The Paradoxes of the American Presidency,* 2nd ed. New York: Oxford University Press, 2006.

Dallek, Robert. *Hail to the Chief: The Making and Unmaking of American Presidents.* New York: Oxford University Press, 2001.

Daynes, Byron W., and Glen Sussman. *The American Presidency and the Social Agenda.* Upper Saddle River, NJ: Prentice Hall, 2001.

Edwards, George C., III, and Stephen J. Wayne. *Presidential Leadership: Politics and Policy Making,* 6th ed. New York: Bedford Books, 2002.

Greenstein, Fred I. *The Presidential Difference: Leadership Style from FDR to George W. Bush,* 2nd ed. Princeton, NJ: Princeton University Press, 2004.

Martin, Janet M. *The American Presidency and Women: Promise, Performance, and Illusion.* College Station: Texas A&M University Press, 2003.

Neustadt, Richard E. *Presidential Power and the Modern Presidents.* New York: Free Press, 1991.

Pfiffner, James P. *The Character Factor: How We Judge America's Presidents.* College Station: Texas A&M University Press, 2004.

———. *The Modern Presidency,* 4th ed. Belmont, CA: Wadsworth, 2004.

Ragsdale, Lyn. *Vital Statistics on the Presidency: Washington to Clinton.* Washington, DC: CQ Press, 1998.

Rossiter, Clinton. *The American Presidency,* reprint ed. Baltimore, MD: Johns Hopkins University Press, 1987.

Skowronek, Stephen. *The Politics Presidents Make: Leadership from John Adams to Bill Clinton.* Cambridge, MA: Harvard University Press, 1997.

Warshaw, Shirley Anne. *The Keys to Power: Managing the Presidency,* 2nd ed. New York: Longman, 2004.

WEB EXPLORATIONS

To learn more about specific presidents, see
http://www.nara.gov/nara/president/address.html

For a chronology of the Clinton impeachment proceedings, see
http://www.washintonpost.com/wp-srv/politics/special/clinton/timeline.htm

For more on the vice president, see
http://www.whitehouse.gov/vicepresident/

To learn more about presidential pardons, go to
http://jurist.law.pitt.edu/pardons0a.htm

For more on the modern White House, see
http://www.whitehouse.gov

For more on first ladies, see
http://www.firstladies.org

To try your hand at balancing the budget, go to
http://www.nathannewman.org/nbs/

For more details on Watergate, see
http://watergate.info/

For more on the White House Project, see
http://www.thewhitehouseproject.org

For more details on the controversy over the War Powers Act, see
http://www.ford.utexas.edu/library/speeches/770411.htm and
http://www.fff.org/comment/com0204a.asp

THE WHITE HOUSE
WASHINGTON

NATIONAL STRATEGY FOR
PANDEMIC
INFLUENZA

IMPLEMENTATION PLAN

Photo courtesy: Ron Edmonds/AP Wide World Photo

THE EXECUTIVE BRANCH AND THE FEDERAL BUREAUCRACY

9

TO MAINTAIN A SECURE HOMELAND, planning is critical. And, at a time when federal resources are stretched to their limit given the high cost of military interventions in Iraq and Afghanistan, the U.S. government—especially its bureaucracy—is trying to prepare for what some are calling the next pandemic: avian flu.

Avian influenza, or H5N1—the designation scientists have given this particular strain of the influenza virus—has infected domesticated and migratory birds in more than fifty nations across Asia, Africa, and Europe. It has infected more than 250 people worldwide, with an astonishingly high death rate of more than 50 percent. Flu viruses mutate rapidly, and experts believe it is highly likely that this particular strain of avian flu could become a global threat to humanity. The last major influenza pandemic occurred in 1918 and killed tens of millions of people worldwide.

Since it takes time to culture a reliable vaccine to protect people from getting a specific strain of flu, a virus like H5N1, if it becomes easily transmittable from person to person, could outpace the abilities of governments to vaccinate their citizens or contain the outbreak. Even if the first widespread infections occurred in China, given the global travel patterns of U.S. citizens, a deadly virus likely would be on the ground in the United States within weeks. "If such an outbreak occurred, hospitals would become overwhelmed, riots would engulf vaccination clinics, and even power and food would be in short supply," concludes a draft of a plan the Bush administration developed as part of its initial planning to handle avian flu.[1]

On May 3, 2006, Frances Townsend, the White House homeland security adviser, issued the administration's Pandemic Influenza Strategic Plan to get the nation ready for a 1918-style flu disaster, which left more than one-half million Americans dead. The new government plan outlined the responsibilities of every federal department and agency should the flu begin to spread quickly among humans. The secretary of health and human services was given major responsibility for health issues, and nonmedical emergency efforts and coordination were given to the secretary of homeland security. The secretary of state was given responsibility for international response issues.[2]

Critics were quick to point out that none of the secretaries were given emergency powers to spend additional monies, such as granting emergency medical coverage to the uninsured. Priorities as to how to allot any vaccines or interventional medicines were also left unanswered, as was any potential role for the military. "The real shortcoming of the plan is that it doesn't say who's in charge," said a top health official who fears the consequences of a disorganized response from the federal government.[3] Possibly further complicating a "national plan of action," the administration's plan places tremendous responsibility on state and local governments, who are often first responders in any emergency, and it has been criticized by the National Association of County and City Health Officials, who view the administration's plan as "the mother of all unfunded mandates."[4]

The plan, which suggests steps that state and local governments can take to prepare for a pandemic, calls for quarantine and travel restrictions, but the administration admits that such steps are largely stopgap measures. Its worst-case scenario foresees the deaths of nearly 2 million Americans and the need to hospitalize an additional 8.5 million.

---

bureaucracy
A set of complex hierarchical departments, agencies, commissions, and their staffs that exist to help a chief executive officer carry out his or her duties. Bureaucracies may be private organizations of governmental units.

IN THE AMERICAN SYSTEM, the **bureaucracy,** or the thousands of federal government agencies and institutions that implement and administer federal laws and programs, can be thought of as the part of the government that makes policy as it links together the three branches of the national government. Although Congress makes the laws, it must rely on bureaucrats in the executive branch to enforce and implement them. These agency determinations, in turn, are often challenged in the courts. Because most administrative agencies that make up part of the bureaucracy enjoy reputations for special expertise in clearly defined policy areas, the federal judiciary routinely defers to bureaucratic administrative decision makers.

A massive pandemic of the sort described in the opening vignette would tax every agency of the federal bureaucracy, whether it was directly involved in health issues or not. If quarantines were put into effect, for example, the U.S. Postal Service would close down, Social Security checks would not be printed or mailed, banks might close, and commerce could come to a stop. Such is the tremendous scope of what the federal government and the bureaucrats and political appointees who run it do.

The federal bureaucracy often is called the "fourth branch of government." But, politicians often charge that the bureaucracy is too large, too powerful, and too unaccountable to the people or even to elected officials. Many politicians, elected officials, and voters also complain that the federal bureaucracy is too wasteful. However, few critics discuss the fact that laws and policies also are implemented by state and local bureaucracies and bureaucrats whose numbers are proportionately far larger, and often far less accountable, than those working for the federal government.

As a result, many Americans are uncomfortable with the large role of the federal government in policy making. Nevertheless, recent studies show that most users of federal agencies rate quite favorably the agencies and the services they receive. Many of those polled by the Pew Research Center were frustrated by complicated rules and the slowness of a particular agency. Still, a majority gave most agencies overall high marks. Most of those polled drew sharp distinctions between particular agencies and the government as a whole. For example, 84 percent of physicians and pharmacists rated the Food and Drug Administration favorably, whereas only one-half of all those sampled were positive about the government in general.[5]

Harold D. Lasswell once defined political science as the "study of who gets what, when, and how."[6] It is by studying the bureaucracy that those questions can perhaps best be answered. To allow you to understand the role of the bureaucracy, this chapter explores the following issues:

- First, we will examine *the origins and growth of the federal bureaucracy.*
- Second, we will examine *the modern bureaucracy* by discussing bureaucrats and the formal organization of the bureaucracy.
- Third, we will discuss *how the bureaucracy works.*
- Finally, we will discuss *making agencies accountable.*

TIMELINE

Evolution of the Federal Bureaucracy

The Origins and Growth of the Federal Bureaucracy

IN 1789, ONLY THREE DEPARTMENTS existed under the Articles of Confederation: Foreign Affairs, War, and Treasury. President George Washington inherited those departments, and soon, the head of each department was called its secretary and Foreign Affairs was renamed the Department of State. To provide the president with legal advice, Congress also created the office of attorney general. From the beginning, individuals appointed as Cabinet secretaries (as well as the attorney general) were subject to approval by the U.S. Senate, but they could be removed from office by the president alone. Even the First Congress realized how important it was that a president be surrounded by those in whom he had complete confidence and trust.

From 1816 to 1861, the size of the federal executive branch and the bureaucracy grew as increased demands were made on existing departments and new departments were created. The Post Office, for example, which Article I constitutionally authorized the Congress to create, was forced to expand to meet the needs of a growing and westward-expanding population. President Andrew Jackson removed the Post Office from the jurisdiction of the Department of the Treasury in 1829 and promoted the postmaster general to Cabinet rank.

Photo courtesy: Rob Crandall/The Image Works

■ The federal bureaucracy encompasses numerous agencies and institutions. Here, an employee of the Bureau of Engraving and Printing checks new U.S. one dollar bills.

Photo courtesy: Bettmann/Corbis

■ A political cartoonist's view of how President Andrew Jackson would be immortalized for his use of the spoils system.

spoils system
The firing of public-office holders of a defeated political party and their replacement with loyalists of the newly elected party.

patronage
Jobs, grants, or other special favors that are given as rewards to friends and political allies for their support.

VIDEO DEBATE
The Merit System

The Post Office quickly became a major source of jobs President Jackson could fill by presidential appointment, as every small town and village in the United States had its own postmaster. In commenting on Jackson's wide use of political positions to reward friends and loyalists, one fellow Jacksonian Democrat commented: "to the victors belong the spoils." From that statement came the term **spoils system,** which describes an executive's ability to fire public office holders of the defeated political party and replace them with party loyalists. The spoils system was a form of **patronage:** jobs, grants, or other special favors given as rewards to friends and political allies for their support. Political patronage often is defended as an essential element of the party system because it provides rewards and inducements for party workers.

THE CIVIL WAR AND THE GROWTH OF GOVERNMENT

As discussed in chapter 3, the Civil War (1861–1865) permanently changed the nature of the federal bureaucracy. As the nation geared up for war, thousands of additional employees were added to existing departments. The Civil War also spawned the need for new government agencies. A series of poor harvests and distribution problems led President Abraham Lincoln (who understood that you need well-fed troops to conduct a war) to create the Department of Agriculture in 1862, although it was not given full Cabinet-level status until more than twenty years later.

After the Civil War, the need for a strong national government continued unabated. The Pension Office was established in 1866 to pay benefits to the thousands of Union veterans who had fought in the war (more than 127,000 veterans initially were eligible for benefits). Justice, headed by the attorney general, was made a department in 1870, and other departments were added through 1900. Agriculture became a full-fledged department in 1889 and began to play an important role in informing farmers about the latest developments in soil conservation, livestock breeding, and planting techniques.

FROM THE SPOILS SYSTEM TO THE MERIT SYSTEM

The spoils system reached a high-water mark during Abraham Lincoln's presidency. By the time James A. Garfield, a former distinguished Civil War officer, was elected president in 1880, many reformers were calling for changes in the patronage system. Garfield's immediate predecessor, Rutherford B. Hayes, had favored the idea of the replacement of the spoils system with a merit system based on test scores and ability. Congress, however, failed to pass the legislation he proposed. Possibly because potential job seekers wanted to secure positions before Congress had the opportunity to act on an overhauled civil service system, thousands pressed Garfield for positions. This siege prompted Garfield to record in his diary: "My day is frittered away with the personal seeking of people when it ought to be given to the great problems which concern the whole country."[7] Garfield resolved to reform the civil service, but his life was cut short by the bullets of an assassin who, ironically, was a frustrated job seeker.

Public reaction to Garfield's death and increasing criticism of the spoils system prompted Congress to pass the Civil Service Reform Act in 1883, more commonly

■ An artist's interpretation of President James A. Garfield's assassination at the hands of an unhappy office seeker.

known as the **Pendleton Act,** named in honor of its sponsor, Senator George H. Pendleton (D–OH). It established the principle of federal employment on the basis of open, competitive exams and created a bipartisan three-member Civil Service Commission, which operated until 1978. Initially, only about 10 percent of the positions in the federal **civil service system** were covered by the law, but later laws and executive orders extended coverage of the act to over 90 percent of all federal employees. This new system was called the **merit system.**

REGULATING THE ECONOMY

As the nation grew, so did the bureaucracy (see Analyzing Visuals: The Ebb and Flow of Federal Employees in the Executive Branch, 1789–2005). In the wake of the tremendous growth of big business (especially railroads), widespread price fixing, and other unfair business practices that occurred after the Civil War, Congress created the Interstate Commerce Commission (ICC). In creating the ICC, Congress was reacting to public outcries over the exorbitant rates charged by railroad companies for hauling freight. It became the first **independent regulatory commission,** an agency outside a major executive department. Independent regulatory commissions such as the ICC, generally concerned with particular aspects of the economy, are created by Congress to be independent of direct presidential authority. Commission members are appointed by the president and hold their jobs for fixed terms, but they are not removable by the president unless they fail to uphold their oaths of office. In 1887, the creation of the ICC also marked a shift in the focus of the bureaucracy from service to regulation. Its creation gave the government—in the shape of the bureaucracy—vast powers over individual and property rights.

When Theodore Roosevelt, a progressive Republican, became president in 1901, the movement toward governmental regulation of the economic sphere was strengthened. The size of the bureaucracy was further increased when, in 1903, Roosevelt asked Congress to establish a Department of Commerce and Labor to oversee employer-employee relations. At the turn of the twentieth century, many workers toiled long hours for low wages in substandard conditions. Many employers refused to recognize the rights of workers to join unions, and many businesses had grown so large and powerful that they could force workers to accept substandard conditions. The

Pendleton Act
Reform measure that created the Civil Service Commission to administer a partial merit system. The act classified the federal service by grades, to which appointments were made based on the results of a competitive examination. It made it illegal for federal political appointees to be required to contribute to a particular political party.

civil service system
The system created by civil service laws by which many appointments to the federal bureaucracy are made.

merit system
The system by which federal civil service jobs are classified into grades or levels, to which appointments are made on the basis of performance on competitive examinations.

independent regulatory commission
An agency created by Congress that is generally concerned with a specific aspect of the economy.

Analyzing Visuals

THE EBB AND FLOW OF FEDERAL EMPLOYEES IN THE EXECUTIVE BRANCH, 1789–2005

As discussed in chapter 8, most major expansions of governmental authority occur during times of war, social crisis, or economic emergency. For example, the federal government grew slowly until the 1930s, when President Franklin D. Roosevelt's New Deal programs were created in response to the high unemployment and weak financial markets of the Great Depression. A more modest spike in the federal workforce occurred in the mid-1960s during President Lyndon B. Johnson's Great Society program.

After reviewing the data and balloons in the line graph and reading the material in this chapter on the origins and development of the executive branch and federal bureaucracy, answer the following critical thinking questions: Before the United States' involvement in World War II, what was the principal reason for the growth in the number of federal employees? The rapid decline in federal employees between 1945 and 1950 resulted from the end of World War II, but why do you think the number of federal employees declined after 1970? What do you think caused the increase in federal employees between 1975 and 1990? Later decreases in the Clinton and George W. Bush administrations?

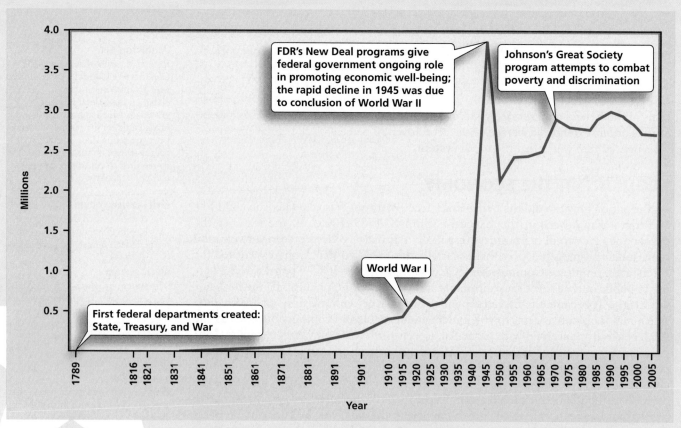

Sources: Office of Personnel Management, *The Fact Book,* http://www.opm.gov/feddata/factbook/2005/factbook2005.pdf.

progressives wanted new government regulations to cure some of the ills suffered by workers and to control the power of the increasingly monopolistic corporations.

In 1913, when it became clear that one agency could not well represent the interests of both employers and employees, President Woodrow Wilson divided the Department of Commerce and Labor, creating two separate departments: Commerce and Labor. One year later, in 1914, Congress created the Federal Trade Commission (FTC). Its function was to protect small businesses and the public from unfair competition, especially from big business. Bureaus within departments also were created to concentrate on a variety of issues.

As discussed in chapter 3, the ratification of the Sixteenth Amendment to the Constitution in 1913 affected the size of government and the possibilities for growth. It gave Congress the authority to implement a federal income tax to supplement the national treasury and provided a huge infusion of funds to support new federal agencies, services, and programs.

THE GROWTH OF GOVERNMENT IN THE TWENTIETH CENTURY

The economy appeared to boom as U.S. involvement in World War I caused an increase in manufacturing, but ominous events were just over the horizon. Farmers were in trouble after a series of bad harvests, the nation experienced a severe slump in agricultural prices, the construction industry went into decline, and, throughout the 1920s, bank failures became common. After stock prices crashed in 1929, the nation plunged into the Great Depression. To combat the resultant high unemployment and weak financial markets, President Franklin D. Roosevelt created hundreds of new government agencies to regulate business practices and various aspects of the national economy. Roosevelt believed that a national economic depression called for national intervention. Thus, the president proposed, and the Congress enacted, far-ranging economic legislation. The desperate mood of the nation supported these moves, as most Americans began to change their ideas about the proper role of government and the provision of governmental services. Formerly, most Americans had believed in a hands-off approach; now they considered it the federal government's job to get the economy going and get Americans back to work.

As the nation struggled to recover from the Depression, the United States was forced into World War II on December 7, 1941, when Japan attacked U.S. ships at Pearl Harbor, Hawaii. The war immediately affected the economy: healthy, eligible men went to war and women went to work at factories or in other jobs to replace the

■ During the New Deal, President Franklin D. Roosevelt suggested and Congress enacted the Emergency Relief Appropriation Act, which authorized the Works Progress Administration (WPA) to hire thousands of unemployed workers to complete numerous public work projects. These WPA workers are widening a road.

Photo courtesy: AP Wide World Photos

men. Factories operated around the clock to produce the armaments, material, and clothes necessary to equip, shelter, and dress an army.

During World War II, the federal government also continued to grow tremendously to meet the needs of a nation at war. Tax rates were increased to support the war, and they never again fell to prewar levels. After the war, this infusion of new monies and veterans' demands for services led to a variety of new programs and a much bigger government. The G.I. (Government Issue) Bill, for example, provided college loans for returning veterans and reduced mortgage rates to allow them to buy homes. The national government's involvement in these programs not only affected more people but also led to its greater involvement in more regulation. Homes bought with Veterans Housing Authority loans, for example, had to meet certain specifications. With these programs, Americans became increasingly accustomed to the national government's role in entirely new areas such as affordable middle-class housing and scholarships that allowed lower- and middle-class men their first opportunities for higher education.

Within two decades after World War II, the civil rights movement and President Lyndon B. Johnson's War on Poverty produced additional growth in the bureaucracy. The Equal Employment Opportunity Commission (EEOC) was created in 1965 by the Civil Rights Act of 1964. The Departments of Housing and Urban Development (HUD) and Transportation were created in 1965 and 1966, respectively. These expansions of the bureaucracy corresponded to increases in the president's power and his ability to persuade Congress that new agencies would be an effective way to solve pressing social problems.

The Modern Bureaucracy

THE NATIONAL GOVERNMENT differs from private business in numerous ways. Governments exist for the public good, not to make money. Businesses are driven by a profit motive; government leaders, but not bureaucrats, are driven by reelection. Businesses get their money from customers; the national government gets its money from taxpayers. Another difference between a bureaucracy and a business is that it is difficult to determine to whom bureaucracies are responsible. Is it the president? Congress? The citizenry? Still, governments can learn much from business, and recent reform efforts have tried to apply business solutions to create a government that works better and costs less.

The different natures of government and business have a tremendous impact on the way the bureaucracy operates. Because all of the incentive in government "is in the direction of not making mistakes," public employees view risks and rewards very differently from their private-sector counterparts.[8] The key to the modern bureaucracy is to understand who bureaucrats are, how the bureaucracy is organized, how organization and personnel affect each other, and how bureaucrats act within the political process. It also is key to understand that government cannot be run like a business. An understanding of these facts and factors can help in the search for ways to motivate positive change in the bureaucracy.

WHO ARE BUREAUCRATS?

Federal bureaucrats are career government employees who work in the executive branch in the Cabinet-level departments and independent agencies that comprise more than 2,000 bureaus, divisions, branches, offices, services, and other subunits of the federal government. There are more than 2.7 million federal workers in the executive branch. Nearly one-third of all civilian employees work in the U.S. Postal Service, as illustrated in Figure 9.1. The remaining federal civilian workers are spread out among the various executive departments and agencies throughout the United States. Most of these federal employees are paid according to what is called the "General Schedule" (GS). They advance within fifteen GS grades (as well as steps within those grades), moving into higher GS levels and salaries as their careers progress.

FIGURE 9.1 DISTRIBUTION OF FEDERAL CIVILIAN EMPLOYMENT, 2004

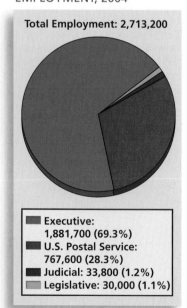

Total Employment: 2,713,200

- Executive: 1,881,700 (69.3%)
- U.S. Postal Service: 767,600 (28.3%)
- Judicial: 33,800 (1.2%)
- Legislative: 30,000 (1.1%)

Source: Office of Personnel Management, 2005 Fact Book.

Global Perspective

BUREAUCRATIC CULTURE IN THE UNITED KINGDOM

Bureaucracies tend to reflect the prevailing political culture of the people they administer, and bureaucratic activity is determined largely by the form of government under which a bureaucracy functions. The United Kingdom (U.K.), or as it often is called, Great Britain, functions as a parliamentary democracy where Parliament, the bicameral British legislature, has the power to enact laws and where elections to Parliament determine the party controlling the government. Unlike their U.S. counterparts, who are considered a part of the executive branch, bureaucrats in Great Britain ultimately answer to Parliament.

This difference affects the relative power that the U.S. president and British prime minister have over political appointees. In the United States, presidents are free to use or discount the policy advice or recommendations of their chosen administrators, who as members of the executive branch work for the president. In the United Kingdom, the leader of the majority party in the House of Commons in Parliament becomes prime minister and works with members of his or her party to appoint the ministers who will form a government to lead the country. Thus, the prime minister and the appointed members of the government are responsible to party members in Parliament.

Both the American and British administrative systems provide continuity. When one party is voted out of office, the bureaucracy ensures that the work of government continues without interruption. The American and British bureaucracies are somewhat different, though, when it comes to free speech rights. Civil servants actively or formerly employed by Great Britain's security services who are accused of leaking classified information may be prosecuted under the British Official Secrets Act of 1989, which provides for broader safeguards of security information than exist in the United States, since the law also allows the British government to prosecute journalists who repeat such disclosures. In the United States, the right of civil servants to inform the public of possibly harmful government operations is considered by many (though not all) to be constitutionally protected based on the First Amendment ideals of a free press, free speech, and the right to petition the government for redress of grievances. No such public interest defense currently exists for British leakers and whistleblowers, unless it can be proved that the leak was intended to prevent an immediate threat to life.

QUESTIONS

1. Should a president or prime minister be expected to follow the advice of political appointees? What are the benefits or drawbacks of having to follow bureaucratic advice?
2. To what extent should civil servants respect the authority of their government with regard to information? Under what circumstances would it be ethical for government information to be leaked to the press?

Sources: CIA World Factbook; U.K. Civil Service, http://www.civilservice.gov.uk; Official Secrets Act of 1989, http://www.opsi.gov.uk; BBC News online, http://news.bbc.co.uk; Sarah Lyall, "Britain Wields Legal Bludgeon in Effort to Stop Leaks," *New York Times* (July 13, 2006); Martin Bright, "Follow My Lead, Says Whistleblower," *Observer* (September 12, 2004), http://observer.guardian.co.uk.

As a result of reforms during the Truman administration that built on the Pendleton Act, most civilian federal governmental employees today are selected by merit standards, which include tests (such as civil service or foreign service exams) and educational criteria. Merit systems also protect federal employees from being fired for political reasons.

At the lower levels of the U.S. Civil Service, most positions are filled by competitive examinations. These usually involve a written test. Mid-level to upper ranges of federal positions do not normally require tests; instead, applicants simply submit a resume, or even apply by phone. Personnel departments then evaluate potential candidates and rank candidates according to how well they fit a particular job opening. Only the names of those deemed "qualified" are then forwarded to the official filling the vacancy. This can be a time-consuming process; it often takes six to nine months before a position can be filled in this manner.

PARTICIPATION

Who Wants To Be a Bureaucrat?

The remaining 10 percent of the federal workforce is made up of persons not covered by the civil service system. These positions generally fall into three categories:

1. Appointive policy-making positions. Nearly 3,000 people are presidential appointees. Some of these, including Cabinet secretaries and under- and assistant secretaries, are subject to Senate confirmation. These appointees, in turn, are

responsible for appointing high-level policy-making assistants who form the top of the bureaucratic hierarchy. These are called "Schedule C" political appointees, and their numbers have been increased by over 300 by the Bush administration. The number of political appointees grew by 33 percent from the Clinton to the Bush administration (1,229 to 2,000). There was also a 50 percent decline in the number of minority political appointees from Clinton to Bush. The proportion of women dropped 20 percent (see Figure 9.2).[9]

FIGURE 9.2 CHARACTERISTICS AND RANK DISTRIBUTION OF FEDERAL CIVILIAN EMPLOYEES, 2004

This bar graph depicts the percentage of the federal civilian workforce in several categories. As you review the data displayed in the graph, consider the trends you observe across GS levels, as well as the under-representation of Hispanics overall, as well as women in some categories.

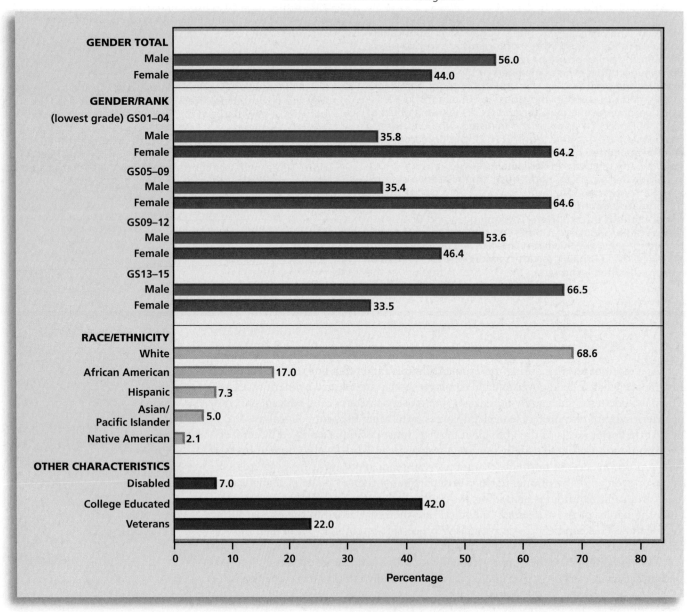

Source: Office of Personnel Management, 2005 Fact Book.

2. Independent regulatory commissioners. Although each president gets to appoint as many as one hundred commissioners, they become independent of his direct political influence once they take office.

3. Low-level, nonpolicy patronage positions. These types of positions generally concern secretarial assistants to policy makers.

Comparing Bureaucracies

More than 15,000 job skills are represented in the federal government, and its workers are perhaps the best trained and most skilled and efficient in the world. (See Global Perspective: Bureaucratic Culture in the United Kingdom for a comparison between the U.S. and British bureaucracies.) Government employees, whose average age is forty-seven years, have an average length of service of seventeen years. They include forest rangers, FBI agents, foreign service officers, computer programmers, security guards, librarians, administrators, engineers, plumbers, lawyers, doctors, postal carriers, and zoologists, among others. The diversity of government jobs mirrors the diversity of jobs in the private sector. The federal workforce, itself, is also diverse but under-represents African Americans and Hispanics, in particular, and the employment of women lags behind that of men. Women still make up more than 60 percent of the lowest GS levels but have raised their proportion of positions in the GS 13–15 ranks from 18 percent in 1990 to over 30 percent in 2004.[10]

The Changing Face of the Federal Bureaucracy

There are about 332,500 federal workers in the nation's capital; the rest are located in regional, state, and local offices scattered throughout the country. To enhance efficiency, the United States is broken up into several regions, with most agencies having regional offices in one city in that region. (See Figure 9.3.) The decentralization of the bureaucracy facilitates accessibility to the public. The Social Security Administration, for example, has numerous offices so that its clients can have a place nearby to take their paperwork, questions, and problems. Decentralization also helps distribute jobs and incomes across the country. Many complain that jobs in the federal government, especially highly skilled ones, are difficult to fill because they pay less than their comparable positions in the private sector. This has become especially true in the Department of Homeland Security. Many employees of its Transportation Safety Agency, for example, leave after only a short time on the job for more lucrative

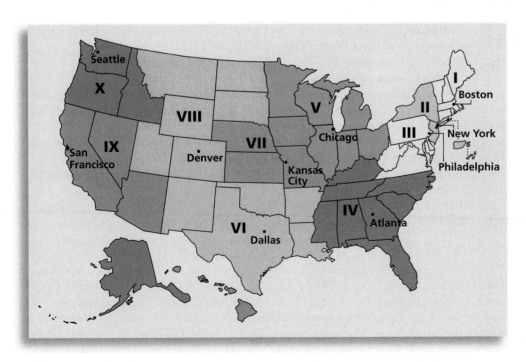

FIGURE 9.3 FEDERAL AGENCY REGIONS AND CITY HEADQUARTERS

Source: Department of Health and Human Services, http://www.hhs.gov/images/regions.gif.

Photo courtesy: Presidential Management Fellows

■ Presidential Management Fellow Denisse Betancourt (left) celebrates her graduation from the program with her sister Diana (center) and Tochukwu Igbo (right), another graduate of the program. Experts hope that graduates like Betancourt and Igbo will help to alleviate the management shortfall the federal bureaucracy is facing.

careers outside government. And, at the Department of State, which once had many of the most highly coveted jobs in the federal bureaucracy, the dangers associated with postings in Iraq and Afghanistan, as well as elsewhere in the Middle East, are making it harder to find well-qualified people to staff critical positions.[11]

The graying of the federal workforce is another problem of concern to many. More than two-thirds of those in the highest nonpolitical positions as well as a large number of mid-level managers are eligible to retire.[12] Many in government hope that the Presidential Management Fellows Program, which was begun in 1977 to hire and train future managers and executives, will be enhanced to make up for the shortfall in experienced managers that the federal government is now facing. Agencies even are contemplating ways to pay the college loans of prospective recruits while at the same time trying to enhance benefits to attract older workers.[13]

The federal government also has devoted resources to shrinking the number of federal employees by hiring outside contractors. The biggest reason for these reforms is that outside contractors often provide cheaper labor than government employees and are not eligible for government benefits and pension plans. The Bush administration, for example, concluded that 850,000 federal jobs are essentially commercial in nature and could be performed more cost-effectively by private corporations, and that half should be outsourced as quickly as possible.[14] Some observers, however, have questioned the contention that privatization saves taxpayers money in all cases. They also argue that privatization can increase cronyism in government and may contribute to the outsourcing of jobs overseas—an ironic turn of events, since the outsourced jobs would be funded by U.S. taxpayers.

FORMAL ORGANIZATION

While even experts can't agree on the exact number of separate governmental agencies, commissions, and departments that make up the federal bureaucracy, there are at least 1,150 civilian agencies.[15] A distinctive feature of the executive bureaucracy is its traditional division into areas of specialization. For example, the Occupational Safety and Health Administration (OSHA) handles occupational safety, and the Department of State specializes in foreign affairs. It is not unusual, however, for more than one agency to be involved in a particular issue or for one agency to be involved in myriad issues. The vast authority and range of activities of the Department of Homeland Security are probably the best example of this phenomenon. In fact, numerous agencies often have authority in the same issue areas, making administration even more difficult.

Agencies fall into four general types: (1) Cabinet departments; (2) government corporations; (3) independent agencies; and, (4) regulatory commissions.

departments
Major administrative units with responsibility for a broad area of government operations. Departmental status usually indicates a permanent national interest in a particular governmental function, such as defense, commerce, or agriculture.

Cabinet Departments The fifteen Cabinet **departments** are major administrative units that have responsibility for conducting a broad area of government operations. (See The Living Constitution: Article II, Section 2, Clause 1.) Cabinet departments account for about 60 percent of the federal workforce. The vice president, the heads of all of the departments, as well as the heads of the Environmental Protection Agency (EPA), Office of Management and Budget (OMB), Office of National Drug Control Policy, the U.S. Trade Representative, and the president's chief of staff make up his formal Cabinet.

The Living Constitution

The President … may require the Opinion, in writing, of the principle Officer in each of the executive Departments, upon any subject relating to the Duties of their respective Office.

—ARTICLE II, SECTION 2, CLAUSE 1

This clause, along with additional language designating that the president shall be the commander in chief, notes that the heads of departments are to serve as advisers to the president. There is no direct mention of the Cabinet in the Constitution.

This meager language is all that remains of the Framers' initial efforts to create a council to guide the president. Those in attendance at the Constitutional Convention largely favored the idea of a council, but could not agree on who should be a part of that body. Some actually wanted to follow the British parliamentary model and create the Cabinet from members of the House and Senate, who would rotate into the bureaucracy; most, however, appeared to support the idea of the heads of departments along with the chief justice, who would preside when the president was unavailable. The resulting language above depicts a one-sided arrangement whereby the heads of executive departments must simply answer in writing questions put to them by the president.

The Cabinet of today differs totally from the structure envisioned by the Framers. George Washington was the first to convene a meeting of what he called his Cabinet. Some presidents have used their Cabinets as trusted advisers; others have used them to demonstrate that they are committed to political, racial, ethnic, or gender diversity, and have relied more on White House aides than particular Cabinet members. Who is included in the Cabinet, as well as how it is used, is solely up to the discretion of the sitting president, although executive departments cannot be created or abolished without Congressional approval.

The executive branch departments depicted in Figure 9.4 are headed by Cabinet members called secretaries (except the Department of Justice, which is headed by the attorney general). The secretaries are responsible for establishing their department's general policy and overseeing its operations. As discussed in chapter 8, Cabinet secretaries are responsible directly to the president but are often viewed as having two masters—the president and those affected by their department. Cabinet secretaries also are tied to Congress, from which they get their appropriations and the discretion to implement legislation and make rules and policy.

Although departments vary considerably in size, prestige, and power, they share certain features. Department status generally signifies a strong permanent national interest to promote a particular function. Each department covers a broad area of responsibility generally reflected by its name. Each secretary is assisted by one or more deputies or undersecretaries who take part of the administrative burden off the secre-

FIGURE 9.4 THE EXECUTIVE BRANCH

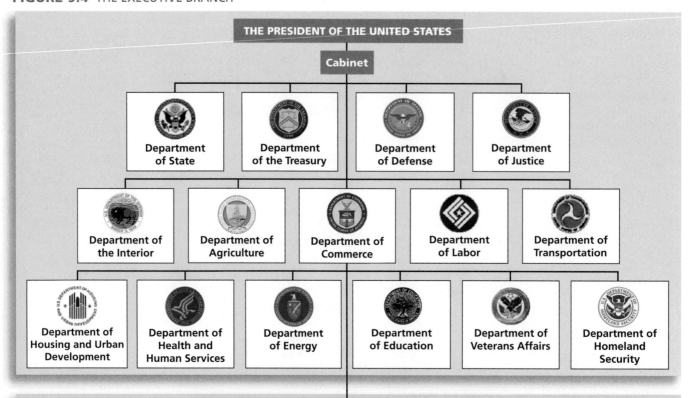

Independent Agencies and Government Corporations

Advisory Council on Historic Preservation
African Development Foundation
American Battle Monuments Commission
Appalachian Regional Commission
Architectural and Transportation
    Barriers Compliance Board
Arctic Research Commission
Armed Forces Retirement Home
Barry M. Goldwater Scholarship and
    Excellence in Education Foundation
Broadcasting Board of Governors
Central Intelligence Agency
Civil Air Patrol Great Lakes Region
Commission on Civil Rights
Commission of Fine Arts
Committee for Purchase from People
    Who Are Blind or Severely Disabled
Commodity Futures Trading Commission
Consumer Product Safety Commission
Corporation for National Service
Defense Nuclear Facilities Safety Board
Delaware River Basin Commission
Environmental Protection Agency
Equal Employment Opportunity Commission
Export-Import Bank of the U.S.
Farm Credit Administration
Federal Communications Commission
Federal Deposit Insurance Corporation
Federal Election Commission
Federal Emergency Management Agency
Federal Energy Regulatory Commission
Federal Housing Finance Board
Federal Labor Relations Authority
Federal Maritime Commission

Federal Mediation and Conciliation Service
Federal Mine Safety and Health Review Commission
Federal Reserve System
Federal Retirement Thrift Investment Board
Federal Trade Commission
General Services Administration
Harry S Truman Scholarship Foundation
Inter-American Foundation
International Boundary and Water Commission,
    United States and Mexico
International Broadcasting Bureau
Interstate Commission on the Potomac River Basin
James Madison Memorial Fellowship Foundation
Japan–United States Friendship Commission
Marine Mammal Commission
Merit Systems Protection Board
National Aeronautics and Space Administration
National Archives and Records Administration
National Capital Planning Commission
National Commission on Libraries and
    Information Science
National Council on Disability
National Credit Union Administration
National Foundation on the Arts
    and the Humanities
National Labor Relations Board
National Mediation Board
National Performance Review
National Railroad Passenger Corporation (Amtrak)
National Science Foundation
National Transportation Safety Board
Nuclear Regulatory Commission
Occupational Safety and Health Review Commission
Office of Government Ethics

Office of Navajo and Hopi Indian Relocation
Office of Personnel Management
Office of Special Counsel
Overseas Private Investment Corporation
Peace Corps
Pension Benefit Guaranty Corporation
Physician Payment Review Commission
Postal Rate Commission
President's Commission on White House
    Fellowships
President's Committee on Employment
    of People with Disabilities
Railroad Retirement Board
Securities and Exchange Commission
Selective Service System
Small Business Administration
Smithsonian Institution
Social Security Administration
Surface Transportation Board
Susquehanna River Basin Commission
Tennesse Valley Authority
Trade Development Agency
U.S. Arms Control and Disarmament Agency
U.S. Chemical Safety and Hazard
    Investigation Board
U.S. Holocaust Memorial Council
U.S. Information Agency
U.S. Institute of Peace
U.S. International Development
    Corporation Agency
U.S. International Trade Commission
U.S. Postal Service
Woodrow Wilson International Center
    for Scholars

tary's shoulders, as well as by several assistant secretaries who direct major programs within the department. In addition, each secretary, just as the president, has numerous assistants who help with planning, budgeting, personnel, legal services, public relations, and their key staff functions. Most departments are subdivided into bureaus, divisions, sections, or other smaller units, and it is at this level that the real work of each agency is done. Most departments are subdivided along functional lines, but the basis for division may be geography, work processes (for example, the new Transportation Security Agency is housed in the Department of Homeland Security), or clientele (such as the Bureau of Indian Affairs in the Department of the Interior). Clientele agencies are particularly subject to outside lobbying from organized interests in Washington. The clientele agencies and groups also are active at the regional level, where the agencies devote a substantial part of their resources to program implementation.

Government Corporations
Government corporations are the most recent addition to the bureaucracy. Dating from the early 1930s, they are businesses established by Congress to perform functions that could be provided by private businesses. The corporations are formed when the government chooses to engage in activities that primarily are commercial in nature, produce revenue, and require greater flexibility than Congress generally allows regular departments. Some of the better-known government corporations include Amtrak and the Federal Deposit Insurance Corporation. Unlike other governmental agencies, government corporations charge for their services. For example, the largest government corporation, the U.S. Postal Service—whose functions could be handled by a private corporation, such as the United Parcel Service (UPS)—exists today to ensure delivery of mail throughout the United States at cheaper rates than those a private business might charge. The U.S. Postal Service is increasingly being challenged by the growing popularity of e-mail correspondence and the lower negotiated rates that delivery services such as United Panel Service (UPS) and Federal Express (FedEx) give to large corporate clients. Similarly, the Tennessee Valley Authority (TVA) provides electricity at reduced rates to millions of Americans in the Appalachian region of the Southeast, generally a low-income area that had failed to attract private utility companies to provide service there.

In cases such as the TVA, where the financial incentives for private industry to provide services are minimal, Congress often believes that it must act. In other cases, it steps in to salvage valuable public assets. For example, when passenger rail service in the United States became unprofitable, Congress stepped in to create Amtrak, nationalizing the passenger-train industry to keep passenger trains running, especially in the Northeast corridor.

Independent Executive Agencies
Independent executive agencies closely resemble Cabinet departments but have narrower areas of responsibility. Generally speaking, independent agencies perform service rather than regulatory functions. The heads of these agencies are ap-

government corporation
Business established by Congress to perform functions that can be provided by private businesses (such as the U.S. Postal Service).

independent executive agency
Governmental unit that closely resembles a Cabinet department but has a narrower area of responsibility (such as the Central Intelligence Agency) and is not part of any Cabinet department.

■ Workers install housing for turbines during the 1941 construction of the Tennessee Valley Authority's Cherokee Dam in Tennessee. Today, the TVA continues to provide electricity at reduced rates to millions of Americans living in the Appalachian region.

Photo courtesy: AP Wide World Photos

■ The Mine Safety and Health Administration, part of the Department of Labor, has been responsible for protecting the safety and health of miners since 1978. A spate of mining disasters in West Virginia in 2006 has led to increased pressure for greater government oversight of mining companies. Here, Senator Robert Byrd (D-WV) meets with family members of Marty Bennet, one of twelve miners killed in the 2006 Sago Mine Explosion.

SIMULATION

You Are the President of MEDICORP

pointed by the president and serve, like Cabinet secretaries, at his pleasure.

Independent agencies exist apart from executive departments for practical or symbolic reasons. The National Aeronautics and Space Administration (NASA), for example, could have been placed within the Department of Defense. Such positioning, however, could have conjured up thoughts of a space program dedicated solely to military purposes, rather than to civilian satellite communication or scientific exploration. Similarly, the Environmental Protection Agency (EPA) could have been created within the Department of the Interior but instead was created as an independent agency in 1970 to administer federal programs aimed at controlling pollution and protecting the nation's environment. As an independent agency, the EPA is less indebted to the president on a day-to-day basis than it would be if it were within a Cabinet department, although the president still has the ability to appoint its director and often intervenes on high-profile decisions.

Independent Regulatory Commissions As Noted on page 319, independent regulatory commissions are agencies created by Congress to exist outside the major departments to regulate a specific economic activity or interest. Because of the complexity of modern economic issues, Congress sought to create commissions that could develop expertise and provide continuity of policy with respect to economic issues because neither Congress nor the courts have the time or specific talents to do so. Examples include the National Labor Relations Board, the Federal Reserve Board, the Federal Communications Commission, and the Securities and Exchange Commission (SEC).[16]

Older boards and commissions, such as the SEC and the Federal Reserve Board, generally are charged with overseeing a certain industry. Most were created specifically to be free from partisan political pressure. Each is headed by a board composed of five to seven members (always an odd number, to avoid tie votes) who are selected by the president and confirmed by the Senate for fixed, staggered terms to increase the chances of a bipartisan board. Unlike executive department heads, they cannot easily be removed by the president. In 1935, the U.S. Supreme Court ruled that in creating independent commissions, the Congress had intended that they be independent panels of experts as far removed as possible from immediate political pressures.[17]

Newer regulatory boards are more concerned with how the business sector relates to public health and safety. The Occupational Safety and Health Administration (OSHA), for example, promotes job safety. These boards and commissions often lack autonomy and freedom from political pressures; they are generally headed by a single administrator who can be removed by the president. Thus, they are far more susceptible to the political wishes of the president who appoints them.

GOVERNMENT WORKERS AND POLITICAL INVOLVEMENT

As the number of federal employees and agencies grew during the 1930s, many Americans began to fear that the members of the civil service would play major roles not only in implementing public policy but also in electing members of Congress and even the president. Consequently, Congress enacted the Political Activities Act of 1939, commonly known as the **Hatch Act,** named in honor of its main sponsor, Senator Carl Hatch (D–NM). It was designed to prohibit federal employees from becoming directly involved in working for political candidates. Although this act allayed many critics' fears, other people argued that the Hatch Act was too extreme.

Today, government employees' political activity is regulated by the **Federal Employees Political Activities Act** of 1993. This liberalization of the Hatch Act allows employees to run for public office in nonpartisan elections, contribute money to political organizations, and campaign for or against candidates in partisan elections. Federal employees still, however, are prohibited from engaging in political activity while on duty, soliciting contributions from the general public, or running for office in partisan elections. See Table 9.1 for more specifics about the Federal Employees Political Activities Act.

Some workers, however, didn't even realize that they were federal employees. The Federal Employees Political Activities Act, for example, had a surprising effect when a teacher in the Washington, D.C., public schools was fired for running for the D.C. city council, a race he lost in a landslide. Prior to 1993, D.C. employees were exempt from the Hatch Act's reach. But, political wrangling led to their being covered in the 1993 act. Thus, because D.C. employees are treated as federal workers, they are not exempt from Federal Employees Political Activities Act provisions that bar federal workers from running for public office in partisan elections. Initially, the teacher was not aware of the prohibition, but he refused to terminate his candidacy even after being notified that it could cost him his job.[18]

Hatch Act
Law enacted in 1939 to prohibit civil servants from taking activist roles in partisan campaigns. This act prohibited federal employees from making political contributions, working for a particular party, or campaigning for a particular candidate.

Federal Employees Political Activities Act
1993 liberalization of the Hatch Act. Federal employees are now allowed to run for office in nonpartisan elections and to contribute money to campaigns in partisan elections.

TABLE 9.1 THE FEDERAL EMPLOYEES POLITICAL ACTIVITIES ACT

Here are some examples of permissible and prohibited activities for federal employees under the Federal Employees Political Activities Act of 1993. Federal Employees:

- **May** be candidates for public office in nonpartisan elections
- **May** assist in voter registration drives
- **May** express opinions about candidates and issues
- **May** contribute money to political organizations
- **May** attend political fund-raising functions
- **May** attend and be active at political rallies and meetings
- **May** join and be active members of a political party or club
- **May** sign nominating petitions
- **May** campaign for or against referendum questions, constitutional amendments, and municipal ordinances
- **May** campaign for or against candidates in partisan elections
- **May** make campaign speeches for candidates in partisan elections
- **May** distribute campaign literature in partisan elections
- **May** hold office in political clubs or parties
- **May not** use their official authority or influence to interfere with an election
- **May not** collect political contributions unless both individuals are members of the same federal labor organization or employee organization and the one solicited is not a subordinate employee
- **May not** knowingly solicit or discourage the political activity of any person who has business before the agency
- **May not** engage in political activity while on duty
- **May not** engage in political activity in any government office
- **May not** engage in political activity while wearing an official uniform
- **May not** engage in political activity while using a government vehicle
- **May not** solicit political contributions from the general public
- **May not** be candidates for public office in partisan elections

Source: U.S. Special Counsel's Office.

How the Bureaucracy Works

GERMAN SOCIOLOGIST MAX WEBER believed bureaucracies were a rational way for complex societies to organize themselves. Model bureaucracies, said Weber, are characterized by certain features, including:

1. A chain of command in which authority flows from top to bottom.
2. A division of labor whereby work is apportioned among specialized workers to increase productivity.
3. Clear lines of authority among workers and their superiors.
4. A goal orientation that determines structure, authority, and rules.
5. Impersonality, whereby all employees are treated fairly based on merit and all clients are served equally, without discrimination, according to established rules.
6. Productivity, whereby all work and actions are evaluated according to established rules.[19]

implementation
The process by which a law or policy is put into operation by the bureaucracy.

iron triangles
The relatively stable relationships and patterns of interaction that occur among an agency, interest groups, and congressional committees or subcommittees.

issue networks
The loose and informal relationships that exist among a large number of actors who work in broad policy areas.

interagency councils
Working groups created to facilitate coordination of policy making and implementation across a host of governmental agencies.

Clearly, this Weberian idea is somewhat idealistic, and even the best-run government agencies don't always work this way, but most are trying.

When Congress creates any kind of department, agency, or commission, it is actually delegating some of its powers listed in Article I, section 8, of the U.S. Constitution. Therefore, the laws creating departments, agencies, corporations, or commissions carefully describe their purpose and give them the authority to make numerous policy decisions, which have the effect of law. Congress recognizes that it does not have the time, expertise, or ability to involve itself in every detail of every program; therefore, it sets general guidelines for agency action and leaves it to the agency to work out the details. How agencies execute congressional wishes is called **implementation,** the process by which a law or policy is put into operation.

Historically, political scientists attempting to study how the bureaucracy made policy investigated what they termed **iron triangles,** a term that was used to refer to the relatively stable relationships and patterns of interaction that occurred among federal workers in agencies or departments, interest groups, and relevant congressional subcommittees (see Figure 9.5). Today, however, iron triangles no longer dominate most policy processes. Some do, however, persist, such as the relationship between the Department of Veterans Affairs, the House Committee on Veterans Affairs, and the American Legion and the Veterans of Foreign Wars, the two largest veterans groups.

Many political scientists examining external influences on the modern bureaucracy prefer to examine **issue networks.** In general, issue networks, like iron triangles, include agency officials, members of Congress (and committee staffers), and interest group lobbyists. But, they also include lawyers, consultants, academics, public relations specialists, and sometimes even the courts. Unlike iron triangles, issue networks constantly are changing as members with technical expertise or newly interested parties become involved in issue areas.

As a result of the increasing complexity of many policy domains, many alliances have also been created within the bureaucracy. One such example is **interagency councils,** working groups that bring together representatives of several departments and agencies to facilitate the coordina-

FIGURE 9.5 AN IRON TRIANGLE

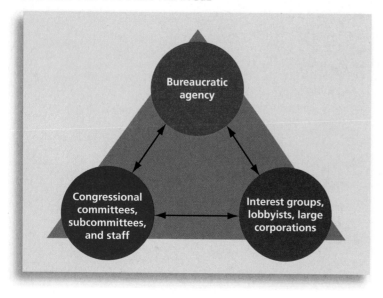

tion of policy making and implementation. Depending on how well these councils are funded, they can be the prime movers of administration policy in any area where an interagency council exists. The U.S. Interagency Council on the Homeless, for example, was created in 1987 to coordinate the activities of the more than fifty governmental agencies and programs that work to alleviate homelessness. How the interagency structure works for national security policy in the Bush administration is illustrated in Figure 9.6.

In areas where there are extraordinarily complex policy problems, recent presidential administrations have created policy coordinating committees (PCCs) to facilitate interaction among agencies and departments at the subcabinet level. These PCCs gained increasing favor as a result of the September 11, terrorist attacks. For example, the PCC on Terrorist Financing, which includes representatives from the Departments of Treasury, State, Defense, and Justice, along with the CIA and FBI, conducted a study that recommended to the president that he ask the Saudi government to take action against alleged terrorist financiers.[20] Similarly, in the wake of the 2003 *Columbia* space shuttle disaster, a PCC on space was created to review NASA's evaluation of why the disaster occurred.[21]

FIGURE 9.6 U.S. INTERAGENCY STRUCTURE FOR NATIONAL SECURITY IN THE GEORGE W. BUSH ADMINISTRATION

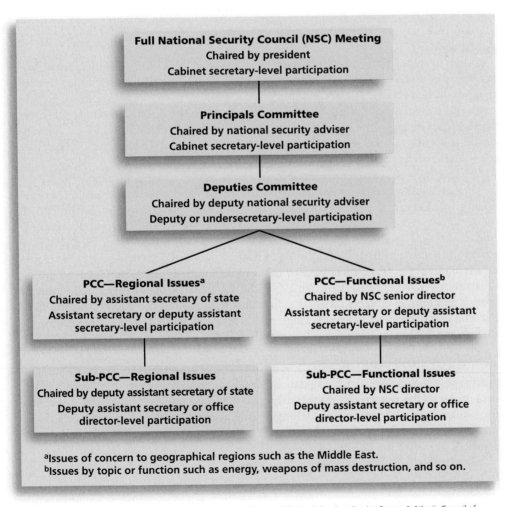

Source: Steven Pifer et al., "Ukraine's Euro-Atlantic Ambitions: Building an Effective Policy Coordination Process," *Atlantic Council of the United States,* February 2006, 5.

MAKING POLICY

The end product of all of these decision-making bodies is policy making. Policy making and implementation take place on both informal and formal levels. Practically, many decisions are left to individual government employees on a day-to-day basis. Department of Justice lawyers, for example, make daily decisions about whether or not to prosecute someone. Similarly, street-level Internal Revenue Service agents make many decisions during personal audits. These street-level bureaucrats make policy on two levels. First, they exercise wide discretion in decisions concerning citizens with whom they interact. Second, taken together, their individual actions add up to agency behavior.[22] Thus, how bureaucrats interpret and how they apply (or choose not to apply) various policies are equally important parts of the policy-making process.

    Administrative discretion, the ability to make choices concerning the best way to implement congressional or executive intentions, also allows decision makers (whether they are in a Cabinet-level position or at the lowest GS levels) a tremendous amount of leeway. It is exercised through two formal administrative procedures: rule making and administrative adjudication.

Rule Making

Rule making is a quasi-legislative administrative process that results in regulations and has the characteristics of a legislative act. **Regulations** are the rules that govern the operation of all government programs and have the force of law. In essence, then, bureaucratic rule makers often act as lawmakers as well as law enforcers when they make rules or draft regulations to implement various congressional statutes. The rule-making process is illustrated in Figure 9.7. Some political scientists say that rule making "is the single most important function performed by agencies of government."[23]

    Because regulations often involve political conflict, the 1946 Administrative Procedures Act established rule-making procedures to give everyone the chance to participate in the process. The act requires that: (1) public notice of the time, place, and nature of the rule-making proceedings be provided in the *Federal Register;* (2) interested parties be given the opportunity to submit written arguments and facts relevant to the rule; and, (3) the statutory purpose and basis of the rule be stated. Once rules are written, thirty days generally must elapse before they take effect.

    Sometimes an agency is required by law to conduct a formal hearing before issuing rules. Evidence is gathered, and witnesses testify and are cross-examined by opposing interests. The process can take weeks, months, or even years, at the end of which agency administrators must review the entire record and then justify the new rules. Although cumbersome, the process has reduced criticism of some rules and bolstered the deference given by the courts to agency decisions. Many Americans are unaware of the opportunities available to them to influence government at this stage. As illustrated in On Campus: Enforcing Gender Equity in College Athletics, women's groups and female athletes testified at hearings held around the country urging then Secretary of Education Roderick Paige not to revise existing Title IX regulations, although the Bush administration ultimately did.

Administrative Adjudication

Administrative adjudication is a quasi-judicial process in which a bureaucratic agency settles disputes between two parties in a manner similar to the way courts resolve disputes. Administrative adjudication is referred to as quasi judicial, because law-making by any body other than Congress or adjudication by any body other than the judiciary would be a violation of the constitutional principle of separation of powers.

    Agencies regularly find that persons or businesses are not in compliance with the federal laws the agencies are charged with enforcing, or that they are in violation of an agency rule or regulation. To force compliance, some agencies resort to administrative adjudication, which generally is less formal than a trial. Several agencies and boards

---

administrative discretion
The ability of bureaucrats to make choices concerning the best way to implement congressional intentions.

rule making
A quasi-legislative administrative process that has the characteristics of a legislative act.

regulations
Rules that govern the operation of a particular government program that have the force of law.

SIMULATION

You Are a Federal Administrator

administrative adjudication
A quasi-judicial process in which a bureaucratic agency settles disputes between two parties in a manner similar to the way courts resolve disputes.

FIGURE 9.7 HOW A REGULATION IS MADE

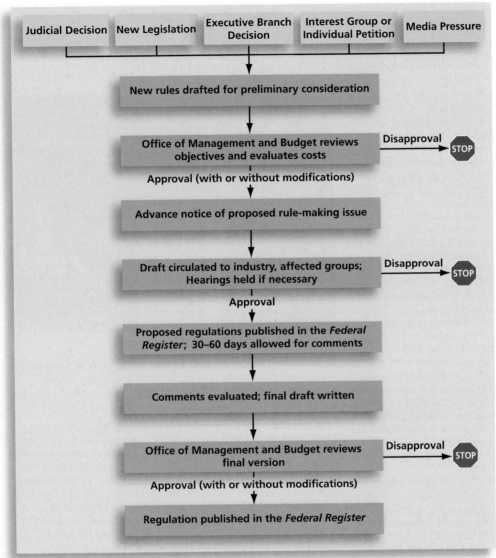

employ administrative law judges to conduct the hearings. Although these judges are employed by the agencies, they are strictly independent and cannot be removed except for gross misconduct. Congress, for example, empowers the Federal Trade Commission to determine what constitutes an unfair trade practice.[24] Its actions, however, are reviewable in the federal courts. So are the findings of the Equal Employment Opportunity Commission and Social Security judges.

Making Agencies Accountable

THE QUESTION OF to whom bureaucrats should be responsible is one that continually comes up in any debate about governmental accountability. Should the bureaucracy be answerable to itself? To organized interest groups? To its clientele? To the president? To Congress? Or to some combination of all of these? At times an agency

VIDEO
ROUNDTABLE

Bureaucratic Reform

On Campus

ENFORCING GENDER EQUITY IN COLLEGE ATHLETICS

In 2004, there were approximately 150,000 female student-athletes, a number up dramatically from 1971, when there were only about 30,000 women participating in collegiate athletics.[a] Male participation has grown much more slowly, while the number of women's teams in the National Collegiate Athletic Association nearly doubled between 1971 and 2002, from 4,776 to 8,414.[b] A major source of that difference? The passage in 1972 of legislation popularly known as Title IX, which prohibits discrimination against girls and women in federally funded education, including athletic programs. This legislation mandates that "No person in the United States shall, on the basis of sex, be excluded from participation in, be denied the benefits of, or be subjected to discrimination under any education program or activity receiving federal financial assistance." It wasn't until December 1978—six years after passage of Title IX—that the Office for Civil Rights in what was then the Department of Health, Education, and Welfare released a policy interpretation of the law, dealing largely with the section that concerned intercollegiate athletics.[c] More than thirty pages of text were devoted to dealing with a hundred or so words from the statute. Football was recognized as unique, because of the huge revenues it produces, so it could be inferred that male-dominated football programs could continue to outspend women's athletic programs. The more than sixty women's groups that had lobbied for equality of spending were outraged and turned their efforts toward seeking more favorable rulings on the construction of the statute from the courts.

Increased emphasis on Title IX enforcement has led many women to file lawsuits to force compliance. In 1991, in an effort to trim expenses, Brown University cut two men's and two women's teams from its varsity roster. Several women students filed a Title IX complaint against the school, arguing that it violated the act by not providing women varsity sport opportunities in relation to their population in the university. The women also argued that cutting the two women's programs saved $62,000, whereas the men's cuts saved only $16,000. Thus, the women's varsity programs took a bigger hit, in violation of federal law.

A U.S. district court refused to allow Brown to cut the women's programs. A U.S. court of appeals upheld that action, concluding that Brown had failed to provide adequate opportunities for its female students to participate in athletics.[d] In 1997, in *Brown University* v. *Cohen,* the U.S. Supreme Court declined to review the appeals court's decision.[e] This put all colleges and universities on notice that discrimination against women would not be tolerated, even when, as in the case of Brown University, the university had expanded sports opportunities for women tremendously since the passage of Title IX.

Women have made significant strides on all college campuses, but true equity in athletics is still a long way away at many colleges and universities. Although the number of women participating in college level sports is increasing, the proportion of women coaches is decreasing (at the same

Photo courtesy: Doug Mills/*The New York Times*

■ Soccer Olympian Julie Foudy lobbies along with female Democratic and Republican members of the Congressional Women's Caucus to save Title IX.

time the pool of women who could be coaches is increasing). Most colleges still provide far fewer opportunities to women, given their numbers in most universities, and enforcement still lags. This disparity has required groups including the National Women's Law Center to take the lead in the *Brown* case and to spend millions of dollars in legal fees to press for fuller enforcement.[f] Individual colleges and universities must comply with the law, aggrieved students must complain of inequities, and the Department of Education's Office of Civil Rights now is charged with enforcing the law.

In early 2003, after holding hearings on Title IX throughout the United States, a commission appointed by the Bush administration recommended to the secretary of education that enforcement of Title IX's requirements that provide opportunities for women in athletics be weakened to account for perceived differences in interest in athletics between male and female college students. In March 2005, the Bush administration announced new rules that would allow colleges to avoid the act's gender equity requirements if a sufficient number of women on any campus fail to return an e-mail survey expressing interest in playing sports.

[a] *Intercollegiate Athletics: Status of Efforts to Promote Gender Equity,* General Accounting Office, October 25, 1996.

[b] Bill Pennington, "Colleges: More Men's Teams Benched as Colleges Level the Playing Field," *New York Times* (May 9, 2002): A1.

[c] See Joyce Gelb and Marian Lief Palley, *Women and Public Policies* (Charlottesville: University of Virginia Press, 1996), ch. 5.

[d] *Cohen* v. *Brown University,* 101 F.3d 155 (1996).

[e] *Cohen* v. *Brown University,* 520 U.S. 1186 (1997).

[f] http://www.edc.org/WomensEquity/resource/title9/report/athletic.html.

becomes so removed from the public it serves that Congress must step in. This is what happened with the Internal Revenue Service (IRS). Throughout 1997 and 1998, Congress held extensive hearings about abuses at the IRS, one of the most hated and feared federal agencies in America. Senate hearings in particular exposed abuses of ordinary citizens who found themselves in a nightmare of bureaucratic red tape and agency employee abuse of power. As a result of these hearings, Congress ordered the new IRS commissioner to overhaul the way the IRS deals with the public.[25] The IRS's attempt to ease online tax filing in 2002 was another example of the use of technology to improve relations with the public. The IRS also redesigned its Web site, http://www.irs.gov. (For more on accessing government information on the Internet, see Politics Now: E-Government.) The public responded positively to these changes, and by 2003, 52 percent of the American public reported that they had confidence in the IRS.[26]

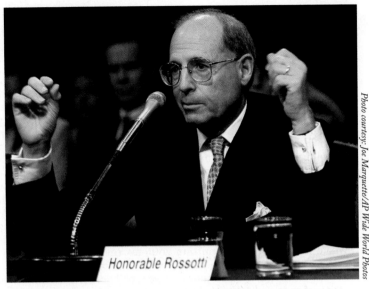

Photo courtesy: Joe Marquette/AP Wide World Photos

Honorable Rossotti

■ Internal Revenue Service Commissioner Charles O. Rossotti appears before the Senate Finance Committee during the 1997–1998 congressional probe into alleged abuses of taxpayers by employees of the IRS. As a result of the hearings, numerous positive changes were made in the way the IRS deals with the public.

Although many critics of the bureaucracy might argue that federal employees should be responsive to the public interest, the public interest is difficult to define. As it turns out, several factors work to control the power of the bureaucracy, and to some degree, the same kinds of checks and balances that operate among the three branches of government serve to check the bureaucracy (see Table 9.2).

Many political scientists argue that the president should be in charge of the bureaucracy because it is up to him to see that popular ideas and expectations are translated into administrative action. But, under our constitutional system, the president is not the only actor in the policy process. Congress creates the agencies, funds them, and establishes the broad rules of their operation. Moreover, Congress continually reviews the various agencies through oversight committee investigations, hearings, and its power of the purse. And, the federal judiciary, as in most other matters, has the ultimate authority to review administrative actions.

TABLE 9.2 MAKING AGENCIES ACCOUNTABLE

The president has the authority to:
- Appoint and remove agency heads and other top bureaucrats.
- Reorganize the bureaucracy (with congressional approval).
- Make changes in an agency's annual budget proposals.
- Ignore legislative initiatives originating within the bureaucracy.
- Initiate or adjust policies that would, if enacted by Congress, alter the bureaucracy's activities.
- Issue executive orders.
- Reduce an agency's annual budget.

Congress has the authority to:
- Pass legislation that alters the bureaucracy's activities.
- Abolish existing programs.
- Refuse to appropriate funds for certain programs.
- Investigate bureaucratic activities and compel bureaucrats to testify about them.
- Influence presidential appointments of agency heads and other top bureaucratic officials.
- Write legislation to limit the bureaucracy's discretion.

The judiciary has the authority to:
- Rule on whether bureaucrats have acted within the law and require policy changes to comply with the law.
- Force the bureaucracy to respect the rights of individuals through hearings and other proceedings.
- Rule on the constitutionality of all challenged rules and regulations.

Politics Now

E-GOVERNMENT

In 1992, the White House first went up on the World Wide Web. Now all government agencies and bureaus have Web sites and provide a plethora of information to the American public that formerly would have taken numerous trips to the library or even Washington, D.C., to obtain.

By 1998, the Government Paperwork Elimination Act required that federal agencies allow persons transacting business with the government to have the option of submitting information or transacting business with them electronically. It is from this act that you or members of your family now have the option of submitting your tax returns electronically.

In 2002, the Bush administration took additional advantage of changing technologies and the increasing number of Americans' access to it, whether in their homes, at local public libraries, or at Internet cafes. The E-Government Act of 2002 was an effort to mandate that all government agencies use "Internet-based information technologies to enhance citizens' access to government information and services."[a]

According to the E-Gov Web site, e-government is not simply about putting forms online; its major purpose is to harness technology to make it easier for citizens to learn more about government services. Through GovBenefits.gov, for example, citizens can find answers to a range of questions dealing with their individual circumstances and will immediately receive a list of government programs for which they may be eligible. Recreation.gov allows individuals to find out about national parks and recreation sites and to make online reservations at those facilities.

One addition to the e-government effort under the Bush administration is its eRulemaking Initiative. Managed by the Environmental Protection Agency, this new use of technology is designed to transform "the federal rule-making process by enhancing the public's ability to participate in their government's regulatory decision making." Regulations.gov was launched in 2002 to allow the public to "search, view, and comment on proposed federal regulations open for comment."[b] While the regulatory process almost exclusively involved interest groups and affected industries, this new initiative allows the public to search proposed regulations easily. Agencies are in the process of posting their proposed regulations on this central site, although some agencies still have their own sites. OMB Watch, a nonprofit group that monitors government actions as they affect citizen participation, has applauded the notion of a centralized, one-stop method to allow concerned citizens input into the policy process.

Even before revelations that the government has collected e-mails, phone records, and other information about millions of Americans, the notion of e-government had become somewhat controversial, despite its original intentions. Earlier surveys revealed that while nearly 50 percent of the public believed that it is permissible for the federal government to search its data bases for information to help track terrorists, 42 percent disagreed, believing that "privacy should be a top priority."[c]

QUESTIONS

1. Will the bureaucracy become more responsive to citizens and less captured by special interests as e-government increases?
2. Studies reveal that many Americans use e-government largely for gathering information. As the government increasingly uses the Web for collecting information about Americans, what problems do you see potentially happening with expansions of e-government?

[a] About E-Gov, http://www.whitehouse.gov/omb/egov/about_leg.htm.

[b] http://www.regulations.gov.

[c] Judy Sarasohn, "Survey Finds Americans Split on 'E-Government,' " *Washington Post* (April 14, 2003): A14.

EXECUTIVE CONTROL

As the size and scope of the American national government, in general, and of the executive branch and the bureaucracy, in particular, have grown, presidents have delegated more and more power to bureaucrats. But, most presidents have continued to try to exercise some control over the bureaucracy, although they have often found that task more difficult than they first envisioned. As president, John F. Kennedy, for example, once lamented that to give anyone at the Department of State an instruction was comparable to putting your request in a dead-letter box.[27] No response would ever be forthcoming.

Recognizing these potential problems, presidents try to appoint the best possible persons to carry out their wishes and policy preferences. Presidents make hundreds of appointments to the executive branch; in doing so, they have the opportunity to appoint individuals who share their views on a range of policies. Although presidential appointments make up a very small proportion of all federal jobs, presidents or the

American Values/American Voices

EXECUTIVE CONTROL OF THE BUREAUCRACY

President George W. Bush, an evangelical Christian, consistently has spoken about the centrality of religious faith and values in his life. In an interview with the *Washington Times* in January 2005, Bush said, "I fully understand that the job of the president is and must always be protecting the great right of people to worship or not worship as they see fit. . . . On the other hand, I don't see how you can be president at least from my perspective, how you can be president, without a relationship with the Lord."[a] Conservative evangelical Christians are a key component of the Republican Party's base, and the president's policies, many of them promoted through administrative actions such as political appointments and executive orders, are very much in line with his faith and values and those of his supporters, who have been known to refer to themselves, members of the GOP, as belonging to "God's Official Party."[b]

President Bush's conservative, evangelical agenda has been furthered by his strategic use of the appointment power and is reflected in those he has appointed. In a departure from previous administrations, Bush administration Cabinet officers, who typically have been allowed to hire their own senior staffs, were given a list of candidates who had been interviewed and approved by the director of the White House Office of Personnel, thus insuring the hiring of only those with a shared commitment to the president's policy positions.[c] The former dean of evangelist Pat Robertson's Regent University was made the director of the Office of Personnel Management. High-profile Bush appointees such as Secretary of Commerce Don Evans and Attorney General John Ashcroft held weekly and sometimes daily prayer meetings in their offices to which political appointees and other staffers were invited. Lester Crawford, who served as commissioner of the Food and Drug Administration, refused to allow emergency contraception to be made available over the counter in spite of positive recommendations by staff and a panel of experts based on his religious beliefs.

The president, like his predecessors, also has used executive orders to further his values agenda within the bureaucracy. Countering President Bill Clinton's pro-choice policy positions, two days after taking office in 2001, President Bush issued an executive order reinstating a ban on funding nongovernmental organizations engaging in abortion-related activities. This global gag rule, which was in effect during President Bush's father's time in office, prevents money from going to any international family planning agencies that mention abortion as an alternative to pregnancy. Thus, only groups that exclusively tout abstinence-only education can receive funding. The president also issued directives severely limiting stem cell research—a move that put him at odds with former First Lady Nancy Reagan, who lost her husband, former President Ronald Reagan, to Alzheimer's disease. Stem cell research may provide a cure for Alzheimer's as well as other illnesses; nevertheless, President Bush, like other pro-life advocates, is against making use of cells from fetuses in scientific experiments because he believes that life begins at conception. One of the president's most controversial actions, discussed in American Values/American Voices: Where's the Wall? in chapter 5, was to create offices of faith-based initiatives in most federal departments. By doing so, the president added to the number of overtly religious political appointments he was able to make.

QUESTIONS

1. What role should the president and the executive branch play in defining what the American values agenda should be?
2. To what extent should the president seek to shape the bureaucracy in order to further his preferred policy agenda without the help of Congress?

[a] James G. Lakely, "President Outlines Role of His Faith," *Washington Times* (January 12, 2005), http://washingtontimes.com.

[b] Michael Crowley, "Base Ball: TNR's Republican Convention Blog," *New Republic Online* (August 30, 2004), http://www.tnr.com.

[c] Shirley Anne Warshaw, "The Administrative Strategies of President George W. Bush," *Extensions* (Spring 2006): 19–20.

Cabinet secretaries usually fill most top policy-making positions. (See American Values/American Voices: Executive Control of the Bureaucracy.)

Presidents, with the approval of Congress, can reorganize the bureaucracy. They also can make changes in an agency's annual budget requests and ignore legislative initiatives originating within the bureaucracy. Several presidents have made it a priority to try to tame the bureaucracy to make it more accountable. Thomas Jefferson was the first president to address the issue of accountability. He attempted to cut waste and bring about a "wise and frugal government." But, it wasn't until the Progressive era (1890–1920) that calls for reform began to be taken seriously. Later, President Calvin Coolidge urged spending cuts and other reforms. His Correspondence Club was designed to reduce bureaucratic letter writing by 30 percent.[28]

executive order
Rule or regulation issued by the president that has the effect of law. All executive orders must be published in the *Federal Register*.

As discussed in chapter 8, presidents also can shape policy and provide direction to bureaucrats by issuing executive orders.[29] **Executive orders** are rules or regulations issued by the president that have the effect of law. For example, even before Congress acted to protect women from discrimination by the federal government, the National Organization for Women convinced President Lyndon B. Johnson to sign a 1967 executive order that amended an earlier one prohibiting the federal government from discriminating on the basis of race, color, religion, or national origin in the awarding of federal contracts, by adding to it the category of "gender." Although the president signed the order, the Office of Federal Contract Compliance, part of the Department of Labor's Employment Standards Administration, failed to draft appropriate guidelines for implementation of the order until several years later.[30] A president can direct an agency to act, but it may take some time for the order to be carried out. Given the many jobs of any president, few can ensure that all their orders will be carried out or that they will like all the rules that are made.

CONGRESSIONAL CONTROL

Congress, too, historically has played an important role in checking the power of the bureaucracy. Constitutionally, it possesses the authority to create or abolish departments and agencies as well as to transfer agency functions, as was the case in the protracted debate over the creation of the Department of Homeland Security. In addition, it can expand or contract bureaucratic discretion. The Senate's authority to confirm (or reject) presidential appointments also gives Congress a check on the bureaucracy. Legally, Congress has considerable oversight over the bureaucracy in several ways. But, as discussed in chapter 8, the Bush administration has been reluctant to cooperate fully even with the Republican-led Congress.

Congress uses many of its constitutional powers to exercise control over the bureaucracy. These include its investigatory powers. It is not at all unusual for a congressional committee or subcommittee to hold hearings on a particular problem and then direct the relevant agency to study the problem or find ways to remedy it. Representatives of the agencies also appear before these committees on a regular basis to inform members about agency activities and ongoing investigations. In the aftermath of Hurricane Katrina, for example, several congressional committees held hearings ordering then Federal Emergency Management Agency chief Michael Brown as well as Secretary Michael Chertoff of the Department of Homeland Security, to appear before them to explain the series of bad decisions that contributed to the disaster, not only for purposes of accountability, but also so that Congress and the administration could learn from the mistakes made. Indeed, the Senate Committee on Homeland Security found FEMA to be so inadequate that it was "beyond repair" and should be replaced with a new agency.[31]

Political scientists distinguish between two different forms of congressional oversight: police patrol and fire alarm oversight.[32] As the names imply, police patrol oversight is proactive and allows Congress to set its own agenda for programs or agencies to review. In contrast, fire alarm oversight is reactive and generally involves a congressional response

■ U.S. Secretary of State Designate Condoleezza Rice shakes hands with Senator Christopher Dodd (D–CT), as Senator Joseph Biden (D–DE) and Senator Barack Obama (D–IL) look on, after her second day of testimony before the U.S. Senate Foreign Relations Committee during her confirmation hearings. On January 26, 2005, Rice was confirmed by the Senate as the first female African American secretary of state.

■ Roy Dillon mows the lawn in front of his FEMA trailer in the Lower Ninth Ward of New Orleans. By late September of 2006, over a year after Hurricane Katrina, the Federal Emergency Management Agency had spent approximately $7.5 billion on trailers and manufactured homes to house people who, like Dillon, had lost their homes in the hurricane. Reports that tens of thousands of empty trailers were warehoused in Arkansas and other states led to calls for increased Congressional oversight of how funds were being spent.

Photo courtesy: Justin Sullivan/Getty Images

VIDEO ROUNDTABLE

Hurricane Katrina and New Orleans

to a complaint filed by a constituent or politically significant actor. (See Join the Debate: Fuel Economy Standards and Government Policy.)

Given the prevalence of iron triangles, issue networks, and policy coordinating committees, it is not surprising that the most frequently used form of oversight is fire alarm oversight and the most effective communication is between House staffers and agency personnel. Various forms of program evaluations make up the next most commonly used forms of congressional control. Members of Congress and their staff routinely conduct evaluations of programs and conduct oversight hearings.

Congress also has the power of the purse. To control the bureaucracy, Congress uses its ability to fund or not to fund an agency's activities much like the proverbial carrot and stick. The House Appropriations Committee routinely holds hearings to allow agency heads to justify their budget requests. Authorization legislation originates in the various legislative committees that oversee particular agencies (such as Agriculture, Veterans Affairs, Education, and Labor) and sets the maximum amounts that agencies can spend on particular programs. While some authorizations, such as those for Social Security, are permanent, others, including the Departments of State and Defense procurements, are watched closely and are subject to annual authorizations. For example, spending on the War in Iraq must be approved by Congress on an annual basis. In fiscal year 2007, Congress allocated more than $200 million for the war.

Once programs are authorized, funds for them must be appropriated before they can be spent. Appropriations originate with the House Appropriations Committee, not the specialized legislative committees. Often the Appropriations Committee allocates sums smaller than those authorized by legislative committees. Thus, the Appropriations Committee, a budget cutter, has an additional oversight function.

To help Congress's oversight of the bureaucracy's financial affairs, in 1921 Congress created the General Accounting Office, now called the Government Accountability Office (GAO), at the same time that the Office of the Budget, now the Office of Management and Budget (OMB), was created in the executive branch. With the establishment of the GAO, the Congressional Research Service (CRS), and later, the Congressional Budget Office (CBO), Congress essentially created its own bureaucracy to keep an eye on what the executive branch and bureaucracy were doing. Today, the GAO not only tracks how money is spent in the bureaucracy, but it also monitors how policies are implemented. The CBO also conducts oversight studies. If it or the GAO uncovers problems with an agency's work, Congress is notified immediately.

Join the Debate

FUEL ECONOMY STANDARDS AND GOVERNMENT POLICY

OVERVIEW: Government bureaucracies influence life in the United States in many beneficial and, sometimes, not so beneficial ways. Government agencies are charged with securing the common good and are dedicated to serving the American public. Administrative agencies, however, do not operate in a vacuum—they have mandates from the government and are ultimately subject to congressional, executive, and judicial supervision. Bureaucratic rule-making is subject to political oversight so as to ensure agencies and departments are held accountable for their activities, though administrative units vary in the extent of their discretion and freedom of action, depending on their mandates. While considered expert in their respective policy domains, bureaucrats may receive politically motivated, ill-conceived, or poorly researched directives from the government that can interfere with an agency's mission or operating efficiency. The intersection between politics, policy, and administrative regulation can be illustrated by the battle over government-mandated fuel economy for America's vehicles under the Corporate Average Fuel Economy (CAFE) program, which was part of the 1975 Energy Policy and Conservation Act (ECPA).

In response to the 1973 Organization of Petroleum Exporting Countries (OPEC) oil embargo and the resulting energy crisis, Congress established the CAFE program to reduce America's dependence on imported oil and consumption of gasoline. The idea was to set fuel efficiency standards for American passenger automobiles and light trucks, with fines to be imposed on automakers whose vehicle lines failed to meet these standards. Congress retained the authority to determine the miles-per-gallon standard for passenger cars, but it gave the Department of Transportation (DOT) the authority to set standards for light trucks (which include minivans and SUVs) and to enforce CAFE regulations. Automakers have opposed CAFE standards from the beginning. The industry claims that CAFE regulations impose an undue cost on automobile production by forcing manufacturers to make products the market does not want. As a result, the Department of Transportation has been thrust into the political battles between auto industry interests, environmental and energy interests, and Congress over whether to increase or repeal the CAFE standards.

CAFE policy has had mixed results. It is undeniable that during the 1980s increased efficiency due to increased standards resulted in a surge of increased fuel economy for new cars and trucks, and that CAFE standards, coupled with tighter emission controls, reduced auto pollutants. But, low gas prices throughout the 1990s and through 2004 allowed Americans to buy less-efficient vehicles (notably trucks and SUVs), and this resulted in an overall increase in American gasoline consumption. As disruptions in the Middle East and global competition contribute to record gas prices in the United States, CAFE standards have once again taken a prominent place in America's energy policy debate. The Bush administration has called on Congress to give the DOT the authority to set new CAFE standards for both light trucks and passenger cars, but Congress has been reluctant to increase the department's rule-making authority due to pressure from the automobile and oil and gas industries.

ARGUMENTS FOR INCREASING FUEL ECONOMY STANDARDS

- **Increased CAFE standards will reduce America's dependence on foreign oil.** One obvious benefit of increased

Legislators also augment their formal oversight of the executive branch by allowing citizens to appeal adverse bureaucratic decisions to agencies, Congress, and even the courts. Congressional review, a procedure adopted by the 104th Congress, by which agency regulations can be nullified by joint resolutions of legislative disapproval, is another method of exercising congressional oversight. This form of oversight is discussed in greater detail in chapter 7.

JUDICIAL CONTROL

Whereas the president's and Congress's ongoing control over the actions of the bureaucracy is very direct, the judiciary's oversight function is less apparent. Still, federal judges, for example, can issue injunctions or orders to an executive agency even before a rule is promulgated formally, giving the federal judiciary a potent check on the bureaucracy.

standards would be to reduce the United States' dependence on foreign oil supplies. Building more fuel-efficient vehicles would allow the United States to decrease oil imports while American energy producers seek alternative fuel sources and the means for cleaner and more efficient oil extraction.

- **Increased CAFE standards will reduce the effect of greenhouse gas emissions.** The Environmental Protection Agency reports that technology improvements to meet CAFE standards have resulted in cleaner vehicles that emit reduced greenhouse gas pollutants. Increasing the standards should create a more environmentally friendly vehicle fleet.
- **Increased CAFE standards will force automakers to seek improved and efficient technologies.** In order to meet increased CAFE standards and remain profitable, automakers will develop automobiles with a view to affordability and efficiency. As a response to America's oil concerns, the hybrid car was developed, and research currently is being directed to explore other alternative energy sources, such as hydrogen fuel cells.

ARGUMENTS FOR REPEALING FUEL ECONOMY STANDARDS

- **CAFE standards have failed to reduce America's oil consumption.** The *Wall Street Journal* reports that as America's autos have become more fuel efficient, Americans have almost *doubled* the number of miles driven each year. The effect is a net increase in oil consumption, and this is contrary to CAFE's policy goals. Many argue that if the government truly is concerned with decreasing fuel consumption, it should increase gas taxes, a strategy that has proven to be effective.

- **CAFE standards have created new environmental problems.** To meet CAFE standards, automakers have made lighter-weight vehicles by using composites and plastics to replace steel, for example. But, the National Research Council has found that new vehicle materials may create a new set of environmental impacts, such as environmental problems with vehicle disposal.
- **Market mechanisms are the best way to reduce fuel consumption and pollutants.** Dramatically increased gasoline prices have created a strong demand for fuel- and energy-efficient hybrid vehicles and have caused American public opinion to coalesce around the idea of pursuing research into alternative fuels and power sources. Automakers are responding by developing the hybrid vehicles the American people are now demanding.

QUESTIONS

1. Should the federal government have a role in directing the automobile industry in regard to fuel efficiency standards? Why or why not?
2. What seems to be the best policy to reduce America's dependence on foreign energy sources? Why?

SELECTED READINGS

Bent, Robert, Lloyd Orr, and Randall Baker, eds. *Energy: Science, Policy, and the Pursuit of Sustainability.* Washington, DC: Island Press, 2002.

National Research Council. *Effectiveness and Impact of Corporate Average Fuel Economy Standards.* Washington, DC: National Academies Press, 2003.

The courts also have ruled that agencies must give all affected individuals their due process rights guaranteed by the U.S. Constitution. A Social Security recipient's checks cannot be stopped, for example, unless that individual is provided with reasonable notice and an opportunity for a hearing. On a more informal, indirect level, litigation, or even the threat of litigation, often exerts a strong influence on bureaucrats. Injured parties can bring suit against agencies for their failure to enforce a law, and can challenge agency interpretations of any law. In general, however, the courts give great weight to the opinions of bureaucrats and usually defer to their expertise.[33]

Research by political scientists shows that government agencies are strategic. They often implement Supreme Court decisions "based on the costs and benefits of alternative policy choices." Specifically, the degree to which agencies appear to respond to Supreme Court decisions is based on the "specificity of Supreme Court opinions, agency policy preferences, agency age, and *amicus curiae* support."[34]

The development of specialized courts has altered the relationship of some agencies with the federal courts, apparently resulting in less judicial deference to agency rulings. Research by political scientists reveals that specialized courts such as the Court of International Trade, because of its jurists' expertise, defer less to agency decisions than do more generalized federal courts. Conversely, decisions from executive agencies are more likely to be reversed than those from more specialized independent regulatory commissions.[35]

Summary

THE BUREAUCRACY plays a major role in America as a shaper of public policy, earning it the nickname the "fourth branch" of government. To explain the evolution and scope of bureaucratic power, in this chapter we have made the following points:

1. **The Origins and Growth of the Federal Bureaucracy**

The federal bureaucracy has changed dramatically since George Washington's time, when the executive branch had only three departments—State, War, and Treasury—through the Civil War. Significant gains occurred in the size of the federal bureaucracy as the government geared up to conduct a war. As employment opportunities within the federal government increased, concurrent reforms in the civil service system assured that more and more jobs were filled according to merit and not by patronage. By the late 1800s, reform efforts led to further increases in the size of the bureaucracy, as independent regulatory commissions were created. In the wake of the Depression, many new agencies were created to get the national economy back on course as part of President Franklin D. Roosevelt's New Deal.

2. **The Modern Bureaucracy**

The modern bureaucracy is composed of more than 2.7 million civilian workers from all walks of life. In general, bureaucratic agencies fall into four categories: departments, government corporations, independent agencies, and independent regulatory commissions.

The political activity of employees in the federal government is regulated by the Federal Employees Political Activities Act.

3. **How the Bureaucracy Works**

The bureaucracy gets much of its power from the Congress delegating its powers. A variety of formal and informal mechanisms have been created to help the bureaucracy work more efficiently. These mechanisms help the bureaucracy and bureaucrats make policy.

4. **Making Agencies Accountable**

Agencies enjoy considerable discretion, but they are also subjected to many formal controls. The president, Congress, and the judiciary all exercise various degrees of control over the bureaucracy.

KEY TERMS

administrative adjudication, p. 334
administrative discretion, p. 334
bureaucracy, p. 316
civil service system, p. 319
departments, p. 326
executive order, p. 340
Federal Employees Political Activities Act, p. 331
government corporation, p. 329
Hatch Act, p. 331
implementation, p. 332
independent executive agency, p. 329
independent regulatory commission, p. 319
interagency councils, p. 332
iron triangles, p. 332
issue networks, p. 332
merit system, p. 319
patronage, p. 318
Pendleton Act, p. 319
regulations, p. 334
rule making, p. 334
spoils system, p. 318

SELECTED READINGS

Aberbach, Joel D., and Bert A. Rockman. *In the Web of Politics: Three Decades of the U.S. Federal Executive.* Washington, DC: Brookings Institution, 2000.

Borrelli, MaryAnne. *The President's Cabinet: Gender, Power, and Representation.* Boulder, CO: Lynne Rienner, 2002.

Brehm, John, and Scott Gates. *Working, Shirking, and Sabotage: Bureaucratic Response to a Democratic Public.* Ann Arbor: University of Michigan Press, 1997.

Dolan, Julie A., and David H. Rosenbloom. *Representative Bureaucracy: Continued Cases and Controversies.* Armonk, NY: M. E. Sharpe, 2003.

Felbinger, Claire L., and Wendy A. Haynes, eds. *Outstanding Women in Public Administration: Leaders, Mentors, and Pioneers.* Armonk, NY: M. E. Sharpe, 2004.

Goodsell, Charles T. *The Case for Bureaucracy: A Public Administration Polemic,* 4th ed. Washington, DC: CQ Press, 2003.

Gormley, William T., and Steven J. Balla. *Bureaucracy and Democracy: Accountability and Performance.* Washington, DC: CQ Press, 2003.

Ingraham, Patricia Wallace. *The Foundation of Merit: Public Service in American Democracy.* Baltimore, MD: Johns Hopkins University Press, 1995.

Ingraham, Patricia Wallace, and Laurence E. Lynn Jr. *The Art of Governance: Analyzing Management and Administration.* Washington, DC: Georgetown University Press, 2004.

Kerwin, Cornelius M. *Rulemaking: How Government Agencies Write Law and Make Policy,* 3rd ed. Washington, DC: CQ Press, 2003.

Peters, B. Guy. *The Politics of Bureaucracy,* 5th ed. New York: Routledge, 2001.

Richardson, William D. *Democracy, Bureaucracy and Character.* Lawrence: University Press of Kansas, 1997.

Stivers, Camilla. *Gender Images in Public Administration: Legitimacy and the Administrative State,* 2nd ed. Thousand Oaks, CA: Sage, 2002.

Twight, Charlotte. *Dependent on DC: The Rise of Federal Control over the Lives of Ordinary Americans.* New York: Palgrave Macmillan, 2002.

Wilson, James Q. *Bureaucracy: What Government Agencies Do and Why They Do It,* reprint ed. New York: Basic Books, 2000.

WEB EXPLORATIONS

To examine the federal workforce by gender, race, and ethnicity, go to
http://www.opm.gov/feddata/factbook/

To see federal agency rules and regulations contained in the *Federal Register,* go to
http://www.gpoaccess.gov/fr/index.html

For more about the IRS and its modernization efforts, see
http://www.irs.gov

To find out more about the Presidential Management Fellows Program, go to
http://www.pmf.opm.gov/index.asp

To view the scorecard of federal agencies trying to implement the president's management agenda, go to
http://www.whitehouse.gov/results/agenda/scorecard.html

For contrasting views on the debate over fuel efficiency standards, go to
http://www.heritage.org/Research/
EnergyandEnvironment/BG1458.cfm
http://www.ppionline.org/documents/clean_cars_0304.pdf

THE JUDICIARY

10

IN THE WAKE OF THE SEPTEMBER 11, 2001, terrorist attacks, Congress passed the Authorization for Use of Military Force, giving the president power to "use all necessary appropriate force" against "nations, organizations, or persons" that he deemed to have "planned, authorized, committed or aided" in the completion of those attacks. The president then sent U.S. troops to Afghanistan to subdue al-Qaeda and to defeat the Taliban regime that was lending it support. Soon thereafter, members of the U.S.-supported Afghani Northern Alliance captured several U.S. citizens in Afghanistan, including Yaser Hamdi, who was later handed over to U.S. forces. The capture of Hamdi opened the door to a number of civil liberties questions, which were eventually resolved by the U.S. Supreme Court, underscoring the major role played by the Court in acting as the arbiter of disputes within the federal system.

After his capture, Hamdi, who although a U.S. citizen had spent much of his life in Saudi Arabia, was sent to a U.S. detention facility at Guantanamo Bay, Cuba, where he was held with no access to the outside world or to an attorney. From there, he was sent to a U.S. military base in Virginia and then to a naval brig in South Carolina. The Department of Justice declined to bring any charges against Hamdi and instead designated him an "enemy combatant."

In July 2002, Hamdi's father filed suit on his son's behalf, seeking a review of the legality of his son's detention. He alleged that the government was holding Hamdi in violation of the Fifth and Fourteenth Amendments. A federal judge ordered the United States to allow an attorney to meet with Hamdi in private. While this decision was being appealed, Hamdi was held in solitary confinement with no access to his lawyer. The case finally ended up before the U.S. Supreme Court, where Hamdi, yet to be charged with a crime, argued that his basic civil liberties as an American citizen were being denied. The U.S. government countered that by designating Hamdi an enemy combatant, it was justified holding him in the United States indefinitely—without formal charges or proceedings—until it decided that access to counsel or other actions were warranted.

In June 2004, the U.S. Supreme Court ruled in *Hamdi et al.* v. *Rumsfeld* that "a state of war is not a blank check for the president" to deny basic civil liberties to U.S. citizens held in captivity. The Court went on to say that citizens must be apprised of the charges against them and allowed access to lawyers.[1] Although the Court affirmed the right of the president to detain citizens as enemy combatants, it reiterated that such prisoners must be given the right to challenge their captivity before a neutral fact finder.

Hamdi was released in October 2004, but as a condition of his release, he had to renounce his U.S. citizenship and return to Saudi Arabia. This outcome meant that Hamdi never was charged formally or brought to trial, despite three years of imprisonment. The question of how the U.S. government should treat enemy combatants was not, however, completely resolved. Thus, in 2006, the Supreme Court revisited the issue in *Hamdan* v. *Rumsfeld.*

Hamdan stemmed from a lawsuit filed by Guantanamo Bay detainee Salim Hamdan, a Yemeni whom the administration accused of being an agent of Osama bin Laden. Continuing the line of reasoning established in *Hamdi,* the Court ruled that the military commissions created by the Bush administration in 2001 to try suspected members of al-Qaeda went far beyond the con-

stitutional powers granted to the president under the U.S. Constitution.[2] A 5–3 majority—Chief Justice John G. Roberts Jr. did not participate in the decision because he had been on the lower court that had upheld the president's actions—found that the commissions, "were neither authorized by federal law nor required by military necessity"[3] and circumvented the Geneva Conventions for dealing with prisoners of war, as well as the U.S. Military Code of Justice.

The *Hamdi* and *Hamdan* cases represent a historically significant rebuke of executive authority in a time of war and underscore the growing authority of the Supreme Court in the federal system. In the past, the Court has often acquiesced to unprecedented claims of executive power, such as those claimed by President Abraham Lincoln during the Civil War or President Franklin D. Roosevelt's internment of Japanese American citizens during World War II. Moreover, the Court's rulings underscore the delicate system of separation of powers established by the Framers. The Supreme Court of the United States—not the president—is the ultimate authority on what the U.S. Constitution means.

IN 1787, WHEN ALEXANDER HAMILTON wrote to urge support of the U.S. Constitution, he firmly believed that the judiciary would prove to be the weakest of the three departments of government. In its formative years, the judiciary was, in Hamilton's words, "the least dangerous" branch. The judicial branch seemed so inconsequential that when the young national government made its move to the District of Columbia in 1800, Congress actually forgot to include any space to house the justices of the Supreme Court! Last-minute conferences with Capitol architects led to the allocation of a small area in the basement of the Senate wing of the Capitol building for a courtroom. No other space was allowed for the justices, however. Noted one commentator, "A stranger might traverse the dark avenues of the Capitol for a week, without finding the remote corner in which justice is administered to the American Republic."[4]

Today, the role of the courts, particularly the Supreme Court of the United States, is significantly different from that envisioned when the national government came into being. The "least dangerous branch" now is perceived by many as having too much power.

Historically, Americans have been unaware of the political power held by the courts. They have been raised to think of the federal courts as above the fray of politics. That, however, has never been the case. Elected presidents nominate judges to the federal courts and justices to the Supreme Court, often to advance their personal politics, and elected senators ultimately confirm (or decline to confirm) presidential nominees to the federal bench. The process by which cases ultimately get heard—if they are heard at all—by the Supreme Court often is political as well. Interest groups routinely seek out good test cases to advance their policy positions. Even the U.S. government, generally through the Department of Justice and the U.S. solicitor general (a political appointee in that department), seeks to advance its version of the public interest in court. Interest groups then often line up on opposing sides to advance their positions, much in the same way lobbyists do in Congress.

In this chapter, we will explore these issues and the scope and development of judicial power:

- First, we will look at *the Constitution and the creation of the federal judiciary*. Article III of the Constitution created a Supreme Court but left it to Congress to create any other federal courts, a task it took up quickly.

- Second, we will discuss *the American legal system* and the concepts of civil and criminal law.

- Third, we will discuss *the federal court system*. The federal court system is composed of specialized courts, district courts, courts of appeals, and the Supreme Court, which is the ultimate authority on all federal law.

- Fourth, we will examine *how federal court judges are selected*. All appointments to the federal district courts, courts of appeals, and the Supreme Court are made by the president and are subject to Senate confirmation.

- Fifth, we will take a look at *the Supreme Court today*. Only a few of the millions of cases filed in courts around the United States every year eventually make their way to the Supreme Court through the lengthy appellate process.

- Sixth, we will examine *judicial philosophy and decision making* and discuss how judicial decision making is based on a variety of legal and extra-legal factors.

- Finally, we will discuss *judicial policy making and implementation*.

A note on terminology: When we refer to the "Supreme Court," the "Court," or the "high Court" here, we always mean the U.S. Supreme Court, which sits at the pinnacle of the federal and state court systems. The Supreme Court is referred to by the name of the chief justice who presided over it during a particular period. (For example, the Marshall Court is the Court presided over by John Marshall from 1801 to 1835, and the Roberts Court is the current Court that began in late 2005.) When we use the term "courts," we refer to all federal or state courts unless otherwise noted.

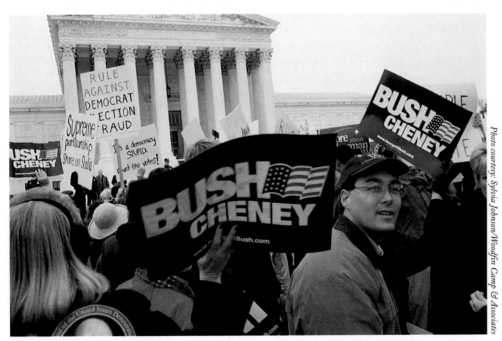

■ The power of the judiciary becomes apparent to most members of the general public only when it decides landmark cases. Here, protesters gather outside the U.S. Supreme Court during arguments in *Bush* v. *Gore* (2000). The Court's decision, in effect, decided the outcome of the 2000 presidential election.

Photo courtesy: Sylvia Johnson/Woodfin Camp & Associates

The Living Constitution

The Judges both of the supreme and inferior Courts, shall . . . receive for their services, a compensation, which shall not be diminished during their continuance in office.

—ARTICLE III, SECTION 1

This section of Article III simply posits the notion that the salaries of all federal judges cannot be reduced during their service on the bench. During the Constitutional Convention, there was considerable debate over how to treat the payment of federal judges. Some believed that Congress should have an extra check on the judiciary by being able to intimidate judges with the threat of reducing their salaries. This provision was a compromise after James Madison suggested that Congress have the authority to bar increases as well as decreases in the salaries of these unelected jurists. The delegates recognized that decreases, as well as no opportunity for raises, could negatively affect the pluses associated with life tenure.

There has not been much controversy over this clause of the Constitution. When the federal income tax was first enacted, some judges unsuccessfully challenged it as a diminution of their salaries. Much more recently, Chief Justices William H. Rehnquist and John G. Roberts Jr. have repeatedly urged Congress to increase salaries for federal judges, who earn less than some of their former clerks do as first-year associates in private law firms. As early as 1989, Rehnquist noted that "judicial salaries are the single greatest problem facing the federal judiciary today." Roberts, in his first state of the judiciary message, pointed out that the comparatively low salaries earned by federal judges drive away many well-qualified and diverse lawyers, compromising the independence of the American judiciary.

More and more federal judges are leaving the bench for more lucrative private practice, which is a relatively recent phenomenon. While a salary of $212,100 (for the chief justice) or $203,300 (for the other justices) may sound like a lot to most people, lawyers in large urban practices routinely earn more than double and often triple that amount each year. Supreme Court clerks, moreover, now regularly receive $200,000 signing bonuses (in addition to large salaries) from law firms anxious to pay for their expertise.

The Constitution and the Creation of the Federal Judiciary

THE DETAILED NOTES James Madison took at the Constitutional Convention in Philadelphia make it clear that the Framers devoted little time to the writing of or the content of Article III, which created the judicial branch of government. The Framers believed that a federal judiciary posed little of the threat of tyranny that they feared from the other two branches. One scholar has even suggested that, for at least some delegates to the Constitutional Convention, "provision for a national judiciary was a matter of theoretical necessity . . . more in deference to the maxim of separation [of powers] than in response to clearly formulated ideas about the role of a national judicial system and its indispensability."[5]

Alexander Hamilton argued in *Federalist No. 78* that the judiciary would be the least dangerous branch of government. Anti-Federalists, however, did not agree with Hamilton. They particularly objected to a judiciary whose members had life tenure and the ability to interpret what was to be "the supreme law of the land," a phrase that Anti-Federalists feared would give the Supreme Court too much power.

As discussed in chapter 2, the Framers also debated the need for any federal courts below the level of the Supreme Court. Some argued in favor of deciding all cases in state courts, with only appeals going before the Supreme Court. Others argued for a system of federal courts. A compromise left the final choice to Congress, and Article III, section 1, begins simply by vesting "The judicial Power of the United States . . . in one supreme Court, and in such inferior Courts as the Congress may from time to time ordain and establish." Although there is some debate over whether the Court should have the power of **judicial review,** which allows the judiciary to review acts of the other branches of government and the states, the question is left unsettled in Article III—and was not finally resolved until *Marbury* v. *Madison* (1803),[6] regarding acts of the national government and *Martin* v. *Hunter's Lessee* (1816), regarding state law.[7]

Article III, section 1, also gave Congress the authority to establish other courts as it saw fit. Section 2 specifies the judicial power of the Supreme Court (see Table 10.1) and discusses the Court's original and appellate jurisdiction. This section also specifies that all federal crimes, except those involving impeachment, shall be tried by jury in the state in which the crime was committed. The third section of the article defines treason, and mandates that at least two witnesses appear in such cases.

Although it is the duty of the chief justice of the United States to preside over presidential impeachments, this is not mentioned in Article III. Instead, Article I, section 3, notes in discussing impeachment, "When the President of the United States is tried, the Chief Justice shall preside."

Had the Supreme Court been viewed as the potential policy maker it is today, it is highly unlikely that the Framers would have provided for life tenure with "good behavior" for all federal judges in Article III. This feature was agreed on because the Framers did not want the justices (or any federal judges) subject to the whims of politics, the public, or politicians. (See The Living Constitution: Article III, Section 1.) Moreover, Alexander Hamilton argued in *Federalist No. 78* that the "independence of judges" was needed "to guard the Constitution and the rights of individuals." Because the Framers viewed the Court as quite powerless, Hamilton stressed the need to place federal judges above the fray of politics.

judicial review
Power of the courts to review acts of other branches of government and the states.

Judicial Review

TABLE 10.1 THE JUDICIAL POWER OF THE UNITED STATES SUPREME COURT

The following are the types of cases the Supreme Court was given the jurisdiction to hear as initially specified in the Constitution:

- All cases arising under the Constitution and laws or treaties of the United States
- All cases of admiralty or maritime jurisdiction
- Cases in which the United States is a party
- Controversies between a state and citizens of another state (later modified by the Eleventh Amendment)
- Controversies between two or more states
- Controversies between citizens of different states
- Controversies between citizens of the same states claiming lands under grants in different states
- Controversies between a state, or the citizens thereof, and foreign states or citizens thereof
- All cases affecting ambassadors or other public ministers

Join the Debate

SENATE ADVICE AND CONSENT AND JUDICIAL NOMINATIONS

OVERVIEW: Article II of the Constitution gives the president sole authority to make judicial and executive appointments, and it gives the Senate the power to confirm the chief executive's choices. Furthermore, Article I of the Constitution gives the Senate authority to determine its own rules; this includes procedural devices such as the filibuster to slow or stop legislative and political action. Any senator can use the filibuster to delay a vote on a political nominee. A two-thirds majority vote is needed to invoke cloture, thereby ending the filibuster, while only a simple majority is needed to confirm a nominee. Historically, the Senate generally has confirmed the president's nominees, and it was only in 1955 that the tradition of judicial appointees regularly appearing before the Senate Judiciary Committee began (the first potential justice to appear before the Senate did so in 1925). Though there were battles over judicial politics (President Thomas Jefferson's supporters came close to impeaching Justice Salmon Chase for political reasons), the Senate has generally played a narrow role in the confirmation process and has usually deferred to the president's wishes. Precedent for filibustering Supreme Court nominees was set in 1968 when President Lyndon B. Johnson's choice for chief justice, Abe Fortas, was blocked by the Republican minority. But it was with the controversial Supreme Court nomination of Judge

Robert H. Bork in 1987 that confirmation politics took a contentious turn. The Senate voted against Bork's nomination after unprecedented pressure from civil and women's rights groups who believed his conservative judicial views would roll back civil liberties protections.

Senate Democrats, while in the minority in 2005 and 2006, argued, argue that the use of the filibuster is necessary to help moderate the ideological make-up of the federal bench, noting that Republicans made similar arguments when they were in the minority and opposed some of former President Bill Clinton's judicial nominees. As a result, the Senate's Republican majority threatened to use the somewhat arcane rules of the chamber to bar filibusters on judicial nominations. Those opposed to judicial filibusters argue that the minority party has no right to thwart the majority's constitutional advice and consent role. They argue that the Constitution requires a simple majority to confirm nominees—the Constitution is explicit when it requires a two-thirds or three-quarters supermajority vote—and judicial filibusters have the effect of denying the Senate majority its right to exercise consent.

ARGUMENTS AGAINST ALLOWING FILIBUSTERS IN THE SENATE'S CONFIRMATION PROCESS

- **Article II of the Constitution gives the president sole authority to make judicial nominations.** Constitutional scholar John Eastman has argued using records of the constitutional and state ratifying conventions that the

---

Some checks on the power of the judiciary were nonetheless included in the Constitution. The Constitution gives Congress the authority to alter the Court's jurisdiction (its ability to hear certain kinds of cases). Congress can also propose constitutional amendments that, if ratified, can effectively reverse judicial decisions, and it can impeach and remove federal judges. In one further check, it is the president who, with the "advice and consent" of the Senate, appoints all federal judges. (See Join the Debate: Senate Advice and Consent and Judicial Nominations.)

THE JUDICIARY ACT OF 1789 AND THE CREATION OF THE FEDERAL JUDICIAL SYSTEM

In spite of the Framers' intentions, the pervasive role of politics in the judicial branch quickly became evident with the passage of the Judiciary Act of 1789. Congress spent nearly the entire second half of its first session deliberating the various provisions of the act to give form and substance to the federal judiciary. As one early observer noted, "The convention has only crayoned in the outlines. It left it to Congress to fill up and colour the canvas."[8]

president has full power over the nomination process. The Senate's role is merely to provide advice and consent on already chosen nominees.

■ **Article I of the Constitution gives the House of Representatives and the Senate the authority to decide their own rules of procedure.** Article I, section 5, gives each chamber the authority to determine its own rules of procedure by a simple majority vote. If the Senate, in order to change with the times, wishes to adapt rules accordingly, it has the full authority of the Constitution behind it. There is nothing in the Constitution creating or giving protection to judicial filibusters.

■ **The Constitution's Framers intended only a simple majority vote for the advice and consent clause.** Alexander Hamilton explains in *Federalist Nos. 76* and *77* that the advice and consent function would be exercised "by the whole body, by [the] entire branch of the legislature." That is, the advice and consent would reflect the majority's will. A faction should not be allowed to thwart a legitimate majority's will.

ARGUMENTS FOR ALLOWING FILIBUSTERS IN THE SENATE'S CONFIRMATION PROCESS

■ **Filibusters are necessary to maintain the ideological balance of the federal courts.** Filibusters on judicial nominees allow the minority party to check a president's attempt to stack the judiciary with one political philosophy. Maintaining ideological diversity will allow different constitutional interpretations and understanding, thus adding depth to our knowledge of constitutional jurisprudence.

■ **The Founders intended for the Senate to be a deliberative body.** The Constitution's writers intended for Senate debate to be slow, deliberate, and reasoned. The idea was to create a small legislative body in which all views would be aired in the marketplace of ideas. The filibuster keeps the debate open. Besides, if two-thirds of the Senate support cloture, the filibuster ends.

■ **Senate rules benefit both political parties and their partisans.** No party remains in the majority forever. History shows that both parties spend significant time in both majority and minority status. Altering the rules to suit partisan politics practically ensures that minority party members will engage in the same tactics and politics once they regain majority standing and the cycle of bitter partisan politics will continue.

QUESTIONS

1. Who has the better argument: those who oppose or support judicial filibusters? Why?
2. Should a president strive to place nonpartisan judges on the federal bench? Why or why not?

SELECTED READINGS

David, Richard. *Electing Justice: Fixing the Supreme Court Nomination Process.* New York: Oxford University Press, 2005.

Epstein, Lee, and Jeffrey A. Segal. *Advice and Consent: The Politics of Judicial Appointments.* New York: Oxford University Press, 2005.

The **Judiciary Act of 1789** established the basic three-tiered structure of the federal court system. At the bottom are the federal district courts—at least one in each state—each staffed by a federal judge. If the people participating in a lawsuit (called litigants) were unhappy with the district court's verdict, they could appeal their case to one of three circuit courts. Each circuit court, initially created to function as a trial court for important cases, was composed of one district court judge and two itinerant Supreme Court justices who met as a circuit court twice a year. It wasn't until 1891 that circuit courts (or, as we know them today, courts of appeals) took on their exclusively appellate function. The third tier of the federal judicial system fleshed out by the Judiciary Act of 1789 was the Supreme Court of the United States. Although the Constitution mentions "the supreme Court," it was silent on its size. In the Judiciary Act, Congress set the size of the Supreme Court at six—the chief justice plus five associate justices. After being reduced to five members in 1801, it later expanded and contracted, and finally the Court's size was fixed at nine in 1869.

When the justices met in their first public session in New York City in 1790, they were garbed magnificently in black and scarlet robes in the English fashion. The elegance of their attire, however, could not make up for the relative ineffectiveness of the

Judiciary Act of 1789
Established the basic three-tiered structure of the federal court system.

Court. Its first session—presided over by John Jay, who was appointed chief justice of the United States by George Washington—initially had to be adjourned when less than half the justices attended. Later, once a sufficient number of justices assembled, the Court decided only one major case—*Chisholm* v. *Georgia* (1793) (discussed below). Moreover, as an indication of its lowly status, one associate justice left the Court to become chief justice of the South Carolina Supreme Court. (Although such a move would be considered a step down today, keep in mind that in the early years of the United States, many viewed the states as more important than the new national government.)

Hampered by frequent changes in personnel, limited space for its operations, no clerical support, and no system of reporting its decisions, the Court and its meager activities did not impress many people. From the beginning, the circuit court duties of the Supreme Court justices presented problems for the prestige of the Court. Few good lawyers were willing to accept nominations to the high Court because circuit court duties entailed a substantial amount of travel—most of it on horseback over poorly maintained roads in frequently inclement weather. Southern justices often rode as many as 10,000 miles a year on horseback. President George Washington tried to prevail on several friends and supporters to fill vacancies on the Court as they appeared, but most refused the "honor." John Adams, the second president of the United States, ran into similar problems. When he asked John Jay to resume the position of chief justice after he resigned to become governor of New York, Jay declined the offer. Jay once had remarked of the Court that it lacked "energy, weight, and dignity" as well as "public confidence and respect."

In spite of all its problems, in its first decade, the Court took several actions to help mold the new nation. First, by declining to give George Washington advice on the legality of some of his actions, the justices attempted to establish the Supreme Court as an independent, nonpolitical branch of government. Although John Jay, as an individual, frequently gave the president private advice, the Court refused to answer questions Washington posed to it concerning the construction of international laws and treaties. The justices wanted to avoid the appearance of prejudging any issues that could arise later before them.

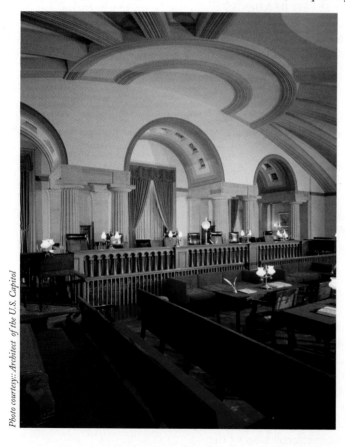

■ The Supreme Court initially met in this small room in the basement of the U.S Capitol building.

Photo courtesy: Architect of the U.S. Capitol

The early Court also tried to advance principles of nationalism and to maintain the national government's supremacy over the states. As circuit court jurists, the justices rendered numerous decisions on such matters as national suppression of the Whiskey Rebellion, which occurred in 1794 after a national excise tax was imposed on whiskey, and the constitutionality of the Alien and Sedition Acts, which made it a crime to criticize national governmental officials or their actions (see chapter 5).

During the ratification debates, Anti-Federalists had warned that Article III extended federal judicial power to controversies "between a State and Citizens of another State"—meaning that a citizen of one state could sue any other state in federal court, a prospect unthinkable to defenders of state sovereignty. Although Federalists, including Alexander Hamilton and James Madison, had scoffed at the idea, the nationalist Supreme Court quickly proved them wrong in *Chisholm* v. *Georgia* (1793). In *Chisholm,* the justices interpreted the Court's jurisdiction under Article III, section 2, to include the right to hear suits brought by a citizen against a state in which he did not reside. Writing in *Chisholm,* Justice James Wilson denounced the "haughty notions of state independence, state sovereignty, and state supremacy."[9] The states' reaction to this perceived attack on their authority led to passage and ratification in 1798 of the Eleventh Amendment to the Constitution, which specifically limited judicial power by stipulating that the authority of the federal courts could not "extend to any suit . . . commenced or prosecuted against one of the United States by citizens of another State."

Finally, in a series of circuit and Supreme Court decisions, the justices paved the way for announcement of the doctrine of judicial review by the third chief justice, John Marshall.[10] Justices riding circuit occasionally held state laws unconstitutional because they violated the U.S. Constitution. In 1796, the Court for the first time evaluated the constitutionality of an act of Congress finding the law, however, to be constitutional.[11]

THE MARSHALL COURT: *MARBURY V. MADISON* (1803) AND JUDICIAL REVIEW

John Marshall, who headed the Court from 1801 to 1835, brought much-needed respect and prestige to the Court through his leadership in a progression of cases and a series of innovations. Marshall was appointed chief justice by President John Adams in 1801, three years after he declined to accept a nomination as associate justice. An ardent Federalist, Marshall has come to be considered the most important justice ever to serve on the high Court. Part of his reputation is the result of the duration of his service and the historical significance of this period in our nation's history.

As chief justice, Marshall instituted several innovations and led the Court to issue a number of important rulings that established the Court as a co-equal branch of government. First, the Marshall Court discontinued the practice of *seriatim* (Latin for "in a series") opinions, which was the custom of the King's Bench in Great Britain. Prior to the Marshall Court, the justices delivered their individual opinions in order. There was no single opinion of the Court, as we are accustomed to today. For the Court to take its place as an equal branch of government, Marshall strongly believed, the justices needed to speak as a Court and not as six individuals. In fact, during Marshall's first four years in office, the Court routinely spoke as one, and the chief justice wrote twenty-four of its twenty-six opinions.

The Marshall Court also established the authority of the Supreme Court over the judiciaries of the various states, including the Court's power to declare state laws invalid in a series of cases from 1810 to 1821 in which states opposed the authority of the national government to review state actions.[12] In addition, the Court established the supremacy of the federal government and Congress over state governments through a broad interpretation of the necessary and proper clause in *McCulloch v. Maryland* (1819), discussed in detail in chapter 3.[13]

Finally, the Marshall Court claimed the right of judicial review, from which the Supreme Court derives much of its day-to-day power and impact on the policy process. This established the Court as the final arbiter of constitutional questions, with the right to declare congressional acts void (*Marbury v. Madison* [1803]).[14]

Photo courtesy: Boston Athenaeum

■ A single person can make a major difference in the development of an institution. Such was the case with John Marshall (1755–1835), who dominated the Supreme Court during his thirty-four years as chief justice. Marshall was born in a log cabin in Virginia, the first of fifteen children of Welsh immigrants. After serving in the Continental Army and acquiring the rank of captain, Marshall taught himself law. More of a politician than a lawyer, Marshall served as a delegate to the Virginia legislature from 1782 to 1785, 1787 to 1790, and 1795 to 1796, and he played an instrumental role in Virginia's ratification of the U.S. Constitution in 1787. He became secretary of state in 1800 under John Adams. When Oliver Ellsworth resigned as chief justice of the United States in 1800, Adams nominated Marshall. Though Marshall was an ardent Federalist, he was a third cousin of Democratic-Republican President Thomas Jefferson, whose administration he faced head on in *Marbury v. Madison* (1803). Marshall served on the Court until the day he died, participating in more than 1,000 decisions and authoring more than 500 opinions.

In *Federalist No. 78*, Alexander Hamilton first publicly endorsed the idea of judicial review, noting, "Whenever a particular statute contravenes the Constitution, it will be the duty of the judicial tribunals to adhere to the latter and disregard the former." Nonetheless, because the power of judicial review is not mentioned in the U.S. Constitution, the actual authority of the Supreme Court to review the constitutionality of acts of Congress was an unsettled question. But, in ***Marbury v. Madison* (1803)**, Chief Justice John Marshall claimed this sweeping authority for the Court by asserting that the right of judicial review was a power that could be implied from the Constitution's supremacy clause.[15]

Marbury v. *Madison* arose amid a sea of political controversy. In the final hours of the Adams administration, William Marbury was appointed a justice of the peace for the District of Columbia. But, in the confusion of winding up matters, Adams's secretary of state failed to deliver Marbury's commission. Marbury then asked James Madison, Thomas Jefferson's secretary of state, for the commission. Under direct orders from Jefferson, who was irate over the Adams administration's last-minute appointment of several Federalist judges (quickly confirmed by the Federalist Senate), Madison refused to turn over the commission. Marbury and three other Adams appointees who were in the same situation then filed a writ of *mandamus* (a legal motion) asking the Supreme Court to order Madison to deliver their commissions.

Political tensions ran high as the Court met to hear the case. Jefferson threatened to ignore any order of the Court. Marshall realized that he and the prestige of the Court could be devastated by any refusal of the executive branch to comply with the decision. Responding to this challenge, in a brilliant opinion that in many sections reads more like a lecture to Jefferson than a discussion of the merits of Marbury's claim, Marshall concluded that although Marbury and the others were entitled to their commissions, the Court lacked the power to issue the writ sought by Marbury. In *Marbury* v. *Madison*, Marshall further ruled that the parts of the Judiciary Act of 1789 that extended the jurisdiction of the Court to allow it to issue writs were inconsistent with the Constitution and therefore unconstitutional.

Although the immediate effect of the decision was to deny power to the Court, its long-term effect was to establish the principle of judicial review. Said Marshall, writing for the Court, "it is emphatically the province and duty of the judicial department to say what the law is." Through judicial review, an implied power, the Supreme Court most dramatically exerts its authority to determine what the Constitution means. Since *Marbury,* the Court has routinely exercised the power of judicial review to determine the constitutionality of acts of Congress, the executive branch, and the states.

***Marbury v. Madison* (1803)**
Case in which the Supreme Court first asserted the power of judicial review in finding that the congressional statute extending the Court's original jurisdiction was unconstitutional.

The Chief Justice of the United States

The American Legal System

Comparing Judiciaries

THE JUDICIAL SYSTEM in the United States can best be described as a dual system consisting of the federal court system and the judicial systems of the fifty states, as illustrated in Figure 10.1 and also described in chapter 4. Cases may arise in either system. Both systems are basically three tiered. At the bottom of the system are **trial courts,** where litigation begins. In the middle are appellate courts in the state systems and the courts of appeals in the federal system. At the top of each pyramid sits a court of last resort. (Some states call their high courts supreme courts; New York and Maryland, however, call it the Court of Appeals; Oklahoma and Texas have a Supreme Court and a separate highest state court for criminal cases called the Court of Criminal Appeals.) The federal courts of appeals and Supreme Court as well as state courts of appeals and supreme courts are **appellate courts** that, with few exceptions, review on appeal only cases that already have been decided in lower courts. These courts generally hear matters of both civil and criminal law.

trial courts
Courts of original jurisdiction where cases begin.

appellate courts
Courts that generally review only findings of law made by lower courts.

FIGURE 10.1 THE DUAL STRUCTURE OF THE AMERICAN COURT SYSTEM

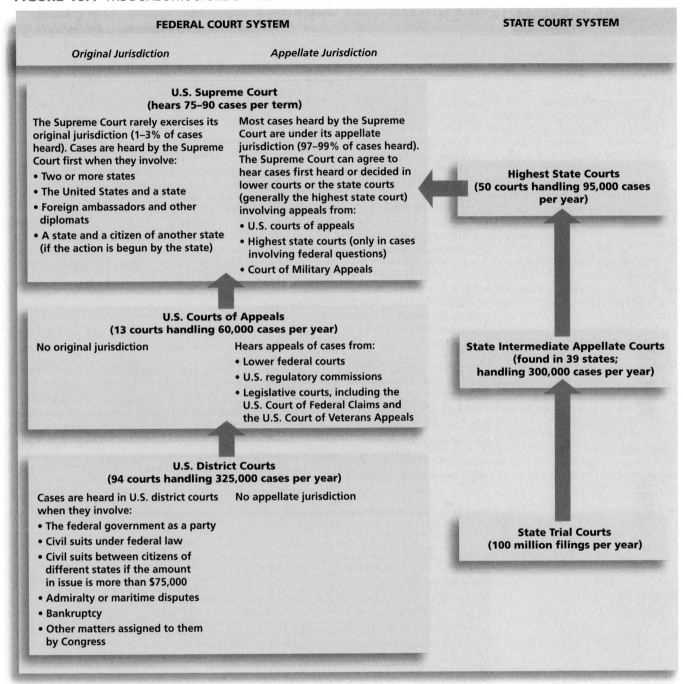

JURISDICTION

Before a state or federal court can hear a case, it must have **jurisdiction,** which means the authority to hear and decide the issues in that case. The jurisdiction of the federal courts is controlled by the U.S. Constitution and by statute. Jurisdiction is conferred based on issues, the amount of money involved in a dispute, or the type of offense. Procedurally, we speak of two types of jurisdiction: original and appellate. **Original jurisdiction** refers to a court's authority to hear disputes as a trial court and may occur on the federal or state level. For example, the child molestation case against Michael Jackson was begun in a California state trial court of original jurisdiction. In contrast,

jurisdiction
Authority vested in a particular court to hear and decide the issues in any particular case.

original jurisdiction
The jurisdiction of courts that hear a case first, usually in a trial. Courts determine the facts of a case under their original jurisdiction.

Global Perspective

THE EUROPEAN COURT OF JUSTICE

The European Union (EU) is composed of twenty-five member nations who have agreed to cede some of their national sovereignty in exchange for the political and economic benefits that belonging to a large, overarching organization provides. Members of the European Union turn to the Court of Justice as their highest court. The Court of Justice consists of twenty-five judges, one from each EU member nation, who serve six-year terms. These judges may sit in a Grand Chamber of thirteen judges or in chambers of three or five judges. Court of Justice proceedings may take place in any of the twenty-one official languages of the European Union.

It is the Court of Justice's role to ensure that EU law and regulations are interpreted uniformly and applied by all member states, regardless of the cultural norms and mores of those nations. For example, when a member state's national court has a question concerning the interpretation or validity of European Union law or policy, it submits a request for clarification to the Court of Justice, and the court then issues a preliminary ruling to all member national courts explaining how to construe and execute the directive in question. The U.S. Supreme Court fulfills a similar role as the ultimate interpreter of federal law but offers no advisory opinions.

Unlike the Supreme Court, however, the Court of Justice is empowered to levy sanctions, including heavy fines, on recalcitrant states to force compliance with EU rules. For example, France was fined $25 million for violating EU fishing regulations and was threatened with fines when it prohibited the importation of British beef. With authority comes accountability, and citizens of some EU member nations question whether too much authority has been taken away from their national courts. For example, when German students began relocating to Austria to take advantage of lower university entrance requirements, many Austrians were outraged and appealed to the high court. The Court of Justice ruled that Austrian university admission policy must give access to citizens of all other EU members, but the Austrian government argued that educational policy is a matter of national sovereignty and that the Court of Justice was engaging in judicial overreach. EU member nation arguments such as this are similar to those offered by states' rights advocates in the United States.

QUESTIONS

1. What similarities and differences can you identify between the European Court of Justice and the U.S. Supreme Court?
2. Identify some of the difficulties associated with the European Court of Justice's role in settling disputes among member nations. Is the Court of Justice's task more or less difficult than that of the U.S. Supreme Court in settling disputes between state governments and the federal government?

Sources: CIA World Factbook, http://www.cia.gov; European Court of Justice, http://curia.europa.eu.

---

appellate jurisdiction
The power vested in an appellate court to review and/or revise the decision of a lower court.

the legal battle over the constitutionality of the federal Partial Birth Abortion Ban Act was begun in several federal district courts. More than 90 percent of all cases, whether state or federal, end in a court of original jurisdiction. **Appellate jurisdiction** refers to a court's ability to review cases already decided by a trial court. Appellate courts ordinarily do not review the factual record; instead, they review legal procedures to make certain that the law was applied properly to the issues presented in the case.

CRIMINAL AND CIVIL LAW

criminal law
Codes of behavior related to the protection of property and individual safety.

Criminal law is the body of law that regulates individual conduct and is enforced by the state and national governments.[16] Crimes are graded as felonies, misdemeanors, or offenses, according to their severity. Some acts—for example, murder, rape, and robbery—are considered crimes in all states. Although all states outlaw murder, their penal, or criminal, codes treat the crime quite differently; some states, for example, allow the death penalty for murder, while others prohibit the use of capital punishment. Other practices—such as gambling—are illegal only in some states.

Criminal law assumes that society itself is the victim of the illegal act; therefore, the government prosecutes, or brings an action, on behalf of an injured party (acting as a plaintiff) in criminal but not civil cases. For example, the charges against Michael Jackson were styled as *The People of the State of California* v. *Michael Joseph Jackson.*

Criminal cases are traditionally in the purview of the states. But, a burgeoning set of federal criminal laws is contributing significantly to delays in the federal courts.

Civil law is the body of law that regulates the conduct and relationships between private individuals or companies. Because the actions at issue in civil law do not constitute a threat to society at large, people who believe they have been injured by another party must take action on their own to seek judicial relief. Civil cases, then, involve lawsuits filed to recover something of value, whether it is the right to vote, fair treatment, or monetary compensation for an item or service that cannot be recovered. Most cases seen on television shows such as *Judge Judy* are civil cases.

Before a criminal or civil case gets to court, much has to happen. In fact, most legal disputes that arise in the United States never get to court. Individuals and companies involved in civil disputes routinely settle their disagreements out of court. Often these settlements are not reached until minutes before the case is to be tried. Many civil cases that go to trial are settled during the course of the trial—before the case can be handed over to the jury or submitted to a judge for a decision or determination of responsibility or guilt.

Each civil or criminal case has a plaintiff, or petitioner, who brings charges against a defendant, or respondent. Sometimes the government is the plaintiff. The government may bring civil charges on behalf of the citizens of the state or the national government against a person or corporation for violating the law, but it is always the government that brings a criminal case. When cases are initiated, they are known first by the name of the petitioner. In *Marbury* v. *Madison*, William Marbury was the plaintiff, suing the defendants, the U.S. government and James Madison as its secretary of state, for not delivering Marbury's judicial commission.

During trials, judges often must interpret the intent of laws enacted by Congress and state legislatures as they bear on the issues at hand. To do so, they read reports, testimony, and debates on the relevant legislation and study the results of other similar legal cases. They also rely on the presentations made by lawyers in their briefs and at trial.

Another important component of most civil and criminal cases is the jury. This body acts as the ultimate finder of fact and plays an important role in determining the culpability of the individual on trial. The composition of juries has been the subject of much controversy in the United States. In the past, women and blacks often were excluded from jury service because many states selected jurors from those registered to vote. Although the Supreme Court ruled in 1888 that African American citizens could not be barred from serving as jurors,[17] it was not until 1979 that the Court extended this ruling to women.[18]

Until recently, however, it was not all that unusual for lawyers to use their peremptory challenges (those made without a reason) systematically to dismiss women or African Americans if they believed that they would be hostile to their case. In two opinions, however, the Supreme Court concluded that race or gender could not be used as reasons to exclude potential jurors.[19] Thus, today, juries are much more likely to be more representative of the community than in the past and capable of offering litigants in civil or criminal trial a jury of their peers.

civil law
Codes of behavior related to business and contractual relationships between groups and individuals.

You Are a Young Lawyer

The Federal Court System

THE FEDERAL DISTRICT COURTS, courts of appeals, and the Supreme Court are called **constitutional** (or Article III) **courts** because Article III of the Constitution either established them (as is the case with the Supreme Court) or authorizes Congress to establish them. Judges who preside over these courts are nominated by the president (with the advice and consent of the Senate), and they serve lifetime terms, as long as they engage in "good behavior."

constitutional courts
Federal courts specifically created by the U.S. Constitution or by Congress pursuant to its authority in Article III.

legislative courts
Courts established by Congress for specialized purposes, such as the Court of Military Appeals.

In addition to constitutional courts, **legislative courts** are set up by Congress, under its implied powers, generally for special purposes. The U.S. territorial courts (which hear federal cases in the territories) and the U.S. Court of Veterans Appeals are examples of legislative courts, or what some call Article I courts. The judges who preside over these federal courts are appointed by the president (subject to Senate confirmation) and serve fixed, limited terms.

DISTRICT COURTS

As we have seen, Congress created U.S. district courts when it enacted the Judiciary Act of 1789. District courts are federal trial courts of original jurisdiction (see Figure 10.1). There are currently ninety-four federal district courts staffed by a total of 678 active judges, assisted by more than 300 retired judges who still hear cases on a limited basis. No district court cuts across state lines. Every state has at least one federal district court, and the most populous states—California, Texas, and New York—each have four (see Figure 10.2).[20]

Federal district courts, where the bulk of the judicial work takes place in the federal system, have original jurisdiction over only specific types of cases, as indicated in Figure 10.1. Although the rules governing district court jurisdiction can be complex, cases heard in federal district courts by a single judge (with or without a jury) generally fall into one of three categories:

1. They involve the federal government as a party.
2. They present a federal question based on a claim under the U.S. Constitution, a treaty with another nation, or a federal statute. This is called federal question jurisdiction and it can involve criminal or civil law.

FIGURE 10.2 THE FEDERAL COURT SYSTEM
This map shows the location of the U.S. courts of appeals and the boundaries of the federal district courts in states with more than one district.

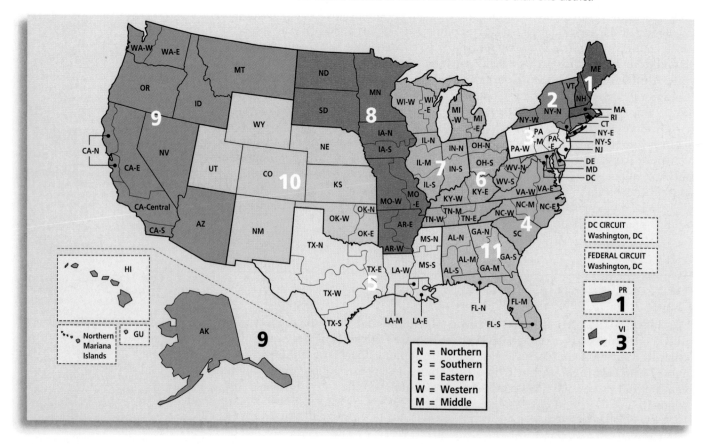

3. They involve civil suits in which citizens are from different states, and the amount of money at issue is more than $75,000.[21]

Each federal judicial district has a U.S. attorney, who is nominated by the president and confirmed by the Senate. The U.S. attorney in each district is that district's chief law enforcement officer. The size of the staff and the number of assistant U.S. attorneys who work in each district depend on the amount of litigation in each district. U.S. attorneys, like district attorneys within the states, have a considerable amount of discretion as to whether they pursue criminal or civil investigations or file charges against individuals or corporations. These highly visible positions often serve as springboards for elective office. Former New York City Mayor Rudy Giuliani earlier was the U.S. attorney for the Southern District of New York.

THE COURTS OF APPEALS

The losing party in a case heard and decided in a federal district court can appeal the decision to the appropriate court of appeals. The United States courts of appeals (known as the circuit courts of appeals prior to 1948) are the intermediate appellate courts in the federal system and were established in 1789 to hear appeals from federal district courts. There are currently eleven numbered courts of appeals (see Figure 10.2). A twelfth, the D.C. Circuit Court of Appeals, handles most appeals involving federal regulatory commissions and agencies, including, for example, the National Labor Relations Board and the Securities and Exchange Commission. The thirteenth federal appeals court is the U.S. Court of Appeals for the Federal Circuit, which deals with patents and contract and financial claims against the federal government.

In 2005, the U.S. courts of appeals were staffed by 179 active judges—assisted by almost 100 retired judges who still hear cases on a limited basis—who were appointed by the president, subject to Senate confirmation. The number of judges within each circuit varies—depending on the workload and the complexity of the cases—and ranges from six to nearly thirty. Each circuit is supervised by a chief judge, the most senior judge in terms of service below the age of sixty-five, who can serve no more than seven years. In deciding cases, judges are divided into rotating three-judge panels, made up of the active judges within the circuit, visiting judges (primarily district judges from the same circuit), and retired judges. In rare cases, all the judges in a circuit may choose to sit together (*en banc*) to decide a case by majority vote.

As shown in Figure 10.1, the courts of appeals have no original jurisdiction. Rather, Congress has granted these courts appellate jurisdiction over two general categories of cases: appeals from criminal and civil cases from the district courts, and appeals from administrative agencies. Criminal and civil case appeals constitute about 90 percent of the workload of the courts of appeals, with appeals from administrative agencies about 10 percent. Because so many agencies are located in Washington, D.C., the D.C. Circuit Court of Appeals hears an inordinate number of such cases. The D.C. Circuit Court of Appeals, then, is considered the second most important court in the nation because its decisions govern the regulatory agencies. Supreme Court Chief Justice John G. Roberts Jr. and Justices Antonin Scalia, Clarence Thomas, and Ruth Bader Ginsburg sat on that court before their nomination to the Supreme Court.

Once a decision is made by a federal court of appeals, a litigant no longer has an automatic right to an appeal. The losing party may submit a petition to the U.S. Supreme Court to hear the case, but the Court grants few of these requests. The courts of appeals, then, are the courts of last resort for almost all federal litigation. Keep in mind, however, that most cases, if they actually go to trial, go no further than the district court level.

In general, courts of appeals try to correct errors of law and procedure that have occurred in lower courts or administrative agencies. Courts of appeals hear no new testimony; instead, lawyers submit written arguments in what is called a **brief** (also

brief
A document containing the legal written arguments in a case filed with a court by a party prior to a hearing or trial.

submitted in trial courts), and they then appear to present and argue the case orally to the court.

precedent

A prior judicial decision that serves as a rule for settling subsequent cases of a similar nature.

stare decisis

In court rulings, a reliance on past decisions or precedents to formulate decisions in new cases.

Decisions of any court of appeals are binding on only the district courts within the geographic confines of the circuit, but decisions of the U.S. Supreme Court are binding throughout the nation and establish national **precedents.** This reliance on past decisions or precedents to formulate decisions in new cases is called *stare decisis* (a Latin phrase meaning "let the decision stand"). The principle of *stare decisis* allows for continuity and predictability in our judicial system. Although *stare decisis* can be helpful in predicting decisions, at times judges carve out new ground and ignore, decline to follow, or even overrule precedents to reach a different conclusion in a case involving similar circumstances. In one sense, that is why there is so much litigation in America today. Parties to a suit know that one cannot always predict the outcome of a case; if such prediction were possible, there would be little reason to go to court.

THE SUPREME COURT

The U.S. Supreme Court, as we saw in the opening vignette, is often at the center of the storm of highly controversial issues that have yet to be resolved successfully in the political process. As the court of last resort at the top of the judicial pyramid, it reviews cases from the U.S. courts of appeals and state supreme courts (as well as other courts of last resort) and acts as the final interpreter of the U.S. Constitution. It not only decides major cases with tremendous policy significance each year, but it also ensures uniformity in the interpretation of national laws and the Constitution, resolves conflicts among the states, and maintains the supremacy of national law in the federal system.

Since 1869, the U.S. Supreme Court has consisted of eight associate justices and one chief justice, who is nominated by the president specifically for that position. There is no special significance about the number nine, and the Constitution is silent about the size of the Court. Between 1789 and 1869, Congress periodically altered the size of the Court. The lowest number of justices on the Court was six; the most, ten. Through January 2007, only 110 justices had served on the Court, and there had been seventeen chief justices (see Appendix IV).

Compared with the president or Congress, the Supreme Court operates with few support staff. Along with the three or four clerks each justice employs, there are about 400 staff members at the Supreme Court.

VIDEO ROUNDTABLE

Selecting Federal Judges

senatorial courtesy

Process by which presidents generally defer selection of district court judges to the choice of senators of their own party who represent the state where the vacancy occurs.

How Federal Court Judges Are Selected

THE SELECTION OF FEDERAL JUDGES is often a very political process with important political ramifications because judges are nominated by the president and must be confirmed by the U.S. Senate. Presidents, in general, try to select well-qualified men and women for the bench. But, these appointments also provide a president with the opportunity to put his philosophical stamp on the federal courts (see Figure 10.3). Nominees, however, while generally members of the nominating president's party, usually are vetted through the senator's offices of the states where the district court or court of appeals vacancy occurs. In the Clinton White House, candidates for district court generally came from recommendations by Democratic senators, "or in the absence of a Democratic senator, from the Democratic members of the House of Representatives or other high ranking Democratic Party politicians."[22] This process, by which presidents generally defer selection of district court judges to the choice of senators of their own party who represent the state where the vacancy occurs, is known as **senatorial courtesy.**

FIGURE 10.3 HOW A PRESIDENT AFFECTS THE FEDERAL JUDICIARY
This figure depicts the number of judges appointed by each president and how
quickly a president can make an impact on the make-up of the Court.

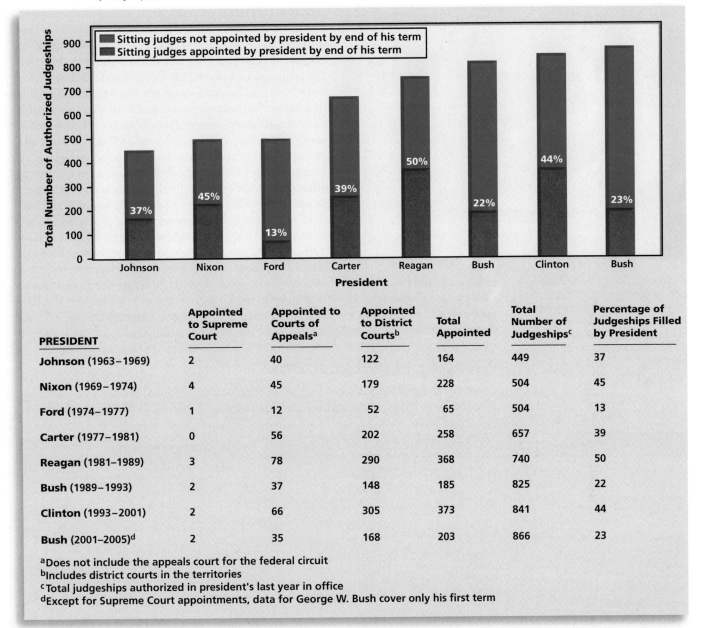

PRESIDENT	Appointed to Supreme Court	Appointed to Courts of Appeals[a]	Appointed to District Courts[b]	Total Appointed	Total Number of Judgeships[c]	Percentage of Judgeships Filled by President
Johnson (1963–1969)	2	40	122	164	449	37
Nixon (1969–1974)	4	45	179	228	504	45
Ford (1974–1977)	1	12	52	65	504	13
Carter (1977–1981)	0	56	202	258	657	39
Reagan (1981–1989)	3	78	290	368	740	50
Bush (1989–1993)	2	37	148	185	825	22
Clinton (1993–2001)	2	66	305	373	841	44
Bush (2001–2005)[d]	2	35	168	203	866	23

[a]Does not include the appeals court for the federal circuit
[b]Includes district courts in the territories
[c]Total judgeships authorized in president's last year in office
[d]Except for Supreme Court appointments, data for George W. Bush cover only his first term

Source: "Imprints on the Bench," CQ Weekly Report (January 19, 2001): 173. Reprinted by permission of Copyright Clearance Center on behalf of Congressional Quarterly, Inc. Updated by authors.

Despite the Clinton administration's attempts to appoint moderate justices, so that they might win approval in a Republican-controlled Senate, the Senate leadership took steps to prevent many of these nominees from winning approval. Thus, when George W. Bush took office in 2001, his judicial nominees were automatically subject to extreme scrutiny. Almost immediately, Senate Democrats charged that many of Bush's appointees were too conservative, and even filibustered several nominations.

Photo courtesy: J. Scott Applewhite/AP Wide World Photos

■ President George W. Bush meets with conservative judge Priscilla Owen, one of his most controversial nominees. It took more than four years to confirm Owen to a position on the Fifth Circuit Court of Appeals.

In 2003, the Republican leadership held a forty-hour talkathon to bring attention to the Senate's failure to confirm these nominees. Although this event received a good deal of press, it achieved little success. President George W. Bush further irritated Senate Democrats when he made several recess appointments of contested appointees, which allowed them to serve for the remainder of the 108th Congress. In 2004, President Bush and Senate Democrats reached an agreement that no further recess appointments would occur if the Senate confirmed twenty-five of the president's nominees.[23] These accords fell apart in 2005 as the Bush administration continued to nominate judges perceived by Democrats as too ideological. As discussed in chapter 7, bitter confrontations over the Democrats' threats as well as use of the filibuster to block votes on several more Bush nominees led a bipartisan "Gang of Fourteen" senators to band together. Their aim was to make sure that well-qualified nominees would be brought to a vote except in extraordinary circumstances, such as when a nominee could be considered to have ideological views far outside the mainstream. This group of moderates from both parties worked across the aisle to prevent the Republican leadership from exercising the "nuclear option" by changing Senate rules so that votes on all judicial nominees would be immune from filibuster.[24]

WHO ARE FEDERAL JUDGES?

Typically, federal district court judges have held other political offices, such as those of state court judge or prosecutor, as illustrated in Table 10.2. Most have been in-

TABLE 10.2	CHARACTERISTICS OF DISTRICT COURT APPOINTEES FROM CARTER TO BUSH				
	Carter	*Reagan*	*Bush*	*Clinton*	*G. W. Bush*[a]
Occupation					
Politics/government	5.0%	13.4%	10.8%	11.5%	8.3%
Judiciary	44.6	36.9	41.9	48.2	50.6
Lawyer	49.9	49.0	45.9	38.7	38.1
Other	0.5	0.7	1.4	2.6	3.0
Experience					
Judicial	54.0%	46.2%	46.6%	52.1%	56.6%
Prosecutorial	38.1	44.1	39.2	41.3	44.0
Neither	30.7	28.6	31.8	28.9	24.4
Political Affiliation					
Democrat	91.1%	4.8%	6.1%	87.5%	6.6%
Republican	4.5	91.7	88.5	6.2	84.5
Other/None	4.5	3.4	5.4	6.2	8.9
ABA Rating					
Extremely/Well Qualified	51.0%	53.5%	57.4%	59.0%	70.8%
Qualified	47.5	46.6	42.6	40.0	27.4
Not Qualified	1.5	—	—	1.0	1.8
Net Worth					
Under $200,000	35.8%	17.6%	10.1%	13.4%	6.0%
200,000–499,999	41.2	37.6	31.1	21.6	19.6
500,000–999,999	18.9	21.7	26.4	26.9	21.4
1,000,000+	4.0	23.1	32.4	32.4	53.0
Average age at nomination (years)	49.6	48.6	48.2	49.5	49.0
Total number of appointees	202	290	148	305	168

Note that percentages do not always add to 100 because some nominees fit in more than one category (i.e., they have been judges and prosecutors).

[a] George W. Bush appointee data are through January 20, 2005.

Source: Sheldon Goldman et al., "W. Bush's Judiciary: The First Term Record," *Judicature* 88 (May/June 2005): 269.

Analyzing Visuals

RACE, ETHNICITY AND GENDER OF DISTRICT COURT APPOINTEES

Traditionally, white males have dominated federal court appointments. Of President Ronald Reagan's 290 appointees to federal district courts, for example, 92.4 percent were white males. Of President Bill Clinton's 305 appointments, however, the percentage of white males was only 52.1 percent. George W. Bush reversed the trend during his first term; 67.3 percent of his appointees were white males. While most presidents in recent years have pledged to appoint more women, Hispanics, and African Americans to the federal bench, Clinton was the most successful. After reviewing the bar graph below, answer the following critical thinking questions: Is there a difference between appointments made by Democratic presidents (Carter and Clinton) and Republican presidents? Which group is most underrepresented in appointments? What factors do presidents consider, in addition to the nominee's gender, race and ethnicity, in making appointments to the federal bench? Should gender, race and ethnicity be considered by a president? Explain your answers.

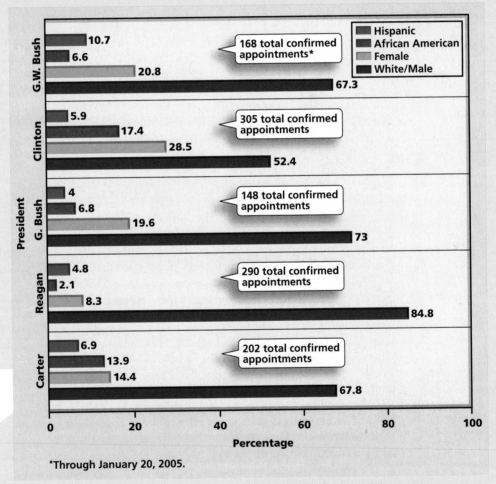

*Through January 20, 2005.

Source: Sheldon Goldman et al., "W. Bush's Judiciary: The First Term Record," *Judicature* 88 (May/June 2005): 269.

volved in politics, which is what usually brings them into consideration for a position on the federal bench. Griffin Bell, a former federal court of appeals judge (who later became U.S. attorney general in the Carter administration), once remarked, "For me, becoming a federal judge wasn't very difficult. I managed John F. Kennedy's presidential campaign in Georgia."[25]

TABLE 10.3 THE SUPREME COURT, 2006

Name	Year of Birth	Year of Appointment	Political Party	Law School	Appointing President	Religion	Prior Judicial Experience	Prior Government Experience
John G. Roberts Jr.	1955	2005	R	Harvard	G.W. Bush	Roman Catholic	U.S. Court of Appeals	Dept. of Justice, White House Counsel
John Paul Stevens	1920	1975	R	Chicago	Ford	Nondenominational Protestant	U.S. Court of Appeals	
Antonin Scalia	1936	1986	R	Harvard	Reagan	Roman Catholic	U.S. Court of Appeals	
Anthony Kennedy	1936	1988	R	Harvard	Reagan	Roman Catholic	U.S. Court of Appeals	
David Souter	1939	1990	R	Harvard	G. Bush	Episcopalian	U.S. Court of Appeals	New Hampshire assistant attorney general
Clarence Thomas	1948	1991	R	Yale	G. Bush	Roman Catholic	U.S. Court of Appeals	Chair, Equal Employment Opportunity Commission
Ruth Bader Ginsburg	1933	1993	D	Columbia	Clinton	Jewish	U.S. Court of Appeals	
Stephen Breyer	1938	1994	D	Harvard	Clinton	Jewish	U.S. Court of Appeals	Chief counsel, Senate Judiciary Committee
Samuel A. Alito Jr.	1950	2006	R	Yale	G.W. Bush	Roman Catholic	U.S. Court of Appeals	U.S. Attorney, Dept. of Justice

Increasingly, most judicial nominees have had prior judicial experience. White males continue to dominate the federal courts, but since the 1970s, most presidents have pledged (with varying degrees of success) to do their best to appoint more African Americans, Hispanics, women, and other underrepresented groups to the federal bench (see Analyzing Visuals: Race, Ethnicity and Gender of District Court Appointees).

APPOINTMENTS TO THE U.S. SUPREME COURT

The Constitution is silent on the qualifications for appointment to the Supreme Court (as well as to other constitutional courts), although Justice Oliver Wendell Holmes once remarked that a justice should be a "combination of Justinian, Jesus Christ and John Marshall."[26] However, like other federal court judges, the justices of the Supreme Court are nominated by the president and must be confirmed by the Senate.

Presidents always have realized how important their judicial appointments, especially their Supreme Court appointments, are to their ability to achieve all or many of their policy objectives. But, even though most presidents have tried to appoint jurists with particular political or ideological philosophies, they often have been wrong in their assumptions about their appointees. President Dwight D. Eisenhower, a moderate conservative, was appalled by the liberal opinions written by his appointee to chief justice, Earl Warren, concerning criminal defendants' rights. Similarly, Justices John Paul Stevens and David Souter, appointed by Presidents Gerald R. Ford and George Bush, respectively, are not as conservative as some predicted. Souter, in particular, has surprised many commentators with his moderate to liberal decisions in a variety of areas, including free speech, criminal rights, race and gender discrimination, and abortion.

Historically, because of the special place the Supreme Court enjoys in our constitutional system, its nominees have encountered more opposition than have district court or court of appeals nominees. As the role of the Court has increased over time, so too has the amount of attention given to nominees. With this increased attention

VIDEO ROUNDTABLE
Chief Justice John Roberts

has come greater opposition, especially to nominees with controversial views. For a discussion of the new justices on the Court, see Politics Now: The Roberts Court.

NOMINATION CRITERIA

Justice Sandra Day O'Connor once remarked that "You have to be lucky" to be appointed to the Court.[27] Although luck is certainly important, over the years nominations to the bench have been made for a variety of reasons. Depending on the timing of a vacancy, a president may or may not have a list of possible candidates or even a specific individual in mind. Until recently, presidents often have looked within their circle of friends or their administration to fill a vacancy. Nevertheless, whether the nominee is a friend or someone known to the president only by reputation, at least six criteria are especially important: competence, ideology or policy preferences, rewards, pursuit of political support, religion, and race and gender.

Competence Most prospective nominees are expected to have had at least some judicial or governmental experience. For example, John Jay, the first chief justice, was one of the authors of *The Federalist Papers* and was active in New York politics. In 2006, all nine sitting Supreme Court justices had prior judicial experience (see Table 10.3).

Ideology or Policy Preferences Most presidents seek to appoint to the Court individuals who share their policy preferences, and almost all have political goals in mind when they appoint a justice. Presidents Franklin D. Roosevelt, Richard M. Nixon, and Ronald Reagan were very successful in molding the Court to their own political beliefs. Roosevelt was able to appoint eight justices from 1937 to his death in 1945, solidifying support for his liberal New Deal programs. In contrast, Reagan was extraordinarily successful in remolding the Court in a conservative image.

Rewards Historically, many of those appointed to the Supreme Court have been personal friends of presidents. Abraham Lincoln, for example, appointed one of his key political advisers to the Court. Lyndon B. Johnson appointed his longtime friend Abe Fortas to the bench. Most presidents also select justices of their own party affiliation. Chief Justice John G. Roberts Jr. and Justice Samuel A. Alito Jr., for example, both Republicans, worked in the Department of Justice during the Reagan and George Bush administrations. Roberts also served as associate White House Counsel under Reagan.

Pursuit of Political Support During Ronald Reagan's successful campaign for the presidency in 1980, some of his advisers feared that the gender gap would hurt him. Polls repeatedly showed that he was far less popular with female voters than with men. To gain support from women, Reagan announced during his campaign that should he win, he would appoint a woman to fill the first vacancy on the Court. When Justice Potter Stewart, a moderate, announced his retirement from the bench, under pressure from women's rights groups, President Reagan nominated Sandra Day O'Connor of the Arizona Court of Appeals to fill the vacancy. Similarly, it probably did not hurt President Bill Clinton that his first appointment (Ruth Bader Ginsburg) was a woman and Jewish (at a time when no Jews served on the Court).

Religion Ironically, religion, which historically has been an important issue, was hardly mentioned during the most recent Supreme Court vacancies. For years, traditionally, there was a Catholic and a Jewish seat on the Court.

Through 2007, of the 110 justices who served on the Court, almost all have been members of traditional Protestant faiths.[28] Only eleven have been Catholic and only seven have been Jewish.[29] Today, more Catholics—Roberts, Scalia, Kennedy, Thomas, and Alito—serve on the court than at any other point in history. Ironically, there was a time in history when no one could have imagined that Roman Catholics could have

Politics Now

THE ROBERTS COURT

At the end of the 2005–2006 term, the first with a new chief justice since 1986, and the first with a new justice since 1994, commentators were anxious to see if John G. Roberts Jr. and Justice Samuel A. Alito Jr., had begun to make their marks on the Court. As posed by the *New York Times* Supreme Court reporter Linda Greenhouse, the question was whether it was the Roberts Court in name as well as in practice. Her answer? "Not yet." Says Greenhouse, a keen observer of the Court, Chief Justice Roberts "was clearly in charge, presiding over the Court with grace, wit and meticulous preparation. But he was not in control."[a]

In major divided Court decisions, Roberts was in the minority nearly as frequently as he was in the majority. Therefore, he was unable to exert influence over the Court's decisions by assigning the writing of many important majority opinions. (By Supreme Court tradition, the most senior justice in the majority assigns the author of the Court's opinion.) Nor was he able to stop the public bickering that has now become a hallmark of some of the justices, particularly Justice Antonin Scalia. Even the Court's quietest member, Justice Clarence Thomas, took the opportunity to announce his dissent in *Hamdan* v. *Rumsfeld* (2006), discussed in the opening vignette. Publicly reading a dissent is a rare practice on the Court. In fact, in fifteen years on the bench, this was the first dissent Thomas delivered orally.[b]

Greenhouse argues that the justice in control on the Roberts Court appears to be Anthony Kennedy, who has a history of being the swing justice in many major cases. As a result, Justice Kennedy's votes often determine the direc-

tion of many of the 5–4 decisions that have become standard for the narrowly divided Court. Greenhouse speculates that the current Court could even be called the Stevens Court after the most senior justice, John Paul Stevens. Justice Stevens assigns the author of the majority opinion any time Chief Justice Roberts is in the minority and Justice Stevens is in the majority. And, Justice Stevens used this authority to author many of the Court's most important decisions, including *Hamdan.*

In short, says Greenhouse, Robert's first term was a time of testing, of battles joined and battles, for the moment, postponed.[c] Still, the frequent agreement of Roberts and Alito—they voted together in 88 percent of all decisions—sends a powerful signal that the Court is heading in a decidedly conservative direction.

QUESTIONS

1. What role should the chief justice play on the Supreme Court?
2. As the Supreme Court becomes more conservative, and with cases on presidential authority, the treatment of prisoners in detainee camps, and abortion on its 2006–2007 calendar, what role do you foresee the Roberts Court playing in national policy?

[a]This feature draws heavily on Linda Greenhouse, "Roberts Is at the Court's Helm, But He Isn't in Control," *New York Times* (July 1, 2006): A1.

[b] *Hamdan v. Rumsfeld*, 548 U.S.___ (2006).

[c] Greenhouse, "Roberts Is at the Court's Helm."

made up a majority of the Court, given historical discrimination against Catholics through the 1950s. Still, with the Bush administration attempting to solidify its Christian fundamentalist base, it is interesting that there are no evangelicals on the Court.

Race, Ethnicity, and Gender   Through 2006, only two African Americans and two women have served on the Court. Race was undoubtedly a critical issue in the appointment of Clarence Thomas to replace Thurgood Marshall, the first African American justice. But, President George Bush refused to acknowledge his wish to retain a black seat on the Court. Instead, he announced that he was "picking the best man for the job on the merits," a claim that was met with considerable skepticism by many observers. Before the appointments of Roberts and Alito, many commentators assumed that Bush would appoint a Hispanic to fill the next vacancy on the bench in recognition of the growing proportion of Hispanics in the general population and their underrepresentation in national politics. This plan, however, was derailed by questions from the right as well as the left about the ideology and activities of the front-runners for the nomination, Attorney General Alberto Gonzales and lawyer Miguel Estrada.

The role of gender, which was crucial to the nomination of Sandra Day O'Connor, seems to have decreased in recent years. The nomination of Ruth Bader Ginsburg, for example, surprised many people because the Clinton administration initially appeared to be considering several men to fill the vacancy.

Several women appeared to be considered by the Bush administration for the vacancy created by Justice O'Connor's resignation. Bush, however, nominated Judge John G. Roberts Jr. When Chief Justice Rehnquist died soon after, Bush nominated Roberts to fill the vacant chief justice position. Though his next choice to fill O'Connor's seat was a woman, White House counsel Harriet Miers, her nomination was short-lived after it met with significant criticism from conservatives. O'Connor's vacancy eventually was filled by a man, Judge Samuel A. Alito Jr., much to O'Connor's public chagrin. The departing justice noted that one woman on the Supreme Court was hardly proportional to women's representation within the legal profession.

THE SUPREME COURT CONFIRMATION PROCESS

The Constitution gives the Senate the authority to approve all nominees to the federal bench. Before 1900, about one-fourth of all presidential nominees to the Supreme Court were rejected by the Senate. In 1844, for example, President John Tyler sent six nominations to the Senate, and all but one were defeated. In 1866, Andrew Johnson nominated his brilliant attorney general, Henry Stanberry, but the Senate's hostility to Johnson led it to reduce the size of the Court from nine to six seats to prevent Johnson from filling any vacancies. Ordinarily, nominations are referred to the Senate Judiciary Committee. This committee investigates the nominees, holds hearings, and votes on its recommendation for Senate action. At this stage, the committee may reject a nominee or send the nomination to the full Senate for a vote. The full Senate then deliberates on the nominee before voting. A simple majority vote is required for confirmation.

Investigation As a president begins to narrow the list of possible nominees to the Supreme Court, those names are sent to the Federal Bureau of Investigation before a nomination formally is made. At the same time, until George W. Bush became president, the names of prospective nominees were forwarded to the American Bar Association (ABA), the politically powerful organization that represents the interests of the legal profession. Republican President Dwight D. Eisenhower started this practice, believing it helped "insulate the process from political pressure."[30] After its own investigation, the ABA rated each nominee, based on his or her qualifications, as Well Qualified (previously "Highly Qualified"), Qualified, or Not Qualified. (The same

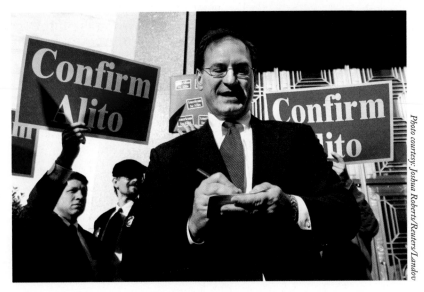

■ Justice Samuel A. Alito Jr. was the subject of a high stakes confirmation battle that involved a number of interest groups in late 2005 and early 2006. Here, Justice Alito signs autographs for ardent supporters on the way to his confirmation hearing.

Photo courtesy: Joshua Roberts/Reuters/Landov

system was used for lower federal court nominees; over the years, however, the exact labels have varied.)

David Souter, George Bush's first nominee to the Court, received a unanimous rating of Highly Qualified from the ABA, as did both of Bill Clinton's nominees, Ruth Bader Ginsburg and Stephen Breyer. In contrast, another Bush nominee, Clarence Thomas, was given only a Qualified rating (well before sexual harassment charges against him became public). Two ABA members even voted him Not Qualified. Unlike the twenty-two previous successful nominees rated by the ABA, Thomas was the first to receive less than a unanimous Qualified rating.

Early in his administration, President George W. Bush announced that the ABA would no longer play this key role. Earlier, the 1996 Republican presidential candidate, Bob Dole, went so far as to pledge, if elected, he would remove the ABA from the selection process.[31] Bush has looked to the more conservative Federalist Society to vet his nominees, and to be a source of nominees as well. Both Chief Justice Roberts and Justice Alito have been affiliated with this organization.

After a formal nomination is made and sent to the Senate, the Senate Judiciary Committee begins its own investigation. (The same process is used for nominees to the lower federal courts, although such investigations generally are not nearly as extensive as for Supreme Court nominees.) To begin its task, the Senate Judiciary Committee asks each nominee to complete a lengthy questionnaire detailing previous work (dating as far back as high school summer jobs), judicial opinions written, judicial philosophy, speeches, and even all interviews ever given to members of the press. Committee staffers also contact potential witnesses who might offer testimony concerning the nominee's fitness for office.

Lobbying by Interest Groups   Although historically the ABA was the only organization that was asked formally to rate nominees, other groups also are keenly interested in the nomination process. Until the 1980s, interest groups played a minor and backstage role in most appointments to the Supreme Court. Although interest groups generally have not lobbied on behalf of any one individual, women's rights groups, as previously noted, successfully urged President Ronald Reagan to honor his campaign commitment to appoint a woman to the high Court in 1981.

It is more common for interest groups to lobby against a prospective nominee, as revealed in Table 10.4. Even this, however, is a relatively recent phenomenon. In 1987, the nomination of Judge Robert H. Bork to the Supreme Court led liberal groups to launch the most extensive radio, television, and print media campaign against a nominee to the U.S. Supreme Court. These interest groups felt that Bork's actions as solicitor general, especially his firing of the Watergate special prosecutor at the request of President Richard M. Nixon, as well as his political beliefs, were abhorrent.

More and more, interest groups are also getting involved in district court and court of appeals nominations. They recognize that these appointments often pave the way for future nominees to the Supreme Court, as was the case with all of the members of the current Court. For example, a coalition of conservative evangelical Christian organizations, including Focus on the Family and the Family Research Council, have held a series of "Justice Sunday" events featuring televangelists and politicians promoting the confirmation of judges with conservative and religious records to coun-

VIDEO DEBATE
Popular Election of Judges

TABLE 10.4	INTEREST GROUPS APPEARING IN SELECTED SENATE JUDICIARY COMMITTEE HEARINGS				
Nominee	Year	Liberal	Conservative	ABA Rating	Senate Vote
Stevens	1976	2	3	Well-Q	98–0
Scalia	1986	5	7	Well-Q	98–0
Bork	1987	18	68	Well-Q[a]	42–58
Kennedy	1987	12	14	Well-Q	97–0
Souter	1990	13	8	Well-Q	90–9
Thomas	1991	30	46	Q[b]	52–48
Ginsburg	1993	6	5	Well-Q	96–3
Breyer	1994	8	3	Well-Q	87–9
Roberts	2005	5	4	Well-Q	78–22
Alito	2005	2	1	Well-Q	58–42

[a] Four ABA committee members evaluated him as Not Qualified.

[b] Two ABA committee members evaluated him as Not Qualified.

Source: Karen O'Connor, Alixandra B. Yanus, and Linda Mancillas Patterson, "Where Have All the Interest Groups Gone? An Analysis of Interest Group Participation in Presidential Nominations to the Supreme Court of the United States," in Allan J. Cigler and Burdett A. Loomis, eds., *Interest Group Politics*, 7th ed. (Washington, DC: CQ Press, 2007).

teract what these groups consider a liberal judiciary hostile to the values that social conservatives espouse.

The Senate Committee Hearings and Senate Vote As the relatively uneventful 1994 hearings of Stephen Breyer attest, not all nominees inspire the kind of intense reaction that kept Bork from the Court and almost blocked the confirmation of Clarence Thomas. Until 1929, all but one Senate Judiciary Committee hearing on a Supreme Court nominee was conducted in executive session—that is, closed to the public. The 1916 hearings on Louis Brandeis, the first Jewish justice, were conducted in public and lasted nineteen days, although Brandeis himself never was called to testify. In 1939, Felix Frankfurter became the first nominee to testify in any detail before the committee.[32]

Since the 1980s, it has become standard for senators to ask the nominees probing questions. Most nominees have declined to answer most of these questions on the grounds that the issues raised ultimately might come before the Court.

After hearings are concluded, the Senate Judiciary Committee usually makes a recommendation to the full Senate. Any rejections of presidential nominees to the Supreme Court generally occur only after the Senate Judiciary Committee has recommended against a nominee's appointment. Few recent confirmations have been close; Clarence Thomas's 52–48 vote in 1991 and Samuel A. Alito Jr.'s 58–42 vote in 2006 were the closest in recent history (see Table 10.4).

Photo courtesy: Patti Longmire/AP Wide World Photos

■ Former Senate Majority Leader Bill Frist, who retired from the Senate in 2006, addresses evangelical Christians attending a 2006 "Justice Sunday" event.

The Supreme Court Today

GIVEN THE JUDICIAL SYSTEM'S vast size and substantial, although often indirect, power over so many aspects of our lives, it is surprising that so many Americans know next to nothing about the judicial system, in general, and the U.S. Supreme Court, in particular.

Even after the recent attention the Supreme Court received during the nominations of John G. Roberts Jr. and Samuel A. Alito Jr., more than half of those Americans surveyed in early 2006 could not name one member of the Court; virtually no one could name all nine members of the Court. As revealed in Table 10.5, Sandra Day O'Connor, the first woman appointed to the Court, was the most well-known justice. Still, only about a quarter of those polled could name her. To fill in any gaps in your knowledge of the current Supreme Court, see Table 10.3.

While much of this ignorance can be blamed on the American public's lack of interest, the Court has also taken great pains to ensure its privacy and sense of decorum. Its rites and rituals contribute to the Court's mystique and encourage a "cult of the robe."[33] Consider, for example, the way Supreme Court proceedings are conducted. Oral arguments are not televised, and deliberations concerning the outcome of cases are conducted in utmost secrecy. In contrast, C-SPAN brings us daily coverage of

TABLE 10.5	DON'T KNOW MUCH ABOUT . . . THE SUPREME COURT
Supreme Court Justice	*Percentage Who Could Name*
Sandra Day O'Connor	27
Clarence Thomas	21
John G. Roberts Jr.	16
Antonin Scalia	13
Ruth Bader Ginsburg	12
Anthony Kennedy	7
David Souter	5
Stephen Breyer	3
John Paul Stevens	3

Source: Findlaw.com poll, January 10, 2006, http://company.findlaw.com/pr/2006/011006.supremes.html.

various congressional hearings and floor debate on bills and important national issues, and Court TV (and sometimes other networks) provides gavel-to-gavel coverage of many important state court trials. The Supreme Court, however, remains adamant in its refusal to televise its proceedings—including public oral arguments, although it now allows the release of same-day audio tapes of oral arguments.

DECIDING TO HEAR A CASE

Case Overload

Over 9,600 cases were filed at the Supreme Court in its 2005–2006 term; 90 were heard, and 88 decisions were issued. In contrast, from 1790 to 1801, the Court heard only 87 cases under its appellate jurisdiction.[34] In the Court's early years, the main of the justices' workload involved their circuit-riding duties. From 1862 to 1866, only 240 cases were decided. Creation of the courts of appeals in 1891 resulted in an immediate reduction in Supreme Court filings—from 600 in 1890 to 275 in 1892.[35] As recently as the 1940s, fewer than 1,000 cases were filed annually. Filings increased at a dramatic rate until the mid 1990s, shot up again in the late 1990s, and have, with but the exception of a few terms, shown steady growth since that time. (See Figure 10.4.) The process by which cases get to the Supreme Court is outlined in Figure 10.5.

Just as it is up to the justices to say what the law is, they can also exercise a significant role in policy making and politics by opting not to hear a case. For example, in

FIGURE 10.4 SUPREME COURT CASELOAD, 1950–2006 TERMS

Cases the Supreme Court chooses to hear (represented by red bars below) represent a tiny fraction of the total number of cases filed with the Court (represented by green bars).

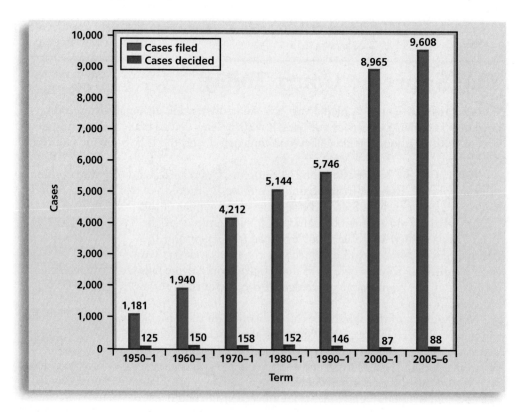

Source: Administrative Office of the Courts; Supreme Court Public Information Office.

FIGURE 10.5 HOW A CASE GETS TO THE SUPREME COURT
This figure illustrates both how cases get on the Court's docket and what happens after a case is accepted for review.

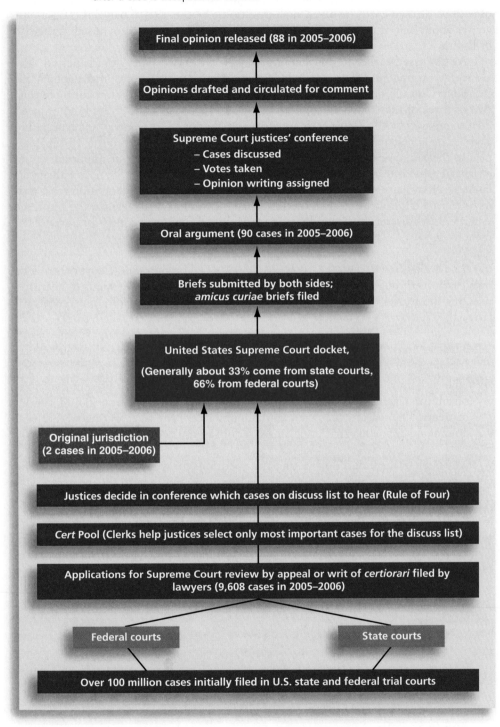

Final opinion released (88 in 2005–2006)

Opinions drafted and circulated for comment

Supreme Court justices' conference
– Cases discussed
– Votes taken
– Opinion writing assigned

Oral argument (90 cases in 2005–2006)

Briefs submitted by both sides;
amicus curiae briefs filed

United States Supreme Court docket,
(Generally about 33% come from state courts, 66% from federal courts)

Original jurisdiction
(2 cases in 2005–2006)

Justices decide in conference which cases on discuss list to hear (Rule of Four)

Cert Pool (Clerks help justices select only most important cases for the discuss list)

Applications for Supreme Court review by appeal or writ of *certiorari* filed by lawyers (9,608 cases in 2005–2006)

Federal courts   State courts

Over 100 million cases initially filed in U.S. state and federal trial courts

late 2004 when it refused to hear an appeal of a Massachusetts Supreme Court decision requiring the state to sanction same-sex marriages, the Court prompted President George W. Bush and others to renew their calls for a constitutional amendment to ban same-sex marriage. The content of the Court's docket is, of course, every bit as significant as its size. During the 1930s, cases requiring the interpretation of constitutional law began to take a growing portion of the Court's workload, leading the Court to take a more important role in the policy-making process. At that time, only 5 percent of the Court's cases involved questions concerning the Bill of Rights. By the late 1950s, one-third of filed cases involved such questions; by the 1960s, half did.[36] More recently, about half of the cases decided by the Court deal with issues raised in the Bill of Rights.[37]

As discussed earlier in the chapter, the Court has two types of jurisdiction. The Court has original jurisdiction in "all Cases affecting Ambassadors, other public Ministers and Consuls, and those in which a State shall be a party." It is rare for more than two or three of these cases to come to the Court in a year. The second kind of jurisdiction enjoyed by the Court is its appellate jurisdiction. The Court is not expected to exercise its appellate jurisdiction simply to correct errors of other courts. Instead, appeal to the Supreme Court should be taken only if the case presents important issues of law, or what is termed "a substantial federal question." Since 1988, nearly all appellate cases that have gone to the Supreme Court arrived there on a petition for a **writ of *certiorari*** (from the Latin "to be informed"), which is a request for the Supreme Court—at its discretion—to order up the records of the lower courts for purposes of review.

writ of *certiorari*
A request for the Court to order up the records from a lower court to review the case.

Writs of *Certiorari* and the Rule of Four

The Supreme Court controls its own caseload through the *certiorari* process, deciding which cases it wants to hear, and rejecting most cases that come to it. All petitions, or writs of *certiorari*, must meet two criteria:

1. The case must come from either a U.S. court of appeals, a special three-judge district court, or a state court of last resort.
2. The case must involve a federal question. Thus, the case must present questions of interpretation of federal constitutional law or involve a federal statute, action, or treaty. The reasons that the Court should accept the case for review and legal argument supporting that position are set out in the petition (also called a brief).

The clerk of the Court's office transmits petitions for writs of *certiorari* first to the chief justice's office, where clerks review the petitions, and then to the individual justices' offices. On the Roberts Court, all of the justices except Justice John Paul Stevens

■ The Roberts Court. Back row, from left to right: Justices Stephen Breyer, Clarence Thomas, Ruth Bader Ginsburg, and Samuel A. Alito Jr. Front row, from left to right: Justice Anthony Kennedy, Justice John Paul Stevens, Chief Justice John G. Roberts Jr., Justice Antonin Scalia and Justice David Souter.

Photo courtesy: Supreme Court Historical Society

(who allows his clerks great individual authority in selecting the cases for him to review) participate in what is called the *cert* pool.[38] Pool participants review their assigned fraction of petitions and share their notes with each other. Those cases that the justices deem noteworthy are then placed on what is called the discuss list prepared by the chief justice's clerks and circulated to the chambers of the other justices. All others are dead listed and go no further unless a justice asks that a case be removed from the dead list and discussed at conference. Only about 30 percent of submitted petitions make it to the discuss list. During one of the justices' weekly conference meetings, the cases on the discuss list are reviewed. The chief justice speaks first, then the rest of the justices, according to seniority. The decision process ends when the justices vote, and by custom, *certiorari* is granted according to the **Rule of Four**—when at least four justices vote to hear a case.

The Role of Clerks

As early as 1850, the justices of the Supreme Court beseeched Congress to approve the hiring of a clerk to assist each justice. Congress denied the request, so when Justice Horace Gray hired the first law clerk in 1882, he paid the clerk himself. Justice Gray's clerk was a top graduate of Harvard Law School whose duties included cutting Justice Gray's hair and running personal errands. Finally, in 1886, Congress authorized each justice to hire a stenographer clerk for $1,600 a year.

Clerks typically are selected from candidates at the top of the graduating classes of prestigious law schools. They perform a variety of tasks, ranging from searching for arcane facts to playing tennis or taking walks with the justices. Clerks spend most of their time researching material relevant to particular cases, reading and summarizing cases, and helping justices write opinions. The clerks also make the first pass through the petitions that come to the Court, undoubtedly influencing which cases get a second look. Just how much help they provide in the writing of opinions is unknown.[39] (See Table 10.6 for more on what clerks do.)

Over time, the number of clerks employed by the justices has increased. Through the 1946 to 1969 terms, most justices employed two clerks. By 1970, most had three clerks, and by 1980 all but three justices had four clerks. In 2006, the nine active justices and retired Justice O'Connor employed a total of thirty-eight clerks. This growth in the number of clerks has had many interesting ramifications for the Court. As the number of clerks has grown, so have the number and length of the Court's opinions.[40] And, until recently, the number of cases decided annually increased as more help was available to the justices.

The relationship between clerks and the justices for whom they work is close and confidential, and many aspects of the relationship are kept secret.[41] Clerks may sometimes talk among themselves about the views and personalities of their justices, but rarely has a clerk leaked such information to the press. In 1998, a former clerk to Justice Harry A. Blackmun broke the silence. Edward Lazarus published a book that shocked many Court watchers by penning an insider's account of how the Court really works.[42] He also charged that the justices give their young, often ideological, clerks far too much power.

HOW DOES A CASE SURVIVE THE PROCESS?

It can be difficult to determine why the Court decides to hear a particular case. Sometimes it involves a perceived national emergency, as was the case with appeals concerning the outcome of the 2000 presidential election. The Court does not offer reasons, and "the standards by which the justices decide to grant or deny review

Rule of Four
At least four justices of the Supreme Court must vote to consider a case before it can be heard.

SIMULATION

You Are a Clerk to Supreme Court Justice Judith Gray

TABLE 10.6 WHAT DO SUPREME COURT CLERKS DO?

Supreme Court clerks are among the best and brightest recent law school graduates. Almost all first clerk for a judge on one of the courts of appeals. After their Supreme Court clerkship, former clerks are in high demand. Firms often pay signing bonuses of up to $200,000 to attract clerks, who often earn over $150,000 their first year in private practice.

Tasks of a Supreme Court clerk include the following:
- Perform initial screening of the 9,000 or so petitions that come to the Court each term
- Draft memos to summarize the facts and issues in each case, recommending whether the case should be accepted by the Court for full review
- Write a "bench memo" summarizing an accepted case and suggesting questions for oral argument
- Write the first draft of an opinion
- Be an informal conduit for communicating and negotiating with other justices' chambers as to the final wording of an opinion

are highly personalized and necessarily discretionary," noted former Chief Justice Earl Warren.[43] Political scientists nonetheless have attempted to determine the characteristics of the cases the Court accepts; not surprisingly, they are similar to those that help a case get on the discuss list. Among the cues are the following:

- The federal government is the party asking for review.
- The case involves conflict among the circuit courts.
- The case presents a civil rights or civil liberties question.
- The case involves ideological and/or policy preferences of the justices.
- The case has significant social or political interest, as evidenced by the presence of interest group *amicus curiae* briefs.

solicitor general

The fourth-ranking member of the Department of Justice; responsible for handling all appeals on behalf of the U.S. government to the Supreme Court.

amicus curiae

"Friend of the court"; *amici* may file briefs or even appear to argue their interests orally before the court.

The Federal Government   One of the most important cues for predicting whether the Court will hear a case is the position the solicitor general takes on it. The **solicitor general,** appointed by the president, is the fourth-ranking member of the Department of Justice and is responsible for handling most appeals on behalf of the U.S. government to the Supreme Court. The solicitor's staff resembles a small, specialized law firm within the Department of Justice. But, because this office has such a special relationship with the Supreme Court, even having a suite of offices within the Supreme Court building, the solicitor general often is referred to as the Court's "ninth and a half member."[44] Moreover, the solicitor general, on behalf of the U.S. government, appears as a party or as an *amicus curiae* in more than 50 percent of the cases heard by the Court each term. *Amicus curiae* means friend of the court. *Amici* may file briefs or even appear to argue their interests orally before the Court.

This special relationship with the Court helps explain the overwhelming success the solicitor general's office enjoys before the Supreme Court. The Court generally accepts 70 to 80 percent of the cases where the U.S. government is the petitioning party, compared with about 5 percent of all others.[45] But, because of this special relationship, the solicitor general often ends up playing two conflicting roles: representing in Court both the president's policy interests and the broader interests of the United States. At times, solicitors find these two roles difficult to reconcile. Former Solicitor General Rex E. Lee (1981–1985), for example, noted that on more than one occasion he refused to make arguments in Court that had been advanced by the Reagan administration (a stand that ultimately forced him to resign his position).[46]

Conflict Among the Circuits   Conflict among the lower courts is apparently another reason that the justices take cases. When interpretations of constitutional or federal law are involved, the justices seem to want consistency throughout the federal court system.

Often these conflicts occur when important civil rights or civil liberties questions arise. As political scientist Lawrence Baum has commented, "Justices' evaluations of lower court decisions are based largely on their ideological position."[47] Thus, it is not uncommon to see conservative justices voting to hear cases to overrule liberal lower court decisions, or vice versa.

Interest Group Participation   A quick way for the justices to gauge the ideological ramifications of a particular civil rights or liberties case is by the nature and amount of interest group participation. Richard C. Cortner has noted that "Cases do not arrive on the doorstep of the Supreme Court like orphans in the night."[48] Instead, most cases heard by the Supreme Court involve either the government or an interest group—either as the sponsoring party or as an *amicus curiae*. Liberal groups such as the American Civil Liberties Union, People for the American Way, or the NAACP Legal Defense Fund, and conservative groups including the Washington Legal Foundation, Concerned Women for America, or the American Center for Law and Justice, routinely sponsor cases or file *amicus* briefs either urging the Court to hear a case or asking it to deny *certiorari.*

The positions of both parties are often echoed or expanded in *amicus curiae* briefs filed by interested parties, especially interest groups. (The vast majority of the cases decided by the Court in the 1990s, for example, had at least one *amicus* brief.) Interest groups also provide the Court with information not necessarily contained in the major-party briefs, help write briefs, and assist in practice oral arguments during moot-court sessions. In these moot-court sessions, the lawyer who will argue the case before the nine justices goes through several complete rehearsals, with prominent lawyers and law professors role playing the various justices.

Since the 1970s, interest groups increasingly have used the *amicus* brief as a way to lobby the Court. Because litigation is so expensive, few individuals have the money (or time or interest) to pursue a perceived wrong all the way to the U.S. Supreme Court. All sorts of interest groups, then, find that joining ongoing cases through *amicus* briefs is a useful way of advancing their policy preferences. Major cases such as *Brown* v. *Board of Education* (1954) (see chapter 6), *Planned Parenthood of Southeastern Pennsylvania* v. *Casey* (1992) (see chapter 5), and *Grutter* v. *Bollinger* (2003) (see chapter 6) all attracted large numbers of *amicus* briefs as part of interest groups' efforts to lobby the judiciary and bring about desired political objectives.[49] (See Table 10.7.)

Research by political scientists has found that "not only does [an *amicus*] brief in favor of *certiorari* significantly improve the chances of a case being accepted, but two, three and four briefs improve the chances even more."[50] Clearly, it's the more the merrier, whether or not the briefs are filed for or against granting review.[51]

HEARING AND DECIDING THE CASE

Once a case is accepted for review, a flurry of activity begins. Lawyers on both sides of the case begin to prepare their written arguments for submission to the Court. In these briefs, lawyers cite prior case law and make arguments as to why the Court should find in favor of their client.

Oral Arguments Once a case is accepted by the Court for full review, and after briefs and *amicus* briefs are submitted on each side, oral argument takes place. The Supreme Court's annual term begins the first Monday in October, as it has since the late 1800s, and runs through late June or early July. Justices hear oral arguments from the beginning of the term until early April. Special cases, such as *U.S.* v. *Nixon* (1974), which involved President Richard M. Nixon's refusal to turn over tapes of Oval Office conversations to a special prosecutor investigating a break-in at the Democratic Party headquarters in the Watergate building, have been heard even later in the year.[52] During the term, "sittings," periods of about two weeks in which cases are heard, alternate with "recesses," also about two weeks long. Oral arguments usually are heard Monday through Wednesday.

Oral argument generally is limited to the immediate parties in the case, although it is not uncommon for the U.S. solicitor general to appear to argue orally as an *amicus curiae.* Oral argument at the Court is fraught with time-honored tradition and ceremony. At precisely ten o'clock every morning when the Court is in session, the Court marshal, dressed in a formal morning coat, emerges to intone "Oyez! Oyez! Oyez!" as the nine justices emerge from behind a reddish-purple velvet curtain to take their places on the raised and slightly angled bench. The chief justice sits in the middle. The remaining justices sit to the left and right alternating in seniority.

TABLE 10.7 *AMICUS CURIAE* BRIEFS IN COMPANION AFFIRMATIVE ACTION CASES: *GRUTTER* V. *BOLLINGER* AND *GRATZ* V. *BOLLINGER* (2003)

For the Petitioners

Asian American Legal Foundation	Claremont Institute Center for	Pacific Legal Foundation
Cato Institute	Constitutional Jurisprudence	Reason Foundation
Center for Equal Opportunity et al.	Law Professors	State of Florida and Governor Jeb Bush
Center for Individual Freedom	Massachusetts School of Law	United States
Center for the Advancement of Capitalism	Michigan Association of Scholars	Ward Connerly
Center for New Black Leadership	National Association of Scholars	

For the Respondents

65 Leading American Businesses	Deans of Law Schools	National Coalition of Blacks for Reparations in
AFL-CIO	General Motors Corporation	America et al.
American Bar Association	Graduate Management Admission Council et al.	National Education Association
American Council on Education et al.	Harvard Black Law Students Association et al.	National School Boards Association
American Educational Research Association et al.	Harvard University et al.	National Urban League et al.
American Jewish Committee et al.	Hayden Family	New America Alliance
American Law Deans Association	Hispanic National Bar Association	New Mexico Hispanic Bar Association et al.
American Media Companies	Howard University	New York City Council Members
American Psychological Association	Human Rights Advocates et al.	New York State Black and Puerto Rican Legislative
American Sociological Association	Indiana University	Caucus
Amherst College et al.	King County Bar Association	Northeastern University
Arizona State University College of Law	Latino Organizations	NOW Legal Defense and Education Fund et al.
Association of American Law Schools	Lawyers Committee for Civil Rights Under	School of Law of the University of North Carolina
Association of American Medical Colleges	Law et al.	Social Scientists
Authors of the Texas Ten Percent Plan	Leadership Conference on Civil Rights et al.	Society of American Law Teachers
Bay Mills Indian Community et al.	Massachusetts Institute of Technology et al.	State of New Jersey
Black Women Lawyers Association of Greater	Members of Congress (3 briefs)	State of Maryland et al.
Chicago	Members of the Pennsylvania General	Students of Howard University Law School
Boston Bar Association et al.	Assembly et al.	UCLA School of Law Students of Color
Carnegie Mellon University et al.	Michigan Black Law Alumni Association	United Negro College Fund et al.
City of Philadelphia et al.	Michigan Governor Jennifer Granholm	University of Michigan Asian Pacific American Law
Clinical Legal Educational Association	Military Leaders	Students Association
Coalition for Economic Equity et al.	MTV Networks	University of Pittsburgh et al.
Columbia University et al.	NAACP Legal Defense and Education Fund et al.	Veterans of the Southern Civil Rights Movement
Committee of Concerned Black Graduates of	National Asian Pacific American Legal	et al.
ABA Accredited Law Schools	Consortium et al.	
Current Law Students at Accredited Law Schools	National Center for Fair and Open Testing	

For Neither Party

Anti-Defamation League	Equal Employment Opportunity Council
BP America	Exxon Mobil Corporation
Criminal Justice Legal Foundation	

Almost all attorneys are allotted one half hour to present their cases, and this time includes that required to answer questions from the bench. As a lawyer approaches the mahogany lectern, a green light goes on, indicating that the attorney's time has begun. A white light flashes when five minutes remain. When a red light goes on, Court practice mandates that counsel stop immediately. One famous piece of Court lore told to all attorneys concerns a counsel who continued talking and reading from his prepared argument after the red light went on. When he looked up, he found an empty bench—the justices had risen quietly and departed while he continued to talk. On another occasion, Chief Justice Charles Evans Hughes stopped a leader of the New York bar in the middle of the word "if."

Although many Court watchers have tried to figure out how a particular justice will vote based on the questioning at oral argument, most researchers find that the nature and number of questions asked do not help much in predicting the outcome of a case. Nevertheless, many scholars believe that oral argument has several important functions. First, it is the only opportunity for even a small portion of the public (who may attend the hearings) and the press to observe the workings of the Court. Second, it assures lawyers that the justices have heard the parties' arguments, and it forces lawyers to focus on arguments believed important by the justices. Last, it provides the Court with additional information, especially concerning the Court's broader political role, an issue not usually addressed in written briefs. For example, the justices can ask how many people might be affected by its decision or where the Court (and country) would be heading if a case were decided in a particular way. Justice Stephen Breyer also notes that oral arguments are a good way for the justices to try to highlight certain issues for other justices.

The Conference and the Vote The justices meet in closed conference once a week when the Court is hearing oral arguments. Since the ascendancy of Chief Justice Roger B. Taney to the Court in 1836, the justices have begun each conference session with a round of handshaking. Once the door to the conference room closes, no others are allowed to enter. The justice with the least seniority acts as the doorkeeper for the other eight, communicating with those waiting outside to fill requests for documents, water, and any other necessities.

Conferences highlight the importance and power of the chief justice, who presides over them and makes the initial presentation of each case. Each individual justice then discusses the case in order of his or her seniority on the Court, with the most senior justice speaking next. Most accounts of the decision-making process reveal that at this point some justices try to change the minds of others, but that most enter the conference room with a clear idea of how they will vote on each case. Although other Courts have followed different procedures, during the Rehnquist Court, the justices generally voted at the same time they discussed each case, with each justice speaking only once. Initial conference votes were not final, and justices were allowed to change their minds before final votes were taken later.

The Roberts Court is much more informal than the Rehnquist Court. The justices' regular Friday conferences now last longer and, unlike the conferences headed by Rehnquist, the new chief justice encourages discussion.[53]

Writing Opinions After the Court has reached a decision in conference, the justices must formulate a formal opinion of the Court. If the chief justice is in the majority, he selects the justice who will write the opinion. This privilege enables him to wield tremendous power and is a very important strategic decision. If the chief justice is in the minority, the assignment falls to the most senior justice in the majority.

The opinion of the Court can take several different forms. Most decisions are reached by a majority opinion written by one member of the Court to reflect the views of at least five of the justices. This opinion usually sets out the legal reasoning justifying the decision, and this legal reasoning becomes a precedent for deciding future cases. The reasoning behind any decision is often as important as the outcome. Under the system of *stare decisis*, both are likely to be relied on as precedent later by lower courts confronted with cases involving similar issues.

In the process of creating the final opinion of the Court, informal caucusing and negotiation often take place, as justices may hold out for word changes or other modifications as a condition of their continued support of the majority opinion. This negotiation process can lead to divisions in the Court's majority. When this occurs, the Court may be forced to decide cases by plurality opinions, which attract the support of three or four justices. While these decisions do not have the precedential value of majority opinions, they nonetheless have been used by the Court to decide many major cases.

Justices who agree with the outcome of the case but not with the legal rationale for the decision may file concurring opinions to express their differing approach. For example, Justice Steven Breyer filed a concurring opinion in *Clinton v. Jones* (1997). Although a unanimous Court ruled that a sitting president was not immune to civil lawsuits, Breyer wanted to express his belief that a federal judge could not schedule judicial proceedings that might interfere with a president's public duties.[54]

Justices who do not agree with the outcome of a case file dissenting opinions. Although these opinions have little direct legal value, they can be an important indicator of legal thought on the Court and are an excellent platform for justices to note their personal and legal disagreements with other members of the Court. Justice Antonin Scalia is often noted for writing particularly stinging dissents. In his dissent in *Webster* v. *Reproductive Health Services* (1989), for example, Scalia wrote that Justice Sandra Day O'Connor's "assertion that a fundamental rule of judicial restraint requires [the Court] to avoid reconsidering *Roe* [v. *Wade*] cannot be taken seriously."[55]

The process of crafting a final opinion is not an easy one, and justices often rely heavily on their clerks to do much of the revision. Neither is the process apolitical. Today, one vote on the Court can be the difference between two very different outcomes.

Judicial Philosophy and Decision Making

JUSTICES DO NOT MAKE DECISIONS in a vacuum. Principles of *stare decisis* dictate that the justices follow the law of previous cases in deciding cases at hand. But, a variety of legal and extra-legal factors have also been found to affect Supreme Court decision making.

JUDICIAL PHILOSOPHY, ORIGINAL INTENT, AND IDEOLOGY

Legal scholars long have argued that judges decide cases based on the Constitution and their reading of various statutes. Determining what the Framers meant—if that is even possible today—often appears to be based on an individual jurist's philosophy.

One of the primary issues concerning judicial decision making focuses on what is called the activism/restraint debate. Advocates of **judicial restraint** argue that courts should allow the decisions of other branches to stand, even when they offend a judge's own sense of principles. Restraintists defend their position by asserting that the federal courts are composed of unelected judges, which makes the judicial branch the least democratic branch of government. Consequently, the courts should defer policy making to other branches of government as much as possible.

Restraintists refer to *Roe* v. *Wade* (1973), the case that liberalized abortion laws, as a classic example of **judicial activism** run amok. They maintain that the Court should have deferred policy making on this sensitive issue to the states or to the other branches of the federal government—the legislative and executive—because their officials are elected and therefore are more receptive to the majority's will.

Advocates of judicial restraint generally agree that judges should be **strict constructionists;** that is, they should interpret the Constitution as it was written and intended by the Framers. They argue that in determining the constitutionality of a statute or policy, the Court should rely on the explicit meanings of the clauses in the document, which can be clarified by looking at the intent of the Framers.

Advocates of judicial activism contend that judges should use their power broadly to further justice, especially in the areas of equality and personal liberty. Activists argue that it is the courts' appropriate role to correct injustices committed by the other

judicial restraint
A philosophy of judicial decision making that argues courts should allow the decisions of other branches of government to stand, even when they offend a judge's own sense of principles.

judicial activism
A philosophy of judicial decision making that argues judges should use their power broadly to further justice, especially in the areas of equality and personal liberty.

strict constructionist
An approach to constitutional interpretation that emphasizes the Framers' original intentions.

branches of government. Explicit in this argument is the notion that courts need to protect oppressed minorities.[56]

Activists point to *Brown* v. *Board of Education* (1954) as an excellent example of the importance of judicial activism.[57] In *Brown,* the Supreme Court ruled that racial segregation in public schools violated the equal protection clause of the Fourteenth Amendment. Segregation nonetheless was practiced after passage of the Fourteenth Amendment. An activist would point out that if the Court had not reinterpreted provisions of the amendment, many states probably would still have laws or policies mandating segregation in public schools.

Although judicial activists are often considered politically liberal and restraintists politically conservative, in recent years a new brand of conservative judicial activism has become prevalent. Unlike their liberal counterparts, whose activist decisions often expanded the rights of political and legal minorities, conservative activist judges view their positions as an opportunity to issue broad rulings that impose conservative political beliefs and policies on the country at large.

Some scholars argue that this increased conservative judicial activism has had an effect on the Court's reliance on *stare decisis* and adherence to precedent. Chief Justice William H. Rehnquist even noted that while "*stare decisis* is a cornerstone of our legal system . . . it has less power in constitutional cases."[58]

MODELS OF JUDICIAL DECISION MAKING

Most political scientists who study what is called judicial behavior conclude that a variety of forces shape judicial decision making. Many have attempted to explain how judges vote by integrating a variety of models to offer a more complete picture of how judges make decisions.[59] Many of those models attempt to take into account justices' individual behavioral characteristics and attitudes as well as the fact patterns of the case. The explanatory power of these models is often difficult to discern, and even those who have built their careers on constructing models note their inadequacies. Passage of time, the internal dynamics of the Court, and assumptions of presumed political values often can wreak havoc with these models.[60] Still, it is important to recognize the ways in which political scientists have attempted to evaluate and predict how justices will vote.

Behavioral Characteristics Originally, some political scientists argued that social background differences, including childhood experiences, religious values, education, earlier political and legal careers, and political party loyalties, are likely to influence how a judge evaluates the facts and legal issues presented in any given case. Justice Harry A. Blackmun's service at the Mayo Clinic often is pointed to as a reason that his opinion for the Court in *Roe* v. *Wade* (1973) was grounded so thoroughly in medical evidence. Similarly, Justice Potter Stewart, who was generally considered a moderate on most civil liberties issues, usually took a more liberal position on cases dealing with freedom of the press. Why? It may be that Stewart's early job as a newspaper reporter made him more sensitive to these claims.

The Attitudinal Model The attitudinal approach links judicial attitudes with decision making.[61] The attitudinal model holds that Supreme Court justices decide cases according to their personal preferences toward issues of public policy. Among some of the factors used to derive attitudes are a justice's party identification,[62] the party of the appointing president, and the liberal/conservative leanings of a justice.[63] For example, under the attitudinal model, a liberal justice appointed by a Democratic president would be more likely to decide an abortion case in favor of the pro-choice point of view. Similarly, a conservative justice appointed by a Republican president would most likely favor measures to support a free-market economy. Both justices would then adapt their interpretations of the law to support these ideological beliefs.

The Strategic Model Some scholars who study the courts believe that judges act strategically, meaning that they weigh and assess their actions against those of other justices to optimize the chances that their preferences will be adopted by the whole Court.[64] Moreover, this approach seeks to explain not only a justice's vote but also the range of forces such as congressional/judicial relations and judicial/executive relations that also affect the outcome of legal disputes.

PUBLIC OPINION

Many political scientists have examined the role of public opinion in Supreme Court decision making. Not only do the justices read legal briefs and hear oral arguments, but they also read newspapers, watch television, and have some knowledge of public opinion—especially on controversial issues.

Whether or not public opinion actually influences some justices, public opinion can act as a check on the power of the courts as well as an energizing factor. Activist periods on the Supreme Court generally have corresponded to periods of social or economic crisis. For example, the Marshall Court supported a strong national government, much to the chagrin of a series of pro–states' rights Democratic-Republican presidents in the early crisis-ridden years of the republic. Similarly, the Court capitulated to political pressures and public opinion when, after 1936, it reversed many of its earlier decisions that had blocked President Franklin D. Roosevelt's New Deal legislation.

The courts, especially the Supreme Court, also can be the direct target of public opinion. When *Webster* v. *Reproductive Health Services* (1989) was about to come before the Supreme Court, the Court was subjected to unprecedented lobbying as groups and individuals on both sides of the abortion issue marched and sent appeals to the Court. Mail at the Court, which usually averaged about 1,000 pieces a day, rose to an astronomical 46,000 pieces per day, virtually paralyzing normal lines of communication.

The Supreme Court also appears to affect public opinion. Political scientists have found that the Court's initial rulings on controversial issues such as abortion or capital punishment positively influence public opinion in the direction of the Court's opinion. However, this research also finds that subsequent decisions have little effect.[65] The extent to which the public and the Court are in agreement on a variety of controversial issues is shown in Table 10.8.

The Court also is dependent on the public for its prestige as well as for compliance with its decisions. In times of war and other emergencies, for example, the Court frequently has decided cases in ways that commentators have attributed to the sway of public opinion and political exigencies. In *Korematsu* v. *U.S* (1944), for example, the high Court upheld the obviously unconstitutional internment of Japanese American

TABLE 10.8 THE SUPREME COURT AND THE AMERICAN PUBLIC

In recent years, the Court's rulings have agreed with or diverged from public opinion on various questions, such as:

Issue	Case	Court Decision	Public Opinion
Should homosexual relations between consenting adults be legal?	*Lawrence* v. *Texas* (2003)	Yes	Maybe (50%)
Should members of Congress be subject to term limits?	*U.S. Term Limits* v. *Thornton* (1995)	No	Yes (77% favor)
Is affirmative action constitutional?	*Grutter* v. *Bollinger* (2003) *Gratz* v. *Bollinger* (2003)	Yes	Yes (64%)
Before getting an abortion, whose consent should a teenager be required to gain?	*Williams* v. *Zbaraz* (1980)	One parent	Both parents (38%) One parent (37%) Neither parent (22%)
Is the death penalty constitutional?	*Gregg* v. *Georgia* (1976)	Yes	Yes (72% favor)

Source: Table compiled from Lexis-Nexis RPOLL.

citizens during World War II.[66] Moreover, Chief Justice William H. Rehnquist himself once suggested that the Court's restriction on presidential authority in *Youngstown Sheet & Tube Co. v. Sawyer* (1952), which invalidated President Harry S Truman's seizure of the nation's steel mills,[67] was largely attributable to Truman's unpopularity in light of the Korean War.[68]

Public confidence in the Court, as with other institutions of government, has ebbed and flowed. Public support for the Court was highest after the Court issued *U.S. v. Nixon* (1974).[69] At a time when Americans lost faith in the presidency due to the Watergate scandal, they could at least look to the Supreme Court to do the right thing. Although the numbers of Americans with confidence in the courts has fluctuated over time, in 2006, 40 percent of those sampled by Gallup International had a "great deal" or "quite a lot" of confidence in the Supreme Court.[70] Recent battles over judicial opinions regarding hot-button social issues have led to blatantly hostile rhetoric toward members of the judiciary on the Internet and even in Congress. This, in turn, has led even some members of the Supreme Court to comment publicly on the continuing need for an independent judiciary. (See American Values/American Voices: Judicial Independence and the Court of World Opinion.)

Judicial Policy Making and Implementation

ALL JUDGES, WHETHER THEY RECOGNIZE IT OR NOT, make policy. The primary way federal judges, and the U.S. Supreme Court, in particular, make policy is through interpreting statutes or the Constitution. This occurs in a variety of ways. Judges can interpret a provision of a statute to cover matters previously not understood to be covered by the law, or they can discover new rights, such as that of privacy, from their reading of the Constitution. They also have literal power over life and death when they decide death penalty cases.

VIDEO ROUNDTABLE

Judges and Politics

This power of the courts to make policy presents difficult questions for democratic theory, as noted by Justice Antonin Scalia in *Webster* v. *Reproductive Health Services* (1989), because democratic theorists believe that the power to make law resides only in the people or their elected representatives. Yet, court rulings, especially Supreme Court decisions, routinely affect policy far beyond the interests of the immediate parties.

POLICY MAKING

One measure of the power of the courts and their ability to make policy is that more than one hundred federal laws have been declared unconstitutional. Although many of these laws have not been particularly significant, others have. For example, in *Ashcroft* v. *Free Speech Coalition* (2002), the Court ruled that the Child Online Protection Act, designed to prevent minors from viewing pornography over the Internet, was unconstitutional.[71]

Another measure of the policy-making power of the Supreme Court is its ability to overrule itself. Although the Court generally abides by the informal rule of *stare decisis,* by one count, it has overruled itself in more than 200 cases.[72] *Brown* v. *Board of Education* (1954), for example, overruled *Plessy* v. *Ferguson* (1896), thereby reversing years of constitutional interpretation concluding that racial segregation was not a violation of the Constitution. Moreover, in the past few years, the Court repeatedly has reversed earlier decisions in the areas of criminal defendants' rights, women's rights, and the establishment of religion, thus revealing its powerful role in determining national policy.

American Values/American Voices

JUDICIAL INDEPENDENCE AND THE COURT OF WORLD OPINION

Although the Framers spent little time on Article III of the U.S. Constitution at the Philadelphia Convention, the provisions they did include regarding Supreme Court justices—life tenure with good behavior and fixed compensation—were included for one major reason: the need to preserve the independence of the Court from all other branches. Alexander Hamilton defended these inclusions extensively in *The Federalist Papers*. In *Federalist No. 78,* for example, Hamilton wrote: "judges under this system will be independent in the strict sense of the word. . . . [T]here is no power above them that can control their decisions, or correct their errors. There is no authority that can remove them from office for any errors or want of capacity, or lower their salaries, and in many cases their power is superior to that of the legislature."

The actions of the Court's earliest chief justices, including John Jay and John Marshall, went a long way toward maintaining an image of independence for the Supreme Court. Even today, most casual observers consider the Court a neutral arbiter of the law that is above outside influence. As this chapter shows, however, the Supreme Court is not entirely insulated from outside forces. Historically, interest groups, public opinion, and even justices' personal experiences have played a role in the justices' decisions. So, too, have the laws and customs of other countries.

As early as 1877, in the case of *Pennoyer* v. *Neff,* Justice Stephen Field used international law to help define the boundaries of the U.S. Constitution's due process clause.[a] Recently, however, drawing on other countries' laws in American courts has become a contentious issue among the justices of the Supreme Court. Justices John Paul Stevens, Ruth Bader Ginsburg, and Steven Breyer sit on one side of the issue. These justices often refer to international law in their opinions and have spoken out in defense of cautiously using international standards for guidance in their decision-making process. Justice Ginsburg, for example, has said: "If U.S. experience and decisions can be instructive to systems that have more recently instituted or invigorated judicial review for constitutionality, so we can learn from others including Canada, South Africa, and most recently the U. K.—now engaged in measuring ordinary laws and executive actions against charters securing basic rights."[b]

On the other side of the issue sit a number of federal and state judges, including Supreme Court Justices Clarence Thomas and Antonin Scalia, who argue that citing international law compromises the independence of the American courts, runs contrary to the intentions of the Framers, and ignores the uniqueness of the American nation. In a 2006 speech to the American Enterprise Institute, for example, Scalia declared: "If there was any thought absolutely foreign to the founders of our country, surely it was the notion that we Americans should be governed the way that Europeans are—and nothing has changed."[c]

The justices' opinions in the 2002 death penalty case of *Atkins* v. *Virginia* illustrate how contentious the use of international law has become on the Supreme Court. Justice Stevens penned the majority opinion, and in footnote 21 he noted, "Moreover, within the world community, the imposition of the death penalty for crimes committed by mentally retarded offenders is overwhelmingly disapproved." In dissent, Justice Scalia attacked his colleague's reference to international norms, noting, "But the Prize for the Court's Most Feeble Effort to fabricate 'national consensus' must go to its appeal (deservedly relegated to a footnote) to the views of . . . the so-called 'world community.' . . . We must never forget that it is a Constitution for the United States of America that we are expounding. . . . [W]here there is not first a settled consensus among our own people, the views of other nations, however enlightened the Justices of this Court may think them to be, cannot be imposed upon Americans through the Constitution."[d]

The *Atkins* case is just one example of the public battles over the use of international law in the U.S. Supreme Court. Justices have used comparative constitutionalism to guide their decisions on a number of civil liberties issues, including affirmative action, homosexual rights, and assisted suicide.[e] And, with an increasingly global community, this is not a trend that is likely to stop anytime soon. The question is whether this international focus compromises the independence of American courts or whether it provides enlightening evidence of progress made in other societies that can be used to make the United States a better place to live.

QUESTIONS

1. Do you think that drawing on international law in framing judicial opinions compromises the independence of American courts? Why or why not?
2. When does it become appropriate for judges and justices to turn to international law and other external factors to help them reach a decision?

[a] Tim Wu, "Should the Supreme Court Care What Other Countries Think?" *Slate* (April 9, 2004), http://www.slate.com.

[b] Ruth Bader Ginsburg, speech at the University of Cape Town, South Africa, February 7, 2006.

[c] Antonin Scalia, speech at the American Enterprise Institute, February 21, 2006.

[d] *Atkins* v. *Virginia,* 536 U.S. 304 (2002).

[e] See *Grutter* v. *Bollinger,* 539 U.S. 306 (2003); *Bowers* v. *Hardwick,* 478 U.S. 186 (1986) and *Lawrence* v. *Texas,* 539 U.S. 558 (2003); and *Washington* v. *Glucksburg,* 521 U.S. 702 (1997).

A measure of the growing power of the federal courts is the degree to which they now handle issues that had been considered political questions more appropriately left to the other branches of government to decide. Prior to 1962, for example, the Court refused to hear cases questioning the size (and population) of congressional districts, no matter how unequal they were.[73] The boundary of a legislative district was considered a political question. Then, in 1962, writing for the Court, Justice William Brennan Jr. concluded that simply because a case involved a political issue, it did not necessarily involve a political question. This opened up the floodgates to cases involving a variety of issues that the Court formerly had declined to address.[74]

IMPLEMENTING COURT DECISIONS

President Andrew Jackson, annoyed about a particular decision handed down by the Marshall Court, is alleged to have said, "John Marshall has made his decision; now let him enforce it." Jackson's statement raises a question: how do Supreme Court rulings translate into public policy? In fact, although judicial decisions carry legal and even moral authority, all courts must rely on other units of government to carry out their directives. If the president or members of Congress, for example, don't like a particular Supreme Court ruling, they can underfund programs needed to implement a decision or seek only lax enforcement. **Judicial implementation** refers to how and whether judicial decisions are translated into actual public policies affecting more than the immediate parties to the lawsuit.

How well a decision is implemented often depends on how well crafted or popular it is. Hostile reaction in the South to *Brown* v. *Board of Education* (1954) and the absence of precise guidelines to implement the decision meant that the ruling went largely unenforced for years. The *Brown* experience also highlights how much the Supreme Court needs the support of both federal and state courts as well as other governmental agencies to carry out its judgments. For example, you probably graduated from high school after 1992, when the Supreme Court ruled that public middle school and high school graduations could not include a prayer, yet your own commencement ceremony may have included one.

The implementation of judicial decisions involves what political scientists call an implementing population and a consumer population.[75] The implementing population consists of those people responsible for carrying out a decision. It varies, depending on the policy and issues in question, but can include lawyers, judges, public officials, police officers and police departments, hospital administrators, government agencies, and corporations. In the case of school prayer, the implementing population could include teachers, school administrators, or school boards. The consumer population consists of those people who might be directly affected by a decision, that is, in this case, students and parents.

For effective implementation of a judicial decision, the first requirement is that the members of the implementing population must act to show that they understand the original decision. For example, the Supreme Court ruled in *Reynolds* v. *Sims* (1964) that every person should have an equally weighted vote in electing governmental representatives.[76] This "one person, one vote" decision might seem simple enough at first glance, but in practice it can be very difficult to understand. The implementing

judicial implementation
Refers to how and whether judicial decisions are translated into actual public policies affecting more than the immediate parties to a lawsuit.

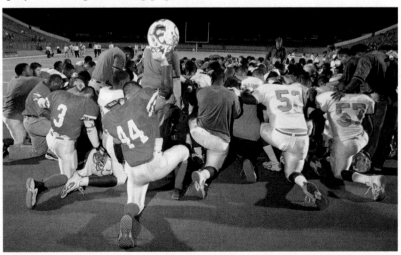

■ This photo, taken in September 2000, illustrates the difficulty in implementing judicial decisions. Although the Supreme Court had ruled in June 2000 that pre-game prayers at public schools were unconstitutional, prayers continued at many public school sporting events across the country after the Court's decision.

Photo courtesy: Joe Raedle/Newsmakers/Getty Images

population in this case consists chiefly of state legislatures and local governments, which determine voting districts for federal, state, and local offices (see chapter 13). If a state legislature draws districts in such a way that African American or Hispanic voters are spread thinly across a number of separate constituencies, the chances are slim that any particular district will elect a representative who is especially sensitive to minority concerns. Does that violate "equal representation"? (In practice, through the early 1990s, courts and the Department of Justice intervened in many cases to ensure that elected officials would include minority representation, only ultimately to be overruled by the Supreme Court.)[77]

The second requirement is that the implementing population actually must follow Court policy. Thus, when the Court ruled that men could not be denied admission to a state-sponsored nursing school, the implementing population—in this case, university administrators and the state board of regents governing the nursing school—had to enroll qualified male students.[78]

Judicial decisions are most likely to be implemented smoothly if responsibility for implementation is concentrated in the hands of a few highly visible public officials, such as the president or a governor. By the same token, these officials also can thwart or impede judicial intentions. Recall from chapter 6, for example, the effect of Governor Orval Faubus's initial refusal to allow black children to attend all-white public schools in Little Rock, Arkansas.

The third requirement for implementation is that the consumer population must be aware of the rights that a decision grants or denies them. Teenagers seeking an abortion, for example, are consumers of the Supreme Court's decisions on abortion. They need to know that most states require them to inform their parents of their intention to have an abortion or to get parental permission to do so. Similarly, criminal defendants and their lawyers are consumers of Court decisions and need to know, for instance, the implications of recent Court decisions for evidence presented at trial.

Summary

THE JUDICIARY AND THE LEGAL PROCESS—on both the national and state levels—are complex and play a far more important role in the setting of policy than the Framers ever envisioned. To explain the judicial process and its evolution, we have made the following points:

1. **The Constitution and the Creation of the Federal Judiciary**
Many of the Framers viewed the judicial branch of government as little more than a minor check on the other two branches, ignoring Anti-Federalist concerns about an unelected judiciary and its potential for tyranny.

The Judiciary Act of 1789 established the basic federal court system we have today. It was the Marshall Court (1801–1835), however, that interpreted the Constitution to include the Court's major power, that of judicial review.

2. **The American Legal System**
Ours is a dual judicial system consisting of the federal court system and the separate judicial systems of the fifty states. In each system there are two basic types of courts: trial courts and appellate courts. Each type

deals with cases involving criminal and civil law. Original jurisdiction refers to a court's ability to hear a case as a trial court; appellate jurisdiction refers to a court's ability to review cases already decided by a trial court.

3. **The Federal Court System**
The federal court system is made up of constitutional and legislative courts. Federal district courts, courts of appeals, and the Supreme Court are constitutional courts.

4. **How Federal Court Judges Are Selected**
District court and court of appeals judges are nominated by the president and subject to Senate confirmation. Supreme Court justices are nominated by the president and must also win Senate confirmation. Presidents use different criteria for selection, but important factors include competence, standards, ideology, rewards, pursuit of political support, religion, race, ethnicity, and gender.

5. **The Supreme Court Today**
Several factors go into the Court's decision to hear a case. Not only must the Court have jurisdiction, but at least four justices must vote to hear the case, and cases with certain characteristics are most likely to be heard.

Once a case is set for review, briefs and *amicus curiae* briefs are filed and oral argument scheduled. The justices meet after oral argument to discuss the case, votes are taken, and opinions are written, circulated, and then announced.

6. **Judicial Philosophy and Decision Making**

Judges' philosophy and ideology have an extraordinary impact on how they decide cases. Political scientists consider these factors in identifying several models for how judges make decisions, including the behavioral, attitudinal, and strategic models.

7. **Judicial Policy Making and Implementation**

The Supreme Court is an important participant in the policy-making process. The process of judicial interpretation gives the Court powers never envisioned by the Framers.

KEY TERMS

amicus curiae, p. 376
appellate courts, p. 356
appellate jurisdiction, p. 358
brief, p. 361
civil law, p. 359
constitutional courts, p. 359
criminal law, p. 358
judicial activism, p. 380
judicial implementation, p. 385
judicial restraint, p. 380
judicial review, p. 351
Judiciary Act of 1789, p. 353
jurisdiction, p. 357
legislative courts, p. 360
Marbury v. *Madison* (1803), p. 356
original jurisdiction, p. 357
precedent, p. 362
Rule of Four, p. 375
senatorial courtesy, p. 362
solicitor general, p. 376
stare decisis, p. 362
strict constructionist, p. 380
trial courts, p. 356
writ of *certiorari*, p. 374

SELECTED READINGS

Abraham, Henry J. *The Judiciary: The Supreme Court in the Governmental Process*, 10th ed. New York: New York University Press, 1996.

Baum, Lawrence. *The Supreme Court*, 8th ed. Washington, DC: CQ Press, 2004.

———. *The Puzzle of Judicial Behavior*. Ann Arbor: University of Michigan Press, 1997.

Clayton, Cornell, and Howard Gillman, eds. *Supreme Court Decision-Making: New Institutionalist Approaches*. Chicago: University of Chicago Press, 1999.

Epstein, Lee, and Jeffrey A. Segal. *Advice and Consent: The Politics of Judicial Appointments*. New York: Oxford University Press, 2005.

Epstein, Lee, et al. *The Supreme Court Compendium*, 3rd ed. Washington, DC: Congressional Quarterly Inc., 2002.

Goldman, Sheldon. *Picking Federal Judges: Lower Court Selection from Roosevelt Through Reagan*. New Haven, CT: Yale University Press, 1997.

Hall, Kermit L., ed. *The Oxford Companion to the Supreme Court of the United States*, 2nd ed. New York: Oxford University Press, 2005.

Hall, Kermit L., and Kevin T. McGuire, eds. *Institutions of American Democracy: The Judicial Branch*. New York: Oxford University Press, 2005.

Lazarus, Edward. *Closed Chambers: The First Eyewitness Account of the Epic Struggles Inside the Supreme Court*. New York: Times Books, 1998.

O'Brien, David M. *Storm Center: The Supreme Court in American Politics*, 7th ed. New York: Norton, 2005.

Perry, H. W. *Deciding to Decide: Agenda Setting in the United States Supreme Court*, reprint ed. Cambridge, MA: Harvard University Press, 2005.

Salokar, Rebecca Mae. *The Solicitor General: The Politics of Law*. Philadelphia: Temple University Press, 1992.

Segal, Jeffrey A., and Harold J. Spaeth. *The Supreme Court and the Attitudinal Model Revisited*. New York: Cambridge University Press, 2002.

Slotnick, Elliot E., and Jennifer A. Segal. *Television News and the Supreme Court: All the News That's Fit to Air*. Boston: Cambridge University Press, 1998.

Sunstein, Cass R. *One Case at a Time: Judicial Minimalism on the Supreme Court*, 2nd ed. Cambridge, MA: Harvard University Press, 2001.

Ward, Artemus, and David L. Weiden. *Sorcerer's Apprentices: 100 Years of Law Clerks at the United States Supreme Court*. New York: New York University Press, 2006.

Woodward, Bob, and Scott Armstrong. *The Brethren: Inside the Supreme Court*, 2nd reprint ed. New York: Avon, 2005.

WEB EXPLORATIONS

To learn more about the workings of the U.S. justice system, see
http://www.usdoj.gov

To learn more about U.S. federal courts, see
http://www.uscourts.gov/UFC99.pdf

To take a virtual tour of the U.S. Supreme Court and examine current cases on its docket, go to
http://www.supremecourtus.gov

To learn about the U.S. Senate Judiciary Committee and judicial nominations currently under review, see
http://judiciary.senate.gov

To learn the extent of the ABA's legislative and government advocacy, go to
http://www.abanet.org

To examine the major Supreme Court decisions from the past to the present, go to
http://supct.law.cornell.edu/supct/index.htm

To examine the recent filings of the office of solicitor general, go to
http://www.usdoj.gov/osg/

Photo courtesy: Bob Daemmrich/Stock Boston

POLITICAL SOCIALIZATION AND PUBLIC OPINION

AT 2:18 A.M. ON NOVEMBER 9, 2000, one of the major television networks made the call that George W. Bush would become the forty-third president of the United States. All the major networks quickly followed suit. But, as we all know now, that was not the end of it. As demands for recounts and litigation went on, one of the longest presidential elections in the nation's history became a field day for pollsters and their critics. In fact, the original call awarding Florida to Democrat Al Gore came early in the evening and was based not on actual vote totals, but on projections from the Voter News Service, an exit poll service used by a consortium of news organizations to hold down costs.

Pollsters sprang into action after Gore decided to retract the concession call he had made to Governor Bush. The Gallup Organization polled Americans to determine if they favored or opposed hand recounts in Florida. Nationwide, on November 11–12, 2000, 55 percent favored a recount: 85 percent of the Gore voters but only 20 percent of those who voted for Bush. Sixty percent believed that those votes should be included in the final totals.[1] On November 26, 2000, when asked whom they considered the real winner in Florida, 51 percent said Bush, but 32 percent were unsure. By then, only 15 percent thought Gore was the real winner. But, after the U.S. Supreme Court's decision that stopped all further vote counting and, in essence, declared George W. Bush the winner, voters were asked on December 15–17, "Just your best guess, if the Supreme Court had allowed the vote recount to continue in Florida, who do you think would have ended up with the most votes in Florida?" Of the national sample, 46 percent said Gore; 45 percent said Bush.

As in the November 11–12 poll, there was a huge chasm between Bush and Gore voters. Nearly three-quarters (74 percent) of the Gore voters continued to believe that he was the rightful winner; 77 percent of the Bush voters believed that their man would have ended up the winner. The same poll found that only 51 percent of those sampled believed that the Electoral College outcome was "fair." Again, huge gaps were evident in Bush and Gore voters. Eighty-five percent of the Bush voters thought the election outcome was fair; only 23 percent of the Gore voters did. Nationally, 68 percent of black voters believed that their votes were less likely to have been counted fairly in Florida than the votes of whites. Still, 61 percent of the public reported their belief that George W. Bush would work hard to "represent the interests of all Americans,"

although only 22 percent of blacks polled agreed with this statement.

Polling gives us a unique view into the psyche of Americans. Polls reflect the different political orientations—a result of political socialization—of myriad groups of voters and others. Moreover, politicians read the polls, as do their advisers. George W. Bush, who prided himself on his good relations with Hispanic and African American communities in Texas, undoubtedly was surprised by the feelings of Gore supporters and African Americans. Some might even argue that the diversity of Bush's first-term Cabinet appointments reflected his concern with bolstering his support among Hispanics, blacks, and even women. These efforts paid off in the 2004 presidential election, when he was able to capture more voters in all those groups.

Comparing Public Opinion

IN 1787, JOHN JAY WROTE GLOWINGLY of the sameness of the American people. He and the other authors of *The Federalist Papers* believed that Americans had more in common than not. Wrote Jay in *Federalist No. 2*, we are "one united people—a people descended from the same ancestors, speaking the same language, professing the same religion, attached to the same principles of government, very similar in manners and customs." Many of those who could vote in Jay's time were of English heritage; almost all were Christian. Moreover, most believed that certain rights—such as freedom of speech, association, and religion—were rights that could not be revoked. Jay also spoke of shared public opinion and of the need for a national government that reflected American ideals.

Today, however, Americans are a far more heterogeneous lot. Election after election and poll after poll reveal this diversity, but, nonetheless, Americans appear to agree on many things. Most want less government, particularly at the national level. So did many citizens in 1787. Most want a better nation for their children. So did the Framers.

political socialization
The process through which individuals acquire their political beliefs and values.

People develop their political views through **political socialization,** "the process through which an individual acquires his particular political orientations—his knowledge, feeling, and evaluations regarding his political world."[2] The political beliefs developed through the political socialization process affect public opinion, which is based on the sum total of a selection of individuals' views on issues, candidates, and various public policies.

The process and role of political socialization and public opinion and their role in the making of public policy are explored in this chapter:

- First, we will discuss *political socialization*, including the broad array of factors that influence this process.
- Second, we will examine *public opinion and polling*, noting the role of political socialization in public opinion formation, and explaining the role of public opinion polls in determining public perception of political issues.
- Third, we will examine *why we form and express political opinions*.
- Fourth, we will describe *the effects of public opinion and polling on government and politics*. Since the writing of *The Federalist Papers*, parties, candidates, and public officials have tried to sway as well as gauge public opinion for political purposes.

Political Socialization

POLITICAL SCIENTISTS BELIEVE that many of our attitudes about issues are grounded in our political values. We learn these values through political socialization. Family, school, peers, and the mass media are often important influences or agents of political socialization. For example, try to remember your earliest memory of the president of the United States. It may have been George Bush or Bill Clinton (older students probably remember earlier presidents). What did you think of the president? Of the Republican or Democratic Party? It is likely that your earliest feelings or attitudes were shaped by what your parents thought about that particular president and his party. Your experiences at school and your friends also probably influence your political beliefs today. Similar processes also apply to your early attitudes about the American flag, or the police. Other factors, too, often influence how political opinions are formed or reinforced. These include religious beliefs, race and ethnicity, gender, age, the region of the country in which you live, and even political events. Your own political knowledge may also shape your ideals.

THE FAMILY

The influence of the family on political socialization can be traced to two factors: communication and receptivity. Children, especially during their preschool years, spend tremendous amounts of time with their parents; early on they learn their parents' political values, even though these concepts may be vague. (See American Values/American Voices: Motherhood, the Framers, and Political Socialization.) One study, for example, found that the most important visible public figures for children under the age of ten were police officers and, to a much lesser extent, the president.[3] Young children almost uniformly view both as "helpful." But, by the age of ten or eleven, children become more selective in their perceptions of the president. By this age, children raised in Democratic households are much more likely to be critical of a Republican president than are those raised in Republican households. In 1988, for example, 58 percent of children in Republican households identified themselves as Republicans, and many had developed strong positive feelings toward Ronald Reagan, the Republican president. Support for and the popularity of Ronald Reagan translated into support for the Republican Party through the 1988 presidential election and also contributed to the decline of liberal ideological self-identification of first-year college students (see Figure 11.1).

SCHOOL AND PEERS

Researchers report mixed findings concerning the role of schools in the political socialization process. (See Join the Debate: Teaching Civics in American High Schools.) There is no question that, in elementary school, children are taught respect for their nation and its symbols. Most school days begin with the Pledge of Allegiance, and patriotism and respect for country are important, although subtle, components of most school curricula. Support for flag and country create a foundation for national allegiance that prevails despite the negative views about politicians and government institutions that many Americans develop later in life. For example, though many Americans initially questioned the U.S. action in Iraq in 2003, large numbers of schoolchildren prepared letters and packages to send to troops there and elsewhere. In some states, teachers were also encouraged to limit anti-war

■ Political values are shaped in childhood.

Photo courtesy: Nancy O'Connor

FIGURE 11.1 THE IDEOLOGICAL SELF-IDENTIFICATION OF FIRST-YEAR COLLEGE STUDENTS

A majority of first-year college students describe themselves as middle of the road; this number has held fairly steady since the early 1990s. The number of students identifying themselves as liberal and far left declined dramatically during the 1970s and early 1980s, while the number of students identifying themselves as conservative and far right increased.

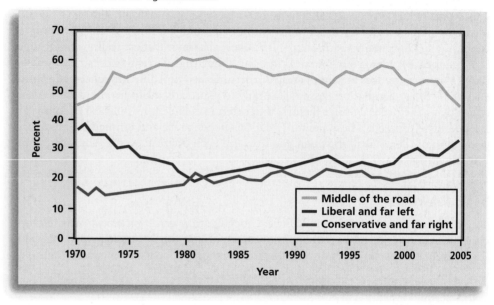

Sources: Reprinted from Howard W. Stanley and Richard G. Niemi, *Vital Statistics on American Politics, 2005–2006* (Washington, DC: CQ Press, 2006), 121. 2005 data from Cooperative Institutional Research Program, "The American Freshman: National Norms for Fall 2005," December 2005.

discussion.[4] Measures such as these, however controversial, help to build a sense of patriotism at a young age.

In 1994, Kids Voting USA was launched nationwide. This civic education project was designed to have a short-term impact on student political awareness and lead to a higher voter turnout among parents. Over 2 million students participate annually, and adult turnout frequently goes up 3 to 5 percent in communities where the program operates.[5] Thus, a school-based program actually uses children to affect their parents.

The *Weekly Reader*, read by elementary students nationwide, not only attempts to present young students with newsworthy stories but also tries to foster political awareness and a sense of civic duty. In presidential election years, students get the opportunity to vote for actual presidential candidates in the nationwide *Weekly Reader* election. These elections, which have been held since 1956, have been remarkably accurate. *Weekly Reader* has been wrong only once, in the 1992 election of Bill Clinton. These returns were skewed by prominent independent candidate Ross Perot.

A child's peers—that is, children about the same age—also seem to have an important effect on the socialization process. Whereas parental influences are greatest from birth to age five, a child's peer group becomes increasingly important as the child gets older, especially as he or she gets into middle school or high school.[6] Groups such as the Girl Scouts of the USA recognize the effect of peer pressure and are trying to influence more young women to participate in, and have a positive view of, politics. The Girl Scouts' Ms. President merit badge encourages girls as young as five to learn "herstory" and to emulate women leaders.

High schools also can be important agents of political socialization. They continue the elementary school tradition of building good citizens and often reinforce

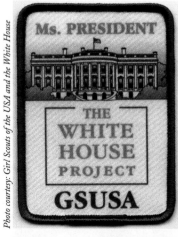

Photo courtesy: Girl Scouts of the USA and the White House

■ To heighten young girls' interest in politics, Girl Scouts of the USA, in conjunction with the White House Project, has created a Ms. President merit badge.

American Values/American Voices

MOTHERHOOD, THE FRAMERS, AND POLITICAL SOCIALIZATION

In the earliest days of the American republic, women were prohibited from voting in most elections and were excluded from many other forms of political participation. This does not mean, however, that the country's early leaders saw no role for women in the creation and development of the new nation. Capitalizing on women's traditional roles as wife and mother, early political leaders urged women to play a role in the country's continued prosperity by educating and developing their sons into the next generation of political leaders. This phenomenon, which was later dubbed "republican motherhood" by historians, represents one of the most obvious acceptances of political socialization—and the family as a source of political socialization—in the American nation. However, the Framers were not the first to envision such a role for women. The republican mother, in fact, had her roots in the Spartan mother of ancient Greece, who raised virtuous and moral sons for the good of the community.[a]

Although her role was considered important for the continued prosperity of the new nation, the republican mother was not a radical actor. Republican mothers did not hold protests in front of the White House demanding the right to vote, as suffragists did in the early twentieth century. However, the mere step of merging domesticity and politics opened the door for women's gradual progress in other spheres.[b] Many of the earliest women's colleges, for example, were founded to educate women so that they would be able to better teach their children. These same schools later produced many of the revolutionaries who demanded greater rights for women.

The gradual expansion of American women's political and social equality has only served to increase their role as agents of political socialization. Voting, for example, is often considered a learned behavior. If children—both male and female—see their parents voting, they are more likely to vote themselves. Since women vote in higher numbers than men, their influence on the next generation of voters cannot be ignored.

Unlike their predecessors, modern mothers may extend their role outside the home. Whether it is through overtly political activity such as running for office, or less political activity such as ascending into upper management at a Fortune 500 company, women who defy traditional sex-role stereotypes set a powerful example for the next generation. These pioneers have the power to change the context and subject matter of some of the biggest policy discussions in the world. Some scholars have even argued that without pioneers who challenge sex-role stereotypes, the United States will never see gender parity in elected representation.[c]

QUESTIONS

1. How is the "republican mother" concept consistent with the ideals traditionally espoused by the Framers? How is it different?
2. How has socialization within your home shaped your political development? Which of your parents or other relatives played a particularly big role in the development of your ideology and why?

[a] Linda Kerber, "The Republican Mother: Women and the Enlightenment—An American Perspective," *American Quarterly* 28 (1976): 187–205.

[b] Kerber, "The Republican Mother."

[c] Richard Fox and Jennifer Lawless, "Entering the Arena: Gender and the Decision to Run for Office," *American Journal of Political Science* 48 (2004): 264–80.

---

textbook learning with trips to the state or national capital. They also offer courses on current U.S. affairs. Many high schools impose a compulsory service learning requirement, which some studies report positively affects later political participation.[7] Although the formal education of many people in the United States ends with high school, research shows that better-informed citizens vote more often as adults. Therefore, presentation of civic information is especially critical at the high school level, where it reinforces views about participation.

At the college level, teaching style often changes. Many college courses and texts like this one are designed in part to provide you with the information necessary to think critically about issues of major political consequence. It is common in college for students to be called on to question the appropriateness of certain political actions or to discuss underlying reasons for certain political or policy decisions. Therefore, most researchers believe that college has a liberalizing effect on students. Since the 1920s, studies have shown that students become more liberal each year they are in college.

Figure 11.1, however, reveals that students entering college in the 1980s were more conservative than in past years. The 1992 and 1996 victories of Bill Clinton and his equally youthful running mate Al Gore, who went out of their way to woo the youth vote, probably contributed to the small bump in the liberal ideological identification of first-year college students in those years. But, in 2005, 25.3 percent of freshmen identi-

Join the Debate

TEACHING CIVICS IN AMERICAN HIGH SCHOOLS

OVERVIEW: Classical, Enlightenment, and contemporary political theories assert that a primary function of the state is the education of citizens; indeed, civic education is understood to be inseparable from public education. Civic education is considered an essential component of political socialization. In many classrooms, for example, children elect the students who will erase chalkboards or serve as class leaders; by participating in classroom elections, students are thus socialized to accept electoral politics as part of legitimate political behavior. All mass democratic societies have some form of civic education, if only to teach citizens social norms, virtues, and the "rules of the game" of the democratic process. Low voter turnout and close election outcomes have been cited by supporters of civic education as a sign that more needs to be done to teach young people the importance of political participation. Recently, civic education requirements have taken on additional urgency in light of debates about immigration policy and questions regarding the extent to which civic education efforts should focus exclusively on U.S. norms or emphasize commonalities and differences among democratic nations worldwide.

It is obvious and accepted that civic education in secondary education has declined over the last thirty years. Many point to the Watergate scandal, the Vietnam War, and racial and social unrest during the civil rights movement as having a negative effect on the teaching of American history and government. The latest National Assessment of Educational Progress (NAEP) determined that only

26 percent of all high school seniors may be considered "proficient" in American political knowledge, and a Roper Survey discovered the majority of graduates from America's elite universities were incapable of identifying James Madison (a principal architect of the Constitution) or words from the Gettysburg Address (Lincoln's reaffirmation of American principles). As a corrective, the federal government has instituted increased spending and guidelines for secondary American history and government education under the National Endowment for the Humanities' We the People Initiative, a program created to reaffirm and reinstitute civic education in America's classrooms.

The noted nineteenth-century commentator on American political society Alexis de Tocqueville argued that without common values and virtues, there can be no common action and social stability. What is the best way to teach American history, government, and political principles so that all who have contributed to the American experiment are recognized? Is a common civic education necessary, or should political socialization be left to the family? What can be done to increase interest in democratic politics and participation, and how can civic knowledge be restored to the American electorate?

ARGUMENTS FOR INCREASED CIVIC EDUCATION IN HIGH SCHOOLS

- **There may be a relationship between the decline in political participation and the lack of civic education.** Research indicates there may be a correlation between political participation and civic education. A Carnegie Corporation study contends that student participation in the management of schools and classroom, as well as in simulations of democratic institutions and processes, may increase involvement in the American political process.

fied themselves as conservative or far right; this was the highest percentage of conservative identifiers in more than thirty years. The number of students identifying themselves as liberal or far left increased from 24.2 percent in 2003 to 32.2 percent in 2005. More students continue to identify themselves as liberal than conservative, as they have done in nearly every year since studies of incoming freshmen began in 1965.[8]

THE MASS MEDIA

The media today are taking on a growing role as socialization agents. Adult Americans spend nearly thirty hours a week in front of their television sets; children spend even more.[9] Television has a tremendous impact on how people view politics, government, and politicians. TV talk shows, talk radio, and online newsletters, magazines, and blogs are important sources of information about politics for many, yet the information that people get from these sources often is skewed.

- **Civic education teaches citizens how to participate in democratic society.** Students become politically socialized by taking part in school elections, activities, and extracurricular activities (such as participating in debate teams and publishing school newspapers). Civic education teaches not only cooperation but tolerance of dissent and opposing views, as well as the means of political compromise. This helps prepare students for the realities of pluralistic democratic life.
- **Civic education is a complement to political socialization.** The primary influence on one's political development comes from family and friends, and mass media and culture also help to shape political values and attitudes. The role of a formal civic education is to teach American history and governmental and political structures and principles, as well as to provide a forum for students to hone their political skills, practice public debate, and learn civic engagement.

ARGUMENTS AGAINST INCREASED CIVIC EDUCATION IN HIGH SCHOOLS

- **Civic education is innately biased by promoting certain values over others.** In a free, multicultural society, it is inherently wrong to press upon individuals a certain political and social view. Modern democratic governments gather their strength from the many diverse cultures and political views that make up their respective social bodies. Teaching one sociopolitical view would stifle the contributions of those from different cultures. To this end, the American Historical Society advocates the teaching of comparative and world history in the nation's classrooms.

- **Parents should be responsible for civic education.** One may assume a government-sanctioned education will be partial to its own interests and views. It is proper that parents introduce their children to political culture and socialization; this will help ensure a diversity of views in regard to the nature of government, thereby fostering debate and compromise in the marketplace of political ideas.
- **In a pluralist society it is difficult to determine what should constitute a civic education curriculum.** Which understanding of American history, politics, and government is to be taught? Different groups have different interpretations and understanding of the historical unfolding of American society. To promote the views of one group over another would be unfair, and to teach all views would be to overwhelm students with information; the effect may be actually to *discourage* political engagement by subjecting students to information overload.

QUESTIONS

1. Is there a correlation between the decline in civic participation and civic education? If so, why? If not, why not?
2. Is it the proper place of public schools to engage in civic education or is this the duty of family and friends?

SELECTED READINGS

Niemi, Richard G., and Jane Junn. *Civic Education: What Makes Students Learn.* New Haven, CT: Yale University Press, 2005.
Ravitch, Diane, ed. *Making Good Citizens: Education and Civil Society.* New Haven, CT: Yale University Press, 2003.

Television also can serve to enlighten voters and encourage voter turnout. For example, MTV began coverage of presidential campaigns in 1992 and had reporters traveling with both major candidates to heighten young people's awareness of the stakes in the campaign. In addition, its "Choose or Lose" and "Rock the Vote" campaigns are designed to change the abysmal turnout rates of young voters.

Over the years, more and more Americans have turned away from traditional sources of news such as nightly news broadcasts on the major networks and daily newspapers in favor of different outlets. In 2004, one study estimated that more than 40 percent of those polled regularly learned about the election or candidates from alternative sources such as *The Tonight Show, The Late Show,* or *The Daily Show.*[10]

Some of the movement toward alternative news sources may be attributed to the growth of the sound bite. In the 2004 election, for example, the average sound bite was just six seconds, which gives the electorate little opportunity to evaluate a candidate. In sharp contrast, talk shows allow candidates ample time to discuss issues and present themselves as people. Thus, in 2004, both George W. Bush and John Kerry appeared on several popular shows and the public saw them unfiltered by packaging. Both candidates even appeared on *Dr. Phil* with their wives to talk about their families.

Since the 2004 presidential election, major party candidates have used another form of media to sway and inform voters: the Internet. Each presidential and most other major and minor campaigns in 2004 launched their own Internet sites, and the major networks and newspapers had their own Internet sites reporting on the election. Moreover, during the 2004 election cycle, more than 50 percent of those polled reported using the Internet to research candidates' positions on the issues.[11]

RELIGIOUS BELIEFS

Throughout our history, religion has played an extraordinary role in political life. Many colonists came to our shores seeking religious liberty, yet many quickly moved to impose their religious beliefs on others and some made participation in local politics contingent on religiosity. Since political scientists began to look at the role of religion, numerous scholars have found that organized religion influences the political beliefs and behaviors of its adherents. The effects of organized religion are magnified in today's society, as 76 percent of all Americans consider religion an important part of their lives.

Through much of the twentieth century, social scientists found that faith-based political activity occurred largely on the left. From the civil rights movement, to efforts to improve the living standards of farmers and migrant workers, to abolition of the death penalty, religious leaders were evident. The civil rights movement, in particular, was led by numerous religious men, including the Reverend Martin Luther King Jr. and the Reverend Andrew Young (who later became mayor of Atlanta, Georgia, and the U.S. Ambassador to the United Nations), as well as more recently the Reverend Jesse Jackson and the Reverend Al Sharpton.

In 1972, for the first time, a religious gap appeared in voting and public opinion. Richard M. Nixon's re-election campaign was designed to appeal to what he termed "the Silent Majority," who wanted a return to more traditional values after the tumult of the 1960s. After Nixon's campaign, conservative religious leaders established organizations whose effective fund-raising and get out the vote efforts allowed them to gain significant national political influence within the Republican Party. In 1979, televangelist Jerry Falwell became the widely recognized face of the Moral Majority, a group of conservative religious political action committees. Reverend Falwell, along with conservative Catholic and Jewish leaders, helped to ensure Republican candidate Ronald Reagan's election to office in 1980. The Moral Majority officially dissolved in 1989 when Falwell decided to focus on the growth of Liberty University, the Christian educational institution he had established in Lynchburg, Virginia, in 1971. Meanwhile, the Reverend Pat Robertson, host of television's widely watched *700 Club*, had established the Christian Coalition as a political advocacy and voter mobilization

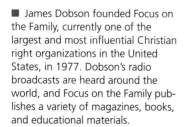

■ James Dobson founded Focus on the Family, currently one of the largest and most influential Christian right organizations in the United States, in 1977. Dobson's radio broadcasts are heard around the world, and Focus on the Family publishes a variety of magazines, books, and educational materials.

Photo courtesy: Jeff Fusco/Getty Images

FIGURE 11.2 THE IDEOLOGICAL SELF-IDENTIFICATION OF PROTESTANTS, CATHOLICS, AND JEWS

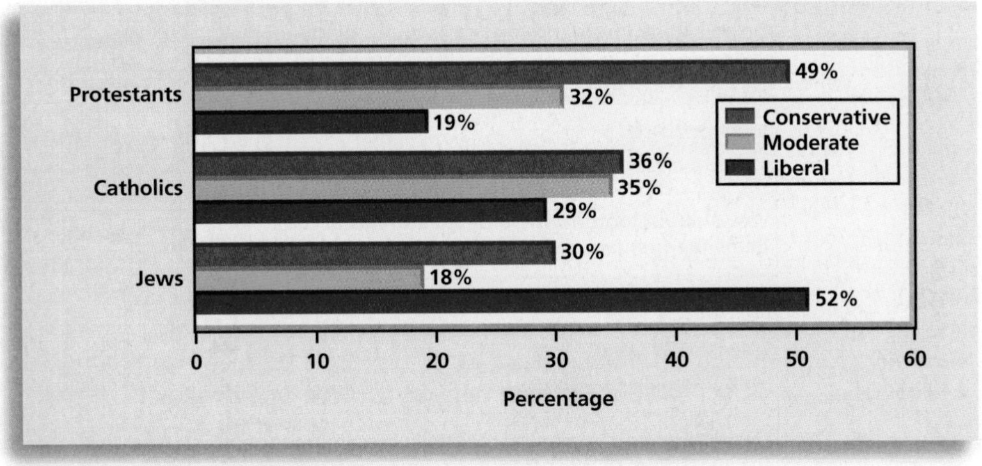

Source: Data compiled and analyzed by Alixandra B. Yanus from the 2004 American National Election Study.

effort after his failed 1988 bid for the U.S. presidency. Each election cycle, the Christian Coalition distributes voter guides evaluating candidates on a range of issues to conservative evangelical churches throughout the United States. Today, religion is the second largest predictor of the vote, after party identification. Regular church-goers have conservative views and vote Republican by a 2 to 1 margin.

In 2006, 54 percent of Americans identified themselves as Protestant, 25 percent as Catholic, 4 percent as Jewish, and 2 percent as other, while 15 percent claimed to have no religious affiliation. As shown in Figure 11.2, Protestants, especially evangelicals, are the most conservative and Jews the most liberal. And, as liberals, Jews tend to vote Democratic.[12] In 2004, for example, John Kerry and his running mate, John Edwards, captured 74 percent of the Jewish vote.[13]

Shared religious attitudes tend to affect voting and stances on particular issues. Catholics as a group, for example, favor aid to parochial schools, while many fundamentalist Protestants support organized prayer in public schools as well as abstinence-only education.

RACE AND ETHNICITY

Differences in political socialization of African Americans and whites appear at a very early age. Young black children, for example, generally show very positive feelings about American society and political processes, but this attachment lessens considerably over time. Black children fail to hold the president in the esteem accorded him by white children; indeed, older African American children in the 1960s viewed the government primarily in terms of the U.S. Supreme Court.[14] These differences continue through adulthood.

Differences in racial attitudes were starkly evident in the wake of Hurricane Katrina. As revealed in Figure 11.3, while both blacks and whites said they believed that the federal government's response to the disaster was slow because most of the affected were poor or black, far more blacks (77 percent) than whites (44 percent) viewed the looters as "mostly desperate people." And, while 67 percent of the whites polled by *USA Today*/Gallup reported they believed that "President Bush cares about black people," only 21 percent of blacks agreed with this statement.[15]

Race and ethnicity are exceptionally important factors in elections and in the study of public opinion. The direction and intensity of African American opinion on

FIGURE 11.3 VIEWS OF WHITES AND BLACKS IN WAKE OF HURRICANE KATRINA

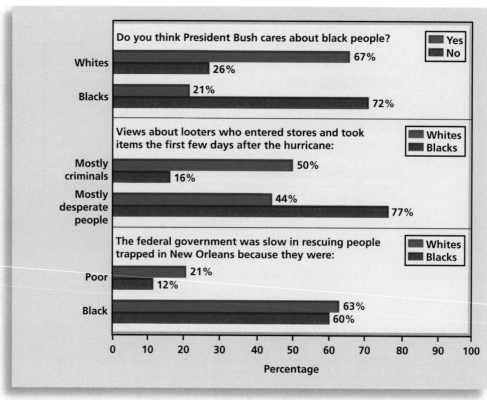

Note: Margins of sampling error: overall results ± 3 percentage points; whites ± 4 percentage points; blacks ± 7 percentage points.

*Source: USA Today/*CNN/Gallup Poll of 1,110 people taken September 8–11, 2005.

a variety of hot-button issues often are quite different from those of whites. As revealed in Analyzing Visuals: Racial and Ethnic Attitudes on Selected Issues, whites are much more likely to support the war in Iraq than are blacks or Hispanics. Likewise, differences can be seen in other issue areas, including support for preferential treatment to improve the position of minorities.[16]

Hispanics, Asians/Pacific Islanders, and American Indians are other identifiable ethnic minorities in the United States who often respond differently to issues than do whites. Generally, Hispanics and American Indians hold similar opinions on many issues, largely because members of these groups often have low incomes and find themselves targets of discrimination. Government-sponsored health insurance for the working poor, for example, is a hot-button issue with Hispanic voters, with 94 percent favoring it. Unlike many other Americans, they also favor bilingual education and liberalized immigration policies.[17]

Within the Hispanic community, however, existing divisions often depend on national origin. Generally, Cuban Americans who cluster in Florida and in the Miami–Dade Country area, in particular, are more likely to be conservative. They fled from communism and Fidel Castro in Cuba, and they generally vote Republican. In contrast, Hispanics of Mexican origin who vote in California, New Mexico, Arizona, Texas, or Colorado are more likely to vote Democratic.[18]

GENDER

Poll after poll reveals that women hold very different opinions from men on a variety of issues, as shown in Table 11.1. Some believe that from an early age, women are

Analyzing Visuals
RACIAL AND ETHNIC ATTITUDES ON SELECTED ISSUES

Political opinions held by racial and ethnic groups in the United States differ on many issues. In the figure below, the opinions of whites, blacks, and Hispanics are compared on a number of political issues. After studying the bar graph and the material in this chapter on race, ethnicity, and public opinion, answer the following critical thinking questions: What do you observe about the differences and similarities in opinions among the different groups? On which issues do blacks and whites, Hispanics and blacks, and Hispanics and whites have similar or diverging opinions? What factors might explain these similarities and differences?

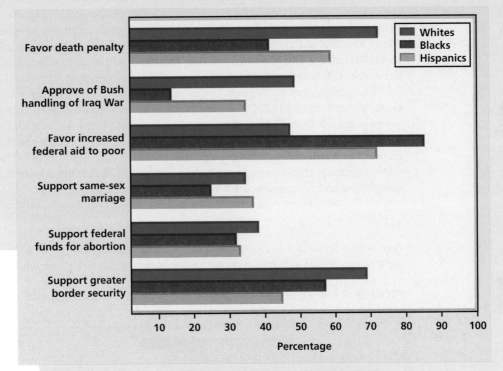

Source: Data compiled and analyzed by Alixandra B. Yanus from the 2004 American National Election Study.

socialized to be more nurturing and caring while men are more aggressive or even warlike. According to this argument, these differences in political socialization lead to different political orientations and often have translated into substantial gaps in the way men and women vote. Women, and particularly unmarried women, are more likely to be Democrats, while white men are increasingly becoming the core of the Republican Party.[19]

From the time that the earliest public opinion polls were taken, women have been found to hold more liberal attitudes about issues touching on social welfare concerns, such as education, juvenile justice, capital punishment, and the environment. Some analysts suggest that women's more nurturing nature and their prominent role as mothers lead women to have more liberal attitudes on issues affecting the family or children. Research by political scientists, however, finds no support for a maternal explanation.[20]

TABLE 11.1 GENDER DIFFERENCES ON POLITICAL ISSUES

Public opinion polls reveal that men and women tend to hold different views on a number of political issues. Yet, as this table reveals, on some political issues, little difference is evident.

	Men (%)	Women (%)
Think Iraq War worth the cost	42	35
Favor increased federal spending on war on terrorism	50	36
Favor increased federal spending on Social Security	57	67
Favor ban on late-term (partial birth) abortion	57	60
Think federal government should make it more difficult to buy guns	48	67
Voted for George W. Bush in 2004	55	48

Source: Data compiled and analyzed by Alixandra B. Yanus from the 2004 American National Election Study.

Historically, public opinion polls have also found that women hold more negative views about war and military intervention. However, the gender gap on military issues began to disappear in the late 1990s, when the United States intervened in Kosovo. Many speculated that this occurred because of the increased participation of women in the workforce and the military, the "sanitized nature of much of the war footage" shown on TV, and the humanitarian reasons for involvement.[21]

The gender gap in military affairs also was not visible following the terrorist attacks of September 11, 2001. Right after the attacks, polls showed that 47 percent of women and 53 percent of men voiced their support for the U.S. military intervention in Afghanistan.[22] However, as the memory of 9/11 has receded, the war in Iraq has resulted in a renewed gender gap on foreign affairs (see Table 11.1). Many commentators speculate that this gap may be the product of increasing concerns about terrorism abroad and national security at home.

AGE

Age seems to have a decided effect on political socialization (see Figure 11.4). Our view of the proper role of government, for example, often depends on the era in which

FIGURE 11.4 COMPARING FOUR AGE COHORTS ON ISSUES, 2004

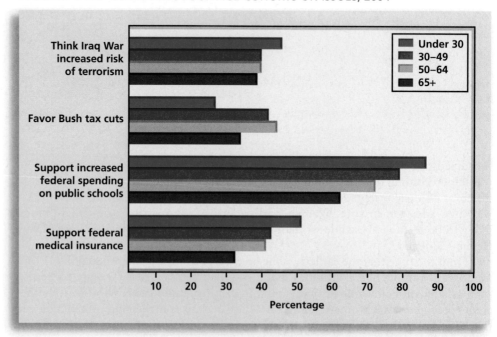

Source: Data compiled and analyzed by Alixandra B. Yanus from the 2004 American National Election Study.

we were born and our individual experiences with a variety of social, political, and economic forces. Older people continue to be affected by having lived through the Depression and World War II. One political scientist predicts that as Baby Boomers age, the age gap in political beliefs about political issues, especially governmental programs, will increase.[23] Young people, for example, resist higher taxes to fund Medicare, while the elderly resist all efforts to limit Medicare or Social Security.

In states such as Florida, to which many northern retirees have flocked seeking relief from cold winters and high taxes, the elderly have voted as a bloc to defeat school tax increases and to pass tax breaks for themselves. As a group, senior citizens are much more likely to favor an increased governmental role in the area of medical insurance.

In the future, the graying of America will have major social and political consequences. As we discuss in chapter 13, those between sixty and seventy years of age vote in much larger numbers than do their younger counterparts. Moreover, the fastest growing age group in the United States is that of citizens over the age of sixty-five. Thus, not only are there more people in this category, but they are more likely to be registered to vote, and often vote conservatively.

REGION

Regional and sectional differences have been important factors in the development and maintenance of political beliefs since colonial times. As the United States developed into a major industrial nation, waves of immigrants with different religious traditions and customs entered the United States and often settled in areas where other immigrants from their region already lived. For example, thousands of Scandinavians settled in Minnesota, and many Irish settled in the urban centers of the Northeast, as did many Italians and Jews. All brought with them unique views about numerous issues, as well as about the role of government. These political views often have been transmitted through generations, and many regional differences continue to affect public opinion today.

One of the most long-standing and dramatic regional differences in the United States is that between the South and the North. Recall that during the Constitutional Convention most Southerners staunchly advocated a weak national government. Nearly a hundred years later, the Civil War was fought in part because of basic differences in philosophy toward government (states' rights in the South versus national rights in the North). As we know from the results of modern political polling, the South has continued to lag behind the rest of the nation on support for civil rights, while continuing to favor return of power to the states at the expense of the national government.

The South also is much more religious than the rest of the nation, as well as more Protestant. Seventy-six percent of the South is Protestant (versus 49 percent for the rest of the nation), and church attendance is highest in the South, where 38 percent report weekly visits. In contrast, only 30 percent of those living in the North and 29 percent of those residing in the West go to church or synagogue on a weekly basis.[24] Given the South's higher churchgoing rates, it is not surprising that the Christian Coalition (also discussed in chapter 16) has been very successful at mobilizing voters in that region.

The West, too, now appears different from other sections of the nation. Some people have moved there to avoid city life; other residents have an anti-government bias. Many who have sought refuge there are staunchly against any governmental action, especially on the national level. One need only look at a map of the vote distribution in the 2004 presidential election to see stark differences in candidate appeal. John Kerry carried almost every large city in America; George W. Bush carried 59 percent of the rural and small-town voters as well as most of America's heartland.[25] Republicans won the South, the West, and much of the Midwest; Democrats carried the Northeast and West Coast.

War, Peace, and
Public Opinion

THE IMPACT OF EVENTS

Key political events play a very important role in a person's political socialization. You probably have some professors who remember what they were doing on the day that President John F. Kennedy was killed—November 22, 1963. This dramatic event is indelibly etched in the minds of virtually all people who were old enough to be aware of it. Similarly, most college students today remember where they were when they heard about the September 11 attacks on the World Trade Center and the Pentagon. These attacks on American shores evoked a profound sense of patriotism and national unity as American flags were displayed from windows, doors, balconies, and cars. For many Americans, the attacks were life-changing political events (see Table 11.2).

One has to go back to 1974 to find a political event that had such a dramatic effect on what people thought about the political process. President Richard M. Nixon's resignation in 1974 made a particular impression on young people, who were forced to realize that their government was not always right or honest. This general distrust of politicians was reignited during the highly publicized investigation of President Bill Clinton and his subsequent impeachment. Interestingly, in an informal survey of a small group of Americans age eighteen to twenty in 2006, respondents failed to report a single political event that affected them during their early school years.[26] The impact of a shared political moment for an age cohort has yet to be studied.

One problem in discussing the impact of events on political socialization is that many of the major studies on this topic were conducted in the aftermath of Watergate, which, along with the civil rights movement and the Vietnam War, produced a marked increase in Americans' distrust of government. The findings reported in Figure 1.7 (see page 26) reveal the dramatic drop-off of trust in government that began in the mid-1960s and continued through the election of Ronald Reagan in 1980.

TABLE 11.2 AMERICA'S COLLECTIVE MEMORY

Memories often define generations, and the memories (and experiencing) of key events often affect how individuals perceive other political events. Today, nearly all Americans know what they were doing when they first heard of the 9/11 attacks.

Early Events Fading		*Events Most Compelling*	
Percentage of public who remember hearing the news of:		*Percentage who remember what they were doing when they heard the news of:*[a]	
Princess Diana's death	87	John F. Kennedy's assassination	90
Oklahoma City bombing	86	Princess Diana's death	87
Challenger explosion	78	Oklahoma City bombing	86
Beginning of 1991 Persian Gulf War	75	Attack on Pearl Harbor	85
President Ronald Reagan shot by John Hinckley	67	*Challenger* explosion	82
Fall of Berlin Wall	59	Neil Armstrong walking on moon	80
Neil Armstrong walking on moon	54	End of World War II	79
President John F. Kennedy's assassination	53	Beginning of 1991 Persian Gulf War	76
President Richard M. Nixon's resignation	53	President Ronald Reagan shot by John Hinckley	72
Reverend Martin Luther King's assassination	43	Franklin D. Roosevelt's death	71
Tiananmen Square, China, massacre	41	President Richard M. Nixon's resignation	67
End of World War II	21	Reverend Martin Luther King's assassination	67
Attack on Pearl Harbor	18	Fall of Berlin Wall	60
President Franklin D. Roosevelt's death	17	N. Korea invading S. Korea	43
N. Korea invading S. Korea	15	Tiananmen Square, China, massacre	42
Paris falling to the Nazis	7	Paris falling to the Nazis	38
1929 stock market crash	4	1929 stock market crash	38

[a] Based on those who are old enough to remember.

Source: "Public Perspectives on the American Century." 1999 *Millennium Survey* 1: Section 4, http://people-press.org/reports/display.ph3?PageID=283.

Global Perspective

KEY CHALLENGES AROUND THE WORLD

Public opinion polls can be used to measure more than just political attitudes and beliefs. They can also provide us with a window on how people feel about a wide range of issues that affect their daily lives. In 2002, the Pew Global Attitudes Project published the results of a poll given to more than 38,000 people in forty-four countries. The results show points of global convergence and divergence with regard to the issues people believe are the biggest problems facing their nation.

In the Pew poll, people were asked to identify the "very big" problems facing their respective nations. Possible answers included crime, AIDS and other diseases, corrupt leaders, terrorism, ethnic conflict, poor drinking water, moral decline, poor schools, immigration, and emigration (people leaving the country). In nineteen of the forty-four countries, people identified crime as the most significant problem affecting their lives. Only in Canada, Jordan, China, and South Korea was crime

viewed as a less serious problem. People in thirteen countries—including eight of ten African nations—rated AIDS and infectious diseases as the principal threat facing their respective nations. Clean water was identified as the greatest problem in Jordan, while in Senegal it was ethnic strife. Although both the United States and India ranked terrorism as the problem of greatest concern, only 50 percent of Americans considered it a significant problem, while 90 percent of Indians did.

QUESTIONS

1. In your opinion, which of the significant national problems identified in the table below is most easily solved and which will be the hardest to solve? Why? What strategies would you use to solve these problems?
2. How do you explain the different responses from citizens in Canada, the United States, and Great Britain?

"VERY BIG" NATIONAL PROBLEMS AROUND THE WORLD

	Crime	AIDS and Other Diseases	Corrupt Leaders	Terrorism	Immigration	Moral Decline
United States	48%	42%	46%	**50%**	37%	49%
Canada	26	31	**32**	19	21	29
Great Britain	**61**	30	21	23	46	33
Russia	**75**	63	61	65	14	47
Poland	**80**	37	70	45	12	36
Pakistan	**84**	63	61	65	26	55
Mexico	**81**	78	73	69	31	45
Venezuela	65	**69**	58	62	26	43
India	86	72	80	**90**	32	44
Japan	**85**	54	**85**	68	21	66
South Korea	35	30	**75**	15	10	38
Kenya	83	**94**	84	42	28	56
Nigeria	84	83	**88**	65	35	59
South Africa	**96**	**96**	75	43	63	59

Note: Bold indicates highest-ranking problem for each country.

Source: Pew Global Attitudes Project, 2002.

Public Opinion and Polling

AT FIRST GLANCE, **public opinion** seems to be a very straightforward concept: it is what the public thinks about a particular issue or set of issues at a particular time. Since the 1930s, governmental decision makers have relied heavily on **public opinion polls**—interviews with samples of citizens that are used to estimate what the public is thinking. According to George Gallup (1901–1983), an Iowan who is considered the founder of modern-day polling, polls have played a key role in defining issues of

public opinion
What the public thinks about a particular issue or set of issues at any point in time.

public opinion polls
Interviews or surveys with samples of citizens that are used to estimate the feelings and beliefs of the entire population.

concern to the public, shaping administrative decisions, and helping "speed up the process of democracy" in the United States.[27]

Gallup further contends that leaders must constantly take public opinion—no matter how short-lived—into account. This does not mean that leaders must follow the public's view slavishly; it does mean that they should have an available appraisal of public opinion and take some account of it in reaching their decisions.[28]

Even though Gallup undoubtedly had a vested interest in fostering reliance on public opinion polls, his sentiments accurately reflect the feelings of many political thinkers concerning the role of public opinion and governance. Some, like Gallup, believe that the government should do what a majority of the public wants done. Others argue that the public as a whole doesn't have consistent opinions on day-to-day issues but that subgroups within the public often hold strong views on some issues. These pluralists believe that the government must allow for the expression of these minority opinions and that democracy works best when these different voices are allowed to fight it out in the public arena.

THE HISTORY OF PUBLIC OPINION RESEARCH

As early as 1824, one Pennsylvania newspaper tried to predict the winner of that year's presidential contest. Later, in 1883, the *Boston Globe* sent reporters to selected election precincts to poll voters as they exited voting booths in an effort to predict the results of key contests. In 1916, *Literary Digest*, a popular magazine, began mailing survey postcards to potential voters in an effort to predict election outcomes. *Literary Digest* drew its survey sample from "every telephone book in the United States, from the rosters of clubs and associations, from city directories, lists of registered voters [and] classified mail order and occupational data."[29] Using data from the millions of postcard ballots it received from all over the United States, *Literary Digest* correctly predicted every presidential election from 1920 to 1932.

But, public opinion polling as we know it today did not begin to develop until the 1930s. Much of this growth was prompted by Walter Lippmann's seminal work,

Public Opinion (1922). In this piece, Lippmann observed that research on public opinion was far too limited, especially in light of its importance. Researchers in a variety of disciplines, including political science, heeded Lippmann's call to learn more about public opinion. Some tried to use scientific methods to measure political thought through the use of surveys or polls. As methods for gathering and interpreting data improved, survey data began to play an increasingly important role in all walks of life, from politics to retailing.

Literary Digest, for example, was a pioneer in the use of **straw polls,** unscientific surveys used to gauge public opinion, to predict the popular vote in those four presidential elections. Its polling methods were hailed widely as "amazingly right" and "uncannily accurate."[30] In 1936, however, its luck ran out. *Literary Digest* predicted that Republican Alfred M. Landon would beat incumbent President Franklin D. Roosevelt by a margin of 57 percent to 43 percent of the popular vote. Roosevelt, however, won in a landslide election, receiving 62.5 percent of the popular vote and carrying all but two states.

Literary Digest's 1936 straw poll had three fatal errors. First, its sample was drawn from telephone directories and lists of automobile owners. This technique oversampled the upper middle class and the wealthy, groups heavily Republican in political orientation. Moreover, in 1936, voting polarized along class lines. Thus, the oversampling of wealthy Republicans was particularly problematic because it severely underestimated the Democratic vote.

Literary Digest's second problem was timing. Questionnaires were mailed in early September. It did not measure the changes in public sentiment that occurred as the election drew closer.

Its third error occurred because of a problem we now call self-selection. Only highly motivated individuals sent back the cards—a mere 22 percent of those surveyed responded. Those who respond to mail surveys (or today, online surveys) are quite different from the general electorate; they often are wealthier and better educated and care more fervently about issues. *Literary Digest*, then, failed to observe one of the now well-known cardinal rules of survey sampling: "One cannot allow the respondents to select themselves into the sample."[31]

At least one pollster, however, correctly predicted the results of the 1936 election: George Gallup. Gallup had written his dissertation in psychology at the University of Iowa on how to measure the readership of newspapers. He then expanded his research to study public opinion about politics. He was so confident about his methods that he gave all of his newspaper clients a money-back guarantee: if his poll predictions weren't closer to the actual election outcome than those of the highly acclaimed *Literary Digest*, he would refund their money. Although Gallup underpredicted Roosevelt's victory by nearly 7 percent, the fact that he got the winner right was what everyone remembered, especially given *Literary Digest*'s dramatic miscalculation.

Through the late 1940s, polling techniques became more sophisticated. The number of polling groups also dramatically increased, as businesses and politicians began to rely on polling information to market products and candidates. But, in 1948, the polling industry suffered a severe, although fleeting, setback when Gallup and many other pollsters incorrectly predicted that Thomas E. Dewey would defeat President Harry S Truman.

straw polls
Unscientific surveys used to gauge public opinion on a variety of issues and policies.

■ Not only did advance polls in 1948 predict that Republican nominee Thomas E. Dewey would defeat Democratic incumbent President Harry S Truman, but based on early and incomplete vote tallies, some newspapers' early editions published the day after the election declared Dewey the winner. Here a triumphant Truman holds aloft the *Chicago Daily Tribune.*

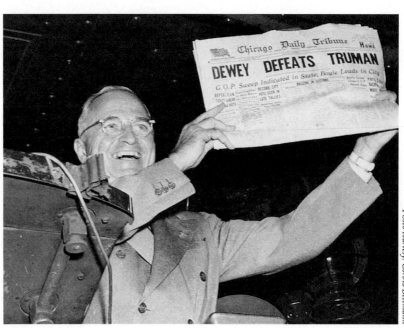

Photo courtesy: Corbis/Bettmann

Nevertheless, as revealed in Figure 11.5, the Gallup Organization, now co-chaired by George Gallup Jr., continues to predict the winners of the presidential popular vote successfully. In 2004, for example, Gallup predicted the winner while under-predicting George W. Bush's popular vote.

Recent efforts to measure public opinion also have been aided by social science surveys such as the National Election Study (NES), conducted by researchers at the University of Michigan since 1952. NES surveys focus on the political attitudes and the behavior of the electorate, and they include questions about how respondents voted, their party affiliation, and their opinions of major political parties and candidates. In addition, NES surveys include questions about interest in politics and political participation.

These surveys are conducted before and after midterm and presidential elections and often include many of the same questions. This format enables researchers to compile long-term studies of the electorate and facilitates political scientists' understanding of how and why people vote and participate in politics.

The Internet also has had an effect on how public opinion is measured. For example, Harris Interactive, an Internet-based marketing firm, used the Internet to achieve a 99 percent accuracy rate in seventy-three political contests in November

FIGURE 11.5 THE SUCCESS OF THE GALLUP POLL IN PRESIDENTIAL ELECTIONS, 1936–2004

As seen here, Gallup's final predictions have been remarkably accurate. Furthermore, in each of the years where there is a significant discrepancy between Gallup's prediction and the election's outcome, there was a prominent third candidate. In 1948, Strom Thurmond ran on the Dixiecrat ticket; in 1980, John Anderson ran as the American Independent Party candidate; in 1992, Ross Perot ran as an independent.

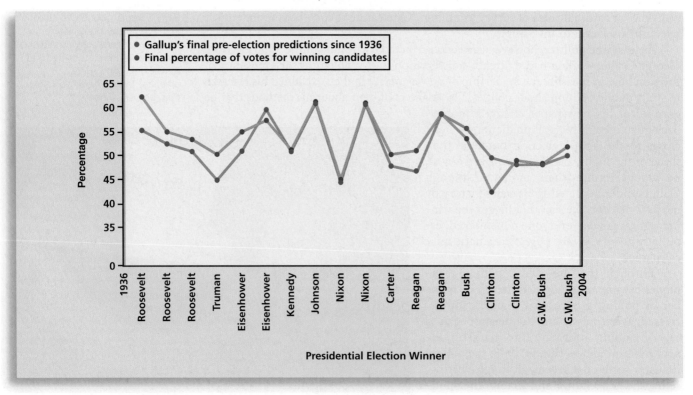

Sources: Marty Baumann, "How One Polling Firm Stacks Up," *USA Today* (October 27, 1992): 13A; 1996 data from Mike Mokrzycki, "Pre-election Polls' Accuracy Varied," *Atlanta Journal and Constitution* (November 8, 1996): A12; 2000 data from Gallup Organization, "Poll Releases," November 7, 2000; 2004 data from *USA Today* and CNN/Gallup Tracking Poll, USAtoday.com.

2000.[32] Still, critics charge that the Internet is far from perfect for polling. Many citizens, especially the poor and the elderly, are not online and therefore are undercounted in Internet polls.

TRADITIONAL PUBLIC OPINION POLLS

The polling process most often begins when someone says, "Let's find out about X and Y." Potential candidates for local office may want to know how many people have heard of them (the device used to find out is called a name recognition survey). Better-known candidates contemplating running for higher office might want to know how they might fare against an incumbent. Polls also can be used to gauge how effective particular ads are or if a candidate is being well (or negatively) perceived by the public. Political scientists have found that public opinion polls are critical to successful presidents and their staffs, who use polls to "create favorable legislative environment(s) to pass the presidential agenda, to win reelection, and to be judged favorably by history."[33] These polls and others have several key phases, including: (1) determining the content and phrasing the questions; (2) selecting the sample; and, (3) contacting respondents.

Determining the Content and Phrasing the Questions Once a candidate, politician, or news organization decides to use a poll to measure the public's attitudes, special care has to be taken in constructing the questions to be asked. For example, if your professor asked you, "Do you think my grading procedures are fair?" rather than asking, "In general, how fair do you think the grading is in your American Politics course?" you might give a slightly different answer. The wording of the first question tends to put you on the spot and personalize the grading style; the second question is more neutral. Even more obvious differences appear in the real world of polling, especially when interested groups want a poll to yield particular results. Responses to highly emotional issues such as abortion, same-sex marriage, and affirmative action often are skewed depending on the wording of a particular question.

Selecting the Sample Once the decision is made to take a poll, pollsters must determine the universe, or the entire group whose attitudes they wish to measure. This universe could be all Americans, all voters, all city residents, all Hispanics, or all Republicans. In a perfect world, each individual would be asked to give an opinion, but such comprehensive polling is not practical. Consequently, pollsters take a sample of the universe in which they are interested. One way to obtain this sample is by **random sampling.** This method of selection gives each potential voter or adult the same chance of being selected. In theory, this sounds good, but it is actually impossible to achieve because no one has lists of every person in any group. Thus, the method of poll taking is extremely important in determining the validity and reliability of the results.

SIMULATION
You Are a Polling Consultant

random sampling
A method of poll selection that gives each person in a group the same chance of being selected.

■ How the questions in an opinion poll are worded can have a profound impact on the results of the poll. Here, the cartoonist questions the polling source itself.

As discussed earlier in the chapter, *Literary Digest* polls suffered from an oversampling of voters whose names were drawn from telephone directories and car registrations; this group was hardly representative of the general electorate in the midst of the Depression. Thus, the use of a nonstratified or nonrepresentative sample led to results that could not be used to predict accurately how the electorate would vote in 1936.

Perhaps the most common form of unrepresentative sampling is the kind of straw poll used today by local television news programs or online services. Many have regular features asking viewers to call in their sentiments (with one phone number for pro and another for con) or asking those logged on to indicate their preferences. The results of these unscientific polls are not very accurate because those who feel very strongly about the issue often repeatedly call in to vote more than once.

A more reliable method is a quota sample, in which pollsters draw their sample based on known statistics. Assume that a citywide survey has been commissioned. If the city is 30 percent African American, 15 percent Hispanic, and 55 percent white, interviewers will use those statistics to determine the proportion of particular groups to be questioned. These kinds of surveys often are conducted in local shopping malls. Perhaps you've wondered why the man or woman with the clipboard has let you pass by but has stopped the next shopper. Now you know it is likely that you did not match the subject profile that the interviewer was instructed to locate. Although this kind of sampling technique can produce relatively accurate results, the degree of accuracy falls short of those surveys based on probability samples. Moreover, these surveys generally oversample the visible population, such as shoppers, while neglecting the stay-at-homes who may be glued to the Home Shopping Network or prefer to buy online.

stratified sampling
A variation of random sampling; census data are used to divide the country into four sampling regions. Sets of counties and standard metropolitan statistical areas are then randomly selected in proportion to the total national population.

Most national surveys and commercial polls use samples of 1,000 to 1,500 individuals and use a variation of the random sampling method called **stratified sampling.** Simple random, nonstratified samples are not very useful at predicting voting because they may undersample (or oversample) key populations that are not likely to vote. To avoid these problems, reputable polling organizations use stratified sampling (the most rigorous sampling technique) based on census data that provide the number of residences in an area and their location. Researchers divide the country into four sampling regions. They then randomly select a set of counties and standard metropolitan statistical areas in proportion to the total national population. Once certain primary sampling units are chosen, they often are used for many years, because it is cheaper for polling companies to train interviewers to work in fixed areas.

About twenty respondents from each primary sampling unit are picked to be interviewed. Generally four or five city blocks or areas are selected, and then four or five target families from each district are used. Large, sophisticated surveys such as the National Election Study and General Social Survey, which produce the data commonly used by political scientists, attempt to sample from lists of persons living in each household. The key to the success of the stratified sampling method is not to let people volunteer to be interviewed—volunteers as a group often have different opinions from those who do not volunteer.

Stratified sampling generally is not used by those who do surveys reported in the *New York Times* and *USA Today* or on network news programs. Instead, those organizations or pollsters working for them randomly place telephone calls to every tenth, hundredth, or thousandth person or household. If those individuals do not answer, they call the next person on the list.

Contacting Respondents After selecting the methodology to conduct the poll, the next question is how to contact those to be surveyed. Television stations often ask people to call in, and some surveyors hit the streets. Telephone polls, however, are becoming the most frequently used mechanism by which to gauge the temper of the electorate.

Model Introduction

Hello, my name is _____ and I'm calling from (company). Today/Tonight we are calling to gather opinions regarding (general subject), and are not selling anything. This study will take approximately (length) and may be monitored (and recorded) for quality purposes. We would appreciate your time. May I include your opinions?

Closing

- At the conclusion of the survey, thank the respondent for his/her time.

- Express the desired intention that the respondent had a positive survey experience and will be willing to participate in future market research projects.

- Remind the respondent that his/her opinions do count.

MODEL CLOSING

Thank you for your time and cooperation. I hope this experience was a pleasant one and you will participate in other market research projects in the future. Please remember that your opinion counts! Have a good day/evening.

Alternative: Participate in collecting respondent satisfaction data to improve survey quality.

Thank you very much for taking part in this survey. Because consumers like you are such a valued part of what we do, I'd like you to think about the survey you just participated in. On a scale from 1 to 10 where ten means "it was a good use of my time", and one means "it was not a good use of my time", which number between 1 and 10 best describes how you feel about your experience today? That's all the questions I have. Please remember that your opinion counts! Have a good day/evening.

Photo courtesy: Council for Marketing and Opinion Research (CMOR)

■ This script provides the general format for a survey conducted by the Council for Marketing and Opinion Research. Note that even in a telephone survey drawn from a random sample, the respondent has the opportunity to self-select out of the sample.

The most common form of telephone polls are random-digit dialing surveys, in which a computer randomly selects telephone numbers to be dialed. Because it is estimated that as many as 95 percent of the American public have telephones in their homes, samples selected in this manner are likely to be fairly representative, although the increasing use of cell phones, especially among young adults, may eventually affect this. In spite of some problems (such as the fact that many people do not want to be bothered, especially at dinner time), most polls done for newspapers and news magazines are conducted in this way. Pollsters, notably, are exempt from federal and state do-not-call lists because poll-taking is a form of constitutionally protected speech.

Individual, in-person interviews are conducted by some groups, such as the National Election Study. Some analysts favor such in-person surveys, but others argue that the unintended influence of the questioner or pollster is an important source of errors. How the pollster dresses, relates to the person being interviewed, and even asks the questions can affect responses. (Some of these factors, such as tone of voice or accent, can also affect the results of telephone surveys.)

POLITICAL POLLS

As polling has become increasingly sophisticated and networks, newspapers, and magazines compete with each other to report the most up-to-the-minute changes in public opinion on issues or politicians, new types of polls have been suggested and put into use. Each type of poll has contributed much to our knowledge of public opinion and its role in the political process.

Push Polls All good polls for political candidates contain push questions. These questions produce information that helps campaigns judge their own strengths and weaknesses as well as those of their opponents.[34] They might, for example, ask if you would be more likely to vote for candidate X if you knew that candidate was a strong environmentalist. These kinds of questions are accepted as an essential part of any poll, but there are concerns as to where to draw the line. Questions that go over the line result in **push**

push polls
Polls taken for the purpose of providing information on an opponent that would lead respondents to vote against that candidate.

polls, which are telephone polls with ulterior motives. Push polls are designed to give respondents some negative or even untruthful information about a candidate's opponent to push them away from that candidate and toward the one paying for the poll. Reputable polling firms eschew these tactics. A typical push poll might ask a question such as "If you knew Candidate X beat his wife, would you vote for him?" Push poll takers don't even bother to record the responses because they are irrelevant. The questions are designed simply to push as many voters away from a candidate as possible. Push poll calls are made to thousands; legitimate polls survey much smaller samples.

Although campaign organizations generally deny conducting push polls, research shows that more than three-quarters of political candidates have been a victim of push polling. These numbers are likely to grow as the Internet becomes a more important campaign tool—unregulated online polls and mass e-mails have the potential to reach thousands of Internet users.

tracking polls
Continuous surveys that enable a campaign to chart its daily rise or fall in support.

Tracking Polls   During the 1992 presidential elections, **tracking polls,** which were taken on a daily basis by some news organizations, were first introduced to allow presidential candidates to monitor short-term campaign developments and the effects of their campaign strategies. Tracking polls involve small samples (usually of registered voters contacted at certain times of day) and are conducted every twenty-four hours. They usually are combined statistically with some other data to produce a statistical average to boost the sample size and therefore statistical reliability.[35] Even though such one-day surveys are fraught with reliability problems and are vulnerable to bias, many major news organizations continue their use. As revealed in Figure 11.6, the 2004 tracking polls, in spite of receiving significant criticism for their performance in 2000, performed quite well and predicted a Bush victory.

exit polls
Polls conducted at selected polling places on Election Day.

Exit Polls   **Exit polls** are polls conducted at selected polling places on Election Day. Generally, large news organizations send pollsters to selected precincts to sample

FIGURE 11.6 A DAILY TRACKING POLL FOR THE 2004 PRESIDENTIAL ELECTION
The day-to-day fluctuations in presidential and congressional races are often shown through tracking polls. This figure shows the ups and downs of the 2004 presidential election.

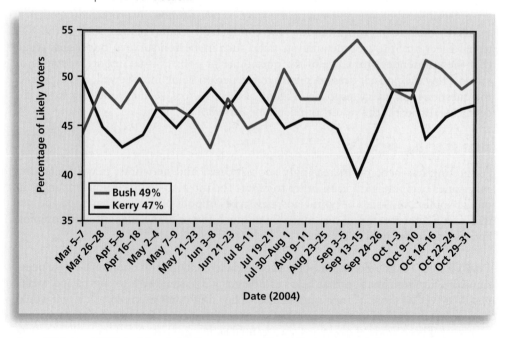

Source: USA Today and CNN/Gallup Poll results, http://www.usatoday.com/news/politicselections/nation/polls/usatodaypolls.htm.

every tenth voter as he or she emerges from the polling site. The results of these polls are used to help the media predict the outcome of key races, often just a few minutes after the polls close in a particular state and generally before voters in other areas— sometimes in a later time zone—have cast their ballots. They also provide an independent assessment of why voters supported particular candidates.

In 1980, President Jimmy Carter's own polling and the results of network exit polls led him to concede defeat three hours before the polls closed on the West Coast. Many Democratic party officials and candidates criticized Carter and network predictions for harming their chances at victories, arguing that with the presidential election already called, voters were unlikely to go to the polls. In the aftermath of that controversy, all networks agreed not to predict the results of presidential contests until all polling places were closed. Exit polls continue to be problematic. In 2000, they led newscasters to inaccurately call Florida in the Gore column, as discussed in our opening vignette and below. In 2004, mid-afternoon exit poll results that were leaked on the Internet made many believe a Kerry victory was at hand. Whether Republicans voted later, Democrats were more willing to be polled, or for other reasons, the exit polls were wrong. In 2006, exit polls were conducted in states with senatorial races and paid for by the major news networks and the Associated Press. Pollsters were sequestered and no results were available until the polls had closed.

SHORTCOMINGS OF POLLING

The information derived from public opinion polls has become an extremely important part of governance. When the results of a poll are accurate, they express the feelings of the electorate in unique way and help guide the creation of public policy. However, when the results of a poll are inaccurate, disastrous consequences often result. For example, during the 2000 presidential election, Voter News Service (VNS), the conglomerate organization that provided the major networks with their exit poll data, made a host of errors in estimating the results of the election in Florida, as noted in our opening vignette. Not only did VNS fail to estimate the number of voters accurately, but it also used an inaccurate exit poll model and incorrectly estimated the number of African American and Cuban voters. These errors came together in VNS's exit poll prediction and caused the major networks to call the state of Florida, and thus the entire presidential election, too early and incorrectly. Early reports on the 2006 midterm elections found the exit polls more reliable than in past years.

It got worse in 2002. VNS, in spite of pledges to improve its act, announced midday that there would be no exit poll data revealed, leaving the networks with no data to project winners or discuss turnout or issues. Finally, in January 2003, VNS was disbanded. In November 2004, the major networks and the Associated Press joined in a new polling consortium, the National Election Pool. Its data, like that of VNS, also were riddled with errors. Its subscribers were quite unhappy and the fate of exit polls on Election Day remains in doubt, given their poor track record in predicting winners in the past three national elections. Early reports on the 2006 midterm elections found the exit polls more reliable than in past years.

Sampling Error The accuracy of any poll depends on the quality of the sample that was drawn. Small samples, if properly drawn, can be very accurate if each unit in the universe has an equal opportunity to be sampled. If a pollster, for example, fails to sample certain populations, his or her results may reflect that shortcoming. Often the opinions of the poor and homeless are underrepresented because insufficient attention is given to making certain that these groups are sampled representatively. For example, in the case of tracking polls, if you choose to sample only on weekends or from 5 p.m. to 9 p.m., you may get more Republicans, who tend to have higher incomes and are less likely to be working shift work or multiple jobs. The 1992 CNN/Gallup poll,

Peter Steiner

Photo courtesy: Peter Steiner/Cartoon Bank

■ Politicians' dependence on public opinion polls are well documented and can provide political cartoonists with an opportunity to poke fun at them, as this cartoon shows.

sampling error or margin of error
A measure of the accuracy of a public opinion poll.

for example, used two different time periods—weekdays 5 p.m. to 9 p.m. and all day on the weekends. Midweek surveys produced candidate distributions that disproportionately favored George Bush over Bill Clinton, while weekend surveys showed the reverse. There comes a point in sampling, however, where increases in the size of the sample have little effect on a reduction of the **sampling error** (also called the **margin of error**), the difference between the actual universe and the sample.

All polls contain errors. Standard samples of approximately 1,000 to 1,500 individuals provide fairly good estimates of actual behavior (in the case of voting, for example). Typically, the margin of error in a sample of 1,500 will be about 3 percent. If you ask 1,500 people "Do you like ice cream?" and 52 percent say yes and 48 percent say no, the results are too close to tell whether more people like ice cream than not. Why? Because the margin of error implies that somewhere between 55 percent (52 + 3) and 49 percent (52–3) of the people like ice cream, while between 51 percent (48 + 3) and 45 percent (48–3) do not. The margin of error in a close election makes predictions very difficult.

Limited Respondent Options Polls can be inaccurate when they limit responses. If you are asked, "How do you like this class?" and are given only like or dislike options, your full sentiments may not be tapped if you like the class very much or feel only so-so about it. The political identification poll reflected in Figure 11.1 provided respondents with five options.

Lack of Information Public opinion polls may also be inaccurate when they attempt to gauge attitudes about issues that some or even many individuals do not care about or about which the public has little information. For example, until the 2000 election, few Americans cared about the elimination of the Electoral College. If a representative sample had been polled prior to 2000, many would have answered pro or con without having given much consideration to the question.

Most academic public opinion research organizations, such as the National Election Study, use some kind of filter question that first asks respondents whether or not they have thought about the question. These screening procedures generally allow surveyors to exclude as many as 20 percent of their respondents, especially on complex issues like the federal budget. Questions on more personal issues such as moral values, drugs, crime, race, and women's role in society get far fewer "no opinion" or "don't know" responses.

Difficulty Measuring Intensity Another shortcoming of polls concerns their inability to measure intensity of feeling about particular issues. Whereas a respondent might answer affirmatively to any question, it is likely that his or her feelings about issues such as abortion, the death penalty, or support for U.S. troops in Afghanistan or Iraq are much more intense than are his or her feelings about the Electoral College or types of voting machines.

Why We Form and Express Political Opinions

OFTEN, THE SENTIMENTS WE EXPRESS in public opinion polls can be traced to our political socialization. However, most people also are influenced by a number of other factors, including: (1) personal benefits; (2) political knowledge; (3) cues from various leaders or opinion makers; and, (4) their political ideology.

PERSONAL BENEFITS

Most polls reveal that Americans are growing more and more "I" centered. This perspective often leads people to agree with policies that will benefit them personally. You've probably heard the adage "People vote with their pocketbooks." Taxpayers generally favor lower taxes, hence the popularity of candidates pledging "No new taxes." Elderly people are likely to support Social Security increases, while people in their thirties or forties, worried about the continued stability of the Social Security program, are not likely to be very supportive of federal retirement programs. Traditional-age college students appear even less willing to support retirement programs. Similarly, African Americans are likely to support strong civil rights laws and affirmative action programs, while a majority of nonminorities will not.

Some government policies, however, don't really affect us individually. Legalized prostitution and the death penalty, for example, are often perceived as moral issues that directly affect few citizens. Individual's attitudes on these issues often are based on underlying values they have acquired through the years.

When we are faced with policies that don't affect us personally and don't involve moral issues, we often have difficulty forming an opinion. Foreign policy is an area in which this phenomenon is especially true. Most Americans often know little of the world around them. Unless moral issues such as prisoner abuse in Iraq are involved, American public opinion is likely to be volatile in the wake of any new information.

POLITICAL KNOWLEDGE

Political knowledge and political participation have a reciprocal effect on one another—an increase in one will increase the other.[36] Knowledge about the political system is essential to successful political involvement, which, in turn, teaches citizens about politics and increases their interest in public affairs.[37] And, although few citizens know everything about all of the candidates and issues in a particular election, they can, and often do, know enough to impose their views and values as to the general direction the nation should take.[38]

Political Knowledge

This is true despite the fact that most Americans' level of knowledge about history and politics is quite low (see Table 11.3). A 2002 U.S. Department of Education report, for example, found that most high school seniors had a poor grasp of history and that levels of knowledge haven't changed in nearly a decade.[39] Fifty-two percent didn't know that Russia was an ally of the United States in World War II, and 63 percent didn't know that President Richard M. Nixon opened diplomatic relations with China. According to the Department of Education, today's college graduates have less civic knowledge than high school graduates did fifty years ago.[40]

Americans also don't appear to know much about foreign policy, and some critics would argue that many Americans are geographically illiterate. One National Geographic Society study done in late 2002, for example, showed that 87 percent of Americans age eighteen to twenty-four could not find Iraq on a map, despite the attention the nation received in the media. Similarly, an astounding 49 percent of young Americans could not find New York on a map, and 10 percent of all Americans could not locate the United States.[41]

There are also significant gender differences in political knowledge. For example, one 2004 study done by the Annenberg Public Policy Center found that men were consistently more able than women to identify the candidates' issue positions.[42] This gender gap in knowledge, which has existed for the last fifty years, perplexes scholars, because women consistently vote in higher numbers than males of similar income and education levels.

TABLE 11.3 AMERICANS' POLITICAL KNOWLEDGE

	Percentage Unable to Identify
Number of senators (2002)	52
Representative in the House (2002)	53
Speaker of the House (2004)	89
British Prime Minister (2004)	35
Chief Justice of the Supreme Court (2004)	69

Sources: "A Nation That Is in the Dark," *San Diego Union-Tribune* (November 3, 2002): E3; John Wilkens, "America Faces a Crisis of Apathy," *San Diego Union-Tribune* (November 3, 2002): E3; and data compiled by Alixandra B. Yanus from the 2004 American National Election Study.

CUES FROM LEADERS

As early as 1966, noted political scientist V. O. Key Jr. argued in *The Responsible Electorate* that voters "are not fools."[43] Still, low levels of knowledge can lead to rapid opinion shifts on issues. The ebb and flow of popular opinion can be affected dramatically (some cynics might say manipulated) by political leaders. Given the visibility of political leaders and their access to the media, it is easy to see the important role they play in influencing public opinion. Political leaders, members of the news media, and a host of other experts have regular opportunities to influence public opinion because of the lack of deep conviction with which most Americans hold many of their political beliefs.[44]

The president, especially, is often in a position to mold public opinion through effective use of the bully pulpit, as discussed in chapter 8.[45] Political scientist John E. Mueller concludes, in fact, that there is a group of citizens—called followers—who are inclined to rally to the support of the president no matter what he does.[46]

According to Mueller, the president's strength, especially in the area of foreign affairs (where public information is lowest), derives from the majesty of his office and his singular position as head of state. Recognizing this phenomenon, presidents often take to television in an effort to drum up support for their programs.[47] President George W. Bush, borrowing a page from Presidents Ronald Reagan and Bill Clinton, clearly realizes the importance of mobilizing public opinion. He took his case for the wars in Afghanistan and Iraq as well as Social Security privatization directly to the public, urging citizens to support his efforts. These efforts, however, are not always successful. The Iraq War, for example, contributed to President Bush's fall in public opinion polls. (See Politics Now: Public Opinion and Political Capital.)

POLITICAL IDEOLOGY

political ideology
The coherent set of values and beliefs about the purpose and scope of government held by groups and individuals.

As discussed in chapter 1, an individual's coherent set of values and beliefs about the purpose and scope of government is called his or her **political ideology.** Americans' attachment to strong ideological positions has varied over time. In sharp contrast to spur-of-the-moment responses, these sets of values, which are often greatly affected by political socialization, can prompt citizens to favor a certain set of policy programs and adopt views about the proper role of government in the policy process.

Conservatives generally are likely to support smaller, less activist governments, limited social welfare programs, and reduced government regulation of business. Increasingly, they also have very strong views on social issues, including abortion and same-sex marriage. In contrast, liberals generally believe that the national government has an important role to play in a wide array of areas, including helping the poor and the disadvantaged. Unlike most conservatives, they generally favor activist governments. Most Americans today, however, identify themselves as moderates.

Political scientists and politicians often talk in terms of conservative and liberal ideologies, and most Americans believe that they hold a conservative or liberal political ideology. When asked by the Roper Center, although 35 percent of Americans responded that their political beliefs were moderate, 30 percent labeled themselves as conservative. A similar number—29 percent—described themselves as liberal. Six percent of those polled "didn't know" or refused to label themselves. (For more information on political ideology, see Figure 1.5, page 22.)

VISUAL LITERACY
Who Are Liberals and Conservatives?

PARTICIPATION
Are You a Liberal or a Conservative?

The Effects of Public Opinion and Polling on Government and Politics

AS EARLY AS THE FOUNDING PERIOD, the authors of *The Federalist Papers* noted that "all government rests on public opinion," and as a result, public opinion inevitably

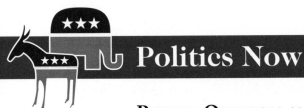

Politics Now

PUBLIC OPINION AND POLITICAL CAPITAL

In early 2006, much was made of President George W. Bush's declining approval ratings—a trajectory that is determined through a series of public opinion polls. And, while any person who has survived high school can understand the dilemmas that come with being unpopular, when you're the president of the United States, these problems are magnified exponentially.

For presidents and other public figures, approval ratings are often used as tacit measures of their political capital: their ability to enact public policy simply because of their name and their office. Presidents who have high approval ratings, as President Bush did in the immediate aftermath of September 11, 2001, are assumed to be more powerful leaders with a mandate for action that comes largely by virtue of the high levels of public support they enjoy. They are often able to use their clout to push controversial legislation, such as the USA Patriot Act, through Congress. A public appearance from a popular president can even deliver a hotly contested congressional seat or gubernatorial contest to the president's party.

In sharp contrast, presidents with low approval ratings are often crippled in the policy arena. Their low ratings can actually prevent favored policies from being enacted on Capitol Hill, even when their party controls the legislature, as many of their partisans locked in close elections shy away from being seen or affiliated with an unpopular president.

Because of the public opinion–political capital connection, President Bush's approval ratings, which hovered around 30 percent in July 2006, were a major concern for his advisers. Not only did the president hope to achieve significant legislative goals such as immigration reform, privatization of Social Security, and a constitutional amendment to ban same-sex marriage, but 2006 was a midterm election year and the House and Senate were within the reach of the Democrats.

Early failures on Social Security reform and the same-sex marriage amendment and the president's initial immigration bill were viewed by many as casualties of Bush's approval ratings and his newfound inability to secure support in Congress. As one Republican pollster commented, "[Bush] has no political capital. Slowly but surely it's been unraveling. There's been a direct correlation between the trajectory of his approval numbers and the—I don't want to call it disloyalty—the independence on the part of the Republicans in Congress."[a]

In spite of, or perhaps because of, these legislative failures, the president and vice president's fund-raising appear-

■ President George W. Bush campaigns for incumbent Senator Rick Santorum (R–PA) in the spring of 2006. Santorum's reelection bid was ultimately unsuccessful.

ances for the Republican Party quickly eclipsed anything they had done during the 2002 midterm elections. Six months before the 2006 midterm elections, Bush had made thirty-two fund-raising stops, and Vice President Dick Cheney had made a remarkable sixty-two.[b]

By the week before the election, President Bush's approval ratings remained below 40 percent. A number of Republican candidates in close elections asked President Bush not to campaign in their districts. The Republican National Committee sent First Lady Laura Bush and more moderate Republicans such as Representative John McCain (R–AZ) to rally supporters instead. Other Republicans in close elections chose to downplay their affiliation with the president and his policies, choosing instead to tout their records of bipartisan support and cooperation with former President Bill Clinton.

[a]Quoted in Peter Baker, "In an Election Year, GOP Wary of Following Bush," *Washington Post* (March 10, 2006): A6.

[b]Peter Baker and Jim VandeHei, "Elections Are Crux of GOP's Strategy," *Washington Post* (May 22, 2006): A1.

---

influences the actions of politicians and public officials. The public's perception of crime as a problem, for example, was the driving force behind the comprehensive crime bill President Bill Clinton submitted to Congress in 1994. The public's concern with crime skyrocketed to an all-time high in 1994, when 37 percent of the public rated crime as the nation's most important problem, and politicians at all levels were quick to convert that concern into a campaign issue.

VIDEO ROUNDTABLE

Public Opinion and Leadership

Although politicians and government officials spend millions of dollars each year taking the pulse of the public, it is difficult to determine how much they rely on this data. Several political scientists have attempted to study whether public policy is responsive to public opinion, with mixed results.[48] As we have seen, public opinion can fluctuate, making it difficult for a politician or policy maker to assess. Some critics of polls and of their use by politicians argue that polls hurt democracy and make leaders weaker. Political scientist Benjamin Ginsberg, one of these critics, argues that widespread use of polling by politicians weakens democracy.[49] He claims that polls allow governments and politicians to say that they have considered public opinion even though polls don't always measure the intensity of feeling on an issue or might over-reflect the views of the public because of responders who lack sufficient information to make educated choices. Ginsberg further argues that democracy is better served by politicians' reliance on telephone calls and letters—active signs of interest—than on the passive voice of public opinion. Some observers worry that politicians rely on poll results rather than a thoughtful debate of the issues to determine their actions, arguing that the outcome of polls determines individual policy positions. In response to this argument, George Gallup retorted, "One might as well insist that a thermometer makes the weather."[50]

Polls can clearly distort the election process by creating what are called bandwagon and underdog effects. In a presidential campaign, an early victory in the Iowa caucuses or the New Hampshire primary, for example, can boost an underdog candidate's standings in the polls as the rest of the nation begins to think of him or her in a more positive light. New supporters jump on the bandwagon. A strong showing in the polls, in turn, can generate more and larger donations, the lifeblood of any campaign. However, the opposite can also happen, turning a front-runner into an underdog. One political scientist has noted that "bad poll results, as well as poor primary and caucus standings, may deter potential donors from supporting a failing campaign."[51]

Summary

PUBLIC OPINION is a subject constantly mentioned in the media, especially in presidential election years or when important policies are under consideration. What public opinion is, where it comes from, how it is measured, and how it is used are aspects of a complex subject. To that end, this chapter has made the following points:

1. **Political Socialization**

   The first step in forming opinions occurs through a process called political socialization. Our family, school, peers, social groups—including religion, race, ethnicity, gender, and age—as well as where we live and the impact of events all affect how we view political events and issues. Even the views of other people affect our ultimate opinions on a variety of issues, including race relations, the death penalty, abortion, and federal taxes.

2. **Public Opinion and Polling**

   Public opinion is what the public thinks about an issue or a particular set of issues. Public opinion polls are used to estimate public opinion. Almost since the beginning of the United States, various attempts have been made to influence public opinion about particular issues or to sway elections. Modern-day polling did not begin until the 1930s, however.

   Over the years, polling to measure public opinion has become increasingly sophisticated and more accurate because pollsters are better able to sample the public in their effort to determine their attitudes and positions on issues. Polls, however, have several shortcomings, including sampling error, limited respondent options, lack of information, and difficulty measuring intensity.

3. **Why We Form and Express Political Opinions**

   Myriad factors enter our minds as we form opinions about political matters. These include a calculation about the personal benefits involved, degree of personal political knowledge, cues from leaders, and political ideology.

4. **The Effects of Public Opinion and Polling on Government and Politics**

   Knowledge of the public's views on issues is often used by politicians to tailor campaigns or to drive policy decisions.

KEY TERMS

SELECTED READINGS

Althaus, Scott L. *Collective Preferences in Democratic Politics: Opinion Surveys and the Will of the People*. New York: Cambridge University Press, 2003.

Alvarez, R. Michael, and John Brehm. *Easy Answers, Hard Choices: Values, Information, and American Public Opinion*. Princeton, NJ: Princeton University Press, 2002.

Asher, Herbert. *Polling and the Public: What Every Citizen Should Know*, 6th ed. Washington, DC: CQ Press, 2004.

Erikson, Robert S., and Kent L. Tedin. *American Public Opinion: Its Origins, Contents, and Impact*, 7th ed. New York: Longman, 2004.

Erikson, Robert S., Michael B. MacKuen, and James A. Stimson. *The Macro Polity*. New York: Cambridge University Press, 2002.

Fishkin, James S. *The Voice of the People: Public Opinion and Democracy*. New Haven, CT: Yale University Press, 1997.

Herbst, Susan. *Numbered Voices: How Opinion Polling Has Shaped American Politics*. Chicago: University of Chicago Press, 1993.

Jamieson, Kathleen Hall. *Everything You Think You Know About Politics . . . And Why You Were Wrong*. New York: Basic Books, 2000.

Key, V. O., Jr. *Public Opinion and American Democracy*. New York: Knopf, 1961.

Manza, Jeff, ed. *Navigating Public Opinion: Polls, Policy, and the Future of American Democracy*. New York: Oxford University Press, 2002.

Mutz, Diana Carole. *Impersonal Influence: How Perceptions of Mass Collectives Affect Political Attitudes*. New York: Cambridge University Press, 1998.

Norrander, Barbara, and Clyde Wilcox, eds. *Understanding Public Opinion*, 2nd ed. Washington, DC: CQ Press, 2001.

Stimson, James A. *The Tides of Consent: How Public Opinion Shapes American Politics*. New York: Cambridge University Press, 2004.

Warren, Kenneth F. *In Defense of Public Opinion Polling*. Boulder, CO: Westview, 2001.

Zaller, John. *The Nature and Origins of Mass Opinions*. New York: Cambridge University Press, 1992.

WEB EXPLORATIONS

To learn more about the Gallup Organization and poll trends, see
http://www.gallup.com

To use NES data sets, go to
http://www.umich.edu/~nes/

For the most recent Roper Center polls, see
http://www.ropercenter.uconn.edu

To test your own political knowledge, go to
http://www.ablongman.com/oconnor

To see an example of a nonstratified poll, go to
http://www.cnn.com

POLITICAL PARTIES

IN JULY 2004, the Democrats used the city of Boston to formally launch the nomination of John Kerry as their candidate for president of the United States. A few weeks later, from New York, the Republicans followed by renaming President George W. Bush their candidate. The televised convention proceedings and morning papers focused on the nominations of these two men and their personal attributes. Relatively little attention, however, was paid to the importance of the party platforms, the official statements that detail each party's positions on key public policy issues. Party platforms are often taken for granted, certainly by the news media, and even by many political activists. They are rarely noted by American voters, many of whom are cynical about the idea that parties stand for anything other than gaining power.

How wrong the cynics are. The Republicans' platform, entitled "A Safer World and a More Hopeful America," strongly defended the policies of the Bush administration, including the invasion of Iraq, a country they described as a "great and gathering" danger to American interests at home and abroad. The Democrats' platform, "Strong at Home, Respected in the World," pointed to the Bush administration's failure to find the weapons of mass destruction that had been said to constitute such a threat, and to the failure of the administration to bring peace to the region.

The platforms were filled with differing policy perspectives. The Republicans insisted that President Bush's 2001 and 2003 tax cuts were essential to rebuilding a weakened American economy. The Democrats argued that the tax cuts had created enormous national deficits to be paid off by future generations and had disproportionately benefited the richest Americans. The Republicans continued their strong pro-life stance on the issue of abortion, their most recent success being a federal ban on the late-term abortion procedure that pro-life groups call partial birth abortion. Democrats made no mention of this ban but reiterated their commitment to a woman's right to make her own choices with regard to pregnancy and reproductive health. The abortion issue had increased salience for the parties as Supreme Court vacancies were forecast by interest groups on both sides and the future of abortion rights (1973) came into question. Republicans were opposed to same-sex marriages, and the party platform sup- ported President Bush's call for a constitutional amendment to ban same-sex marriage. Democrats opposed amending the Constitution and asserted their belief that marriage should be defined at the state level. (See Table 12.1 for excerpts from the party platforms.)

LONG AFTER MEMORIES of the national conventions have faded, the issues embodied by the party platforms persist. In the first half of his second term, President George W. Bush aggressively pursued the foreign policy objectives laid out in his party's platform by continuing the war on terrorism abroad and by pursuing an equally aggressive domestic policy against terrorism. Consistent with the party platform, the president fought for pro-business policies and a preservation of the current tax cuts, as well as the partial privatization of Social Security. He pursued the Republican Party's stated social issues, most notably by nominating conservative jurists John G. Roberts Jr. and Samuel A. Alito Jr. to fill vacancies on the Supreme Court.

In fact, the policy differences outlined in the platforms and pursued by the president stretch well beyond presidential politics, as these same themes echoed throughout the country in the 2006 midterm elections. Once again the parties differed on issues related to foreign policy and national security, taxation, and social issues such as same-sex marriage and abortion. Republicans lost six Senate races, giving Democrats control of the chamber for the first time since 2000. In the House, Republicans fared even worse, especially in battleground states like Pennsylvania and Ohio, losing a total of 30 seats and the majority.

As this chapter will discuss, party positions really matter, as they give voters important choices in the electoral process and help guide the direction of the nation. Political parties have been influencing American life for over two centuries and, in one form or another, they will most likely continue to direct American politics in the future. In this chapter we will address contemporary party politics by examining them from many vantage points. Our discussion of political parties will trace their development from their infancy in the late 1700s to their status today:

- First, we will answer the question, *what is a political party?*
- Second, we will look at *the evolution of the American party system.*
- Third, we will examine *the functions of the American party system.*
- Fourth, we will explore the formal structure of *the party organization.*
- Fifth, we will uncover *the party in government,* the office holders and candidates who govern under a party's banner.
- Sixth, we will look at *the party in the electorate,* showing the parties' tenuous hold on the electorate.
- Finally, we will discuss the likely future of party influence in the United States as we explore the question, *is the party over or has it just begun?*

	TABLE 12.1 **PARTY PLATFORMS: MODERATE BUT DIFFERENT**	

As most Americans have moderate political views and the aim of political parties is to attract voters, the platforms of the two dominant parties tend to be moderate in tone and sometimes similar in substance, though the differences below the rhetoric are often profound.

	Democratic Platform	*Republican Platform*
Environment	For generations, Americans of all political beliefs have understood that the protection of our environment and the stewardship of our land are vital to the strength of our nation. God gave America extraordinary natural gifts; it is our responsibility to protect them. The health of our families, the strength of our economy, and the well-being of our world all depend upon a clean environment.	Republicans know that economic prosperity is essential to environmental progress. That belief is supported by compelling historical evidence. For example, over the last 30 years, air pollution from the six major pollutants decreased substantially, even as our population grew, our energy consumption increased, and the economy expanded.
Abortion	We will defend the dignity of all Americans against those who would undermine it. Because we believe in the privacy and equality of women, we stand proudly for a woman's right to choose, consistent with *Roe* v. *Wade*, and regardless of her ability to pay. We stand firmly against Republican efforts to undermine that right. At the same time, we strongly support family planning and adoption incentives. Abortion should be safe, legal, and rare.	As a country, we must keep our pledge to the first guarantee of the Declaration of Independence. That is why we say the unborn child has a fundamental individual right to life which cannot be infringed. We support a human life amendment to the Constitution and we endorse legislation to make it clear that the Fourteenth Amendment's protections apply to unborn children.
Marriage	We support full inclusion of gay and lesbian families in the life of our nation and seek equal responsibilities, benefits, and protections for these families. In our country, marriage has been defined at the state level for 200 years, and we believe it should continue to be defined there. We repudiate President Bush's divisive effort to politicize the Constitution by pursuing a "federal Marriage Amendment." Our goal is to bring Americans together, not divide them apart.	We strongly support President Bush's call for a constitutional amendment that fully protects marriage, and we believe that neither federal nor state judges nor bureaucrats should force states to recognize other living arrangements as equivalent to marriage. We believe, and social science confirms, that the well-being of children is best accomplished in the environment of the home, nurtured by their mother and father anchored by the bonds of marriage.
Taxation	First, we must restore our values to our tax code. We want a tax code that rewards work and creates wealth for more people, not a tax code that hoards wealth for those who already have it. With the middle class under assault like never before, we simply cannot afford the massive Bush tax cuts for the very wealthiest.	We believe that good government is based on a system of limited taxes and spending. Furthermore, we believe that the federal government should be limited and restricted to the functions mandated by the United States Constitution. The taxation system should not be used to redistribute wealth or fund ever-increasing entitlements and social programs.

Note: Excerpts are taken directly from the relevant sections of the 2004 party platforms.

Sources: http://www.gop.com/media/2004platform.pdf and http://www.democrats.org/pdfs/2004platform.pdf.

What Is a Political Party?

AT THE MOST BASIC LEVEL, a **political party** is an organized effort by office holders, candidates, activists, and voters to pursue their common interests by gaining and exercising power through the electoral process. Notice how pragmatic this concept of party is. The goal is to win office so as to exercise power, not just to compete for office. While the party label carries with it messages about ideology and issue positions, political parties are not narrowly focused interest groups—organized groups that try to influence public policy (see chapter 16). Interest groups exist to pursue issue outcomes, while political parties have traditionally existed to win elections. Stated differently, interest groups use elections to pursue their policy objectives, while parties make use of issues to pursue their electoral goals. The difference is a matter of emphasis, with parties stressing the role of elections in gaining and exercising power. Indeed, as

political party
An organized effort by office holders, candidates, activists, and voters to pursue their common interests by gaining and exercising power through the electoral process.

one observer noted, parties and interest group allies now work together so closely that "the traditional lines of demarcation between parties and interest groups are no longer clear."[1]

Political scientists sometimes describe political parties as consisting of three separate but related entities: (1) the office holders who organize themselves and pursue policy objectives under a party label (the **governmental party**); (2) the workers and activists who make up the party's formal organization structure (the **organizational party**); and, (3) the voters who consider themselves allied or associated with the party (the **party in the electorate**).[2] In this chapter, we examine all three components of political parties—the organizational party, the governmental party, and the party in the electorate. First, however, we turn to the history and development of political parties in the United States.

governmental party
The office holders who organize themselves and pursue policy objectives under a party label.

organizational party
The workers and activists who make up the party's formal organization structure.

party in the electorate
The voters who consider themselves allied or associated with the party.

The Evolution of the American Party System

IT IS ONE OF THE GREAT IRONIES of the early republic that George Washington's public farewell, which warned the nation against parties, marked the effective end of the brief era of partyless politics in the United States (see Figure 12.1). Washington's unifying influence ebbed as he stepped off the national stage, and his vice president and successor, John Adams, occupied a much less exalted position. To win the presidency in 1796, Adams narrowly defeated his arch-rival Thomas Jefferson, who according to the existing rules of the Constitution became vice president. Over the course of Adams's single term, two competing congressional factions, the Federalists and Democratic-Republicans, gradually organized around these clashing men and their principles: Adams and his Federalist allies supported a strong central government; the Democratic-Republicans of Thomas Jefferson and his allies inherited the mantle of the Anti-Federalists (see chapter 2) and preferred a federal system in which the states retained the balance of power. (Jefferson actually preferred the simpler name "Republicans," a very different group from today's party of the same name, but Alexander Hamilton, a leading Federalist, insisted on calling the group "Democratic-Republicans," an attempt to disparage the group by linking them to the radical democrats of the French Revolution.) In the presidential election of 1800, the Federalists supported Adams's bid for a second term, but this time the Democratic-Republicans prevailed with their nominee, Jefferson, who became the first U.S. president elected as the nominee of a political party. (See The Living Constitution)

Jefferson was deeply committed to the ideas of his party but not nearly as devoted to the idea of a party system. He regarded his party as a temporary measure necessary to defeat Adams, not a long-term political tool or an essential element of democracy. Jefferson's party never achieved widespread loyalty among the citizenry akin to that of today's Democrats and Republicans. Although Southerners were overwhelmingly partial to the Democratic-Republicans and New Englanders favored the Federalists, no broad-based party organizations existed to mobilize popular support. Rather, the congressional factions organized around Adams and Jefferson were primarily governmental parties designed to settle the dispute over how strong the new federal government would be.[3] Just as the nation was in its infancy, so, too, was the party system.

THE EARLY PARTIES FADE

After the spirited confrontations of the republic's early years, political parties faded somewhat in importance for a quarter of a century. The Federalists ceased nominating

FIGURE 12.1 AMERICAN PARTY HISTORY AT A GLANCE

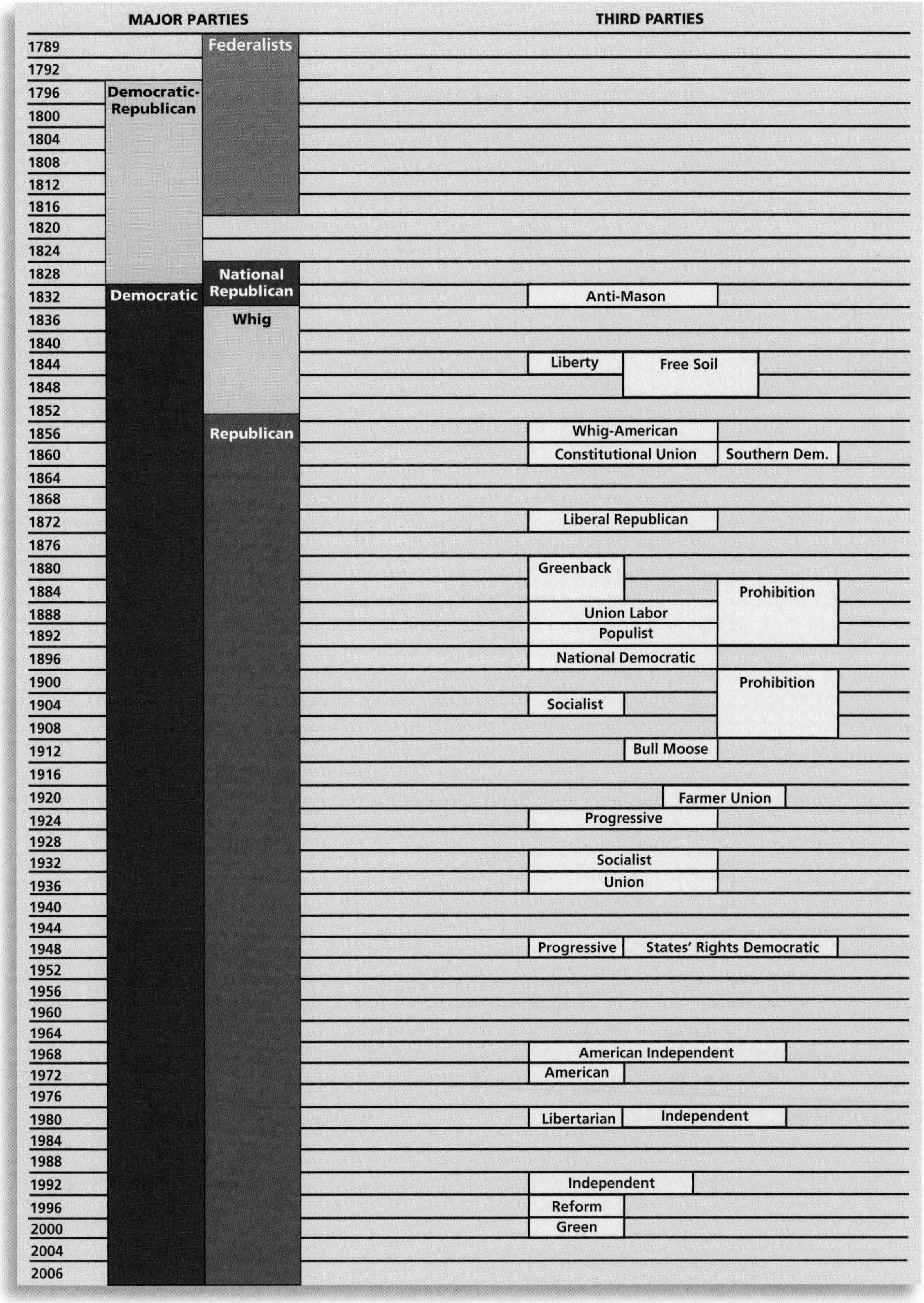

	MAJOR PARTIES		THIRD PARTIES
1789		Federalists	
1792			
1796	Democratic-Republican		
1800			
1804			
1808			
1812			
1816			
1820			
1824			
1828		National Republican	
1832	Democratic		Anti-Mason
1836		Whig	
1840			
1844			Liberty Free Soil
1848			
1852			
1856		Republican	Whig-American
1860			Constitutional Union Southern Dem.
1864			
1868			
1872			Liberal Republican
1876			
1880			Greenback
1884			Prohibition
1888			Union Labor
1892			Populist
1896			National Democratic
1900			Prohibition
1904			Socialist
1908			
1912			Bull Moose
1916			
1920			Farmer Union
1924			Progressive
1928			
1932			Socialist
1936			Union
1940			
1944			
1948			Progressive States' Rights Democratic
1952			
1956			
1960			
1964			
1968			American Independent
1972			American
1976			
1980			Libertarian Independent
1984			
1988			
1992			Independent
1996			Reform
2000			Green
2004			
2006			

Note: Chart lists political parties that received at least 1 percent of the presidential vote.

Source: Harold W. Stanley and Richard G. Niemi, Vital Statistics on American Politics, 2005–2006 (Washington, DC: CQ Press, 2006).

The Living Constitution

It is difficult to imagine modern American politics without the political parties, but where in the text of Constitution do we find the provision to establish them?

Nowhere in the Constitution do we find a provision establishing political parties. Some might point out that the First Amendment establishes the right to assemble as a Constitutional right, and this right certainly helps to preserve and protect parties from governmental oppression during rallies and conventions. However, the right to assembly is not the same as permission for two organizations to mediate elections. Furthermore, James Madison, in *Federalist No. 10*, feared that one of the greatest dangers to the new American republic was a majority tyranny created by the domination of a single faction fighting for one set of interests, so he hoped that extending the sphere of representation among many members of Congress would prevent a majority of representatives from coming together to vote as a bloc.

Of course, parties are *not* like the factions Madison describes. Parties today seem to embody Madison's principle of the extended sphere of representation. Neither of the two major political parties is monolithic in its beliefs; rather, both parties constantly reconsider their platforms in light of the changes of the various constituencies they try to represent. The Republicans have both Senator Olympia Snowe (ME), who is pro-choice and pro-environment, and Representative Roy Blunt (MO), who is pro-life and pro-business. Democrats have both Representative Dennis Kucinich (OH), who advocates withdrawal from the North American Free Trade Agreement, and Governor Bill Richardson (NM), who balances various racial/ethnic concerns and business interests while trying to protect the border between the U.S. and Mexico. Both comparisons yield differences in interests, the kind of things Madison wanted.

Finally, Madison himself actually belonged to two early American political parties during his public service, first the Federalists and later the Democratic-Republicans. In fact, it is because of the Federalist Party that we have a Constitution today. Federalists compromised with Anti-Federalists to provide a Bill of Rights so long as the Anti-Federalists would stop opposing ratification of the Constitution. So parties are not so much *in* the Constitution as *behind* the Constitution, first behind its ratification and, today, behind its preservation of diverse interests.

presidential candidates by 1816, having failed to elect one of their own since Adams's victory in 1796, and by 1820 the party had dissolved. James Monroe's presidency from 1817 to 1825 produced the so-called Era of Good Feeling, when party politics was nearly suspended at the national level. Even during Monroe's tenure, though, party organizations continued to develop at the state level. Party growth was fueled in part by the enormous increase in the electorate that took place between 1820 and 1840, as the United States expanded westward and most states abolished property requirements as a condition of white male suffrage. During this twenty-year period, the number of votes cast in presidential contests rose from 300,000 to more than 2 million.

At the same time, U.S. politics was being democratized in other ways. By the 1820s, all the states except South Carolina had switched from state legislative selection of presidential electors to popular election of Electoral College members. This change helped transform presidential politics. No longer just the concern of society's upper crust, the election of the president became a matter for all qualified voters to decide.

Party membership broadened along with the electorate. After receiving criticism for being elitist and undemocratic, the small caucuses of congressional party leaders that had previously nominated candidates gave way to nominations at large party conventions. In 1832, the Democratic Party, which succeeded the old Jeffersonian Democratic-Republicans, held the first national presidential nomination convention. Formed around President Andrew Jackson's popularity, the Democratic Party attracted most of the newly enfranchised voters, who were drawn to Jackson's charismatic style. His strong personality helped to polarize politics, and opposition to the president coalesced into the Whig Party. Among the Whig Party's early leaders was Henry Clay, the Speaker of the House from 1811 to 1820. The incumbent Jackson, having won a first term as president in 1828, defeated Clay in the 1832 presidential contest. Jackson was the first chief executive who won the White House as the nominee of a truly national, popularly based political party.

The Whigs and the Democrats continued to strengthen after 1832, establishing state and local organizations almost everywhere. Their competition was usually fierce and closely matched, and they brought the United States the first broadly supported two-party system in the Western world.[4] Unfortunately for the Whigs, the issue of slavery sharpened the many divisive tensions within the party, which led to its gradual dissolution and replacement by the new Republican Party. Formed in 1854 by anti-slavery activists, the Republican Party set its sights on the abolition (or at least the containment) of slavery. After a losing presidential effort for John C. Frémont in 1856, the party was able to assemble enough support primarily from former Whigs and anti-slavery northern Democrats to win the presidency for Abraham Lincoln in a fragmented 1860 vote. In that year, the South voted solidly Democratic, beginning a tradition so strong that not a single southern state voted Republican for president again until 1920.

DEMOCRATS AND REPUBLICANS: THE GOLDEN AGE

From the presidential election of 1860 to this day, the same two major parties, the Republicans and the Democrats, have dominated elections in the United States, and control of an electoral majority has seesawed between them. Party stability, the dominance of party organizations in local and state governments, and the impact of those organizations on the lives of millions of voters were the central traits of the era called the "Golden Age" of political parties. This era, which spanned the years 1874–1912, from the end of post–Civil War Reconstruction until the reforms of the Progressive era, featured remarkable stability in the identity of the two major political parties. Such stability has been exceptionally rare in democratic republics around the world.

Emigration from Europe (particularly from Ireland, Italy, and Germany) fueled the development in America of big-city party organizations that gained control of local and state government during this time. These big-city party organizations were called **machines.** A political machine is a party organization that uses tangible incentives such as jobs and favors to win loyalty among voters. Machines are also characterized by a high degree of leadership control over member activity. Party machines were a central element of life for millions of people in the United States during the Golden

VIDEO ROUNDTABLE

Difference Between Democrats and Republicans

machine
A party organization that recruits voter loyalty with tangible incentives and is characterized by a high degree of control over member activity.

Photo courtesy: Museum of the City of New York/Hulton Archive/Getty Images

■ William March "Boss" Tweed of the Tammany Hall political machine ran New York City politics until his conviction on graft charges in 1873.

direct primary
The selection of party candidates through the ballots of qualified voters rather than at party nomination conventions.

civil service laws
These acts removed the staffing of the bureaucracy from political parties and created a professional bureaucracy filled through competition.

issue-oriented politics
Politics that focuses on specific issues rather than on party, candidate, or other loyalties.

ticket-split
To vote for candidates of different parties for various offices in the same election.

candidate-centered politics
Politics that focuses directly on the candidates, their particular issues, and character, rather than on party affiliation.

Age. For city-dwellers, their party and their government were virtually interchangeable during this time. Party organizations sponsored community events and provided social services to those in immediate need, all in exchange for loyalty to party bosses and their candidates.

Political parties thus not only served the underlying political needs of the society but also supplemented the population's desire for important services. In addition to providing housing, employment, and even food to many voters, parties in most major cities provided entertainment by organizing torchlight parades, weekend picnics, socials, and the like. Many citizens—even those who weren't particularly "political"—attended, thereby gaining some allegiance to one party or the other. The parties offered immigrants not just services but also the opportunity for upward social mobility as they rose in the organization. As a result, parties engendered intense devotion among their supporters and office holders that helped to produce startlingly high voter turnouts—75 percent or better in all presidential elections from 1876 to 1900—compared with today's 50–60 percent.[5]

THE MODERN ERA

The modern era seems very different from the Golden Age of parties. Many social, political, technological, and governmental changes have contributed to changes in the nature of the national parties since the 1920s. Historically, the government's gradual assumption of important functions previously performed by the parties, such as printing ballots, conducting elections, and providing social welfare services, had a major impact. Beginning in the 1930s with Franklin Roosevelt's New Deal, social services began to be seen as a right of citizenship rather than as a privilege extended in exchange for a person's support of a party. Also, as the flow of immigrants slowed dramatically in the 1920s, party organizations gradually shrank in many places.

A **direct primary** system, in which party nominees were determined by the ballots of qualified voters rather than at party conventions, gained widespread adoption by the states in the first two decades of the twentieth century. Direct primaries, which were championed by the Progressive movement, which flourished in the first two decades of the twentieth century, removed the power of nomination from party leaders and workers and gave it instead to a much broader and more independent electorate, thus loosening the tie between party nominees and the party organization.

Additional Progressive movement reforms also contributed to reduced party influence in the United States. **Civil service laws,** for example, which require appointment on the basis of merit and competitive examinations, removed opportunities for much of the patronage used by the parties to reward their followers. The development of the civil service is discussed in greater detail in chapter 9.

In the post–World War II era, extensive social changes also contributed to the move away from strong parties. A weakening of the party system gave rise to candidate and **issue-oriented politics,** politics that focuses on the individuals running for office and specific issues, such as civil rights, tax cutting, or environmentalism, rather than on party platforms. Interest groups and lobbyists have stepped into the void that weaker parties have left behind, and candidates compete for endorsements and contributions from a variety of multi-issue as well as single-issue organizations. Issue politics tends to cut across party lines and encourages voters to **ticket-split**—to vote for candidates of different parties in the same election (a phenomenon we discuss in greater depth in chapter 13). Parties' diminished control over issues and campaigns have also left candidates considerable power in how they conduct themselves during election season and how they seek resources. This new **candidate-centered politics** is an outgrowth of voters focusing directly on the candidates, their particular issues, and character, rather than on their party affiliation.

Another post–World War II social change that has affected the parties is the population shift from urban to suburban locales. Millions of people have moved from the cities to the suburbs, where a sense of privacy and detachment can deter the most energetic party organizers. In addition, population growth in the last half-century has created districts with far more people, making it less feasible to knock on every door or shake every hand.

REALIGNMENT

Periodically in congressional elections, voters will make dramatic shifts in partisan preference that will drastically alter the political landscape. During these **party realignments,**[6] existing party affiliations are subject to upheaval: many voters may change parties, and the youngest age group of voters may permanently adopt the label of the newly dominant party.

Preceding a major realignment are one or more **critical elections,** which may polarize voters around new issues and personalities in reaction to crucial developments, such as a war or an economic depression. Three tumultuous eras in particular have produced significant critical elections. First, Thomas Jefferson, in reaction against the Federalist Party's agenda of a strong, centralized federal government, formed the Democratic-Republican Party, which took the presidency and Congress in 1800. Second, in reaction to the growing crisis over slavery, the Whig Party gradually dissolved and the Republican Party gained strength and ultimately won the presidency in 1860. Third, the Great Depression of the 1930s caused large numbers of voters to repudiate Republican Party policies and embrace the Democratic Party. Each of these cases resulted in fundamental and enduring alterations in the party equation. See Figure 12.2 for the electoral results of these three critical elections.

The last confirmed major realignment, then, happened in the 1928–1936 period, as Republican Herbert Hoover's presidency was held to one term because of voter anger about the Depression. In 1932, Democrat Franklin D. Roosevelt swept to power as the electorate decisively rejected Hoover and the Republicans. This dramatic vote of "no confidence" was followed by substantial changes in policy by the new president. The majority of voters responded favorably to Roosevelt's New Deal policies, accepted his vision of society, and ratified their choice of the new president's party in subsequent presidential and congressional elections.

The idea that party realignments occurred on a predictable, periodic basis beguiled many political scientists in the 1960s and 1970s, and much attention was focused on awaiting the next sea change in partisan alignment.[7] However, no uniform shift in partisan alignment has occurred in American politics since the election of Franklin D. Roosevelt in 1932. In fact, divided partisan government has been a dominant outcome of elections since World War II. Many scholars today question the value of party realignments in understanding partisanship and policy change. While critical elections share some degree of similarity, each is precipitated by distinctive political changes that are linked to the particular period and issues.[8] Nonetheless, party realignments offer a useful basis for understanding how pivotal elections may lastingly alter the direction of American politics.

A critical election is not the only occasion when changes in partisan affiliation are accommodated. In truth, every election produces realignment to some degree, since some individuals are undoubtedly pushed to change parties by events and by their reactions to the candidates. Research suggests that partisanship is much more responsive to current issues and personalities than had been believed earlier, and that major realignments are just extreme cases of the kind of changes in party loyalty registered every year.[9]

SECULAR REALIGNMENT

Although the term *realignment* is usually applied only if momentous events such as war or economic depression produce enduring and substantial alterations in the party

party realignment
A shifting of party coalition groupings in the electorate that remains in place for several elections.

critical election
An election that signals a party realignment through voter polarization around new issues.

FIGURE 12.2 ELECTORAL COLLEGE RESULTS FOR THREE REALIGNING PRESIDENTIAL CONTESTS

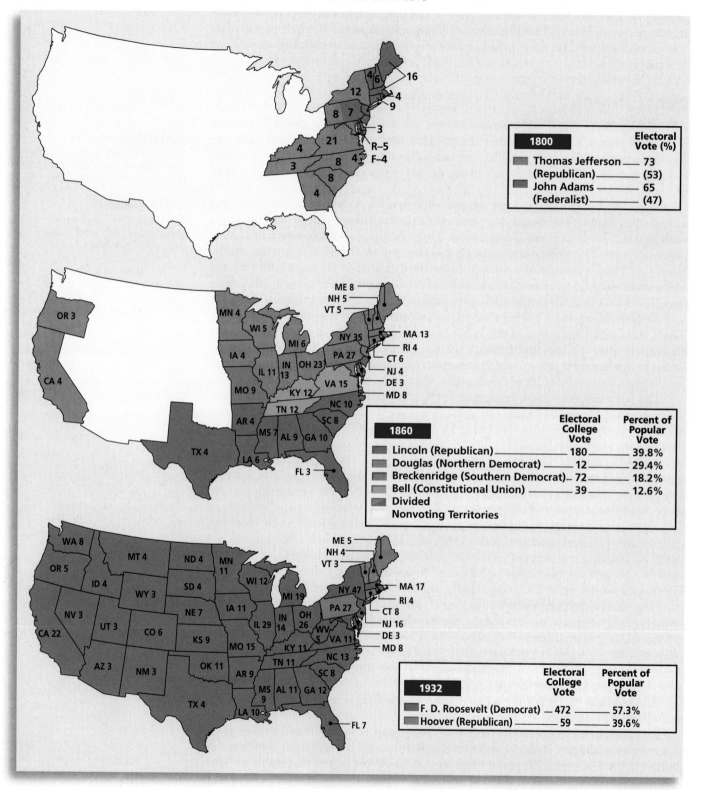

1800	Electoral Vote (%)
Thomas Jefferson (Republican)	73 (53)
John Adams (Federalist)	65 (47)

1860	Electoral College Vote	Percent of Popular Vote
Lincoln (Republican)	180	39.8%
Douglas (Northern Democrat)	12	29.4%
Breckenridge (Southern Democrat)	72	18.2%
Bell (Constitutional Union)	39	12.6%
Divided		
Nonvoting Territories		

1932	Electoral College Vote	Percent of Popular Vote
F. D. Roosevelt (Democrat)	472	57.3%
Hoover (Republican)	59	39.6%

coalitions, political scientists have long recognized that a more gradual rearrangement of party coalitions can occur.[10] Called **secular realignment,** this piecemeal process depends not on convulsive shocks to the political system but on slow, almost barely discernible demographic shifts—the shrinking of one party's base of support and the enlargement of the other's, for example—or simple generational replacement (that is, the dying off of the older generation and the maturing of the younger generation). According to one version of this theory, in an era of weaker party attachments (such as we currently are experiencing), a dramatic, full-scale realignment may not be possible.[11] Still, a critical mass of voters may be attracted for years to one party's banner in waves or streams, if that party's leadership and performance are consistently exemplary.

The prospect of a national realignment is unlikely as long as party ties remain tenuous for so many voters.[12] However, regionally there have been slow but stable partisan realignments that have affected the power bases of the major parties. During the 1990s, the southern states, traditionally Democratic stalwarts since the Civil War, shifted dramatically toward the Republican Party. The Northeast, a longtime reliable voting bloc for Republicans, became increasingly Democratic during the same period. Many factors have contributed to these gradual regional shifts in party allegiance. Southern Democrats were the most conservative of the New Deal coalition, favoring the social status quo and opposing civil rights reform. As the Democratic Party shifted its platform toward more liberal social causes such as civil rights and social spending, many southern voters and politicians shifted their allegiance toward the Republicans. In a region where voting for a Republican was once considered taboo, the South is now one of the most reliable blocs of Republican voters.[13]

secular realignment

The gradual rearrangement of party coalitions, based more on demographic shifts than on shocks to the political system.

SIMULATION

You Are Redrawing the Districts in Your State

The Functions of the American Party System

FOR 150 YEARS, the two-party system has served as the mechanism American society uses to organize and resolve social and political conflict. Political parties often are the chief agents of change in our political system. They provide vital services to society, and it would be difficult to envision political life without them.

MOBILIZING SUPPORT AND GATHERING POWER

Party affiliation is enormously helpful to elected leaders. They can count on support among their fellow party members not just in times of trouble and times when they need to gather support for tight votes, but also on general political and legislative matters. Therefore the parties aid office holders by giving them room to develop their policies and by mobilizing support for them. When the president addresses the nation and requests support for his policies, for example, his party's members are usually the first to respond to the call, perhaps by flooding Congress with e-mails and phone calls urging action on the president's agenda.

Because there are only two major parties in the United States, citizens who are interested in politics or public policy are mainly attracted to one or the other party, creating natural majorities or near majorities for party office holders to command. The party generates a community of interest that bonds disparate groups over time into a **coalition.** This continuing mutual interest eliminates the necessity of forming a new coalition for every campaign or every issue. Imagine the constant chaos and mad scrambles for public support that would ensue without the continuity provided by the parties.

coalition

A group made up of interests or organizations that join forces for the purpose of electing public officials.

It remains an open debate whether or not party activities that are designed to mobilize voters actually increase political participation among the general public. It is easy to see how party efforts such as voter registration drives and get out the vote (GOTV) efforts might increase voter participation. The Republican Party in particular has been very successful in identifying likely voters and getting them to turn up on Election Day. In these GOTV drives, parties spend tremendous resources to identify their base voters and then motivate these people to cast a ballot through the mail or at the ballot box. GOTV drives have been an increasingly effective means of winning elections, helping to drive up the number of committed partisan voters going to the polls.[14] But, the overall effect of increasing the numbers of registered voters or motivating those unaffiliated with political parties to vote is not as pronounced. While the 2004 presidential election showed an upswing in both voter turnout and partisan affiliation, it is too soon to state whether these statistics point to an emerging trend toward party alignment within the electorate. However, they are encouraging signals of partisan resurgence after a historically long period of party weakness.

A FORCE FOR STABILITY AND MODERATION

As mechanisms for organizing and containing political change, the parties are a potent force for stability. They represent continuity in the wake of changing issues and personalities, anchoring the electorate in the midst of the storm of new political policies and people. Because of its overarching desire to win elections (not just to contest them), each party in a sense acts to moderate public opinion. Traditionally, parties have tamed their own extreme elements by pulling them toward an ideological center in order to attract a majority of votes on Election Day. But, an increasingly polarized political landscape has diminished the moderating effects of partisan competition.[15] (For an overview of where the parties stand on certain issues, see American Values/American Voices: Democrats, Republicans, Independents, and Shared Values.)

The parties encourage stability in the type of coalitions they form. There are inherent contradictions in these coalitions that, oddly enough, strengthen the nation even as they strain party unity. Franklin D. Roosevelt's Democratic New Deal coalition, for example, included many African Americans and most southern whites, opposing groups nonetheless joined in common political purpose by economic hardship and, in the case of better-off Southerners, in longtime voting habits. A recent study determined that the liberalization of the formerly conservative southern Democratic Party was a direct result of the growth of the viable and conservative southern Republican Party and the extension of greater voting rights to African Americans.[16] As many white Southerners abandoned the Democratic Party for the GOP, the Democrats became even more dependent on black votes, and their policy positions changed in order to retain those votes.[17]

While parties still serve to moderate the turbulent passions of democracy, both the Republicans and Democrats have come close to parity in Congress, and many politicians have become increasingly more strident in their partisan attacks in their struggle for power and influence in the electorate. The wrangling in the Senate over President Bush's judicial nominations, which inspired extended and rancorous debate over the survival of the filibuster, led many to decry a lack of decorum and moderation in party politics. However, as discussed in chapter 7, a coalition of moderate senators from both parties averted any changes to the rules governing the filibuster. Despite the tribulations of public opinion or partisan passions, the party system still manages to organize and direct effective political action.

UNITY, LINKAGE, AND ACCOUNTABILITY

Parties are the glue that holds together the disparate elements of the U.S. governmental and political apparatus. The Framers designed a system that divides and subdivides

American Values/American Voices

DEMOCRATS, REPUBLICANS, INDEPENDENTS, AND SHARED VALUES

The rancor and tumult of partisan politics can sometimes blind Americans to the common values they share and hide much of what is not up for debate. Compared to their European compatriots, Americans are very close in their assumptions about individual responsibility, the place of religion, and other social issues. While Republicans and Democrats regularly feud over the place of government in people's lives and the size and extent of the social safety net, American partisan assumptions about what the government should provide and what individuals should take responsibility for are very similar and in striking contrast to European expectations. For example, on the question of whether the government should help or the individual take responsibility in feeding, clothing, and housing children under eighteen, Americans overall were 25 percent more likely than Europeans to believe it was all the responsibility of the

individual, with only a 10 percent difference between Republicans and Democrats.

The issue of the government providing retirement benefits was more divisive between parties, with Republicans preferring individual responsibility for retirement by 15 percent. America's long experience with Social Security and the oldest generation of Americans identifying strongly with the New Deal and the Democratic Party may explain some of this difference, but even Democrats were 12 percent more supportive of individual responsibility for retirement than Europeans.

In foreign affairs, American partisans are very much aligned in how America should position itself on the world stage. Whereas in the past the Republican Party was known for a more isolationist stance toward world affairs, both Republicans and Democrats overwhelmingly believe America should seek a position of shared world leadership.

Individual vs. Government Responsibility	Total U.S.	Republicans	Democrats	Independents	European Avg.
To provide food, clothes, and housing for their children under age 18					
Individual entirely responsible	82%	89%	79%	82%	57%
Expects the government to help	11	6	14	12	29
To save enough money to meet at least their basic expenses in retirement					
Individual entirely responsible	59	69	54	59	42
Expects the government to help	33	25	37	33	45

Source: Pew Research Center for the People and the Press, 2005.

U.S. Global Leadership Role	Total U.S.	Republican	Democrat	Independent
Leadership role for the United States in the world?				
Single world leader	11%	14%	8%	13%
Shared world leadership	74	76	76	72
No leadership role	9	5	10	10

Source: Pew Research Center for the People and the Press, 2004.

power, making it possible to preserve individual liberty but difficult to coordinate and produce action in a timely fashion. Parties help compensate for this drawback by linking the executive and legislative branches. Although rivalry between these two branches of U.S. government is inevitable, the partisan affiliations of the leaders of each branch constitute a common basis for cooperation, as the president and his fellow party members in Congress usually demonstrate daily. When President George W. Bush proposed a major new program of tax cuts, Republican members of Congress were the first to speak up in favor of the program and to orchestrate efforts for its passage. Not surprisingly, presidential candidates and presidents are inclined to push policies similar to those advocated by their party's congressional leaders.[18]

Even within each branch, there is intended fragmentation, and the party once again helps narrow the differences between the House of Representatives and the Senate, or between the president and the department heads in the executive bureaucracy. Similarly, the division of national, state, and local governments, while always an invitation to conflict, is made more workable and more easily coordinated by the intersecting party relationships that exist among office holders at all levels. Party affiliation, in other words, is a basis for mediation and negotiation laterally among the branches of government and vertically among national, state, and local layers.

The party's linkage function does not end there. Party identification and organization foster communication between the voter and the candidate, as well as between the voter and the office holder. The party connection is one means of increasing accountability in election campaigns and in government. Candidates on the campaign trail and elected party leaders in office are required from time to time to account for their performance at party-sponsored forums, nominating primaries, and conventions.

THE ELECTIONEERING FUNCTION

The election, proclaimed author H. G. Wells, is "democracy's ceremonial, its feast, its great function," and the political parties assist this ceremony in essential ways. First, the parties help to funnel eager, interested individuals into politics and government. While most candidates are self-recruited, some are also recruited each year by the two parties, as are many of the candidates' staff members—the people who manage the campaigns and go on to serve in key governmental positions once the election has been won.

Elections can have meaning in a democracy only if they are competitive, and in the United States they probably could not be competitive without the parties. (When we use the term *competitive*, we mean that both parties have sufficient organization, money, and people to run a vigorous election campaign, and to sustain their arguments through the period of governance.)

PARTY AS A VOTING AND ISSUE CUE

A voter's party identification can act as an invaluable filter for information, a perceptual screen that affects how he or she digests political news. Parties try to cultivate a popular image and help inform the public about issues through advertising and voter contact. Therefore, party affiliation provides a useful cue for voters, particularly for the least informed and least interested, who can use the party label as a shortcut or substitute for interpreting issues and events they may not fully comprehend. Better-educated and more involved voters also find party identification helpful. After all, no one has the time to study every issue carefully or to become fully knowledgeable about every candidate seeking public office.

POLICY FORMULATION AND PROMOTION

national party platform
A statement of the general and specific philosophy and policy goals of a political party, usually promulgated at the national convention.

VISUAL LITERACY
State Control and National Platforms

As discussed at the beginning of this chapter, the **national party platform** is the most visible instrument that parties use to formulate, convey, and promote public policy. Every four years, each party writes for the presidential nominating conventions a lengthy platform explaining its positions on key issues. In a two-party system, a platform not only explains what a party supports, but it also delineates important differences between the two dominant parties, giving voters meaningful policy choices through the electoral process. In other words, a party platform not only explains the party's policy preferences but also argues why its preferences are superior to those of the rival party. This is particularly true for contentious social issues on which there is little room for compromise and which divide the electorate, like abortion and same-sex marriage (see Table 12.1 on p. 421).

Scholarship suggests that about two-thirds of the promises in the victorious party's presidential platform have been completely or mostly implemented. Moreover, about one-half or more of the pledges of the losing party also tend to find their way into public policy, a trend that no doubt reflects the effort of both parties to support broad policy positions that enjoy widespread support in the general public.[19] For example, continuing the war in Iraq, which a majority of Americans supported leading into the 2004 presidential election, was endorsed in both party platforms. Both parties also supported the larger war on terrorism and the focus on homeland security, which has led some critics to point out that the two-party system, and its preference for broadly supported issues, can severely limit voter choice.

The party platform also has great influence on a new presidential administration's legislative program and on the president's State of the Union Address. While party affiliation is normally the single most important determinant of voting in Congress and in state legislatures,[20] the party–vote relationship is even stronger when party platform issues come up on the floor of Congress.

Besides mobilizing Americans on a permanent basis, then, the parties convert the cacophony of hundreds of identifiable social and economic groups into a two-part semi-harmony that is much more comprehensible, if not always on key and pleasing to the ears. The simplicity of two-party politics may be deceptive, given the enormous variety in public policy choices, but a sensible system of representation in the American context might be impossible without it.

CRASHING THE PARTY: MINOR PARTIES IN THE AMERICAN TWO-PARTY SYSTEM

Unlike many European countries that use **proportional representation** (awarding legislative seats according to the percentage of votes a political party receives), the United States has a "single-member, plurality" electoral system, often referred to as a **winner-take-all system** (a system in which the party that receives at least one more vote than any other party wins the election). In contrast, countries that use proportional representation often guarantee legislative seats to any faction securing as little as 5 percent of the vote. To paraphrase the legendary football coach Vince Lombardi, finishing first is not everything, it is the *only* thing in U.S. politics; placing second, even by a smidgen, doesn't count. The winner-take-all system encourages the grouping of interests into as few parties as possible (the democratic minimum being two). Moreover, the two parties will often move to the left or right on issues in order to gain popular support. Some observers claim that parties in the United States have no permanent positions at all, only permanent interests—winning elections. Regardless of one's position on this issue, it is clear that the adaptive nature of the two parties further forestalls the growth of third parties in the United States.

Despite their lack of electoral strength, minor parties based on causes often neglected by the major parties have had an important impact on American politics. (See Join the Debate: Third Parties: Good or Bad for the American Political System?) Third parties find their roots in sectionalism (as did the South's states' rights Dixiecrats, who broke away from the Democrats in 1948), in economic protest (such as the agrarian revolt that fueled the Populists, an 1892 prairie-states party), in specific issues (such as the Green Party's support of the environment), in ideology (the Socialist, Communist, and Libertarian Parties are examples), and in appealing, charismatic personalities (Theodore Roosevelt's affiliation with the Bull Moose Party in 1912 is perhaps the best case). Many minor parties have drawn strength from a combination of these sources. The American Independent Party enjoyed a measure of success because of a dynamic leader (George Wallace in 1968), a firm geographic base (the South), and an emotional issue (civil rights). In 1992, Ross Perot, the billionaire with a folksy Texas manner, was a charismatic leader whose campaign was fueled by the deficit issue (as well as by his personal fortune).

proportional representation
A voting system that apportions legislative seats according to the percentage of the vote won by a particular political party.

winner-take-all system
An electoral system in which the party that receives at least one more vote than any other party wins the election.

VIDEO ROUNDTABLE

Third Parties

Join the Debate

THIRD PARTIES: GOOD OR BAD FOR THE AMERICAN POLITICAL SYSTEM?

OVERVIEW: Third parties are a recurring political phenomenon in the United States, and they originate for one of two reasons: (1) to express an alternative political platform to those held by the two major parties or (2) to launch an alternative candidate for public office.

The Socialist Party favored a dismantling of the American capitalist system and a complete overhaul of the government. The Dixiecrats, who believed in continued racial segregation, broke from the Democratic Party because it was beginning to abandon this position. These parties emerged to express ideas lacking support in the Republican and Democratic Parties.

The Reform Party and the Bull Moose Party illustrate how third parties can offer an alternative presidential candidate. In 1992, Ross Perot founded the Reform Party with the sole purpose of running for president. Similarly, in 1911, the Bull Moose Party—known officially as the Progressive Party—was conceived to support Theodore Roosevelt's 1912 presidential campaign. The Green Party, on the other hand, courted Ralph Nader, a well-known consumer advocate and political activist, to be their presidential candidate in 2000 in order to increase their exposure among voters nationwide. These parties, and the candidates that bore their standard, gained popularity and support based on a dissatisfaction with the candidates and trends in the two major parties at the time. They offered alternatives to the established Republican and Democratic Parties, and they claimed to have nominees who would achieve greater success as president due to their lack of strong party ties. Despite their failures at the ballot box, they all exerted pressure on the two major parties and helped tip the balance in the elections they ran in.

While single issues and popular candidates are successful ingredients for the creation of third parties, they lack the power to sustain a party's viability over time. In addition, the trouble with single-issue parties is that the issue is usually specific to a certain group of people or a certain area of the nation that is too small to impact a national election. If these third parties fought for more local or state representation, they would have better chances of winning, as the Vermont Socialists did when one of their own, Bernard Sanders, was elected to the U.S. House of Representatives in 1990 as an independent. Repeatedly reelected, Sanders caucuses with the Democrats.

The trouble with candidate-oriented third parties is that they depend utterly on their candidate. When interest in Ross Perot declined, the support for the Reform Party seemed to evaporate with it, until former professional wrestler and popular independent governor of Minnesota, Jesse Ventura, became the new candidate on which the party could focus. When arch-conservative and former Republican insider Pat Buchanan received the Reform Party nomination for president, in hopes that he could also shine beneath the party's limelight, Ventura and his independent voters backed out, leaving the Reform Party in ruins.

ARGUMENTS FOR THIRD PARTIES

- **Third parties benefit the United States because they allow for a greater diversity of opinion, beyond that of Democrats and Republicans.** Often the issues promoted by third parties and the candidates that represent them gain popular support, and the major parties are then forced to address them. For example, several of the reforms proposed by the GOP's 1994 Contract with America had been part of Ross Perot's campaign platform in 1992. In cases like this, third parties are essential in guaranteeing that all voices are heard.

Third Parties in American History

Minor-party and independent candidates are not limited to presidential elections. Many also run in congressional elections, and the numbers appear to be growing. In the 2006 congressional elections, for example, nearly 350 minor-party and independent candidates ran for seats in the House and Senate—almost three and half times as many as in 1968 and one and a half times the number that ran in 1980. Only one member of the 110th Congress, Senator Bernie Sanders of Vermont, who caucuses with the Democrats, is an independent. Senator Joe Lieberman lost the Democratic primary but won reelection as an independent in Connecticut. Lieberman refers to himself as an "Independent Democrat". Minor-party candidates for the House are most likely to emerge under three conditions: (1) when a House seat becomes open; (2) when a minor-party candidate has previously competed in the district; and, (3) when partisan competition between the two major parties in the district is close.[21]

- **The two-party system is not integral to a successful representative democracy.** While American democracy quickly evolved into a political system characterized by two major parties, many other successful democracies operate with multiparty systems. Spain, Germany, South Korea, and Israel, for example, have stable democratic governments that continue to provide successful leadership and progress for their citizens.
- **Third parties can provide useful solutions to political problems on the local and regional level.** While the major parties must incorporate a broad range of issues in order to maintain national appeal, third parties are able to focus on a single issue or on a few issues specific to a state or locality. While there has never been a third-party president, there have been several third-party state governors in recent history.

ARGUMENTS AGAINST THIRD PARTIES

- **Third parties can be composed of political extremists who are uninterested in real politics.** With an intense focus on a specific issue or agenda, some third parties and their candidates have been known to disregard the idea of compromise that characterizes the American political system and is the basis for progress. To energize supporters, they may use rhetoric and emotional appeals that many find repulsive, resulting in disenchantment with the system and less participation in the process.
- **Some third parties exhibit strongly anti-democratic tendencies.** In the 1940s, the Dixiecrats wanted to preserve the Jim Crow South, where African Americans were legally discriminated against and states required businesses and public buildings to separate white patrons from black patrons. Earlier in the twentieth century, the Bull Moose Party nearly became a cult of personality for

Theodore Roosevelt. His supporters' hero worship went beyond political support and prevented the party from focusing simply on the issue positions that he represented.

- **Third parties may impact elections and produce an outcome contrary to the popular sentiment.** Frequently a third-party will arise out of dissatisfaction within a major party on a specific issue, or among individuals with particular political leanings. As a result, the third party can drain support disproportionately from voters of the major party on Election Day, leading to a victory for a candidate who would not have had a majority in a two-candidate race. Ross Perot is often credited with costing then-President George Bush a second term in 1992, by appealing to a large number of conservative voters who might otherwise have voted for Bush. Likewise, in the 2000 presidential election, many cite Ralph Nader as the primary reason for Al Gore's defeat, because he pulled much of his support from liberal voters.

QUESTIONS

1. In what ways has the current political climate benefited from the presence of third parties? How have third parties harmed the system?
2. How did third-party candidates impact the outcome of the 2004 presidential election? Do you think third parties had anything to do with the outcome of recent previous elections?

SELECTED READINGS

Bibby, John, and L. Sandy Maisel. *Two Parties—Or More? The American Party System*. Boulder, CO: Westview, 2002.

Disch, Lisa Jane. *The Tyranny of the Two Party System*. New York, NY: Columbia University Press, 2002.

Above all, third parties make electoral progress in direct proportion to the failure of the two major parties to incorporate new ideas or alienated groups or to nominate attractive candidates as their standard-bearers. Third parties do best when declining trust in the two major political parties plagues the electorate.[22] Usually, though, third parties are eventually co-opted by one of the two major parties, each of them eager to take the politically popular issue that gave rise to the third party and make it theirs in order to secure the allegiance of the third party's supporters. For example, the Republicans of the 1970s absorbed many of the states' rights planks of George Wallace's 1968 presidential bid. Both major parties have also more recently attempted to attract independent voters by sponsoring reforms of the governmental process, such as Senators John McCain and Russ Feingold's successful reform of campaign finance law.

The Party Organization

ALTHOUGH THE DISTINCTIONS might not be as clear today as they were two or three decades ago, the two major parties remain fairly loosely organized, with national, state, and local branches (see Figure 12.3). The different levels of each party represent diverse interests in Washington, D.C., state capitals, and local governments throughout the nation.

NATIONAL COMMITTEES

The first national party committees were skeletal and formed some years after the creation of the presidential nominating conventions in the 1830s. First the Democrats in 1848 and then the Republicans in 1856 established national governing bodies—the Democratic National Committee, or DNC, and the Republican National Committee, or RNC—to make arrangements for the national conventions and to coordinate the subsequent presidential campaigns. In addition, to serve their interests, the congressional party caucuses in both houses organized their own national committees, loosely allied with the DNC and RNC. The National Republican Congressional Committee (NRCC) was started in 1866 when the Radical Republican congressional

FIGURE 12.3 POLITICAL PARTY ORGANIZATION IN AMERICA: FROM BASE TO PINNACLE

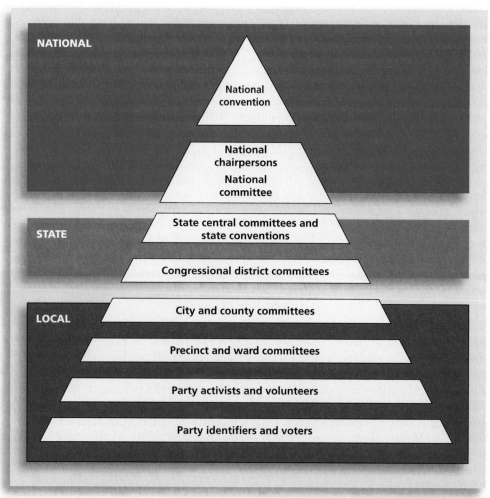

delegation was feuding with Abraham Lincoln's moderate successor, President Andrew Johnson, and wanted a counterweight to his control of the RNC. At the same
time, House and Senate Democrats set up a similar committee.

After the popular election of U.S. senators was initiated in 1913 with the ratification of the Seventeenth Amendment to the Constitution, both parties organized separate Senate campaign committees. This three-part arrangement of national party committee, House party committee, and Senate party committee has
persisted in both parties to the present day, and each party's three committees are
located in Washington, D.C. There is, however, an informal division of labor
among the national committees. Whereas the DNC and RNC focus primarily on
aiding presidential campaigns and conducting general party-building activities, the
congressional campaign committees work primarily to maximize the number of
seats held by their respective parties in Congress. In the past two decades, all six
national committees have become major, service-oriented organizations in American politics.[23]

LEADERSHIP

The key national party official is the chairperson of the national committee. Although
the chair is formally elected by the national committee, he or she is usually selected by
the sitting president or newly nominated presidential candidate, who is accorded the
right to name the individual for at least the duration of his or her campaign. Only the
post-campaign, out-of-power party committee actually has the authority to appoint a
chairperson independently. The committee-crowned chairpersons generally have the
greatest impact on the party, because they come to their posts at times of crisis when a
leadership vacuum exists. (A defeated presidential candidate is technically the head of
the national party until the next nominating convention, but the reality is naturally
otherwise as a party attempts to shake off a losing image.)

The chair often becomes the prime spokesperson and arbitrator for the party during the four years between elections. He or she is called on to damp down factionalism, negotiate candidate disputes, and prepare the machinery for the next presidential
election. Perhaps most critically, the chair is called upon to raise funds and keep the
party financially strong. Balancing the interests of all potential White House contenders is a particularly difficult job, and strict neutrality is normally expected from
the chair.

NATIONAL CONVENTIONS

Every four years, each party holds a **national convention** to nominate its presidential and vice presidential candidates. Much of any party chairperson's work involves
planning the presidential nominating convention, the most publicized and vital
event on the party's calendar. Until 1984, gavel-to-gavel coverage was standard
practice on all national television networks. Recently, however, television networks
have cut back convention air time to no more than one hour a day, during which the
most important speaker speaks as much to viewers as he or she does to convention
attendees. Most of the recent party chairpersons, in cooperation with the incumbent president or likely nominee, have tried to orchestrate every minute of the conventions in order to project just the right image. By and large, they have succeeded,
though at the price of draining spontaneity and excitement from the convention
process.

In addition to nominating the presidential ticket, the convention also fulfills its
role as the ultimate governing body for the party. The rules adopted and the party
platform that is passed serve as durable guidelines that steer the party until the next
convention.

national convention
A party conclave (meeting) held in
the presidential election year for the
purposes of nominating a presidential and vice presidential ticket and
adopting a platform.

■ Democratic National Committee Chair Howard Dean greets voters at an appearance in Texas prior to the 2006 midterm elections. Dean's decision to fund grassroots organizing even in typically "red" states like Texas was controversial with some party leaders, but many attributed at least some of his party's successes in 2006 to this effort.

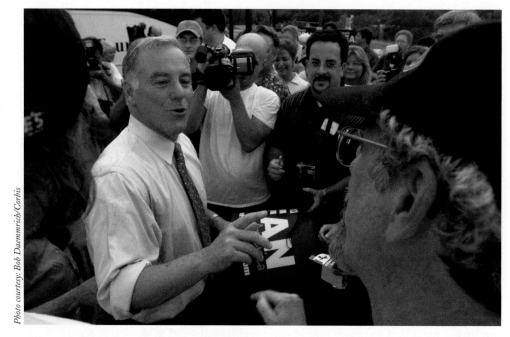

Photo courtesy: Bob Daemmrich/Corbis

STATES AND LOCALITIES

Although national committee activities of all kinds attract most of the media attention, the party is structurally based not in Washington, D.C., but in the states and localities. Except for the campaign finance arena, virtually all government regulation of political parties is left to the states. Most importantly, the vast majority of party leadership positions are filled at subnational levels.

The arrangement of party committees provides for a broad base of support. The smallest voting unit, the precinct, usually takes in a few adjacent neighborhoods and is the fundamental building block of the party. There are more than 100,000 precincts in the United States. The precinct committee members are the foot soldiers of any party, and their efforts are supplemented by party committees above them in the wards, cities, counties, towns, villages, and congressional districts.

The state governing body supervising this collection of local party organizations is usually called the state central (or executive) committee. Its members come from all major geographic units, as determined by and selected under state law. Generally, state parties are free to act within the limits set by their state legislatures without interference from the national party, except in the selection and seating of presidential convention delegates. National Democrats have been particularly inclined to regulate this aspect of party life. With the decline of big-city political machines, few local parties are strong enough to defy national party policy positions or to select nominees against the national party's wishes. However, in 2006, New Hampshire resisted when the Democratic National Committee attempted to change the order of the early primaries and caucuses by placing Nevada's caucus before the New Hampshire primary and threatening to not seat delegates from states that violated the party's schedule. New Hampshire was able to secure several candidates' pledges that, despite the proposed penalties, they would participate even if the state deviated from the DNC schedule.

Although weaker in respect to how they affect the national party, state and local parties have become significantly more effective over the past three decades in terms of fund-raising, campaign events, registration drives, publicity of party and candidate activity, and the distribution of campaign literature.[24] Examining separately the national, state, and local parties should not lead us to overlook the increasing integration of these committees. The national parties have also become fund-raising power-houses during the last two decades, and they now channel significant financial support to state parties. This financial support has given the national parties considerable leverage over the state committees—many of which have become dependent on the funding—and the national parties have increasingly used the state committees to help execute national campaigns.

The growing reliance of state parties on national party funding has changed fundamentally the balance of power in the American party system. Whereas power previously flowed up from the state and local parties to the national committees, the national committees now enjoy considerable leverage over state and local parties.[25] That said, the relationships among the national, state, and local party committees are now being altered because of the passage of the Bipartisan Campaign Reform Act (BCRA) that took effect following the 2002 midterm elections (see chapter 14 for details of the BCRA). New organizations called 527 groups, named after a provision of the federal tax code, have been formed to circumvent the new regulations and played a prominent role in the 2004 campaign (see chapter 14). Well-funded 527 groups, like the liberal group MoveOn.org and the conservative group Swift Boat Veterans for Truth, poured millions of dollars into the 2004 elections. Unfettered by the contribution limits placed on donors to candidates and political parties, wealthy contributors, like George Soros on the left and Bob Perry on the right, contributed more than $23 million and $8 million respectively to 527 groups during the 2004 election cycle.

INFORMAL GROUPS

The formal structure of party organization is supplemented by numerous official and semi-official groups that attempt to affect politics through the formal party organization. Both the DNC and RNC have affiliated organizations of state and local party women (the National Federation of Democratic Women and the National Federation of Republican Women), as well as numerous college campus organizations, including the College Democrats of America and the College Republican National Committee. The youth divisions (the Young Democrats of America and the Young Republicans' National Federation) have a generous definition of "young," up to and including age thirty-five. State governors in each party have their own party associations, too: the Democratic Governors Association and the Republican Governors Association.

Just outside the party orbit are the supportive interest groups and associations that often provide money, labor, or other forms of assistance to the parties. Labor unions, progressive political action committees (PACs), teachers, African American and liberal women's groups, and the Americans for Democratic Action are some of the Democratic Party's organizational groups. Business PACs, the U.S. Chamber of Commerce, fundamentalist Christian organizations, and some anti-abortion groups work closely with the Republicans.

Each U.S. party has several institutionalized sources of policy ideas. Though unconnected to the parties in any official sense, these **think tanks** (institutional collections of policy-oriented researchers and academics) influence party positions and platforms. Republicans have dominated the world of think tanks, with prominent conservative groups including the Hudson Institute, American Enterprise Institute, and Heritage Foundation. And, the libertarian Cato Institute is closely aligned with the Republican Party. While generally fewer in number and enjoying far less funding than their conservative counterparts,

think tank
Institutional collection of policy-oriented researchers and academics who are sources of policy ideas.

■ The close relationship between conservative think tanks and the Republican Party insures the appearance of high-profile members of the Bush administration at their events. Here, Secretary of State Condoleezza Rice walks off stage after delivering a speech about the Iraq War and the upcoming 2006 midterm elections at the Heritage Foundation.

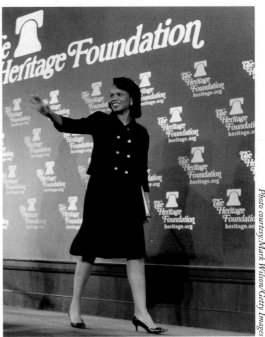

Photo courtesy:Mark Wilson/Getty Images

prominent think tanks that generally align with the Democratic Party include the Center for National Policy and Open Society Institute. The Brookings Institution, founded in 1916, prides itself on a scholarly and nonpartisan approach to public policy.

THE TRANSFORMATION OF THE PARTY ORGANIZATION

Both major political parties have supplemented labor-intensive, person-to-person operations with modern technological and communication strategies, and both parties are similar in the objectives they pursue to achieve political power. Nevertheless, each party has its strengths and weaknesses.

The contemporary national Republican Party has considerable organizational prowess, often surpassing the Democrats in fund-raising by large margins (see Figure 12.4). In recent election cycles, Democrats have worked hard to compete with the Republican Party fund-raising machine, which is fueled by a large number of wealthy donors. In 2004, the Republican Party out raised the Democratic Party, but the Democrats came closer to matching the Republicans than in any other modern election season. This was true even after **soft money,** the virtually unregulated money funneled through political parties under the auspice of party building, was banned following passage the Bipartisan Campaign Reform Act in 2002 (campaign finance reform efforts will be discussed in more detail in chapter 14). As Republicans had long enjoyed a substantial advantage in raising **hard money,** funds that can be used for direct electioneering but that are limited and regulated by the Federal Elections Commission, many Democrats feared that banning soft money would give Republicans a clear fund-raising advantage in 2004. No doubt this fear aided the Democrats in their fund-raising efforts, providing donors a strong incentive to increase their contributions and, in fact, helping to shrink the GOP fund-raising advantage in 2004. During the 2006 midterm elections, the Democrats came closer to matching the Republicans than in any other modern election. Still, the Republican Party and its congressional campaign committees raised $438 million—$100 million more than the Democrats—in 2006.

The parties raise so much money because they have developed networks of donors reached by a variety of methods. Both parties have highly successful mail solicitation lists. The Republican effort to reach donors through the mail dates back to the early 1960s and accelerated in the mid-1970s, when postage and production costs were relatively low. The national Republican Party has expanded its mailing list of proven donors to several million. Republicans also pioneered the use of interactive technologies to attract voters. The RNC's award-winning "Main Street" Internet site has offered "chats" with the RNC chair and links to sites of interest to voters. As a presidential candidate in the 2004 Democratic primaries, former Vermont governor Howard Dean used an Internet Web site to coordinate "meet-ups" and to bring in an unprecedented sum of online campaign contributions. When his candidacy ended in defeat, Dean and his network of activist-contributors became a fundraising resource for Democrats, a fact that Dean later trumpeted during his successful bid to chair the DNC.[26]

The national Republican and Democratic Committees have spent millions of dollars for national, state, and local public opinion surveys, and they have accumulated an enormous storehouse of data on American attitudes in general and on marginal districts in particular. Many of the surveys are provided to party nominees at a cut-rate cost. In important contests, the party frequently commissions tracking polls to chart its daily rise or fall. The information provided in such polls is invaluable in the tense concluding days of an election. Both parties operate sophisticated media divisions that specialize in the design and production of television advertisements for party nominees at all levels. And both parties train the armies of the political volunteers and paid operatives who run the candidates' campaigns. Early in each election

soft money
The virtually unregulated money funneled through political parties under the auspice of party building.

hard money
Funds that can be used for direct electioneering but that are limited and regulated by the Federal Elections Commission.

FIGURE 12.4 POLITICAL PARTY FINANCES, 1991–2006

Note how the Republican Party has consistently taken in higher receipts than its Democratic competitor and how the receipts for both parties have substantially increased over time, even following the 2002 Bipartisan Campaign Reform Act (BCRA), which outlawed soft-money contributions (shown in the top graph) to the parties.

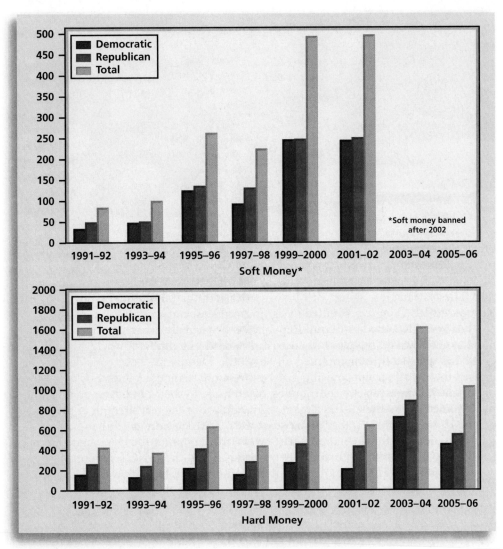

Sources: 2003–2006 from Center for Responsive Politics (http://www.opensecrets.org), and earlier years from Harold W. Stanley and Richard Niemi, *Vital Statistics on American Politics, 2003–2004* (Washington, DC: CQ Press, 2004).

cycle, the national parties also help prepare voluminous research reports on opponents, analyzing their public statements, votes, and attendance records.

The RNC manages a sophisticated fund-raising data base and helps coordinate national GOTV efforts. Many observers credit the success of the Bush campaign in 2004 to a well-organized and costly GOTV effort by the Republican Party. Because Democrats were the majority party in Congress for decades throughout the twentieth century, they have been late in creating similar programs. Electoral defeats prior to 2006 made Democrats realize that their party needed to revitalize its organization. Thus was born the commitment to technological and fund-raising modernization that

■ Staffers call on the party faithful to vote on Election Day. Phone banks, like the ones shown here, have become a major part of party-related activity around election time.

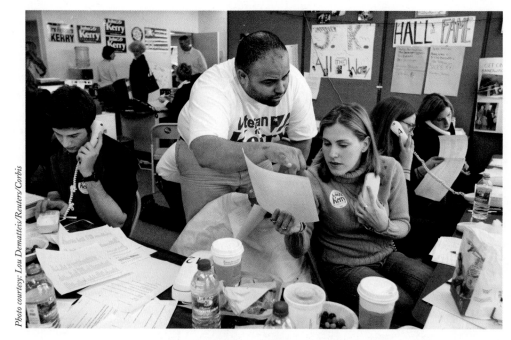

Photo courtesy: Lou Dematteis/Reuters/Corbis

drives the Democratic Party today. In 2006, Democrats focused on fielding competitive candidates in nearly every race and the DNC provided organizing funds to Democrats in traditionally Republican states as part of a 50-state grassroots organizing effort. These strategies, along with low approval ratings for President Bush and the Republican-led Congress, resulted in significant Democratic victories in 2006.

For now, Democrats still trail Republicans by virtually every significant measure of party activity. Yet, the party finances can be read in a different way. Although the GOP has consistently maintained an edge, the Democrats have considerably increased their total receipts, raising many times more than just a few years ago. More importantly, Democrats are contributing much more to their candidates and have actually come close to the GOP's larger total recently. But the real strength of the Democratic Party is in the number of party activists. The decision in 1981 to begin a direct-mail program for the national party was a turning point for Democrats. From a list of only 25,000 donors before the program began, the DNC's support base has grown to 500,000. Democratic National Committee Chair Howard Dean made grassroots organization and fund-raising a priority for the Democratic Party, and made increasing local party activity a priority for the 2006 congressional elections.

The Party in Government

IN ADDITION TO THEIR ROLE in mobilizing voters, political parties are used to organize the branches and layers of American government.

THE CONGRESSIONAL PARTY

In no segment of U.S. government is the party more visible or vital than in the Congress. In this century, political parties have dramatically increased the sophistication and impact of their internal congressional organizations. Prior to the beginning of every session, the parties in both houses of Congress gather (or "caucus") separately to select party leaders (House Speaker and minority leader, Senate majority and minority leaders, party whips, and so on) and to arrange for the appointment of members of each chamber's committees. In effect, then, the parties organize and operate the Congress. Their management systems have grown quite elaborate; the web of deputy and assistant whips for House Democrats now extends to about one-fourth of the party's entire membership. Although not invulnerable to pressure from the minority, the majority party in each house generally holds sway, even fixing the size of its majority on all committees—a proportion frequently in excess of the percentage of seats it holds in the house as a whole.

Congressional party leaders enforce a degree of discipline in their party members in various ways. Even though seniority traditionally determined committee assignments, increasingly choice assignments have been given to the loyal or withheld from the rebellious, regardless of seniority. The Senate majority leader can decide whether a member's bill is given priority in the legislative agenda or will be dismissed with barely a hearing. Pork-barrel projects—government projects yielding rich patronage benefits that sustain many a legislator's electoral survival—may be included or deleted during the appropriations process. Small favors and perquisites (such as the allocation of desirable office space or the scheduling of floor votes for the convenience of a member) can also be useful levers. Then, too, there are the campaign aids at the command of the leadership: money from party sources, endorsements, appearances in the district or at fund-raising events, and so on.

There are, however, limits to coordinated, cohesive party action. For example, the separate executive branch, the bicameral power sharing, and the extraordinary decentralization of Congress's work all constitute institutional obstacles to effective party action. Moreover, party discipline is hurt by the individualistic nature of U.S. politics: campaigns that are candidate centered rather than party oriented; diverse electoral constituencies to which members of Congress must understandably be responsive; the largely private system of election financing that indebts legislators to wealthy individuals and nonparty interest groups more than to their parties; and the importance to lawmakers of attracting the news media's attention—often more easily done by showmanship than by quiet, effective labor within the party system.

Indeed, given the barriers to coordinated party activity, it is impressive to discover that party labels have consistently been the most powerful predictor of congressional roll-call voting. In the last few years, party voting has increased noticeably, as reflected in the upward trend by both Democrats and Republicans shown in Figure 12.5. Although not invariably predictive, a member's party affiliation proved to be the indicator of his or her votes about 90 percent of the time in 2005; that is, the average representative or senator sided with his or her party on about 90 percent of the votes that divided a majority of Democrats from a majority of Republicans that year. In most recent years, unanimous party-line votes have become increasingly common, with Democrats recording a record 151 unanimous roll-call votes in 2005.[27]

There are many reasons for the recent growth of congressional party unity. Both congressional parties, for instance, have gradually become more ideologically homogeneous and internally consistent. Southern Democrats today are typically moderate or liberal like their northern counterparts. Similarly, the vast majority of Republicans in Congress identify themselves as conservative. Partisan gerrymandering (see Figure 13.6 on p. 495), redrawing congressional lines so as to create safe districts, has also increased party cohesion, as members of Congress increasingly represent congressional districts that strongly favor a single party. The political party campaign committees have also played a role in the renewed cohesiveness. Each national party committee has been recruiting and training House and Senate candidates as never before, and devising themes and issues aimed at targeted districts. With the numbers so close in each chamber of Congress, each party has a singular focus on electing a majority of legislators.

■ Senator Lindsay Graham (R-SC) is generally a consistent supporter of his party's policy agenda. Graham has criticized the Bush administration's treatment of detainees in the War on Terrorism, however, based on his past experience as an active duty Air Force lawyer and as a Staff Judge Advocate for the South Carolina Air National Guard. Graham is currently a member of the U.S. Air Force Reserves.

Photo courtesy: Alex Wong/Getty Images

FIGURE 12.5 CONGRESSIONAL PARTY UNITY SCORES, 1959–2005

Note how party-based voting has increased conspicuously since the 1970s.

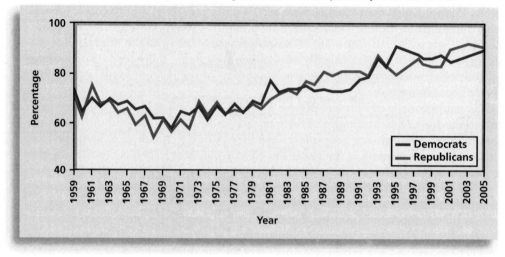

Source: Congressional Quarterly Almanacs (Washington, DC: CQ Press).

THE PRESIDENTIAL PARTY

Political parties may be more central to the operation of the legislative branch than the executive branch, but it is the party of the president that captures the public imagination and shapes the electorate's opinion of the two parties. Voters' perceptions of the incumbent president and the presidential candidates determine to a large extent how citizens perceive the parties. The chief executive's successes are his party's successes; his failures are borne by the party as much as by the individual. The image a losing presidential candidate projects is incorporated into the party's contemporary portrait, whether wanted or not.

It is not easy for a president to juggle contradictory roles. Expected to bring the country together as ceremonial chief of state and also to forge a ruling consensus as head of government, the president must also be an effective commander of a sometimes divided party. Along with the inevitable headaches party leadership brings, though, are clear and compelling advantages. Foremost among them is a party's ability to mobilize support among voters for a president's program. Also, the executive's legislative agenda might be derailed more quickly without the common tie of party label between the chief executive and many members of Congress; all presidents appeal for some congressional support on the basis of shared party affiliation, and—depending on circumstances and their executive skill—they generally receive it.

Presidents reciprocate the support they receive in many ways. In addition to compiling a record for the party and giving substance to its image, presidents appoint many activists to office, recruit candidates, raise money for the party treasury, and campaign extensively for party nominees during election seasons.

Some presidents have taken their party responsibilities more seriously than have others. In general, most presidents since Franklin D. Roosevelt have been less supportive of their respective political parties than were earlier presidents.[28] Dwight D. Eisenhower elevated nonpartisanship to a virtual art form; while this may have preserved his personal popularity, it proved a disaster for his party. Despite his full two-term occupancy of the White House, the Republican Party remained mired in minority status among the electorate, and Eisenhower never really attempted to transfer his high ratings to the party. Lyndon Johnson, Richard M. Nixon, and Jimmy Carter all showed similar neglect of their parties, often drawing on their party's organization for personal uses.

Photo courtesy: Bettmann/Corbis

■ Despite winning two consecutive terms as president, Republican Dwight D. Eisenhower, here shown in 1952 surrounded by Republican Committee women from eleven states, failed to help his party achieve majority status.

Nevertheless, some presidents have taken their party responsibilities extremely seriously. Democrats Woodrow Wilson and Franklin D. Roosevelt were dedicated to building their party electorally and governmentally. Republican Ronald Reagan exemplified the "pro-party" presidency, as has George W. Bush.

THE PARTIES AND THE JUDICIARY

While it is true that legislators tend to be much more partisan than judges and that legal restrictions and judicial norms often limit the partisan activities of judges, it would be wrong to assume that judges reach decisions wholly independently of partisan values. First, judges are creatures of the political process, and their posts are considered patronage plums. Judges who are not elected are appointed by presidents or governors for their abilities but also as members of the executive's party and increasingly as representatives of a certain philosophy of or approach to government. Most recent presidents have appointed judges overwhelmingly from their own party. Furthermore, Democratic executives are naturally inclined to select for the bench more liberal individuals who may be friendly to social programs or labor interests. Republican executives generally lean toward conservatives for judicial posts, hoping they will be tough on criminal defendants, opposed to abortion, and support business interests. President George W. Bush saw many of his judicial appointments, such as Miguel Estrada and Priscilla Owens, blocked by Senate Democrats, who refused to allow a vote on the nominations. This tactic provided not only a way for Democrats to exact revenge on the Republicans, who had used similar measures during the Clinton administration, but also a means to forestall ideological changes that can last far beyond the next election cycle.

Research has long indicated that party affiliation is a moderately good predictor of judicial decisions in some areas.[29] One specific example involves judicial approval of new congressional districts created by state legislatures every ten years based on the U.S. Census. Judges tend to favor redistricting plans passed by their partisans in state legislatures rather than those of the opposition party.[30] Not surprisingly, jurists who are elected to office are often more partisan than those who are appointed. In a majority of states, at least some judicial positions are filled by election, and fourteen states hold outright partisan elections, with both parties nominating opposing candidates and running hard-hitting campaigns. In some rural counties across the United States, local judges are not merely partisan elected figures; they are the key public officials, controlling many patronage jobs and the party machinery. In other words, party matters in the judiciary just as it does in the other two branches of government.

THE PARTIES AND STATE GOVERNMENTS

Most of the conclusions just discussed about the party's relationship to the legislature, the executive, and the judiciary apply to those branches at the state level as well. The national parties, after all, are organized around state units, and the basic structural arrangement of party and government is much the same in Washington and the state capitals. Remarkably, too, the major national parties are the dominant political forces in all fifty states. This has been true consistently; unlike Great Britain or Canada, the United States has no regional or state parties that displace one or both of the national parties in local contests. Occasionally in U.S. history, a third party has proven locally potent, as did Minnesota's Farmer-Labor Party and Wisconsin's Progressives, both of which elected governors and state legislative majorities in the twentieth century. But, over time, no such party has survived,[31] and every state's two-party system mirrors national party dualism, at least as far as labels are concerned.

Governors in many states have greater influence over their parties' organizations and legislators than do presidents. Many governors have more patronage positions at their command than does a president, and these material rewards and incentives give governors added clout with party activists and office holders. In addition, tradition in some states permits the governor to play a role in selecting the legislature's committee chairs and party floor leaders, and some state executives even attend and help direct the party legislative caucuses, activities no president would ever undertake. Moreover, forty-one governors possess the power of the line-item veto, which permits the governor to veto single items (such as pork-barrel projects) in appropriations bills. The line-item veto has given governors enormous leverage with legisla-

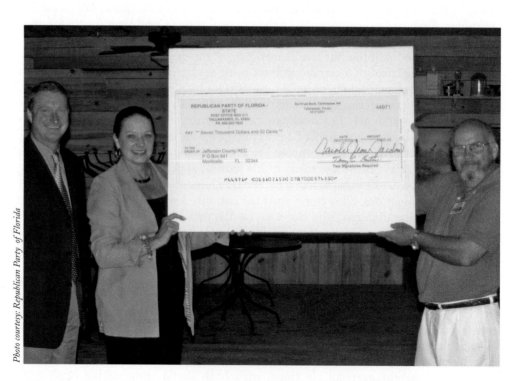

■ State parties often provide valuable financial assistance to party organizations at the local level. Here, Florida Republican Party Chair Carole Jean Jordan presents Jefferson County Republicans with a check for $7,000 in matching funds for party development.

Photo courtesy: Republican Party of Florida

tors, as they can now remove pork-barrel projects from members who oppose the governor's agenda.

After the 2006 elections, Democrats controlled a majority of state legislatures. Parties often have significant legislative influence at the state level, so the repercussions of this increase in Democratic control may be significant. Most state legislatures surpass the U.S. Congress in partisan unity and cohesion, with a number of state legislatures (including Massachusetts, New York, Ohio, and Pennsylvania) achieving party voting levels of 70 percent or better in some years. Not all states display party cohesion of this magnitude, of course. Nebraska has a nonpartisan legislature, elected without party labels on the ballot.

One other party distinction is notable in many state legislatures. Compared with the Congress, state legislative leaders have much more authority and power; this is one reason party unity is usually higher in the state capitols.[32] State legislative leaders, for example, often have considerable discretion in appointing committee chairs and members.

Party leaders and caucuses as well as the party organizations have more influence over legislators at the state level. State legislators depend on their state and local parties for election assistance much more than their congressional counterparts. Whereas members of Congress have large government-provided staffs and lavish perquisites to assist (directly or indirectly) their reelection efforts, state legislative candidates need party workers and, increasingly, the party's financial support and technological resources at election time.

The Party in the Electorate

A POLITICAL PARTY is much more than its organizational shell, however dazzling the technologies at its command, and its reach extends well beyond the small number of men and women who are the party in government. In any democracy, where power is derived directly from the people, the party's real importance and strength must come from the citizenry it attempts to mobilize. The party in the electorate—the mass of potential voters who identify with the Democratic or Republican labels—is a crucial element of the political party, providing the foundation for the organizational and governmental parties. But, in some respects, it is the weakest of the components of the U.S. political party system. In recent decades, fewer citizens have been willing to pledge their loyalty to the major parties, and many of those who have declared their loyalties have done so with less intensity. Increasingly, Americans are choosing not to identify themselves with political parties; over 38 percent of voters declared themselves independents in 2004. Partisan identification is a more reliable indicator of likely voting choices today than it once was, but fewer voters choose to identify themselves with a party. (For a more detailed explanation of patterns in American vote choice, see chapter 13.)

COMPARATIVE

Comparing
Political Parties

PARTY IDENTIFICATION

Most American voters identify with a party but do not belong to it. Universal party membership does not exist in the United States: the voter pays no prescribed dues; no formal rules govern an individual's party activities; and voters assume no enforceable obligations to the party even when they consistently vote for its candidates. A party has no real control over its adherents, and the party's voters subscribe to few or none of the commonly accepted tenets of organizational membership, such as regular participation and some measure of responsibility for the group's welfare. Rather, **party identification** or affiliation is an informal and impressionistic exercise whereby a

party identification
A citizen's personal affinity for a political party, usually expressed by his or her tendency to vote for the candidates of that party.

Analyzing Visuals

PARTY IDENTIFICATION, 1952–2004

This table indicates the responses of a representative sample of Americans to the question, "Generally speaking, do you consider yourself a Republican, a Democrat, an Independent, or what?" Looking at the data, how would you describe the general trend in the number of Americans who identify strongly or weakly as Democrats? As Republicans? The table shows that the number of self-identified independents has risen significantly over the years, reaching a high point of 40 percent in 2000. When "leaners," independents who normally support one party over the other, are included as partisans, however, what can be said about the number of true independents, sometimes referred to as hard or stubborn independents? What can be said about the relative strength of the Democratic and Republican Parties when you include the percentage of independent leaners along with those who identify weakly or strongly with each party?

PARTISAN IDENTIFICATION, NATIONAL ELECTION STUDIES, 1952–2004 (PERCENT)

| | Democrat | | | | Republican | | |
Year	Strong	Weak	Independent	Independent	Independent	Weak	Strong
1952	22	25	10	6	7	14	14
1954	22	25	9	7	6	14	13
1956	21	23	6	9	8	14	15
1958	27	22	7	7	5	16	11
1960	20	25	6	10	7	14	16
1962	23	23	7	8	6	16	12
1964	27	25	9	8	6	14	11
1966	18	28	9	12	7	15	10
1968	20	25	10	11	9	15	10
1970	20	24	10	13	8	15	9
1972	15	26	11	13	10	13	10
1974	17	21	13	15	9	14	8
1976	15	25	12	15	10	14	9
1978	15	24	14	14	10	13	8
1980	18	23	11	13	10	14	9
1982	20	24	11	11	8	14	10
1984	17	20	11	11	12	15	12
1986	18	22	10	12	11	15	10
1988	17	18	12	11	13	14	14
1990	20	19	12	10	12	15	10
1992	18	18	14	12	12	14	11
1994	15	19	13	11	12	15	15
1996	18	19	14	9	12	15	12
1998	19	18	14	11	11	16	10
2000	19	15	15	12	13	12	12
2002	16	17	15	8	13	16	14
2004	16	16	17	10	12	12	16

Note: Question: Generally speaking, do yo consider yourself a Republican, a Democrat, an Independent or what?" If Republican or Democrat: "Would you call yourself a strong (R/D) or a not very strong (R/D)? If Independent or other: "Do you think of yourself as closer to the Republican or Democratic party?"

Source: Calculated by the editors from National Election Studies data, Center for Political Studies, University of Michigan, Ann Arbor (http://www.umich.edu/~nes), as of June 25, 2005.

Source: Harold W. Stanley and Richard G. Niemi, *Vital Statistics on American Politics, 2005–2006* (Washington, DC: CQ Press, 2006).

PARTICIPATION

Deciding on a Political Party

citizen acquires a party label and accepts its standard as a summary of his or her political views and preferences. (For trends in party identification, see Analyzing Visuals: Party Identification, 1952–2004.)

For those Americans who do firmly adopt a party label, their party often becomes a central political reference symbol and perceptual screen, a prism or filter through

Politics Now

A PURPLE ELECTORATE?

Journalists, pundits, and their like have generally assumed that the growing political divisions in the United States are between so-called "blue" and "red" states. Blue states are largely composed of New England, New York, the Pacific Coast, and a few Midwestern states. Red States make up the South, the Midwest, Southwest, the Rockies, and Alaska. The electoral map of the 2000 presidential election reflected this striking geographical continuity, which was generally duplicated in the 2004 presidential election. Many suppose that the stark contrast on the political map indicates a growing division among the American people, but the reality is that Americans are not as ideologically rigid as the map might indicate. Polling from after the 2004 election indicates that most Americans do not fit neatly into the categories of liberal or conservative, with most respondents demonstrating inconsistent or ambivalent views on many issues that clearly divide partisans. Increasingly pundits and scholars are referring to the American political landscape as being more "purple," or a complex combination of both liberal and conservative beliefs.

There is a tendency for people to pay more attention to those who make the most noise; subsequently, activists and extremists receive more attention, giving us the impression that everyone is an activist and an extremist. Looking at the survey results at right, it's clear that Americans are more "in sync" with regard to social issues like the death penalty, making English the official language, and school vouchers than one would otherwise suppose. Still, the results at right do reveal that there are some important differences between voters in red and blue states. Red state voters tend to be somewhat more conservative and more likely to be evan-

gelical Christians than blue state voters. With results like these, it is hard to discount entirely the belief in a cultural division among Americans.

RED VERSUS BLUE

Survey responses from voters in "red states" (states won by the Republican George W. Bush) and "blue states" (states won by the Democrat Al Gore) in the 2000 presidential election.

	Blue	Red
Party		
Democratic self-ID	40	32
Republican self-ID	25	34
Ideology		
Liberal	20	11
Conservative	24	31
Religion		
Evangelical Christian	28	45
Religion is important	62	74
Issues		
Do whatever it takes to protect the environment	70	64
Homosexuality should be accepted in society	57	45
Favor death penalty	70	77
Abortion always legal	48	37
Stricter gun control	64	52
Make English official language	70	66
Favor school vouchers	51	54

Sources: National survey, Pew Research Center for the People and the Press (2000); and Morris P. Fiorina et al., *Culture War? The Myth of a Polarized America* (New York: Longman, 2005).

which the world of politics and government flows and is interpreted. For these partisans, party identification is a significant aspect of their political personality and a way of defining and explaining themselves to others. The loyalty generated by the label can be as intense as any enjoyed by sports teams and alma maters. (But, see Politics Now: A Purple Electorate?)

Individual party identifications are reinforced by the legal institutionalization of the major parties. Because of restrictive ballot laws, campaign finance rules, the powerful inertia of political tradition, and many other factors, voters for all practical purposes are limited to a choice between a Democrat and a Republican in almost all elections—a situation that naturally encourages the pragmatic choosing up of sides. About half of the states require a voter to state a party preference (or independent status) when registering to vote, and they restrict voting in a party primary only to registrants in that particular party, making it an incentive for voters to affiliate themselves with a party.[33]

Whatever the societal and governmental forces responsible for party identification, the explanations of partisan loyalty at the individual's level are understandably more personal. Not surprisingly, parents are the single greatest influence in establishing a person's first party identification. Politically active parents with the same party loyalty raise children who will be strong party identifiers, whereas parents without party affiliations or with mixed affiliations produce offspring more likely to be independents (see chapter 11).

Early socialization is hardly the last step in an individual's acquisition and maintenance of a party identity; marriage, economic status, and other aspects of adult life can change one's loyalty. Charismatic political personalities, particularly at the national level (such as Franklin D. Roosevelt and Ronald Reagan) can influence party identification, as can cataclysmic events (the Civil War and the Great Depression are the best examples). Hot-button social issues (for instance, abortion and same-sex marriage) can also influence party ties. Social class remains a powerful indicator of likely partisan choice in the United States, with wealthy Americans tending to prefer the Republican Party and working-class Americans tending to favor the Democratic Party, though the relationship is weaker than in other Western democracies. Not only are Americans less inclined than Europeans to perceive class distinctions, preferring instead to see themselves and most other people as members of an exceedingly broad middle class, but other factors, including sectionalism and candidate-oriented politics, tend to blur class lines in voting.

GROUP AFFILIATIONS

Just as individuals vary in the strength of their partisan choice, so, too, do groups vary in the degree to which they identify with the Democratic Party or the Republican Party. Variations in party identification are particularly noticeable when geographic region, gender, race and ethnicity, age, social and economic status, religion, marital status, and ideology are examined. (See Table 12.2.)

Geographic Region In modern American politics, the geographic regions are relatively closely contested between the parties. The South, which was solidly Democratic as a result of party attachments that were cultivated in the nineteenth century and hardened in the fires of the Civil War, is now a competitive two-party region. While Democrats still outdo Republicans in local elections in the South, in the 2004 elections, Southerners elected Republicans to a majority of the U.S. House seats representing the states of the old Confederacy, and Republican presidential candidates have come to rely on strong support in southern states.

Gender Some political scientists argue that the difference in the way men and women vote first emerged in 1920, when newly enfranchised women registered overwhelmingly as Republicans. It was not until the 1980 presidential election, however, that a noticeable and possibly significant gender gap emerged. When Ronald Reagan trounced incumbent Democratic President Jimmy Carter, he did so with the support of 54 percent of the men who voted but only 46 percent of the women voters. The 2004 election showed that the gender gap was smaller but still present (see Figure 12.6). While polls leading up to November 2, 2004, hinted at a possible change, the results illustrated that women still favored Democrats, and men still favored Republicans. George W. Bush received 55 percent of the men's vote versus 44 percent for Kerry, while Bush received 48 percent of the women's vote versus Kerry's 51 percent.

One of the biggest challenges facing Republicans is how to gain the support of women without alienating their male base. Besides abortion and women's rights issues, women's concerns for peace and social justice may provide much of the gap's distance. For instance, women are usually less likely than men to favor American military action and are generally more supportive of education and social welfare spending. Most researchers now explain the gender gap not by focusing on the Republican Party's difficulties in attracting female voters, but rather on the Democratic Party's inability to attract the votes of males. In other words, as one study notes, the

TABLE 12.2 **PARTY IDENTIFICATION BY GROUP AFFILIATION**

		Democratic Party	Independent Party	Republican Party
Region	North East	30	43	22
	North Central	29	30	30
	South	35	29	30
	West	30	35	30
Gender	Male	25	38	30
	Female	37	29	38
Race	Asian	18	39	36
	Black	61	33	2
	Hispanic	36	36	15
	White	25	32	36
Age	<30	31	42	21
	30-49	29	32	30
	50 +	34	30	31
Income	<35,000	33	35	25
	35,000-69,999	34	29	33
	70,000 +	26	30	38
Education	High School or	32	36	25
	College	29	30	34
	Advanced Degree	39	25	32
Union Member	Yes	36	38	20
Religion Type	Protestant	31	31	32
	Catholic	32	33	30
	Jewish	60	20	17
Religious Attendance	Weekly or >	31	29	34
	Monthly	31	32	32
	< Monthly	38	31	25
Marital Status	Married	28	29	36
	Single	32	42	20
	Divorced	33	35	25
Ideology	Conservative	18	28	48
	Moderate	29	37	30
	Liberal	51	39	6

Note: In this table, independent leaners are collapsed into the independent column. Partisans and strong partisans are collapsed into the party columns. Due to rounding, not all rows equal 100 percent.

Source: National Election Study 2004.

gender gap exists because of the lack of support for the Democratic Party among men and the corresponding male preference for the Republican Party, stemming from differences in opinions about social welfare and military issues.[34]

Race and Ethnicity African Americans are the most dramatically split population subgroup in party terms. The 50-percent-plus advantage they offer the Democrats dwarfs the edge given to either party by any other significant segment of the electorate, and their proportion of strong Democrats (about 40 percent) is three times that of whites. African Americans account almost entirely for the slight lead in party affiliation that Democrats normally enjoy over Republicans, since the GOP has recently been able to attract a narrow majority of whites to its standard. Perhaps as a reflection of the massive party chasm separating blacks and whites, the two races differ greatly on many policy issues, with blacks overwhelmingly on the liberal side and whites closer to the conservative pole. The belief of most blacks that their fate is

FIGURE 12.6 THE GENDER GAP: MEN AND WOMEN'S VOTE CHOICES IN THE 2004
PRESIDENTIAL ELECTION

The vote choices of men and women have consistently shown clear differences in
the last twenty years, with Republicans consistently lagging behind Democrats in
the number of women voters. The election of 2004 proved no different, as an estimated 7 percent more women than men voted for John Kerry nationwide. There
are variations throughout the country in the intensity of the gender gap, as is illustrated in this map based on exit polling for the 2004 presidential election.

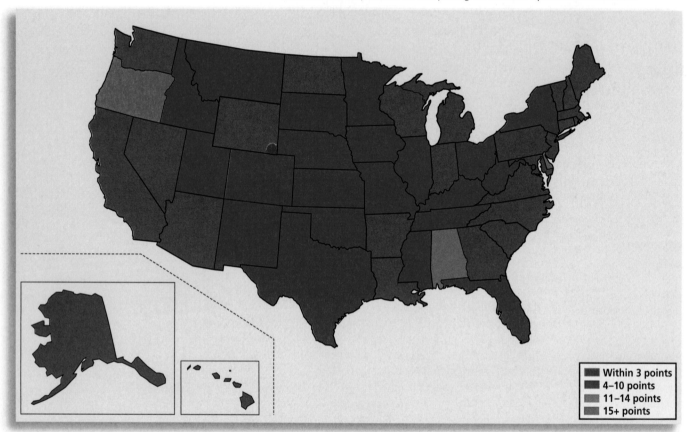

Legend:
- Within 3 points
- 4–10 points
- 11–14 points
- 15+ points

Source: Election 2004 exit polling, CNN, http://www.cnn.com.

linked causes upper-income blacks generally to vote the same as lower-income blacks.
Whites see no such class-based obligation.[35] An exception, incidentally, is abortion
and gay rights, where religious beliefs lead many African Americans to adopt more
conservative stances than their white Democratic counterparts.

Hispanics supplement African Americans as Democratic stalwarts; by more
than three to one, Hispanics prefer the Democratic Party. Voting patterns of Puerto
Ricans are very similar to those of African Americans, while Mexican Americans
favor the Democrats by smaller margins. An exception is the Cuban American population, whose anti–Fidel Castro tilt leads to support for the Republican Party. In a
2004 preelection survey, 81 percent of Cuban American respondents said they supported President Bush.[36] As the Hispanic population has increased rapidly in recent
years and now exceeds that of African Americans, Republicans have fought to make
inroads with Hispanic voters. President Bush made a high-ranking Hispanic appointment when he selected former Texas Supreme Court Justice Alberto Gonzales
to serve as attorney general. Governor Jeb Bush of Florida, President Bush's brother,

Photo courtesy: Stefan Zaklin/epa/Corbis

■ In July of 2006, President George W. Bush presided over a naturalization ceremony at Walter Reed Army Medical Center for three Hispanic soldiers who were injured in Iraq. The president signed an executive order after the September 11, 2001, terrorist attacks making non-citizens immediately eligible for citizenship when they served on active duty in the U.S. military. Bush's support for legislation that would have allowed many illegal immigrants currently living in the United States to achieve legal status met with significant opposition from his own party.

speaks fluent Spanish and often campaigns with Hispanic groups on behalf of the Republican Party. Recent debates and legislation regarding immigration have focused both parties on the importance of the emerging Hispanic vote, with Republicans cautiously attempting to satisfy their base with restrictions and increased enforcement without alienating a potentially supportive new voting bloc. Karl Rove, president Bush's political adviser, has strongly advocated attracting Hispanic voters to the Republican Party, believing the party's social conservatism would appeal to many new immigrants. However, in some states with high immigrant populations such as California, the Republican Party has not had much success in finding a balance between attracting new immigrant voters and appeasing those within the party who support stringent immigration enforcement measures.[37]

Age Age has long been associated with party identification, as most voters develop their partisan affiliations based on formative political experiences growing up. For example, many voters who were alive during the Great Depression identify strongly with the Democratic Party, whereas many who were young during the Reagan years identify with the Republican Party. Today, generally the very youngest and very oldest voters tend to prefer the Democratic Party, while middle-aged voters disproportionately favor the Republican Party. The Democratic Party's more liberal positions on social issues tend to resonate with today's moderate, but socially progressive, young adults. (For a discussion of the evolution of the youth vote, see On Campus: Party Affiliation Among College Students.) The nation's oldest voters, who tend to focus on Social Security and Medicare, tend to favor the Democratic Party's consistent support for these programs and are generally skeptical of privatization plans supported by many Republicans. Middle-aged voters, often at the height of their careers and consequently at the height of their earnings potential, tend to favor the low taxes and fiscal conservatism often championed by Republicans.

On Campus

PARTY AFFILIATION AMONG COLLEGE STUDENTS

The political turmoil over the reinstitution of the draft during the Vietnam War created a movement among young citizens for a lowering of the legal voting age to eighteen, leading to ratification of the Twenty-Sixth Amendment to the Constitution in 1971. Since that time, the vote of college-age students has been important to American politics, with each party vying for the attention of these newly eligible voters. Traditionally, these youngest voters voted the least, despite efforts by public and private organizations to register and encourage participation. Happily, in the 2004 presidential election, turnout among those age eighteen to twenty-four surged to 47 percent, or 11 percent more than in 2000. It is too soon to tell if this is an emerging trend, but it is nonetheless encouraging that younger voters are engaging in American politics in greater numbers.

During the 1970s, the youth vote was predominately liberal and oriented toward the Democratic Party. By the end of the 1980s, after President Ronald Reagan's two terms in office, the eighteen- to twenty-four-year-old age group was one of the most Republican of all, marking what many believed was the beginning of a secular realignment.

Young people began to swing back to the Democrats in 1992. President Bill Clinton, who aggressively courted the youth vote, ran strongly among eighteen- to twenty-four-year-olds. In 1996, young voters voted 53 percent for President Clinton and only 34 percent for Republican Senator Bob Dole. In 2000, young voters were almost evenly split: 48 percent voted for Al Gore and 46 percent voted for George W. Bush. In 2004, however, John Kerry won the youth vote by almost ten points, garnering 54 percent to George W. Bush's 45 percent.

It might be that young voters are more candidate centered and less loyal to a political party than are older voters. It may also be that young voters have been neglected by the political parties. Another line of thinking suggests that neither party currently provides a solid fit with the issues that are important to young voters. Young voters tend to hold more liberal positions on social issues, like abortion rights and same-sex marriage, while at the same time they tend to favor traditionally conservative positions like low taxes and strong national security.[a] If parties could once again find issues that capture the imagination of young voters, then perhaps young voters might become more loyal to a party.

---

[a] For more information on issues, turnout, and other statistics on the youth vote, see the Center for Information and Research on Civic Learning and Engagement's Web site on youth voting: http://www.civicyouth.org/quick/youth_voting.htm.

VIDEO DEBATE

Poverty and Political Parties

Social and Economic Factors Occupation, income, and education also influence party affiliation. The GOP remains predominant among executives, professionals, and white-collar workers, whereas the Democrats lead substantially among trial lawyers, educators, and blue-collar workers. Labor union members are also Democratic by nearly two to one. Women who do not work outside the home are less liberal and Democratic than those who do. Occupation, income, and education are closely related, of course, so many of the same partisan patterns appear in all three classifications. Democratic support drops as one climbs the income scale. Those with a college education tend to support the Republican Party, while those with advanced degrees tend to be Democratic.

Religion Party preferences by religion are also traditional, but with modern twists. White Protestants—especially Methodists, Presbyterians, and Episcopalians—favor the Republicans, whereas Catholics and, even more so, Jewish voters tend to favor the Democratic Party. Decreased polarization is apparent all around, though.[38] Democrats have made inroads among many liberal Protestant denominations over the past three decades, and Republicans can now sometimes claim up to 25 percent of Jewish voters and a nearly equal share of the Catholic vote. Evangelical Christians are somewhat less Republican than commonly believed. The GOP usually has just a 10 percent edge among them, primarily because so many African Americans, who are strongly pro-Democrat, are also members of this group.

Marital Status   Even marital status reveals something about partisan affiliation. People who are married, a traditionally more conservative group, tend to favor the Republican Party, while single people who have never married tend to favor the Democratic Party. Taken as a group, the widowed lean toward the Democrats, probably because there are many more widows than widowers; here, the gender gap is again expressing itself. The divorced and the separated, who may be experiencing economic hardship, appear to be more liberal than the married population.

Ideology   Ideologically, there are few surprises. When asked to rate each party on an ideological 7-point scale where 1 was liberal and 7 was conservative, over 40 percent of voters rated Democrats a 2, at the liberal end of the continuum, and Republicans a 6, at the conservative end of the continuum, thus providing support for the belief that both parties are ideologically distinct.[39] Not surprisingly, liberals are overwhelmingly Democratic and conservatives are staunchly Republican in most surveys and opinion studies.

Is The Party Over or Has It Just Begun?

OVER THE PAST TWO DECADES, numerous political scientists as well as other observers, journalists, and party activists have become increasingly anxious about **dealignment,** a general decline in partisan identification and loyalty in the electorate.[40] Since parties traditionally provide political information and serve as an engine of political participation, it has been feared that weakening party attachments are undermining political involvement.

> **dealignment**
> A general decline in partisan identification and loyalty in the electorate.

As the table in Analyzing Visuals: Party Identification, 1952–2004 (p. 449) illustrates, many public opinion surveys have shown an increase in independents at the expense of the two major parties. The Center for Political Studies/Survey Research Center (CPS/SRC) of the University of Michigan has charted the rise of self-described independents from a low of 19 percent in 1958 to a peak of 40 percent in 2000, with percentages in recent years consistently hovering just below the high-water mark of 40 percent. Before the 1950s (although the evidence for this research is more circumstantial because of the scarcity of reliable survey research data), it is believed that independents were far fewer in number and party loyalties were considerably firmer than is the case today.

Currently, the Democratic and Republican Parties can claim a roughly equal percentage of self-identified partisans, with levels fluctuating around one-third of the population each. This can seem inconsistent with voting behavior and election results, but one must pay close attention to the manner in which these data are collected. When pollsters ask for party identification information, they generally proceed in two stages. First, they inquire whether a respondent considers himself or herself to be a Democrat, Republican, or independent. Then the party identifiers are asked to categorize themselves as "strong" or "not very strong" supporters, while the independents are pushed to reveal their "leanings" with a question such as "Which party do you normally support in elections, the Democrats or the Republicans?" It may be true that some independent respondents are thereby prodded to pick a party under the pressure of the interview situation, regardless of their true feelings. But, research has demonstrated that independent "leaners" in fact vote very much like real partisans, in some elections more so than the "not very strong" party identifiers. There is reason to count the independent leaners as closet partisans, though voting behavior is not the equivalent of real partisan identification.

VIDEO ROUNDTABLE

Declining Political
Parties

In fact, the reluctance of leaners to admit their real party identities reveals a significant change in attitudes about political parties and their role in our society. Being a socially acceptable, integrated, and contributing member of one's community once almost demanded partisan affiliation; it was a badge of good citizenship signifying that one was a patriot. Today, many voters consider such labels an offense to their individualism, and many Americans insist that they vote for "the person, not the party."

The reasons for these anti-party attitudes are not hard to find. The growth of issue-oriented politics that cut across party lines for voters who feel intensely about certain policy matters is partly the cause. So, too, is the emphasis on personality politics by the mass media and political consultants.

Although the underlying partisanship of the American people has not declined significantly since 1952, voter-admitted partisanship has dropped considerably. From 1952 to 1964, about three-fourths or more of the electorate volunteered a party choice without prodding, but since 1970 an average of less than two-thirds has been willing to do so. Professed independents (including leaners) have increased from around one-fifth of the electorate in the 1950s to over one-third during the last three decades. In recent years, the number of voters who identify with parties has stabilized, but the number still lags far behind historical norms.

Despite the challenges described above, however, the parties' decline can easily be exaggerated. When we view parties in the broad sweep of U.S. history, several strengths of parties become clear.

First, although political parties have evolved considerably and changed form from time to time, they usually have been reliable vehicles for mass participation in a representative democracy. In fact, parties orchestrated the gradual but steady expansion of suffrage in order to incorporate new supporters into the party fold.[41] Keep in mind, however, the notable exceptions in which parties attempted to contract the electorate. Southern Democrats, for example, worked to exclude African American political participation from the end of Reconstruction through the civil rights movement of the 1960s, in an effort to maintain their political power in the region.

Second, the parties' journeys through U.S. history have been characterized by the same ability to adapt to prevailing conditions that is often cited as the genius of the Constitution. Both major parties exhibit flexibility and pragmatism, which help ensure their survival and the success of the society they serve.

Third, despite massive changes in political conditions and frequent dramatic shifts in the electorate's mood, the two major parties not only have achieved remarkable longevity but also have almost always provided strong competition for each other and the voters at the national level. (See Global Perspective: The Emergence of New Parties for information on how America's experience with parties differs from that of most European nations.) Of the thirty presidential elections from 1884 to 2004, for instance, the Republicans won seventeen and the Democrats fourteen. Even when calamities have beset the parties—the Great Depression in the 1930s or the Watergate scandal of 1973–1974 for the Republicans (see chapter 8), and the Civil War for the Democrats—the two parties have proved tremendously resilient, sometimes bouncing back from landslide defeats to win the next election.

Fourth, while the party in the electorate might have waned in recent years, depending on whether you look at the relatively modest rise in pure independents or more robust increase in independent leaners, the party in government and the party organizations are stronger than ever. The sharp rise in party unity scores in Congress discussed earlier in the chapter suggests the party in government is alive and well, while the unprecedented fund-raising of the party organizations suggests that political parties are here to stay.

Perhaps most of all, history teaches us that the development of parties in the United States has been inevitable, as James Madison predicted. Human nature alone guarantees conflict in any society; in a free state, the question is simply how to contain and channel conflict productively without infringing on individual liberties. The

Global Perspective

THE EMERGENCE OF NEW PARTIES

As we have seen in this chapter, the American political party system essentially is a two-party system. Occasionally, third parties or independent candidates surface and make a bid to win public office, but for all practical purposes, Americans remain wedded to the Republican and Democratic parties. Such long-standing allegiances are not the case in Western Europe. There, support for new political parties (those founded since 1960) has been growing steadily over the past four decades at the expense of older established political parties, regardless of whether we look at presidential systems or parliamentary ones. The emergence of these new parties is tied to voter dissatisfaction with existing parties and the ability of new parties to tap into very specific complaints and concerns on the part of citizens.

In the 1960s, new parties received only 3.9 percent of the vote across Western Europe. They were most successful in France (16.3 percent) and least successful in Great Britain (0 percent) and Ireland (0.3 percent). Their percentage of the vote increased to 9.7 percent in the 1970s and to 15.3 percent in the 1980s. In the 1990s, new parties received 23.7 percent of all votes cast in Western Europe—a 19.8 percent increase.

The following table shows the growth of support for new parties in selected Western European states. Only in Great Britain have they failed to increase their share of the vote.

MEAN PERCENTAGE OF VOTE RECEIVED BY NEW PARTIES

	1960s	1970s	1980s	1990s
Finland	1.6	8.2	13.7	22.3
France	16.3	29.1	27.1	41.7
Germany	4.3	0.5	7.5	13.9
Great Britain	0	0.8	11.6	2.3
Italy	9.5	3.3	7.1	66.8
Netherlands	2.3	26.6	44.5	45.9

Even more significant than the growth in support for new parties in Western Europe is the growing support over the past two decades for extremist parties—political parties at the ideological ends of the political spectrum. Those on the political left are most easily identified today as Green parties. They advocate a clearly defined and aggressive pro-environmental agenda. Those on the political right tend to be more difficult to classify. Many of the most visible ones, such as the National Front in France or the Freedom Party in Austria, advocate strongly nationalistic and anti-immigration policies that critics characterize as racist and anti-Semitic.

Jean-Marie Le Pen, leader of the French National Front, scored a surprising 16.86 percent of the vote in the 2002 presidential elections, enough for Le Pen to go on to a second round of voting with the incumbent Jacques Chirac. Having such a marginal and extreme party make it to a second round of voting was a first for French politics and sent shock waves throughout Europe and the world. Le Pen and the National Front's fortunes did not last far beyond the first round of voting, however, as Chirac easily won the second round with a convincing 82 percent of the vote. In Austria, the Freedom Party, led by Jörg Haider, gradually gained support during the 1990s, eventually becoming part of a coalition government in 2000. Many outside of Austria, especially Jewish groups, fear the Freedom Party's influence because of its strident anti-immigrant, anti-European Union, and nationalistic political history. While the party lost a good deal of support in the 2002 elections, and Haider has stepped down as leader, the party persists. In 2004, Haider was elected governor of the Austrian province of Carinthia with over 42 percent of the vote.

MEAN PERCENTAGE OF VOTE RECEIVED BY EXTREMIST PARTIES

	Green Vote		Right-Wing Vote	
	1980s	1990s	1980s	1990s
Finland	2.7	7.0	0	0.3
France	0.9	8.4	6.7	14.2
Germany	5.1	6.4	0.3	2.5
Great Britain	0.3	0.3	0.1	0
Italy	1.3	2.7	6.6	20.9
Netherlands	1.1	5.6	0.6	1.8

QUESTIONS

1. Under what conditions might new parties develop in the United States and get the type of support that they have in Western Europe?
2. Which type of extremist parties are more likely to become electorally successful in the United States, ones on the political left or the political right? Why?

Source: Hans Keman, ed., *Comparative Democratic Politics* (London: Sage, 2002), 134, 137.

Framers' utopian hopes for the avoidance of partisan faction, Madison's chief concern, have given way to an appreciation of the parties' constructive contributions to conflict definition and resolution during the years of the American republic. Political parties have become the primary means by which society addresses its irreconcilable differences, and as such they play an essential role in democratic society.

Summary

A POLITICAL PARTY is an organized effort by office holders, candidates, activists, and voters to pursue their common interests by gaining and exercising power through the electoral process. Parties encompass three separate components: (1) the governmental party comprises office holders who organize themselves and pursue policy objectives under a party label; (2) the party organization comprises the workers and activists who comprise the party's formal structure; and, (3) the party in the electorate refers to the voters who consider themselves allied or associated with the party. In this chapter, we have made the following points:

1. **What Is a Political Party?**

   A political party is an organized effort by office holders, candidates, activists, and voters to pursue their common interests by gaining and exercising power through the electoral process. The goal is to win office so as to exercise power and pursue common policy objectives.

2. **The Evolution of the American Party System**

   The evolution of U.S. political parties has been remarkably smooth, and the stability of the Democratic and Republican groupings is a wonder, considering all the social and political tumult in U.S. history.

3. **The Functions of the American Party System**

   For 150 years, the two-party system has served as the mechanism American society uses to organize and resolve social and political conflict. The Democratic and Republican Parties, through lengthy nominating processes, provide a screening mechanism for those who aspire to office, helping to weed out unqualified individuals, expose and test candidates' ideas on important policy questions, and ensure a measure of long-term continuity and accountability.

4. **The Party Organization**

   The basic structure of the major parties is complex and amorphous. The state and local parties are generally more important than the national ones, though campaign technologies and fund-raising concentrated in Washington, D.C., have helped to centralize power within national party committees. Political parties' use of modern technologies and communication strategies has begun to be tempered by a renewed focus on get out the vote drives, canvassing, and voter identification. Nevertheless, the capabilities of the party organizations vary widely from place to place.

5. **The Party in Government**

   Political parties are not restricted to their role as grassroots organizations of voters; they also have another major role *inside* government institutions. The party in government comprises the office holders who organize themselves and pursue policy objectives under a party label.

6. **The Party in the Electorate**

   The party in the electorate refers to the voters who consider themselves allied or associated with a particular party. This significant political party element provides the foundation for the organizational and governmental parties.

7. **Is the Party Over or Has It Just Begun?**

   While dealignment, a general decline in partisan identification and loyalty in the electorate, has undoubtedly occurred over the last fifty years, the future of the party system is not in doubt. Parties remain strong, adaptive, and essential players in the political process and are likely to remain so in the future.

KEY TERMS

candidate-centered politics, p. 426
civil service laws, p. 426
coalition, p. 429
critical election, p. 427
dealignment, p. 455
direct primary, p. 426
governmental party, p. 422
hard money, p. 440
issue-oriented politics, p. 426
machine, p. 425
national convention, p. 437
national party platform, p. 432
organizational party, p. 422
party identification, p. 447
party in the electorate, p. 422
party realignment, p. 427
political party, p. 421
proportional representation, p. 433
secular realignment, p. 429
soft money, p. 440
think tank, p. 439
ticket-split, p. 426
winner-take-all system, p. 433

SELECTED READINGS

Abramowitz, Alan, and Jeffrey A. Segal. *Senate Elections*. Ann Arbor: University of Michigan Press, 1997.

Aldrich, John Herbert. *Why Parties? The Origin and Transformation of Political Parties in America*. Chicago: University of Chicago Press, 1995.

Corrado, Anthony, et al. *The New Campaign Finance Sourcebook*. Washington, DC: Brookings Institution Press, 2005.

Cox, Gary W., and Mathew McCubbins, *Setting the Agenda*. New York: Cambridge University Press, 2005.

Fiorina, Morris P. *Divided Government*. Boston: Allyn and Bacon, 1996.

Fiorina, Morris P., et al., *Culture War? The Myth of a Polarized America*. New York: Longman, 2005.

Green, Donald, Bradley Palmquist, and Eric Schickler. *Partisan Hearts and Minds*. New Haven: Yale University Press, 2002.

Hershey, Marjorie. *Party Politics in America*, 12th ed. New York: Pearson Longman, 2007.

Jacobson, Gary C. *The Politics of Congressional Elections*, 6th ed. New York: Longman, 2004.

Jewell, Malcolm E., and Sarah M. Morehouse. *Political Parties and Elections in American States*, 4th ed. Washington: CQ Press, 2001.

Key, V. O., Jr. *Politics, Parties, and Pressure Groups*, 5th ed. New York: Crowell, 1964.

Maisel, L. Sandy, ed. *The Parties Respond*, 4th ed. Boulder, CO: Westview, 2002.

Mayhew, David R. *Placing Parties in American Politics*. Princeton, NJ: Princeton University Press, 1986.

Milkis, Sidney M. *The President and the Parties: The Transformation of the American Party System Since the New Deal*. New York: Oxford University Press, 1993.

Reichley, James. *The Life of the Parties: A History of American Political Parties*. Lanham, MD: Rowman and Littlefield, 2000.

Riordan, William L., ed. *Plunkitt of Tammany Hall*. New York: Dutton, 1963.

Rosenstone, Steven J., Roy L. Behr, and Edward H. Lazarus. *Third Parties in America*, 2nd ed. Princeton, NJ: Princeton University Press, 1996.

Sabato, Larry J., and Howard R. Ernst. *Encyclopedia of American Parties and Elections*. New York: FactsOnFile, 2005.

Sabato, Larry J., and Bruce A. Larson. *The Party's Just Begun: Shaping Political Parties for America's Future*, 2nd ed. New York: Longman, 2002.

Schattschneider, E. E. *Party Government*. New York: Holt, Rinehart and Winston, 1942.

Shea, Daniel M. *Transforming Democracy: Legislative Campaign Committees and Political Parties*. Albany: SUNY Press, 1995.

Wattenberg, Martin P. *The Decline of American Political Parties, 1952–1996*. Cambridge, MA: Harvard University Press, 1998.

WEB EXPLORATIONS

To evaluate how the "Big Two" political parties portray their platform issues and use political language to present their policies, go to
http://www.democrats.org and
http://www.rnc.org

To learn about the campaign finances of the political parties, go to
http://www.tray.com

To explore the partisan and ideological agendas of unaffiliated think tanks and search for connections to specific parties or politicians, go to
http://www.heritage.org
http://www.cato.org
http://www.ppionline.org

To compare the planks of several minor parties and find one that represents your views, go to
http://www.reformparty.org
http://www.gp.org
http://www.lp.org

To learn about the informal factions and interest groups that strive for influence with the major parties, go to
http://www.adaction.org/www.cc.org
http://www.moveon.org

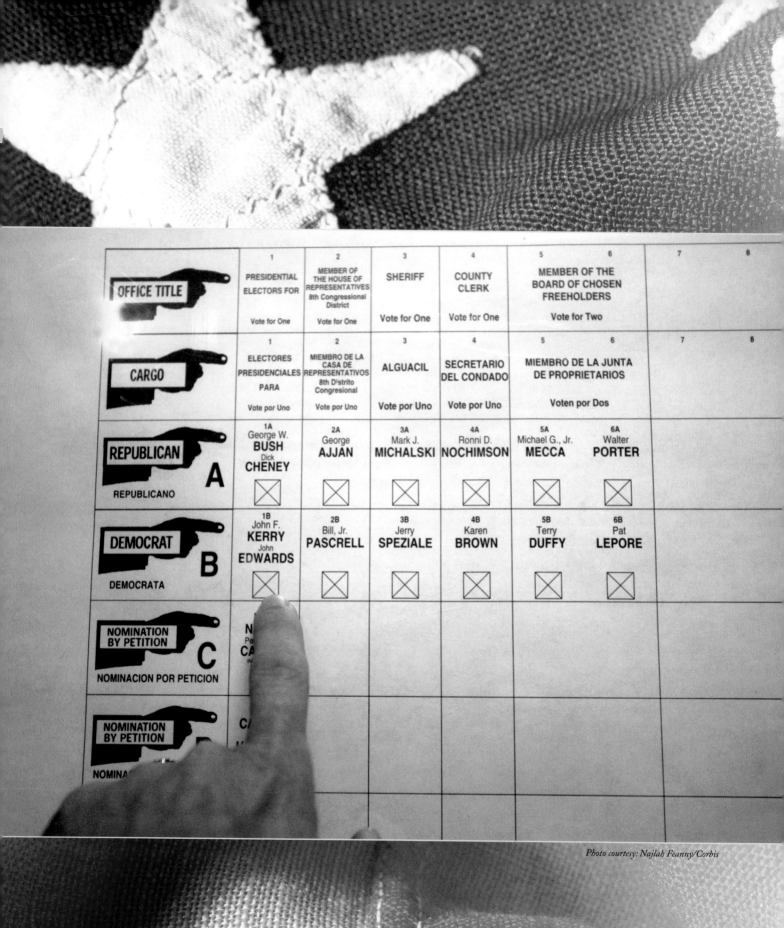

Photo courtesy: Najlah Feanny/Corbis

VOTING AND ELECTIONS

13

DURING THE MONTHS leading up to the 2004 presidential election, no one doubted that the race between Republican President George W. Bush and the Democratic challenger, Massachusetts Senator John Kerry, would be close. The question everyone wanted answered was exactly how close it would be. Although the presidential election is national, both candidates focused on specific states that showed either narrow margins or even ties. Many of these "battleground states" were located in the Rust Belt—Wisconsin, Michigan, Ohio, and Pennsylvania. Others—such as Minnesota, Iowa, Florida, New Hampshire, New Mexico, and Hawaii—were spread across the country.

Of these several battleground states, three stood out because of their razor-thin margins of victory in 2000 and their large number of electoral votes. Pennsylvania, a state the 2000 Democratic candidate Al Gore won by 220,000 votes, had twenty-one electoral votes. Florida, with the minuscule and heavily contested 537-vote margin for Bush in 2000, had twenty-seven electoral votes. Finally, there was Ohio with twenty electoral votes, a state no Republican candidate has lost and still been able to go on to win the presidency. By Election Day, it was conventional wisdom that a candidate had to win at least two of these three states in order to win the election. By early evening, it was clear that Bush would take Florida by a much wider margin than in 2000, and Kerry would narrowly win Pennsylvania. This left the election up to Ohio, which both candidates had visited more than twenty-five times in 2004. Throughout the night, Bush appeared to hold a 2 percent voter margin over Kerry, leading some networks—FOX News and NBC—to call the state for Bush, while others—such as ABC, CBS, and CNN— left it too close to call. However, fears that Ohio might become the 2004 version of Florida quickly abated when it became clear that Kerry could not rely on provisional and absentee ballots to overtake Bush's voter lead. By the morning after Election Day, Bush was declared the winner in Ohio.

Bush also won the battleground states of New Mexico and Iowa (states Gore carried in 2000), but he lost New Hampshire to Kerry. The remaining

CHAPTER OUTLINE

- ⭐ Voting Behavior
- ⭐ Elections in the United States
- ⭐ Presidential Elections
- ⭐ Congressional Elections
- ⭐ The 2006 Midterm Elections
- ⭐ Reforming the Electoral Process

battleground states also went to Kerry, but they did not collectively have enough Electoral College votes for him to win. When looking at how the 2004 Electoral College map changed from the 2000 map, one can see that the division of coastal "blue" (Democratic) states and "red" (Republican) states became even more contiguous. Like the Pacific states (except Alaska), New England is now completely Democratic in terms of Electoral College votes, while the South from Florida to Arizona is solidly Republican. The general regional divisions between red and blue remained in 2006. Still, Republicans lost ground across the country in the 2006 midterm elections, with upsets in red states like Virginia, Texas, and Florida providing Senate and House Democrats with control of both chambers for the first time since 1994.

EVERY FOUR YEARS, on the Tuesday following the first Monday in November, a plurality of voters, simply by casting ballots peacefully across a continent-sized nation, reelects or replaces politicians at all levels of government—from the president of the United States, to members of the U.S. Congress, to state legislators. Americans tend to take this process for granted, but in truth it is a marvel. Many other countries do not enjoy the benefit of competitive elections and the peaceful transition of political power made possible through the electoral process. American political institutions have succeeded in maintaining peaceful elections, even when they are closely contested, as was the case with the 2000 presidential election. Elections take the pulse of average people and gauge their hopes and fears; they provide direction for government action; and they hold the nation's leaders accountable.

The United States of America, judging from its frequent elections at all levels of government for more offices than any other nation on earth, is committed to democracy. The nation has steadily increased the size of the electorate (those citizens eligible to vote) by removing restrictions based on property ownership, religion, race, and gender. But despite the increased access to the ballot box, and the various direct democratic devices such as primaries and initiatives opened to the public in the last century, voter turnout remains historically low. After all the blood spilled and energy expended to expand voting rights, little more than half of eligible voters bother to go to the polls.

This chapter focuses on patterns of voting over time, the purposes served by elections, and the various kinds of elections held in the United States. Presidential and congressional elections are given special attention, as their rich histories tell us a great deal about the American people and their changing hopes and needs. We conclude by returning to contemporary presidential elections and addressing key aspects of electoral reform.

- First, we will discuss *voting behavior*, focusing on distinct patterns in voter turnout and vote choice.
- Second, we will examine *the purposes and types of elections*, pointing out that elections at all levels confer a legitimacy on regimes better than any other method of change.
- Third, we will take a closer look at the elements of *presidential elections*, including primaries, conventions, and the Electoral College.
- Fourth, we will explore how *congressional elections*, although they share similarities with presidential elections, are really quite different.
- Fifth, we will discuss *the 2006 midterm elections* and their similarities and differences with other recent midterm elections.
- Finally, we will present arguments for *reforming the electoral process* and explore the potential benefits and unintended consequences of electoral change.

Voting Behavior

BY FAR THE MOST ACCEPTED and common method of political participation in the United States is voting in an election at the local, state, or national level. Voting is the most widespread example of **conventional political participation**—political participation that attempts to influence the political process through well-accepted and often moderate forms of persuasion, such as writing letters to government officials, making political contributions, and, as noted above, voting.

The war in Iraq has caused a great deal of political tension and revived a venerable American tradition of protest and demonstration. **Unconventional political participation** in the United States—political participation that attempts to influence the political process through unusual or extreme measures such as protests, boycotts, and picketing—is older than the nation itself and has been carried out during every period of American history. The Boston Tea Party and Shays's Rebellion are but two prominent early examples.

Elections are more common today than rebellions, however, and political scientists have focused significant time and energy looking at voting behavior. Research on voting behavior seeks primarily to explain two phenomena: voter turnout (that is, what factors contribute to an individual's decision to vote or not to vote) and vote choice (once the decision to vote has been made, what leads voters to choose one candidate over another). In this section, we will discuss patterns in voter turnout and analyze the relatively low level of voter participation in the United States; we will then turn our attention to patterns in vote choice.

PATTERNS IN VOTER TURNOUT

Turnout is the proportion of the voting-age public that votes. About 40 percent of the eligible adult population in the United States votes regularly, whereas 25 percent are occasional voters and 35 percent rarely or never vote. According to the International Institute for Democracy and Electoral Assistance, this places the United States far below nations such as Italy, Australia, and Sweden, which regularly have voting rates that exceed 80 percent. (See Global Perspective: Political Participation Around the World.)

As discussed in chapter 12, turnout is especially important in American elections because candidates are elected in a winner-take-all system, where an election's outcome can be influenced by a single voter. The presidential election of 2000 that resulted in George W. Bush becoming president is a classic example of the power of an individual's single vote. As recount succeeded recount in several states, and the fate of the presidency rested on razor-thin margins, many nonvoters in Florida, New Mexico, and Oregon must have wished they had taken the trouble to exercise their right to choose their leader. Some of the factors known to influence voter turnout include education, income, age, gender, race and ethnicity, and interest in politics.

Education People who vote are usually more highly educated than nonvoters. Other things being equal, college graduates are much more likely to vote than those with less education, and people with advanced degrees are the most likely to vote. People with more education tend to learn more about politics, are less hindered by registration requirements, and are more self-confident about their ability to affect public life.[1] Therefore, one might argue that

conventional political participation
Political participation that attempts to influence the political process through well-accepted, often moderate forms of persuasion.

unconventional political participation
Political participation that attempts to influence the political process through unusual or extreme measures, such as protests, boycotts, and picketing.

turnout
The proportion of the voting-age public that votes.

■ Anti-war activist Cindy Sheehan has been one of the most visible embodiments of unconventional political participation during the Iraq War. Sheehan, whose son Casey was killed in Iraq in 2004, has sought for over a year to meet with President Bush to convince him to withdraw troops.

Photo courtesy: Jason Reed/Reuters/Corbis

Global Perspective

POLITICAL PARTICIPATION AROUND THE WORLD

The table shows the average percentage of the voting age population that voted in national elections between 1945 and 2005.

Country	Vote Percentage
Italy	93
Iceland	90
New Zealand	86
Netherlands	85
Australia	84
Denmark	84
Sweden	83
Germany	81
Israel	80
Norway	80
Finland	79
Romania	77
Spain	77
Ireland	75
United Kingdom	75
Japan	69
Canada	68
France	67
India	61
Switzerland	49
United States	48

Source: International Institute for Democracy and Electoral Assistance, "Global Database," http://www.idea.int/vt/survey/voter_turnout_pop2.cfm.

From a global perspective, voting rates in the United States are embarrassingly low. While other Western democracies have average voting rates that often exceed 70 percent, the number generally is less than 50 percent for the United States. Italy, the nation with the highest average voting rate since 1945, exceeds 90 percent, while the average voting rate among all the countries in the International Institute for Democracy and Electoral Assistance data base was 65 percent.

While voting rates in the United States are unquestionably low, the figures might not be as discouraging as they suggest. Voting in the United States remains a voluntary activity, but voting is compulsory in a number of countries—for example, in Australia, Italy, Uruguay, Belgium, and Cyprus, all of which enjoy rates of over 70 percent participation. Few countries with compulsory voting laws have strict enforcement requirements, however, with the most strict penalties usually being only a modest fine. Moreover, voters in the United States and Switzerland, with their lower turnout numbers, are called on to vote far more often than in other nations. Between 1945 and 2005, the United States held thirty national elections in addition to several local and state elections, while Italy held only fourteen, Iceland held sixteen, and Portugal held nine. Switzerland's canton system holds countless local elections for a variety of candidates and issues. And, while voting rates are low in the United States for any given election, when one takes into account the number of elections that take place in the United States, Americans are frequent participators in the electoral process.

There is additional evidence to suggest that voting rates in the United States are not as dismal as they first appear. The 2000 and 2004 presidential elections saw increases in voter participation. In the 2004 presidential race, more than 122 million Americans cast ballots, more than in any other election in U.S. history, though the voting rate as a percentage of eligible voters remained relatively low, at 57 percent. In comparison, in 1960, the year with the highest voter participation rate in the twentieth century (65 percent), fewer than 69 million people voted in the presidential race. Moreover, through the 1970s, there were substantial differences between the voting rates in the American South and the rest of the nation, differences that have been dramatically reduced in recent elections.

QUESTIONS

1. How often should elections be held? Can they be held too frequently? Explain your reasoning.
2. Should the United States make voting compulsory, as it is in Australia and Belgium? Why or why not?

---

institutions of higher education provide citizens with opportunities to learn about and become interested in politics.

Income There is also a strong relationship between income and voting. A considerably higher percentage of citizens with annual incomes over $65,000 vote than do citizens with incomes under $35,000. Income level, to some degree, is connected to education level, as wealthier people tend to have more opportunities for higher education, and more education also may lead to higher income. Wealthy citizens are more likely than poor ones to think that the "system" works for them and that their votes make a difference. People with higher incomes are more likely to recognize their direct financial stake in the decisions of the government, thus spurring them into action.[2]

On Campus

STUDENTS AND VOTING

In the 2004 presidential election, 47 percent of eligible voters aged 18 – 24 voted—11 percent more than in the 2000 presidential election.[a] While midterm elections typically draw fewer voters than presidential elections, exit polls suggested that the "surge" in the youth vote continued in 2006, when 26 percent of young people voted—two million more than in the 2002 midterms.[b] Still, when compared to the approximately 66 percent of voters 25 and over who voted in the last presidential election, 47 percent can only be described as low.

This low level of turnout should disturb young voters, since their low turnout directly impacts what issues state and federal governments address. Ongoing military action in Iraq and Afghanistan, the federal deficit, concerns about rising health costs, and concerns about the long-term financial stability of Social Security are all issues likely to affect young voters—if not now then in the future. Rising tuition costs and the extent to which government supports higher education are issues that hit even closer to home, since many students already must work to pay their tuition bills and are likely to have loans to repay when they graduate. The stakes are high for young voters, so why aren't they voting?

According to one survey, young voters said they did not vote because they believed their vote does not make a difference, they did not have enough information to make a decision, or they were too busy.[c] Nearly half of the students sampled claimed not to discuss politics with their parents, and over half of them said schools did not sufficiently educate them on how to vote! Of course, if you do not know how to vote, then you do not vote, and if you never vote, then you never discover that your vote does make a difference.

A number of get out the vote efforts focus on informing young voters about how to vote. Rock the Vote, for instance, provides young voters with registration kits and election schedules. However, those with the most to gain from securing the young vote, the two major political parties, remain on the sidelines. Another study shows that over 53 percent of undergraduates claim that neither party contacted them during the 2004 presidential campaign.[d] If one of the parties chooses to fill this gap, it could tilt the balance in their favor in future elections. That would be good not only for the party but for young voters, since they could use their influence to affect legislation.

[a] National Election Pool exit polls, http://www.cnn.com/ELECTION/2004/pages/results/states/US/P/00/epolls.0.html

[b] See http://www.civic youth.org/quick/youth_voting.htm for information on youth voting drawn from exit poll results in 2002, 2004, and 2006.

[c] http://www.stateofthevote.org/factsheet.html.

[d] Richard Niemi and Michael Hamner, Circle Fact Sheet: College Students in the 2004 Election, http://www.civicyouth.org/PopUps/FactSheets/FS_College_Voting.pdf.

By contrast, lower-income citizens often feel alienated from politics, possibly believing that conditions will remain the same no matter who holds office. American political parties may contribute to this feeling of alienation. As discussed in chapter 12, unlike parties in many other countries that tend to associate themselves with specific socioeconomic classes, U.S. political parties are less directly linked to socioeconomic class. One consequence of "classless" parties is that the poor may believe their interests are unrepresented, feeding feelings of alienation and apathy.

Age A strong correlation exists between age and voter participation rates. The Twenty-Sixth Amendment to the Constitution, ratified in 1971, lowered the voting age to eighteen. While this amendment obviously increased the number of *eligible* voters, it did so by enfranchising the group that is least likely to vote. A much higher percentage of citizens age thirty and older vote than do citizens younger than thirty, although voter turnout decreases over the age of seventy, primarily due to difficulties some older voters have getting to the polling location. Regrettably, less than half of eligible eighteen- to twenty-four-year-olds are even registered to vote. The most plausible reason for this is that younger people are more mobile; they have not put down roots in a community. Because voter registration is not automatic, people who relocate have to make an effort to register. Therefore, the effect of adding this low-turnout group to the electorate has been to lower the overall turnout rate. As young people marry, have children, and settle down in a community, their likelihood of voting increases.[3] In the 2004 presidential election, turnout among those age eighteen to twenty-four surged to 47 percent, or 11 percent more than in 2000. Turnout among young voters was up in 2006, as well, suggesting that more young American voters are engaging in politics. (See On Campus: Students and Voting.)

VIDEO ROUNDTABLE

Political Participation and the Young

Gender With passage of the Nineteenth Amendment in 1920, women gained the right to vote in the United States (see chapter 6). While early polling numbers are not reliable enough to shed light on the voting rate among women in the years immediately following their entry into the voting process, it is generally accepted that in the period following ratification of the Nineteenth Amendment, women voted at a lower rate than men. Recent polls suggest that today women vote at the same or a slightly higher rate than men. Since women comprise slightly more than 50 percent of the U.S. population, they now account for a majority of the American electorate.

Race and Ethnicity Despite substantial gains in voting rates among minority groups, especially African Americans, race remains an important factor in voter participation. Whites still tend to vote more regularly than do African Americans, Hispanics, and other minority groups. This was evident in the 2004 presidential election. Although turnout was up in general—from the 51 percent of 2000 to 57 percent in 2004—turnout increased less among African Americans than among whites.[4] Turnout among whites was slightly over 60 percent in 2004; among African Americans, it hovered in the mid-50 percent range, depending on the locality; among Hispanics, turnout was just under 40 percent.

Several factors help to explain the persistent difference in voting rates between white and black voters. One reason is the relative income and educational levels of the two racial groups. African Americans tend to be poorer and to have less formal education than whites; as mentioned earlier, both of these factors affect voter turnout. Significantly, though, highly educated and wealthier African Americans are as likely to vote as whites of similar background, and sometimes more likely.[5] Another explanation focuses on the long-term consequence of the voting barriers that African American's historically faced in the United States, especially in areas of the Deep South (see chapter 6).

FIGURE 13.1 THE SOUTH VERSUS THE NON-SOUTH FOR PRESIDENTIAL VOTER TURNOUT

After a century-long discrepancy caused by discrimination against African American voters in the South, regional voting turnouts have grown much closer together with the increasing enfranchisement of these voters.

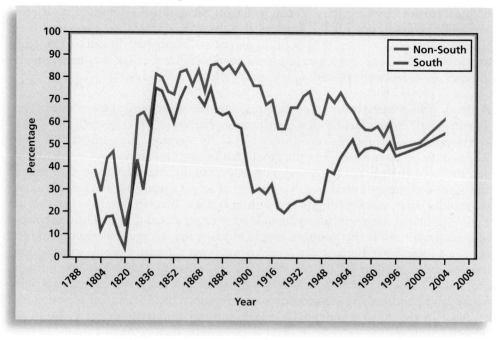

Source: Compiled from data contained in the Center for the Study of the American Electorate 2004 Election Report, November 4, 2004.

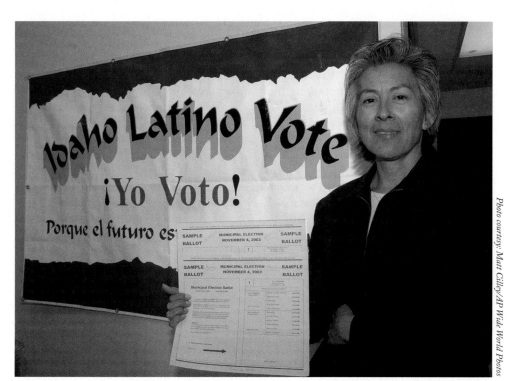

■ Maria Gonzales Mabbutt, Director of Idaho Latino Vote, holds a sample ballot flyer from Nampa, Idaho. The project "Get the Vote Out" was created to inform the Hispanic community where and when to vote, as well as who the candidates are.

Race also helps explain why the South has long had a lower turnout than the rest of the country (see Figure 13.1). As discussed in chapter 6, in the wake of Reconstruction, the southern states made it extremely difficult for African Americans to register to vote, and only a small percentage of the eligible African American population was registered throughout the South until the 1960s. The Voting Rights Act (VRA) of 1965 helped to change this situation. Often now heralded as the most successful piece of civil rights legislation ever passed, VRA was intended to guarantee voting rights to African Americans nearly a century after passage of the Fifteenth Amendment. VRA, key provisions of which were extended for another twenty-five years in 2006, targets states that once used literacy or morality tests or poll taxes to exclude minorities from the polls. The act bans any voting device or procedure that interferes with a minority citizen's right to vote and requires approval for any changes in voting qualifications or procedures in certain areas where minority registration was not in proportion to the racial composition of the district. It also authorizes the federal government to monitor all elections in areas where discrimination was found to be practiced or where less than 50 percent of the voting-age public was registered to vote in the 1964 election.

The 2000 Census revealed that the Hispanic community in the United States is now slightly larger in size than the African American community; thus, Hispanics have the potential to wield enormous political power. In California, Texas, Florida, Illinois, and New York, five key electoral states, Hispanic voters have emerged as powerful allies for candidates seeking office. However, just as voter turnout among African Americans is historically much lower than among whites, the turnout among Hispanics is much lower than turnout among African Americans.[6] In 2004, 55 percent of African Americans voted in the presidential election; only 38 percent of Hispanics turned out to vote.

Like any voting group, Hispanics are not easily categorized and voting patterns cannot be neatly generalized. However, several major factors play out as key decision-making variables: one's point of origin, length of time in the United States, and income levels. Although Hispanics share a common history of Spanish colonialism and similar patterns of nation building, they differ in political processes and agendas. Despite having citizenship, Puerto Ricans can vote in a presidential election only if they live on the mainland and establish residency. Cuban Americans are concentrated in south Florida and tend to be conservative and vote for GOP candidates. Mexican American's favor Democrats, but their voting patterns are very issue-oriented, and vary according to income levels, length of time in the United States, and age.[7]

As more Hispanic candidates run for office, the excitement level and participation of Hispanic voters is likely to increase. The 2004 elections featured several high-profile Hispanic candidates, including Colorado's Salazar brothers: Ken, who won a Senate seat, and John, who won a seat in the House and was reelected in 2006. Mel Martinez ran for a Senate seat in Florida and won as well. The highest profile Hispanic candidate to win in 2006 was Democratic Senator Bob Menendez of New Jersey. Democrat Patricia Madrid narrowly lost to incumbent Republican Representative Heather Wilson. House Republican incumbent Henry Bonilla of Texas lost to Democrat Ciro D. Rodriguez in a closely watched runoff election for Texas's 23rd Congressional District, while brothers Lincoln and Mario Diaz-Balart of Florida, both Republicans, easily won reelection in 2006.

Interest in Politics An interest in politics must also be included as an important factor for voter turnout. Many citizens who vote have grown up in families interested and active in politics. There is also a strong relationship between interest in politics and age, income, and education, factors discussed above that are also known to increase the likelihood of voter participation. Independent of these relationships, it is believed that interest serves as a gateway that leads people to gather information about candidates and to more fully participate in the political process, including voting. People who are highly interested in politics constitute only a small minority of the U.S. population. For example, the most politically active Americans—party and issue-group activists—make up less than 5 percent of the country's more than 300 million people. Those who contribute time or money to a party or a candidate during a campaign make up only about 10 percent of the total population. On the other hand, although these percentages appear low, they translate into millions of Americans who contribute more than just votes to the system.

VISUAL LITERACY

Voting Turnout: Who Votes?

■ Citizen Change is one of many organizations that endeavors to educate, register, and turn out young voters in national elections. Here, Sean "Diddy" Combs wears a shirt featuring the group's much-publicized slogan.

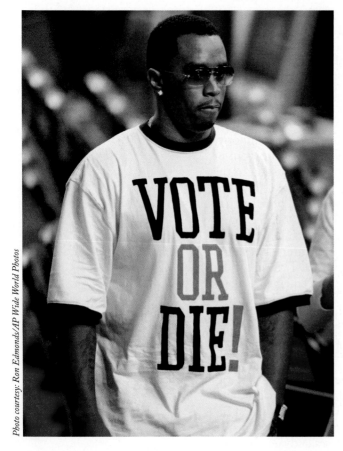

Photo courtesy: Ron Edmonds/AP Wide World Photos

WHY IS VOTER TURNOUT SO LOW?

The United States has one of the lowest voter participation rates of any nation in the industrialized world. In 1960, 62 percent of the eligible electorate voted in the presidential election, but by 1996, American voter participation had fallen to a record low of 48.8 percent—the lowest general presidential election turnout in modern times. In 2004, participation climbed to 57 percent, the highest it has been since 1968. Figure 13.2 shows several reasons U.S. nonvoters give for not voting. A number of contributing factors are discussed below.

Too Busy Over 90 million eligible voters did not cast a ballot in the 2004 presidential election. According to the U.S. Census Bureau, 20 percent of registered nonvoters reported they did not vote in a recent election because they were too busy or had conflicting work or school schedules (see Figure 13.2). Another 15 percent said they did not vote because they were ill, disabled, or had a family emergency. While these reasons seem to account for a large portion of the people surveyed, they may also reflect the respondents'

FIGURE 13.2 WHY PEOPLE DON'T VOTE

According to the U.S. Census Bureau's Current Population Survey taken after the 2004 elections, "too busy" was the single biggest reason Americans gave for not voting on Election Day. Anger toward politicians and disenchantment with the current political system also drove Americans away from the polls.

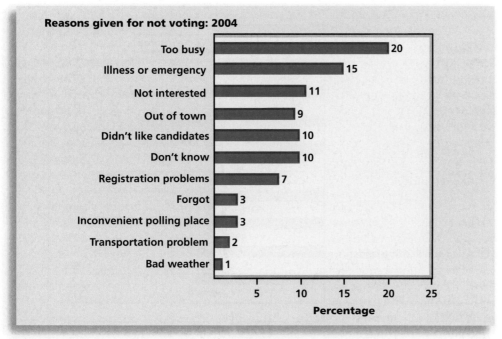

Source: U.S. Census Bureau, Current Population Survey, November 2004.

desire not to seem uneducated about the candidates and issues or apathetic about the political process. Although some would-be voters are undoubtedly busy, infirm, or otherwise unable to make it to the polls, it is likely that many of these nonvoters are offering an easy excuse and have another reason for failing to vote.

Difficulty of Registration Of those citizens who are registered, the overwhelming majority vote. A major reason for lack of participation in the United States remains the relatively low percentage of the adult population that is registered to vote (see Figure 13.3 for an overview of the percentage of registered voters by age, race, and gender). There are several reasons for the low U.S. registration rate. First, while nearly every other democratic country places the burden of registration on the government rather than on the individual, in the United States the registration process still requires individual initiative—a daunting impediment in this age of political apathy. Thus, the cost (in terms of time and effort) of registering to vote is higher in the United States than it is in other industrialized democracies. Second, many nations automatically register all of their citizens to vote. In the United States, however, citizens must jump the extra hurdle of remembering on their own to register. Indeed, it is no coincidence that voter participation rates dropped markedly after reformers, desiring to combat voter fraud, pushed through strict voter registration laws in the early part of the twentieth century. Correspondingly, several recent studies of the effects of relaxed state voter registration laws show that easier registration leads to higher levels of turnout.[8] When states adopted Election Day registration of new voters, large and significant improvements in turnout occurred among younger voters and the poor.[9]

The National Voter Registration Act of 1993, commonly known as the Motor Voter Act, was a recent attempt to ease the bureaucratic hurdles associated with

FIGURE 13.3 PERCENTAGE OF REGISTERED VOTERS BY AGE, RACE/ETHNICITY, AND GENDER, 2004

Older Americans continue to register at a much higher rate than younger voters. While increasing their representation at the ballot box, minorities still lag behind white voters in registration.

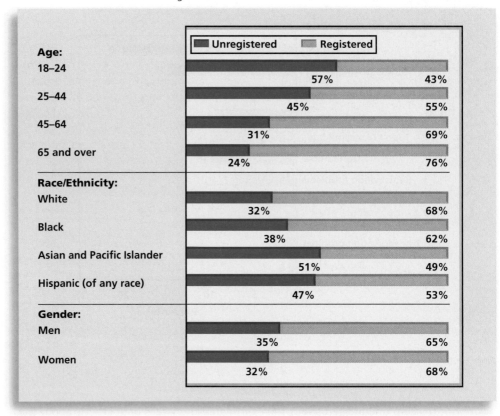

Source: U.S. Census Bureau, Current Population Survey.

registering to vote. The law requires states to provide the opportunity to register through drivers' license agencies, public assistance agencies, and the mail. While a large number of Americans have yet to take advantage of the Motor Voter Act, it is likely that the law is at least partially responsible for the increases in voter participation experienced in 2000 and 2004.

Difficulty of Absentee Voting Stringent absentee ballot laws are another factor in low voter turnout for the United States. Many states, for instance, require citizens to apply in person for absentee ballots, a burdensome requirement given that one's inability to be present in his or her home state is often the reason for absentee balloting in the first place. Recent literature in political science links liberalized absentee voting rules and higher turnout. One study, for instance, concluded that generous absentee voting guidelines reduced the "costs of voting" and increased turnout when the parties mobilized their followers to take advantage of such absentee voting rules.[10]

Number of Elections Another explanation for low voter turnout in the United States is the sheer number and frequency of elections. According to a study by the International Institute for Democracy and Electoral Assistance, the United States typically holds twice as many national elections as other Western democracies, a consequence of the relatively short two-year term of office for members of the House of Representatives.[11] American federalism (see chapter 3), with its separate elections at the local, state, and national levels, and its use of primary elections for the selection of candidates, also contributes to the number of elections in which Americans are called on to participate. With so many elections, even the most active political participants may skip part of the electoral process from time to time.

Voter Attitudes Although some low voter participation is due to the institutional factors we have just described, voter attitudes play an equally important part. Some voters are alienated, and others are just plain apathetic, possibly because of a lack of pressing issues in a particular year, satisfaction with the status quo, or uncompetitive (even uncontested) elections. Furthermore, many citizens may be turned off by the quality of campaigns in a time when petty issues and personal mudslinging are more prevalent than ever. Divided government can also affect voter turnout, with turnout declining by 2 percent in each consecutive election conducted when the presidency and Congress are controlled by different parties.[12] Some nations, such as Australia and Belgium, try to get around the effects of voter attitudes with compulsory voting laws. Not surprisingly, voter turnout rates in Australia and Belgium are often greater than 90 percent, as these nations fine citizens who fail to vote.

Weakened Influence of Political Parties Political parties today are not as effective as they once were in mobilizing voters, ensuring that they are registered, and getting them to the polls. As we discussed in chapter 12, the parties once were grass-roots organizations that forged strong party–group links with their supporters. Today, candidate-centered campaigns and the growth of expansive party bureaucracies have resulted in a somewhat more distant party with which fewer people identify very strongly. While efforts have been made in recent elections to bolster the influence of parties, in particular through sophisticated get out the vote efforts, the parties' modern grassroots activities pale in comparison to their earlier efforts.

EFFORTS TO IMPROVE VOTER TURNOUT

Reformers have proposed many ideas to increase voter turnout in the United States. Always on the list is raising the political awareness of young citizens, a reform that inevitably must involve our nation's schools. The rise in formal education levels among Americans has played a significant role in preventing an even greater decline in voter turnout.[13] No less important, and perhaps simpler to achieve, are institutional reforms, though many of the reforms discussed below, if enacted, may result in only a marginal increase in turnout. (For a related discussion, see Join the Debate: Does Low Turnout Matter?)

■ A worker at a state motor vehicles office displays the form that makes it easy to register to vote.

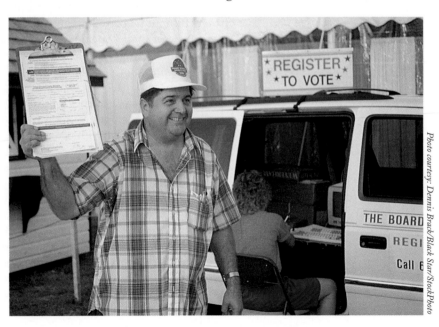

Photo courtesy: Dennis Brack/Black Star/StockPhoto

Easier Registration and Absentee Voting Registration laws vary by state, but in most states, people must register prior to Election Day. Six states now permit same-day registration—Minnesota, Maine, Wisconsin, New Hampshire, Wyoming, and Idaho—which allows people to register to vote on Election Day. Turnout in these same-day registration states averaged 10 percentage points

Join the Debate

DOES LOW VOTER TURNOUT MATTER?

OVERVIEW: While voting rates in the United States have spiked during the last two presidential elections, they remain significantly lower than in other Western democracies and abysmally low in nonpresidential years. It is not uncommon for candidates in midterm elections to win office with support from less than 20 percent of the eligible voters.

In 2004, nationwide voter turnout was just over 60 percent of the voting-age population, nearly 9 percentage points up from 51 percent in 2000.

In 2006, a post-election analysis from American University's Center for the Study of the American Electorate estimated that 40.4 percent of the electorate voted in the 2006 midterm elections—up from 39.7 percent in the 2002 midterms and the highest turnout since 1982.

The 2004 surge in voter turnout, which seems to have continued somewhat in 2006, was the product of considerable effort and unique circumstances. The major political parties and nonpartisan groups had been registering voters throughout the year and in unprecedented numbers. Voters also had much to motivate them with the election predicted to be as close as in 2000 and featuring critical issues such as the war in Iraq, the fate of Social Security, and possible appointments to the Supreme Court. Even under these extraordinary circumstances, nearly 40 percent of eligible voters chose not to participate in 2004. the nation's persistently low level of political participation pose a threat to democracy in America?

ARGUMENTS THAT LOW VOTER PARTICIPATION IS NOT A PROBLEM

■ **The preferences of nonvoters are not much different from those who do vote.** While higher voting rates are desirable in theory, in practice they might not make a difference in election outcomes and are unlikely to justify the expense associated with costly reform plans designed to increase voter participation.

higher in 2000 and 2004 than in other states, supporting the long-held claim by reformers that voter turnout could be increased if registering to vote were made simpler for citizens. Better yet, all U.S. citizens could be registered automatically at the age of eighteen. Another proposal is that states could make it easier to obtain absentee ballots by eliminating the in-person requirement. Oregon has become the first state in the nation to eliminate polling places, switching to all-mail balloting; after the change, turnout increased. More and more voters are choosing to receive mail-in ballots because of their convenience, and election administrators are encouraging them because of the savings to taxpayers.

The motor-voter bill discussed above, which requires states to permit individuals to register by mail, also allows citizens to register to vote when they visit any motor vehicles office, public assistance agency, or military recruitment office. When the legislation was initially proposed, supporters said it would result in the registration of roughly 49 million Americans of voting age with driver's licenses or identification cards. Opponents claimed the law was yet another unfunded federal mandate burdening state governments. The widespread adoption of motor-voter by the various states has increased voter registration rates an estimated 5 to 9 percent, especially among young voters, and confirms the value of innovative election reform for state and federal lawmakers.[14]

Make Election Day a Holiday Besides removing an obstacle to voting (the busy workday), making Election Day a national holiday might focus more voter attention on the contests in the critical final hours. The strategy might backfire, however, as people might use the day off to extend vacations or long weekends. The tradition of Tuesday elections in this country should reduce this risk.

- **Legal barriers that once restricted voting among disenfranchised groups (African Americans, women, and those eighteen to twenty years old) have been eliminated.** In the absence of restrictions, nonvoting is voluntary and indicates an acceptance of things as they are.

- **Low voter turnout increases the quality of voter participation.** Since nonvoters tend to be less well educated and less informed than voters, low voting rates might increase the quality of political participation in the United States.

ARGUMENTS THAT LOW VOTER PARTICIPATION IS A PROBLEM

- **Voters do not represent the interests of nonvoters.** The socioeconomic composition and attitudes of present-day nonvoters are significantly different from those of voters. Even if their expressed preferences about politics do not look very distinctive, their objective circumstances and their need for government services differ from the majority of those who do vote.

- **Low voting rates perpetuate racial imbalances within government.** Since voting rates remain lower for Hispanic, African American, and other minority groups than for whites, the racial composition of elected officials remains far from representative of the nation as a whole.

- **Low voter rates delegitimize the political process.** Voting rates that dip below 50 percent challenge the very legitimacy of the political system, as elected officials cannot claim a clear mandate, or even the support of a substantial segment of society.

SELECTED READINGS

Conway, M. Margaret. *Political Participation in the United States*, 3rd ed. Washington, DC: CQ Press, 2000.

Patterson, Thomas E. *The Vanishing Voter: Public Involvement in an Age of Uncertainty*. New York: Vintage, 2003.

Strengthen Parties Reformers have long argued that strengthening the political parties would increase voter turnout, because parties have historically been the organizations in the United States best suited for and most successful at mobilizing citizens to vote. During the late 1800s and early 1900s, the country's "Golden Age" of powerful political parties, one of their primary activities was getting out the vote on Election Day. Even today, the parties' Election Day get out the vote drives increase voter turnout by several million in national contests. The Democratic National Committee undertook an initiative proposed by its chair, Howard Dean, to canvass all fifty states prior to the 2006 election, even putting resources in states that have traditionally not been receptive to Democratic politics in an attempt to reinvigorate the party nationwide.

Other Suggestions Other ideas to increase voter turnout are less practical or feasible. For example, holding fewer elections might sound appealing, but it is difficult to see how this could be accomplished without diluting many of the central tenets of federalism and separation of powers that the Framers believed essential to the protection of liberty. One proposal to increase voter turnout is the use of a proportional representation system for congressional elections to encourage third parties and combat voter apathy toward the two major parties. Other proposals include changing Election Day to Saturday or Sunday, making voting mandatory, or providing a tax credit for those who vote. Other, perhaps more promising ideas include allowing for a longer period of time to vote (perhaps an election week), using Internet technology to ease the burden of voting, increasing the availability of mail-in voting, or simply increasing the availability of voting places.[15]

VIDEO DEBATE
Compulsory Voting

PATTERNS IN VOTE CHOICE

Just as there are certain predictable patterns when it comes to American voter turnout, so, too, are there predictable patterns of vote choice. Some of the most prominent correlates of vote choice include partisan identification, race and ethnicity, gender, income, ideology, issues, and campaign-specific developments.

Party Identification　Party identification remains the most powerful predictor of voter behavior. Stated simply, self-described Democrats tend to vote for Democratic candidates and self-described Republicans tend to vote for Republican candidates. Still, although intense partisanship has increased over the last ten years, many voters continue to be more independent of party in their vote choice. The practice of **ticket-splitting,** voting for candidates of different parties for various offices in an election, rose dramatically during the 1960s and 1970s.[16] In 1972, a year with a particularly high level of ticket-splitting, 30 percent of voters split their tickets between their presidential vote and their vote for U.S. representative. The National Elections Study estimates ticket-splitting was at 26 percent in the 2004 election, with 55 percent of respondents stating they preferred to have party control split between the president and Congress.[17]

Scholars have posited several potential explanations for ticket-splitting. One explanation is that voters split their tickets, consciously or not, because they trust neither party to govern.[18] Under this interpretation, ticket-splitters are aware of the differences between the two parties and split their tickets to augment the checks and balances already present in the Constitution. Alternatively, voters split their tickets possibly because partisanship has become less relevant as a voting cue.[19] Other explanations for ticket-splitting abound. The growth of issue-oriented politics, the mushrooming of single-interest groups, the greater emphasis on candidate-centered personality politics, and broader-based education are all often cited.

Race and Ethnicity　Just as voter turnout varies according to race and ethnicity, so does vote choice. The different racial and ethnic groups tend to vote in distinct patterns. While whites have shown an increasing tendency to vote Republican in recent elections, African American voters remain overwhelmingly Democratic in both their partisan identification and in their voting decisions. Despite the best efforts of the Republican Party to garner African American support, this pattern shows no signs of waning. In 2004, for example, 88 percent of the votes cast by African Americans were cast for Kerry, while Bush received a mere 11 percent of the African American vote.[20]

In the wake of Hurricane Katrina in 2005 and the Bush administration's failure to provide timely relief to New Orleans' majority black population, African American resentment reached an all-time high, with at least one poll showing a measly 2 percent approval rating for President Bush among African Americans.

Hispanics also tend to identify with and vote for Democrats, although not as monolithically as do African Americans.[21] In 2004, for example, Kerry received 53 percent of the votes cast by Hispanics; Bush received only 44 percent. The Asian American segment of the electorate is less monolithic and more variable in its voting than either the Hispanic or the African American communities. It is worth noting

ticket-splitting
Voting for candidates of different parties for various offices in the same election.

■ President George W. Bush greets members of the NAACP after addressing organization members at their annual convention on July 20, 2006, the same day that the Senate approved a 25-year extension of the Voting Rights Act. Up until this occasion, Bush had been the first president since Herbert Hoover to refuse to address the group.

Photo courtesy: Win McNamee/Getty Images

the considerable political diversity within this group: Chinese Americans tend to prefer Democratic candidates, but Vietnamese Americans, with a strong anti-communist leaning, tend to support Republicans. A typical voting split for the Asian American community in general, though, might run about 60 percent Democratic and 40 percent Republican, though it can reach the extreme of a 50–50 split, depending on the election.

Gender There have been elections throughout the twentieth century in which gender was touted as a factor, although precise data are not always available to prove the conventional wisdom. For example, journalists in 1920 claimed that women—in their first presidential election after passage of the Nineteenth Amendment granted women suffrage—were especially likely to vote for Republican presidential candidate Warren G. Harding due to Harding's good looks and purported charm.

Women act and react differently from men to some candidacies, including those of other women. For instance, Democratic women were more likely than Democratic men to support Walter Mondale's presidential ticket in 1984, a fact that some observers believe resulted from Mondale's selection of Representative Geraldine Ferraro (D–NY) for the second slot on his presidential ticket. However, Republican women at the time were more likely than GOP men to support Ronald Reagan's candidacy, as Republican women were opposed to Ferraro's liberal voting record and views. Since 1980, the gender gap, the difference between the voting choices of men and women, has become a staple of American politics (see chapter 12).

Simply put, in most elections today, women are more likely to support the Democratic candidate and men are more likely to support the Republican candidate. The size of the gender gap varies considerably from election to election, though normally the gender gap is between 5 and 7 percentage points. That is, women support the average Democrat 5 to 7 percent more than men. Some elections result in an expanded gender gap though, such as the presidential election of 1996. Bob Dole narrowly won among men in 1996, while Bill Clinton scored a landslide among women. In 2004, Bush won 55 percent of the male vote, while Kerry received 51 percent of the female vote.[22]

Income Over the years, income has been a remarkably stable correlate of vote choice. The poor vote more Democratic; the well-to-do vote heavily Republican.[23] Indeed, in the 2004 presidential election, those voters who earned less than $15,000 yearly voted for Kerry over Bush by 63 percent to 36 percent, whereas those voters who earned more than $100,000 yearly supported Bush over Kerry by 59 to 41 percent.[24]

Ideology Ideology represents one of the most significant cleavages in contemporary American politics. Liberals, generally speaking, favor government involvement in social programs (like Social Security, public education, and Medicare) and are committed to the ideals of tolerance and social justice. Liberals tend to view government as an instrument of social progress. Conservatives, on the other hand, tend to favor defense and police protection as the top priorities of government and believe that private and faith-based organizations are better suited to provide social programs than the government. Conservatives are dedicated to the ideals of individualism and market-based competition, and they tend to view government as a necessary evil rather than an agent of social improvement. Moderates, who comprise the bulk of the American electorate, lie somewhere between liberals and conservatives on the ideological spectrum.

Not surprisingly, ideology is very closely related to vote choice. Liberals tend to vote for Democrats, and conservatives tend to vote for Republicans. In 2004, 85 percent of self-described liberals voted for Kerry, whereas only 13 percent voted for Bush. Conservatives, on the other hand, voted for Bush over Kerry at a rate of 84 to 15 percent.[25]

Issues In addition to the underlying influences on vote choice discussed above, individual issues can have important effects in any given election year. In 1992, when Bill Clinton's chief political adviser, James Carville, established "it's the economy stupid" as Clinton's campaign mantra, he was confirming a well-established idea in American politics: perceptions of the economy drive voter decisions.[26] Voters tend to reward the party in government, usually the president's party, during good economic times and punish the party in government during periods of economic downturn. When this occurs, the electorate is exercising **retrospective judgment;** that is, voters are rendering judgment on the performance of the party in power by judging whether the economy has improved under its governance. At other times, voters might use **prospective judgment;** that is, they vote based on what they perceive to be the future direction of the economy. By looking forward, voters can evaluate if a party's positions are likely to serve their interests, while not holding the ruling party accountable for economic conditions that might be beyond the party's control (for example, the economic effects of a hurricane or terrorist attack).

Whether voters use retrospective or prospective judgment, there is little doubt that the economy is one of the most important issues in voters' minds. Consider for a moment how voters retrospectively and prospectively judged recent presidential administrations in reaching their ballot decisions:

> *1992:* A prolonged recession, weak job growth, and Ross Perot's candidacy—which split the Republican base—denied a second term to George Bush, despite many significant foreign policy triumphs. In the end, voters decided to vote retrospectively and gamble on little-known Arkansas Governor Bill Clinton.
>
> *1996:* A healthy economy prompted Americans to retrospectively support President Bill Clinton in his quest for reelection over Bob Dole. Voters also looked prospectively at the two candidates and again registered their support for President Clinton and his vision for the country's future.
>
> *2000:* Eight years of peace and record economic prosperity should have worked in favor of Vice President Al Gore. While he received more votes than any Democratic candidate in U.S. history, and slightly more than his opponent, Gore's Clinton-era baggage and credibility questions helped to nullify any advantage over Texas Governor George W. Bush, an opponent with an undistinguished record but no significant liabilities. Given the unusual circumstances of the actual election, it is difficult to say more precisely to what extent the outcome represents a retrospective or prospective political opinion.
>
> *2004:* Ordinarily, incumbent reelections become a referendum on the incumbent's performance, making Americans likely to think retrospectively. However, economic conditions, which were slowly recovering following the September 11, terrorist attacks and the subsequent war on terrorism, offered no clear direction to voters. While President Bush, the incumbent, encouraged prospective evaluations by arguing his opponent would bring a tax-and-spend philosophy to the White House, economic factors seemed to be of secondary importance in this election. The ongoing war on terrorism led voters to consider how their choice of president would affect the next four years of American military policy, and Bush won with a higher percentage of the popular vote than he had received in 2000.

Prospective and retrospective judgments aside, the 2004 election had two major campaign-specific issues: Iraq and the war on terrorism. Early in the campaign, George W. Bush attempted to link the two issues together with the hope that the general support he received in his handling of the war on terrorism could help boost flagging ratings for his handling of the war in Iraq. The Kerry campaign's efforts to keep the two issues separate, however, succeeded. Exit polls showed that voters who considered terrorism the most important issue voted 86 to 14 percent for Bush, while

retrospective judgment
A voter's evaluation of the performance of the party in power.

prospective judgment
A voter's evaluation of a candidate based on what he or she pledges to do about an issue if elected.

those who considered Iraq the most important issue voted 73 to 26 percent for Kerry. Amazingly, while terrorism and Iraq dominated the 2004 election, and even the 2004 Democratic primaries, voters actually cited the economy (20 percent of respondents) and moral values (22 percent) as the most important issues. (Terrorism and Iraq were cited by 19 and 15 percent, respectively.) Those voters citing the economy as most important voted 82 to 18 percent in favor of Kerry, and those stating moral values as most important voted 80 to 20 percent in favor of Bush. In the end, the campaign-specific issues ran side by side with the perennial problems Americans and their representatives face every day.

Elections in the United States

BOTH THE BALLOT AND THE BULLET are methods of governmental change around the world, and surely the former is preferable to the latter. Although the United States has not escaped the bullet's awful effects, the election process is responsible for most leadership change in this country. Regular free elections guarantee mass political action and enable citizens to influence the actions of their government. Societies that cannot vote their leaders out of office are left with little choice other than to force them out by means of strikes, riots, or coups d'état.

THE PURPOSES OF ELECTIONS

Popular election confers on a government the legitimacy that it can achieve no other way. Elections confirm the very concept of popular sovereignty, the idea that legitimate political power is derived from the consent of the governed (see chapter 1), and they serve as the bedrock for democratic governance. Even **authoritarian systems,** such as those in North Korea, Syria, and China, which base their rule on force rather than the consent of the governed, recognize this fact and sometimes attempt to create the appearance of fair and open elections to justify their rule. From time to time, they hold "referenda" to endorse their regimes or one-party elections, even though these so-called elections offer no real choice that would ratify their rule. The symbolism of elections as mechanisms to legitimize change, then, is important, but so is their practical value.

> **authoritarian system**
> A system of government that bases its rule on force rather than consent of the governed.

After all, in a democratic society, elections are the primary means to fill public offices and staff the government. The voters' choice of candidates and parties helps to organize government as well. Regular elections ensure that government is accountable to the people it serves. At fixed intervals, the **electorate** —citizens eligible to vote—is called on to judge those in power. Even though the majority of office holders in the United States win reelection (see The Incumbency Advantage, page 492), some office holders inevitably lose power, and all candidates are exposed to the sobering effect of elections. The threat of elections keeps policy makers concerned with public opinion and promotes ethical behavior, as nothing makes an incumbent more vulnerable than a scandal (see Scandals, page 496).

> **electorate**
> The citizens eligible to vote.

Because candidates advocate certain policies, elections also involve a choice of platforms and point the society in certain directions on a wide range of issues, from abortion to civil rights to national defense to the environment. If current office holders are reelected, they may continue their policies with renewed resolve. Should office holders be defeated and their challengers elected, however, a change in policies will likely result. Either way, the winners will claim a **mandate** (literally, a command) from the people to carry out their platform.

> **mandate**
> A command, indicated by an electorate's votes, for the elected officials to carry out their platforms.

Often the claim of a mandate is suspect because voters are not so much endorsing one candidate and his or her positions as rejecting his or her opponent. Moreover, elections that are won by razor-thin margins, as has been the case in recent presidential contests, cannot qualify as an electoral mandate. This was particularly true in 1992 when the presence of third-party candidate Ross Perot enabled Bill Clinton to win the presidency with less than 50 percent of the vote, and in 2000 when George W. Bush lost the popular vote but won the Electoral College vote as a result of a Supreme Court ruling.

On rare occasions, off-year congressional elections can produce mandates. In 1994, backlash against President Clinton's policy direction helped Representative Newt Gingrich (R–GA) lead Republicans to gain control of the House of Representatives and claim a mandate for his "Contract with America," a series of popular policy proposals supported by Gingrich and his followers. The fact that the House Republicans were unified in support of a set policy platform and that they were able to pick up fifty-two seats in the House helped them build a strong case that the election represented a rare off-year mandate.

TYPES OF ELECTIONS

So far, we have referred mainly to general elections at the national level, but in the U.S. system, elections happen at various levels (national, state, and local) and come in numerous types (primary elections, general elections, initiatives, referenda, and recalls). (See The Living Constitution for a discussion of age qualifications for the different levels of national elected office.)

Primary Elections
In **primary elections,** voters decide which of the candidates within a party will represent the party's ticket in the general elections. There are different kinds of primaries. For example, **closed primaries** allow only a party's registered voters to cast a ballot, and **open primaries** allow independents and sometimes members of the other party to participate. Closed primaries are considered healthier for the party system because they prevent members of one party from influencing the primaries of the opposition party. Studies of open primaries indicate that **crossover voting**—participation in the primary of a party with which the voter is not affiliated—occurs frequently.[27] Nevertheless, the research shows little evidence of much **raiding**—an *organized* attempt by voters of one party to influence the primary results of the other party.[28]

When none of the candidates in the initial primary secures a majority of the votes, most states have a **runoff primary,** a contest between the two candidates with the greatest number of votes. Louisiana has a novel twist on the primary system. There, all candidates for office appear on the ballot, and if one candidate receives over 50 percent of the vote, the candidate wins and no general election is necessary. If no candidate wins a majority of the vote, the top two candidates, even if they belong to the same party, face each other in a runoff election. Such a system blurs the lines between primary and general election and all but removes the political party from the selection process.

General Elections
Once party members vote for their party candidates for various offices, each state holds its general election. In the **general election,** voters decide which candidates will actually fill the nation's elective public offices. These elections are held at many levels, including municipal, county, state, and national. Whereas primaries are contests between the candidates within each party, general elections are contests between the candidates of opposing parties.

Initiative, Referendum, and Recall
Three other types of elections are the initiative, the referendum, and the recall. Taken together, the initiative and referendum processes are collectively known as ballot measures. **Ballot measures** provide the electorate a direct voice in the political process by allowing voters to enact public policy. An **initiative** is a process that allows citizens to propose legislation or

---

primary election
Election in which voters decide which of the candidates within a party will represent the party in the general election.

closed primary
A primary election in which only a party's registered voters are eligible to vote.

open primary
A primary in which party members, independents, and sometimes members of the other party are allowed to vote.

crossover voting
Participation in the primary of a party with which the voter is not affiliated.

raiding
An organized attempt by voters of one party to influence the primary results of the other party.

runoff primary
A second primary election between the two candidates receiving the greatest number of votes in the first primary.

general election
Election in which voters decide which candidates will actually fill elective public offices.

ballot measure
An election option such as the initiative or referendum that enables voters to enact public policy.

initiative
An election that allows citizens to propose legislation and submit it to the state electorate for popular vote.

The Living Constitution

No Person shall be a Representative who shall not have attained to the Age of twenty five Years.

—ARTICLE I, SECTION 2

No Person shall be a Senator who shall not have attained to the Age of thirty Years.

—ARTICLE I, SECTION 3

...neither shall any person be eligible to that Office [of the Presidency] who shall not have attained to the Age of thirty five Years.

—ARTICLE II, SECTION 1

There was little debate among the Framers at the Constitutional Convention that elected officials should have enough experience in life and in politics before being qualified to take on the responsibility of representing the interests of the nation and of their district or state. It is likely that they concurred, as they so often did, with John Locke, who stated in section 118 of his *Second Treatise of Government*, "*a Child is born a Subject of no Country or Government*. He is under his Father's Tuition and Authority, till he come to Age of Discretion." However, a minor, who is not subject to the authority of the state in the same way as a full citizen, also could not possibly be qualified to vote. The Framers added age requirements higher than the age when one becomes a full citizen as a guarantee that individuals with the necessary experience would be elected. Notice how the age limits scale upward according to the amount of deliberation and decision making that the position involves. House members need to be only twenty-five, but the president must be at least thirty-five, giving whoever would run for that office plenty of time to acquire the political experience necessary for the central role he or she will play.

State governments usually employ similar requirements. For instance, Virginia requires that candidates for the state's House of Delegates and Senate be at least twenty-one years old, while candidates for the state's three most powerful executive positions—governor, lieutenant governor, and attorney general—must be at least thirty years old. South Dakota, however, sets the minimum age limit for its most important executive officers—governor and lieutenant governor—at twenty-one.

Amazingly, the Framers did not impose an age limit on Supreme Court justices, not even the chief justice. Perhaps the Framers thought that the president was not likely to appoint minors to the bench, or at least that they would not be approved by the Senate. Looking at the nine justices today, it is obvious that the Framers were right not to worry.

referendum

An election whereby the state legislature submits proposed legislation to the state's voters for approval.

recall

An election in which voters can remove an incumbent from office by popular vote.

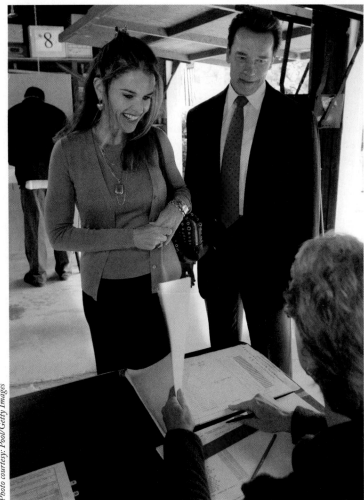

■ Governor Arnold Schwarzenegger and his wife Maria Schriver prepare to vote in California's 2005 special election. Schwarzenegger failed to convince voters to support his slate of referendum measures.

Photo courtesy: Pool/Getty Images

state constitutional amendments by submitting them directly to the state electorate for popular vote, provided the initiative supporters receive a certain number of signatures on petitions supporting the placement of the proposal on the ballot. The initiative process is used in twenty-four states and the District of Columbia. A **referendum** is an election whereby the state legislature submits proposed legislation or state constitutional amendments to the state's voters for approval. Although both the referendum and the initiative provide for more direct democracy, they are not free from controversy.

Ballot measures have been the subject of heated debate in the past decades. Critics charge that ballot measures—which were intended to give citizens more direct control over policy making—are now unduly influenced by interest groups and "the initiative industry"—"law firms that draft legislation, petition management firms that guarantee ballot access, direct-mail firms, and campaign consultants who specialize in initiative contests."[29] Moreover, critics often question the ability of voters to deal with the numerous complex issues that appear on the ballot. In the 1990 elections, for instance, California had so many referenda and initiatives on its ballot that the state printed a lengthy two-volume guide to explain them all to voters. In addition, the wording of the ballot measure in question can have an enormous impact on the outcome. In some cases, a "yes" vote will bring about a policy change; in other cases, a "no" vote will cause a change.[30] Moreover, ballot initiatives are not subject to the same campaign contribution limits that limit donations in candidate campaigns. Consequently, a single wealthy individual can bankroll a ballot measure and influence public policy in a manner that is not available to the individual through the normal policy process.

Supporters of ballot measures argue that critics have overstated their case, and they point out that the process has historically been used to champion popular issues that were resisted at the state level by entrenched political interests. Initiatives, for example, have been instrumental in popular progressive causes such as banning child labor, promoting environmental laws, expanding suffrage to women, and passing campaign finance reform. The process has also been used to pass popular conservative proposals such as tax relief and banning affirmative action policies.[31] Supporters point out that ballot measures can heighten public interest in elections and can increase voter participation. In general, the supporters have far more confidence in the ability of the voting public to understand and judge public policy than do the critics.

The third type of election (or "deelection") found in many states is the **recall,** in which voters can remove an incumbent from office prior to the next scheduled election. Recall elections are very rare, and sometimes they are thwarted by the official's resignation or impeachment prior to the vote. In 2003, under intense national media attention, Californians recalled Governor Grey Davis (a Democrat) and replaced him with movie star (and Republican) Arnold Schwarzenegger. Davis, who had won reelection against a weak Republican candidate, Bill Simon, faced intense criticism for his handling of the state's slumping economy and looming energy crisis. Immediately following the recall, commentators feared that voters in California had set a precedent for the people of a state to recall governors whenever things are not going well. This fear has proven unjustified, since no additional governors were removed from office following the Davis recall and only two governors have ever been removed from office through the recall process (California's Grey Davis in 2003 and North Dakota's Lynn J. Frazier in 1921).

Presidential Elections

VARIETY ASIDE, NO U.S. ELECTION can compare to the presidential contest. This spectacle, held every four years, brings together all the elements of politics and attracts the most ambitious and energetic politicians to the national stage. Voters in a series of state contests that run through the winter and spring of the election year select delegates who will attend each party's national convention. Following the national convention for each party, held in mid and late summer, there is a final set of fifty separate state elections all held on the Tuesday after the first Monday in November to select the president. This lengthy process exhausts candidates and voters alike, but it allows the diversity of the United States to be displayed in ways a shorter, more homogeneous presidential election process could not.

The state party organizations use several types of methods to elect national convention delegates and ultimately select the candidates who will run against each other in the general election:

1. *Winner-take-all primary:* Under this system the candidate who wins the most votes in a state secures all of that state's delegates. While Democrats no longer permit its use because it is viewed as less representative than a proportional system, Republicans generally prefer this process as it enables a candidate to amass a majority of delegates quickly and shortens the divisive primary season.

2. *Proportional representation primary:* Under this system, candidates who secure a threshold percentage of votes are awarded delegates in proportion to the number of popular votes won. Democrats now strongly favor this system and use it in many state primaries, where they award delegates to anyone who wins more than 15 percent in any congressional district. Although proportional representation is probably the fairest way of allocating delegates to candidates, its downfall is that it renders majorities of delegates more difficult to accumulate and thus can lengthen the contest for the presidential nomination.

3. *Caucus:* Under this system, party members meet in small groups throughout a state to discuss and select the party's delegates to the national convention. While less common in recent years than in the past, this method maintains some of the characteristics of the era in which party bosses selected candidates. The first in the nation contest, the Iowa caucus, serves as the first test of candidate strength and receives a remarkable level of attention by both the candidates and the media.

PRIMARIES VERSUS CAUCUSES

The mix of preconvention contests has changed over the years, with the most pronounced trend being the shift from caucuses to primary elections. Only seventeen states held presidential primaries in 1968; the number increased to thirty-eight in 1992, forty-two in 1996, forty-three in 2000, and thirty-eight in 2004. In recent years, the vast majority of delegates to each party's national convention have been selected through the primary system (see Figure 13.4).

The caucus is the oldest, most party-oriented method of choosing delegates to the national conventions. Traditionally, the caucus was a closed meeting of party activists

FIGURE 13.4 METHODS OF SELECTING DEMOCRATIC PARTY PRESIDENTIAL
DELEGATES
This map illustrates the range of methods used to select party delegates to the national conventions. It shows the methods used to select Democratic delegates in
2004.

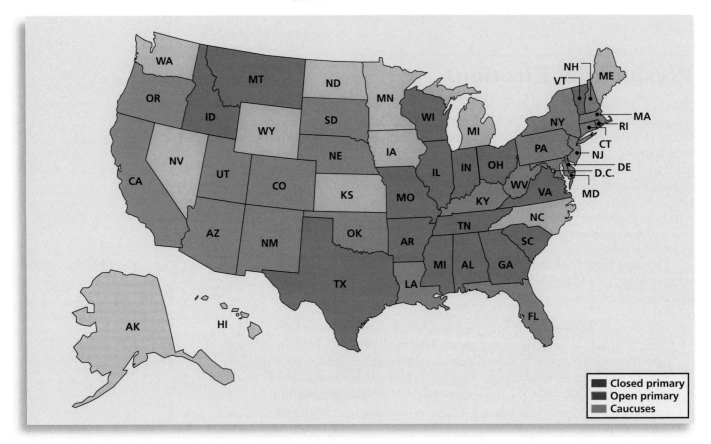

Closed primary
Open primary
Caucuses

: Methods of selection are current as of May 2006.

Source: Federal Election Commission, http://www.fec.gov; the Reform Institute, http://reforminstitute.org.

in each state who selected the party's choice for presidential candidate. In the late
nineteenth and early twentieth centuries, however, many people viewed these caucuses
as elitist and anti-democratic, and reformers succeeded in replacing them with direct
primaries in most states. Although there are still presidential nominating caucuses today (in Iowa, for example, as noted above), they are now more open and attract a wider
range of the party's membership. Indeed, new participatory caucuses more closely resemble primary elections than they do the old, exclusive party caucuses.[32]

Some people support the increase in the number of primaries because they believe
that this type of election is more democratic. The primaries are open not only to party
activists, but also to anyone, wealthy or poor, urban or rural, northern or southern,
who wants to vote. Related to this idea, advocates argue that presidential primaries
are the most representative means by which to nominate presidential candidates. They
are a barometer of a candidate's popularity with the party rank and file. While conventional wisdom holds that both primaries and caucuses attract more extreme voters
in each party, recent research posits that primaries help nominate more moderate and
appealing candidates—those that primary voters believe can win in the general election. For instance, scholars describe "sophisticated voting," where primary voters vote
for their second or third choice because they believe the candidate will more easily win
in November than will their first choice—perhaps because of less extreme policy positions.[33] Finally, the proponents of presidential primaries claim that they constitute a

rigorous test for the candidates, a chance to display under pressure some of the skills needed to be a successful president.

Critics of presidential primaries argue that although primaries may attract more participants than do caucuses, this quantity does not substitute for the quality of information held by caucus participants. At a caucus, participants spend several hours learning about politics and the party. They listen to speeches by candidates or their representatives and receive advice from party leaders and elected officials, then cast a well-informed vote. Critics of the primary system argue that primary voters tend to make their decisions based on campaign advertisements or a candidate's popularity among media elites.

Critics also argue that the unfair scheduling of primaries affects their outcomes. For example, the earliest primary takes place in New Hampshire, a small, heavily white, and historically conservative state. Some argue that New Hampshire receives much more media coverage than it deserves simply because its primary is first in the nation. Such excessive coverage undoubtedly skews voter opinions in more populous states that hold their primaries later. Additionally, critics believe that the qualities tested by the primary system are by no means a complete list of those a president needs to be successful. For instance, skill at handling national and local media representatives is by itself no guarantee of an effective presidency. The exhausting primary schedule may be a better test of a candidate's stamina than of his or her brain power.

The primary schedule has been altered by a phenomenon often referred to as **front-loading,** the tendency of states to choose an early date on the primary calendar. Seventy percent of all the delegates to both party conventions are now chosen before the end of March. This trend is hardly surprising, given the added press emphasis on the first contests and the voters' desire to cast their ballots before the competition is decided. The focus on early contests (such as the Iowa caucus and the New Hampshire primary), coupled with front-loading, can result in a party's selecting a nominee too quickly, before press scrutiny and voter reflection separate the wheat from the chaff.

Front-loading has other important effects on the nomination process. First, a front-loaded primary schedule generally benefits the front-runner, since opponents have little time to turn the contest around once they fall behind. Second, front-loading gives an advantage to the candidate who can raise the bulk of the money *before* the

front-loading
The tendency of states to choose an early date on the primary calendar.

■ Senator John Kerry (D–MA) and former Governor Howard Dean of Vermont shake hands at a joint rally. Dean, the early front-runner in the 2004 Democratic presidential primaries, later supported Kerry, the Democratic candidate, who was defeated by Republican George W. Bush. Dean's showing in the 2004 primaries later helped his efforts to become the chair of the Democratic National Committee.

Photo courtesy: Kevin Lamarque/Reuters/Corbis

nomination season begins, since there will be little opportunity to raise money once the primaries begin and since candidates will need to finance campaign efforts simultaneously in many states. In 2004, Internet fund-raising emerged as a means to soften this advantage; its use will continue and expand in future presidential elections. Finally, front-loading has amplified the importance of the "invisible primary"—the year or so prior to the start of the official nomination season when candidates begin raising money and unofficially campaigning.[34] For the 2008 race for president, the Democratic National Committee introduced a very crowded opening by adding Nevada's caucus between the contests in Iowa and New Hampshire, with South Carolina following closely behind.

THE PARTY CONVENTIONS

The seemingly endless nomination battle does have a conclusion: the national party convention held in the summer of presidential election years. The out-of-power party traditionally holds its convention first, in late July, followed in mid-August by the party holding the White House. Preempting an hour or more of prime-time network television for four nights and monopolizing the cable networks such as CNN, FOX News, and C-SPAN, these remarkable conclaves give the civically engaged viewer a chance to learn about the candidates.

Yet, the conventions once were much more: they were composed of party members who made actual decisions, where party leaders held sway and deals were sometimes cut in "smoke-filled rooms" to deliver nominations to little-known contenders called "dark horses." This era predated the modern emphasis on reform, primaries, and proportional representation, all of which have combined to make conventions the place where parties choose one of several nominees who has been preselected through the various primaries and caucuses.[35]

Today, the convention is fundamentally different from what it was in the past. First, its importance as a party conclave, at which compromises on party leadership and policies can be worked out, has diminished. Second, although the convention still formally selects the presidential ticket, most nominations are settled well in advance. Third, three preconvention factors have lessened the role of the current parties and conventions: delegate selection, national candidates and issues, and the news media.

Delegate Selection As mentioned in the previous section, the selection of delegates to the conventions is no longer the function of party leaders but of primary elections and grassroots caucuses. Moreover, recent reforms, especially by the Democratic Party, have generally weakened any remaining control by local party leaders over delegates. A prime example of such reform is the Democrats' abolition of the **unit rule,** a traditional party practice under which the majority of a state delegation (say, twenty-six of fifty delegates) could force the minority to vote for its candidate. Another new Democratic Party rule decrees that a state's delegates be chosen in proportion to the votes cast in its primary or caucus (so that, for example, a candidate who receives 30 percent of the vote gains about 30 percent of the convention delegates). This change has had the effect of requiring delegates to indicate their presidential preference at each stage of the selection process. Consequently, the majority of state delegates now come to the convention already committed to a candidate. Before 1972, most delegates to a Democratic National Convention were not bound by primary results to support a particular candidate for president. This freedom to maneuver meant that conventions could be exciting and somewhat unpredictable gatherings, where last-minute events and deals could sway wavering delegates.

In sum, the many complex changes in the rules of delegate selection have contributed to the loss of decision-making powers by the convention. Even though the Democratic Party initiated many of these changes, the Republicans were carried along as many Democratic-controlled state legislatures enacted the reforms as state laws.

unit rule
A traditional party practice under which the majority of a state delegation can force the minority to vote for its candidate.

There have been new rules to counteract some of these changes, however. For instance, since 1984, the number of unpledged delegate slots reserved for elected Democratic Party officials—**superdelegates**—has been increased. The creation of superdelegates was an attempt to maintain some level of party control over the selection process, while still allowing most delegates to be selected through the electoral process. Typically, these superdelegates include members of the Democratic National Committee, governors, members of Congress, and other distinguished party leaders. Of the 4,322 delegates that attended the Democratic National Convention in 2004, 802 were unpledged superdelegates. Republicans do not bind delegates to select the candidate the party members chose during the primary; thus, delegates can vote against the will of the state party and the use of superdelegates is unnecessary. Who the delegates are, a topic that is less important today than it was when delegates enjoyed more power in the selection process, still reveals interesting differences between the political parties. Both parties draw their delegates from an elite group whose income and educational levels are far above the average American's. Nearly 40 percent of delegates at the 2004 Democratic convention were minorities, and half were women. (For some historic "firsts" for women at the conventions, see Table 13.1.) Only 17 percent of the delegates to the Republican convention were minorities; however, this actually marks the GOP's concerted effort to increase minority representation at its convention, since only 9 percent of the 2000 delegates were minorities.

The contrast in the two parties' delegations is no accident; it reflects not only the differences in the party constituencies, but also conscious decisions made by party leaders. After the tumultuous 1968 Democratic National Convention, which was torn by dissent over the Vietnam War, Democrats formed a commission to examine the condition of the party and to propose changes in its structure. As a direct consequence of the commission's work, the 1972 Democratic convention was the most broadly representative ever of women, African Americans, and young people, because the party required these groups to be included in state delegations in rough proportion to their numbers in the population of each state. (State delegations failing this test were not seated.) This new mandate was very controversial, and it has since been watered down considerably. Nonetheless, women and minority groups are still more fully represented at Democratic conventions than at Republican conventions. GOP leaders have placed much less emphasis on proportional representation; instead of procedural reforms, Republicans have concentrated on strengthening their state organizations and fund-raising efforts, a strategy that clearly paid off at the polls in the elections of 1980, 1984, and 1988, which saw Republicans elected as president. Yet, overall, the representation of women and minorities at the convention is largely symbolic, as delegates no longer have a great deal of power in selecting the nominee.

superdelegate
Delegate slot to the Democratic Party's national convention that is reserved for an elected party official.

TABLE 13.1   HISTORIC MOMENTS FOR WOMEN AT THE CONVENTIONS

Since 1980, Democratic Party rules have required that women constitute 50 percent of the delegates to its national convention. The Republican Party has no similar quota. Nevertheless, both parties have tried to increase the role of women at the convention. Some "firsts" and other historic moments for women at the national conventions include:

1876	First woman to address a national convention
1890	First women delegates to conventions of both parties
1940	First woman to nominate a presidential candidate
1951	First woman asked to chair a national party
1972	First woman keynote speaker
1984	First major-party woman nominated for vice president (Democrat Geraldine Ferraro)
1996	Wives of both nominees make major addresses
2000	Daughter of a presidential candidate nominates her father
2004	Both candidates introduced by their daughters

Source: Center for American Women in Politics. Updated by authors.

National Candidates and Issues The political perceptions and loyalties of voters are now influenced largely by national candidates and issues, a factor that has undoubtedly served to diminish the power of state and local party leaders at the convention. The national candidates have usurped the autonomy of state party leaders with their preconvention ability to garner delegate support. Issues, increasingly national in scope, remain central to the convention. The conventions still provide the parties with a forum for drafting their platforms and for debating their future direction (see chapter 12). But, the party professionals, who prior to the late 1960s had a monopoly on the management of party affairs, are no longer able to dominate the process.

You Are a Presidential Campaign Consultant

The News Media The media have helped transform the national conventions into political extravaganzas for the television audience's consumption. They have also helped to preempt the convention, by keeping count of the delegates committed to the candidates; as a result, well before the convention, the delegates and even the candidates have much more information about nomination politics than they did in the past. From the strategies of candidates to the commitments of individual delegates, the media cover it all. Even the bargaining within key party committees, formerly done in secret, is now subject to some public scrutiny, thanks to open meetings.

Television coverage has shaped the business of the convention. Desirous of presenting a unified image to kick off a strong general election campaign, the parties assign important roles to attractive speakers, and most crucial party affairs are saved for prime-time viewing hours. During the 1990s, the networks gradually began to reduce their convention coverage, citing low viewer ratings. In 2004, the major networks changed their coverage slightly, providing no prime-time coverage on some days, and extending coverage to as much as three hours on the final day of each convention. While this likely reflects a change in the political culture away from meaningful convention activity overall, the increased final-night coverage indicates a greater interest in the candidates themselves. The cable networks (CNN, FOX, MSNBC, and others) have more than made up for the reduced prime-time coverage from the networks, and C-SPAN still gives gavel-to-gavel coverage.

Extensive media coverage of the convention has its pros and cons. On the one hand, such exposure helps the party launch its presidential campaign with fanfare, usually providing a boost to the party's candidate. President George W. Bush received a considerable 13-point bounce following the 2004 Republican convention; the Kerry-Edwards campaign received a far smaller bounce following the Democratic convention. On the other hand, media coverage can expose rifts within a party, as happened in 1968 at the Democratic convention in Chicago. Dissension was obvious when "hawks," supporting the Vietnam War and President Lyndon B. Johnson, clashed with the anti-war "doves" both on the convention floor and in street demonstrations outside the convention hall. Whatever the case, it is obvious that saturation media coverage of preelection events has led to the public's loss of anticipation and exhilaration about convention events.

Some reformers have spoken of replacing the conventions with national direct primaries, but it is unlikely that the parties would agree to this. Although its role in nominating the presidential ticket has often been reduced to formality, the convention is still valuable. After all, it is the only real arena

■ The 1968 Democratic Convention was beset by violent protests over the Vietnam War and clashes with Chicago police, which were extensively covered by the three major television networks' news divisions.

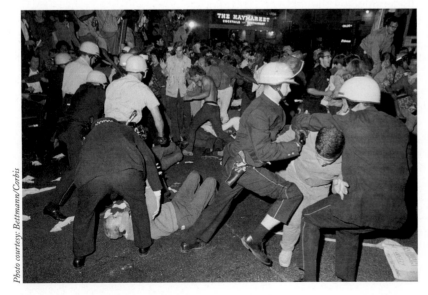

Photo courtesy: Bettmann/Corbis

where the national political parties can command a significant audience while they celebrate past achievements and project their hopes for the future.

THE ELECTORAL COLLEGE: HOW PRESIDENTS ARE ELECTED

Given the enormous amount of energy, money, and time expended to nominate two major-party presidential contenders, it is difficult to believe that the general election could be more arduous than the nominating contests, but it usually is. The actual campaign for the presidency (and other offices) is described in chapter 14, but the object of the exercise is clear: winning a majority of the **Electoral College.** This uniquely American institution consists of representatives of each state who cast the final ballots that actually elect a president. The total number of **electors**—the members of the Electoral College—for each state is equivalent to the number of senators and representatives that state has in the U.S. Congress. And, the District of Columbia is accorded three electoral votes. With 538 votes cast in the Electoral College, the magic number for winning in the presidency is 270. Win 270 votes in the Electoral College and you become arguably the most influential person in the world; win anything less and you gain no power.

The Electoral College was the result of a compromise between those Framers who argued for selection of the president by the Congress and those who favored selection by direct popular election. The Electoral College compromise, although not a perfect solution, had practical benefits. Since there were no mass media in those days, common citizens, even reasonably informed ones, were unlikely to know much about a candidate from another state. On the one hand, this situation could have left voters with no choice but to vote for someone from their own state, thus making it improbable that any candidate would secure a national majority. On the other hand, the electors would be men of character with a solid knowledge of national politics who were able to identify, agree on, and select prominent national statesmen. There are three essentials to understanding the Framers' design of the Electoral College. The system was constructed (1) to work without political parties; (2) to cover both the nominating and electing phases of presidential selection; and, (3) to produce a nonpartisan president.

The Electoral College machinery as originally designed by the Framers was somewhat complex. Each state designated electors (through appointment or popular vote) equal in number to the sum of its representation in the House and Senate. The electors met in their respective states. Each elector had two votes to cast in the Electoral College's selection for the president and vice president, although electors could not vote for more than one candidate from their state. The rules of the college stipulated that each elector was allowed to cast only one vote for any single candidate, and by extension obliged each elector to use his second vote for another candidate. There was no way to designate votes for president or vice president; instead, the candidate with the most votes (provided he also received votes from a majority of the electors) won the presidency and the runner-up won the vice presidency. If two candidates received the same number of votes and both had a majority of electors, the election was decided in the House of Representatives, with each state delegation acting as a unit and casting one vote. If no candidate secured a majority, the election would also be decided in the House, with each state delegation casting one vote for any of the top five electoral vote-getters. In both these scenarios, the candidate needed a majority of the total number of states for victory.

This system seems almost insanely unpredictable, complex, and unwieldy until one remembers that the Framers devised it specifically for the type of political system that existed when they framed the Constitution and that they (erroneously) foresaw for America in perpetuity: a nonpartisan, consensus-based, indirectly representative, multicandidate system. In such a system, the Electoral College would function ad-

Electoral College
Representatives of each state who cast the final ballots that actually elect a president.

elector
Member of the Electoral College chosen by methods determined in each state.

VIDEO ROUNDTABLE

The Electoral College

mirably. In practice, the Framers hoped that electors with a common basic political understanding would arrive at a consensus preference for president, and most, if not all, would plan to cast one of their votes for that candidate, thereby virtually guaranteeing one clear winner, who would become president (a tie was an unlikely and unhappy outcome). Each would then plan to cast his remaining vote for another candidate, the one whom the elector implicitly preferred for vice president. Consensus on the vice presidency would presumably be less clear than for the more important position of president, so there might be a closer spread among the runners-up. But, in any case, the eventual president and vice president—indeed, all the candidates—would still have been members of the same one party.

The Electoral College in the Nineteenth Century   The republic's fourth presidential election revealed a flaw in the Framers' Electoral College plan. In 1800, Thomas Jefferson and Aaron Burr were, respectively, the presidential and vice presidential candidates advanced by the Democratic-Republican Party, and supporters of the Democratic-Republican Party controlled a majority of the Electoral College. Accordingly, each Democratic-Republican elector in the states cast one of his two votes for Jefferson and the other one for Burr, a situation that resulted in a tie for the presidency between Jefferson and Burr, since there was no way under the constitutional arrangements for electors to earmark their votes separately for president and vice president. Even though most understood Jefferson to be the actual choice for president, the Constitution mandated that a tie be decided by the House of Representatives. It was, of course, and in Jefferson's favor, but only after much energy was expended to persuade lame-duck Federalists not to give Burr the presidency.

The Twelfth Amendment, ratified in 1804 and still the constitutional foundation for presidential elections, was an attempt to remedy the confusion between the selection of vice presidents and presidents that beset the election of 1800. The amendment provided for separate elections for each office, with each elector having only one vote to cast for each. In the event of a tie or when no candidate received a majority of the total number of electors, the election still went to the House of Representatives; now, however, each state delegation would have one vote to cast for one of the three candidates who had received the greatest number of electoral votes.

The Electoral College modified by the Twelfth Amendment has fared better than the college as originally designed, but it has not been problem free. On three occasions during the nineteenth century, the electoral process resulted in the selection of a president who received fewer votes than his opponent. In 1824, neither John Quincy Adams nor Andrew Jackson secured a majority of electoral votes, throwing the election into the House. Although Jackson had more electoral and popular votes than Adams, the House voted for the latter as president. In the 1876 contest between Republican Rutherford B. Hayes and Democrat Samuel J. Tilden, no candidate received a majority of electoral votes; the House decided in Hayes's favor even though he had only one more (disputed) electoral vote and 250,000 fewer popular votes than Tilden. In the election of 1888, President Grover Cleveland secured about 100,000 more popular votes than did Benjamin Harrison, yet Harrison won a majority of the Electoral College vote, and with it the presidency.

The Electoral College in the Twentieth and Twenty-First Centuries
Several near crises pertaining to the Electoral College occurred in the twentieth century. The election of 1976 was almost a repeat of those nineteenth-century contests in which the candidate with fewer popular votes won the presidency. Even though Democrat Jimmy Carter received about 1.7 million more popular votes than Republican Gerald Ford, a switch of some 8,000 popular votes in Ohio and Hawaii would have secured for Ford enough votes to win the Electoral College, and hence the presidency. Had Ross Perot stayed in the 1992 presidential contest, he could have thrown the

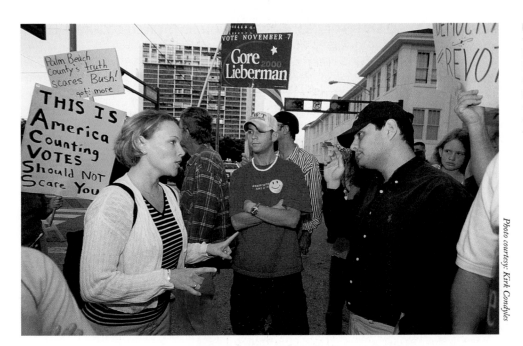

Photo courtesy: Kirk Condyles

election into the House of Representatives. His support had registered from 30 percent to 36 percent in the polls in early 1992, prior to his dropping out of the race. When he reentered the race, some of that backing had evaporated, and he finished with 19 percent of the vote and carried no states. However, Perot drained a substantial number of Republican votes from George Bush, thus splitting the GOP base and enabling Bill Clinton to win many normally GOP-leaning states.[36]

Throughout the 2000 presidential campaign, many analysts foresaw that the election would likely be the closest since the 1960 race between John F. Kennedy and Richard M. Nixon. Few realized, however, that the election would be so close that the winner would not be officially declared for more than five weeks after Election Day. And, no one could have predicted that the Electoral College winner, George W. Bush, would lose the popular vote and become president after the Supreme Court's controversial decision in *Bush* v. *Gore* (2000) stopped the recount in Florida. With the margin of the Electoral College results so small (271 for Bush, 267 for Gore), a Gore victory in any number of closely contested states could have given him a majority in the Electoral College. As it turned out, Al Gore became only the fourth person to win the popular vote and lose the presidency.

Keep in mind that through **reapportionment,** representation in the House of Representatives and consequently in the Electoral College is altered every ten years to reflect population shifts. Reapportionment is simply the reallocation of the number of seats in the House of Representatives that takes place after each decennial census. The number of House seats has been fixed at 435 since 1910. Since that time, the average size of congressional districts has tripled in population, from 211,000 following the 1910 Census to 647,000 in the 2000 Census.[37] Following the 2000 Census, Arizona, Florida, Georgia, and Texas each gained two congressional districts, and therefore two additional seats in the House of Representatives and two additional votes in the Electoral College. California, Colorado, Nevada, and North Carolina each picked up one seat and one vote. Two states, New York and Pennsylvania, each lost two seats and two votes, while eight states each lost a single seat and electoral vote. The census figures show a sizeable population shift from the Northeast to the South and West. (Figure 13.5 shows the gains and losses in Electoral College votes per state.) Recent reapportionment has favored the Republicans.

TIMELINE

And the Winner Is . . . Close Calls in Presidential Elections

reapportionment
The reallocation of the number of seats in the House of Representatives after each decennial census.

FIGURE 13.5 THE STATES DRAWN IN PROPORTION TO THEIR ELECTORAL COLLEGE VOTES

This map visually represents the respective electoral weights of the fifty states in the 2004 presidential election. For each state, the gain or loss of Electoral College votes based on the 2000 Census is indicated in parentheses.

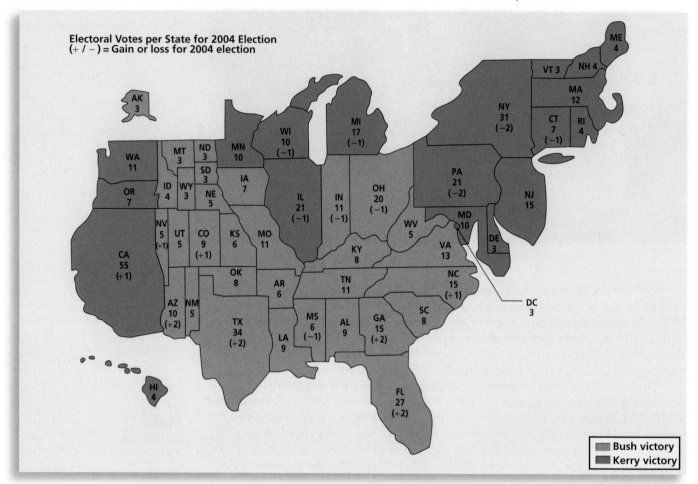

Note: States drawn in proportion to number of electoral votes. Total electoral votes: 538.

Source: *New York Times,* 2004 Election Guide, http://www.nytimes.com.

With the exception of California, George W. Bush carried all of the states that gained seats in 2000. Had Bush won the same states in 2004 that he won in 2000, he would have gained 6 additional electoral votes.

The 2000 Presidential Election

The Electoral College Reconsidered Given the Electoral College's imperfections, especially those exposed by the 2000 election, reformers have seized the opportunity to suggest several proposals for improving the presidential selection process. Three major reform ideas have developed; each is described below.

Popular Vote This reform would abolish the Electoral College entirely and have the president selected by popular vote, eliminating the chance of someone losing the presidency after winning the popular vote. Many critics believe that the Electoral College is archaic and that it distorts the popular vote while failing to provide the benefits that the Framers originally envisioned. The critics argue that the United States, with its

Politics Now

SHOULD WE ABOLISH THE ELECTORAL COLLEGE?

Since the passage of the Twelfth Amendment to the U.S. Constitution in 1804, there has been no major constitutional change to the system of electing the president. The original system the Framers envisioned to manage the choice of president, the Electoral College, is still in place. Many at the Constitutional Convention worried that unscrupulous men who would incite the people and destroy liberty could be elected president if the election were based on the popular vote. As Alexander Hamilton remarked, the Constitution would prevent politicians with "talents for low intrigue, and the little arts of popularity" from ever attaining the office of president. It is also the case that the drafters of the Constitution, under the idea of federalism, understood the states as electing the president, either through their legislatures or through a popular vote within the state, not individual voters through their status as U.S. citizens. At various times, however, there have been calls to abolish the Electoral College in favor of a national popular vote, with the loudest shouts coming in the wake of the Florida voting debacle in 2000.

A group called National Popular Vote (NPV) has been working within several states to get state legislatures and federal elected officials to endorse abolishing the Electoral College and instituting fully popular elections in its place. Because of the extreme difficulty associated with gathering enough support for a constitutional amendment, and the opposition from smaller states that fear a dilution of their representation, serious attempts have rarely been successful. However, NPV has devised a clever way to circumvent the necessity of an amendment. The group proposes that states change their election laws to give their electoral votes not to the winners in their states, but the winner of the popular vote in all fifty states. If NPV can convince enough state legislatures—enough to reach a combined total of at least 270 electoral votes, the number needed to elect a president—this would eliminate the power of the Electoral College to determine a president. A total of 29 states, including California, have sponsors lined up to introduce NPV legislation in 2007. The California Legislature approved NPV legislation in 2006, but the bill was vetoed by Governor Arnold Schwarzenegger. .

QUESTIONS

1. Has the nature of politics or the sophistication of the American people changed sufficiently to eliminate the need for the Electoral College? Explain your answer.
2. Given the election disaster in Florida in 2000 over a handful of votes, do you think electing a president through the popular vote would cause a nationwide political disaster if another close election were to occur? Why or why not?

Sources: National Popular Vote, http://www.nationalpopularvote.com/; FairVote: The Center for Voting and Democracy, http://www.fairvote.org/.

mature party system and tradition of democratic governance, no longer benefits from an electoral process that was designed to operate in the absence of parties and that was designed to distance the presidency from the electorate.

While this is the most democratic reform, it is by far the least likely to be enacted, given that the Constitution of the United States would have to be amended to abolish the Electoral College. Even assuming that the House of Representatives could muster the two-third majority necessary to pass an amendment, the proposal would almost certainly never pass the Senate. Small states have the same representation in the Senate as populous ones, and the Senate thus serves as a bastion of equal representation for all states, regardless of population—a principle generally reinforced by the existing configuration of the Electoral College, which ensures a minimum of electoral influence for even the smallest states. California, the most populous state and one that would benefit electorally from the elimination of the Electoral College, passed a bill through assembly in May 2006 endorsing the popular election of the president. Certain organizations such as National Popular Vote continue to promote Electoral College reform. (See Politics Now: Should We Abolish the Electoral College?). However, if the national crisis over electoral votes in Florida in 2000 could not motivate a national outcry for reform, the chances of a constitutional amendment seem remote.

Congressional District Plan Under this plan, each candidate would receive one electoral vote for each congressional district that he or she wins in a state, and the winner of the overall popular vote in each state would receive two bonus votes (one for each senator) for that state. Take for example Virginia, which has eleven representatives and two senators for a total of thirteen electoral votes. If the Democratic candidate wins five congressional districts, and the Republican candidate wins the other six districts and also the statewide majority, the Democrat wins five electoral votes and the Republican wins a total of eight. This reform could be adopted without a constitutional amendment. This electoral system currently exists only in Maine and Nebraska, though neither state has ever split its electoral votes. Any state can adopt this system on its own because the Constitution gives states the right to determine the place and manner by which it selects its electors.

The congressional district plan has some unintended consequences. First, the winner of the popular vote might still lose the presidency under this plan. Under a congressional district plan, Richard M. Nixon would have won the 1960 election instead of John F. Kennedy. George W. Bush would have likely won by a wider margin if the entire nation used this system in 2000. Second, this reform would further politicize the redistricting process that takes place every ten years according to U.S. Census results. Fair and objective redistricting already suffers at the hands of many political interests; if electoral votes were at stake, it would suffer further as the parties made nationwide efforts to maximize the number of safe electoral districts for their presidential nominee while minimizing the number of competitive districts. The third consequence of state-by-state adoption is that the nation would quickly come to resemble a patchwork of different electoral methods, with some states being awarded by congressional districts and some states awarded solely by popular vote. Finally, candidates would quickly learn to focus their campaigning on competitive districts while ignoring secure districts, since secure districts would contribute electoral votes only through the senatorial/statewide-majority component.

PARTICIPATION

The Electoral College

Keep the College, Abolish the Electors This proposal calls for the preservation of the college as a statistical electoral device but would remove all voting power from actual human electors and their legislative appointers. It would eliminate the threat of so-called faithless electors—that is, electors who are appointed by state legislators to vote for the candidate who won that state's vote but who then choose, for whatever reason, to vote for a different candidate. Most Americans are comfortable with making this change, although the problem of faithless electors is only a secondary and little-realized liability of the Electoral College. While in the history of presidential elections there have been 157 instances in which electors have cast their ballots in a different manner than they were directed by the state legislature, no faithless elector has ever changed the outcome of an election. The most recent incident occurred in 2000, when Barbara Lett-Simmons from the District of Columbia refused to cast her ballot for the Gore-Lieberman ticket as a protest against the District's lack of congressional representation.[38]

The fate of these three reform proposals has yet to be determined. Any change in the existing system would inevitably have a profound impact on the way that candidates go about the business of seeking votes for the U.S. presidency.

Congressional Elections

COMPARED WITH PRESIDENTIAL ELECTIONS, congressional elections receive scant national attention. Unlike major-party presidential contenders, most candidates for Congress labor in relative obscurity. There are some celebrity nominees for Congress—television stars, sports heroes, even local TV news anchors. In 2000, First

Lady Hillary Rodham Clinton made history with her Senate campaign and gained the nation's attention by becoming the only first lady to win elected office. The vast majority of party nominees for Congress, however, are little-known state legislators and local office holders who receive remarkably limited coverage in many states and communities. For them, just establishing name identification in the electorate is the biggest battle.

THE INCUMBENCY ADVANTAGE

The current circumstances enhance the advantages of **incumbency** (that is, already being in office). Those people in office tend to remain in office. Of the 399 incumbents running for the House in 2004, only seven lost.[39] In a "bad" year for House incumbents, such as the Democratic wave of 2006, "only" 94 percent of incumbents will win, but the senatorial reelection rate can drop much lower on occasion (79 percent in 2006). To the political novice, these reelection rates might seem surprising, as public trust in government and satisfaction with Congress has remained remarkably low during the very period that reelection rates have been on the rise. To understand the nature of the incumbency advantage it is necessary to explore its primary causes.

Staff Support Members of the U.S. House of Representatives are permitted to hire eighteen permanent and four nonpermanent aides to work in their Washington and district offices. Senators typically enjoy far larger staffs, with the actual size determined by the number of people in the state they represent, and both House and Senate members enjoy the additional benefits provided by the scores of unpaid interns who assist with office duties. Many of the activities of staff members directly or indirectly promote the legislator by means of generating free mass mailings and *constituency services,* the term used to describe a wide array of assistance provided by a member of Congress to voters in need (for example, tracking a lost Social Security check, helping a veteran receive disputed benefits, or finding a summer internship for a college student). Having a responsive constituent service program contributes strongly to incumbency. If a House incumbent helped solve a problem for a constituent, that constituent rated the incumbent more favorably than constituents who were not assisted by the incumbent,[40] therefore providing the incumbent a great advantage over any challenger.

Media and Travel In addition to these institutional means of self-promotion, most incumbents are highly visible in their districts. They have easy access to local media, cut ribbons galore, attend important local funerals, and speak frequently at meetings and community events. Moreover, convenient schedules and generous travel allowances increase the local availability of incumbents. Nearly a fourth of the people in an average congressional district claim to have met their representative, and about half recognize their legislator's name without prompting. This visibility has an electoral payoff, as research shows district attentiveness is at least partly responsible for incumbents' electoral safety.[41]

The "Scare-off" Effect Research also identifies an indirect advantage of incumbency: the ability of the office holder to fend off challenges from strong opposition candidates, something scholars refer to as the "scare-off" effect.[42] Incumbents have the ability to scare off high-quality challengers because of the institutional advantages of office, such as high name recognition, large war chests, staffs attached to legislative offices, and overall experience in running a successful campaign. Potential strong challengers facing this initial uphill battle will wait until the incumbent retires rather

Photo courtesy: David McNew/Newsmakers/Getty Images

■ U.S. Senator Edward Kennedy (D–MA) knows full well the advantages of incumbency. Elected to the Senate in 1962 to complete the term of his brother, President John F. Kennedy, Edward Kennedy has been reelected every term since. His name recognition and campaign war chest enabled him to handily defeat Republican challenger Kenneth Chase 69 percent to 31 percent in the 2006 election.

incumbency
The holding of an office.

than challenge him or her. This tendency only strengthens the arguments for advantages to reelection related to incumbency.[43]

The "scare-off" effect also helps to explain why reelection rates tend to be lower in the Senate than in the House. Studies show that the quality of the challengers in Senate races is higher than in House races, making it more likely that an incumbent could be upset.[44] While it is impossible to say whether high-quality challengers cause the lower reelection rates, or whether the lower reelection rates attract high-quality challengers, it is clear that Senate elections attract strong challengers, and incumbents often lose reelections in the Senate.

Redistricting   Because the Constitution requires that representation in the House be based on state population, and that each state have at least one representative, congressional districts must be redrawn by state legislatures to reflect population shifts, so that each member in Congress will represent approximately the same number of residents. Exceptions to this rule are states such as Wyoming and Vermont, whose statewide populations are less than average congressional districts. This process of redrawing congressional districts to reflect increases or decreases in seats allotted to the states, as well as population shifts within a state, is called **redistricting.**

Redistricting is a largely political process that the majority party in a state uses to ensure formation of voting districts that protect their majority. For example, in 2003, ten Texas Democratic state senators left the capitol in Austin for Albuquerque, New Mexico, in order to break the state Senate quorum necessary to pass a Republican-sponsored redistricting bill. The Republicans, who had gained control of the state government following the 2002 election, desired to redraw the district lines that had been crafted by the judiciary when the legislature, then divided, failed to redraw the lines in time for the 2002 election. At one point in the standoff, state police were ordered to begin a search for the errant state senators. The efforts of the ten Democrats failed after one of them, John Whitmire, returned to the Texas Senate, believing that the Democrats were going to lose any future legal action against them. In the end, the Republican plan was adopted and Republicans gained seats in the 2004 election. As we discuss in greater detail below, a 2006 Supreme Court ruling upheld all but one of the redrawn districts. Hoping to avoid this sort of political high theater, some states, including Iowa and Arizona, appoint nonpartisan commissions or use some other independent means of drawing district lines. Although the processes vary in detail, most states require legislative approval of redistricting plans.

This redistricting process often involves what is called **gerrymandering** (see Figure 13.6). The term is derived by combining the last name of the Massachusetts governor first credited with politicizing the process, Elbridge Gerry, and the word salamander, which signifies the oddly shaped district that Gerry created. Because of enormous population growth, the partisan implications of redistricting, and the requirement under the Voting Rights Act for minorities to get an equal chance to elect candidates of their choice, legislators end up drawing oddly shaped districts to achieve their goals.[45] Redistricting plans routinely meet with court challenges across the country. Following the 2000 Census and the subsequent redistricting in 2002, the courts threw out legislative maps in a half-dozen states, primarily because of state constitutional concerns about compactness. The circuitous boundaries of improper districts often cut across county lines or leap over natural barriers and split counties and long-standing communities.[46]

Over the years, the Supreme Court has ruled that:

- Congressional as well as state legislative districts must be apportioned on the basis of population.[47]

- District lines must be contiguous; you must be able to draw the boundaries of the district with one unbroken line.

- Purposeful gerrymandering of a congressional district to dilute minority strength is illegal under the Voting Rights Act of 1965.[48]

redistricting
Redrawing congressional districts to reflect increases or decreases in seats allotted to the states as well as population shifts within a state.

gerrymandering
The legislative process through which the majority party in each statehouse tries to assure that the maximum number of representatives from its political party can be elected to Congress through the redrawing of legislative districts.

FIGURE 13.6 GERRYMANDERING

Two drawings—one a mocking cartoon, the other all too real—show the bizarre geographical contortions that result from gerrymandering.

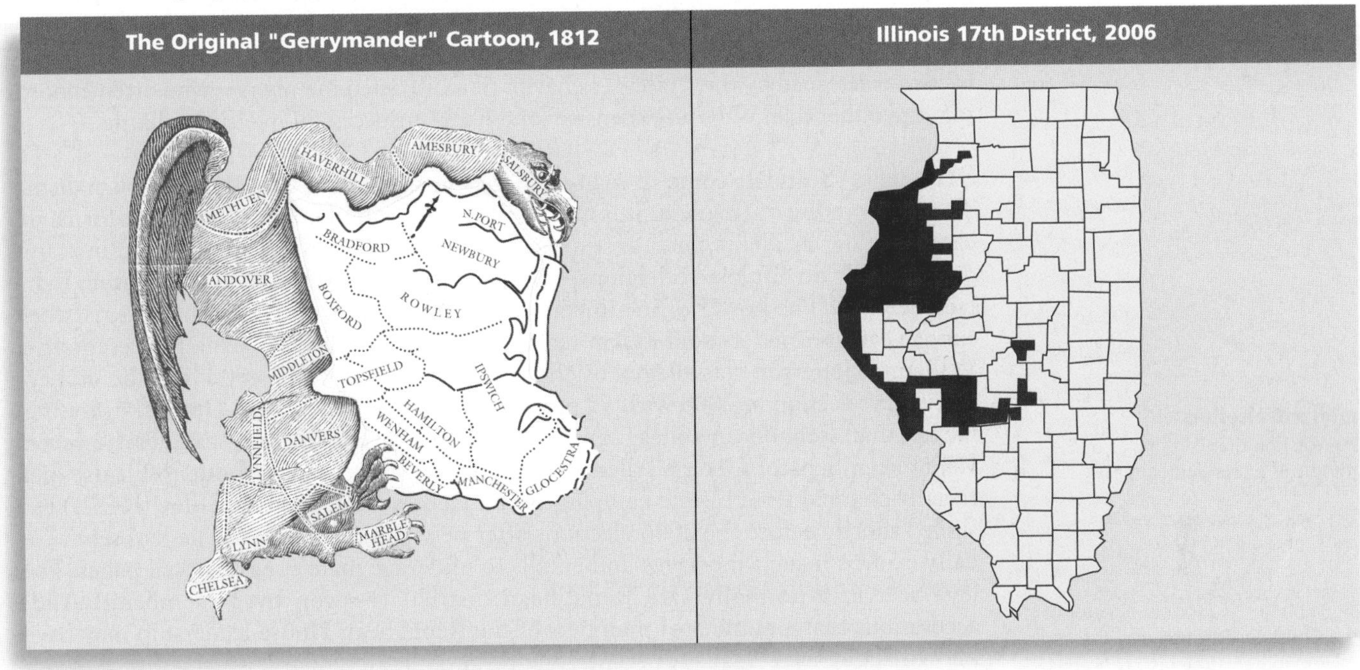

Sources: David Van Biema, "Snakes or Ladders?" *Time* (July 12, 1993) © 1993, Time Inc. Reprinted by permission. Illinois General Assembly.

- Redrawing of districts for obvious racial purposes to enhance minority representation is constitutional if race is not the "predominate" factor over all other factors that are part of traditional redistricting, including compactness.[49]

The dominant party often uses redistricting to make their incumbents safer. This can also happen in a state with divided government, in which one party controls one part of state government and another party controls a different branch of government. In this situation, neither party has sufficient power to redistrict for partisan advantage, and consequently, both parties often work together to achieve what in the political world is the next best thing to partisan advantage, safe districts. The Supreme Court has for a long time considered political redistricting based on partisan considerations to be a political question that was not a matter of Constitutional law, but rather a question to be worked out through the regular political process.[50] However, the Court recently upheld most of the 2003 political gerrymander of Texas by state Republicans that cost Democrats five seats in Congress in the 2004 election. The same decision found that Texas's 23rd congressional district was unconstitutional because it violates federal voting rights protections for Hispanics.[51] Conservatives on the Supreme Court continue to contend that gerrymandering is primarily a political and not a judicial question, and with President Bush's two conservative appointments, it seems likely the Court will continue to affirm this position.

COUNTERVAILING FORCES TO THE INCUMBENCY ADVANTAGE

Despite the fact that most incumbents win reelection, in every election cycle some members of Congress lose their positions to challengers. For the relatively few incumbent members of Congress who lose their reelection bids, there are four major reasons: redistricting efforts, scandals, presidential coattails, and midterm elections.

Redistricting Efforts

While redistricting can be used to secure incumbent advantage (as discussed above), it can also be used to punish incumbents in the out-of-power party. Some incumbents can be put in the same districts as other incumbents, or the base of other representatives can be weakened by adding territory favorable to the opposition party. The number of incumbents who actually lose their reelections because of redistricting is lessened by the strategic behavior of redistricted members—who often choose to retire rather than wage an expensive (and likely unsuccessful) reelection battle.[52]

Scandals

Scandals come in many varieties in this age of investigative journalism. The old standby of financial impropriety has been supplemented by other forms of career-ending incidents, such as sexual improprieties. Incumbents implicated in scandals typically do not lose reelections—because they simply choose to retire rather than face defeat.[53] The power of incumbency is so strong, however, that many legislators survive even serious scandal to win reelection. For example, Louisiana Representative William J. Jefferson was alleged by the FBI to have taken $100,000 in bribe money, but won reelection in 2006 with 57 percent of the vote. Jefferson, a Democrat, was far luckier than Republican colleagues implicated in a variety of 2006 scandals, however. Republican Senator George Allen of Virginia lost his seat in part due to his use of a racially charged term on the campaign trail. Representative Mark Foley (R–FL) resigned shortly before the 2006 elections after newspaper reports that he had sent sexually explicit instant messages and emails to underage male congressional pages. Foley's seat in a normally safe Republican district was won by a Democrat. And, accusations that a number of members of the Republican House leadership may have known about the e-mails for some time resulted in an embarrassing series of ethics hearings conducted in the run-up to the elections.

Presidential Coattails

The defeat of a congressional incumbent can also occur as a result of the presidential coattail effect. Successful presidential candidates usually carry into office congressional candidates of the same party in the year of their election. Notice the overall decline in the strength of the coattail effect in modern times, however, as party identification has weakened and the powers and perks of incumbency have grown. Whereas Harry S Truman's party gained seventy-six House seats and nine additional Senate seats in 1948, George W. Bush's party actually lost two House seats and four Senate berths in 2000, and saw only modest gains in 2004. The gains can be minimal even in presidential landslide reelection years, such as 1972 (Nixon) and 1984 (Reagan). Occasionally, though, when the issues are emotional and the voters' desire for change is strong enough, as in Reagan's original 1980 victory, the coattail effect can still be substantial.

midterm election

An election that takes place in the middle of a presidential term.

■ Ralph Reed, a former director of the Christian Coalition and successful Republican strategist, concedes defeat in the Republican primary for Georgia lieutenant governor in 2006. The revelation that Reed had accepted money provided by Indian clients of lobbyist Jack Abramoff in order to mount anti-gambling campaigns targeting competitors of Abramoff's clients cost him the race. Reed was just one of a number of high-profile Republican casualties who lost races or resigned from office in the wake of Abramoff's guilty pleas on charges of fraud, tax evasion, and bribery.

Photo courtesy: Ric Feld/AP Wide World Photos

MIDTERM ELECTIONS

Elections in the middle of presidential terms, called **midterm elections,** present a threat to incumbents of the president's party. Just as the presidential party usually gains seats in presidential election years, it usually loses seats in off years (see Table 13.2). The problems and tribulations of governing normally cost a president some popularity, alienate key groups, or cause the public to want to send the president a message of one sort or another. An economic downturn or presidential scandal can underline and expand this circumstance, as the Watergate scandal of 1974 and the recession of 1982 demonstrated. The 2002 midterm elections, however, bucked that trend, marking the first time since 1934 and Franklin D. Roosevelt that a first-term

TABLE 13.2 CONGRESSIONAL ELECTION RESULTS, 1948–2006

The party of the president in power almost always loses seats in midterm elections, especially in the midterm election of the second term. In a phenomenon sometimes called the "sixth-year itch," voters are tired of the incumbent president and reward the opposition party with big gains in Congress. The recent exceptions showed the American people's unhappiness with impeachment efforts against Bill Clinton and their support for George W. Bush due to concerns related to the war on terrorism.

| | Gain (+) or Loss (-) for President's Party | | | | |
| | Presidential Election Years | | | Midterm Election Years | |
President/Year	House	Senate	Year	House	Senate
Truman (D): 1948	+76	+9	1950	−29	−6
Eisenhower (R): 1952	+24	+2	1954	−18	−1
Eisenhower (R): 1956	−2	0	1958	−48	−13
Kennedy (D): 1960	−20	−2	1962	−4	+3
Johnson (D): 1964	+38	+2	1966	−47	−4
Nixon (R): 1968	+7	+5	1970	−12	+2
Nixon (R): 1972	+13	−2	Ford (R): 1974	−48	−5
Carter (D): 1976	+2	0	1978	−15	−3
Reagan (R): 1980	+33	+12	1982	−26	+1
Reagan (R): 1984	+15	−2	1986	−5	−8
G. Bush (R): 1988	−3	−1	1990	−9	−1
Clinton (D): 1992	−10	0	1994	−52	−9[a]
Clinton (D): 1996	+10	−2	1998	+5	0
G. W. Bush (R): 2000	−2	−4	2002	+6	+2
G. W. Bush (R): 2004	+3	+4	2006	-30	-6

[a]Includes the switch from Democrat to Republican of Alabama U.S. Senator Richard Shelby.

president gained seats for his party in a midterm election. The 2002 election was likely an anomaly, as it was the first election following the September 11 terrorist attacks, and voters most likely sought political stability by supporting the president's party.

Most apparent is the tendency of voters to punish the president's party much more severely in the sixth year of an eight-year presidency, a phenomenon associated with retrospective voting. After only two years, voters are still willing to "give the guy a chance," but after six years, voters are often restless for change.

In what many saw as a referendum on President George W. Bush's policy in Iraq, for example, the Republican Party lost control of both chambers of Congress in the 2006 election. This midterm election was typical of the sixth-year itch, with voters looking for a change and punishing the incumbent president's party in Congress.

Senate elections are less inclined to follow these off-year patterns than are House elections, although that was not the case in 2006 elections, in which Republicans lost six Senate seats. The idiosyncratic nature of Senate contests is due to their intermittent scheduling (only one-third of the seats come up for election every two years) and the existence of well-funded, well-known candidates who can sometimes swim against whatever political tide is rising. Also worth remembering is that midterm elections typically have a much lower voter turnout than presidential elections. (See Analyzing Visuals: Voter Turnout in Presidential and Midterm Elections.)

The 2006 Midterm Elections

Midterm Elections 2006

IN 2006, CONGRESSIONAL REPUBLICANS were beset by setbacks during the election relating to scandal, corruption charges, President Bush's low approval numbers, and the deteriorating situation in Iraq. Stacking the odds further against the Republicans was the sixth-year itch—the pattern in American elections, discussed earlier, where the incumbent president's party typically loses seats during the midterm of his second term. This election proved to be no exception: Republicans lost thirty seats in the

Analyzing Visuals
VOTER TURNOUT IN PRESIDENTIAL AND MIDTERM ELECTIONS

Various factors influence voter turnout in the United States. The high percentage of 1960 occurred in an open race (that is, when no incumbent was running). Moreover, the first televised presidential debates energized and engaged the electorate. Following the controversial 2000 presidential election, in which the outcome was essentially determined by the Supreme Court, few were surprised to see higher voter turnout in 2004. Take a few moments to study the graph below, and then answer the following critical thinking questions: What general trend do you notice about voter turnout since 1948? What is generally true about turnout in midterm elections as opposed to turnout in presidential elections? Drawing on what you've learned from this and other chapters, why do you think voter turnout, generally speaking, has remained relatively low in the United States?

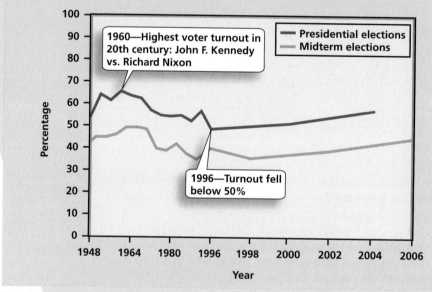

Source: Adapted from Harold W. Stanley and Richard G. Niemi, *Vital Statistics on American Politics, 2005–2006* (Washington, DC: CQ Press, 2006).

House and six in the Senate, giving the Democrats control of both houses of Congress for the first time since 1994.

Fundraising was at a record level in 2006, with congressional candidates from both parties raising over $1.14 billion, an increase of 30 percent over congressional spending in 2004. 527 committees (see chapter 14) played a larger role in 2006, contributing over $320 million to candidates, a 40 percent increase from the 2002 midterm election. The biggest fundraiser of any congressional candidate was Senator Hillary Clinton (D–NY), who raised over $38 million for her re-election bid. The biggest fundraiser in the House was Vernon Buchanan, running for the open seat left by Rep. Katherine Harris (R–FL), who amassed over $6 million to keep the seat Republican.

Democrats' convincing sweep of the House in 2006 saw a takeover of nearly twice the number of seats they had needed to win control of the body, changing a 203–232 deficit into a 233-202 seat majority for the 110th Congress. Democrats captured eight open Republican seats and defeated 22 GOP incumbents, including many moderate Republican officeholders from northeastern states. The pro-Democratic wave that washed over the lower chamber did not discriminate by seniority: only two GOP freshmen suffered defeat; 14 of the 22 incumbent Republican casualties had served in Congress for longer than ten years, and 4 of those 14 had served for longer than twenty. Democrats were buoyed by success on the turf most politically favorable to them: they reaped gains in 10 districts where President Bush had trailed John Kerry in votes in the 2004 presidential election. In fact, Democrats picked up more than the fifteen seats they needed to win a House majority in just six states east of the Mississippi: Connecticut (2), Florida (2), Indiana (3), New Hampshire (2), New York (3), and Pennsylvania (4).

While a Democratic takeover of the House was all but assured prior to election day, the battle for control of the Senate was far from certain. Of the 33 seats up for election in 2006, Democrats needed not only to hold control of competitive seats in New Jersey and Maryland, but they also needed to pick up six of seven Republican-held seats to create a majority. On election night, four Republican incumbents became early casualties of the sixth year itch. The hotly contested open seat race in Tennessee stayed in the GOP column. Two races remained too close to call on election night: Democrats needed to win in both

Photo courtesy: Ann Heisenfelt/AP Wide World Photos

■ Congressional races for open seats often lead to spirited electoral contests. Here, the Democratic and Republican candidates for Minnesota's open senate seat, Amy Klobuchar and Mark Kennedy, pose for the cameras at a campaign debate. While Republicans had high hopes for picking up the senate seat being vacated by one-term Democrat Mark Dayton, low approval ratings for the Republican-led Congress and President Bush translated into a decisive win for Klobuchar.

TABLE 13.3 RESULTS OF SELECTED ELECTIONS, 2006

State	Contest	Winner	Loser	Significance
Arizona	House	Harry Mitchell(D)	J.D. Hayworth (R)	Challenger Harry Mitchell received high-profile Republican endorsements and had momentum throughout the very bitter race. Hayworth, a leading supporter of immigration reform, suffered from the late push by Democrats in Arizona.
Florida	House	Tim Mahoney (D)	Joe Negron (R)	Joe Negron's defeat in a highly Republican district was largely due to the negative stigma associated with Mark Foley's name appearing on the ballot. Negron's campaign used the slogan "Punch Foley for Joe" to great last-minute effect, but it simply was not enough.
Illinois	House	Peter Roskam (R)	Tammy Duckworth (D)	Tammy Duckworth, a disabled Iraq war veteran, drew national attention in her House bid, but Roskam pulled out the win in a traditionally Republican district.
Missouri	Senate	Claire McCaskill (D)	Jim Talent (R)	In the "Show Me" state, the advantage of a stem cell research question on the ballot (and not a same-sex marriage question) helped Democrat Claire McCaskill defeat incumbent Jim Talent.
Montana	Senate	Jon Tester (D)	Conrad Burns (R)	Conrad Burns, an embattled incumbent with ties to indicted lobbyist Jack Abramoff, portrayed Jon Tester as well left of Montana's mainstream, but the taint of scandal proved insurmountable for Burns in this nail-biter.
North Carolina	House	Heath Shuler (D)	Charles Taylor (R)	Ex-Redskins quarterback Heath Shuler, a conservative Blue Dog Democrat, hammered incumbent Charles Taylor over ethical issues and picked up an important seat for Democrats in the South.
Ohio	Senate	Sherrod Brown (D)	Mike DeWine (R)	DeWine's defeat serves as the best example of just how drastically the Republican Party's fortunes faded over the course of 2006. Brown's aggressive campaign benefited from voter dissatisfaction with scandals associated with Republican Gov. Bob Taft and Rep. Bob Ney.
Tennessee	Senate	Bob Corker (R)	Harold Ford (D)	Although Ford proved a more charismatic candidate than Corker, his race and single status – highlighted by a controversial RNC ad – may have hurt him in the closing weeks of this very tough campaign.
Texas	House	Nick Lampson (D)	Shelley Sekula-Gibbs (R)	In another scandal-plagued House race, Republican majority leader Tom DeLay resigned from Congress too late for an official replacement to be placed on the ballot. Former Democratic congressman Nick Lampson defeated Republican Shelley Sekula-Gibbs's write-in campaign.
Virginia	Senate	Jim Webb (D)	George Allen (R)	Allen's missteps and allegations of racial insensitivity throughout the campaign gave Webb, a former Navy Secretary under Reagan, a big win for Democrats and control of the Senate.

Virginia and Montana to take control of the Senate. On Wednesday, Democrat John Tester claimed a narrow victory over Republican Conrad Burns in Montana, and the next day, Republican George Allen of Virginia conceded defeat to Democratic challenger Jim Webb. Including the seats of Joe Lieberman of Connecticut and Bernie Sanders of Vermont, who ran as independents, the Democrats won a governing majority of 51 seats, reclaiming the U.S. Senate for the first time since 2002, and overall control of Congress for the first time in twelve years.

What is in store for the last two years of the Bush presidency? It is difficult to know the exact implications of the 2006 midterms, but it is clear that the new Congress will need to be responsive to the mandate from voters to address the situation in Iraq. The resignation of Secretary of Defense Donald Rumsfeld following the election may be the first signal of a change in strategy for the war. As discussed in chapter 7, the 110th Congress will see its very first female Speaker of the House in Nancy Pelosi (D–CA). The ability of Speaker Pelosi and the Democrats to accomplish domestic legislative goals in a closely divided Congress will have a tangible impact as their party tries to capture the main prize—the presidency—in 2008.

Comparing Voting and Elections

Reforming the Electoral Process

THE LEGITIMACY OF THE ELECTORAL OUTCOMES and the legitimacy of the political institutions that elections serve ultimately rest in the health of the electoral process. (See American Values/American Voices: Protecting the Electoral Process.) While Americans might disagree with the policy preferences of a particular president, they take comfort in the fact that the president was chosen in a fair and open system and that they will have the chance to influence the direction of the country by participating in future elections. When the legitimacy of the electoral process itself comes into question, as was the case with the 2000 presidential contest and, to a significantly lesser extent, the 2004 presidential election, the very foundation of democratic governance can be shaken to its core.

Because of the Electoral College's ability to distort public input, many proposals for electoral reform in America center on the Electoral College, as discussed earlier. What the numerous ideas for reforming the electoral process have in common is the desire for elections to serve as a clearer reflection of public preference. Abolition of the Electoral College, the establishment of a congressional district plan, or the elimination of electors are at once the most dramatic and apparently urgent reform options, especially in light of the events of the 2000 election. They are also the least likely to succeed, given entrenched interests and the difficulty of amending the Constitution. Changes to the Electoral College, however, are not the only ways in which the election of public officials in America might be improved. Several of the numerous other plans that merit attention are described below; each is designed to cure an existing weakness in the current system.

REGIONAL PRIMARIES

regional primary
A proposed system in which the country would be divided into five or six geographic areas and all states in each region would hold their presidential primary elections on the same day.

Electoral reforms that focus on the presidential nominating process often attempt to cure the uneven playing field that currently exists among states. These reform proposals attempt to remove the disproportionate attention that some states receive by holding their contests early in the primary season. One proposal is to hold a series of **regional primaries** throughout the United States during the first week of each month, beginning in February of a presidential election year. Under this system, the country would be divided into five regions: the Southeast, Southwest, Far West, Midwest, and Northeast. In December of the year prior to the presidential election, states would hold a lottery to determine the order of the primaries, with all regional contests held on the first of every month from February through

American Values/American Voices

PROTECTING THE ELECTORAL PROCESS

Fair and open elections are the bedrock upon which the legitimacy of any democratic system rests. Are American elections as secure and free of fraud and corruption as many would like to believe?

Following the contentious presidential election of 2000, Democrats and Republicans alike have been quick to allege fraud and tampering in closely contested races. In 2002, the Republican Party decried what they claimed was widespread fraud in registering Native American voters in the South Dakota senatorial election. Meanwhile, in the closely contested 2002 New Hampshire Senate race, state Republican efforts to jam a Democratic phone bank led to a guilty plea and prison term for the New Hampshire Republican Party's executive director and a Virginia-based Republican consultant. In 2004, Democratic groups, especially Internet bloggers, cried foul about a host of alleged vote fraud and voter intimidation in Ohio and other states. While these are isolated examples, many groups worry that increased use of mail-in ballots and electronic voting machines, and proposals for Internet voting, will open American elections to a host of abuses.

There have been some famous examples of vote fraud in American history. In the late nineteenth century, political bosses such as William M. Tweed—better known as Boss Tweed—were found to have bought votes, stuffed ballot boxes, and generally abused the trust of voters in New York and other major cities. The end of machine politics in big cities did not end vote fraud, however. In the 1960 presidential election, the campaigns of both John F. Kennedy and Richard M. Nixon were accused of questionable activities in Illinois and Texas, pivotal states in the closest election of the century. However, while a handful of convictions were handed down in Chicago for election fraud, subsequent investigations were unable to find enough electoral misdeeds to change the outcome of the election.[a]

In the 2004 presidential election, many Democrats accused Republicans and the Bush campaign of organized voter intimidation or ballot manipulation in several states. Kathy Dopp, a mathematician and Webmaster of ustogether.org, was quick to point to gains for Bush in traditionally Democratic counties in Florida where new optical scanning equipment was in use.[b] Subsequent investigations by a group of academics found that these patterns were not evidence of fraud, and that there was "no current evidence of irregularities of sufficient magnitude or scope to change the popular vote."[c]

The recent trend in the Northwest toward mail-in balloting has opened up potential for fraud. In 2004, in the incredibly close Washington State gubernatorial election, where 129 votes ended up determining the winner, several irregularities plagued the recount. Several boxes of ballots were unsecured or misplaced and went uncounted initially, while a handful of ballots were found to have been sent in fraudulently. As more states begin to adopt mail-in balloting, electronic voting, and other new technologies, the potential for misconduct will continue to rise. However, despite some incompetence and certain isolated incidents of fraud, most modern elections in the United States appear to be free and fair.

QUESTIONS

1. Some have suggested that allowing voters to use the Internet to cast their ballots would encourage many more to participate. Do you think the Internet is a safe and responsible technology to use for elections? What is the potential for fraud and abuse?
2. Since partisans usually run state elections and oversee the election process, is there too much potential for conflicts of interest in counting and administering elections? Should there be a nonpartisan government agency to oversee U.S. elections? Why or why not?

[a]David Greenberg, "Was Nixon Robbed? The Legend of the Stolen 1960 Presidential Election," *Slate* (October 16, 2000).

[b]Tom Zeller Jr., "Vote Fraud Theories, Spread by Blogs, Are Quickly Buried," *New York Times* (November 12, 2004).

[c]National Research Commission on Elections and Voting, "Alleged Irregularities in the United States Presidential Election of 2 November 2004" (New York: Social Science Research Council, 2004).

June. The goals of this reform would be twofold. First, it would end the current "permanent campaign" by preventing candidates from "camping out" in Iowa and New Hampshire for one to two years in the hopes of winning or doing better than expected in these small, unrepresentative states. Second, some rational order would be imposed on the nomination process, more equitably distributing the influence of states in the nomination process and allowing candidates to focus on each region's concerns.

CAMPAIGN FINANCE REFORM

Another perennial election concern focuses on the corrupting influence of money in the electoral process. The electoral reform that has attempted to address this issue and that has gained the most attention in recent years involves campaign finance reform. The Bipartisan Campaign Reform Act (BCRA), sponsored by Senators John McCain (R–AZ) and Russ Feingold (D–WI), was signed into law in March 2002. This legislation banned unregulated "soft money" donations to political parties, restricted the use of political ads, and increased political contribution limits for private individuals. Supporters heralded its passage as a major victory in lessening the influence of big money on politics. Unfortunately, political consultants have found ways around the legislation, leaving many voters to wonder what improvement the BRCA brought, if any. Campaign finance will be discussed more thoroughly in chapter 14.

PARTICIPATION

**Democracy and
the Internet**

ONLINE VOTING

The quest for a secure, reliable, fraud-free voting mechanism continues to elude the American voter. In the nineteenth century, political parties ran the elections, supplying not only paper ballots but also many of the poll watchers and election judges. This was a formula for fraud, of course—there was not even a truly secret ballot, as people voted on ballots of different colors, depending on their choice of party. The twentieth century saw widespread improvements in election practices and technology. The states now oversee the election process through official state boards of election, and the use of voting machines, nearly universal in America by the 1970s, permits truly secret mechanical voting. These measures helped effect enormous reductions in fraud and electoral ambiguity—though as the problems of the 2000 and 2004 elections proved, there is still a long way to go.

As more and more Americans become computer savvy, and as computer technology continues to evolve, Internet voting has become a likely way to cast votes in the coming years. Rightly or wrongly, many Americans equate Internet voting with the ideals of instant democracy and greater citizen participation. Many states are formally studying the feasibility and impact of Internet voting. In 2000, Arizona pioneered online balloting by allowing citizens to vote via the Internet in the state's Democratic presidential primary. In 2004, Michigan made a similar attempt during its presidential caucus. In both cases, fears of computer hacking and voter fraud, as well as technical difficulties, limited the success of the experiments.

In 2004, the U.S. military attempted the most ambitious use of Internet voting in the nation's history. The $22 million program, know as Secure Electronic Registration

■ New electronic voting systems are being rolled out across the country as an alternative to traditional paper and punch-card balloting. Here, the ESlate System is demonstrated in Austin, Texas.

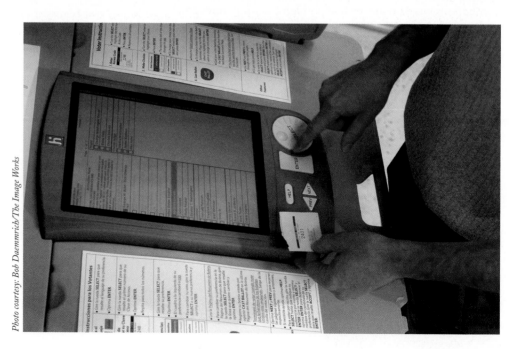

Photo courtesy: Bob Daemmrich/The Image Works

and Voting Experiment (SERVE), was intended to allow 100,000 overseas U.S. military personnel to vote online in the 2004 presidential race. Due to security concerns and the inability to adequately protect against voter fraud and computer hackers, the program was scrapped prior to the election. To date, persistent security concerns have hampered widespread adoption of online voting practices.

VOTING BY MAIL

As noted earlier in the chapter, over a quarter of eligible voters who failed to vote in the 2002 election cited "too busy" as their reason. Reformers who seek to increase turnout note that the process is inconvenient and time consuming, especially having to show up at a specific polling place on a particular day. The use of mail-in ballots, whereby registered voters are mailed ballots and given several weeks to mail them back with their votes, has been found to increase participation. Currently, Oregon is the only state that votes entirely by mail-in ballots. However, most states have a system of absentee balloting through which voters can request that they receive their ballots at home. Voters then mail back their completed ballots. Political parties have encouraged their voters to register by absentee ballot, as it increases turnout and allows the party more time to follow up with voters and make sure they have returned their ballots.

While the all-mail system remains popular in Oregon and is credited with increasing voting rates in that state, voting by mail has its down side. One problem with such an approach is that it delays elections results. Oregon did not have its 2000 presidential results finalized until several weeks after Election Day. The state of Washington, which has extremely liberal laws regarding mail-in votes, was also much later than the rest of the country in announcing its presidential and congressional winners. Additionally, there are concerns about decreased ballot security and increased potential for fraud with mail-in elections.

MODERNIZING THE BALLOT

The use of electronic voting machines has increased rapidly since 2000 (see Figure 13.7). Following the 2004 presidential election, many states replaced their paper ballots with electronic devices. Indeed, prior to the 2002 midterm elections, the Florida legislature undertook massive voting reforms, including banning punch-card ballots and investing $30 million in new touch-screen voting systems, with the individual counties spending tens of millions more. Unfortunately, problems plagued the 2002 Democratic gubernatorial primary. Confusion abounded as voters and poll workers misused the expensive new machines. Election administrators had difficulty tabulating the electronic votes, leading to a week-long delay in naming an official winner. Everyone learned an important lesson: technology is not a panacea that will cure all election problems.

Supporters of electronic voting believe that emphasis must be placed on training poll workers, administrators, and voters on how to effectively use the new equipment. Critics believe that the lack of a paper trail leaves electronic machines vulnerable to fraud and worry that the machines could crash during an election. Still other critics cite the expense of the machines. Reflecting these concerns, in the months leading up to the 2006 midterm elections, lawsuits targeting electronic voting were filed in a number of states, including Arizona, California, Colorado, Florida, Ohio, and Pennsylvania. Observers agree that updating election equipment and ensuring fair elections across the country should be a legislative priority. As Charles M. Vest, the president of the Massachusetts Institute of Technology, noted, "A nation that can send a man to the moon, that can put a reliable ATM machine on every corner, has no excuse not to deploy a reliable, affordable, easy-to-use voting system."

FIGURE 13.7
PERCENTAGE OF VOTERS USING ELECTRONIC VOTING MACHINES, 2000–2006
Since the 2000 election disaster in Florida, where problems with voting equipment and ballot design prevented many votes from being properly counted, more areas are adopting electronic voting machines.

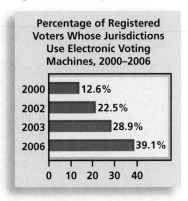

Percentage of Registered Voters Whose Jurisdictions Use Electronic Voting Machines, 2000–2006

Year	Percentage
2000	12.6%
2002	22.5%
2003	28.9%
2006	39.1%

Source: Election Data Services.

Summary

ELECTIONS CONTINUE TO BE the cornerstone of American government, a continual reaffirmation of the right of the people to rule. Despite lingering voter apathy, many reforms have increased citizens' access to elections. Moreover, the relatively high turnout in the 2004 presidential election demonstrated a reassuring increase in the interest and intensity of American elections. In our efforts to explain the complex and multilayered U.S. electoral system, we covered these points in this chapter:

1. **Voting Behavior**
   Whether they are casting ballots in congressional or presidential elections, voters behave in certain distinct ways and exhibit unmistakable patterns to political scientists who study them.

2. **Elections in the United States**
   Regular elections guarantee mass political action and governmental accountability. They also confer legitimacy on regimes better than any other method of change. When it comes to elections, the United States has an embarrassment of riches. There are various types of primary elections in the country, as well as general elections, initiatives, referenda, and recall elections.

3. **Presidential Elections**
   Variety aside, no U.S. election can compare to the presidential contest. This spectacle, held every four years, brings together all the elements of politics and attracts the most ambitious and energetic politicians to the national stage. The parties select presidential candidates through either primary elections or caucuses, with the primary process culminating in each party's national convention, after which the general election campaign begins.

4. **Congressional Elections**
   Many similar elements are present in different kinds of elections. Candidates, voters, issues, and television advertisements are constants. But, there are distinctive aspects of each kind of election as well. Compared with presidential elections, congressional elections are a different animal.

5. **The 2006 Midterm Elections**
   The sixth-year itch was in full force during the 2006 midterm elections as voters rejected Republicans by returning Democrats to control of both chambers of Congress for the first time since 1994. Beset by scandals, corruption, an unpopular president, and the deteriorating situation in Iraq, Republicans lost 30 seats in the House and 6 seats in the Senate.

6. **Reforming the Electoral Process**
   The American political system uses indirect electoral representation in the form of the Electoral College.

Events of the 2000 election renewed calls for change in the Electoral College. Other suggested reforms are regional primaries, campaign finance limits, online voting, and voting by mail. Some states have promoted electronic voting technologies to eliminate problems with punch-card ballots, but critics point to the possibility of voter fraud.

KEY TERMS

authoritarian system, p. 477
ballot measure, p. 478
closed primary, p. 478
conventional political participation, p. 463
crossover voting, p. 478
elector, p. 487
Electoral College, p. 487
electorate, p. 477
front-loading, p. 483
general election, p. 478
gerrymandering p. 494
incumbency, p. 493
initiative, p. 478
mandate, p. 477
midterm election, p. 496
open primary, p. 478
primary election, p. 478
prospective judgment, p. 476
raiding, p. 478
reapportionment, p. 489
recall, p. 480
redistricting, p. 494
referendum, p. 480
regional primary, p. 500
retrospective judgment, p. 476
runoff primary, p. 478
superdelegate, p. 485
ticket-splitting, p. 474
turnout, p. 463
unconventional political participation, p. 463
unit rule, p. 484

SELECTED READINGS

Campbell, Angus, Philip E. Converse, Warren E. Miller, and Donald E. Stokes, reprint ed. *The American Voter.* Chicago: University of Chicago, 1980.

Conway, M. Margaret. *Political Participation in the United States,* 3rd ed. Washington, DC: CQ Press, 2000.

Conway, M. Margaret, David W. Ahern, and Gertrude A. Steuernagel. *Women and Political Participation: Cultural Change in the Political Arena,* 2nd ed. Washington, DC: CQ Press, 2004.

Darcy, Robert, Susan Welch, and Janet Clark. *Women, Elections, and Representation,* 2nd ed. Lincoln: University of Nebraska Press, 1994.

Fiorina, Morris P. *Retrospective Voting in American National Elections.* New Haven, CT: Yale University Press, 1999.

Herrnson, Paul S. *Congressional Elections: Campaigning at Home and in Washington,* 4th ed. Washington, DC: CQ Press, 2000.

Jacobson, Gary C. *The Politics of Congressional Elections,* 6th ed. New York: Longman, 2003.

Key, V. O., Jr., with Milton C. Cummings. *The Responsible Electorate.* Cambridge, MA: Harvard University Press, 1966.

Lupia, Arthur, and Matthew D. McCubbins. *The Democratic Dilemma: Can Citizens Learn What They Need to Know?* Political Economy of Institutions and Decisions. Cambridge: Cambridge University Press, 1998.

Nie, Norman H., Sidney Verba, and John R. Petrocik. *The Changing American Voter.* Cambridge, MA: Harvard University Press, 1980.

Niemi, Richard G., and Herbert F. Weisberg. *Classics in Voting Behavior.* Washington, DC: CQ Press, 1992.

———. *Controversies in Voting Behavior,* 4th ed. Washington, DC: CQ Press, 2001.

Patterson, Thomas E. *The Vanishing Voter: Public Involvement in an Age of Uncertainty.* New York: Vintage, 2003.

Sabato, Larry J. *The Sixth Year Itch: The Rise and Fall of George W. Bush's Presidency.* New York: Longman, 2007.

Sabato, Larry J., and Howard R. Ernst, eds. *The Encyclopedia of American Political Parties and Election.* New York: FactsOnFile, 2006.

Stanley, Harold W., and Richard G. Niemi. *Vital Statistics on American Politics, 2005–2006.* Washington, DC: CQ Press, 2005.

Teixeira, Ruy. *The Disappearing American Voter.* Washington, DC: Brookings Institution, 1992.

Verba, Sidney, Kay Lehman Schlozman, and Henry E. Brady. *Voice and Equality: Civic Voluntarism in American Politics.* New York: Belknap, 1996.

Wayne, Stephen J. *The Road to the White House,* 6th ed. New York: Wadsworth, 2003.

Weisberg, Herbert F., ed. *Democracy's Feast: Elections in America.* Chatham, NJ: Chatham House, 1995.

WEB EXPLORATIONS

To select, evaluate, and debate upcoming referenda or initiatives currently under consideration, go to
http://www.iandrinstitute.org

To see how presidential candidates presented themselves in the technology age of the 2004 race, see the official sites of some of the past, and possibly future, candidates:
http://www.johnkerry.com
http://www.gop.com

To learn about the functions of the Federal Election Commission, the government agency that monitors and enforces campaign finance and election laws, see
http://www.fec.gov

To access the most up-to-date, high-quality data on voting, public opinion, and political participation, go to
http://www.gallup.com

To learn more about the Electoral College, go to
http://www.fec.gov/pages/ecmenu2.htm

To explore campaign contributions and election results, see
http://www.opensecrets.org

To learn more about candidates so you can make informed choices, go to
http://www.vote-smart.org

To look at what voters said before going to the polls and whom they actually voted for, go to
http://www.pollingreport.com

THE CAMPAIGN PROCESS

14

WHILE IT IS IMPOSSIBLE TO MARK the exact beginning of the 2008 presidential contest, it is likely that the 2008 race was on the minds of several presidential hopefuls prior to the conclusion of the 2004 contest. Senator John McCain's belated endorsement in 2004 of George W. Bush, his arch rival from the 2000 presidential primary, was certainly influenced by McCain's desire to gain support among the party faithful for a 2008 bid. Senator and former First Lady Hillary Rodham Clinton's decision not to run in 2004 was undoubtedly influenced by her upcoming bid for reelection to the Senate in 2006, as well as the fact that the 2008 presidential election, unlike the 2004 race, is likely be highly contested by both parties, since Vice President Dick Cheney is unlikely to run for president given his health and low approval ratings.

By the fall of 2005, fully three years prior to the next presidential election, the contest had begun in earnest, as hopefuls jockeyed for position. By this time, Republican Senator George Allen from Virginia had made more than ten trips to early primary states since the 2004 election, and Republican Senator John McCain had made more than fourteen trips. Other GOP hopefuls camped out in early primary states included Senator Bill Frist (thirteen trips), former Speaker of the House Newt Gingrich (thirteen trips), former New York City Mayor Rudy Giuliani (thirteen trips). On the Democratic side, Senator Hillary Rodham Clinton had already made sixteen trips to early primary states. And, when the would-be candidates were not racking up frequent flyer miles, they were competing for coveted television airtime.

All the while, the pundits were writing books about an election that was years in the future, identifying not only the likely candidates but detailing the likely winner. Dick Morris, former political adviser to Bill Clinton, published the best-selling *Condi v. Hillary* in the fall of 2005. Morris made the bold prediction that Senator Clinton would not only win the Democratic nomination but most likely would win the presidency in 2008. The sentiment was echoed in political futures markets, in which investors buy stock in a

CHAPTER OUTLINE

- The Nature of Modern Political Campaigns
- The Key Players: The Candidate and the Campaign Staff
- Coverage of the Game: The Media's Role in Defining the Playing Field
- The Rules of the Game: Campaign Finance
- The Main Event: The 2004 Presidential Campaign

507

candidate based on the likelihood of the candidate winning a future election. By November 2006, in the largest of such markets, Intrade.com, investors were paying more than $50 per share for stock that predicted Clinton would be the 2008 Democratic nominee for president. The stock for the leading Republican front-runner, John McCain, was selling at a little over $44 per share—all this two years prior to the Iowa caucus.

MODERN POLITICAL CAMPAIGNS enjoy all the trappings of a major-league sporting event, plus the added intrigue that comes from knowing that election outcomes can quite literally alter the course of history. Though campaigns have become high-stakes, high-priced extravaganzas, the basic purpose of modern electioneering remains intact: one person asking another for support.

The art of modern campaigning involves the management of a large budget and staff, the planning of sophisticated voter outreach efforts, and the creation of sophisticated Internet sites that provide continuous communication updates and organize voter and donor support. Campaigning also involves the diplomatic skill of unifying disparate individuals and groups to achieve a fragile but election-winning majority. How candidates perform these exquisitely difficult tasks is the subject of this chapter, in which we discuss the following topics:

- First, we will explore *the nature of modern campaigns*, which are often described in terms of military strategy or sports competitions and are generally segmented into nomination and general election campaigns.

- Second, we will look at *the key players in the modern campaign*, the people who run for office and the paid and volunteer staffs who constitute the campaign organization.

- Third, we will examine *the coverage of the game: the media's role in defining the playing field*—exploring how conventional and new types of media depict the political landscape and how campaigns attempt to influence media coverage.

- Fourth, we will analyze *the rules of the game: campaign finance*—giving special attention to the impact of the Bipartisan Campaign Reform Act of 2002.

- Finally, we will assess *the main event: the 2004 presidential campaign* and its important lessons.

FIGURE 14.1
THE ELEMENTS OF A POLITICAL CAMPAIGN
Several elements combine to shape the character of a political campaign, with candidates left to navigate this often intricate political dynamic in their attempt to win.

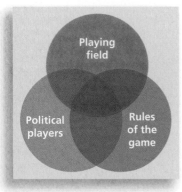

The Nature of Modern Political Campaigns

"CAMPAIGN" IS THE MILITARY term for an armed struggle to achieve a specific objective. The language of modern campaigning is filled with military words. For example, political campaigns are "launched," and they include "tactics and strategy." Incumbents amass considerable "war chests," while challengers attempt to "raid" votes from the incumbent. Common sports metaphors have also infiltrated the lexicon of campaigning, with candidates "scoring touchdowns," "hitting home runs," and "landing knockout punches" when they perform well against their opponents. And, as in sports, there are the big leagues (presidential, gubernatorial, and U.S. Senate races), as well as minor leagues (state and local contests). There is a campaign "season," and ultimately every campaign has its "winners" and "losers."

No two political campaigns are the same: the players change, the political landscape evolves, and even the rules change from time to time. Each aspect of the campaign (see Figure 14.1) interacts with the other aspects to create a dynamic set of circumstances that make campaigns unpredictable and add to their excitement. Despite the unique qualities of each race, however, electoral contests are similar in structure, consisting of some form of nomination campaign and a general election.

THE NOMINATION CAMPAIGN

The **nomination campaign** begins as soon as the candidate has decided to run—sometimes years prior to an official announcement, as discussed in the opening vignette—and ends the night of the party primary or convention. During the nomination campaign, the candidate targets the leaders and activists who choose nominees in primaries or conventions. Party leaders are concerned with electability, while party activists are often ideologically and issue oriented, so a candidate must appeal to both bases.

The nomination campaign gives new candidates an opportunity to get their sea legs early on. As they seek their party's nomination, candidates learn to adjust to the pressure of being in the spotlight day in and day out. This is the time for the candidates to learn that a single careless phrase could end the campaign or guarantee a defeat. This is also the time to seek the support of party leaders and interest groups and to test out themes, slogans, and strategies. The press and public take much less notice of shifts in strategy at this time than they will later in the general election campaign.

The nomination campaign is a critical time for gaining and maintaining an aura of support both within the party and with the larger electorate. In the months leading up to the 2000 Republican convention, George W. Bush, the eventual Republican nominee for president, won support through a variety of means. Much of this support grew out of Bush's early fund-raising success and the sense of inevitability a steady flow of cash supplies in politics—not necessarily out of support for Bush's issue positions or campaign themes.[1] In the 2004 campaign for the Democratic Party nomination, John Kerry also benefited from the momentum of early fund-raising success and the perception of inevitability. By the end of the nominating period, his former competitors for the Democratic ticket, such as Dick Gephardt and Howard Dean, were campaigning alongside Kerry, and his toughest opponent, John Edwards, had become his vice presidential nominee.

COMPARATIVE

Comparing Political Campaigns

nomination campaign
That part of a political campaign aimed at winning a primary election.

■ Democratic Presidential nominee John Kerry responds to supporters at a rally in Pittsburgh, Pennsylvania, in July 2004. During his speech, Kerry announced that Senator John Edwards would be his vice presidential running mate. Kerry lost the 2004 presidential election, but some political observers believe he will seek the Democratic nomination again in 2008.

Photo courtesy: Kat Wade/San Francisco Chronicle/Corbis

A danger not always heeded by candidates during the nomination campaign is that, in the quest to win the party's nomination, a candidate can move too far to the right or left and appear too extreme to the electorate in November. Party activists are generally more ideologically extreme than party-identified voters in the general electorate, and activists participate in primaries and caucuses at a relatively high rate. If a candidate tries too hard to appeal to their interests, he or she jeopardizes the ultimate goal of winning the election. Conservative Barry Goldwater, the 1964 Republican nominee for president, and liberal George McGovern, the 1972 Democratic nominee for president, both fell victim to this phenomenon in seeking their party's nomination—Goldwater going too far right, and McGovern going too far left—and they were handily defeated in the general elections by Presidents Lyndon B. Johnson and Richard M. Nixon, respectively.

THE GENERAL ELECTION CAMPAIGN

general election campaign
That part of a political campaign aimed at winning a general election.

After earning the party's nomination, candidates embark on the **general election campaign.** They must seek the support of interest groups and a majority of voters and decide on the issues they will emphasize. When courting interest groups, a candidate seeks both money and endorsements, although the results are mainly predictable: liberal, labor, and minority groups usually back Democrats, while social conservatives and business organizations usually support Republicans. The most active groups often coalesce around emotional issues such as abortion and gun control, and these organizations can produce a bumper crop of money and activists for favored candidates. (See Politics Now: Wedge Issues and Campaign Strategy.)

Virtually all candidates adopt a brief theme, or slogan, to serve as a rallying cry in their quest for office. In 2004, the Kerry-Edwards campaign adopted the slogan "A Stronger America" in order to emphasize the security issue. Most slogans can fit many candidates ("He's on our side," "She hears you," "New leadership for a change"). Candidates try to avoid controversy in their selection of slogans, and some openly eschew ideology. (An ever popular one of this genre is "Not left, not right—forward!") The clever candidate also attempts to find a slogan that cannot be lampooned easily. In 1964, Barry Goldwater's handlers may have regretted their choice of "In your heart, you know he's right" when Lyndon B. Johnson's supporters quickly converted it into "In your guts, you know he's nuts." (Democrats were trying to portray Goldwater as a warmonger after the Republican indicated a willingness to use nuclear weapons.)

■ 1964 Republican candidate Barry Goldwater's famous slogan, "In your heart, you know he's right," was quickly lampooned by incumbent Democratic opponent President Lyndon B. Johnson's campaign as "In your guts, you know he's nuts."

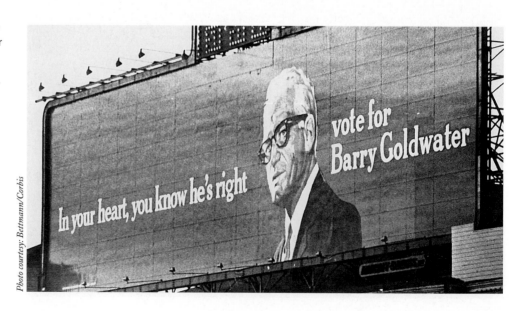

Photo courtesy: Bettmann/Corbis

Politics Now

WEDGE ISSUES AND CAMPAIGN STRATEGY

With the rise of interest group politics, many partisan voters are strongly attached to supporting single issues that often outweigh their party loyalty. These issues are usually controversial social issues, such as abortion, same-sex marriage, or mandated prayer in the public schools. Some candidates, in formulating their campaign strategy, exploit these issues in order to divide their opponent's supporters and win the election. When an issue is used to divide electoral opinion for tactical campaign purposes, it is known as a wedge issue, driving a wedge between party loyalty and support for a particular social issue.

For many years, Democrats have used abortion as a wedge issue against pro-choice Republican candidates, driving away religious conservatives and weakening moderate Republicans' base of support. In 2006, Democratic strategists found that many Americans strongly support the use of contraceptives and sex education. Trying to capitalize on this fact, Democratic senators crafted a wedge-issue strategy in an attempt to isolate Republicans as too conservative on family planning. Harry Reid (D–NV) sponsored the Prevention First Act, which also had the support of Democratic presidential front-runner Senator Hillary Clinton (D–NY). The bill would require health care insurers to cover the costs of contraceptive devices and related care, as well as make federally supported clinics and hospitals disseminate information on contraception.[a] Democrats believed that forcing a vote on this bill would draw moderate Republican voters away from conservative Republican candidates who do not support the bill, while driving religious conservatives away from moderate Republicans who do.

Same-sex marriage is a wedge issue Republicans have deployed to divide Democrats, since many socially conservative Democrats oppose the marriage of same-sex couples, while liberal members of the Democratic Party are more supportive of the idea. President Bush's support of a constitutional amendment banning same-sex marriage was seen by many political observers as a wedge-issue strategy that would work against Democrats in the 2006 midterm election, as was the Senate roll-call vote on the issue in June 2006. Overall, Americans oppose same-sex marriage by a significant majority, but among Americans with religious commitments, the disapproval soars to 74 percent, with only 18 percent in support.[b] While few expected that the Senate would support such an amendment, forcing a vote on the issue gave Republicans ammunition to use against weak Democratic candidates in races in more conservative regions. Same-sex marriage did not prove overly successful as a wedge issue in 2006, however. Arizona became the first state to reject such a ban, and several Republican incumbents who had supported the ban were defeated.

[a]Alexander Bolton, "Senate Dems to Pursue New Strategy on Abortion," *The Hill* (April 5, 2006).

[b]Pew Forum on Religious and Public Life, http://pewforum.org/gay-marriage/.

In addition to deciding on the issues to focus on during the campaign, the candidate must also define his or her stance on other topics of interest to voters. A variety of factors influence candidates' positions and core issues, including personal conviction, party platform, and experience in a certain area. Candidates also use public opinion polling to gauge whether the issues that they care about are issues that the voters care about.

The Key Players: The Candidate and the Campaign Staff

MOST OBSERVERS AGREE that the most important aspect of any campaign is the quality of the candidate and the attributes of the campaign team. The ability to convey ideas in a persuasive manner, the cornerstone of all political campaigns, ultimately rests in the hands of the candidate. The ability to package and project the candidate's message in the most effective and persuasive manner, the work of the campaign staff, requires expertise in media and public relations. The ability to raise funds, which in turn provide volume to the campaign message, requires the combined effort of a strong candidate and experienced campaign staff.

American Values/American Voices

FROM THE BATTLEFIELD AND ONTO THE BALLOT

A willingness to die to protect the United States' security and freedom is considered by the majority of Americans to be the ultimate measure of patriotism. Not surprisingly, there is a long tradition in American politics of former soldiers running for and winning political office. Starting with George Washington, many former generals such as Andrew Jackson, Ulysses S. Grant and Dwight D. Eisenhower have risen from the top ranks of the military to the highest office in the land. Citizen-soldiers, many agree, epitomize values of democratic leadership and so are uniquely qualified to serve as their fellow citizens' elected representatives.

In the 109th Congress that convened in 2005, 26 percent of the members were veterans, far higher than the 12 percent of the U.S. population with military experience, but significantly lower than the number of veterans who served in the 95th Congress in 1977 and 1978—a high for the post–World War II era of 77 percent. The majority of veterans serving in the 109th Congress were Republicans, but Democrats, who traditionally have been viewed as weaker on defense and security issues, sought attention for the more than fifty veterans running for Congress as Democrats in the 2006 midterm election.

While many of the veterans who ran for office in 2006 had completed their military service decades earlier, a number were recently off the battlefield in Afghanistan or Iraq. In a contrast to the bitter days of the Vietnam War, citizens warmly welcomed these recent veterans, whose experiences gave them a unique perspective on the situation in Iraq and the war on terrorism. Approximately ten veterans from the military actions in Iraq and Afghanistan ran for House seats in 2005 and 2006; all but one of them, Repub-

lican Van Taylor in Texas's 17th congressional district, ran as Democrats.

One of the first veterans of the war in Iraq to receive widespread media coverage was Democrat Paul Hackett of Ohio, who made an unsuccessful bid for Congress in 2005. Hackett, a marine reservist, traded heavily on his war experience, trying to convince a heavily Republican district of his unique qualifications to represent them on the war. Although his campaign was unsuccessful, he came amazingly close to defeating his Republican opponent.

Other recent veterans have been candidates not only for the U.S. Congress but also for state and local offices. In one particularly surprising turn, Major Mike McNamara, a member of the Marine Corps Reserve stationed in Iraq, managed to win a June 2006 city council seat in Grand Forks, North Dakota. McNamara beat three other candidates, all of whom had the advantage of actually being in the city during the election.

Of the 2006 Democratic challengers, two Pennsylvania veterans managed to unseat incumbent Republican congressmen. Chris Carney defeated Don Sherwood by six percent in Pennsylvania's 10th Congressional District, and Patrick Murphy narrowly defeated Mike Fitzpatrick by only 1,500 votes in Pennsylvania's 8th Congressional District. L. "Tammy" Duckworth of Illinois and Eric Massa of New York, both touted as two of the strongest Democratic veteran challengers, narrowly lost their election bids in heavily Republican districts.

Sources: Brady Dennis, "Soldiers' New Battles: Fighting for Votes," *St. Petersburg Times State* (June 19, 2006); Linda Feldmann, "Now Running for Office: An Army of Iraq Veterans," *Christian Science Monitor* (February 22, 2006); Andrea Stone, "War Vets Ready for New Battle: Politics," *USA Today* (January 23, 2006).

THE CANDIDATE

Before there can be a campaign there must be candidates. Candidates run for office for any number of reasons, including personal ambition, the desire to promote ideological objectives or to pursue specific public policies, or simply because they think they can do a better job than their opponents.[2] (See American Values/American Voices: From the Battlefield and onto the Ballot.) In any case, to be successful, candidates must spend a considerable amount of time and energy in pursuit of their desired office, and all candidates must be prepared to expose themselves to public scrutiny and the chance of rejection by the voters.

In the effort to show voters that they are hardworking, thoughtful, and worthy of the office they seek, candidates try to meet personally as many citizens as possible in the course of a campaign. To some degree, such efforts are symbolic, especially for presidential candidates, since it only possible to have direct contact with a small fraction of the more than 100 million people who are likely to vote in a presidential contest. Moreover, at the presidential level, these "one-on-one" meetings are often staged events, meant more for the television audience than the actual participants. But, one should not discount the value of visiting numerous localities to both increase media coverage and to motivate local activists who are working for the candidate's campaign.

In a typical campaign, a candidate for high office maintains an exhausting schedule. The day may begin at 5 a.m. at the entrance gate to an auto plant with an hour or two of handshaking, followed by similar glad-handing at subway stops until 9 a.m. Strategy sessions with key advisers and preparation for upcoming presentations and forums may fill the rest of the morning. A luncheon talk, afternoon fundraisers, and a series of television and print interviews crowd the afternoon agenda. Cocktail parties are followed by a dinner speech, perhaps telephone or neighborhood canvassing of voters, and a civic-forum talk or two. More meetings with advisers and planning for the next day's events can easily take a candidate past midnight. Following only a few hours of sleep, the candidate starts all over again. The hectic pace of campaigning can strain the candidate's family life and leaves little time for reflection and long-range planning. After months of this grueling pace, candidates may be functioning on automatic pilot and often commit gaffes, from referring to the wrong city's sports team to fumbling an oft-repeated stump speech.

THE CAMPAIGN STAFF

Paid staff, political consultants, and dedicated volunteers work behind the scenes to support the candidate. Collectively, they plan strategy, conduct polls, write speeches, craft the campaign's message, organize dinners and other fund-raising events, and design television advertisements, radio spots, and direct mail pieces. The staff, professional and volunteer, keeps the candidate on message and manages the campaign's near-infinite details. The size and nature of the organizational staff varies significantly depending on the type of race. Senate and gubernatorial races, for example, are able to hire for many staff positions and employ a number of different consultants and pollsters, whereas races for state legislatures will likely have a paid campaign manager and rely more heavily on volunteer workers. Presidential campaign organizations, not surprisingly, have the most elaborate structure (see Figure 14.2 for an organizational chart of President George W. Bush's 2004 reelection campaign).

Volunteer Campaign Staff Volunteers are the lifeblood of every national, state, and local campaign. Volunteers answer phone calls, staff candidate booths at festivals and county fairs, copy and distribute campaign literature, and serve as the public face of the campaign. They go door to door to solicit votes, or use computerized telephone banks to call targeted voters with scripted messages, two basic methods of **voter canvass.** Most canvassing, or direct solicitation of support, takes place in the month before the election, when voters are most likely to be paying attention. Closer to Election Day, volunteers begin vital **get out the vote (GOTV)** efforts, calling and e-mailing supporters to remind them to vote and arranging for their transportation to the polls if necessary.

The Candidate's Professional Staff Nearly every campaign at the state and national level is run by a **campaign manager,** who coordinates and directs the campaign. The campaign manager is the person closest to the candidate, the person who delivers the good and bad news about the condition of the campaign and makes the essential day-to-day decisions, such as whom to hire and when to air which television

Photo courtesy: Ronen Zilberman/AP Wide World Photos

■ Competing in an extremely crowded field of ten Democratic primary candidates in Hawaii's 2nd Congressional District, Mazie Hirono, a former Lt. Governor, won by a razor thin 844 votes

SIMULATION

You Are a Professional Campaign Manager

voter canvass
The process by which a campaign reaches individual voters, either by door-to-door solicitation or by telephone.

get out the vote (GOTV)
A push at the end of a political campaign to encourage supporters to go to the polls.

campaign manager
The individual who travels with the candidate and coordinates the many different aspects of the campaign.

FIGURE 14.2 BUSH CAMPAIGN ORGANIZATIONAL CHART

The modern presidential campaign requires an incredible amount of organization and personnel, as is reflected in this organizational chart from George W. Bush's 2004 campaign.

President George W. Bush's Campaign Organization

Bush Cheney '04, Inc.

General
Chairman: Marc Racicot
Campaign Manager: Ken Mehlman
Deputy to the Campaign Manager for
   Campaign Operations: Kelley McCullough
Deputy Campaign Manager: Mark Wallace
Chief Financial Officer: Sandra Pack
General Counsel: Thomas J. Josefiak
Counsel (outside): Ben Ginsberg

Political
Political Director: Terry Nelson
Regional Political Directors
Northeast: Mike DuHaime
Central: Dave DenHerder
Southeast: Heath Thompson
Midwest: Karen Slifka
Northwest: Cary Evans
Southwest: Rudy Fernandez
Director of Coalitions: Jafar Karim
National Youth Director: Jordan Sekulow
Legislative Director: Elise Finley

Field
Field Director: Coddy Johnson

Communications
Communications Director: Nicolle Devenish
Press Secretary: Terry Holt

e-Campaign
Director: Michael Turk

Policy
Policy Director: Tim Adams

Vice Presidential
Director of Vice Presidential Operations:
   Mary Cheney

Finance
Finance Chairman: Mercer Reynolds
Deputy Finance Chairman: Jack Oliver
National Finance Director: Travis Thomas
Senior Strategist (includes polling):
   Matthew Dowd
Deputy to the Chief Strategist:
   Sara Taylor

Media
Mark McKinnon, Maverick Media
14-person creative team headed up
   by McKinnon

Regional
11 Regional Chairpersons

States
Leadership Team Chairpersons
Leadership Team Co-chairpersons
Executive Directors

---

finance chair
A professional who coordinates the fund-raising efforts for the campaign.

pollster
A professional who takes public opinion surveys that guide political campaigns.

direct mailer
A professional who supervises a political campaign's direct mail fund-raising strategies.

communications director
The person who develops the overall media strategy for the candidate, blending free press coverage with paid TV, radio, and mail media.

---

advertisement. The campaign manager helps to determine the campaign's overall strategy, and equally important, works to keep the campaign on message throughout the race.

Other key paid positions, depending on the race, include the **finance chair,** who is responsible for bringing in the large contributions that fund the campaign, the **pollster,** who takes public opinion surveys to learn what issues voters want candidates to address in speeches, and the **direct mailer,** who supervises direct mail fund-raising. The **communications director** develops the overall media strategy for the candidate, carefully blending press coverage with paid TV, radio, and mail media, not to mention advertisements on Web sites visited by those likely to favor the candidate's positions.

The **press secretary** is charged with interacting and communicating with journalists on a daily basis. It is the press secretary's job to be quoted in the newspapers or on TV explaining the candidate's positions or reacting to the actions of the opposing candidate. Good news is usually announced by the candidate. Bad news, including responding to attacks from the other side, is the preserve of the press secretary (better to have someone not on the ballot doing the dirty work of the campaign).

An increasingly indispensable part of modern political campaigns is the campaign's **Internet team,** which manages the campaign's communications, outreach, and fund-raising via the Internet, and increasingly tries to manage the candidate's visibility on blogs popular with the party faithful. Howard Dean's technology guru, Joe Trippi, took Internet campaigning to new levels in the 2004 election. Dean surged to an early lead in the polls thanks in large part to Trippi's tremendously successful Internet-based fund-raising strategy. Tens of thousands of small online donations bolstered the more than $50 million in individual contributions that the Dean campaign eventually raised. Since making an online appeal for campaign contributions costs significantly less than raising funds through expensive direct mail campaigns or pricey fund-raising events—the standard means of attaining campaign resources—the Internet is radically altering the way candidates raise funds for their campaigns. The importance of the Internet team is likely to expand in future elections.

The Candidate's Hired Guns
Campaign consultants are the private-sector professionals and firms who sell the technologies, services, and strategies many candidates need to get elected. Consultants' numbers have grown exponentially since they first appeared in the 1930s, and their specialties and responsibilities have increased accordingly, to the point that campaign consultants are now an obliga-

Photo courtesy: AFP/Getty Images

■ Ken Mehlman, President George W. Bush's campaign manager, answers reporters' questions in Allentown, New Jersey, less than a month before the 2004 election.

press secretary
The individual charged with interacting and communicating with journalists on a daily basis.

Internet team
The campaign staff that makes use of Web-based resources to communicate with voters, raise funds, organize volunteers, and plan campaign events.

campaign consultant
A private-sector professional who sells to a candidate the technologies, services, and strategies required to get that candidate elected.

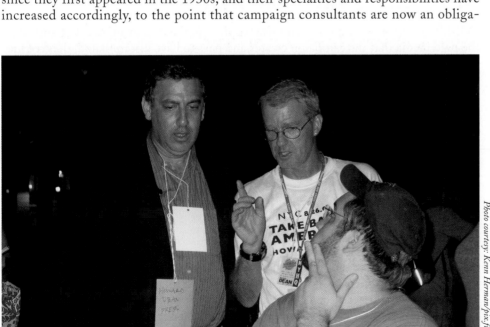

Photo courtesy: Kenn Herman/pix-filter.com

■ Joe Trippi, far left, discussing the Dean campaign's blog with Webmaster Nicco Mele (center). Dean's Internet team managed to help the campaign to an early lead thanks to their innovative fundraising strategy.

■ Karl Rove is best known for his role as the political adviser to President George W. Bush. Rove's relationship with the president predates his White House tenure; he assisted Bush's two successful gubernatorial races in Texas prior to orchestrating Bush's two successful presidential campaigns. Rove is widely characterized as both a masterful political operative for whom there is no modern rival and a Machiavellian trickster intent on ensuring Republican successes without regard to tactics or scruples.

media consultant
A professional who produces candidates' television, radio, and print advertisements.

SIMULATION
You Are a Media Consultant to a Political Candidate

paid media
Political advertisements purchased for a candidate's campaign.

free media
Coverage of a candidate's campaign by the news media.

new media
New technologies, such as the Internet, that blur the line between paid and free media sources.

positive ad
Advertising on behalf of a candidate that stresses the candidate's qualifications, family, and issue positions, without reference to the opponent.

negative ad
Advertising on behalf of a candidate that attacks the opponent's platform or character.

tory part of campaigns at the state and national level.[3] Candidates generally hire specialized consultants who focus on only one or two areas, such as fund-raising, polling, mass mailings, media relations, advertising, Internet outreach, and speech writing.

Media consultants design TV, radio, and direct mail advertisements. More than one consultant or even an advertising company or two may be assigned to this fundamental part of the modern political campaign. The communications director, with frequent involvement from the campaign manager, pollster, and sometimes even the candidate, works with the media consultant to craft the campaign's advertising message and address key issues.

The Candidate's Personal Advisers Figure 14.2 shows the organizational chart for the George W. Bush reelection campaign. The reelection committee was headed by Ken Mehlman, who worked at the White House for three years before resigning in mid-2003 to head the reelection committee. An important player in the campaign is not on the chart, however. Karl Rove, a longtime friend and colleague of Bush, masterminded Bush's nomination and general election in 2000 and performed the same function in 2004 while remaining in the White House. Mehlman, who became chair of the Republican National Committee after the 2004 election, clearly answered to Rove.

Coverage of the Game: The Media's Role in Defining the Playing Field

WHAT VOTERS ACTUALLY SEE and hear of the candidate is primarily determined by the **paid media** that the campaign creates and pays to have disseminated, the **free media** that result from stories about the campaign that the media choose to broadcast, and the **new media** that blur the lines between paid and free media sources. The campaign staff and media consultants discussed above determine the amount, form, and content of paid media. Free media consists of independent press coverage—all the media outlets covering the candidate and his or her run for office. The new media, made possible by a wide array of technological innovations, is generated in part by the campaign but is also driven by individuals from outside the campaign who either contribute to the candidate's existing online effort or who maintain Web sites and blogs of their own.

PAID MEDIA

Within the media campaign, candidates and their media consultants decide on how to use the paid media; that is, which ads to air to support the campaign's strategies. **Positive ads** stress the candidate's qualifications, family and personal ties, and issue positions with no direct reference to the opponent. Positive ads are usually favored by the incumbent candidate. **Negative ads** attack the opponent's character and platform. And, with the exception of the candidate's brief, legally required statement that he or she approved the ad, a negative ad may not even mention the candidate who is paying for the airing. **Contrast ads** compare the records and proposals of the candidates, with a bias toward the candidate sponsoring the ad. In 2004, Senator John Kerry, relatively unknown to people outside of his home state of Massachusetts, sought to define himself by releasing positive ads stating his position on taxes and health care. In a television ad called "Patriot Act," the Bush campaign sought to use contrast ads to portray Kerry as indecisive for his reversal of support for the USA Patriot Act after receiving criticism from fellow Democrats. While the lines between different types of ads are not always clear, a classic example of a negative advertisement aired in the 2005 New Jersey gubernatorial race between Republican Doug Forrester and Democrat John Corzine. Forrester's campaign aired a smear ad using a quote from his opponent's ex-wife suggesting that Corzine had let down his family and would likely let down the voters of New Jersey.

Most paid advertisements are short **spot ads** that range from ten to sixty seconds long. In the past, when air time was less expensive, some ads ran as long as thirty minutes and took the form of documentaries.

Although negative advertisements have grown dramatically in number during the past two decades, they have been a part of American campaigns for some time. In 1796, Federalists portrayed presidential candidate Thomas Jefferson as an atheist and a coward. In Jefferson's bid for a second term in 1800, Federalists again attacked him, this time spreading a rumor that he was dead. The effects of negative advertising are well documented. Voters frequently vote *against* the other candidate, and negative ads can provide the critical justification for such a vote.

Before the 1980s, well-known incumbents usually ignored negative attacks from their challengers, believing that the proper stance was to be above the fray. But, after some well-publicized defeats of incumbents in the early 1980s in which negative television advertising played a prominent role,[4] incumbents began attacking their challengers in earnest. The new rule of politics became "An attack unanswered is an attack agreed to." In a further attempt to stave off brickbats from challengers, incumbents began anticipating the substance of their opponents' attacks and airing **inoculation ads** early in the campaign to protect themselves in advance from the other side's spots. Inoculation advertising attempts to counteract an anticipated attack from the opposition before such an attack is launched. For example, a senator who fears a broadside about her voting record on veterans issues might air advertisements featuring veterans or their families praising her support.

Although paid advertising remains the most controllable aspect of a campaign's strategy, the news media are increasingly having an impact on it. Major newspapers throughout the country have taken to analyzing the accuracy of television advertisements aired during campaigns—a welcome and useful addition to journalists' scrutiny of politicians.

FREE MEDIA

While candidates have control over what advertisements are run (paid media), they have little control over how journalists will cover their campaign and convey it to voters. During campaign season, the news media constantly report political news. What they report is largely based on news editors' decisions of what is newsworthy or "fit to print." The press often reports what candidates are doing, such as giving speeches, holding fundraisers, or meeting with party leaders. Even better from the candidate's perspective, the news media may report on a candidate's success, perhaps giving that candidate the brand of a "winner," making him or her that much more difficult to beat. Reporters may also investigate rumors of a candidate's misdeeds or unflattering personal history, such as run-ins with the law or a failed marriage.

Analysts observe that not all media practices are conducive to fair and unbiased coverage of campaigns. For example, the news media often regard political candidates

contrast ad
Ad that compares the records and proposals of the candidates, with a bias toward the sponsor.

spot ad
Television advertising on behalf of a candidate that is broadcast in sixty-, thirty-, or ten-second duration.

Television and Presidential Campaigns

inoculation ad
Advertising that attempts to counteract an anticipated attack from the opposition before the attack is launched.

with suspicion—looking for possible deception even when a candidate is simply trying to share his or her message with the public. This attitude makes it difficult for candidates to explain their positions to the news media without being on the defensive. In addition, many studies have shown that the media are obsessed with the horse-race aspect of politics—who's ahead, who's behind, who's gaining—to the detriment of the substance of the candidates' issues and ideas. Public opinion polls, especially tracking polls, many of them taken by the news outlets themselves, dominate coverage, especially on network television, where only a few minutes a night are devoted to politics.

The media's expectations can have an effect on how the public views the candidates. Using poll data, journalists often predict the margins by which they expect contenders to win or lose. A clear victory of 5 percentage points can be judged a setback if the candidate had been projected to win by 12 or 15 points. The tone of the media coverage—that a candidate is either gaining or losing support in polls—can affect whether people decide to give money and other types of support to a candidate.[5]

One final area in which the media tend to portray candidates in a biased way is in overemphasizing trivial parts of the campaign, such as a politician's minor gaffe, hairstyle, or private-life indiscretions. This superficial coverage displaces serious journalism on the issues. These subjects are discussed in detail in the next chapter, which deals specifically with the media.

THE NEW MEDIA

Since candidates began experimenting with electronic media to reach out directly to voters, the nature of campaigns has changed drastically. Labor-intensive community activities have been replaced by carefully targeted messages disseminated through the mass media, and candidates today are able to reach voters more quickly than at any time in our nation's history. The results of this technological transformation, which skyrocketed with the advent of personal computers and the Internet, are candidate-centered campaigns in which candidates build well-financed, finely tuned organizations centered around their personal aspirations, and political parties play a secondary role in the election process.

Contemporary campaigns have an impressive new array of weapons at their disposal: faster printing technologies, reliable data bases, instantaneous Internet publishing and mass e-mail, fax machines, video technology, and enhanced telecommunications and teleconferencing. As a result, candidates can gather and disseminate information more quickly and effectively than ever.

One outcome of these changes is the ability of candidates to employ "rapid-response" techniques: the formulation of prompt and informed responses to changing events on the campaign battlefield. In response to breaking news of a scandal or issue, for example, candidates can conduct background research, implement an opinion poll and tabulate the results, devise a containment strategy and appropriate "spin," and deliver a reply. This makes a strong contrast with the campaigns of the 1970s and early 1980s, dominated primarily by radio and TV advertisements, which took much longer to prepare and had little of the flexibility enjoyed by the contemporary e-campaign.[6]

In 2002, many candidates increasingly turned to recorded phone messages targeted to narrow constituencies. Florida Governor Jeb Bush used a fund-raising technique many might question; the governor recorded a message asking for money, which was autodialed to contributors to the 2000 presidential campaign of his brother, George W. Bush. President Bush's victory was due, in part, to the cohesive use of this kind of new and effective tactic. This practice was much more widespread in 2004, as both parties used politicians and celebrities to contact voters through prerecorded phone messages. Democrats heard from John Kerry, Bill Clinton, Wesley Clark, and comedian Chris Rock, for example, while Republicans heard from Rudy Giuliani, Arnold Schwarzenegger, and actress Janine Turner.[7]

The first widespread use of the Internet in national campaigning came in 1996. Republican presidential candidate Bob Dole urged voters to log onto his Web site, and many did. According to one source, during the 2004 election 37 percent of the adult population and 61 percent of all Americans with Internet access regularly logged on to get campaign and election information.[8] On Election Day 2004, traffic on the CNN Web site increased by 110 percent, while the FOX News site saw a 134 percent jump.[9] All of the candidates for the 2004 presidential campaign and the 2006 midterm elections made use of Web sites, even when their candidacies were only in the exploratory stage.

With the advent of blogs, a candidate's Web site can take on a life of its own. Blogs enable supporters and the occasional stealthy opponent to post messages on the candidate's Web site and to engage in a nearly contemporaneous exchange of ideas with other supporters and with the candidate's Internet team. Even after the campaign has concluded, online networks can persist and keep supporters abreast of a candidate's future direction. After failing to win the 2004 presidential election, John Kerry has been able to keep his base informed by maintaining his Web site and sending a steady flow of mass e-mails to supporters.

■ Senator John McCain (R–AZ) has taken the same theme he used aboard his campaign bus, the "Straight Talk Express", during his unsuccessful bid for the Republican presidential nomination in 2000 and applied it to his current campaign. McCain is a leading Republican candidate for the 2008 presidential nomination.

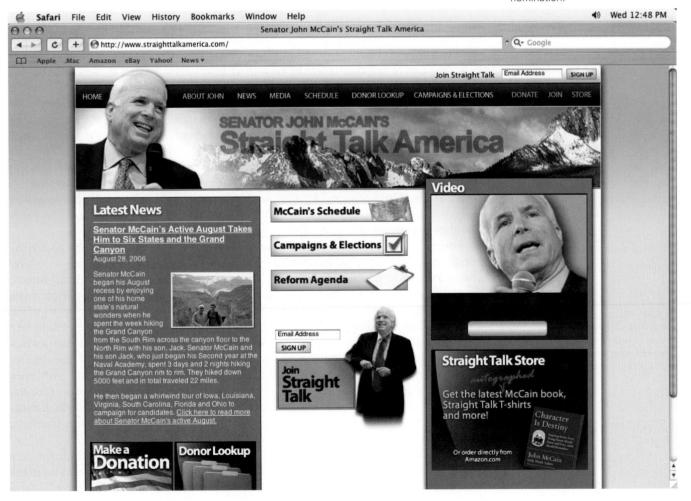

CAMPAIGN STRATEGIES TO CONTROL MEDIA COVERAGE

Candidates, of course, want favorable media coverage but realize that they can afford to buy only a limited amount of coverage. Moreover, voters consider the news media more credible sources of information than paid advertisements or what they read on a candidate's or party's Web site. In an effort to obtain favorable coverage, candidates and their media consultants use various strategies to attempt to influence the press.

First, the campaign staff members often seek to isolate the candidate from the press, thus reducing the chances that reporters will bait a candidate into saying something that might damage his or her cause. Naturally, journalists are frustrated by such a tactic, and they demand open access to candidates. During John McCain's presidential bid in 2000, he was able to take advantage of the media's frustration with tight-lipped candidates by inviting reporters on his bus tour and providing them with virtually unlimited access. The move undoubtedly earned McCain favorable coverage, but it was risky, as a candidate is always one gaffe away from an embarrassing headline.

Second, the campaign stages media events: activities designed to include brief, clever quotes called *sound bites* and staged with appealing backdrops so that they will be covered on the television news and in the newspaper. In this fashion, the candidate's staff can successfully fill the news hole reserved for campaign coverage. In this area, the incumbent president always has a tremendous advantage. The president's news events are almost always newsworthy and consequently covered by the mainstream press. This well-established fact allows sitting presidents to package news in a way that virtually guarantees positive coverage.

Third, campaign staff and consultants have cultivated a technique termed *spin*—they put the most favorable possible interpretation for their candidate (and the most negative for their opponent) on any circumstance occurring in the campaign, and they work the press to sell their point of view or at least to ensure that it is included in the reporters' stories. Early in the 2004 Democratic primaries, Howard Dean was the front-runner, a position he won by portraying himself as the indignant or "angry" candidate, which worked well with the Democratic base voting in the primaries; yet, he lost the Iowa caucus vote. Dean tried to spin the loss as playing to his strengths, since Dean had achieved front-runner status after starting at the back of the pack. Spin can spin both ways, however, and Dean's spin spun out of control when he tried to show strength in rallying his supporters by letting out a high-pitched yelp, now famously known as the "Dean scream." While the outburst certainly helped rally the troops, it also gave competing candidates the proof they needed to spin Dean as not the angry candidate but the "crazy" candidate.[10]

Fourth, candidates have found ways to circumvent the news media by appearing on talk shows such as *The Oprah Winfrey Show* and *Larry King Live*, where they have an opportunity to present their views and answer questions in a less critical forum. They also make regular appearances on comedy shows, such as *Saturday Night Live*, *The Late Show*, and Jon Stewart's *Daily Show*.

candidate debate
Forum in which political candidates face each other to discuss their platforms, records, and character.

Candidate debates are a surprisingly recent aspect of presidential elections and were not a staple of electoral politics until the twentieth century. The first face-to-face presidential debate in U.S. history did not occur until 1960, and face-to-face debates did not become a regular part of presidential campaigns until the 1980s. However, they are now an established feature of presidential campaigns, as well as races for governor, U.S. senator, and many other offices, and serve as a fifth means by which campaigns seek to control (or at least to influence) media coverage. (See On Campus: Presidential Debates: Coming to a Campus Near You?)

Candidates and their staffs recognize the importance of debates as a tool not only for consolidating their voter base but also for correcting misperceptions about the candidate's suitability for office. However, while candidates have complete control

On Campus

PRESIDENTIAL DEBATES: COMING TO A CAMPUS NEAR YOU?

Since the nation's first televised presidential debate in 1960, debates have offered the American electorate a unique opportunity to see and hear the candidates for the presidency. They are a means by which millions of Americans gather information regarding each candidate's personality and platform. Recognizing the profound educational value of these debates to the voting public, two bipartisan national study groups recommended that steps be taken to establish an organization whose main function was the sponsorship of presidential and vice presidential debates during the general election period. In response to the recommendations put forward by the two study groups, the Commission on Presidential Debates was established in 1987.

The commission's formal charge is to ensure that debates are a permanent part of every general election and that they provide the best possible information to viewers and listeners. The organization sponsored all the presidential debates since 1988, heavily favoring institutions of higher learning as the host sites. The last five presidential elections have included seventeen debates sponsored by the commission, thirteen of which have been held on college campuses. In 2004, the University of Miami, Case Western Reserve, Washington University in St. Louis, and Arizona State University were the sites for the presidential debates.

Prospective debate hosts must conform to a rigorous set of criteria as dictated by the commission. The selection criteria encompass a broad range of categories, including the physical structure of the debate hall (over 17,000 square feet with a 35-foot ceiling and 65-foot stage), the transportation and lodging networks available, and the ability to raise $550,000 to cover production costs.

Why would a college or university go through so much trouble to host a presidential debate, especially since only a relatively small percentage of students are able to attend, and an even smaller percentage of students are permitted to ask candidates questions? The answer is that the benefits are plentiful and diverse. The host sites inevitably bring in revenue with masses of people migrating into town, purchasing community services and products. The colleges gain immediate international exposure, perhaps becoming a more attractive option to prospective students. And, students and professors benefit from firsthand exposure to a very important aspect of the American political process.

Source: Commission on Presidential Debates, http://www.debates.org.

over what they say in debates, they do not have control over what the news media will highlight and focus on after the debates. Therefore, even though candidates prepare themselves by rehearsing their responses, they cannot avoid the perils of spontaneity. Errors or slips of the tongue in a debate can affect election outcomes. President Gerald R. Ford's erroneous insistence during an October 1976 debate with Jimmy Carter that Poland was not under Soviet domination (when in fact it was) may have cost him a close election. George Bush's bored expression and watch gazing during his 1992 debate with Bill Clinton certainly did not help Bush's electoral hopes. In an effort to put the best possible spin on debates, teams of consultants and staffers for each participant swarm the press rooms to declare victory even before their candidates finish their closing statements.

The presidential debates of 2004 confirm the importance of debates, as public opinion surveys showed that Kerry's strong performance in the first debate spurred him to a temporary lead in the polls. While the debates did not alter the results of this election, they did tend to increase knowledge about the candidates and their respective personalities and issue positions, especially among voters who had not previously paid attention to the campaign.

Sometimes debates affect voters only by confirming or denying the public preconceptions of the candidates. The two major presidential contenders in 2004 offered a classic example of spin before and after their first debate. George W. Bush was widely believed to have benefited from low expectations in the 2000 presidential debates. The Bush and Kerry campaigns remembered this phenomenon, and each at-

Photos courtesy: Bettmann/Corbis; Rich Wilking/Reuters/Corbis

■ Presidential debates have come a long way—at least in terms of studio trappings—since the ill-at-ease Richard M. Nixon was visually bested by John F. Kennedy in the first televised debate. John Kerry's strong performances in the three presidential debates of 2004 helped him stay within striking distance of President Bush's lead going into the final weeks of the campaign.

tempted to paint their opponent as a superior debater going into the debate. Bush strategist Matthew Dowd called Kerry "the best debater since Cicero." The Kerry campaign countered that Bush had never lost a debate. Each campaign tried to spin the press to call its opponent the superior debater, hoping that its candidate would then be perceived as "exceeding expectations."

The Rules of the Game: Campaign Finance

TO RUN ALL ASPECTS of a campaign successfully requires a great deal of money. More than $1.7 billion was raised by the Democratic and Republican parties through November 2004, a 37 percent increase in fund-raising over the totals of the 2000 election cycle. Presidential candidates in 2004 raised a record $880 million in support of their campaigns. John Kerry raised over $320 million, with 225 million coming from individual donors and nearly $75 million coming from the federal funds set aside for presidential candidates. George W. Bush raised $367 million (a new record in presidential fund-raising), with nearly $272 million coming from individual donors and $75 million coming from the federal funds. Democratic incumbents in the Senate raised an average of $9.7 million, while Republican incumbents in the Senate raised an average of $6.7 million. Their challengers, in contrast, raised an average of $889,000.[11] As humorist Will Rogers once remarked early in the twentieth century, "Politics has got so expensive that it takes lots of money even to get beat with."

While the amount expended in a single election season has recently increased, in the past the cost of elections in the United States has been less than or approximately the same as in some other nations if measured on a per-voter basis. For example, the per capita cost of Canada's 2004 elections is estimated at almost $9 per person, whereas in the United States it was around $5.50.[12] (The Living Constitution feature examines campaign finance and free speech concerns.)

The Living Constitution

Congress shall make no law…abridging the freedom of speech.

—FIRST AMENDMENT

When the nation's Framers set about writing the Constitution and the Bill of Rights, they were not specific in their definition of free speech in the First Amendment. Therefore it has been up to subsequent Congresses, presidents, Supreme Courts, and others to interpret and expand on their very simple, elegant statement. Today, we have an elaborate campaign finance system that tries to balance free speech with the need to prevent political corruption. The Supreme Court has repeatedly addressed that difficult balance in cases such as *Buckley* v. *Valeo* (1976) and *McConnell* v. *Federal Election Commission* (2003).

Essentially, the Framers looked at campaigning as crass and beneath the dignity of office holders. At least theoretically, they believed that the office should seek the person, although in practice many of them were very ambitious and intensely sought high elected office. They did not do so in the context of a mass electorate, but rather by means of the aristocratic gentry that acted through the Electoral College to select the president and vice president.

In this era of ultra-democracy, when everyone expects to have a voice, the system must operate very differently. As a result, candidates campaign by raising hundreds of millions of dollars, visiting television studio after television studio for news coverage, holding media events, taping paid television and radio advertisements, and using the Internet for communication with their supporters. The candidates' free speech is augmented by the free speech of those interested in seeing one candidate elected and the other defeated in a particular race. Thus, political parties raise money and carry out organizational and electioneering activies as described in chapter 12.

Also being heard are political action committees (PACs)—the contributing arms of special interest groups on the left, on the right, and in the middle. And, because of loopholes in the Bipartisan Campaign Reform Act of 2002, there are 527 committees, which form to attack a candidate through television and radio ads as well as individual voter contact. Finally, there are completely independent political committees that can raise and spend whatever they want, for whatever interests they support—so long as they have no direct or indirect contact with any campaign organizations.

It is amazing that all of these aspects have developed from the powerful words of the First Amendment regarding free speech. The Framers could hardly have imagined what massive enterprises campaigns would become, and what the few words they penned on parchment would create with the passing of two centuries.

THE ROAD TO REFORM

The United States has struggled to achieve effective campaign finance rules for well over one hundred years. One early attempt to regulate the way candidates raise campaign resources was enacted in 1883, when Congress passed civil service reform legislation that prohibited solicitation of political funds from federal workers, attempting to halt a corrupt and long-held practice. In 1907, the Tillman Act prohibited corporations from making direct contributions to candidates for federal office. The Corrupt Practices Acts (1910, 1911, and 1925), Hatch Act (1939), and Taft-Hartley Act (1947) all attempted to regulate the manner in which federal candidates finance their campaigns and to some extent limit the corrupting influence of campaign spending.

In the early 1970s, Congress enacted its most ambitious round of campaign laws to date. The Federal Election Campaign Act (FECA) and its later amendments established disclosure requirements, established the Presidential Public Funding Program, which provides partial public funding for presidential candidates who meet certain criteria, and created the Federal Elections Commission (an independent federal agency tasked with enforcing the nation's election laws).

The most recent bout of reforms was set in motion by Senators John McCain (R–AZ) and Russell Feingold (D–WI). McCain ran for the 2000 Republican presidential nomination on a platform to ban unregulated soft-money contributions and to take elections out of the hands of the wealthy. McCain lost to George W. Bush, who ironically used soft money in the primaries to defeat McCain. However, McCain's credibility on the issue skyrocketed. Once corporate soft-money donors at Enron, WorldCom, and Global Crossing (to name a few) became embroiled in accounting scandals and alleged criminal behavior, the possibility of electoral corruption became too strong for Congress to ignore. McCain and Feingold co-sponsored the Bipartisan Campaign Reform Act (BCRA) of 2002 in the Senate, while Representatives Chris Shays (R–CT) and Martin Meehan (D–MA) sponsored the House version. On Valentine's Day, the bills passed, and in March 2002, President George W. Bush signed BCRA into law. Included within BCRA was a "fast track" provision that any suits challenging the constitutionality of the reforms would be immediately placed before a U.S. District Court, and giving appellate powers to the U.S. Supreme Court. The reason for this provision was simple: to thwart the numerous lobbying groups and several high-profile elected officials who threatened to tie up BCRA in the courts for as long as they could. No sooner did President Bush sign BCRA than U.S. Senator Mitch McConnell (R–KY) and the National Rifle Association separately filed lawsuits claiming that the BCRA violated free speech rights.

In May 2003, a three-judge panel of the U.S. District Court for the District of Columbia found that the BCRA restrictions on soft-money donations violated free speech rights, although the BCRA restrictions on political advertising did not.[13] The decision was immediately appealed to the Supreme Court. In their 5–4 decision in *McConnell v. Federal Election Commission* (2003), the Court held that the government's interest in preventing political-party corruption overrides the free speech rights to which the parties would otherwise be entitled.[14] In other words, the Supreme Court very narrowly upheld the BCRA measures restricting speech both in the form of political contributions (soft money) and in political advertising. (For a broader view, see Global Perspective: The Impact of Funding and Free and Fair Elections on the Campaign Process.)

Campaign Finance Reform

CURRENT RULES

The Supreme Court's *McConnell* decision in 2003 means that political money is now regulated by the federal government under the terms of the Bipartisan Campaign Reform Act (BCRA) of 2002, which supplanted most of the provisions of the Federal Election Campaign Act (FECA). The BCRA outlaws unlimited and unregulated contributions to parties, known as soft money, and limits the amounts that individuals, interest groups, and political parties can give to candidates for president, U.S.

Global Perspective

THE IMPACT OF FUNDING AND FREE AND FAIR ELECTIONS ON THE CAMPAIGN PROCESS

Few Americans would argue with the proposition that, for elections to matter, they must be free and fair. But, what is a "free and fair" election? Although no clear answer exists to this question, we can identify conditions that contribute to protecting the integrity of the electoral system. Elections are likely to be free to the extent that we find freedom of speech, freedom of association, freedom from coercion, free access to the polls, and the freedom to vote in secret. Elections are likely to be fair when elections are administered in a nonpartisan fashion, there is balanced reporting by the media, votes are counted in an open and transparent fashion, and there is equitable access to the resources needed to run a campaign.

This last point, access to campaign funds, is particularly problematic today, given the high costs of running for office. Some election observers have concluded that corruption related to the financing of parties and candidates is among the most common dangers facing democracies around the world today. The negative consequences of unequal access to campaign funds include the beliefs that only the rich can run for public office, that large contributors get preferential treatment by public officials, and that because incumbents can raise money more easily than challengers, they do not have to be responsive to voters.

Many different ways exist for trying to ensure an even-handed access to campaign funds for all parties and candidates. In some cases this involves limiting the amount of money that can be spent. New Zealand forbids parties from spending more than $1 million plus $20,000 per candidate nominated by the party in the three months preceding the election. Some countries try to limit the source of campaign funds. Canadian parties and candidates may accept contributions only from Canadian citizens or permanent residents—corporations and associations not doing business in Canada are not allowed to make contributions. France places limits on the size of campaign contributions and reimburses some of the costs. Individuals may not contribute more than $5,000 to a legislative race (corporations and other organizations may not make contributions). All parties that get more than 5 percent of the vote are reimbursed the cost of the paper and printing of their official ballots, posters, and campaign circulars.

Other nations employ a combination of measures. Brazil seeks to limit the length of the election campaign and the amount of money spent, and provides reasonable access to the media. All elections at the national, regional, and local level are held on the first Sunday in October. Election materials can be distributed only after July 5. Candidates may buy advertising space in newspapers, but radio and television airtime is free and allocated equally among the registered political parties. Limits are placed on how many candidates a party may run in an election. They may only field candidates equal to 150 percent of the positions to be filled in an election.

Japan also seeks to put multiple restrictions in place. Here a distinction is made between political activities that try to make the public aware of a party's position on issues and political activity designed to obtain votes for a particular candidate. Door-to-door political canvassing is illegal. Campaign materials cannot be posted until six months before one's term has expired or one day after parliament is dissolved. All candidates receive a specified amount of free advertising in newspapers.

Political parties in Japan face more lenient restrictions, however. Neither candidates nor parties may advertise in the mass media until twelve days before the election. But, there is no limit on how much can be spent in these twelve days. Japanese parties are required to report all campaign contributions of more than $500, and their recipients. Political contributions from corporations and organizations are banned. Japanese parties are eligible to obtain public funding if they have at least five members in the lower house of parliament or have received at least 2 percent of the vote in a recent national election.

To be effective, laws must be enforced. Even on paper, great variation exists. In Brazil, a court reviews compliance with campaign laws, but there are no legal or financial penalties. In Japan, failure to report contributions by individuals can result in a five-year prison term and a $10,000 fine.

QUESTIONS

1. Which do you think is the most effective way to make an election fair: regulate the source of campaign funds, limit campaign expenditures, or require greater public disclosure of sources?
2. How does the United States compare with other countries in regard to the above criteria for having free and fair elections?

---

senator, and U.S. representative (see Table 14.1). The goal of all limits is the same: to prevent any single group or individual from gaining too much influence over elected officials, who naturally feel indebted to campaign contributors.

Individual Contributions Individual contributions are donations from individual citizens. The current maximum allowable contribution under federal law for con-

TABLE 14.1 INDIVIDUAL CONTRIBUTION LIMITS PER ELECTION CYCLE BEFORE AND AFTER BIPARTISAN CAMPAIGN REFORM ACT (2002)

	Before	After*
Contributions per candidate	$1,000	$2,000
Contributions per national party committee	$20,000	$26,700
Total contributions per 2-year cycle	$50,000	$101,400
Soft money	Unlimited	Banned

*These limits are for 2006. BCRA limits are adjusted in odd-numbered years to account for inflation.
Source: Campaign Finance Institute, http://www.cfinst.org/studies/ElectionAfterReform/pdf/EAR_Appendix1.pdf.

gressional and presidential elections is $2,100 per election to each candidate, adjusted for inflation, with primary and general elections considered separately. Individuals are also limited to a total of $50,700 in gifts to all candidates, political action committees, and parties combined in each calendar year. Most candidates receive a majority of all funds directly from individuals, and most individual gifts are well below the maximum level. Finally, individuals who spend over $10,000 to air "electioneering communication," that is, "any broadcast, cable, or satellite communication which refers to a clearly identified candidate for Federal office" within sixty days of a general election or thirty days of a primary election, is now subject to a strict disclosure law. The rationale behind the last regulation is that spending on an ad favoring a candidate is effectively the same as a contribution to the candidate's campaign and requires the same scrutiny as other large donations.

Political Action Committee (PAC) Contributions When interest groups such as labor unions, corporations, trade unions, and ideological issue groups seek to make donations to campaigns, they must do so by establishing **political action committees (PACs).** PACs are officially recognized fund-raising organizations that are allowed by federal law to participate in federal elections. (Some states have similar requirements for state elections.) Under current rules, a PAC can give no more than $5,000 per candidate per election (primary, general, and special election), and $15,000 each year to each of the units of the national parties.

Approximately 4,000 PACs are registered with the Federal Election Commission—the government agency charged with administering the election laws. In 2004, PACs contributed $294 million to Senate and House candidates, while individuals donated $693 million. On average, PAC contributions account for 57 percent of the war chests (campaign funds) of House candidates and 67 percent of the treasuries of Senate candidates. Incumbents benefit the most from PAC money; incumbents received $228 million, much more than the $66 million given to challengers during the 2004 election cycle.[15] By making these contributions, PACs hope to secure entrée to candidates after they have been elected in order to influence them on issues important to the PAC, since they might reciprocate campaign donations with loyalty to the cause. Corporate PACs give primarily to incumbents because incumbents tend to win, and lobbyists want to guarantee access for their clients. Single-issue and more ideologically based PACs are often willing to support challengers and more untried candidates who pledge to support their positions if elected.[16]

Because donations from a small number of PACs make up such a large proportion of campaign war chests, PACs have influence disproportionate to that of individuals. Studies, in fact, have shown that PACs effectively use contributions to punish legislators and affect policy, at least in the short run.[17] Legislators who vote contrary to the wishes of a PAC see their donations withheld, but those who are successful in legislating as the PAC wishes are rewarded with even greater donations.[18] However, contribution limits keep the influence of PACs to $5,000 per candidate per year, and while this amount may substantially aid an incumbent's reelection, it pales in comparison to the total budget required for victory in federal elections.

In an attempt to control PACs, the BCRA has a limit on the way PACs attempt to influence campaigns. The law strictly forbids PACs from using corporate or union funds for the electioneering communications discussed earlier. PACs can use corporate or labor contributions

political action committee (PAC)
Federally mandated, officially registered fund-raising committee that represents interest groups in the political process.

■ Former EPA Administrator Christine Todd Whitman launched It's My Party Too PAC in February of 2005 to bolster the electoral chances of centrist Republican candidates. Whitman has consistently taken a moderate stance on social issues such as reproductive choice.

Photo courtesy: Bill Boyce/AP Wide World Photos

only for administrative costs. The purpose of the limit is to prevent corporations or unions from having an undue influence on the outcome of elections by heavily advertising toward specific audiences in the weeks leading up to elections.

PACs remain one of the most controversial parts of the campaign financing process. Some observers claim that PACs are the embodiment of corrupt special interests that use campaign donations to buy the votes of legislators. Furthermore, they argue that the less affluent and minority members of society do not enjoy equal access to these political organizations. These charges are serious and deserve consideration. Although the media relentlessly stress the role of money in determining policy outcomes, the evidence that PACs buy votes is not well supported by research.[19] Political scientists have conducted many studies to determine the impact of interest group PAC contributions on legislative voting, and the conclusions reached by these studies have varied widely.[20] Whereas some studies have found that PAC money affects legislators' voting behavior, other studies have uncovered no such correlation. It may be, of course, that interest group PAC money has an impact at earlier stages of the legislative process. One innovative study found that PAC money had a significant effect on legislators' participation in congressional committees on legislation important to the contributing group.[21] Thus, interest group PAC money may mobilize something more important than votes—the valuable time and energy of members.

Although a good number of PACs of all persuasions existed prior to the 1970s, it was during the 1970s—the decade of campaign finance reform—that the modern PAC era began. Spawned by the Watergate-inspired revisions of the campaign finance laws, PACs grew in number from 113 in 1972 to 4,268 by the late 1980s. While the number of PACs now remains stable at about 4,000, their contributions to congressional candidates multiplied almost thirty-fold, from $8.5 million in 1971 and 1972 to $330 million in 2006 (see Figure 14.3). But, these numbers should not obscure a basic truth about the PAC system:

FIGURE 14.3 GROWTH IN TOTAL CONTRIBUTIONS BY PACS TO HOUSE AND SENATE CANDIDATES

The growth of campaign spending by PACs has roughly paralleled the increasing number of PACs over their thirty-year history.

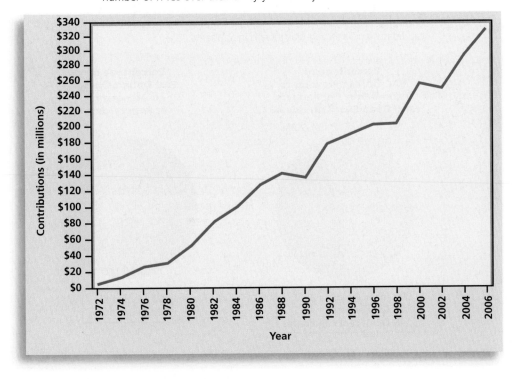

Note: Contributions are for two-year election cycles ending in years shown.

Source: Center for Responsive Politics, http://www.opensecrets.org.

that a very small group of PACs conducts the bulk of total PAC activity. Indeed, as political scientist Paul Herrnson observes, a mere 6 percent of all PACs contributed a full 62 percent of the total dollars given to congressional candidates by PACs during the 2001–2002 election cycle.[22]

Although the widespread use of the PAC structure is relatively new, special-interest money of all types has always found its way into politics. Before the 1970s, it did so in less traceable and much more disturbing and unsavory ways, because little of the money given to candidates was regularly disclosed to public inspection. Although it is true that PACs contribute a massive sum to candidates in absolute terms (see Figure 14.4), it is not clear that there is proportionately more interest group money in the system than earlier. The proportion of House and Senate campaign funds provided by PACs has certainly increased since the early 1970s, but individuals, most of whom are unaffiliated with PACs, together with the political parties still supply more than 60 percent of all the money spent by or on behalf of House candidates, 75 percent of the campaign expenditures for Senate contenders, and 85 percent of the campaign expenditures for presidential candidates.[23] So, while the importance of PAC spending has grown, PACs clearly remain secondary as a source of election funding and therefore pose no overwhelming threat to the system's legitimacy.

Political Party Contributions Candidates also receive donations from the national and state committees of the Democratic and Republican Parties. As mentioned in chapter 12, political parties can give substantial contributions to their congressional nominees. Under the current rules, national parties can give up to $5,000 to a House candidate in their general election and $37,000 to a Senate candidate.

In 2006, the Republican and Democratic parties funneled over $768 million to their standard-bearers, via direct contributions and coordinated expenditures. In

FIGURE 14.4 EXPENDITURES BY PACS IN THE 2004 ELECTION CYCLE
PACs contributed a total of $290 million to candidates competing in the 2004 election. Notice how PACs used a majority of their expenditures to support congressional candidates and how PAC spending has a slight bias toward Republican candidates and a strong bias toward incumbents.

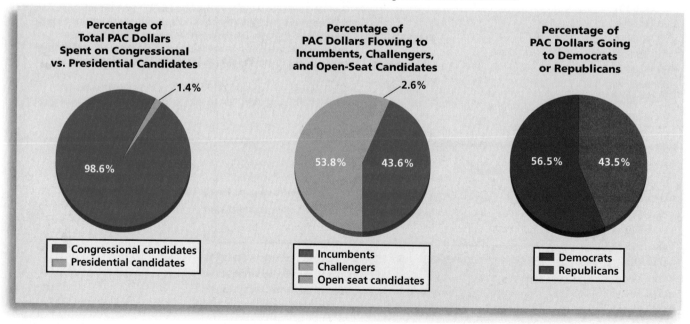

Source: Federal Election Commission, http://www.fec.gov; Political Money Line, http://www.tray.com.

competitive races, the parties may provide 15–17 percent of their candidates' total war chests. In addition to helping elect party members, campaign contributions from political parties have another, less obvious benefit: helping to ensure party discipline in voting. One study of congressional voting behavior in the 1980s, for instance, found that those members who received a large percentage of their total campaign funds from their party voted with their party more often than they were expected to.[24]

Member-to-Candidate Contributions

In Congress and in state legislatures, well-funded, electorally secure incumbents now often contribute campaign money to their party's needy incumbent and nonincumbent legislative candidates.[25] This activity began in some state legislatures (notably California), but it is now well-established at the congressional level.[26] Generally, members contribute to other candidates in one of two ways. First, some members have established their own PACs—informally dubbed "leadership" PACs—through which they distribute campaign support to candidates. For example, through the 2006 general election cycle, a PAC established by Senator Barbara Boxer (D–CA) contributed $71,500 to Democratic House candidates and $161,000 to Democrats running for Senate seats. In total, Boxer's PAC For A Change spent nearly $300,000 in an attempt to help the Democrats win back the Senate and House.[27]

These contributions from members, whether individually or via a PAC, can add up. In 2004, the U.S. House race in South Dakota saw a tremendous influx of member-to-candidate money, with Republican challenger Larry Diedrich receiving the most, at over $423,000. He lost the race to first-term Democratic incumbent Stephanie Herseth, who received an impressive $293,000 of these donations.[28] In 2006, Herseth won her reelection bid in a race against Republican Bruce Whalen. As an incumbent, Herseth had little difficulty with fundraising, amassing almost $1.4 million dollars for her re-election bid. Whalen, who only managed to raise $129,000, lost badly with only 29 percent of the vote.

In general, members give their contributions to the same candidates who receive the bulk of congressional campaign committee resources. Thus, member contributions at the congressional level have emerged as a major supplement to the campaign resources contributed by the party campaign committees.[29]

Candidates' Personal Contributions

Candidates and their families may donate to the campaign. The U.S. Supreme Court ruled in *Buckley* v. *Valeo* (1976) that no limit could be placed on the amount of money candidates can spend from their own families' resources, since such spending is considered a First Amendment right of free speech.[30] (See Join the Debate: Campaign Finance: Freedom of Speech or License to Corrupt.) For wealthy politicians, this allowance may mean personal spending in the millions. In 2006, for example, the top two self-financers were candidates for the Senate, Republican Pete Ricketts of Nebraska and Democrat Ned Lamont of Connecticut. Both lost their bids despite each spending over $10 million of their own money on their campaigns. While Lamont ran a competitive campaign, Ricketts only managed to receive 36 percent of the vote against incumbent Democrat Ben Nelson. While self-financed candidates often garner a great deal of attention, most candidates commit much less than $100,000 in family resources to their election bids.[31]

Public Funds

Public funds are donations from general tax revenues to the campaigns of qualifying candidates. Only presidential candidates (and a handful of state and local contenders) receive public funds. Under the terms of the FECA (which first established public funding of presidential campaigns), a candidate for president can become eligible to receive public funds during the nominating contest by raising at least $5,000 in individual contributions of $250 or less in each of twenty states. The candidate can apply for federal **matching funds,** whereby every dollar raised from individuals in amounts less than $251 is matched by the federal treasury on a dollar-for-dollar basis. Of course, this assumes there is enough money in the Presidential Election Campaign Fund to do so.

public funds
Donations from the general tax revenues to the campaigns of qualifying presidential candidates.

matching funds
Donations to presidential campaigns from the federal government that are determined by the amount of private funds a qualifying candidate raises.

Join the Debate

CAMPAIGN FINANCE: FREEDOM OF SPEECH OR LICENSE TO CORRUPT

OVERVIEW: Campaigns are not free. A candidate has to employ an army of staff to engage in a number of activities, from scheduling campaign stops to ordering pizza deliveries. Unless a candidate is massively wealthy, the money to pay for campaign staff and services has to come from other people, namely donors. Aside from the instrumental value of money, there is a symbolic value. Many donors believe that their contributions make a statement about their beliefs. The question is, therefore, whether campaign finance regulations are merely controlling the sources and use of money to prevent political corruption or are also prohibiting the right to free speech that belongs to all Americans.

Both the National Rifle Association and the American Civil Liberties Union agree that the regulation of campaign contributions amounts to a government violation of the very rights the government is supposed to protect. If organizations wish to air ads on behalf of an issue that interests them, then they should be able to do so under the First Amendment. Organizations such as Common Cause, however, say that the problem with the "money equals speech" argument is that money actually replaces speech. Too often, groups lacking funds are squeezed out of meetings with elected officials, who need the money for reelection more than they need to hear about the complaints of constituents.

Disallowing organizations from engaging in the political process is by definition an infringement of political freedom, but perhaps it was a freedom so thoroughly abused that it had to be taken away to protect the republic. Furthermore, there is no guarantee that increasing government regulation will make the process any more democratic, just more regulated, meaning more complicated and bureaucratic. The scope of campaign finance is broad, and the implications of regulating it are far reaching. While the Supreme Court continues to give limited free-speech protections to campaign contributors, it upheld the ban on soft money and the regulation of "sham issue ads" in the recent Bipartisan Campaign Reform Act of 2002. Many interest groups believe the legislation limits free-speech rights by placing restrictions on when and what type of political ads may air before elections.

ARGUMENTS FOR CAMPAIGN FINANCE REFORM

- **A government beholden to a small group of wealthy and mobilized interests is, by definition, an oligarchy and undemocratic.** With millions of dollars to spare, large organizations such as unions and corporations can control candidate agendas by demanding loyalty in exchange for donations. The result is that a candidate, once elected, represents not ordinary constituents but those who got him or her elected. This is nothing more than bribery.
- **Prohibiting large organizations from dominating the attention of elected officials creates greater grassroots**

VIDEO DEBATE
Public Campaign Financing

The fund is accumulated by taxpayers who designate $3 of their taxes for this purpose each year when they send in their federal tax returns. (Only about 20 percent of taxpayers check off the appropriate box, even though participation does not increase their tax burden.) During the 2004 Democratic primaries, John Kerry and Howard Dean, like George W. Bush in 2000, both opted out of the federal matching funds, allowing them to raise considerably more money than the government would have provided.

For the general election, the two major-party presidential nominees can accept a $75 million lump-sum payment from the federal government after the candidate accepts his or her nomination. If the candidate accepts the money, it becomes the sole source for financing the campaign. A candidate could refuse the money and be free from the spending cap the government attaches to it, though this has never happened. Because the Democratic convention occurred five weeks before the Republican convention in 2004, John Kerry actually had five weeks more than Bush during which he had to stretch out the $75 million the government provided. Kerry first considered forgoing the public funding and later considered not accepting his party's nomination until after the Republican convention, but neither option proved popular and he eventually decided to accept the public funding and abide by the spending limit.[32]

political involvement. If candidates cannot count on big donors to finance their elections, they will have to find ways of appealing to larger numbers of people. That forces candidates back into their local communities to listen to their concerns and promise to address them. Then, communities can organize to fund-raise for certain candidates. The winner is bound to address the local community's interests, which is what representative government is supposed to do in the first place.

■ **Campaign finance reform opens up the door for new challengers.** Curbing the influence of wealthy interests creates a more even playing field for candidates. If incumbents must run against strong challengers, they become more accountable and, if necessary, more easily replaced.

ARGUMENTS AGAINST CAMPAIGN FINANCE REFORM

■ **Campaign contributions are political speech, the most hallowed and protected speech under the First Amendment.** All Americans have a right to freely state their political beliefs; just because one group has more money than another doesn't make a difference.

■ **Bureaucracy is never the better answer to a market-driven problem.** While the intentions behind campaign finance reform are usually good, they are based on the assumption that the way to solve political problems is through regulations. More regulations create a forever expanding labyrinth of quickly out-of-date rules that only years of debate and wrangling will fix, followed by implementing more quickly outgrown rules requiring another round of wrangling. Regulation is a dog chasing its tail.

■ **Campaign finance reform actually assists incumbents, not challengers.** Incumbents benefit from free media, since they have name recognition and greater credibility from their experience "on the Hill." A challenger needs money to counteract this and other advantages of incumbency. Regulating campaign finance limits a challenger's competitiveness, making the government less democratic as a result.

QUESTIONS

1. Can money, in the form of campaign contributions, be considered protected speech under the First Amendment? Why or why not?
2. Is it more democratic to centralize control of elections in order to allow more interests to be heard, or to let interests compete for attention without government interference? Explain your reasoning.

SELECTED READINGS

Lubenow, Gerald C., ed. *A User's Guide to Campaign Finance Reform.* Lanham, MD: Rowman and Littlefield, 2001.

Smith, Bradley A. *Unfree Speech: The Folly of Campaign Finance Reform.* Princeton, NJ: Princeton University Press, 2001.

A third-party candidate receives a smaller amount proportionate to his or her November vote total if that candidate gains a minimum of 5 percent of the vote. Note that in such a case, the money goes to third-party campaigns only *after* the election is over; no money is given in advance of the general election. Only two third-party candidates have qualified for public campaign funding: John B. Anderson in 1980, gaining 7 percent of the vote, and colorful Texas billionaire Ross Perot in 1992, gaining 19 percent of the vote.

THE FALL OF THE SOFT-MONEY LOOPHOLE AND THE RISE OF THE 527 LOOPHOLE

Soft money is campaign money raised and spent by political parties for expenses such as overhead and administrative costs and for grassroots activities such as political education and GOTV efforts. In a 1978 advisory opinion, the Federal Election Commission ruled that political parties could raise these funds without regulation. Then, in 1979, Congress passed an amendment allowing parties to *spend* unlimited sums on

soft money
The virtually unregulated money funneled by individuals and political committees through state and local parties.

**American
Electoral Rules:
How Do They
Influence
Campaigns?**

hard money
Legally specified and limited contributions that are clearly regulated by the Federal Election Campaign Act and by the Federal Election Commission.

527 political committees
Nonprofit and unregulated interest groups that focus on specific causes or policy positions and attempt to influence voters.

■ Rear Admiral Roy Hoffman, who commanded a swiftboat during the Vietnam War, appearing in an ad by the 527 group Swift Boat Veterans for Truth. These ads, which attacked John Kerry's character and service in Vietnam and questioned his honor and truthfulness, had a significant impact on the 2004 election.

these same activities.[33] In the years immediately following the rule changes, the national parties began raising five- and six-figure sums from individuals and interest groups to pay for expenses such as rent, employee salaries, and building maintenance. The national parties also began transferring large sums of soft money to state parties in order to help pay for grassroots activities (such as get out the vote drives) and campaign paraphernalia (such as yard signs and bumper stickers).

However, the line separating expenditures that influence federal elections from those that do not proved to be quite blurry, and this blurriness resulted in a significant campaign finance loophole. The largest controversy came in the area of campaign advertisements. The federal courts ruled that only campaign advertisements that use explicit words or phrases—for example, "vote for," "vote against," "elect," or "support"— qualify as *express advocacy* advertisements. Political advertisements that do not use these words were considered *issue advocacy* advertisements.[34] Because express advocacy advertisements were openly intended to influence federal elections, they could be paid for only with strictly regulated **hard money.** Issue advocacy advertisements, on the other hand, were paid for with unregulated soft money. The parties' response to these rules was to create issue advocacy advertisements that very much resemble express advocacy ads, for such advertisements call attention to the voting record of the candidate supported or opposed and are replete with images of the candidate. However, the parties ensured that the magic words "vote for" or "vote against" were never uttered in the advertisements, allowing them to be paid for with unregulated soft rather than hard money.

Soft-money donations are now prohibited under the BCRA, and third-party issue ads, if coordinated with a federal candidate's campaign, can now be considered campaign contributions and are thus regulated by the FEC. The last election cycle for the parties to use soft money was 2001–2002, and the amount raised, nearly $430 million for Republican and Democrats combined,[35] highlights why the reform seemed necessary. Republicans raised $219 million in soft money from pharmaceutical, insurance, and energy companies. Democrats came in just under $211 million in soft money from unions and law firms. With soft money banned, the hope was that wealthy donors and interest groups would be deprived of their privileged and potentially corrupting influence on parties and candidates. The hope was that, like every other citizen, they would have to donate within the hard-money limits placed on individuals and PACs. Unfortunately, these reforms have not worked, and the 2004 election revealed the latest campaign finance loophole.

The most significant unintended result of the BRCA in 2004 was the emergence of political entities known as **527 political committees**—the numbers come from the provisions of the Internal Revenue tax code that establish their legal status. The 501(c)(3) committees are nonprofit interest groups, and 527s are essentially unregulated interest groups that focus on specific causes or policy positions and attempt to influence voters. (See Analyzing Visuals: The Ten Most Active 527 Groups in 2004.)

According to the tax code, 527s may not directly engage in advocacy for or against a candidate, but they can advocate on behalf of political issues. This allowed them to circumvent the direct advocacy prohibition by creating what detractors called "sham issue ads" naming a particular candidate and stating how the candidate supported or harmed a particular interest, but without directly stating the 527 group's opinion on how to vote in the election. Thus, money that would have entered the system as unregulated soft money in previous election cycles

Photo courtesy: Swiftvets/AP Wide World Photos

Analyzing Visuals

THE TEN MOST ACTIVE 527 GROUPS IN 2004

After the Bipartisan Campaign Reform Act of 2002 outlawed soft-money contributions to political parties, Democratic and Republican political operatives were quick to find alternative ways to funnel money into the political process. The tool of choice following the 2002 reforms was the previously underutilized 527 political committees, named after their designation in the Internal Revenue Service code. Looking at the information in the table, what conclusions can you draw about the relative success of Democratic and Republican fund-raising efforts with regard to 527 groups? Given what you know about some of the individual 527s listed at right, a number of which are discussed in the text, what conclusions can you draw about the effectiveness of various 527 strategies with regard to the 2004 presidential election?

Committee	Expenditures	Pro-Democratic	Pro-Republican
America Coming Together	$78,040,480	✓	
Joint Victory Campaign 2004	$72,588,053	✓	
Media Fund	$57,694,580	✓	
Service Employees International Union	$47,730,761	✓	
Progress for America	$35,631,378		✓
American Federation of State/County/Municipal Employees	$26,170,411	✓	
Swift Boat Veterans for Truth	$22,565,360		✓
MoveOn.org	$21,565,803	✓	
College Republican National Committee	$17,260,655		✓
New Democrat Network	$12,524,063	✓	

Source: http://www.opensecrets.org.

ended up in the hands of 527 organizations in 2004, funding several television advertisements and direct mailings.[36] To limit the influence of such ads on voters, the BCRA now forbids their airing in the thirty days before a primary and sixty days before a general election.

The 527s exist in both political camps, though the Democrats, the party out of power, were first to aggressively pursue them in 2004. Two of the largest pro-Democratic committees in the 2004 election were the Media Fund and Americans Coming Together (ACT), both raising millions of dollars from people eager to see a Democrat in the White House. These committees bought TV, radio, and print advertising to sell their message, focusing on the battleground or "swing" states that were not firmly in the Bush or Kerry camps. Even though most political observers predicted that President Bush would easily outspend Senator Kerry in the presidential contest, the Democratic 527s considerably aided the Democratic campaign. Through the end of the 2004 election, pro-Democratic 527 groups spent more than $200 million, more than double that of their Republican counterparts. Groups on both sides saw large donations from wealthy individuals, including billionaire George Soros, who gave $23.4 million to Democratic organizations, and Texas developer Bob Perry, who donated $8 million to Republican groups.[37] As fund-raising records in almost every category were shattered in 2004, the campaign reform law clearly had no effect on overall spending or in limiting the amount that wealthy individuals can contribute to influence the process (see Table 14.2). 527 committees contributed almost $300 million to House and Senate candidates in 2006, with the Service Employees International Union's 527 contributing the most at over $26 million. Bob Perry's 527 topped the list of individual contributors, giving over $5 million to Republican groups.

Reformers will once again attempt to reform their reforms, but the abolition of 527 committees is highly unlikely—and the money supporting them would most likely reappear in some other way. Overall, however, one lesson of the Bipartisan

TABLE 14.2 MOST ACTIVE CONTRIBUTORS TO 527 GROUPS, 2004

The Bipartisan Campaign Reform Act of 2002 failed to place reasonable contribution limits on wealthy political donors. Rather than close the soft-money loophole, it exposed an even bigger flaw in the current system, the entirely unregulated world of 527 contributions. The top three Democratic political supporters alone were able to use 527 groups to funnel more than $55 million into the 2004 election. While no individual Republican donor came close to the level of giving achieved by the top Democratic donors, Republicans also made considerable contributions. Texas developer Bob Perry gave more than $8 million, much of which went to fund the Swift Boat Veterans for Truth, arguably the most effective 527 group in the 2004 election cycle.

Contributor	Total Contribution	Pro-Democratic	Pro-Republican
George Soros Soros Fund Management	$23,450,000	✓	
Peter Lewis Peter B Lewis/Progressive Corp	$22,997,220	✓	
Steven Bing Shangri-La Entertainment	$13,852,031	✓	
Herb & Marion Sandler Golden West Financial	$13,008,459	✓	
Bob Perry Perry Homes	$8,085,199		✓
Alex Spanos AG Spanos Companies	$5,000,000		✓
Ted Waitt Gateway Inc	$5,000,000	✓	
Dawn Arnall Ameriquest Capital	$5,000,000		✓
T Boone Pickens BP Capital	$4,600,000		✓
Andrew and Deborah Rappaport August Capital	$4,268,400	✓	

Source: http://www.opensecrets.org/527s/527indivs.asp?cycle=2004.

The Debate Over Campaign Finance Reform

Campaign Reform Act is obvious: no amount of clever legislating will rid the American system of campaign money. Interested individuals and groups will always find ways to have their voices heard. The challenge is to find a way to force contributors to disclose their contributions in a timely fashion, so that the public may take this information into account when deciding how to vote. Information regarding political contributions, when revealed to the public by the press in advance of an election, provides the voters with an invaluable cue for evaluating candidates. What better way to understand who supports a candidate and who does not? As always, disclosure is the ultimate check on potential misbehavior in the realm of political money.

The Main Event: The 2004 Presidential Campaign

THE 2004 ELECTION for president may go down in history for how extremely it divided the nation. An entire month before the election, polls showed that only 3 percent of Americans remained undecided on a candidate. Despite his status as an incumbent, implementation of tax cuts, and reputation for decisiveness, President George W. Bush faced an incredibly heated race against Massachusetts Senator John Kerry. At the most basic level, Americans knew that John Kerry had the knowledge and experience to serve in the highest office in the nation. Many were also unhappy with America's involvement in Iraq, job losses, and health care costs. However, Americans were also mindful of the September 11, 2001, terrorist attacks and were casting their first presidential vote in the post-9/11 world. Many had reservations about electing a president whose leadership during a national security crisis had not yet been proven.

THE PARTY NOMINATION BATTLE

Although few Americans were aware of it, the Republican Party *did* hold presidential primaries in 2004. Few noticed, as is usually the case when there is an incumbent candidate, because there was no significant opposition within the party to George W. Bush's reelection.

The Democrats, meanwhile, had ten candidates competing for their party's nomination (see Table 14.3). Democratic Party veterans Representative Dick Gephardt (MO), Senator and 2000 vice presidential nominee Joseph Lieberman (CT), Senator Bob Graham (FL), and Senator John Kerry (MA) joined the five other "original" candidates: Senator John Edwards (NC); former Illinois Senator Carol Moseley Braun, the first African American woman in the Senate; former Vermont Governor Howard Dean; Representative Dennis Kucinich (OH); and the Reverend Al Sharpton, an African American activist from New York. Retired General Wesley Clark entered late in the race after some Democrats ran a "Draft Clark" effort.

TABLE 14.3 2004 DEMOCRATIC CANDIDATES AND THEIR STRATEGIES

Wesley Clark: to use his record as Supreme Allied Commander in Europe in 1997–2000, during which time he successfully managed a multilateral military effort ousting Serbian dictator Slobodan Milosevic, thus neutralizing Bush's claim to expertise in national defense and foreign diplomacy; to appeal to male voters who otherwise tend to vote Republican.

Howard Dean: to relieve the dissatisfaction of many Democratic interest groups that opposed the dominance of moderates in party decision making; to tap into desire for true liberalism; to capitalize on the newest form of political organization and fund-raising, the Internet.

John Edwards: to market himself as a fresh, new leader unconnected to inside-the-Beltway disputes and corruption; to represent the South, a necessary group of states to capture in order to win.

Richard Gephardt: to capitalize on his long experience in public office (in Congress since 1977; presidential candidate in 1988; minority leader in U.S. House 1995–2002); to capture the imagination of the Democratic Party with a comprehensive health care package.

Bob Graham: to capitalize on the Democratic obsession with the state of Florida that emerged following the close presidential election in 2000; to put forward a dovish foreign policy.

John Kerry: to use both his military service in Vietnam and significant foreign policy experience in the Senate to convince voters that he had the credentials to challenge President Bush on any issue in the general election.

Dennis Kucinich: to promote liberal and progressive issues important to the far left of the Democratic voter base, while also articulating opposition to the war in Iraq and anti-Bush sentiments popular among liberal voters.

Joseph Lieberman: to capitalize on his service as vice presidential candidate in 2000; to satisfy interests of conservative Democrats with his socially conservative views and as a foreign policy hawk.

Carol Moseley Braun: to capitalize on her historic position as the first African American woman elected to the Senate; to promote the roles of minorities and women in Democratic office.

Al Sharpton: to present himself as the new Jesse Jackson and to have a "seat at the table" for decision making within the party; to advocate African American interests within the Democratic Party.

The Democratic candidates spent the spring and summer of 2003 in the typical primary season fashion: fund-raising, debating, giving speeches, and concentrating on the key states of Iowa and New Hampshire. By autumn, a full year prior to the general election, Senator Graham had dropped out of the race, citing fund-raising problems and proving the old adage that the first votes in any campaign are cast with dollars, not ballots. Autumn also brought the rise of the once "fringe" candidate Howard Dean. Dean's solid stance against the war in Iraq and pointed criticism of President Bush appealed to Democratic partisans, providing him with impressive grassroots support and a large war chest. Although in the spring of 2003 Democratic insiders were predicting that John Kerry would emerge as the front-runner, the fall brought Howard Dean the endorsements of party leaders such as Iowa Senator Tom Harkin and former Vice President Al Gore.

Initially, the Democrats' campaigns were focused on contrasting themselves with President Bush. However, as Dean emerged as the apparent front-runner, his rivals began aiming many of their attacks in his direction rather than at the president. The former governor's third-place finish in the Iowa caucuses, behind both John Kerry and John Edwards, may be partially attributed to these attacks. Others blamed the Iowa upset on the campaign's mismanagement of Dean's resources—not spending enough on ads and appearances and overspending on other items. Dean would win only one primary, in Vermont, and he dropped out of the race in February.

After Iowa, the race centered on Kerry and Edwards. Edwards, the charismatic first-term senator from North Carolina, hoped to energize the party and find support in the South. Edwards gave one of the most memorable stump speeches of the 2004 presidential election. In this speech, called "The Two Americas," Edwards discussed how the wealthy minority of Americans live in stark contrast to the majority of working and middle-class Americans. The contrast was not to provoke a "hate the rich" politics of envy but to demonstrate how the disparity between the two groups was detrimental to American democracy and could be closed only by improving state services, repealing tax breaks for the rich, and giving greater tax relief to the middle class.

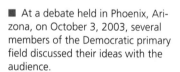
■ At a debate held in Phoenix, Arizona, on October 3, 2003, several members of the Democratic primary field discussed their ideas with the audience.

Photo courtesy: Matt York/AP Wide World Photos

Kerry relied on his experience and his support among party loyalists, capitalizing on anti-Bush sentiment and the perception that he was the best candidate to defeat Bush in the general election. In the end, Democratic voters sided with Kerry, and Edwards dropped out of the race in March, leaving Kerry the presumptive Democratic candidate. Democrats appeared united, at least in their determination to defeat George W. Bush in the general election. For this reason, many suggest, they chose a candidate quickly and channeled their energies toward winning in the fall.

The 2004 election indicated that left-leaning voters had become risk-averse after their experience in 2000. Whereas in 2000 some left-leaning voters complained that there was not much of a difference between Bush and Gore and thus voted for Ralph Nader, four years of a Bush presidency contributed to a mentality that came to be known as "anything but Bush." Anything-but-Bush adherents were not necessarily enthusiastic about John Kerry, but they were so determined to get President Bush out of office that they gave Kerry their votes. The "Nader effect" in 2004 was a mere 1 percent nationally, not enough to swing any states.

THE DEMOCRATIC CONVENTION

As the 2004 Democratic National Convention approached, polls showed Kerry and Bush in a virtual tie. Kerry and Edwards would use the convention to define their candidacy, woo new voters, and rally their party faithful. The convention was held July 26–29 in Boston, Massachusetts, Kerry's home state and solid Democratic territory. The first night started with a flourish: former Presidents Bill Clinton and Jimmy Carter took center stage, joined by former Vice President Al Gore. With polls that showed Americans giving Bush higher marks than Kerry on national security issues, Clinton sought to highlight the Democratic nominee's credentials in this area.

The speaker who stole the spotlight on the convention's second night was Barack Obama, a Democratic Senate candidate from Illinois. The multiracial son of a Kenyan immigrant father and Kansas-born mother, Obama used his own story, of "a skinny kid with a funny name who believes that America has a place for him too," to illustrate his party's hope for creating opportunity and unity in America. This appearance launched Obama into fame on the national political scene, and he would go on to win the seat in the U.S. Senate.

The overarching theme of the Democrats' convention was "Respected abroad, stronger at home." This emphasis on national security was most prominent on the final night of the convention, which featured testimonials from former Senator Max Cleland and Kerry's Vietnam swiftboat crewmates. In Kerry's speech, foreign affairs and his personal biography vastly overshadowed other topics. The biographical portion was most likely in response to polls that showed Kerry as not yet having established a personal connection with Americans. Kerry also used his speech as an opportunity to defend against GOP accusations that he was a "flip-flopper" on key issues. In one of his most direct attacks on the integrity of President Bush, Kerry pledged that his leadership would "start by telling the truth to the American people."

Despite what most analysts considered a solid performance, Kerry-Edwards received only a small post-convention "bounce" in the polls. Not since George McGovern in 1972 had a convention yielded such a small bounce. In their candidate's defense, the Kerry campaign argued that challengers historically run behind incumbents by about 15 points heading into a convention, whereas Kerry entered the convention already polling neck and neck with Bush.

■ President George W. Bush receiving the Republican presidential nomination at the 2004 Republican Convention. While conventions were turbulent and contentious in the past, today they are highly orchestrated events intended to sell the party's candidate to a national audience.

THE REPUBLICAN CONVENTION

The 2004 Republican National Convention was held from August 30 to September 2, beginning a full month after the Democratic National Convention ended. It was held in Madison Square Garden in New York City, considered one of the most heavily liberal, Democratic locales in the nation and most certainly Kerry territory. It was clear that the GOP picked New York City not to win over its residents but rather in an effort to use the symbolism of the 9/11 terrorist attacks to their advantage.

Under the theme "A Nation of Courage," the convention had an unmistakable focus on showcasing moderate Republicans. The right-wing branch of the Republican Party that had captured the stage at past conventions would stand aside as the more moderate Arnold Schwarzenegger, Rudy Giuliani, and John McCain spoke on behalf of their party and President Bush. The convention would be a delicate balancing act between reaching out to swing voters (who were charmed in 2000 by Bush's "compassionate conservative" agenda) without alienating the socially conservative Republican base.

The most surprising speaker at the Republican convention was undoubtedly Georgia Democratic Senator Zell Miller. Miller, who was by then thought of as a Democrat in name only, sharply attacked John Kerry and the Democratic Party's positions on national defense. Vice President Dick Cheney also took the stage on the third night of the convention, accepting his party's nomination for a second term. In harmony with the Bush campaign strategy, he sought to portray Kerry as a "flip-flopper." "On Iraq, Senator Kerry has disagreed with many of his fellow Democrats. But Senator Kerry's liveliest disagreement is with himself," he said. Although the vice president made mention of domestic issues such as reforming medical liability laws, job creation, and health care, his speech reflected the general focusof the convention: the war on terrorism, Iraq, and homeland security.

The 2004 Republican National Convention was not only a depiction of the Republican Party's agenda and campaign strategy but also a vivid demonstration of how polarized the nation had become. Thousands of New Yorkers and protesters from other states took to the streets during the convention for primarily peaceful protests against Bush, the war in Iraq, and the Republican Party. Still, the GOP had reason to be pleased with its convention performance. Whereas the Democratic National Convention did not give Kerry an advantage in the public opinion polls, Bush left New York with the prize of a modest 2 percent post-convention bounce, giving him the support of 52 percent of likely voters.

THE PRESIDENTIAL DEBATES

The first presidential debate took place on September 30, 2004, at the University of Miami in Coral Gables, Florida. The format for this event featured questions posed by the moderator, PBS host Jim Lehrer, with responses and rebuttals by the candidates. During the discussion on foreign policy, Bush and Kerry clashed sharply on the war in Iraq and on fighting terrorism. Television ratings were exceptionally high, with the first debate being watched by 62.5 million viewers, the most since 1992. Viewers generally found Kerry had won the debate, and many pundits commented on Bush's lack of energy and focus.

A town-hall format was used for the second presidential debate. Registered voters found to be undecided by the Gallup polling organization were allowed to ask questions of each candidate in turn. Reacting against the criticism that he seemed tired and unfocused in the earlier debate, Bush was extremely forthright and energetic throughout the night. The candidates met for the last time on October 13 in Tempe, Arizona. This debate followed a structure similar to that for the first debate, with the candidates standing behind podiums and answering questions in turn from CBS News anchor Bob Schieffer. For the first time during the debates, the questions were geared toward domestic issues. The public and media commentators generally considered the last debate to have been won by Kerry. Ultimately, Kerry—with his debate performances—seemed to even the playing field going into the final days of the campaign.

THE FALL CAMPAIGN AND GENERAL ELECTION

In the final weeks of the campaign, public opinion was deadlocked, and many Americans began to fear that the closeness and uncertainty of 2000 were again possible in 2004. There was even the real possibility of a tie in the Electoral College, which would throw the election into the House of Representatives. The election was especially close in the key battleground states of Ohio, Florida, Pennsylvania, New Mexico, Iowa, and Wisconsin.

Bush stayed on message during the last days of the campaign, emphasizing the need to continue the effort in Iraq and to strongly prosecute the war on terrorism. Kerry continued to hack away at the president's choice to invade Iraq as misguided and without a plan for victory. Kerry especially criticized Bush's handling of foreign relations, mentioning the bad blood in Europe and around the world created out of his Iraq policy. Kerry promised a change in international relations in which the United States would be more attuned to the concerns of allies and would expend more effort building alliances to fight the global war on terrorism. In a number of television commercials, and in public appearances, Bush fought back, continuing to paint Kerry as a "flip-flopper" who frequently switched his positions to follow public opinion. To attack Kerry's credibility on defense, Bush also used a *New York Times* interview in which Kerry likened terrorism before 9/11 to a "nuisance" like illegal gambling or prostitution.

Despite the efforts of each campaign, public opinion remained very divided in key states like Ohio and Florida up until the election. Realizing this, both candidates made a marathon sprint through battleground states in the last few days before the election. Bush covered several states in the final week but spent seven consecutive days traveling through Ohio, including Election Day. Kerry visited Michigan, Wisconsin, Florida, and Ohio in the final days of the campaign. After voting in his home state of Texas, Bush flew back to Washington to await the election results. Kerry returned to Massachusetts to cast his vote and follow an Election Day tradition of lunch at a Boston oyster bar. With the election close, and both candidates confident of their chances, the afternoon wore on in anticipation of the first exit polls.

ELECTION RESULTS

Network and cable news bureaus proceeded with caution on Election Night and did not call states for a candidate until the outcome was clear. As the night wore on and more states began to close their polls, Bush began to show a convincing lead in the key battleground state of Florida. However, the networks remained extremely cau-

TABLE 14.4 2004 ELECTION RESULTS (POPULAR VOTE PERCENTAGE)

	Bush (%)	Kerry (%)		Bush (%)	Kerry (%)
Alabama	63	37	Montana	59	39
Alaska	62	35	Nebraska	66	33
Arizona	55	44	Nevada	51	48
Arkansas	54	45	New Hampshire	49	50
California	45	54	New Jersey	46	53
Colorado	52	47	New Mexico	50	49
Connecticut	44	54	New York	40	58
Delaware	46	53	North Carolina	56	44
District of Columbia	9	90	North Dakota	63	36
Florida	52	47	Ohio	51	49
Georgia	58	41	Oklahoma	66	34
Hawaii	45	54	Oregon	48	52
Idaho	68	30	Pennsylvania	49	51
Illinois	45	55	Rhode Island	39	60
Indiana	60	39	South Carolina	58	41
Iowa	50	49	South Dakota	60	39
Kansas	62	37	Tennessee	57	43
Kentucky	60	40	Texas	61	38
Louisiana	57	42	Utah	71	27
Maine	45	54	Vermont	39	59
Maryland	43	56	Virginia	54	45
Massachusetts	37	62	Washington	46	53
Michigan	48	51	West Virginia	56	43
Minnesota	48	51	Wisconsin	49	50
Mississippi	60	40	Wyoming	69	29
Missouri	54	46	Total	51	48

Source: Official election results from CNN, http://www.cnn.com/ELECTION/2004/.

tious. As midnight approached, Florida was called for Bush, but Ohio still remained too close to call for some networks, despite a significant lead by the president. By early the next morning, neither candidate had captured the necessary 270 electoral votes. Despite a lead of over a hundred thousand votes for Bush in Ohio, the Kerry campaign believed there might be enough late votes to turn the tide.

Later on Wednesday morning, the Bush campaign was confident that they had carried the election, and they informed the Kerry campaign that they would be declaring victory. (Table 14.4 shows the candidates' popular vote percentages in each state.) Allowing Kerry the courtesy of giving his concession speech first, the Bush campaign waited until the early afternoon for Kerry to speak. Kerry conceded formally at historic Faneuil Hall in Boston, emphasizing the need for unity after such a divisive campaign. About an hour later, Bush gave his victory speech at the Ronald Reagan building in Washington, DC, also speaking of the need for unity but emphasizing his victory as ratification by the people of his policies.

ANALYZING THE OUTCOME OF THE 2004 ELECTION

One distinguishing characteristic of the 2004 election was that it had the highest voter turnout rate since 1968, with 60.7 percent of eligible citizens participating, or an estimated 122 million votes. Millions more Americans voted in 2004 than in 2000, despite long lines that kept some voters waiting for over seven hours. Not surprisingly, the largest turnouts occurred in swing states, where a majority of campaign time and resources were spent. The major partisan divide is seen as a primary cause for such high numbers. See Figure 14.5 for an overview of group-identified voting patterns in the 2004 election.

In many other ways, the 2004 election was similar to the 2000 election. For the most part, "red states" remained red and "blue states" remained blue. Most of the action and campaign spending took place in the handful of competitive states, which once again determined the outcome of the election. While 2004 was the most expensive presidential race in the nation's history, this was merely a continuation of long-standing modern trends. And, after years of debating campaign finance reform and enacting the much touted Bipartisan Campaign Reform Act of 2002, the spending by interest groups and wealthy individuals continued unabated.

Perhaps the most amazing aspect of the 2004 election was that while 60 million people left the election disappointed, some profoundly so, as their preferred candidate was defeated, the event unfolded without incident. Americans continue to accept and take comfort in the results of their nation's democratic process.

FIGURE 14.5 GROUP-IDENTIFIED VOTING PATTERNS IN THE 2004 PRESIDENTIAL ELECTION
Race, ideology, and religion all figured prominently among specific demographics in determining support for Senator John Kerry. Except for conservatives, George W. Bush's support was similar across several groups.

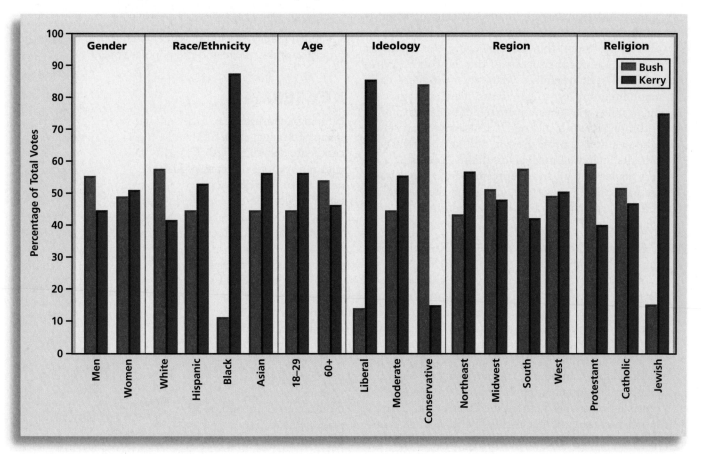

Source: CNN Exit Polls, http://www.cnn.com/election/2004/pages/results/states/us/p/00/epolls.0.html.

Summary

WITH THIS CHAPTER, we switched our focus from voting and the election decision and turned our attention to the actual campaign process. What we have seen is that while campaign rules and media coverage have a profound impact on elections, campaigns still tend to rise and fall on the strength of the individual candidate and his or her campaign team. In this chapter we have stressed the following observations:

1. **The Nature of Modern Political Campaigns**
   While each campaign has its own unique aspects, in modern campaigns there is a predictable pathway toward elections that involves a nomination and general election strategy. At the nomination phase it is essential for candidates to secure the support of people within their party, interest groups, and political activists. In the general election the candidates must focus on the voters and defining their candidacy in terms acceptable to a majority of voters in the district or state.

2. **The Key Players: The Candidate and the Campaign Staff**
   The candidate makes appearances, meets voters, raises funds, holds press conferences, gives speeches, and is ultimately responsible for conveying the campaign message and for the success of the campaign. A professional staff organizes volunteers, produces campaign literature, organizes events, plans strategy, conducts polls, produces advertisements, raises money, and interacts with the media. Campaign staffs combine volunteers, professionals, and key political consultants including media consultants, a pollster, a direct mailer, and an Internet team. Media consultants are particularly important, and given the cost of advertising, campaign media budgets consume the lion's share of available resources.

3. **Coverage of the Game: The Media's Role in Defining the Playing Field**
   Candidates for public office seek to gain favorable coverage in the media. They gain access with paid media, purchasing ad time on television and ad space in print media, and with free media, television, and print media news coverage. Because candidates cannot easily control media coverage, they cannot rely on free media alone. Candidates, therefore, must spend campaign dollars on creating advertisements that deliver campaign messages without media criticism. The Internet increasingly makes this possible, since candidates can use it as a cheap medium to relate directly to voters and activists.

4. **The Rules of the Game: Campaign Finance**
   Since the 1970s, campaign financing has been governed by the terms of the Federal Election Campaign Act (FECA). Because of the rise of soft money, the FECA was amended in 2002 by the Bipartisan Campaign Reform Act (BCRA), which was promptly challenged and upheld with very few exceptions by the Supreme Court. Though BCRA was successful in banning the unregulated soft money that flowed through the political parties, it exposed another loophole in the existing campaign finance laws, the unregulated money that now flows through 527 groups.

5. **The Main Event: The 2004 Presidential Campaign**
   A very competitive Democratic primary season, which had Howard Dean leading for much of the winter, ended in victory for John Kerry in Iowa. Kerry's momentum carried him to a quick primary victory, and he began the unofficial general campaign far in advance of the summer. Public opinion remained extremely close until the conventions, where President Bush benefited from a well-orchestrated effort by the Republicans. Bush's slight lead over Kerry was diminished by a lackluster performance during three televised debates, and the end of the race was a photo finish. Turnout was very brisk, and President Bush managed a close but convincing win in both the Electoral College and the popular vote.

KEY TERMS

campaign consultant, p. 515
campaign manager, p. 513
candidate debate, p. 520
communications director, p. 514
contrast ad, p. 517
direct mailer, p. 514
finance chair, p. 514
527 political committees, p. 532
free media, p. 516
general election campaign, p. 510
get out the vote (GOTV), p. 513
hard money, p. 532
inoculation ad, p. 517
Internet team, p. 515
matching funds, p. 529
media consultant, p. 516
negative ad, p. 516
new media, p. 516
nomination campaign, p. 509
paid media, p. 516
political action committee (PAC), p. 526
pollster, p. 514

positive ad, p. 516
press secretary, p. 515
public funds, p. 529
soft money, p. 531
spot ad, p. 517
voter canvass, p. 513

SELECTED READINGS

Abramson, Paul R., John H. Aldrich, and David W. Rohde. *Change and Continuity in the 2000 and 2002 Elections.* Washington, DC: CQ Press, 2003.

Ansolabehere, Stephen, and Shanto Iyengar. *Going Negative: How Political Ads Shrink and Polarize the Electorate.* New York: Free Press, 1997.

Caeser, James W., and Andrew E. Busch. *Red over Blue: The Elections and American Politics.* Lanham, MD: Rowman and Littlefield, 2005.

Fenno, Richard F., Jr. *Senators on the Campaign Trail: The Politics of Representation.* Norman: University of Oklahoma Press, 1998.

Greive, R. R. Bob. *The Blood, Sweat, and Tears of Political Victory . . . And Defeat.* Lanham, MD: University Press of America, 1996.

Herrnson, Paul S. *Congressional Elections: Campaigning at Home and in Washington,* 4th ed. Washington, DC: CQ Press, 2003.

Holbrook, Thomas M. *Do Campaigns Matter?* Thousand Oaks, CA: Sage, 1996.

Mayer, William G., ed. *In Pursuit of the White House 2000: How We Choose Our Presidential Nominees.* Chatham, NJ: Chatham House, 2000.

Nelson, Michael, ed. *The Elections of 2004.* Washington, DC: CQ Press, 2005.

Pomper, Gerald M., ed. *The Election of 2000: Reports and Interpretations.* Washington, DC: CQ Press, 2001.

Sabato, Larry J. *Divided States of America: The Slash and Burn Politics of the 2004 Presidential Election.* New York: Longman, 2005.

———. *Overtime! The Election 2000 Thriller.* New York: Longman, 2001.

Sabato, Larry J., and Howard Ernst. *Encyclopedia of American Political Parties and Elections.* New York: Facts on File, 2006.

Sabato, Larry J., and Glenn R. Simpson. *Dirty Little Secrets: The Persistence of Corruption in American Politics.* New York: Random House, 1996.

Sorauf, Frank J. *Inside Campaign Finance,* reissue ed. New Haven, CT: Yale University Press, 1994.

Thurber, James A., and Candice J. Nelson. *Campaign Warriors: Political Consultants in Elections.* Washington, DC: Brookings Institution, 2000.

Trippi, Joe. *The Revolution Will Not Be Televised.* New York: HarperCollins, 2004.

Troy, Gil. *See How They Ran: The Changing Role of the Presidential Candidate,* revised ed. Cambridge, MA: Harvard University Press, 1996.

WEB EXPLORATIONS

To compare the development of presidential candidates, go to http://www.cnn.com/ALLPOLITICS/

To view past presidential campaign commercials, go to http://livingroomcandidate.movingimage.us/index.php

To get an insider's look at the detail and urgency with which campaigns are now covered, go to http://www.cnn.com/ELECTION/2006/

To keep track of political futures markets, go to http://www.intrade.com/jsp/intrade/contractSearch/

To find out more about current political developments in campaign finance reform, visit Common Cause's site on Money in Politics at http://www.commoncause.org

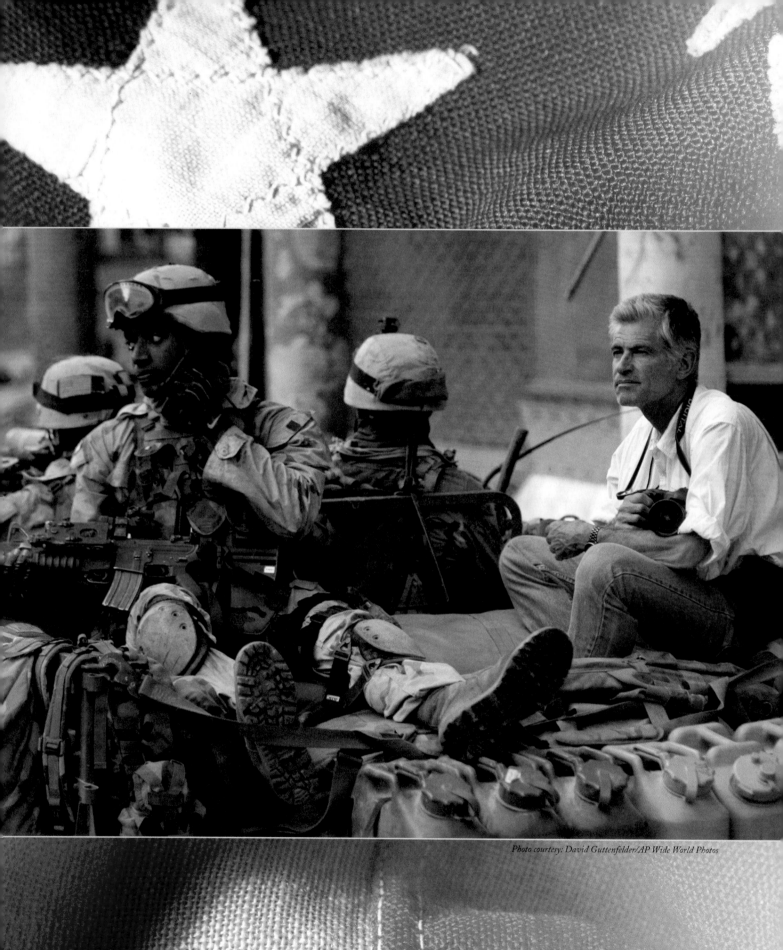

Photo courtesy: David Guttenfelder/AP Wide World Photos

THE MEDIA

PHOTO OPPORTUNITIES RUN AMOK and embarrassing images have hounded President George W. Bush in a way that few other administrations have experienced. In May 2003, there was the jet landing on the USS *Abraham Lincoln*, with the president dressed in a green flight suit and helmet, and his speech under the now infamous "Mission Accomplished" banner. There were the horrific images of prisoner abuse at Abu Ghraib in April 2004, and the troubling images from New Orleans following Hurricane Katrina in the summer of 2005. In October 2005, the White House tried to pass off a staged media event as an authentic question-and-answer exchange between the president and troops in Iraq.

The media coverage also featured Lewis "Scooter" Libby, Vice President Dick Cheney's chief of staff. Libby was indicted on five charges related to a leak that exposed the identity of an undercover CIA operative whose husband had written an unflattering editorial in the *New York Times* that challenged the veracity of information the president reported in his State of the Union Address. There were also widespread reports that the administration had paid Iraqi reporters to run pro-U.S. stories, stories that undoubtedly received less coverage than the stories about the payments. In another public image nightmare, Vice President Dick Cheney accidentally shot and wounded a fellow hunter, not revealing the incident to the press until the next day, and then only to a small local Texas newspaper. The publication of an unflattering book about the Bush White House by veteran reporter Bob Woodward in September 2006, a little over a month before the 2006 Midterm elections, led to furious media attention and a parade of former officials willing to acknowledge their disagreements with the President and his Cabinet.

The Bush administration has its own complaints about the media. In June 2006, the president angrily reacted to a *New York Times* story that revealed the administration's secret monitoring program that was tracking the flow of terrorist funds around the world. Bush claimed the *Times* was undermining the war on terrorism and being irresponsible in choosing to print the story. The Bush administration, despite its reputation for being one of the most media-savvy administrations in modern times, as well as one of the most tight-lipped, has time and again been stung by media that remain beyond its control. The Bush presidency has shown that in a world with twenty-four-hour news coverage and highly competitive private media outlets, there are few secrets in Washington. Moreover, attempts to control or manage the media stand the risk of backfiring and leading to unwanted media scrutiny.

CHAPTER OUTLINE

- ⭐ The Evolution of News Media in the United States

- ⭐ Current Media Trends

- ⭐ Rules Governing the Media

- ⭐ How the Media Cover Politics

- ⭐ The Media's Influence on the Public

IN A LETTER WRITTEN IN 1787, Thomas Jefferson explained that if he was forced to decide between a "government without newspapers or newspapers without a government," he "would not hesitate a moment to prefer the latter." Jefferson, like many of the nation's founders, realized the profound importance of a free press in a free society. So important was this idea that it was canonized in the First Amendment with the simple words "Congress shall make no law . . . abridging the freedom of speech, or of the press," an idea that has shaped the American republic as much as any other idea in the Constitution. With the Constitution's sanction, as interpreted by the Supreme Court over two centuries, a vigorous and highly competitive press has emerged. This freedom has been crucial in facilitating the political discourse and education necessary to maintain democracy.

A free press is a necessary component of a democratic society because it informs the public, giving them the information they need in order to choose their leaders and influence the direction of public policy. In fact, the American media have been called the "fourth branch of government" because their influence is often as great as that of the three constitutional branches: the executive, the legislative, and the judiciary. However, this term is misleading because the American media are composed of many competing private enterprises.

Throughout the world, mass media are organized around different principles from those in the United States and can serve different purposes. Under authoritarian regimes, the media serve as a carefully controlled outlet for "approved" messages from those in charge to those being governed without consent. In constitutional monarchies, the media cooperate with the monarchy in a mutually beneficial relationship. The media get interesting stories about the royal family, while the family helps support the media. In the turbulent Middle East, where there is no more influential network than al-Jazeera, news is reported from a distinct perspective, often providing militants a venue to express their ideas and casting U.S. involvement in the region in the darkest possible light.

This chapter traces the historical development of the news media in the United States and then explores recent developments affecting the media. The rules under which the news media operate, the ways in which government regulates aspects of the media, and the manner in which the media cover politics are also discussed. Finally, the chapter discusses how the media influence public opinion, giving special attention to how competition among media outlets can distort the news, and to the issue of bias in the news. In discussing the changing role and impact of the media, we will address the following:

- First, we will discuss *the evolution of news media in the United States*, from the founding of the country to the modern period.
- Second, we will examine *current media trends*.
- Third, we will consider *rules governing the media*, both self-imposed rules of conduct and government regulations affecting radio, television, and the Internet.
- Fourth, we will discuss *how the media cover politics*.
- Finally, we will investigate *the media's influence on the public*, including the issue of media bias.

The Evolution of News Media in the United States

mass media
The entire array of organizations through which information is collected and disseminated to the general public.

THE MASS MEDIA—the entire array of organizations through which information is collected and disseminated to the general public—have become a colossal enterprise in the United States. The mass media include print sources, movies, television, radio, and Web-based material. Collectively the mass media make use of broadcast, cable, and satellite technologies to distribute information, which reaches every corner of the United States. The mass media are a powerful tool for both entertaining and informing the public. They reflect American society, but they are also the primary lens through which citizens view American culture and American politics. The **news media,** which are one component of the larger mass media, provide the public with new information about subjects of public interest and play a vital role in the political process.[1] Although often referred to as a large, impersonal whole, the media are made up of diverse personalities and institutions, and they form a spectrum of opinion. Through the various outlets that make up the news media—from printed page to electronic blog—journalists inform the public, influence public opinion, and affect the direction of public policy in our democratic society.

Throughout American history, technological advances have had a major impact on the way in which Americans receive their news. (See Table 15.1.) High-speed presses and more cheaply produced paper made mass-circulation daily newspapers possible. The telegraph and then the telephone made newsgathering easier and much faster. When radio became widely available in the 1920s, millions of Americans could hear national politicians instead of merely reading about them. With television—first introduced in the late 1940s, and nearly a universal fixture in U.S. homes by the mid-1950s—citizens could see and hear political candidates and presidents. And now with the rise of Web-based media, the process is once again undergoing a transformation. Never before has information been more widely distributed, and never have the lines between news producer and consumer been less clear.

news media
Media providing the public with new information about subjects of public interest.

TIMELINE

**Three Hundred
Years of American
Mass Media**

PRINT MEDIA

The first example of news media in America came in the form of newspapers, which were published in the colonies as early as 1690. The number of newspapers grew throughout the 1700s, as colonists began to realize the value of a press free from government oversight and censorship. The battle between Federalists and Anti-Federal-

TABLE 15.1 LANDMARKS OF THE AMERICAN NEWS MEDIA	
1760	First newspaper published.
1789	First party newspapers circulated.
1833	First penny press.
1890	Yellow journalism spreads.
1900	Muckraking in fashion.
1928	First radio broadcast of election.
1948	First election results to be covered by television.
1952	First presidential campaign advertisements aired on television.
1960	Televised presidential campaign debates.
1979	The Cable Satellite Public Affairs Network (C-SPAN) is founded, providing live, round-the-clock coverage of politics and government.
1980	Cable News Network (CNN) is founded by media mogul Ted Turner, making national and international events available instantaneously around the globe.
1992	Talk-show television circumvents traditional media outlets, allowing candidates to go around journalists to reach the voting public directly.
1996	Official candidate home pages appear on the World Wide Web, containing candidate profiles, issue positions, campaign strategy and slogans, and more.
2000	Explosion of the Web as a primary campaign tool for candidates and a twenty-four-hour source of news.
2002	Web logs, or "blogs," create a popular forum for the disbursement of political news and commentary.
2004	The Internet plays its largest role yet as a source for elections information: 37 percent of the adult population and 61 percent of all Americans with Internet access regularly log on to get campaign and election information during the 2004 presidential election.

ists over ratification of the Constitution, discussed in chapter 2, played out in various partisan newspapers in the late eighteenth century. Thus, it was not surprising that one of the Anti-Federalists' demands was a consitutional amendment guaranteeing the freedom of the press (see The Living Constitution).

The partisan press eventually gave way to the penny press. In 1833, Benjamin Day founded the *New York Sun,* which cost a penny at the newsstand. Beyond its low price, the *Sun* sought to expand its audience by freeing itself from the grip of a single party. Inexpensive and politically independent, the *Sun* was the forerunner of modern newspapers, which rely on mass circulation and commercial advertising to produce profit. By 1861, the penny press had so supplanted partisan papers that President Abraham Lincoln announced that his administration would have no favored or sponsored newspaper.

Although print media was becoming less partisan, it was not necessarily becoming more respectable. Mass-circulation dailies sought wide readership, attracting readers with the sensational and the scandalous. The sordid side of politics became the entertainment of the times. One of the best-known examples occurred in the presidential campaign of 1884, when the *Buffalo Evening Telegraph* headlined "A Terrible Tale" about Grover Cleveland, the Democratic nominee.[2] The story alleged that Cleveland, an unmarried man, had fathered a child in 1871, while sheriff of Buffalo, New York. Even though paternity was indeterminate because the child's mother had been seeing other men, Cleveland willingly accepted responsibility, since all the other men were married, and he had dutifully paid child support for years. The strict Victorian moral code that dominated American values at the time made the story even more shocking than it would be today. Fortunately for Cleveland, another newspaper, the *Democratic Sentinel,* broke a story that helped to offset this scandal: Republican presidential nominee James G. Blaine and his wife had had their first child just three months after their wedding.

Throughout the nineteenth century, payoffs to the press were common. Andrew Jackson, for instance, gave one in ten of his early appointments to loyal reporters.[3] During the 1872 presidential campaign, the Republicans slipped cash to about 300 newsmen.[4] Wealthy industrialists also sometimes purchased investigative cease-fires for tens of thousands of dollars.

In the late 1800s and early 1900s, prominent publishers such as William Randolph Hearst and Joseph Pulitzer expanded the reach of newspapers in their control by practicing what became known as **yellow journalism**—sensationalized reporting that lowered journalistic standards in order to increase readership. Hearst's and Pulitzer's newspapers featured pictures and comics printed in color and sensationalized news stories designed to increase their readership and to capture a share of the burgeoning immigrant population market.

The Progressive Movement, discussed in chapter 4, gave rise to a new type of journalism in the early 1920s. **Muckraking** journalists—so named by President Theodore Roosevelt after a special rake designed to collect manure—were devoted to exposing misconduct by government, business, and individual politicians.[5] For Roosevelt, muckraking was a derogatory term used to describe reporters who focused on the carnal underbelly of politics rather than its more lofty pursuits. Nevertheless, much good came from these efforts. Muckrakers stimulated demands for anti-trust regulations—laws that prohibit companies, like large steel companies, from controlling an entire industry—and exposed deplorable working conditions in factories, as well as outright exploitation of workers by business owners. An unfortunate side effect of this emphasis on crusades and investigations, however, was the frequent publication of gossip and rumor without sufficient proof.

As the news business grew, its focus increasingly shifted to maintaining and increasing its profitability. Newspapers became more careful in their reporting to avoid alienating the advertisers and readers who produced their revenues, and reporting became less harsh and more objective.

yellow journalism
A form of newspaper publishing in vogue in the late nineteenth century that featured pictures, comics, color, and sensationalized, oversimplified news coverage.

muckraking
A form of journalism, in vogue in the early twentieth century, concerned with reforming government and business conduct.

SIMULATION
You Are the News Editor

The Living Constitution

Congress shall make no law respecting an establishment of religion, or prohibiting the free exercise thereof; or abridging the freedom of speech, or of the press; or the right of the people peaceably to assemble, and to petition the government for a redress of grievances.

—FIRST AMENDMENT

The Framers knew that no democracy is easy, that a republic requires a continuous battle for rights and responsibilities. One of those rights is the freedom of the press, preserved in the First Amendment to the Constitution. To protect the press, the Framers were wise enough to keep the constitutional language simple—and a good thing, too. Their view of the press, and its required freedom, was almost certainly less broad than we conceive of the press today.

It is difficult today to appreciate what a leap of faith it was for the Framers to grant freedom of the press when James Madison brought the Bill of Rights before Congress. Newspapers were largely run by disreputable people, since at the time editors and reporters were judged as merely purveyors of rumor and scandal, the reason Madison, as well as Alexander Hamilton and John Jay, published their newspaper articles advocating the ratification of the Constitution, *The Federalist Papers*, under the pseudonym "Publius."

The printed word was one of the few mediums of political communication in the young nation—it was critical for keeping Americans informed about issues. Therefore, the Framers had to hope that giving freedom for the press to print all content, although certain to give rise to tabloids, would also produce high-quality newspapers. Nevertheless, we should note that the Framers were not above using journalism as a way of promoting their political agendas. For example, Thomas Jefferson created a newspaper, the *National Gazette,* to report news favoring his Democratic-Republican Party. Giving the press freedom was also giving opposing politicians an open forum to attack each other.

Not much has changed since the Framers instituted the free press. We still have tabloids and partisan publications in which politicians attack each other, and we still rely on the press to give us important political information with which we make voting decisions. The First Amendment declares the priority of free expression. The Framers recognized that all kinds of information would have to be allowed, in order to create as many opportunities for solid information to be reported, the fear being that regulations in response to what offends some people might be the first step on the slippery slope to censorship. In other words, protecting the *New York Times* and the *Wall Street Journal* means protecting the "paparazzi" or else we will have neither. Although the vices and virtues of a free press have not changed, the number of media has. But, the simple yet powerful protection the Framers created in the First Amendment made their invention and implementation merely a continuation of a freedom we all enjoy.

"Uncle Sam's Next Campaign—the War Against the Yellow Press." In this 1898 cartoon in the wake of the Spanish-American War, yellow journalism is attacked for its threats, insults, filth, grime, blood, death, slander, gore, and blackmail, all of which are "lies." The cartoonist suggests that, after winning the foreign war, the government ought to attack its own yellow journalists at home.

Photo courtesy: Stock Montage, Inc.

RADIO NEWS

The advent of radio in the early part of the twentieth century was a media revolution and a revelation to the average American who rarely, if ever, had heard the voice of a president, governor, or senator. The radio became the center of most homes in the evening, when national networks broadcast the news as well as entertainment shows. Calvin Coolidge was the first president to appear on radio on a regular basis, but President Franklin D. Roosevelt made the radio appearance a must-listen by presenting "fireside chats" to promote his New Deal. The soothing voice of Roosevelt made it difficult for most Americans to believe that what the president wanted could be anything other than what was best for America.

News radio, which had begun to take a back seat to television by the mid-1950s, regained popularity with the development of AM talk radio in the mid-1980s. Controversial radio host Rush Limbaugh began the trend with his unabashed conservative views, opening the door for other conservative commentators such as Laura Ingraham, Sean Hannity, and Michael Reagan (son of the former president). Statistics show that these conservative radio hosts have resurrected the radio as a news medium by giving the information that they broadcast a strong ideological bent. In 1997, 12 percent of Americans reported getting their news from talk radio; by 2005, 22 percent did.[6] Liberal groups have attempted to break into the AM market, but to date liberal programming, like Air America, which was established in 2004 but declared bankruptcy in 2006, has had limited success. The impact of fee-based satellite radio services on news radio remains to be seen. Sirius Satellite Radio, for example, offers both a conservative and a liberal political talk channel and recieved significant publicity when radio personality Howard Stern moved his show to Sirius's network in early 2006.

TELEVISION NEWS

Television was first demonstrated in the United States at the 1939 Worlds Fair in New York, but it did not take off as a news source until after World War II. While television had expanded into most homes by the early 1960s, it would take several years for television to replace print and radio as the nation's chief news provider. In 1963, most networks provided only fifteen minutes of news per day; only two major networks provided thirty minutes of news coverage. During this period, a substantial majority of Americans still received most of their news from newspapers, but in 2005,

74 percent of Americans claimed to get their news from television, whereas only 44 percent read newspapers (see Figure 15.1).

There is, however, an important distinction between network and cable news stations. Network news has lost viewers since 1980, with the loss becoming even steeper after the advent of cable news. Between 2000 and 2004, viewership for all network news programming declined from 45 percent to 35 percent.[7] Cable news has seen an increase in viewership, from 34 percent in 2000 to 38 percent in 2004. This increase is due in large part to the increased availability of services providing twenty-four-hour news channels. By 2006, 58 percent of all U.S. households were subscribed to a cable service, and 29 percent of households were using a direct broadcast satellite (such as DirectTV or DISH Network).[8] Thus, the vast majority of Americans receive cable news in addition to their broadcast stations.

Cable and satellite providers give consumers access to a less glitzy and more unfiltered source of news with C-SPAN, a basic cable channel that offers gavel-to-gavel coverage of congressional proceedings, as well as major political events when Congress is not in session. It also produces some of its own programming, such as *Washington Journal,* which invites scholars and journalists to speak about topics pertaining to their areas of expertise. C-SPAN expanded its brand to include C-SPAN2 and C-SPAN3, which air programming such as academic seminars and book presentations in a series titled *BookTV.* C-SPAN benefits from having no sponsors distracting (with commercials or banners) or possibly affecting what it broadcasts. Because the content of C-SPAN can be erudite, technical, and sometimes downright tedious (such as the fixed camera shot of the Senate during a roll-call vote), audiences tend to be very small, but they are very loyal and give C-SPAN its place as a truly content-driven medium.

The latest development in television news is the growth in popularity of comedy news programs. While *Saturday Night Live* and other late-night comedy programs, like those hosted by Jay Leno and David Letterman, have mocked politicians and the

VIDEO ROUNDTABLE
Soft News vs. Hard News

FIGURE 15.1 DISTRIBUTION OF NEWS SOURCE USAGE BY INDIVIDUALS
While the dominant, mainstream media outlets are still used by the greatest number of consumers, growth areas include ethnic, alternative, and online media.

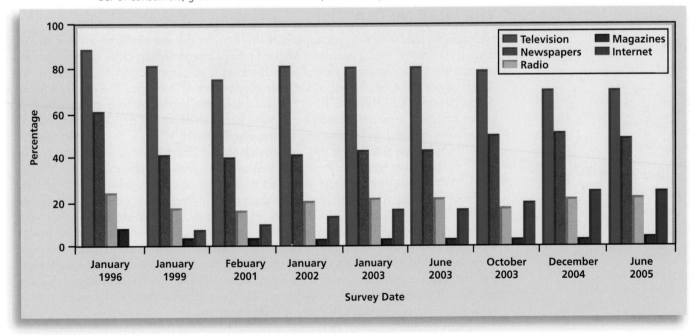

Source: Pew Research Center for the People and the Press, "Public More Critical of Press, but Goodwill Persists," http://people-press.org.

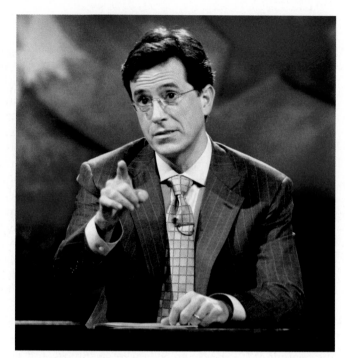

■ Bill O'Reilly (seen at left), host of the FOX News program *The O'Reilly Factor*, is one of the country's most visible conservative commentators. O'Reilly received some unforeseen competition from Comedy Central's Stephen Colbert (right) with the launch of *The Colbert Report*, a spin-off of *The Daily Show* that lampoons O'Reilly's conservative views and blustering approach to reporting the news.

news for years, more recent programs like Jon Stewart's *Daily Show* and Stephen Colbert's *Colbert Report*—a satire of FOX News's *The O'Reilly Factor*—dedicate their entire program to poking fun at world leaders and current issues. One study conducted by the Annenberg Public Policy Center of the University of Pennsylvania revealed comedy programs actually inform viewers as well as entertain them. Regular viewers of the *Daily Show* were found to know more about world events than nonviewers, even when education, party identification, watching cable news, and other factors were taken into consideration.[9]

THE NEW MEDIA

Increasingly, media consumers, especially those under the age of thirty-five, are abandoning traditional media outlets in favor of other sources. While cable news networks are still the most regularly viewed, the Internet is gaining ground.[10] The Internet, which began as a Department of Defense project named Advanced Research Projects Agency Network (ARPANET) in the late 1960s, has grown into an unprecedented source of public information for people in all parts of the world. In 2000, 9 percent of Americans claimed to receive news from the Internet, whereas 24 percent did in 2005.[11] Of course, few people rely exclusively on the Internet for news, although it is likely in the future that many citizens will use the video components of the World Wide Web to substitute for television news watching or newspaper reading. Already, all major networks and newspapers offer their news online. Major cable news stations, such as CNN, MSNBC, and FOX News, each have their own Web sites that are also used to promote their television programming as well as provide up-to-date news. The *New York Times* and *Washington Post* are available online for free to users who register. Access to older articles (and, in the case of the *Times*, op-ed pieces) requires a fee. Political magazines such as the conservative *National Review* and liberal *Nation* provide all online content free of charge; like the online newspapers, they earn revenue from advertising through pop-up and banner ads.

Many people wonder if newspapers and television stations currently offering free Web sites are cutting into their own subscription revenues. However, there is very

On Campus

WHERE DO COLLEGE STUDENTS GET THEIR CAMPAIGN NEWS?

In January 2004, the Pew Research Center for the People and the Press stated in a press release that Americans increasingly believed there is partisan bias in cable news.[a] Also buried in the release was the report that young voters (age eighteen to twenty-nine) increasingly rely on two sources for campaign news: the Internet and comedy television shows, such as *The Daily Show* and *Saturday Night Live*. Twenty-one percent of young voters, 16 percent of voters age thirty to forty-nine, and 7 percent of voters age fifty or older use the Internet for campaign news; 21 percent of young voters use comedy television shows, much higher than the 6 percent of those between thirty to forty-nine and 3 percent of those fifty or older. The fact that young voters might make voting decisions based on a quip from Steven Colbert or Seth Meyers's impression of John Kerry upset many in the media, generating a flurry of articles. One journalist called the age bracket "the Young and the Newsless."[b]

But there is more to the data than reported. What Pew actually revealed was that where voters get their news affects how well informed they are. For voters of all ages, if the regular source of 2004 campaign news was a television comedy show, they were very badly informed about the campaign. For voters using new Internet Web sites as their regular source of campaign news, knowledge of the

campaign was actually higher than average. Pew raises the issue of age because young voters use both comedy shows and the Internet more frequently than any other age demographic, a finding indicating that well-informed young voters gravitate to newer technologies for learning about politics. At the same time, while comedy viewers may claim to get their news from sketches and satire, it is clear that the content is only entertaining and not informing them.

So when Jon Stewart reminds the audience, as he often does, that he anchors a fake news show, the audience will listen and perhaps, after the "Moment of Zen" segment, check the headlines at a major news Web site or even pick up a local newspaper. After all, when told that *The Daily Show* could be confused with an old form of satire or a new kind of journalism, Stewart said, "Well, then, that either speaks to the sad state of comedy or the sad state of the news."[c]

---

[a] Pew Research Center for the People and the Press, "Cable and Internet Loom Large in Fragmented Political News Universe: Perceptions of Partisan Bias Seen as Growing, Especially by Democrats," January 11, 2004, http://www.pewinternet.org.

[b] Melanie McFarland, "Young People Turning Comedy Shows into Serious News Source," *Seattle Post-Intelligencer,* January 22, 2004, http://seattlepi.nwsource.com.

[c] Jon Stewart interview by Bill Moyers, *NOW,* July 11, 2003, http://www.pbs.org.

---

little evidence that this is happening. By and large, the people who use media Web sites are highly informed voters who devour additional information about politics and government and use the Web for updates and supplements to their traditional media services. Indeed, a 2003 study discovered that out of light, medium, and heavy users of online news sites, heavy users read newspapers the most, while light users read newspapers the least. In short, heavy users, those most interested in the news, will take their news any way they can get it.[12] (See On Campus: Where Do College Students Get Their Campaign News?)

In an attempt to assert an online presence, the U.S. government provides its own news, frequently publishing its press releases on Web sites it has set up for its major departments, as well as for both houses of Congress and the president. These Web sites offer basic information regarding the history and function of the respective bodies, and current issues before them. Web users who access the Senate or House site can enter their zip code to find out the identity of their elected representatives. Users can also access the complete voting record of individual members of Congress on the Senate and House sites and use the contact information found there to contact any representatives or senators.

The Internet also offers access to foreign news media previously unavailable to most Americans. The British Broadcasting Channel (BBC) has a Web site entirely devoted to news and available in over forty languages. International newspapers offer online content, although usually in their native languages. Al-Jazeera, a major Arabic television news source, has an English-language Web site providing news concerning the Middle East (see Global Perspective: Al-Jazeera: The CNN of the Arab World?)

COMPARATIVE

Comparing News Media

Global Perspective

AL-JAZEERA: THE CNN OF THE ARAB WORLD?

Few Americans other than those of Arabic descent had heard of al-Jazeera before October 7, 2001. On that day, less than one month following the 9/11 terrorist attacks on the World Trade Center and the Pentagon, Osama bin Laden spoke to the world for six and one-half minutes via a tape shown on al-Jazeera's television network. It was not the first time al-Jazeera carried bin Laden's image or his words, nor would it be the last. In June 1999 it broadcast a ninety-minute interview with him, and several bin Laden tapes have been aired since then. Some critics have taken these interviews, as well as the airing of graphic videos showing the execution of Western prisoners by al-Qaeda operatives in Iraq, as evidence that al-Jazeera is little more than a mouthpiece for al-Qaeda's anti-American propaganda, or at least an accomplice, but the answer is undoubtedly more complicated.

Al-Jazeera (which means "the island" or "the peninsula" in Arabic), is an independent station that broadcasts from the tiny, oil-rich, Islamic country of Qatar in the Persian Gulf. Qatar is a member of the Organization of Petroleum Exporting Countries (OPEC) and is ruled by a progressive emir (prince) who is pro-Western. The emir allowed American troops to use Qatar as a staging point for the 1991 Persian Gulf War and the invasion of Iraq. He funded al-Jazeera when it was founded in 1996. Al-Jazeera emerged out of the failure of a British Broadcasting Corporation (BBC) news service, after a Saudi Arabian–owned radio and television network reportedly terminated its financial support because the news service had aired a documentary about executions in Saudi Arabia.

Al-Jazeera immediately set a course that separated it from its competitors in the region. Most of them were owned either by Middle Eastern governments or by powerful individuals within those countries, and their standard of offerings emphasized entertainment and limited news that amounted to state propaganda. A typical newscast would do little more than follow the morning-to-night public schedule of a leading official. Sensitive political and social issues were ignored for fear of the controversy they would create.

In contrast, the trail that al-Jazeera chose to follow was pioneered by Cable News Network (CNN). Like CNN, al-Jazeera focuses its political reporting on two staples. The first is on-the-scene coverage of conflicts or other world events. Just as CNN was the only television network to broadcast out of Baghdad in the Persian Gulf War, al-Jazeera had a monopoly of live reporting from Kabul during the war in Afghanistan against the Taliban. Three Western news agencies, including CNN, also received permission from the Taliban government in 1999 to establish offices in Afghanistan, but only al-Jazeera did so. In 2001, al-Jazeera's office in Kabul was bombed by U.S. forces, as was the network's Baghdad office in 2003. In both cases, Pentagon officials insisted the bombings were accidents. Al-Jazeera also covers the Palestinian conflict extensively, receiving heavy criticism from the West for referring to Palestinians killed by Israeli forces as martyrs and showing extensive footage of Palestinian casualties.

A second programming staple is political talk shows that often feature call-ins from viewers. Among the most popular are *The Opposite Direction,* a live weekly two-hour show modeled after CNN's now defunct *Crossfire,* and *Without Frontiers,* in which an individual discusses a current topic in depth. Segments aired on these programs have often angered Middle Eastern governments where there is little tradition of a free press. Libya and Kuwait both threatened to recall their ambassadors to Qatar in protest over critical stories aired by al-Jazeera. Saudi Arabia did so and prohibited al-Jazeera from covering the annual pilgrimage to Mecca. The government of Algeria created a blackout in the capital city to prevent the airing of a story on its civil war. Saddam Hussein once criticized al-Jazeera's broadcasts as too "pro-American" and expelled two al-Jazeera reporters during the U.S.-led invasion of Iraq because of its coverage.

President George W. Bush, British Prime Minister Tony Blair, and U.S. government figures such as Colin Powell, Condoleezza Rice, and Donald Rumsfeld have all been interviewed by al-Jazeera. Osama bin Laden was interviewed after the 9/11 attacks, though the network decided against airing the interview when faced with strong criticism from U.S. officials. An interview with Israeli Prime Minster Ariel Sharon was cancelled because of criticism from Palestinian officials.

QUESTIONS

1. Spend some time looking at the Web site of al-Jazeera (aljazeera.net). How does its coverage compare with that of American networks?
2. How do the sources quoted in al-Jazeera's articles differ from those quoted in U.S. news articles?

By visiting alternative news sources like these, individuals gain a more nuanced and informed understanding of global issues.

The future relationship between the Internet and politics remains hard to predict. Some analysts believe that as today's computer-literate children and young people become adult voters, the Web is likely to become the primary means by which America informs itself about politics and government. (Table 15.2 shows the public's media

TABLE 15.2 THE NEWS GENERATION GAP				
	18–29 %	30–49 %	50–64 %	65+ %
Regularly watch/listen to				
Nightly network news	18	26	43	56
Cable TV news	29	37	40	46
Local TV news	46	58	64	70
C-SPAN	5	4	6	8
National Public Radio	11	19	19	12
Morning news show	16	22	26	26
Larry King Live	2	2	6	11
The O'Reilly Factor	5	7	10	11
Did yesterday				
Read a newspaper	23	39	52	60
Watched TV news	44	58	67	74
Read a magazine	26	24	23	27

Source: Pew Research Center for the People and the Press, "News Audiences Increasingly Polarized," June 8, 2004, http://people-press.org.

choices by age group.) Others assert that "it appears unlikely that more than a small portion of the existing audience for traditional news media will abandon those media for Internet news sources."[13] Scholars debate whether all the information available on the Web will be good for politics or not. Some believe that the availability of all this information makes for a better-informed and more active electorate, whereas others think that this remains to be seen.[14] One obvious question is whether citizens will devote the time necessary to find valid and balanced data amidst the almost unlimited information available through the Internet, or if instead they will refer to only a few favorite sites that support their views.

Current Media Trends

THE EDITORS OF THE FIRST partisan newspapers could scarcely have imagined what their profession would become more than two centuries later. The number and diversity of media outlets today are stunning. The **print media** consist of many thousands of daily and weekly newspapers, magazines, newsletters, and journals. **Broadcast media** encompass traditional radio and television stations, as well as satellite and cable services. The **new media** are the latest technologies, such as the Internet, that blur the lines between media sources and create new opportunities for the dissemination of news and other information.

THE INFLUENCE OF MEDIA GIANTS

Every newspaper, radio station, television station, and Web site is influential in its own area, but only a handful of media outlets are influential nationally, and an even smaller number of media giants have international influence. The United States has no nationwide daily newspapers to match the influence of Great Britain's *Times*, *Guardian*, and *Daily Telegraph*, all of which are avidly read in virtually every corner of the United Kingdom. The national orientation of the British print media can be traced to the smaller size of the country and also to London's role as both the national capital and that nation's largest cultural metropolis. The vastness of the United States and the existence of many large cities effectively preclude a nationally united print medium in this country.

print media
The traditional form of mass media, comprising newspapers, magazines, newsletters, and journals.

broadcast media
Television, radio, cable, and satellite services.

new media
Technologies, such as the Internet, that blur the line between media sources and create new opportunities for the dissemination of news and other information.

network
An association of broadcast stations (radio or television) that share programming through a financial arrangement.

affiliates
Local television stations that carry the programming of a national network.

wire service
An electronic delivery of news gathered by the news service's correspondents and sent to all member news media organizations.

However, the *New York Times*, the *Wall Street Journal, USA Today,* and the *Christian Science Monitor* are distributed nationally, and other newspapers, such as the *Washington Post* and the *Los Angeles Times,* have substantial influence from coast to coast. These six newspapers also have a pronounced effect on what the major national broadcast **networks** (ABC, CBS, NBC, and FOX) air on their evening news programs, and what the major cable news networks (CNN, FOX News, MSNBC, and CNBC) air around the clock. In turn, these media giants influence news around the globe, as regional and local media outlets follow their lead. A major story that breaks in one of these papers is nearly guaranteed to be featured on one or more of the network news shows and be discussed around the globe. The news shows are carried by hundreds of local stations—called **affiliates**—that are associated with the national networks and may choose to carry their programming. **Wire services,** such as the Associated Press (AP), Reuters, and United Press International (UPI) distribute news around the globe. Most newspapers subscribe to at least one of these services, which not only produce their own news stories but also put on the wire major stories produced by other media outlets.

Several national news magazines, whose subscribers number in the millions, supplement the national newspapers, wire services, and broadcast networks. *Time, Newsweek,* and *U.S. News and World Report* bring the week's news into focus and headline one event or trend for special treatment. Other news magazines stress commentary from an ideological viewpoint, including the *Nation* (left-wing), *New Republic* (moderate-liberal), and the *Weekly Standard* (conservative). These last three publications have much smaller circulations, but because their readerships are composed of activists and opinion leaders, they have disproportionate influence. There are now some good, exclusively Web-based magazines, such as Salon.com and Slate.com. These Web sites direct their content to a hipper, generally younger audience by emphasizing cultural forces at work within day-to-day political events.

MEDIA CONSOLIDATION

Private ownership of the media in the United States has proven to be a mixed blessing. While private ownership assures media independence, something that cannot be said about state-controlled media in the former Soviet Union or in present-day China, it also brings market pressures to journalism that do not exist in state-run systems. The news media in the United States are multibillion-dollar, for-profit businesses that ultimately are driven by the bottom line. As with all free-market enterprises, the pressure in privately owned media is to increasingly consolidate media ownership, so as to reap the benefits that come from larger market shares and fewer large-scale competitors.

Unlike traditional industries, where the primary concern associated with consolidation is the manipulation of prices made possible by monopolies or near monopolies, the consolidation of the media poses a far greater potential risk. Should the news media become dominated by a few mega-corporations, the fear is that these groups could limit the flow of information and the free flow of ideas that form the very essence of a free society and that make democracy possible. While it is unlikely that profit-driven media chains intentionally manipulate the news in favor of specific political perspectives, it is possible that market forces, aimed at expanding market shares and pleasing advertisers, lead to the focus on sensational issues, news as entertainment, and avoidance of issues that could bore or alienate their audiences.

In 1923, over 500 cities had competing daily newspapers; by 2005, that number was down to a mere twelve. Most of the dailies are owned by large media conglomerates called chains, such as Gannett, McClatchy, and the Tribune Company. The top ten chains account for 54 percent of daily circulation, while only 280 of the nearly 1,460 daily newspapers are independently owned; thus, chains own over 80 percent of the daily newspapers.[15]

As it currently stands, none of the three original networks remain independent entities: General Electric owns NBC, Viacom owns CBS, and Walt Disney owns ABC. In the print media, Gannett, the parent company of *USA Today* and roughly 100 other newspapers in the United States, enjoys the nation's largest circulation rate. From the mid-1970s to the current period, the number of owners of full-power TV stations and daily newspapers has been cut by more than half. And in radio a single company, Clear Channel, which owns and operates more than 1,200 radio stations, accounts for roughly 18 percent of the total market. While government officials continue to grapple with the consequences of a market-driven media industry (see the section on Government Regulation of the Electronic Media below), the media outlets continue to exert considerable pressure on policy makers, demanding more, not less, media consolidation.

INCREASING USE OF EXPERTS

Most journalists know a little bit about many subjects but do not specialize in any one area and certainly do not possess enough knowledge to fill the hours of airtime made possible by cable's twenty-four-hour news cycle. Therefore, especially on cable stations, the news media like to employ expert consultants from a number of different disciplines ranging from medical ethics to political campaigning. These experts, also referred to as pundits, or the more derogatory term "talking heads," are hired to discuss the dominant issues of day. For example, during the proceedings of the 9/11 Commission, which investigated the September 11 terrorist attacks on the United States, and after the release of the commission's report, with its recommendations on how to improve security and intelligence gathering, one could not turn on the television or read a newspaper without encountering a stable full of government officials, former intelligence officers, and other experts giving their thoughts.

One 1992 study about how experts affect the views of Americans toward foreign policy says that "news from experts or research studies is estimated to have almost as great an impact [as anchorpersons, reporters in the field, or special commentators]." Such findings are both good and bad for Americans. On the one hand, the "strong effects by commentators and experts are compatible with a picture of a public that engages in collective deliberation and takes expertise seriously." On the other, "one might argue that the potency of media commentators and of ostensibly nonpartisan TV 'experts' is disturbing. Who elected them to shape our views of the world? Who says they are insightful or even unbiased?"[16]

The lesson is clear. Viewers and readers must rely on the networks and newspapers to choose experts wisely. Rarely is there much discussion of the backgrounds and the credentials of the individuals who are placed on the screen. There may be biases in the commentary of these experts, but it is the hope that a diversity of expert opinion is reflected on each subject throughout the media. Nonetheless, biases do break through, and many critics claim that various media outlets consciously represent unobjective points of view in their reportage, which will be discussed later in the chapter.

NARROWCASTING

In recent years, fierce competition to attract viewers and the availability of additional television channels made possible by cable and satellite television have led media outlets to move toward **narrowcasting**—targeting media programming at specific populations within society. Within the realm of cable news, the two ratings leaders, CNN and FOX News, have begun engaging in this form of niche journalism. The two stations divide audiences by ideology. FOX News emphasizes a conservative viewpoint and CNN increasingly stresses a more liberal perspective, although the FOX view is often more pronounced.[17] Table 15.3 indicates where Republicans, Democrats, and independents prefer to get their news about political campaigns.

narrowcasting
Targeting media programming at specific populations within society.

TABLE 15.3 MAIN SOURCE OF CAMPAIGN NEWS BY PARTY AFFILIATION

Percentage who regularly watch/listen	Total %	Rep. %	Dem. %	Ind. %
FOX News	25	35	21	22
CNN	22	19	28	22
MSNBC	11	10	12	12
CNBC	10	9	12	9
NBC Nightly News	17	15	18	19
CBS Evening News	16	13	19	17
ABC World News	16	15	20	12
NPR	16	13	19	17
NewsHour (PBS)	5	4	5	5
O'Reilly Factor	8	16	3	6
Rush Limbaugh	6	14	2	4
Larry King	5	5	6	3
Daily Show	3	3	3	3

Note: Figures add to more than 100% because respondents could list more than one source.

Source: Pew Research Center for the People and the Press, Early January 2004 Political Communications Study.

The nation has also seen the rise of Spanish-language news programs on stations such as Univision and Mundovision, as well as news programming geared toward African American viewers on cable's Black Entertainment Television (BET). In fact, well before cable television, African Americans benefited from a lengthy history of newspapers published specifically for the African American community (see chapter 6). And for Christian conservatives, Pat Robertson's Christian Broadcasting Network (CBN), with its flagship *700 Club*, has been narrowcasting news for over forty years.

While narrowcasting can help to promote the interests of parts of the population, especially racial and ethnic minorities who may ordinarily be left out of mainstream media coverage, it comes with a social cost. Narrowcasting increases the chance that group members will rely on news that is appealing to their preexisting views. By limiting one's exposure to a broad range of information or competing views, narrowcasting could result in the further polarization of public opinion. The polarization made possible by narrowcasting is particularly problematic when it comes to programs that are narrowcasted in a specific ideological direction.

PUBLIC DISCONTENT WITH THE MEDIA

In one survey, Americans found media election coverage biased, but those most likely to report a bias were on the ideological extremes: liberal Democrats reported a Republican bias and conservative Republicans reported a Democratic bias. While partisans are most likely to perceive ideological bias in the media, the news media have increasingly been the subject of broader public discontent and criticism. A 2005 survey by the Pew Research Center for the People and the Press, which has been studying public opinion of the media since 1984, found that the perceived believability of network TV news declined 23 percent since 1984. A majority of Americans perceive the media to be politically biased, believe the media stand in the way of solving society's problems, and think the media usually report inaccurately and are unwilling to admit mistakes.[18]

Despite the obvious displeasure that the majority of Americans express about political bias and sensationalism, credibility ratings for the national news media have remained relatively high. Broadcast news outlets tend to get higher believability ratings than print, with CNN, C-SPAN, and the major networks leading the way. But, the *Wall Street Journal* consistently ranks with CNN at the top of credibility polls. In 2002, anchors Tom Brokaw, Dan Rather, and Peter Jennings were rated as the most trusted journalists (around 80 percent positive ratings), while cable journalist Geraldo

Rivera ranked at the bottom (less than 9 percent believed all or most of what he says).[19] Following the death of Peter Jennings and the retirements of Dan Rather and Tom Brokaw, a new generation of lead anchors entered the national news arena. With the diversity of news outlets on television and the Internet, it seems less likely this new generation of network anchors will have as influential a hold on the public as their predecessors.

The terrorist attacks of September 11 caused a temporary shift in the public's attitude toward the media—Americans followed the news more closely and relied heavily on cable network coverage of the attacks and the war on terrorism. Among Americans polled, 69 percent believed that the news media defend America abroad, and the professionalism rating of the news media soared to 73 percent. During this period of extreme stress, however, Americans appeared simply to have united behind their institutions against an unknown threat. The bounce in media popularity was short lived. By July 2002, less than a year after the attacks, the public's perception and support of the media were essentially back at pre-9/11 levels. However, Americans continue to value the watchdog role that the media serve, with 59 percent believing that press scrutiny keeps political leaders from doing things they should not do. In addition, a substantial majority thinks that the media's influence is increasing, rather than decreasing.[20]

TECHNOLOGICAL INNOVATION

While technological innovation has been a constant throughout American history and has regularly transformed the way information travels, it is not always possible to recognize the full significance of technological changes while society is in the midst of technological upheaval, as we are today. The technological transformation that the world has experienced in the last decade, with the explosion of Web resources and electronic media outlets, is most likely to provide only a glimpse of things to come.

To date, we have seen how the new media can simultaneously work to consolidate the flow of news and to disperse news. The new media give the media giants, discussed above, the ability to project their news messages to local and regional news outlets around the world, which are often eager to reproduce or at least respond to the message of the dominant media. As technology continues to reduce the cost of producing news, making anyone with a personal computer, Internet connection, and something to say a potential news source, the value of reliable and high-quality information may continue to grow in importance, further adding to the influence of the existing media giants. Since time is limited and the available news options made possible by the new media are virtually unlimited, it is likely that information misers (information seekers who want the news but do not have time to waste) will continue to be drawn to reliable news outlets.

Ironically, the same technology that has given rise to media giants also has the ability to increase the diversity of available news (see Figure 15.2). **Blogs**, which have rapidly grown in popularity in recent years, are Web-based journal entries that provide an editorial and news outlet for citizens. They have become webs of information linking together people with common ideological or issue-specific interests. They also provide unprecedented access to events as they are unfolding. One of the more interesting phenomena to unfold in the blogosphere in recent years has been war blogs, where soldiers serving in Afghanistan and Iraq provide firsthand accounts of their war experiences.

In some instances, information made public on blogs has been picked up by mainstream news outlets, revealing how the new media provides unprecedented opportunities for the flow of information. Following FEMA's slow response to Hurricane Katrina during the summer of 2005, bloggers on sites like Daily KOS railed against FEMA director Michael Brown for his questionable credentials and his handling of disaster relief in New Orleans. Bloggers pointed out that Brown, who prior

blog
Web-based journal entries that provide an editorial and news outlet for citizens.

FIGURE 15.2 BLOGS VERSUS MAINSTREAM MEDIA INTERNET LINKS

The figure provides insight into a media outlet's influence on the Web, as measured by the number of Web sites that link to blogs and mainstream media sites. The figure reveals that while conventional media sources continue to dominate the world of electronic media, blogs also are well represented.

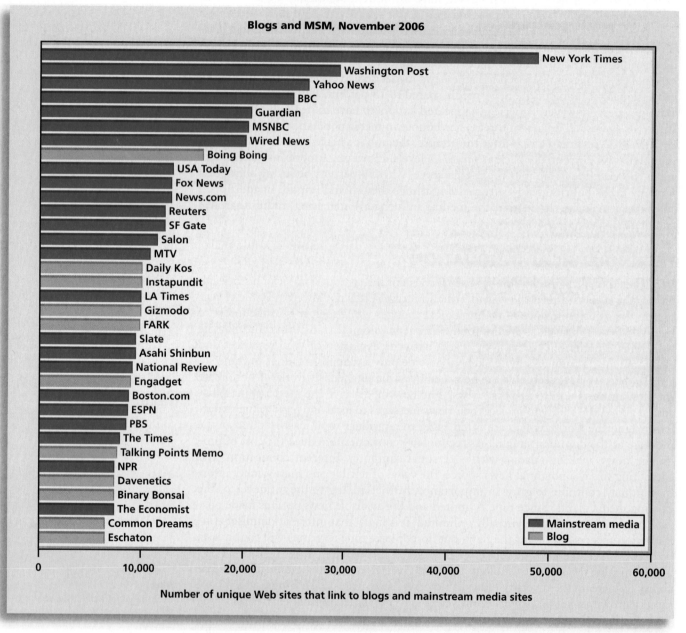

Blogs and MSM, November 2006

New York Times
Washington Post
Yahoo News
BBC
Guardian
MSNBC
Wired News
Boing Boing
USA Today
Fox News
News.com
Reuters
SF Gate
Salon
MTV
Daily Kos
Instapundit
LA Times
Gizmodo
FARK
Slate
Asahi Shinbun
National Review
Engadget
Boston.com
ESPN
PBS
The Times
Talking Points Memo
NPR
Davenetics
Binary Bonsai
The Economist
Common Dreams
Eschaton

Mainstream media
Blog

0   10,000   20,000   30,000   40,000   50,000   60,000

Number of unique Web sites that link to blogs and mainstream media sites

Source: Technorati, November 2006, http://www.technorati.com.

to heading FEMA had served as the head of the International Arabian Horse Association, lacked disaster relief experience, a fact that was later echoed in the mainstream press.

Many blogs are devoted to ideological rabble-rousing and rumormongering, while others provide reasoned discourse. The right-leaning Drudge Report (www.drudgereport.com) pioneered the spreading of newsworthy rumors during the second Clinton administration. Well-known right-leaning political Web sites include

Red State (www.redstate.org) and Power Line (www.powerlineblog.com). On the left are Daily KOS (www.dailykos.com), the Huffington Post (www.huffingtonpost.com), and AmericaBlog (www.americablog.blogspot.com).

While the future of the new media remains as unpredictable as the latest blog entry it is likely that the new media will continue to blur the lines between print and broadcast, consumer and producer, commentary and fact, and entertainment and news. The distinctions between the Internet and broadcast and cable news are likely to shrink as the technologies merge. Wireless handheld devices that allow users to send e-mail and text messages, make phone calls, browse the Internet, and download music and video clips are increasing in popularity. The growth of virtual social networks like MySpace and Facebook, as well as sites like YouTube that allow users to share videos, including campaign commercials and political commentary, are also affecting the ways in which Americans share and consume the news.

■ Markos Moulitsas, founder of the popular blog Daily KOS, is pictured here at the YearlyKos 2006 Convention in Las Vegas. YearlyKos brought pro-Democratic bloggers together with reporters and aspiring congressional and presidential candidates.

Rules Governing the Media

THE FIRST AMENDMENT to the U.S. Constitution, which prohibits Congress from abridging the freedom of the press, does not provide the media with unlimited print and broadcast freedom. A wide array of internal and external checks governs the behavior of the modern media.

JOURNALISTIC STANDARDS

The heaviest restrictions placed on reporters do not come from government regulations but from the industry's own professional norms and each journalist's level of integrity, as well as from the oversight provided by editors who are ultimately responsible for the accuracy of the news they produce. To help guide the ethical behavior of journalists, the Society of Professional Journalists publishes a detailed "Code of Ethics" for journalists that includes principles and standards governing issues like avoiding conflicts of interest, dealing ethically with sources, and verifying the information being reported.

As with any profession, journalism has its fair share of unscrupulous actors, people who disregard professional ethics in pursuit of self-interest. In the early 1980s, *Washington Post* reporter Janet Cook won a Pulitzer Prize for her gripping, but thoroughly fabricated story about an eight-year-old boy addicted to heroin. More recently, Stephen Glass of the *New Republic* was fired after it was discovered he had made a habit adding colorful quotes and edgy facts that were not grounded in reality. Glass went so far as to fake notes and sources, so as to deceive his own editors. Jayson Blair, another ethically challenged young reporter, was fired from the *New York Times* in 2003 after it was discovered that he, too, had made up quotes and interviews to pad his reporting.

While blatant examples of journalistic fraud are obvious and rare, journalists often grapple with less obvious ethical dilemmas. Whether the issue is how to make use of a confidential source, how to deal with "off the record" comments, or simply determining what information is newsworthy, journalists are in the business of balancing

VIDEO ROUNDTABLE
The Role of the Press

competing pressures. In their highly competitive world, the pressure to get the story right is often weighed against the pressure to get the story first, or at the very least to get the story finished before the next deadline. The twenty-four-hour news cycle, brought to life by cable news stations and nourished by the expansion of Web-based media, has only heightened the pressure to produce interesting copy in a timely manner.

In order to assure professional integrity, several major newspapers and magazines, including the *Washington Post* and the *Boston Globe,* have hired media critics, who assess how the media are performing their duties. Some nonprofits, such as the Center for Media and Public Affairs in Washington, D.C., conduct scientific studies of the news and entertainment media. Other groups, including the conservative watchdog group Accuracy in Media (AIM) and its liberal counterpart Fairness and Accuracy in Reporting (FAIR), critique news stories and attempt to set the record straight on important issues that they believe have received biased coverage. All of these organizations have a role in ensuring that the media provide fair and objective coverage of topics that are of importance to citizens.

GOVERNMENT REGULATION OF THE ELECTRONIC MEDIA

The U.S. government regulates the electronic component of the media. Unlike radio or television, the print media are exempt from most forms of government regulation, although even print media must not violate community standards for obscenity, for instance. There are two reasons for this unequal treatment. First, the airwaves used by the electronic media are considered public property and are leased by the federal government to private broadcasters. Second, those airwaves are in limited supply; without some regulation, the nation's many radio and television stations would interfere with one another's frequency signals. It was not, in fact, the federal government but rather private broadcasters, frustrated by the numerous instances in which signal jamming occurred, that initiated the call for government regulation in the early days of the electronic media.

In 1996, Congress passed the sweeping Telecommunications Act, deregulating whole segments of the electronic media. The Telecommunications Act sought to provide an optimal balance of competing corporate interests, technological innovations, and consumer needs. It appeared to offer limitless opportunities for entrepreneurial companies to provide enhanced services to consumers. The result of this deregulation was the sudden merger of previously distinct kinds of media in order to create a more "multimedia" approach to communicating information and entertainment. This gave us multimedia corporations such as Viacom, Time Warner and Comcast.

VIDEO DEBATE

Censorship and the FCC

In June 2003, the Federal Communications Commission (FCC) attempted to push through a series of reforms that would further deregulate the media by enabling media corporations to own more of different kinds of media in a given media market. For instance, the FCC overturned a 1975 regulation that had banned newspapers and broadcast companies from cross-ownership. They also overturned a 1970 rule that similarly prevented radio and television stations from cross-ownership. These bans were replaced with a formula based on the number of outlets in the market. Also, the FCC granted corporations, under certain conditions, the ability to own two or even three television stations in a given market, effectively allowing corporations to own all or nearly all of the television content in those markets.[21] Finally, the FCC increased the limit to the total national audience a corporation could reach from 35 percent to 45 percent. Since total national audience is measured by how many stations a corporation owns, this increase would allow corporations to own more television stations. All this deregulation made it possible for one media corporation to control large chunks of the radio, print, and television programming available in a community.

Both Republicans and Democrats in Congress opposed the FCC changes, arguing that the country needs more and not less media diversification, given the increasing media outlet consolidation. Furthermore, many ideologically opposing groups also argued against media consolidation: conservative religious groups believe that large media corporations purvey immoral content, and liberal groups believe that less diversification kills community-based media. Finally, there was a general public outcry, with legislators receiving angry letters and e-mails demanding Congress stop the FCC.[22] By July 2003, a huge bipartisan majority in the House voted 400–21 to block the FCC policy changes. By December, Congress had passed an appropriations bill that raised the 35 percent cap on a national audience to 39 percent, a compromise that allowed the largest corporations to retain their current share—the largest corporation, Viacom, had 38.9 percent of the national audience—but prohibited any further expansion.[23]

CONTENT REGULATION

The government also subjects the electronic media to substantial **content regulation** that, again, does not apply to the print media. Charged with ensuring that the airwaves "serve the public interest, convenience, and necessity," the FCC has attempted to promote equity in broadcasting. For example, the **equal time rule** requires that broadcast stations sell air time equally to all candidates in a political campaign if they choose to sell it to any, which they are under no obligation to do. An exception to this rule is a political debate: stations may exclude from this event less well-known and minor-party candidates.

Until 2000, FCC rules required broadcasters to give candidates the opportunity to respond to personal attacks and to political endorsements by the station. In October 2000, however, a federal court of appeals found these rules, long criticized by broadcasters as having a chilling effect on free speech, to be unconstitutional when the FCC was unable to justify these regulations to the court's satisfaction.[24]

Perhaps the most controversial FCC regulation was the **fairness doctrine.** Implemented in 1949 and in effect until 1985, the fairness doctrine required broadcasters to be "fair" in their coverage of news events—that is, they had to cover the events adequately and present contrasting views on important public issues. Many broadcasters disliked this rule, claiming that fairness is simply too difficult to define and that the rule abridged their First Amendment freedoms. They also argued that it ultimately forced broadcasters to decrease coverage of controversial issues out of fear of a deluge of requests for air time from interest groups involved in each matter.

The 1969 U.S. Supreme Court case of *Red Lion Broadcasting Co., Inc.* v. *FCC* confirmed the power and legitimacy of the fairness doctrine. In that case, a station in Pennsylvania, licensed by Red Lion Co., had aired a "Christian Crusade" program wherein an author, Fred J. Cook, was attacked. When Cook requested time to reply in keeping with the fairness doctrine, the station refused. Upon appeal to the FCC, the commission declared that there was a personal attack and the station had failed to meet its obligation. The station appealed and eventually the case wound its way to the Supreme Court. The court ruled for the FCC, giving sanction to the fairness doctrine.[25]

In a hotly debated 1985 decision, the FCC, without congressional consent, abolished the fairness doctrine (and subsequently won a 1986 appeal), arguing that the growth of the electronic media in the United States during the preceding forty years had created enough diversity among the stations to render unnecessary the ordering of diversity within them. Congress passed a bill to write the fairness doctrine into law, but President Reagan vetoed it, citing his First Amendment concerns about government regulation of the news media. The abolition of the fairness doctrine has by no means ended debate over its merit, however. Proponents, still trying to reinstate the doctrine, argue that its elimination results in a reduction of quality programming on public issues. Opponents of the fairness doctrine, on the other hand, continue to call for decreased regulation, arguing that the broadcast media should be as free as the print media.

content regulation
Government attempts to regulate the substance of the mass media.

equal time rule
The rule that requires broadcast stations to sell air time equally to all candidates in a political campaign if they choose to sell it to any.

fairness doctrine
Rule in effect from 1949 to 1985 requiring broadcasters to cover events adequately and to present contrasting views on important public issues.

The most recent controversy over regulation of media content has involved the communications industry and Internet service providers. Common carriers as defined by the Communications Act of 1934, such as telephone companies, are required to be neutral in the content they carry over their networks and cannot limit or censor individuals or organizations they may disagree with. Internet service providers (ISPs) are not subject to the common carrier definition and therefore may legally block transmission through their networks of content they find objectionable. Many free speech advocates are lobbying Congress for "net neutrality," which would define ISPs as common carriers and place the same obligations of content neutrality that telephone companies must adhere to. These advocates worry especially about the ability of some ISPs to block or hinder the free and open communication of political ideas.[26]

EFFORTS TO REGULATE MEDIA PRACTICES

In the United States, only government officials can be prosecuted for divulging classified information; no such law applies to journalists. Nor can the government, except under extremely rare and confined circumstances, impose prior restraints on the press—that is, the government cannot censor the press. This principle was clearly established in *New York Times Co.* v. *U.S.* (1971).[27] In this case, the Supreme Court ruled that the government could not prevent publication by the *New York Times* of the Pentagon Papers, classified government documents about the Vietnam War that had been stolen, photocopied, and sent to the *Times* and the *Washington Post* by Daniel Ellsberg, a government employee. "Only a free and unrestrained press can effectively expose deception in the government," Justice Hugo Black wrote in a concurring opinion for the Court. "To find that the President has 'inherent power' to halt the publication of news by resort to the courts would wipe out the First Amendment."

VIDEO DEBATE

Self Censorship and the News

Similar concerns arose in the United States during the 1991 Persian Gulf War. Reporters were upset that the military was not forthcoming about events on and off the battlefield, while some Pentagon officials and many persons in the general public accused the press of telling the enemy too much in their dispatches. The U.S. government attempted to isolate offending reporters by keeping them away from the battlefield. This maneuver was highly controversial and very unpopular with news correspondents because it directly interfered with their job of reporting the news. Defenders of efforts to curb media coverage in war zones cite safety and intelligence concerns. Critics of the military's public affairs strategies during times of war resent its emphasis on controlling information and view it as an attempt to manipulate public support. Critics argue that civilian and military officials alike have a keen awareness of and desire to avoid "Vietnam syndrome," where widespread resistance to the war, some have argued, grew out of the media's unfettered access to the front lines and broadcasts of graphic footage on television.

The George W. Bush administration provided an interesting compromise to this dilemma when it gave journalists the opportunity to be embedded with various parts of the military and report about the experiences of each unit when U.S.-led forces invaded Iraq in 2003. Organizations such as the Project for Excellence in Journalism found that embedded journalists typically provided only anecdotal stories, lacked the overall context of the war, and stressed American successes without much coverage of Iraqi civilian casualties. While conceding these limitations, some scholars maintain that an embedded journalist is better than no journalist at all, especially since journalists of foreign news organizations, like al-Jazeera, will cover the events from different perspectives.[28]

Not all Western democracies provide their media the same level of freedom. In Great Britain, the state-run British Broadcasting Company (BBC) and the privately

American Values/American Voices

HOW MUCH FREEDOM SHOULD THE PRESS BE ALLOWED?

According to constitutional scholar Alexander Bickel in his analysis of the First Amendment's protections for the freedom of the press, "not everything is fit to print."[a] Bickel cautions against the press printing information that is inaccurate, indecent, or potentially dangerous to the national interest. What is the line to be drawn between national security and the freedom of the press? In 1943, Robert McCormick of the *Chicago Tribune*, a staunch political enemy of President Franklin Roosevelt, printed that the United States had broken secret Japanese military codes, thus potentially revealing to the enemy that the United States could read their secret communications. Under the Espionage Act of 1917, it was possible to prosecute journalists who endangered the defense of the country. When the Roosevelt administration decided against prosecuting the case so as not to draw more attention to the story, they helped to set a precedent against prosecuting journalists. In a democracy with strong protections for free speech and freedom of the press, there is an uneasy balance between the public's right to know and the government's interest in defending the country.

In 2006, the *New York Times* revealed that the Bush administration, in cooperation with a Belgian banking cooperative know as Swift, was secretly monitoring financial transactions. The *Times* had decided to print the article despite protests from the Bush administration. The administration reacted angrily to the story, stating that the *Times* had negatively affected the government's ability to fight terrorism. *Times* publisher Arthur Sulzberger Jr. defended the paper's decision to print the story based on the public's right to

know about the secret monitoring of financial transactions by the administration. *Times* executive editor Bill Keller and the editor of the *Los Angeles Times,* Dean Baquet, which had also printed the story, defended their decision to print the story in an editorial that ran in both papers, claiming they had the best interests of the country in mind and were doing their duty as journalists to let the public decide.[b] Quoting Justice Hugo Black's defense of the press's First Amendment rights in *New York Times Co.* v. *U.S.* (1971), they wrote "The government's power to censor the press was abolished so that the press would remain forever free to censure the government. The press was protected so that it could bare the secrets of the government and inform the people."

The *Wall Street Journal* had also carried the story of the administration's monitoring. However, the *Journal's* editorial board and other more right-leaning newspapers charged that the *Times* printed the story because of a political agenda against the Bush administration and its war on terrorism.[c] Meanwhile, the Bush administration wanted an investigation into who in the government had disclosed the information to the press. While there are no prosecutions pending in this case, the administration's reaction underlines the delicate balance that the press must consider as they make their daily decisions about what news is fit to print.

---

[a]Alexander Bickel, *The Morality of Consent* (New Haven, CT: Yale University Press, 1975).

[b]Dean Baquet and Bill Keller, "When Do We Publish a Secret?" *New York Times* (July 1, 2006). [c]"Fit and Unfit to Print," *Wall Street Journa,* (June 30, 2006).

---

owned media are subject to unusually strict regulation on the publication of governmental secrets. For example, the sweeping Official Secrets Act of 1911 makes it a criminal offense for a Briton to publish any facts, material, or news collected in that person's capacity as a public minister or civil servant. The act was invoked when the British government banned the publication of *Spy Catcher,* a 1987 novel written by Peter Wright, a former British intelligence officer, who undoubtedly collected much of the book's information while on the job. On the other hand, Great Britain applies a far more liberal standard of indecency to its broadcasters, who exercise considerably more freedom than Americans with regard to explicit content. To assist the media in determining what is and is not publishable, Great Britain provides a system called D-notice, which allows journalists to submit questionable material to a review committee before its publication. (See American Values/American Voices: How Much Freedom Should the Press Be Allowed?)

Whatever one's specific quarrel with the American news media, most Americans would probably prefer that the media tell them too much rather than not enough. Totalitarian and authoritarian societies have a tame journalism, after all, so media excesses may be the price of popular sovereignty.

How the Media Cover Politics

THE NEWS MEDIA focus an extraordinary amount of attention on our politicians and the day-to-day operations of our government. Since 1983, the number of print (newspaper and magazine) reporters accredited at the U.S. Capitol jumped from 2,300 to more than 4,100.[29] On the campaign trail, a similar phenomenon has occurred. In the 1960s, a presidential candidate in the primaries would attract a press entourage of at most a few dozen reporters, but today a hundred or more journalists can be seen tagging along with a front-runner. When a victorious candidate reaches the White House, he doesn't simply see the media for big events; in 2004, sixty-three journalists were credentialed as daily White House correspondents.[30] Consequently, a politician's every public utterance is reported and intensively scrutinized and interpreted in the media.

HOW THE PRESS AND PUBLIC FIGURES INTERACT

The type of communication between elected officials or public figures and the media may take different forms. A **press release** is a written document offering an official comment or position on an issue or news event; it is usually printed on paper and handed directly to reporters, or increasingly, released by e-mail or fax. A **press briefing** is a relatively restricted live engagement with the press, with the range of questions limited to one or two specific topics. In a press briefing, a press secretary or aide represents the elected official or public figure, who does not appear in person. In a full-blown **press conference,** an elected official appears in person to talk with the press at great length about an unrestricted range of topics. Press conferences provide a field on which reporters struggle to get the answers they need and public figures attempt to retain control of their message and spin the news and issues in ways favorable to them.

On some occasions, candidates and their aides will go on background to give trusted newspersons juicy morsels of negative information about rivals. **On background**—meaning that none of the news can be attributed to the source—is one of several journalistic devices used to elicit information that might otherwise never come to light. **Deep background** is another such device; whereas background talks can be attributed to unnamed senior officials, deep background news must be completely unsourced, with the reporter giving the reader no hint about the origin of the information. A journalist may also obtain information **off the record,** which means that nothing the official says may be printed. (If a reporter can obtain the same information elsewhere, however, he or she is free to publish it.) By contrast, if a session is **on the record,** as in a formal press conference, every word an official utters can be printed—and used against that official. It is no wonder that office holders often prefer the other alternatives!

Clearly, these rules regarding source information are necessary for reporters to do their basic job—informing the public. Ironically, the same rules keep the press from fully informing their readers and viewers. Every public official knows that journalists are pledged to protect the confidentiality of their sources, and therefore the rules can sometimes be used to an official's own benefit. In 2005, *New York Times* reporter Judith Miller was jailed for eighty-five days when she refused to reveal her source for a leak that exposed the identity of an undercover CIA operative. (See Politics Now: When the Media Become the Story.)

Politicians and media also interact in a variety of other ways. Politicians hire campaign consultants who use focus groups and polling in an attempt to gauge how to present the candidate to the media and to the public. Additionally, politicians can attempt to bypass the national news media through paid advertising and by appearing on talk shows and local news programs. (Some of these and other techniques for

press release
A document offering an official comment or position.

press briefing
A relatively restricted session between a press secretary or aide and the press.

press conference
An unrestricted session between an elected official and the press.

on background
Information provided to a journalist that will not be attributed to a named source.

deep background
Information provided to a journalist that will not be attributed to any source.

off the record
Information provided to a journalist that will not be released to the public.

on the record
Information provided to a journalist that can be released and attributed by name to the source.

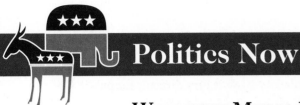

Politics Now

WHEN THE MEDIA BECOME THE STORY

The Watergate scandal of the Nixon administration had a profound impact on press conduct. Watergate began a chain reaction that today allows for intense media scrutiny of public officials' private lives and shifted the orientation of journalism away from mere description (providing an account of happenings) and toward prescription—helping to set the campaign's (and society's) agenda by focusing attention on the candidates' shortcomings as well as on certain social problems. After Watergate, people increasingly saw the press as a powerful agent entrusted with keeping government accountable to the people and exposing political corruption.

For years, stories about George W. Bush's service in the National Guard during the Vietnam War had percolated in the political system, occasionally becoming front-page news but generally lying below the surface. The issue of Bush's military record resurfaced in 2004 when Bill Burkett, a Texan who had served in the National Guard at about the same time as Bush and knew some of the key players, turned over documents to CBS that apparently proved Bush had violated the terms of his National Guard agreement relating to the scheduling of a physical examination and reporting for drill.

In a hastily prepared piece for *60 Minutes* produced by Mary Mapes that was broadcast during a critical juncture in the general campaign, Dan Rather reported, "Mr. Bush may have received preferential treatment in the Guard after not fulfilling his commitments." Within hours of the broadcast, conservative bloggers had dissected the documents and were claiming that they were produced on computers unavailable in the early 1970s. Initially, Rather, Mapes, and CBS held firm, saying, "you couldn't have a starker contrast between the multiple layers of check and balances [at *60 Minutes*] and a guy sitting in his living room in his pajamas writing." But, when media reporters from major outlets such as the *Washington Post* and *USA Today* confirmed the bloggers' allegations, CBS launched a major investigation. The investigation report indicated that CBS had been negligent and that Rather and Mapes had not fulfilled their journalistic obligations in verifying the authenticity of the documents provided by Burkett. Mapes and several CBS employees lost their jobs as a result, and Rather announced his retirement even before the report was released.

Sometimes a journalist's commitment to not revealing sources can make national news. In 2003, Robert Novak wrote a newspaper column that identified Valerie Plame as a CIA operative, based on information from anonymous senior administration sources. Plame's husband, former ambassador Joseph Wilson, had criticized the Bush administration's claim that Iraq had attempted to purchase uranium ore from Niger. Many observers assumed that the administration revealed Plame's identity in retaliation for her husband's criticisms. *New York Times* reporter Judith Miller was thought to know who in the administration leaked Plame's identity, but she refused to testify before a federal grand jury. Eventually, Lewis "Scooter" Libby, chief of staff to Vice President Dick Cheney, gave Miller permission to break confidentiality and reveal that he was her source. Miller, after a long and unpleasant dispute over her handling of the affair with her editors, chose to leave the *Times* shortly after her testimony to the grand jury, stating, "I have chosen to resign because over the last few months, I have become the news, something a *New York Times* reporter never wants to be."[a] Libby was indicted in October 2005 for misleading the investigators, and he resigned his post as the vice president's chief of staff.

[a] Katherine Seelye, "Times Reporter Agrees to Leave the Paper," *New York Times* (November 10, 2005).

dealing with the media during a campaign are discussed in greater detail in chapter 14.) Politicians also use the media to attempt to retain a high level of name recognition and to build support for their ideological and policy ideas.

In the past, a reporter would think twice about filing a story critical of a politician's character, and the editors probably would have killed the story had the reporter been foolish enough to do so. The reason? Fear of a libel suit. (Recall from chapter 5 that libel is written defamation of character that unjustly injures a person's reputation.) The first question editors would ask about even an ambiguous or suggestive phrase about a public official was, "If we're sued, can you prove beyond a doubt what you've written?"

Such inhibitions were ostensibly lifted in 1964, when the Supreme Court ruled in *New York Times Co. v. Sullivan* that simply publishing a defamatory falsehood is not enough to justify a libel judgment.[31] Henceforth, a public official would have to prove "actual malice," a requirement extended three years later to all public figures, such as Hollywood stars and prominent athletes.[32] As discussed in chapter 5, the Supreme

New York Times Co. v. Sullivan (1964)
The Supreme Court concluded that "actual malice" must be proved to support a finding of libel against a public figure.

Court declared that the First Amendment requires elected officials and candidates to prove that the publisher either believed the challenged statement was false or at least entertained serious doubts about its truth and acted recklessly in publishing it in the face of those doubts. The actual malice rule has made it very difficult for public figures to win libel cases.

COVERING THE PRESIDENCY

The three branches of the U.S. government—the executive, the legislative, and the judicial—are roughly equal in power and authority. But, in the world of media coverage, the president is first among equals. All television cables lead to the White House, and a president can address the nation on all networks almost at will. On television, Congress and the courts appear to be divided and confused institutions—different segments contradicting others—whereas the commander in chief is in clear focus as chief of state and head of government. The situation is scarcely different in other democracies. In Great Britain, for example, all media eyes are on No. 10 Downing Street, the office and residence of the prime minister.

Since Franklin D. Roosevelt's time, chief executives have used the office and presidential press conference as a bully pulpit to shape public opinion and explain their actions (see Figure 15.3). The presence of the press in the White House enables a president to appear even on very short notice and to televise live, interrupting regular programming. The White House's press briefing room is a familiar sight on the evening news, not just because presidents use it fairly often, but also because the presidential press secretary has almost daily question and answer sessions there.

The post of press secretary to the president has existed only since Herbert Hoover's administration (1929–1933), and the individual holding it is the president's main disseminator of information to the press. For this vital position, some presidents choose close aides with whom they have worked previously and who are familiar with

FIGURE 15.3 PRESIDENTIAL PRESS CONFERENCES
Modern presidents have been holding increasingly fewer press conferences and rely more on their press secretaries and Cabinet officers to brief the media.

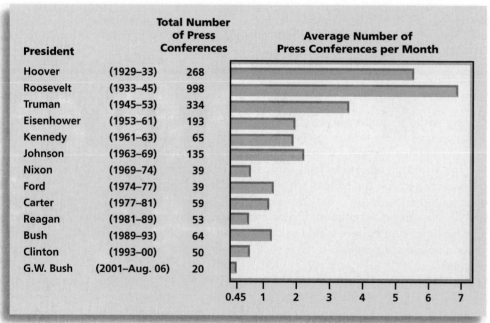

Source: White House press office.

their thinking. Press secretaries must be very adept at dealing with the press; some worked as journalists prior to becoming a press secretary, and many go on to press jobs after their stint in the White House. For example, Lyndon B. Johnson's press secretary, Bill Moyers, now hosts many PBS documentaries. The first female press secretary, Dee Dee Myers, served under Bill Clinton and used her experience to launch a career in political punditry. George W. Bush's first press secretary, Ari Fleischer, resigned in 2003 after twenty-one years working in politics to establish his own corporate communications firm. When Fleischer's successor, Scott McClellan, resigned in May 2006, in an unusual move the Bush administration hired political journalist and FOX News commentator Tony Snow to take his place.

Photo courtesy: Jim Young/Reuters/Landov

■ George W. Bush chose former FOX News commentator Tony Snow as his third press secretary. Here, Snow fileds questions in the White House press briefing room, which opened in 1970 on the former site of President Franklin D. Roosevelt's swimming pool. The briefing room was closed for extensive renovations in August of 2006. Given the traditionally testy relationship between presidential administrations and members of the press, some journalists reacted with suspicion to the renovation, worrying that they would be banned from the West wing permanently.

In deciding what *does* become news, presidents and the press engage in a continuous "debate about newsworthiness." This debate occurs not only between the White House and the news media but within the two entities as well, and it involves "what gets covered, who gets asked about a story, and how and for how long the story is covered."[33]

While the president receives the vast majority of the press's attention, much of this focus is unfavorable. Dwight Eisenhower once opened up a press conference by inviting the press to "nail him to the cross" as they usually did, and this approach suggests the way most presidents approach their formal encounters with the press. A study in the early 1990s found coverage of George Bush's handling of important national problems was almost solely negative.[34] Analysis of the coverage of Bill Clinton's turbulent presidency found a frenzy of negative media coverage immediately following the Lewinsky scandal, followed by a longer period of more even-handed coverage.[35]

The media have faced a more difficult challenge in covering the administration of George W. Bush, a president who prides himself on the tight-lipped, no leaks nature of his White House. No member of his staff appears on television or in print without prior permission, while Bush himself held a record-low number of thirteen formal press conferences during his first term. The Bush communications team continues to keep the president's direct contact with the press to a minimum, with his press conference the day after the 2006 midterm elections counting as only the eleventh of his second term. Compared to his father, who held sixty-four during his four years as president, Bush clearly has tried to control his image by controlling how much the press directly encounters him and by speaking at highly staged media events, quite often at military settings, where he delivers a scripted message and presents an interesting visual, but answers no questions from the media.[36]

COVERING CONGRESS

With 535 voting members representing distinct geographic areas, covering Congress poses a difficult challenge for the media. Nevertheless, the congressional press corps has more than 3,000 members.[37] Most news organizations solve the size and decentralization problems inherent in covering news developments in the legislative branch by concentrating coverage on three groups of individuals. First, the leaders of both parties in both houses receive the lion's share of attention be-

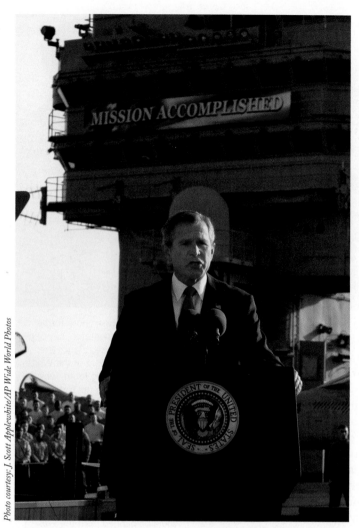

Photo courtesy: J. Scott Applewhite/AP Wide World Photos

■ Staged photo opportunities are a mainstay of presidential media events. On May 1, 2003, President George W. Bush heralded the end of the "hot war" in Iraq by landing on the deck of the aircraft carrier *Abraham Lincoln* in a fighter jet and giving a speech to military personnel on board with a giant banner headlined "Mission Accomplished" in the background, as the photo shows. Even though Bush was careful to note that the work in Iraq was not finished, the picture overwhelmed the president's words. Since then, a tough guerrilla war has taken the lives of thousands of U.S. military personnel and tens of thousands of Iraqis. At the time this photo was taken, almost every observer saw the aircraft-carrier speech as a brilliant stroke that would nearly guarantee Bush's reelection in 2004. Ironically, the Mission Accomplished image came to symbolize the administration's unrealistic expectations and mismanagement of the Iraq invasion and occupation.

cause only they can speak for a majority of their party's members. Usually the majority and minority leaders in each house and the Speaker of the House are the preferred spokespersons, but the whips also receive a substantial share of air time and column inches. Second, key committee chairs command center stage when subjects in their domain are newsworthy. Heads of the most prominent committees (such as Ways and Means or Armed Services) are guaranteed frequent coverage, but even the chairs and members of minor committees or subcommittees can achieve fame when the time and issue are right. Third, local newspapers and broadcast stations normally devote some resources to covering their local senators and representatives, even when these legislators are junior and relatively lacking in influence. Most office holders, in turn, are mainly concerned with meeting the needs of their local media contingents, since these reporters are the ones who directly and regularly reach the voters in their home constituencies.

As with coverage of the president, media coverage of Congress is disproportionately negative. Much media attention given to the House and Senate focuses on conflict among members. Some political scientists believe that such reporting is at least partially responsible for the public's negative perceptions of Congress.[38]

Coverage of Congress has been greatly expanded through cable channels C-SPAN and C-SPAN2, which provide coverage of House and Senate sessions as well as many committee hearings. For the first time, Americans can watch their representatives in action without editing or interpretation.

One other kind of congressional news coverage is worth noting: investigative committee hearings. Occasionally, a sensational scandal leads to televised congressional committee hearings that transfix and electrify the nation. In the early 1950s, Senator Joseph R. McCarthy (R–WI) held a series of hearings to root out what he claimed were Communists in the Department of State and other U.S. government agencies, as well as in Hollywood's film industry. The senator's investigations, which involved wild charges made without proof and the smearing and labeling of opponents as Communists, gave rise to the term *McCarthyism*. In 2002, Congress investigated several high-profile corporate scandals, including the collapse of prominent companies such as Enron and WorldCom. More recently investigations addressed the abuse of Iraqi prisoners in Abu Ghraib, the use of steroids in major league baseball, the government's ineffective response to Hurricane Katrina, and immigration issues. With the election of a Democratic Congress, the number and intensity of hearings is expected to rise.

COVERING THE SUPREME COURT

While the President and Congress interact with the media on a regular basis, the Supreme Court remains a virtual media vacuum. Despite persistent efforts by C-

SPAN and other media outlets to gain access, television cameras have never been permitted to record Supreme Court proceedings. Citing the need to protect the public's perception of the Supreme Court as a nonpolitical and autonomous entity, the justices have given little evidence to suggest that they are eager to reverse their broadcast media ban. Instead, at the end of each term, they release written transcripts and audio recordings of the proceedings, which lack both the visuals and timeliness that could make them fodder for the modern press. Since 2000, however, reporters have been granted on a case-by-case basis the ability to make use of same-day audio recordings. The first instance of this occurred during *Bush* v. *Gore* (2000), which decided the presidential vote in Florida. Since this case, reporters have been granted limited audio access to the Court.

While print and broadcast reporters are granted access to the Court, even if their cameras are not, coverage of the Court remains severely limited when compared with coverage of the executive and legislative branches. There are less than a dozen full-time reporters covering the Supreme Court, and the amount of space dedicated to Court-related stories has continued to shrink. Stories involving complex legal issues are not as easy to sell as graphic-intense stories related to the Congress or president. [39] Not surprisingly, Americans typically know less about the Court than any other branch of government and, as discussed in chapter 10, can rarely identify the name of the chief justice (John G. Roberts Jr.), never mind the other eight justices.

The Media's Influence on the Public

THERE ARE MANY important questions concerning the media's influence on the public. For instance, how much influence do the media actually have on public opinion? Do the media have a discernable ideological bent or bias, as some people suggest? Are people able to resist information that is inconsistent with their preexisting beliefs?

MEDIA EFFECTS

**Use of the Media
By the American
Public**

In most cases, the press has surprisingly little effect on what people believe. To put it bluntly, people tend to see what they want to see; that is, human beings will focus on parts of a report that reinforce their own attitudes and ignore parts that challenge their core beliefs. Most people also selectively tune out or ignore reports that contradict their preferences in politics and other fields. Therefore, a committed Democrat will remember certain portions of a televised news program about a current campaign—primarily the parts that reinforce his or her own choice—and an equally committed Republican will recall very different sections of the report or remember the material in a way that supports the GOP position. In other words, most voters are not empty vessels into which the media can pour their own beliefs. Indeed, many studies from the 1940s and 1950s, an era when partisan identification was very strong, suggested that the media had no influence at all on public opinion. During the last forty years, however, the decline in political identification[40] has opened the door to greater media influence. Although research had indicated for some time that the media have a minimal effect on changing public opinion, more recent studies show that the media have a definite effect on shaping public opinion, especially during elections.[41]

Some political scientists argue that the content of network television news accounts for a large portion of the volatility and change in policy preferences of Americans, when measured over relatively short periods of time.[42] These changes are called **media effects.** Let's examine how these media-influenced changes might occur.

media effects
The influence of news sources on public opinion.

First, reporting can sway people who are uncommitted and have no strong opinion in the first place. So, for example, the media have a greater influence on political independents than on strong partisans.[43] That said, the sort of politically unmotivated individual who is subject to media effects may not vote in a given election, in which case the media influence may be of little particular consequence.

Second, it is likely that the media have a greater impact on topics far removed from the lives and experiences of readers and viewers. News reports can probably shape public opinion about events in foreign countries fairly easily. Yet, what the media say about domestic issues such as rising prices, neighborhood crime, or child rearing may have relatively little effect, because most citizens have personal experience of and well-formed ideas about these subjects.

agenda setting
The constant process of forming the list of issued to be addressed by government.

Third, in a process often referred to as **agenda setting,** news organizations can help tell us what to think about, even if they cannot determine what we think. Indeed, the press often sets the agenda for a campaign or for government action by focusing on certain issues or concerns. For example, nationwide in 2003, the media reported the abduction and recovery of fifteen-year-old Utah resident Elizabeth Smart. Many in the press and in the Utah government attributed the success in finding Smart to the use of the state's Amber alert—a system in which law enforcement uses the media to notify the public of a kidnapping. Soon after, there were calls for a national Amber alert system, which Congress quickly passed as the Protection Act of 2003 and the president just as quickly signed. Before the Smart story, child kidnapping had not been a national issue. It was only after sustained media coverage put Smart and the Amber alert system in headlines that the problem received national attention.

framing
The process by which a news organization defines a political issue and consequently affects opinion about the issue

Fourth, the media influence public opinion through a subtle process referred to as **framing**—the process by which a news organization defines a political issue and consequently affects opinion about the issue. For example, an experiment conducted by one group of scholars found that if a news story about a Ku Klux Klan rally was framed as a civil rights story (i.e., a story about the right of a group to express their ideas, even if they are unpopular ideas), viewers were generally tolerant of the rally. However, the same story, if framed as a law and order issue (i.e., a story about how the actions of one group disrupted a community and threatened public safety), decreased public tolerance for the rally. In either case, the media exert subtle influence over the way people respond to the same information.[44]

Fifth, the media have the power to indirectly influence the way the public views politicians and government. For example, voters' choices in presidential elections are often related to their assessments of the economy. In general, a healthy economy motivates voters to reelect the incumbent president, whereas a weak economy motivates voters to choose the challenger. Hence, if the media paint a consistently dismal picture of the economy, that picture may well hurt the incumbent president seeking reelection. In fact, one study convincingly shows that the media's relentlessly negative coverage of the economy in 1992 shaped voters' retrospective assessments of the economy, which in turn helped lead to George Bush's defeat in the 1992 presidential election.[45]

MEDIA BIAS

Are the Media
Biased?

Whenever the media break an unfavorable story about a politician, the politician usually counters with a cry of "biased reporting"—a claim that the press has told an untruth, has told only part of the truth, or has reported facts out of the complete context of the event. (See Join the Debate: Objective Versus Bias Reporting.) Some research suggests that candidates may charge the media with bias as a strategy for dealing with the press, and that bias claims are part of the dynamic between elected officials and reporters. If a candidate can plausibly and loudly decry bias in the media as the source of his negative coverage, for example, reporters might temper future negative stories or give the candidate favorable coverage to mitigate the calls of bias.[46]

Are journalists biased? The answer is simple and unavoidable. Of course they are. Journalists, like all human beings, have values, preferences, and attitudes galore—some conscious, others subconscious, but all reflected at one time or another in the subjects selected for coverage or the portrayal of events or content communicated. (See Analyzing Visuals: Partisan Bias in Media Reporting?) Given that the press is biased, in what ways is it biased and when and how are the biases shown?

For much of the 1980s and 1990s, the argument was that the media had a liberal bias because of the sheer number of journalists who leaned to the left. Studies in the 1980s showed that professional journalists were drawn heavily from the ranks of highly educated social and political liberals.[47] To this day, journalists are substantially Democratic in party affiliation and voting habits, progressive and anti-establishment in political orientation, and to the left of the general public on many economic, foreign policy, and social issues (such as abortion, affirmative action, gay rights, and gun control). Indeed, a 2004 survey revealed that, whereas 33 percent of the general public describes themselves as being ideologically conservative, only 7 percent of those in the media would do the same.[48] In addition, dozens of the most influential reporters and executives entered (or reentered) journalism after stints of partisan participation in campaigns or government. Many of these people worked for Democrats. Since 1994, however, an increasing number have worked for Republicans.

Some scholars argue that corporate interests play a significant role in what journalists report and counter the liberal leanings of reporters. During legislative debate over the Telecommunications Act of 1996, the passage of which would benefit media corporations with television holdings, scholars found that articles appearing in newspapers owned by media corporations with television interests typically failed to report the possible negative impact resulting from passage of the act. These scholars concluded that "very different pictures of the likely effects of this legislation were being painted by the different newspapers examined, pictures that served to further the interests of the newspapers' corporate owners rather than the interests of their readers in a fair and complete coverage of an important policy issue."[49]

Many media critics have focused on the national news media's lack of skepticism about the Bush administration's arguments for waging a war in Iraq during the run-up to that conflict in 2002–2003. As we now know, those in the administration who believed the Iraqis would acquiesce to a U.S. occupation were dead wrong, as were those who believed that Saddam Hussein possessed weapons of mass destruction. It is now clear that the *New York Times,* the *Washington Post,* the networks, and other news outlets did not question the administration enough about the evidence for Iraqi weapons of mass destruction and ties to terrorism. But it is also clear that the intelligence system failed in this situation and that members of the Congress, both Democrats and Republicans, failed to push the issue. Left with little conflict to report, the press echoed Washington's consensus.

Media Bias

It seems that much of the more recent media bias is intentional and a response to increasing fragmentation and competition among media. One-sided media, a type of narrowcasting, is gaining in popularity as networks intentionally market a one-sided message to secure a competitive edge in niche markets. Not all networks are forthright with their leanings, however. For example, the moniker for FOX News is "fair and balanced," while the reporting has a distinctly conservative bias. A comprehensive study of the news media reports that audiences are aware of news bias and seek out particular perspectives in the news they consume. While "mainstream, general interest newspapers, network television and local television news" are slowly losing audiences, "online, ethnic and alternative media are growing markedly" and "share the same strength—the opportunity for audiences to select tailored content and, in the case of the Internet, to do it on demand."[50] In order for various media to compete, they have

Join the Debate

OBJECTIVE VERSUS BIASED REPORTING

OVERVIEW: Throughout the second half of the twentieth century, the national news media made the claim that their journalists had fully developed the professionalism they needed to be objective in their reporting. Journalistic objectivity is the reporting of the facts of an event without imposing a political or ideological slant. The objectivity of journalists is crucial, since the vast majority of Americans rely on the news media for the information they need to make political decisions. To charge bias against the news media, then, is to explode a whole learning model for American citizenship. Rather than allowing American citizens to make political decisions based on facts, the media would make the decisions for them by either reporting only certain aspects of a story or not reporting the story at all. The media would control what you know or how you know it, making all the political decisions of average Americans merely an outcome of the original bias.

Is there a systemic bias in the news media? Conservative critics charge that the media have a liberal bias because up to 90 percent of journalists vote Democratic.[a] Moreover, they contend that many of the political reporters and analysts are hired not merely because of their political experience but also because of their Democratic experience. For example, ABC News hired former Clinton White House adviser George Stephanopoulos to host the Sunday morning political talk show *This Week*. Liberals argue in return that conservatives have no right to talk, since FOX News reports news for conservatives.[b] Moreover, other critics charge that the corporate interests of companies that own the media, regarded as fiscally conservative and strongly hesitant to

criticize possible sponsors, operate as much stronger biases than do the personal beliefs of journalists.[c]

The difficulty of proving bias is that one's own biases inform one's opinion of bias. While the conservative watchdog group Accuracy in Media believes that the media reports stories of Iraqi violence too often, liberal watchdog group Fairness and Accuracy in Reporting believes that media intentionally suppress stories about Iraqi civilian casualties and prisoner abuse. However, editors have to make decisions on what to report based on newsworthiness and audience demand, not merely their own politics, in order to keep viewers watching or readers reading. Otherwise, editors would simply drive their paper or program into the ground. Therefore, to prove bias, one must disprove alternatives, such as newsworthiness, a standard as frustratingly subjective as bias itself.

ARGUMENTS ASSERTING MEDIA BIAS

- **Since journalists have their own personal bias, claims of professional objectivity are absurd.** Journalistic professionalism is a myth sustained only by those who wish to conceal a personal agenda. Even if journalists feel bound to be objective, it is hard to believe that all of them are all of the time, especially when audiences have no other information with which to corroborate stories the media report. Since they are unaccountable, journalists may be fearless in imposing their beliefs on unsuspecting American audiences.
- **Corporate demands for the news media to make profits preclude the reporting of otherwise newsworthy stories.** Huge corporations demand that papers, television programs, and Web sites report only the stories that attract viewers rather than educating them, and that attract sponsors rather than holding them accountable. The result is that tabloid journalists report on

to differentiate themselves from the rest, and their current method of choice is in the bias infused within their content.

Recent survey data show that Democrats are more likely to watch CNN than Republicans and Republicans are nearly twice as likely to watch FOX News as Democrats (see Table 15.3). With cable news becoming a crowded field of competitors fighting over audience share, stations have tried to differentiate themselves in order to attract audiences. The trend, however, goes beyond cable news. Research shows that nearly 40 percent of Democrats watch network news, while less than 20 percent of Republicans do. Republicans are more likely to watch cable news and listen to AM talk radio. Democrats, on the other hand, are more likely to listen to National Public Radio (NPR), which typically caters to a more liberal palate. Finally, there is only a small disparity in newspaper reading between Republicans and Democrats (38 to 43

minor scandals and not human rights abuses or the negative effects of corporate mergers, leading to further audience ignorance of important issues.

■ **Ideological bias aside, the American media insufficiently report news from other regions of the world.** Americans lack sufficient knowledge about global events. This void is dangerous, since these events directly affect American interests. Television reports on global events are nothing more than "Around the World in 80 Seconds," while newspapers typically relegate world news not immediately pertaining to American interests to the back pages. This downplay creates an unfounded bias among audiences that places America at the center of world affairs.

ARGUMENTS DENYING MEDIA BIAS

■ **Bias is not systemic but a problem only with particular journalists.** Even if a certain journalist is unprofessional, it does not follow that all journalists are. The vast majority of journalists have done nothing to lead us to believe that they are somehow politically biased. Accusations of systemic bias are sometimes the product of bias, and the practice of uncovering media bias may be nothing more than a witch hunt.

■ **Bias is a misunderstanding of the niche journalism trend.** Recently, all news media have begun tailoring their content to specific audiences because audiences for news have fractured into tinier and tinier pieces. Some media direct content toward specific ideologies. Calling certain newspapers or cable stations biased is wrong, not because it is not factually true, but because the stations, rather openly, have begun presenting information about matters important to liberals or to conservatives. That's how the free market works.

■ **There are simply too many sources of news for an audience to suffer the influence of media bias.** Perhaps there was once a media bias, when there were only a few television stations and national newspapers from which to derive political information. Now, however, there are dozens of magazines, news Web sites, and smaller circulation newspapers that allow audiences different views of subjects. Bias, in this context, is understood. Individual citizens have the option of viewing or reading multiple competing sources and then critically evaluating the information they have gathered in order to make informed opinions.

QUESTIONS

1. What other kinds of biases might exist in the news media, aside from a regional or ideological one? Do these seriously impact American audiences? If so, how could these biases be corrected without violating the First Amendment?
2. What does it mean for a journalist to be "objective"?

SELECTED READINGS
Alterman, Eric. *What Liberal Media? The Truth About Bias and the News.* New York: Basic Books, 2004.
Goldberg, Bernard. *Bias: A CBS Insider Exposes How the Media Distort the News.* Washington, DC: Regnery, 2001.

[a]Accuracy in Media, http://www.aim.org.

[b]The Pew Research Center for the People and the Press, "News Audiences Increasingly Politicized: Online News Audience Larger, More Diverse," June 8, 2004, http://people-press.org.

[c]Fairness and Accuracy in Reporting, http://www.fair.org.

percent, respectively). However, like radio, newspapers can be subdivided by ideology; for instance, the *Washington Times* offers more conservative fare than its rival the *Washington Post.*

The ideological fragmentation of the media should give pause to those who believe that mass media are essential to providing the facts to educate the public about policies our local, state, and federal governments consider. If those facts are reported with bias (or worse, not reported at all because of bias), then portions of the public learn only the facts they want to learn, making consensus among the public and, thus, their representatives increasingly difficult.

The deepest bias among political journalists is the desire to get to the bottom of a good campaign story—which is usually negative news about a candidate. The fear of missing a good story, more than bias, leads media outlets to develop similar headlines

Analyzing Visuals
PARTISAN BIAS IN MEDIA REPORTING?

Late in the summer of 2004, the Center for Media and Public Affairs conducted a study of the media's coverage of the presidential campaign by comparing the number of positive and negative stories on each candidate. They examined the evening news programs on the major broadcast television networks and on FOX News, a cable news outlet that debuted in 1996 and quickly reached a level of viewership comparable to—and sometimes better than—that of CNN.

While the question of media bias is not a new one, several incidents in 2004 brought greater attention to the issue and heightened the debate over whether a news organization or its journalists favored one candidate over another and the degree to which that favoritism is evidenced. In September

2004, CBS faced harsh criticism for airing a negative story about President Bush's National Guard service that turned out to be based on forged documents. In October 2004, FOX News was forced to apologize for several unflattering quotes they had attributed to John Kerry but that were actually fabricated by one of its correspondents.

After examining the graph of positive stories aired about each candidate, answer the following critical thinking questions: What do you notice about the results for each network? Given that data were collected from each network during the same time period, what explanations might exist for the differences you see in the graph? Should it always be the goal of a network to have an equal number of positive and negative stories about each candidate?

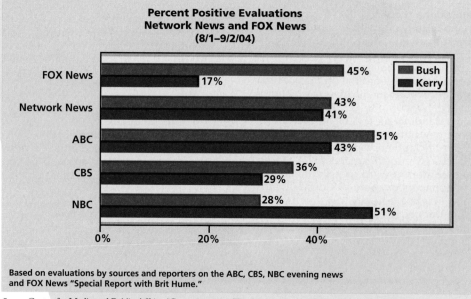

Based on evaluations by sources and reporters on the ABC, CBS, NBC evening news and FOX News "Special Report with Brit Hume."

Source: Center for Media and Public Affairs, "Campaign 2004: The Media Agenda," September 9, 2004, http://www.cmpa.com.

and to frame their stories in a similar fashion. In the absence of a good story, news people may attempt to create a horse race where none exists. News people, whose lives revolve around the current political scene, naturally want to add spice and drama, minimize their boredom, and increase their audience. While the horse-race components of elections are intrinsically interesting, the limited time that television devotes to politics is disproportionately given to the competitive aspects of politics, leaving less time for adequate discussion of public policy.

Other human biases are also at work in reporting on politics. Whether the press likes or dislikes a candidate personally is often vital. In 2000, the press gave Senator

John McCain considerable amounts of favorable coverage, making him a more viable although inevitably defeated candidate for the Republican presidential nomination. Former Governor Howard Dean became a media darling during the 2004 Democratic primaries because his fiery speeches made for good stories, putting him on the cover of *Time* and other news magazines. His rapid fall from grace after his poor showing in Iowa and his subsequent and much criticized "scream" at a rally gave rise to the speculation that the press can make then break their favorite candidates. Richard M. Nixon and Jimmy Carter—both aloof politicians—were disliked by many reporters who covered them, and they suffered from a harsh and critical press. The higher a politician's profile, the more open he or she is to scrutiny, and the more care he or she must take in handling the press.

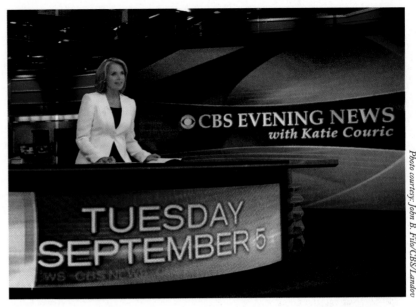

Photo courtesy: John B. Filo/CBS/Landov

■ Celebrity journalist Katie Couric became anchor and managing editor of the CBS Evening News in September 2006.

One other source of bias, or at least of nonobjectivity, is the increasing celebrity status of many people who report the news. In an age of media stardom and blurring boundaries between forms of entertainment, journalists in prominent media positions have unprecedented opportunities to attain fame and fortune, of which they often take full advantage. Already commanding multimillion-dollar salaries, these celebrity journalists can often secure lucrative speaker's fees. Especially in the case of journalists with highly ideological perspectives, close involvement with wealthy or powerful special-interest groups can blur the line between reporting on policy issues and influencing them. Some journalists find work as political consultants or members of government—which seems reasonable, given their prominence, abilities, and expertise, but which can become problematic when they move between spheres not once, but repeatedly. A good example of this revolving-door phenomenon is the case of Pat Buchanan, who has repeatedly and alternately enjoyed prominent positions in media (as a host of CNN's *Crossfire* and later as a commentator on MSNBC) and politics (as a presidential candidate). If American journalism is to retain its integrity, it is essential that key distinctions between private enterprise and conscientious public service continue to command our respect.

Summary

THE SIMPLE WORDS of the First Amendment, that "Congress shall make no law . . . abridging the freedom of speech, or of the press," have shaped the American republic as much as or more than any others in the Constitution. With the Constitution's sanction, as interpreted by the Supreme Court over two centuries, today's vigorous and highly competitive news media have emerged. In this chapter we examined the following topics:

1. **The Evolution of News Media in the United States**
   News media, a component of the larger mass media, provide the public with key information about subjects of public interest and play a crucial role in the political process. The news media consist of print, broadcast, and new media. The nation's first newspaper was published in 1690. Until the mid to late 1800s, when independent papers first appeared, newspapers were partisan; that is, they openly supported a particular party. In the twentieth century, first radio in the late 1920s and then television in the late 1940s revolutionized the transmission of political information. The growth of the Internet over the past few decades has fueled the rise of the new media, which consist of online news information from a variety of sources.

2. **Current Media Trends**
   Trends affecting the modern media include the growth of media conglomerates and an attendant

consolidation of media outlets, the increasing use of experts, and narrowcasting in order to capture particular segments of the population. Public opinion regarding the media continues to be largely critical, though Americans continue to rate media credibility highly. Increasingly, the lines between media types are blurred by technological innovations that continue to transform the way media is produced and distributed, as well as the way that the public perceives the media.

3. Rules Governing the Media

While the media continue to be governed by institutional norms, the government has gradually loosened restrictions on the media. The Federal Communications Commission (FCC) licenses and regulates broadcasting stations but has been quite willing to grant and renew licenses and has reduced its regulation of licensees. Content regulations have loosened, with the courts using a narrow interpretation of libel. The Telecommunications Act of 1996 further deregulated the communications landscape, and the rise of embedded journalists during the 2003 invasion of Iraq showed the government's willingness to cooperate with the media.

4. How the Media Cover Politics

The media cover every aspect of the political process, including the executive, legislative, and judicial branches of government, though the bulk of media attention focuses on the president. Congress, with its 535 members and complex committee system, poses a challenge to the modern media, as does the Supreme Court, with its complex rulings and aversion to media attention. Politicians have developed a symbiotic relationship with the media, both feeding the media a steady supply of news and occasionally being devoured by the latest media feeding frenzy.

5. The Media's Influence on the Public

By controlling the flow of information, framing issues in a particular manner, and setting the agenda, the media have the potential to exert influence over the public, though generally have far less influence than people believe. While the media do possess biases, a wide variety of news options are available in the United States, providing savvy news consumers an unprecedented amount of information from which to choose.

KEY TERMS

SELECTED READINGS

Broder, David S. *Behind the Front Page,* reprint ed. New York: Simon and Schuster, 2000.

Crouse, Timothy. *The Boys on the Bus,* reprint ed. New York: Random House, 2003.

Entman, Robert M. *Projections of Power: Framing News, Public Opinion, and U.S. Foreign Policy.* Chicago: University of Chicago Press, 2003.

Farnsworth, Stephen J., and S. Robert Lichter. *The Nightly News Nightmare: Network Television's Coverage of U.S. Presidential Elections, 1988–2000.* Lanham, MD: Rowman and Littlefield, 2002.

Graber, Doris A. *Mass Media and American Politics,* 7th ed. Washington, DC: CQ Press, 2005.

———. *Processing Politics: Learning from Television in the Internet Age.* Chicago: University of Chicago Press, 2001.

Hamilton, John Maxwell. *Hold the Press: The Inside Story on Newspapers,* reprint ed. Baton Rouge: Louisiana State University Press, 1997.

Iyengar, Shanto, and Donald R. Kinder. *News That Matters,* reprint ed. Chicago: University of Chicago Press, 1989.

Jamieson, Kathleen Hall, and Paul Waldman. *The Press Effect: Politicians, Journalists, and the Stories That Shape the Political World.* Oxford: Oxford University Press, 2002.

Kerbel, Matthew Robert. *If It Bleeds It Leads: An Anatomy of Television News.* Boulder, CO: Westview, 2001.

Lichter, S. Robert, and Stephen J. Farnsworth. *The Nightly News Nightmare: Network Television's Coverage of U.S. Presidential Elections, 1988–2000.* Lanham, MD: Rowman and Littlefield, 2002.

McChesney, Robert W. *The Problem of the Media: U.S. Communication Politics in the Twenty-First Century.* New York: Monthly Review Press, 2004.

Sabato, Larry J. *Feeding Frenzy: Attack Journalism and American Politics,* updated ed. Baltimore, MD: Lanahan, 2000.

Sabato, Larry J., Mark Stencel, and S. Robert Lichter. *Peepshow: Media and Politics in an Age of Scandal.* Lanham, MD: Rowman and Littlefield, 2001.

Starr, Paul. *The Creation of the Media.* New York: Basic Books, 2004.

West, Darrell M. *Air Wars: Television Advertising in Election Campaigns, 1952–1996.* Washington, DC: CQ Press, 2000.

Zaller, John. *The Nature and Origins of Mass Opinion.* Cambridge: Cambridge University Press, 1992.

WEB EXPLORATIONS

For examples of nineteenth-century yellow journalism, go to
http://alt.tnt.tv/movies/tntoriginals/roughriders/jour.home.html

To see how the media are diversifying and repackaging themselves through the use of pundits, go to
http://www.publicagenda.org

For examples of popular blogs, go to
http://www.redstate.org

http://www.powerlineblog.com
http://www.dailykos.com
http://www.huffingtonpost.com/theblog and
http://www.americablog.blogspot.com

To see which newspapers, magazines, and networks have a Web presence and how that complements their standard coverage, go to
http://www.nationaljournal.com
http://www.washingtonpost.com and
http://www.cnn.com/ALLPOLITICS

To learn more about the debate on cameras in the courtroom, particularly the Supreme Court, go to
http://5pj.org/news.asp?REF=68

To compare news coverage on a particular news story for evidence of political bias, go to
http://hometown.aol.com/gopbias/ and
http://new.mrc.org/cyberalerts/1999/cyb19990125.asp#1

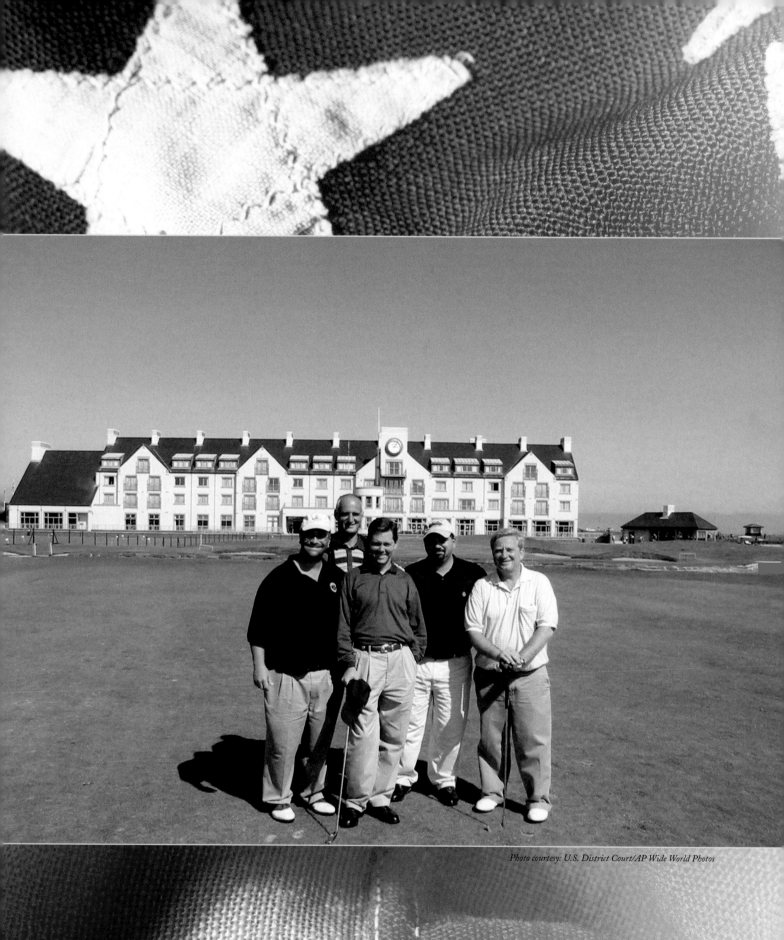

INTEREST GROUPS

16

WASHINGTON, DC, LOBBYIST JACK ABRAMOFF looked for two qualities in prospective clients: lots of money and naivete. Abramoff, who struck a plea bargain with Department of Justice investigators on charges of conspiracy, fraud, and tax evasion in 2006, found a perfect client in a number of Indian tribes whom he and his associates, including Michael Scanlon, former communications aide to then Republican House Majority Leader Tom DeLay (R–TX), reportedly charged approximately $85 million in fees to protect the tribes' gambling interests. Abramoff and Scanlon grossly overbilled their clients, who were new to the lobbying scene, and unethically took on Indian clients whose interests clearly opposed those of existing clients. Other Abramoff clients included eLottery, an Internet gambling firm seeking to "kill a bill that would outlaw most online gambling."[1] The company paid Abramoff $2 million, and he used Christian groups to defeat the bill under the pretense that it did not go far enough in preventing gambling on the Internet. Another major client paid Abramoff $9 million in fees to make sure that textile workers in the Mariana Islands, a commonwealth in political union with the United States, would not be covered by U.S. minimum wage laws.

Abramoff's connections in Congress were extensive.[2] He opened his own restaurant near Capitol Hill to provide free food and a place for congressional fund-raising events. It is estimated that nearly $4.5 million went to lawmakers or their staffers in the form of illegal or highly questionable donations and gifts.

Several members of Congress, including DeLay and Representative Robert Ney (R–OH), who both resigned from Congress in 2006, as well as prominent Republican consultants and interest-group leaders such as Grover Norquist, head of Americans for Tax Reform, have been implicated in Abramoff's dealings. Ralph Reed, former head of the Christian Coalition and a major Republican strategist, was found by the Senate Committee on Indian Affairs to have engaged in extensive anti-gambling lobbying efforts that benefited and were ultimately funded by Abramoff's casino-rich Indian clients.[3] Reed has denied knowing that the payments came from gambling interests, but the ongoing revelations of his close ties with Abramoff are believed to have cost him the primary race for Georgia lieutenant governor in July 2006. The release of a photo of Abramoff with Reed, Ney, and David H. Safavian, the former head of federal procurement in the White House Office

CHAPTER OUTLINE

- ✪ What Are Interest Groups?

- ✪ The Origins and Development of American Interest Groups

- ✪ What Do Interest Groups Do?

- ✪ What Makes an Interest Group Successful?

of Management and Budget on an expensive golf junket in Scotland became emblematic to many of a widespread culture of corruption in the nation's capital.

While the Abramoff scandal brought renewed debate on the need for lobbying reform and raised public awareness of the often fine line between ethical and unethical—or even illegal—lobbying practices, hiring federal lobbyists has become a must for nearly any business, special interest, or even governmental unit eager to win favor with members of the legislative or executive branch who control the distribution of billions of federal dollars. The small town of Treasure Island, Florida, for example, was rebuffed

every year as it sought federal assistance to help it rebuild its crumbling infrastructure. As soon as it hired a DC lobbyist for $5,000 a month, it found that it had secured a $50 million appropriation in the federal budget—called an earmark because funds are designated for a particular purpose—when the city had only sought $15 million!⁴ With results like these, it isn't surprising that since 1998, the number of towns and cities hiring private lobbyists, also called K Street representatives because so many lobbyists have offices there, has nearly doubled. And, as might be expected, the number of earmarks has tripled since 1998.

LOBBYING IS JUST ONE FORM of interest group politics, yet one that often gives a bad name to interest groups in general. Still, citizen participation in political or civic interest groups is critical to a well-functioning civil society and offers myriad opportunities for political engagement.

The face of interest group politics in the United States is changing as quickly as laws, political consultants, and technology allow. Big business and trade groups are increasing their activities and engagement in the political system at the same time that there is conflicting evidence concerning whether ordinary citizens join political groups. In an influential 1995 essay and later in a 2000 book, political scientist Robert Putnam argued that fewer Americans are joining groups, a phenomenon he labelled "bowling alone."⁵ Others have faulted Putnam, concluding that America is in the midst of an "explosion of voluntary groups, activities and charitable donations [that] is transforming our towns and cities."⁶ Although bowling leagues, which were a very common means of bringing people together, have withered, other groups such as volunteer groups, soccer associations, health clubs, and environmental groups are flourishing. Older groups such as the Elks Club and the League of Women Voters, whose membership was tracked by Putnam, no longer are attracting members, but this does not necessarily mean that people aren't joining groups; they just aren't joining the ones studied by Putnam, as revealed in Politics Now: Civic Engagement and New Technologies.

social capital
The myriad relationships that individuals enjoy that facilitate the resolution of community problems through collective action.

civic virtue
The tendency to form small-scale associations for the public good.

Why is this debate so important? Political scientists believe that involvement in these kinds of community groups and activities enhances the level of **social capital,** "the web of cooperative relationships between citizens that facilitates resolution of collective action problems."⁷ The more social capital that exists in a given community, the more citizens are engaged in its governance and well-being, and the more likely they are to work for the collective good.⁸ This tendency to form small-scale associations for the public good, or **civic virtue,** as Putnam calls it, creates fertile ground within communities for improved political and economic development.⁹ Thus, if Americans truly are joining fewer groups, we might expect the overall quality of government and its provision of services to suffer.

Interest groups are also important because they give the unrepresented or underrepresented an opportunity to have their voices heard, thereby making the government and its policy-making process more representative of diverse populations and perspectives. Additionally, interest groups offer powerful and wealthy interests even greater access to, or influence on, policy makers at all levels of government. To explore

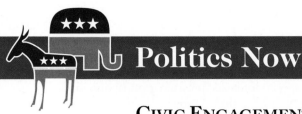

Politics Now

CIVIC ENGAGEMENT AND NEW TECHNOLOGIES

In 2005, ten years after political scientist Robert Putnam's now classic essay "Bowling Alone" was published to much fanfare and distress over the demise of the connectedness of Americans in the new economy, some commentators began to document a new spirit of civic engagement. Take the Cudney family in Vienna, Virginia, for example. Although the family has three children, and James Cudney manages fifteen Homeland Security programs and is a frequent traveler, he and his wife continue to find time to lead their son's Cub Scout troop. In times gone by, the Cudneys would have needed a telephone tree to keep the troop running. Now, says Cudney, "I would not be able to be involved if it wasn't for the Internet. . . . I don't have time to do traditional phone trees and calendars by hand."[a] Today, cell phones, Blackberries, instant text messaging, and e-mails allow people to stay connected, be it for organizing an interest group, working on a local committee, or staying up to date on issues of concern. These new technologies, used by young people, single and married workers, and retirees alike, are changing the face of interest group politics. "People are physically more connected to their community because of Internet use," notes the director of Pew's Internet and American Life Project.[b]

A political scientist who has studied the new ways that Americans are connecting notes that Putnam is correct that classic community organizations such as the Lions Club or Elks are not increasing their membership bases. "People are not members of the old hierarchy organizations," says Ronald Inglehart of the University of Michigan's Institute for Social Research, which surveys social values worldwide.[c] Instead, they have much looser ties to more groups than ever before.

MoveOn.org, a liberal interest group, offers activists the opportunity to use text messaging to organize protests as events occur. In days gone by, it would have taken months of planning and thousands of dollars to organize similar events. MeetUp.com, a Web site that was used by Howard Dean's Internet guru Joe Trippi to organize grassroots support for Dean's failed 2004 presidential bid, offers a venue for individuals with common interests to find each other and organize meetings online quickly and with a minimum of effort. Gone from many activists' calendars are fixed monthly or weekly meetings. Today, technology allows individuals to meet when they need to meet and dispatch with numerous housekeeping issues efficiently via e-mail.

Other types of groups also are taking the place of those interest groups historically studied by scholars. Community associations are creating new forms of activity. They are often founded or their membership spikes when changes are proposed in building codes, township fees, or other items that could affect the quality of life of a community's residents. In 1970, 2.1 million people belonged to homeowners' associations; by 2005, nearly 55 million people were members.[d] Seniors are also volunteering in record numbers in their communities. As the average retirement age has dropped and people are living longer, many seniors now are giving back to their communities. Involvement in what some call "megachurches" also is upping the numbers of citizens involved in public interest activities. While religious organizations have always been a source of volunteer associations, megachurches offer a variety of opportunities for social connections formerly offered by more formal, secular groups. These churches offer calendars and newsletters online, podcasted and televised church services, and mission work in their communities. New technologies open up new ways of interaction and cannot be ignored as we try to understand the interest group culture that has so long permeated the American political, social, and cultural scene.

QUESTIONS

1. What other forms of interest group activity have changed in response to recent technological changes?
2. Do these new technology-based groups offer the same opportunities to develop social capital as their predecessors?

---

[a]This feature draws heavily from Haya El Nasser, "Beyond Kiwanis: Internet Builds New Communities," *USA Today* (June 2, 2005): 1–2A.

[b]El Nasser, "Beyond Kiwanis."

[c]El Nasser, "Beyond Kiwanis."

[d]El Nasser, "Beyond Kiwanis."

---

the impact of interest groups on policy and the political process, in this chapter we will look at the following issues:

- First, we will answer the question, *what are interest groups?*
- Second, we will explore *the origins and development of American interest groups.*
- Third, we will answer the question *what do interest groups do* by looking at the various strategies and tactics used by organized interests.
- Finally, we will analyze *what makes an interest group successful.*

What Are Interest Groups?

interest group
An organized group that tries to influence public policy.

INTEREST GROUPS go by various names: special interests, pressure groups, organized interests, nongovernmental organizations (NGOs), political groups, lobby groups, and public interest groups. David B. Truman, one of the first political scientists to study interest groups, defines an organized interest as "any group that, on the basis of one or more shared attitudes, makes certain claims upon other groups in society for the establishment, maintenance, or enhancement of forms of behavior that are implied by shared attitudes."[10] Interest groups are differentiated from political parties largely by the fact that interest groups do not run candidates for office.

disturbance theory
Political scientist David B. Truman's theory that interest groups form in part to counteract the efforts of other groups.

Truman explained the formation of interest groups through what he termed **disturbance theory.** He hypothesized that groups arise, in part, to counteract the activities of other groups or of organized special interests. According to Truman, the government's role is to provide a forum in which the competing demands of groups and the majority of the U.S. population can be heard and balanced.[11]

Political scientist Robert Salisbury expanded on Truman's theories by arguing that groups form when resources—be they clean air, women's rights, or rights of the unborn, for example—are inadequate or scarce. Unlike Truman, Salisbury stresses the role that leaders, or what he terms "entrepreneurs," play in the formation of groups.[12]

KINDS OF ORGANIZED INTERESTS

public interest group
An organization that seeks a collective good that will not selectively and materially benefit group members.

In this book, we use interest group as a generic term to describe the numerous organized groups that try to influence government policy. Thus, interest groups may be public interest groups, business and economic groups, governmental units such as state and local governments, and political action committees (PACs). These groups can be further delineated as single or multi-issue.

economic interest group
A group with the primary purpose of promoting the financial interests of its members.

With the exception of PACs, most of these groups lobby on behalf of their members. Many also hire D.C.-based lobbying firms to lead or supplement their efforts.

Public Interest Groups Political scientist Jeffrey M. Berry defines **public interest groups** as organizations "that seek a collective good, the achievement of which will not selectively and materially benefit the membership or activists of the organization."[13] Public interest groups do not tend to be particularly motivated by the desire to achieve goals that necessarily benefit their members. For example, many Progressive era groups were created by upper- and middle-class women to solve the varied problems of new immigrants and the poor. Today, civil rights and liberties groups, environmental groups, good government groups such as Common Cause, peace groups, church groups, and groups that speak out for those who cannot (such as children, the mentally ill, or animals) and even MoveOn.org are examples of public interest groups.

■ Geography often determines the kinds of special interests that are most common in a given region.

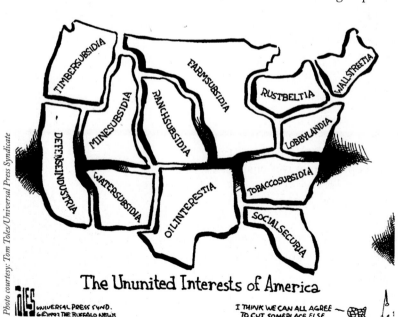

The Ununited Interests of America

Economic Interest Groups Most groups have some sort of economic agenda, even if it only involves acquiring enough money in donations to pay the telephone bill or to send out the next mailing. **Economic interest groups** are, however, a special type of interest group whose primary purpose is to promote the economic interests of their members. Historically, the big three of economic interest groups were business groups (including trade and professional groups such as the American Medical Association), labor organizations (such as the AFL-CIO), and organizations representing the interests of farmers. The influence of farmers and labor unions is on the decline, however, as big businesses such as Halliburton and Altria (formerly Philip Morris) spend increasingly large amounts contributing to campaigns and hiring lobbyists.

Groups that mobilize to protect particular economic interests generally are the most fully and effectively organized of all the types of interest groups.[14] They exist to make profits and to obtain economic benefits for their members. To achieve these goals, however, they often find that they must resort to political means rather than trust the operation of economic markets to produce outcomes favorable for their members.

Governmental Units

State and local governments are becoming strong organized interests as they lobby the federal government or even charitable foundations for money for a vast array of state and local programs. The big intergovernmental associations and state and local governments want to make certain that they get their fair share of federal dollars in the form of block grants or pork-barrel projects. Most states retain lobbyists in Washington, D.C., to advance their interests or to keep them informed about legislation that could affect them as they seek money from the federal budget designated to go back to the states in a variety of forms, including money for roads, schools, and anti-poverty programs. In fact, as discussed in the opening vignette, states and local governments may spend a significant proportion of their revenues trying to win federal **earmarks,** monies specifically targeted for programs within a state or specific congressional district to fund basic programs for building roads, schools, enhancing parks or waterways, or other public works projects. The "Big Seven" intergovernmental associations listed in Table 4.5 in chapter 4 also lobby extensively on behalf of their members.

earmark
Funds that an appropriations bill designates for a particular purpose within a state or congressional district.

Political Action Committees

In 1974, amendments to the Federal Election Campaign Act made it legal for corporations, labor unions, and interest groups to form what were termed **political action committees (PACs),** which could make contributions to candidates for national elections (see chapter 14 for more on this subject). Technically, a PAC is a political arm of a business, labor, trade, professional, or other interest group legally authorized to raise funds on a voluntary basis from employees or members in order to contribute to a political candidate or party. Unlike interest groups, PACs do not have formal members; they simply have contributors who seek to influence public policy by electing legislators sympathetic to their aims. In contrast, 527 political groups, discussed in chapter 14, have members.

political action committee (PAC)
Federally mandated, officially registered fund-raising committee that represents interest groups in the political process.

Political Action Committees

Multi-Issue Versus Single-Issue Groups

Political scientists often talk of interest groups as single-issue or multi-issue. Many organizations, while founded around a single guiding principle such as the NAACP's interest in advancing the cause of civil rights, or the Christian Coalition's concern with conservative family values, actually are involved in a wide range of issue areas, including education (school vouchers, organized prayer in schools), television ratings, and abortion. Thus, multi-issue groups often must have expertise in a wide array of areas and be prepared to work on the local, state, and national levels to advance their interests.

Single-issue groups differ from multi-issue groups in both the range and intensity of their interests. Concentration on one area generally leads to greater zeal in a group's lobbying efforts. Probably the most visible single-issue groups today are those organized on either side of the abortion and gun control debates. Right-to-life groups such as the National Right to Life Committee and pro-choice

Pluralism

■ The National Rifle Association is a clear-cut example of a single-issue interest group. Here, Vice President Dick Cheney inspects a flintlock rifle given to him by National Rifle Association officers, including (from left to right) Sandra Froman, Wayne LaPierre, and Kayne Robinson. The vice president appeared at the NRA's annual convention to voice the Bush administration's support for the rights of gun owners.

Photo courtesy: Jeff Swensen/Getty Images

groups such as NARAL Pro-Choice America are good examples of single-issue groups, as are the National Rifle Association (NRA) and the Campaign for Tobacco Free Kids. Table 16.1 categorizes a number of prominent interest groups by their area of concentration.

The Origins and Development of American Interest Groups

POLITICAL SCIENTISTS HAVE LONG DEBATED how and why interest groups arise, their nature, and their role in a democratic society. Do they contribute to the betterment of society, or are they an evil best controlled by government? From his days in the Virginia Assembly, James Madison knew that factions occurred in all political systems and that the struggle for influence and power among such groups was inevitable in the political process. This knowledge led him and the other Framers to tailor a governmental system of multiple pressure points to check and balance these factions, or what today we call interest groups, in the natural course of the political process. As we discuss in chapter 2, Madison and many of the other Framers were intent on creating a government of many levels—local, state, and national—with the national government consisting of three branches. It was their belief that this division of power would prevent any one individual or group of individuals from becoming too influential. They also believed that decentralizing power would neutralize the effect of special interests, who would not be able to spread their efforts throughout so many different levels of government. Thus, the "mischief of faction" could be lessened. But, farsighted as they were, the Framers could not have envisioned the vast sums of money or technology that would be available to some interest groups as the nature of these groups evolved over time. (See The Living Constitution: First Amendment.)

TABLE 16.1 PROFILES OF SELECTED INTEREST GROUPS

Name (Founded)	Single- or Multi-Issue	Members	PAC	2005–2006 Election Cycle PAC Donation*
Economic Groups				
AFL-CIO (1886)	M	13 million	AFL-CIO	$512,300
American Medical Association (AMA) (1847)	M	250,000	AMA PAC	$654,700
Association of Trial Lawyers of America (1946)	M	50,000	ATLA PAC	$1.6 million
National Association of Manufacturers (NAM) (1895)	M	14,000 companies 350 associations	no	n/a
U.S. Chamber of Commerce (1912)	M	3 million companies	U.S. Chamber of Commerce PAC	$67,000
Public Interest Groups				
AARP (1958)	M	35 million	no	n/a
Concerned Women for America (1974)	M	500,000	CWA Legislative Action Committee/PAC	$1,500
Focus on the Family (1977)	M	1.2 million	no	n/a
League of United Latin American Citizens (LULAC) (1929)	M	115,000	no	n/a
NARAL Pro-Choice America (1969)	S	500,000	NARAL- Pro Choice America PAC	$279,500
National Association for the Advancement of Colored People (NAACP) (1909)	M	500,000	no	n/a
Human Rights Campaign (1980)	S	600,000	HRC PAC	$399,705
National Right to Life Committee (1973)	S	400,000	National Right to Life PAC	$0
Environmental Groups				
Environmental Defense Fund (1967)	S	400,000	no	n/a
Greenpeace USA (1971)	S	350,000	no	n/a
Sierra Club (1892)	S	700,000	Sierra Club Political Committee	$11,454
Good Government Groups				
Common Cause (1970)	S	300,000	no	n/a
Public Citizen, Inc. (1971)	M	160,000	no	n/a
MoveOn.org (1998)	M	3.3 million	MoveOn PAC	$286,588

*2005–2006 data through June 1, 2006.

Source: http:www.opensecrets.org.

NATIONAL GROUPS EMERGE (1830–1889)

Although all kinds of local groups proliferated throughout the colonies and in the new states, it was not until the 1830s, as communications networks improved, that the first groups national in scope emerged. Many of these first national groups were single-issue groups deeply rooted in the Christian religious revivalism that was sweeping the nation. Concern with humanitarian issues such as temperance (total abstinence from alcoholic beverages), peace, education, and slavery led to the founding of numerous associations dedicated to solving these problems. Among the first of these groups was the American Anti-Slavery Society, founded in 1833 by William Lloyd Garrison.

After the Civil War, more groups were founded. For example, the Women's Christian Temperance Union (WCTU) was created in 1874 with the goal of outlawing the sale of liquor. Its members, many of them quite religious, believed that the consumption of alcohol was an evil injurious to family life because many men drank away their paychecks, leaving no money to feed or clothe their families. The WCTU's activities took conventional and nonconventional forms, including organizing prayer groups, lobbying for prohibition legislation, conducting peaceful marches, and engaging in more violent protests such as the destruction of saloons. Like the WCTU, the Grange also was formed during the period following the Civil War. The Grange was created as an educational society for farmers to teach them about the latest agricultural

The Living Constitution

Congress shall make no law respecting ... the right of the people peaceably to assemble, and to petition the Government for a redress of grievances.

—FIRST AMENDMENT

This amendment prohibits the national government from enacting laws dealing with the right of individuals to join together to make their voices known about their positions on a range of political issues. There was little debate on this clause in the U.S. House of Representatives and none was recorded in the Senate. James Madison, however, warned of the perils of "discussing and proposing abstract propositions," which this clause was for many years.

The concept of freedom of association, a key concept that allows Americans to organize and join a host of political groups, grew out of a series of cases decided by the Supreme Court in the 1950s and 1960s when many southern states were trying to limit the activities of the National Association for the Advancement of Colored People (NAACP). From the right to assemble and petition the government, along with the freedom of speech, the Supreme Court construed the right of people to come together to support or to protest government actions. First, the Court ruled that states could not compel interest groups to provide their membership lists to state officials. Later, the Court ruled that Alabama could not prohibit the NAACP from urging its members and others to file lawsuits challenging state discriminatory practices. Today, although states and localities can require organized interests to apply for permits to picket or protest, they cannot in any way infringe on their ability to assemble and petition in peaceable ways.

---

developments. Although its charter formally stated that the Grange was not to become involved in politics, in 1876 it formulated a detailed plan to pressure Congress to enact legislation favorable to farmers.

After the Civil War, business interests began to play even larger roles in both state and national politics. A popular saying of the day noted that the Standard Oil Company did everything to the Pennsylvania legislature except refine it. Increasingly large trusts, monopolies, business combinations, and corporate conglomerations in the oil, steel, and sugar industries became sufficiently powerful to control many representatives in the state and national legislatures.

Perhaps the most effective organized interest of the day was the railroad industry. In a move that couldn't take place today because of its clear impropriety, the Central Pacific Railroad sent its own **lobbyist** to Washington, D.C., in 1861, where he eventually became the clerk (staff administrator) of the committees of both houses of Congress that were charged with overseeing regulation of the railroad industry. Subsequently, Congress awarded the Central Pacific Railroad (later called the Southern

lobbyist
Interest group representative who seeks to influence legislation that will benefit his or her organization or client through political persuasion.

Pacific) vast grants of lands along its route and large subsidized loans. The railroad company became so powerful that it later went on to have nearly total political control of the California state legislature.

THE PROGRESSIVE ERA (1890–1920)

By the 1890s, a profound change had occurred in the nation's political and social outlook. Rapid industrialization, an influx of immigrants, and monopolistic business practices created a host of problems including crime, poverty, squalid and unsafe working conditions, and widespread political corruption. Many Americans began to believe that new measures would be necessary to impose order on this growing chaos and to curb some of the more glaring problems. The political and social movement that grew out of these concerns was called the Progressive movement.

Not even the Progressives themselves could agree on what the term "progressive" actually meant, but their desire for reform led to an explosion of all types of interest groups, including single-issue, trade, labor, and the first public interest groups. Politically, the movement took the form of the Progressive Party, which sought on many fronts to limit or end the power of the industrialists' near-total control of the steel, oil, railroad, and other key industries.

In response to the pressure applied by Progressive-era groups, the national government began to regulate business. Because businesses had a vested interest in keeping wages low and costs down, more business groups organized to consolidate their strength and to counter Progressive moves. Not only did governments have to mediate Progressive and business demands, but they also had to accommodate the role of organized labor, which often allied itself with Progressive groups against big business.

Organized Labor Until the creation of the American Federation of Labor (AFL) in 1886, there was not any real national union activity. The AFL brought skilled workers from several trades together into one stronger national organization for the first time. As the AFL grew in power, many business owners began to press individually or collectively to quash the unions. As business interests pushed states for what are called open shop laws to outlaw unions in their factories, the AFL became increasingly political. It also was forced to react to the success of big businesses' use of legal injunctions to prohibit union organization. In 1914, massive lobbying by the AFL and its members led to passage of the Clayton Act, which labor leader Samuel Gompers hailed as the Magna Carta of the labor movement. This law allowed unions to organize free from prosecution and also guaranteed their right to strike, a powerful weapon against employers.

Business Groups and Trade Associations The National Association of Manufacturers (NAM) was founded in 1895 by manufacturers who had suffered business reverses in the economic panic of 1893 and who believed that they were being affected adversely by the growth of organized labor. NAM first became active politically in 1913 when a major tariff bill was under congressional consideration. NAM's tactics were "so insistent and abrasive" and its expenditures of monies so lavish that President Woodrow Wilson was forced to denounce its lobbying tactics as an "unbearable situation."[15] Congress immediately called for an investigation of NAM's activities but found no member of Congress willing to testify that he had ever even encountered a member of NAM (probably because many members of Congress had received illegal contributions and gifts).

The second major business organization came into being in 1912, when the U.S. Chamber of Commerce was created with the assistance of the Department of Commerce and Labor. (The Chamber was created before that department was split into the Department of Commerce and the Department of Labor.) NAM, the Chamber of Commerce, and other **trade associations** representing specific industries were

trade association
A group that represents a specific industry.

effective spokespersons for their member companies. They were unable to defeat passage of the Clayton Act, but groups such as the Cotton Manufacturers planned elaborate and successful campaigns to overturn key provisions of the act in the courts.[16] Aside from the Clayton Act, innumerable pieces of pro-business legislation were passed by Congress, whose members continued to insist that they had never been contacted by business groups.

In 1928, the bubble burst for some business interests. At the Senate's request, the Federal Trade Commission (FTC) undertook a massive investigation of the lobbying tactics of the business community. The FTC's examination of Congress revealed extensive illegal lobbying by yet another group, the National Electric Light Association (NELA). Not only did NELA lavishly entertain members of Congress, but it also went to great expense to educate the public on the virtues of electric lighting. Books and pamphlets were produced and donated to schools and public libraries to sway public opinion. Needy teachers and ministers who were willing to advocate electricity were helped with financial grants. Many considered these tactics unethical and held business in disfavor. These kinds of activities led the public to view lobbyists in a negative light.

THE RISE OF THE INTEREST GROUP STATE

During the 1960s and 1970s, the Progressive spirit reappeared in the rise of public interest groups. Generally, these groups devoted themselves to representing the interests of African Americans, women, the elderly, the poor, and consumers, or to working on behalf of the environment. Many of their leaders and members had been active in the civil rights and anti–Vietnam War movements of the 1960s. Other groups, such as the American Civil Liberties Union (ACLU) and the NAACP gained renewed vigor. Many of them had as their patron the liberal Ford Foundation, which helped to bankroll numerous groups, including the Women's Rights Project of the ACLU, the Mexican American Legal Defense and Education Fund, the Puerto Rican Legal Defense and Education Fund, and the Native American Rights Fund (as discussed in chapter 6).[17] The American Association of Retired Persons, now simply called AARP, also came to prominence in this era.

The civil rights and anti-war struggles left many Americans feeling cynical about a government that they believed failed to respond to the will of the majority. They also believed that if citizens banded together, they could make a difference. Thus, two major new public interest groups—Common Cause and Public Citizen, Inc.—were founded. Common Cause, a good-government group that acts as a watchdog over the federal government, is similar to some of the early Progressive movement's public interest groups. Common Cause effectively has challenged aspects of the congressional seniority system, successfully urged the passage of sweeping campaign financing reforms, and played a major role in the enactment of legislation authorizing federal financing of presidential campaigns. It continues to lobby for accountability in government and for more efficient and responsive governmental structures and practices.

Perhaps more well known than Common Cause is Public Citizen, Inc., the collection of groups headed by Ralph Nader (who later went on to run as a candidate for president in 1996, 2000, and 2004). In 1965, the publication of Nader's *Unsafe at Any Speed* thrust the young lawyer into the limelight. In this book, he charged that the Corvair, a General Motors (GM) car, was unsafe to drive; he produced voluminous evidence of how the car could flip over at average speeds on curved roads. In 1966, he testified about auto safety before Congress and then learned that GM had spied on him in an effort to discredit his work. The $250,000 that GM subsequently paid to Nader in an out-of-court settlement allowed him to establish the Center for the Study of Responsive Law in 1969. The center analyzed the activities of regulatory agencies and concluded that few of them enforced anti-trust regulations or cracked down on deceptive advertising practices. Nader then turned again to lobbying Congress, which

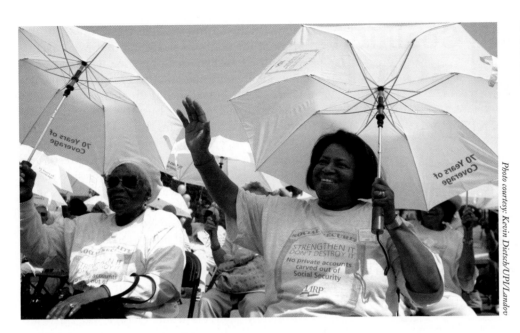

Photo courtesy: Kevin Dietsch/UPI/Landov

■ AARP members have often been a potent political force. Here, members participate in a rally to prevent the Social Security privatization plan favored by the Bush administration.

led him to create Public Citizen, Inc., which would act as an umbrella organization for what was to be called the "Nader Network" of groups.

Conservative Response: Religious and Ideological Groups During the 1960s and 1970s, various public interest groups and civil rights and women's rights movements grew and achieved success in shaping and defining the public agenda. Conservatives, concerned by the activities of these liberal groups, responded by forming religious and ideological groups that became a potent force in U.S. politics. In 1978, the Reverend Jerry Falwell founded the first major new religious group, the Moral Majority. The Moral Majority was widely credited with assisting in the election of Ronald Reagan as president in 1980 as well as with the defeats of several liberal Democratic senators that same year. Falwell claimed to have sent 3 to 4 million newly registered voters to the polls.[18]

In 1990, televangelist Pat Robertson, host of the popular television program *The 700 Club*, formed a new group, the Christian Coalition. Since then, it has grown in power and influence. The Christian Coalition played an important role in the Republicans' winning control of the Congress in 1994. In 2004, the group distributed more than 100 million voter guides in churches throughout the United States. The Christian Coalition also lobbies Congress and the White House. The group had the sympathetic ear of President George W. Bush, whom it helped elect. In fact, one of Bush's first moves as president was to create an Office of Faith-Based and Community Initiatives to work with religious groups to effect policy change.

The Christian Coalition is not the only conservative interest group to play an important role in the policy process as well as in elections at the state and national level. The National Rifle Association (NRA), an active opponent of gun control legislation, saw its membership rise in recent years (see Figure 16.1), as well as its importance in Washington, D.C. The NRA and its political action committee spent $20 million to reelect President George W. Bush in 2004. Similarly, another conservative group, Focus on the Family, was a leader in organizing the Justice Sunday events discussed in chapter 10. And, conservative groups such as Students for Academic Freedom have made their views known in the area of higher education. (See On Campus: Speaking Up.)

Business Groups, Corporations, and Associations Conservative, religious-based groups were not the only ones organized in the 1970s to advance their

2004 Christian Coalition

VOTER GUIDE

PRESIDENTIAL
Election

George W. Bush (R)	ISSUES	John F. Kerry (D)
Supports	Passage of a Federal Marriage Protection Amendment	Opposes
Supports	Permanent Extension of the $1,000 Per Child Tax Credit	Opposes
Supports	Educational Choice for Parents (Vouchers)	Opposes
Opposes	Unrestricted Abortion on Demand	No Response
Supports	Federal Funding for Faith-Based Charitable Organizations	No Response
Supports	Permanent Elimination of the Marriage Penalty Tax	Opposes
Supports	Permanent Elimination of the Death Tax	Opposes
Supports	Banning Partial Birth Abortions	Opposes
Opposes	Public Financing of Abortions	Supports
Opposes	Federal Firearms Registration & Licensing of Gun Owners	No Response
Opposes	Adoption of Children by Homosexuals	No Response
Supports	Prescription Drug Benefits for Medicare Recipients	Supports
Opposes	Placing US Troops Under UN Control	No Response
Opposes	Affirmative Action Programs that Provide Preferential Treatment	Supports
Supports	Allowing Younger Workers to Invest a Portion of their Social Security Tax in a Private Account	Opposes

www.georgewbush.com   www.johnkerry.com

Each candidate was sent a 2004 Federal Issue Survey by certified mail and/or facsimile machine. When possible, positions of candidates on issues were verified or determined using voting records and/or public statements.

Authorized by the Christian Coalition of America; PO Box 37030 - Washington, DC 20013

The Christian Coalition of America is a pro-family, citizen action organization. This voter guide is provided for educational purposes only and is not to be construed as an endorsement of any candidate or party.

Please visit our website at www.cc.org, and the Texas website at www.texascc.org

Vote on November 2   F

Photo courtesy: Christian Coalition of America

■ Voter guides like this one were distributed in conservative churches around the United States as well as at public places and events to let voters see the major candidates' positions on a variety of issues of concern to the Christian Coalition.

views. Many business people, dissatisfied with the work of the National Association of Manufacturers or the Chamber of Commerce, decided to start new, more politically oriented organizations to advance their political and financial interests in Washington, D.C. The Business Roundtable, for example, was created in 1972. The Roundtable, whose members head about 150 large corporations, is "a fraternity of powerful and prestigious business leaders that tells 'business's side of the story' to legislators, bureaucrats, White House personnel, and other interested public officials."[19] It urges its members to engage in direct lobbying to influence the course of policy formation. In 1998, for example, the Business Roundtable's Environment Task Force lobbied hard against the Kyoto Protocol on Climate Change out of concern over its impact on American businesses. These efforts ultimately paid off when George W. Bush announced that his administration would not support the Kyoto agreement. Another indication of the Roundtable's close ties to the federal government is the new communications network the group set up to enable its member CEOs to communicate with appropriate government officials in the wake of another terrorist attack.[20]

Most large corporations, in addition to having their own governmental affairs departments, employ D.C.-based lobbyists to keep them apprised of legislation that may affect them, or to lobby bureaucrats for government contracts. In the past, large corporations also gave significant sums of soft money to favored politicians or political candidates. While campaign finance reforms (discussed in greater detail in chapter 14) have prohibited such corporate donations, businesses still channel money to favored candidates through political action committees, 527s, and individual donations from employees and their families, as well as through state parties. In the 2004 election, for example, 527 groups, which receive corporate as well as individual donations, contributed $409 million to candidates for president and other national offices.[21]

These corporate interests also have far-reaching tentacles and ties to lawmakers. A number of congressional spouses as well as sons, daughters, and in-laws, are registered lobbyists. Moreover, as discussed later in the chapter, many lawmakers become lobbyists after leaving office.

Organized Labor   As revealed in Figure 16.2, membership in labor unions held steady throughout the early and mid-1900s and then skyrocketed toward the end of the Depression. By then, organized labor began to be a potent political force as it was able to turn out its members in support of particular political candidates.

Labor became a stronger force in U.S. politics when the American Federation of Labor (AFL) merged with the Congress of Industrial Organizations (CIO) in 1955. Concentrating its efforts largely on the national level, the new AFL-CIO immediately turned its energies to pressuring the government to protect concessions won from employers at the bargaining table and to other issues of concern to its members,

FIGURE 16.1 NRA MEMBERSHIP

The National Rifle Association (NRA), a single-issue interest group, lobbies against any law that would restrict an individual's right to bear arms. NRA membership tends to increase in reaction to proposed gun control legislation or near an election. Interestingly, following the 1999 Columbine High School shooting in Colorado, in which twelve people were killed and several others were wounded, membership increased dramatically. NRA membership also took a jump after the 9/11 terrorist attacks.

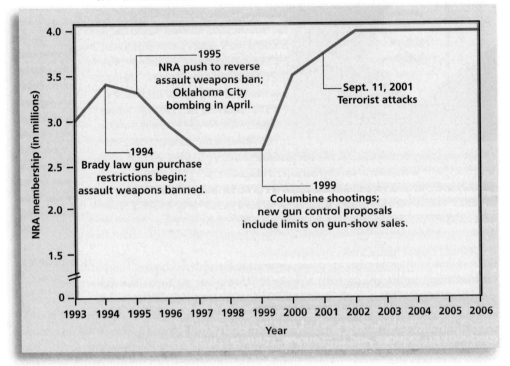

PARTICIPATION

**Gun Rights and
Gun Control**

Sources: Genevieve Lynn, "How the NRA Membership Has Risen." *USA Today* (May 18, 2000): 1A © 2000, USA Today. Reprinted with permission. Updated by the authors using Harold R. Stanley and Richard G. Niemi, *Vital Statistics on American Politics, 2005–2006* (Washington, DC: CQ Press, 2006).

including minimum wage laws, the environment, civil rights, medical insurance, and health care.

More recently, the once fabled political clout of organized labor has been on the wane at the national level. As Figure 16.2 shows, union membership plummeted as the nation changed from a land of manufacturing workers and farmers to a nation of white-collar professionals and service workers. Thus, unions and agricultural organizations no longer have the large memberships or the political clout they once held in governmental circles. Organized labor recognized its troubles and has tried to recapture some of its lost political clout within the rank-and-file members of the Democratic Party. Nevertheless, its electoral weaknesses were clearly evident in the 2004 Democratic presidential primaries. In spite of significant labor backing, Representative Dick Gephardt (D–MO) was forced to withdraw from the presidential race when he came in fourth in the Iowa caucuses.

Even worse for the future of the labor movement, at least in the short run, is the split that occurred at the AFL-CIO's 2005 annual meeting, ironically the fiftieth anniversary of the joining of the two unions. Plagued by reduced union membership, and mired in disagreement about how much money to devote to the campaigns of Democrats at a time when Republicans controlled two branches of government, three of the largest member unions ceded from the AFL-CIO. With the head of the Service Employees International Union (SEIU) noting that the

FIGURE 16.2 LABOR UNION MEMBERSHIP

After reaching an all-time high in 1950, labor union membership and political clout have steadily declined.

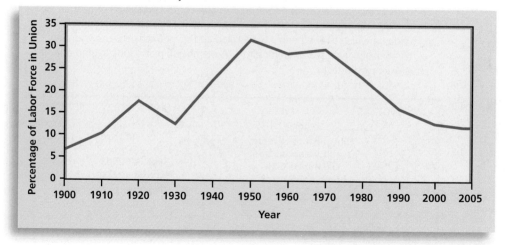

Source: Harold W. Stanley and Richard G. Niemi, eds. *Vital Statistics on American Politics, 2005–2006* (Washington, DC: CQ Press, 2006), 405. Updated by the authors.

AFL-CIO had grown "pale, male, and stale," the SEIU, the Teamsters, and the United Food and Commercial Workers Union left to form the Change to Win Coalition.[22] The AFL-CIO lost 167,775 members from 2003 to 2004, whereas it had lost 39,439 the year before.[23] Losses such as these, as well as disagreement over the millions that were spent on unsuccessful candidates in the 2004 election, prompted the split. This split, coupled with the fact that 84 percent of all labor union members live in but twelve states, makes it difficult to predict whether labor will renew its presence nationwide.[24]

■ The Change to Win Coalition was formed in 2005 when seven unions broke away from the AFL-CIO. Here, Andrew Stern, president of the Service Employees International Union, (SEIU) speaks with reporters. To his far left is Teamsters President James Hoffa.

Photo courtesy: Jim West/Zuma Press

On Campus

SPEAKING UP

Many conservative college students believe that their voices are being stifled on campuses across the United States. Some charge that there is discrimination by professors and a lack of respect of diverse views in the classroom. Others say that the hiring process favors liberal professors. Some charge a bias in the selection of campus speakers and funding of groups.

A 2002 study by the Center for the Study of Popular Culture revealed that at the nation's top thirty-two universities, Democratic professors greatly outnumbered Republicans. Said Harvey Mansfield, a conservative Harvard political scientist, "We have sixty members in the department of government. Maybe three are Republicans. How could that be just by chance? How could that be fair?"[a]

The Center for the Study of Popular Culture has drafted an Academic Bill of Rights that it is urging colleges and universities to adopt. This document requests institutions of higher learning to "include both liberal and conservative viewpoints in their selection of campus speakers and syllabuses for courses and to choose faculty members 'with a view toward fostering a plurality of methodologies and perspectives.'"[b] It also notes a variety of ways in which students' academic freedom can be compromised, including:

- Mocking national or religious leaders.
- Forcing students to take a particular point of view in assignments.
- Requiring readings that cover only one side of an issue.

University administrators and the American Association of University Professors (AAUP) have been nearly unanimous in their disapproval of the center's proposed Academic Bill of Rights. "The danger of such guidelines," says the AAUP, "is that they invite diversity to be measured by political standards that diverge from the academic criteria of the scholarly profession." The AAUP points out that to comply with this Academic Bill of Rights, a professor professing a Nazi philosophy would need to be hired even "if that philosophy is not deemed a reasonable scholarly option within the discipline."[c]

Former Reagan White House lawyer David Horowitz, president of the Center for the Study of Popular Culture in California, has penned *The Professors: The 101 Most Dangerous Academics in America,* profiling the professors he considers among the most liberal in America and accusing them of "poisoning the minds of today's college students."[d] His group, Students for Academic Freedom, has chapters on more than 150 college campuses around the nation and works to pass state academic freedom legislation. It also works with many campus College Republican chapters. Its work has proven effective, especially in drawing the attention of conservative lawmakers to the problems that Horowitz and many other conservatives see as the liberal orthodoxy on college campuses. The Pennsylvania legislature, for example, approved a resolution calling on its fourteen state colleges to make sure that their campuses are free from what the center calls "the imposition of ideological orthodoxy."[e]

At some schools, including the University of Colorado, students can post alleged discrimination by liberal professors on special student-created Web sites.[f] The University of Texas at Austin has a "Professor Watch List," and NoIndoctrination.org allows students from all over the country to post complaints about particular professors. Many professors view this as a form of blacklisting similar to that which existed in the 1950s when professors who were suspected of being members of or sympathetic to the Communist Party were barred from teaching positions.

QUESTIONS

1. On some campuses, rewards of up to $100 have been posted for lecture notes and recordings of liberal professors' lectures. Are these legitimate interest group tactics or violations of basic principles of academic freedom?
2. Getting issues on the public agenda is often as important for groups as the actual passage of legislation or rules. How successful have conservative student groups been on your campus in having issues of classroom bias addressed?

---

[a]Quoted in Yilu Zhao, "Taking the Liberalism Out of Liberal Arts," *New York Times* (April 3, 2004): B9.

[b]Zhao, "Taking the Liberalism Out."

[c]http://www.aaup.org.

[d]David Horowitz, *The Professors: The 101 Most Dangerous Academics in America* (New York: Regnery, 2006).

[e]Bob Kemper, "Conservatives Gain Foothold on Campus," *Atlanta Journal-Constitution* (October 9, 2005): 1C.

[f]Dave Curtin, "Students' Site Solicits Allegations of CU Bias," *Denver Post* (January 20, 2004): A1.

What Do Interest Groups Do?

NOT ALL INTEREST GROUPS are political, but they may become politically active when their members believe that a government policy threatens or affects group goals. Interest groups also enhance political participation by motivating like-minded

**Comparing
Interest Groups**

individuals to work toward a common goal. Legislators often are much more likely to listen to or be concerned about the interests of a group as opposed to the interests of any one individual.

Just as members of Congress are assumed to represent the interests of their constituents in Washington, D.C., interest groups are assumed to represent the interests of their members to policy makers at all levels of government. In the 1950s, for example, the National Association for the Advancement of Colored People (NAACP) was able to articulate and present the interests of African Americans to national decision makers even though as a group they had little or no electoral clout, especially in the South. Without the efforts of the civil rights groups discussed in chapter 6, it is unlikely that either the courts or Congress would have acted as quickly to make discrimination illegal. By banding together with others who have similar interests, all sorts of individuals—from railroad workers to women to physical therapists to campers to homosexuals to mushroom growers—can advance their collective interests. Getting celebrity support or hiring a lobbyist to advocate those interests in Washington, D.C., or a state capital also increases the likelihood that issues of concern to them will be addressed and acted on favorably.

There is a downside to interest groups, however. Because groups make claims on society, they can increase the cost of public policies. The elderly can push for more costly health care and Social Security programs; people with disabilities, for improved access to public buildings; industry, for tax loopholes; and veterans, for improved benefits. Many Americans believe that interest groups exist simply to advance their own selfish interests, with little regard for the rights of other groups or, more importantly, of people not represented by any organized group.

Whether good or bad, interest groups play an important role in U.S. politics. In addition to enhancing the democratic process by providing increased representation and participation, they increase public awareness about important issues, help frame the public agenda, and often monitor programs to guarantee effective implementation. Most often, they accomplish these things through some sort of lobbying activities as well as participating in elections. But, as the rich and powerful appear to be spending far more than those groups representing poor and working-class interests, there is increasing cause for concern.

LOBBYING

MOST INTEREST GROUPS put lobbying at the top of their agendas. **Lobbying** is the process by which interest groups attempt to assert their influence on the policy-making process. The exact origin of the term lobbying is disputed. In mid-seventeenth-century England, there was a room located near the floor of the House of Commons where members of Parliament would congregate and could be approached by their constituents and others who wanted to plead a particular cause. Similarly, in the United States, people often waited outside the chambers of the House and Senate to speak to members of Congress as they emerged. Because they waited in the lobbies to argue their cases, by the nineteenth century they were commonly referred to as lobbyists. Another piece of folklore explains that when Ulysses S. Grant was president, he would frequently walk from the White House to the Willard Hotel on Pennsylvania Avenue just to relax in its comfortable and attractive lobby. Interest group representatives and those seeking favors from Grant would crowd into that lobby and try to press their claims. Soon they were nicknamed lobbyists.

Not only do large, organized interests have their own lobbyists, but other groups, including colleges, trade associations, cities, states, and even foreign nations, also hire lobbying firms (some law firms have lobbying specialists) to represent them in the halls of Congress or to get through the bureaucratic maze.

Most politically active groups use lobbying to make their interests heard and understood by those who are in a position to influence or cause change in governmental

lobbying
The activities of a group or organization that seeks to influence legislation and persuade political leaders to support the group's position.

policies. (See Global Perspective: Fighting HIV/AIDS.) Depending on the type of group and on the role it is looking to play, lobbying can take many forms. You probably have never thought of the Boy Scouts or Girl Scouts as political. Yet, when Congress began debating the passage of legislation dealing with discrimination in private clubs, representatives of both organizations testified in an attempt to persuade Congress to allow them to remain single-sex organizations. Similarly, you probably don't often think of golf clubs as political. Yet, when the Augusta National Golf Course refused to allow women to become members, the National Council of Women's Organizations, an umbrella organization of more than 200 organizations, made that decision political by contacting sponsors of the Masters Tournament and asking them to withdraw their sponsorship.

As Table 16.2 indicates, there are at least twenty-three legal ways for lobbyists and organizations to influence policy on the state and national level. Almost all interest groups lobby by testifying at hearings and contacting legislators. Other groups also provide information that decision makers might not have the time, opportunity, or interest to gather on their own. Of course, information these groups provide is designed to present the group's position in a favorable light, although a good lobbyist for an interest group also will note the downside to proposed legislation. Interest groups also file lawsuits to lobby the courts, and some even engage in

Photo courtesy: Dennis Cook/AP Wide World Photos

■ Julia Roberts testifies before the House Appropriations Subcommittee on Labor, Health and Human Services to appeal for money to fight Rett's Syndrome. Several stars including George Clooney, Michael J. Fox, and the late Christopher Reeve have also used their celebrity status to lobby Congress on behalf of issues of personal concern.

TABLE 16.2 GROUPS AND LOBBYISTS USING EACH LOBBYING TECHNIQUE (PERCENTAGE)

| | State-Based Groups | | Washington, D.C.- |
Technique	Lobbyists (n = 595)	Organizations (n = 301)	Based Groups (n = 175)
1. Testifying at legislative hearings	98	99	99
2. Contacting government officials directly to present point of view	98	97	98
3. Helping to draft legislation	96	88	85
4. Alerting state legislators to the effects of a bill on their districts	96	94	75
5. Having influential constituents contact legislator's office	94	92	80
6. Consulting with government officials to plan legislative strategy	88	84	85
7. Attempting to shape implementation of policies	88	85	89
8. Mounting grassroots lobbying efforts	88	86	80
9. Helping to draft regulations, rules, or guidelines	84	81	78
10. Raising new issues and calling attention to previously ignored problems	85	83	84
11. Engaging in informal contacts with officials	83	81	95
12. Inspiring letter-writing or telegram campaigns	82	83	84
13. Entering into coalitions with other groups	79	93	90
14. Talking to media	73	74	86
15. Serving on advisory commissions and boards	58	76	76
16. Making monetary contributions to candidates	—	45	58
17. Attempting to influence appointment to public office	44	42	53
18. Doing favors for officials who need assistance	41	36	56
19. Filing suit or otherwise engaging in litigation	36	40	72
20. Working on election campaigns	—	29	24
21. Endorsing candidates	—	24	22
22. Running advertisements in media about position	18	21	31
23. Engaging in protests or demonstrations	13	21	20

Source: State-Based Groups: Anthony J. Nownes and Patricia Freeman, "Interest Group Activity in the States," *Journal of Politics* 60 (1998): 92. Washington, D.C.-Based Groups: Kay Lehman Schlozman and John Tierney, "More of the Same: Washington Pressure Group Activity in a Decade of Change," *Journal of Politics* 45 (1983): 358.

Global Perspective

FIGHTING HIV/AIDS

The number of people worldwide living with HIV/AIDS rose from approximately 8 million in 1990 to nearly 39 million in 2005 and continues to grow. An estimated 63 percent of people living with HIV/AIDS reside in sub-Saharan Africa, a region suffering from high rates of poverty and where nations lack the funding and infrastructure to effectively prevent the spread of the disease and care for those living with it. In his January 2003 State of the Union Address, President George W. Bush asked Congress to commit an unprecedented $15 billion over a five-year period to address global HIV/AIDS. This initiative, called the President's Emergency Plan for AIDS Relief, or PEPFAR, has focused on channeling money to HIV/AIDS relief groups in fifteen countries, twelve of them in sub-Saharan Africa.

AIDS prevention groups have clashed over a U.S. preference for prevention programs stressing the ABC (Abstain, Be Faithful, use a Condom) approach. Domestic and international relief groups have criticized ABC's deemphasis of condom use, citing research that an emphasis on condom use saves lives. While a third of prevention funds were initially to be used to promote abstinence/being faithful programs (often called AB programs, since they generally ignore condom use as a preventive measure), a December 2005 document revealed a new requirement for 2006 that two-thirds of prevention funds be spent on AB programs. This preference for funding groups that promote abstinence reflects the influence social conservatives have within the administration and the Republican Party generally.

Groups critical of PEPFAR's funding of abstinence/being faithful programs argue that moral judgments regarding sexual activity have no place in international AIDS relief work, since people with HIV/AIDS—especially those in developing nations— are already subject to stigma and discrimination. Moral judgments, these groups argue, tend to intensify and provide a basis for justifying ongoing discrimination and even violence against people living with HIV/AIDS.

Groups accepting PEPFAR funds must abide by U.S. guidelines that require them to openly oppose sex trafficking and prostitution and that direct them to provide medically accurate information on condom use, including the public health benefits and failure rates of condom use.

Nevertheless, in keeping with the Bush administration's emphasis on faith-based initiatives, otherwise eligible groups cannot be required to endorse or use a prevention method or treatment program to which they have a religious or moral objection.

Some groups and nations have refused to accept PEPFAR funding because they believe that adopting an explicit policy condemning prostitution and sex trafficking will make it difficult for them to provide outreach and help to prostitutes and sex workers, groups in dire need of their help. Brazil, for example, turned down $40 million in PEPFAR funds, citing ethical and human rights principles.

A U.S. Government Accountability Office report in April 2006 found that current policies are less effective than they could be because disbursement rules do not take into account local and regional differences. For example, while U.S. government rules require that 20 percent of relief aid be dedicated to prevention measures, in some areas prevention efforts are doing well and the funds would be more effective if used to purchase necessary medicine or supplies.

Controversies aside, the impact of PEPFAR funds on the AIDS pandemic is significant. PEPFAR supported care for over 1.7 million people living with HIV/AIDS through March 2005. By the end of September 2005, the number of people helped by PEPFAR funds had reached nearly 3 million.

QUESTIONS

1. To what extent should religious and moral values influence U.S. policy toward HIV/AIDS relief?
2. If you were a U.S. policy maker, to what extent would you allow the nations and groups receiving U.S. funds determine how those funds would be allocated to provide HIV/AIDS relief?

Sources: UNAIDS/WHO 2006 Report on the Global AIDS Epidemic; Government Accountability Office Report: Spending Requirement Presents Challenges for Allocating Prevention Funding Under the President's Emergency Plan for AIDS Relief, April, 2006; http://www.avert.org; and "Action Today, a Foundation for Tomorrow: Second Annual Report to Congress on the President's Emergency Plan for AIDS Relief, February 2006."

protests or demonstrations as a form of lobbying public opinion or decision makers. Figure 16.3 illustrates how much some groups and businesses spend on lobbying, including contributions to political campaigns.

Lobbying Congress Efforts to reform lobbying continue to plague members of Congress who are the targets of a wide variety of lobbying activities: congressional testimony on behalf of a group, individual letters from interested constituents, campaign contributions, trips, speaking fees, or the outright payment of money for votes. Of course, the last item is illegal, but there are numerous documented instances of money

FIGURE 16.3 TOP LOBBYING EXPENDITURES

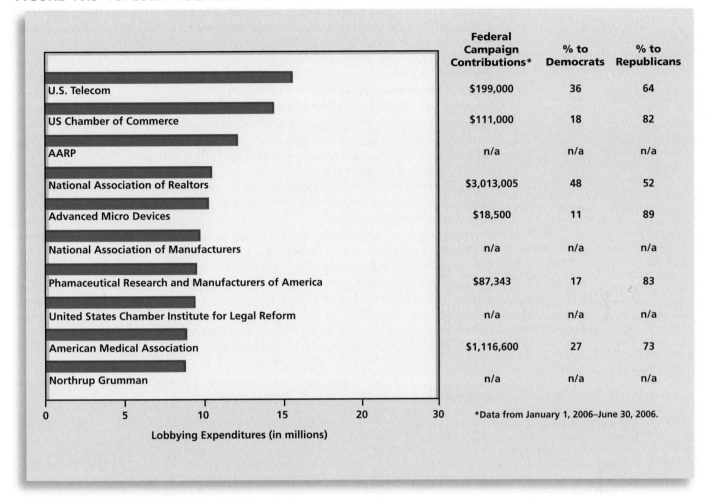

	Federal Campaign Contributions*	% to Democrats	% to Republicans
U.S. Telecom	$199,000	36	64
US Chamber of Commerce	$111,000	18	82
AARP	n/a	n/a	n/a
National Association of Realtors	$3,013,005	48	52
Advanced Micro Devices	$18,500	11	89
National Association of Manufacturers	n/a	n/a	n/a
Phamaceutical Research and Manufacturers of America	$87,343	17	83
United States Chamber Institute for Legal Reform	n/a	n/a	n/a
American Medical Association	$1,116,600	27	73
Northrup Grumman	n/a	n/a	n/a

Lobbying Expenditures (in millions)

*Data from January 1, 2006–June 30, 2006.

Source: Political Moneyline, http://www.tray.com; Center for Responsive Politics, http://www.opensecrets.org.

changing hands for votes. Because, as discussed in chapter 7, lobbying plays such an important role in Congress, many effective lobbyists often are former members of that body, former staff aides, former White House officials or Cabinet officers, or other Washington insiders. This type of lobbyist frequently drops in to visit members of Congress or their staff members and often takes them to lunch, to play golf, or to parties.

Lobbying Congress and issue advocacy are skills that many people have developed over the years. In 1869, for example, women gathered in Washington, D.C., for the second annual meeting of the National Woman Suffrage Association and marched to Capitol Hill to hear one of their members (unsuccessfully) ask Congress to pass legislation to enfranchise women under the terms of the Fourteenth Amendment. Practices such as these floor speeches are no longer permitted.

Today, lobbyists try to develop close relationships with senators and House members in an effort to enhance their access to the policy-making process. A symbiotic relationship between members of Congress, interest group representatives, and affected bureaucratic agencies often develops. In these iron triangles and issue networks (discussed in chapter 9), congressional representatives and their staff members, who face an exhausting workload and legislation they frequently know little about, often look to lobbyists for information. "Information is the currency on Capitol Hill, not dollars," said one lobbyist.[25] According to one aide: "My boss demands a speech and a

SIMULATION

You Are a Lobbyist

statement for the *Congressional Record* for every bill we introduce or co-sponsor—and we have a lot of bills. I just can't do it all myself. The better lobbyists, when they have a proposal they are pushing, bring it to me along with a couple of speeches, a *Record* insert, and a fact sheet."[26]

Not surprisingly, lobbyists work most closely with representatives who share their interests.[27] A lobbyist from the NRA, for example, would be unlikely to try to influence a liberal representative who was on record as strongly in favor of gun control. It is much more effective for a group such as the NRA to provide useful information for its supporters and to those who are undecided. Good lobbyists also can encourage members to file amendments to bills favorable to their interests. They also can urge their supporters in Congress to make speeches (often written by the group) and to pressure their colleagues in the chamber.

A lobbyist's effectiveness depends largely on his or her reputation for fair play and provision of accurate information. No member of Congress wants to look uninformed. As one member noted: "It doesn't take very long to figure out which lobbyists are straightforward, and which ones are trying to snow you. The good ones will give you the weak points as well as the strong points of their case. If anyone ever gives me false or misleading information, that's it—I'll never see him again."[28]

Capitol Hill is often a stepping stone to a career as a lobbyist. As illustrated in Figure 16.4, a 2005 study found that 43 percent of the 198 members of the House and Senate who left office since 1998 became registered lobbyists. Retiring to become a lobbyist was unusual as recently as two decades ago, say congressional historians.[29] But, over the past decade, House leaders in particular urged many members

FIGURE 16.4 LEAVING CONGRESS FOR LOBBYING CAREERS

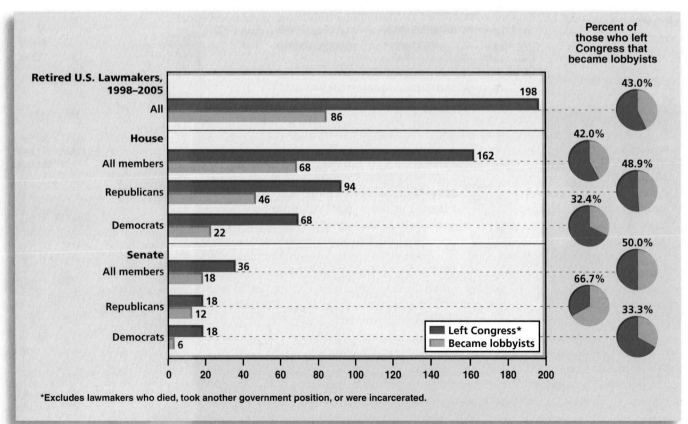

*Excludes lawmakers who died, took another government position, or were incarcerated.

Sources: Public Citizen; *Washington Post* (July 27, 2005): A19.

and their staffers to follow this route. In fact, in the mid-1990s, Republican House Majority Leader Tom DeLay (R–TX) even devised what initially was called a K Street Strategy and later the K Street Project to punish lobbying firms that hired any Democrats, thus paving the way for a huge influx of Republicans into lobbying shops. Underscoring the effectiveness of that plan, after the 2000 presidential elections, 62 percent of the Republicans but only 15 percent of the Democrats joined lobbying firms.[30]

Lobbying the Executive Branch

As the scope of the federal government has expanded and legislation often originates in the executive branch, lobbying that branch has increased in importance and frequency. Groups often target one or more levels of the executive branch be-

Photo courtesy: By permission of Mike Luckovich and Creators Syndicate, Inc.

■ This cartoon presents one popular, although not always correct, view of how legislation gets enacted on Capitol Hill.

cause there are so many potential access points, including the president, White House staff, and the numerous levels of the executive-branch bureaucracy. Groups try to work closely with the administration to influence policy decisions at their formulation and later implementation stages. As with congressional lobbying, the effectiveness of a group often depends on its ability to provide decision makers with important information and a sense of where the public stands on the issue.

Historically, group representatives have met with presidents or their staff members to urge policy directions. Most presidents also have set up staff positions to provide interest groups or organizations with access to the administration. Many of these offices, such as those dealing with consumer affairs, the environment, minority affairs, or women's issues, are routinely the target of organized interests.

An especially strong link exists between interest groups and regulatory agencies (see chapter 9). Because of the highly technical aspects of much regulatory work, many groups employ Washington attorneys and lobbying firms to deal directly with the agencies. So great is interest group influence in the decision-making process of these agencies that many people charge that the agencies have been captured by the interest groups.

Groups often monitor the implementation of the laws or policies they advocated. The National Women's Law Center, for example, has been instrumental in seeing that Title IX, which was passed by Congress to mandate educational equity for women and girls, be enforced fully. It has successfully sued several colleges and universities that have failed to provide equity in athletic funding for men and women.

Lobbying the Courts

The courts, too, have proved a useful target for interest groups.[31] Although you might think that the courts decide cases that affect only the U.S. parties involved or that they should be immune from political pressures, interest groups for years have recognized the value of lobbying the courts, especially the Supreme Court, and many political scientists view it as a form of political participation.[32] As shown in Table 16.2, 72 percent of the Washington D.C.-based groups surveyed participated in litigation as a lobbying tool.

Generally, interest group lobbying of the courts can take two forms: direct sponsorship or the filing of *amicus curiae* briefs. When a case a group is interested in but not actually sponsoring comes before a court, the organization often will file an *amicus* brief—either alone or with other like-minded groups—to inform the justices of the group's policy preference, generally offered in the guise of legal arguments. Over the years, as the number of both liberal and conservative groups viewing litigation as a useful tactic has increased, so has the number of briefs submitted to the courts. Most major Supreme Court cases noted in this book have been sponsored by an interest group, or one or both of the parties in the case have been supported by an *amicus curiae* brief. Interest groups also file cases in state supreme courts, but in much lower numbers.

In addition to litigating, interest groups try to influence who is nominated to the federal courts. For example, they play an important role in judicial nominees' Senate confirmation hearings, as discussed in chapter 10. In 1991, for example, 112 groups testified or filed prepared statements for or against the controversial nomination of Clarence Thomas to the U.S. Supreme Court.[33] Although interest group activity was more subdued during the 2005 nominations of John G. Roberts Jr. and Samuel A. Alito Jr., groups still spent significant sums of money and other resources advocating for the confirmation or defeat of these nominees.

Litigation and efforts to influence the outcome of judicial nominations to the federal courts are not the only ways that interest groups lobby jurists. It is becoming increasingly more common for interest groups of all persuasions to pay for trips for judges to attend "informational conferences" or simply to interact with judges by paying for club memberships and golf outings, as highlighted in American Values/American Voices: Trips for Judges? In fact, many commentators criticized the absence of Justice Antonin Scalia from the swearing in of Chief Justice Roberts, because Scalia was on a golf outing at the Ritz Carleton in Bachelor Gulf, Colorado. This outing was part of a legal conference sponsored by the Federalist Society, a group that, as noted in chapter 10, has been increasingly influential in the appointment process of federal judges during the Bush administration.[34]

Grassroots Lobbying As the term implies, grassroots lobbying is a form of pressure-group activity that attempts to involve individuals who contact their representatives directly in an effort to affect policy.[35] Although it often involves door-to-door informational or petition drives—a tried and true method of lobbying—the term also encompasses more modern forms such as fax and Internet lobbying of lawmakers. As early as the 1840s, women (who could not vote) used petition campaigns to persuade state legislators to enact Married Women's Property Acts that gave women control of their earnings and a greater legal say in the custody of their children. Petitioning has come a long way since then. It is now routine for interest groups to e-mail their members and to provide a direct Web link as well as suggested text that citizens can use to lobby their legislators.

VIDEO DEBATE
Lobbyists

Interest groups regularly try to inspire their members to engage in grassroots activity, hoping that lawmakers will respond to those pressures and the attendant publicity. In essence, the goal of many organizations is to persuade ordinary voters to serve as their advocates. In the world of lobbying, there are few things more useful than a list of committed supporters. Radio talk-show hosts such as Rush Limbaugh try to stir up their listeners by urging them to contact their representatives in Washington, D.C. Other interest groups now run carefully targeted and costly television advertisements pitching one side of an argument. Some of these undefined masses, as they join together on the Internet or via faxes, may be mobilized into one or more groups.

Protests and Radical Activism An occasional though highly visible tactic used by some groups is protest activity. Although it is much more usual for a group's members to opt for more conventional forms of lobbying or to influence policy through the electoral process, when these forms of pressure-group activities are unsuccessful, some groups (or individuals within groups) resort to more forceful measures to attract attention to their cause. Since the Revolutionary War, violent, illegal protest has been one tactic of organized interests. The Boston Tea Party, for example, involved breaking all sorts of laws, although no one was hurt physically. Other forms of protest, such as Shays's Rebellion, ended in tragedy for

American Values/American Voices

TRIPS FOR JUDGES

As noted in American Values/American Voices: Judicial Independence and the Court of World Opinion in chapter 10, the independence of the federal judiciary is a core American value that is now, according to many, coming under attack. What was not discussed in chapter 10 is the growing concern that interest groups are affecting the judiciary, and even how judges and justices vote, by offering them the same sort of trips and gifts that are used to influence legislators. Justice Antonin Scalia's notable absence from the swearing in of the new Chief Justice of the Supreme Court, John G. Roberts Jr., added fuel to the debate over the propriety of what critics call judicial junkets and the question of whether or not they violate basic American values.

Although ABC News recorded Scalia playing tennis, fishing, and socializing with members of the Federalist Society, when asked later why he missed Roberts's swearing in, he was reluctant to say any more about his absence other than that he had a "commitment that I couldn't break." The event invitation, however, offered attendees an exclusive and "rare opportunity to spend time, both socially and intellectually with Scalia."[a] He even attended a cocktail party hosted by the lobbying firm where Jack Abramoff had worked, which was packed with lawyers who regularly do business with the Supreme Court. Scalia also gave ten hours of lectures to more than hundred lawyers on issues of separation of powers.[b] He appeared to have no second thoughts about his attendance at the event, even though earlier he was resoundingly criticized for going on a hunting trip with Vice President Dick Cheney just before the Court heard a case involving the vice president.

Disclosure forms that Supreme Court justices must submit annually reveal that five of the nine justices accepted "tens of thousands of dollars in valuable gifts." Justice Clarence Thomas, for example, accepted golf club memberships, scholarships to help pay for his nephew's education, and even a rare Bible estimated to be worth nearly $20,000.[c] Interestingly, rules about what kinds of gifts jurists can accept apply only to lower federal court judges, but many critics believe that the justices of the Supreme Court should, by action and public pronouncements, follow a higher ethical standard.

The Community Rights Counsel (CRC), a liberal group that tracks what it calls "junketing judges," notes that it is conservative, anti-regulatory organizations that dominate the provision of exclusive, free trips for judges. The "big three"—the Law and Economics Center (LEC), the Foundation for Research on Economics and the Environment (FREE), and the Liberty Fund—provided trips for 125 judges and have conducted seminars attended by about 14 percent of federal judiciary that advance a conservative/libertarian approach to economic and environmental issues.[d] The CRC's Web page notes that "there is considerable evidence that the education judges receive at "big three" seminars is influencing judicial opinions." It believes that attendance at these seminars makes judges more likely to practice a "new strand of judicial activism that is distinctly pro-market, clearly hostile to environmental regulations and decidedly in keeping with the curriculum of FREE seminars."[e] Funding for all three groups comes from private foundations as well as corporations with business before the Court, including Exxon Mobile, Ford Motor Company, and Proctor and Gamble.[f] The CRC, however, has been criticized because it does not offer similar criticisms of trips paid for by more moderate groups such as the Aspen Institute.[g]

Former Chief Justice William H. Rehnquist had defended these conferences, saying that judges "are getting valuable education unavailable elsewhere."[h] In a sharply contrasting voice, Senator Russell Feingold (D–WI) asked John G. Roberts Jr. during his confirmation hearings to study the ethics problems posed by these seminars. While Roberts pledged to do so, it is unlikely that any moves will be made to restrict these trips. While many looked to the American Bar Association, yet another interest group, to weigh in with proposed changes to its Model Code of Judicial Conduct to tighten travel rules, its first draft did nothing to suggest ending judicial junkets.[i]

QUESTIONS

1. What value can you see to these kinds of trips for judges?
2. Should there be an equal-time rule requiring judges to attend courses offered by groups on both sides of the ideological divide, or should judges continue to attend courses of their own choosing?

---

[a]Brian Ross, "Supreme Court Ethics Problem?" *Nightline,* ABC News, January 23, 2006.

[b]Karen Abbott, "Scalia Takes Heat for 'Junket'; Lawyers Defend His Teaching of a Course at Colorado Resort," *Rocky Mountain News* (January 25, 2006): 9A.

[c]Abbott, "Scalia Takes Heat for 'Junket.'"

[d]"Who's Junketing the Judges," Trips for Judges, http://tripsforjudges.com.

[e]"Why Junkets Matter," Trips for Judges, http://tripsforjudges.com.

[f]"Funding Sources and Litigation Ties," Trips for Judges, http://tripsforjudges.com.

[g]"Judicial Seminars Are Not Always Junkets," *Tampa Tribune* (May 25, 2006): 16.

[h]"Rehnquist Defends Groups' Trips for Judges," *Milwaukee Journal Sentinel* (May 15, 2001): 4A.

[i]"Time to Ban Judicial Junkets," *New York Times* (October 15, 2005): A18: and Dorothy Samuels, "Judiciary, Too, Has a Lobbying Scandal," *Sacramento Bee* (January 22, 2006): E4.

---

some participants. Much more recently, anti-war protestors have been willing to march and risk detention and jail in the United States. And, protesters regularly try to picket or protest meetings of the International Monetary Fund or the World Bank. Political conventions as well as inaugurations also routinely are targeted by protesters.

SIMULATION

You Are the
Leader of
Concerned
Citizens for
World Justice

Animal rights activists such as People for the Ethical Treatment of Animals (PETA) and some pro-life groups such as Operation Rescue often rely on illegal protest activities to draw attention to their cause. Members of the Animal Liberation Front, for example, stalked the wife of a pharmaceutical executive, broke into her car, stole her credit cards, and then made over $20,000 in unauthorized charitable donations.[36] Some radical groups post the names of those they believe to be engaging in wrongful activity on the Web, along with their addresses and threats. As a result, some groups have faced federal terrorism charges.

Regulating Lobbying Practices For the first 150 years of our nation's history, federal lobbying practices went unregulated. While the courts remain largely free of lobbying regulations, reforms have altered the state of affairs in Congress and the executive branch. In 1946, in an effort to limit the power of lobbyists, Congress passed the Federal Regulation of Lobbying Act, which required anyone hired to lobby any member of Congress to register and file quarterly financial reports. For years, few lobbyists actually filed these reports and numerous good government groups continued to argue for the strengthening of lobbying laws. Until 1995, however, their efforts were blocked by civil liberties groups such as the ACLU, who argued that registration provisions violate the First Amendment's protections of freedom of speech and of the right of citizens to petition the government.

But, by 1995, public opinion polls began to show that Americans believed the votes of members of Congress were available to the highest bidder. Thus, in late 1995, after nearly fifty years of inaction, Congress passed the first effort to regulate lobbying since the 1946 act. The Lobbying Disclosure Act employs a strict definition of lobbyist (one who devotes at least 20 percent of a client's or employer's time to lobbying activities). It also requires lobbyists to: (1) register with the clerk of the House and the secretary of the Senate; (2) report their clients and issues and the agency or house they lobbied; and, (3) estimate the amount they are paid by each client. These reporting requirements make it easier for watchdog groups or the media to monitor lobbying activities. In fact, a comprehensive analysis by the Center for Responsive Politics revealed that by June 2005, 32,890 lobbyists were registered. Nearly $4 million was spent on lobbying for every member of Congress.[37]

TABLE 16.3 THE ETHICS IN GOVERNMENT ACT

The key provisions of the Ethics in Government Act deal with: (1) financial disclosure and (2) employment after government service.

(1) Financial disclosure: The president, vice president, and top-ranking executive employees must file annual public financial disclosure reports that list:

- The source and amount of all earned income; all income from stocks, bonds, and property; any investments or large debts; the source of a spouse's income, if any.
- Any position or offices held in any business, labor, or nonprofit organizations.

(2) Employment after government services: Former executive branch employees may not:

- Represent anyone before an agency for two years after leaving government service on matters that came within the former employees' sphere or responsibility (even if they were not personally involved in the matter).
- Represent anyone on any matter before their former agency for one year after leaving it, even if the former employees had no connection with the matter while in the government.

Source: Congressional Quarterly Weekly Report (October 28, 1978): 3121.

As noted in our opening vignette, after lobbyist Jack Abramoff pleaded guilty to extensive corruption charges, Congress pledged to re-examine the role of lobbyists in the legislative process and to pass major reforms to current lobbying laws. Nevertheless, while legislators said they wanted higher standards set and Democrats complained about "the GOP culture of corruption" no lobbying reform measures were passed in either house prior to the November 2006 election.

Formal lobbying of the executive branch is not governed by the restrictions in the 1995 Lobbying Disclosure Act. Executive branch employees are, however, constrained by the 1978 Ethics in Government Act (see Table 16.3). Enacted in the wake of the Watergate scandal, this act attempted to curtail questionable moves by barring members of the executive branch from representing any clients before their agency for one year after leaving governmental service. Thus, someone who worked in air pollution policy for the Environmental Protection Agency and then went to work for the Environmental Defense Fund would have to wait a year before lobbying his or her old agency.

ELECTION ACTIVITIES

In addition to trying to achieve their goals (or at least draw attention to them) through the conventional and unconventional forms of lobbying, many interest groups also become involved more directly in the electoral process. The 2004 Republican and Democratic presidential nominating conventions were the targets of significant organized interest group protests concerning each party's stance on a variety of issues, including the U.S.-led war in Iraq, same-sex marriage, the environment, gun control laws, and reproductive rights, among others.

Candidate Recruitment and Endorsements

Many interest groups claim to be nonpolitical. But, some interest groups recruit, endorse, and/or provide financial or other forms of support for political candidates. EMILY's List (EMILY stands for "Early money is like yeast—it makes the dough rise") was founded to support pro-choice Democratic women candidates, especially during party primary election contests. It now, however, like its Republican counterpart the WISH List (WISH stands for Women in the House and Senate), recruits and trains candidates in addition to contributing to their campaigns. EMILY's List, in 2004, for example, solicited volunteers to work on Betty Castor's campaign in Florida for the U.S. Senate. It paid the airfare and expenses for hundreds of volunteers from all over the nation to work in Florida in the four days leading up to the election. In 2006, it supported her daughter Kathy's successful bid for a U.S. House seat.

TIMELINE

Interest Groups and Campaign Finance

Democratic Leader Nancy Pelosi (D-CA) credited EMILY's List with the election of a record number of Democratic women to Congress in 2006. In a phone call to supporters the day after the election, Pelosi noted the critical role of the group's direct financial support to pro-choice Democratic women candidates and the support of its extensive on the ground get-out-the-vote efforts. Victories by over 50 Democratic women were key to giving Democrats control of the House and Senate.

Getting Out the Vote Many interest groups believe they can influence public policy by putting like-minded representatives in office. To that end, many groups across the ideological spectrum, such as the Christian Coalition and EMILY's List, launch massive get out the vote (GOTV) efforts. These include identifying prospective voters and getting them to the polls on Election Day. Well-financed interest groups such as MoveOn.org and Progress for America often produce issue-oriented ads for newspapers, radio, and television designed to educate the public as well as increase voter interest in election outcomes.

Rating the Candidates or Office Holders Many liberal and conservative ideological groups rate candidates to help their members (and the general public) evaluate the voting records of members of Congress. The American Conservative Union (conservative) and the Americans for Democratic Action (liberal)—two groups at ideological polar extremes—routinely rate candidates and members of Congress based on their votes on key issues (see Analyzing Visuals: Interest Group Ratings of Selected Members of Congress). These scores help voters know more about their representatives' votes on issues that concern them.

VISUAL LITERACY

PACs and the Money Trail

Political Action Committees As discussed in chapter 14, corporations, labor unions, and interest groups are allowed to form political action committees (PACs). PACs allow these interests to raise money to contribute to political candidates in national elections. Unlike some contributions to interest groups, contributions to PACs are not tax deductible, and PACs generally don't have members who call legislators; instead, PACs have contributors who write checks specifically for the purpose of campaign donations. PAC money plays a significant role in the campaigns of many congressional incumbents, often averaging over half a House candidate's total campaign spending. PACs generally contribute to those who have helped them before and who serve on committees or subcommittees that routinely consider legislation of concern to that group.

What Makes an Interest Group Successful?

THROUGHOUT OUR NATION'S HISTORY, all kinds of interests in society have organized to pressure the government for policy change. Some have been successful, and some have not. Political scientist E. E. Schattschneider once wrote, "Pressure politics is essentially the politics of small groups. . . . Pressure tactics are not remarkably successful in mobilizing general interests."[38] He was correct; historically, corporate interests often prevail over the concerns of public interest groups such as environmentalists.

VIDEO ROUNDTABLE

Successful interest Groups

All of the groups discussed in this chapter have one thing in common: they all want to shape the public agenda, whether by winning elections, maintaining the status quo, or obtaining favorable legislation or rulings from Congress, executive agencies, or the courts.[39] For powerful groups, simply making sure that certain issues never get discussed may be the goal. In contrast, those opposed to random stops of African

Analyzing Visuals

INTEREST GROUP RATINGS OF SELECTED MEMBERS OF CONGRESS

Among the election activities of interest groups are the endorsement of candidates for public office and the rating of candidates and incumbents. Interest groups inform their members, as well as the public generally, of the voting records of office holders, helping voters make an informed voting decision. The table displays the 2005 ratings of selected members of Congress by eight interest groups that vary greatly in their ideological tendencies. Each group rates the members of Congress on issues that are important to the group. For example, the AFL-CIO bases its rating on a member's votes in support of labor unions. After reviewing the table, answer the following critical thinking questions: Which members of the Senate would you consider the most liberal? Which groups' ratings did you use to reach your conclusion? Which members of the House would you consider the most conservative? Which groups' ratings did you use to reach your conclusion? Would it be important to know which of a representative's votes were used by each group to determine the rating? Explain your answer.

Member	ACU	ACLU	ADA	AFL-CIO	CC	CoC	LCV	NARAL
Senate								
Dianne Feinstein (D–CA)	12	78	95	69	0	50	90	100
Mitch McConnell (R–KY)	100	25	5	7	100	94	0	0
Kay Bailey Hutchison (R–TX)	95	22	15	7	100	94	5	20
Ted Kennedy (D–MA)	0	86	95	100	0	28	95	100
House								
John Boehner (R–OH)	100	0	0	13	91	88	0	0
Sheila Jackson Lee (D–TX)	14	95	100	93	7	56	61	100
Ileana Ros-Lehtinen (R–FL)	88	17	10	20	80	93	11	0
Henry Waxman (D–CA)	0	95	100	93	15	38	100	100

Key
ACU = American Conservative Union
ACLU = American Civil Liberties Union
ADA = Americans for Democratic Action
AFL-CIO = American Federation of Labor–Congress of Industrial Organizations
CC = Christian Coalition
CoC = Chamber of Commerce
LCV = League of Conservation Voters
NARAL = NARAL Pro-Choice America
Members are rated on a scale from 1 to 100, with 1 being the lowest and 100 being the highest support of a particular group's policies.

American or Middle Eastern drivers win when the issue becomes front-page news and law enforcement officials feel pressured to investigate, if not to stop altogether, the discriminatory practice of racial or ethnic profiling.

Groups often claim credit for winning legislation, court cases, or even elections individually or in coalition with other groups.[40] They also are successful when their leaders become elected officials or policy makers in any of the three branches of the government. For example, Representative Rosa DeLauro (D–CT) was a former political director of EMILY's List, and Senator Hillary Clinton (D–NY) was a former board member of the Children's Defense Fund. Associate Justice Ruth Bader Ginsburg was a former ACLU board member and the director of its Women's Rights Project. President George W. Bush's Secretary of Education Margaret Spellings was formerly associate executive director of the Texas Association of School Boards. Lynne Cheney, the wife of George W. Bush's vice president, Dick Cheney, is a senior fellow at the conservative American Enterprise Institutute and a former board member of the conservative Independent Women's Forum.

VIDEO ROUNDTABLE

Interest Groups and Representation

Political scientists have studied several phenomena that contribute in varying degrees—individually and collectively—to particular groups' successes. These include: (1) leaders; (2) patrons and funding; and, (3) a solid membership base.

LEADERS

Interest group theorists frequently acknowledge the key role that leaders play in the formation, viability, and success of interest groups while noting that leaders often vary from rank-and-file members on various policies.[41] Without the powerful pen of William Lloyd Garrison in the 1830s, who knows whether the abolitionist movement would have been as successful? Other notable prime movers include Frances Willard of the WCTU, Marian Wright Edelman of the Children's Defense Fund in 1968, and the Reverend Pat Robertson of the Christian Coalition in the 1990s. Most successful groups, especially public interest groups, are led by charismatic individuals who devote most of their energies to the cause.

The role of an interest-group leader is similar to that of an entrepreneur in the business world. Leaders of groups must find ways to attract members. As in the marketing of a new product, an interest-group leader must offer something attractive to persuade members to join. Potential members of the group must be convinced that the benefits of joining outweigh the costs. Union members, for example, must be persuaded that the cost of their union dues will be offset by the union's winning higher wages for them.

PATRONS AND FUNDING

All interest groups require adequate funding to build their memberships as well as to advance their policy objectives. Governments, foundations, and wealthy individuals can serve as **patrons,** providing crucial start-up funds for groups, especially public interest groups.[42] Advertising, litigating, and lobbying are expensive. Without financiers, few public interest groups could survive their initial start-up period. Many interest groups rely on membership dues, direct-mail solicitations, and patrons to remain in business. Charismatic leaders often are especially effective fundraisers and recruiters of new members.

MEMBERS

Organizations usually are composed of three kinds of members. At the top are a relatively small number of leaders who devote most of their energies to the single group. The second tier of members generally is involved psychologically as well as organizationally. They are the workers of the group—they attend meetings, pay dues, and chair committees to see that things get done. In the bottom tier are the rank and file, members who don't actively participate. They pay their dues and call themselves group members, but they do little more. Most group members fall into this last category.

In 1960, E. E. Schattschneider noted that the interest group system in the United States had a decidedly "upper-class bias," and he concluded that 90 percent of the population did not participate in an interest group, or what he called the pressure-group system.[43] Since the 1960s, survey data have revealed that group membership is drawn primarily from people with higher income and education levels. Individuals who are wealthier can afford to belong to more organizations because they have more money and, often, more leisure time. Money and education also are associated with greater confidence that one's actions will bring results, a further incentive to devote time to organizing or supporting interest groups. These elites often are more involved in politics and hold stronger opinions on many political issues. (See Join the Debate: Should There Be Limits on Interest Group Participation?)

patron
A person who finances a group or individual activity.

People who do belong to groups often belong to more than one. Overlapping memberships often can affect the cohesiveness of a group. Imagine, for example, that you are an officer in the College Republicans. If you call a meeting, people may not attend because they have academic, athletic, or social obligations. Divided loyalties and multiple group memberships frequently can affect the success of a group, especially if any one group has too many members who simply fall into the dues-paying category.

Groups vary tremendously in their ability to enroll what are called potential members (see Table 16.4). According to economist Mancur Olson Jr., all groups provide some **collective good**—that is, something of value, such as money, a tax write-off, a good feeling, or a better environment, that can't be withheld from a nonmember.[44] If one union member at a factory gets a raise, for example, all other workers at that factory will, too. Therefore, those who don't join or work for the benefit of the group still reap the rewards of the group's activity. The downside of this phenomenon is called the **free rider problem.** As Olson asserts, potential members may be unlikely to join a group because they realize that they will receive many of the benefits the group achieves, regardless of their participation. Not only is it irrational for free riders to join any group, but the bigger the group, the greater the free rider problem. Thus, groups need to provide a variety of other material benefits to convince potential members to join. The American Automobile Association, for example, offers roadside assistance and trip planning services to its members. Similarly, AARP offers a wide range of discount programs to its 35 million members over the age of fifty. Many of those members do not necessarily support all of the group's positions but simply want to take advantage of its discounts.

Several scholars examining why individuals join groups have found that a group's attempt to pursue a collective good is not always a mere by-product of the group's ability to provide selective material incentives, as Olson has argued. Specifically, they found that several factors help groups overcome the free rider problem. One factor is that members representing other groups or institutions are much more likely than individuals to value efforts to obtain collective goods. Another factor is that once a policy environment appears to threaten existing rights, many individuals come to realize those threats and join groups in exchange for only collective benefits.[45] Moreover, Olson, an economist, fails to consider that many political, Washington D.C.-based groups count other groups, and not just individuals, as their members. These alliances often are considered carefully by organized interests much in the way some individuals calculate their membership in groups.[46]

These alliances have important implications.[47] Although interest groups do work together in alliances, they also carve out policy niches to differentiate themselves to potential members as well as policy makers. While the National Women's Law Center, for example, vigorously pursues enforcement of Title IX through litigation, the National Organization for Women, although very supportive of Title IX, is more

collective good
Something of value that cannot be withheld from a nonmember of a group, for example, a tax write-off or a better environment.

free rider problem
Potential members fail to join a group because they can get the benefit, or collective good, sought by the group without contributing the effort.

TABLE 16.4 POTENTIAL VERSUS ACTUAL INTEREST GROUP MEMBERS

The goal of most groups is to mobilize all potential members, but as Mancur Olson Jr. points out, the larger the group, the more difficult it is to mobilize. To illustrate the potential versus actual membership phenomenon, here are several examples of groups and their potential memberships.

Population	Group	Number of Potential Members	Number of Actual Members
Governors	National Governors Association (includes territories)	55	55
Political Science Faculty	American Political Science Association	17,000	14,000
Physicians	American Medical Association (AMA)	775,000	250,000
African Americans	National Association for the Advancement of Colored People (NAACP)	37,500,000	500,000
Women	National Organization for Women (NOW)	150,000,000	500,000
Christians	Christian Coalition	207,980,000	350,000

Join the Debate

SHOULD THERE BE LIMITS ON INTEREST GROUP PARTICIPATION?

OVERVIEW: The First Amendment to the Constitution guarantees the right to freedom of speech, press, association, and the right to "petition the government for a redress of grievances." These are necessary rights in a democracy because they guarantee the right of the people—within the framework of law—to have their voice heard by the government. Grievances can be political or social in nature, and all citizens have the right to petition the government to have their (sometimes narrow) interest or issue addressed. This right includes expressing policy preferences. While political speech and activity as well as the actions of government are regulated by law to prevent the encroachment of undue influence and corruption, the line between appropriate regulation and rights violations often is difficult to discern. Additionally, in order for government to fulfill its functions, it must attempt to balance fairly the claims of very diverse competing interests. Because the framework within which interest groups and government must operate is contentious, regulation is necessary. But, when a group lobbies to change government policies, can the government require full disclosure of the group's activities and finances?

Depending on what is done with the information gathered from interest group disclosure requirements, the government may be acting in the public interest. For example, part of the mandate from the Lobbying Disclosure Act of 1995 (LDA) is to facilitate public access to information about lobbying groups as well as about the government's knowledge of their activities. The goal is to allow concerned citizens to verify accountability of both group and government activity—this allows government watchdog groups such as OpenSecrets to correlate lobbying activities with perceived government response. Moreover, insisting that groups disclose information allows both government and the public to know what individuals or groups are behind a lobby's agenda.

The political nature of lobbying activity may mean that interest groups are subject to a higher standard of disclosure and scrutiny. Just as the American people demand transparency in government activity, it seems reasonable that they be provided with information regarding those interest groups monitoring (or supporting) the government. To that end, requiring disclosure of group information is rational. But, what about the right to privacy? Should interest groups have the same right to privacy as individuals? After all, citizens are not required to disclose the reasons behind their votes or why they engage in political activity the way they do. Why should interest groups be denied this standard of privacy?

ARGUMENTS FOR REGULATING INTEREST GROUP ACTIVITIES

- **Interest groups are not given a constitutional role to make or influence policy.** Though individuals and groups have the right to lobby the government, they have no unrestricted right to do so. Given literally thousands of interests, the government must have some means to prioritize and determine the legitimacy of various groups. For example, should a local 4H group have the same voice and access to national policy makers as the National Dairy Association?

involved in welfare reform as it affects women. Similarly, one study of gay and lesbian groups found that they avoided direct competition by developing different issue niches.[48] Some concentrate on litigation; others lobby for marriage law reform or open inclusion of gays in the military.

Small groups often have an organizational advantage because, for example, in a small group such as the National Governors Association, any individual's share of the collective good may be great enough to make it rational for him or her to join.

- **Regulation is necessary to ensure the public knows why and in what capacity an interest group is acting.** LDA's regulatory mandate is to ensure accountability in the lobbying process. The American public needs to know about corruption or misinformation not only coming from the government, but coming from interest groups as well. For instance, the Rainbow Push Coalition was implicated in lobbying the City of Chicago to keep an after-hours dance club open in which a fire subsequently caused twenty-one deaths. The club owners, Rainbow Push, and certain Chicago politicians were known to have a business relationship.
- **Regulation of interest groups allows the government to level the playing field.** Research published by the American Political Science Association (APSA) contends that inequality and unequal access to wealth harms the American democratic process. APSA implies that wealthier groups have a larger voice and thus more access to policy makers. By regulating interest groups, the federal government can ensure relative equality of access—and voice—to policy makers.

ARGUMENTS AGAINST REGULATING INTEREST GROUP ACTIVITIES

- **Government regulation of interest groups may stifle political speech.** For example, the U.S. Supreme Court upheld the Bipartisan Campaign Reform Act's provision prohibiting groups from issue advertising sixty days prior to a general election. Many scholars and legal experts believe that this is a fundamental violation of political speech rights, as it is now believed that money gives "voice" to the political process—and to deny groups the right to political advertisement is to deny political speech.
- **Regulation of groups essentially creates approved speech and politics.** By using regulation to determine which groups have the right to lobby the government, the government is in effect establishing which groups are legitimate (in both their activities and speech) and which are not. It is not the government's role to conclude whether a group's political activity and speech are more or less legitimate or important.
- **Government regulation of interest groups is not necessary.** In an open, pluralistic society, interest groups are subject to market dynamics. That is, those groups that truly represent broad or important interests will have their views heard over those that do not. Thus, a natural voice is given to those groups deemed by the American people to represent important interests and issues.

QUESTIONS

1. Is compelling disclosure of group information a violation of privacy rights? How can this be reconciled with the public's right to know?
2. Does the political nature of lobbyist activity demand a higher level of governmental scrutiny?

SELECTED READINGS

Herrnson, Paul S., Ronald G. Shaiko, and Clyde Wilcox, editors. *The Interest Group Connection, Second Edition.* Washington, D.C.: CQ Press, 2004.

Rozell, Mark J., Clyde Wilcox, David Madland. *Interest Groups in American Campaigns: The New Face of Electioneering, Second Edition.* Washington, D.C.: CQ Press, 2005.

Patrons, be they large foundations such as the Ford Foundation or individuals such as wealthy financier George Soros (who contributed over $15.8 million to new progressive organizations, including Americans Coming Together, MoveOn.org, and Campaign for America's Future, in an effort to defeat President George W. Bush in 2004), often eliminate the free rider problem for public interest groups.[49] They make the costs of joining minimal because they contribute much of the group's necessary financial support.[50]

Summary

INTEREST GROUPS LIE at the heart of the American social and political system. National groups first emerged in the 1830s. Since that time, the type, nature, sophistication, and tactics of groups have changed dramatically. In this chapter, we have made the following points:

1. What Are Interest Groups?

Those who study interest groups have offered a variety of definitions to explain what they are. Most definitions revolve around notions of associations or groups of individuals who share some sort of common interest or attitude and who try to influence or engage in activity to affect governmental policies or the people in government. Political scientists find it helpful to categorize interest groups in several ways. They study multi-issue versus single-issue groups. They also examine economic, public interest, and governmental units as participants in the interest group process.

2. The Origins and Development of American Interest Groups

Interest groups, national in scope, did not begin to emerge until around the 1830s. Later, from 1890 to 1920, the Progressive movement emerged. The 1960s saw the rise of a wide variety of liberal interest groups. By the 1970s through the 1980s, legions of conservatives were moved to form new groups to counteract those efforts. Business groups, corporations, and unions established their presence in Washington, D.C.

3. What Do Interest Groups Do?

Interest groups often fill voids left by the major political parties and give Americans opportunities to make claims, as a group, on government. The most common activity of interest groups is lobbying, which takes many forms. Groups routinely pressure members of Congress and their staffs, the president and the bureaucracy, and the courts; they use a variety of techniques to educate and stimulate the public to pressure key governmental decision makers. Interest groups also attempt to influence the outcome of elections; some run their own candidates for office. Others rate elected officials to inform their members how particular legislators stand on issues of importance to them. Political action committees (PACs), a way for some groups to contribute money to candidates for office, are another method of gaining support from elected officials and ensuring that supportive officials stay in office.

4. What Makes an Interest Group Successful?

Interest group success can be measured in a variety of ways, including a group's ability to get its issues on the public agenda, winning key pieces of legislation in Congress or executive branch or judicial rulings, or backing successful candidates. Several factors contribute to interest group success, including leaders and patrons, funding, and committed members.

KEY TERMS

civic virtue, p. 582
collective good, p. 609
disturbance theory, p. 584
earmark, p. 585
economic interest group, p. 584
free rider problem, p. 609
interest group, p. 584
lobbying, p. 596
lobbyist, p. 588
patron, p. 608
political action committee (PAC), p. 585
public interest group, p. 584
social capital, p. 582
trade association, p. 590

SELECTED READINGS

Baumgartner, Frank, and Beth Leech. *Basic Interests.* Princeton, NJ: Princeton University Press, 1998.

Berry, Jeffrey M. *The Interest Group Society,* 4th ed. New York: Addison Wesley, 2001.

Cigler, Allan J., and Burdett A. Loomis, eds. *Interest Group Politics,* 7th ed. Washington, DC: CQ Press, 2007.

Grossman, Gene M., and Elhanan Helpman. *Special Interest Politics.* Cambridge, MA: MIT Press, 2001.

Herrnson, Paul S., Ronald G. Shaiko, and Clyde Wilcox, eds. *The Interest Group Connection,* 2nd ed. Washington, DC: CQ Press, 2005.

Kollman, Ken. *Outside Lobbying: Public Opinion and Interest Group Strategies.* Princeton, NJ: Princeton University Press, 1998.

McGlen, Nancy E., et al. *Women, Politics, and American Society,* 4th ed. New York: Longman, 2004.

Nownes, Anthony. *Total Lobbying: What Lobbyists Want (and How They Try to Get It).* New York: Cambridge University Press, 2006.

Olson, Mancur, Jr. *The Logic of Collective Action: Public Goods and the Theory of Groups.* Cambridge, MA: Harvard University Press, 1965.

Sirota, David. *Hostile Takeover: How Big Money and Corruption Conquered Our Government—and How We Take It Back.* New York: Crown, 2006.

Truman, David B. *The Governmental Process: Political Interests and Public Opinion.* New York: Knopf, 1951.

Wright, John R. *Interest Groups and Congress: Lobbying, Contributions, and Influence.* New York: Longman, 2002.

WEB EXPLORATIONS

For more on NOW and the NRA, see
http://www.now.org and http://www.nra.org

For more about Common Cause and Public Citizen, Inc., see
http://www.commoncause.org and http://www.publiccitizen.org

For more on the Christian Coalition of America and other conservative Christian groups, see
http://www.cc.org and
http://www.focusonthefamily.org

For more on the AFL-CIO and SEIU, see
http://www.aflcio.org and http://www.seiu.org

To experience how the lobbying process works, go to
http://www.meyersandassociates.com/lobbyist.html

To learn more about the issue positions of selected groups mentioned in this chapter, see
http://www.adaction.org http://www.conservative.org and
http://www.aclu.org

Rx KEEPING OUR PROMISE TO SENIORS

SOCIAL WELFARE POLICY

17

IN 2003, THE UNITED STATES federal government assumed a new major responsibility in the area of health care for its citizens. Following years of agitation and national debate over the high cost of prescription drugs, President George W. Bush signed into law the Medicare Prescription Drug, Improvement, and Modernization Act. Hotly debated in Congress because of its expensive price tag and its controversial aspects, the legislation was hailed by President Bush as "the greatest advance in health care coverage for America's seniors since the founding of Medicare."[1] Seniors choosing to participate received drug discount cards in 2004, with the more extensive subsidized prescription benefit taking effect in 2006. The cost for the first ten years of this new government benefit was originally projected at $400 million, but shortly after the legislation was signed, the cost was recalculated to be significantly higher.

This was not the first time the federal government had taken on health care responsibilities. In 1965, the expensive new programs of Medicare (for the elderly) and Medicaid (for the poor) were established as part of an overall expansion of government programs to promote social welfare. Medicare became a sacred program in the decades that followed, and it achieved considerable success in improving the health of the nation's senior citizens.

However, the absence of a drug benefit as part of Medicare left many older Americans with decreased ability to pay for the prescription drugs they depend on to maintain their well-being. Prescription drug costs rose at double-digit rates in the late 1990s, and it was estimated in 2002 that approximately two-fifths of American retirees were without insurance to help pay for the escalating costs of essential medicine. This led to increasing demands for government action. Letters, calls, and petitions from constituents pressed members of Congress to act on the high cost of prescription drugs. Media stories about older Americans going bankrupt to pay for needed medications pushed the issue further onto center stage, and public hearings by Congress provided an additional spotlight. President Bush signed the prescription drug benefit into law in December 2003, and today millions of seniors are enrolled in the federal government's program.

While getting the prescription drug bill into law was an arduous task, implementing the legislation proved even more challenging. The provisions of the plan were difficult for many senior citizens to understand, and states struggled with administering the program. As the prescription benefits went into effect in early 2006, senior citizens expressed considerable disillusionment with the program. According to a survey by the Kaiser Family Foundation, American seniors were almost twice as likely to say they view the prescription drug benefit unfavorably (45 percent) as favorably (23 percent).[2] Such attitudes from the very individuals that the program was designed to assist had to be discouraging to the Bush administration, which had banked on the program as a key component of its domestic policy agenda.

Does establishing such an expensive new government program serve the national interest? For many seniors the answer was yes: it appeared that the passage of this new benefit meant that Congress and the president were finally addressing a serious concern in their lives. Other observers, however, were more skeptical: where will the money come from to pay the hundreds of billions of dollars this prescription drug benefit will cost just over its first ten years? According to one critic, "The drug benefit is a blatant pitch for the votes of the elderly that worsens the long-term budget outlook and will be paid for by the young."[3] Some opponents of the program argued that the new drug benefit was really a boon to pharmaceutical and insurance companies and didn't provide enough help to seniors. Was the government being responsible or irresponsible in establishing this new program? What obligation does the government owe to promoting the social welfare of its people?

---

social welfare policy
Government programs designed to improve quality of life.

SOCIAL WELFARE POLICY is a term that designates a broad and varied range of government programs designed to provide people with protection from poverty and hunger, to improve their health and physical well-being, provide education and employment training opportunities, and otherwise enable them to lead more secure, satisfying, and productive lives. In a nutshell, social welfare policies are intended to enhance the quality of life by acting as a safety net for citizens in need of assistance. They are meant to benefit all segments of society, but especially the less fortunate members, who often find it more difficult to provide for themselves and their families.

To examine the progress of social welfare policy, this chapter will explore the following issues:

- First, we will consider the nature of *the policy-making process*, presenting a model that provides a manageable way of dissecting the policy-making process and examining its components.

- Second, we will examine *the origins of social welfare policy* and describe how the government's commitment expanded in the twentieth century.

- Finally, we will examine *social welfare policies today*, including income security, health care, and public education.

The Policy-Making Process

WHILE THE FOCUS OF THIS CHAPTER is on social welfare policy, we begin with a more general look at the broader process of making government policy. **Public policy** is an intentional course of action followed by government in dealing with some problem or matter of concern.[4] Public policies are thus governmental policies, based on law; they are authoritative and binding on people. Individuals, groups, and even government agencies that do not comply with policies can be penalized through fines, loss of

public policy
An intentional course of action followed by government in dealing with some problem or matter of concern.

benefits, or even jail terms. The phrase "course of action" implies that policies develop or unfold over time. They involve more than a legislative decision to enact a law or a presidential decision to issue an executive order. Also important is how the law or executive order is carried out. The impact or meaning of a policy depends on whether it is vigorously enforced, enforced only in some instances, or not enforced at all.

THEORIES OF PUBLIC POLICY

Political scientists and other social scientists have developed many theories and models to explain the formation of public policies. According to elite theory, the chosen few or elite make all-important decisions in society. A proponent of elite theory, political scientist Thomas R. Dye, contends that all societies are divided into elites and masses.

Photo courtesy: Tom Toles/Universal Press Syndicate

The elites have power to make and implement policy, while the masses simply respond to the desires of the elites. Elite theorists believe that an unequal distribution of power in society is normal and inevitable.[5] Elites, however, are not believed to be immune from public opinion, nor do they by definition oppress the masses. Dye argues that in complex societies such as the United States, only a tiny minority of people serve as the elites.

In contrast to elite theory are other views of public policy, such as bureaucratic theory, interest group theory, and pluralist theory. According to bureaucratic theory, all institutions, governmental and nongovernmental, have fallen under the control of a large and ever growing bureaucracy that carries out policy using standardized procedures. This growing complexity of modern organizations has empowered bureaucrats, who become dominant as a consequence of their expertise and competence. Eventually, the bureaucrats wrest power from others, especially elected officials.

According to interest group theory, interest groups—not elites or bureaucrats—control the governmental process. The noted interest group theorist David B. Truman believed that there are so many potential pressure points in the three branches of the federal government, as well as at the state level, that interest groups can step in on any number of competing sides. The government then becomes the equilibrium point in the system as it mediates among competing interests.[6]

Many political scientists subscribe to the pluralist perspective. For example, Robert Dahl argues that political resources in the United States are scattered so widely that no single elite group could ever gain monopoly control over any substantial area of policy.[7] According to political scientist Theodore Lowi, participants in every political controversy get something; thus, each has some impact on how political decisions are made. Lowi contends that governments in the United States rarely say no to any well-organized interest, noting that since all organized interests receive some benefits, the public interest—what is good for the public at large—often tends to lose out in the American system.[8]

A MODEL OF THE POLICY-MAKING PROCESS

A popular model used to describe the policy-making process views it as a sequence of stages or functional activities. (This model, depicted in Figure 17.1, can be used

■ One of the most significant yet controversial pieces of legislation passed during the George W. Bush administration was the 2003 Medicare Prescription Drug, Improvement and Modernization Act. This law provided millions of the nation's senior citizens with financial benefits to help defray the skyrocketing costs of prescription drugs in the United States. While the benefits provided by this new program were welcomed by many elderly Americans, the Prescription Drug law was widely criticized for its complexity and escalating price tag for the federal government.

FIGURE 17.1 STAGES OF THE PUBLIC POLICY PROCESS

One of the best ways to understand public policy is to examine the process by which policies are made. While there are many unique characteristics of policy making at the various levels of government, there are commonalities that define the process from which public policies emerge. In the figure, the public policy process is broken down into seven steps. Each step has distinguishing features, but it is important to remember that the steps often merge into one another in a less distinct manner.

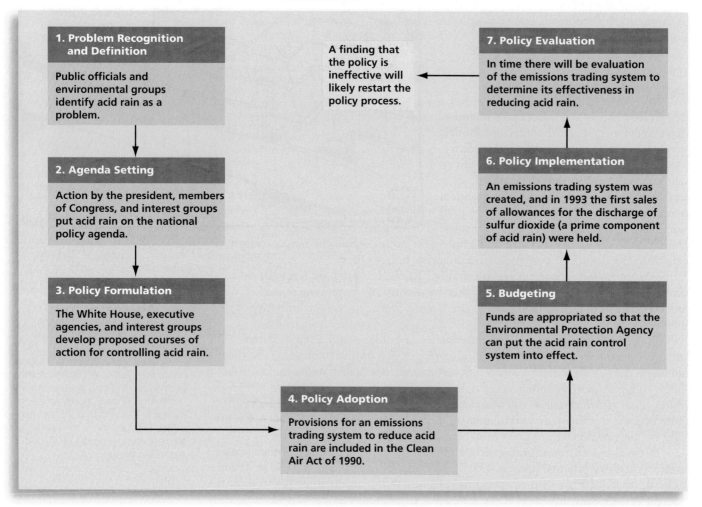

to analyze any of the issues discussed in this book.) Public policies do not just happen; rather, they are typically the products of a predictable pattern of events. Models for analyzing the policy-making process do not always explain *why* public policies take the specific forms that they do, however. That depends on the political struggles over particular policies. Nor do models necessarily tell us *who* dominates or controls the formation of public policy.

Policy making typically can be thought of as a process of sequential steps that are included in the following list:

- **Problem recognition**—identification of an issue that disturbs the people and leads them to call for governmental intervention.

- **Agenda setting**—government recognition that a problem is worthy of consideration for governmental intervention.

- **Policy formulation**—identification of alternative approaches to addressing the problems placed on government's agenda.
- **Policy adoption**—the formal selection of public policies through legislative, executive, judicial, and bureaucratic means.
- **Budgeting**—the allocation of resources to provide for the proper implementation of public policies.
- **Policy implementation**—the actual administration or application of public policies to their targets.
- **Policy evaluation**—the determination of a policy's accomplishments, consequences, or shortcomings.

With this overview in mind, let's now look in more detail at the various stages of the policy process or cycle.

PROBLEM RECOGNITION AND DEFINITION

At any given time, there are many conditions that disturb or distress people, such as polluted air and water, the outsourcing of jobs overseas, rising rates of childhood obesity, natural disasters, the rising cost of college tuition, lewdness or violence on television, and possible terrorist attacks. All disturbing conditions do not automatically become problems in need of public policy solutions, however. Some of them may be accepted as trivial, inevitable, or beyond the control of government.

For a condition to become a problem, there must be some criterion—a standard or value—that leads people to believe that the condition does not have to be accepted or acquiesced to and, further, that it is something with which government can deal effectively and appropriately. For example, natural disasters such as hurricanes are unlikely to be identified as a policy problem because there is little that government can do about them directly. The consequences of hurricanes—the human distress and property destruction that they bring—are another matter. Relief from the devastation of natural disasters can be a focus of government action, and agencies such as the Federal Emergency Management Agency (FEMA) have been set up to reduce these hardships. When these agencies fail to fulfill their roles, as FEMA did in the wake of Hurricane Katrina in 2005, the public requires answers for why government has not done its job.

Perceptions toward government responsibilities also change over time. For example, conditions that were once considered beyond government's responsibility may at a later time be identified as problems because of changes in public outlooks. At one time, care of children was considered the sole prerogative of parents. This perspective, however, began to change in the late 1880s in response to newspaper accounts of child abuse. During the 1960s, a time of social activism and concern about people's rights, all of the state legislatures enacted laws requiring the reporting of child abuse. In 1974, Congress enacted legislation requiring states to create child protection agencies. In 1993, President Bill Clinton signed the National Child Abuse Prevention Act, which established a national data base to track child abusers and prevent them from working in childcare centers. In this first decade of the twenty-first century, protection of children is clearly recognized as a public-sector responsibility.

Usually there is not a single, agreed-on definition of a problem. Indeed, political struggle often occurs at this stage because how the problem is defined helps determine what sort of action is appropriate. Consider one example. If we define access to transportation for people with disabilities as a transportation problem, then an acceptable solution is to provide people with disabilities with transportation by adapting the regular transportation system or by establishing other means of transport, such as a special van service. If we define access to transportation as a civil rights problem, however, then people with disabilities are entitled to equal access to the regular transportation system. Solving a problem once defined as a civil right might require extensive and expensive alterations to make *all* public transport accessible to people with disabilities. After some wavering between these definitions in the 1980s, the national government appeared to be moving toward the transportation view of the problem. But, the civil rights view triumphed with congressional passage of the Americans with Disabilities Act in 1990. The legislation mandated that local and state governments must make transportation accessible to the elderly and to all people with disabilities.

Problems differ not only in their definitions but also in the difficulty of resolving them. For instance, it is more difficult to tackle problems that affect large numbers of people or that require behavioral change than problems that have more focused solutions. (See Politics Now: The Politics of Immigration Reform.) In the area of environmental protection, there have been major improvements in surface water quality in the United States since the 1970s.[9] These improvements have been achieved because the solutions were relatively easy to reach through improved sewage treatment plants and stricter wastewater requirements for businesses. No substantial behavioral changes were required of the average U.S. citizen to achieve these accomplishments. In contrast, the issue of global warming stands as a policy problem with no easy solutions. In order to reduce the greenhouse gas emissions that have been linked to climate change, individuals will need to make behavioral adjustments—for example, in the amount of miles they drive and the size and performance of their vehicles. For elected officials eager to show tangible results to their constituents, it makes political sense to work on problems in which improvements can be made quickly and without direct costs to the public.

Note that public policies themselves are frequently viewed as problems or the causes of other problems. Thus, for some people, gun control legislation is a solution to gun violence. To the National Rifle Association (NRA), however, any law that restricts gun ownership is a problem because the NRA views such laws as inappropriately infringing on an individual's constitutional right to keep and bear arms. To social conservatives, legal access to abortion is a problem; for social liberals, laws restricting abortion access fall into the problem category.

AGENDA SETTING

Once a problem is recognized and defined as such by a significant segment of society, it must be brought to the attention of public officials and it must secure a place on an agenda.

Defining Agendas
An **agenda** is a set of issues to be discussed or given attention. In the area of public policy, there are two basic types of agendas: the systemic agenda and the governmental or institutional agenda.[10] The **systemic agenda** is essentially a discussion agenda; it comprises "all issues that are commonly perceived by the members of the political community as meriting public attention and as involving matters within the legitimate jurisdiction" of governments.[11] Every political community—national, state, and local—has a systemic agenda.

A **governmental** or **institutional agenda** includes only problems to which legislators or other public officials feel obliged to devote active and serious attention. Not all problems that attract the attention of officials are likely to have been widely discussed by the general public, or even the "attentive" public—those who follow certain issues closely. Acid rain was a widely discussed public problem in the 1980s that was addressed by the Clean Air Act of 1990, but there was little public awareness of the Pollution Prevention Act, also adopted in 1990. This act set priorities for pollution control programs in an attempt to improve their effectiveness.

Problems or issues (an issue emerges when disagreement exists over what should be done about a problem) may move onto an institutional agenda, whether from the

VIDEO DEBATE
**illegal
Immigration**

agenda
A set of issues to be discussed or given attention.

systemic agenda
All public issues that are viewed as requiring governmental attention; a discussion agenda.

governmental (institutional) agenda
The changing list of issues to which governments believe they should address themselves.

Politics Now

THE POLITICS OF IMMIGRATION REFORM

On May 1, 2006, the streets of America's cities were filled with nearly one million individuals protesting initiatives in Congress that would crack down on illegal immigration in the United States. In addition to marching, many of these protesters did not go to work that day and boycotted shopping to call attention to the positive economic impact that immigrants have on the nation. As Congress considered tightening the borders and stiffening penalties on illegal aliens, members of many immigrant communities sought to demonstrate the numerous contributions that immigrants, both legal and illegal, bring to the quality of life in the United States. Indeed, there is evidence that the estimated 12 million illegal immigrants living in the United States do make substantial contributions to the U.S. economy.[a] By working primarily for low wages, illegal immigrants help to keep down the costs of many goods and services in the United States, including agricultural products, construction, and restaurant meals. In turn, these lower costs increase consumer demand, and the overall economy is enhanced. In addition, some argue that illegal immigrants often take jobs that Americans do not want, and therefore help to provide valuable labor that would not otherwise be available. The Pew Hispanic Center has found that a majority of Americans believe that illegal immigrants are taking jobs that their fellow citizens won't do.[b]

But even as most economists agree that the proliferation of low-wage illegal immigrants helps to keep prices down in the United States, there are also significant costs incurred by the presence of undocumented laborers in America. Harvard economist George Borjas contends that the primary losers in regard to illegal immigration are U.S. citizens who do not have high school diplomas, particularly poorer African Americans and native-born Hispanic Americans. Others contend that the biggest burden of illegal immigration falls on American taxpayers who pay for government programs that benefit both illegal immigrants and their dependents. The Center for Immigration Studies (CIS), a Washington-based group that advocates tougher immigration policies, used Census Bureau figures to argue that illegal immigrants contribute far less in taxes than the cost of government services they use. According to a 2004 CIS report, households headed by illegal aliens accounted for more than $26 billion in costs to the federal government in 2002 through government services, including Medicaid, medical treatment for the uninsured, food assistance programs, and federal aid to public schools.[c]

There have been many proposals to limit government services to illegal aliens. In 2005 and 2006, numerous bills were taken up by state legislatures to limit illegal immigrant access to taxpayer-funded social services such as drug rehabilitation, childcare programs, and mental health centers. Meanwhile, Congress focused more of its efforts on trying to stop the entry of illegal aliens by passing legislation to construct a wall along the U.S. Mexican border. President Bush signed this bill into law in 2006.

The overall impact of illegal immigration on the nation's economic, fiscal, and social well-being will in all likelihood remain a subject of heated debate. What is certain is that the political controversies surrounding illegal immigration will continue to occupy a prominent role in American politics in both the near and long term.

[a]Mary Fitzgerald, "Illegal Immigrants' Cost to Government Studied," *Washington Post* (August 26, 2004): A21; Nell Henderson, "Effect of Immigration on Jobs, Wages Is Difficult for Economists to Nail Down," *Washington Post* (April 15, 2006): D1.
[b]The Pew Hispanic Center, "The State of American Public Opinion on Illegal Immigration in Spring 2006," http://pewhispanic.org/files/factsheets/18.pdf,
[c]Center for Immigration Studies,
The High Cost of Cheap Labor: Illegal Immigration and the Federal Budget,
http://www.cis.org/articles/2004/fiscalexec.html.

---

systemic agenda or elsewhere, in several ways. The congressional agenda represents issues that demand both legislative attention and official consideration.

Getting on the Congressional Agenda **Agenda setting** is a competitive process. Congress, for instance, does not have the time or the money to take on all the problems and issues it is called on to handle. Whether because of their influence or skill in developing political support, some people or groups are more successful than others in steering items onto the agenda. Chance plays a small role in agenda setting, except in cases of accidents or natural disasters.

As discussed in chapter 8, the president is an important agenda-setter for Congress. In the State of the Union Address, proposed budget, and special messages, the president presents Congress with a legislative program for its consideration. Much of Congress's time is spent deliberating presidential recommendations, although by no

agenda setting
The constant process of forming the list of issues to be addressed by government.

means does Congress always respond as the president might wish. Congress can be recalcitrant even when the president and congressional majorities come from the same party. This scenario was very apparent in 2006 when the Republican-controlled Congress blocked President Bush's plan to allow Dubai Ports World, a company owned by the United Arab Emirates, to take over operations at six major U.S. ports. Citing fears that national security would be threatened, Congress successfully pressured the president to take the deal off the table.[12]

Interest groups are major actors and initiators in the agenda-setting process. Interest groups and their lobbyists frequently ask Congress to legislate on problems of special concern to them. Environmentalists, for instance, call for government action on such issues as global warming, the protection of wetlands, and the reduction of air pollution. Business groups may seek protection against foreign competitors, restrictions on product liability lawsuits, or government financial bailouts.

Problems may secure agenda status because of some crisis, natural disaster, or other extraordinary event. The attacks on the World Trade Center and the Pentagon on September 11, 2001, placed the issue of homeland security at the top of the policy agenda. Efforts to create a new agency for homeland security were a direct consequence of the attack. Some problems and issues draw the attention of the news media and consequently gain agenda status, more salience, or both. The cost of prescription drugs for the elderly (described in the chapter opener) is an example of an issue that received significant media attention. The problem of soaring gas prices, coupled with record oil-company profits, grabbed national headlines in 2006, prompting a variety of proposals designed to lower the cost of gas or increase taxes on the profits of oil companies.

Individual private citizens, members of Congress, and other officials acting as policy entrepreneurs may push issues onto the congressional agenda. In the 1960s, Ralph Nader's book *Unsafe at Any Speed* and Rachel Carson's *Silent Spring* brought motor vehicle safety and the misuse of pesticides, respectively, to the attention of Congress and many citizens. Representative Leonor Sullivan (D–MO) worked for a decade to secure the adoption in 1964 of a permanent food stamp program to help the needy. The actors Michael J. Fox, who has Parkinson's disease, and Christopher Reeve, who fought courageously to overcome a severe spinal injury, appeared in front of congressional committees and used their celebrity status to push for greater funding of medical research. Music celebrities Don Henley of the Eagles and Kevin Richardson of the Backstreet Boys testified before Congress on issues ranging from environmental policies to copyright infringement. While books and testimony are themselves important, it is ultimately the media's converage of the activities that will have the greatest impact on drawing broad public attention to an issue.

Finally, political changes may contribute to agenda setting. The landslide election of Democratic President Lyndon B. Johnson in 1964, along with strong, favorable Democratic majorities in Congress, made possible the enactment of a flood of Great Society legislation. The intent of this legislation was to mitigate social welfare problems such as poverty and inadequate medical care for the elderly and needy and to provide education for disadvantaged children. Similarly, the election of Republican President Ronald Reagan, who in his 1981 inaugural address asserted that "Government is not the solution; government is the problem," brought issues concerning the size and activities of government onto national policy agendas. Reagan's

■ Actor Salma Hayak addresses the Senate Judiciary Committee on violence against women.

Photo courtesy: Chris Kleponis/Reuters

administration, however, had only limited success in cutting back the size of the government.[13]

POLICY FORMULATION

Policy formulation is the crafting of appropriate and acceptable proposed courses of action to ameliorate or resolve public problems. It has both political and technical components. The political aspect of policy formulation involves determining generally what should be done to reduce acid rain, for example—whether standard setting and enforcement or emissions testing should be used. The technical facet involves correctly stating in specific language what one wants to authorize or accomplish, so as to adequately guide those who must implement policy and to prevent distortion of legislative intent. Political scientist Charles O. Jones suggests that formulation may take different forms.[14]

policy formulation
The crafting of appropriate and acceptable proposed courses of action to ameliorate or resolve public problems.

1. *Routine formulation* is "a repetitive and essentially changeless process of reformulating similar proposals within an issue area that is well established on the government agenda." For instance, the formulation of policy for veterans' benefits represents a standard process of drafting proposals similar to those established in the past.
2. *Analogous formulation* handles new problems by drawing on experience with similar problems in the past. What has been done in the past to cope with the activities of terrorists? What has been done in other states to deal with child abuse or divorce law reform?
3. *Creative formulation* involves attempts to develop new or unprecedented proposals that represent a departure from existing practices and that will better resolve a problem. For example, plans to develop an anti-missile defense system to shoot down incoming missiles represents a departure from previous defense strategies of mutual destruction.

Policy formulation may be undertaken by various players in the policy process: the president, presidential aides, agency officials, specially appointed task forces and commissions, interest groups, private research organizations (or "think tanks"), and legislators and their staffs. The people engaged in formulation are usually looking ahead toward policy adoption. Particular provisions may be included or excluded from a proposal in an attempt to enhance its likelihood of adoption. To the extent that formulators think in this strategic manner, the formulation and adoption stages of the policy process often overlap.

In many cases elected officials and nongovernmental organizations work as partners in the formulation of public polices. A prime example of these partnerships was the tight relationship between the libertarian Cato Institute and the Bush administration in the construction of the president's Social Security reform efforts.[15]

POLICY ADOPTION

Policy adoption is the approval of a policy proposal by the people with requisite authority, such as a legislature or chief executive. This approval gives the policy legal force. Because most public policies in the United States result from legislation, policy adoption frequently requires the building of majority coalitions necessary to secure the enactment of legislation.

In chapter 7, we discuss how power is diffused in Congress and how the legislative process comprises a number of roadblocks or obstacles—House subcommittee, House committee, House Rules Committee, and so on—that a bill must successfully navigate before it becomes law. A majority is needed to clear a bill through each of these obstacles; hence, not one majority but a series of majorities is needed for

policy adoption
The approval of a policy proposal by the people with the requisite authority, such as a legislature.

congressional policy adoption. To secure the needed votes, a bill may be watered down or modified at each of these decision points. Or, the bill may fail to win a majority at one of them and die, at least for the time being.

The adoption of major legislation, such as the Medicare Prescription Drug Act of 2003, requires much negotiation, bargaining, and compromise. In some instances, years or even decades may be needed to secure the enactment of legislation on a controversial matter. Congress considered federal aid to public education off and on over several decades before it finally won approval in 1965. At other times, the approval process may move quickly.

The tortuous nature of congressional policy adoption has some important consequences. First, complex legislation may require substantial periods of time in order to pass. Second, the legislation passed is often incremental, making only limited or marginal changes in existing policy. Third, legislation is frequently written in general or ambiguous language, as in the Clean Air Act. The Clean Air Act provided amorphous instructions to administrators in the Environmental Protection Agency to set air quality standards that would allow for an "adequate margin of safety" to protect the public health. Phrases such as "adequate margin" are highly subjective and open to a wide range of interpretations. Language such as this may provide considerable discretion to the people who implement the law and also leave them in doubt as to its intended purposes.

Not all policy adoption necessitates formation of majority coalitions. Presidential decision-making on foreign affairs, military actions, and other matters is often unilateral. Although a president has many aides and advisers and is bombarded with information and advice, the final decision rests with him or her. Ultimately, too, it is the president who decides whether to veto a bill passed by Congress. Sometimes a president can get concessions from Congress by threatening to veto legislation. For example, George W. Bush was able to secure some changes to a post-9/11 spending bill by simply raising the specter of a veto. Ironically, Bush is the first president since Thomas Jefferson not to use a single veto during his first term in office.

BUDGETING

VISUAL LITERACY

Where the Money Goes . . .

Most policies require money in order to be carried out; some policies, such as those providing income security, essentially involve the transfer of money from taxpayers to the government and back to individual beneficiaries. Funding for most policies and agencies is provided through the budgetary process (discussed in chapter 18). Whether a policy is well funded or poorly funded has a significant effect on its scope, impact, and effectiveness.

A policy can be nullified by a refusal to fund, which was the fate of the Homeownership and Opportunity for People Everywhere (Hope VI) program. In 2006, the Bush administration decided not to seek funds for HOPE VI, a program within the Department of Housing and Urban Development (HUD) that demolishes obsolete and severely distressed public housing, while introducing community service and self-sufficiency initiatives. President Bush had tried to eliminate HOPE VI twice before by not funding it, but each time Congress directed financial resources to HUD to keep the program alive. However, in 2006, Congress followed the president's lead, and HOPE VI was terminated.[16]

Other policies or programs often suffer from inadequate funding. Thus, the Occupational Safety and Health Administration (OSHA) can afford to inspect annually only a small fraction of the workplaces within its jurisdiction. Similarly, the Department of Housing and Urban Development has funds sufficient to provide rent subsidies only to approximately 20 percent of the eligible low-income families.

The budgetary process also gives the president and the Congress an opportunity to review the government's many policies and programs, to inquire into their administration, to appraise their value and effectiveness, and to exercise some influence on their conduct. Not all of the government's hundreds of programs are fully examined every year. But, over a period of several years, most programs come under scrutiny.

In a given year, most agencies experience only limited or marginal changes in their funding. Still, budgeting is a vital part of the policy process that helps determine the impact and effectiveness of public policies. Having the potential to curb funding can be a powerful tool for congressional committee chairs.

POLICY IMPLEMENTATION

Policy implementation is the process of carrying out public policies, most of which are implemented by administrative agencies. Some, however, are enforced in other ways. Product liability and product dating are two examples. Product liability laws such as the Food and Drug Act of 1906, the National Traffic and Motor Vehicle Safety Act of 1966, and the Consumer Product Safety Act of 1972 are typically enforced by lawsuits initiated in the courts by injured consumers or their survivors. In contrast, state product-dating laws are implemented more by voluntary compliance when grocers take out-of-date products off their shelves or when consumers choose not to buy food products after the use dates stamped on them expire. The courts also get involved in implementation when they are called on to interpret the meaning of legislation, review the legality of agency rules and actions, and determine whether institutions such as prisons and mental hospitals conform to legal and constitutional standards.

In areas like environmental policy, the courts are regularly asked to determine if government agencies are properly enforcing the nation's laws. During President George W. Bush's second term, a number of state governments throughout the Northeast filed suit against the Environmental Protection Agency (EPA) to get that agency to stiffen its rules regarding mercury emissions. Contending that the EPA's standards regarding mercury were too lax to meet the air quality goals established by the Clean Air Act and its amendments, the states asked the federal courts to make the EPA impose stronger restrictions.[17]

Administrative agencies may be authorized to use a number of techniques to implement the public policies within their jurisdictions. These techniques can be categorized as authoritative, incentive, capacity, or hortatory, depending on the behavioral assumptions on which they are based.[18]

policy implementation
The process of carrying out public policy through governmental agencies and the courts.

1. *Authoritative techniques* for policy implementation rest on the notion that people's actions must be directed or restrained by government in order to prevent or eliminate activities or products that are unsafe, unfair, evil, or immoral. Consumer products must meet certain safety regulations, and radio stations can be fined heavily or have their broadcasting licenses revoked if they broadcast obscenities. Many government agencies have authority to issue rules and set standards to regulate such matters as meat and food processing, the discharge of pollutants into the environment, the healthfulness and safety of workplaces, and the safe operation of commercial airplanes. Compliance with these standards is determined by inspection and monitoring, and penalties may be imposed on people or companies that violate the rules and standards set forth in a particular policy. For example, under Title IX, the federal government can terminate funds to colleges or universities that discriminate against female students. Its detractors sometimes stigmatize this pattern of action as "command and control regulation," although in practice it often involves much education, bargaining, and persuasion in addition to the exercise of authority. In the case of Title IX, for instance, the Department of Education will try to negotiate with a school to bring it into compliance before funding is terminated.

2. *Incentive techniques* for policy implementation encourage people to act in their own best interest by offering payoffs or financial inducements to get them to

comply with public policies. Such policies may provide tax deductions to encourage charitable giving or the purchase of alternative fuel vehicles such as hybrid automobiles. Farmers receive subsidies to make their production (or nonproduction) of wheat, cotton, and other goods more profitable. Conversely, sanctions such as high taxes may discourage the purchase and use of such products as tobacco or liquor, and pollution fees may reduce the discharge of pollutants by making this action more costly to businesses.

3. *Capacity techniques* provide people with information, education, training, or resources that will enable them to participate in desired activities. The assumption underlying the provision of these techniques is that people have the incentive or desire to do what is right but lack the capacity to act accordingly. Job training may enable able-bodied people to find work, and accurate information on interest rates will enable people to protect themselves against interest-rate gouging. Financial assistance can help the needy acquire better housing and warmer winter coats and perhaps allow them to lead more comfortable lives.

4. *Hortatory techniques* encourage people to comply with policy by appealing to people's "better instincts" in an effort to get them to act in desired ways. In this instance, the policy implementers assume that people decide how to act according to their personal values and beliefs on matters such as right and wrong, equality, and justice. During the Reagan administration, First Lady Nancy Reagan implored young people to "Just say no" to drugs. Hortatory techniques also include the use of highway signs that tell us "Don't Be a Litterbug" and "Don't Mess with Texas" to discourage littering. Slogans such as "Only You Can Prevent Forest Fires" are meant to encourage compliance with fire and safety regulations in national parks and forests.

Effective administration of public policies depends partly on whether an agency is authorized to use appropriate implementation techniques. Many other factors also come into play, including the clarity and consistency of policies' statutory mandates, adequacy of funding, political support, and the will and skill of agency personnel. Often government will turn to a combination of authoritative, incentive, capacity, and hortatory approaches to reach their goals. For example, public health officials employ all of these tools in their efforts to reduce tobacco use. These techniques include laws prohibiting smoking in public places, taxes on the sales of tobacco products, warning labels on packs of cigarettes, and anti-smoking commercials on television. There is no easy formula that will guarantee successful policy implementation; in practice, many policies only partially achieve their goals.

POLICY EVALUATION

policy evaluation
The process of determining whether a course of action is achieving its intended goals.

Practitioners of **policy evaluation** seek to determine what a policy is actually accomplishing. They may also try to determine whether a policy is being fairly or efficiently administered. Policy evaluation may be conducted by a variety of players: congressional committees, through investigations and other oversight activities; presidential commissions; administrative agencies themselves; university researchers; private research organizations, such as the Brookings Institution and the American Enterprise Institute; and the Government Accountability Office (GAO), formerly named the General Accounting Office.

The GAO, created in 1921, is an important evaluator of public policies. Every year, the GAO conducts hundreds of studies of government agencies and programs, either at the request of members of Congress or on its own initiative. The titles of three of its 2006 evaluations convey a notion of the breadth of its work: *Military Housing: Management Issues Require Attention as the Privatization Program Matures; Ryan White Care Act: Changes Needed to Improve Distribution of Funding; Internal Control:*

Improvements Needed in Federal Drug Administration's Post-market Decision-making and Oversight Process.

Social scientists and qualified investigators design studies to measure the societal impact of programs and to determine whether these programs are achieving their specified goals or objectives. The national executive departments and agencies often have officials and units responsible for policy evaluation; so do state governments. Evaluation research and studies can stimulate attempts to modify or terminate policies and thus restart the policy process. Legislators and administrators may formulate and advocate amendments designed to correct problems or shortcomings in a policy. In 1988, for example, legislation was adopted to correct weaknesses in the enforcement of the Fair Housing Act of 1968, which banned discrimination in the sale or rental of most housing. Policies are also terminated as a result of the evaluation process; for example, through the Airline Deregulation Act of 1978, Congress eliminated the Civil Aeronautics Board and its program of economic regulation of commercial airlines. This action was taken on the assumption that competition in the marketplace would better protect the interests of airline users. Competition indeed reduced the cost of flying on many popular routes.

The demise of programs is relatively rare, however; more often, a troubled program is modified or allowed to limp along because it provides a popular service. For example, the nation's passenger rail system, Amtrak, has been consistently unable to survive without significant government subsidies. While its northeastern lines are financially self-sufficient, many of Amtrak's longer distance routes are not able to operate without significant subsidies. Nevertheless, the more rural routes remain popular with legislators in western states, and thus Amtrak continues to receive federal support.[19]

While policy evaluation has become more rigorous, systematic, and objective over the past few decades, judgments by policy makers still are often based on anecdotal and fragmentary evidence rather than on solid facts and thorough analyses. Sometimes a program is judged to be a good program simply because it is politically popular or fits the ideological beliefs of an elected official. For example, despite very limited empirical evidence that "abstinence-only" education reduces the level of sexual engagement among teenagers, the administration of President George W. Bush has sought increased federal funding for this approach to fight teen pregnancy.[20] Having described the policy-making process on a general level, we now turn our attention to the roots of social welfare policy.

The Origins of Social Welfare Policy

TIMELINE

The Evolution of Social Welfare Policy

TODAY WE TAKE FOR GRANTED the fact that the federal government plays a major role in providing social services. Yet, most social welfare programs in the United States are largely a product of the twentieth century. In the early history of the country, people did not want or expect the national government to provide social welfare beyond some limited assistance to promote public education or to provide for veterans of American wars. (See The Living Constitution: Preamble.) When the nation experienced economic downturns, it was widely accepted that everyone should tighten their belts and await economic recovery. Limited help was occasionally available through local governments, but Americans relied heavily on private charity to help the neediest.

This attitude began to change, gradually, in the late nineteenth century, as many farmers and rural Americans sought government help to protect them against falling commodity prices and exploitation by railroads and other corporations. Then, with the very severe economic depression of the mid-1890s, other Americans began to ask the government for help. A group of several hundred unemployed individuals, led by

The Living Constitution

We the People of the United States, in Order to form a more perfect Union, establish Justice, insure domestic Tranquility, provide for the common defence, promote the general Welfare, and Secure the Blessings of Liberty to ourselves and our Posterity, do ordain and establish this Constitution for the United States of America.

—PREAMBLE

The Preamble of the U.S. Constitution lets posterity know the purpose and ends of the Constitution, and Supreme Court Justice Joseph Story—who served on the Court from 1812 to 1845, during its formative years—held that the Preamble also provides the "best key to the true interpretation" and spirit of the United States' fundamental law. Though the seemingly austere Preamble is not a source of rights or powers for the federal government, its inclusion in the Constitution was not without comment. Story, an Anti-Federalist, argued that the language of the Preamble could allow for an expansive judicial interpretation of the Constitution, and could do so in such a manner that the federal government would be given the authority of "general and unlimited powers of legislation in all cases."

It is true that the extent and authority of both the federal and state governments have increased, but the Preamble is understood to declare that "the People" are the source of all constitutional authority, and it is they, through constitutional institutions, who determine what constitutes justice and the "general Welfare." Constitutional government, it may be said, should strive to secure the well-being and happiness of all citizens, and it is to this end that social policy in the United States is directed.

The federal government is the only American government with the authority and means to ensure that social policy is fairly applied across the states, and it does faithfully attempt to pursue social policy that reflects the prevailing sentiments of the American people. For example, in 1996, social welfare in the United States was radically transformed to reflect a new understanding of how best to help the unfortunate, and it was done so with the intent to promote the general welfare of all Americans—to balance the interests not only of those whose taxes support the social welfare, but also of those for whom public support is necessary. Thus understood, the Preamble gives expression and guidance to the desires and will of the American people.

Jacob Coxey of Ohio, marched to Washington, D.C., in 1894 asking for government assistance. While unsuccessful in their effort, "Coxey's Army" reflected an unprecedented new willingness of individuals and groups to ask for help from the federal government to provide assistance in hard times. The severity of the depression of the mid-1890s, in fact, led many to reassess their attitude about the government's

■ In 1894, during a severe economic depression, Jacob Coxey led a group of several hundred—known as Coxey's Army—on a march from Ohio to Washington, D.C., in an unsuccessful attempt to push the federal government to provide assistance to the unemployed.

Photo courtesy: The Granger Collection

responsibility to protect Americans from calamity. "In prosperous times, Americans had thought of unemployment as the result of personal failure, affecting primarily the lazy and immoral. . . . In the midst of [the 1890s] depression, such views were harder to maintain, since everyone knew people who were both worthy and unemployed."[21] While attitudes were beginning to change, it would take another, more severe depression for that change to result in government action.

This gradual change in attitude toward government responsibilities also reflected broader social changes in the United States and abroad. As U.S. society became more urban and industrial, self-sufficiency declined and people became more interdependent and reliant on a vast system of production, distribution, and exchange. The ostentation of the very wealthy and the suffering of the many on the bottom rung of the social ladder created fears of an economic revolution if the gap between rich and poor was not reduced. Some industrialized European countries, where class-consciousness ran stronger, established new social welfare programs around this time, with those governments assuming more of a direct responsibility for the well-being of their people. The Great Depression of the 1930s reinforced the notion that hard work alone would not provide economic security for everyone, and showed that the state governments and private charities lacked adequate resources to alleviate economic want and distress. Beginning with the Social Security Act of 1935, which we will describe below, a variety of national programs aimed at providing economic security have emerged.

INCOME SECURITY

The economic turmoil known as the Great Depression produced massive shock waves throughout American society. To many, only the Civil War was more socially destructive and disruptive to the United States than the Great Depression.[22]

Although there had been earlier signs of business trouble, the start of this long and steep economic decline is commonly associated with the great stock market crash of October 1929. Unlike previous economic panics, there seemed to be no bottom to the market sell-off. By 1933, the value of stock on the New York Stock Exchange was less than a fifth of what it had been at its peak in 1929. As might be expected, the decline in the stock market coincided with a more general collapse in the American economy. At the depth of the Great Depression in 1933, the gross national product (GNP) had declined by 25 percent and unemployment reached almost 25 percent, a dramatic increase from the 3 percent level of unemployment in 1929.[23] In some communities that relied on hard-hit industries such as farming or tourism, unemployment reached well over 50 percent.

As a consequence of the Great Depression, social and economic thinking began to change far more intensely and broadly than it had even in the 1890s. Prior to 1929, most modern economic theorists had focused on the value of limited government and a "hands-off" economic policy for government to follow. After 1929, and the collapse of confidence in the private sector, the idea that government could and should be used as a positive influence in society gained widespread approval.[24]

With the election of Franklin D. Roosevelt as president in 1932, the federal government began to play a more active role in addressing hardships and turmoil growing out of the Great Depression. An immediate challenge facing the Roosevelt administration was massive unemployment. The problems of unemployment were viewed as having a corrosive effect on the economic well-being and moral character of American citizens. In Roosevelt's words, an array of programs to put people back to work would "eliminate the threat that enforced idleness brings to spiritual and moral stability."[25]

To address the issue of unemployment, Roosevelt issued an executive order in November 1933 that created the Civil Works Administration (CWA). The intent of the CWA was to put people to work as quickly as possible for the stated goal of building public works projects. Within a month of its start, CWA had hired 2.6 million people; at its peak in January 1934, it employed more than 4 million workers. Wages averaged about $15 a week, a sum that was approximately two and one-half times the typical relief payment given through the Federal Emergency Relief Administration (FERA). While the CWA assisted in building moral and economic capital, critics claimed that it was too political and rife with corruption. In response to such criticisms, Roosevelt ordered the CWA disbanded in 1934.

In 1935, the notion of federal works programs was revived in the form of the Works Progress Administration (WPA). The WPA paid a wage of about $55 a month, about twice the amount of a direct relief payment, yet below what would be available in the private sector. Such a wage would reward work over the dole but would not discourage individuals from seeking market-based employment. A number of concrete accomplishments were attained through the WPA. About 30 percent of the unemployed were absorbed; the WPA also constructed or improved more than 20,000 playgrounds, schools, hospitals, and airfields.[26] These jobs programs did not become permanent, but they established the notion that, in extreme circumstances, the government might become the employer of last resort.

A more permanent and important legacy of the New Deal was the creation of Social Security. The intent of Social Security was to go beyond the various "emergency" programs such

■ The Great Depression, beginning in late 1929 and continuing throughout the 1930s, dramatically pointed out to average Americans the need for a broad social safety net and gave rise to a host of income, health, and finance legislation.

Photo courtesy: Bettmann/Corbis

as the WPA and provide at least a minimum of economic security for all Americans. Due to the nature of this commitment, passage of the **Social Security Act** in 1935 represented the beginning of a permanent welfare state in America and a dedication to the ideal of greater equity.[27] The act consisted of three major components: (1) old-age insurance (what we now call Social Security); (2) public assistance for the needy, aged, blind, and families with dependent children (later, people with disabilities were added); and, (3) unemployment insurance and compensation.

The core of the Social Security Act was the creation of a compulsory old-age insurance program funded equally by employer and employee contributions. The act imposed a payroll tax, collected from the employer, equal to 1 percent from both employee and employer starting in 1937. Payroll taxes were to rise a point a year up to 3 percent from both employer and employee, and the payroll tax was applied to the first $3,000 of income. The law originally exempted many categories of workers, including government employees, farm workers, domestic service workers, and casual labor. At the age of sixty-five, workers would receive payments that were based on their lifelong earnings. In 1940, the maximum old-age pension was $85 a month. It was believed that funding Social Security through payroll deductions would ensure its survival, because once average workers contributed their own money to the program, they would view it as a "sacred trust" rather than a form of welfare.[28] Critics of Social Security branded it as "creeping socialism" and something that would lead to an unwanted expansion of government.

The Social Security Act also addressed the issue of unemployment, requiring employers to pay 3 percent of a worker's salary into an insurance fund. If workers became unemployed, they could draw from this fund for a given period of time. During the time laid-off workers drew from the insurance fund, they were required to seek other jobs. This component of the Social Security Act served two basic purposes: on the individual level, it provided income to laid-off workers, expanding the social safety net; on the broader economic level, it acted as an automatic stabilizer, increasing the amount of money in the nation's economy when financial resources were scarce.

Social Security is credited with replacing a piecemeal collection of local programs with a national system. This national system was widely praised but also was perceived to contain two basic flaws: the payroll tax was regressive (the tax fell disproportionately on lower-income contributors), and some workers were excluded from the program. Over the next decades, Social Security was expanded to include a much greater

Social Security Act
A 1935 law that established old-age insurance (Social Security) and assistance for the needy, children, and others, and unemployment insurance.

■ Franklin D. Roosevelt's New Deal expanded the role of the federal government in profound ways, including the establishment of Social Security in 1935.

Photo courtesy: AP Wide World Photos

percentage of American workers. The program also became one of the most successful and popular government programs. In the 1930s, poverty rates were highest among the elderly. Today, seniors have the lowest rate of poverty among any age group in the United States.

HEALTH CARE

Governments in the United States have long been active in the health care field. Local governments began to establish public health departments in the first half of the nineteenth century, and state health departments followed in the second half. Discoveries related to the bacteriological causes of diseases and human ailments discovered in the late nineteenth and early twentieth centuries led to significant advances in improving public health. Public sanitation and clean-water programs, pasteurization of milk, immunization programs, and other activities reduced greatly the incidence of infectious and communicable diseases. Public health policies have also been highly effective in reducing the incidence of infectious diseases such as measles, infantile paralysis (poliomyelitis), and smallpox. The increase in American life expectancy from forty-seven in 1900 to nearly seventy-eight in 2005 is tightly linked to public health programs.

Beginning in 1798 with the establishment of the National Marine Service (NMS) for "the relief of sick and disabled seamen," which was the forerunner of the Public Health Service, the national government has provided health care for some segments of the population. Continuous efforts have been made to expand coverage of health care to all Americans with plans such as that for national health insurance.

National health insurance was considered at the time Social Security legislation was passed. Because of the strong opposition of the American Medical Association (AMA), which was the dominant force in American medicine at the time, health insurance was omitted from the Social Security Act. It was feared that addressing this social need would jeopardize adoption of other important elements of the program. Health insurance remained on the back burner for many years.

The AMA and its allies typically were distrustful of government intervention in their affairs and fearful that regulations would limit their discretion as well as their earnings. In particular, they feared that the intrusion of government into the health care field could limit physician charges, confine the amount of time approved for specific types of hospital visits, and place a lid on charges for prescription drugs. Members of the health care industry viewed these outcomes unfavorably. More generally, conservatives opposed the expansion of government power and contended that such extensions could be harmful to the ideal of individual liberty.

Liberal political leaders did not lose interest in national health insurance, however. In 1958, a bill was introduced in Congress that covered the hospital costs of elderly people receiving Social Security. The AMA again weighed in against this proposal, but by focusing on the aged, the proponents of health insurance changed the terms of the struggle. Strong support developed for providing medical assistance to the elderly, and in 1960, Congress passed legislation benefiting the needy aged. This provision, however, did not satisfy liberals and other supporters of a broader program. The issue was resolved by the 1964 elections, which produced sufficient votes in Congress to enact Medicare and Medicaid, programs that sharply increased access to care for both the elderly (in the case of Medicare) and the poor (in the case of Medicaid).

The national government's role in health care expanded dramatically with the enactment of these two programs. The share of health care expenditures financed by public spending rose from under 25 percent in 1960 to almost 40 percent in 1970. During this time, public expenditures on health care as a percent of total gross domestic product (GDP) rose by more than 100 percent, from 1.3 percent to 2.7 percent. Total expenditures rose from 5.3 percent of GDP in 1960 to 7.4 percent in 1970.[29] As we will discuss later in the chapter, costs associated with health care have continued to rise, and policy debates related to containing costs and providing comprehensive coverage continue unabated.

PUBLIC EDUCATION

Public education was almost the exclusive province of state and local governments until well into the twentieth century. Some commentators and critics argue that education was one area the Framers intended to be reserved to the states by the Tenth Amendment. Others pointed out that the national government has been somewhat involved in education since passage of the Northwest Ordinance in 1785, which formed the basis of many state and local governments. Constitutional justification for the national government's involvement with public education rests on a broad view of its delegated powers, such as taxing and spending for the general welfare. National financial aid for the public schools was an agenda item during the twentieth century and is now a permanent aspect of public school funding.

Historically, responsibility for public education has been vested in the local community. In the Massachusetts Bay Colony, the Puritans (having fled from a highly centralized Church of England) set up a system of local autonomy. Massachusetts laws of the mid-seventeenth century required every Massachusetts town of at least fifty families to hire a teacher, setting a precedent of public responsibility for education. During this time, schooling was restricted to a few years of instruction, with the primary goal of assuring that children could read the Bible. Only sons of the upper classes were able to attend secondary schools that prepared them for leadership in politics or the ministry. Over time, access to education expanded. Reformers such as Horace Mann advocated the development of publicly financed education for the masses. In the 1830s, Mann argued that an educated citizenry would improve the standard of living for all. By 1860, over one-half of school-age children in the United States were enrolled in school. States gave local school districts the responsibility for financing schools, appointing and removing teachers, selecting classroom materials, and resolving conflicts among teachers and parents. Property taxes became the major means of supporting local schools.[30]

■ Traditionally, public education has been left to state and local governments. Children of all ages were often schooled together, in settings such as this nineteenth-century, one-room schoolhouse.

Photo courtesy: Charles Redmond/The Denver Public Library

Beginning in 1944 with the GI Bill, which paid for college for many World War II veterans, the federal government has helped students secure the funds they need to continue their education beyond high school. During the Cold War, the feared "missile gap" caused by the Soviet launch of *Sputnik* in 1957 led Congress to allocate some federal funds to bolster science and math programs in American public schools. Then, as part of Lyndon Johnson's program for creating a "Great Society," federal spending for elementary and secondary education became more significant. Also at that time, new programs were established to help make college education more affordable to a greater number of Americans. Some college assistance programs, such as Pell Grants, were aimed at students from poorer families, while loan guarantee and other programs were made available to more affluent students. Loan guarantees reduce the risk of default to lenders because the federal government guarantees to pay interest on student loans as long as the recipient remains in school. The U.S. Department of Education indicates that the

Photos courtesy: left, Bob Daemmrich/Stock Boston; right, Bob Daemmrich/Photo Edit, Inc.

■ School districts have traditionally raised revenue mostly from property taxes. As a result, richer districts spend more per pupil than poorer districts, leaving a disparity in the quality of education that students receive. In one poor school district in Texas, left, a bucket is used as a basketball hoop. In contrast, a wealthy district in Texas has state-of-the-art equipment and supplies.

volume of student loans has doubled over the last decade, with over $62 billion directed to this area of financial aid during the 2004–2005 academic year alone.[31]

Reliance on local property taxes to fund schools led to vast disparities among the different districts. Schools in wealthy suburban districts (such as Beverly Hills in California or Scarsdale in New York) enjoyed stronger financing than schools located in South Central Los Angeles or the South Bronx. To counterbalance this funding inequity, many states enacted education "equalization" formulas whereby additional state funding would be provided to low-wealth districts. Despite this addition of state money, large funding disparities still exist between school districts.[32] Disparities in funding and the realization that per capita spending by itself did not guarantee high performance led to willingness on the part of educators to experiment with new concepts such as charter schools and vouchers.[33]

While local control remains the norm, and most school and college funding is derived from local sources, the federal government today assumes far more responsibility for public education than at any point in the nation's past. As was true with income security and health care, expansion of such government involvement in social welfare was a huge legacy of the twentieth century. We turn our attention next to the current policies and debates that derive from this involvement.

Social Welfare Policies Today

PARTICIPATION
Making a Difference: Welfare Reform

THIS SECTION FOCUSES on three areas of social welfare policy today: income security, health care, and public education. Each area encompasses many complex policies and programs. Although all levels of government (national, state, and local) are involved with the development and implementation of social welfare policies, we emphasize the national government's role.

INCOME SECURITY PROGRAMS

Income security programs protect people against loss of income because of retirement, disability, unemployment, or death or absence of the family breadwinner. Although cases of total deprivation are now rare, many people are unable to provide a minimally decent standard of living for themselves and their families. They are poor in a relative if not an absolute sense. In 2006, the poverty threshold for a four-person family unit was $19,307.[34]

Income security programs fall into two general categories. Social insurance programs are **non-means-based programs** that provide cash assistance to qualified

non-means-based program
Program such as Social Security where benefits are provided irrespective of the income or means of recipients.

beneficiaries. **Means-tested programs** require that people must have incomes below specified levels to be eligible for benefits (see Table 17.1). Benefits of means-tested programs may come either as cash or in-kind benefits, such as food stamps.

means-tested program
Income security program intended to assist those whose incomes fall below a designated level.

Social Insurance: Non-Means-Based Programs Social insurance programs operate in a manner somewhat similar to private automobile or life insurance. Contributions are made by or on behalf of the prospective beneficiaries, their employers, or both. When a person becomes eligible for benefits, the monies are paid as a matter of right, regardless of the person's wealth or unearned income (for example, from dividends and interest payments).

Old Age, Survivors, and Disability Insurance As mentioned earlier, this program began as old-age insurance, providing benefits only to retired workers. Its coverage was extended to survivors of covered workers in 1939 and to the permanently disabled in 1956. Customarily called Social Security, it is not, as many people believe, a pension program that collects contributions from workers, invests them, and then returns them with interest to beneficiaries. Instead, the current workers pay taxes that directly go toward providing benefits for retirees. In 2006, an employee tax of 7.65 percent was levied on the first $94,200 of wages or salaries and placed into the Social Security Trust Fund. An equal tax was levied on employers. Nearly all employees and most of the self-employed (who pay a 15.3 percent tax) are now covered by Social Security. People earning less than $94,200 pay a greater share of their income into the Social Security Fund, since wages or salaries above that amount are not subject to the Social Security tax. The Social Security tax therefore is considered a regressive tax because it captures larger proportions of incomes from lower- and middle-income individuals than from high-wage earners.

People born before 1938 are eligible to receive full retirement benefits at age sixty-five. The full retirement age gradually rises until it reaches sixty-seven for persons born in 1960 or later. Individuals can opt to receive reduced benefits as early as age sixty-two. In January 2006, the average monthly Social Security benefit for retired workers was $1,002, with the maximum monthly benefit set at $2,053. Social Security is the primary source of income for many retirees and keeps them from living in poverty. However, eligible people are entitled to Social Security benefits regardless of how much *unearned* income (for example, dividends and interest payments) they also receive. Beginning with a change in 2004, Social Security recipients between the age of sixty-two and sixty-four had one dollar withheld from their earnings for every two dollars earned after a specific amount of earnings was reached. For recipients age

TABLE 17.1 **RECIPIENTS OF SOCIAL INSURANCE PROGRAMS, 2004**

Program	Number of Recipients (millions)	Percentage of U.S. Population
Non-Means-Tested[a]		
Social Security (OASDI)	47.7	16.2
Medicare (hospital insurance)	41.6	14.1
Veterans' Disability Benefits	2.6	0.9
Unemployment Benefits	3.3	1.1
Means-Tested		
Medicaid	46.8	15.9
Supplemental Security Income	6.9	2.4
Temporary Assistance for Needy Families	4.7	1.6
Food Stamps	23.9	8.1

[a]"Means-tested" refers to the requirement of demonstrated financial need.

Sources: Social Security Administration, http://www.ssa.gov; Department of Health and Human Services, http://acf.dhhs.gov; Food Research Action Center, http://www.frac.org; Department of Veterans Affairs, http://www.va.gov; Bureau of Labor Statistics, http://www.bls.gov.

sixty-five, one dollar was withheld for every three dollars earned after the threshold was reached. Social Security recipients older than sixty-five were allowed to earn an unlimited amount of money without any reduction of Social Security benefints.[35]

The trustees of the Social Security Trust Fund predicted in 2006 that, starting about 2010, Social Security Fund expenditures would begin to increase rapidly as the Baby Boom generation (roughly speaking, those born in the two decades immediately following World War II) reached retirement age. It was estimated that by 2017, payments would exceed revenues collected. Viewing costs and revenues as a proportion of taxable payrolls (to correct for the value of the dollar over time), one can see that projected revenues remain relatively constant over time, while costs are projected to rise substantially (see Figure 17.2). Aside from the retirement of Baby Boomers, other factors pressuring the fund include increased life expectancies and low fertility rates. In other words, Americans are living longer and having fewer children who as workers would contribute to the Social Security Fund.

After George W. Bush was elected in 2000, he promoted his vision of privatizing Social Security through investments in stocks and bonds, and he created a President's Commission to Strengthen Social Security. This panel consisted of sixteen members, with the former Democratic senator from New York, Daniel Patrick Moynihan, and Richard Parsons, co-chief operating officer of AOL Time Warner, serving as co-chairs. By the end of 2001, the panel disappointed proponents of privatization with their set of recommendations. The panel provided three options: (1) allowing workers to invest up to 2 percentage points of their payroll tax in personal accounts; (2) allowing workers to invest up to 4 percentage points of their payroll tax in personal accounts, to a maximum of $1,000 per year; and, (3) allowing workers to invest an additional 1 percent of their earnings in a personal account. Proponents of privatization had hoped for a single recommendation. Congress ignored the recommendations, no doubt influenced by the slump in the stock market and unpopular panel observations. The panel noted they believed that ultimately benefits would have to be cut or more money would have to be assigned to the program. Following his reelection in 2004, Bush reaffirmed his support for Social Security privatization.

Despite controlling both houses of Congress and the presidency after the 2004 elections, Republicans have been unable to achieve any substantial reform of Social

FIGURE 17.2 SOCIAL SECURITY COSTS AND REVENUES, 1970–2080 (AS PERCENTAGE OF TAXABLE PAYROLL)

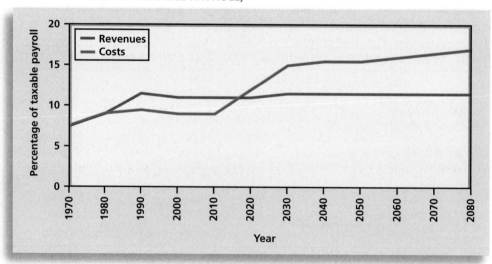

Source: Social Security Administration, Status of the Social Security and Medicare Programs, Summary of the 2004 Annual Reports, http://www.ssa.gov.

Security. This may be explained by continued public skepticism regarding the president's plan. According to a 2005 poll by the Pew Research Center for the People and the Press, only about four in ten Americans supported the concept of individualized accounts as part of the Social Security system.[36] Given the central role that these accounts play in Bush's reform efforts, it was not a surprise that his plan was unable to gather the necessary support in Congress. Simply put, many Republican legislators could not risk aligning themselves with the president because of the possibility of a backlash at the polls. In fact, Democratic candidates used President Bush's support for Social Security privatization against their Republican opponents with some success in the 2006 midterm elections.

While the future of the Social Security system is quite uncertain, it is not a risky prediction to contend that Social Security will continue to be an election issue well beyond 2006.

Unemployment Insurance As mentioned earlier, unemployment insurance is financed by a payroll tax paid by employers. The program pays benefits to workers who are covered by the government plan and are unemployed through no fault of their own. The Social Security Act provided that if a state set up a comparable program and levied a payroll tax for its support, most of the federal tax would be forgiven (not collected). The states were thus accorded a choice: either set up and administer an acceptable unemployment program, or let the national government handle the matter. Within a short time, all states had their own programs.

Unemployment insurance covers employers of four or more people, but not part-time or occasional workers. Benefits are paid to unemployed workers who have neither been fired for personal faults nor quit their jobs, and who are willing and able to accept suitable employment. State unemployment programs differ considerably in levels of benefits, length of benefit payment, and eligibility for benefits. For example, in 2004, average weekly benefit payments ranged from $508 in Massachusetts and $496 in Washington to $210 in both Alabama and Mississippi.[37] In general, less generous programs exist in southern states, where labor unions are less powerful. Nationwide, only about half of the people who are counted as unemployed at any given time are receiving benefits.

In July 2006, the unemployment rate stood at 4.8 percent. (See Analyzing Visuals: Unemployment Rates by State.) While unemployment rates under 5 percent are considered good by historical standards, there is considerable difference in employment conditions across the nation. In Hawaii and Wyoming, unemployment rates were below 3 percent, while levels of unemployment in states such as Michigan, Mississippi, and Alaska were over 6.5 percent. There is also considerable variation in unemployment rates across races and by age. For example, levels of unemployment for African American males are approximately twice that of whites, with unemployment rates of 25 percent or greater common among young African American males.[38]

Social Insurance: Means-Tested Programs Means-tested income security programs are intended to help the need; that is, individuals or families whose incomes fall below specified levels, such as a percentage of the official poverty line. Included in the means-tested categories are the Supplemental Security Income (SSI), Temporary Assistance for Needy Families (TANF), and food stamp programs (see Table 17.1).

Supplemental Security Income This program began under the Social Security Act as a grant-in-aid program to help the needy aged or blind. Grants were financed jointly by the national and state governments, but the states played a major role in determining standards of eligibility and benefit levels. In 1950, Congress extended coverage to needy people who were permanently and totally disabled.

With the support of the Nixon administration, Congress reconfigured the grant programs into the Supplemental Security Income (SSI) program in 1974. Primary

Analyzing Visuals

UNEMPLOYMENT RATES BY STATE

This map shows the rates of unemployment across the United States the summer of 2006. According to the Bureau of Labor Statistics, the U.S. unemployment rate was 4.8 percent percent in July 2006, down from a high of 6 percent in 2003. As can be seen on the map, certain states and regions have rates far higher than the national average. Based on your analysis of this map and your understanding of the chapter discussion, answer the following critical thinking questions: Which states are currently suffering from the highest levels of unemployment, and why do you think that is so? Why do you think unemployment rates vary substantially from state to state? Do you detect any similarities among states with the lowest rates of unemployment? What role do you think the unemployment rate will play in the 2008 presidential elections?

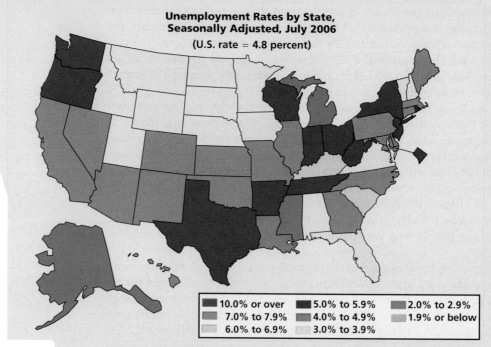

Unemployment Rates by State, Seasonally Adjusted, July 2006

(U.S. rate = 4.8 percent)

■ 10.0% or over	■ 5.0% to 5.9%	■ 2.0% to 2.9%
■ 7.0% to 7.9%	■ 4.0% to 4.9%	■ 1.9% or below
■ 6.0% to 6.9%	■ 3.0% to 3.9%	

Source: Bureau of Labor Statistics, Local Area Unemployment Statistics, http://www.bls.gov/lau/#tables.

funding for SSI is provided by the national government, which prescribes uniform benefit levels throughout the nation. To be eligible, beneficiaries can own only a limited amount of possessions. In 2006, monthly payments were about $603 for an individual, $904 for a married couple.[39] The states may choose to supplement the federal benefits, and forty-eight states do.

For years, this program generated little controversy, as modest benefits go to people who obviously cannot provide for themselves. However, there was a growing perception among conservatives as well as Democratic President Bill Clinton that many social welfare programs were flawed. In 1996, access to SSI and other programs was limited by legislation. Under George W. Bush's administration, funding for SSI has remained fairly stable, with about $35 billion directed to the program in fiscal year 2005.[40]

Family and Child Support In 1950, Aid to Families with Dependent Children (AFDC), the predecessor to the Temporary Assistance for Needy Families (TANF) program, was broadened to include not only dependent children without fathers but also mothers themselves or other adults with whom dependent children were living. The AFDC rolls expanded greatly since 1960 because of the increasing numbers of children born to unwed mothers, the growing divorce rate, and the migration of poor people to cities, where they are more likely to apply for and be provided with benefits.

Because of its clientele, the AFDC program was the focus of much controversy. Critics who pointed to the rising number of recipients claimed that it encouraged promiscuity, out-of-wedlock births, and dependency that resulted in a permanent class of welfare families. To restrict the availability of aid, to ferret out fraud and abuse, and to hold down cost, public officials sought to reform the program. These efforts eventually led to major legislative changes.

In 1988, during President Ronald Reagan's second term, Congress passed legislation to reform AFDC. Titled the Family and Child Support Act, the law sought to move people off welfare and into productive jobs. Each state operated a Job Opportunities and Basic Skills (JOBS) program to provide education, training, and job experience for members of welfare families. Most adult welfare recipients were enrolled, with the states providing childcare and other services necessary to facilitate participation. The national and state governments shared funding for JOBS, which was successful in helping people gain employment and in reducing public assistance payments. Some analysts, however, questioned whether job training programs for welfare mothers significantly increased the income of mothers or enhanced the well-being of their children.[41]

States were required by the Family and Child Support Act to participate in the AFDC-UP program, which provided benefits for two-parent families in which the principal wage earner was unemployed. A workfare provision included at the insistence of the Reagan administration required one parent in a recipient family to work at least sixteen hours weekly. Other provisions of the act called for stronger enforcement of court orders for child support payments and greater efforts to establish paternity for children born out of wedlock.

The Family and Child Support Act represented significant reform of the welfare system. Because its provisions were phased in, it was not fully implemented until the early 1990s.[42] By 1992, however, some 500,000 persons were participating in the act's education and training programs, a number that exceeded the required level of participation.[43] Some states, however, had difficulty providing welfare recipients with sufficient job and training opportunities.[44]

Conservatives generally believe that the poor should do more to help themselves. Liberals, on the other hand, generally support income security programs; they believe that poverty results more from social causes than from personal shortcomings. But, in the 1990s, even some liberals questioned the effectiveness of income security programs and began to call for reforms that would help the poor become more self-sufficient. Accepting the need for reform, President Bill Clinton promised to "end welfare as we know it." The Republican majority in Congress was also anxious to reform welfare policies and supported the president's efforts.

In what was hailed as the biggest shift in social policy since the Great Depression, a new welfare bill, the Personal Responsibility and Work Opportunity Reconciliation Act (PRWORA) of 1996, created the Temporary Assistance for Needy Families (TANF) pro-

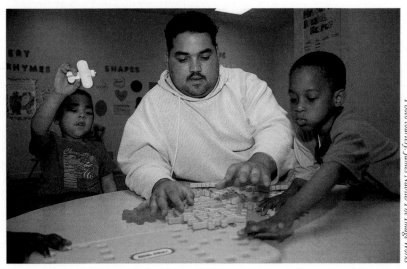

■ Workfare is a welfare strategy that gives adults the opportunity to learn skills that can lead to employment. Here, one workfare recipient tends to children at his day-care-center job.

Photo courtesy: James Nubile/The Image Works

gram to replace AFDC. The shift from AFDC to TANF was meant to foster a new philosophy of work rather than welfare dependency. The most fundamental change enacted in the new law was the switch in funding for welfare from an open-ended matching program to a block grant to the states. PRWORA also gave states more flexibility in reforming their welfare programs toward work-oriented goals.

Significant features of the welfare plan included: (1) a requirement for single mothers with a child over five years of age to work within two years of receiving benefits; (2) a provision that unmarried mothers under the age of eighteen were required to live with an adult and attend school in order to receive welfare benefits; (3) a five-year lifetime limit for aid from block grants; (4) a requirement that mothers must provide information about a child's father in order to receive full welfare payments; (5) cutting off food stamps and Supplemental Security Income for legal immigrants; (6) cutting off cash welfare benefits and food stamps for convicted drug felons; and, (7) limiting food stamps to three months in a three-year period for persons eighteen to fifty years old who are not raising children and not working.[45]

The TANF program established guidelines for states to follow. For example, the federal legislation requires states to have a specific proportion of TANF recipients participating in work activities. (Single mothers head most families covered by TANF.) Work activities are broadly defined and can include private-sector employment, subsidized public-sector employment, job readiness assistance, community service, child-care services, education, and other activities. Benefits and conditions differ from state to state, however, with some states providing more generous cash benefits and having fewer eligibility requirements.

In 2002, the Bush administration released a detailed plan for TANF reauthorization. The plan proposed to strengthen work rules to ensure that all welfare families were engaged in meaningful activities that would lead to self-sufficiency. These meaningful activities included not only work but also allowed "individuals participating in substance abuse treatment, rehabilitative services, and work-related training" to qualify for TANF benefits.[46] The administration proposed increasing the proportion of TANF families that would have to participate in work activities and increasing the number of hours of required work.[47] Between 2002 and 2006, Congress passed a number of extensions to keep the TANF program in operation, with President Bush signing a reauthorization in February 2006. This reauthorization did not address the issue of increased work hours but did strengthen enforcement of child support provisions and provided over $150 million to encourage married couples to remain together.[48] (See Join the Debate: Marriage, Family, and the Federal Government.)

Earned Income Tax Credit Program Designed to help the working poor, this program was created in 1975 at the insistence of Senator Russell Long (D–LA). It helps the working poor by subsidizing their wages, and it also provides an incentive for people to go to work. Drawing extensive support from both Democrats and Republicans in Congress, the Earned Income Tax Credit (EITC) is frequently described as being "pro-work and pro-family." The EITC results in a net cash rebate for many low-income taxpayers who pay no federal income tax.

The intent of the EITC was to enhance the value of working and encourage families to move from welfare to work. Advocates also claimed that the program would enhance spending, which would in turn stimulate the economy. In addition to this stimulus, supporters of the EITC had two other objectives: (1) to increase work incentives among the welfare population; and, (2) to refund indirectly part or all of the Social Security taxes paid by workers with low incomes. In theory, the EITC would serve to ease the regressive nature of the Social Security payroll tax.[49]

To claim the EITC on tax returns, a person must have earned income during the year. During 2005, the earned income had to be less than $11,750 if there were no qualifying children, $31,030 with one qualifying child, and $35,263 with more than one qualifying child. In 2003, over 22 million families filing federal income tax returns (roughly one tax return in six) claimed the federal EITC. The success of the federal EITC in reducing poverty has led a number of states to enact state Earned Income Tax Credits.[50]

Food Stamp Program The initial food stamp program (1939–1943) was primarily an effort to expand domestic markets for farm commodities. Food stamps provided the poor with the ability to purchase more food, thus increasing the demand for American agricultural produce. Attempts to reestablish the program during the Eisenhower administration failed, but in 1961, a $381,000 pilot program began under the Kennedy administration. It was made permanent in 1964 and extended nationwide in 1974. Although strongly opposed by Republicans in Congress, Democrats put together a majority coalition when urban members agreed to support a wheat and cotton price support program wanted by rural and southern Democrats in return for their support of food stamps.

In the beginning, recipients had to pay cash for food stamps, but this practice ceased in 1977. Benefiting low-income families, the program has helped to combat hunger and reduce malnutrition.

While the food stamp program remains an essential element of the government's social welfare program, its phenomenal growth in the 1970s and 1980s led to calls for reining it in by the mid-1990s. Evidence of fraudulent practices by some food stamp recipients and local businesses in several communities also led to greater skepticism about its worthiness. Nonetheless, food stamps continue to play an important part in the government's welfare program. Food stamps went to more than 25 million beneficiaries in 2005 at a cost of $31 billion.[51] The average participant received $93 worth of stamps per month.[52] In 2005, families of four earning less than $2,043 in gross monthly income or $1,571 in net monthly income qualified for food stamps.[53] In 2005, congressional Republicans initiated a plan that would significantly reduce the number of individuals eligible for food stamps. According to the nonpartisan Congressional Budget Office, the cuts in food stamp funding would eventually knock nearly 300,000 people off nutritional assistance programs, including 70,000 legal immigrants.[54]

The national government operates several other food programs for the needy. These programs include a special nutritional program for women, infants, and children (WIC); a school breakfast and lunch program; and an emergency food assistance program.

■ Food stamps remain an important component of the federal government's safety net for low-income Americans.

The Effectiveness of Income Security Programs
Many of the income security programs, including Social Security, Supplemental Security Income, and food stamps, are **entitlement programs.** That is, Congress sets eligibility criteria—such as age, income level, or unemployment—and those who meet the criteria are legally "entitled" to receive benefits. Unlike such programs as public housing, military construction, and space exploration, spending for entitlement programs is mandatory. Year after year, funds *must* be provided for them unless the laws creating the programs are changed. This feature of entitlement programs has made it difficult to control spending for them.

Income security programs have not eliminated poverty and economic dependency, but they have improved the lives of large numbers of people. Millions of elderly people in the United States would be living below the poverty line were it not for So-

entitlement program
Income security program to which all those meeting eligibility criteria are entitled.

Join the Debate

MARRIAGE, FAMILY, AND THE FEDERAL GOVERNMENT

OVERVIEW: Historically, the states have been chiefly responsible for social policy. Since the New Deal of the 1930s and the Great Society programs of the 1960s, however, the American people have decided it is proper for the federal government to engage in social policy within defined limits such as Social Security. More recently, with the launching of President George W. Bush's Healthy Marriage Initiative (HMI) in 2002, and his administration's support in 2004 (strongly reaffirmed in a speech by President Bush in June 2006) of an amendment to the U.S. Constitution to bar same-sex marriage, the institutions of marriage and family have been put at the vanguard of social policy debate. The Bush administration requested $1.5 billion for HMI over five years in the welfare reform authorization bill, to promote research and fund programs that aim to give individuals receiving social welfare the skills needed to maintain or enter into a marriage. The administration's assumption is that households headed by two parents, one male and one female, are less likely to rely on social welfare, and that a stable marriage fosters self-sufficiency and improves emotional well-being.

Many Americans believe that in order for all Americans to enjoy the rights and liberties offered by life in the United States, government has a role in helping those who are somehow disadvantaged. Americans generally accept the fact that government programs are necessary to provide social welfare and to help secure the well-being of citizens. Social conservatives believe that in order to secure this well-being, the traditional male father/female mother family structure should be protected and encouraged. Social liberals, on the other hand, question government efforts to limit the definition of family or use tax dollars to support one family structure over other family structures.

The Bush administration framed the debate over its Healthy Marriage Initiative in such a way that those who are opposed to it (particularly Democrats) are seen as being opposed to family responsibility and accountability. Republicans who believe in limited government find themselves opposed to this initiative because they believe that the federal government should not fund these programs or violate the right of the states to determine family law.

Is legislation defining or attempting to strengthen individual marriages a proper duty of government? The Healthy Marriage Initiative is an attempt to encourage social and individual responsibility by attempting to lower rates of out-of-wedlock births and the number of single-parent households. The vast majority (approximately 80 percent) of children living below the poverty line come from single-parent households. What social scientists and interest groups cannot agree on, however, is whether this statistic is a result of being raised in single-parent households, or whether single-parent households are the result of economic instability, lack of education, and a dearth of affordable transportation and childcare. In other words, are single-parent families a cause or merely a result of existing social inequities?

This debate aside, where does the proper constitutional authority for family and marriage law lie—with the people, the states, or the federal government? Should the government have a final say in what defines a marriage or family? Are acts of government in the social arena—such as the Healthy Marriage Initiative and the proposed amendment to the Constitution to bar same-sex marriage—legitimate in a society that values individual liberty and freedom for all?

ARGUMENTS IN FAVOR OF HMI

- **Research from both ends of the political spectrum suggests children and parents benefit from the institution**

---

cial Security. While often a matter of considerable debate, a range of income security programs is a characteristic of all democratic industrial societies.

HEALTH CARE

Currently, many millions of people receive medical care through the medical branches of the armed forces, the hospitals and medical programs of the Department of Veterans Affairs, and the Indian Health Service. The government spent $69.2 billion in 2004 for health and human services and estimated that it would spend $68.9 billion in the 2006 fiscal year for health and human services, the construction and operation of facilities, and the salaries of doctors and other medical personnel.[55]

Comparing Social
Welfare Policy

The national government finances most medical research, primarily through the National Institutes of Health (NIH). The National Cancer Institute, the National Heart, Lung, and Blood Institute, the National Institute of Allergy and Infectious Diseases, and

of marriage. Social studies from both liberal and conservative groups suggest that two-parent households are less likely to go onto, or remain on, social welfare. Furthermore, children in single-parent households are seven times more likely to live in poverty than those who live with two parents. Studies show that children in two-parent households are more likely to do better in school, and they have higher graduation rates as well.

- **The Healthy Marriage Initiative is cost effective.** According to the Heritage Foundation, a conservative think tank, research indicates the benefits from funding HMI programs outweigh the projected costs of traditional welfare programs such as Temporary Aid to Needy Families and food stamps. The end result will be lowered federal expenditures for social welfare programs while increasing parental responsibility and familial self-sufficiency.
- **The Healthy Marriage Initiative is voluntary.** Supporters of HMI argue that it does not constitute an impermissible government intrusion into the private lives of those receiving social welfare because it is a purely voluntary program. Proponents say it is designed for those who desire a strengthened marriage as a means to extricate the family from government and social dependence.

ARGUMENTS AGAINST HMI

- **HMI does not address the true needs of social welfare recipients.** Opponents of HMI argue that most families do not need counseling but do need education, jobs and job programs, day care, and low-cost transportation. In addition, stricter enforcement of child support laws would help relieve the economic burden on those receiving social welfare.
- **Social policy regarding families and marriage is the constitutional responsibility of the states.** Many opponents of HMI argue that marriage and family policy falls under the proper authority of state governments. When discussing the federal marriage amendment before Congress, former Republican congressman Bob Barr argued that to interfere with a state's right to regulate marriage is to sacrifice the Constitution to social engineering.
- **The Healthy Marriage Initiative does not address the evolving nature of the family structure.** HMI assumes the two-parent household of a married man and woman is the norm. Critics charge that changing family structures, including the growing number of committed heterosexual couples choosing to live together without marrying, make it unreasonable to assume that HMI can ultimately be as effective as its adherents claim. Moreover, critics argue that HMI represents a hypocritical approach to supporting marriage as an institution, since it seeks to strengthen heterosexual marriage at the same time that HMI supporters are attempting to limit the ability of same-sex couples to avail themselves of the protections and benefits of marriage.

QUESTIONS

1. Will the Healthy Marriage Initiative be as effective as its proponents claim? If so, why? If not, why not?
2. Which level of government—local, state, or federal—is best suited to address family needs? Why?

SELECTED READINGS

Albelda, Randy. *Lost Ground: Welfare Reform, Poverty, and Beyond.* Cambridge, MA: South End, 2002.
Duncan, Greg J., and P. Lindsay Chase-Lansdale. *For Better and for Worse: Welfare Reform and the Well-Being of Children and Families.* New York: Russell Sage, 2004.

the other NIH institutes and centers spend more than $10 billion annually on biomedical research. NIH scientists and scientists at universities, medical schools, and other research facilities receiving NIH research grants conduct the research. Most Americans accept and support extensive government spending on medical research. Congress, in fact, often appropriates more money for medical research than the president recommends.

The United States spends significant sums of money on public health, a larger proportion of its gross domestic product than most other industrialized democracies. (See Global Perspective: Quality of Life Around the World.) Much of the increase in funding for health care has gone to the Medicare and Medicaid programs. Reasons for growth in medical spending include the public's increased expectations, increased demand for services, advances in health care technology, the perception of health care as a right, and the third-party payment system.[56] In many ways the issue of soaring health care costs underlies most of the current problems affecting the American health care system and limits the range of alternatives available to government officials.

A quick review of the increase in health care costs over the past fifteen years helps to demonstrate the magnitude of the problem. Per capita spending on health care in the United States increased by 123 percent in the fourteen-year period between 1990 and 2004. But, per capita income in America increased by only 59 percent during the same time frame, meaning that individual financial resources grew at less than half the rate of the cost of health care. Behind this dramatic increase in health care costs are a number of important factors. First, more people are living longer and are requiring costly and extensive care in their declining years. Second, the range and sophistication of diagnostic practices and therapeutic treatments, which are often quite expensive, have increased. Third, the expansion of private health insurance, along with Medicare and Medicaid, has reduced the direct costs of health care to most people and increased the demand for services. More people, in short, can afford care. They may also be less aware of the costs of care. Fourth, the costs of health care have also increased because of its higher quality and because labor costs have outpaced productivity in the provision of hospital care.[57] Fifth, U.S. health care focuses less on preventing illnesses and more on curing them, which is more costly.

While all areas of health care experienced significant increases in cost since 1990, there were areas within the broader health field that underwent the sharpest spike in prices. Figure 17.3 demonstrates that prescription drug costs increased at rates even greater than those for physicians and hospital stays, thus increasing the pressure for the federal government to adopt the prescription drug program discussed at the beginning of this chapter. Because government health care programs such as Medicare

FIGURE 17.3 U.S. HEALTH CARE SPENDING, 1994–2004

One of the greatest challenges facing health care in the United States is the tremendous growth in the cost of medical services. Since the mid-1990s, health care costs have increased at rates far exceeding national rates of inflation. Prescription drugs, the area of health care with the greatest increases, experienced double-digit growth in costs for much of the past decade. While the cost increases for prescription drugs have come down to the level of other health care services such as physicians and hospitals, overall health care costs continue to increase at very high rates.

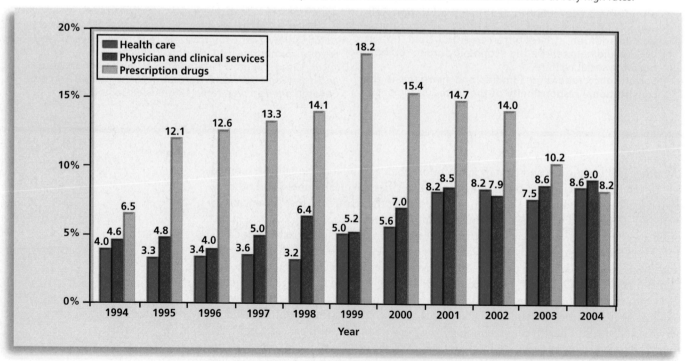

Source: Kaiser Family Foundation, "Trends and Indicators in the Changing Health Care Marketplace," http://www.kff.org.

Global Perspective

QUALITY OF LIFE AROUND THE WORLD

A major purpose of public policy programs in the United States is to improve the quality of life of Americans. How should we think about the quality of life in the United States? Are Americans better off than citizens of other countries? Much better off? And, what does it mean to be better or worse off than others? Since 1975, through the construction of a Human Development Index (HDI), an attempt has been made to answer these questions not only for Americans, but also for citizens of other countries.[a] The HDI measures the achievements of a country along three different dimensions.

The first dimension concerns the quality of health care, measured by average life expectancy. The second dimension addresses the quality and breadth of educational opportunities in a country, measured by looking at the adult literacy rate. This rate is defined as the percentage of individuals age fifteen and above who can read. The final dimension seeks to establish the extent to which individuals in a country enjoy a "decent" standard of living. The HDI measures this dimension by dividing a country's gross domestic product (GDP) by its population. Gross domestic product refers to the total value of good and services produced by residents working in a country. If we divide this number by the population of a country, we get the per capita GDP. The assumption is that the more money individuals have on average, the more they can spend on things other than the fundamental necessities of food, clothing, and shelter.

There are problems with each of these measures. For example, we should know the impact of gender on life expectancy and literacy. We should also know how evenly distributed income is across a society or how many people live below the poverty line. In its full report, the HDI provides additional information on these concerns.[b]

Where does the United States rank in regard to these dimensions? In 2005, the United States was judged to have the tenth highest quality of life. Norway was judged to have the highest quality of life, followed by Iceland, Australia, Luxembourg, Canada, Sweden, Switzerland, Ireland, and Belgium. Fifty-seven countries qualified as having a high human development score. Eighty-nine countries fell into the medium development category, and thirty-one were judged to be low human development countries. Niger had the lowest HDI score. The charts below show how the countries in these three groupings compare in terms of their average life expectancy, adult literacy levels, and standard of living.

QUESTIONS

1. What would you add to the Human Development Index to give a fuller picture of the quality of life in a country? Do you think any of the HDI dimensions are more important than others? Explain.
2. What responsibility do the high-ranking states have to those in the bottom two categories to improve the quality of life in those countries?

[a]Human Development Index, United Nations Development Programme, 2006.

[b]Human Development Report 2005, available at http://www.hdr.org/reports/global/2005.

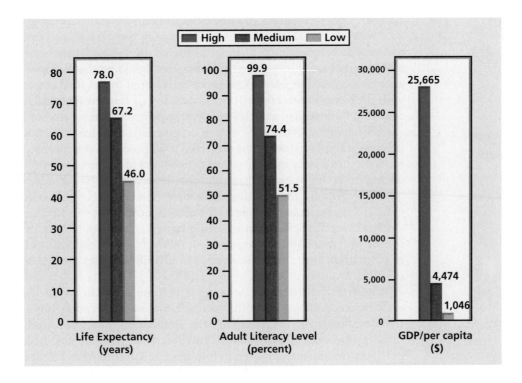

TABLE 17.2 **THE RISING COST OF ENTITLEMENT AND OTHER PROGRAMS**

	2005	2011 estimate	% change
Outlays (in billions of dollars)			
Means-tested Entitlements[a]	$356	$454	28%
Social Security	519	722	39%
Defense	473	499	6%
Nondefense Discretionary	465	455	– 2%

[a]Includes Medicaid, food stamps, Supplemental Security Income, child nutrition programs, earned income tax credits, Temporary Assistance to Needy Families, and other programs.

Source: United States Budget, Fiscal Year 2007, Historical Tables, http://www.gpoaccess.gov/usbudget/fy07/sheets/hist11z3.xlsles, Section 8, Outlays by Budget Enforcement Act Category.

Medicare

The federal program established in the Lyndon B. Johnson administration that provides medical care to elderly Social Security recipients.

Medicaid

An expansion of Medicare, this program subsidizes medical care for the poor.

and Medicaid are directly affected by soaring prices, policy makers have been challenged to keep these programs fully funded. In 2005, national expenditures for both the Medicare and Medicaid programs were $515 billion. Projected increases for Medicare and Medicaid are expected to grow between 2005 and 2011 at a faster pace than other key areas of the federal budget (see Table 17.2).

In the next sections, we explore these two key federal health care programs in greater detail, as well as the impact of government-sponsored health care programs on public health.

Medicare Medicare, which covers persons receiving Social Security benefits, is administered by the Center for Medicare and Medicaid Services in the Department of Health and Human Services. Medicare coverage has two components, Parts A and B. Benefits under Part A come to all Americans automatically at age sixty-five, when they qualify for Social Security. It covers hospitalization, some skilled nursing care, and home health services. Individuals have to pay about $700 in medical bills before they are eligible for Part A benefits. Medicare is financed by a payroll tax of 1.45 percent paid by both employees and employers on the total amount of one's wages or salary.

Part B, which is optional, covers payment for physicians' services, outpatient and diagnostic services, X-rays, and some other items not covered by Part A. Excluded from coverage are eyeglasses, hearing aids, and dentures. This portion of the Medicare program is financed partly by monthly payments from beneficiaries and partly by general tax revenues.

As noted in the chapter-opening vignette, a new Medicare benefit provides some prescription drug coverage for recipients who opt to participate. Since January 2006, American seniors have been able to participate. Those who choose to participate have to pay a monthly premium of approximately $35; after a $250 annual deductible, they have 75 percent of their prescription costs paid for. For those whose annual prescription drug costs exceed $5,100, the new program pays 95 percent of prescription costs over that amount. There are some odd gaps in the prescription drug coverage, however. Many congressional Democrats found the bill too weak in helping the average senior and claimed its primary beneficiaries would be the pharmaceutical and insurance industries. But even some Democrats voted for its final passage, as they agreed with the leaders of the American Association of Retired Persons (AARP) that it was time to do something, and this seemed the only plan with a chance to pass.[58]

The addition of the prescription drug benefit troubled many budget conservatives because of the added costs it is projected to impose on a system that, whatever its merits, is extraordinarily expensive. The actual costs of this new program were understated during the congressional debate, and that leads many to wonder how the federal budget can withstand the additional pressure. Medicare itself has become a costly program because people live longer, the elderly need more hospital and physicians' services, and medical care costs are rising rapidly. Attempts to limit or cap expenditures for the program have had only marginal effects. With millions of Baby Boomers set to retire in the next fifteen years, the system will be under even greater strain.

Medicaid Enacted into law at the same time as Medicare, the **Medicaid** program provides comprehensive health care, including hospitalization, physician services, prescription drugs, and long-term nursing-home care (unlike Medicare) to all who qualify as needy under TANF and SSI. In 1986, Congress extended Medicaid coverage to pregnant women and children in low-income families whose total earnings were less than 133 percent of the official poverty level. The states were also accorded the option of extending coverage to all pregnant women and to all children under one year of age in families with incomes below 185 percent of the poverty level. By 1993, twenty-nine states had chosen to provide this coverage. In 2005, Medicaid served over 52 million people at a cost of $184.2 billion.[59] Nursing facility services, in-patient general hospital services, home health services, and prescription drugs represented major categories of spending within the Medicaid program.

Medicaid is financed by the national and state governments. The national government pays 50 to 79 percent of Medicaid costs, based on average per capita income, which awards more financial support to poor than to wealthy states. Each state is responsible for the administration of its own program and sets specific standards of eligibility and benefit levels for Medicaid recipients within the boundaries set by national guidelines. In some states, nearly all needy people are covered by Medicaid, while in others, only one-third or so of the needy are protected. Some states also award coverage to the "medically indigent," that is, to people who do not qualify for welfare but for whom large medical expenses would constitute a severe financial burden.

While the average amount paid for by the states varies, the portion of state budgets going to Medicaid is similar—ever upward. If Medicaid expenditures continue to grow at their present rate, the proportion of funding that is available for other programs will be reduced.

Public Health In addition to funding large portions of the nation's health care costs, government plays a major role in managing the growth of both infectious and chronic disease. From AIDS to obesity, public policy makers have attempted to use government power to fight threats to the nation's health. Among the tools employed by government are immunizations, education, advertisements, and regulations. For many contagious diseases such as polio, measles, and chickenpox, the government requires young children to be immunized if they are to be enrolled in day care, preschool, or elementary school. Public health officials also use vaccines in the adult population to manage the spread of diseases such as influenza (the flu). While not requiring citizens to receive flu shots, the government recommends that high-risk

■ In 2006 Massachusetts became the first state to pass legislation that guaranteed health insurance to all its residents. The problem of health insurance coverage for the 45 million uninsured Americans has plagued government for decades. Massachusetts' efforts to address this problem relied on a bipartisan effort between Republican Governor Mitt Romney (center of photo) and the state's Democratic legislature under the leadership of House Speaker Salvatore DiMasi. The two political leaders are pictured at the April 2006 signing of the legislation.

Photo courtesy: Elise Amendola/AP Wide World Photos

groups (infants, senior citizens) receive immunizations and also subsidizes vaccines for low-income populations.

The process of getting a nation immunized against a disease may be more difficult than it seems. The case of the avian (bird) flu helps demonstrate these difficulties. The emergence of this particularly deadly strain of influenza in 2003 has put pressure on public health officials to prepare the U.S for a possible pandemic. This preparation is extremely challenging for public health officials because the flu strain may quickly mutate, thus making current vaccines incapable of blocking the spread of the virus. With the possibility of having no vaccine ready at the onset of an avian flu outbreak, the Bush administration's disease response plan relies on other policy tools, such as educating the public on how to minimize exposure to the disease, prohibiting individuals from traveling, and closing schools.[60] For diseases such as AIDS, which is at present incurable and for which no vaccines have been developed, public health officials expend much of their energy attempting to educate the public and thereby alter behaviors that put individuals at risk for becoming infected with AIDS or spreading it to others.

As with many facets of public policy, the deep-seated attachment of Americans to personal liberty limits the types of tools government can employ. The case of obesity illustrates this point. Widely accepted as the second biggest threat to the health of Americans (behind only tobacco), obesity poses a difficult challenge for public health officials. With almost 60 million Americans defined as obese by the Centers for Disease Control and Prevention (CDC), public health officials are expecting an increase in the prevalence of obesity-related illnesses such as heart disease and diabetes.[61] In combating this emerging public health threat, the U.S. government is very constrained in the types of tools it can use. Trying to limit the food intake of Americans is a very difficult task because of the personal nature of the activity. It is hard to imagine government attempting to ban certain foods as they have narcotics. Instead, policy makers have attacked obesity through channels that do not directly threaten individual choice. Of the 140 obesity-related bills that came before state legislatures in 2003, most dealt with bettering public understanding of the nutritional value of food or reducing access to fast food and soft drinks within the public school systems. A few bills included increased taxes on soda and junk food, but no bill directly limited the sales of unhealthy food to the general public.[62]

Public opinion polls indicate that most people are satisfied with the quality of health care services provided by physicians and hospitals, but a substantial majority express dissatisfaction over the costs and accessibility of health care.[63] There is, as a consequence, a strong belief in the need to improve the nation's health care system, but some substantial hindrances block easy reform in this area. Most notably, the desire of individuals to maintain control over their health care decisions limits the policy solutions to which government can turn. (See American Values/American Voices: Liberty and Health Care for All.)

PUBLIC EDUCATION

In 2003, national, state, and local governments in the United States collected more than $400 billion to spend on public (elementary and secondary) education. Of this amount, 48.7 percent came from the state governments, 42.8 percent from local governments, and 8.5 percent from the national government. (See Figure 17.4.) There is much variation among states, and among school districts within states, on educational expenditures, as measured by spending on a per-student basis. Some states spend two or three times as much as other states according to this measure. Federal dollars are the smallest share of public school funding, but these dollars are still vital to school systems that are usually financially strapped and sometimes in dire need of additional revenue.

Federal Aid to Education   The national government assisted public education in minor ways up until the mid-twentieth century, leaving it to states and local govern-

FIGURE 17.4 ELEMENTARY AND SECONDARY SCHOOL REVENUE SOURCES, 2002–2003
The national government provides only a fraction of total spending on public schools.

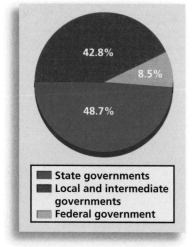

Source: U.S. Department of Education, Education Finance Statistics Center, http://nces.ed.gov.

American Values/American Voices

LIBERTY AND HEALTH CARE FOR ALL

Americans hate to be told what to do. As noted in chapter 1, personal liberty is one of the most important characteristics of American democracy. Since the nation's founding, its citizens have been vigilant about keeping government from interfering in their ability to make their own choices. In recent years, this deep cultural attachment to individual liberty has played a major role in the area of health care provision.

According to the U.S. Census Bureau, 45.8 million Americans lacked health care insurance in 2004. Among these uninsured were millions of individuals who worked full time but did not receive health insurance from their employers and were ineligible for Medicaid because they earned too much. The current number of uninsured is higher than at any time since the 1930s, and the number of uninsured Americans has been growing for some time.

During the early 1990s, the Clinton administration proposed a major federal policy that would provide at least some health insurance coverage to all Americans. Despite public opinion polls that supported federal efforts to address the problem of the uninsured, Clinton's plan ended in a notable defeat for his administration. Among the main causes of its demise was a rise in public concern over the impact of the plan on the ability of individuals to choose their own physicians. In order to reach its goal of universal health care coverage, the Clinton reform called for restrictions on individual choices in order to help control the spiraling costs of health services. The declining public support for the Clinton plan was undoubtedly aided by a series of television ads funded by the health insurance industry that warned Americans they would lose control of their health care under the Clinton proposal. Arguments against the Clinton plan were summed up in a statement by then Republican Senator Bob Dole, who told the *Washington Post*, "More cost. Less choice. More taxes. Less quality. More government control. Less control for you and your family. That's what the president's government-run plan is likely to give you."[a]

Since the demise of the Clinton health care plan, the problems of the health care system have not gone away. In fact, the costs of health care have risen even faster than in the early 1990s, and the number of uninsured has increased by millions. With the public's deep-seated resistance to losing personal liberty narrowing the choices available to policy makers in the area of health care reform, government officials have had to come up with creative options to address the ongoing problem.

In 2006, Massachusetts passed a state law requiring every individual in the Commonwealth to purchase health insurance by July 1, 2007. For the approximately 500,000 individuals who were uninsured in Massachusetts, this will mean different things. First, about 100,000 state residents are eligible for Medicaid but are not receiving this benefit because they have not enrolled in the program. Another 200,000 residents who made too much money to get Medicaid but have been unable to afford health insurance will receive assistance on an income-based sliding scale to buy insurance policies without deductibles. Another 200,000 Massachusetts residents with incomes above the federal poverty line will be able to purchase lower-cost policies in the private market. The financial assistance for health insurance will be financed by redirecting much of the $1 billion spent by state government on the uninsured.

But, how can government make someone purchase health insurance, especially given the American attachment to personal liberty? The answer is through economic disincentives. Beginning in 2008, failure by individuals to purchase health insurance will result in the loss of their state tax refund equal to 50 percent of an affordable health insurance premium. Thus, failure to use the government assistance will actually come at a price for those without health insurance.

While it is too early to say if the Massachusetts health insurance reforms will work, the approach taken in the Bay State may be a model for national reform. The Massachusetts plan does place limits on personal choice, but only among those without health insurance. The plan does not limit options for the majority of individuals who already have insurance, and thus it did not draw the same harsh public reaction that the Clinton reform plan received in the 1990s. This may explain why the legislation was approved by a bipartisan 154–2 margin in the Massachusetts House of Representatives and a 37–0 vote in the state Senate.

QUESTIONS

1. What major factors have led to the high number of Americans without any form of health insurance?
2. Do you support the Massachusettes health insurance plan? Why or why not?

[a]Ann Devroy , "President Insists Congress Enact Reforms in Welfare, Health Care," *Washington Post* (January 26, 1994): A1.

Sources: U.S. Census Bureau, "Income, Poverty, and Health Insurance Coverage in the United States: 2004," August 2005, http://www.census.gov; Theda Sckopol, *Boomerang: Health Care Reform and the Turn Against Government* (New York: Norton, 1997); Ann Devroy, "President Insists Congress Enact Reforms in Welfare, Health Care," *Washington Post* (January 26, 1994): A1; Kaiser Commission on Medicaid and the Uninsured, "Massachusetts Health Care Reform Fact Sheet," http://www.kff.org/uninsured/upload/7494.pdf; Steve LeBlanc, "Mass Lawmakers Pass Bill to Require Health Insurance for All," *Boston Globe* (April 4, 2006).

ments to fund and administer their own schools. In the two decades following World War II, the school-age population doubled. Classroom shortages became so severe that many urban schools operated on two shifts. At the same time, technological knowledge was expanding rapidly, further challenging the adequacy of public education. Many people came to view federal financial assistance (more simply, federal aid) as a necessary part

On Campus

STUDENT LOAN RELIEF

If you are reading this book as a student at an American college, you are likely to be the recipient of some form of student financial aid. In the 2004–2005 academic year, $129 billion in aid was distributed to students at higher education institutions in the United States. These funds were needed to help college students keep up with the soaring costs of a postsecondary education. According to the College Board, the cost of tuition for a public university increased by 7 percent between 2004 and 2005, and the costs of a private university rose by 5.9 percent. While these increases are substantial, they are actually smaller than the double-digit increases in tuition that students have experienced in most years since 2000.[a]

With higher tuition burdens facing college students, financial aid demands have escalated in recent years. Government has continued to help students meet their financial needs, but in a different manner than in the past. Between 1996 and 2002, students increasingly received financial aid in the form of grants-in-aid rather than student loans. In 2004–2005, the percentage of total undergraduate aid in the form of grants declined for the third year in a row, with loans accounting for a greater share of aid than grants for the first time since 1997.

Greater dependence on loans to finance higher education has implications for both students and the broader society. Obviously, increased levels of student loans mean increased financial burdens for students as they enter the workforce. In 2004, two out of three public university graduates had student loan debt, with the median amount of money borrowed topping $15,000. The level of debt is even higher for the three out of four graduates of private universities who take out loans, with median debt burdens just under $20,000 in 2004.[b]

Student loan debt may be seen as a great long-term investment for individuals because of the beneficial effect of a college degree on lifetime earnings. Census Bureau statistics from 2000 indicate that college graduates earn nearly twice as much as high school graduates, making higher loan levels a necessary evil for many students.[c] But, growing student loan debt may be excluding graduates from taking jobs in low-paying public service jobs. Faced with the prospect of repaying student loans shortly after graduation, financially constrained individuals will most likely seek higher paying jobs in the private sector rather than lower paying jobs in government or nonprofit organizations.

To make public service more financially attainable to students with high levels of debt, the federal government has created numerous incentive programs. In 2001, the federal government's Office of Personnel Management (OPM) enacted rules that allowed federal agencies to set up debt relief programs for specific employees. Agencies such as the Department of Energy, General Services Administration, NASA, and the Department of Health and Human Services adopted the programs in efforts to attract or retain talented individuals. Under the new OPM rules, federal government agencies could relieve as much as $6,000 a year in a person's student loan obligations. To receive benefits, applicants would have to sign an agreement to remain in the service of the agency for at least three years.[d]

Other debt relief programs are available. For workers who provide services to low-income, high-risk children and their families, debt would be completely cancelled after five years. Loan relief is also available for individuals who teach in high-demand fields such as math, science, foreign languages, and bilingual education, and to workers in career fields such as nursing, law enforcement, corrections, and medicine. Members of the U.S. armed forces can have up to 50 percent of their loans canceled if they serve in hazardous areas. Vista and Peace Corps volunteers also qualify for debt relief. Through these programs, government may be able to persuade a critical mass of young professionals to take on jobs that serve the greater public interest.

---

[a]College Board, "2005–2006 College Costs," http://www.collegeboard.com.
[b]Steven Barr, "Repayment Program's Slow Start May Be a Matter of Timing," Washington Post (July 2, 2002):B2.
[c]Kimberly Lankford, "Fringe Benefit," Kiplinger's Personal Finance 56 (July 2002): 94.
[d]Beth Kobliner, "Learn Now, Pay Back (Somewhat Less) Later," New York Times (June 30, 2002): A12; and Jim McTague, "Sallie Forth," Barron's 82 (June 24, 2002): 35.

---

of the solution to the inadequacies of public education. Consequently, federal aid to education has been an item on the national policy agenda almost continually since the early 1950s. (See On Campus: Student Loan Relief.)

In 1988, President George Bush and the nation's governors agreed to a program called Goals 2000 to improve the nation's schools. In 1994, Congress enacted the Goals 2000: Educate America Act to help all children achieve higher educational standards. For the first time, national standards were established, but compliance with these standards by the states was voluntary. According to Goals 2000, high school graduates should possess certain skills such as the ability to use a calculator, knowledge of the function of the United Nations, the ability to use an atlas or map, understanding of heredity, and knowledge of how to use a thesaurus.

In 2002, President George W. Bush signed legislation aimed at raising standards and promoting achievement in all public schools. Called No Child Left Behind, the law requires the states to monitor all school districts in order to verify that students are showing educational progress. Districts and specific schools administer proficiency tests to their students to verify satisfactory progress. Those schools where students don't perform well are identified to the public so parents can provide pressure or consider other school choices. Poorly performing schools are then given more oversight, along with some additional resources. While No Child Left Behind may lead to greater accountability for school performance, the program has many critics. In particular it has been argued that schools structure their classes to help students pass proficiency tests rather than focusing on more meaningful content. Nevertheless, supporters argue that the program is especially needed to raise standards of poorly performing schools and narrow the great disparity in performance among America's public schools.

Other national legislation may impose requirements on the public schools that are mandatory but not fully funded by the national government. An example is education for children with disabilities. Several million school-age children currently have disabilities that can range from mild physical disability to severe mental retardation. In the past, many of the more handicapped children were excluded from the regular public school systems; some were enrolled in special state institutions or schools.

Beginning in the 1960s, the education of children with learning disabilities moved from the state to the national policy agenda. In 1975, Congress passed what is now called the Individuals with Disabilities Education Act to mandate that the states educate children with disabilities.[64] This law stated that every such child is entitled to a "free appropriate public education" provided through the regular public school system, which, for children with severe disabilities, can be a costly task. Because national funding covers only about one-fifth of the costs of educating children with disabilities, the state and local school districts bear the major costs of this unfunded federal mandate.

Inequality in Spending Among School Districts

The revenues raised by most local school districts come mostly from property taxes. Because of substantial differences among districts in the value of the taxable property within their boundaries, some communities are able to generate much more revenue than others, even with lower tax rates. This variation is then reflected in spending disparities among schools when measured on a per-pupil basis. Within a given state, some districts may spend more than twice as much per pupil as others. Many parents, educators, and public officials believe that such unequal spending results in significant disparities in the quality of the education that students receive.

SIMULATION

You Are a State Legislator

A challenge to inequality in education spending arose out of the Texas public school system and was decided in 1973 by the U.S. Supreme Court.[65] The five-justice majority ruled that the right to an education was not of such fundamental character that differences in per-pupil spending among districts violated the Fourteenth Amendment's equal protection clause. Although concerned about the inequalities in school funding, the Court held that this was a problem for the state governments to resolve.

Most conflicts concerning the quality of education that a state must provide have been solved through state administrative procedures. In some situations, however, disputes have ended up in the U.S. Supreme Court. In 1993, for example, the Court ruled that a school district must provide a sign language interpreter for a deaf child attending a Catholic school.[66] In 1994, however, the U.S. Supreme Court ruled that a New York school district had gone too far to accommodate religious needs. The creation of a new school district to educate the special-needs children of the Satmar Hasidim, a strict Jewish sect, was found to violate the First Amendment's establishment clause.[67]

■ A crowded classroom at the Frey School in Edgewood, Texas. Lacking the funds to build new schools, many school districts face overcrowding.

Photo courtesy: Bob Daemmrich/The Image Works

In some states, inequality in expenditures among districts has been held to violate the state constitution. In New Jersey, for instance, the state court practically forced the legislature to adopt an income tax to finance the schools.[68] School finance has been a volatile and vexing issue in many other states. Most people want good schools, but paying for good schools, particularly if this requires raising taxes, stirs up much opposition in a time when "no new taxes" is a mantra with wide popular appeal.

Voucher Plans and Charter Schools Supporters of education vouchers believe that free market competition can improve the quality of American education by forcing underperforming schools to improve. In theory, if parents received vouchers for children to attend schools of their choice, the better-performing schools would grow and expand while the poorer-performing schools would close their doors. Proponents argue that free choice of schools would create greater efficiencies as parents "shopped wisely" and sent their children to better-performing schools. Opponents of vouchers argue that they would undermine public education by siphoning money to private secular and religious schools.

In 1988, a handful of active voucher programs could be found in Milwaukee and Cleveland, cities with the two largest programs serving low-income children. Cleveland's voucher program covered approximately 3,000 students, and Milwaukee's program served about 15,000 children. Both programs experienced moderate success as math and reading scores improved in each location. Partially in response to these successes, voucher proposals were prepared in 1998 for about half of the nation's fifty states.

Popular opinion, especially among minorities, seemed to fuel the drive for vouchers. In a recent Columbia University survey of African American voters under the age of thirty-five, 66 percent indicated support for school vouchers.[69] One explanation for the fairly strong support of vouchers among minority populations is that younger blacks and Hispanics were more likely to have children who attended failing public schools. It is unlikely that lower-income minorities would be able to send their children to other schools without the aid of programs (such as vouchers) that would lower the cost. Empirical evidence also exists concerning the value of voucher pro-

PARTICIPATION

The Courts and School Vouchers

grams. For example, a study by Harvard University's Paul Peterson concluded that black elementary school students who were enrolled in a privately funded voucher program (to attend New York private schools from 1997 to 2000) rose two grade levels beyond black students who stayed in public schools.[70]

Organized interest groups such as the National Association for the Advancement of Colored People (NAACP) and teachers' unions were in the forefront in their opposition to vouchers. Opponents feared that poorer urban public schools would be stigmatized, possibly even abandoned, if vouchers were implemented. Democratic politicians, in general, also voiced strong reservations about these plans. In 1998, President Clinton vetoed a bill that would have provided vouchers to selected poor children in Washington, D.C.[71] In 2002, support for school voucher programs was invigorated by a Supreme Court decision upholding a high-profile voucher plan in Cleveland. President George W. Bush hailed the ruling as a landmark decision, and school choice proponents promised to intensify their efforts for voucher plans in a number of states.

In addition to vouchers, the concept of charter schools also gained support in recent years. Charter schools permit some institutions (those with charters) to operate beyond the reach of school boards. In theory, charter schools break the monopoly exercised by centralized school boards and allow students as well as parents to exercise choice. Costs for these schools are still paid by the taxpayer, and charter schools are relatively free to choose what to teach, what to spend money on, and whom to hire.

In 1998, only six years after the first charter school was opened in Minneapolis, there were approximately 800 independent charter schools educating more than 165,000 students in twenty-three states and the District of Columbia. President Clinton endorsed the concept of charter schools, calling for an increase in their number to 3,000 by the year 2000. By 2006, forty-one states approved charter school laws, making these schools eligible for federal funds.[72] Some states, such as Maryland, have had difficulty passing charter legislation because of teacher union concern about hiring underqualified teachers.[73]

Concerns about charter schools were raised after a review of experiences in Arizona and Washington, DC. While a few charter schools in Arizona were noted for their exemplary performance, the high-performing schools were outnumbered by institutions perceived to be beset with problems as bad as, and in many cases worse than, those plaguing traditional public schools. Private companies took advantage of the fact that the state required high school students to attend school only four hours a day. Companies ran two or three four-hour sessions in a day, often in rooms of commercial buildings without library facilities, and they substituted self-paced computer instruction for regular teachers. Some courses lasted only a few weeks, there was no homework, and many students received credit for after-school work. Private education companies typically targeted low achievers, truants, and those with discipline problems with promises of an easy route to graduation.[74]

In Washington, D.C., the Board of Education voted unanimously to close two charter schools in the summer of 2002. The board stated that the two schools failed to provide basic services to children. The failure of basic services was assigned for various reasons, including a lack of instructional material and inattention to students with special needs.[75]

Some promising hybrid versions of charter schools have shown early signs of success. Boston's "pilot schools" remain part of the formal school system but are granted charter-like powers over budgets, hiring, and curriculum. These schools remain in the public realm but escape the rigid bureaucracies that often restrict public schools from quickly adapting to changing circumstances.[76]

Summary

THIS CHAPTER EXAMINED the policy-making process and social welfare policies. To that end, we made the following points:

1. **The Policy-making Process**

   The policy-making process can be viewed as a sequence of functional activities beginning with the identification and definition of public problems. Once identified, problems must get on the governmental agenda. Other stages of the process include policy formulation, policy adoption, budgeting for policies, policy implementation, and the evaluation of policy.

2. **The Roots of Social Welfare Policy**

   The origins of social welfare policy can be traced back to early initiatives in the nation's history. Only after the Great Depression, however, was a public-sector role in the delivery of social services broadly accepted. Programs initiated in the Great Depression became a model for greater public-sector responsibilities in the area of social welfare.

3. **Social Welfare Policies Today**

   Governments at all levels are involved in the policy process. The social welfare policies highlighted here are income security, health care, and education. Income security programs to relieve economic dependency and poverty were mostly handled by state and local governments, albeit in minimal fashion, through the nineteenth century. Most income security programs generally take two forms: non-means-based programs and means-tested programs, which indicate that all people who meet eligibility criteria are automatically entitled to receive benefits. Governments in the United States have a long history of involvement in the health of Americans. Most state and local governments have health departments, and the U.S. government has several public health and medical research divisions. Medicare and Medicaid are the two most prominent national programs. As the cost of health care has risen, however, new demands have been made to restrain the rate of growth in costs. Despite those concerns, a new program to provide seniors some assistance with their prescription drug costs was added to Medicare in 2003. Public education was the province of state and local governments through the nineteenth century. Through a variety of federal laws, Congress has attempted to improve educational standards, especially for disadvantaged students and also for people with disabilities. Today, the national government provides a modest but vital share of the financing for public schools. Notable recent efforts to improve the education system have included school voucher programs and charter schools.

KEY TERMS

agenda, p. 620
agenda setting, p. 621
entitlement program, p. 641
governmental (institutional) agenda, p. 620
means-tested program, p. 635
Medicaid, p. 646
Medicare, p. 646
non-means-based program, p. 634
policy adoption, p. 623
policy evaluation, p. 626
policy formulation, p. 623
policy implementation, p. 625
public policy, p. 616
Social Security Act, p. 631
social welfare policy, p. 616
systemic agenda, p. 620

SELECTED READINGS

Brooks, Robin, and Assaf Razin. *Social Security Reform: Financial and Political Issues in International Perspective.* Cambridge, MA: Cambridge University Press, 2005.

Chubb, John, and Terry Moe. *Politics, Markets, and America's Schools.* Washington, DC: Brookings Institution, 1990.

Feldstein, Paul. *Health Policy Issues: An Economic Perspective on Health Reform,* 3rd ed. Chicago: Health Administration Press, 2002.

Gilens, Martin. *Why Americans Hate Welfare: Race, Media, and the Politics of Antipoverty Policy.* Chicago: University of Chicago Press, 2001.

Gill, Brian, P. Michael Timpane, Karen E. Ross, and Dominic J. Brewer. *Rhetoric Versus Reality: What We Know and What We Need to Know About Vouchers and Charter Schools.* Santa Monica, CA: Rand, 2001.

Handler, Joel. *The Poverty of Welfare Reform.* New Haven, CT: Yale University Press, 1995.

Isaacs, Stephen, and James Knickman, eds. *To Improve Health and Health Care.* Vol. 8. San Francisco: Jossey-Bass, 2005.

Kahlenberg, Richard D. *Public School Choice vs. Private School Vouchers.* New York: Century Foundation, 2003.

Kotlikoff, Laurence J., and Scott Burns. *The Coming Generational Storm: What You Need to Know About America's Economic Future.* Cambridge, MA: MIT Press, 2004.

Lindbloom, Charles E., and Edward J. Woodhouse. *The Policy-Making Process,* 3rd ed. Englewood Cliffs, NJ: Prentice-Hall, 1993.

Longest, Beaufort B. *Health Policymaking in the United States,* 3rd ed. Chicago: Health Administration Press, 2002.

Marmor, Theodore. *Understanding Health Care Reform.* New Haven, CT: Yale University Press, 1994.

Mead, Lawrence M., ed. *The New Paternalism: Supervisory Approaches to Poverty.* Washington, DC: Brookings Institution, 1997.

Oberlander, Jonathan. *The Political Life of Medicare.* Chicago: University of Chicago Press, 2003.

Rich, Robert, and William White. *Health Policy, Federalism, and the American States.* Washington, DC: Urban Institute, 1996.

Rushefsky, Mark, and Kant Patel. *Politics, Power, and Policy Making: The Case of Health Care Reform in the 1990s.* Armonk, NY: M. E. Sharpe, 1998.

Sherraden, Michael. *Inclusion in the American Dream: Assets Poverty and Public Policy.* Oxford: Oxford University Press, 2005.

Skocpol, Theda. *The Missing Middle: Working Families and the Future of American Social Policy.* New York: Norton, 2000.

Thompson, Frank, and John J. DiIulio Jr. *Medicaid and Devolution: A View from the States.* Washington, DC: Brookings Institution, 1998.

Weil, Alan, and Kenneth Finegold, eds. *Welfare Reform: The Next Act.* Washington, DC: Urban Institute, 2002.

Wilson, Steven F. *Learning on the Job: When Business Takes on Public Schools.* Cambridge, MA: Cambridge University Press, 2006.

Wilson, William J. *The Bridge over the Racial Divide: Rising Inequality and Coalition Politics.* Berkeley, CA: University of California Press, 1999.

WEB EXPLORATIONS

To understand how public policies are prioritized and analyzed, go to
http://www.ncpa.org

To see an overview of the legislative process for public policy, go to
http://www.house.gov/house, Tying_it_all.html
http://thomas.loc.gov/home/lawsmade.toc.html

To understand how public policy laws are made, go to
http://thomas.loc.gov/home/thomas.html

To learn more about how public policies are budgeted, go to
http://www.cbpp.org

To learn about the research institutes and organizations that evaluate policies, go to
http://www.aei.org and http://www.brookings.org

To learn more about the most current Social Security benefits and statistics, go to
http://www.ssa.gov

To learn more about current welfare provisions, go to
http://www.progress.org

For other health care policy initiatives and consumer health information, go to
http://www.nih.gov

To learn about other educational policies, go to
http://nces.ed.gov

Photo courtesy: Scott Tufankjian/AP Wide World Photos

ECONOMIC POLICY

18

SINCE THE 1970S, millions of manufacturing jobs in the United States have been lost in the textile, apparel, steel, electronics, and other industries as manufacturers move their plants abroad or simply shut them down, unable to compete with less expensive foreign imports. Displaced American workers and business owners in these industries have decried this trend, fearful for their own plight, while others have expressed concern about the national impact of the elimination of jobs that have helped to sustain a large middle class. However, most economists and political leaders have argued that the United States must accept the global reality of comparative advantage. As manufacturing jobs are shipped overseas, they say, the United States should concentrate on training Americans in more technologically sophisticated white-collar jobs where the nation has a significant competitive advantage.

But, since 2003, a steady stream of media and think tank reports have described a growing business phenomenon: American companies are outsourcing a significant number of "brainpower" jobs—accounting, engineering, technology, and other white-collar positions—to workers in other countries, especially India. Analysts have estimated that, with advances in technology and telecommunications, a computer programmer, data-entry specialist, or customer service operator working for an American company from India or another low-wage country can save the parent company between 30 to 70 percent in costs.[1] One analyst predicted in 2003 that over 3 million white-collar jobs and $136 billion in wages would shift from the United States to foreign countries by 2015, and a report in May 2004 indicated that the actual figure might be considerably higher.[2] While the U.S. economy recovered from recession in 2004, the threat of outsourcing made many workers insecure. In February 2004, Gregory Mankiw, then chair of President George W. Bush's Council of Economic Advisers, downplayed the significance of this new outsourcing of white-collar jobs, calling it "probably a plus." Immediately, labor leaders, Democrats, and even some Republicans lashed out at Mankiw's comments, and President Bush felt the need to distance himself from them. Mankiw subsequently apologized for leaving the "wrong impression."[3]

At the same time, a study sponsored by the Information Technology Association of America (ITAA) claimed that IT outsourcing created over 257,000 net new jobs in 2005 and is expected to create 337,000 net new jobs by 2010. The report claimed that global sourcing of IT services and software contributed to a $68 billion gain in GDP in 2005. The expected GDP gain in 2010 is estimated, according to this study, at $147 billion more than in a situation that would not allow for software and IT outsourcing.[4]

President Bush, on a March 2006 visit to India, strongly promoted the idea of free trade and open markets, even if it meant short-term adjustment costs for workers in the United States. He reiterated that the United States would not give in to protectionist pressures.[5]

SHOULD THE U.S. GOVERNMENT do something to protect American workers and stop what some economists consider merely a "natural" trend? Would interference by the government harm the nation's larger economic interests? In a global economy, should a national government protect its workers or industries against foreign competition? More broadly, what should the role of the federal government be in the nation's economic affairs? The last question has been asked, in different ways, ever since the nation began.

There continues to be a lively debate over the proper role of the government in the economy. Those favoring limited government participation are pitted against others who believe the government is responsible for managing the economy through policy. In this chapter, we consider those viewpoints as we describe the policies the government uses to achieve its economic goals.

In this chapter, we will examine the following:

- First, we will take a historical look at *the origins of government involvement in the economy.*

- Second, we will examine the government's role in *stabilizing the economy,* sometimes called "macroeconomic regulation."

- Finally, we will look at *the economics of environmental regulation* as an example of one important area of "microeconomic regulation."

The Origins of Government Involvement in the Economy

DURING THE NATION'S FIRST CENTURY, the states were responsible for managing economic affairs. The national government defined its economic role narrowly, although it did collect tariffs (taxes on imported goods), fund public improvements, and encourage private development. (See The Living Constitution: Sixteenth Amendment.) Congress became active in setting economic policy and enacting economic regulation only after people realized that the states alone could not solve the problems affecting the economy.

THE NINETEENTH CENTURY

Although the U.S. economic system is a mixed free-enterprise system characterized by the private ownership of property, private enterprise, and marketplace competition, the national government has long played an important role in fostering economic development through its tax, tariff, public lands disposal, and public works policies, and also through the creation of a national bank (see chapter 3). For much of the nineteenth cen-

The Living Constitution

The Congress shall have power to lay and collect taxes on incomes, from whatever source derived, without apportionment among the several States, and without regard to any census or enumeration.

—SIXTEENTH AMENDMENT

Ratified on February 3, 1913, the Sixteenth Amendment modified the Article I prohibition against levying a "direct tax" on individual property, unless the tax in question addresses the rule of apportionment as set forth in Article I, sections 2 and 9. This amendment was yet another revision made to the Constitution in response to a U.S. Supreme Court decision, namely the 1895 *Pollock* v. *Farmers' Loan & Trust Co.*—a judgment in which a divided Court held that Congress could not tax incomes uniformly throughout the United States.

The authority to tax is one of the fundamental rights inherent in legitimate government, and it is the hallmark of good and just governance to tax citizens fairly and equitably. The Constitution gives the House of Representatives sole authority to originate revenue bills, since the Framers believed the House, as the institution that directly represents the people, should determine how taxes should be raised and apportioned. Indeed, during the ratification debates, concern was expressed in regard to the Senate's ability to amend revenue bills as being a potential means for unjust taxation, since the Senate would not directly represent the people in its political capacity.

As the nineteenth century drew to a close, the Supreme Court became aware that in the new industrial age, the *Pollock* decision could threaten national solvency. As a result, the Court began to redefine "direct taxation" so as to help the federal government adapt to the new era. For example, the Court held in 1911 that corporate income could be taxed as an "excise measured by income." And, in its first appraisal of the newly ratified Sixteenth Amendment, the Court began to view income taxes as a form of indirect taxation. The Sixteenth Amendment has thus guaranteed the federal government a consistent and continuous revenue stream, and it is up to the Congress and the president to ensure fair taxation for all Americans.

tury, however, national regulatory programs were few and were restricted to such tasks as steamboat inspection and the regulation of trade with American Indian tribes.

In contrast, the state governments were quite active in promoting and regulating private economic activity. They constructed such public works as the Erie Canal, built roads, and subsidized railroads to encourage trade within and among the states; they also carried on many licensing, inspection, and regulatory programs. For example, the states issued licenses to certify public school teachers and other professionals and established building inspection programs to protect the public interest.

Following the Civil War, the United States entered a period of rapid economic growth. The rise of industrial capitalism brought about the creation of large-scale

business cycles
Fluctuations between expansion and recession that are a part of modern capitalist economies.

laissez-faire
A French term literally meaning "to allow to do, to leave alone." It is a hands-off governmental policy that is based on the belief that government involvement in the economy is wrong.

manufacturing enterprises. Many people began working in factories for wages and crowded into large cities. New problems resulted from industrialization—industrial accidents and disease, labor–management conflict, unemployment, and the emergence of huge corporations that could exploit workers and consumers. Another problem was the hardship that resulted from downturns in the business cycle, which became more severe in the new industrial society. **Business cycles** involve fluctuations between growth and recession, or periods of "boom and bust," and are an inherent part of modern capitalist economies. During recessions, people lose their jobs and income, and the economy experiences a low or even negative growth rate.

Disturbed by the problems resulting from industrialization, many people turned to government for help. Because the states, with their limited jurisdictions, appeared inadequate to cope with industrial problems, the national government was called on to control these new forces. Businesses and conservatives who had welcomed government intervention to aid economic development in the early decades of the nineteenth century, however, now proclaimed their faith in **laissez-faire.** Based on Adam Smith's *The Wealth of Nations* (published in 1776), the doctrine of laissez-faire holds that active governmental involvement in the economy is wrong and that the role of government should be limited to the maintenance of order and justice, the conduct of foreign affairs, and the provision of necessary public works such as roads or lighthouses, which are not profitable for private persons to provide. Beyond that, individuals should be left free to pursue their self-interest. Market-based competition and the laws of supply and demand, according to this view, will control individual behavior and ensure that self-interest does not get out of hand. Furthermore, reliance on market forces, instead of government, will deliver the greatest amount of welfare for the greatest amount of people in society.

While opposed to regulation of their activities, businesses did not shun other forms of government intervention in the economy. They strongly supported tariffs that provided protection from foreign competitors. Other favored policies included the giveaway of public lands, subsidies for railroad construction, and the use of armed force to put down strikes. Essentially, what businesses and their supporters considered laissez-faire was an economic system and a set of government policies that would encourage business profits.[6]

The first major government effort to regulate business was caused by growing concern over the power of the railroads. After nearly two decades of pressure from

■ Public works projects such as construction of the Erie Canal spurred settlement and building throughout the state of New York.

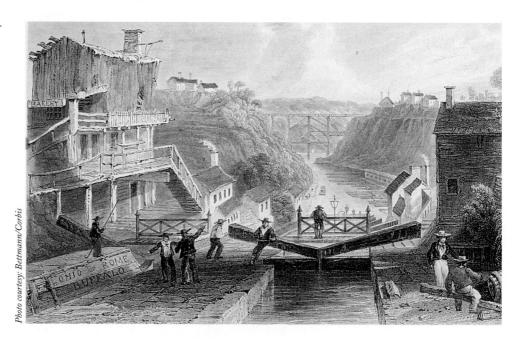

Photo courtesy: Bettmann/Corbis

■ Here, a political cartoonist depicts the perception that the U.S. government was dominated by various trusts in the nineteenth century.

Photo courtesy: Bettmann/Corbis

farmers, owners of small businesses, and reformers in the cities, Congress adopted the Interstate Commerce Act in 1887 to regulate the railroad industry. Enforced by the new Interstate Commerce Commission (ICC), the act required that railroad rates should be "just and reasonable."[7] The act also prohibited such practices as pooling (rate agreements), rate discrimination, and charging more for a short haul than for a long haul of goods.

Three years later, Congress dealt with the problem of "trusts," the name given to large-scale, monopolistic businesses that dominated many industries, including oil, sugar, whiskey, salt, and meatpacking. The Sherman Anti-Trust Act of 1890 prohibits all restraints of trade, including price-fixing, bid-rigging, and market allocation agreements. It also prohibits all monopolization or attempts to monopolize, including domination of a market by one company or a few companies. The act was to be enforced by the Anti-Trust Division of the Department of Justice, which was empowered to sue violators in the federal courts.

The Interstate Commerce Act and the Sherman Anti-Trust Act marked a break from the past and were the key legislative responses of the national government to the new industrialization. The Sherman Anti-Trust Act has been invoked in recent times, as in the Department of Justice lawsuit against the computer software giant Microsoft.

During the nineteenth century, government influence grew in the field of agriculture, the largest sector of the economy at that time. The year 1862 was significant: it saw the establishment of the Department of Agriculture, which gained Cabinet status in 1889; the adoption of the Homestead Act, which gave 160 acres of public land in the West free to people willing to live on the land and improve it; and passage of the Morrill Land Grant Act, which subsidized the establishment of state colleges ("land grant schools"). Subsequent legislation set up agricultural experiment stations and established programs to deal with such farm problems as pesticides, commodity standards, and the rail shipment of livestock.

THE PROGRESSIVE ERA

The Progressive movement drew much of its support from the middle class and sought to reform the political, economic, and social systems of U.S. society. There was a desire to bring corporate power under the control of government and make it more responsive to democratic ends. Progressive administrations under presidents Theodore Roosevelt and Woodrow Wilson established or strengthened regulatory programs to protect consumers and to control railroads, business, and banking.

The Pure Food and Drug Act and the Meat Inspection Act, both enacted in 1906, marked the beginning of consumer protection as a major responsibility of the national government. These laws prohibited adulteration and mislabeling of food and drugs and set sanitary standards for the food industry.

To control banking and regulate business, Congress passed three acts. The Federal Reserve Act (1913) created the Federal Reserve System to regulate the national banking system and to provide for flexibility in the money supply in order to better meet commercial needs and to combat financial panics. Passage of the Federal Trade Commission (FTC) Act and Clayton Act of 1914 strengthened anti-trust policy. The FTC Act created the Federal Trade Commission and authorized it to prevent "unfair methods of competition," including price discrimination, exclusive dealing contracts, and corporate mergers that lessened competition. These statutes, like the Sherman Anti-Trust Act, sought to prevent businesses from forming monopolies or trusts.

Throughout the nineteenth century, the national government was able to raise the revenue it needed by levying protective tariffs and a few excise taxes, such as those on alcoholic beverages. These additional revenues allowed for generous government pensions for Union veterans of the Civil War and ample spending on internal infrastructure improvements.

As the national government's functions expanded in the late nineteenth and early twentieth century, fiscal constraints forced the public officials to focus on the income tax as a way to raise money. In 1895, the Supreme Court held that the income tax was a direct tax, which, according to the U.S. Constitution, had to be allocated among the states in proportion to their population.[8] This ruling made the income tax a political and administrative impossibility. Consequently, the Sixteenth Amendment to the Constitution was adopted in 1913 to reverse that decision. The Sixteenth Amendment authorized the national government "to lay and collect taxes on incomes, from whatever source derived" without being apportioned among the states. Personal and corporate income taxes have since become the national government's major source of general revenues. Income taxes and particularly the tax burden have also been a source of continued political controversy.

THE GREAT DEPRESSION AND THE NEW DEAL

Growth of the Budget and Federal Spending

America's entry into World War I brought the Progressive era to an end. During the 1920s, in the Republican administrations of Presidents Warren G. Harding, Calvin Coolidge, and Herbert Hoover, the federal government reduced its role in restricting private business activities.[9] The economy grew at a rapid pace, and many Americans assumed that the resulting prosperity would last forever. But, "forever" came to an end in October 1929, when the stock market collapsed and the catastrophic worldwide economic decline known as the Great Depression set in. Although the Depression was worldwide in scope, the United States was especially hard hit. All sectors of the economy suffered and no economic group or social class was spared, although some fared better than others.

The initial response of the Hoover administration was to declare that the economy was fundamentally sound, a claim few believed. Investors, businesspeople, and others lost confidence in the economy. Prices dropped, production declined, and unemployment rose. According to Bureau of Labor Statistics estimates, about one-fourth of the civilian workforce was unemployed in 1933.[10] Many other people worked only part-time or at jobs below their skill levels. The economic distress produced by the Great Depression, which lasted for a decade, was unparalleled before or since that time.

Calling for a "New Deal" for the American people, Franklin D. Roosevelt overwhelmed Herbert Hoover and the Republican Party in the 1932 presidential election. Roosevelt favored strong government action to relieve economic distress and to reform the capitalist economic system while preserving its basic features.

The Depression and the New Deal marked a major turning point in U.S. history in general and in U.S. economic history in particular. During the 1930s, the laissez-faire state was replaced with an **interventionist state,** in which the government began to play an active and extensive role in guiding and regulating the private economy. Until the 1930s, the national government's role in the economy was consistent with a broad interpretation of laissez-faire doctrine in that the government mostly provided a framework of rules within which the economy was left alone to operate. The New Deal, however, established the national government as a major regulator of private businesses, as a provider of Social Security (see chapter 17), and as ultimately responsible for maintaining a stable economy.

While the New Deal was not (and is not) without critics, most people today accept the notion that the government should play a role in the economy. The New Deal brought about a number of reforms in almost every area, including finance, agriculture, labor, and industry.

interventionist state
Alternative to the laissez-faire state; the government takes an active role in guiding and managing the private economy.

Financial Reforms The first actions of the New Deal were directed at reviving and reforming the nation's financial system. Because of bad investments and poor management, many banks failed in the early 1930s. To restore confidence in the banks, Roosevelt declared a bank holiday the day after he was inaugurated, closing all of the nation's banks. On the basis of emergency legislation passed by Congress, only financially sound banks were permitted to reopen. Many unsound banks were closed for good and their depositors paid off.

Major New Deal banking laws included the Glass-Steagall Act (1933). The Glass-Steagall Act required the separation of commercial and investment banking and set up the Federal Deposit Insurance Corporation (FDIC) to insure bank deposits, originally for $5,000 per account. Legislation was also passed to control abuses in the stock markets. The Securities Act (1933) required that prospective investors be given full and accurate information about the stocks or securities being offered to them. The Securities Exchange Act (1934) created the Securities and Exchange Commission (SEC), an independent regulatory commission. The SEC was authorized to regulate the stock exchanges, to enforce the Securities Act, and to reduce the number of stocks bought on margin (that is, with borrowed money).

Agriculture The economic condition of U.S. agriculture, which had been weak even during the prosperous 1920s, became much worse during the Depression. The Agricultural Adjustment Act (AAA) of 1933 sought to boost farm income by restricting agriculture production in order to bring it into better balance with demand. Farmers who reduced their crop production in line with the program were eligible to receive cash payments and other benefits. In 1936, however, the Supreme Court held the AAA unconstitutional on the grounds that the national government lacked authority to regulate farming through any of its powers set out in Article I, section 8.[11] Congress quickly replaced the AAA with the Soil Conservation and Domestic Allotment Act, which paid farmers for taking land out of crop production and devoting it to soil conservation purposes. The crops taken out of production generally were those whose prices the AAA had been designed to increase. This plan did not work very well to increase farm income.

In 1938, Congress adopted the second Agricultural Adjustment Act. The second AAA provided subsidies to farmers raising crops such as corn, cotton, and wheat who grew no more than their allotted acreage. Direct payments and commodity loans were also available from the government to participating farmers. The Supreme Court upheld the constitutionality of the second AAA, finding it an appropriate exercise of

PARTICIPATION

Farm Subsidies and Domestic Policy

Photo courtesy: Bettmann/Corbis

More Oklahomans reach Calif. via the cotton fields of Ariz.

■ Okies fleeing the Dust Bowl during the Great Depression.

Congress's power to regulate interstate commerce.[12] The overall effect of the New Deal agricultural legislation was to protect farmers through extensive government intervention. Some saw this as a needed reform, while others thought it was wasteful and promoted inefficient agricultural choices.

Labor Anti-labor public officials and public policies had long handicapped organized labor in its relationships with management. The fortunes of labor unions, which were strong supporters of the New Deal, improved significantly in 1935 when Congress passed the National Labor Relations Act. Better known as the Wagner Act after its sponsor, Senator Robert Wagner (D–NY), this statute guaranteed workers' rights to organize and bargain collectively through unions of their own choosing. The act prohibited a series of "unfair labor practices," such as discriminating against employees because of their union activities. The National Labor Relations Board (NLRB) was created to carry out the act and to conduct elections to determine which union, if any, employees wanted to represent them. Unions prospered under the protection provided by the Wagner Act.

The last major piece of New Deal economic legislation passed by Congress was the Fair Labor Standards Act (FLSA) of 1938. Intended to protect the interests of low-paid workers, the law set twenty-five cents per hour and forty-four hours per week as initial minimum standards. Within a few years, wages rose to forty cents per hour, and hours declined to forty per week. The act also banned child labor. The FLSA did not cover all employees, however; it exempted farm workers, domestic workers, and fishermen, for example.

Industry Regulations During the New Deal, Congress established new or expanded regulatory programs for several industries. The Federal Communications Commission (FCC), created in 1934 to replace the old Federal Radio Commission, was given extensive jurisdiction over the radio, telephone, and telegraph industries. The Civil Aeronautics Board (CAB) was put in place in 1938 to regulate the commercial aviation industry. The Motor Carrier Act of 1935 put the trucking industry under the jurisdiction of the Interstate Commerce Commission (ICC). Like railroad regulation, the regulation of industries such as trucking and commercial aviation extended to such matters as entry into the business, routes of service, and rates. To a substantial extent, government regulation, as a protector of the public interest, replaced competition in these industries. Supporters of these programs believed they were necessary to prevent destructive or excessive competition. Critics warned that limiting competition resulted in users having to pay more for the services.

The Legacy of the New Deal Era Just as World War I brought down the curtain on the Progressive era, the outbreak of World War II diverted Americans' attention from domestic reform, and brought an end to the New Deal era. Many of the New Deal programs, however, became permanent parts of the American public policy landscape. Moreover, the New Deal established the legitimacy and viability of national governmental intervention in the economy. Passive government was replaced with activist government.

economic regulation
Government regulation of business practices, industry rates, routes, or areas serviced by particular industries.

THE SOCIAL REGULATION ERA

Economists and political scientists frequently distinguish between economic regulation and social regulation. **Economic regulation** focuses on such matters as control of entry into a business, prices or rates businesses charge, and service routes or areas. Economic regulation is usually tailored to the conditions of particular industries, such as railroads or stock exchanges. In contrast, **social regulation** sets standards for the quality and safety of products and the conditions under which goods are produced and services rendered. Social regulation strives to protect and enhance the quality of life.

Most of the regulatory programs established through the 1950s fell into the category of economic regulation. From the mid-1960s to the mid-1970s, however, the national government passed social regulatory legislation affecting consumer protection, health and safety, and environmental protection. Congress based this legislation on its commerce clause authority.

This legislation set up several major new regulatory agencies to implement these new social regulations. These agencies include the Consumer Product Safety Commission, the Occupational Safety and Health Administration (OSHA), the Environmental Protection Agency (EPA), the Mining Enforcement and Safety Administration, and the National Transportation Safety Administration (see chapter 9).

The social regulatory statutes took various forms. Some had specific targets and goals, such as the Egg Product Inspection Act and the Lead-Based Paint Poison Prevention Act. Others were loaded with specific standards, deadlines, and instructions for the administering agency. Examples are the Clean Air Act of 1970 and the Employee Retirement Income Security Act of 1974 (intended to protect workers' pensions provided by private employers). Other statutes conferred broad substantive discretion on the implementing agency. Thus, the Occupational Safety and Health Act guarantees workers a safe and healthful workplace, but it contains no health and safety standards with which workplaces must comply. These standards are set through rule-making proceedings conducted by the Occupational Safety and Health Administration, which also has responsibility for their enforcement.

As a consequence of this flood of social regulation, many industries that previously had limited dealings with government found they now had to comply with government regulation in the conduct of their operations. For example, the automobile industry, which previously had been lightly touched by anti-trust, labor relations, and other general statutes, found that its products were now affected by motor vehicle emissions standards and federally mandated safety standards.

Why the surge of social regulation? There are four major reasons.[13] First, the late 1960s and early 1970s were a time of social activism; the consumer and environmental movements were at the peak of their influence. Public interest groups such as the Consumers Union, Common Cause, the Environmental Defense Fund, the Sierra Club, and Ralph Nader's numerous organizations were effective voices for consumer, environmental, and other programs (see chapter 16). Strong support also came from organized labor.

Second, the public had become much more aware of the dangers to health, safety, and the environment associated with various modern products. There was, noted one observer, "a level of public consciousness about environmental, consumer, and occupational hazards that appears to be of a different order of magnitude from public outrage over such issues during both the Progressive era and the New Deal."[14]

Third, members of Congress saw the advocacy of social regulation as a way to gain visibility and national prominence and thus to enhance their election prospects. Senator Edmund Muskie (D–ME), for example, took the lead on environmental issues, while Senator Warren Magnuson (D–WA) successfully pushed for a number of consumer protection laws.

social regulation
Government regulation of the quality and safety of products as well as the conditions under which goods and services are produced.

■ The Ford Pinto was manufactured for years despite internal company studies revealing that it had serious safety flaws.

Basic is when a car goes a long way on a little gas.

One of the reasons the Model A was so good was that it gave generous gas mileage. No doubt economy has a lot to do with Pinto's popularity, too. And this year all those extra miles per gallon come with a number of improvements. They're all good reasons why the closer you look, the better we look.

A bigger engine than last year's: First and foremost is a little bigger 2000cc 4-cylinder overhead cam engine as standard. It's been developed for good gas mileage. And for those of you who want even a bit more pep, there's an optional 2300cc engine.

Refined front and rear suspension: We've refined the suspension both front and rear with a new package specifically developed for the '74 model.

Better brakes: Standard front disc brakes for '74 give you efficient and fade resistant braking, and little pedal effort.

Other basics: Still standard for '74 is rack-and-pinion steering, a 4-speed fully synchronized transmission, a body welded into one solid piece of steel, steel guard rails in the doors, and steel reinforcements in the roof.

See the Pinto at your Ford Dealer's: 2-door sedan, 3-door Runabout, and the popular Pinto Wagon. With improved basics for 1974.

When you get back to basics, you get back to Ford.

FORD PINTO
FORD DIVISION

Photo courtesy: Gaslight Archives

Fourth, the presidents in office during most of this period—the Democrat Lyndon B. Johnson and the Republican Richard M. Nixon—each gave support to the social regulation movement. For them, it was good politics to be in favor of health, safety, and environmental legislation. In most instances, the direct costs to the government of this legislation were minimal.

DEREGULATION

deregulation
A reduction in market controls (such as price fixing, subsidies, or controls on who can enter the field) in favor of market-based competition.

Beginning in the 1950s and 1960s, economists, political scientists, and journalists began to point out defects in some economic regulatory programs and promoted deregulation of the economy.[15] **Deregulation** is the reduction in market controls (such as price fixing, subsidies, or controls on who can enter the field) in favor of market-based competition. Advocates of deregulation contended that regulation often encouraged lack of competition and monopolistic exploitation, discrimination in services, and inefficiency in operation of regulated industries. For instance, regulatory standards meant that no new major commercial airline was permitted to enter the industry after the Civil Aeronautics Board (CAB) began to regulate the industry in 1938. Consequently, consumers paid higher prices for airfares and had fewer choices than they would in a more competitive market. Critics contended that regulatory commissions like the CAB and the Interstate Commerce Commission were more responsive to the interests of the regulated firms than to the public interest.

For some time, there were no changes in economic regulation despite these criticisms. In the mid-1970s, however, President Nixon's successor, Republican President Gerald R. Ford, decided to make deregulation a major objective of his administration. He saw regulation as one cause of the high inflation that existed at the time. At about this time, Senator Edward M. Kennedy (D–MA) became chair of a subcommittee of the Senate Judiciary Committee. Kennedy decided to use his new position to hold hearings on airline deregulation. The combined actions of Ford and Kennedy put deregulation on the national policy agenda and got the deregulatory movement underway. Democrats and Republicans, liberals and conservatives, all found deregulation to be an appealing political issue.[16]

■ One of the most noted scandals to rock the corporate world involved the Houston based energy giant, Enron. In 2006 the company's former CEO Jeffrey Skilling (seen here, center left, leaving court) was found guilty on nineteen counts of fraud and conspiracy related to his work at Enron and sentenced to over 24 years in prison. The Enron scandal, along with others at WorldCom and Global Crossing, served as a catalyst for tighter federal government oversight of business and accounting practices in the United States.

Photo courtesy: Dave Einsel/Getty Images

Deregulation was also a high priority for Ford's successor, Democratic President Jimmy Carter. Legislation that deregulated commercial airlines, railroads, motor carriers, and financial institutions was enacted during Carter's term as president. All successive presidents have maintained an active deregulatory agenda. The effects of deregulation have been mixed, as illustrated by the airline, communication, and agricultural sectors.

The Airline Deregulation Act of 1978 completely eliminated economic regulation of commercial airlines over several years. Although many new passenger carriers flocked into the industry when barriers to entry were first removed, they were unable to compete successfully with the existing major airlines. All of the original new entrants have now disappeared, as have some of the major airlines that were operating at the time of deregulation. Consequently, there are now fewer major carriers than under the regulatory regime, although new airlines, such as Jet Blue, continue to emerge. Competition has lowered some passenger rates, but there is disagreement as to the extent to which passengers have benefited. For example, by 2002, it was clear that since enactment of the Airline Deregulation Act, small communities were losing service. Despite Congress's promise to maintain service to small communities, thirty-eight communities lost air service between 1978 and 2002.[17]

As the government removed or modified long-standing regulations in other industries, there was public disagreement over who benefited the most. The landmark Telecommunications Act of 1996 deregulated the radio industry. This act allowed companies to own an unlimited number of stations nationwide, erasing the previous forty-station limit. Deregulation strengthened the position of efficient companies and drove the less efficient into bankruptcy. Radio station owners such as Jacor Communications went from possessing fifty stations in 1996 to 204 in 1998. The large media enterprise CBS owned 160 stations in 1998, and Capstar Broadcasting Partners owned 229. Negative consequences, however, can also be linked to deregulation and the resulting industry consolidation. It was estimated that between March 1996 and February 1998, the number of individual owners dropped 14 percent, minority ownership declined, and diversity of content suffered.

In June 2003, the Federal Communications Commission (FCC) passed a ruling that would have allowed for further deregulation of the media. This ruling would have permitted broadcast networks' ownership of TV stations to reach 45 percent of the national audience instead of the current 35 percent. The ruling was met with opposition in the courts and in Congress. Congress voted to overturn the ruling. Politicians and citizens alike have expressed concern about concentrated corporate ownership of the media industry. As Representative Maurice Hinchey (D–NY) wrote in February 2006, "Over the past three decades the number of major U.S. media companies fell by more than half; most of the survivors are controlled by fewer than ten huge media conglomerates."[18] Corporate corruption has also raised concerns about such powerful conglomerates. (See Politics Now: Corporate Scandals.)

In agriculture, too, deregulation has had an impact. There has been significant rethinking of programs begun during the New Deal era. In the 1980s and 1990s, agricultural price support programs came under increasing attack from conservatives, who claimed that such government price supports promote inefficiency. Republicans, who took control of Congress in 1995, sought to phase out crop supports as part of the effort to curb federal spending. In 1996, Congress passed a landmark agriculture bill with the aim of phasing out crop subsidies by the year 2002 and to make prices more dependent upon the workings of the free market. By 1997, however, Congress was moving away from the intent of the landmark bill, appropriating significant sums of money to rescue farmers from bad weather, crop disease, and falling commodity prices. The 2002 farm bill actually increased agricultural subsidies by 70 percent as part of a ten-year, $180 billion package. The political pressure coming from large-scale farms and agribusinesses was obvious. According to one analyst: "Nearly three-quarters of these funds will go to the wealthiest 10 percent of farmers—most of whom earn more than $250,000 per year."[19]

The global backlash against agricultural subsidies in rich countries was visible at the 2003 Cancun Conference of the World Trade Organization. A new bloc—the

Politics Now

CORPORATE SCANDALS

When the founder of one of the nation's largest cable companies and two of his sons were arrested in July 2002, the general public was getting used to the idea of wrongdoing by corporate executives. Prior to the arrest of John Rigas and his sons, Samuel D. Waksal, the former chief executive of the biotechnology company ImClone Systems, was arrested at his Manhattan home and charged with insider trading. L. Dennis Kozlowski, the former chair and chief executive of the conglomerate Tyco International, was indicted on charges of evading more than $1 million of sales taxes on six paintings. The large media company AOL Time Warner disclosed that the Securities and Exchange Commission (SEC) had begun an investigation into the accounting at its America Online division.[a] The press castigated accounting firm Arthur Andersen for shredding "tons" of documents, and many of its former clients, such as Dynergy, Qwest Communications, WorldCom, and Global Crossing, were accused of using questionable accounting practices.

In July 2002, WorldCom became the largest bankruptcy in U.S. history, far surpassing the size of Enron's December 2001 bankruptcy, previously the largest. It was revealed that WorldCom's chief financial officer, Scott D. Sullivan, had devised a strategy that improperly accounted for $3.5 billion of expenses. The questionable accounting practice was discovered by an internal auditor and led to further distrust of accounting firm Arthur Andersen. Andersen, WorldCom's former accounting firm, had not detected these irregularities. As WorldCom declared bankruptcy in 2002, it prepared to lay off 17,000 employees, about one-fifth of its workforce. A federal jury in Houston, Texas, had already convicted the Arthur Andersen accounting firm on one felony count of obstructing the SEC's investigation into Enron's collapse. The corporate scandals of 2001–2002 reinforced the need for greater government oversight and regulation.[b]

Lynn E. Turner, chief accountant for the SEC from 1998 to 2001, asserted that accounting problems represented more than a "few bad apples." According to Turner, it is small wonder that auditors overlooked enormous errors in companies' financial statements since the system was stoked by the need to generate high consulting and underwriting fees. In 2001, a record high number of public companies restated their earnings. Turner concluded that in order to fix the problem, the Department of Justice needed more money to bring criminal cases against financial crooks. In addition, she contended that auditors had to be more independent from companies they audited. Banning auditing companies from receiving payments for consulting and legal services would increase their independence.[c]

By 2004, news about corporate scandals ceased to figure prominently in the media. Many have credited the strong-willed William Donaldson, chair of the SEC from February 2003 to June 2005, for restoring the SEC's credibility and morale, as well as investor confidence. His effective stance on mutual-fund governance and hedge-fund regulation "restored confidence in the markets and forced Corporate America and Wall Street to watch their step in keeping the books and managing conflicts of interest."[d]

SEC Chair Christopher Cox, while testifying before the Senate Banking Committee in April 2006, outlined the SEC's initiatives to improve financial disclosures for investors and stated that the SEC has "full authority to investigate and bring enforcement action against hedge funds."[e] It is reassuring that the SEC has taken steps to curtail corporate corruption. At the same time it should be noted that it will take further action from the executive and legislative branches to build a transparent and accountable framework that will keep businesses honest in the long run. SEC steps notwithstanding, the American public remains seriously concerned about the health of public and private pension plans.

---

[a]Andrew Sorkin, "Founder of Adelphia and 2 Sons Arrested," *New York Times* (July 25, 2002): A1; David Kirkpatrick, "AOL Accounts Under Scrutiny from the S.E.C.," *New York Times* (July 25, 2002): A1.

[b]"Auditor's Ruling: Andersen Win Lifts U.S. Case," *Wall Street Journal* (June 17, 2002): A1; Kurt Eichenwald and Simon Romero, "Inquiry Appears to Bolster Fraud Case," *New York Times* (June 28, 2002): A1.

[c]Lynn E. Turner, "Just a Few Rotten Apples? Better Audit Those Books," *Washington Post* (July 14, 2002): B1.

[d]"Donaldson: A Legacy That May Not Last," http://www.businessweek.com.

[e]"Chairman Cox Outlines SEC Agenda," http://www.bondmarkets.com.

G20—was formed when a group of developing countries united in their opposition to unfair trade practices created by agricultural subsidies. In the face of their opposition, trade talks collapsed at Cancun. Price supports and tariffs are other targets of those who favor deregulation in the agricultural sector. In 2005, the U.S. government spent approximately $21 billion in price supports for agricultural products. U.S. Trade Representative Rob Portman proposed reducing that figure to $12 billion, provided the European Union (EU), Japan, and other nations also lowered trade barriers. The United States, the EU, and many poorer nations have kept farm tariffs at an average of 40 percent, which is significantly higher than the approximately 5 percent average tariffs levied on manufactured goods.[20] U.S. Trade Representative Susan Schwab was quoted on September 10, 2006, as stating: "we are willing to do more in terms of cutting our agricultural support, but we could only do so in response to more market access." She also remarked that the United States had signaled its flexibility.[21] It remains to be seen whether the government can regulate the economy effectively in spite of powerful political pressure to distort the market prices through subsidies and tariff protection.

In spite of the mixed record, economic deregulation has remained a top policy priority among American politicians. (For a related issue, see Join the Debate: File Sharing and Protecting Intellectual Property Rights.) The same cannot be said of deregulation efforts in the social sphere. Strong support continues for social regulation to protect consumers, workers, and the environment. Moreover, in some areas in which economic deregulation occurred, there have been calls to "reregulate." This has occurred in the airline industry because of concern about safety and industry domination by a small number of companies.

In the next sections of this chapter, we take a detailed look at two areas of government economic regulation. The first is macroeconomic regulation, the government's role in stabilizing the economy through policies that influence the overall performance of the economy. The second is microeconomic regulation to control environmental pollution.

Stabilizing the Economy

UNTIL THE EARLY 1930S, the prevailing view in the United States was that government intervention in the economy could disrupt natural economic laws but could not improve them. The massive scale and the persistence of the Great Depression challenged that notion, as the economic doctrine promoted by the English economist John Maynard Keynes gained more traction. In his *General Theory of Employment, Interests, and Money* (1936), Keynes argued that deficit spending by a government could supplement the total or aggregate demand for goods and services, especially during recessions. The government's intervention in the economy rose with the New Deal and World War II. The economy expanded, production rose, unemployment fell to less than 2 percent. But the budget deficit grew. The government had essentially assumed responsibility for economic stability.

Economic stability is a condition in which there is economic growth, a rising national income, high employment, and a steadiness in the general level of prices. Conversely, economic instability involves either inflation or recession. **Inflation** occurs when there is too much demand for the available supply of goods and services, with the consequence that general price levels rise as buyers compete for the available supply. Prices may also rise if large corporations and unions have sufficient economic power to push prices and wages above competitive levels. A **recession** is marked by a decline in the economy. Investment sags, production falls off, and unemployment increases.

The government manages the economy through monetary and fiscal policies. Monetary policies influence the economy through changes in the money supply, while fiscal policies influence the behavior of consumers and businesses through government spending and taxing decisions. How does the government use these policy tools?

MONETARY POLICY: CONTROLLING THE MONEY SUPPLY

The government conducts **monetary policy** by managing the nation's money supply and influencing interest rates. In an industrialized economy, all those making exchanges—consumers, businesses, and government—use money. That is, prices of goods and services are set in **money**

economic stability
A situation in which there is economic growth, rising national income, high employment, and steadiness in the general level of prices.

inflation
A rise in the general price levels of an economy.

recession
A short-term decline in the economy that occurs as investment sags, production falls off, and unemployment increases.

monetary policy
A form of government regulation in which the nation's money supply and interest rates are controlled.

money
A system of exchange for goods and services that includes currency, coins, and bank deposits.

■ British economist John Maynard Keynes led a revolution in economics, arguing that government deficit spending during economic downturns could stimulate spending and lead to recovery.

Photo courtesy: Time Life Pictures/Getty Images

Join the Debate

FILE SHARING AND PROTECTING INTELLECTUAL PROPERTY RIGHTS

OVERVIEW: The U.S. Constitution, in Article I, section 8, gives Congress the authority to "promote the Progress of Science and the useful Arts, by securing to Authors and Inventors the exclusive Right to their respective Writings and Discoveries." According to legal scholars, the idea behind this clause is twofold: first, it recognizes that works of the mind, such as those produced in the arts and sciences, can bring great benefits to society at large; second, it recognizes not only that intellectual property can greatly impact the nation's finances in terms of real property (just think what the personal computer has done to revolutionize the economy), but also that inventors and artists should reap the rewards of their efforts. The government must balance competing claims with regard to what constitutes legitimate intellectual property and what belongs to the public domain. In some instances, this balancing act may have dramatic consequences for the nation in general. The controversy involving the entertainment industry and those (by some estimates) 60 million Americans engaged in peer-to-peer file sharing illustrates how the government must balance these competing claims. Peer-to-peer file sharing bypasses the need for central servers by allowing all computers to communicate and share resources as equals. This technology has allowed for a boom in music file sharing and instant messaging.

The Recording Industry Association of America (RIAA) testified that file sharing cost the music industry an 8 percent loss in sales in 2002 and a 9 percent drop in CD unit sales during that same period. In part due to perceived economic losses owing to file-sharing activity, the RIAA sued Internet service providers in order to gain access to users who were file sharing illegally. In *Verizon* v. *RIAA* (2003), the RIAA won access to peer-to-peer programs and the ability to sue—without the approval of a judge—those engaged in illegal file sharing. Users, for their part, argue that hard drives are personal property and are subject to requisite privacy rights, and what they do with their personal property (as long as no one is "harmed") is not the business of RIAA or government.

In *Metro-Goldwyn-Mayer Studios Inc. et al.* v. *Grokster, Ltd. et al.* (2005), a case brought by twenty-eight of the world's largest entertainment companies against the manufacturers of Morpheus, Grokster, and Kazaa file-sharing software, the Supreme Court's unanimous ruling was a defeat for the manufacturers of peer-to-peer interface software that allows for sharing music and video files. Justice Souter wrote the majority opinion: "We hold that one who distributes a device with the object of promoting its use to infringe copyright, as shown by clear expression or other affirmative steps taken to foster infringement, is liable for the resulting acts of infringement."[a] The debate over the decision continues today, since many have argued that such an interpretation of copyright laws will stifle innovation. In effect, the Supreme Court deemed that Grokster was liable for inducing copyright infringement. As one advocacy group inquired: "When should the distributor of a multi-purpose tool be held liable for the infringements that may be committed by end-users of the tool?"[b] The broader question is whether an innovator is responsible for all infringements by the end user.

As the above case shows, the rapid pace of change in computer, Internet, and affiliated technologies has created questions regarding rights, economics, and law that are difficult to answer. These technologies have dramatically altered and enlarged the public domain. What constitutes intellectual property? What constitutes the public domain? What are the implications of an unregulated Internet? How much regulation will suffocate creative, intellectual, and economic activity?

---

units (dollars), and the amount of money in circulation influences the quantity of goods and services demanded, the number of workers hired, the decisions to build factories, and so on. Money is more than just the currency and coin in our pockets: it includes balances in our checkbooks, deposits in bank accounts, and the value of other assets.

The Federal Reserve System is responsible for changing the money supply. As it makes these changes, it attempts to promote economic stability. The **Board of Governors** has responsibility for the formation and implementation of monetary policy because of its ability to control the credit-creating and lending activities of the nation's

Board of Governors
In the Federal Reserve System, a seven-member board that sets member banks' reserve requirements, controls the discount rate, and makes other economic decisions.

ARGUMENTS FOR ALLOWING FILE SHARING

- **File sharing fosters creativity and innovation.** Once an idea is out in the public domain, others can take the original concept and improve it. This may improve a social good and increase economic productivity as well. For example, the first personal computers could not multitask and could run only one application at a time. The development of multitasking greatly increased the viability of the computer as a tool and means of communication to increase economic productivity.
- **Files are private property.** Hard-drive files are created by the user. Once a user creates a file, it becomes his or her property and should have the legal protection of such. The right to privacy and property are understood to be two fundamental rights in the American system, and the Fourth Amendment's prohibition against unwarranted searches and seizures should apply.
- **Peer-to-peer file sharing improves the quality of life for the economically disadvantaged.** What better way to ensure that the economically disadvantaged have access to music, entertainment, and information than to allow services such as Kazaa and Napster? File sharing allows those without means to access programs not only for entertainment but for work and productivity as well.

ARGUMENTS AGAINST ALLOWING FILE SHARING

- **Sharing entertainment, literature, and software files constitutes theft of intellectual property.** The products of artists and inventors are protected by federal copyright law. To use a product under copyright protection without permission or payment may be a criminal offense. The fine for copyright violation when downloading music can be a maximum of $150,000 per song.
- **File sharing without paying for service or content reduces incentives for innovators to create.** Free-market economic theory contends that those who do not benefit from their efforts, whether artists, writers, musicians, or software engineers, are more likely to switch to other employment to meet their living needs. This may deprive society of artistic, intellectual, or technological goods.
- **Illegal peer-to-peer file sharing constitutes "free riding" and causes economic harm.** Those who download or upload music files that they have not bought are benefiting from purchases by other consumers and are lowering income and incentives for those who produce intellectual property. This has the effect of reducing resources devoted to producing content. Paying customers are crucial to spur investment in content and technology.

QUESTIONS

1. Does peer-to-peer file sharing increase innovation and productivity? Why, or why not?
2. Does intellectual property need added or different protections? What makes intellectual property different from real property?

SELECTED READINGS

Bouchoux, Deborah. *Protecting Your Company's Intellectual Property: A Practical Guide to Trademarks, Copyrights, Patents, and Trade Secrets.* New York: American Management Association, 2001.

Lessig, Lawrence. *The Future of Ideas: The Fate of the Commons in the Connected World.* New York: Vintage, 2002.

---

[a]*"Supreme Court Rules Against File Swapping,"* http://news.com.com/Supreme+Court+rules+against+file+swapping/2100-1030_3-5764135.html.
[b]*MGM v. Grokster,* 545 U.S. ___ (2005).

---

banks. When individuals and corporations deposit their money in financial institutions such as commercial banks (which accept deposits and make loans) and savings and loan associations (S&Ls), these deposits serve as the basis for loans to borrowers. In effect, the loaning of money creates new deposits or financial liabilities—new money that did not previously exist. But, we are getting ahead of our story. First, we'll look at the Federal Reserve System and its authority

The Federal Reserve System   Created in 1913 to adjust the money supply to the needs of agriculture, commerce, and industry, the Federal Reserve System comprises the Federal Reserve Board (FRB) (formally, the Board of Governors of the Federal Reserve System; informally, "the Fed"), the Federal Open Market Committee (FOMC), the twelve Federal Reserve Banks in regions throughout the country, and other member banks.[22] (See Figure 18.1.)

The president appoints (subject to Senate confirmation) the seven members of the Board of Governors, who serve fourteen-year, overlapping terms. The president can remove a member for stated causes, but this has never occurred. The president designates one board member to serve as chair for a four-year term, which runs from the midpoint of one presidential term to the midpoint of the next to ensure economic stability during a change of administrations. The current chair, Ben S. Bernanke, was sworn in on February 1, 2006. Prior to this appointment, he served as chair of President George W. Bush's Council of Economic Advisers. Formally, the FRB has much independence from the executive branch, ostensibly so that monetary policy will not be influenced by political considerations. Defenders of the FRB's independent position assert that monetary policy is too important, complex, and technical to be under the day-to-day control of elected public officials, who might be inclined to make inflationary monetary decisions to advance their own short-term political interests (such as being reelected). Bernanke's prior position at the White House may raise some skeptical eyebrows regarding the Fed's independence from the current administration. It should be noted, however, that his predecessor at the Fed, Alan Greenspan, served during Republican and Democratic administrations for almost two decades.

FIGURE 18.1 THE FEDERAL RESERVE SYSTEM

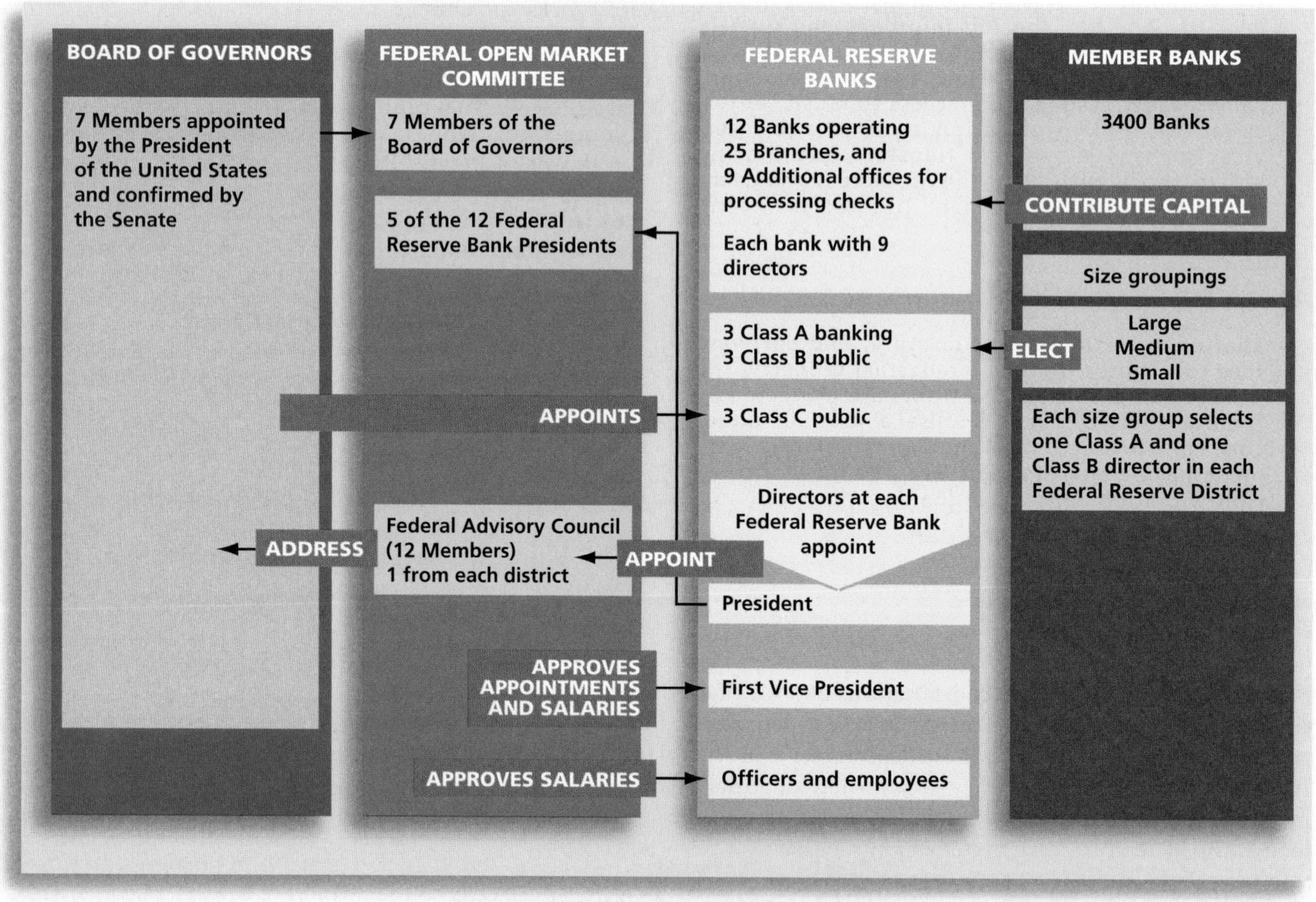

Source: Board of Governors of the Federal Reserve System.

Greenspan, like Bernanke, had also served as a chair of the Council of Economic Advisers (under President Gerald R. Ford). It is expected that Bernanke, like Greenspan before him, will pursue monetary policies that foster low-inflation, macroeconomic growth over the long term, and that he will withstand political pressure from the White House and Congress.

At the base of the Federal Reserve System are the twelve Federal Reserve Banks. These are "bankers' banks"; they are formally owned by the Federal Reserve System member banks in each region, and they do not do business with the public.

Monetary authority is allocated to the FRB, the Federal Reserve Bank boards of directors, and the FOMC. In actuality, however, all three are dominated by the FRB and its chair. Public officials and the financial community pay great attention to the utterances of the Fed's chair for clues to the future course of monetary policy. The primary monetary policy tools are the setting of reserve requirements for member banks, control of the discount rate, and open market operations.

Reserve requirements set by the Federal Reserve designate the portion of the banks' deposits that most banks must retain as backing for their loans. The reserves determine how much or how little banks can lend to businesses and consumers. For example, if the FRB changed the reserve requirements and allowed banks to keep $10 on hand rather than $15 for every $100 in deposits that it held, it would free up some additional money for loans. The **discount rate** is the rate of interest at which the Federal Reserve Board lends money to member banks. Lowering the discount rate would encourage local member banks to increase their borrowing from the Fed and extend more loans at lower rates. This would expand economic activity, since when rates are lower, more people should be able to qualify for large purchases by taking out car loans or housing mortgages. As a consequence of cheaper interest rates, more large durable goods (such as houses and cars) should be produced and sold.

In **open market operations,** the FRB buys and sells government securities in the open market. The Federal Open Market Committee meets periodically to decide on purchases or sale of government securities to member banks. When member banks buy long-term government bonds, they make dollar payments to the Fed and reduce the amount of money available for loans. Fed purchases of securities from member banks in essence give the banks an added supply of money. This action increases the availability of loans and should decrease interest rates. As described above, decreases in interest rates stimulate economic activity.

The FRB can also use "moral suasion" to influence the actions of banks and other members of the financial community by suggestion, exhortation, and informal agreement. Because of its commanding position as a monetary policy maker, the media, economists, and market observers pay attention to verbal signals about economic trends and conditions emitted by the FRB and its chair.

How the FRB uses these tools depends in part on its views of the state of the economy. If inflation appears to be the problem, then the Fed would likely restrict or tighten the money supply. If a recession with rising unemployment appears to threaten the economy, then the FRB would probably act to loosen or expand the money supply in order to stimulate the economy.

The FRB and the Executive and Legislative Branches

Although the public generally holds the president responsible for maintaining a healthy economy, he does not really possess adequate constitutional or legal authority to meet this obligation. The president shares

reserve requirements
Government requirements that a portion of member banks' deposits must be retained to back loans made.

discount rate
The rate of interest at which member banks can borrow money from their regional Federal Reserve Bank.

open market operations
The buying and selling of government securities by the Federal Reserve Bank in the securities market.

■ Ben S. Bernanke, center, after President Bush announced Bernanke's nomination to replace Federal Reserve Board Chair Alan Greenspan, at left.

responsibility for fiscal policy with Congress, and Congress authorizes the FRB to make monetary policy. In terms of pressing the Fed to adjust its monetary policy, presidential power is, at its best, "the power to persuade." There are many formal and informal contacts between the White House and the FRB, however, to discuss monetary policy. During formal meetings, the FRB chair can convey some of his views on the economy to the administration. The result is that the president customarily accepts the monetary policy made by the FRB, even if it is not precisely what he would prefer.[23]

FISCAL POLICY: TAXING AND SPENDING

fiscal policy
Federal government policies on taxes, spending, and debt management, intended to promote the nation's macroeconomic goals, particularly with respect to employment, price stability, and growth.

Fiscal policy is the deliberate use of the national government's taxing and spending policies to influence the overall operation of the economy and maintain economic stability. The president and Congress formulate fiscal policy and conduct it through the federal budget process. The powerful instruments of fiscal policy are budget surpluses and deficits. These are achieved by manipulating the overall or "aggregate" levels of revenue and expenditures.

According to the Keynesian theory behind fiscal policy, there is a level of total or aggregate spending at which the economy will operate at full employment. Total spending is the sum of consumer spending, private investment spending, and government spending. If consumer and business spending does not create demand sufficient to cause the economy to operate at full employment, then the government should make up the shortfall by increasing spending in excess of revenues. This was essentially what Keynes recommended for the national government during the Great Depression. If inflation is the problem confronting policy makers, then government can reduce demand for goods and services by reducing its expenditures and running a budget surplus.[24]

One type of fiscal policy is discretionary fiscal policy, which involves deliberate decisions by the president and Congress to run budget surpluses or deficits. This can be done by increasing or decreasing spending while holding taxes constant, by increasing or cutting taxes while holding spending stable, or by some combination of changes in taxing and spending.

The first significant application of fiscal policy theory occurred in 1964. President John F. Kennedy, a Democrat committed to getting the country "moving again," brought Keynesian economists to Washington as his economic advisers. These advisers believed that increased government spending, even at the expense of an increase in the budget deficit, was needed to stimulate the economy in order to achieve full employment. Many conservatives opposed budget deficits as bad public policy. President Kennedy's advisers decided that many conservatives and members of the business community would find deficits more palatable, or less objectionable, if they were achieved by cutting taxes rather than by increasing government spending. Furthermore, a tax cut, they reasoned, would increase private-sector spending on goods and services.

The result was the adoption of the Revenue Act of 1964, which reduced personal and corporate income tax rates. This variant of fiscal policy, which was more acceptable to business, has been labeled "commercial Keynesianism." The tax-cut stimulus contributed to the expansion of the economy through the remainder of the 1960s and reduced the unemployment rate to less than 4 percent, its lowest peacetime rate and what many people then considered to be full employment.[25] President Reagan in 1981 and President George W. Bush in 2001 and 2003 pushed tax cuts through Congress in part to stimulate a faltering economy.

There remains a serious partisan division over tax politics. By and large, Republicans have remained steadfast supporters of tax cuts, while Democrats have remained committed to tax revenues as the means of funding government programs. In September 1999, President Bill Clinton vetoed a $792 billion tax-cut proposal backed by

Republicans because he considered it "wrong for Medicare, wrong for Social Security, wrong for education and wrong for the economy."[26] In May 2006, President George W. Bush was pressing for action on stalled legislation that would ensure a 15 percent tax rate on dividends and capital gains through 2010. In his words, "tax increase would be disastrous for business, disastrous for families, and disastrous for the economy."[27] Democrats argued that the proposed tax legislation overwhelmingly benefited wealthy investors and not the middle class.

THE EFFECTS OF GLOBALIZATION

Before we turn to how the budgetary process works, it is important to consider another context for fiscal policy: the international economy. Advances in transportation, communication, and technology have strengthened the link between the United States and the rest of the world. (See Global Perspective: Economic Freedom Around the World.) International affairs influence business decisions of American companies that wish to reduce labor costs as well as expand their markets. Free trade has, on balance, had a beneficial impact on the U.S. economy because the competition created by free trade limits price increases on American goods and services, thereby benefiting consumers. In addition, free trade expands the market for high-quality American products that are in demand in the global economy. By 1999, the U.S. economy was enjoying more than eight years of uninterrupted growth, the third longest expansion in the nation's history. Reflecting this growth, the stock market soared by more than 300 percent between 1990 and 1999. Many believed that the higher stock prices were driven by lower labor costs and the relocation of manufacturing to low-wage nations. Lower labor costs can expand profits, which drive stock prices higher.

**Comparing
Economic Policy**

The 2001 recession and the "jobless recovery" did not immediately dampen the enthusiasm for economic globalization. Between July 2000 and January 2004, however, the manufacturing sector lost 3 million jobs. This trend cannot be explained exclusively by globalization and international trade. Productivity gains in the manufacturing sector, a shift in U.S. consumer demand away from manufactured goods, the rising U.S. trade deficit, and the outsourcing of manufacturing jobs help explain the loss of jobs over the past decades.[28] It is overseas competition, however, that is the frequent target of labor unions and politicians favoring protectionist policies.

Labor unions in the United States are among the strongest critics of free trade. Union leaders warn that free trade with nations such as China or Mexico means that American workers must compete against workers in nations where wages are low, where human rights violations exist, and where environmental restrictions are ineffective or nonexistent. They argue that opening up production to large infusions of new workers drives down wages in the higher-cost nation while improving wages in the lower-cost countries. Union leaders have also stressed the need to restrict "dumping" low-priced foreign goods onto American markets and the need to open other nations to more American goods.

Loss of real, or inflation-adjusted, income has become a serious concern in the United States. In September 1997, the minimum wage was raised from $4.75 to $5.15, and it remains at that rate as of early 2006. Inflation since 1997 has devalued the wages of many that have not been able to make adequate advancements in earnings. One analysis estimates a 4 percent loss of real median American household income from 2000 to 2004, in spite of economic expansion in the years of 2002, 2003, and 2004. The same analysis posited that only the top 5 percent of households gained in real income in the 2003–2004 fiscal year, while 5.4 million more Americans fell into poverty between 2000 and 2004.[29] Figure 18.2 shows the growth of the minimum wage since its creation.

A number of analysts have warned of globalization's impact on income distribution. Globalization appears to further segment the market into economic winners and losers. During the 1990s, Fortune 500 companies achieved huge gains, yet many of

Global Perspective

ECONOMIC FREEDOM AROUND THE WORLD

Economic globalization is blurring the territorial boundaries that separate countries. In the process, it is creating a single world economy. Significant differences still remain among countries, however, in regard to their political and economic systems. These differences are important to investors because they affect investors' ability to earn profits and their decisions on where to set up new businesses or expand existing ones. Important considerations include tax rates, communication and transportation systems, regulations governing investments, and labor costs. The last of these has been particularly influential for certain businesses. Between 2000 and 2003, the United States lost 455,000 jobs in the computer and electronics industry. It is not hard to understand why. Salaries for computer programmers in the United States, for example, ranged from $60,000 to $80,000 per year. In Ireland, the range was $23,000 to $34,000; in India, it was $5,880 to $11,000. A more recent evaluation of data published by the Bureau of Labor Statistics, however, suggests a more optimistic picture: the IT unemployment rate was 2.5 percent in early 2006, the lowest it has been since early 2001. The analysis provided by *Information Week* suggests that there has been a 20 percent decline in computer programmer employment in the United States, while the number of software engineers employed increased by 15 percent. The former requires less expertise and can be outsourced with greater ease.[a]

Outsourcing, of course, is a concern for all countries that stress economic freedom. Market friendly legislation and institutions in developing countries help attract much needed foreign investments to promote economic development. Developing countries face economic and political pressure from donor countries and organizations such as the World Bank and the International Monetary Fund to promote economic freedom. We can get a quick picture of how hospitable a country is to business by looking at its ranking on the *Economic Freedom of the World* index prepared by the Economic Freedom Network. The group's 2006 report (based on 2004 data) evaluated 130 countries on a 10-point scale, with 10 being the highest score.[b] The measure scores a country's performance on thirty-seven different dimensions, including a legal system that pro-

tects an individual's private property, a stable currency, patent rights protections, the freedom to compete in labor and product markets, and tax policies that encourage investment. According to the study, economic freedom does not lead to greater income inequality and tends to appear where there are high individual income levels, high rates of economic growth, and long life expectancy. The 2006 report found that the average economic freedom score was 6.5 in 2004—up from 5.99 in 1995. Overall, economic freedom declined during the 1970s and reached a low of 5.1 in 1980. Since then, economic freedom has been on the rise, especially with the collapse of the Soviet Union.

In 2004, Hong Kong, a special trade area within China, had the highest economic freedom ranking (8.7). The United States ranked third (8.2). Mexico was sixtieth (6.6). The highest-ranking South American country was Chile at twentieth (7.4). African and Latin American countries as well as countries that emerged from the former Soviet Union tended to congregate at the bottom of the rankings. Botswana was the highest-ranking African country at thirty-fifth (7.1).

The 2006 report found that nations in the top quartile in economic freedom have an average per capita GDP of $24,402, compared to only $2,998 for those countries in the bottom quartile. Similarly, the nations in the top quartile far outperform those in the bottom quartile in terms of life expectancy, employment rates, and other quality of life indicators.

QUESTIONS

1. What political factors most directly impact a nation's economic performance?
2. What is the difference between economic freedom and political freedom?

---

[a]Eric Chabrow, "More U.S. Workers Have IT Jobs Than Ever Before," *Information Week*, April 24, 2006, http://www.informationweek.com.

[b]Economic Freedom of the World, 2005 Annual Report: Executive Summary, http://www.freetheworld.com.

---

those gains appeared to come at the expense of smaller businesses and workers. By the late 1990s, money was flowing to corporations with high concentrations of financial, legal, marketing, and other professional expertise and away from manufacturing production. Average workers witnessed an erosion of income while professionals and those with information technology skills reaped huge benefits. In 1999, analysts found that the average real after-tax income of the middle 60 percent of Americans was lower than it was in 1977.[30] Furthermore, the debate over outsourcing white-collar professional and technological jobs to foreign countries, discussed at the beginning of

FIGURE 18.2 GROWTH IN THE MINIMUM WAGE OVER TIME

The minimum wage rose from 25 cents an hour in 1938 to $5.15 in 1997. Once inflation is considered, however, workers earned their highest minimum wages in the 1960s and 1970s.

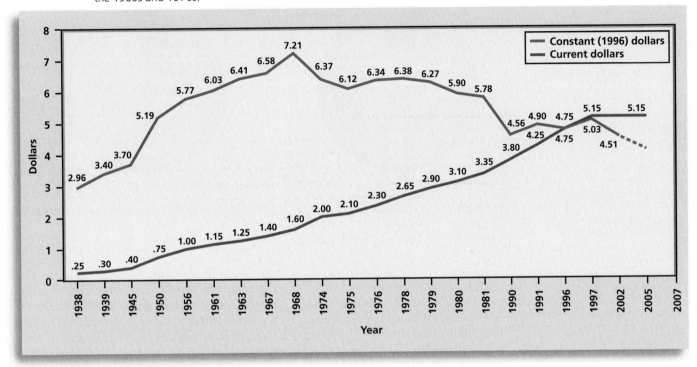

this chapter, raises additional concerns about the global economy's negative impact on American jobs.

In general, economists do not share the protectionist views expressed by unions and some politicians. A member of President Bush's Council of Economic Advisers stated in January 2006: "There are many here in Washington and elsewhere who are calling for more barriers to international commerce. These calls for protectionism are at odds with the evidence that decades of trade liberalization have played an important role in helping raise average U.S. living standards. American companies that are globally engaged—through exporting, importing, and foreign direct investment—tend to be the most-productive, highest-paying companies in the United States."[31]

THE BUDGET PROCESS

The primary purpose of the federal budget is funding government programs, but manipulating the budget can also be used as part of fiscal policy to stabilize the economy and to counteract fluctuations. Because federal budget planning begins roughly a year and a half before the beginning of the fiscal year in which it takes effect, its immediate influence on the economy is limited. Once a budget is adopted, it takes time to implement the provisions. Because of the difficulty in predicting the future, the budget is not a precise instrument for manipulating the economy. Furthermore, the budget process is complex and disjointed.

VISUAL LITERACY

Evaluating Federal Spending and Economic Policy

How the Federal Government Raises and Spends Money
The federal government raises money from a variety of sources, with individual income taxes and social insurance and retirement receipts representing over 80 percent of the funds received (see Figure 18.3). Social insurance and retirement receipts include Social Secu-

FIGURE 18.3 RECEIPTS AND OUTLAYS OF THE FEDERAL GOVERNMENT

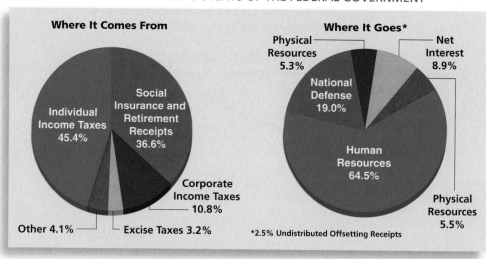

Source: United States Budget, Fiscal Year 2006, http://www.gpoaccess.gov.

rity, hospital insurance, and other taxes. Between 1991 and 2001, individual income taxes rose from 44.3 percent of total receipts to 49.9 percent. By calendar year 2006, due primarily to tax cuts supported by the Bush administration and approved by the Republican-led Congress, individual income taxes accounted for 37.6 percent of total federal government income. This significant reduction in the share of individual income taxes may have resulted in the 15.2 percent of borrowed funds that account for the federal budget deficit.[32]

Most government spending is directed toward national defense and human resources. Defense spending consists primarily of maintaining the U.S. armed forces and developing the weapons the military needs. Human resources include the spending categories of health, income security, and social security. The human resources share of total outlays grew significantly from its 1991 share of 52.1 percent to 59.1 percent in calendar year 2006.[33]

Congress and the Budget Process The Budget and Accounting Act of 1921 gave the president authority to prepare an annual budget and submit it to Congress for approval. A staff agency now called the Office of Management and Budget (OMB) was created to assist the president and handle the details of budget preparation (see also chapter 8). The budget runs for a single fiscal year, beginning on October 1 of one calendar year and running through September 30 of the following calendar year. The fiscal year takes its name from the calendar year in which it ends; thus the time period from October 1, 2007, through September 30, 2008, is designated fiscal year (FY) 2008.

The president sends a budget proposal to Congress in January or February of each year (see Table 18.1). Work on the budget within the executive branch will have begun nine or ten months earlier, however. Acting in accordance with presidential decisions on the general structure of the budget, the OMB provides the various departments and agencies with instructions and guidance on presidential priorities to help them in preparing their budget requests. The departments and agencies then proceed to develop their detailed funding requests. The OMB reconciles the discrepancies between presidential and agency preferences, but it should be remembered that the OMB's mission is to defend the presidential budgetary agenda.[34]

Article I of the Constitution provides that "no money shall be drawn from the Treasury, but in consequence of appropriations made by law." Congress and its leg-

TABLE 18.1 THE FEDERAL BUDGET PROCESS

First Monday in February	Congress receives the president's budget.
February 15	Congressional Budget Office (CBO) reports to the budget committees on fiscal policy and budget priorities, including an analysis of the president's budget.
February 25	Congressional committees submit views and estimates on spending to the budget committees.
April 1	Budget committees report concurrent resolution on the budget, which sets a total for budget outlays, an estimate of expenditures for major budget categories, and the recommended level of revenues. This resolution acts as an agenda for the remainder of the budget process.
April 15	Congress completes action on concurrent resolution on the budget.
May 15	Annual appropriations bills may be considered in the House.
June 10	House Appropriations Committee completes action on regular appropriations bills.
June 15	Congress completes action on reconciliation legislation, bringing budget totals into conformity with established ceilings.
June 30	House completes action on all appropriations bills.
October 1	The new fiscal year begins.

Source: Adapted from Howard E. Shuman, *Politics and the Budget,* 3rd ed. © 1992. Reprinted by permission of Prentice Hall, Inc., Upper Saddle River, NJ.

islative committees (such as those on resources, education and educational opportunities, and national security) may authorize spending on programs, but it is Congress and the appropriations committees in each chamber that actually provide the funding needed to carry out these programs. The appropriations committees often deny some, and once in a while all, of the funding authorized by the legislative committees. Consequently, the legislative committees sometimes have resorted to backdoor spending—authorizing agencies to borrow money from the Treasury or creating entitlement programs that make funding mandatory in order to circumvent the appropriations committees.[35]

To give itself more control over the budget process, Congress initiated and enacted the Budget and Impoundment Control Act of 1974. The act establishes a budget process that includes setting overall levels of revenues and expenditures, the size of the budget surplus or deficit, and priorities among different "functional" areas (for example, national defense, transportation, agriculture, foreign aid, and health). The House and Senate established new budget committees to perform these tasks and authorized the Congressional Budget Office (CBO), a professional staff of technical experts, to assist the budget committees and to provide members of Congress with their own source of budgetary information so they would be more independent of the OMB.

Typically, budget committees hold hearings on the president's proposed budget and set targets for overall revenue and spending and a ceiling for individual categories of spending. Other committees evaluate requests by various agencies. In most years, reconciliation legislation is necessary to ensure that targets are met. Changes in existing law can be proposed in reconciliation bills. Changes can be proposed in tax rates or benefit levels of entitlement programs. The growth of entitlement spending is a major source of concern to policy makers. As shown in Figure 18.4, growth in spending for entitlements has far exceeded growth in discretionary programs.

Legislative action on all appropriations bills is supposed to be completed by October 1, the start of the fiscal year. It is rare, however, for Congress to pass all appropriations bills by this date. For programs still unfunded at the start of the fiscal year, Congress can pass a continuing resolution, which authorizes agencies to continue operating on the basis of last year's appropriation until approval of their new budget. This procedure can cause some uncertainty in agency operations. When the president

FIGURE 18.4 ENTITLEMENTS AND DISCRETIONARY SPENDING, 1963–2007
(IN BILLIONS OF 1996 DOLLARS)
*Projections.

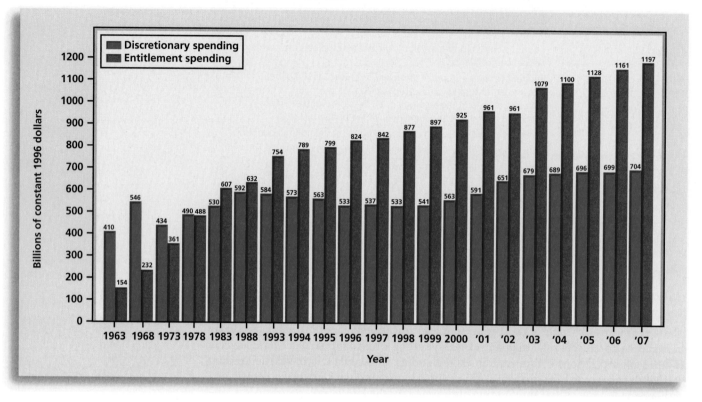

Source: United States Budget, Fiscal Year 2007, http://www.gpo.gov.

and Congress cannot agree, some programs may be shut down until the terms for a continuing resolution are worked out.

Major Budget Conflicts Conflict often develops between Congress and the president over the details of the budget and its overall dimensions, such as the size of the deficit, the balance between military and domestic spending, and international agreements affecting domestic economics. Uncertainty also arises over the political feasibility of funding very specific initiatives. Throughout the 1980s, there was conflict between the Democrats in Congress, who favored more domestic spending and less military spending, and President Ronald Reagan and his administration, who favored less domestic spending and more spending on defense. In 1993, the Clinton administration touched off a partisan political struggle in Congress with its budget deficit reduction plan because it included tax increases.

The 1993 struggle between Congress and the president, however, was a love fest compared to the 1995–1996 stalemate. Under the leadership of House Speaker Newt Gingrich, the first Republican congressional majority in forty years devised a plan to balance the budget in seven years. While President Clinton also professed a desire to eliminate annual deficits, he and Congress clashed over which programs to cut to balance the budget. In 1995, 1996, and 1999, Clinton vetoed appropriations bills that he believed cut social programs too severely.

SIMULATION
You Are Trying to Get a Tax Cut

Budget Initiatives of the George W. Bush Administration Significant budget changes were adopted when George W. Bush signed the Economic Growth and Tax Relief Reconciliation Act of 2001. While the bill passed the Republican-controlled Congress by a healthy margin, it was not universally embraced. Critics claimed the bill would squander budget surpluses, represented a giveaway to the rich, and would starve the government of needed funds. Supporters viewed it as a reasonable response to high rates of taxation.

The bill lowered income tax rates across the board, expanded deductions, and provided taxpayers with rebates in the summer and early fall of 2001. Rebate checks amounted to up to $300 for single tax filers, $500 for heads of households, and $600 for married couples. It was estimated that by 2011 (when all of the tax cuts and deductions from the bill would be in place), Americans would pay considerably less in taxes. Table 18.2 indicates how much money could be saved by taxpayers under different income and household scenarios.[36]

In 2003, the American economy remained stagnant, and President Bush won congressional approval for another round of income tax cuts. The short-term goal of these cuts was to stimulate the economy by providing taxpayers with more of their own money to spend. Tax withholdings were lowered in the summer of 2003 to reflect the lower rates, and rebate checks were sent to most taxpayers with dependent children. The short-term effect of these cuts was considerable: the GDP rose over 7 percent in the third quarter of 2003 as consumer spending increased. The economy continued to expand, posting a nearly 5 percent growth rate in the first quarter of 2006.

Aside from the tax cuts, George W. Bush also focused attention on combating terrorism and fighting wars in Afghanistan and Iraq. In 2002, a supplemental request was made for an additional $27.1 billion for war-fighting activities of the Department of Defense and for homeland security. Congress overwhelmingly approved Bush's proposal to create a Department of Homeland Security to meet new threats to the nation's security (see chapter 19) and, with some dissent, authorized billions of dollars to fund military operations in Iraq.

The tax rebate checks of 2001 and 2003 represent examples of how changes in legislation and public policy impact our lives. Many Americans no doubt were happy to get money back from the government. The long-term impact of the cuts, however, remains murky. Deficit hawks point to the fact that these cuts, coupled with the high cost of military operations in Iraq and Afghanistan, will likely cause deficits to soar in the next few years. Other critics charge that these cuts "have conferred the most benefits, by far, on the highest-income households—those least in need of additional resources—at a time when [wealth] already is exceptionally concentrated at the top of the income spectrum."[37] But, congressional Republicans and many conservatives hail these cuts as indicative of a philosophical desire to limit government and stimulate the economy. As previously mentioned, President Bush urged Congress to make the 2001 and 2003 tax cuts permanent. (See American Values/American Voices: The Taxation Conundrum.)

According to official estimates, the projected budget deficit for 2006 increased slightly to 3.2 percent of GDP, or $423 billion. The Bush administration stated that the unanticipated costs of Hurricanes Katrina and Rita in 2005 and the new Medicare prescription drug benefit accounted for this increase. The president's 2007 budget proposal aimed to cut the deficit to 2.4 percent of GDP in 2007 and to 1.4 percent of GDP by 2009. A centerpiece of this policy is reduction of discretionary spending by government. The president argued that Social Security and Medicare are fiscally un-

TABLE 18.2 SAMPLE TAX SAVINGS BASED ON 2001 RATE CUTS

These savings come from a combination of specific deductions enacted with the Economic Growth and Tax Relief Reconciliation Act of 2001 and general across-the-board reductions in all income tax rates. Tax reductions benefited all groups, but the reduction in rates disproportionately benefited upper-income groups.

Type of Household	Tax Cut
Case 1 Single taxpayer making $29,960	$345
Case 2 Married taxpayers with no children making $60,000	$1,571
Case 3 Married taxpayers with two children making $40,000	$1,750
Case 4 Married taxpayers with three children making $100,000	$1,915
Case 5 Married taxpayers making $1,000,000	$259,234

Sources: Heritage Foundation, http://www.taxation.org; Radie Bunn, G. E. Whittenburg, and Carol F. Venable, "Analysis of the Economic Growth and Tax Relief Reconciliation Act of 2001," National Public Accountant (October 2001): 8–12, http://proquest.umi.com.

American Values/American Voices

THE TAXATION CONUNDRUM

As chapter 1 has shown, Americans cherish personal liberty and individualism as defining characteristics of their political culture. That political culture also stresses political, if not economic, equality. The tension between liberty and equality has driven much of American political life since 1776. The notion of popular sovereignty and a distrust of an intrusive government have also shaped American political values. Election campaigns in America are replete with promises of tax cuts or promises not to raise taxes. Yet, it pays to examine American values when it comes to the taxation issue. In an October 2005 survey conducted by the Pew Research Center for the People and the Press, a plurality of those polled believe that reducing the budget deficit should be a top priority (42 percent), but only 26 percent favor raising taxes as a means to address this issue. According to the poll, lowering domestic nondefense spending is favored by 47 percent of respondents as a solution for budget deficits.[a]

It seems that Americans prefer government spending cuts over tax cuts. A November 2004 Ipsos Public Affairs poll found that 66 percent of respondents preferred balancing the budget, while 31 percent preferred tax cuts. At the same time, 55 percent of respondents preferred spending more on education, health care, and economic development, while 44 percent preferred balancing the budget.[b] Such a multiplicity of views raises questions about whether Americans can have their cake and eat it too.

Any serious discussion about taxation and tax reform also has to consider public attitudes on the fairness of the tax system. In this context, it is worth mentioning that in 2003, the top 5 percent of income earners accounted for over 31 percent of the nation's adjusted gross income and contributed over 54 percent of federal individual tax revenues. The bottom 50 percent of income earners, on the other hand, accounted for just below 14 percent of the nation's adjusted gross income and just 2.95 percent of federal individual income tax revenues.[c] In an April 2006 Gallup Poll that asked respondents whether they regarded their income tax as fair, 60 percent reported that their tax rate is fair. The same poll asked respondents to evaluate the federal income tax rate as it affected them in 2006. The poll results demonstrate that while the perception that taxes are too high remains high, the share of those agreeing to that proposition declined quite significantly between 2001 and 2003, from 65 percent in April 2001 to 48 percent in April 2006. Correspondingly, the share of those who felt that the federal income tax rate they would be paying was about right rose during the same period from 31 percent to 44 percent. It seems that a large number of Americans think the federal tax rate is fair and yet too high for them.[d]

Given the minuscule number of citizens that consider federal taxes too low, it would seem unlikely that politicians would suggest higher tax rates and win elections. At the same time, with the highly unequal distribution of income in America, the conservative versus liberal tax debate often revolves over redistributive issues and focuses on themes relating to the size versus share of the economic pie. Some economists contend that lower tax burdens provide incentives for economic growth by promoting competition, innovation, and efficiency and thereby increase the size of the economic pie. Other economists support a strong role for the government in regulating the markets and providing public goods including health, education, and social safety nets to promote economic growth and an equitable social system. Their understanding of the role of the government in macroeconomic management assumes a higher tax burden.

The debate over progressive, regressive, or flat rates of taxation has often been very ideological and has focused on equity versus efficiency issues. Many have come to assume that progressive taxes are linked with large and liberal government, while regressive or flat taxes are related to small and conservative government—but the political reality is more complex than those simple assumptions. The United States saw a budget surplus under Democratic President Bill Clinton and large deficits under Republican President George W. Bush. Deficits also grew under Republican President Ronald Reagan. Irrespective of ideology, Republican and Democratic presidencies alike have to deal with tax issues and the fiscal sustainability of government expenditures ranging from defense and infrastructure development to education and health. The debate over Social Security reform is tied, in large part, to questions of fiscal sustainability as Baby Boomers begin to retire in 2011. The tax debate will continue to galvanize politics, given popular antipathy toward higher tax rates coupled with high expectations for government services in health care, education, Social Security, and other areas.

QUESTIONS

1. Are there any conditions that would make Americans more accepting of higher taxes? Explain.
2. Why do most Americans believe that the overall federal tax rates are fair but that they pay too much taxes?

---

[a]Pew Research Center for the People and the Press, October 2005 poll, http://www.pollingreport.com/budget.htm.

[b]Associated Press–Ipsos Poll, November 3–5, 2004, http://www.pollingreport.com/budget.htm.

[c]Summary of Federal Individual Income Tax Data, http://www.taxfoundation.org/news/show/250.html.

[d]Gallup Poll, April 10–13, 2006, http://www.pollingreport.com/budget.htm.

---

sustainable and are in need of urgent reform.[38] At the same time, the 2007 budget proposes a $439 billion base budget—representing a 7 percent increase over 2006—for the Department of Defense. In addition, the budget requests another $50 billion to support the military's efforts in Iraq and Afghanistan for the 2007 fiscal year.[39] In contrast, the 2007 budget proposal requests a total of discretionary and mandatory spending for the Department of Education in the amount of $63.4 billion—significantly lower than the 2006 figure of $88.9 billion.[40]

Not all Republicans approve of large budget deficits. With President Bush's approval ratings hovering in the low 30s in mid-2006, and with the midterm elections in November 2006 and the 2008 presidential election in mind, some Republicans began to distance themselves from the "mushrooming government spending and soaring deficits on [the president's] watch."[41]

THE BUDGET DEFICIT AND THE DEBT

Large annual budget deficits and a rapidly growing national debt (which is the sum of the annual budget deficits) characterized government finance from the early 1980s through the early 1990s. Several factors contributed to this situation: a severe recession in the early 1980s, the large tax cut enacted in 1981, sharply increased spending for national defense during the 1980s, and continuously expanding spending on such entitlement programs as Social Security, Medicare, and Medicaid.[42] Annual **federal budget deficits,** or the amount by which federal expenditure exceeds federal revenue, which rarely exceeded $60 billion before 1980 and usually were much less than that, averaged $150 billion during the 1980s. These dollar figures have increased in part because of inflation. One way to account for inflation when comparing budget deficits is to express the deficits as a percentage of **gross domestic product (GDP).** The U.S. GDP is the total market value of all goods and services produced in the United States during a year. During the 1960s, the budget deficit typically was less than 1 percent of GDP, whereas the deficit rose to between 3 percent and 5 percent of GDP during the 1980s. So, the 2006 budget deficit at 3.2 percent of the GDP is not a historic high.

Yearly deficits, however, help to increase total debt. The national debt tripled during the 1980s. Standing at $909 billion in 1980, it soared beyond $2.87 trillion in 1989. By 1996, the national debt was nearly $5 trillion. In May 2006, the national debt stood at an astounding $8.37 trillion, and interest payments on the debt constituted a serious budget expense. In 2005, the government paid $352 billion in interest on the national debt.

While deficits have long been recognized for their potentially negative impact on economies, acceptance of Keynesian economic perspectives since the 1930s has led economists to impute some value to deficits. Federal deficits are justified as a means of stimulating economic growth in periods of decline. In contrast to state governments, the federal government (because of its size and macroeconomic responsibilities) legitimizes deficit spending. It is believed that such spending is needed from time to time to stimulate economic recovery and keep vital social and defense-related expenses intact. Deficits are justified in times of recession; however, they are criticized if they are viewed as "structural" or built into the economy even in times of prosperity.

Deficit Reduction Legislation

Budget surpluses from 1998 to 2002 resulted from several key congressional acts: the Gramm-Rudman-Hollings Act of 1985, the Budget Enforcement Act of 1990, and the Omnibus Budget Reconciliation Act of 1993. The Gramm-Rudman-Hollings Act was the most significant of these. Called "a bad idea whose time had come," the act was named after its three Senate sponsors: Phil Gramm (R–TX), Warren Rudman (R–NH), and Ernest Hollings (D–SC). The initial deficit reduction effort represented in the Gramm-Rudman-Hollings Act was not very successful in reducing budget deficits, but it represented an early attack on the deficit and paved the way for other initiatives.

The Budget Enforcement Act of 1990 represented another attempt to bring expenditures into line with revenues. The act set limits on discretionary spending and created a "pay as you go" procedure, requiring that increases in spending be offset by decreases in other appropriations so there would be no increase in the deficit. The Omnibus Budget Reconciliation Act of 1993 incorporated a mix of tax increases and entitlement reductions. Under the provisions of this act, the top income tax rate was increased and those with very high incomes were assessed a surcharge. There were increases in corporate taxes and increases in the tax that high-income Social Security

VIDEO ROUNDTABLE

Deficit Spending

federal budget deficit
The amount by which federal expenditure exceeds federal revenue.

gross domestic product (GDP)
The total market value of all goods and services produced in a country during a year.

Analyzing Visuals

PROJECTING FEDERAL BUDGET DEFICITS: WHOSE NUMBERS ARE RIGHT?

In the late 1990s, after years of annual deficits, the federal government began to operate in the black, taking in slightly more money than it paid out. However, the economic downturn from 2000–2003, the terrorist attacks of September 11, 2001, the price of fighting wars in Afghanistan and Iraq, growing costs of government programs such as Medicare, and income tax cuts in 2001 and 2003 all fueled rising deficits. According to the Congressional Budget Office (CBO), President George W. Bush's 2007 budget proposal suggests the deficit will be in the vicinity of $355 billion, or 2.6 percent of GDP in 2007. The optimistic estimate suggests that the budget deficit will start to decline in 2008 until it stabilizes at about 1 percent annually through the year 2016. The CBO admits that these figures do not include any

appropriations for military operations in Iraq or Afghanistan after 2007. Critics charge that both the CBO and the president's budgets vastly understate the likely deficits in the years ahead. The Concord Coalition, a bipartisan organization committed to balanced budgets, contends that the budget deficits will actually worsen after 2008. Why do you think the predictions are so far apart? Based on the graph and your understanding of the chapter discussion, answer the following critical thinking questions: How soon will we know which of these predictions is the most valid? What events could significantly alter the projected lines on the graph? Should Americans be concerned about the high deficits that even the CBO sees over the next several years? What impact do these deficits have on the American economy?

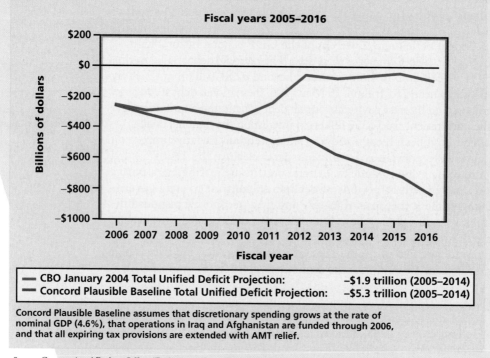

Concord Plausible Baseline assumes that discretionary spending grows at the rate of nominal GDP (4.6%), that operations in Iraq and Afghanistan are funded through 2006, and that all expiring tax provisions are extended with AMT relief.

Sources: Congressional Budget Office, "Preliminary Analysis of the President's Budget Request for 2007," http://www.cbo.gov; and Concord Coalition, http://www.concordcoalition.org.

recipients would pay. To reduce the growth of entitlements, the Reconciliation Act placed limits on the Medicare program.[43]

Following the Clinton budget and the Reconciliation Act of 1993, significant declines in the deficit were attained. Total income tax receipts rose nearly 25 percent from 1992 to 1995, despite predictions by some economists that higher taxes enacted in the 1993 act would actually produce less revenue. After peaking at $290 billion in

1992, deficits declined to $22 billion in 1997 and turned into a surplus in 1998. (See Analyzing Visuals: Projecting Federal Budget Deficits.)

Budget Surplus and Renewed Deficits The budget surplus that emerged in 1998 was a testament to a variety of factors. The growing economy prompted substantial revenue growth and a slowing of recession-impacted entitlements. The slowdown in military spending, an aggressive monetary policy, and legislation enacted by Congress also contributed to the new budget environment. The years of budget surpluses, however, would not endure, and by fiscal year 2003, deficits reappeared. The Bush administration acknowledged the budget deficit would be over $500 billion in 2004 but argued that, sparked by tax cuts, economic growth would return and the deficits would disappear within a decade. Critics were not so sure. Tom Daschle, then Democratic minority leader of the U.S. Senate, warned: "Unless we get back on the right track soon, these record deficits could undercut growth and job creation for decades to come." While cautioning against overly alarmist fears, then Federal Reserve Chair Alan Greenspan also warned that the return of large deficits represents "a significant obstacle to long-term stability."[44] Current Federal Reserve Chair Ben Bernanke voiced concern as well that the rising budget deficit would put future living standards at risk.[45] In February 2006, President Bush signed the Deficit Reduction Act of 2005, which aims to reduce direct spending by the government by $40 billion between 2006 and 2010. This includes a reduction in Medicare spending by $5 billion over the five-year period.

The Economics of Environmental Regulation

AS WE HAVE SEEN, many of the national government's economic policies place direct control or restrictions on private economic activity. These economic regulatory policies are intended to prevent or mitigate actions and conditions regarded as unfair, undesirable, unhealthy, or immoral. Collectively, they create an extensive framework of rules governing the conduct of private (and occasionally public) economic activity. Here, we focus on one important segment of regulatory policies: regulation of environmental activity to protect the public health and the national environment.

Until the late 1960s, the national government was only minimally involved in the control of environmental pollution. The national government had long been concerned with the conservation of natural resources and the management of public lands—national forests, national parks, and Western grazing lands. Air and water pollution were considered matters for the state and local governments to handle, if they so chose. But, many states did little or nothing, as pollution was not perceived as a pressing problem.

Since 1970, Congress has enacted a large volume of pollution control legislation intended to help clean up the nation's air and water and to regulate the disposal of hazardous and toxic wastes. Among the most prominent environmental laws were the Clean Air Act (1970) and the Clean Water Act (1972), which helped establish federal regulations for emission of pollutants in the nation's air and water. These landmark acts also established minimum quality standards for the nation's air and surface water bodies. Over the next decade, Congress enacted further legislation targeting the proliferation of toxic substances in the environment. These acts included the Federal Insecticide, Fungicide, and Rodenticide Act (1972), the Toxic Substances Control Act (1976), and the Resource Conservation and Recovery Act (1976). Responsibility for the implementation of these laws rests primarily with the Environmental Protection Agency, to which we now turn.

THE ENVIRONMENTAL PROTECTION AGENCY

Congress established the Environmental Protection Agency (EPA) in 1970 to take charge of environmental programs previously overseen in five executive departments. As an independent agency, the EPA reports directly to the president. The EPA consolidated responsibility for water pollution, air pollution, solid waste management, radiation control, and hazardous and toxic substance control. Its administrator is appointed by the president, with the approval of the Senate.

The EPA is the nation's largest regulatory agency, issuing permits, establishing and overseeing environmental standards, and enforcing relevant federal statutes and rules. The EPA's activities include research, rule making, and enforcement. The agency conducts much research on the effects of various pollutants on human health and the natural environment in order to provide evidence for its rule making. Rules are necessary to convert the goals and requirements of pollution control legislation into standards and specifications that can be implemented. For example, the Clean Air Act—originally enacted in the 1960s, then significantly revised and updated in 1990—directs the EPA to set ambient air standards (ambient air is air that circulates around us) for such pollutants as carbon dioxide, ozone, and lead that will provide an "adequate margin of safety" to protect public health. The standards, stated in terms of parts per million, are enforced against potential polluters.

With the cooperation and supervision of EPA regional offices, state pollution control agencies do much of the actual enforcement. Pollution control enforcement is thus basically a two-step process. The EPA must encourage state agencies to act in appropriate ways, and the state agencies must then secure compliance from the companies and individuals to whom the pollution standards apply.

There have been four major eras in the political life of the EPA.[46] The first era, which extended through the 1970s, was characterized by growth in the EPA's budget and number of employees, expansion of its legislative authority, and substantial efforts to gain compliance with pollution control standards, both through legal enforcement and voluntary compliance. The second era began with the inception of the Reagan administration in 1981 and lasted through 1983. Opposed to strong pollution control programs, the Reagan administration appointed people to top-level EPA positions who were hostile or indifferent to its goals. Substantial cuts were made in the agency's budget and personnel, and many employees became demoralized.

The third era began in late 1983 and continued through the presidencies of George Bush and Bill Clinton. The EPA's budget and personnel levels were increased, but environmental protection was to be balanced against its economic cost. This balancing act reflected the view that overzealous enforcement of environmental regulations could be detrimental to the economy. Nonetheless, polls show that most Americans want to protect their environment.

The succession of George W. Bush to the presidency in 2001 ushered in a fourth era with significant similarities to the second era during the Reagan administration. Environmental preservation came into greater conflict with the administration's pro-business policies and energy development efforts. A key aspect of this conflict was the debate regarding vigorous exploration and drilling for oil in the Arctic National Wildlife Refuge (ANWR) in Alaska. The president argued that this project would reduce the nation's dependence on foreign oil and stimulate economic growth. Environmentalists and others contended that pristine areas such as parts of

SIMULATION

You Are an Environmental Activist

■ Environmental Protection Agency (EPA) director Stephen L. Johnson (right) photographed during a 2006 visit to a thermal power plant in Shanghai, China. As the federal government's most prominent official in the area of environmental matters, Johnson is responsible for a wide range of pollution control and abatement functions that affect both the nation's health and economic interests.

Photo courtesy: Liu Ying/Xinhua/AP Wide World Photos

Alaska should be preserved in their natural beauty and that research into new technologies and alternative energy sources should be vigorously pursued in order to reduce America's dependence on foreign oil.

ENVIRONMENTAL PROTECTION: TWO EXAMPLES

Two key environmental concerns in recent years are the disposal of hazardous and toxic waste and transboundary atmospheric pollution and its impact on climate change. The economic cost of these problems can be significant. Improper handling of hazardous and toxic waste can despoil land and reduce its value. In addition, diseases such as cancer have been linked to toxic chemicals. Such diseases increase health care costs in the nation and deprive employers of productive workers. Acid rain, a by-product of atmospheric pollution, can harm fish and plant life and affect the economic self-sufficiency of entire communities, while climate change has the potential to disrupt the global economy as well as significantly affect the biosphere. An examination of these problems can highlight both the difficulties and politics of protecting the environment.

Hazardous and Toxic Wastes The increase in the production and use of chemicals has contributed to a higher standard of living in the United States, but not without social and environmental costs. Safe disposal of waste chemicals is a major problem. Whether emitted into the air, injected into the ground, dumped into bodies of water, or incinerated, chemicals pose risks to human health and to the environment.

National policy to control hazardous wastes takes three approaches: prevention, safe disposal, and cleanup. The Toxic Substances Control Act (1976) takes a preventive approach. The act is designed to regulate the manufacture and distribution of toxic substances in order to identify hazardous chemicals and keep them out of the environment. The EPA is authorized to suspend production of a chemical permanently when the agency has "a reasonable basis to conclude that the chemical will present an unreasonable risk of injury to the health of the environment."

The Resource Conservation and Recovery Act (1976) is focused on ensuring the safe disposal of hazardous wastes currently being produced. The EPA is directed to develop criteria for environmentally safe hazardous-waste disposal sites and for identifying hazardous wastes. The EPA is also authorized to create a "manifest system" (that is, a system of receipts) that would permit tracking hazardous wastes from their points of origin to their final, safe disposal. This "cradle to grave" regulation was intended to eliminate "midnight dumping" and other unsafe forms of waste disposal. In 1984, amendments to the act provided for the elimination of leaking underground storage tanks, such as might be found at gasoline stations. If their enforcement programs meet national standards, state agencies can implement these regulations.

In 1980, Congress enacted the Comprehensive Environmental Response, Compensation, and Liability Act, creating what is commonly referred to as the Superfund, to provide for the cleanup of abandoned hazardous-waste sites, of which there are tens of thousands in the United States. One such site was Love Canal, near Niagara Falls in upstate New York. In the 1940s and 1950s, the Hooker Chemical Company used the dry canal bed as a disposal site for hazardous chemical wastes. The canal was then covered with a layer of earth and later donated as a site for a public school and homes. In the 1970s, chemicals began to ooze to the surface, and noxious fumes entered people's homes. Adults and children suffered from a variety of medical ailments. These occurrences led to a major controversy and to the eventual evacuation of people from the area. In time, the site was cleaned up at a cost of more than $300 million.

The Love Canal disaster contributed to Congress's hurried enactment of the Superfund legislation in late 1980. The EPA was directed to compile a National Priority List (NPL) of hazardous-waste sites urgently in need of cleanup. If the responsible parties could not be located or failed to clean up a site, the EPA would do so. A Hazardous Substance Response Fund, financed mostly by a tax on oil, chemical, and other

Photo courtesy: Jim Raymen/UPI/Landov

■ Former Vice President Al Gore and his wife Tipper promoting his 2006 documentary "An Inconvenient Truth." Gore's movie called worldwide attention to the issue of global warming and the problems associated with increasing levels of greenhouse gases from the burning of fossil fuels.

industries, was set up to pay the costs of cleaning up hazardous-waste sites. Subsequent amendments increased the size of the Superfund to more than $15 billion.

Superfund cleanups have been slow and tedious because of problems in determining financial liability for cleaning up waste sites (which often entails litigation), in deciding how clean each site must be, and in designing and carrying out remedial work. As of late 2005, 1,498 sites were on the NPL list, of which approximately 70 percent had been fully cleaned up. The EPA's annual evaluation in 2005 indicated that it lacked resources to address numerous projects that remained on the NPL.[47]

An important issue related to hazardous and toxic waste regulation that is currently confronting the EPA is environmental civil rights. By 1998, the EPA had received over fifty petitions from minority groups claiming that state officials did not consider the impact of pollution on the health of African Americans living near industrial plants. Critics, however, worried that additional assessment would prevent communities from attracting business. In 2001, a federal appeals court dealt a blow to environmental justice advocates who sought to prevent companies from locating industrial facilities in communities that already were exposed to disproportionate amounts of pollution. The decision by the Third Circuit Court of Appeals in Trenton, New Jersey, was interpreted as a victory for industrial groups. The court ruled that only federal agencies, and not private litigants, had the right to sue to enforce environmental justice laws. Nevertheless, the issue of environmental justice remains one of the more controversial and difficult aspects of environmental policy in the United States.

Atmospheric Pollution, Acid Rain, and Climate Change

Pollution of the atmosphere by emissions from power plants has been a matter of public concern for decades. U.S. government efforts to curb a serious problem stemming from such pollution, acid rain, began in the late 1980s. More recently, the accrual of scientific data on the impact of greenhouse gas emissions on the world's climate has led concerned scientists and policy makers to pressure the EPA to further regulate industrial pollution of the atmosphere.

Acid rain is a by-product of the consumption of fossil fuels, especially high-sulfur coal. It occurs when sulfur and nitrogen oxides combine with water vapor in the atmosphere and later fall to earth as rain, snow, mist, or particulate matter. The acidity of the precipitation harms fish and plant populations.

Acid rain was not recognized as a problem in 1970, when the Clean Air Act was adopted. Indeed, the tall smokestacks (200 to 800 feet in height) built at coal-burning electric utility plants in the Midwest and elsewhere as a result of the passage of the Clean Air Act were found to contribute to the production of acid rain. These smokestacks spewed sulfur and nitrogen oxides higher into the atmosphere, which improved the quality of air in their vicinity and helped localities comply with air quality standards under the Clean Air Act. The smokestacks, however, also increased the likelihood that pollutants would fall to earth somewhere downwind.[48] The sulfur and nitrogen oxides emitted by electric utility plants, particularly in the Midwest, fall to earth as acid rain in the northeastern United States and in eastern Canada.

The Reagan administration delayed taking regulatory action on acid rain on the grounds that more research was needed to better understand its causes and consequences. Electric utility companies, high-sulfur coal producers, and other businesses endorsed this point of view. As research findings accumulated, however, it became increasingly clear that action on the acid rain problem was necessary. In early 1989,

President George Bush called for major amendments to the Clean Air Act, including action on acid rain.

As part of the strategy to control acid rain, the Clean Air Act Amendments of 1990 authorized an emissions trading system. Some economists have argued that the use of economic incentives, as in an emissions trading system, will be more effective in controlling pollution than the traditional standard setting and enforcement pattern of regulation.[49] The argument asserts that economic incentives will provide companies with positive motivation—the pursuit of their self-interest—to reduce the discharge of pollutants. Each of the 110 electric utility plants named in the act, most of which are located in the Midwest, was allocated a specified number of "allowables." Effective in 1995, an allowable authorized a utility plant to discharge legally one ton of sulfur dioxide. In 2000, stricter limitations on sulfur dioxide emissions were phased in. If a company reduced its emissions below its specified level by burning low-sulfur coal, installing smoke-stack scrubbers, or using other pollution control methods, it could "bank" its excess allowables or sell them to other utility companies. A company that exceeds its specified limit and does not buy allowables to cover its excess emissions is subject to heavy fines. The Chicago Board of Trade, a large commodity exchange, has been authorized by the EPA to establish a market for the purchase and sale of sulfur dioxide allowables.

In the 1990s, various utility companies appeared to violate the Clean Air Act by expanding coal-fired power plants without installing scrubbers or other anti-pollution equipment. In 1999, the Clinton administration began a crackdown on these utility companies, leading to litigation against nine companies that operated fifty-one power plants. Since the election of George W. Bush in 2000, however, no new legal action against major utility companies has been pursued.

Global warming refers to the impact of carbon emissions on the world's climate. In particular, the burning of fossil fuels, such as oil and coal, is linked to increasing global temperatures that may have dramatic impacts on weather patterns, ocean levels, wildlife habitat, and the world's population and economy.

In 1997, most of the world's industrial nations ratified the Kyoto Protocol, whereby they agreed to reduce greenhouse gas emissions. Despite the Clinton administration's support for the Kyoto Protocol, the United States has never ratified the agreement. The administration of George W. Bush has steadfastly refused to join with other major economies by signing the treaty, citing the adverse effects of the act on the economy of the United States. Instead, the Bush administration endorsed an initiative termed Clear Skies, which called for only voluntary steps to reduce carbon dioxide. This stance was viewed as consistent with the Bush administration's rejection of the Kyoto Protocol. The Clear Skies initiative was unveiled in 2002 with promises to require a two-thirds reduction in most power plant emissions by 2018. Trades of emission credits would be used to accomplish emission reduction goals.[50] Critics of the Clear Skies proposals have noted that the expansion of the pollution trading system would not be fully in place for many years, during which time additional pollutants would be released. They also criticized the plan for weakening provisions of the Clean Air Act.[51]

A legislative proposal that sought to make the president's Clear Skies initiative law failed to make it out of committee when members deadlocked in a 9–9 vote in March 2005. Moderate Republican Lincoln Chafee of Rhode Island and Independent James Jeffords of Vermont joined seven committee Democrats to vote against the bill. Since the bill's failure, the Bush administration has sought to implement key aspects of the initiative administratively through the EPA.

The Bush administration's decision not to regulate carbon dioxide pollution has been met with legal action from the states and environmental interest groups. In July 2005, a three-judge panel upheld the EPA's decision not to regulate carbon dioxide emissions from vehicles as part of the Clean Air Act. In late April 2006, however, ten states joined by Washington, D.C., the City of New York, and three environmental groups sued the EPA in order to require it to regulate carbon dioxide emissions by

VIDEO ROUNDTABLE
Energy Policy

global warming
The increase in global temperatures that results from carbon emissions from burning fossil fuels such as oil and coal.

power plants.[52] The Supreme Court agreed to review whether the Bush administration must regulate carbon dioxide emissions under the Clean Air Act.[53] Beyond lawsuits, some states are addressing climate change unilaterally. In August 2006, California announced that it would begin to restrict carbon dioxide emissions within its borders.[54]

Summary

THE NATURE AND ROLE of the government in the economy, especially the national government, have changed significantly since the nation's founding. In analyzing these developments, this chapter has made the following points:

1. **The Origins of Government Involvement in the Economy**

   Efforts by the national government to regulate the economy began with anti-monopoly legislation. Under President Franklin D. Roosevelt, the interventionist state replaced the laissez-faire state. After World War II, many areas of economic policy were settled. Full employment, employee–employer relations, and social regulation became new concerns of government. Even before social regulation began to ebb, economic deregulation, which involves reducing market controls, emerged as an attractive political issue.

2. **Stabilizing the Economy**

   The national government continues to shape monetary policy by regulating the nation's money supply and interest rates. Monetary policy is controlled by the Board of Governors. Fiscal policy, which involves the deliberate use of the national government's taxing and spending policies, is another tool of the national government and involves the president and Congress setting the national budget. Although the budget is initially suggested by the president, Congress has constitutional authority over the process.

3. **The Economics of Environmental Regulation**

   The environment is one area in which the national government has used its economic regulatory powers to alter business practices. Conflicts over environmental regulation frequently pit the business community against environmental groups. The Environmental Protection Agency (EPA), which was created as an independent agency, is the nation's largest regulatory agency.

KEY TERMS

Board of Governors, p. 670
business cycles, p. 660
deregulation, p. 666
discount rate, p. 673
economic regulation, p. 664
economic stability, p. 669
federal budget deficit, p. 683
fiscal policy, p. 674
global warming, p. 689
gross domestic product (GDP), p. 683
inflation, p. 669
interventionist state, p. 663
laissez-faire, p. 660
monetary policy, p. 669
money, p. 669
open market operations, p. 673
recession, p. 669
reserve requirements, p. 673
social regulation, p. 665

SELECTED READINGS

Chernow, Ron. *Alexander Hamilton*. New York: Penguin Press, 2004.

Derthick, Martha, and Paul J. Quirk. *The Politics of Deregulation*. Washington, DC: Brookings Institution, 1985.

Devine, Robert S. *Bush Versus the Environment*. New York: Anchor Books, 2004.

Greider, William. *One World, Ready or Not: The Manic Logic of Global Capitalism*. New York: Simon and Schuster, 1997.

Harr, Jonathan. *A Civil Action*. New York: Random House, 1995.

Keech, William. *Economic Politics: The Costs of Democracy*. Cambridge: Cambridge University Press, 1995.

Kettl, Donald F. *Deficit Politics: Public Budgeting in Its Institutional and Historical Context*. New York: Macmillan, 1992.

Krugman, Paul. *The Great Unraveling: Losing Our Way in the New Century*. New York: Norton, 2003.

Phillips, Kevin. *Wealth and Democracy: A Political History of the American Rich*. New York: Broadway, 2002.

Rabe, Barry. *The Emerging Politics of American Climate Change Policy*. Washington, DC: Brookings Institution, 2004.

Rubin, Robert E., with Jacob Weisberg. *In an Uncertain World: Tough Choices from Wall Street to Washington*. New York: Random House, 2003.

Schiller, Robert. *Irrational Exuberance*. Princeton, NJ: Princeton University Press, 2000.

Switzer, Jacqueline Vaughn. *Environmental Politics: Domestic and Global Dimension*, 4th ed. Belmont, CA: Wadsworth, 2004.

Thurmaier, Kurt M., and Katherine G. Willoughby. *Policy and Politics in State Budgeting*. Armonk, NY: M. E. Sharpe, 2001.

Tonelson, Alan. *The Race to the Bottom: Why a Worldwide Worker Surplus and Uncontrolled Free Trade Are Sinking American Living Standards*. Boulder, CO: Westview, 2002.

Tuccile, Jerome. *Alan Shrugged: Alan Greenspan, the World's Most Powerful Banker*. San Francisco: Jossey-Bass, 2002.

Young, James Harvey. *Pure Food: Securing the Federal Food and Drugs Act of 1906*. Princeton, NJ: Princeton University Press, 1990.

WEB EXPLORATIONS

To learn about the government bureau for economic analysis, go to
http://www.bea.doc.gov

To compare various business cycle indicators, go to
http://www.tcb-indicators.org

To access the most current labor and wages data for your state or region, go to
http://www.bls.gov/ncs/

To learn about current economic policy, go to
http://www.nber.org

To learn more about regulation of financial markets via the Federal Reserve Board, go to
http://www.federalreserve.gov

To learn about current fiscal policy, go to
http://www.gpoaccess.gov/usbudget/index.html

To compare the current fiscal budget with budgets from prior years, go to
http://www.whitehouse.gov/omb

To compare the federal budget with the national debt, go to
http://www.gpoaccess.gov/usbudget/fy06/index.html

To examine current EPA laws, regulations, projects, and programs, go to
http://www.epa.gov

FOREIGN AND DEFENSE POLICY

19

THE WAR ON TERRORISM declared by President George W. Bush after the September 11, 2001, attacks on the United States is a multifaceted, global undertaking that includes military action overseas, increased security measures at home, cooperation among domestic and international intelligence agencies, diplomacy, and the prevention of terrorists' access to weapons of mass destruction. It involves domestic strategies, such as efforts to improve homeland security, as well as international activities, such as the promotion of democracy abroad, military strikes against terrorist organizations and the states that sponsor them, and diplomatic initiatives designed to thwart the spread of religious extremism. In the context of the war on terrorism, the division of U.S. policies into "foreign affairs" and "domestic affairs" is somewhat artificial.

After the events of September 11, striking the appropriate balance between foreign and domestic affairs so that American interests and objectives are achieved and the American public is protected remains a continuing challenge for the president and others involved in the foreign and defense policy process. For example, three days after the 9/11 attacks, President Bush authorized the National Security Administration (NSA) to eavesdrop on telephone calls and e-mails between American citizens and foreigners suspected of terrorist ties without first seeking a court warrant. When it was disclosed, the NSA's spying program created a great deal of controversy because the 1978 Foreign Intelligence Surveillance Act (FISA) requires a special court to approve any interception of communications involving U.S. citizens. The program has generated debate in Congress over the legality of President Bush's decision to order the NSA to conduct warrantless surveillance of Americans' communications. The Department of Justice, however, has argued that the president's constitutional role as commander in chief provides adequate justification for his authorization of such a program. Critics argue that the program violates U.S. law, that the president is unnecessarily extending the reach of the federal government, and that the NSA's limited resources should be targeted at more precise threats to national security.

CHAPTER OUTLINE

- ⭐ The Development of U.S. Foreign and Defense Policy
- ⭐ The United States as a World Power
- ⭐ Foreign and Defense Policy Decision Making
- ⭐ Twenty-First-Century Challenges

The debate intensified in the wake of revelations of a much larger data-mining project designed to track the domestic phone records of millions of ordinary U.S. citizens and analyze them for signs that Americans are communicating with suspected terrorists. In a White House press briefing on May 11, 2006, President Bush strongly defended his administration's surveillance and monitoring efforts: "We're not mining or trolling through the personal lives of millions of innocent Americans," he stated. "Our efforts are focused on links to al-Qaeda and their known affiliates."[1] But, the NSA's domestic surveillance program blurs the distinction between domestic and foreign policies and raises complicated constitutional questions about the reach of the federal government in the context of combating terrorism.

Domestic issues, such as the privacy rights of ordinary Americans, have become part of the discussion of how best to pursue a defense policy that will effectively thwart terrorism here and abroad. The war on terrorism has dramatically changed how the United States conducts foreign and defense policy, ushering in a period of unprecedented unilateral military action abroad, aggressive detention practices for those suspected of terrorist activities, and controversial spying programs at home.

FOLLOWING THE END OF THE COLD WAR (1947–1991), the collapse of the Soviet Union in 1991, and the expulsion of Iraqi forces from Kuwait in the 1991 Persian Gulf War, U.S. foreign policy began a period of transition. Many wondered what role the United States would play in a multipolar world with only one remaining superpower. Most hoped that the world would be a safer place in the new millennium. After September 11, 2001, however, the United States recognized a new and deadly adversary: terrorism. More Americans began to pay attention to foreign policy and defense issues. Many wondered how the United States, with its superior military resources and unchallenged supremacy in the world order, could be susceptible to a devastating series of terrorist attacks on a single fateful day.

To explore the most important elements of U.S. foreign and defense policy, this chapter will cover four major topics:

- First, we will trace *the development of U.S. foreign and defense policy* in the years before the United States became a world power.
- Second, we will detail U.S. policy during and after the Cold War, examining *the United States as a world power*.
- Third, we will study *foreign and defense policy decision making* and the role of the executive branch, Congress, and other groups in foreign policy making.
- Fourth, we will examine *twenty-first-century challenges* in foreign and defense policy.

The Development of U.S. Foreign and Defense Policy

LIKE SOCIAL AND ECONOMIC POLICY, U.S. foreign and defense policy has evolved. Today, the United States is the most powerful and influential country in the world. No other country has as large an economy, as powerful a military, or plays as influential a role in world affairs as the United States. It was not always this way. When the United States was founded, it was a weak country on the margins of world affairs, with an uncertain future.

Even so, the United States was fortunate. Separated from Europe and Asia by vast oceans, it had abundant resources and industrious people. The United States often stood apart from world engagements, following a policy of **isolationism,** that is, avoiding participation in foreign affairs. However, isolationism was rarely total. Even in its early years, the United States engaged in foreign affairs, and it always was a trading nation. Another consistent hallmark of U.S. policy was **unilateralism,** that is, acting without consulting others. **Moralism** was also central to U.S. self-image in foreign policy, with most Americans believing their country had higher moral standards than European and other countries. Many Americans were also proud of their **pragmatism**—their ability to find ways to take advantage of a situation. Thus, when Europe was at war, Americans sold goods to both sides and profited handsomely. When opportunities to acquire more land arose, Americans aggressively pursued them.

To understand how and why the United States emphasized isolationism, unilateralism, moralism, and pragmatism, we must examine the history of U.S. foreign policy from the Constitution until the beginning of World War II.

THE CONSTITUTION

When the Framers of the U.S. Constitution met in Philadelphia in 1789 to write a new governing document for the thirteen states, they wanted the stronger national government to keep the United States out of European affairs and to keep Europe out of American affairs. As a result, the power to formulate and implement foreign policy was given to the national government rather than the states. In addition, many foreign and military powers not enumerated in the Constitution are generally accorded to the national government. (See The Living Constitution.)

The Framers of the Constitution divided authority for many foreign and military policy functions between the president and Congress. The Framers named the president commander in chief of the armed forces but gave Congress power to fund the army and navy and to declare war. The president has authority to negotiate and sign treaties, but treaties only take effect after the Senate ratifies them by a two-thirds majority. Similarly, the president appoints ambassadors and other key foreign and military affairs officials, but the Senate grants advice and consent on the appointments.

This division of responsibility for foreign and military policy stood in marked contrast to the way the European powers of the eighteenth century made foreign policy. In Great Britain and France, the ability to formulate and implement foreign policy resided almost exclusively with the ruling monarch and his or her advisers.

THE EARLY HISTORY OF U.S. FOREIGN AND DEFENSE POLICY

Following the creation of the Constitution, the United States delved gingerly into foreign affairs. As the United States took its place among the family of nations, it remained hesitant about engaging with other countries. George Washington emphasized this in his 1796 Farewell Address, his final address as president, when he asserted that it was the United States' "true policy to steer clear of permanent alliances with any portion of the foreign world." Washington, however, was not an isolationist. While he believed that U.S. democracy and security depended on remaining apart from Europe, he accepted the need for trade—and trade the United States did. Throughout the late eighteenth and nineteenth centuries, American ships plied the world's sea lanes, bringing large profits to U.S. merchants.

Trade led to conflicts. In the 1790s, the United States fought an undeclared naval war with France because France was seizing U.S. ships trading with France's enemies.

isolationism
A national policy of avoiding participation in foreign affairs.

unilateralism
A national policy of acting without consulting others.

moralism
The policy of emphasizing morality in foreign affairs.

pragmatism
The policy of taking advantage of a situation for national gain.

The Living Constitution

To provide for calling forth the Militia to execute the Laws of the Union, suppress Insurrections and repel Invasions;

To provide for organizing, arming, and disciplining, the Militia, and for governing such Part of them as may be employed in the Service of the United States, reserving to the States respectively, the Appointment of the Officers, and the Authority of training the Militia according to the discipline proscribed by Congress;

—ARTICLE I, SECTION 8

With the Constitution's Article I militia clauses, a significant defect of the Articles of Confederation was corrected. A fundamental weakness of the earlier document was that it did not grant the central U.S. government adequate means for national defense, and this defect was understood to hamper the Revolutionary War effort. In the view of the Framers, a government without the force to administer its laws or to defend its citizens was either a weak government or no government at all, and these clauses consequently give the federal government authority to call up the state militias in times of national emergency or distress.

Joseph Story, an associate justice of the Supreme Court from 1812 to 1845, commented that the militia clauses passed the Constitutional Convention "by a declared majority" because the delegates understood that the power to call up the militia would be necessary in providing for the common defense and in securing domestic peace. The clauses address the understanding that military training, proficiency, and organization should be uniform across state and national forces so as to ensure effectiveness and efficiency in military operations.

Many Anti-Federalists, however, were concerned that the federal government could call together the state militias for unjust ends. They held the position that state governments should control their militias in order to prevent any perfidy on the part of the federal government. To this end, the states were given authority to name militia officers and train their forces. During the War of 1812—to the consternation of President James Madison—two state governments withheld their militias, because they believed it was the purview of the state to set the terms for the use of its guards. The Supreme Court has since held that, except for constitutional prohibitions, the Congress has "unlimited" authority over the state militias. The National Defense Act of 1916 mandated the use of the term "National Guard" and gave the president the authority to mobilize the National Guard during times of national emergency or war.

Throughout U.S. history, the National Guard has proved effective and essential in defending the United States. With the extensive use of the National Guard to assist American efforts in Iraq and in the struggle against terrorism, its role has expanded. The militia clauses ensure the unity, effectiveness, and strength of the United States military not only during wartime, but also during other national emergencies.

Shortly thereafter, the United States fought the Barbary Wars against North African Barbary states, which since the 1780s had captured American and other ships, holding sailors for ransom.

In the early 1800s, the British naval practice of impressment, that is, stopping ships to seize suspected deserters of the Royal Navy who were working as merchant sailors, angered the American public. Despite U.S. protests, Great Britain refused to end the practice. Thus, in 1807, Congress passed the **Embargo Act,** which prevented U.S. ships from leaving for foreign ports without the approval of the federal government. President Thomas Jefferson believed that European states, embroiled in the continuing Napoleonic Wars, depended so much on U.S.-provided supplies and raw materials that Great Britain would stop impressment. Jefferson was wrong. U.S. exports fell, the economy suffered, and inflation soared. U.S.-British relations continued to deteriorate, fueled by impressments and by U.S. designs on Canada. These conditions led to the War of 1812 between the United States and Great Britain. Peace talks began even before the first battles were fought, but the war ended only after Great Britain decided to concentrate on defeating Napoleon. The 1814 Treaty of Ghent ended the war, with Great Britain and the United States accepting prewar borders and treaty obligations.

In 1815, Napoleon was defeated, and Europe was at peace for the first time in almost two decades. Europeans celebrated, but the United States feared that European powers, especially France in Latin America and Russia in Alaska and the Northwest, would try to expand their control in the Western Hemisphere. To prevent these actions, President James Monroe in 1823 declared that "the American continents, by the free and independent condition which they have assumed and maintain, are henceforth not to be considered as subjects for future colonization by any European power." This declaration became known as the **Monroe Doctrine.** In reality, the Monroe Doctrine was a preference more than a policy, since the United States had little capability to enforce it. However, Great Britain also wanted to keep other European powers out of the Americas. The Royal Navy thus protected British interests and promoted U.S. preferences.

Embargo Act
Passed by Congress in 1807 to prevent U.S. ships from leaving U.S. ports for foreign ports without the approval of the federal government.

Monroe Doctrine
President James Monroe's 1823 pledge that the United States would oppose attempts by European states to extend their political control into the Western Hemisphere.

■ During the War of 1812, the British set fire to many buildings in Washington, D.C., including the U.S. Capitol and the White House. Both buildings were repaired and refurbished shortly after the war.

THE UNITED STATES AS AN EMERGING POWER

Throughout most of the nineteenth century, the United States gained territory, developed economically, and began to emerge as a world power. This process centered on three areas: trade policy and commerce, continental expansion and manifest destiny, and during the last half of the century, interests beyond the Western Hemisphere.

Trade Policy and Commerce As early as 1791, Alexander Hamilton in his *Report on Manufactures* urged Congress to protect domestic industries from foreign competition. However, Hamilton's advice was often ignored as the U.S. government relied on the principles of trade reciprocity and most favored nation (MFN) status. Reciprocity meant that the United States would treat foreign traders in the same way that foreign countries treated U.S. traders, and MFN status meant that U.S. exports would face the lowest **tariffs,** or taxes on imports, offered to any other country.

For most of the early years of the United States' existence, this worked well. However, at the end of the Napoleonic Wars, global peace meant increased competition, and the United States adopted protectionist tariffs designed to keep the home market for domestic producers, as Hamilton had suggested years before. Congress passed the first protectionist tariff in 1816.

Over the next eight years, Congress adopted the "American System" of trade protection by increasingly higher tariffs. Tariffs often were 20 to 30 percent of the value of an import, sometimes as high as 100 percent.[2] High protectionist tariffs were the American norm well into the twentieth century. While high tariffs protected the U.S. market for American producers, they also cut off foreign markets for American producers as foreign countries retaliated with their own high tariffs.

Continental Expansion and Manifest Destiny In 1800, the United States consisted of the original thirteen states and a few others that had just joined the union. During the nineteenth century, the United States acquired immense quantities of land in various ways. It took land from Native Americans in wars against the Creek, Seminole, Sioux, Comanche, Apache, and other tribes. It bought territory from the French, Spanish, and Russians. It fought the 1846 Mexican War, acquiring a large expanse of Mexican territory in the American Southwest and California. By the end of the century, the United States stretched from the Atlantic to the Pacific.

Some called this expansion **manifest destiny,** believing the United States had a divinely mandated obligation to expand across North America to the Pacific and "overspread the continent allotted by Providence for the free development of our multiplying millions."[3] Manifest destiny permitted Americans to rationalize expansion as legitimate and moral. Even though most Americans criticized the overseas expansionism of others as colonialism, most did not consider U.S. expansion in North America as colonialism because the acquired territory was connected to the United States.

Interests Beyond the Western Hemisphere The United States did not limit its economic ambitions to North America. By the mid-nineteenth century, the United States concluded a commercial treaty with China, limited Europe's ability to restrict U.S. trade with China, and opened Japan to Western trade. U.S. trade with China and Japan expanded as clipper ships plied the sea lanes in record time between Asia and the United States. The U.S. Civil War reduced American trade in the Pacific for a time, but soon the United States was once again trading with Asian nations. As American economic interests in the Pacific expanded, so, too, did U.S. interest in acquiring Pacific islands to support expansion. Thus, in the 1890s, the United States acquired the Hawaiian Islands, Midway Island, Wake Island, and part of Samoa.

The 1898 Spanish-American War, fought between the United States and Spain over Spanish policies and presence in Cuba, made the world take note of the United States as a rising power. The United States won an easy victory, in the process acquiring Puerto Rico, the Philippines, Guam, and for a few years, Cuba. Not only had the

---

tariffs
Taxes on imports used to raise government revenue and to protect infant industries.

manifest destiny
Theory that the United States was divinely mandated to expand across North America to the Pacific Ocean.

United States defeated an established European power, albeit one in decline, but it also acquired heavily populated overseas territory. The United States had clearly become a colonial power.

This did not sit well with all Americans. Throughout most of the post–Civil War era, Americans did not agree on the U.S. role in world affairs. Both major political parties were generally against colonialism but divided on free trade and whether to intervene overseas. Disagreement became even more heated in 1899 when Filipinos revolted against U.S. rule. The United States sent nearly 200,000 troops to the islands over the next three years. When fighting finally ended in 1903, tens of thousands of Filipinos had died, along with five thousand Americans. The costs of empire were considerable.

THE ROOSEVELT COROLLARY

In 1903, President Theodore Roosevelt sent a naval squadron to Panama to help it win independence from Colombia. The following year, the United States initiated construction of the Panama Canal, which opened in 1914. The canal helped trade and enabled the U.S. Navy to move ships quickly from the Atlantic to the Pacific and back again. Roosevelt's legacy also included the **Roosevelt Corollary** to the Monroe Doctrine, which stated:

> Chronic wrongdoing, or an impotence which results in the general loosening of the ties of civilized society, may in America, as elsewhere, ultimately require intervention by some civilized nation, and in the Western Hemisphere the adherence of the United States to the Monroe Doctrine may force the United States . . . to the exercise of an international police power.[4]

Under the Roosevelt Corollary, the United States intervened in the Caribbean and Latin America many times as Roosevelt and subsequent U.S. presidents sent U.S. troops into Cuba, the Dominican Republic, Haiti, Nicaragua, Panama, Mexico, and elsewhere. During this era, many Latin Americans came to regard the United States as "the Colossus of the North," intervening in Latin American affairs whenever it wanted.

Roosevelt Corollary
Concept developed by President Theodore Roosevelt early in the twentieth century that it was the U.S. responsibility to assure stability in Latin America and the Caribbean.

Photo courtesy: Bettmann/Corbis

■ A cartoon depicting President Theodore Roosevelt's support of building the Panama Canal to strengthen the U.S. naval presence in the world.

WORLD WAR I

When World War I broke out in Europe in 1914, the United States at first remained neutral. It was a European war, according to most Americans, and no U.S. interests were involved. In addition, the United States was largely a nation of European immigrants, and Americans were deeply divided about whom to support. It thus made sense for both foreign policy and domestic political reasons to stay out of the war. Indeed, when President Woodrow Wilson ran for a second term in 1916, he used the slogan "He kept us out of war" to win reelection.

Nevertheless, several events, especially Germany's policy of unrestricted submarine warfare, under which German subs sank U.S. ships carrying cargo to Great Britain and France, caused immense problems in U.S.-German relations. Finally, declaring that the United States was fighting "a war to end all wars," Wilson in 1917 led the nation into the conflict. American troops and supplies began to arrive just when the human and material resources of the United States' main allies, Great Britain and France, were nearly exhausted. Even though the United States entered the war late, its armed forces and economic assistance swung the tide of victory to the Allies' side.

After World War I, Wilson put great faith in **collective security** to maintain the peace. To Wilson, collective security was based on the premise that if one country attacked another, then other countries in the international community should all unite

collective security
The concept that peace would be secured if all countries collectively opposed any country that invaded another.

against the attacking country. Countries would thus ensure their security collaboratively.

At the Paris Peace Conference following the war, Wilson was instrumental in creating a new international organization, the **League of Nations,** to implement collective security. However, he failed to build support for the League in the United States. A Democratic president with a Senate controlled by Republicans, Wilson failed to include GOP senators among the U.S. delegates to the peace conference. Besides partisan reasons, many senators believed that U.S. membership in the League of Nations would fly in the face of traditional U.S. isolationism and unilateralism. The Senate thus refused to give the necessary two-thirds vote to ratify the Treaty of Versailles, which formalized the terms of the end of the war, and the United States never joined the League.

League of Nations
Created in the peace treaty that ended World War I, it was an international governmental organization dedicated to preserving peace.

THE INTERWAR YEARS

Following rejection of the Treaty of Versailles, most Americans thought that U.S. interests were best served by isolationism and unilateralism. Nonetheless, new U.S. industries sought more raw materials from foreign countries and American businesses sought new markets overseas. During the 1920s, the United States became the world's leading source of credit and goods as the American economy prospered.

As Europeans rebuilt their economies, they presented a challenge to U.S. industry. Consequently, the Republican-controlled Congress during the 1920s raised tariffs to protect U.S. industry from foreign competition. In 1930, Congress passed the extremely high Smoot-Hawley Tariff, and other countries responded by raising their tariffs. The impact that higher tariffs had on world trade, in conjunction with the Great Depression, was dramatic. By 1932, trade dropped to about one-third its former level.[5]

As the Great Depression of the 1930s worsened, some Americans concluded that isolationism and unilateralism were wrong. They argued that the Depression was worse than it may have been because of the decline in trade brought about by high tariffs. Some also attributed the rise of Germany's Adolf Hitler and Japanese and Italian leaders bent on world domination to the economic turmoil of the times. In addition, they argued that without the United States, the League of Nations had proven incapable of preserving peace.

The United States and the rest of the world did little to oppose German, Japanese, and Italian aggression in the 1930s, and the world slid toward war. Congress was particularly isolationist, passing Neutrality Acts to keep the United States from becoming involved in foreign conflicts. President Franklin D. Roosevelt occasionally warned against this mentality, but he also knew that the American people and Congress were unwilling to get pulled into another world war without a more direct threat to America itself.

The United States as a World Power

ANY DOUBT ABOUT WHETHER the world was headed toward war disappeared on September 1, 1939, when Nazi Germany invaded Poland. Great Britain and France immediately declared war on Germany, and World War II began. In the United States, strong isolationist sentiment persisted. The country remained formally neutral even though it tilted more and more toward Great Britain. Despite the tilt, the United States stayed out of the war for over two years after it had begun in Europe. This changed on December 7, 1941, when Japan bombed **Pearl Harbor,** a U.S. naval base in Hawaii. The next day, the United States declared war on Japan. A few days later, Germany and Italy declared war on the United States, and the United States re-

Pearl Harbor
Naval base in Hawaii attacked by Japan on December 7, 1941, initiating U.S. entry into World War II.

sponded in kind. The United States was then fully engaged in a global war, participating in the Grand Alliance of the United States, Great Britain, the Soviet Union, and several other allied nations against the Axis powers of Japan, Germany, and Italy.

This global conflict transformed the United States' role in the world. Before World War II, the United States was an essentially isolationist country with a sizeable power base that it rarely used. By the end of the war, the United States was the leader of the most powerful military coalition that the world had ever seen. What is more, the United States had the only major economy in the world that had not been decimated by war. These realities forced the United States to reassess the principles that had guided its foreign and military policy for the previous century and a half.

From Stand-Alone to Superpower: The Evolution of Foreign Policy

WORLD WAR II AND ITS AFTERMATH: 1941–1947

After the United States entered World War II, it took a phenomenal industrial and military mobilization to secure victory. The war transformed American society, cost tens of billions of dollars, and cost the lives of more than 400,000 members of the American armed forces. The war ended in Europe on May 8, 1945 (V-E Day), with the Allies bruised but victorious. The war against Japan ended after the United States dropped two atomic bombs on Japan, one on Hiroshima on August 6, 1945, and the other on Nagasaki three days later. On August 15, Japan surrendered, and the Allies celebrated V-J Day and the end to World War II. The birth of the nuclear age made it all the more important that, in building the postwar world, the victorious powers somehow find a way to keep the peace.

One way to do this, many believed, was to create an improved version of the League of Nations, this time with the participation of all of the world's great powers, including the United States. Thus, even before the war ended, the United States and fifty-one of its allies met in San Francisco to create the **United Nations (UN),** an **international governmental organization (IGO),** whose purpose was to guarantee the security of member states when attacked and to promote economic, physical, and social well-being around the world. Successful operations of the UN depended on the postwar cooperation of the "Big Three" of the Grand Alliance (the United States, Britain, and the Soviet Union) as well as China and France, which had the five permanent seats on the new UN Security Council. The UN, like all IGOs, was created by its member states to achieve the international purposes that they designate.[6]

Believing that the collapse of international trade in the 1930s created conditions that led to the rise of dictators and the beginning of World War II, the victorious powers also created new international economic organizations to encourage trade. Meeting in Bretton Woods, New Hampshire, before the war ended, the victorious powers finalized the **Bretton Woods Agreement.**[7] This agreement established the **International Monetary Fund (IMF)** to stabilize exchange rates among major currencies and set their value in terms of the dollar and gold, and the International Bank for Reconstruction and Development, also called the **World Bank,** tasked to help the world recover economically from the destruction of World War II.

The allies also hoped to create an international trade organization at Bretton Woods, but the U.S. Congress feared that the creation of such an organization would lead to international control over the U.S. economy. Given this fear, the most that could be achieved was a **General Agreement on Tariffs and Trade (GATT),** a set of agreements that over the years led to negotiations that substantially reduced tariffs. GATT remained in place until the World Trade Organization was created in 1995. The IMF and the World Bank continue to operate today.

The U.S. intention to participate in these institutions indicated a shift in U.S. attitudes regarding isolationism and unilateralism. To participate in these institutions, the United States had to be less isolationist and less unilateralist than before the war. Gradually, then, the country moved toward internationalism and **multilateralism**—a belief that foreign and military policy actions should be taken in cooperation with other states.

United Nations (UN)
An international governmental organization created shortly before the end of World War II to guarantee the security of nations and to promote global economic, physical, and social well-being.

international governmental organization (IGO)
An organization created by the governments of at least two and often many countries that operates internationally with the objectives of achieving the purposes that the member countries agree upon.

Bretton Woods Agreement
International financial agreement signed shortly before the end of World War II that created the World Bank and the International Monetary Fund.

International Monetary Fund (IMF)
International governmental organization created shortly before the end of World War II to stabilize international financial relations through fixed monetary exchange rates.

World Bank
International governmental organization created shortly before the end of World War II to provide loans for large economic development projects.

General Agreement on Tariffs and Trade (GATT)
Devised shortly after World War II as an interim agreement until a World Trade Organization could be created to help lower tariffs and increase trade.

multilateralism
The U.S. foreign policy that actions should be taken in cooperation with other states after consultation.

THE COLD WAR AND CONTAINMENT: 1947–1960

Although the United States and the Soviet Union were allies during World War II, cooperation between them was strained. After the war, the situation deteriorated as the Soviets imposed communist governments in Eastern Europe and supported revolutionary movements and left-wing political parties throughout the world. Many Americans concluded that the Soviet Union was bent on dominating the world. How should the United States respond?

This question was answered early in 1947 when both Greece and Turkey were threatened with communist takeover. President Harry S Truman addressed Congress, presenting the **Truman Doctrine:** "I believe that it must be the policy of the United States to support peoples who are resisting attempted subjugation by armed minorities or by outside pressures."[8] Under the Truman Doctrine, the United States provided economic and military aid to Greece and Turkey. A few weeks later, U.S. Secretary of State George Marshall proposed that the United States provide economic assistance to France, Germany, Great Britain, and other European states struggling to rebuild their economies. Congress supported the idea. In its first year of operation (1948–1949), the **Marshall Plan** provided more than $6 billion to European states to rebuild.[9] The Marshall Plan provided the basis for European economic recovery, which prevented communist parties from winning elections throughout Western Europe.

The Truman Doctrine and the Marshall Plan were the linchpins of the strategy of **containment.** As postulated by diplomat George Kennan, who like many Americans believed that the Soviet Union wanted to dominate the world, the United States would apply "counterforce" wherever the Soviet Union applied pressure: "The Soviet pressure against the free institutions of the Western World is something that can be contained by the adroit and vigilant application of counterforce at a series of constantly shifting geographical and political points, corresponding to the shifts and maneuvers of Soviet policy."[10]

Containment had other key elements. In 1949, the United States and eleven other countries signed the North Atlantic Treaty, which stated that all signatories considered an attack against one an attack against all.[11] This was the first occasion when the United States joined a political and military alliance during peacetime. The following year, treaty members created the **North Atlantic Treaty Organization (NATO),** a defense alliance to implement the treaty. Figure 19.1 depicts the strategic alliances of NATO and the Warsaw Pact, a defensive group the Soviets established with their Eastern European satellite countries to counter NATO. The United States would eventually dispatch hundreds of thousands of troops to Europe to deter any potential Soviet attack.

In 1950, North Korea invaded South Korea. Taken by surprise, the United States sent troops under UN auspices to defend South Korea. When U.S. forces arrived, they pushed back the North Korean forces, but the United States then changed its war aims from defending South Korea (containment) to unifying Korea (liberation). When U.S. forces drove north and approached Korea's border with China, however, China entered the war and pushed the Americans back. Fighting dragged on indecisively for months. Finally, the warring parties reached a truce in 1953, dividing Korea almost exactly where it had been divided before North Korea's invasion. It remains divided today, with U.S. troops deployed along the border to protect South Korea.

Starting in the 1950s, much of the U.S. military strategy was based on nuclear weapons and deterrence. Deterrence was the theory that, if a potential enemy wanted to attack but knew that it would in turn be attacked, it would not attack. During the 1950s and 1960s, as the United States and the Soviet Union developed large nuclear arsenals, a new version of deterrence developed called mutual assured destruction (MAD). Under MAD, both the United States and the Soviet Union were deterred

Margin glossary

Truman Doctrine
U.S. policy initiated in 1947 of providing economic assistance and military aid to countries fighting against communist revolutions or political pressure.

Marshall Plan
European Recovery Program, named after Secretary of State George C. Marshall, of extensive U.S. aid to Western Europe after World War II.

containment
Strategy to oppose expansion of Soviet power, particularly in Western Europe and East Asia, with military power, economic assistance, and political influence.

North Atlantic Treaty Organization (NATO)
The first peacetime military treaty the United States joined, NATO is a regional political and military organization created in 1950.

FIGURE 19.1 COLD WAR ALLIANCES IN EUROPE

In 1949, the United States sponsored the creation of the North Atlantic Treaty Organization (NATO), an alliance of Western European nations, the United States, and Canada. Greece and Turkey were formally admitted to NATO membership in 1952, West Germany in 1955, and Spain in 1982. In response to the creation of NATO, the Soviet Union and seven other communist countries established a rival alliance, the Warsaw Pact, in 1949.

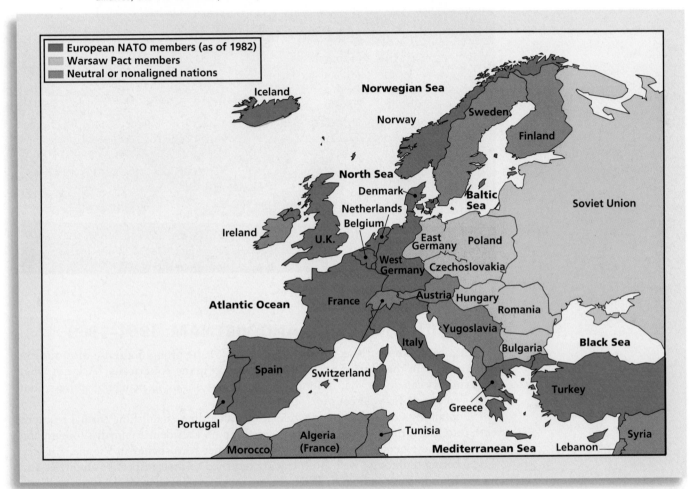

from launching a nuclear attack because each knew that if they attacked first, the other would still have enough nuclear weapons remaining to destroy the attacker as a functioning society. U.S. President Dwight D. Eisenhower and Soviet President Nikita Khrushchev held summit meetings in the 1950s to address their differences, but tensions often flared between the two superpowers.

Throughout the 1950s and into the 1960s, the world seemed divided into two camps, one led by the United States and the other by the Soviet Union. Containment was the core U.S. foreign and military policy. With some modifications, it remained so until the Cold War ended. Meanwhile, moralism and pragmatism remained key principles of U.S. foreign and military policy. Most Americans despised communism as dangerous and dictatorial. Most accepted that containment required the United States to adopt pragmatic policies such as supporting authoritarian governments that opposed communism. Isolationism and unilateralism had been discarded as principles of foreign and military policy. While some Americans called for their return, most accepted internationalism and multilateralism.

■ During much of the Cold War, the United States and the Soviet Union carried on testing of nuclear weapons. The rapid expansion of nuclear arsenals resulted in a stalemate position known as mutually assured destruction (MAD), whereby a first strike by either superpower would result in a devastating counterstrike.

Photo courtesy: National Archives and Records Administration

CONTAINMENT, CUBA, AND VIETNAM: 1961–1969

When John F. Kennedy became president in 1961, he brought a sense of optimism and activism to the United States that captivated many Americans. "Ask not what your country can do for you," Kennedy urged Americans in his inaugural address, "but what you can do for your country."[12]

Containing the Soviet Union while at the same time establishing cordial relations with it to lessen the peril of nuclear war was high on President Kennedy's foreign and military policy agenda. Thus, in 1961, Kennedy met Khrushchev in Vienna, Austria. The meeting did not go well. Both leaders returned to their respective countries and increased military spending. In 1962, the Soviet Union began to deploy intermediate-range ballistic missiles in Cuba, only ninety miles from Florida, leading to the **Cuban Missile Crisis**.[13] The United States reacted strongly, placing a naval blockade around Cuba and warning the Soviet Union to withdraw the missiles or suffer the consequences. After several days during which the world was closer to nuclear war than it had ever been, Khrushchev backed down and withdrew the missiles. The world breathed a sigh of relief.

The Cuban Missile Crisis led to a period of improved U.S.-Soviet relations. During the crisis, the United States and the Soviet Union had marched to the edge of nuclear war, and neither liked what they had seen. Thus, in 1963, the two nations concluded a partial nuclear test ban treaty and installed a "hot line" between Washington and Moscow to allow the leaders of the two countries to talk directly during crises.

The Cuban Missile Crisis confirmed the majority of Americans' belief that the Soviet Union was an expansionist power. Despite its dangers, most Americans believed that containment was the correct strategy, and that the United States remained the moral defender of liberty and justice, acting pragmatically but always with restraint to prevent communist expansion. Few questioned the morality of containment, the necessity for pragmatism, or the need for internationalism and American-led multilateralism.

Cuban Missile Crisis
The 1962 confrontation that nearly escalated into war between the United States and the Soviet Union over Soviet deployment of medium-range ballistic missiles in Cuba.

SIMULATION

**You Are President
John F. Kennedy**

Then came the **Vietnam War.**[14] The United States sought to contain communism from spreading from North Vietnam into South Vietnam starting in the 1950s, but it was in the mid-1960s that U.S. bombing and ground operations began, and they escalated quickly. While many in South Vietnam were grateful for U.S. assistance, others were actively supporting the communists. The United States became embroiled in a civil war in which it was difficult to determine friend from foe. Eventually, the U.S. presence in Vietnam grew to more than 500,000 troops, 58,000 of whom were killed. As deaths mounted and costs grew, many Americans asked questions they had rarely asked before. Was the United States on the side of justice in Vietnam, or had it only replaced France there as a colonial power? How much killing and how great a cost would the United States bear to prevent the expansion of communism? Was communism still the enemy it had been? Increasingly, U.S. citizens became less persuaded that their mission in Vietnam was moral or that communism was universally dangerous. By the end of the 1960s, Americans were not as sure of their moral superiority as they had been, nor were they sure that containment was the proper strategy on which to base their foreign and military policy. President Lyndon B. Johnson, who had presided over the massive U.S. military escalation in Vietnam, became so unpopular by 1968 that he chose not to run for reelection.

Vietnam War
Between 1965 and 1973, the United States deployed up to 500,000 troops to Vietnam to try to prevent North Vietnam from taking over South Vietnam; the effort failed and was extremely divisive within the United States.

DÉTENTE AND HUMAN RIGHTS: 1969–1981

When Richard M. Nixon was inaugurated as president in 1969, he declared it was time to move from "an era of confrontation" to "an era of negotiation" in relations with the Soviet Union.[15] Recognizing that nuclear war would destroy life as it existed, searching for a way to exit Vietnam, and trying to improve East–West relations without conceding international leadership or renouncing containment, Nixon undertook policies that began this transformation. The improvement in U.S.-Soviet relations was called **détente.**[16]

As Nixon calculated how to achieve these objectives, some criticized his approach as cynical. Emphasizing pragmatism to the virtual exclusion of moralism, Nixon's approach reminded many of old-style European power politics that the United States

détente
The relaxation of tensions between the United States and the Soviet Union that occurred during the 1970s.

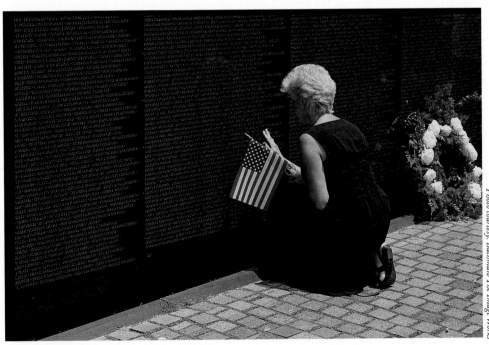

■ Many Americans continue to visit the Vietnam War Memorial in Washington, D.C., to grieve for those in the U.S. military who gave their lives during the conflict in Southeast Asia.

Photo courtesy: Bachman/The Image Works

Nixon Doctrine
The policy implemented at the end of the Vietnam War that the United States would provide arms and military equipment to countries but not do the fighting for them.

human rights
The belief that human beings have inalienable rights such as freedom of speech and freedom of religion.

Carter Doctrine
Policy announced after the 1979 Soviet invasion of Afghanistan that the Persian Gulf area was a vital U.S. interest and the United States would fight to maintain access to it.

Reagan Doctrine
Policy that the United States would provide military assistance to anti-communist groups fighting against pro-Soviet governments.

had rejected since its earliest days. Critics pointed to the **Nixon Doctrine**—that the United States would provide military aid to countries but not do the fighting for them—as evidence of this cynicism. Under the Nixon Doctrine, the United States expanded military aid to South Vietnam and accelerated bombing even as negotiations for American withdrawal proceeded. To many, this showed that Nixon ignored morality. Others supported Nixon's approach, arguing that it would get the United States out of Vietnam, open relations with China, and improve relations with the Soviet Union.

The changed nature of U.S.-Soviet relations brought about by détente was best illustrated by the frequency of summit meetings. From 1972 to 1979, American and Soviet leaders met six times, but détente was more than summitry. It also included increased trade, arms control agreements such as the Strategic Arms Limitation Treaty and the Anti-Ballistic Missile Treaty, and cultural exchanges. Détente improved East–West relations in Europe as well. For example, the heads of government of almost every nation in Europe and North America attended a meeting in Helsinki, Finland, in 1975.

When Jimmy Carter became president in 1977, he too intended to pursue détente. However, he rejected Nixon's foreign policy cynicism. Carter instead emphasized **human rights,** that is, the protection of people's basic freedoms and needs. This found a sympathetic ear among many Americans. Once again, they believed, the United States would emphasize morality in foreign policy. Some Americans wondered, however, if Carter's emphasis on human rights was misdirected and was weakening the United States.[17]

Concern about American weakness grew in 1979 when radical Iranians, with the support of Iran's fundamentalist Islamic government, overran the U.S. embassy in Tehran and held the embassy staff captive. The Iranian hostage crisis eroded Carter's support in the United States. For over a year, the country was powerless to win the hostages' release. A failed rescue attempt added to American humiliation. (The hostages were not released until the day that Carter left office in 1981.)

Détente finally died in 1979 when the Soviet Union invaded Afghanistan. Described by Carter in his 1980 State of the Union Address as "the most serious threat to peace since the Second World War,"[18] the Soviet invasion led to an immediate increase in U.S. defense spending. Carter also adopted a more hard-line approach to foreign policy, announcing the **Carter Doctrine** under which the United States would fight to prevent any further Soviet expansion toward the Persian Gulf.

CONTAINMENT REVISITED AND RENEWED: 1981–1989

The tense U.S.-Soviet relations during Jimmy Carter's last year as president became confrontational during President Ronald Reagan's first term in office. Reagan accelerated the U.S. arms buildup and initiated an activist foreign policy in response to Soviet influence in developing countries including the invasion of Grenada, a pro-Soviet island nation in the Caribbean, and support for the Contras, an insurgency attempting to overthrow the pro-Soviet Sandinista government in Nicaragua in Central America. In addition, Reagan emphasized morality in American foreign policy and pushed to create an open international economic system.[19]

By 1984, however, relations between the United States and the Soviet Union were beginning to improve. The two countries upgraded their hotlines and agreed to expand arms-control talks. Most importantly, the rhetoric from both capitals deescalated. What happened? First, the 1984 U.S. presidential election constrained U.S. rhetoric. Although most Americans supported the arms buildup, they were concerned about confrontation with the Soviets. In response, Reagan moderated his statements. Second, U.S. foreign and military policy initiatives had an impact on Moscow as, in addition to its arms buildup, the United States implemented the **Reagan Doctrine,** under which the United States provided arms to anti-Soviet movements fighting pro-

Soviet governments in Afghanistan, Angola, Mozambique, and Nicaragua. These programs increased the cost of Soviet involvement there and led Soviet leaders to rethink their foreign policy. Finally, the Soviet Union had serious internal problems. Its economy was performing poorly and it had a leadership crisis, with three Soviet leaders dying between 1982 and 1985. These problems had to be addressed. To do this, the Soviet Union needed a less confrontational relationship with the United States.

Recognizing this, Soviet President Mikhail Gorbachev worked with Reagan to improve relations after Gorbachev became the Soviet leader in 1985. Even before Gorbachev's reforms took hold, Gorbachev and Reagan laid the groundwork for a transformation in relations.[20] At the third of five summit meetings, the two leaders signed an agreement to destroy all intermediate-range nuclear weapons. Gorbachev introduced "perestroika"—reforms in domestic, foreign, and military policies that transformed the Soviet Union and U.S.-Soviet relations. Although the reforms were intended to address the serious problems that the Soviet Union faced, they eventually led to the end of the Cold War and the demise of the Soviet Union.[21]

Photo courtesy: Tannen Murray/The Image Works

■ After several tense years in U.S.-Soviet relations, the emergence of Mikhail Gorbachev as Soviet premier in 1985 led to the adoption of stunning reforms in the Soviet Union and a series of increasingly friendly summit meetings between Gorbachev and U.S. President Ronald Reagan.

SEARCHING FOR A NEW INTERNATIONAL ORDER: 1989–2001

George Bush, vice president during President Reagan's two terms, assumed the presidency in 1989 pledging to continue Reagan's foreign policy directions. However, the pace and scope of change in Eastern Europe and the Soviet Union raised questions about the entire direction of U.S. foreign policy. The first question came from Eastern Europe. In 1989, the people of many Eastern European states revolted against their governments. During previous rebellions, Soviet troops stationed in Eastern Europe subdued the rebellions. This time, Gorbachev ordered Soviet troops to remain in their barracks. The rebellions continued, and in every communist country in Eastern Europe, the government fell.

The United States was not quite sure how to respond. At first, Bush proceeded cautiously. As it became clear that the revolutions were irreversible, the United States and other democratic states helped the new noncommunist Eastern European states try to establish democratic political and free market economic systems. Remarkably, in a matter of months, the so-called "Iron Curtain" in Europe had collapsed, with almost no serious bloodshed.

The 1990 Iraqi invasion of Kuwait produced a new challenge. The Bush administration believed that the invasion threatened vital U.S. interests, and the United Nations passed a resolution authorizing the use of force to expel Iraq from Kuwait. Shortly after Congress voted to support the use of military force against Iraq, the Persian Gulf War began in January 1991. In an attack called Operation Desert Storm, U.S. and allied forces defeated Iraq in a matter of weeks. The objective—expelling Iraq from Kuwait—had been achieved with few U.S. casualties.[22] The conduct of Operation Desert Storm reflected the principles of the **Powell Doctrine** articulated by Colin Powell, President Bush's chair of the Joint Chiefs of Staff.

Meanwhile, startling events were unfolding in the Soviet Union. Under Gorbachev, the Soviet Union posed less and less of a threat as the United States and Soviet Union forged an increasingly close relationship. Weakened by a failed coup attempt against Gorbachev in the summer of 1991, its economy in shambles, and torn

Powell Doctrine
The Powell Doctrine advocates an all-or-nothing approach to military intervention. Among other criteria, it emphasizes the use of overwhelming force to ensure a quick and decisive victory, and the adoption of an exit strategy prior to any intervention.

by internal dissent and the desires of nationalities for independence, the Soviet Union collapsed.[23] The Cold War was over, as was the need for containment. Once again Americans asked questions: What would U.S. strategy now be? With the Cold War over, should the United States cut defense spending, and if so, how much? How much aid should the United States send to its former enemy to help it survive its collapse? What criteria would guide decisions about where and when to employ U.S. forces abroad in a world with only one remaining superpower?

These were the complex questions Bill Clinton faced when he assumed the presidency in 1993. Defining the American role in this world presented a challenge. Clinton's agenda centered on implementing engagement and enlargement, shaping new international economic relationships, deciding when U.S. armed forces should be used overseas, and puzzling over what role the United States should play in the post–Cold War world. (See Politics Now: The United States and the International Criminal Court.) **Engagement** meant that the United States would not retreat into isolationism as it did after World War I and for a short time after World War II. Engagement implied that the United States relied on negotiations and cooperation rather than confrontation and conflict, although it would use force when necessary. **Enlargement** meant that the United States would promote democracy, open markets, and other Western political, economic, and social values. In practice, engagement and enlargement led to the implementation of the Partnership for Peace program with former communist states in Eastern Europe and the former Soviet Union and the expansion of NATO.

Deciding when to use U.S. armed forces overseas is a vexing problem. As we have seen, from the end of World War II to the collapse of the Soviet Union, U.S. military intervention was usually tied to containing communism. With the Soviet Union gone, this easy benchmark for deciding when to intervene no longer existed. Thus, the Clinton administration had to clarify when and under what conditions the United States would intervene abroad. The administration faced different types of crises in countries in Africa, Eastern Europe, Asia, the Middle East, and the Caribbean and intervened militarily in a number of those countries, but no pattern was evident about the use of U.S. military force overseas in those crises. In some cases, the U.S. response was largely humanitarian, other situations dictated peacekeeping or peace enforcement efforts, and still others involved combat activities.

International economic issues were another focus of Clinton's activities. With help from members of his own Democratic Party as well as congressional Republicans, he guided the **North American Free Trade Agreement (NAFTA)** into law, establishing the free flow of goods among Canada, Mexico, and the United States. The United States under Clinton also played a major role in initiating two other major free trade areas: the Free Trade Area of the Americas and the Asia-Pacific Economic Cooperation agreement, as well as creating the **World Trade Organization (WTO),** charged with overseeing world trade, judging trade disputes, and lowering tariffs.[24]

THE WAR ON TERRORISM: 2001 TO THE PRESENT

During his first months as president, George W. Bush conducted an active foreign policy, traveling to other countries and ordering several changes to policy. As a Texan, Bush placed high priority on U.S. relations with Mexico and other Latin American states. Indeed, his first trip outside the United States as president was to Mexico to discuss immigration, anti-drug policies, economic development, and border issues. By September 2001, the Bush administration had a full foreign policy agenda. Relations with Latin America, Europe, Russia, and China all loomed large, as did security, international economics, immigration, drugs, and the environment. However, the new administration had not sorted through this considerable agenda to determine which items it considered most important. Suddenly and unexpectedly, on the morning of September 11, the Bush administration's foreign and defense priorities became clear.

On September 11, 2001, members of **al-Qaeda,** a terrorist network founded and funded by Muslim fundamentalist Osama bin Laden, hijacked four jetliners, flying

engagement
Policy implemented during the Clinton administration that the United States would remain actively involved in foreign affairs.

enlargement
Policy implemented during the Clinton administration that the United States would actively promote the expansion of democracy and free markets throughout the world.

North American Free Trade Agreement (NAFTA)
Agreement that promotes free movement of goods and services among Canada, Mexico, and the United States.

World Trade Organization (WTO)
International governmental organization created in 1995 that manages multilateral negotiations to reduce barriers to trade and settle trade disputes.

al-Qaeda
Worldwide terrorist organization led by Osama bin Laden; responsible for numerous terrorist attacks against U.S. interests, including 9/11 attacks against the World Trade Center and the Pentagon.

Politics Now

THE UNITED STATES AND THE INTERNATIONAL CRIMINAL COURT

In 1998, a United Nations conference finalized a treaty establishing an International Criminal Court (ICC) that would have jurisdiction over crimes against humanity, war crimes, and genocide once sixty states ratified it. By 2001, 139 states had signed the treaty. The United States was not one of them.

The United States opposes crimes against humanity, war crimes, and genocide. In the mid-1990s, it deployed thousands of troops to Bosnia to help prevent genocide. In the late 1990s, it supported the creation of a UN tribunal that indicted Yugoslav President Slobodan Milosevic for war crimes and convicted other Serbs of crimes against humanity for their ethnic-cleansing campaign against Bosnian Muslims. In 1999, the United States contributed most of the armed forces for NATO's military operation against ethnic cleansing in Kosovo.

Why then did the United States not support the ICC? Some conservative Americans believed that the powers the ICC statutes gave the court might lead to politically motivated prosecutions of U.S. military personnel involved in peacekeeping missions, fearing that frivolous charges might be made against U.S. personnel engaged in legitimate activities. For example, Former U.S. Senator Jesse Helms (R–NC) argued that a government that committed human rights abuses against its citizens might charge that a member of the U.S. armed forces trying to prevent such abuses was violating the rights of its citizens and bring charges against him or her in the ICC. Defenders of the ICC asserted that this could not occur, because the ICC statutes allowed the United States and other peacekeeping states to preempt the ICC by first trying anyone so accused in their own national courts.

The United States under President Bill Clinton signed the treaty in 2000, but the Senate never ratified it. When George W. Bush took office in 2001, he renounced the treaty. As the International Criminal Court neared operational status in 2002, Bush threatened to oppose all UN peacekeeping missions if the ICC began operations, to refuse to provide U.S. funding for such operations if approved, and to refuse to have U.S. forces participate in any peacekeeping efforts. The Bush administration also initiated an extensive diplomatic offensive designed to conclude one-on-one agreements with other countries that they would not prosecute or bring changes against U.S. peacekeepers. The United States threatened to cut off military aid to countries that refused to sign bilateral agreements. By 2004, ninety-two countries had signed such agreements.

The U.S. diplomatic effort was widely criticized outside the United States as an attempt to circumvent the ICC. For example, the European Union and many of its members chastised the United States, and Amnesty International called the effort an attempt to undermine the ICC.

Despite U.S. resistance, the ICC was established at the Hague, in the Netherlands, and prepared to conduct investigations, trials, and appeals procedures for cases involving war crimes and other crimes against humanity. By 2006, the Court completed elections for eighteen judgeships organized into three divisions: pre-trial, trial, and appeals. On March 17, 2006, Thomas Lubanga Dyilo, a Congolese national accused of war crimes, was arrested and transferred to the International Criminal Court where he awaits a trial. He is the first person to be arrested and transferred to the court since its entry into force in 2002. The ICC has also issued arrest warrants for several Ugandan individuals and is investigating allegations of genocide in the Darfur region of Sudan as requested by the United Nations Security Council.

---

two into the twin towers of New York's World Trade Center. The impact destroyed the towers and killed almost 3,000 people. Another hijacked plane slammed into the Pentagon, killing 189 individuals. The fourth plane headed toward Washington, D.C., but crashed into a field in Pennsylvania after passengers charged the hijackers and forced them to lose control of the plane.[25]

After the 9/11 attacks, President Bush, declaring a **war on terrorism,** as discussed in the chapter opening, organized a coalition of nations to combat the threat posed by terrorist groups such as al-Qaeda. He also demanded that Afghanistan's **Taliban** government, which had provided safe haven for bin Laden and al-Qaeda's terrorist training camps, turn bin Laden over to the United States. When the Taliban refused, the Bush administration launched Operation Enduring Freedom against al-Qaeda and the Taliban regime in October 2001. The military operation included air strikes against Taliban and al-Qaeda targets and support for the Northern Alliance, an Afghani opposition force battling Taliban control. By the end of 2001, the Taliban were overthrown and the United States was committed to peace enforcement in Afghanistan and assistance with the transition to a democratic government.

war on terrorism
Initiated by George W. Bush after the September 11, 2001, attacks to weed out terrorist operatives throughout the world, using diplomacy, military means, improved homeland security, stricter banking laws, and other means.

Taliban
Fundamentalist Islamic government of Afghanistan that provided terrorist training bases for al-Qaeda.

VIDEO ROUNDTABLE
9-11-2001

■ The south tower of the World Trade Center collapses September 11, 2001, after it was struck by a hijacked airplane. The north tower, also struck by a hijacked plane, collapsed shortly after. The tragic 9/11 terrorist attacks caused enormous loss of life and had a profound impact on U.S. foreign and defense policy.

Photo courtesy: Thomas Nilsson/Getty Images

Bush Doctrine
Policy advocated by President George W. Bush of using preemptive military action against a perceived threat to U.S. interests.

weapons of mass destruction (WMDs)
Biological, chemical, and nuclear weapons, which present a sizeable threat to U.S. security.

Ironically, the 9/11 attacks drew the United States and Russia closer together as Russia helped the United States gain access to military bases in Central Asia. The United States also muted its criticism of Russian policies in Russia's breakaway province of Chechnya, and Russian President Vladimir Putin indicated a willingness to modify the 1972 Anti-Ballistic Missile Treaty, thereby removing ballistic missile defense as a stumbling block in U.S.-Russian relations. The United States and Russia made so much progress on strategic arms discussions that during Bush's May 2002 trip to Moscow, the United States and Russia signed the Strategic Offensive Arms Reduction Treaty, under which both sides agreed to cut their strategic nuclear arsenals to the lowest total in decades.[26]

The terrorist attacks of September 11, 2001, had a profound impact on U.S. foreign policy. Despite its superpower status and nuclear superiority, the United States appeared vulnerable in a way it had not previously. President Bush responded by inaugurating a global campaign against terrorists and their supporters. Like other presidents before him, George W. Bush was putting his distinctive stamp on how the country should address threats to national security. Bush and his foreign policy team concluded that a more ambitious, "muscular" posture was needed to fight threats to U.S. interests. Instead of relying on the reactive strategies of deterrence and containment, the Bush administration advocated a proactive doctrine of preemptive military action. This bold but controversial strategy is commonly referred to as the **Bush Doctrine.**

When the United States launched its war against Saddam Hussein's regime in Iraq in March 2003, it signaled the implementation of the Bush Doctrine. In past conflicts of this magnitude, the United States had intervened militarily in response to a direct attack (such as Pearl Harbor), or to defend other countries that had been invaded (such as South Korea or Kuwait). The 2003 U.S.-led invasion of Iraq was part of a new strategy that sought to promote American security through preemptive military strikes against potentially dangerous nations. Believing that the Hussein regime was developing **weapons of mass destruction (WMDs)**—nuclear, chemical, or biological weapons—and that Iraq was a safe harbor and potential breeding ground for terrorists, the U.S. government chose to act even though the UN Security Council refused to endorse the recourse to war, and even without the support of key allies such

President George W. Bush holds a meeting with his national security team on September 12, 2001. From left are Secretary of Defense Donald Rumsfeld, Secretary of State Colin Powell, Bush, Vice President Dick Cheney, and Henry Shelton, chair of the Joint Chiefs of Staff.

Photo courtesy: Kevin LaMarque/Reuters

as France and Germany. The failure of the United States to win approval from the Security Council for the 2003 invasion of Iraq led to vigorous debate at home and abroad, and U.S. actions created hard feelings among many of America's traditional allies. (See Join the Debate: Should the United States Pull Out of the United Nations?)

The overthrow of Saddam Hussein's government in the spring of 2003 was relatively quick. The U.S.-led bombing campaign destroyed much of the military and governmental infrastructure in Iraq within days. The Iraqi armed forces seemed helpless and disorganized. Within weeks, U.S. and other allied forces entered Hussein's palaces, tore down statues of the dictator around the country, and began to create a post-Saddam government in Iraq. American forces ultimately captured Saddam Hussein himself on December 13, 2003.

Over time, coalition forces failed to find evidence of an active nuclear weapons program in Iraq—the original justification provided by the Bush administration for a preemptive military strike—but it is clear that Hussein possessed chemical weapons, engaged in genocide, and brutally oppressed the Shiite majority in Iraq.[27] As evidence of WMDs failed to materialize, the Bush administration changed its justification for war, arguing that Saddam Hussein posed a severe danger to the world because of his long history of brutality, and emphasizing the goal of promoting democracy in the Middle East through his removal from power.

In the months after President Bush declared an end to major combat, soldiers from the United States and its allies found themselves under attack from mortar fire, roadside bombings, and suicide missions by various insurgents. As the American military presence in Iraq continued, war deaths and injuries mounted. By the end of 2006, more than 2,900 U.S. service men and women had lost their lives in Iraq and more than 22,000 had been injured.[28]

VIDEO DEBATE

Americans in Iraq

A positive development, however, was the January 2005 election in which the Iraqi people chose representatives for a 275-member National Assembly. The election marked an important step in the process of turning over control of the country from the U.S.-led coalition to the Iraqis themselves. But hopes for an end to the growing civil unrest and a withdrawal of U.S. troops declined. On August 14, 2005, the

Join the Debate

SHOULD THE UNITED STATES PULL OUT OF THE UNITED NATIONS?

OVERVIEW: The United Nations came into existence in 1945 in the wake of two world wars and the desire of most nations for an international organization dedicated to pursuing global justice, peace, and human rights. To back up its mandate, the United States and the United Nations have worked together to help maintain relative global security. For example, UN member nations helped defend South Korea from invasion by North Korea, provided a blueprint to help mediate peace in the Middle East, and voted for sanctions against South Africa to help end racial apartheid. The UN has also helped millions living in famine, as well as aided countless refugees fleeing war and natural disasters by providing food, shelter, clothing, and medical relief.

Since the end of the Cold War, the United States and the United Nations have developed competing and sometimes antagonistic views with regard to the UN's mandate and global role. In 1992, for example, the UN released a bold initiative—the Agenda for Peace—to recast the UN's peacekeeping role. The move was viewed by some U.S. policy makers as giving the UN control over U.S. military and foreign policy resources and it received a great deal of criticism in Congress.

Furthermore, due to disagreements with the United States over a variety of issues, including its military and foreign policy role in the Middle East, its refusal to ratify the Kyoto climate change treaty, and its opposition to a treaty to abolish land mines, the UN voted the United States off the UN Human Rights Commission in 2001. This action infuriated the Bush administration, because countries that engage in human rights violations, such as Sudan, Libya, and

Cuba, retained their seats on the commission. The United States walked out of the UN conference on racism in 2001 because it objected to criticisms of Israel in a draft of the conference's final declaration. The strain between the Bush administration and the United Nations increased even more in 2003 when the UN Security Council refused to sanction military action against Iraq. The UN also faced criticism for a major financial scandal involving its Oil for Food program, which had been created during Saddam Hussein's regime in order to give the Iraqi people humanitarian aid while sanctions against Hussein's government were in place. Nearly $1 billion disappeared into hidden bank accounts and fake corporations, and the U.S. Congress launched an investigation into where the money went.

To what extent should the United States support the diplomatic and peacekeeping efforts of the United Nations? Should the United States have a dominant role in determining UN policy and actions, given its dominant role in the world? Many U.S. conservatives support a full U.S. withdrawal from the United Nations. Would this decision help or hurt the United States' interests in the long run?

ARGUMENTS IN FAVOR OF THE UNITED STATES PULLING OUT OF THE UNITED NATIONS

- It is difficult for the United Nations to act, and even when it does, it is incapable of enforcing its own resolutions. In 2006, Iran made public its intention to develop nuclear weapons, but the UN could not forge a consensus regarding how to respond. China and Russia balked at imposing sanctions on Iran, creating an impasse within the Security Council. Getting the global community to act with one voice can be extremely difficult, given the diverse interests of the countries that are represented on the Security Council and within the larger UN body.

Washington Post quoted a dismal assessment of the situation in Iraq from an anonymous U.S. senior official: "the United States no longer expects to see a model new democracy, a self-supporting oil industry, or a society in which the majority of people are free from serious security or economic challenges. . . . What we expected to achieve was never realistic given the timetable or what unfolded on the ground."[29] Throughout 2006, Iraqi insurgents and foreign terrorists continued their attacks against the U.S.-led coalition forces, and increasing sectarian violence led many observers to conclude that Iraq was embroiled in a civil war. The resignation of Secretary of Defense Donald Rumsfeld after the 2006 elections suggests the administration intends to adjust its policy in Iraq in response to rising violence and waning public support.

- **The United States is not accountable to international organizations when pursuing its own interests.** The United States and the United Nations have divergent interests and understandings of international law and diplomacy. Placing members of the American armed forces under UN command cedes control to an organization that may not always act in the best interests of the United States. The United States must maintain its ability to act in whatever way it sees fit to defend its interests at home and abroad.
- **Adhering to UN resolutions results in giving up American sovereignty.** Some supporters of U.S. withdrawal from the United Nations believe the UN is attempting to create a "world government" and that to accede to UN mandates and resolutions is to relinquish U.S. sovereignty and U.S. control over its own citizens. Many see the UN as one more instance of the international community trying to institute international government.

ARGUMENTS AGAINST THE UNITED STATES PULLING OUT OF THE UNITED NATIONS

- **The UN engages in peacekeeping and nation building when the United States will not.** The UN is currently engaged in about fifteen peacekeeping operations, with more than 72,000 uniformed personnel from member nations in places such as Lebanon, Haiti, and Sudan. The UN can provide peacekeeping support when the United States is either unable or unwilling, thus preventing humanitarian disaster and conflict. This is an essential function if global security and stability are to be maintained.
- **The United States must lead by example.** Because the United States has a unique world, military, and economic position, it can use its various strengths and principles to promote global peace and justice. Why should other nations respond to UN resolutions and decrees when the United States does not? By acceding to UN requests, the United States can set an example for other nations to follow, and this may help facilitate other nations' compliance with UN wishes to ensure global security.
- **International institutions provide global stability and promote peaceful conflict resolution.** Since the establishment of the United Nations, there have been no worldwide wars. The UN was able to provide security for South Korea and it acts as an international forum for conflict mediation. Though imperfect, the UN affords a medium in which human rights policy is debated and developed and international security and stability discussed. For example, the UN has taken on the cause of disarmament and elimination of WMDs and thereby provides legitimacy in this policy domain, whereas the United States cannot. Because the United States is a world power, its membership in the UN gives the organization credibility and validity.

QUESTIONS

1. Does adhering to UN mandates mean giving up national sovereignty? Explain.
2. What can be done to reconcile U.S. and UN interests? Do the United States and the United Nations have similar interests? If not, what is to be done?

SELECTED READINGS

Jett, Dennis. *Why Peacekeeping Fails.* New York: Palgrave Macmillan, 2001.
Weiss, Thomas, ed. *United Nations and Changing World Politics.* Boulder, CO: Westview, 2004.

The September 11 terrorist attacks gave the United States two overarching foreign and defense policy priorities: defense of the homeland and pursuing the global war on terrorism. Few Americans disagree with these priorities. But, disagreements and controversies continue regarding the means to these ends and the effectiveness of government policies. (See On Campus: The Impact of the War on Terrorism on American Campuses.) Moreover, other foreign and defense policy issues, such as the threat of a nuclear-armed Iran, hostilities between Israel and Lebanon, and the humanitarian crisis in Sudan, have also captured the public's attention.

Having discussed the history of U.S. foreign policy during the twentieth century and the new direction foreign policy has taken during the presidency of George W. Bush, we turn to how foreign policy is made and the major players involved.

On Campus

THE IMPACT OF THE WAR ON TERRORISM ON AMERICAN CAMPUSES

The September 11 terrorist attacks on the World Trade Center and the Pentagon had an immense impact on the United States. American colleges and universities were not immune from that impact. Some effects were predictable. Colleges and universities across the United States reported increased enrollment in courses on Islam, international affairs, and terrorism. ROTC programs on many campuses experienced renewed interest. Security at information technology facilities and other sensitive sites was increased on most campuses. Unfortunately, a few campuses also experienced anti-Arab and anti-Islamic incidents.

American campuses also became a focus of the effort to improve homeland security, a part of the U.S. global war on terrorism. Even though most of the 9/11 hijackers were on tourist or work visas, two were in the United States on student visas. Concern over terrorists on student visas increased more when, several months after the attacks, the Immigration and Naturalization Service (INS) admitted it had processed a pre-9/11 visa application from one of the hijackers and granted a student visa to him even after he had conducted one of the attacks and died.*

The most notable impact on campuses of the effort to improve homeland security was the full implementation of the Student and Exchange Visitor Information System (SEVIS) required by the USA Patriot Act of 2001. SEVIS is a Web-based registration and tracking system operated by the INS to monitor foreign students and scholars on certain types of visas. SEVIS allows the INS to rapidly integrate information on foreign students and scholars with other information collected by the INS, U.S. intelligence agencies, and the Departments of State and Defense. Even so, SEVIS is no panacea. Only about 2 percent of the foreign nationals who enter the United States each year, or about 600,000 people, enter as scholars or students.

In 2002, the administration of President George W. Bush proposed the creation of the Interagency Panel for Advanced Science Security (IPASS) in order to "prohibit certain international students from receiving any training in sensitive areas, including areas of study with direct application to the development and use of weapons of mass destruction." The panel closely scrutinizes visa applications from prospective students from certain countries who are engaged in particularly sensitive fields of study.

Some efforts to improve homeland security could significantly alter campus life. In Georgia, one legislator introduced a bill that would require professors to report to the INS any foreign student who missed class for two weeks. Although well intentioned, this would have converted professors into INS agents. Other legislators recognized this, and the bill died in committee. Other states had similar experiences.

*On March 1, 2003, service and benefit functions of The U.S. Immigration and Naturalization Service transitioned into The Department of Homeland Security as the U.S. Citizenship and Immigration Services (USCIS).

Sources: U.S. House of Representatives, Committee on Science, "Dealing with Students and Scholars in an Age of Terrorism: Visa Backlogs and Tracking Systems," Full Committee Hearing, March 26, 2003; and Homeland Security Presidential Directive 2, October 2001.

Foreign and Defense Policy Decision Making

THE EXECUTIVE BRANCH is the most powerful branch of government in the formulation and implementation of U.S. foreign and defense policy. The Congress also influences and shapes policy, as do the military-industrial complex, the news media, and the public.

THE EXECUTIVE BRANCH

The executive branch is the locus for creating and implementing U.S. foreign and defense policy; within the executive branch, the president is the most important individual. Among executive departments, the Department of State is primarily responsible for diplomatic activity and the Department of Defense for military policy. Other executive agencies, such as the National Security Council, the Joint Chiefs of Staff, and the Central Intelligence Agency provide additional resources for the president. The relatively new Department of Homeland Security has a role to play in foreign and defense policy making as well.

The President   The president is preeminent in foreign and defense policy for several reasons. The president alone is in charge of all executive-branch resources. The president has greater access to and control over information, and the president alone can act with little fear that his actions will be countermanded.

American presidents have often used their authority to order U.S. armed forces to engage in actions without seeking approval from others. Ronald Reagan ordered air strikes against Libya and the invasion of Grenada; George Bush ordered the invasion of Panama; and Bill Clinton ordered cruise missile attacks against Afghanistan, Iraq, and Sudan. Although these presidents informed congressional leaders of their intended actions, they made the decisions and undertook the actions on their own authority. For far more extensive and serious military commitments—such as the 1991 Persian Gulf War and the 2003 U.S.-led invasion of Iraq—the president sought and received congressional approval in advance.

The president has exclusive sources of information—Department of State diplomats, military attaches working for the Department of Defense, CIA agents, and technical means of gathering information, such as satellites—that others do not have. Private citizens, companies, interest groups, Congress, and the media cannot match the president's sources for information.

The Departments of State and Defense   The Departments of State and Defense have responsibility for implementing U.S. diplomatic and military policy respectively. The **Department of State** is the oldest executive department, established originally in 1781 under the Articles of Confederation and reorganized during the administration of President George Washington. Today there are more than 30,000 personnel within the Department of State who gather information on foreign political, economic, social, and military situations; represent the United States in negotiations and international organizations; staff U.S. embassies and consulates in more than 180 countries, and manage numerous international assistance programs.

Funding for foreign affairs programs directed by the Department of State was approximately $18.5 billion in 2006, including funding for economic development, disease prevention, nuclear nonproliferation, anti-terrorism, the Peace Corps, and global peacekeeping capabilities.

The **Department of Defense** contributes to policy formulation and provides the forces to undertake military operations. It was created after World War II when Congress consolidated the Departments of War, Army, Navy, and Air Force into a single department. Under the secretary of defense and other appointed civilian officials, the Department of Defense directs U.S. forces from the Pentagon, a complex across the Potomac River from Washington, D.C. With thousands of civilian employees and millions of active-duty, National Guard, and reserve military personnel, the Department of Defense is among the most influential executive departments. The department is also home to some of the nation's most sophisticated intelligence organizations. For example, the **National Security Agency (NSA)** gathers intelligence from electronic and other sources and undertakes code breaking. Other resources include the Defense Intelligence Agency, the National Imagery and Mapping Agency, and the intelligence units of each branch of the military.

Within the Department of Defense, the **Joint Chiefs of Staff** is an important advisory body to the president, the secretary of defense, and the National Security Council. The Joint Chiefs of Staff provides a link between senior civilian leadership in the Department of Defense and the professional military, and the office often assists with the coordination of the various branches of the armed forces.

You Are the President

Evaluating Defense Spending

Department of State
Chief executive-branch department responsible for formulation and implementation of U.S. foreign policy.

Department of Defense
Chief executive-branch department responsible for formulation and implementation of U.S. military policy.

National Security Agency (NSA)
Intelligence agency primarily responsible for gathering intelligence from electronic and nonelectronic sources and for breaking foreign information transmission codes.

Joint Chiefs of Staff
Advisory body to the president that includes the army chief of staff, the air force chief of staff, the chief of naval operations, and the marine commandant.

Photo courtesy: Shawn Thew/epa/Corbis

■ General John Abizaid, head of U.S. Central Command, Secretary of Defense Donald Rumsfeld, and General Peter Pace, head of the Joint Chiefs of Staff, testifying at a hearing before the Senate Armed Services Committee on August 3, 2006. During his testimony, General Abizaid acknowledged that Iraq might slide into civil war. In the wake of increasing criticism concerning the course of the war in Iraq, Secretary Rumsfeld resigned his post the day after the November 2006 midterm elections.

Central Intelligence Agency (CIA)

Executive agency responsible for collection and analysis of information and intelligence about foreign countries and events.

National Security Council (NSC)

Executive agency responsible for advising the president about foreign and defense policy and events.

The **Central Intelligence Agency (CIA)** and the **National Security Council (NSC)** were established by Congress in 1947. The CIA collects and analyzes information necessary to meet national security requirements, and the NSC advises the president on foreign and military affairs. The CIA is the most well-known intelligence agency, but it is only one of many government organizations engaged in intelligence work. In the United States, the intelligence community consists of fifteen agencies, including the CIA. Many of these reside within the Department of Defense, but the Departments of State, Homeland Security, Treasury, and Energy also maintain intelligence units. The CIA is an independent agency and its head, the director of central intelligence, reports directly to the president. The Intelligence Reform and Terrorism Prevention Act of 2004 established a director of national intelligence who oversees the entire intelligence community (see Figure 19.2).

During the Cold War, the CIA ran covert operations to try to alter political events in many countries.[30] At times, these operations undermined broader U.S. objectives by supporting assassinations, corruption, and other scandalous activities. In the 1970s, Congress criticized the CIA and mandated changes in procedures to provide more congressional oversight to its secret operations. In the 1990s, the CIA's failure to predict the fall of the Soviet Union and the penetration of the agency by foreign agents raised congressional interest in reforming the CIA. After the 9/11 terrorist attacks, the CIA and the rest of the intelligence community were criticized for failing to identify clues that could have prevented the attacks and for relying too heavily on electronic means of gathering intelligence and not heavily enough on human sources. Controversy over faulty intelligence about Iraq, the agency's serious lack of human intelligence sources in a number of trouble spots, and its connection to secret prisons has generated a great deal of criticism on Capitol Hill and among the public.[31]

The National Security Council was set up to institutionalize the system by which the U.S. government integrates foreign and military policy and to coordinate U.S. activities on a range of foreign policy and defense issues. Former NSC advisers include Henry Kissinger, Colin Powell, and Condoleeza Rice. The NSC includes the president, the vice president, the secretaries of state and defense, the chair of the Joint Chiefs of Staff, and the director of the CIA. The special assistant for national security affairs manages the NSC and is often one of the president's closest advisers.

The NSC staff is relatively small when compared with the large bureaucracies of the Departments of State or Defense. The NSC is located in the west wing of the White House and provides advice on foreign and military affairs directly to the president. As an advisory body, it is closely connected to the president and is shielded from media scrutiny more than other agencies in the executive bureaucracy. Because of its physical proximity to the president and the close personal relationship that is often present between the NSC adviser and the president, the heads of other departments must often compete with the NSC for the president's attention.

VIDEO ROUNDTABLE

The Department of Homeland Security

The Department of Homeland Security Following the 9/11 terrorist attacks on the United States, the Office of Homeland Security was created by executive order and tasked to coordinate the executive branch's efforts to "detect, prepare for, prevent, protect against, respond to, and recover from terrorist attacks against the United States." Legislation in late 2002 converted this office into the cabinet-level

FIGURE 19.2 THE UNITED STATES INTELLIGENCE COMMUNITY

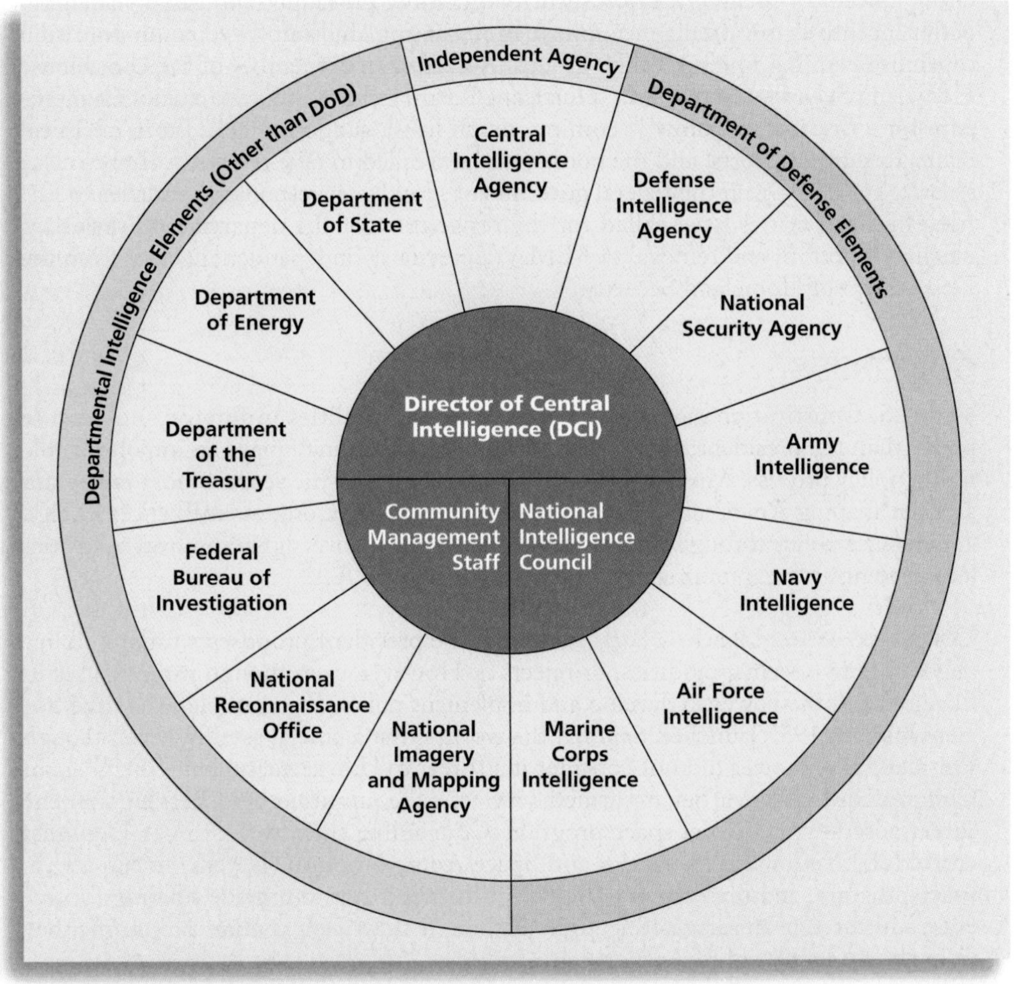

Source: Central Intelligence Agency, http://www.odci.gov/ic/icroll.htm.

Department of Homeland Security (DHS). This was the largest reorganization of the federal government since the creation of the Department of Defense in 1947. The homeland security reorganization process brought the functions of twenty-two existing agencies, approximately thirty newly created agencies or offices, and 180,000 employees under a single department. The mission of the department is to protect the American public from future acts of terror by engaging in activities designed to thwart terrorist activities and respond to any future crises.

The department is the locus for federal, state, and local homeland security coordination. Staff members work with state, local, and private sector partners to identify threats, determine vulnerabilities, and target resources. The department includes the Transportation Security Administration (TSA), the organization responsible for aviation security; the Federal Emergency Management Agency (FEMA), the primary federal disaster relief organization; Customs and Border Protection; the Coast Guard; the Secret Service; and immigration services and enforcement.

Since its creation, the Department of Homeland Security has been the subject of a great deal of criticism. The National Commission on Terrorist Attacks upon the United States—more commonly known as the **9/11 Commission**—was critical of government preparedness; their 2004 report advised a number of corrective measures. In 2005, the 9/11 Public Discourse Project, the successor to the 9/11 Commission,

Department of Homeland Security
Cabinet department created after the 9/11 attacks to coordinate domestic U.S. security efforts against terrorism.

9/11 Commission
National Commission on Terrorist Attacks upon the United States; this bipartisan, independent group was authorized by Congress and President Bush in 2002 to study the circumstances surrounding the September 11 terrorist attacks, including preparedness and the immediate response. Its 2004 report includes recommendations designed to guard against future attacks.

issued a scathing report concerning the nation's efforts to prevent terrorists attacks, citing a need for greater aviation security including passenger and cargo screening, better incentives for intelligence information sharing, and improved communication capabilities among first responder groups. According to a member of the U.S. House Homeland Security Committee, "Hurricane Katrina showed that we cannot even prepare for a disaster we know is coming, much less a sudden attack. From chemical plants to subways, ports, and the border, we have failed to take the steps need to close security gaps."[32] Given the federal government's lackluster response to Hurricane Katrina in 2005, critics have called for the resignation of the department's secretary, Michael Chertoff, and removal of FEMA, a previously independent agency, from the Department of Homeland Security.

CONGRESS

The U.S. Constitution gave Congress fewer responsibilities in foreign and defense policy than the president; nevertheless, the legislative branch plays an important role in the policy process. Most would agree that Congress is the second most important actor in shaping American foreign and defense policy.[33] Congress influences foreign and defense policy through its congressional leadership, oversight, approval of treaties and appointments, appropriations, and the War Powers Act.

Congressional Leadership Normally the president proposes a foreign policy and Congress accepts, modifies, or rejects it. However, even though it rarely uses it, Congress has the power to develop and implement policy. For example, when the Soviet Union in 1957 launched *Sputnik,* the world's first artificial satellite, even though President Eisenhower did not consider it a threat to U.S. security, some members of Congress did. Thus, a Senate armed services subcommittee held hearings on the threat posed by the Soviet space program. Concluding there was a threat, Congress created the National Aeronautics and Space Administration (NASA) to run a U.S. space program, and the National Defense Education Act to provide funding for science and foreign-language education. Although they were civilian programs, they were closely connected to defense.

Congressional Oversight Congress oversees foreign and defense policy in many ways. We describe below the role of Congress in appointments, appropriations, and the War Powers Act. Congress's other oversight powers include the ability to conduct hearings on foreign and defense policy and to have the president and CIA inform congressional committees about covert operations.

From World War II until the late 1960s, Congress deferred to the president and the military on foreign and defense issues and rarely exercised its oversight responsibilities outside appropriations. The Vietnam War changed this. As questions emerged about U.S. policy toward Vietnam, Congress questioned executive leadership in other areas of foreign and military policy as well. This expanded oversight is now the norm. For example, in 2005 and 2006, the Senate Foreign Relations Committee questioned Bush administration officials and military leaders about growing sectarian violence in Iraq and the NSA's domestic spying program.

Treaties and Executive Agreements The Constitution gives the Senate explicit power to approve treaties, but the Senate has rejected treaties only twenty times in U.S. history.[34] The Senate's power to approve treaties is not inconsequential, however. Presidents want to avoid the embarrassment of Senate rejection of a treaty, the delay of a filibuster, or senatorial refusal to consider a treaty.

Presidents can avoid the treaty process by using executive agreements, which unlike treaties do not require Senate approval. Prior to 1972, the president did not have to inform Congress of the text of these accords. Normally presidents use executive agreements for routine business matters, but executive agreements have also been used for more substantial policy commitments. The expansion of the U.S. role in world affairs after World War II, the increase in the number of independent countries, and the growing complexity of global relations explains why presidents have used executive agreements more frequently over time. (Table 8.4 in chapter 8 illustrates this greater use.)

Appointments Although the Constitution gives the president the power to appoint ambassadors and others involved in foreign and defense policy, it gives the Senate the responsibility to provide advice and consent on these appointments. Frequently, important appointees to these foreign and defense policy posts have close connections to Congress.

Senators can put a hold on the confirmation process to express concern about issues or a specific appointee. Individual senators also have the ability to derail a nomination through other means. For example, in 1997, Senator Jesse Helms (R–NC), chair of the Foreign Relations Committee, refused to hold nomination hearings for William Weld, a former Republican governor of Massachusetts, as ambassador to Mexico. Helms blocked the nomination because Weld supported the medical use of marijuana, a position that Helms opposed. In 2005, President Bush nominated John R. Bolton to serve as the U.S. ambassador to the United Nations. Bolton, a former State Department official, has close ties to the Bush family and pursued aggressive tactics against the 2000 presidential vote recount in Florida. His nomination as ambassador to the UN caused a prolonged filibuster by Senate Democrats, who opposed Bolton for a number of reasons, including his skepticism of the United Nations, his opposition to the International Criminal Court, and his aggressive management tactics. Ultimately President Bush installed him as ambassador via a congressional recess appointment that lasted until a new Congress convened in January 2007.

Appropriations Congress has a key role in shaping foreign and defense policy through its power to appropriate funds and influences when and where the United States fights through its control of the budget. While the power to go to war is shared by the executive and legislative branches of government, the power to appropriate funds belongs to the legislature alone (see Figure 19.3 for information on U.S. defense spending since 1940). Congress has been careful about using this power. For example, in 1982, Congress used its appropriation power to limit U.S. involvement in Nicaragua, where a revolutionary group called the Sandinistas had come to power in 1979. By 1982, the Sandinistas received aid from Cuba and the Soviet Union, and usually sided with the Soviet Union on international issues. The Reagan administration therefore provided military aid to the Contras, a group of Nicaraguans fighting the Sandinistas. Many U.S. citizens opposed funding the Contras. After much debate, Congress voted to cut appropriations to the group.

The Contra example also shows how the executive branch's ability to act can limit the impact that congressional control of appropriations may have on the conduct of U.S. foreign and military policy. After Congress cut funding for the Contras, some senior Reagan administration officials felt so strongly about funding the Contras that they contacted foreign nations to provide funds to purchase weapons for the Contras. In addition, they arranged arms sales to Iran, overcharging Iran for the weapons and using the surplus funds to buy weapons for the Contras.[35]

Sometimes, Congress approves more for foreign and military affairs than the president requests, as occurred during the Clinton administration when Congress sometimes appropriated additional funds for weapons purchases. Thus, Congress in 1999 approved about twice as much as Clinton requested for the fighting in Kosovo, much of the greater amount intended for weapons purchases.[36]

FIGURE 19.3 U.S. DEFENSE SPENDING, 1940–2010

The figure shows the percentage change from the prior year in the amount of current dollars spent on U.S. defense. As the figure illustrates, nothing in modern American history compares to the increase in spending after the United States entered World War II in 1941. Other significant increases in defense spending were related to the Cold War in the early 1950s and the Vietnam War in the mid to late 1960s. President George W. Bush's defense increases to fight the war on terrorism after 2001 are the highest since the end of the Cold War in the 1980s.

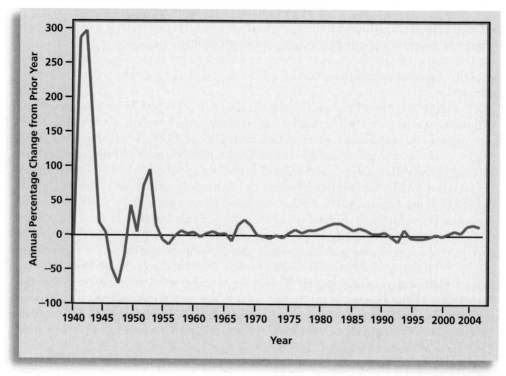

Source: Harold W. Stanley and Richard G. Niemi, eds., *Vital Statistics on American Politics, 2005–2006* (Washington, DC: CQ Press, 2006). Reprinted by permission.

The War Powers Act Funding the Contras in Nicaragua was not the first time the executive supported military action against congressional will. Throughout American history, there have been cases where Congress and the executive branch disagreed on U.S. military actions overseas. During the Vietnam War, Congress tried to define and limit the president's ability to engage U.S. forces in military action overseas.

As we have seen, for most of the post–World War II period, Congress acceded to presidential preferences in foreign and military affairs. One example of this was the 1964 Gulf of Tonkin Resolution, which granted President Lyndon Johnson broad authority to conduct military actions in Vietnam but stopped short of declaring war. As support for the war dwindled in the late 1960s, Congress grew frustrated with its inability to influence policy on Vietnam. Thus, in 1973, during the Nixon administration, Congress passed the **War Powers Act** to try to prevent future interventions overseas without specific congressional approval. Under the act, the president is required to consult with Congress before deploying American troops into hostile situations. Under certain conditions, the president is required to report to Congress within forty-eight hours of the deployment. A presidential report can trigger a sixty-day clock that requires congressional approval for any continued military involvement past the sixty-day window. If Congress does not give explicit approval within sixty days, the president then has thirty days to withdraw the troops. Under the act, the president could respond to an emergency such as rescuing endangered Americans but could not engage in a prolonged struggle without congressional approval.

War Powers Act
Passed by Congress in 1973; the president is limited in the deployment of troops overseas to a sixty-day period in peacetime (which can be extended for an extra thirty days to permit withdrawal) unless Congress explicitly gives its approval for a longer period.

The War Powers Act is controversial and has not been an effective restraint on presidential military adventurism. When first passed, President Nixon vetoed it, but Congress overrode the president's veto. Nixon then claimed the act was unconstitutional, but such a claim has yet to be formally tested. Only President Ford has reported military activity so as to trigger the War Powers Act's sixty-day clock. Subsequent presidents, including President George W. Bush, have reported military activities to Congress but have failed to do so in a way that triggers the provisions of the act. The fundamental weakness of the War Powers Act is the requirement that the president, not Congress, start the sixty-day clock.

THE MILITARY-INDUSTRIAL COMPLEX

Before World War II, the United States during peacetime maintained a small military force and required few weapons and supplies. After World War II, this changed as the United States became a global superpower with major responsibilities, a large military, and the capability to go to war at a moment's notice. Consequently, a close relationship developed between the Department of Defense and the industries that provided the immense quantities of weapons and supplies. This close relationship also created the danger that the military and defense industries would acquire, because of their shared interests, influence over foreign and military policy.

President Eisenhower, a former general who commanded allied forces during World War II, warned in his 1961 farewell address that the United States had developed a **military-industrial complex** that included the military and defense industries. This complex, Eisenhower feared, could become an increasingly dominant factor in U.S. politics with "potential for the disastrous rise of misplaced power."[37]

military-industrial complex
The grouping of the U.S. armed forces and defense industries.

The military-industrial complex has the potential to acquire power for several reasons. First, it has economic clout. During the Cold War, as much as 7 percent of the U.S. gross national product was spent on defense. Second, it has access to technical expertise and political information. Third, the military and defense industries share many interests. For example, both benefited economically when tensions between the United States and the Soviet Union increased. Fourth, personal and professional relationships between the military and defense industries are close, with many military officers on retirement going to work for defense industries. Finally, the military and defense industry officials work closely with legislators and their staffs. Planned or unplanned, undue influence can accompany close working relations. In 2005, for example, it became known that a number of defense contractors had paid Representative Randy "Duke" Cunningham (R–CA) in order to obtain lucrative defense and intelligence contracts from the federal government. The scandal generated interest in lobbying reform (see chapter 16) and new questions about the extent of the defense industry's influence on the legislative process. For his role in the scandal, Cunningham was sentenced to more than eight years in prison in 2006, the longest jail sentence ever given to a member of Congress.[38]

THE NEWS MEDIA

The news media are important to our understanding of foreign and defense policy because media reports provide information on government actions and policy initiatives. As discussed in greater depth in chapter 15, the media influence the course of foreign policy but do not determine it.

From World War II to the Vietnam War, the press tended to support the president in foreign and defense policy. As a rule, editors assumed that government statements were true and printed them as fact. In the mid-1960s, this changed as U.S. involvement in Vietnam grew and reporters based in Vietnam realized that the daily military briefings at times were untrue. This led many journalists to investigate government statements as opposed to accepting them. Some observers complain that since Vietnam and the Watergate scandal during Richard M. Nixon's presidency, the news media have become too intent on investigating and challenging the government, but others argue that freedom of the press is a crucial, constitutionally protected right in the United States and that investigative reporting is critical for a full accounting of government activities.

The U.S. military learned a hard lesson as coverage of the dismal course of the Vietnam War was relayed to Americans during nightly news broadcasts. As a result, contemporary military operations have been closely guarded and media access highly managed. The military has also grown more adept at controlling the agenda and using the media for strategic advantage.

During the 1991 Persian Gulf War, the military provided the media extensive access to marines in landing ships off the shore of Kuwait. The Pentagon hoped that Iraq would monitor the broadcasts and that the news coverage would convince Iraq to keep its best divisions on the Kuwaiti coast, awaiting the marines while the actual attack came far inland. The ruse worked. Iraq monitored the broadcasts and kept its best divisions on the coast, waiting for the landing that never came. The assault far inland went perfectly. The U.S. government had used the media to gain a military advantage.

More recently, in Iraq, the media broke the news about abuse of prisoners at Abu Ghraib prison by military personnel, launching a public outcry and government investigations. (See Analyzing Visuals: Abu Ghraib Prisoner Abuse.) Also, media outlets revealed that the Department of Defense paid Pentagon contractors to plant articles written by American soldiers in Iraqi publications, and in some instances Iraqi journalists were paid to provide positive coverage of conditions in the country and U.S. reconstruction efforts. The Department of Defense has since launched an investigation of this practice because it undermines the concept of a free press in Iraq and distorts the journalistic process into a propaganda effort.[39]

As discussed in chapter 15, the media are able to influence what topics the public thinks about with regard to foreign policy, although it does not necessarily influence people's opinions on those topics except in cases where people know little about the topic and have not already formed an opinion. Even in cases where the media raise public awareness about an issue that leads to a public outcry, the media do not determine policy. For example, despite extensive media coverage, ethnic cleansing in Bosnia and Kosovo went on for years before the United States responded militarily. Our opening vignette in chapter 6 describing government policies toward Darfur also underscores this view.

THE PUBLIC

Public opinion also influences U.S. foreign and defense policy. Some scholars argue that public opinion on issues of foreign and defense policy has two dimensions, militarism/nonmilitarism and isolationism/internationalism, creating four opinion groups.[40] Others say that a third dimension, unilateralism/multilateralism, is also important. The public is not equally divided among these opinion groups, but foreign and defense policy usually has to appeal across these dimensions to two or more groups to achieve widespread popular support. The presence of these dimensions also means that most foreign or defense policies have a core group of people in opposition.

As a rule, the American public is more interested in domestic affairs than foreign and defense policy (see Figure 19.4). Nevertheless, public opinion is often on the president's mind when creating or implementing foreign or defense policy. Public opinion rarely determines what an administration does, but it often influences the emphasis that an administration places on a foreign or defense initiative.

In the United States and other democracies, foreign policy or defense crises generally increase presidential popularity, but sometimes the increase is temporary. President George W. Bush's approval ratings skyrocketed from 51 percent to 86 percent

FIGURE 19.4 THE MOST IMPORTANT PROBLEM: DOMESTIC OR FOREIGN, 1947–2005

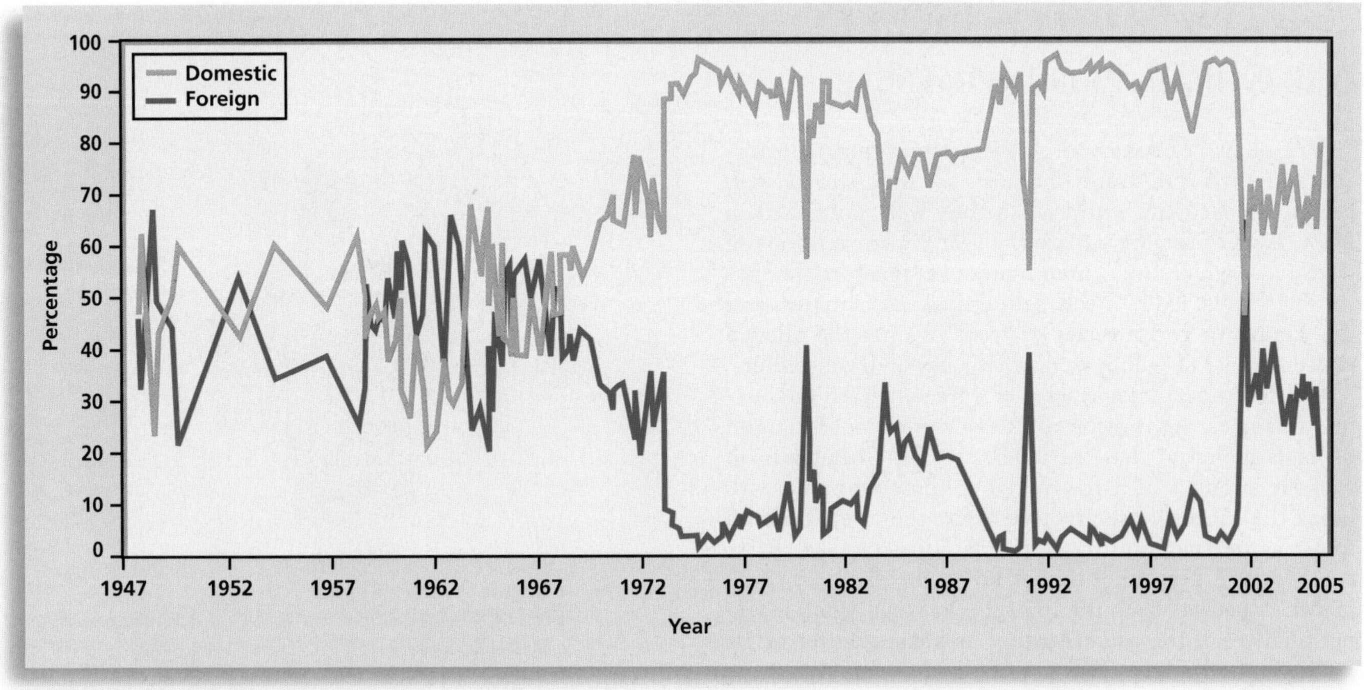

Note: Typical question: "What do you think is the most important problem facing this country today?"

Source: Harold W. Stanley and Richard G. Niemi, eds., *Vital Statistics on American Politics, 2005–2006* (Washington, DC: CQ Press, 2006). Reprinted by permission.

shortly after September 11, 2001—the largest "rally effect" ever reported by the Gallup polling organization. Bush's popularity remained high during the war in Afghanistan, fell somewhat at the beginning of the war against Iraq in 2003, and then declined significantly as the war in Iraq dragged on following the president's "Mission Accomplished" event on an aircraft carrier in May 2003. By 2006, Bush's job approval rating had fallen to a low of 31 percent. Experts agree that the president's precipitous fall in the polls was due in large part to difficulties in managing growing civil conflict in Iraq and the federal government's poor response to Hurricane Katrina. In addition to public opinion, the American public affects foreign and defense policy in elections and through public action.

Elections In the U.S. system, citizens exercise electoral control on presidential power in only the crudest of ways and only at set intervals: every fourth year during a presidential election. Even then, voters can express their approval or disapproval of an existing policy, but they can send no clear message for an alternative. For example, in 1952, Eisenhower was elected on a vague promise to end the Korean War. With such a vague promise, he was as free to end the war by using nuclear weapons as he was to end it by negotiating a truce. He chose the latter. In a similar vein, Nixon won the 1968 election in part because he claimed he had a "secret plan to end the war" in Vietnam.

Public Action Public action sometimes shapes foreign and defense policy, as in the widespread resistance to the draft during the Vietnam War. Growing public opposition to the war over time made it difficult to draft soldiers and reach the personnel levels that the military desired. Opposition to the draft also helped move the United States toward an all-volunteer military.

Analyzing Visuals

ABU GHRAIB PRISONER ABUSE

The photos of American soldiers demeaning, taunting, and torturing Iraqi detainees in the Abu Ghraib prison shocked the world when they were published in 2004. Acts of torture violate the Geneva conventions of warfare, to which the United States is a signatory. The resulting scandal led to investigations by both Congress and the Pentagon and a series of trials against the alleged abusers, most of whom were young, lower-level soldiers. Ultimately, nine Army reservists were convicted of abusing detainees; eight received prison sentences. Pentagon officials maintain that the abuse at Abu Ghraib prison was the product of a few rogue soldiers who chose to break the rules. Those involved argue they were ordered to use aggressive interrogation techniques by CIA interrogators and personnel higher up in the chain of command. What has been the impact—nationally and internationally—of the use of torture on suspected terrorists by the United States? Taking place at the same time were kidnappings and beheadings of nonmilitary Westerners by various insurgent groups in Iraq. Are there instances in which you would condone torture of an enemy? Why or why not?

Photo courtesy: The New Yorker Magazine

■ This detainee held at Abu Ghraib prison had wires attached to his body and was told that he would be electrocuted if he moved his arms or fell off the box. This particular photo was published worldwide and quickly became emblematic of the prisoner abuse scandal.

nongovernmental organization (NGO)
An organization that is not tied to a government.

Political activists also influence U.S. policy, especially when they join or work with **nongovernmental organizations (NGOs),** international organizations that have members from several countries who seek a set of objectives but are not formally connected to a government. Amnesty International, for example, monitors human rights violations worldwide and seeks to galvanize world opinion to influence the behaviors of the most offending governments.

Congress, the military-industrial complex, the news media, and the public influence U.S. foreign and defense policy, but only rarely are they as important as the executive branch and president. Combining the roles of head of government and head of state, with access to immense amounts of information and the ability to act, the president is unrivaled in power in foreign and military affairs. It is not surprising that Congress, the military-industrial complex, the news media, and the public look to the president as national leader.

Twenty-First-Century Challenges

COMPARATIVE
Comparing Foreign and Security Policies

AS PRESIDENT, GEORGE W. BUSH has grappled with many of the same issues as his two predecessors. When should the United States intervene militarily overseas? When should the United States act unilaterally and when should it act multilaterally? (See Global Perspective: U.S. Foreign Policy and the United Nations.) How should the United States handle China's emergence as a world power? What can the United States do to promote peace between Israelis and Palestinians? What is the best way to

Global Perspective

U.S. FOREIGN POLICY AND THE UNITED NATIONS

Most American presidents have had what amounts to a love-hate relationship with the United Nations (UN) since its creation following World War II. More than one U.S. administration has simultaneously been drawn to the UN and turned its back on it—in large part because of the different perspectives on U.S. foreign policy goals and the role of the UN. The United States sees itself as an international reformer and understands that the UN can be an important ally in democracy promotion. Viewed in this light, the United States and United Nations have similar policy goals: the Declaration of Independence, the U.S. Constitution, and the United Nations' Universal Declaration of Human Rights espouse a commitment to securing freedom, justice, and consensual government as positive human goods.

In March 2006, the Bush administration released its National Security Strategy in which it noted that the goal of U.S. foreign policy is to end tyranny and secure human dignity. To pursue these ends, the president advocated a policy of diplomacy, but with the option of using preemptive military force if diplomatic efforts failed. Similarly, at the end of the Cold War, the United Nations delivered its Agenda for Peace, a 1992 policy statement in which the United Nations declared that its post–Cold War mission is to help secure freedom, justice, and human rights. Though they have congruent goals, the United States and the United Nations are often at odds on how much of a say the United States, the world's one remaining superpower, should have in the UN's peacekeeping missions.

When the UN was founded, it was hoped that the permanent members of the Security Council—the United States, Great Britain, France, China, and the Soviet Union—would be able to work together to keep international peace. This hope was soon dashed by the outbreak of the Cold War. In the mid 1950s, in an effort to lessen the intensity of the Cold War in the developing world and to reestablish a role for itself in settling international disputes, the UN moved forward with the twin ideas of preventive diplomacy and peacekeeping. Before a conflict turned into open fighting, the UN would try to mediate and settle the dispute. If its efforts failed, it could send UN peacekeeping forces to stabilize a situation. The presence of UN peacekeepers, known as "blue helmets," was governed by three rules. First, UN peacekeepers must be invited into a country by its government. Second, they must be neutral in the conflict. Third, they must leave when asked. Both the United States and the Soviet Union were willing to accept the presence of UN peacekeepers as a second-best solution in a conflict. It meant that although neither side had won, neither side had lost to the other.

With the end of the Cold War, U.S.-Soviet rivalry for influence around the world diminished. Conflicts between states and within states, however, continued. Some states devolved into chaos, with citizens caught between warring factions. To address such crises, the UN reworked the ground rules of peacekeeping. Under it, UN blue helmets would not have to be invited into a country by the government or have to leave when asked. Once in a country, they are not expected to be neutral and stay above the conflict. They are there to help bring an end to hostilities and reestablish peace and order. Though the United States provides the bulk of financial and material support, American policy makers believe that other nations can make up for their relative lack of monetary support by providing the necessary troops—and this they in fact do.

As the table highlights, an inherent tension is built into UN peacekeeping efforts. The states that provide the most money for peacekeeping are not those that provide the most troops. Both sets of states believe they should have the major say in how these troops are used.

Top Five Providers of Assessed Contributions to UN Peacekeeping Budget as of January 1, 2006	
United States	27%
Japan	19%
Germany	9%
United Kingdom	7%
France	7%

Top Five Troop Contributors to UN Missions as of March 31, 2006	
Bangladesh	10,255 troops
Pakistan	9,638 troops
India	9,061 troops
Jordan	3,723 troops
Nepal	3,498 troops

Source: United Nations Department of Peacekeeping Operations Fact Sheet, http://www.un.org.

QUESTIONS

1. Who should have the most say in UN peacekeeping operations, those who contribute the money for them or those who provide the personnel? Why?
2. Under what circumstances is the United States likely to support UN interventions? Under what circumstances is the United States likely to pursue its own military solutions?

prevent nuclear proliferation and the attempts of rogue states like Iran to develop nuclear capabilities? As the international community has grown more interconnected over time, forging U.S. foreign and defense policies that both protect American interests and benefit those outside our borders has become more consequential and increasingly challenging.

IDENTIFYING POLICIES TO PURSUE IN THE NATIONAL INTEREST

Throughout the post–World War II era, most Americans agreed that it was in the United States' national interest to attain economic prosperity, defend the homeland, and protect American values. Further, with occasional exceptions such as the Vietnam War, they generally agreed with the policies put into place to attain these goals. In the post–Cold War era, prosperity, homeland defense, and protecting national interests remain key elements of U.S. foreign policy.

Before the 9/11 terrorist attacks, there was disagreement about what policies should be adopted in pursuit of these interests. Post-9/11 consensus regarding the need for strong homeland defense and for effective prosecution of the war on terrorism has largely eclipsed earlier debates about which foreign policy to prioritize. Nevertheless, the Bush administration's support of preemptive military action has generated debate about how to address emerging threats that include saber-rattling from North Korea, Iran's quest for enriched uranium, humanitarian crises such as the genocide in the Darfur region of Sudan, and the reemergence of the Taliban and its regime of violent intimidation in rural regions of Afghanistan. In addition, how involved should the United States be in trying to resolve the Israeli-Palestinian dispute or countering Iran's attempts at hegemony in the Middle East? These are a few of the questions that policy makers ponder as they debate which policies to implement in the national interest.

DECIDING WHEN TO INTERVENE OVERSEAS

Economic Sanctions and Cuba

Between the end of World War II and the demise of the Soviet Union, U.S. military intervention overseas usually was tied to the containment of communism. But, the demise of the Soviet Union eliminated this easy benchmark for deciding when to intervene. Following the Cold War, Presidents George Bush, Bill Clinton, and George W. Bush all faced the problem of when to use the U.S. military overseas, and none of these presidents hesitated to commit U.S. forces to overseas action.

In 2001, the decision to intervene was relatively easy in the case of Afghanistan, whose Taliban government supported and sheltered Osama bin Laden and al-Qaeda terrorist training camps. The Bush administration's preemptive defense strategy aroused more debate when the United States and several partner countries invaded Iraq in March 2003. This intervention was controversial with many U.S. allies and fueled criticism in the United States. Supporters of the U.S. action in Iraq argued that the display of American resolve would be an object lesson for other countries that were not behaving as the United States wanted. According to Richard Perle, a senior adviser to the Bush administration, "It's always been at the heart of the Bush Doctrine that a more robust policy would permit us to elicit greater cooperation from adversaries."[41] When Libyan leader Muammar Qaddafi indicated his willingness to abandon the development of weapons of mass destruction in late 2003, some viewed this as proof that the Bush Doctrine worked.

Critics, however, believe the Bush Doctrine is misguided for several reasons. First, they point to the frightening precedent of launching preemptive wars, and the dangerous lesson that might teach other countries (for instance, Pakistan and India) who fear and hate their adversaries. Second, they question the morality of invading another country based solely on what it *might* do. Senator Robert Byrd (D–WV), a staunch opponent of the Iraq War, referred to the U.S. action as "an unprovoked invasion of a sovereign nation."[42] Third, they question whether such an aggressive strategy might create lasting problems with allies (the governments of Canada, Mexico, France, Germany, and Russia, for example, were among those who opposed the invasion of Iraq), and a deepening hatred of the United States by adversaries. By attacking an Arab government in Iraq, was the United States creating, as Egyptian President Hosni Mubarak warned, many more Osama bin Ladens?

Beyond the war on terrorism, the same quandaries confront U.S. policy makers after the 9/11 attacks that they struggled with before. Should the United States intervene overseas to stop human rights violations? Should the United States intervene overseas to overthrow dictatorial governments or support democratic governments? Except for the Bush administration's strategic doctrine of preemptive defense, there are no easy guidelines, and decisions will undoubtedly be made on a case by case basis.

Photo courtesy: AFP/Getty Images

PROMOTING DEMOCRACY IN THE MIDDLE EAST

■ Although they disagreed with the United States about the U.S.-led invasion of Iraq, leaders of the G-8 countries meet regularly to discuss trade, world debt, terrorism, and other international issues. President Bush and Russian President Vladimir Putin share a private moment at a meeting held in St. Petersburg, Russia, in July 2006.

Promoting democracy in the Middle East is a difficult task that can have unexpected consequences. In a surprising outcome, the Islamic resistance movement Hamas won a decisive victory in Palestinian elections in early 2006. Long identified as a terrorist organization by the United States and the European Union because of its commitment to the destruction of Israel, Hamas gained control of the majority of seats in a democratically elected parliament. The United States has refused to do business with a Hamas-controlled government unless it renounces violence and agrees to recognize Israel as a legitimate nation.

Though the Hussein government in Iraq was easily toppled in 2003, the situation there is far less secure than initially predicted by the Bush administration. Many Iraqis, even those glad to be free of Hussein's tyrannical rule, are troubled by the lawlessness unleashed by Hussein's overthrow. Many resent the U.S. occupation and remain skeptical of the democratically elected government's ability to manage the growing violence. Some attacks appear to be the work of individuals who entered Iraq specifically to fight U.S. forces, but increasingly the violence has been characterized by sectarian warfare and the marks of civil war. While some parts of Iraq are successfully rebuilding and remain relatively calm thanks to help from the U.S.-led coalition, the overall situation remains enormously volatile. Oil pipelines are routinely sabotaged, Iraqi police forces often come under attack, and Iraqis face great uncertainty about the future.

The election of representatives to the National Assembly in 2005 gave some life to the democratic process despite the fact that the election was boycotted by most Sunni Iraqis. After the swearing in of the al-Maliki national government in May 2006, the United States began serious talks with Iraq officials about increasingly turning over control of security to Iraqi forces to decrease the violence by insurgents opposed to the presence of U.S. and other coalition forces. Whether the new Iraqi government has the capacity and the legitimacy to reverse the country's slide toward civil war is an open question.

Iraq remains an unfinished piece of business, as does Afghanistan. As Iraq struggles with continued insurgent and sectarian violence, Afghanistan is under assault from reorganized Taliban militias. It is unclear how long the United States will need to station troops or how many more Americans will die in the struggle to make Iraq and Afghanistan democratic havens in the Arab world. President Bush continues to defend the Iraq War despite the failure to locate weapons of mass destruction and the escalating costs (in dollars and human lives) associated with a continued U.S. military presence. It is unlikely that in the near future the United States will go to war with such a preemptive strike given the high cost and the difficulty of sustaining long-term military operations without international help.

TRANSNATIONAL THREATS TO PEACE

Terrorist organizations represent an ever evolving threat that is not easily contained or defeated with traditional military activities. Operating as nonstate actors, terrorists "blur the line between civilians and the military" and "confound war plans and diplomatic practices based upon enemies with fixed territory and political sovereignty."[43] Some groups, such as al-Qaeda, possess sophisticated economic, political, and military resources and are actively seeking to obtain weapons of mass destruction—nuclear, chemical, or biological weapons. Meeting these threats is a key element of the war on terrorism, which the Bush administration has repeatedly cautioned will be both long and costly.

Because of its reliance on computers, the United States is vulnerable to information warfare: attacks on information systems. These threats have led officials to warn about the danger of an "electronic Pearl Harbor" in which information warfare could bring some sectors of the United States to a halt. Indeed, computers and Web sites used by the U.S. government as well as businesses such as CNN, Home Depot, and Amazon.com often have come under attack from individual hackers.

How serious is the threat of information warfare? Government studies have highlighted the vulnerabilities of U.S. infrastructures, including communications and telephones, banking, power grids, water systems, fuel supply networks, and other systems that rely on computers.[44] Indeed, in a 1997 war game, government hackers penetrated computers on military bases, gained access to computers on a navy cruiser, could have closed down the U.S. electric power grid, and positioned themselves to disable the emergency 911 network.[45]

DRUG AND ENVIRONMENTAL PROBLEMS

During the late twentieth century, international efforts to address the illegal drug trade and the quality of the world's environment emerged as issues that challenged U.S. policy makers. The United States has a mixed record on both.

American policy makers use three tactics against illegal drugs. The first concentrates on reducing demand in the United States and rarely is involved with foreign and defense affairs. The second emphasizes stopping the flow of drugs into the United States. It includes seizing drug-running planes and ships and stopping drug smuggling at U.S. and foreign ports and airports. A third tactic is helping countries stop drug production within their borders. The United States provides economic and military help. For example, in 2000, the United States began a $1.3 billion anti-drug military aid program to Colombia. Although Colombia has a long way to go in eradicating cocaine production, U.S. assistance has helped to reduce coca production in Colombia, Peru, and Bolivia.

Since the U.S. overthrow of the Taliban regime in Afghanistan in 2001, opium production has surged. U.S. government officials have identified the resurgence in opium production and trafficking as one of the greatest challenges currently facing Afghanistan.[46] Today, Afghanistan is the world's largest producer of opium. According to the IMF, drug revenue accounts for roughly 60 percent of the country's economy and opium trafficking has contributed to government corruption at all levels. The United States has committed millions to counter-narcotics programs in Afghanistan and continues to work with the Afghani government to eradicate opium production.

Environmental issues such as global warming, ocean pollution, deforestation, desertification, and the loss of biodiversity moved onto the foreign policy agenda in the late twentieth century. At times, the United States has been a leader in international efforts to address environmental issues. When it became clear that the growth of the hole in the ozone layer was related to chlorofluorocarbon (CFC) use, the United States quickly supported and signed the 1987 Montreal Protocol to reduce the use of CFCs. In 1992, however, the United States opposed many environmental proposals at the UN Rio Earth Summit, arguing that they endangered economic growth. Eventually, the United States supported most of the measures, but only after they were weakened. Since the United States is responsible for approximately one-third of the pollutants that are thought to contribute to global warming, it is an especially important player in any international efforts to improve climate conditions. Under the Clinton administration, the United States supported a treaty passed at the 1997 Kyoto Conference on Global Climate Change designed to reduce the emission of greenhouse gases that contribute to global warming. However, many in Congress as well as U.S. business interests claimed it would be too costly to implement.[47]

As discussed in chapter 18, George W. Bush opposes the Kyoto agreements and withdrew U.S. support when he became president. As the European community has moved forward with the implementation of the Kyoto Protocol, the United States has continued to distance itself from international efforts to limit greenhouse gas emissions. In 2002, the European Union, Canada, and Japan ratified the Kyoto Protocol, but for its provisions to become internationally binding, participation by the United States or Russia was necessary. In 2004, Russia formally ratified the treaty. Because the United States is not a signatory to the treaty, the United States is not bound by its provisions. However, support among the American public and at the state level—including Bush's home state of Texas—for limiting carbon dioxide emissions and for renewable energy programs means that global climate issues are bound to remain a part of the political agenda for the foreseeable future.

CHOOSING BETWEEN UNILATERALISM AND MULTILATERALISM

Since the United States is economically and militarily the most powerful country in the world, why should it not do what it wants to do in foreign and defense affairs? Why should it limit its actions to only those with which other countries and international organizations like NATO and the UN agree? The easy response is that the United States should always act to protect its national interests, aligning its actions and policies with the UN and other international and nongovernmental organizations when possible, but not allowing those institutions to constrain U.S. actions and policies. On another level, the challenge revolves around the issue of what kind of world the United States wants to have develop. Should it be one where might determines right, or one where mutual agreement determines the course of action?

This is a difficult problem for policy makers. In the end, deciding whether unilateralism or multilateralism will predominate is a political issue. (See American Values/American Voices: Multilateralism and Unilaterism in American Foreign Policy.) Throughout this chapter, we have seen cases where the United States acted only in the presence of international support and agreement and other cases, most notably the war in Iraq, where the United States chose to undertake military action despite the opposition of key allies. The challenge is to make U.S. interests and the interests of the global community coincide, and when this is impossible, to promote U.S. interests without damaging the United States' status in the global community.

In the twenty-first century, the United States remains the world's only superpower, but it is vulnerable to terrorist attack even as it confronts other foreign and

VIDEO ROUNDTABLE

Unilateralism and Multilateralism

American Values/American Voices

MULTILATERALISM AND UNILATERISM IN AMERICAN FOREIGN POLICY

Since its creation, the United States has considered itself an exceptional nation. Established against great odds, to this day the nation represents a beacon of hope for the oppressed, disenfranchised, or those people simply searching for a better life. The fact that the nation currently reigns as the world's only superpower adds to America's sense of exceptionalism. The conduct of American foreign policy is rooted in the belief that the United States represents a role model for the rest of the world and its values and ideals are universal and worthy of emulation by others. President Ronald Reagan often referred to America as "the shining house on the hill"—an example of what other countries should strive to achieve.

The fall of the Soviet Union and the end of communism in Eastern Europe fueled numerous foreign policies designed to advance democracy and democratic principles abroad. President Bill Clinton emphasized "enlargement of democracy" through the promotion, militarily and economically, of democratic governments around the world. His successor, President George W. Bush, identified "the global expansion of democracy" as a key pillar of American security. In the context of Afghanistan and Iraq, President Bush has vigorously pursued the exportation of democracy as a central component of American foreign policy.

While the presidencies of George Bush, Bill Clinton, and George W. Bush all share an interest in the global promotion of democratic values, compared to his father's presidency and that of Clinton, George W. Bush has relied to a much greater degree on unilateral action to accomplish his foreign policy goals—including the spread of democracy to the Middle East. Whereas his two predecessors emphasized a multilateral approach—what one scholar has called "the preference for seeking international consensus and multilateral implementation of solutions to world problems"—George W. Bush has often pursued a strategy of unilateralism when dealing with global issues—"the preference for seeking *American* solutions to international problems, even if these are at odds with international norms."[a]

The unilateralist approach is evident in the Bush administration's 2001 renunciation of the Kyoto Protocol, an international agreement that commits industrialized nations to reductions in greenhouse emissions; its 2002 refusal to participate in the International Criminal Court despite legal obligations arising from President Clinton's signature on the treaty that established the court; and the 2003 decision to withdraw a resolution requesting United Nations approval for U.S. military action against Saddam Hussein because of international opposition to an American invasion of Iraq. In an address to the nation on March 19, 2003, when preemptive U.S. military action commenced against Iraq, President Bush announced that the United States was acting unilaterally "to disarm Iraq, to free its people, and to defend the world from grave danger." In response to criticism of his go-it-alone approach, Bush declared in his 2004 State of the Union Address that the United States would never ask the international community for a "permission slip" to act in defense of national interests.

Proponents of the unilateralist approach argue that when American interests collide with those of the international community, the United States must be willing to engage in unilateral action in order to protect vital national interests—regardless of the level of opposition to those activities by other countries. Unilateralism provides the president with a great deal more flexibility in crafting and executing foreign policy than does a multilateral approach and is certainly an important option during times of a national emergency. Multilateralism requires a commitment to a process of give-and-take with regard to international consensus building and awareness that the United States will not always be able to dictate the rules of play. Critics of the Bush administration's unilateralist tendencies argue that preemptive military action in Iraq has done little to dampen the nuclear ambitions of Iran and North Korea. During his second administration, Bush has begun to move away from unilateralism and has made diplomatic overtures to Iran and emphasized a multilateral approach to dealing with North Korea's missile tests.

QUESTIONS

1. Under what conditions is a unilateralist approach to the conduct of foreign policy more suitable than a multilateral solution? When might multilateralism be a more suitable approach?
2. Does the United States have a special responsibility to lead the rest of the world, or is it simply one of several important world leaders such as China, Russia, and the European community?

[a]Donald M. Snow, *United States Foreign Policy: Politics Beyond the Water's Edge,* 3rd ed. (Belmont, CA: Thomson Wadsworth, 2005).

defense policy challenges. How the United States manages homeland defense, the war on terrorism, and appropriate responses to future international crises is the greatest challenge for twenty-first-century U.S. policy makers. Lessons learned from the war in Iraq will likely have a profound influence over how U.S. foreign policy evolves. Notably, most Americans still accept internationalism, multilateralism, moralism, and pragmatism as the basis for U.S. foreign and defense policy. Most also recognize that the United States faces foreign policy and defense challenges in addition to terrorism.

Summary

FOREIGN AND DEFENSE POLICY are important functions of the U.S. government. This chapter stressed the evolution of foreign and defense policy over time, the role of public and private agencies, and the challenges that American policy makers face in the twenty-first century. In examining these issues, this chapter made the following points:

1. **The Development of U.S. Foreign and Defense Policy**
   From the earliest days, isolationism, unilateralism, moralism, and pragmatism were central elements of U.S. foreign and defense policy. Foreign and defense policy played a minor role in American politics for most of the nation's first century. As U.S. economic interests expanded, the United States intervened more and more overseas, especially in Latin America. After a delayed entry into World War I, America retreated into isolation but was unable to avoid World War II.

2. **The United States as a World Power**
   After World War II, foreign and defense policy often dominated the American political agenda, and defense spending became one of the biggest items in the national budget. Foreign and defense policy became major concerns, especially issues such as U.S.-Soviet relations, nuclear weapons, and the Vietnam War. Despite debate, an underlying consensus existed that American policy should focus on containing the Soviet Union. After the Soviet Union collapsed, no immediate consensus emerged on the direction of U.S. foreign policy. The events of terrorist attacks that took place on September 11, 2001, caused the United States to focus much of its energy on the war against terrorism.

3. **Foreign and Defense Policy Decision Making**
   Balances found in other parts of the U.S. political system are generally absent in foreign and defense policy. The executive branch of government dominates foreign and defense policy, with the Departments of State and Defense being particularly important. Within the executive branch, the president is preeminent. Until the War Powers Act, few constraints were placed on presidential prerogatives in foreign and defense policy. Presidential power has experienced a post-9/11 resurgence as concerns about national security have often eclipsed executive accountability and the protection of civil liberties. Institutions outside the executive also play a role in U.S. foreign and defense policy. These include Congress, the military-industrial complex, the news media, and the public.

4. **Twenty-First-Century Challenges**
   The United States faces major challenges in foreign and defense policy during the twenty-first century, especially homeland defense and the global war on terrorism. Other challenges include identifying other national interests, balancing foreign and domestic issues, deciding when to intervene overseas, how best to promote democratic values globally, meeting the threats of transnational terrorism, addressing drug and environmental problems, and choosing between unilateral and multilateral action. How well the United States succeeds in meeting these challenges will go a long way toward determining how the country fares in the twenty-first century.

KEY TERMS

al-Qaeda, p. 708
Bush Doctrine, p. 710
Bretton Woods Agreement, p. 701
Carter Doctrine, p. 706
Central Intelligence Agency (CIA), p. 716
collective security, p. 699
containment, p. 702
Cuban Missile Crisis, p. 704
Department of Defense, p. 715
Department of Homeland Security, p. 717
Department of State, p. 715
détente, p. 705
Embargo Act, p. 697
engagement, p. 708
enlargement, p. 708
General Agreement on Tariffs and Trade (GATT), p. 701
human rights, p. 706
international governmental organization (IGO), p. 701

SELECTED READINGS

Allison, Graham F., and Philip Zelikow. *Essence of Decision: Explaining the Cuban Missile Crisis,* 2nd ed. New York: Pearson, 1999.

Ambrose, Stephen, and Douglas Brinkley (contributor). *Rise to Globalism: American Foreign Policy Since 1938,* 8th ed. New York: Penguin, 1997.

Axelrod, Alan. *American Treaties and Alliances.* Washington, DC: CQ Press, 2000.

Bacevich, Andrew J. *American Empire: The Realities and Consequences of U.S. Diplomacy.* Cambridge: Harvard University Press, 2002.

Boot, Max. *The Savage Wars of Peace: Small Wars and the Rise of American Power.* New York: Basic Books, 2002.

Byman, Daniel, and Matthew C. Waxman. *The Dynamics of Coercion: American Foreign Policy and the Limits of Military Might.* Cambridge: Cambridge University Press, 2002.

Clarke, Richard A. *Against All Enemies: Inside America's War on Terror.* New York: Free Press, 2004.

Eckes, Alan E., Jr. *Opening America's Markets: U.S. Foreign Trade Policy Since 1776.* Chapel Hill: University of North Carolina Press, 1995.

Ervin, Clark Kent. *Open Target: Where America Is Vulnerable to Attack.* New York: Palgrave Macmillan, 2006.

Forsythe, David P., Patrice C. McMahon, and Andrew Wedeman. *American Foreign Policy in a Globalized World.* New York: Routledge, 2006.

Goldstein, Joshua S. *International Relations,* 5th ed. New York: Longman, 2005.

Halberstam, David. *War in a Time of Peace: Bush, Clinton, and the Generals.* New York: Scribner's, 2001.

Hook, Steven W. *U.S. Foreign Policy: The Paradox of World Power.* Washington, DC: CQ Press, 2005.

Howard, Russell D., James J. F. Forest, and Joanne C. Moore. *Homeland Security and Terrorism: Readings and Interpretations.* New York: McGraw-Hill, 2006.

Huntington, Samuel P. *The Clash of Civilizations and the Remaking of World Order.* New York: Touchstone, 1998.

Johnson, Loch K. *Seven Sins of American Foreign Policy.* New York: Longman, 2007.

Kennan, George F. *American Diplomacy, 1900–1950.* Chicago: University of Chicago Press, 1951.

Kissinger, Henry. *Diplomacy.* New York: Touchstone, 1995.

Lowenthal, Mark M. *Intelligence: From Secrets to Policy,* 2nd ed. Washington, DC: CQ Press, 2003.

Mann, Robert A. *A Grand Delusion: America's Descent into Vietnam.* New York: Basic Books, 2001.

Nye, Joseph S., Jr. *The Paradox of American Power: Why the World's Only Superpower Can't Go It Alone.* New York: Oxford University Press, 2002.

Papp, Daniel S. *Contemporary International Relations,* 6th ed. New York: Longman, 2002.

———. *The Impact of September 11 on Contemporary International Relations.* New York: Longman, 2003.

Paterson, Thomas G., et al. *American Foreign Relations: A History to 1920,* 6th ed. Boston: Houghton Mifflin, 2005.

Talbott, Strobe, and Nayan Chanda, eds. *The Age of Terror: America and the World After September 11.* New York: Basic Books, 2002.

Veseth, Michael. *Globaloney: Unraveling the Myths of Globalization.* Lanham, MD: Rowman and Littlefield, 2005.

WEB EXPLORATIONS

To see the reach and worldwide involvement of the United Nations, go to
http://www.unsystem.org

To learn about the specific workings of the IMF and World Bank, go to
http://www.imf.org and http://www.worldbank.org

To learn more about U.S. military operations around the globe, go to
http://www.defenselink.mil

To learn more about the CIA and the larger intelligence community, go to
http://www.cia.gov

To learn more about key congressional committees in military and foreign affairs, go to

http://www.house.gov/hasc

http://www.senate.gov/~armed_services/

http://www.house.gov/international_relations

http://www.senate.gov/~foreign

To visit the official site of the International Criminal Court, go to

http://www.icc-cpi.int

To learn more about the Kyoto Protocol and its implementation, go to

http://unfccc.int

To learn more about strategic security, nuclear nonproliferation, and weapons of mass destruction, among other national security issues, visit the Federation of American Scientists at

http://www.fas.org

The Declaration of Independence

In Congress, July 4, 1776
The Unanimous Declaration of the Thirteen United States of America

When in the Course of human events it becomes necessary for one people to dissolve the political bands which have connected them with another, and to assume, among the powers of the earth, the separate and equal station to which the Laws of Nature and of Nature's God entitle them, a decent respect to the opinions of mankind requires that they should declare the causes which impel them to the separation.

We hold these truths to be self-evident, that all men are created equal, that they are endowed by their Creator with certain unalienable Rights, that among these are Life, Liberty and the pursuit of Happiness. That to secure these rights, Governments are instituted among Men, deriving their just powers from the consent of the governed. That whenever any Form of Government becomes destructive of these ends, it is the Right of the People to alter or to abolish it, and to institute new Government, laying its foundation on such principles and organizing its powers in such form, as to them shall seem most likely to effect their Safety and Happiness. Prudence, indeed, will dictate that Governments long established should not be changed for light and transient causes; and accordingly all experience hath shewn that mankind are more disposed to suffer, while evils are sufferable, than to right themselves by abolishing the forms to which they are accustomed. But when a long train of abuses and usurpations, pursuing invariably the same Object evinces a design to reduce them under absolute Despotism, it is their right, it is their duty, to throw off such Government, and to provide new Guards for their future security.—Such has been the patient sufferance of these Colonies; and such is now the necessity which constrains them to alter their former Systems of Government. The history of the present King of Great Britain is a history of repeated injuries and usurpations, all having in direct object the establishment of an absolute Tyranny over these States. To prove this, let Facts be submitted to a candid world.

He has refused his Assent to Laws, the most wholesome and necessary for the public good.

He has forbidden his Governors to pass Laws of immediate and pressing importance, unless suspended in their operation till his Assent should be obtained; and when so suspended, he has utterly neglected to attend to them.

He has refused to pass other Laws for the accommodation of large districts of people, unless those people would relinquish the right of Representation in the Legislature, a right inestimable to them and formidable to tyrants only.

He has called together legislative bodies at places unusual, uncomfortable, and distant from the depository of their Public Records, for the sole purpose of fatiguing them into compliance with his measures.

He has dissolved Representative Houses repeatedly, for opposing with manly firmness his invasions on the rights of the people.

He has refused for a long time, after such dissolutions, to cause others to be elected; whereby the Legislative Powers, incapable of Annihilation, have returned to the People at large for their exercise, the State remaining in the mean time exposed to all the dangers of invasion from without, and convulsions within.

He has endeavored to prevent the population of these States; for that purpose obstructing the Laws of Naturalization of Foreigners; refusing to pass others to encourage their migration hither, and raising the conditions of new Appropriations of Lands.

He has obstructed the Administration of Justice, by refusing his Assent to Laws for establishing Judiciary powers.

He has made Judges dependent on his Will alone, for the tenure of their offices, and the amount and payment of their salaries.

He has erected a multitude of New Offices, and sent hither swarms of Officers to harass our people, and eat out their substance.

He has kept among us, in times of peace, Standing Armies without the Consent of our legislatures.

He has affected to render the Military independent of and superior to the Civil power.

He has combined with others to subject us to a jurisdiction foreign to our constitution, and unacknowledged by our laws, giving his Assent to their Acts of pretended Legislation:

For quartering large bodies of armed troops among us:

For protecting them, by a mock Trial, from punishment for any Murders which they should commit on the Inhabitants of these States:

For cutting off our Trade with all parts of the world:

For imposing Taxes on us without our Consent:

For depriving us in many cases, of the benefits of Trial by Jury:

For transporting us beyond Seas to be tried for pretended offences:

For abolishing the free System of English Laws in a neighboring Province, establishing therein an Arbitrary government, and enlarging its Boundaries so as to render it at once an example and fit instrument for introducing the same absolute rule into these Colonies:

For taking away our Charters, abolishing our most valuable Laws, and altering fundamentally the Forms of our Governments:

For suspending our own Legislatures, and declaring themselves invested with power to legislate for us in all cases whatsoever.

He has abdicated Government here, by declaring us out of his Protection and waging War against us.

He has plundered our seas, ravaged our Coasts, burnt out towns, and destroyed the lives of our people.

He is at this time transporting large Armies of foreign Mercenaries to compleat the works of death, desolation and tyranny, already begun with circumstances of Cruelty and perfidy scarcely paralleled in the most barbarous ages, and totally unworthy the Head of a civilized nation.

He has constrained our fellow Citizens taken Captive on the high Seas to bear Arms against their Country, to become the executioners of their friends and Brethren, or to fall themselves by their Hands.

He has excited domestic insurrections amongst us, and has endeavored to bring on the inhabitants of our frontiers, the merciless Indian Savages, whose known rule of warfare, is an undistinguished destruction of all ages, sexes and conditions.

In every stage of these Oppressions We have Petitioned for Redress in the most humble terms: Our repeated Petitions have been answered only by repeated injury: A Prince, whose character is thus marked by every act which may define a Tyrant, is unfit to be the ruler of a free people.

Nor have We been wanting in attention to our British brethren. We have warned them from time to time of attempts by their legislature to extend an unwarrantable jurisdiction over us. We have reminded them of the circumstances of our emigration and settlement here. We have appealed to their native justice and magnanimity; and we have conjured them by the ties of our common kindred to disavow these usurpations, which would inevitably interrupt our connections and correspondence. They too have been deaf to the voice of justice and consanguinity. We must, therefore, acquiesce in the necessity, which denounces our Separation, and hold them, as we hold the rest of mankind, Enemies in War, in Peace Friends.

We, therefore, the Representatives of the United States of America, in General Congress, Assembled, appealing to the Supreme Judge of the world for the rectitude of our intentions, do, in the Name, and by Authority of the good People of these Colonies, solemnly publish and declare, That these United Colonies are, and of Right ought to be Free and Independent States; that they are Absolved from all Allegiance to the British Crown, and that all political connection between them and the State of Great Britain, is and ought to be totally dissolved: and that as Free and Independent States, they have full power to levy War, conclude Peace, contract Alliances, establish Commerce, and to do all other Acts and Things which Independent States may of right do. And for the support of this Declaration, with a firm reliance on the protection of Divine Providence, we mutually pledge to each other our Lives, our Fortunes and our sacred Honor.

JOHN HANCOCK

NEW HAMPSHIRE
Josiah Bartlett
William Whipple
Matthew Thornton

MASSACHUSETTS BAY
Samuel Adams
John Adams
Robert Treat Paine
Elbridge Gerry

RHODE ISLAND
Stephen Hopkins
William Ellery

CONNECTICUT
Roger Sherman
Samuel Huntington
William Williams
Oliver Wolcott

NEW YORK
William Floyd
Philip Livingston
Francis Lewis
Lewis Morris

NEW JERSEY
Richard Stockton
John Witherspoon
Francis Hopkinson
John Hart
Abraham Clark

PENNSYLVANIA
Robert Morris
Benjamin Rush
Benjamin Franklin
John Morton
George Clymer
James Smith
George Taylor
James Wilson
George Ross

DELAWARE
Caesar Rodney
George Read
Thomas McKean

MARYLAND
Samuel Chase
William Paca
Thomas Stone
Charles Carroll

VIRGINIA
George Wythe
Richard Henry Lee
Thomas Jefferson
Benjamin Harrison
Thomas Nelson, Jr.
Francis Lightfoot Lee
Carter Braxton

NORTH CAROLINA
William Hooper
Joseph Hewes
John Penn

SOUTH CAROLINA
Edward Rutledge
Thomas Heyward, Jr.
Thomas Lynch, Jr.
Arthur Middleton

GEORGIA
Button Gwinnett
Lyman Hall
George Walton

Federalist No. 10

November 22, 1787
James Madison

TO THE PEOPLE OF THE STATE OF NEW YORK.

Among the numerous advantages promised by a well constructed Union, none deserves to be more accurately developed than its tendency to break and control the violence of faction. The friend of popular governments, never finds himself so much alarmed for their character and fate, as when he contemplates their propensity to this dangerous vice. He will not fail therefore to set a due value on any plan which, without violating the principles to which he is attached, provides a proper cure for it. The instability, injustice and confusion introduced into the public councils, have in truth been the mortal diseases under which popular governments have every where perished; as they continue to be the favorite and fruitful topics from which the adversaries to liberty derive their most specious declamations. The valuable improvements made by the American Constitutions on the popular models, both ancient and modern, cannot certainly be too much admired; but it would be an unwarrantable partiality, to contend that they have as effectually obviated the danger on this side as was wished and expected. Complaints are every where heard from our most considerate and virtuous citizens, equally the friends of public and private faith, and of public and personal liberty; that our governments are too unstable; that the public good is disregarded in the conflicts of rival parties; and that measures are too often decided, not according to the rules of justice, and the rights of the minor party; but by the superior force of an interested and over-bearing majority. However anxiously we may wish that these complaints had no foundation, the evidence of known facts will not permit us to deny that they are in some degree true. It will be found indeed, on a candid review of our situation, that some of the distresses under which we labor, have been erroneously charged on the operation of our governments; but it will be found, at the same time, that other causes will not alone account for many of our heaviest misfortunes; and particularly, for that prevailing and increasing distrust of public engagements, and alarm for private rights, which are echoed from one end of the continent to the other. These must be chiefly, if not wholly, effects of the unsteadiness and injustice, with which a factious spirit has tainted our public administrations.

By a faction I understand a number of citizens, whether amounting to a majority or minority of the whole, who are united and actuated by some common impulse of passion, or of interest, adverse to the rights of other citizens, or to the permanent and aggregate interests of the community.

There are two methods of curing the mischiefs of faction: the one, by removing its causes; the other, by controlling its effects.

There are again two methods of removing the causes of faction: the one by destroying the liberty which is essential to its existence; the other, by giving to every citizen the same opinions, the same passions, and the same interests.

It could never be more truly said than of the first remedy, that it is worse than the disease. Liberty is to faction, what air is to fire, an aliment without which it instantly expires. But it could not be a less folly to abolish liberty, which is essential to political life, because it nourishes faction, than it would be to wish the annihilation of air, which is essential to animal life, because it imparts to fire its destructive agency.

The second expedient is as impracticable, as the first would be unwise. As long as the reason of man continues fallible, and he is at liberty to exercise it, different opinions will be formed. As long as the connection subsists between his reason and his self-love, his opinions and his passions will have a reciprocal influence on each other; and the former will be objects to which the latter will attach themselves. The diversity in the faculties of men from which the rights of property originate, is not less an insuperable obstacle to a uniformity of interests. The protection of these faculties is the first object of Government. From the protection of different and unequal faculties of acquiring property, the possession of different degrees and kinds of property immediately results: and from the influence of these on the sentiments and views of the respective proprietors, ensues a division of the society into different interests and parties.

The latent causes of faction are thus sown in the nature of man; and we see them everywhere brought into different degrees of activity, according to the different circumstances of civil society. A zeal for different opinions concerning religion, concerning Government and many other points, as well of speculation as of practice; an attachment to different leaders ambitiously contending for pre-eminence and power; or to persons of other descriptions whose fortunes have been interesting to the human passions, have in turn divided mankind into parties, inflamed them with mutual animosity, and rendered them much more disposed to vex and oppress each other, than to cooperate for their common good. So strong is this propensity of mankind to fall into mutual animosities, that where no substantial occasion presents itself, the most frivolous and fanciful distinctions have been sufficient to kindle their unfriendly passions, and excite their most violent conflicts. But the most common and durable source of factions, has been the various and unequal distribution of property. Those who hold, and those who are without property, have ever formed distinct interests in society. Those who are creditors, and those who are debtors, fall under a like discrimination. A landed interest, a manufacturing interest, a mercantile interest, a monied interest, with many lesser interests, grow up of necessity in civilized nations, and divide them into different classes, actuated by different sentiments and views. The regulation of these various and interfering interests forms the principal task of modern Legislation, and involves the spirit of party and faction in the necessary and ordinary operations of Government.

No man is allowed to be a judge in his own cause; because his interest would certainly bias his judgment, and, not improbably, corrupt his integrity. With equal, nay with greater reason, a body of men, are unfit to be both judges and parties, at the same time; yet, what are many of the most important acts of legislation, but so many judicial determinations, not indeed concerning the rights of single persons, but concerning the rights of large bodies of citizens, and what are the different classes of legislators, but advocates and parties to the causes which they determine? Is a law proposed concerning private debts? It is a question to which the creditors are parties on one side, and the debtors on the other. Justice ought to hold the balance between them. Yet the parties are and must be themselves the judges; and the most numerous party, or, in other words, the most powerful faction must be expected to prevail. Shall domestic manufactures be encouraged, and in what degree, by restrictions on foreign manufactures? are questions which would be differently decided by the landed and the manufacturing classes; and probably by neither, with a sole regard to justice and the public good. The apportionment of taxes on the various descriptions of property, is an act which seems to require the most exact impartiality; yet, there is perhaps no legislative act in which greater opportunity and temptation are given to a predominant party, to trample on the rules of justice. Every shilling with which they over-burden the inferior number, is a shilling saved to their own pockets.

It is in vain to say, that enlightened statesmen will be able to adjust these clashing interests, and render them all subservient to the public good. Enlightened statesmen will not always be at the helm: Nor, in many cases, can such an adjustment be made at all, without taking into view indirect and remote considerations, which will rarely prevail over the immediate interest which one party may find in disregarding the rights of another, or the good of the whole.

The inference to which we are brought, is, that the *causes* of faction cannot be removed; and that relief is only to be sought in the means of controlling its *effects*.

If a faction consists of less than a majority, relief is supplied by the republican principle, which enables the majority to defeat its sinister views by regular vote: It may clog the administration, it may convulse the society; but it will be unable to execute and mask its violence under the forms of the Constitution. When a majority is included in a faction, the form of popular government on the other hand enables it to sacrifice to its ruling passion or interest, both the public good and the rights of other citizens. To secure the public good, and private

rights, against the danger of such a faction, and at the same time to preserve the spirit and the form of popular government, is then the great object to which our enquiries are directed: Let me add that it is the great desideratum, by which alone this form of government can be rescued from the opprobrium under which it has so long labored, and be recommended to the esteem and adoption of mankind.

By what means is this object attainable? Evidently by one of two only. Either the existence of the same passion or interest in a majority at the same time, must be prevented; or the majority, having such co-existent passion or interest, must be rendered, by their number and local situation, unable to concert and carry into effect schemes of oppression. If the impulse and the opportunity be suffered to coincide, we well know that neither moral nor religious motives can be relied on as an adequate control. They are not found to be such on the injustice and violence of individuals, and lose their efficacy in proportion to the number combined together; that is, in proportion as their efficacy becomes needful.

From this view of the subject, it may be concluded, that a pure Democracy, by which I mean, a Society, consisting of a small number of citizens, who assemble and administer the Government in person, can admit of no cure for the mischiefs of faction. A common passion or interest will, in almost every case, be felt by a majority of the whole; a communication and concert results from the form of Government itself; and there is nothing to check the inducements to sacrifice the weaker party, or an obnoxious individual. Hence it is, that such Democracies have ever been spectacles of turbulence and contention; have ever been found incompatible with personal security, or the rights of property; and have in general been as short in their lives, as they have been violent in their deaths. Theoretic politicians, who have patronized this species of Government, have erroneously supposed, that by reducing mankind to a perfect equality in their political rights, they would, at the same time, be perfectly equalized and assimilated in their possessions, their opinions, and their passions.

A republic, by which I mean a government in which the scheme of representation takes place, opens a different prospect, and promises the cure for which we are seeking. Let us examine the points in which it varies from pure democracy, and we shall comprehend both the nature of the cure and the efficacy which it must derive from the union.

The two great points of difference, between a democracy and a republic, are, first, the delegation of the government, in the latter, to a small number of citizens, elected by the rest; secondly, the greater number of citizens, and greater sphere of country, over which the latter may be extended.

The effect of the first difference is, on the one hand, to refine and enlarge the public views, by passing them through the medium of a chosen body of citizens, whose wisdom may best discern the true interest of their country, and whose patriotism and love of justice, will be least likely to sacrifice it to temporary or partial considerations. Under such a regulation, it may well happen, that the public voice, pronounced by the representatives of the people, will be more consonant to the public good, than if pronounced by the people themselves, convened for the purpose. On the other hand the effect may be inverted. Men of factious tempers, of local prejudices, or of sinister designs, may by intrigue, by corruption, or by other means, first obtain the suffrages, and then betray the interest of the people. The question resulting is, whether small or extensive republics are most favorable to the election of proper guardians of the public weal, and it is clearly decided in favor of the latter by two obvious considerations.

In the first place, it is to be remarked that, however small the republic may be, the representatives must be raised to a certain number, in order to guard against the cabals of a few; and that however large it may be, they must be limited to a certain number, in order to guard against the confusion of a multitude. Hence, the number of representatives in the two cases not being in proportion to that of the constituents, and being proportionally greatest in the small republic, it follows, that if the proportion of fit characters be not less in the large than in the small republic, the former will present a greater option, and consequently a greater probability of a fit choice.

In the next place, as each Representative will be chosen by a greater number of citizens in the large than in the small Republic, it will be more difficult for unworthy candidates to practise with success the vicious arts, by which elections are too often carried; and the suffrages of the people being more free, will be more likely to center on men who possess the most attractive merit, and the most diffusive and established characters.

It must be confessed, that in this, as in most other cases, there is a mean, on both sides of which inconveniences will be found to lie. By enlarging too much the number of electors, you render the representatives too little acquainted with all their local circumstances and lesser interests; as by reducing it too much, you render him unduly attached to these, and too little fit to comprehend and pursue great and national objects. The Federal Constitution forms a happy combination in this respect; the great and aggregate interests being referred to the national, the local and particular, to the state legislatures.

The other point of difference is, the greater number of citizens and extent of territory which may be brought within the compass of Republican, than of Democratic Government; and it is this circumstance principally which renders factious combinations less to be dreaded in the former, than in the latter. The smaller the society, the fewer probably will be the distinct parties and interests composing it; the fewer the distinct parties and interests, the more frequently will a majority be found of the same party; and the smaller the number of individuals composing a majority, and the smaller the compass within which they are placed, the more easily will they concert and execute their plans of oppression. Extend the sphere, and you take in a greater variety of parties and interests; you make it less probable that a majority of the whole will have a common motive to invade the rights of other citizens; or if such a common motive exists, it will be more difficult for all who feel it to discover their own strength, and to act in unison with each other. Besides other impediments, it may be remarked, that where there is a consciousness of unjust or dishonorable purposes, communication is always checked by distrust, in proportion to the number whose concurrence is necessary.

Hence it clearly appears, that the same advantage, which a Republic has over a Democracy, in controlling the effects of faction, is enjoyed by a large over a small Republic—is enjoyed by the Union over the States composing it. Does this advantage consist in the substitution of Representatives, whose enlightened views and virtuous sentiments render them superior to local prejudices, and to schemes of injustice? It will not be denied, that the Representation of the Union will be most likely to possess these requisite endowments. Does it consist in the greater security afforded by a greater variety of parties, against the event of any one party being able to outnumber and oppress the rest? In an equal degree does the increased variety of parties, comprised within the Union, increase this security? Does it, in fine, consist in the greater obstacles opposed to the concert and accomplishment of the secret wishes of an unjust and interested majority? Here, again, the extent of the Union gives it the most palpable advantage.

The influence of factious leaders may kindle a flame within their particular States, but will be unable to spread a general conflagration through the other States: a religious sect, may degenerate into a political faction in a part of the Confederacy but the variety of sects dispersed over the entire face of it, must secure the national Councils against any danger from that source: a rage for paper money, for an abolition of debts, for an equal division of property, or for any other improper or wicked project, will be less apt to pervade the whole body of the Union, than a particular member of it; in the same proportion as such a malady is more likely to taint a particular county or district, than an entire State.

In the extent and proper structure of the Union, therefore, we behold a Republican remedy for the diseases most incident to Republican Government. And according to the degree of pleasure and pride, we feel in being Republicans, ought to be our zeal in cherishing the spirit, and supporting the character of Federalists.

PUBLIUS

Federalist No. 51

February 6, 1788
James Madison

TO THE PEOPLE OF THE STATE OF NEW YORK.

To what expedient then shall we finally resort for maintaining in practice the necessary partition of power among the several departments, as laid down in the constitution? The only answer that can be given is, that as all these exterior provisions are found to be inadequate, the defect must be supplied, by so contriving the interior structure of the government, as that its several constituent parts may, by their mutual relations, be the means of keeping each other in their proper places. Without presuming to undertake a full development of this important idea, I will hazard a few general observations, which may perhaps place it in a clearer light, and enable us to form a more correct judgment of the principles and structure of the government planned by the convention.

In order to lay a due foundation for that separate and distinct exercise of the different powers of government, which to a certain extent, is admitted on all hands to be essential to the preservation of liberty, it is evident that each department should have a will of its own; and consequently should be so constituted, that the members of each should have as little agency as possible in the appointment of the members of the others. Were this principle rigorously adhered to, it would require that all the appointments for the supreme executive, legislative, and judiciary magistracies, should be drawn from the same fountain of authority, the people, through channels, having no communication whatever with one another. Perhaps such a plan of constructing the several departments would be less difficult in practice than it may in contemplation appear. Some difficulties however, and some additional expense, would attend the execution of it. Some deviations therefore from the principle must be admitted. In the constitution of the judiciary department in particular, it might be inexpedient to insist rigorously on the principle; first, because peculiar qualifications being essential in the members, the primary consideration ought to be to select that mode of choice, which best secures these qualifications; secondly, because the permanent tenure by which the appointments are held in that department, must soon destroy all sense of dependence on the authority conferring them.

It is equally evident that the members of each department should be as little dependent as possible on those of the others, for the emoluments annexed to their offices. Were the executive magistrate, or the judges, not independent of the legislature in this particular, their independence in every other would be merely nominal.

But the great security against a gradual concentration of the several powers in the same department, consists in giving to those who administer each department, the necessary constitutional means, and personal motives, to resist encroachments of the others. The provision for defense must in this, as in all other cases, be made commensurate to the danger of attack. Ambition must be made to counteract ambition. The interest of the man must be connected with the constitutional right of the place. It may be a reflection on human nature, that such devices should be necessary to control the abuses of government. But what is government itself but the greatest of all reflections on human nature? If men were angels, no government would be necessary. If angels were to govern men, neither external nor internal controls on government would be necessary. In framing a government which is to be administered by men over men, the great difficulty lies in this: You must first enable the government to control the governed; and in the next place, oblige it to control itself. A dependence on the people is no doubt the primary control on the government; but experience has taught mankind the necessity of auxiliary precautions.

This policy of supplying by opposite and rival interests, the defect of better motives, might be traced through the whole system of human affairs, private as well as public. We see it particularly displayed in all the subordinate distributions of power; where the constant aim is to divide and arrange the several offices in such a manner as that each may be a check on the other; that the private interest of every individual, may be a sentinel over the public rights. These inventions of prudence cannot be less requisite in the distribution of the supreme powers of the state.

But it is not possible to give to each department an equal power of self defense. In republican government the legislative authority, necessarily, predominates. The remedy for this inconveniency is, to divide the legislature into different branches; and to render them by different modes of election, and different principles of action, as little connected with each other, as the nature of their common functions, and their common dependence on the society, will admit. It may even be necessary to guard against dangerous encroachments by still further precautions. As the weight of the legislative authority requires that it should be thus divided, the weakness of the executive may require, on the other hand, that it should be fortified. An absolute negative, on the legislature, appears at first view to be the natural defense with which the executive magistrate should be armed. But perhaps it would be neither altogether safe, nor alone sufficient. On ordinary occasions, it might not be exerted with the requisite firmness; and on extraordinary occasions, it might be perfidiously abused. May not this defect of an absolute negative be supplied, by some qualified connection between this weaker department, and the weaker branch of the stronger department, by which the latter may be led to support the constitutional rights of the former, without being too much detached from the rights of its own department? If the principles on which these observations are founded be just, as I persuade myself they are, and they be applied as a criterion, to the several state constitutions, and to the federal constitution, it will be found, that if the latter does not perfectly correspond with them, the former are infinitely less able to bear such a test.

There are moreover two considerations particularly applicable to the federal system of America, which place that system in a very interesting point of view.

First. In a single republic, all the power surrendered by the people, is submitted to the administration of a single government; and usurpations are guarded against by a division of the government into distinct and separate departments. In the compound republic of America, the power surrendered by the people, is first divided between two distinct governments, and then the portion allotted to each, subdivided among distinct and separate departments. Hence a double security arises to the rights of the people. The different governments will control each other; at the same time that each will be controlled by itself.

Second. It is of great importance in a republic, not only to guard the society against the oppression of its rulers; but to guard one part of the society against the injustice of the other part. Different interests necessarily exist in different classes of citizens. If a majority be united by a common interest, the rights of the minority will be insecure. There are but two methods of providing against this evil: The one by creating a will in the community independent of the majority, that is, of the society itself, the other by comprehending in the society so many separate descriptions of citizens, as will render an unjust combination of a majority of the whole, very improbable, if not impracticable. The first method prevails in all governments possessing an hereditary or self appointed authority. This at best is but a precarious security; because a power independent of the society may as well espouse the unjust views of the major, as the rightful interests, of the minor party, and may possibly be turned against both parties. The second method will be exemplified in the federal republic of the United States. While all authority in it will be derived from and dependent on the society, the society itself will be broken into so many parts, interests and classes of citizens, that the rights of individuals or of the minority, will be in little danger from interested combinations of the majority. In a free government, the security for civil rights must be the same as for religious rights. It consists in the one case in the multiplicity of interests, and in the other, in the multiplicity of sects. The degree of security in both cases will depend on the number of interests and sects; and this may be presumed to depend on the extent of country and number of people comprehended under the same government. This view of the subject must particularly recommend a proper federal system to all the sincere and considerate friends of republican government: Since it shows that in exact proportion as the territory of the union may be formed into more circumscribed confederacies or states, oppressive combinations of a majority will be facilitated, the best security under the republican form, for the rights of every class of citizens, will be diminished; and consequently, the stability and independence of some member of the government, the only other security, must be proportionally increased. Justice is the end of government. It is the end of civil society. It ever has been, and ever will be pursued, until it be obtained, or until liberty be lost in the pursuit. In a society under the forms of which the stronger faction can readily unite and oppress the weaker, anarchy may as truly be said to reign, as in a state of nature where the weaker individual is not secured against the violence of the stronger: And as in the latter state even the stronger individuals are prompted by the uncertainty of their condition, to submit to a government which may protect the weak as well as themselves: So in the former state, will the more powerful factions or parties be gradually induced by a like motive, to wish for a government which will protect all parties, the weaker as well as the more powerful. It can be little doubted, that if the state of Rhode Island was separated from the confederacy, and left to itself, the insecurity of rights under the popular form of government within such narrow limits, would be displayed by such reiterated oppressions of factious majorities, that some power altogether independent of the people would soon be called for by the voice of the very factions whose misrule had proved the necessity of it. In the extended republic of the United States, and among the great variety of interests, parties and sects which it embraces, a coalition of a majority of the whole society could seldom take place on any other principles than those of justice and the general good; and there being thus less danger to a minor from the will of the major party, there must be less pretext also, to provide for the security of the former, by introducing into the government a will not dependent on the latter; or in other words, a will independent of the society itself. It is no less certain than it is important, notwithstanding the contrary opinions which have been entertained, that the larger the society, provided it lie within a practicable sphere, the more duly capable it will be of self government. And happily for the *republican cause,* the practicable sphere may be carried to a very great extent, by a judicious modification and mixture of the *federal principle.*

PUBLIUS

Presidents, Congresses, and Chief Justices: 1789–2007

Term	President and Vice President	Party of President	Congress	Majority Party		Chief Justice of the United States
				House	Senate	
1789–1797	**George Washington** John Adams	None	1st 2nd 3rd 4th	(N/A) (N/A) (N/A) (N/A)	(N/A) (N/A) (N/A) (N/A)	John Jay (1789–1795) John Rutledge (1795) Oliver Ellsworth (1796–1800)
1797–1801	**John Adams** Thomas Jefferson	Federalist	5th 6th	(N/A) Fed	(N/A) Fed	Oliver Ellsworth (1796–1800) John Marshall (1801–1835)
1801–1809	**Thomas Jefferson** Aaron Burr (1801–1805) George Clinton (1805–1809)	Democratic- Republican	7th 8th 9th 10th	Dem-Rep Dem-Rep Dem-Rep Dem-Rep	Dem-Rep Dem-Rep Dem-Rep Dem-Rep	John Marshall (1801–1835)
1809–1817	**James Madison** George Clinton (1809–1812)[a] Elbridge Gerry (1813–1814)[a]	Democratic- Republican	11th 12th 13th 14th	Dem-Rep Dem-Rep Dem-Rep Dem-Rep	Dem-Rep Dem-Rep Dem-Rep Dem-Rep	John Marshall (1801–1835)
1817–1825	**James Monroe** Daniel D. Tompkins	Democratic- Republican	15th 16th 17th 18th	Dem-Rep Dem-Rep Dem-Rep Dem-Rep	Dem-Rep Dem-Rep Dem-Rep Dem-Rep	John Marshall (1801–1835)
1825–1829	**John Quincy Adams** John C. Calhoun	National- Republican	19th 20th	Nat'l Rep Dem	Nat'l Rep Dem	John Marshall (1801–1835)
1829–1837	**Andrew Jackson** John C. Calhoun (1829–1832)[c] Martin Van Buren (1833–1837)	Democratic	21st 22nd 23rd 24th	Dem Dem Dem Dem	Dem Dem Dem Dem	John Marshall (1801–1835) Roger B. Taney (1836–1864)
1837–1841	**Martin Van Buren** Richard M. Johnson	Democratic	25th 26th	Dem Dem	Dem Dem	Roger B. Taney (1836–1864)
1841	**William H. Harrison**[a] John Tyler (1841)	Whig				Roger B. Taney (1836–1864)
1841–1845	**John Tyler** (VP vacant)	Whig	27th 28th	Whig Dem	Whig Whig	Roger B. Taney (1836–1864)
1845–1849	**James K. Polk** George M. Dallas	Democratic	29th 30th	Dem Whig	Dem Dem	Roger B. Taney (1836–1864)
1849–1850	**Zachary Taylor**[a] Millard Fillmore	Whig	31st	Dem	Dem	Roger B. Taney (1836–1864)

Term	President and Vice President	Party of President	Congress	Majority Party		Chief Justice of the United States
				House	Senate	
1850–1853	**Millard Fillmore** (VP vacant)	Whig	32nd	Dem	Dem	Roger B. Taney (1836–1864)
1853–1857	**Franklin Pierce** William R. D. King (1853)[a]	Democratic	33rd 34th	Dem Rep	Dem Dem	Roger B. Taney (1836–1864)
1857–1861	**James Buchanan** John C. Breckinridge	Democratic	35th 36th	Dem Rep	Dem Dem	Roger B. Taney (1836–1864)
1861–1865	**Abraham Lincoln**[a] Hannibal Hamlin (1861–1865) Andrew Johnson (1865)	Republican	37th 38th	Rep Rep	Rep Rep	Roger B. Taney (1836–1864) Salmon P. Chase (1864–1873)
1865–1869	**Andrew Johnson** (VP vacant)	Republican	39th 40th	Union Rep	Union Rep	Salmon P. Chase (1864–1873)
1869–1877	**Ulysses S. Grant** Schuyler Colfax (1869–1873) Henry Wilson (1873–1875)[a]	Republican	41st 42nd 43rd 44th	Rep Rep Rep Dem	Rep Rep Rep Rep	Salmon P. Chase (1864–1873) Morrison R. Waite (1874–1888)
1877–1881	**Rutherford B. Hayes** William A. Wheeler	Republican	45th 46th	Dem Dem	Rep Dem	Morrison R. Waite (1874–1888)
1881	**James A. Garfield**[a] Chester A. Arthur	Republican	47th	Rep	Rep	Morrison R. Waite (1874–1888)
1881–1885	**Chester A. Arthur** (VP vacant)	Republican	48th	Dem	Rep	Morrison R. Waite (1874–1888)
1885–1889	**Grover Cleveland** Thomas A. Hendricks (1885)[a]	Democratic	49th 50th	Dem Dem	Rep Rep	Morrison R. Waite (1874–1888) Melville W. Fuller (1888–1910)
1889–1893	**Benjamin Harrison** Levi P. Morton	Republican	51st 52nd	Rep Dem	Rep Rep	Melville W. Fuller (1888–1910)
1893–1897	**Grover Cleveland** Adlai E. Stevenson	Democratic	53rd 54th	Dem Rep	Dem Rep	Melville W. Fuller (1888–1910)
1897–1901	**William McKinley**[a] Garret A. Hobart (1897–1899)[a] Theodore Roosevelt (1901)	Republican	55th 56th	Rep Rep	Rep Rep	Melville W. Fuller (1888–1910)
1901–1909	**Theodore Roosevelt** (VP vacant, 1901–1905) Charles W. Fairbanks (1905–1909)	Republican	57th 58th 59th 60th	Rep Rep Rep Rep	Rep Rep Rep Rep	Melville W. Fuller (1888–1910)
1909–1913	**William Howard Taft** James S. Sherman (1909–1912)[a]	Republican	61st 62nd	Rep Dem	Rep Rep	Melville W. Fuller (1888–1910) Edward D. White (1910–1921)
1913–1921	**Woodrow Wilson** Thomas R. Marshall	Democratic	63rd 64th 65th 66th	Dem Dem Dem Rep	Dem Dem Dem Rep	Edward D. White (1910–1921)
1921–1923	**Warren G. Harding**[a] Calvin Coolidge	Republican	67th	Rep	Rep	William Howard Taft (1921–1930)
1923–1929	**Calvin Coolidge** (VP vacant, 1923–1925) Charles G. Dawes (1925–1929)	Republican	68th 69th 70th	Rep Rep Rep	Rep Rep Rep	William Howard Taft (1921–1930)
1929–1933	**Herbert Hoover** Charles Curtis	Republican	71st 72nd	Rep Dem	Rep Rep	William Howard Taft (1921–1930) Charles Evans Hughes (1930–1941)

Term	President and Vice President	Party of President	Congress	Majority Party House	Majority Party Senate	Chief Justice of the United States
1933–1945	**Franklin D. Roosevelt**[a] John Nance Garner (1933–1941) Henry A. Wallace (1941–1945) Harry S Truman (1945)	Democratic	73rd 74th 75th 76th 77th 78th	Dem Dem Dem Dem Dem Dem	Dem Dem Dem Dem Dem Dem	Charles Evans Hughes (1930–1941) Harlan F. Stone (1941–1946)
1945–1953	**Harry S Truman** (VP vacant, 1945–1949) Alben W. Barkley (1949–1953)	Democratic	79th 80th 81st 82nd	Dem Rep Dem Dem	Dem Rep Dem Dem	Harlan F. Stone (1941–1946) Frederick M. Vinson (1946–1953)
1953–1961	**Dwight D. Eisenhower** Richard M. Nixon	Republican	83rd 84th 85th 86th	Rep Dem Dem Dem	Rep Dem Dem Dem	Frederick M. Vinson (1946–1953) Earl Warren (1953–1969)
1961–1963	**John F. Kennedy**[a] Lyndon B. Johnson (1961–1963)	Democratic	87th	Dem	Dem	Earl Warren (1953–1969)
1963–1969	**Lyndon B. Johnson** (VP vacant, 1963–1965) Hubert H. Humphrey (1965–1969)	Democratic	88th 89th 90th	Dem Dem Dem	Dem Dem Dem	Earl Warren (1953–1969)
1969–1974	**Richard M. Nixon**[b] Spiro Agnew (1969–1973)[c] Gerald R. Ford (1973–1974)[d]	Republican	91st 92nd	Dem Dem	Dem Dem	Earl Warren (1953–1969) Warren E. Burger (1969–1986)
1974–1977	**Gerald R. Ford** Nelson A. Rockefeller[d]	Republican	93rd 94th	Dem Dem	Dem Dem	Warren E. Burger (1969–1986)
1977–1981	**Jimmy Carter** Walter Mondale	Democratic	95th 96th	Dem Dem	Dem Dem	Warren E. Burger (1969–1986)
1981–1989	**Ronald Reagan** George Bush	Republican	97th 98th 99th 100th	Dem Dem Dem Dem	Rep Rep Rep Dem	Warren E. Burger (1969–1986) William H. Rehnquist (1986–2005)
1989–1993	**George Bush** Dan Quayle	Republican	101st 102nd	Dem Dem	Dem Dem	William H. Rehnquist (1986–2005)
1993–2001	**Bill Clinton** Al Gore	Democratic	103rd 104th 105th 106th	Dem Rep Rep Rep	Dem Rep Rep Rep	William H. Rehnquist (1986–2005)
2001–2009	**George W. Bush** Dick Cheney	Republican	107th 108th 109th 110th	Rep Rep Rep Dem	Dem Rep Rep Dem	William H. Rehnquist (1986–2005) John G. Roberts Jr. (2005–)

[a]Died in office.
[b]Resigned from the presidency.
[c]Resigned from the vice presidency.
[d]Appointed vice president.

Selected Supreme Court Cases

- *Agostini* v. *Felton (1997):* The Court agreed to permit public school teachers to go into parochial schools during school hours to provide remedial education to disadvantaged students because it was not an excessive entanglement of church and state.

- *Ashcroft* v. *Free Speech Coalition* (2002): The Court ruled that the Child Online Protection Act of 1998 was unconstitutional because it was too vague in its reliance on "community standards" to define what is harmful to minors.

- *Atkins* v. *Virginia* (2002): Execution of the mentally retarded is prohibited by the Eighth Amendment's cruel and unusual punishment clause.

- *Avery* v. *Midland* (1968): The Court declared that the one-person, one-vote standard applied to counties as well as congressional and state legislative districts.

- *Ayotte* v. *Planned Parenthood of Northern New England* (2006): A New Hampshire abortion law that did not provide an exception for the woman's health was unconstitutional.

- *Baker* v. *Carr* (1962): Watershed case establishing the principle of one person, one vote, which requires that each legislative district within a state have the same number of eligible voters so that representation is equitably based on population.

- *Barron* v. *Baltimore* (1833): Decision that limited the application of the Bill of Rights to the actions of Congress alone.

- *Batson* v. *Kentucky* (1986): Peremptory challenges cannot be used to exclude all people of a given race (in this case, African Americans) from a jury pool.

- *Benton* v. *Maryland* (1969): Incorporated the Fifth Amendment's double jeopardy clause.

- *Board of Regents* v. *Southworth* (2000): Unanimous ruling from the Supreme Court which stated that public universities could charge students a mandatory activities fee that could be used to facilitate extracurricular student political speech so long as the programs are neutral in their application.

- *Boerne* v. *Flores* (1997): The Court ruled that Congress could not force the Religious Freedom Restoration act upon the state governments.

- *Bowers* v. *Hardwick* (1986): Unsuccessful attempt to challenge Georgia's sodomy law. The case was overturned by *Lawrence* v. *Texas* in 2003.

- *Bradwell* v. *Illinois* (1873): In this case, a woman argued that Illinois's refusal to allow her to practice law despite the fact that she had passed the bar violated her citizenship rights under the privileges and immunities clause of the Fourteenth Amendment; the justices denied her claim.

- *Bragdon* v. *Abbott* (1998): The Court ruled that individuals infected with HIV but not sick enough to qualify as having AIDS were protected from discrimination by the 1990 Americans with Disabilities Act (ADA).

- *Brandenburg* v. *Ohio* (1969): The Court fashioned the direct incitement test for deciding whether certain kinds of speech could be regulated by the government. This test holds that advocacy of illegal action is protected by the First Amendment unless imminent action is intended and likely to occur.

- *Brown* v. *Board of Education* (1954): Supreme Court decision holding that school segregation is inherently unconstitutional because it violates the Fourteenth Amendment's guarantee of equal protection; marked the end of legal segregation in the United States.

- *Brown* v. *Board of Education II* (1955): Follow-up to *Brown* v. *Board of Education*, this case laid out the process for school desegregation and established the concept of dismantling segregationist systems "with all deliberate speed."

- *Brown University* v. *Cohen* (1997): Landmark Title IX case that put all colleges and universities on notice that discrimination against women would not be tolerated, even when, as in the case of Brown University, the university had tremendously expanded sports opportunities for women.

- *Buckley* v. *Valeo* (1976): The Court ruled that money spent by an individual or political committee in support or opposition of a candidate (but independent of the candidate's campaign) was a form of symbolic speech, and therefore could not be limited under the First Amendment.

- *Bush* v. *Gore* (2000): Controversial 2000 election case that made the final decision on the Florida recounts, and thus determined the result of the 2000 election.

- *Cantwell* v. *Connecticut* (1940): The case in which the Supreme Court incorporated the freedom of religion, ruling that the freedom to believe is absolute, but the freedom to act is subject to the regulation of society.

- *Chandler* v. *Miller* (1997): The Supreme Court refused to allow Georgia to require all candidates for state office to pass a urinalysis thirty days before qualifying for nomination or election, concluding that this law violated the search and seizure clause.

- *Chaplinsky* v. *New Hampshire* (1942): Established the Supreme Court's rationale for distinguishing between protected and unprotected speech.

- *Chicago, B&Q R.R. Co.* v. *Chicago* (1897): Incorporated the Fifth Amendment's just compensation clause.

- *Chisholm* v. *Georgia* (1793): The Court interpreted its jurisdiction under Article III, section 2, of the Constitution to include the right to hear suits brought by a citizen of one state against another state.

- *City of Cleburne* v. *Cleburne Living Center* (1985): Established that zoning restrictions against group homes for the retarded have a rational basis.

- *Civil Rights Cases* (1883): Name attached to five cases brought under the Civil Rights Act of 1875. In 1883, the Supreme Court decided that discrimination in a variety of public accommodations, including theaters, hotels, and railroads, could not be prohibited by the act because it was private and not state discrimination.

- *Clinton* v. *City of New York* (1998): The Court ruled that the line-item veto was unconstitutional because it gave powers to the president denied him by the U.S. Constitution.

- *Clinton* v. *Jones* (1997): The Court refused to reverse a lower court's decision that allowed Paula Jones's civil case against President Bill Clinton to proceed.

- *Cohens* v. *Virginia* (1821): The Court defined its jurisdiction to include the right to review all state criminal cases; additionally, this case built on *Martin* v. *Hunter's Lessee*, clarifying the Court's power to declare state laws unconstitutional.

- *Colorado Republican Federal Campaign Committee* v. *Federal Election Commission* (1996): The Supreme Court extended its ruling in *Buckley* v. *Valeo* to also include political parties.

- *Cooper* v. *Aaron* (1958): Case wherein the Court broke with tradition and issued a unanimous decision against the Little Rock School Board, ruling that the district's evasive schemes to avoid the *Brown II* decision were illegal.

- *Craig* v. *Boren* (1976): The Court ruled that keeping drunk drivers off the roads may be an important governmental objective, but allowing women aged eighteen to twenty-one to drink alcoholic beverages while prohibiting men of the same age from drinking is not substantially related to that goal.

- *Cruzan by Cruzan* v. *Director, Missouri Department of Health* (1990): The Court rejected any attempt to extend the right to privacy into the area of assisted suicide. However, the Court did note that individuals could terminate medical treatment if they were able to express, or had done so in writing, their desire to have medical treatment terminated in the event they became incompetent.

- *DeJonge* v. *Oregon* (1937): Incorporated the First Amendment's right to freedom of assembly.

- *Doe* v. *Bolton* (1973): In combination with *Roe* v. *Wade*, established a woman's right to an abortion.

- *Dred Scott* v. *Sandford* (1857): Concluded that the U.S. Congress lacked the constitutional authority to bar slavery in the territories; this decision narrowed the scope of national power while it enhanced that of the states. This case marks the first time since *Marbury* v. *Madison* that the Supreme Court found an act of Congress unconstitutional.

- *Duncan* v. *Louisiana* (1968): Incorporated the Sixth Amendment's trial by jury clause.

- *Engel* v. *Vitale* (1962): The Court ruled that the recitation in public classrooms of a nondenominational prayer was unconstitutional and a violation of the establishment clause.
- *Fletcher* v. *Peck* (1810): The Court ruled that state legislatures could not make laws that voided contracts or grants made by earlier legislative action.
- *Furman* v. *Georgia* (1972): The Supreme Court used this case to end capital punishment, at least in the short run. (The case was overturned by *Gregg* v. *Georgia* in 1976.)
- *Garcia* v. *San Antonio Metropolitan Transport Authority* (1985): In this case, the court ruled that Congress has the broad power to impose its will on state and local governments, even in areas that have traditionally been left to state and local discretion.
- *Georgia* v. *Randolph* (2006): The Court ruled that both residents of a home must consent to a search before that search is regarded as constitutional.
- *Gibbons* v. *Ogden* (1824): The Court upheld broad congressional power over interstate commerce.
- *Gideon* v. *Wainwright* (1963): Granted indigents the right to counsel.
- *Gitlow* v. *New York* (1925): Incorporated the free speech clause of the First Amendment, ruling that the states were not completely free to limit forms of political expression.
- *Gonzales* v. *O Centro Espirita Beneficente União do Vegetal* (2006): Under the Religious Freedom Restoration Act, the government has to make an exception to the Controlled Substances Act for a substance used in religious services.
- *Gonzales* v. *Oregon* (2006): Held that the Justice Department does not have the authority to block physician assisted suicides.
- *Gonzales* v. *Raich* (2005): Upheld power of Congress to ban and prosecute the possession and use of marijuana for medical purposes, even in states that permitted it.
- *Gratz* v. *Bollinger* (2003): The Court struck down the University of Michigan's undergraduate point system, which gave minority applicants twenty automatic points simply because they were minorities.
- *Gray* v. *Sanders* (1963): The Court held that voting by unit systems is unconstitutional.
- *Gregg* v. *Georgia* (1976): Overturning *Furman* v. *Georgia*, the case ruled that Georgia's rewritten death penalty statute is constitutional.
- *Griswold* v. *Connecticut* (1965): Supreme Court case that established the Constitution's implied right to privacy.
- *Grutter* v. *Bollinger* (2003): The Court voted to uphold the constitutionality of the University of Michigan law school's affirmative action policy, which gave preference to minority students.
- *Hamdan* v. *Rumsfeld* (2006): The Court ruled that detainees in the war on terrorism were entitled to the protections of the Geneva Convention and the procedural rights of the Uniform Code of Military Justice, since Congress had not approved of President George W. Bush's system of military tribunals. Congress passed the Military Commissions Act in 2006 to address the Court's ruling in *Hamdan*.
- *Hamdi et al* v. *Rumsfeld* (2004): The government does not have the authority to detain a U.S. citizen charged as an enemy combatant in the war on terrorism without providing basic due process protections under the Fifth Amendment.
- *Harris* v. *Forklift Systems* (1993): The Court ruled that a federal civil rights law created a "broad rule of workplace equality."
- *Hill* v. *McDonough* (2006): Challenging the form of execution prescribed in a defendant's sentence is not a proper use of a *habeas corpus* petition.
- *House* v. *Bell* (2006): A Tennessee death-row inmate who had otherwise exhausted his federal appeals was provided an exception due to the availability of DNA evidence suggesting his innocence; the case recognized the potential exculpatory power of DNA evidence.
- *Hoyt* v. *Florida* (1961): The Court ruled that an all-male jury did not violate a woman's rights under the Fourteenth Amendment.
- *Hudson* v. *Michigan* (2006): Evidence obtained in violation of the "knock and announce" rule is not subject to the restrictions of the exclusionary rule.

- *Hunt* v. *Cromartie* **(1999, 2001):** Continuation of redistricting litigation begun with *Shaw* v. *Reno* (1993). The Court reversed district court conclusions that the North Carolina legislature had used race-driven criteria in violation of the equal protection clause to redraw district lines.

- *Immigration and Naturalization Service* v. *Chadha* **(1983):** The Court ruled that the legislative veto as it was used in many circumstances was unconstitutional because it violated the separation of powers principle.

- *J.E.B.* v. *Alabama* **(1994):** The use of peremptory challenges to exclude jurors of a particular gender is unconstitutional.

- *Kelo* v. *New London* **(2004):** The Court ruled that government could take private property and then sell it to private developers so long as that property was slated for economic development that would benefit the surrounding community.

- *Klopfer* v. *North Carolina* **(1967):** Incorporated the Sixth Amendment's right to a speedy trial.

- *Korematsu* v. *U.S.* **(1944):** In this case, the Court ruled that the internment of Japanese Americans during World War II was not unconstitutional.

- *Lawrence* v. *Texas* **(2003):** The Court reversed its 1986 ruling in *Bowers* v. *Hardwick* by finding a Texas statute that banned sodomy to be unconstitutional.

- *League of United Latin American Citizens et al.* v. *Perry* **(2006):** Part of the 2004 Texas redistricting plan violated the Voting Rights Act because it deprived Hispanic citizens of the right to elect a representative of their choosing.

- *Lemon* v. *Kurtzman* **(1971):** The Court determined that direct government assistance to religious schools is unconstitutional. In the majority opinion, the Court created what has become known as the "Lemon Test" for deciding if a law is in violation of the establishment clause.

- *Lynch* v. *Donnelly* **(1984):** In a defeat for the ACLU, the Court held that a city's inclusion of a crèche in its annual Christmas display in a private park did not violate the establishment clause.

- *Malloy* v. *Hogan* **(1964):** Incorporated the Fifth Amendment's self-incrimination clause.

- *Mapp* v. *Ohio* **(1961):** Incorporated a portion of the Fourth Amendment by establishing that illegally obtained evidence cannot be used at trial.

- *Marbury* v. *Madison* **(1803):** Case in which the Court first asserted the power of judicial review in finding that a congressional statute extending the Court's original jurisdiction was unconstitutional.

- *Martin* v. *Hunter's Lessee* **(1816):** The Court's power of judicial review in regard to state law was clarified in this case.

- *Maryland* v. *Craig* **(1990):** The confrontation clause of the Sixth Amendment does not guarantee defendants an absolute right to come face to face with their accusers.

- *Ex parte McCardle* **(1869):** Post–Civil War case that reinforced Congress's power to determine the jurisdiction of the Supreme Court.

- *McCleskey* v. *Kemp* **(1987):** The Court ruled that the imposition of the death penalty did not violate the equal protection clause.

- *McCleskey* v. *Zant* **(1991):** On this appeal of the 1987 *McCleskey* case, the Court produced new standards designed to make it much more difficult for death-row inmates to file repeated appeals.

- *McConnell* v. *FEC* **(2003):** Generally speaking, the Bipartisan Campaign Finance Reform Act of 2002 does not violate the First Amendment.

- *McCreary County* v. *ACLU of Kentucky* **(2005):** The Court ruled that the display of the Ten Commandments in public schools and courthouses violated the establishment clause.

- *McCulloch* v. *Maryland* **(1819):** The Court upheld the power of the national government and denied the right of a state to tax the bank. The Court's broad interpretation of the necessary and proper clause paved the way for later rulings upholding expansive federal powers.

- *Miller* v. *California* **(1973):** Case wherein the Supreme Court began to formulate rules designed to make it easier for states to regulate obscene materials and to return to communities a greater role in determining what is obscene.

- *Minor* v. *Happersett* (1875): The Supreme Court once again examined the privileges and immunities clause of the Fourteenth Amendment, ruling that voting was not a privilege of citizenship.

- *Miranda* v. *Arizona* (1966): The Fifth Amendment requires that individuals arrested for a crime must be advised of their right to remain silent and to have counsel present.

- *Morrison* v. *U.S.* (2000): The Court ruled that Congress has no authority under the commerce clause to enact a provision of the Violence Against Women Act providing a federal remedy to victims of gender-motivated violence.

- *Muller* v. *Oregon* (1908): Case that ruled Oregon's law barring women from working more than ten hours a day was constitutional; also an attempt to define women's unique status as mothers to justify their differential treatment.

- *Near* v. *Minnesota* (1931): By ruling that a state law violated the freedom of the press, the Supreme Court incorporated the free press provision of the First Amendment.

- *Nebraska Press Association* v. *Stuart* (1976): Prior restraint case; the Court ruled that a trial judge could not prohibit the publication or broadcast of information about a murder trial.

- *Nevada Department of Human Resources* v. *Hibbs* (2003): The court upheld the ability of state employees to sue under the Family and Medical Leave Act.

- *New York Times Co.* v. *Sullivan* (1964): Supreme Court ruling that simply publishing a defamatory falsehood is not enough to justify a libel judgment. "Actual malice" must be proved to support a finding of libel against a public figure.

- *New York Times Co.* v. *U.S.* (1971): Also called the Pentagon Papers case; the Supreme Court ruled that any attempt by the government to prevent expression carried "a heavy presumption" against its constitutionality.

- *NLRB* v. *Jones and Laughlin Steel Co.* (1937): Case that upheld the National Labor Relations Act of 1935, marking a turning point in the Court's ideology toward the programs of President Franklin D. Roosevelt's New Deal.

- *In re Oliver* (1948): Incorporated the Sixth Amendment's right to a public trial.

- *Palko* v. *Connecticut* (1937): Set the Court's rationale of selective incorporation, a judicial doctrine whereby most but not all of the protections found in the Bill of Rights are made applicable to the states via the Fourteenth Amendment.

- *Parker* v. *Gladden* (1966): Incorporated the Sixth Amendment's right to an impartial trial.

- *Planned Parenthood* v. *Casey* (1992): This case was an unsuccessful attempt to challenge Pennsylvania's restrictive abortion regulations.

- *Plessy* v. *Ferguson* (1896): *Plessy* challenged a Louisiana statute requiring that railroads provide separate accommodations for blacks and whites. The Court found that separate but equal accommodations did not violate the equal protection clause of the Fourteenth Amendment.

- *Pointer* v. *Texas* (1965): Incorporated the Sixth Amendment's right to confrontation of witnesses.

- *Printz* v. *U.S.* (1997): The Court found that Congress lacks the authority to compel state officers to execute federal laws, specifically relating to background checks on handgun purchasers.

- *Quilici* v. *Village of Morton Grove* (1983): The Supreme Court refused to review a lower court's ruling upholding the constitutionality of a local ordinance banning handguns against a Second Amendment challenge.

- *R.A.V.* v. *City of St. Paul* (1992): The Court concluded that St. Paul, Minnesota's Bias-Motivated Crime Ordinance violated the First Amendment because it regulated speech based on the content of the speech.

- *Reed* v. *Reed* (1971): Turned the tide in terms of constitutional litigation, ruling that the equal protection clause of the Fourteenth Amendment prohibited unreasonable classifications based on sex.

- *Regents of the University of California* v. *Bakke* (1978): A sharply divided Court concluded that the university's rejection of Bakke as a student had been illegal because the use of strict affirmative action quotas was inappropriate.

- *Reno* v. *American Civil Liberties Union* (1997): The Court ruled that the 1996 Communications Decency Act prohibiting transfer of obscene or indecent materials over the Internet to minors violated the First Amendment because it was too vague and overbroad.

- *Reynolds* v. *Sims* (1964): The Court decided that every person should have an equally weighted vote in electing governmental representatives.

- *Robinson* v. *California* (1962): Incorporated the Eighth Amendment's right to freedom from cruel and unusual punishment.

- *Roe* v. *Wade* (1973): The Supreme Court found that a woman's right to an abortion was protected by the right to privacy that could be implied from specific guarantees found in the Bill of Rights and the Fourteenth Amendment.

- *Romer* v. *Evans* (1996): A Colorado constitutional amendment precluding any legislative, executive, or judicial action at any state or local level designed to bar discrimination based on sexual preference was ruled not rational or reasonable.

- *Rompilla* v. *Beard* (2005): Counsel must make a reasonable effort to examine information pertaining to the case they are trying.

- *Roper* v. *Simmons* (2005): Execution of minors violates the Eighth Amendment's prohibition on cruel and unusual punishment.

- *Roth* v. *U.S.* (1957): The Court held that in order to be obscene, material must be "utterly without redeeming social value."

- *Santa Fe Independent School District* v. *Doe* (2000): The Court ruled that student-led, student-initiated prayer at high school football games violated the establishment clause.

- *Schenck* v. *U.S.* (1919): Case in which the Supreme Court interpreted the First Amendment to allow Congress to restrict speech that is "of such a nature as to create a clear and present danger that will bring about the substantive evils that Congress has a right to prevent."

- *Seminole Tribe* v. *Florida* (1996): Congress cannot impose a duty on states forcing them to negotiate with Indian tribes; the state's sovereign immunity protects it from a congressional directive about how to do business.

- *Shaw* v. *Reno* (1993): First in a series of redistricting cases in which the North Carolina legislature's reapportionment of congressional districts based on the 1990 Census was contested because the plan included an irregularly shaped district in which race seemed to be a dominant consideration. The Court ruled that districts created with race as the dominant consideration violated the equal protection clause of the Fourteenth Amendment.

- *In re Sindram* (1991): The Court chastised Michael Sindram for filing his petition *in forma pauperis* to require the Maryland courts to expedite his request to expunge a $35 speeding ticket from his record.

- *The Slaughterhouse Cases* (1873): The Court upheld Louisiana's right to create a monopoly on the operation of slaughterhouses, despite the Butcher's Benevolent Association's claim that this action deprived its members of their livelihood and the privileges and immunities granted by the Fourteenth Amendment.

- *Smith* v. *Massachusetts* (2005): Double jeopardy clause prohibits judges from reconsidering verdicts reached earlier in a trial, even in light of new evidence.

- *South Dakota* v. *Dole* (1987): The Court ruled that it was permissible for the federal government to require states that wanted transportation funds to pass laws setting twenty-one as the legal drinking age.

- *Stenberg* v. *Carhart* (2000): The Court ruled that a Nebraska "partial birth" abortion statute was unconstitutionally vague and unenforceable, calling into question the laws of twenty-nine other states.

- *Stromberg* v. *California* (1931): The Court overturned the conviction of a director of a Communist youth camp under a state statute prohibiting the display of a red flag.

- *Swann* v. *Charlotte-Mecklenburg School District* (1971): The Supreme Court ruled that all vestiges of *de jure* discrimination must be eliminated at once.

- *Tennessee* v. *Lane* (2004): Upheld application of the Americans with Disabilities Act to state courthouses.

- *Texas* v. *Johnson* **(1989):** The Court overturned the conviction of a Texas man found guilty of setting fire to an American flag.
- *Thornburg* v. *Gingles* **(1986):** At-large election of state legislators violates the Voting Rights Act because it dilutes the voting strength of African Americans.
- *Tinker* v. *Des Moines Independent School District* **(1969):** Upheld student's rights to express themselves by wearing black armbands symbolizing protest of the Vietnam War.
- *Tory* v. *Cochran* **(2005):** Prohibiting defamation of an individual after that person's death is an overly broad exercise of prior restraint.
- *U.S.* v. *Curtiss-Wright Export Corporation* **(1936):** The Court upheld the rights of Congress to grant the president authority to act in foreign affairs and to allow the president to prohibit arms shipments to participants in foreign wars.
- *U.S.* v. *Grubbs* **(2006):** A warrant does not need to describe the reason for its existence, only the person and things to be seized.
- *U.S.* v. *Lopez* **(1995):** The Court invalidated a section of the Gun Free School Zones Act, ruling that regulating guns did not fall within the scope of the commerce clause, and therefore was not within the powers of the federal government. Only states have the authority to ban guns in school zones.
- *U.S.* v. *Miller* **(1939):** The last time the Supreme Court addressed the constitutionality of the Second Amendment; ruled that the amendment was only intended to protect a citizen's right to own ordinary militia weapons.
- *U.S.* v. *Nixon* **(1974):** In a case involving President Richard M. Nixon's refusal to turn over tape recordings of his conversations, the Court ruled that executive privilege does not grant the president an absolute right to secure all presidential documents.
- *U.S.* v. *Patane* **(2004):** Physical evidence obtained in un-Mirandized voluntary statements is admissible in court.
- *U.S. Term Limits* v. *Thornton* **(1995):** The Supreme Court ruled that states do not have the authority to enact term limits for federal elected officials.
- *Washington* v. *Glucksberg* **(1997):** A state ban on physician assisted suicide does not violate the Fourteenth Amendment's due process clause.
- *Washington* v. *Texas* **(1967):** Incorporated the Sixth Amendment's right to a compulsory trial.
- *Webster* v. *Reproductive Health Services* **(1989):** In upholding several restrictive abortion regulations, the Court opened the door for state governments to enact new restrictions on abortion.
- *Weeks* v. *U.S.* **(1914):** Case wherein the Supreme Court adopted the exclusionary rule, which bars the use of illegally obtained evidence at trial.
- *Westberry* v. *Sanders* **(1964):** Established the principal of one person, one vote for congressional districts.
- *Wolf* v. *Colorado* **(1949):** The Court ruled that illegally obtained evidence did not necessarily have to be eliminated from use during trial.
- *Youngstown Sheet & Tube Co.* v. *Sawyer* **(1952):** The Court invalidated President Harry S Truman's seizure of the nation's steel mills.
- *Zelman* v. *Simmons-Harris* **(2002):** The Court concluded that governments can give money to parents to allow them to send their children to private or religious schools.

CHAPTER 1

1. Thomas Byrne Edsall, "The Era of Bad Feelings," *Civilization* (March/April 1996): 37.
2. Jack C. Plano and Milton Greenberg, *The American Political Dictionary*, 6th ed. (New York: Holt, Rinehart and Winston, 1982).
3. Frank Michelman, "The Republican Civic Tradition," *Yale Law Journal* 97 (1988): 1503.
4. The United States Agency for International Development, "Agency Objectives: Civil Society."
5. Thomas Carothers, "Democracy Promotion: A Key Focus in a New World Order," *Issues of Democracy* (May 2000): online.
6. Pew Forum on Religion and Public Life, "Growing Number of Americans Say Islam Encourages Violence," press release, July 24, 2003.
7. Pew Forum on Religion and Public Life.
8. Richard Allen Greene, "Religion and Politics in America," *BBC News,* (September 15, 2004).
9. Susan A. MacManus, *Young v. Old: Generational Combat in the 21st Century* (Boulder, CO: Westview Press, 1995), 3.
10. MacManus, *Young v. Old*, 4.
11. Dennis Cauchon, "Who Will Take Care of an Older Population?" *USA Today* (October 25, 2005): 1–2B.
12. Kavita Varma, "Family Values," *USA Today* (March 11, 1997): 6D.
13. Fox News/Opinion Dynamics Poll, April 6, 2006, Lexis-Nexis RPOLL.
14. CBS News Poll, February 27, 2006, http://www.cbsnews.com/ntdocs/pdf/poll_katrina_022706.pdf.
15. This discussion draws heavily from Terence Ball and Richard Dagger, *Political Ideologies and the Democratic Ideal*, 5th ed. (New York: Longman, 2004).
16. Ball and Dagger, *Political Ideologies and the Democratic Ideal*, 2.
17. Isaiah Berlin, *The Crooked Timber of Humanity: Chapters in the History of Ideas* (New York: Vintage Books, 1992), 1.
18. William Safire, *Safire's New Political Dictionary* (New York: Random House, 1993), 144–45.
19. Jack C. Plano and Milton Greenberg, *The American Political Dictionary*, 9th ed. (Fort Worth, TX: Harcourt Brace, 1993), 16.
20. Philip E. Converse, "The Nature of Belief Systems in Mass Publics," in David E. Apter, ed., *Ideology and Discontent* (New York: Free Press, 1964), 206–21.
21. Roper Center for Public Opinion Research, University of Connecticut, June 29, 2005, Lexis-Nexis RPOLL.
22. Scott Shepard, "Non-voters: Too Busy or Apathetic?" *Palm Beach Post* (August 1998): 6A.

CHAPTER 2

1. See Richard B. Bernstein with Jerome Agel, *Amending America* (New York: New York Times Books, 1993), 138–40.
2. *Oregon* v. *Mitchell*, 400 U.S. 112 (1970).
3. Bernstein with Agel, *Amending America*, 139.
4. For an account of the early development of the colonies, see D. W. Meining, *The Shaping of America*, vol. 1: *Atlantic America, 1492–1800* (New Haven, CT: Yale University Press, 1986).
5. For an excellent chronology of the events leading up to the writing of the Declaration of Independence and the colonists' break with Great Britain, see Calvin D. Lonton, ed., *The Bicentennial Almanac* (Nashville, TN: Thomas Nelson, 1975).
6. See Garry Wills, *Inventing America: Jefferson's Declaration of Independence* (New York: Random House, 1978). Wills argues that the Declaration was signed solely to secure foreign aid for the ongoing war effort.
7. See Gordon S. Wood, *The Creation of the American Republic, 1776–1787*, reissue ed. (New York: Norton, 1993).
8. For more about the Articles of Confederation, see Merrill Jensen, *The Articles of Confederation* (Madison: University of Wisconsin Press, 1940).
9. Charles A. Beard, *An Economic Interpretation of the Constitution of the United States*, reissue ed. (Mineola, NY: Dover, 2004).
10. Quoted in Richard N. Current et al., *American History: A Survey*, 6th ed. (New York: Knopf, 1983), 170.
11. John Patrick Diggins, "Power and Authority in American History: The Case of Charles A. Beard and His Critics," *American Historical Review* 86 (October 1981): 701–30; Robert Brown, *Charles Beard and the Constitution: A Critical Analysis of "An Economic Interpretation of the Constitution"* (Princeton, NJ: Princeton University Press, 1956).
12. Jackson Turner Main, *The Anti-Federalists: Critics of the Constitution, 1781–1788* (Chapel Hill: University of North Carolina, 2004).
13. Wood, *Creation of the American Republic*.
14. For more on the political nature of compromise at the convention, see Calvin C. Jillson, *Constitution Making: Conflict and Consensus in the Federal Constitution of 1787* (New York: Agathon, 1988).
15. Quoted in Doris Faber and Harold Faber, *We the People* (New York: Charles Scribner's Sons, 1987), 31.
16. Quoted in Current et al., *American History,* 168.
17. Bernard Bailyn, *The Ideological Origins of the American Revolution* (Cambridge, MA: Belknap Press, 1967).
18. *U.S. Term Limits* v. *Thornton*, 514 U.S. 779 (1995).
19. Richard E. Neustadt, *Presidential Power: The Politics of Leadership from FDR to Carter* (New York: Macmillan, 1980), 26.
20. Quoted in Faber and Faber, *We the People,* 51–52.
21. Federal Republicans favored a republican or representative form of government (do not confuse this term with the modern Republican Party, which came into being in 1854; see chapter 12). Ultimately, the word *federal* referred to the form of government embodied in the new Constitution, and *confederation* referred to a "league of states," as under the Articles, and later was applied in the "Confederacy" of 1861–1865.
22. See Ralph Ketcham, ed., *The Anti-Federalist Papers and the Constitutional Debates* (New York: New American Library, 1986).
23. See Herbert J. Storing, *What the Anti-Federalists Were For* (Chicago: University of Chicago Press, 1981), for a fuller discussion of Anti-Federalist views.
24. See Alan P. Grimes, *Democracy and the Amendments to the Constitution* (Lexington, MA: Lexington Books, 1978).
25. David E. Kyvig, *Repealing National Prohibition* (Chicago University of Chicago Press, 1978).
26. See Jane J. Mansbridge, *Why We Lost the ERA* (Chicago: University of Chicago Press, 1986).
27. *Marbury* v. *Madison, 5* U.S. 137 (1803).
28. Speech by Attorney General Edwin Meese III before the American Bar Association, July 9, 1985, Washington, DC. See also Antonin Scalia and Amy Gutman, eds. *A Matter of Interpretation: Federal Courts and the Law* (Princeton, NJ: Princeton University Press, 1998).
29. Speech by Associate Justice William J. Brennan Jr. at Georgetown University, Text and Teaching Symposium, October 10, 1985, Washington, DC.
30. Mark V. Tushnet, *Taking the Constitution Away from the Courts.* Princeton, NJ: Princeton University Press, 2000.
31. Bruce Ackerman, *We the People: Foundations* (Cambridge, MA: Belknap Press, 1991).

CHAPTER 3

1. Evan Thomas, "How Bush Blew It," *Newsweek* (September 19, 2005), http://www.msnbc.msn.com/id/9287434/site/newsweek/page/3/.
2. See Spencer S. Hsu, "Katrina Report Spreads Blame: Homeland Security, Chertoff Singled Out," *Washington Post* (January 12, 2006): A1.

3. In *City of Burbank* v. *Lockheed Air Terminal*, 411 U.S. 624 (1973), the U.S. Supreme Court ruled that the city could not impose curfews on plane takeoff or landing times. The Court said that one uniform national standard was critical for safety and the national interest.
4. *Missouri* v. *Holland*, 252 U.S. 416 (1920).
5. Oral argument in *Baker by Thomas* v. *General Motors Corporation*, 522 U.S. 222 (1998), noted in Linda Greenhouse, "Court Weighs Whether One State Must Obey Another's Courts," *New York Times* (October 16, 1997): A25.
6. John Mountjoy, "Interstate Cooperation: Interstate Compacts Make a Comeback," *Council of State Governments*, available online at http://www.csg.org.
7. *McCulloch* v. *Maryland*, 17 U.S. 316 (1819).
8. *Gibbons* v. *Ogden*, 22 U.S. 1 (1824).
9. *Dred Scott* v. *Sandford*, 60 U.S. 393 (1857).
10. *Plessy* v. *Ferguson*, 163 U.S. 537 (1896).
11. *Panhandle Oil Co.* v. *Knox*, 277 U.S. 218, 223 (1928).
12. *Indian Motorcycle Co.* v. *U.S.*, 238 U.S. 570 (1931).
13. *Pensacola Telegraph* v. *Western Union*, 96 U.S. 1 (1877).
14. *U.S.* v. *E. C. Knight*, 156 U.S. 1 (1895).
15. *Pollock* v. *Farmers Loan and Trust*, 157 U.S. 429 (1895); and *Springer* v. *U.S.*, 102 U.S. 586 (1881).
16. John O. McGinnis, "The State of Federalism," testimony before the Senate Government Affairs Committee, May 5, 1999.
17. *NLRB* v. *Jones and Laughlin Steel Co.*, 301 U.S. 1 (1937).
18. *U.S.* v. *Darby Lumber Co.*, 312 U.S. 100 (1941).
19. *Wickard* v. *Filburn*, 317 U.S. 111 (1942).
20. Morton Grodzins, "Centralization and Decentralization in the American Federal System," in Robert A. Goldwin, ed., *A Nation of States* (Chicago: Rand McNally, 1963), 3–4.
21. Alice M. Rivlin, *Reviving the American Dream* (Washington, DC: Brookings Institution, 1992), 92.
22. Rivlin, *Reviving the American Dream*, 98.
23. Richard P. Nathan et al., *Reagan and the States* (Princeton, NJ: Princeton University Press, 1987), 4.
24. T. R. Reid, "States Feel Less Pinch in Budgets, Services," *Washington Post* (May 9, 2004): A3.
25. Marianne Arneberg, "Cuomo Assails Judicial Hodgepodge," *Newsday* (August 15, 1990): 15.
26. *Webster* v. *Reproductive Health Services*, 492 U.S. 490 (1989).
27. *Stenberg* v. *Carhart*, 530 U.S. 914 (2000).
28. *Ayotte* v. *Planned Parenthood of Northern New England* 546 U.S. _____ (2006).
29. *U.S.* v. *Lopez*, 514 U.S. 549 (1995).
30. *Seminole Tribe* v. *Florida*, 517 U.S. 44 (1996).
31. *Boerne* v. *Flores*, 521 U.S. 507 (1997).
32. *Printz* v. *U.S.*, 521 U.S. 898 (1997).
33. *Florida Prepaid* v. *College Savings Bank*, 527 U.S. 627 (1999).
34. Linda Greenhouse, "The Rehnquist Court and Its Imperiled States' Rights Legacy," *New York Times* (June 12, 2005): A3.
35. Linda Greenhouse, "In a Momentous Term, Justices Remake the Law and the Court," *New York Times* (July 1, 2003): A18.
36. *Nevada Department of Human Resources* v. *Hibbs*, 538 U.S. 72 (2003).
37. *Gonzales* v. *Raich*, 545 U.S. 1 (2005).
38. *Gonzales* v. *Oregon*, 546 U.S. _____ (2006).

CHAPTER 4

1. Peter K. Eisinger, *The Rise of the Entrepreneurial State* (Madison: University of Wisconsin Press, 1988).
2. Albert L. Sturm, "The Development of American State Constitutions," *Publius* 12 (Winter 1982): 62–68.
3. Albert L. Kohlmeier, *The Old Northwest as the Keystone of the Arch of the American Federal Union* (Bloomington, IN: Principia, 1938), and *Pathways to the Old Northwest* (Indianapolis: Indiana Historical Society, 1988).
4. George E. Mowry, *The Progressive Era, 1900–1920* (Washington, DC: American Historical Association, 1972).

5. Janice C. May, "Constitutional Amendment and Revision Revisited," *Publius* 12 (Winter 1982): 153–79.
6. Charles Wiggins, "Executive Vetoes and Legislative Overrides in the American States," *Journal of Politics* 54 (November 1980): 42. Also see Glenn Abney and Thomas Lauth, "The Line-Item Veto in the States," *Public Administration Review* 45 (January/February 1985): 66–79.
7. F. Ted Hebert, Jeffrey L. Brudney, and Deil S. Wright, "Gubernatorial Influence and State Bureaucracy," *American Politics Quarterly* 11 (April 1983): 37–52; and Glenn Abney and Thomas Lauth, "The Governor as Chief Administrator," *Public Administration Quarterly* 3 (January/February 1983): 40–49.
8. Thad L. Beyle and Robert Dalton, "Appointment Power: Does It Belong to the Governor?" *State Government* 54:1 (1981): 6.
9. Leon W. Blevins, *Texas Government in National Perspective* (Englewood Cliffs, NJ: Prentice Hall, 1987), 169.
10. James L. Garnett, *Reorganizing State Government: The Executive Branch* (Boulder, CO: Westview, 1980), 8–9; and Diane Kincaid Blair, "The Gubernatorial Appointment Power: Too Much of a Good Thing?" *State Government* 55 (Summer 1982): 88–91.
11. Timothy O'Rourke, *The Impact of Reapportionment* (New Brunswick, NJ: Transaction, 1980).
12. Council of State Governments, *Book of the States, 2000–2001* (Lexington, KY: Council of State Governments, 2000), 49.
13. "Schwarzenegger Wants Part-time Legislature," April 7, 2004, http://sfgate.com.
14. Diana Gordon, "Citizen Legislators—Alive and Well," *State Legislatures* 20 (January 1994): 24–27.
15. Earl M. Maltz, "Federalism and State Court Activism," *Intergovernmental Perspective* (Spring 1987): 23–26.
16. Thomas E. Cronin, *Direct Democracy* (Cambridge, MA: Harvard University Press, 1989); and David B. Magleby, *Direct Legislation* (Baltimore, MD: Johns Hopkins University Press, 1984).
17. Patrick McMahon, "Voters Like Recall Idea, but Few Want One," *USA Today* (October 14, 2003): 3A; Andy Bowers, "Can You Recall Your Governor?" *Slate,* July 30, 2003, http://slate.msn.com.
18. Alexis de Tocqueville, *Democracy in America*, ed. Phillips Bradley (New York: Knopf, 1945), 40.
19. *City of Clinton* v. *Cedar Rapids and Missouri River Railroad Co.* (Iowa, 1868).
20. Steven P. Erie, *Rainbow's End: Irish-Americans and the Dilemmas of Urban Machine Politics, 1840–1985* (Berkeley: University of California Press, 1988); Alfred Steinberg, *The Bosses* (New York: New American Library, 1972); Seymour Mandelbaum, *Boss Tweed's New York* (New York: Wiley, 1955); and Milton Rakove, *Don't Make No Waves—Don't Back No Losers: An Insider's Analysis of the Daley Machine* (Bloomington: Indiana University Press, 1975).
21. Samuel P. Hays, "The Politics of Reform in Municipal Government in the Progressive Era," *Pacific Northwest Quarterly* 55 (October 1964): 157–66.
22. Raymond Wolfinger, "Reputation and Reality in the Study of Community Power," *American Sociological Review* 25 (October 1960): 636–44; Nelson Polsby, *Community Power and Political Theory* (New Haven, CT: Yale University Press, 1963); and Robert E. Agger, Daniel Goldrich, and Bert Swanson, *The Rulers and the Ruled: Political Power and Impotence in American Communities* (New York: Wiley, 1964).
23. Laura R. Woliver, *From Outrage to Action: The Politics of Grass-Roots Dissent* (Urbana: University of Illinois Press, 1993); and Matthew A. Crenson, *Neighborhood Politics* (Cambridge, MA: Harvard University Press, 1983).
24. Sharon O'Brien, *American Indian Tribal Governments* (Norman: University of Oklahoma Press, 1989), 261–97.
25. U.S. Census Bureau, *Government Finances in 1993–1994* (Washington, DC: Government Printing Office, 1994), 12–19.
26. National Governors Association, http://www.nga.org.
27. Dennis Cauchon, "States Getting Budgets Under Control," *USA Today* (November 12, 2003): 3A.
28. Steven Ginsberg and Chris L. Jenkins, "Vote Quiets Anti-Tax Clarion Call in Virginia," *Washington Post* (April 29, 2004): A1.

CHAPTER 5

1. Sudarsan Raghaven, "Crisis in Darfur Is Expected to Draw Thousands to Mall; Rallies Promoting End to Genocide Planned in 17 Other Cities," *Washington Post* (April 30, 2006): C3.
2. Raghaven, "Crisis in Darfur Is Expected to Draw Thousands to Mall."
3. Sudarsan Raghaven, "Divisions Cast Aside in Cry for Darfur; Mall Rally Highlights Growing Concern," *Washington Post* (May 1, 2006): A1.
4. Farah Stockman, "Americans Rally for Darfur; Protests Push Action on Genocide," *Boston Globe* (May 1, 2006): A1.
5. The absence of a bill of rights led Mason to refuse to sign the proposed Constitution, noting that he "would sooner chop off his right hand than put it to the Constitution as it now stands." Quoted in Eric Black, *Our Constitution: The Myth That Binds Us* (Boulder, CO: Westview, 1988), 75.
6. Quoted in Jack N. Rakove, "Madison Won Passage of the Bill of Rights but Remained a Skeptic," *Public Affairs Report* (March 1991): 6.
7. *Barron v. Baltimore*, 32 U.S. 243 (1833).
8. *Allgeyer v. Louisiana*, 165 U.S. 578 (1897).
9. *Gitlow v. New York*, 268 U.S. 652 (1925).
10. *Near v. Minnesota*, 283 U.S. 697 (1931). For more about *Near*, see Fred W. Friendly, *Minnesota Rag: The Dramatic Story of the Landmark Case That Gave New Meaning to Freedom of the Press* (New York: Random House, 1981).
11. *Palko v. Connecticut*, 302 U.S. 319 (1937).
12. Continental Congress to the People of Great Britain, October 21, 1774, in Philip Kurland and Ralph Lerner, eds., *The Founders' Constitution*, vol. 5 (Chicago: University of Chicago Press, 1987), 61.
13. *Reynolds v. U.S.*, 98 U.S. 145 (1879).
14. *Cantwell v. Connecticut*, 310 U.S. 296 (1940).
15. *Zobrest v. Catalina Foothills School District*, 506 U.S. 813 (1992).
16. *Engel v. Vitale*, 370 U.S. 421 (1962).
17. *Lee v. Weisman*, 505 U.S. 577 (1992).
18. *Lemon v. Kurtzman*, 403 U.S. 602 (1971).
19. "An Eternal Debate," *Omaha World-Journal* (November 27, 2002): 6B.
20. *Widmar v. Vincent*, 454 U.S. 263 (1981).
21. *Board of Education v. Mergens*, 496 U.S. 226 (1990).
22. *Lamb's Chapel v. Center Moriches Union Free School District*, 508 U.S. 384 (1993).
23. *Rosenberger v. University of Virginia*, 515 U.S. 819 (1995).
24. *Agostini v. Felton*, 521 U.S. 203 (1997).
25. *Mitchell v. Helms*, 530 U.S. 793 (2000).
26. *Zelman v. Simmons-Harris*, 536 U.S. 639 (2002).
27. Charles Lane, "Court Upholds Ohio School Vouchers," *Washington Post* (June 28, 2002): A1, A11.
28. *McCreary County v. ACLU of Kentucky*, 545 U.S. 844 (2005).
29. Alan Cooperman, "Judge Bars Tax-Funded Religious Jail Project," *Washington Post* (June 3, 2006): A2.
30. *Church of the Lukumi Babalu Aye v. Hialeah*, 508 U.S. 525 (1993).
31. *Employment Division, Dept. of Human Resources of Oregon v. Smith*, 494 U.S. 872 (1990).
32. *Boerne v. Flores*, 521 U.S. 507 (1997).
33. *Gonzales v. O Centro Espirita Beneficente União do Vegetal*, 546 U.S. ____ (2006).
34. *U.S. v. Seeger*, 380 U.S. 163 (1965).
35. *Cruz v. Beto*, 405 U.S. 319 (1972).
36. *O'Lone v. Shabazz*, 482 U.S. 342 (1987).
37. Tony Mauro, "Stern's Raunch Is Better than Silence," *USA Today* (May 12, 2004): 13A.
38. *Ex parte McCardle*, 74 U.S. 506 (1869).
39. David M. O'Brien, *Constitutional Law and Politics*, vol. 2: *Civil Rights and Civil Liberties* (New York: Norton, 1991), 345.
40. See Frederick Siebert, *The Rights and Privileges of the Press* (New York: Appleton-Century, 1934), 886, 931–40.
41. *Schenck v. U.S.*, 249 U.S. 47 (1919).
42. *Brandenburg v. Ohio*, 395 U.S. 444 (1969).
43. *New York Times Co. v. U.S.*, 403 U.S. 713 (1971).
44. *Nebraska Press Association v. Stuart*, 427 U.S. 539 (1976).
45. *Tory v. Cochran*, 544 U.S. ____ (2005).
46. *Abrams v. U.S.*, 250 U.S. 616 (1919).
47. *Stromberg v. California*, 283 U.S. 359 (1931).
48. *Tinker v. Des Moines Independent Community School District*, 393 U.S. 503 (1969).
49. *Texas v. Johnson*, 491 U.S. 397 (1989).
50. *U.S. v. Eichman*, 496 U.S. 310 (1990).
51. Harry Kalven Jr., *Negro and the First Amendment* (Chicago: University of Chicago Press, 1966).
52. Henry Louis Gates Jr., "Why Civil Liberties Pose No Threat to Civil Rights," *New Republic* (September 20, 1993).
53. *R.A.V. v. City of St. Paul*, 505 U.S. 377 (1992).
54. *Virginia v. Black*, 538 U.S. 343 (2003).
55. *Chaplinsky v. New Hampshire*, 315 U.S. 568 (1942).
56. *New York Times Co. v. Sullivan*, 376 U.S. 254 (1964).
57. *Masson v. New Yorker Magazine*, 501 U.S. 496 (1991).
58. Geraldine Sealy, "Calling Someone 'Gay' May Not Be Slanderous for Long," ABCNews.com (January 16, 2003).
59. "Justin Timberlake Accepts Libel Damages," FemaleFirst.com (August 28, 2005).
60. *Chaplinsky v. New Hampshire*, 315 U.S. 568 (1942).
61. *Cohen v. California*, 403 U.S. 15 (1971).
62. *Regina v. Hicklin*, L.R. 2 Q.B. 360 (1868).
63. *Roth v. U.S.*, 354 U.S. 476 (1957).
64. *Miller v. California*, 413 U.S. 15 (1973).
65. *Barnes v. Glen Theater*, 501 U.S. 560 (1991).
66. *National Endowment for the Arts v. Finley*, 524 U.S. 569 (1998).
67. *Reno v. American Civil Liberties Union*, 521 U.S. 844 (1997).
68. *Ashcroft v. Free Speech Coalition*, 535 U.S. 234 (2002).
69. David G. Savage, "Ban on 'Virtual' Child Porn Is Upset by Court," *Los Angeles Times* (April 17, 2002): A1.
70. Lyle Denniston, "Court Puts 2D Pornography Law on Hold: A Majority Doubt Giving Localities an Internet Veto," *Boston Globe* (May 14, 2002): A2.
71. Nick Anderson and Elizabeth Levin, "Crime Bill Passes Easily in Congress: Measure Includes Expansion of Amber Alert System," *Los Angeles Times* (April 11, 2003): A36.
72. *Ashcroft v. American Civil Liberties Union*, 542 U.S. 656 (2004).
73. *DeJonge v. Oregon*, 229 U.S. 353 (1937).
74. *Barron v. Baltimore*, 32 U.S. 243 (1833).
75. *Dred Scott v. Sandford*, 60 U.S. 393 (1857).
76. *U.S. v. Miller*, 307 U.S. 174 (1939).
77. *Quilici v. Village of Morton Grove*, 104 U.S. 194 (1983).
78. *Printz v. U.S.*, 514 U.S. 898 (1997).
79. *Stein v. New York*, 346 U.S. 156 (1953).
80. *Wilson v. Arkansas*, 514 U.S. 927 (1995).
81. *Hudson v. Michigan*, 547 U.S. ____ (2006).
82. *U.S. v. Sokolov*, 490 U.S. 1 (1989).
83. *U.S. v. Knights*, 534 U.S. 112 (2001).
84. *U.S. v. Matlock*, 415 U.S. 164 (1974).
85. *Georgia v. Randolph*, 547 U.S. ____ (2006).
86. *Johnson v. U.S.*, 333 U.S. 10 (1948).
87. *Winston v. Lee*, 470 U.S. 753 (1985).
88. *South Dakota v. Neville*, 459 U.S. 553 (1983).
89. *Michigan v. Tyler*, 436 U.S. 499 (1978).
90. *Hester v. U.S.*, 265 U.S. 57 (1924).
91. *Kyllo v. U.S.*, 533 U.S. 27 (2001).
92. David G. Savage, "Court Says No to Home Snooping," *Los Angeles Times* (June 12, 2001): A1.
93. *Carroll v. U.S.*, 267 U.S. 132 (1925).
94. *U.S. v. Arvizu*, 534 U.S. 266 (2002).
95. *Skinner v. Railway Labor Executives' Association*, 489 U.S. 602 (1989).
96. *Vernonia School District v. Acton*, 515 U.S. 646 (1995).
97. *Board of Education of Independent School District No. 92 of Pottawatomie County v. Earls*, 536 U.S. 822 (2002).
98. *Chandler v. Miller*, 520 U.S. 305 (1997).
99. John Wefing, "Employer Drug Testing: Disparate Judicial and Legislative Responses," *Albany Law Review* 63 (2000): 799–801.
100. *Ferguson v. City of Charleston*, 532 U.S. 67 (2001).

101. *Counselman* v. *Hitchcock*, 142 U.S. 547 (1892).
102. *Brown* v. *Mississippi*, 297 U.S. 278 (1936).
103. *Lynumm* v. *Illinois*, 372 U.S. 528 (1963).
104. *Rhode Island* v. *Innis*, 446 U.S. 291 (1980).
105. *Arizona* v. *Fulminante*, 500 U.S. 938 (1991).
106. *Dickerson* v. *U.S.*, 530 U.S. 428 (2000).
107. *U.S.* v. *Patane*, 542 U.S. 630 (2004).
108. *Smith* v. *Massachusetts*, 543 U.S. 462 (2005).
109. *Weeks* v. *U.S.*, 232 U.S. 383 (1914).
110. *Mapp* v. *Ohio*, 367 U.S. 643 (1961).
111. *Stone* v. *Powell*, 428 U.S. 465 (1976).
112. *U.S.* v. *Grubbs*, 547 U.S. _____ (2006).
113. *Johnson* v. *Zerbst*, 304 U.S. 458 (1938).
114. *Powell* v. *Alabama*, 287 U.S. 45 (1932).
115. *Gideon* v. *Wainwright*, 372 U.S. 335 (1963).
116. *Argersinger* v. *Hamlin*, 407 U.S. 25 (1972).
117. *Scott* v. *Illinois*, 440 U.S. 367 (1979).
118. *Alabama* v. *Shelton*, 536 U.S. 654 (2002).
119. *Rompilla* v. *Beard*, 545 U.S. 347 (2005).
120. *Strauder* v. *West Virginia*, 100 U.S. 303 (1880).
121. *Taylor* v. *Louisiana*, 419 U.S. 522 (1975).
122. *Batson* v. *Kentucky*, 476 U.S. 79 (1986).
123. *J.E.B.* v. *Alabama*, 511 U.S. 127 (1994).
124. *Maryland* v. *Craig*, 497 U.S. 836 (1990).
125. *Hallinger* v. *Davis*, 146 U.S. 314 (1892).
126. *O'Neil* v. *Vermont*, 144 U.S. 323 (1892).
127. See Michael Meltsner, *Cruel and Unusual: The Supreme Court and Capital Punishment* (New York: Random House, 1973).
128. *Furman* v. *Georgia*, 408 U.S. 238 (1972).
129. *Gregg* v. *Georgia*, 428 U.S. 153 (1976).
130. *McCleskey* v. *Kemp*, 481 U.S. 279 (1987).
131. *McCleskey* v. *Zant*, 499 U.S. 467 (1991).
132. *Atkins* v. *Virginia*, 536 U.S. 304 (2002).
133. *Roper* v. *Simmons*, 543 U.S. 551 (2005).
134. Henry Weinstein, "Inmate Seeks to Halt Execution for DNA Tests," *Los Angeles Times* (April 28, 2002): A20.
135. Henry Weinstein, "Judge Leans Toward Declaring Death Penalty Unconstitutional," *Los Angeles Times* (April 26, 2002): A22.
136. *House* v. *Bell*, 547 U.S. _____ (2006).
137. *Hill* v. *McDonough*, 547 U.S. _____ (2006).
138. *Olmstead* v. *U.S.*, 277 U.S. 438 (1928).
139. *Griswold* v. *Connecticut*, 381 U.S. 481 (1965).
140. *Eisenstadt* v. *Baird*, 410 U.S. 113 (1972).
141. *Roe* v. *Wade*, 410 U.S. 113 (1973).
142. *Beal* v. *Doe*, 432 U.S. 438 (1977); and *Harris* v. *McRae*, 448 U.S. 297 (1980).
143. *Webster* v. *Reproductive Health Services*, 492 U.S. 490 (1989).
144. *Planned Parenthood of Southeastern Pennsylvania* v. *Casey*, 502 U.S. 1056 (1992).
145. Karen O'Connor, *No Neutral Ground: Abortion Politics in an Age of Absolutes* (Boulder, CO: Westview, 1996).
146. "House Sends Partial Birth Abortion Bill to Clinton," *Politics USA* (March 28, 1996): 1.
147. *Stenberg* v. *Carhart*, 530 U.S. 914 (2000).
148. *Ayotte* v. *Planned Parenthood of Northern New England*, 546 U.S. _____ (2006).
149. *Bowers* v. *Hardwick*, 478 U.S. 186 (1986).
150. *Lawrence* v. *Texas*, 539 U.S. 558 (2003).
151. *Cruzan* v. *Director, Missouri Dept. of Health*, 497 U.S. 261 (1990).
152. *Vacco* v. *Quill*, 521 U.S. 793 (1997).
153. Office of the Attorney General, Memorandum for Asa Hutchinson, Administrator, the Drug Enforcement Administration, November 6, 2001.
154. William McCall, "Oregon Suicide Law Gets Longer Reprieve: Court Allows US Senate 5 Months to Ready Arguments," *Boston Globe* (November 21, 2001): A8.
155. *Oregon* v. *Ashcroft*, 192 F. Supp. 2d 1077 (2002); and Kim Murphy, "U.S. Cannot Block Oregon Suicide Law, Judge Rules," *Los Angeles Times* (April 18, 2002): A1.
156. Attorney General's petition for a writ of certiorari, *Gonzales* v. *Oregon*, 2005.
157. *Gonzales* v. *U.S.* 546 U.S. _____ (2006).

CHAPTER 6

1. Dan Eggen, "Civil Rights Focus Shift Roils Staff at Justice," *Washington Post* (December 13, 2005): A1. This vignette draws heavily from this article.
2. Eggen, "Civil Rights Focus Shift Roils Staff at Justice."
3. Dan Eggen, "Politics Alleged in Voting Cases," *Washington Post* (January 23, 2006): A1.
4. David E. Rosenbaum et al., "New Twist in Texas Districting Dispute," *New York Times* (December 3, 2005).
5. League of United Latin American Citizens v. Perry, 547 U.S. _____ (2006).
6. *Civil Rights Cases*, 109 U.S. 3 (1883).
7. *Plessy* v. *Ferguson*, 163 U.S. 537 (1896).
8. Jack Greenberg, *Judicial Process and Social Change: Constitutional Litigation* (St. Paul, MN: West, 1976), 583–86.
9. Juan Williams, *Eyes on the Prize: America's Civil Rights Years, 1954–1965* (New York: Penguin, 1987), 10.
10. *Williams* v. *Mississippi*, 170 U.S. 213 (1898); *Cummins* v. *Richmond County Board of Education*, 175 U.S. 528 (1899).
11. *Muller* v. *Oregon*, 208 U.S. 412 (1908).
12. *Missouri ex Rel. Gaines* v. *Canada*, 305 U.S. 337 (1938).
13. Richard Kluger, *Simple Justice* (New York: Vintage, 1975), 268.
14. *Sweatt* v. *Painter*, 339 U.S. 629 (1950); and *McLaurin* v. *Oklahoma*, 339 U.S. 637 (1950).
15. *Sweatt* v. *Painter*, 339 U.S. 629 (1950).
16. *Brown* v. *Board of Education*, 347 U.S. 483 (1954).
17. But see Gerald Rosenberg, *The Hollow Hope: Can Courts Bring About Social Change?* (Chicago: University of Chicago Press, 1991).
18. Quoted in Williams, *Eyes on the Prize*, 10.
19. *Brown* v. *Board of Education II*, 349 U.S. 294 (1955).
20. Quoted in Williams, *Eyes on the Prize*, 37.
21. *Cooper* v. *Aaron*, 358 U.S. 1 (1958).
22. *Heart of Atlanta Motel* v. *U.S.*, 379 U.S. 241 (1964).
23. *Swann* v. *Charlotte-Mecklenburg School District*, 402 U.S. 1 (1971).
24. *Freeman* v. *Pitts*, 498 U.S. 1081 (1992); *Missouri* v. *Jenkins*, 515 U.S. 70 (1995).
25. "UPI NewsTrack TopNews," (January 20, 2006): NEXIS.
26. *Griggs* v. *Duke Power Co.*, 401 U.S. 424 (1971).
27. Jo Freeman, *The Politics of Women's Liberation* (New York: Longman, 1975), 57.
28. *Hoyt* v. *Florida*, 368 U.S. 57 (1961).
29. Betty Friedan, *The Feminine Mystique* (New York: Dell, 1963).
30. *Korematsu* v. *U.S.*, 323 U.S. 214 (1944). This is the only case involving race-based distinctions applying the strict scrutiny standard where the Court has upheld the restrictive law.
31. *Reed* v. *Reed*, 404 U.S. 71 (1971).
32. *Craig* v. *Boren*, 429 U.S. 190 (1976).
33. *Mississippi University for Women* v. *Hogan*, 458 U.S. 718 (1982).
34. *Craig* v. *Boren*, 429 U.S. 190 (1976).
35. *Orr* v. *Orr*, 440 U.S. 268 (1979).
36. *J.E.B* v. *Alabama TB*, 440 U.S. 268 (1979).
37. *U.S.* v. *Virginia*, 518 U.S. 515 (1996).
38. *Nguyen* v. *INS*, 533 U.S. 53 (2001).
39. *Rostker* v. *Goldberg*, 453 U.S. 57 (1981).
40. *Michael M.* v. *Superior Court of Sonoma County*, 450 U.S. 464 (1981).
41. *Rostker* v. *Goldberg*, 453 U.S. 57 (1981).
42. *U.S.* v. *Virginia*, 518 U.S. 515 (1996).
43. *Meritor Savings Bank* v. *Vinson*, 477 U.S. 57 (1986).
44. *Oncale* v. *Sundowner Offshore Services, Inc.*, 523 U.S. 75 (1998).
45. *Hishon* v. *King & Spalding*, 467 U.S. 69 (1984).
46. *Johnson* v. *Transportation Agency*, 480 U.S. 616 (1987).
47. *Davis* v. *Monroe County Board of Education*, 526 U.S. 629 (1999).
48. Joyce Gelb and Marian Lief Palley, *Women and Public Policies* (Charlottesville: University of Virginia Press, 1996).

49. Erik Brady, "Small Interest Could Be Big Deal," *USA Today* (May 17, 2005): 1C.
50. Christine Marie Sierra, "Hispanics and the Political Process," in Pastora San Juan Cafferty and David W. Engstrom, eds., *Hispanics in the United States* (New Brunswick, NJ: Transaction, 2000), ch. 10.
51. *White* v. *Register*, 412 U.S. 755 (1973).
52. *San Antonio Independent School District* v. *Rodriguez*, 411 U.S. 1 (1973).
53. *Edgewood Independent School District* v. *Kirby*, 777 SW.2d 391 (1989).
54. "MALDEF 'Pleased with Settlement of California Public Schols Inequity Case, *Williams* v. *California*,'" August 13, 2004.
55. MALDEF, "U.S. Supreme Court to Hear MALDEF's Appeal of Texas Redistricting Case," December 12, 2005.
56. *League of United Latin American Citizens* v. *Perry*, 547 U.S. _____ (2006).
57. Randall C. Archibold, "Immigrants Take to U.S. Streets in Show of Strength," *New York Times* (May 1, 2006): A1.
58. Judy Keen, "From Coast to Coast, 'We Need to Be Heard,'" *USA Today* (May 2, 2006): 3A.
59. "Best-Selling Book Challenges Long-Held Theories About Life in America," Voice of America News, October 7, 2005.
60. Rennard Strickland, "Native Americans," in Kermit Hall, ed., *The Oxford Companion to the Supreme Court of the United States* (New York: Oxford University Press, 1992), 557.
61. Strickland, "Native Americans," 579.
62. *Employment Division of the Oregon Department of Human Resources* v. *Smith*, 494 U.S. 872 (1990).
63. *Boerne* v. *Flores*, 521 U.S. 507 (1997).
64. Dee Brown, *Bury My Heart at Wounded Knee* (New York: Holt, Rinehart and Winston, 1971).
65. *Cobell* v. *Norton*, 204 F.3d 1081 (2001). For more on the Indian trust, see http://www.indiantrust.com/overview.cfm.
66. Richard Luscombe, "Tribes Go on Legal Warpath," *The Observer* (April 25, 2004): 20.
67. Michael McNutt, "Group Supports Indians in Office," *Daily Oklahoman* (May 15, 2006).
68. Diane Helene Miller, *Freedom to Differ: The Shaping of the Gay and Lesbian Struggle for Civil Rights* (New York: New York University Press, 1998).
69. Sarah Brewer, David Kaib, and Karen O'Connor, "Sex and the Supreme Court: Gays, Lesbians, and Justice," in Craig A. Rimmerman, Kenneth D. Wald, and Clyde Wilcox, eds., *The Politics of Gay Rights* (Chicago: University of Chicago Press, 2000).
70. Evan Gerstmann, *The Constitutional Underclass: Gays, Lesbians, and the Failure of Class-Based Equal Protection* (Chicago: University of Chicago Press, 1999).
71. Deborah Ensor, "Gay Veterans Working for Change," *San Diego Union* (April 13, 2002): B1.
72. John White, "'Don't Ask' Costs More than Expected," *Washington Post* (February 14, 2006): A4.
73. *Romer* v. *Evans*, 517 U.S. 620 (1996).
74. *Lawrence* v. *Texas*, 539 U.S. 558 (2003).
75. Joan Biskupic, "Court's Opinion on Gay Rights Reflects Trends," *USA Today* (July 18, 2003): 2A.
76. David Pfeiffer, "Overview of the Disability Movement: History, Legislative Record and Political Implications," *Policy Studies Journal* (Winter 1993): 724–42; and "Understanding Disability Policy," *Policy Studies Journal* (Spring 1996): 157–74.
77. Joan Biskupic, "Supreme Court Limits Meaning of Disability," *Washington Post* (June 23, 1999): A1.
78. *Sutton* v. *United Air Lines, Inc.*, 527 U.S. 471 (1999).
79. *Tennessee* v. *Lane*, 541 U.S. 509 (2004).
80. American Association of People with Disabilities, www.aapd-dc.org.
81. *Regents of the University of California* v. *Bakke*, 438 U.S. 265 (1978).
82. *Johnson* v. *Santa Clara County*, 480 U.S. 616 (1987).
83. Ruth Marcus, "Hill Coalition Aims to Counter Court in Job Bias," *Washington Post* (February 8, 1990): A10.
84. *Adarand Constructors* v. *Pena*, 515 U.S. 200 (1995).
85. Cert. denied, *Texas* v. *Hopwood*, 518 U.S. 1033 (1996). See also Terrance Stutz, "UT Minority Enrollment Tested by Suit: Fate of Affirmative Action in Education Is at Issue," *Dallas Morning News* (October 14, 1995).
86. *Grutter* v. *Bollinger*, 539 U.S. 306 (2003).
87. *Gratz* v. *Bollinger*, 539 U.S. 306 (2003).
88. *Grutter* v. *Bollinger*, 539 U.S. 306 (2003).
89. Victoria Colliver, "Class Action Considered in Wal-Mart Suit," *San Francisco Chronicle* (September 25, 2003): B1.
90. "Wal-Mart's Immigrant Labor Problem," *Tampa Tribune* (November 14, 2003): 10.

CHAPTER 7

1. For an outstanding account of Pelosi's campaign for the whip post, see Juliet Eilperin, "The Making of Madam Whip: Fear and Loathing—and Horse Trading—The Race for the House's No. 2 Democrat," *Washington Post* (January 6, 2002): W27.
2. "Mother of All Whips," *Pittsburgh Post-Gazette* (February 9, 2002): A11.
3. Steven S. Smith and Eric D. Lawrence, "Party Control of Congress in the Republican Congress," in Lawrence C. Dodd and Bruce I. Oppenheimer, eds., *Congress Reconsidered*, 6th ed. (Washington, DC: CQ Press, 1997), 163–4. For more on the role of parties in the organization of Congress, see Forrest Maltzman, *Competing Principals: Committees, Parties, and the Organization of Congress* (Ann Arbor: University of Michigan Press, 1997) ; and Marc J. Hetherington and William J. Keefe, *Parties, Politics, and Public Policy in America*, 10th ed. (Washington, DC: CQ Press, 2006).
4. "What Is the Democratic Caucus?" http://dcaucusweb.house.gov/about/what_is.asp.
5. Barbara Hinckley, *Stability and Change in Congress*, 3rd ed. (New York: Harper and Row, 1983), 166.
6. Katharine Seelye, "Congressional Memo: New Speaker, New Style, Old Problem," *New York Times* (March 12, 1999): A18.
7. Charles Babbington, "Pelosi Seeks House Minority 'Bill of Rights,' Hastert Dismisses Democrats' Complaint, Saying GOP Record Is Better than Foes'," *Washington Post* (June 24, 2004): A23.
8. Barbara Sinclair, "The Struggle over Representation and Law-making in Congress: Leadership Reforms in the 1990s," in James A. Thurber and Roger H. Davidson, eds., *Remaking Congress: Change and Stability in the 1990s* (Washington, DC: CQ Press, 1995), 105.
9. Quoted in Donald R. Matthews, *U.S. Senators and Their World* (Chapel Hill: University of North Carolina Press, 1960), 97–8.
10. Woodrow Wilson, *Congressional Government: A Study in American Government* (New York: Meridian Books, 1956; originally published in 1885), 79.
11. Roger H. Davidson, "Congressional Committees in the New Reform Era: From Combat to the Contract," in Thurber and Davidson, *Remaking Congress*, 28.
12. See E. Scott Adler, *Why Congressional Reforms Fail: Reelection and the House Committee System* (Chicago: University of Chicago Press, 2002).
13. See Thomas Mann and Norman Ornstein, *The Broken Branch* (New York: Oxford University Press, 2006), 34–45; and Paul Quirk, "Deliberation and Decision Making," in Paul Quirk and Sarah Binder, eds., *Legislative Branch* (New York: Oxford University Press, 2005), 330–342.
14. For more about committees, see Christopher Deering and Steven S. Smith, *Committees in Congress*, 3rd ed. (Washington, DC: CQ Press, 1997).
15. Woodrow Wilson, *Congressional Government*. (New York: Houghton Mifflin, 1885).
16. Kenneth A. Shepsle, *The Giant Jigsaw Puzzle: Democratic Committee Assignments in the Modern House* (Chicago: University of Chicago Press, 1978).
17. Tim Groseclose and Charles Stewart III, "The Value of Committee Seats in the House, 1947–91," *American Journal of Political Science* 42 (April 1998): 453–74.
18. Charles S. Bullock III, "House Careerists: Changing Patterns of Longevity and Attrition," *American Political Science Review* 66 (December 1972): 1295–1300.

19. Michael K. Moore and John R. Hibbing, "Situational Dissatisfaction in Congress: Explaining Voluntary Departures," *Journal of Politics* 60 (November 1998): 1088–1107.

20. Helen Dewar, "Retiring Senators Look Beyond the Beltway; Eschewing Washington's Revolving Door, Many Instead Turn to Home-State Classrooms," *Washington Post* (December 29, 1996): A4.

21. Juliet Eilperin, "Ex Lawmakers' Edge Is Access," *Washington Post* (September 13, 2003): A1.

22. Jeffrey H. Birnbaum, "Hill a Stepping Stone to K Street for Some," *Washington Post* (July 27, 2005): A19.

23. Jim Drinkard, "Sponsored Trips Fall Amid Lobbying Debate," *USA Today* (May 3, 2006): 1A.

24. Richard F. Fenno Jr., "U.S. House Members in Their Constituencies: An Exploration," *American Political Science Review* 71 (September 1977): 883–917.

25. Richard F. Fenno Jr., *Home Style: House Members in Their Districts* (Boston: Little, Brown, 1978), 32.

26. Hedrick Smith, *The Power Game* (New York: Ballantine Books, 1989), 108.

27. Gary W. Cox and Jonathan N. Katz, "Why Did the Incumbency Advantage in U.S. House Elections Grow?" *American Journal of Political Science* 40 (May 1996): 478–97; Kenneth N. Bickers and Robert M. Stein, "The Electoral Dynamics of the Federal Pork Barrel," *American Journal of Political Science* 40 (November 1996): 1300–26; and Diana Evans, *Greasing the Wheels: Using Pork Barrel Projects to Build Majority Coalitions in Congress* (New York: Cambridge University Press, 2004).

28. Marjorie Randon Hershey, "Congressional Elections," in Gerald M. Pomper et al., *The Election of 1992: Reports and Interpretations* (Chatham, NJ: Chatham House, 1993), 159.

29. Alan I. Abramowitz, "Incumbency, Congressional Spending, and the Decline of Competition in House Elections," *Journal of Politics* 53 (February 1991): 34–56.

30. Mildred L. Amer, "Membership of the 108th Congress: A Profile." Congressional Research Service (March 20, 2003).

31. Amy Keller, "The Roll Call 50 Richest: For Richer or Poorer Thanks to Spouses, Kerry Keeps Top Spot and Clinton Joins List," *Roll Call* (September 9, 2002).

32. Andrea Stone, "War Vets Ready for New Battle: Politics," *USA Today* (January 23, 2006): 1A.

33. Warren E. Miller and Donald Stokes, "Constituency Influence in Congress," *American Political Science Review* 57 (March 1963): 45–57.

34. Public Opinion Online, Accession Number 0363310, Question Number 054, June 14–18, 2000, Lexis-Nexis RPOLL.

35. Nancy E. McGlen et al., *Women, Politics and America Society,* 4th ed. (New York: Longman, 2004).

36. See also Cindy Simon Rosenthal, *Women Transforming Congress* (Norman: University of Oklahoma Press, 2003); Karen O'Connor, *Women and Congress: Winning, Running, and Ruling* (Binghamton, N.Y.: Haworth Press, 2003); and Susan J. Carroll, ed., *The Impact of Women in Public Office* (Bloomington: Indiana University Press, 2002).

37. Michele L. Swers, *The Difference Women Make* (Chicago: University of Chicago Press, 2002).

38. *Congressional Quarterly Weekly Report* (January 6, 2001).

39. David E. Price, "Reflections on *Congressional Government* at 120 and Congress at 216," speech delivered at the Wilson Center, November 14, 2005.

40. Norman Ornstein, "GOP Moderates Can Impact Policy—If They Dare," *Roll Call* (February 12, 2003).

41. Byron York, "Bored by Estrada? Owen May Be a Reprise," *The Hill* (March 19, 2003): 43.

42. Price, "Reflections on *Congressional Government* at 120 and Congress at 216."

43. See L. Martin Overby, "The Senate and Justice Thomas: A Note on Ideology, Race, and Constituent Pressures," *Congress and the Presidency* 21 (Autumn 1994): 131–6.

44. John W. Kingdon, *Congressmen's Voting Decisions,* 3rd ed. (Ann Arbor: University of Michigan Press, 1989).

45. Kingdon, *Congressmen's Voting Decisions.* See also Lee Sigelman, Paul J. Wahlbeck, and Emmett H. Buell Jr., "Vote Choice and the Preference for Divided Government: Lessons of 1992," *American Journal of Political Science* 41 (July 1997): 879–94.

46. Ken Kollman, "Inviting Friends to Lobby: Interest Groups, Ideological Bias, and Congressional Committees," *American Journal of Political Science* 41 (April 1997): 519–44. See also Marie Hojnacki and David C. Kimball, "Organized Interests and the Decision of Whom to Lobby in Congress," *American Political Science Review* 92 (December 1998): 775–90.

47. Robert Beirsack, Paul Herrnson, and Clyde Wilcox, *After the Revolution: PACs, Lobbies and the Republican Congress* (Boston: Allyn and Bacon, 1999).

48. Barbara S. Romzek and Jennifer A. Utter, "Congressional Legislative Staff: Political Professionals or Clerks?" *American Journal of Political Science* 41 (October 1997): 1251–79; Susan Webb Hammond, "Recent Research on Legislative Staffs," *Legislative Studies Quarterly* (November 1996): 543–76; and Michael T. Heaney, "Brokering Health Policy: Coalitions, Parties, and Interest Group Influence," *Journal of Health Politics, Policy, and Law* 31 (October 2006): 887–944.

49. Keith Krehbiel, "Cosponsors and Wafflers from A to Z." *American Journal of Political Science* 39 (November 1995): 906–23.

50. Don Phillips, "Biden Stalls Transportation Picks," *Washington Post* (March 28, 2002): A4.

51. David E. Sanger, "Rounding Out a Clear Clinton Legacy," *New York Times* (May 25, 2000): A1.

52. Sanger, "Rounding Out," A1, A10.

53. Eric Schmitt, "How a Hard-Driving G.O.P. Gave Clinton a Trade Victory," *New York Times* (May 26, 2000): A1.

54. John Burgess, "A Winning Combination: Money, Message, and Clout," *Washington Post* (May 25, 2000): A4.

55. David E. Rosenbaum, "With Smiles and Cell Phones, a Last-Minute Assault on the Undecided," *New York Times* (May 25, 2000): A11.

56. Schmitt, "How a Hard-Driving."

57. Schmitt, "How a Hard-Driving."

58. Sanger, "Rounding Out," A1, A10.

59. Andrew Beadle, "Up Against a Wall? Election-Year Politics and a New Trade Dispute Pose a Challenge to Otherwise Strong Relations Between the US and China," *Journal of Commerce* (April 5, 2004): 24.

60. Paul Blustein, "U.S. Takes Parts Fight with China to WTO," *Washington Post* (March 31, 2006): D5.

61. Dan Eggen and Peter Baker, "A Defiant Stance in Jefferson Probe," *Washington Post* (May 27, 2006): A1, A10.

62. Joel D. Aberbach, *Keeping a Watchful Eye: The Politics of Congressional Oversight* (Washington, DC: Brookings Institution, 1990).

63. William F. West, "Oversight Subcommittees in the House of Representatives, *Congress and the Presidency* 25 (Autumn 1998): 147–60.

64. Price, "Reflections on *Congressional Government* at 120 and Congress at 216," 10.

65. Mann and Ornstein, *The Broken Branch,* 1–22.

66. This discussion draws heavily on Steven J. Balla, "Legislative Organization and Congressional Review," paper delivered at the 1999 meeting of the Midwest Political Science Association.

67. Cindy Skrzycki, "Reforms' Knockout Act, Kept Out of the Ring," *Washington Post* (April 18, 2006): D1.

68. *Wall Street Journal* (April 13, 1973): 10.

69. Craig Gilbert, "Use of Force Is President's Call," *Milwaukee Journal Sentinel* (April 18, 2002): A8.

70. Note from Senator Jay Rockefeller to Vice President Dick Cheney, July 13, 2003, reprinted in Charles Babington and Dafna Linzer, "Senator Sounded Alarm in '03" *Washington Post* (December 20, 2005): A10.

71. Quoted in Stewart M. Powell, "Lee Fight Signals Tougher Battles Ahead on Nomination," *Commercial Appeal* (December 21, 1997): A15.

CHAPTER 8

1. "Two Hundred Years of Presidential Funerals," *Washington Post* (June 10, 2004): C14.

2. "The Fold: Presidential Funerals; Farewell to the Chiefs," *Newsday* (June 9, 2004): A38.

3. Gail Russell Chaddock, "The Rise of Mourning in America," *Christian Science Monitor* (June 11, 2004): 1.

4. Richard E. Neustadt, *Presidential Power and the Modern Presidency* (New York: Free Press, 1991).

5. Edward S. Corwin, *The President: Office and Powers, 1787–1957,* 4th ed. (New York: New York University Press, 1957), 5.

6. Quoted in Corwin, *The President,* 11.

7. Winston Solberg, *The Federal Convention and the Formation of the Union of the American States* (Indianapolis, IN: Bobbs-Merrill, 1958), 235.

8. James P. Pfiffner, "Recruiting Executive Branch Leaders," *Brookings Review* 19 (Spring 2001): 41–43.

9. Benjamin I. Page and Mark P. Petracca, *The American Presidency* (New York: McGraw-Hill, 1983), 262.

10. Page and Petracca, *The American Presidency,* 268.

11. Jim Lobe, "Bush 'Unsigns' War Crimes Treaty," AlterNet.com, May 6, 2002. See also Lincoln P. Bloomfield Jr., "The U.S. Government and the International Criminal Court," Remarks to the Parliamentarians for Global Action, Consultative Assembly of Parliamentarians for the International Criminal Court and the Rule of Laws, address delivered at the United Nations, New York, September 12, 2003.

12. Quoted in Solberg, *The Federal Convention,* 91.

13. *Clinton v. City of New York,* 524 U.S. 417 (1998).

14. "War Powers: Resolution Grants Bush Power He Needs," *Rocky Mountain News* (September 15, 2001): B6.

15. *Public Papers of the Presidents* (1963), 889.

16. Quoted in Neustadt, *Presidential Power,* 9.

17. Quoted in Paul F. Boller Jr., *Presidential Anecdotes* (New York: Penguin Books, 1981), 78.

18. Lyn Ragsdale and John Theis III, "The Institutionalization of the American Presidency, 1924–1992," *American Journal of Political Science* 41 (October 1997): 1280–1318.

19. Quoted in Page and Petracca, *The American Presidency,* 57.

20. Alfred Steinberg, *The First Ten: The Founding Presidents and Their Administrations* (New York: Doubleday, 1967), 59.

21. See Louis Fisher, *Constitutional Conflicts Between Congress and the President,* 4th ed. (Lawrence: University Press of Kansas, 1997).

22. Franklin D. Roosevelt, Press Conference, July 23, 1937.

23. Lyndon B. Johnson, *The Vantage Point* (New York: Holt, Rinehart and Winston, 1971), 448.

24. Morris Fiorina, *Divided Government,* Longman Classics (New York: Longman, 2002); and David R. Mayhew, *Divided We Govern: Party Control, Lawmaking, and Investigations, 1946–2002,* 2nd ed. (New Haven, CT: Yale University Press, 2005).

25. See Lance LeLoup and Steven Shull, *The President and Congress: Collaboration and Conflict in National Policymaking* (Boston: Allyn and Bacon, 1999).

26. See Cary Covington, J. Mark Wrighton, and Rhonda Kinney, "A 'Presidency-Augmented' Model of Presidential Success on House Roll Call Votes," *American Journal of Political Science* 39 (November 1995): 1001–24; and Wayne P. Steger, "Presidential Policy Initiation and the Politics of Agenda Control," *Congress and the Presidency* 24 (Spring 1997): 102–14.

27. Quoted in Thomas E. Cronin, *The State of the Presidency,* 2nd ed. (Boston: Little, Brown, 1980), 169.

28. Robert A. Caro, *Master of the Senate: The Years of Lyndon Johnson* (New York: Knopf, 2002).

29. Paul C. Light, *The President's Agenda: Domestic Policy Choice from Kennedy to Carter* (Baltimore, MD: Johns Hopkins University Press, 1983).

30. Mary Leonard, "Bush Begins Talks on Human Cloning," *Boston Globe* (January 17, 2002): A6.

31. "Resisting Secrecy," *Plain Dealer* (April 30, 2002): B8.

32. Richard Reeves, "Writing History to Executive Order," *New York Times* (November 16, 2001): A25.

33. Samuel Kernell, *New Strategies of Presidential Leadership,* 2nd ed. (Washington, DC: CQ Press, 1993), 3.

34. Jeffrey Cohen, "Presidential Rhetoric and the Public Agenda," *American Journal of Political Science* 39 (February 1995): 87–107.

35. George Reedy, *The Twilight of the Presidency* (New York: New American Library), 38–39.

36. Neustadt, *Presidential Power,* 1–10.

37. Samuel Kernell, *Going Public: New Strategies of Presidential Leadership,* 3rd ed. (Washington, DC: CQ Press, 1997).

38. Dan Balz, "Strange Bedfellows: How Television and Presidential Candidates Changed American Politics," *Washington Monthly* (July 1993).

39. William E. Gibson, "Job Approval Ratings Steady: Personal Credibility Takes a Hit," *News and Observer* (August 19, 1998): A16.

CHAPTER 9

1. Gardiner Harris, "Bush Plan Shows U.S. Is Not Ready for Deadly Flu," *New York Times* (October 8, 2005).

2. Anita Manning and David Jackson, "Bird Flu Plan Lacks a Key Detail," *USA Today* (May 4, 2006): 2A.

3. Harris, "Bush Plan Shows U.S. Is Not Ready for Deadly Flu."

4. Harris, "Bush Plan Shows U.S. Is Not Ready for Deadly Flu."

5. Stephen Barr, "Users Mostly Rate Agencies Favorably," *Washington Post* (April 13, 2000): A29.

6. Harold D. Lasswell, *Politics: Who Gets What, When and How* (New York: McGraw-Hill, 1938).

7. Quoted in Robert C. Caldwell, *James A. Garfield* (Hamden, CT: Archon Books, 1965).

8. David Osborne and Ted Gaebler, *Reinventing Government* (Reading, MA: Addison-Wesley, 1992), 20–21.

9. U.S. House of Representatives Committee on Government Reform, Minority Staff Special Investigation Division, "The Growth of Political Appointees in the Bush Administration," May 3, 2006, 2.

10. Office of Personnel Management, *The Fact Book,* http://www.opm.gov/feddata/factbook/2005/factbook2005.pdf.

11. Barbara Slavin, "State Department Having Staffing Trouble," *USA Today* (December 2005): 10A.

12. Stephen Barr, "Some Trainees Voice Frustration with Presidential Management Intern Program," *Washington Post* (November 26, 2001): B2.

13. Kenneth J. Cooper, "U.S. May Repay Loans for College," *Washington Post* (December 13, 2001): A45.

14. Edward Walsh, "OMB Details 'Outsourcing' Revisions; Unions Denounce New Rules Aimed at Competition," *Washington Post* (May 30, 2003): A24.

15. "A Century of Government Growth," *Washington Post* (January 3, 2000): A17. On the difficulty of counting the exact number of government agencies, see David Nachmias and David H. Rosenbloom, *Bureaucratic Government: U.S.A.* (New York: St. Martin's Press, 1980).

16. The classic work on regulatory commissions is Marver Bernstein, *Regulating Business by Independent Commission* (Princeton, NJ: Princeton University Press, 1955).

17. *Humphrey's Executor v. U.S.,* 295 U.S. 602 (1935).

18. Avram Goldstein, "Teacher to Lose Job Under Hatch Act," *Washington Post* (April 15, 2002): A8.

19. H. H. Gerth and C. Wright Mills, *From Max Weber* (New York: Oxford University Press, 1958).

20. Karen DeYoung, "Saudis Detail Steps on Charities; Kingdom Seeks to Quell Record on Terrorist Financing," *Washington Post* (December 3, 2002): A1.

21. Mike Allen, "White House to Defer to NASA Investigation; Work on Space Policy to Await Probe's End," *Washington Post* (February 5, 2003): A14.

22. Michael Lipsky, *Street-Level Bureaucracy: Dilemmas of the Individual in Public Services* (New York: Russell Sage Foundation, 1980).

23. Cornelius M. Kerwin, *Rulemaking: How Government Agencies Write Law and Make Policy,* 2nd ed. (Washington, DC: CQ Press, 1999), xv.

24. Jack C. Plano and Milton Greenberg, *The American Political Dictionary,* 6th ed. (New York: Holt, Rinehart and Winston, 1982), 236.

25. Stephen Barr, "For IRS, a Deadline to Draft a Smile," *Washington Post* (January 31, 1999): H1.

26. FOX News, Opinion Dynamics Poll, May 20, 2003, Lexis-Nexis RPOLL.

27. Quoted in Arthur Schlesinger Jr., *A Thousand Days* (Greenwich, CT: Fawcett Books, 1967), 377.

28. Thomas V. DiBacco, "Veep Gore Reinventing Government—Again!" *USA Today* (September 9, 1993): 13A.

29. George A. Krause, "Presidential Use of Executive Orders, 1953–1994," *American Politics Quarterly* 25 (October 1997): 458–81.

30. Irene Murphy, *Public Policy on the Status of Women* (Lexington, MA: Lexington Books, 1974).

31. "By Any Other Name: Whatever FEMA Is Ultimately Called, It's Still an Agency in Need of Profound Reform," *Washington Post* (May 10, 2006): A24.

32. Mathew McCubbins and Thomas Schwartz, "Congressional Oversight Overlooked: Police Patrols Versus Fire Alarms," *American Journal of Political Science* 28 (1987): 165–79.

33. Rosemary O'Leary, *Environmental Change: Federal Courts and the EPA* (Philadelphia: Temple University Press, 1993).

34. James F. Spriggs III, "The Supreme Court and Federal Administrative Agencies: A Resource-Based Theory and Analysis of Judicial Impact," *American Journal of Political Science* 40 (November 1996): 1122.

35. Wendy Hansen, Renee Johnson, and Isaac Unah, "Specialized Courts, Bureaucratic Agencies, and the Politics of U.S. Trade Policy," *American Journal of Political Science* 39 (August 1995): 529–57.

CHAPTER 10

1. *Hamdi et al.* v. *Rumsfeld,* 542 U.S. 507 (2004).

2. *Hamdan* v. *Rumsfeld,* 548 U.S. _____ (2006)

3. Charles Lane, "High Court Rejects Detainees Tribunals," *Washington Post* (June 30, 2006): A1.

4. Bernard Schwartz, *The Law in America* (New York: American Heritage, 1974), 48.

5. Julius Goebel Jr., *History of the Supreme Court of the United States,* vol. 1: *Antecedents and Beginnings to 1801* (New York: Macmillan, 1971), 206.

6. *Marbury* v. *Madison,* 5 U.S. 137 (1803).

7. *Martin* v. *Hunter's Lessee,* 14 U.S. 304 (1816).

8. Quoted in Goebel, *History of the Supreme Court,* 280.

9. *Chisholm* v. *Georgia,* 2 U.S. 419 (1793).

10. Oliver Ellsworth served from 1796 to 1800.

11. In *Hylton* v. *U.S.,* 3 U.S. 171 (1796), the Court ruled that a congressional tax on horse-drawn carriages was an excise tax and not a direct tax and therefore it need not be apportioned evenly among the states (as direct taxes must be, according to the Constitution).

12. *Fletcher* v. *Peck,* 10 U.S. 87 (1810); *Martin* v. *Hunter's Lessee,* 14 U.S. 304 (1816); *Cohens* v. *Virginia,* 19 U.S. 264 (1821).

13. *McCulloch* v. *Maryland,* 17 U.S. 316 (1819).

14. *Marbury* v. *Madison,* 5 U.S. 137 (1803).

15. *Marbury* v. *Madison,* 5 U.S. 137 (1803).

16. This discussion draws heavily on Jack C. Plano and Milton Greenberg, *The American Political Dictionary,* 10th ed. (Fort Worth, TX: Harcourt Brace, 1996), 247.

17. *Strauder* v. *West Virginia,* 100 U.S. 303 (1888).

18. *Duren* v. *Missouri,* 439 U.S. 357 (1979).

19. *Batson* v. *Kentucky,* 476 U.S. 79 (1986) (African Americans), and *JEB* v. *Alabama,* 511 U.S. 127 (1994) (women).

20. David W. Neubauer, *Judicial Process: Law, Courts, and Politics* (Pacific Grove, CA: Brooks/Cole, 1991), 57.

21. Cases involving citizens from different states can be filed in state or federal court.

22. Sheldon Goldman and Elliot E. Slotnick, "Clinton's First Term Judiciary: Many Bridges to Cross," *Judicature* (May/June 1997): 254–55.

23. Neil Lewis, "Deal Ends Impasse over Judicial Nominees," *New York Times* (May 19, 2004): A19.

24. Dan Balz and Amy Goldstein, "Filibuster Showdown Looms in Senate: Democrats Prepare for Next Court Pick," *Washington Post* (September 28, 2005): A4.

25. Quoted in Nina Totenberg, "Will Judges Be Chosen Rationally?" *Judicature* (August/September 1976): 93.

26. Quoted in Judge Irving R. Kaufman, "Charting a Judicial Pedigree," *New York Times* (January 24, 1981): A23.

27. Quoted in Lawrence Baum, *The Supreme Court,* 3rd ed. (Washington, DC: CQ Press, 1989), 108.

28. See Barbara A. Perry, *A Representative Supreme Court? The Impact of Race, Religion, and Gender on Appointments* (New York: Greenwood Press, 1991).

29. Clarence Thomas was raised a Catholic but attended an Episcopalian church at the time of his appointment, having been barred from Catholic sacraments because of his remarriage. He again, however, is attending Roman Catholic services.

30. Amy Goldstein, "Bush Set to Curb ABA's Role in Court Appointments," *Washington Post* (March 18, 2001): A2.

31. Saundra Torry, "ABA's Judicial Panel Is a Favorite Bipartisan Target," *Washington Post* (April 29, 1996): F7.

32. Subsequent revelations about Brandeis's secret financial payments to Frankfurter to allow him to handle cases of social interest to Brandeis (while Brandeis was on the Court and couldn't handle them himself) raise questions about the fitness of both Frankfurter and Brandeis for the bench. Still, no information about Frankfurter's legal arrangements with Brandeis was unearthed during the committee's investigations or Frankfurter's testimony.

33. John Brigham, *The Cult of the Court* (Philadelphia: Temple University Press, 1987).

34. Stephen L. Wasby, *The Supreme Court in the Federal Judicial System,* 4th ed. (Chicago: Nelson-Hall, 1988), 194.

35. Wasby, *The Supreme Court in the Federal Judicial System,* 194.

36. Wasby, *The Supreme Court in the Federal Judicial System,* 199. Much of this change occurred as the result of an increase in state criminal cases, of which nearly 100 percent concerned constitutional questions.

37. Data compiled by authors for 2001–2002 term of the Court.

38. Justice Stevens chooses not to join this pool. According to one former clerk, "He wanted an independent review," but Stevens examines only about 20 percent of the petitions, leaving the rest to his clerks. Tony Mauro, "Ginsburg Plunges into the Cert Pool," *Legal Times* (September 6, 1993): 8.

39. Paul Wahlbeck, James F. Spriggs II, and Lee Sigelman, "Ghostwriters on the Court? A Stylistic Analysis of U.S. Supreme Court Opinion Drafts," *American Politics Research* 30 (March 2002): 166–92. Wahlbeck, Spriggs, and Sigelman note that "between 1969 and 1972— the period during which the justices each became entitled to a third law clerk . . . the number of opinions increased by about 50 percent and the number of words tripled."

40. Richard A. Posner, *The Federal Courts: Crisis and Reform* (Cambridge, MA: Harvard University Press, 1985), 114.

41. Todd C. Peppers, *Courtiers of the Marble Palace: The Rise and Influence of the Supreme Court Law Clerk* (Palo Alto, CA: Stanford University Press, 2006).

42. Edward Lazarus, *Closed Chambers: The First Eyewitness Account of the Epic Struggles Inside the Supreme Court* (New York: Random House, 1998).

43. "Retired Chief Justice Warren Attacks . . . Freund Study Group's Composition and Proposal," *American Bar Association Journal* 59 (July 1973): 728.

44. Kathleen Werdegar, "The Solicitor General and Administrative Due Process," *George Washington Law Review* (1967–1968): 482.

45. Rebecca Mae Salokar, *The Solicitor General: The Politics of Law* (Philadelphia: Temple University Press, 1992), 3.

46. Quoted in Elder Witt, *A Different Justice: Reagan and the Supreme Court* (Washington, DC: CQ Press, 1986), 133.

47. Lawrence Baum, *The Supreme Court,* 4th ed. (Washington, DC: CQ Press, 1992), 106.

48. Richard C. Cortner, *The Supreme Court and Civil Liberties* (Palo Alto, CA: Mayfield, 1975), vi.

49. *Brown* v. *Board of Education,* 347 U.S. 483 (1954); *Planned Parenthood of Southeastern Pennsylvania* v. *Casey,* 585 U.S. 833 (1992); *Grutter* v. *Bollinger,* 539 U.S. 306 (2003).

50. Gregory A. Caldeira and John R. Wright, "*Amicus Curiae* Before the Supreme Court: Who Participates, When and How Much?" *Journal of Politics* 52 (August 1990): 803.

51. See also John R. Hermann, "American Indians in Court: The Burger and Rehnquist Years," Ph.D. dissertation, Emory University, 1996.

52. *U.S.* v. *Nixon,* 418 U.S. 683 (1974).

53. Linda Greenhouse, "With O'Connor Retirement and a New Chief Justice Comes an Awareness of Change," *New York Times* (January 28, 2006): A10.

54. *Clinton* v. *Jones,* 520 U.S. 681 (1997).

55. *Webster* v. *Reproductive Health Services,* 492 U.S. 490 (1989).

56. Donald L. Horowitz, *The Courts and Social Policy* (Washington, DC: Brookings Institution, 1977), 538.

57. *Brown* v. *Board of Education,* 347 U.S. 483 (1954).

58. *Webster* v. *Reproductive Health Services,* 492 U.S. 490 (1989).

59. See, for example, Tracey E. George and Lee Epstein, "On the Nature of Supreme Court Decision Making," *American Political Science Review* 86 (1992): 323–37; Melinda Gann Hall and Paul Brace, "Justices' Responses to Case Facts: An Interactive Model," *American Politics Quarterly* (April 1996): 237–61; Lawrence Baum, *The Puzzle of Judicial Behavior* (Ann Arbor: University of Michigan Press, 1997); and Gregory N. Flemming, David B. Holmes, and Susan Gluck Mezey, "An Integrated Model of Privacy Decision Making in State Supreme Courts," *American Politics Quarterly* 26 (January 1998): 35–58.

60. Lee Epstein and Jeffrey A. Segal, "Changing Room: The Court's Dynamics Have a Way of Altering a Justice's Approach to the Law," *Washington Post* (November 20, 2005): B1.

61. Jeffrey A. Segal and Harold J. Spaeth, *The Supreme Court and the Attitudinal Model Revisited* (New York: Cambridge University Press, 2002).

62. Gerard Gryski, Eleanor C. Main, and William Dixon, "Models of State High Court Decision Making in Sex Discrimination Cases," *Journal of Politics* 48 (1986): 143–55; and C. Neal Tate and Roger Handberg, "Time Binding and Theory Building in Personal Attribute Models of Supreme Court Voting Behavior, 1916–1988," *American Political Science Review* 35 (1991): 460–80.

63. Donald R. Songer and Sue Davis, "The Impact of Party and Region on Voting Decisions in the U.S. Courts of Appeals, 1955–86," *Western Political Quarterly* 43 (1990): 830–44.

64. See, generally, Lee Epstein and Jack Knight, "Field Essay: Toward a Strategic Revolution in Judicial Politics: A Look Back, a Look Ahead," *Political Research Quarterly* 53 (September 2000): 663–76.

65. Timothy R. Johnson and Andrew D. Martin, "The Public's Conditional Response to Supreme Court Decisions," *American Political Science Review* 92 (June 1998): 299–309.

66. *Korematsu* v. *U.S.,* 323 U.S. 214 (1944).

67. *Youngstown Sheet & Tube Co.* v. *Sawyer,* 343 U.S. 579 (1952).

68. The Supreme Court ruled that President Truman's seizure and operation of U.S. steel mills in the face of a strike threat were unconstitutional, because the Constitution implied no such broad executive power. See Alan Westin, *Anatomy of a Constitutional Law Case* (New York: Macmillan, 1958); and Maeva Marcus, *Truman and the Steel Seizure Case* (New York: Columbia University Press, 1977).

69. *U.S.* v. *Nixon,* 418 U.S. 683 (1974).

70. Gallup Poll, June 1–4, 2006, Lexis–Nexis RPOLL.

71. *Ashcroft* v. *Free Speech Coalition,* 535 U.S. 234 (2002).

72. "Supreme Court Cases Overruled by Subsequent Decision," U.S. Government Printing Office. Accessed online at http://www.gpoaccess.gov/constitution/pdf/con041.pdf.

73. See *Colegrove* v. *Green,* 328 U.S. 549 (1946), for example.

74. *Baker* v. *Carr,* 369 U.S. 186 (1962).

75. Charles Johnson and Bradley C. Canon, *Judicial Policies: Implementation and Impact,* 2nd ed. (Washington, DC: CQ Press, 1998), ch. 1.

76. *Reynolds* v. *Sims,* 377 U.S. 533 (1964).

77. *Hunt* v. *Cromartie,* 546 U.S. 541 (1999).

78. *Mississippi University for Women* v. *Hogan,* 458 U.S. 718 (1982).

CHAPTER 11

1. The Gallup Organization, "Poll Releases: The Florida Recount Controversy from the Public's Perspective: 25 Insights," http://www.gallup.com/poll/releases. All data discussed here are drawn from this compendium of polls concerning the Florida recount.

2. Richard Dawson et al., *Political Socialization,* 2nd ed. (Boston: Little, Brown, 1977), 33.

3. Robert D. Hess and David Easton, "The Child's Changing Image of the President," *Public Opinion Quarterly* 14 (Winter 1960): 632–42; and Fred I. Greenstein, *Children and Politics* (New Haven, CT: Yale University Press, 1965).

4. Laura Pappano, "Potential War Poses Threat to Teachers," *Boston Globe* (March 9, 2003): B9.

5. "Kids Voting USA Gains Support in Two Congressional Actions: Rep. Pastor Praised for His Continued Efforts," http://www.kidsvoteusa.org/march1502.htm.

6. James Simon and Bruce D. Merrill, "Political Socialization in the Classroom Revisited: The Kids Voting Program," *Social Science Journal* 35 (1998): 29–42.

7. Simon and Merrill, "Political Socialization in the Classroom Revisited."

8. Howard W. Stanley and Richard G. Niemi, *Vital Statistics on American Politics, 2005–2006* (Washington, DC: CQ Press, 2006).

9. *Statistical Abstract of the United States, 1997* (Washington, DC: Government Printing Office, 1997), 1011.

10. Princeton Research Survey Associates Poll, accessed through LEXIS, Question ID USPSRA.011104, R19, December 19, 2003–January 3, 2004.

11. Princeton Research Survey Associates Poll, accessed through LEXIS, Question ID USPSRA.032504, RIT06B, March 17–21, 2004.

12. Steven M. Cohen and Charles S. Liebman, "American Jewish Liberalism," *Public Opinion Quarterly* 61 (1997): 405–30.

13. USA Today and CNN/Gallup Tracking Poll, USAToday.com.

14. Edward S. Greenberg, "The Political Socialization of Black Children," in Edward S. Greenberg, ed., *Political Socialization* (New York: Atherton Press, 1970), 181.

15. Susan Page and Maria Puente, "Views of Whites, Blacks Differ Starkly on Disaster," *USA Today* (September 13, 2005): A1, A2.

16. Elaine J. Hall and Myra Marx Ferree, "Race Differences in Abortion Attitudes," *Public Opinion Quarterly* 50 (Summer 1986): 193–207; and Jon Hurwitz and Mark Peffley, "Public Perceptions of Race and Crime: The Role of Racial Stereotypes," *American Journal of Political Science* 41 (April 1997): 375–401.

17. Elaine S. Povich, "Courting Hispanics: Group's Votes Could Shift House Control," *Newsday* (April 21, 2002): A4.

18. Alejandro Portest and Rafael Mozo, "The Political Adaptation Process of Cubans and Other Ethnic Minorities in the United States: A Preliminary Analysis," in F. Chris Garcia, ed., *Latinos and the Political System* (Notre Dame, IN: University of Notre Dame Press, 1988), 161.

19. Karen M. Kaufmann and John Petrocik, "The Changing Politics of American Men: Understanding Sources of the Gender Gap," *American Journal of Political Science* 43 (July 1999):/864–87.

20. Margaret Trevor, "Political Socialization, Party Identification, and the Gender Gap," *Public Opinion Quarterly* 63 (Spring 1999): 62–89.

21. Alexandra Marks, "Gender Gap Narrows over Kosovo," *Christian Science Monitor* (April 30, 1999): 1.

22. Pew Research Center for People and the Press, 2002.

23. Susan A. MacManus, *Young v. Old: Generational Combat in the 21st Century* (Boulder, CO: Westview, 1995).

24. "Church Pews Seat More Blacks, Seniors, and Republicans," http://www.gallup.com/POLL_ARCHIVES/970329/html.

25. CNN Exit Polls, www.cnn.com/election/2004/pages/results/states/us/p/oo/epolls.o.html.

26. Survey of 125 students in Karen O'Connor's Politics in the U.S. class, spring 2006.

27. Allan M. Winkler, "Public Opinion," in Jack Greene, ed., *The Encyclopedia of American Political History* (New York: Charles Scribner's Sons, 1988), 1038.

28. Quoted in *Public Opinion Quarterly* 29 (Winter 1965–1966): 547.

29. *Literary Digest* 122 (August 22, 1936): 3.

30. *Literary Digest* 125 (November 14, 1936): 1.

31. Robert S. Erikson, Norman Luttbeg, and Kent Tedin, *American Public Opinion: Its Origin, Contents, and Impact* (New York: Wiley, 1980), 28.

32. "2000 Election Winners: George W. Bush and Online Polling," *Business Wire* (December 14, 2000).

33. Diane J. Heith, "Staffing the White House Public Opinion Apparatus 1969–1988," *Public Opinion Quarterly* 62 (Summer 1998): 165.

34. Francis J. Connolly and Charley Manning, "What 'Push Polling' Is and What It Isn't," *Boston Globe* (August 16, 2001): A21.

35. Michael W. Traugott, "The Polls in 1992: Views of Two Critics: A Good General Showing, but Much Work Needs to Be Done," *Public Perspective* 4 (November/December 1992): 14–16.

36. Suzanne Soule, "Will They Engage? Political Knowledge, Participation and Attitudes of Generations X and Y," paper prepared for the 2001 German and American Conference, 6.

37. Soule, "Will They Engage?" quoting Richard G. Niemi and Jane Junn, *Civic Education* (New Haven, CT: Yale University Press, 1998).

38. Quoted in Everett Carll Ladd, "Fiskin's 'Deliberative Poll' Is Flawed Science and Dubious Democracy," *Public Perspective* (December/January 1996): 41.

39. Tamara Henry, "Kids Get 'Abysmal' Grade in History," *USA Today* (May 10, 2002): 1A.

40. "Don't Know Much About . . ." *Christian Science Monitor* (May 16, 2002): 8.

41. "Don't Know Much About History, Geography . . ." *Pittsburgh Post-Gazette* (January 22, 2003): E2; Laurence D. Cohen, "Geography for Dummies," *Hartford Courant* (December 8, 2002): C3.

42. "Gender Gap in Political Knowledge Persists in 2004, National Annenberg Election Survey Shows," http://www.nacs.org/.

43. V. O. Key Jr., *The Responsible Electorate: Rationality in Presidential Voting, 1936–1960* (Cambridge, MA: Belknap Press of Harvard University, 1966).

44. Richard Nodeau et al., "Elite Economic Forecasts, Economic News, Mass Economic Judgments and Presidential Approval," *Journal of Politics* 61 (February 1999): 109–35.

45. Michael Towle, Review of *Presidential Responsiveness and Public Policymaking: The Public and the Policies* by Jeffrey E. Cohen, *Journal of Politics* 61 (February 1999): 230–2.

46. John E. Mueller, *War, Presidents, and Public Opinion* (New York: Wiley, 1973), 69.

47. Roderick P. Hart, *The Sound of Leadership: Presidential Communication in the Modern Age* (Chicago: University of Chicago Press, 1987).

48. See, for example, Benjamin Page and Robert Shapiro, "Effects of Public Opinion on Policy," *American Political Science Review* 57 (March 1983): 175–90; Alan D. Monroe, "Public Opinion and Public Policy, 1980–1993," *Public Opinion Quarterly* 62 (Spring 1998): 6–28; and Kathleen M. McGraw, Samuel Best, and Richard Timpone, "'What They Say or What They Do?' The Impact of Elite Explanation and Policy Outcomes on Public Opinion," *American Journal of Political Science* 39 (February 1995): 53–74.

49. Benjamin Ginsberg, *The Captive Public* (New York: Basic Books, 1986), ch. 4.

50. "George Gallup Is Dead at 82," *New York Times* (July 28, 1984): A1.

51. Herbert Asher, *Polling and the Public: What Every Citizen Should Know* (Washington, DC: CQ Press, 1988), 109.

CHAPTER 12

1. John F. Bibby, "Party Networks: National-State Integration, Allied Groups, and Issue Activists," in John C. Green and Daniel M. Shea, eds., *The State of the Parties: The Changing Role of Contemporary American Parties*, 3rd ed. (Lanham, MD: Rowman and Littlefield, 1999).

2. This conception of a political party was originally put forth by V. O. Key Jr. in *Politics, Parties, and Pressure Groups* (New York, Crowell, 1958).

3. John H. Aldrich, *Why Parties? The Origin and Transformation of Party Politics in America* (Chicago: University of Chicago Press, 1995).

4. By contrast, Great Britain did not develop truly national, broad-based parties until the 1870s.

5. See *Historical Statistics of the United States: Colonial Times to 1970*, part 2, series Y-27-28 (Washington, DC: Government Printing Office, 1975), based on unpublished data prepared by Walter Dean Burnham.

See also Harold W. Stanley and Richard G. Niemi, *Vital Statistics on American Politics 2005–2006* (Washington, DC: CQ Press, 2006), for contemporary turnout figures.

6. On the subject of party realignment, see Walter Dean Burnham, *Critical Elections and the Mainsprings of American Politics* (New York: Norton, 1970); Kristi Andersen, *The Creation of a Democratic Majority* (Chicago: University of Chicago Press, 1979); and John R. Petrocik, "Realignment: New Party Coalitions and the Nationalization of the South," *Journal of Politics* 49 (May 1987): 347–75.

7. See Walter Dean Burnham, *Critical Elections and the Mainsprings of American Politics* (New York: Norton, 1970), for a defense of realignment theory.

8. For a perspective on reconsidering the relevance and validity of critical realignments, see David Mayhew, *Electoral Realignments* (New Haven, CT: Yale University Press, 2004).

9. Morris P. Fiorina, *Retrospective Voting in American National Elections* (New Haven, CT: Yale University Press, 1981); and Charles H. Franklin and John E. Jackson, "The Dynamics of Party Identification," *American Political Science Review* 77 (1983): 957–73.

10. See, for example, V. O. Key Jr., "A Theory of Critical Elections," *Journal of Politics* 17 (February 1955): 3–18.

11. See Everett Carll Ladd, "The Brittle Mandate: Electoral Dealignment and the 1980 Presidential Election," *Political Science Quarterly* 96 (1981): 1–25.

12. Everett Carll Ladd, "Like Waiting for Godot: The Uselessness of 'Realignment' for Understanding Change in Contemporary American Politics," in Byron Shafer, ed., *The End of Realignment? Interpreting American Electoral Eras* (Madison: University of Wisconsin Press, 1991).

13. For a discussion of secular realignment in the South, see Jeffrey M. Stonecash, "Class and Party: Secular Realignment and the Survival of Democrats Outside the South," *Political Research Quarterly* 53:4 (2000): 731–52.

14. M. V. Hood, Quentin Kidd, and Irwin L. Morris, "Of Byrds and Bumpers: Using Democratic Senators to Analyze Political Change in the South, 1960–1995," *American Journal of Political Science* 43 (April 1999): 465–87.

15. For a discussion of the disruptive effects of polarization, see David R. Jones, "Party Polarization and Legislative Gridlock," *Political Research Quarterly* 54 (2001): 125–41.

16. Earl Black and Merle Black, *The Rise of Southern Republicans* (Cambridge, MA: Harvard University Press, 2002).

17. Kelly D. Patterson, *Political Parties and the Maintenance of Liberal Democracy* (New York: Columbia University Press, 1996).

18. For a discussion of how the Bush campaign's 2004 efforts to increase turnout paid off in Florida, see Abby Goodnough, "Bush Secured Victory by Veering from Beaten Path," *New York Times* (November 7, 2004).

19. See David E. Price, *Bringing Back the Parties* (Washington, DC: CQ Press, 1984), 284–8.

20. See, for example, Sarah McCally Morehouse, "Legislatures and Political Parties," *State Government* 59 (1976): 23.

21. Christian Collet and Martin P. Wattenberg, "Strategically Unambitious: Minor Party and Independent Candidates in the 1996 Congressional Elections," in John C. Green and Daniel M. Shea, eds., *The State of the Parties: The Changing Role of Contemporary American Parties*, 3rd ed. (Lanham, MD: Rowman and Littlefield, 1999).

22. Marc J. Hetherington, "The Effect of Political Trust on the Presidential Vote, 1968–1992," *American Political Science Review* 93 (1999): 311–26.

23. John Clifford Green, Paul S. Herrnson, and John C. Green, eds., *Responsible Partisanship: The Evolution of American Political Parties Since the 1950s* (Lawrence: University Press of Kansas, 2003).

24. Cornelius P. Cotter, James L. Gibson, John F. Bibby, and Robert J. Huckshorn, *Party Organizations in American Politics* (Pittsburgh: University of Pittsburgh Press, 1989).

25. Bibby, "Party Networks."

26. Mark Leibovich, "Howard Dean: He Still Has the Power," *Washington Post* (January 18, 2005).

27. Martin Kady II, "Party Unity: Learning to Stick Together," *CQ Weekly* (January 9, 2006): 92.

28. Sidney M. Milkis, *The President and the Parties: The Transformation of the American Party System Since the New Deal* (New York: Oxford University Press, 1993).

29. See S. Sidney Ulmer, "The Political Party Variable on the Michigan Supreme Court," *Journal of Public Law* 11 (1962): 352–62; Stuart Nagel, "Political Party Affiliation and Judges' Decisions," *American Political Science Review* 55 (1961): 843–50; David W. Adamany, "The Party Variable in Judges' Voting: Conceptual Notes and a Case Study," *American Political Science Review* 63 (1969): 57–73; Sheldon Goldman, "Voting Behavior on the United States Courts of Appeals, 1961–1964," *American Political Science Review* 60 (1966): 374–83; and Robert A. Carp and C. K. Rowland, *Policymaking and Politics in the Federal District Courts* (Knoxville: University of Tennessee Press, 1983).

30. Randall D. Lloyd, "Separating Partisanship from Party in Judicial Research: Reapportionment in the U.S. District Courts," *American Political Science Review* 89 (June 1995): 413–20.

31. The Farmer-Labor Party did survive in a sense; having endured a series of defeats, it merged in 1944 with the Democrats, and Minnesota's Democratic candidates still officially bear the standard of the Democratic-Farmer-Labor (DFL) Party. At about the same time, also having suffered severe electoral reversals, the Progressives stopped nominating candidates in Wisconsin. The party's members either returned to the Republican Party, from which the Progressives had split early in the century, or became Democrats.

32. Morehouse, "Legislatures and Political Parties," 19–24.

33. See Steven E. Finkel and Howard A. Scarrow, "Party Identification and Party Enrollment: The Difference and the Consequence," *Journal of Politics* 47 (May 1985): 620–42.

34. Karen M. Kaufmann and John R. Petrocik, "The Changing Politics of American Men: Understanding the Sources of the Gender Gap," *American Journal of Political Science* 43 (July 1999): 864–87.

35. Michael Dawson, *Behind the Mule: Race and Class in African-American Politics* (Princeton, NJ: Princeton University Press, 1994); and Louis Bolce, Gerald DeMaio, and Douglas Muzzio, "Blacks and the Republican Party: The 20 Percent Solution," *Political Science Quarterly* 107 (Spring 1992): 63–79.

36. Abby Goodnough, "Hispanic Vote in Florida: Neither a Bloc nor a Lock," *New York Times* (October 17, 2004).

37. For a look at how supporting restricting immigration has imperiled California Republicans' appeal to Hispanic voters, see Shaun Bowler, Stephen P. Nicholson, and Gary M. Segura, "Earthquakes and Aftershocks: Race, Direct Democracy, and Partisan Change," *American Journal of Political Science* 50:1 (2006): 146–59.

38. The presidential election of 1960 may be an extreme case, but John F. Kennedy's massive support among Catholics and Richard M. Nixon's less substantial but still impressive backing by Protestants demonstrates the polarization that religion could once produce. See Philip E. Converse, "Religion and Politics: The 1960 Election," in Angus Campbell et al., *Elections and the Political Order* (New York: Wiley, 1966), 96–124.

39. Pew Research Center for the People and the Press, calculated from the 2000 National Election Studies.

40. For a discussion of recent trends in party strength, see Morris P. Fiorina, "Parties and Partisanship: A 40-Year Retrospective," *Political Behavior* 24 (2002): 93–115.

41. Elmer E. Schattschneider, *Party Government* (New York: Farrar and Rinehart, 1942).

CHAPTER 13

1. William A. Galston, "Civic Education and Political Participation," *Political Science and Politics* 37 (2004): 263–6.

2. Steven J. Rosenstone and John Mark Hanson, *Mobilization, Participation, and Democracy in America* (New York: Macmillan, 1993).

3. See, for example, Laura Stoker and M. Kent Jennings, "Life-Cycle Transitions and Political Participation: The Case of Marriage," *American Political Science Review* 89 (1995): 421–36; and Paul R.

Abramson, John H. Aldrich, and David W. Rohde, *Change and Continuity in the 1996 Elections* (Washington, DC: CQ Press, 1998).

4. Martin P. Wattenberg. "Elections: Turnout in the 2004 Presidential Election," *Presidential Studies Quarterly* 35 (March 2005): 138–46.

5. Thomas M. Guterbock and Bruce London, "Race, Political Orientation, and Participation: An Empirical Test of Four Competing Theories," *American Sociological Review* 48 (1983): 439–53.

6. Carol A. Cassel, "Hispanic Turnout: Estimates from Validated Voting Data," *Political Science Quarterly* 55 (June 2002): 391–408.

7. League of United Latin American Citizens, http://www.lulac.org.

8. Benjamin Highton, "Easy Registration and Voter Turnout," *Journal of Politics* 59 (1997): 565–75.

9. Stephen Knack and J. White, "Election-Day Registration and Turnout Inequality," *Political Behavior* 22 (March 2000): 29–44.

10. J. Eric Oliver, "The Effects of Eligibility Restrictions and Party Activity on Absentee Voting and Overall Turnout," *American Journal of Political Science* 40 (May 1996): 498–513.

11. International Institute for Democracy and Electoral Assistance, "Global Database," http://www.idea.int/vt/survey/voter_turnout_pop2.cfm.

12. Marg N. Franklin and Wolfgang P. Hirczy, "Separated Powers, Divided Government, and Turnout in U.S. Presidential Elections," *American Journal of Political Science* 42 (January 1998): 316–26.

13. Steven J. Rosenstone and John Marc Hansen, *Mobilization, Participation, and Democracy in America* (New York: Macmillan, 1993).

14. Benjamin Highton and Raymond E. Wolfinger, "Estimating the Effects of the National Voter Registration Act of 1993," *Political Behavior* 20:2 (1998), 79–104.

15. Arend Lijphart, "Unequal Participation: Democracy's Unsolved Dilemma," *American Political Science Review* 91 (March 1997): 1–14.

16. Gary C. Jacobson, *The Politics of Congressional Elections*, 5th ed. (New York: Addison Wesley, 2000).

17. Harold W. Stanley and Richard G. Niemi, *Vital Statistics on American Politics 2005–2006* (Washington, DC: CQ Press, 2006).

18. Morris P. Fiorina, *Divided Government* (Boston: Allyn and Bacon, 1996).

19. Martin P. Wattenberg, *The Decline of American Political Parties, 1952–1994* (Cambridge, MA: Harvard University Press, 1996).

20. Cable News Network, 2004 election results, http://www.cnn.com.

21. Henry Cisneros, "Winning the Crucial Hispanic Vote in 2000," *Campaigns and Elections* (August 1, 1999.)

22. Voter News Service Exit Poll, http://www.cnn.com.

23. Warren E. Miller and J. Merrill Shanks, *The New American Voter* (Cambridge, MA: Harvard University Press, 1996), 270.

24. Voter News Service Exit Poll, http://www.cnn.com.

25. Voter News Service Exit Poll, http://www.cnn.com.

26. Michael S. Lewis-Beck and Mary Stegmaier, "Economic Determinants of Electoral Outcomes," *Annual Review of Political Science* 3 (2000): 183–219.

27. Paul Allen Beck, *Party Politics in America*, 8th ed. (New York: Longman, 1998); David Adamany, "Cross-over Voting and the Democratic Party's Reform Rules," *American Political Science Review* 70 (1976): 536–41; Ronald Hedlund and Meredith W. Watts, "The Wisconsin Open Primary: 1968 to 1984," *American Politics Quarterly* 14 (1986): 55–74; and Gary D. Wekkin, "The Conceptualization and Measurement of Crossover Voting," *Western Political Quarterly* 41 (1988): 105–14.

28. Gary D. Wekken, "Why Crossover Voters Are Not 'Mischievous' Voters," *American Politics Quarterly* 19 (1991): 229–47; and Todd L. Cherry and Stephan Kroll, "Crashing the Party: An Experimental Investigation of Strategic Voting in Primary Elections," Public Choice 114 (2003): 387–420.

29. Shaun Bowler, Todd Donovan, and Caroline Tolbert, eds., *Citizens as Legislators: Direct Democracy in the United States* (Columbus: Ohio State University Press, 1998).

30. For a more in-depth discussion of initiative, referendum, and recall voting, see Larry J. Sabato, Howard R. Ernst, and Bruce Larson, *Dangerous Democracy? The Battle over Ballot Initiatives in America* (Lanham, MD: Rowman and Littlefield, 2001); and David S. Broder

Democracy Derailed: Initiative Campaigns and the Power of Money (New York: Harcourt, 2000).

31. Howard R. Ernst, "The Historical Role of Narrow-Material Interests in Initiative Politics," in Larry J. Sabato, Howard R. Ernst, and Bruce Larson, eds., *Dangerous Democracy? The Battle over Ballot Initiatives in America* (Lanham, MD: Rowman and Littlefield, 2001).

32. Elaine Ciulla Kamarck and Kenneth M. Goldstein, "The Rules Matter: Post-Reform Presidential Nominating Politics," in L. Sandy Maisel, *The Parties Respond: Changes in American Parties and Campaigns* (Boulder, CO: Westview, 1994), 174.

33. Paul R. Abramson, John H. Aldrich, Phil Paolino, and David W. Rohde, "'Sophisticated' Voting in the 1998 Presidential Primaries," *American Political Science Review* 86 (March 1992): 55–69.

34. Larry J. Sabato, "Presidential Nominations: The Front-loaded Frenzy of 1996," in Larry J. Sabato, ed., *Toward the Millennium: The Elections of 1996* (New York: Allyn and Bacon, 1997).

35. Byron Shafer, *Bifurcated Politics: Evolution and Reform in the National Party Convention* (Cambridge, MA: Harvard University Press, 1988).

36. R. Michael Alvarez and Jonathan Nagler, "Economics, Issues, and the Perot Candidacy: Voter Choice in the 1992 Presidential Election," *American Journal of Political Science* 39 (1995): 714–44.

37. U.S. Census Bureau, Census 2000 and earlier censuses.

38. For more information, visit the Center for Voting and Democracy's page on "Faithless Electors": http://www.fairvote.org/e_college/faithless.htm.

39. Common Cause, redistricting issues, http://www.commoncause.org.

40. George Serra, "What's in It for Me? The Impact of Congressional Casework on Incumbent Evaluation," *American Politics Quarterly* 22 (1994): 403–20.

41. Glenn R. Parker and Suzanne L. Parker, "Correlates and Effects of Attention to District by U.S. House Members," *Legislative Studies Quarterly* 10 (May 1985): 223–42.

42. Jamie L. Carson, "Strategy, Selection, and Candidate Competition in U.S. House and Senate Elections," *Journal of Politics* 67 (2005): 1–28.

43. Gary W. Cox and Jonathan N. Katz, "Why Did the Incumbency Advantage in U.S. House Elections Grow?" *American Journal of Political Science* 40 (May 1996): 478–97.

44. Jonathan Krasno, *Challengers, Competition, and Reelection: Comparing Senate and House Elections* (New Haven, CT: Yale University Press, 1994).

45. "How to Rig an Election," *The Economist* (April 25, 2002).

46. Matthew Mosk and Lori Montgomery, "Md. Court Spurns Assembly Map: Glendening Plan Ruled Unconstitutional; Judges to Redraw Lines," *Washington Post* (June 12, 2002).

47. *Wesberry* v. *Sanders*, 376 U.S. 1 (1964).

48. *Thornburg* v. *Gingles*, 478 U.S. 30 (1986).

49. *Shaw* v. *Reno*, 113 S.Ct. 2816 (1993).

50. In *Davis v. Bandemer*, 478 U.S. 109 (1986), the Court found that gerrymandering was not a political question but was unable to determine a standard by which to judge constitutionality.

51. *League of United Latin American Citizens et al.* v. *Perry*, No. 05-204 (2006).

52. Sunhil Ahuja et al., "Modern Congressional Election Theory Meets the 1992 House Elections," *Political Research Quarterly* 47 (1994): 909–21; and Paul S. Herrnson, *Congressional Elections: Campaigning at Home and in Washington*, 2nd ed. (Washington, DC: CQ Press, 1998).

53. Gary C. Jacobson and Michael A. Dimock, "Checking Out: The Effects of Bank Overdrafts on the 1992 House Elections," *American Journal of Political Science* 38 (1994): 601–24; and Herrnson, *Congressional Elections*.

CHAPTER 14

1. Patrick J. Kenney and Tom W. Rice, "The Psychology of Political Momentum," *Political Research Quarterly* 47 (December 1994): 923–38.

2. See "Candidates and Nominations," in Paul S. Herrnson, *Congressional Elections: Campaigning at Home and in Washington*, 4th ed. (Washington, DC: CQ Press, 2004), 35–68.

3. Dennis W. Johnson, *No Place for Amateurs: How Political Consultants Are Reshaping American Democracy* (New York: Routledge, 2001).

4. Five liberal Democratic U.S. senators, including George McGovern of South Dakota, were defeated in this way in 1980, for example.

5. Diana C. Mutz, "Effects of Horse-Race Coverage on Campaign Coffers: Strategic Contributing in Presidential Primaries," *Journal of Politics* 57 (November 1995): 1015–42.

6. See "Media, Old and New," in Johnson, *No Place for Amateurs*, 115–47.

7. Dennis J. Willard et al. "Quiet Push Wins Ohio for GOP," *Akron Beacon Journal* (November 4, 2004).

8. Pew Internet and American Life Project, http://www.pewinternet.org.

9. http://www.cyberjournalist.net/news/001705.php.

10. Carla Marinucci, "'Iowa Yell' Stirring Doubts About Dean," *San Francisco Chronicle* (January 21, 2004): A1.

11. http://www.opensecrets.org.

12. "What an Election Costs," Canadian Broadcasting Corporation, March 17, 2004.

13. *McConnell* v. *Federal Election Commission*, 251 F.Supp.2d 176, 251 F.Supp.2d 948 (2003).

14. *McConnell* v. *Federal Election Commission*, 540 U.S. 93 (2003).

15. http://www.opensecrets.org.

16. See "The Internet Campaign," in Herrnson, *Congressional Elections*.

17. Steven T. Engel and David J. Jackson, "Wielding the Stick Instead of Its Carrot: Labor PAC Punishment of Pro-NAFTA Democrats," *Political Research Quarterly* 51 (September 1998): 813–28.

18. Janet M. Box-Steffensmeier and J. Tobin Grant, "All in a Day's Work: The Financial Rewards of Legislative Effectiveness," *Legislative Studies Quarterly* 24 (November 1999): 511–23.

19. Frank Sorauf, *Inside Campaign Finance: Myths and Realities* (New Haven, CT: Yale University Press, 1992), ch. 6.

20. Richard A. Smith, "Interest Group Influence in the U.S. Congress," *Legislative Studies Quarterly* 20 (1995): 89–139. See also Christopher Magee, "Do Political Action Committees Give Money to Candidates for Electoral or Influence Motives?" *Public Choice* 112 (2004): 373–99.

21. Richard L. Hall and Frank W. Wayman, "Buying Time: Moneyed Interests and the Mobilization of Bias in Congressional Committees," *American Political Science Review* 84 (1990): 797–820.

22. http://www.opensecrets.org.

23. Herrnson, *Congressional Elections*, 133.

24. Kevin M. Leyden and Stephen A. Borrelli, "An Investment in Goodwill: Party Contributions and Party Unity Among U.S. House Members in the 1980s," *American Politics Quarterly* 22 (October 1994): 421–52.

25. Amy Keller, "Helping Each Other Out: Members Dip into Campaign Funds for Fellow Candidates," *Roll Call* (June 15, 1998): 1.

26. For member contribution activity at the state level, see Jay K. Dow, "Campaign Contributions and Intercandidate Transfers in the California Assembly," *Social Science Quarterly* 75 (1994): 867–80. For member contribution activity at the congressional level, see Bruce A. Larson, "Ambition and Money in the U.S. House of Representatives: Analyzing Campaign Contributions from Incumbents' Leadership PACs and Reelection Committees" (Ph.D. dissertation, University of Virginia, 1998). For a briefer account, see Paul S. Herrnson, "Money and Motives: Spending in House Elections," in Lawrence C. Dodd and Bruce I. Oppenheimer, eds., *Congress Reconsidered*, 6th ed. (Washington, DC: CQ Press, 1997).

27. Federal Election Commission, http://www.fec.gov.

28. Opensecrets.org 2004 Election Overview: Candidate to Candidate Giving, http://www.opensecrets.org.

29. Larson, "Ambition and Money in the U.S. House of Representatives."

30. *Buckley* v. *Valeo*, 424 U.S. 1 (1976).

31. Jeffrey Milyo and Thomas Groseclose, "The Electoral Effects of Incumbent Wealth," *Journal of Law and Economics* 42 (1999): 699–722.

32. Marisa Katz, "Matching Funds" *New Republic Online*, July 13, 2004, http://www.tnr.com.

33. Anthony Corrado, "Party Soft Money," in Anthony Corrado et al., eds., *Campaign Finance Reform: A Sourcebook* (Washington, DC: Brookings Institution, 1997).

34. Trevor Potter, "Issue Advocacy and Express Advocacy," in Anthony Corrado et al., eds., *Campaign Finance Reform: A Sourcebook* (Washington, DC: Brookings Institution, 1997).
35. http://www.commoncause.org.
36. Federal Election Commission Release, "Party Financial Activity Summarized," December 14, 2004, http://www.fec.gov.
37. Michael Janofsky, "Advocacy Groups Spent Record Amount on 2004 Election," *New York Times* (December 17, 2004).

CHAPTER 15

1. See Mitchell Stephens, *A History of News: From the Drum to the Satellite* (New York: Viking, 1989).
2. For a delightful rendition of this episode, see Shelley Ross, *Fall from Grace* (New York: Ballantine, 1988), ch. 12.
3. Richard L. Rubin, *Press, Party, and Presidency* (New York: Norton, 1981), 38–9.
4. Stephen Bates, *If No News, Send Rumors* (New York: St. Martin's, 1989), 185.
5. See Doris A. Graber, *Mass Media and American Politics*, 3rd ed. (Washington, DC: CQ Press, 1989), 12; and Thomas C. Leonard, *The Power of the Press: The Birth of American Political Reporting* (New York: Oxford University Press, 1986), ch. 7.
6. Pew Research Center for the People and the Press, "Cable and Internet Loom Large in Fragmented Political News Universe: Perceptions of Partisan Bias Seen as Growing, Especially by Democrats," January 11, 2004.
7. Pew Research Center, "Cable and Internet Loom Large."
8. J. D. Power and Associates report, "Although Cable Continues to Lose Market Share to Satellite Providers, Cable Subscribers Are Switching to Digital Service at a Rapid Pace," http://www.jdpower.com.
9. Annenberg National Election Study, 2004, http://www.annenbergpublicpolicycenter.org.
10. Pew Research Center for the People and the Press, Political Communications Study, January 11, 2004, http://people-press.org.
11. Pew Research Center, "Public More Critical of Press, but Goodwill Persists," June 26, 2005.
12. UCLA Center for Communication Policy, "The UCLA Internet Report: Surveying the Digital Future," January 2003; PEJ Research.
13. Scott L. Althaus and David Tewksbury, "Patterns of Internet and Traditional News Media Use in a Networked Community," *Political Communication* 17 (2000): 21–45.
14. Bruce Bimber, "The Search for Effects of Information Technology at the Individual Level," *Political Research Quarterly* 54 (2001): 53–67.
15. Newspaper Association of America; Journalism.org, "The State of the News Media 2006," http://www.stateofthenewsmedia.org.
16. Donald L. Jorand and Benjamin I. Page, "Shaping Foreign Policy Opinions: The Role of TV News," *Journal of Conflict Resolution* 36 (June 1992): 227–41.
17. Andrew Kohut, *The Biennial Pew Media Survey: How News Habits Changed in 2004*, Brookings/Pew Research Center Forum, Washington, D.C., June 8, 2004, http://www.brookings.edu.
18. Pew Research Center, "Public More Critical of Press, but Goodwill Persists."
19. Pew Research Center for the People and the Press, "News Media's Improved Image Proves Short-Lived," August 4, 2002, http://people-press.org.
20. Pew Research Center, "News Media's Improved Image Proves Short-Lived."
21. FCC News Release, "FCC Sets Limits on Media Concentration: Unprecedented Public Record Results in Enforceable and Balanced Broadcast Ownership Rules," June 2, 2003.
22. Christopher Stern, "FCC Chairman's Star a Little Dimmer," *Washington Post* (July 25, 2003): E01, http://www.washingtonpost.com.
23. Mark K. Miller. "On Hold: Rankings Change Little as Regulatory Uncertainty Keeps Station Trading in Neutral," *Broadcasting and Cable* (April, 19, 2004): 50.
24. *RTNDA* v. *FCC*, 229 F3d 269 (DC Cir. 2000).
25. See http://www.museum.tv/archives/etv/F/htmlF/fairnessdoct/fairness doct.htm.
26. For arguments in support of Internet neutrality, see Save the Internet, http://www.savetheinternet.com.
27. *New York Times Co.* v. *U.S.*, 403 U.S. 713 (1971).
28. Jillian Harrison, "Embedded Journalism Limited in Perspective, Tufts U. Professors Say," *University Wire*, April 15, 2003.
29. U.S. Senate press gallery and U.S. House of Representatives radio-television correspondents gallery.
30. List of White House correspondents, http://www.washingtonpost.com.
31. *New York Times Co.* v. *Sullivan*, 376 U.S. 254 (1964). See also Steven Pressman, "Libel Law: Finding the Right Balance," *Editorial Research Reports* 2 (August 18, 1989): 462–71.
32. *Curtis Publishing Co.* v. *Butts*, 388 U.S. 130 (1967); *Associated Press* v. *Walker*, 388 U.S. 130 (1967).
33. Timothy E. Cook and Lyn Ragsdale, "The President and the Press: Negotiating Newsworthiness at the White House," in Michael Nelson, ed., *The Presidency and the Political System*, 5th ed. (Washington DC: CQ Press, 1998), 323.
34. Thomas Patterson, *Out of Order* (New York: Vintage, 1994).
35. John R. Zaller, "Monica Lewinsky's Contribution to Political Science," *PS: Political Science and Politics* 31 (June 1998) 182–9.
36. Lori Robertson, "In Control," *American Journalism Review* (February/March 2005).
37. Harold W. Stanley and Richard G. Niemi, *Vital Statistics on American Politics*, 4th ed. (Washington, DC: CQ Press, 1994), 28.
38. John R. Hibbing and Elizabeth Theiss-Morse, *Congress as Public Enemy: Political Attitudes Toward American Political Institutions* (New York: Cambridge University Press, 1995).
39. Karen Aho, "Broadcasters Want Access, but Will They Deliver Serious Coverage?" *Columbia Journalism Review* 5 (September/October 2003), http://www.cjr.org.
40. Martin P. Wattenberg, *The Decline of American Political Parties, 1952–1994* (Cambridge, MA: Harvard University Press, 1996).
41. Larry Bartels, "Messages Received: The Political Impact of Media Exposure," *American Political Science Review* 87 (June 1993): 267–85.
42. Benjamin I. Page, Robert Y. Shapiro, and Glenn R. Dempsey, "What Moves Public Opinion?" *American Political Science Review* 81 (March 1987): 23–44.
43. Shanto Iyengar and Donald R. Kinder, *News That Matters*, reprint ed. (Chicago: University of Chicago Press, 1989).
44. Thomas E. Nelson, Rosalee A. Clawson, and Zoe M. Oxley, "Media Framing of a Civil Liberties Conflict and Its Effect on Tolerance," *American Political Science Review* 92 (September 1997) 567–83.
45. Marc Hetherington, "The Media's Role in Forming Voters' National Economic Evaluations in 1992," *American Journal of Political Science* 40 (May 1996): 372–95.
46. David Domke, David P. Fan, Dhavan V. Shah, and Mark D. Watts, "The Politics of Conservative Elites and the 'Liberal Media' Argument," *Journal of Communication* 49 (Fall 1999): 35–58.
47. American Society of Newspaper Editors, *The Changing Face of the Newsroom* (Washington, DC: ASNE, 1989), 33; William Schneider and I. A. Lewis, "Views on the News," *Public Opinion* 8 (August/September 1985): 6–11, 58–9; and S. Robert Lichter, Stanley Rothman, and Linda S. Lichter, *The Media Elite* (Bethesda, MD: Adler and Adler, 1986).
48. Pew Research Center for the People and the Press, "How Journalists See Journalists, 2004."
49. Martin Gilens and Craig Hertzman. "Corporate Ownership and News Bias: Newspaper Coverage of the 1996 Telecommunication Act," *Journal of Politics* 62 (May 2000), 369–86.
50. See http://www.stateofthenewsmedia.org/narrative_overview_audience.asp?media=1.

CHAPTER 16

1. Karen Tumulty, "The Man Who Brought Down Washington," *Time* (January 16, 2006): 30–44.

2. Susan Schmidt, James V. Garamaldi, and R. Jeffrey Smith, "Investigating Abramoff—Special Report," *Washington Post,* http://www.washingtonpost.com.

3. Philip Shenon, "Senate Report Lists Lobbyist's Payments to Ex-Leader of Christian Coalition," *New York Times* (June 23, 2006): B2.

4. Jodi Rudoren and Aron Pilhofer, "Hiring Federal Lobbyists, Towns Learn Money Talks," *New York Times* (July 2, 2006): A1.

5. Robert D. Putnam, "Bowling Alone: America's Declining Social Capital," *Journal of Democracy* 6 (1995): 650–65; and Putnam, *Bowling Alone: The Collapse and Revival of American Community* (New York: Simon and Schuster, 2000).

6. Everett Carll Ladd, quoted in Richard Morin, "Who Says We're Not Joiners," *Washington Post* (May 2, 1999): B5.

7. John Brehm and Wendy Rahn, "Individual-Level Evidence for the Causes and Consequences of Social Capital," *American Journal of Political Science* 41 (July 1997): 999.

8. Mark Schneider et al., "Institutional Arrangements and the Creation of Social Capital: The Effects of Public School Choice," *American Political Science Review* 91 (March 1997): 82–93.

9. Nicholas Lemann, "Kicking in Groups," *Atlantic Monthly* (April 1996), NEXIS.

10. David B. Truman, *The Governmental Process: Political Interests and Public Opinion* (New York: Knopf, 1951), 33.

11. Truman, *The Governmental Process,* ch. 16.

12. Robert H. Salisbury, "An Exchange Theory of Interest Groups," *Midwest Journal of Political Science* 13 (1969): 1–32.

13. Jeffrey M. Berry, *Lobbying for the People: The Political Behavior of Public Interest Groups* (Princeton, NJ: Princeton University Press, 1977), 7.

14. Jeffrey M. Berry, *Lobbying for the People,* 7.

15. Quoted in Grant McConnell, "Lobbies and Pressure Groups," in Jack Greene, ed., *Encyclopedia of American Political History,* vol. 2 (New York: Macmillan, 1984), 768.

16. Lee Epstein, *Conservatives in Court* (Knoxville: University of Tennessee Press, 1985).

17. Jack L. Walker, "The Origins and Maintenance of Interest Groups in America," *American Political Science Review* 77 (June 1983): 390–406.

18. Peter Steinfels, "Moral Majority to Dissolve: Says Mission Accomplished," *New York Times* (June 12, 1989): A14.

19. David Mahood, *Interest Groups Participation in America: A New Intensity* (Englewood Cliffs, NJ: Prentice Hall, 1990), 23.

20. Bill Miller, "CEOs Plan Network to Link Them in Attack," *Washington Post* (March 13, 2002): E1.

21. Political Moneyline, http://www.tray.com.

22. Chris Kutalik, "What Does the AFL-CIO Split Mean?" Labor Notes, September 2005, http://www.labornotes.org.

23. "AFL-CIO Membership Falls Below 13 Million, Sowing Net Decrease of 167,775 Members," LaborNET, http://www.labornet.org.

24. Thomas B. Edsall, "Labor's Divisions Widen as Membership Declines," *Washington Post* (March 7, 2005): A2.

25. Michael Wines, "For New Lobbyists, It's What They Know," *New York Times* (November 3, 1993): B14.

26. Quoted in Kay Lehman Schlozman and John T. Tierney, *Organized Interests and American Democracy* (New York: Harper and Row, 1986), 85.

27. Ken Kollman, "Inviting Friends to Lobby: Interest Groups, Ideological Bias, and Congressional Committees," *American Journal of Political Science* 41 (April 1997): 519–44.

28. Quoted in Norman J. Ornstein and Shirley Elder, *Interest Groups, Lobbying and Policy Making* (Washington, DC: CQ Press, 1978), 77.

29. Jeffrey H. Birnbaum, "Hill a Steppingstone to K Street for Some," *Washington Post* (July 27, 2005): A19.

30. Birnbaum, "Hill a Steppingstone to K Street for Some."

31. Some political scientists speak of "iron rectangles," reflecting the growing importance of a fourth party, the courts, in the lobbying process.

32. Clement E. Vose, "Litigation As a Form of Pressure Group Activity," *Annals* 319 (September 1958): 20–31.

33. Karen O'Connor, "Lobbying the Justices or Lobbying for Justice?" in Paul Herrnson, Ronald G. Shaiko, and Clyde Wilcox, eds., *The Interest Group Connection,* 2nd ed., (Washington, DC: CQ Press, 2006), 267–88.

34. Brian Ross, "Supreme Court Ethics Problem?" *Nightline,* ABC News, January 23, 2006.

35. Robert A. Goldberg, *Grassroots Resistance: Social Movement in Twentieth Century America* (Belmont, CA: Wadsworth, 1991).

36. Michelle Garcia, "Animal Rights Activists Step Up Attacks in N.Y.," *Washington Post* (May 9, 2005): A3.

37. Center for Responsive Politics, http://www.opensecrets.org.

38. E. E. Schattschneider, *The Semi-Sovereign People* (New York: Holt, Rinehart, and Winston, 1960), 51.

39. Ken Kollman, *Outside Lobbying: Public Opinion and Interest Group Strategies* (Princeton, NJ: Princeton University Press, 1998); and Karen O'Connor, *Women's Organizations' Use of the Courts* (Lexington, MA: 1980).

40. Marie Hojnacki, "Interest Groups' Decisions to Join Alliances or Work Alone," *American Journal of Political Science* 41 (January 1997): 61–87.

41. Lee Ann Banaszak, *Why Movements Succeed or Fail: Opportunity, Culture, and the Struggle for Woman Suffrage* (Princeton, NJ: Princeton University Press, 1996); Frank R. Baumgartner and Beth L. Leech, *Basic Interests: The Importance of Groups in Politics and in Political Science* (Princeton, NJ: Princeton University Press, 1999); Nancy E. McGlen, Karen O'Connor, Laura Van Assendelft, and Wendy Gunther-Canada, *Women, Politics, and American Society,* 4th ed. (New York: Longman, 2004); Robert H. Salisbury, "An Exchange Theory of Interest Groups," *Midwest Journal of Political Science* 13:1–32; Jack Walker, *Mobilizing Interest Groups in America: Patrons, Professions, and Social Movements* (Ann Arbor: University of Michigan Press, 1991).

42. Walker, *Mobilizing Interest Groups in America.*

43. Schattschneider, *The Semi-Sovereign People,* 35.

44. Mancur Olson Jr., *The Logic of Collective Action: Public Goods and the Theory of Groups* (Cambridge, MA: Harvard University Press, 1965).

45. David C. King and Jack L. Walker, "The Provision of Benefits by Interest Groups in the United States," *Journal of Politics* 54 (May 1992): 394.

46. Hojnacki, "Interest Groups' Decisions."

47. William Browne, "Organized Interests and Their Issue Niches: A Search for Pluralism in a Policy Domain," *Journal of Politics* 52 (May 1990): 477.

48. Donald P. Haider-Markel, "Interest Group Survival: Shared Interests Versus Competition for Resources," *Journal of Politics* 59 (August 1997): 903–12.

49. Leslie Wayne, "And for His Next Feat, Billionaire Sets Sights on Bush," *New York Times* (May 31, 2004): A14.

50. Walker, "The Origins and Maintenance of Interest Groups," 390–406.

CHAPTER 17

1. The White House, "President Signs Medicare Legislation," news release, December 8, 2003, http://www.whitehouse.gov.

2. Kaiser Family Foundation, Kaiser Health Poll Report Survey—Selected Findings on Seniors' Views of the Medicare Prescription Drug Benefit, February 17, 2006, http://www.kff.org.

3. Robert J. Samuelson, "Medicare as Pork Barrel," *Newsweek* (December 1, 2003): 47.

4. James E. Anderson, *Public Policymaking: An Introduction,* 2nd ed. (Boston: Houghton Mifflin, 1994), 5. This discussion draws on Anderson's study.

5. Thomas R. Dye, *Who's Running America?* (Englewood Cliffs, NJ: Prentice Hall, 1976).

6. David B. Truman, *The Governmental Process* (New York: Knopf, 1951).

7. Robert Dahl. *Who Governs?* (New Haven, CT: Yale University Press, 1961).

8. Theodore J. Lowi, *The End of Liberalism* (New York: Norton, 1979).

9. Environmental Protection Agency, "Overview of the National Water Program," http://www.epa.gov.

10. Roger W. Cobb and Charles D. Elder, *Participation in American Politics: The Dynamics of Agenda-Building,* 2nd ed. (Baltimore, MD: Johns Hopkins University Press, 1983), ch. 5.

11. Cobb and Elder, *Participation in American Politics,* 85.

12. Linda Feldmann and Gail Russell Chaddock, "Why the Dubai Deal Collapsed," *Christian Science Monitor* (March, 10, 2006).

13. Charles O. Jones, ed., *The Reagan Legacy: Promise and Performance* (Chatham, NJ: Chatham House, 1988).

14. Charles O. Jones, *An Introduction to the Study of Public Policy*, 3rd ed. (Monterey, CA: Brooks/Cole, 1984), 87–89.

15. Donald Lambro, "Social Security Reform Mulled," *Washington Times* (December 2, 2004), http://www.washingtontimes.com.

16. Judy Sarasohn, "Bush's '06 Budget Would Scrap or Reduce 154 Programs," *Washington Post* (February 22, 2005): A13.

17. Mark Clayton, "States Take on Feds over the Environment," *Christian Science Monitor* (October 6, 2005).

18. This discussion draws on Anne Schneider and Helen Ingram, "Behavioral Assumptions of Policy Tools," *Journal of Politics* 52 (May 1990): 510–29.

19. Government Accountability Office, "Amtrak Management: Systematic Problems Require Actions to Improve Efficiency, Effectiveness, and Accountability," GAO-06-145, April 2005, http://www.gao.gov.

20. Douglas Kirby, "Emerging Answers: Research Findings on Programs to Reduce Teen Pregnancy," National Campaign to Prevent Teen Pregnancy, 2001.

21. Robert Divine et al., *America Past and Present*, 5th ed. (New York: Longman, 1999), 456.

22. Jeffrey Cohen, *Politics and Economic Policy in the United States*, 2nd ed. (Boston: Houghton Mifflin, 2000), 49.

23. Cohen, *Politics and Economic Policy in the United States*.

24. Thomas Lynch, *Public Budgeting in America*, 4th ed. (Englewood Cliffs, NJ: Prentice Hall, 1995), 24.

25. Ronald Edsforth, *The New Deal: America's Response to the Great Depression* (Oxford: Blackwell, 2000), 137.

26. Robert McElvaine, *The Great Depression: America 1929–1941* (New York: Times Books, 1984), 265.

27. Edsforth, *The New Deal*, 231.

28. McElvaine, *The Great Depression*, 257.

29. Robert Rich and William White, "Health Care Policy and the American States: Issues of Federalism," in Rich and White, eds., *Health Policy, Federalism, and the American States* (Washington, DC: Urban Institute Press, 1996), 20.

30. Louann A. Bierlein, *Controversial Issues in Educational Policy* (Newbury Park, CA: Sage, 1993), 6.

31. College Board, "Trends in Student Aid 2004–2005," http://www.collegeboard.com.

32. Bierlein, *Controversial Issues in Educational Policy*, 31.

33. Steven G. Koven, *Public Budgeting in the United States: The Cultural and Ideological Setting* (Washington, DC: Georgetown University Press, 1999), 92.

34. Department of Health and Human Services, http://aspe.hhs.gov.

35. Fact Sheet, Social Security, http://www.ssa.gov.

36. Pew Research Center for the People and the Press, "Survey Finds Bush Failing in Social Security Reform," March 3, 2005.

37. Economic Policy Institute, "State Unemployment Insurance Policies as of June 2004," http://www.epinet.org.

38. Bureau of Labor Statistics, "Employment Situation Summary," http://www.bls.gov.

39. Social Security Administration, http://ssa-custhelp.ssa.gov.

40. Budget of the United States Government, Fiscal Year 2007, Historical Tables, Section 11, Outlays for Payments, http://www.whitehouse.gov/omb/budget/fy2007/pdf/hist.pdf.

41. H. Carl McCall, "New York State's Job Training and Job Creation Programs: Prospects for Welfare Reform," Controllers Report, November 21, 1996.

42. *BNA Daily Labor Report* (March 16, 1994).

43. *Congressional Quarterly Weekly Report* 50 (March 28, 1992): 809–10.

44. Christopher Conte, "A Special News Report on People and Their Jobs in Offices, Fields, and Factories," *Wall Street Journal* (March 9, 1993): A1.

45. Steven G. Koven, Mack C. Shelley II, and Bert E. Swanson, *American Public Policy: The Contemporary Agenda* (Boston: Houghton Mifflin, 1998), 271.

46. The White House, "Working Toward Independence," news release, February 2002, http://www.whitehouse.gov.

47. Nanette Relave, "TANF Reauthorization and Work Requirements," *Reauthorization Resource*, February 2002, http://www.welfareinfo.org.

48. Department of Health and Human Services, "Welfare Reform Reauthorized," February 8, 2006, http://www.hhs.gov.

49. Colin Campbell and William Pierce, *The Earned Income Credit* (Washington, DC: American Enterprise Institute, 1980).

50. Center on Budget and Policy Priorities, *The Earned Income Tax Credit: Boosting Employment, Aiding the Working Poor*, http://www.cbpp.org.

51. Department of Agriculture, "Food Stamp Program Annual Summary," March 24, 2006, http://www.fns.usda.gov.

52. Department of Agriculture, "Food Stamp Program Annual Summary."

53. Department of Agriculture, "Food Stamp Program," October 1, 2005, http://www.fns.usda.gov.

54. Jonathan Weisman, "Food Stamp Cuts Are on the Line," *Washington Post* (November 3, 2005): A1.

55. "Fiscal Year 2006: Mid-Session Review Budget of the U.S. Government," July 13, 2005, http://www.whitehouse.gov/omb/budget/fy2006/pdf/06msr.pdf.

56. Mark Rushefsky and Kant Patel, *Politics, Power, and Policy Making: The Case of Health Care Reform in the 1990s* (Armonk, NY: M. E. Sharpe, 1998), 27.

57. Henry J. Aaron, *Serious and Unstable Condition: Financing America's Health Care* (Washington, DC: Brookings Institution, 1991), ch. 2.

58. John F. Dickerson, "Can We Afford All This?" *Time* (December 8, 2004), 48–51; Edward Walsh and Bill Brubaker, "Drug Benefits Impact Detailed," *Washington Post* (December 8, 2003): A10.

59. Congressional Budget Office, "Medicaid: Federal Outlays in Billions of Dollars," 2005, http://www.house.gov; Kaiser Family Foundation, "HIV/AIDS Policy Fact Sheet," September 2005, http://www.kff.org.

60. The White House, "President Outlines Pandemic Influenza Preparations and Response," news release, http://www.whitehouse.gov.

61. Center for Disease Control and Prevention, Obesity Home Page, http://www.cdc.gov/nccdphp/dnpa/obesity/.

62. Ceci Connolly, "Public Policy Targeting Obesity," *Washington Post* (August 10, 2003): A1.

63. Marilyn Werber Serafina, "Medicrunch," *National Journal* 27 (July 29, 1995): 1937.

64. Erwin L. Levine and Elizabeth M. Wexler, *PL94-142: An Act of Congress* (New York: Macmillan, 1981).

65. *San Antonio Independent School District* v. *Rodriguez*, 411 U.S. 1 (1973).

66. *Zobrest* v. *Catalina Foothills School District*, 113 S.Ct. 2462 (1993).

67. *Board of Education of Kiriass Joel Village School District* v. *Grumet*, 114 S.Ct. 2481 (1994).

68. John J. Harrigan, *Policy and Politics in States and Communities*, 3rd ed. (Glenview, IL: Scott, Foresman, 1988), 300–1.

69. Star Parker, "In Support of School Vouchers for New Orleans Children," Townhall.com, http://www.townhall.com/opinion/columns/StarParker/2005/10/31/173440.html

70. Daniel Golden and Robert Tomsho, "School-Voucher Debate Frays Traditional Alliances: Civil-Rights Organizations See Some Members Break Ranks to Back School-Choice Programs," *Wall Street Journal* (July 1, 2002): B1.

71. Sari Horwitz, "Poll Finds Backing for D.C. School Vouchers; Blacks Support Idea More Than Whites," *Washington Post* (May 23, 1998): F1.

72. Department of Education, "ESEA: Charter Schools Grants FY 2006," December 28, 2005, http://www.ed.gov.

73. David Snyder, "More Work Ahead on Charter School: Site Approval, Hiring on Group's Agenda," *Washington Post* (June 20, 2002): T22.

74. Thomas Toch, "The New Education Bazaar," *U.S. News and World Report* (April 27, 1998): 35–46.

75. Justin Blum, "Citing Failures, D.C. Board Shuts Two Charter Schools," *Washington Post* (June 20, 2002): B3.

76. Neal Pearce, "Boston's 'Pilot Schools': Breakthrough Formula for Cities?" *Washington Post* (March 26, 2006), http://www.postwritersgroup.com/archives/peir0326.htm.

CHAPTER 18

1. Council on Foreign Relations, "Trade: Outsourcing Jobs," http://www.cfr.org.

2. Pete Engardio, Aaron Bernstein, and Manjeet Kripalani, "The New Global Job Shift," *Business Week* (February 3, 2003), http://www.businessweek.com; John Shinal, "Jobs Flying Faster from U.S.," *San Francisco Chronicle* (May 18, 2004): C1.

3. "Bush Adviser Backs Off Pro-outsourcing Comment," http://www.cnn.com.

4. Information Technology Association of America, "Executive Summary: The Comprehensive Impact of Offshore Software and IT Services Outsourcing on the U.S. Economy and the IT Industry," http://www.itaa.org.

5. "Bush: Outsourcing Painful, but Remedy Is Worse," http://edition.cnn.com.

6. Howard R. Smith, *Government and Business* (New York: Ronald Press, 1958), 99.

7. After 108 years of operation, the ICC expired at the end of 1995 as part of the effort by congressional Republicans to reduce federal regulations and allow market forces more freedom in which to operate.

8. *Pollack* v. *Farmers' Loan and Trust Co.*, 158 U.S. 429 (1895).

9. This discussion of the New Deal draws on Louis M. Hacker and Helene S. Zahler, *The United States in the Twentieth Century* (New York: Appleton-Century-Crofts, 1952); and William E. Leuchtenberg, *Franklin D. Roosevelt and the New Deal* (New York: Harper and Row, 1963).

10. http://www.dol.gov/asp/programs/history/chapter5.htm.

11. *U.S.* v. *Butler*, 297 U.S. 1 (1936).

12. *Wickard* v. *Filburn*, 317 U.S. 111 (1942).

13. Larry Gerston, Cynthia Fraleigh, and Robert Schwab, *The Deregulated Society* (Pacific Grove, CA: Brooks/Cole, 1988), 32–34.

14. David Vogel, "The 'New' Social Regulation in Historical and Comparative Perspective," in Thomas K. McCraw, ed., *Regulation in Perspective* (Cambridge, MA: Harvard University Press, 1981), 160.

15. A leading study is Martha Derthick and Paul J. Quirk, *The Politics of Deregulation* (Washington, DC: Brookings Institution, 1985).

16. Derthick and Quirk, *The Politics of Deregulation*, chs. 1, 2; and Dorothy Robyn, *Braking the Special Interests: Trucking Deregulation and the Politics of Policy Reform* (Chicago: University of Chicago Press, 1987), ch. 4.

17. "Is Small Community Air Service Near Extinction?" *Commuter/Regional Airline News* 20:23, 1, http://proquest.umi.com/pdqweb/.

18. Maurice Hinchey, "More Media Owners," *Nation* (February 6, 2006), http://www.thenation.com.

19. Sara Fitzgerald, "Liberalizing Agriculture: Why the U.S. Should Look to New Zealand and Australia," http://www.heritage.org.

20. "Farmings Front and Center at the Talks: Negotiators Slog Away in the Advance of WTO Meeting," *USA Today* (November 11, 2005), http://www.usatoday.com.

21. For Susan Schwab remarks, see http://www.iht.com/articles/2006/09/10/business/trade.php.

22. About 38 percent of the nation's commercial banks are members of the Federal Reserve System. See http://www.richmondfed.org.

23. This is the conclusion reached by John T. Woolley, *Monetary Politics: The Federal Reserve and the Politics of Monetary Policy* (New York: Cambridge University Press, 1984).

24. James E. Anderson, David W. Brady, Charles S. Bullock III, and Joseph Stewart Jr., *Public Policy and Politics in America*, 2nd ed. (Monterey: Brooks/Cole, 1984), 38–40.

25. James D. Savage, *Balanced Budgets and American Politics* (Ithaca, NY: Cornell University Press, 1988), 176–9.

26. "Clinton Vetoes Tax Bill; Republicans Vow to Press for Cuts", http://www.cnn.com.

27. "Bush Makes Case for Extending Cuts," http://www.cbsnews.com.

28. Congressional Budget Office, "What Accounts for the Decline in Manufacturing Employment?" *Economic and Budget Issue Brief* (February 18, 2004), http://www.cbo.gov.

29. "Economy Up, People Down: Declining Earnings Undercut Income Growth," http://www.epi.org.

30. Kevin Phillips, *Wealth and Democracy: A Political History of the American Rich* (New York: Broadway, 2002), 111, 412.

31. Matthew Slaughter, "The Economic Outlook," http://www.whitehouse.gov.

32. Concord Coalition, "The Federal Budget 2006," http://www.concordcoalition.org.

33. Concord Coalition, "The Federal Budget 2006."

34. This discussion on budgeting draws on James E. Anderson, *Public Policymaking: An Introduction*, 2nd ed. (Boston: Houghton Mifflin, 1994), ch. 5.

35. Donald F. Kettl, *Deficit Politics: Public Budgeting in Its Institutional and Historical Context* (New York: Macmillan, 1993).

36. Heritage Foundation, "Tax Reform Now!" http://www.taxation.org; and Radie Bunn, G. E. Whittenburg, and Carol Venable, "Analysis of the Economic Growth and Tax Relief Reconciliation Act of 2001," *National Public Accountant* (October 2001): 8–12, http://proquest.umi.com/pdqweb.

37. Isaac Shapiro and Joel Friedman, "Tax Returns: A Comprehensive Assessment of the Bush Administration's Record on Cutting Taxes," Center on Budget and Policy Priorities, http://www.cbpp.org.

38. "Overview of the President's 2007 Budget," http://www.gpoaccess.gov.

39. Budget of the United States Government, Fiscal Year 2007, http://www.gpoaccess.gov.

40. U.S Department of Education, Fiscal Year 2007 Budget Summary, February 6, 2006, http://www.ed.gov.

41. "Republicans Split on Immigration and Deficits," http://www.cbsnews.com.

42. Paul E. Peterson, "The New Politics of Deficits," in John E. Chubb and Paul E. Peterson, eds., *The New Direction in American Politics* (Washington, DC: Brookings Institution, 1985), ch. 13.

43. Aaron Wildavsky and Naomi Caiden, *The New Politics of the Budgetary Process*, 4th ed. (New York: Addison Wesley Longman, 2001): 146–8.

44. Edmund Andrews, "Federal Deficit Alarm Sounded," *San Francisco Chronicle* (May 7, 2004): C1–2.

45. "Bernanke Voices US Deficit Fears," http://news.bbc.co.uk.

46. Kent E. Portnoy, *Controversial Issues in Environmental Policy: Science vs. Economics vs. Politics* (Newbury Park, CA: Sage, 1992), 47–49.

47. Environmental Protection Agency, http://www.epa.gov.

48. James L. Regens and Robert W. Rycroft, *The Acid Rain Controversy* (Pittsburgh: University of Pittsburgh Press, 1988), 45–47.

49. See Charles I. Schultze, *The Public Use of Private Interest* (Washington, DC: Brookings Institution, 1977).

50. Eric Pianin, "U.S. Weighs Pollution Cases Against Big Utilities: White House Stresses Action in Response to Charges of Lax Enforcement of Clean Air Act," *Washington Post* (May 16, 2002): A2; Katherine Q. Seelye, "Bush to Seek Unlikely Allies in Bid to Alter Clean Air Act," *New York Times* (June 8, 2002): 1, 26.

51. "Facts About the Bush Administration's Plan to Weaken the Clean Air Act," http://www.sierraclub.org.

52. "10 States Sue EPA over Warming, Power Plants," http://www.msnbc.msn.com.

53. Michael Janofsky, "Justices Agree to Consider New Case on Emissions," *New York Times* (July 26, 2006).

54. Juliet Eilperin, "California Tightens Rules on Emissions," *Washington Post* (September 1, 2006).

CHAPTER 19

1. "President Bush Discusses NSA Surveillance Program," White House press briefing, May 11, 2006, http://www.whitehouse.gov.

2. Alfred E. Eckes Jr., *Opening America's Market: U.S. Foreign Trade Policy Since 1776* (Chapel Hill: University of North Carolina Press, 1995).

3. John L. O'Sullivan, writing in 1845, quoted in Julius W. Pratt, "The Ideology of American Expansion," in Avery Craven, ed., *Essays in Honor of William E. Dodd* (Chicago: University of Chicago Press, 1935), 343–4.

4. Fred L. Israel, *The State of the Union Messages*, vol. 2 (New York: Chelsea House, 1967), 2134.

5. Charles P. Kindleberger, *The World in Depression, 1929–1939* (Berkeley: University of California Press, 1986).

6. For a good description of the UN and its early years, see Ruth B. Russell, *A History of the United Nations Charter: The Role of the United States, 1940–1945* (Washington, DC: Brookings Institution, 1958).

7. See W. M. Scammell, *The International Economy Since 1945* (New York: St. Martin's, 1980); and Richard N. Gardner, *Sterling-Dollar Diplomacy in Current Perspective: The Origins and Prospects of Our International Economic Order* (New York: Columbia University Press, 1980).

8. Harry S Truman, speech before a joint session of Congress, March 12, 1947.

9. Corrected for inflation, this is over $100 billion in 2004.

10. George F. Kennan ("X"), "The Sources of Soviet Conduct," *Foreign Affairs* (July 1947): 566–82.

11. The North Atlantic Treaty's original signatory states were Belgium, Canada, Denmark, France, Great Britain, Iceland, Italy, Luxembourg, the Netherlands, Norway, Portugal, and the United States. As of 2004, NATO had twenty-six members.

12. John F. Kennedy, inaugural address, January 20, 1961, Public Papers of the Presidents of the United States (Washington, DC: Government Printing Office).

13. See Graham Allison, *Essence of Decision: Explaining the Cuban Missile Crisis* (Boston: Little, Brown, 1971).

14. For a discussion of U.S., Soviet, and Chinese views of the Vietnam War, see Daniel S. Papp, *Vietnam: The View from Moscow, Beijing, Washington* (Jefferson, NC: McFarland, 1981).

15. Richard M. Nixon, inaugural address, January 20, 1969, Public Papers of the Presidents of the United States (Washington, DC: Government Printing Office).

16. Michael Froman, *The Development of the Idea of Détente* (New York: St. Martin's, 1982).

17. R. C. Schroeder, "Human Rights Policy," *CQ Research Reports* 1 (1979), CQ Researcher Online, http://library.cqpress.com.

18. Jimmy Carter, State of the Union Address, January 21, 1980, Public Papers of the Presidents of the United States (Washington, DC: Government Printing Office).

19. See Colin S. Gray, "Strategic Forces," in Joseph Kruzel, ed., *1986–1987 American Defense Annual* (Lexington, MA: Lexington Books, 1986). For a discussion of Reagan's early international economic policies, see Jeffrey E. Garten, "Gunboat Economics," *Foreign Affairs* 63 (1985): 538–99.

20. See Stephen E. Ambrose, *Rise to Globalism: American Foreign Policy Since 1938*, 8th revised ed. (New York: Penguin, 1998); Steven W. Hook and John Spanier, *American Foreign Policy Since World War II*, 15th ed. (Washington, DC: CQ Press, 2000); Richard Mandelbaum and Strobe Talbott, *Reagan and Gorbachev* (New York: Vintage, 1987); and Richard A. Melanson, *American Foreign Policy Since the Vietnam War*, 3rd ed. (Armonk, NY: M. E. Sharpe, 2000).

21. Karen Brutents and Larisa Galperin, "Origins of the New Thinking," *Russian Social Science Review* 47:1 (2006): 73–102; David Laibman, "The Soviet Demise: Revisionist Betrayal, Structural Defect, or Authoritarian Distortion?" *Science and Society* 69:4 (2005): 594–606; and John Muelle, "What Was the Cold War About? Evidence from Its Ending," *Political Science Quarterly* 119:4 (2004/2005): 609–31.

22. For good discussions of the events that led to the decline and fall of the Soviet Union, see William Head and Earl H. Tilford Jr., *The Eagle in the Desert: Looking Back on U.S. Involvement in the Persian Gulf War* (Westport, CT: Praeger, 1996).

23. See Geoffrey Hosking, *The Awakening of the Soviet Union* (Cambridge, MA: Harvard University Press, 1990); David Remnick, *Lenin's Tomb: The Last Days of the Soviet Empire* (New York: Random House, 1993); and Jeffrey T. Checkel, *Ideas and International Political Change: Soviet/Russian Behavior and the End of the Cold War* (New Haven, CT: Yale University Press, 1997).

24. Jeffrey J. Schott, *The WTO After Seattle* (Washington, DC: Institute for International Economics, 2000); and Bhagirath L. Das, *World Trade Organization: A Guide to New Frameworks for International Trade* (New York: St. Martin's, 2000).

25. See Daniel S. Papp, *The Impact of September 11 on Contemporary International Relations* (New York: Pearson, 2003).

26. Strategic Offensive Arms Reduction Treaty, U.S. Department of State, May 24, 2002.

27. Dana Priest and Walter Pincus, "U.S. 'Almost All Wrong' on Weapons," *Washington Post* (October 7, 2004): A1; Hans Blix, *Disarming Iraq* (New York: Pantheon, 2004); Richard A. Clarke, *Against All Enemies: Inside America's War on Terror* (New York: Free Press, 2004); and Kenneth M. Pollack, *The Threatening Storm: The Case for Invading Iraq* (New York: Random House, 2002).

28. The U.S. Department of Defense provides figures for confirmed U.S. military deaths and other casualties but does not maintain records of Iraqi military or civilian casualties. Information concerning Iraqi deaths is compiled largely from various news reports. During 2006 alone, it is estimated that 5,000–10,000 Iraqi police and military and 15,000–20,000 civilians lost their lives.

29. Robin Wright and Ellen Knickmeyer, "U.S. Lowers Sights on What Can Be Achieved in Iraq," *Washington Post* (August 14, 2005): A1.

30. See Loch K. Johnson, *America's Secret Power: The CIA in a Democratic Society* (New York: Oxford University Press, 1989).

31. U.S. Senate, Select Committee on Intelligence, Report of the Select Committee on Intelligence on the U.S. Intelligence Community's Prewar Intelligence Assessments on Iraq (Washington, DC: Government Printing Office, 2004); Josh Meyer and Greg Miller, "The Prisoner Problem," *Los Angeles Times* (September 7, 2006): A1; and David Stout, "Senate Panel Defies Bush on Detainee Bill," *New York Times* (September 14, 2006): A10.

32. Representative Bennie Thompson (D–MS), quoted in a prepared statement given December 5, 2005, before the U.S. House of Representatives, Committee on Homeland Security.

33. James M. Lindsay, "Congress, Foreign Policy, and the New Institutionalism," *International Studies Quarterly* 38 (June 1994): 281–304.

34. *Congress A to Z*, 4th ed. (Washington, DC: CQ Press, 2003).

35. In the mid-1980s, the Democratic-controlled Congress enacted a series of amendments, known collectively as the Boland Amendments, prohibiting the Department of Defense and the Central Intelligence Agency, or any other government agency, from providing military aid to the Contras in Nicaragua. The Reagan administration circumvented these limitations by using the National Security Council, which was not explicitly covered by the law, to supervise covert military aid to the Contras. Under the direction of Robert McFarlane and John Poindexter, the NSC raised private and foreign funds for the Contras. This operation was directed by NSC staffer Marine Lt. Col. Oliver North and included a plan to secretly ship arms to Iran despite a U.S. trade and arms embargo. The profits from the arms sales were intended for the Contras. In early November 1986, scandal erupted when news reports forced the Reagan administration to disclose the Iranian arms deals. Poindexter resigned and North was fired. Select congressional committees held joint hearings, and in December 1986, Lawrence E. Walsh was named as special prosecutor to investigate what became known as the Iran-Contra Affair. President Reagan claimed to have been uninformed about the details of the secret program, and no evidence was found to link him to any crime. The special prosecutor was critical of the NSC, while congressional hearings uncovered a web of official deception, mismanagement, and illegal activity.

36. William S. Cohen, Secretary of Defense, *Annual Report to the President and Congress* (Washington, DC: Department of Defense, 1999).

37. For Eisenhower's thoughts on the subject, see Dwight D. Eisenhower, *The White House Years* (Garden City, NY: Doubleday, 1963–1965).

38. Roxana Tiron, "Cunningham Sentenced to Eight Years, Four Months," *The Hill* (March 3, 2006).

39. David S. Cloud, "U.S. Urged to Stop Paying Iraqi Reporters," *New York Times* (May 24, 2006): A19.

40. Eugene R. Wittkopf, "On the Foreign Policy Beliefs of the American People: A Critique and Some Evidence," *International Studies Quarterly* 30 (December 1986): 425–55.

41. Dana Milbank, "The 'Bush Doctrine' Experiences Shining Moments," *Washington Post* (December 21, 2003): A26.

42. Robert C. Byrd, "The Truth Will Emerge," Senate Speeches, U.S. Senate, May 21, 2003, http://byrd.senate.gov.

43. Steven W. Hook, *U.S. Foreign Policy: The Paradox of World Power* (Washington, DC: CQ Press, 2005), 319.

44. President's Commission on Critical Infrastructure Protection, *Critical Foundations: Protecting America's Infrastructures,* (Washington, DC: Government Printing Office, 1997).

45. John Christensen, "Bracing for Guerrilla Warfare in Cyberspace," CNN Interactive, April 6, 1999; and Kenneth H. Bacon, Department of Defense news briefing, April 16, 1998.

46. Testimony of U.S. Ambassador Maureen Quinn, Afghanistan coordinator at the Department of State; Mary Beth Long, deputy assistant secretary of defense for counter-narcotics; and Michael A. Braun, chief of operations for the Drug Enforcement Administration before the U.S. House of Representatives Committee on International Relations, March 17, 2005.

47. See R. Coppock, "Implementing the Kyoto Protocol," *Issues in Science and Technology* (Spring 1998): 66–74; B. Bolin and A. P. Loeb, "Act Now to Slow Climate Change," *Issues in Science and Technology* (Fall 1998): 18–22; U.S. Department of State, "The Kyoto Protocol," fact sheet released by the Bureau of Oceans and International Environmental and Scientific Affairs, November 2, 1998; and United Nations press release, "84 Signatories to the Kyoto Protocol," March 16, 1999.

★★★ Glossary

A

administrative adjudication: A quasi-judicial process in which a bureaucratic agency settles disputes between two parties in a manner similar to the way courts resolve disputes.

administrative discretion: The ability of bureaucrats to make choices concerning the best way to implement congressional intentions.

advisory referendum: A process in which voters cast nonbinding ballots on an issue or proposal.

affiliates: Local television stations that carry the programming of a national network.

affirmative action: Policies designed to give special attention or compensatory treatment to members of a previously disadvantaged group.

agenda: A set of issues to be discussed or given attention.

agenda setting: The constant process of forming the list of issues to be addressed by government.

al-Qaeda: Worldwide terrorist organization led by Osama bin Laden, responsible for numerous attacks against U.S. interests, including 9/11 attacks against the World Trade Center and the Pentagon.

American dream: An American ideal of a happy, successful life, which often includes wealth, a house, a better life for one's children, and, for some, the ability to grow up to be president.

amicus curiae: "Friend of the court"; a third party to a lawsuit who files a legal brief for the purpose of raising additional points of view in an attempt to influence a court's decision.

Anti-Federalists: Those who favored strong state governments and a weak national government; opposed the ratification of the U.S. Constitution.

appellate courts: Courts that generally review only findings of law made by lower courts.

appellate jurisdiction: The power vested in an appellate court to review and/or revise the decision of a lower court.

apportionment: The process of allotting congressional seats to each state following the decennial census according to the state's proportion of the population.

Articles of Confederation: The compact among the thirteen original states that was the basis of their government. Written in 1776, the Articles were not ratified by all the states until 1781.

authoritarian system: A system of government that bases its rule on force rather than consent of the governed.

B

ballot measure: An election option such as the initiative or referendum that enables voters to enact public policy.

bicameral legislature: A legislature divided into two houses; the U.S. Congress and the state legislatures are bicameral except Nebraska, which is unicameral.

bill: A proposed law.

bill of attainder: A law declaring an act illegal without a judicial trial.

Bill of Rights: The first ten amendments to the U.S. Constitution, which largely guarantee specific rights and liberties.

Black Codes: Laws denying most legal rights to newly freed slaves; passed by southern states following the Civil War.

block grant: Broad grant with few strings attached; given to states by the federal government for specified activities, such as secondary education or health services.

blog: A Web log; Web-based journal entries that provide an editorial and news outlet for citizens.

Bretton Woods Agreement: International financial agreement signed shortly before the end of World War II that created the World Bank and the International Monetary Fund.

brief: A document containing the legal written arguments in a case filed with a court by a party prior to a hearing or trial.

broadcast media: Television, radio, cable, and satellite services.

Brown v. _Board of Education_ (1954): U.S. Supreme Court decision holding that school segregation is inherently unconstitutional because it violates the Fourteenth Amendment's guarantee of equal protection; marked the end of legal segregation in the United States.

bureaucracy: A set of complex hierarchical departments, agencies, commissions, and their staffs that exist to help a chief executive officer carry out his or her duties. Bureaucracies may be private organizations or governmental units.

Bush Doctrine: Policy advocated by President George W. Bush of using preemptive military action against a perceived threat to U.S. interests.

business cycles: Fluctuations between expansion and recession that are a part of modern capitalist economies.

C

Cabinet: The formal body of presidential advisers who head the fifteen executive departments. Presidents often add others to this body of formal advisers.

campaign consultant: The private-sector professionals and firms who sell to a candidate the technologies, services, and strategies required to get that candidate elected.

campaign manager: The individual who travels with the candidate and coordinates the many different aspects of the campaign.

candidate-centered politics: Politics that focuses directly on the candidates, their issues, and character rather than party affiliation.

candidate debate: Forum in which political candidates face each other to discuss their platforms, records, and character.

Carter Doctrine: Policy announced after the 1979 Soviet invasion of Afghanistan that the Persian Gulf area was a vital U.S. interest and the United States would fight to maintain access to it.

categorical grant: Grant for which Congress appropriates funds for a specific purpose.

Central Intelligence Agency: Executive agency responsible for collection and analysis of information and intelligence about foreign countries and events.

checks and balances: A governmental structure that gives each of the three branches of government some degree of oversight and control over the actions of the others.

citizen: Member of the political community to whom certain rights and obligations are attached.

civic virtue: The tendency to form small-scale associations for the public good.

civil law: Codes of behavior related to business and contractual relationships between groups and individuals.

civil liberties: The personal guarantees and freedoms that the federal government cannot abridge by law, constitution, or judicial interpretation.

civil rights: The government-protected rights of individuals against arbitrary or discriminatory treatment by governments or individuals based on categories such as race, sex, national origin, age, religion, or sexual orientation.

Civil Rights Act of 1964: Legislation passed by Congress to outlaw segregation in public facilities and racial discrimination in employment, education, and voting; created the Equal Employment Opportunity Commission.

Civil Rights Cases (1883): Name attached to five cases brought under the Civil Rights Act of 1875. In 1883, the Supreme Court decided that discrimination in a variety of public accommodations, including theaters, hotels, and railroads, could not be prohibited by the act because it was private, not state, discrimination.

civil service laws: These acts removed the staffing of the bureaucracy from political parties and created a professional bureaucracy filled through competition.

civil service system: The system created by civil service laws by which many

769

appointments to the federal bureaucracy are made.

civil society: Society created when citizens are allowed to organize and express their views publicly as they engage in an open debate about public policy.

clear and present danger test: Test articulated by the Supreme Court in *Schenck v. U.S.* (1919) to draw the line between protected and unprotected speech; the Court looks to see "whether the words used . . ." could "create a clear and present danger that they will bring about substantive evils" that Congress seeks "to prevent."

closed primary: A primary election in which only a party's registered voters are eligible to vote.

cloture: Mechanism requiring sixty senators to vote to cut off debate.

coalition: A group made up of interests or organizations that join forces for the purpose of electing public officials.

collective good: Something of value that cannot be withheld from a nonmember of a group, for example, a tax write-off or a better environment.

collective security: The concept that peace would be secured if all countries collectively opposed any country that invaded another.

Committees of Correspondence: Organizations in each of the American colonies created to keep colonists abreast of developments with the British; served as powerful molders of public opinion against the British.

communications director: The person who develops the overall media strategy for the candidate, blending the free press coverage with the paid TV, radio, and mail media.

concurrent powers: Authority possessed by both the state and national governments that may be exercised concurrently as long as that power is not exclusively within the scope of national power or in conflict with national law.

confederation: Type of government where the national government derives its powers from the states; a league of independent states.

conference committee: Joint committee created to iron out differences between Senate and House versions of a specific piece of legislation.

congressional review: A process whereby Congress can nullify agency regulations by a joint resolution of legislative disapproval.

conservative: One thought to believe that a government is best that governs least and that big government can only infringe on individual, personal, and economic rights.

constitution: A document establishing the structure, functions, and limitations of a government.

constitutional courts: Federal courts specifically created by the U.S. Constitution or by Congress pursuant to its authority in Article III.

containment: Strategy to oppose expansion of Soviet power, particularly in Western Europe and East Asia, with military power, economic assistance, and political influence.

content regulation: Governmental attempts to regulate the electronic media.

contrast ad: Ad that compares the records and proposals of the candidates, with a bias toward the sponsor.

conventional political participation: Political participation that attempts to influence the political process through well-accepted, often moderate forms of persuasion, such as writing letters to government officials, making political contributions, and voting.

cooperative federalism: The relationship between the national and state governments that began with the New Deal.

criminal law: Codes of behavior related to the protection of property and individual safety.

critical election: An election that signals a party realignment through voter polarization around new issues.

crossover voting: Participation in the primary of a party with which the voter is not affiliated.

Cuban Missile Crisis: The 1962 confrontation that nearly escalated into war between the United States and Soviet Union over Soviet deployment of medium-range ballistic missiles in Cuba.

D

de facto **discrimination:** Racial discrimination that results from practice (such as housing patterns or other social factors) rather than the law.

de jure **discrimination:** Racial segregation that is a direct result of law or official policy.

dealignment: A general decline in partisan identification and loyalty in the electorate.

Declaration of Independence: Document drafted by Thomas Jefferson in 1776 that proclaimed the right of the American colonies to separate from Great Britain.

deep background: Information provided to a journalist that will not be attributed to any source.

delegate: Role played by elected representatives who vote the way their constituents would want them to, regardless of their own opinions.

democracy: A system of government that gives power to the people, whether directly or through elected representatives.

Department of Defense: Chief executive-branch department responsible for formulation and implementation of U.S. military policy.

Department of Homeland Security: Cabinet department created after the 9/11 attacks to coordinate domestic U.S. security efforts against terrorism.

Department of State: Chief executive-branch department responsible for formulation and implementation of U.S. foreign policy.

departments: Major administrative units with responsibility for a broad area of government operations. Departmental status usually indicates a permanent national interest in a particular governmental function, such as defense, commerce, or agriculture.

deregulation: A reduction in market controls (such as price fixing, subsidies, or controls on who can enter a field) in favor of market-based competition.

détente: The relaxation of tensions between the United States and the Soviet Union that occurred during the 1970s.

direct democracy: A system of government in which members of the polity meet to discuss all policy decisions and then agree to abide by majority rule.

direct incitement test: A test articulated by the Supreme Court in *Brandenberg* v. *Ohio* (1969) that holds that advocacy of illegal action is protected by the First Amendment unless imminent lawless action is intended and likely to occur.

direct mailer: A professional who supervises a political campaign's direct-mail fund-raising strategies.

direct primary: The selection of party candidates through the ballots of qualified voters rather than at party nomination conventions.

discharge petition: Petition that gives a majority of the House of Representatives the authority to bring an issue to the floor in the face of committee inaction.

discount rate: The rate of interest at which member banks can borrow money from their regional Federal Reserve Bank.

disturbance theory: Political scientist David B. Truman's theory that interest groups form in part to counteract the efforts of other groups.

divided government: The political condition in which different political parties control the White House and Congress.

domestic dependent nation: A type of sovereignty that makes an Indian tribe in the United States outside the authority of state governments but reliant on the federal government for the definition of tribal authority.

double jeopardy clause: Part of the Fifth Amendment that protects individuals from being tried twice for the same offense.

dual federalism: The belief that having separate and equally powerful levels of government is the best arrangement.

due process clause: Clause contained in the Fifth and Fourteenth Amendments. Over the years, it has been construed to guarantee to individuals a variety of rights ranging from economic liberty to criminal procedural rights to protection from arbitrary governmental action.

due process rights: Procedural guarantees provided by the Fourth, Fifth, Sixth, and Eighth Amendments for those accused of crimes.

E

earmark: Funds that an appropriations bill designates for a particular purpose within a state or congressional district.

economic interest group: A group with the primary purpose of promoting the financial interests of its members.

economic regulation: Government regulation of business practices, industry rates, routes, or areas serviced by particular industries.

economic stability: A situation in which there is economic growth, rising national income, high employment, and steadiness in the general level of prices.

Eighth Amendment: Part of the Bill of Rights that states: "Excessive bail shall not be required, nor excessive fines imposed, nor cruel and unusual punishments inflicted."

elector: Member of the Electoral College chosen by methods determined in each state.

Electoral College: Representatives of each state who cast the final ballots that actually elect a president.

electorate: Citizens eligible to vote.

Embargo Act: Passed by Congress in 1807 to prevent U.S. ships from leaving U.S. ports for foreign ports without the approval of the federal government.

engagement: Policy implemented during the Clinton administration that the United States would remain actively involved in foreign affairs.

enlargement: Policy implemented during the Clinton administration that the United States would actively promote the expansion of democracy and free markets throughout the world.

entitlement program: Income security program to which all those meeting eligibility criteria are entitled.

enumerated powers: Seventeen specific powers granted to Congress under Article I, section 8, of the U.S. Constitution; these powers include taxation, coinage of money, regulation of commerce, and the authority to provide for a national defense.

Equal Employment Opportunity Commission: Federal agency created to enforce the Civil Rights Act of 1964, which forbids discrimination on the basis of race, creed, national origin, religion, or sex in hiring, promotion, or firing.

equal protection clause: Section of the Fourteenth Amendment that guarantees that all citizens receive "equal protection of the laws."

Equal Rights Amendment: Proposed amendment that would bar discrimination against women by federal or state governments.

equal time rule: The rule that requires broadcast stations to sell air time equally to all candidates in a political campaign if they choose to sell it to any.

establishment clause: The first clause in the First Amendment; it prohibits the national government from establishing a national religion.

ex post facto **law:** Law passed after the fact, thereby making previously legal activity illegal and subject to current penalty; prohibited by the U.S. Constitution.

exclusionary rule: Judicially created rule that prohibits police from using illegally seized evidence at trial.

executive agreement: Formal government agreement entered into by the president that does not require the advice and consent of the U.S. Senate.

Executive Office of the President (EOP): Establishment created in 1939 to help the president oversee the executive branch bureaucracy.

executive order: Rule or regulation issued by the president that has the effect of law. All executive orders must be published in the *Federal Register*.

executive privilege: An implied presidential power that allows the president to refuse to disclose information regarding confidential conversations or national security to Congress or the judiciary.

exit polls: Polls conducted at selected polling places on Election Day.

extradition clause: Part of Article IV that requires states to extradite, or return, criminals to states where they have been convicted or are to stand trial.

F

fairness doctrine: Rule in effect from 1949 to 1985 requiring broadcasters to cover events adequately and to present contrasting views on important public issues.

federal budget deficit: The amount by which federal expenditure exceeds federal revenue.

Federal Employees Political Activities Act: 1993 liberalization of the Hatch Act. Federal employees are now allowed to run for office in nonpartisan elections and to contribute money to campaigns in partisan elections.

Federal Reserve Board: A seven-member board that sets member banks' reserve requirements, controls the discount rate, and makes other economic decisions.

federal system: System of government where the national government and state governments share some powers, derive all authority from the people, and the powers of the national government are specified in a constitution.

The Federalist Papers: A series of eighty-five political papers written by John Jay, Alexander Hamilton, and James Madison in support of ratification of the U.S. Constitution.

Federalists: Those who favored a stronger national government and supported the proposed U.S. Constitution; later became the first U.S. political party.

Fifteenth Amendment: One of the three Civil War amendments; specifically enfranchised newly freed male slaves.

Fifth Amendment: Part of the Bill of Rights that imposes a number of restrictions on the federal government with respect to the rights of persons suspected of committing a crime. It provides for indictment by a grand jury, protection against self-incrimination, and prevents the national government from denying a person life, liberty, or property without the due process of law. It also

prevents the national government from taking property without fair compensation.

fighting words: Words that, "by their very utterance inflict injury or tend to incite an immediate breach of peace." Fighting words are not subject to the restrictions of the First Amendment.

filibuster: A formal way of halting action on a bill by means of long speeches or unlimited debate in the Senate.

finance chair: A professional who coordinates the fund-raising efforts for the campaign.

First Amendment: Part of the Bill of Rights that imposes a number of restrictions on the federal government with respect to the civil liberties of the people, including freedom of religion, speech, press, assembly, and petition.

First Continental Congress: Meeting held in Philadelphia from September 5 to October 26, 1774, in which fifty-six delegates (from every colony except Georgia) adopted a resolution in opposition to the Coercive Acts.

fiscal policy: Federal government policies on taxes, spending, and debt management, intended to promote the nation's macroeconomic goals, particularly with respect to employment, price stability, and growth.

527 political committees: Nonprofit and unregulated interest groups that focus on specific causes or policy positions and attempt to influence voters.

Fourteenth Amendment: One of the three Civil War amendments; guarantees equal protection and due process of the laws to all U.S. citizens.

Fourth Amendment: Part of the Bill of Rights that reads: "The right of the people to be secure in their persons, houses, papers, and effects, against unreasonable searches and seizures, shall not be violated, and no Warrants shall issue, but upon probable cause, supported by Oath or affirmation, and particularly describing the place to be searched, and the persons or things to be seized."

framing: The process by which a news organization defines a political issue and consequently affects opinion about the issues.

free exercise clause: The second clause of the First Amendment. It prohibits the U.S. government from interfering with a citizen's right to practice his or her religion.

free media: Coverage of a candidate's campaign by the news media.

free rider problem: Potential members fail to join a group because they can get the benefit, or collective good, sought by the group without contributing to the effort.

front-loading: The tendency of states to choose an early date on the primary calendar.

full faith and credit clause: Section of Article IV of the Constitution that ensures judicial decrees and contracts made in one state will be binding and enforceable in any other state.

fundamental freedoms: Those rights defined by the Court to be essential to order, liberty, and justice.

G

General Agreement on Tariffs and Trade: Devised shortly after World War II as an interim agreement until a World Trade Organization could be created to help lower tariffs and increase trade.

general election: Election in which voters decide which candidates will actually fill elective public offices.

general election campaign: That part of a political campaign aimed at winning a general election.

gerrymandering: The legislative process through which the majority party in each statehouse tries to assure that the maximum number of representatives from its political party can be elected to Congress through the redrawing of legislative districts.

get out the vote (GOTV): A push at the end of a political campaign to encourage supporters to go to the polls.

Gibbons v. Ogden **(1824):** The Court upheld broad congressional power over interstate commerce. The Court's broad interpretation of the Constitution's commerce clause paved the way for later rulings upholding expansive federal powers.

global warming: The increase in global temperatures that results from carbon emissions from burning fossil fuels such as oil and coal.

government: The formal vehicles through which policies are made and affairs of state are conducted.

government corporation: Business established by Congress to perform functions that can be provided by private businesses (such as the U.S. Postal Service).

governmental (institutional) agenda: The changing list of issues to which governments believe they should address themselves.

governmental party: The office holders and candidates who run under a political party's banner.

governor: Chief elected executive in state government.

grandfather clause: Voting qualification provision in many Southern states that allowed only those whose grandfathers had voted before Reconstruction to vote unless they passed a wealth or literacy test.

Great Compromise: A decision made during the Constitutional Convention to give each state the same number of representatives in the Senate regardless of size; representation in the House was determined by population.

gross domestic product (GDP): The total market value of all goods and services produced in a country during a year.

H

hard money: Legally specified and limited contributions that are clearly regulated by the Federal Election Campaign Act and by the Federal Election Commission.

Hatch Act: Law enacted in 1939 to prohibit civil servants from taking activist roles in partisan campaigns. This act prohibited federal employees from making political contributions, working for a particular party, or campaigning for a particular candidate.

hold: A tactic by which a senator asks to be informed before a particular bill is brought to the floor. This stops the bill from coming to the floor until the hold is removed.

human rights: The belief that human beings have inalienable rights such as freedom of speech and freedom of religion.

I

ideology: A set or system of beliefs that shapes the thinking of individual and how they view the world.

impeachment: The power delegated to the House of Representatives in the Constitution to charge the president, vice president, or other "civil officers," including federal judges, with "Treason, Bribery, or other High Crimes and Misdemeanors." This is the first step in the constitutional process of removing such government officials from office.

implementation: The process by which a law or policy is put into operation by the bureaucracy.

implied powers: Powers derived from the enumerated powers and the necessary and proper clause. These powers are not stated specifically but are considered to be reasonably implied through the exercise of delegated powers.

impressment: The British practice in the early eighteenth century of stopping ships at sea to seize sailors suspected of having deserted the Royal Navy.

incorporation doctrine: An interpretation of the Constitution that holds that the due process clause of the Fourteenth Amendment requires that state and local governments also guarantee those rights.

incumbency: The holding of an office.

independent executive agency: Governmental unit that closely resembles a Cabinet department but has a narrower area of responsibility (such as the Central Intelligence Agency) and is not part of any Cabinet department.

independent regulatory commission: An agency created by Congress that is generally concerned with a specific aspect of the economy.

indirect (representative) democracy: A system of government that gives citizens the opportunity to vote for representatives who will work on their behalf.

inflation: A rise in the general price levels of an economy.

inherent powers: Powers that belong to the national government simply because it is a sovereign state.

initiative: A process that allows citizens to propose legislation and submit it to the state electorate for popular vote.

inoculation ad: Advertising that attempts to counteract an anticipated attack from the opposition before the attack is launched.

interagency councils: Working groups created to facilitate coordination of policy making and implementation across a host of governmental agencies.

interest group: An organized group that tries to influence public policy.

international governmental organization (IGO): An organization created by the governments of at least two and often many countries that operates internationally with the objectives of achieving the purposes that the member countries agree on.

International Monetary Fund: International governmental organization created shortly before the end of World War II to stabilize international financial relations through fixed monetary exchange rates.

Internet team: Campaign staff that uses Web-based resources to communicate with voters, raise funds, organize volunteers, and plan events.

interstate compacts: Contracts between states that carry the force of law; generally now used as a tool to address multistate policy concerns.

interventionist state: Alternative to the laissez-faire state; the government takes an active role in guiding and managing the private economy.

iron triangles: The relatively stable relationships and patterns of interaction that occur among an agency, interest groups, and congressional committees or subcommittees.

isolationism: A national policy of avoiding participation in foreign affairs.

issue networks: The loose and informal relationships that exist among a large number of actors who work in broad policy areas.

issue-oriented politics: Politics that focuses on specific issues rather than on party, candidate, or other loyalties.

J

Jim Crow laws: Laws enacted by southern states that discriminated against blacks by creating "whites only" schools, theaters, hotels, and other public accommodations.

Joint Chiefs of Staff: Advisory body to the president that includes chief of staff of the army, chief of staff of the air force, chief of naval operations, and marine commandant.

joint committee: Includes members from both houses of Congress, conducts investigations or special studies.

judicial activism: A philosophy of judicial decision making that argues judges should use their power broadly to further justice, especially in the areas of equality and personal liberty.

judicial implementation: Refers to how and whether judicial decisions are translated into actual public policies affecting more than the immediate parties to a lawsuit.

judicial restraint: A philosophy of judicial decision making that argues courts should allow the decisions of other branches of government to stand, even when they offend a judge's own sense of principles.

judicial review: Power of the courts to review acts of other branches of government and the states.

Judiciary Act of 1789: Established the basic three-tiered structure of the federal court system.

jurisdiction: Authority vested in a particular court to hear and decide the issues in any particular case.

L

laissez-faire: A French term literally meaning "to allow to do, to leave alone." It is a hands-off governmental policy that is based on the belief that government involvement in the economy is wrong.

League of Nations: Created in the peace treaty that ended World War I, it was an international governmental organization dedicated to preserving peace.

legislative courts: Courts established by Congress for specialized purposes, such as the Court of Military Appeals.

libel: False written statements or written statements tending to call someone's reputation into disrepute.

liberal: One considered to favor extensive governmental involvement in the economy and the provision of social services and to take an activist role in protecting the rights of women, the elderly, minorities, and the environment.

libertarian: One who favors a free market economy and no governmental interference in personal liberties.

line-item veto: The authority of a chief executive to delete part of a bill passed by the legislature that involves taxing or spending. The legislature may override a veto, usually with a two-thirds majority of each chamber.

lobbying: The activities of a group or organization that seeks to influence legislation and persuade political leaders to support the group's position.

lobbyist: Interest group representative who seeks to influence legislation that will benefit his or her organization through political persuasion.

logrolling: Vote trading; voting yea to support a colleague's bill in return for a promise of future support.

M

machine: A party organization that recruits its members with tangible incentives and is characterized by a high degree of control over member activity.

majority leader: The elected leader of the party controlling the most seats in the House of Representatives or the Senate; is second in authority to the Speaker of the House and in the Senate is regarded as its most powerful member.

majority party: The political party in each house of Congress with the most members.

majority rule: The central premise of direct democracy in which only policies that collectively garner the support of a majority of voters will be made into law.

manager: A professional executive hired by a city council or county board to manage daily operations and to recommend policy changes.

mandate: A command, indicated by an electorate's votes, for the elected officials to carry out their platforms.

manifest destiny: Theory that the United States was divinely mandated to expand across North America to the Pacific Ocean.

Marbury v. Madison (1803): Supreme Court first asserted the power of judicial review in finding that the congressional statute extending the Court's original jurisdiction was unconstitutional.

margin of error: A measure of the accuracy of a public opinion poll.

markup: A process in which legislative committee members offer changes to a bill before it goes to the floor in either house for a vote.

Marshall Plan: European Recovery Program, named after Secretary of State George C. Marshall, of extensive U.S. aid to Western Europe after World War II.

mass media: The entire array of organizations through which information is collected and disseminated to the general public.

matching funds: Donations to presidential campaigns from the federal government that are determined by the amount of private funds a qualifying candidate raises.

McCulloch v. Maryland (1819): The Supreme Court upheld the power of the national government and denied the right of a state to tax the bank. The Court's broad interpretation of the necessary and proper clause paved the way for later rulings upholding expansive federal powers.

means-tested program: Income security program intended to assist those whose incomes fall below a designated level.

media consultant: A professional who produces political candidates' television, radio, and print advertisements.

media effects: The influence of news sources on public opinion.

Medicaid: An expansion of Medicare, this program subsidizes medical care for the poor.

Medicare: The federal program established in the Lyndon B. Johnson administration that provides medical care to elderly Social Security recipients.

mercantilism: An economic theory designed to increase a nation's wealth through the development of commercial industry and a favorable balance of trade.

merit system: The system by which federal civil service jobs are classified into grades or levels, to which appointments are made on the basis of performance on competitive examinations.

midterm election: Election that takes place in the middle of a presidential term.

military-industrial complex: The grouping of the U.S. armed forces and defense industries.

minority leader: The elected leader of the party with the second highest number of elected representatives in the House of Representatives or the Senate.

minority party: The political party in each house of Congress with the second most members.

Miranda rights: Statements that must be made by the police informing a suspect of his or her constitutional rights protected by the Fifth Amendment, including the right to an attorney provided by the court if the suspect cannot afford one.

Miranda v. Arizona (1966): A landmark Supreme Court ruling that held the Fifth Amendment requires that individuals arrested for a crime must be advised of their right to remain silent and to have counsel present.

monarchy: A form of government in which power is vested in hereditary kings and queens who govern in the interests of all.

monetary policy: A form of government regulation in which the nation's money supply and interest rates are controlled.

money: A system of exchange for goods and services that includes currency, coins, and bank deposits.

Monroe Doctrine: President James Monroe's 1823 pledge that the United States would oppose attempts by European states to extend their political control into the Western Hemisphere.

moralism: The policy of emphasizing morality in foreign affairs.

muckraking: A form of journalism, in vogue in the early twentieth century, concerned with reforming government and business conduct.

multilateralism: The U.S. foreign policy that actions should be taken in cooperation with other states after consultation.

N

narrowcasting: Targeting media programming at specific populations within society.

national convention: A party conclave (meeting) held in the presidential election year for the purposes of nominating a presidential and vice presidential ticket and adopting a platform.

national party platform: A statement of the general and specific philosophy and policy goals of a political party, usually promulgated at the national convention.

National Security Agency (NSA): Intelligence agency responsible for gathering intelligence from electronic and other sources and for code breaking.

National Security Council (NSC): Executive agency responsible for advising the president about foreign and defense policy and events.

natural law: A doctrine that society should be governed by certain ethical principles that are part of nature and, as such, can be understood by reason.

necessary and proper clause: The final paragraph of Article I, section 8, of the U.S. Constitution, which gives Congress the authority to pass all laws "necessary and proper" to carry out the enumerated powers specified in the Constitution; also called the elastic clause.

negative ad: Advertising on behalf of a candidate that attacks the opponent's platform or character.

network: An association of broadcast stations (radio or television) that share programming through a financial arrangement.

New Deal: The name given to the program of "Relief, Recovery, Reform" begun by President Franklin D. Roosevelt in 1933 to bring the United States out of the Great Depression.

New Federalism: Federal/state relationship proposed by Reagan administration during the 1980s; hallmark is returning administrative powers to the state governments.

New Jersey Plan: A framework for the Constitution proposed by a group of small states; its key points were a one-house legislature with one vote for each state, the establishment of the acts of Congress as the "supreme law" of the land, and a supreme judiciary with limited power.

new media: Technologies such as the Internet that blur the line between media sources and create new opportunities for the dissemination of news and other information.

New York Times Co. v. Sullivan (1964): The Supreme Court concluded that "actual malice" must be proved to support a finding of libel against a public figure.

news media: Media providing the public with new information about subjects of public interest.

9/11 Commission: The National Commission on Terrorist Attacks upon the United States; a bipartisan, independent group authorized by Congress and President Bush in 2002 to study the circumstances surrounding the September 11, 2001, terrorist attacks, including preparedness and response. Its 2004 report includes recommendations for guarding against future attacks.

Nineteenth Amendment: Amendment to the Constitution that guaranteed women the right to vote.

Ninth Amendment: Part of the Bill of Rights that reads "The enumeration in the Constitution, of certain rights, shall not be construed to deny or disparage others retained by the people."

Nixon Doctrine: The policy implemented at the end of the Vietnam War that the United States would provide arms and military equipment to countries but not do the fighting for them.

nomination campaign: That part of a political campaign aimed at winning a primary election.

nongovernmental organization (NGO): An organization that is not tied to a government.

non-means-based program: Program such as Social Security where benefits are provided irrespective of the income or means of recipients.

North American Free Trade Agreement (NAFTA): Agreement that promotes free movement of goods and services among Canada, Mexico, and the United States.

North Atlantic Treaty Organization (NATO): The first peacetime military treaty the United States joined, NATO is a regional political and military organization created in 1950.

O

off the record: Information provided to a journalist that will not be released to the public.

Office of Management and Budget (OMB): The office that prepares the president's annual budget proposal, reviews the budget and programs of the executive departments, supplies economic forecasts, and conducts detailed analyses of proposed bills and agency rules.

oligarchy: A form of government in which the right to participate is conditioned on the possession of wealth, social status, military position, or achievement.

on background: Information provided to a journalist that will not be attributed to a named source.

on the record: Information provided to a journalist that can be released and attributed by name to the source.

open market operations: The buying and selling of government securities by the Federal Reserve Bank in the securities market.

open primary: A primary in which party members, independents, and sometimes members of the other party are allowed to vote.

organizational party: The workers and activists who staff the party's formal organization.

original jurisdiction: The jurisdiction of courts that hear a case first, usually in a trial. Courts determine the facts of a case under their original jurisdiction.

oversight: Congressional review of the activities of an agency, department, or office.

P

paid media: Political advertisements purchased for a candidate's campaign.

pardon: The authority of a government to cancel someone's conviction of a crime by a court and to eliminate all sanctions and punishments resulting from conviction.

party caucus or conference: A formal gathering of all party members.

party identification: A citizen's personal affinity for a political party, usually expressed by his or her tendency to vote for the candidates of that party.

party in the electorate: The voters who consider themselves allied or associated with the party.

party realignment: A shifting of party coalition groupings in the electorate that remains in place for several elections.

patron: Person who finances a group or individual activity.

patronage: Jobs, grants, or other special favors that are given as rewards to friends and political allies for their support.

Pearl Harbor: Naval base in Hawaii attacked by Japan on December 7, 1941, initiating U.S. entry into World War II.

Pendleton Act: Reform measure that created the Civil Service Commission to administer a partial merit system. The act classified the federal service by grades, to which appointments were made based on the results of a competitive examination. It made it illegal for federal political appointees to be required to contribute to a particular political party.

personal liberty: A key characteristic of U.S. democracy. Initially meaning freedom from governmental interference, today it includes demands for freedom to engage in a variety of practices free from governmental discrimination.

Plessy v. Ferguson (1896): Plessy challenged a Louisiana statute requiring that railroads provide separate accommodations for blacks and whites. The Court found that separate but equal accommodations did not violate the equal protection clause of the Fourteenth Amendment.

pocket veto: If Congress adjourns during the ten days the president has to consider a bill passed by both houses of Congress, without the president's signature, the bill is considered vetoed.

policy adoption: The approval of a policy proposal by the people with the requisite authority, such as a legislature.

policy evaluation: The process of determining whether a course of action is achieving its intended goals.

policy formulation: The crafting of appropriate and acceptable proposed courses of action to ameliorate or resolve public problems.

policy implementation: The process of carrying out public policy through governmental agencies and the courts.

political action committee (PAC): Federally mandated, officially registered fund-raising committee that represents interest groups in the political process.

political culture: Commonly shared attitudes, beliefs, and core values about how government should operate.

political equality: The principle that all citizens should participate equally in government; implied by the phrase "one person, one vote".

political ideology: The coherent set of values and beliefs about the purpose and scope of government held by groups and individuals.

political party: A group of office holders, candidates, activists, and voters who identify with a group label and seek to elect to public office individuals who run under that label.

political socialization: The process through which individuals acquire their political beliefs and values.

politico: Role played by elected representatives who act as trustees or as delegates, depending on the issue.

politics: The study of who gets what, when, and how—or how policy decisions are made.

poll tax: Tax levied in many southern states and localities that had to be paid before an eligible voter could cast a ballot.

pollster: A professional who takes public opinion surveys that guide political campaigns.

popular consent: The idea that governments must draw their powers from the consent of the governed.

popular sovereignty: The notion that the ultimate authority in society rests with the people.

pork: Legislation that allows representatives to bring home the bacon to their districts in the form of public works programs, military bases, or other programs designed to benefit their districts directly.

positive ad: Advertising on behalf of a candidate that stresses the candidate's qualifications, family, and issue positions, without reference to the opponent.

Powell Doctrine: An all-or-nothing approach to military intervention advocated by Colin Powell: use overwhelming force for quick, decisive victory, and have an exit strategy before any intervention.

pragmatism: The policy of taking advantage of a situation for national gain.

precedent: Prior judicial decision that serves as a rule for settling subsequent cases of a similar nature.

preemption: A concept derived from the Constitution's supremacy clause that allows the national government to override or preempt state or local actions in certain areas.

president pro tempore: The official chair of the Senate; usually the most senior member of the majority party.

press briefing: A relatively restricted session between a press secretary or aide and the press.

press conference: An unrestricted session between an elected official and the press.

press release: A document offering an official comment or position.

press secretary: The individual charged with interacting and communicating with journalists on a daily basis.

primary election: Election in which voters decide which of the candidates within a party will represent the party in the general election.

print media: The traditional form of mass media, comprising newspapers, magazines, newsletters, and journals.

prior restraint: Constitutional doctrine that prevents the government from prohibiting speech or publication before the fact; generally held to be in violation of the First Amendment.

privileges and immunities clause: Part of Article IV of the Constitution guaranteeing that the citizens of each state are afforded the same rights as citizens of all other states.

proportional representation: A voting system that apportions legislative seats according to the percentage of the vote won by a particular political party.

prospective judgment: A voter's evaluation of a candidate based on what he or she pledges to do about an issue if elected.

public funds: Donations from the general tax revenues to the campaigns of qualifying presidential candidates.

public interest group: An organization that seeks a collective good that will not selectively and materially benefit the members of the group.

public opinion: What the public thinks about a particular issue or set of issues at any point in time.

public opinion polls: Interviews or surveys with samples of citizens that are used to estimate the feelings and beliefs of the entire population.

public policy: An intentional course of action followed by government in dealing with some problem or matter of concern.

push polls: "Polls" taken for the purpose of providing information on an opponent that would lead respondents to vote against that candidate.

R

raiding: An organized attempt by voters of one party to influence the primary results of the other party.

random sampling: A method of poll selection that gives each person in a group the same chance of being selected.

Reagan Doctrine: Policy that the United States would provide military assistance to anti-communist groups fighting against pro-Soviet governments.

reapportionment: The reallocation of the number of seats in the House of Representatives after each decennial census.

recall: A process in which voters can petition for a vote to remove office holders between elections.

recession: A short-term decline in the economy that occurs as investment sags, production falls off, and unemployment increases.

redistricting: The redrawing of congressional districts to reflect population changes or for political advantage.

referendum: An election whereby the state legislature submits proposed legislation to the state's voters for approval.

regional primary: A proposed system in which the country would be divided into five or six geographic areas and all states in each region would hold their presidential primary elections on the same day.

regulations: Rules that govern the operation of a particular government program that have the force of law.

republic: A government rooted in the consent of the governed; a representative or indirect democracy.

reservation land: Land designated in a treaty that is under the authority of an Indian nation and is exempt from most state laws and taxes.

reserve (or police) powers: Powers reserved to the states by the Tenth Amendment that lie at the foundation of a state's right to legislate for the public health and welfare of its citizens.

reserve requirements: Government requirements that a portion of member banks' deposits must be retained to back loans made.

retrospective judgment: A voter's evaluation of the performance of the party in power.

right to privacy: The right to be let alone; a judicially created doctrine encompassing an individual's decision to use birth control or secure an abortion.

***Roe v. Wade* (1973):** The Supreme Court found that a woman's right to an abortion was protected by the right to privacy that could be implied from specific guarantees found in the Bill of Rights applied to the states through the Fourteenth Amendment.

Roosevelt Corollary: Concept developed by President Theodore Roosevelt early in the twentieth century that it was the U.S. responsibility to assure stability in Latin America and the Caribbean.

rule making: A quasi-legislative administrative process that has the characteristics of a legislative act.

Rule of Four: At least four justices of the Supreme Court must vote to consider a case before it can be heard.

runoff primary: A second primary election between the two candidates receiving the greatest number of votes in the first primary.

S

sampling error or margin of error: A measure of the accuracy of a public opinion poll.

Second Continental Congress: Meeting that convened in Philadelphia on May 10, 1775, at which it was decided that an army should be raised and George Washington of Virginia was named commander in chief.

secular realignment: The gradual rearrangement of party coalitions, based more on demographic shifts than on shocks to the political system.

select (or special) committee: Temporary committee appointed for specific purpose, such as conducting a special investigation or study.

selective incorporation: A judicial doctrine whereby most but not all of the protections found in the Bill of Rights are made applicable to the states via the Fourteenth Amendment.

senatorial courtesy: Process by which presidents, when selecting district court judges, defer to senators of their own party who represent the state where the vacancy occurs; also the process by which a governor, when selecting an appointee, defers to the state senator in whose district the nominee resides.

seniority: Time of continuous service on a committee.

separation of powers:
A way of dividing power among three branches of government in which members of the House of Representatives, members of the Senate, the president, and the federal courts are selected by and responsible to different constituencies.

Seventeenth Amendment: Made senators directly elected by the people; removed their selection from state legislatures.

Shays's Rebellion: A 1786 rebellion in which an army of 1,500 disgruntled and angry farmers led by Daniel Shays marched to Springfield, Massachusetts, and forcibly restrained the state court from foreclosing mortgages on their farms.

Sixteenth Amendment: Authorized Congress to enact a national income tax.

Sixth Amendment: Part of the Bill of Rights that sets out the basic requirements of procedural due process for federal courts to follow in criminal trials. These include speedy and public trials, impartial juries, trials in the state where crime was committed, notice of the charges, the right to confront and obtain favorable witnesses, and the right to counsel.

slander: Untrue spoken statements that defame the character of a person.

social capital: The myriad relationships that individuals enjoy that facilitate the resolution of community problems through collective action.

social conservative: One who believes that traditional moral teachings should be supported and furthered by the government.

social contract: An agreement between the people and their government signifying their consent to be governed.

social contract theory: The belief that people are free and equal by God-given right and that this in turn requires that all people give their consent to be governed; espoused by John Locke and influential in the writing of the Declaration of Independence.

social regulation: Government regulation of the quality and safety of products as well as the conditions under which goods and services are produced.

Social Security Act: A 1935 law that established old-age insurance (Social Security) and assistance for the needy, children, and others, and unemployment insurance.

social welfare policy: Government programs designed to improve quality of life.

soft money: The virtually unregulated money funneled by individuals and political committees through state and local parties.

solicitor general: The fourth-ranking member of the Department of Justice;

responsible for handling all appeals on behalf of the U.S. government to the Supreme Court.

sovereign immunity: The right of a state to be free from lawsuit unless it gives permission to the suit. Under the Eleventh Amendment, all states are considered sovereign.

Spanish-American War: Brief 1898 war against Spain because of Spanish policies and presence in Cuba and U.S. desire to attain overseas territory.

Speaker of the House: The only officer of the House of Representatives specifically mentioned in the Constitution; elected at the beginning of each new Congress by the entire House; traditionally a member of the majority party.

spoils system: The firing of public-office holders of a defeated political party and their replacement with loyalists of the newly elected party.

spot ad: Television advertising on behalf of a candidate that is broadcast in sixty-, thirty-, or ten-second duration.

Stamp Act Congress: Meeting of representatives of nine of the thirteen colonies held in New York City in 1765, during which representatives drafted a document to send to the king listing how their rights had been violated.

standing committee: Committee to which proposed bills are referred.

stare decisis: In court rulings, a reliance on past decisions or precedents to formulate decisions in new cases.

stratified sampling: A variation of random sampling; Census data are used to divide a country into four sampling regions. Sets of counties and standard metropolitan statistical areas are then randomly selected in proportion to the total national population.

straw polls: Unscientific surveys used to gauge public opinion on a variety of issues and policies.

strict constructionist: An approach to constitutional interpretation that emphasizes the Framers' original intentions.

strict scrutiny: A heightened standard of review used by the Supreme Court to determine the constitutional validity of a challenged practice.

substantive due process: Judicial interpretation of the Fifth and Fourteenth Amendments' due process clause that protects citizens from arbitrary or unjust laws.

suffrage movement: The drive for voting rights for women that took place in the United States from 1890 to 1920.

superdelegate: Delegate slot to the Democratic Party's national convention that is reserved for an elected party official.

supremacy clause: Portion of Article VI of the U.S. Constitution mandating that national law is supreme to (that is, supercedes) all other laws passed by the states or by any other subdivision of government.

suspect classification: Category or class, such as race, that triggers the highest standard of scrutiny from the Supreme Court.

symbolic speech: Symbols, signs, and other methods of expression generally also considered to be protected by the First Amendment.

systemic agenda: All public issues that are viewed as requiring governmental attention; a discussion agenda.

T

Taliban: Fundamentalist Islamic government of Afghanistan that provided terrorist training bases for al-Qaeda.

tariffs: Taxes on imports used to raise government revenue and to protect infant industries.

Tenth Amendment: Part of the Bill of Rights that reiterates powers not delegated to the national government are reserved to the states or to the people.

think tank: Institutional collection of policy-oriented researchers and academics who are sources of policy ideas.

Thirteenth Amendment: One of the three Civil War amendments; specifically bans slavery in the United States.

Three-Fifths Compromise: Agreement reached at the Constitutional Convention stipulating that each slave was to be counted as three-fifths of a person for purposes of determining population for representation in the U.S. House of Representatives.

ticket-split: To vote for candidates of different parties for various offices in the same election.

Title IX: Provision of the Educational Amendments of 1972 that bars educational institutions receiving federal funds from discriminating against female students.

totalitarianism: A form of government in which power resides in a leader who rules according to self-interest and without regard for individual rights and liberties.

tracking polls: Continuous surveys that enable a campaign to chart its daily rise or fall in support.

trade association: A group that represents a specific industry.

trial courts: Courts of original jurisdiction where a case begins.

Truman Doctrine: U.S. policy initiated in 1947 of providing economic assistance and military aid to countries fighting against communist revolutions or political pressure.

trustee: Role played by elected representatives who listen to constituents' opinions and then use their best judgment to make final decisions.

turnout: The proportion of the voting-age public that votes.

Twenty-Fifth Amendment: Adopted in 1967 to establish procedures for filling vacancies in the office of president and vice president as well as providing for procedures to deal with the disability of a president.

Twenty-Second Amendment: Adopted in 1951, prevents a president from serving more than two terms or more than ten years if he came to office via the death or impeachment of his predecessor.

U

unconventional political participation: Political participation that attempts to influence the political process through unusual or extreme measures, such as protests, boycotts, and picketing.

unfunded mandates: National laws that direct states or local governments to comply with the federal rules or regulations (such as clean air or water standards) but contain no federal funding to defray the cost of meeting these requirements.

unilateralism: A national policy of acting without consulting others.

unitary system: System of government where the local and regional governments derive all authority from a strong national government.

unit rule: A traditional party practice under which the majority of a state delegation can force the minority to vote for its candidate.

United Nations (UN): An international governmental organization created shortly before the end of World War II to guarantee the security of nations and to promote global economic, physical, and social well-being.

***U.S. v. Nixon* (1974):** Key Supreme Court ruling on power of the president, finding that there is no absolute constitutional executive privilege to allow a president to refuse to comply with a court order to produce information needed in a criminal trial.

V

veto: The formal, constitutional authority of the chief executive to reject bills passed by both houses of the legislative body, thus preventing their becoming law without further legislative action.

veto power: The formal, constitutional authority of the president to reject bills passed by both houses of Congress, thus preventing their becoming law without further congressional action.

Vietnam War: Between 1965 and 1973, the United States deployed up to 500,000 troops to Vietnam to try to prevent North Vietnam from taking over South Vietnam; the effort failed and was extremely divisive within the United States.

Virginia Plan: The first general plan for the Constitution, proposed by James Madison and Edmund Randolph. Its key points were a bicameral legislature, an executive chosen by the legislature, and a judiciary also named by the legislature.

voter canvass: The process by which a campaign gets in touch with individual voters, either by door-to-door solicitation or by telephone.

W

war on terrorism: Initiated by President George W. Bush after the 9/11 attacks to weed out terrorist operatives throughout the world, using diplomacy, military means, improved homeland security, stricter banking laws, and other means.

War Powers Act: Passed by Congress in 1973; the president is limited in the deployment of troops overseas to a sixty-day period in peacetime (which can be extended for an extra thirty days to permit withdrawal) unless Congress explicitly gives its approval for a longer period.

weapons of mass destruction: Biological, chemical, and nuclear weapons, which present a sizeable threat to U.S. security.

whip: One of several representatives who keep close contact with all members and take nose counts on key votes, prepare summaries of bills, and in general act as communications links within the party.

winner-take-all system: An electoral system in which the party that receives at least one more vote than any other party wins the election.

wire service: An electronic delivery of news gathered by the news service's correspondents and sent to all member news media organizations.

World Bank: International governmental organization created shortly before the end of World War II to provide loans for large economic development projects.

World Trade Organization: International governmental organization created in 1995 that manages multilateral negotiations to reduce barriers to trade and settle trade disputes.

writ of *certiorari*: A request for the Court to order up the records from a lower court to review the case.

writ of *habeas corpus*: A court order in which a judge requires authorities to prove that a prisoner is being held lawfully and that allows the prisoner to be freed if the judge is not persuaded by the government's case. *Habeas corpus* rights imply that prisoners have a right to know what charges are being made against them.

Y

yellow journalism: A form of newspaper publishing in vogue in the late nineteenth century that featured pictures, comics, color, and sensationalized, oversimplified news coverage.